HMH | into Literature™

TEACHER'S EDITION

GRADE 6

Program Consultants:
Kylene Beers
Martha Hougen
Elena Izquierdo
Carol Jago
Erik Palmer
Robert E. Probst

Front Cover Photo Credits: (t overlay): ©Carlos Caetano /Shutterstock, (outer ring): ©Willyam Bradberry/Shutterstock, (inner ring): ©Jeep5d/Shutterstock, (c) ©Carrie Garcia/Houghton Mifflin Harcourt, (tc overlay): ©Eyewire/Getty Images, (b overlay): ©elenamiv/Shutterstock
Back Cover Photo Credits: (Units 1-6): ©Michal Bednarek/Photocreo/Shutterstock; ©Digital Vision/Getty Images; ©Everett Historical/Shutterstock; ©Yulia Grigoryeva/Shutterstock; ©nazmoo/Fotolia; ©Photoraidz/Shutterstock

Printed in the U.S.A.
ISBN 978-1-328-47484-1

2 3 4 5 6 7 8 9 10 0690 27 26 25 24 23 22 21 20 19

4500752975 B C D E F G

into Literature

Teacher's Edition Table of Contents

into Literature

PROGRAM CONSULTANTS

Kylene Beers

Nationally known lecturer and author on reading and literacy; coauthor with Robert Probst of *Disrupting Thinking, Notice & Note: Strategies for Close Reading,* and *Reading Nonfiction*; former president of the National Council of Teachers of English. Dr. Beers is the author of *When Kids Can't Read: What Teachers Can Do* and coeditor of *Adolescent Literacy: Turning Promise into Practice*, as well as articles in the *Journal of Adolescent and Adult Literacy*. Former editor of *Voices from the Middle,* she is the 2001 recipient of NCTE's Richard W. Halle Award, given for outstanding contributions to middle school literacy. She recently served as Senior Reading Researcher at the Comer School Development Program at Yale University as well as Senior Reading Advisor to Secondary Schools for the Reading and Writing Project at Teachers College.

Martha Hougen

National consultant, presenter, researcher, and author. Areas of expertise include differentiating instruction for students with learning difficulties, including those with learning disabilities and dyslexia; and teacher and leader preparation improvement. Dr. Hougen has taught at the middle school through graduate levels. In addition to peer-reviewed articles, curricular documents, and presentations, Dr. Hougen has published two college textbooks: *The Fundamentals of Literacy Instruction and Assessment Pre-K–6* (2012) and *The Fundamentals of Literacy Instruction and Assessment 6–12* (2014). Dr. Hougen has supported Educator Preparation Program reforms while working at the Meadows Center for Preventing Educational Risk at The University of Texas at Austin and at the CEEDAR Center, University of Florida.

Elena Izquierdo

Nationally recognized teacher educator and advocate for English language learners. Dr. Izquierdo is a linguist by training, with a Ph.D. in Applied Linguistics and Bilingual Education from Georgetown University. She has served on various state and national boards working to close the achievement gaps for bilingual students and English language learners. Dr. Izquierdo is a member of the Hispanic Leadership Council, which supports Hispanic students and educators at both the state and federal levels. She served as Vice President on the Executive Board of the National Association of Bilingual Education and as Publications and Professional Development Chair.

Carol Jago

Teacher of English with 32 years of experience at Santa Monica High School in California; author and nationally known lecturer; former president of the National Council of Teachers of English. Ms. Jago currently serves as Associate Director of the California Reading and Literature Project at UCLA. With expertise in standards assessment and secondary education, Ms. Jago is the author of numerous books on education, including *With Rigor for All* and *Papers, Papers, Papers*, and is active with the California Association of Teachers of English, editing its scholarly journal *California English* since 1996. Ms. Jago also served on the planning committee for the 2009 NAEP Reading Framework and the 2011 NAEP Writing Framework.

Erik Palmer

Veteran teacher and education consultant based in Denver, Colorado. Author of *Well Spoken: Teaching Speaking to All Students* and *Digitally Speaking: How to Improve Student Presentations with Technology*. His areas of focus include improving oral communication, promoting technology in classroom presentations, and updating instruction through the use of digital tools. He holds a bachelor's degree from Oberlin College and a master's degree in curriculum and instruction from the University of Colorado.

Robert E. Probst

Nationally respected authority on the teaching of literature; Professor Emeritus of English Education at Georgia State University. Dr. Probst's publications include numerous articles in *English Journal* and *Voices from the Middle*, as well as professional texts including (as coeditor) *Adolescent Literacy: Turning Promise into Practice* and (as coauthor with Kylene Beers) *Disrupting Thinking, Notice & Note: Strategies for Close Reading,* and *Reading Nonfiction.* He regularly speaks at national and international conventions including those of the International Literacy Association, the National Council of Teachers of English, the Association for Supervision and Curriculum Development, and the National Association of Secondary School Principals. He has served NCTE in various leadership roles, including the Conference on English Leadership Board of Directors, the Commission on Reading, and column editor of the NCTE journal *Voices from the Middle.* He is also the 2004 recipient of the CEL Exemplary Leadership Award.

Lead and Learn

Students who communicate...

- **Listen** actively
  - **Present** effectively
    - **Expand** vocabulary
      - **Question** appropriately
        - **Engage** constructively

Present an Argument

You will now adapt your argument to create a video presentation for your classmates. You will also listen to their presentations, ask questions to better understand their ideas, and help them improve their work.

SPEAKING AND LISTENING TASK

Go to **Giving a Presentation** in the **Speaking and Listening Studio** to learn more.

1 Adapt Your Argument for Presentation

Use the chart below to guide you as you create a script for a video "news editorial" based on your argument, with you as the speaker.

Presentation Planning Chart

Title and Introduction	• How will you revise your title and introduction to capture the listener's attention? • Is there a way to state your claim aloud that is more engaging for video?
Audience	• Who is your audience? What do you want them to understand? • Are your tone, word choices, and visual elements or graphics appropriate for persuading this audience?
Effective Language and Organization	• Is your script logically organized? Is it interesting to listen to? Should parts be rearranged or excluded? • Where can you add evidence, persuasive language, or interesting examples to strengthen your argument? • Do you address a counter argument?
Visuals	• What type of media or visual elements will you use? • What type of audio elements will you use? What text will appear on screen?

Present an Argument   167

SPEAKING AND LISTENING STUDIO

What Makes a Dynamic Presentation?

This Speaker was assigned to give an informal demonstration of the verbal and noverbal elements of speech delivery. View each segment of her presentation and respond to the questions.

Question and Respond

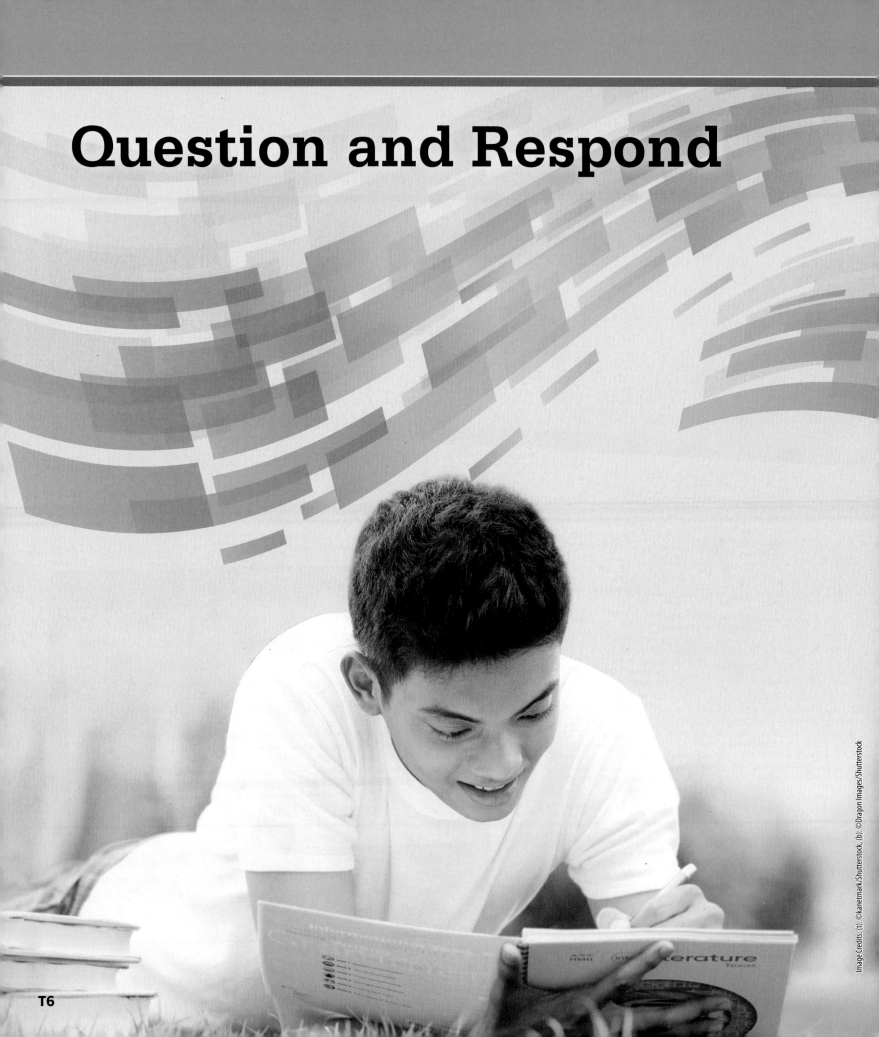

Students who read...

- **Acquire** fluency
- **Choose** independently
- **Monitor** understanding
- **Annotate** and use evidence
- **Write** and discuss within and across texts

ANNOTATION MODEL

NOTICE & NOTE

As you read, notice and note signposts, including **Again and Again, Memory Moments,** and **Contrasts and Contradictions.** The following example shows how one reader responded to the opening of *Pax.*

1   The fox felt the car slow before the boy did, as he felt everything first. Through the pads of his paws, along his spine, in the sensitive whiskers at his wrists. By the vibrations, he learned also that the road had grown coarser. He stretched up from his boy's lap and sniffed at threads of scent leaking in through the window, which told him they were now traveling into woodlands.

> I see lots of description of what the fox senses here.
>
> The narrator repeatedly describes what the fox senses through touch and smell.

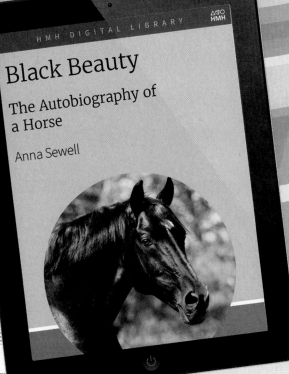

HMH DIGITAL LIBRARY

Black Beauty
The Autobiography of a Horse

Anna Sewell

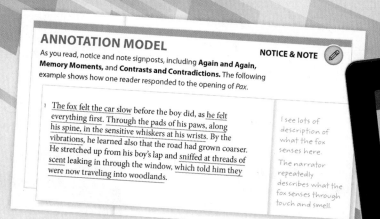

ACADEMIC VOCABULARY

Academic Vocabulary words are words you use when you discuss an
In this unit, you will learn and practice using five words.

☑ benefit   ❑ distinct   ❑ environment   ❑ illustrate

Study the Word Network to learn more about the word **benefit.**

SYNONYMS
help, advantage

DEFINITION
something that provides help
or improves something else

benefit
(běn´ə-fĭt)
n.

ANT
drawback

CLARIFYING EXAMPLE
There are many benefits to
reading your writing aloud.

WORD
comes from th
beneficium, m
a servic

RELATED WORDS
beneficial, benefiting

Write and Discuss Discuss the completed Word Network with a partner, ma
to talk through all of the boxes until you both understand the word, its synon
antonyms, and related forms. Then, fill out Word Networks for the remaining fo
Use a dictionary or online resource to help you complete the activity.

Go online to access the Word Networks.

RESPOND TO THE ESSENTIAL QUESTION

In this unit, you will explore what can be learned by seeing the
world through an animal's eyes. As you read, you will revisit
the **Essential Question** and gather your ideas about it in the
Response Log that appears on page R2. At the end of the unit,
you will write an **argument** about what you can learn by seeing
the world from an animal's perspective. You will also **present an
argument.** Filling out the Response Log will help you prepare
for these tasks.

You can also go online to access the Response Log.

UNIT 2

THROUGH AN ANIMAL'S EYES

? **ESSENTIAL QUESTION:**

What can you learn by seeing the world through an animal's eyes?

> " I have wished that I could . . . look out onto the world through the eyes, with the mind, of a chimpanzee. "
>
> Jane Goodall

90   Unit 2

Through an Animal's Eyes   91

Connect
Reading and Writing

ANALYZE & APPLY

GENRE:
Novel

from
PAX

Novel by **Sara Pennypacker**

? ***ESSENTIAL QUESTION:***

What can you learn by seeing the world through an animal's eyes?

94 Unit 2

GENRE:
Informational Text

ANALYZE

from
ANIMAL SNOOPS: THE WONDROUS WORLD OF WILDLIFE SPIES

Informational Text by **Peter Christie**

? ***ESSENTIAL QUESTION:***

What can you learn by seeing the world through an animal's eyes?

Students who explore genre...

- **Analyze** features

  - **Understand** effects of authors' choices

    - **Emulate** craft

      - **Use** mentor texts

        - **Synthesize** ideas

GENRE ELEMENTS: INFORMATIONAL TEXT

- provides factual information
- includes evidence to support ideas
- often contains text features
- includes many forms, such as news articles and essays
- includes science writing, which explains complex scientific topics in language that is easy to understand

Image Credits: (t): ©kanetmark/Shutterstock, (b): ©MSSA/Shutterstock

QUICK START

Have you ever had a sneaking suspicion that your family pet or the pet of someone you know has been spying on you or listening in on your conversations? Share your experience with the class.

ANALYZE TEXT STRUCTURE

An **anecdote** is a short account of an event that is usually intended to entertain or make a point. Authors use anecdotes to introduce or illustrate important ideas in a way that is easy to understand and remember. As you read the following informational text, note how the author uses anecdotes to structure and present his ideas. Think about how the anecdotes help explain those ideas in a humorous and entertaining way.

DETERMINE KEY IDEAS

To develop and deepen your understanding of what you read, you need to be able to determine key ideas and evaluate details of the text. A **key idea** is a very important idea about a topic in the text. As you read, write down key ideas of the text in the graphic organizer below. Include important details from the text that support each key idea.

KEY IDEA	SUPPORTING DETAILS

Animal Snoops: The Wondrous World of Wildlife Spies   117

WRITING STUDIO

Ways to Organize Reasons and Evidence

Every argument must include reasons and evidence to support a claim. There are several effective ways you can organize that support. Check out some of those ways here.

Read the following techniques that will help you achieve cohesion, or coherence, in your writing.

Order of Importance

Least to most important

Claim: Homewood must switch from a volunteer fire

GENRE: Poem

COLLABORATE & COMPARE

POEM
ANIMAL WISDOM
by **Nancy Wood**
pages 133–135

COMPARE THEMES
As you read, focus on discovering themes, or messages about life or human nature, that both poems share. What ideas are communicated by each poem? Which ideas do they have in common?

? ***ESSENTIAL QUESTION:***
What can you learn by seeing the world through an animal's eyes?

POEM
THE LAST WOLF
by **Mary TallMountain**
pages 136–137

Craft and Communicate

Students who compose...

- **Inform,** argue, and connect
- **Create** in a literary genre
- **Imitate** mentor texts
- **Apply** conventions
- **Use** process and partners

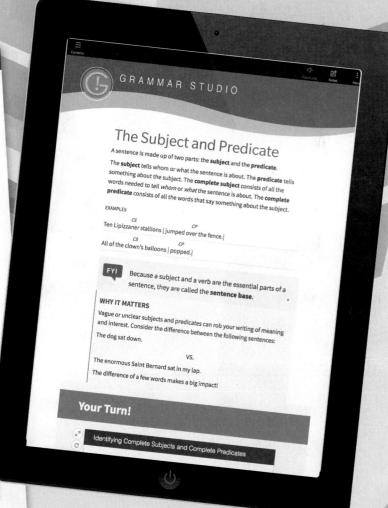

Write an Argument

WRITING TASK

Go to the **Writing Studio** for help writing an argument.

This unit focuses on what we can learn by seeing the world through the eyes of animals. For this writing task, you will write an argumentative essay on a topic related to seeing the world from the perspective of an animal. For examples of arguments that you can use as mentor texts, review "Wild Animals Aren't Pets" and "Let People Own Exotic Animals."

As you write your argument, use the notes from your ... filled out after reading the texts in this unit.

THROUGH AN ANIMAL'S EYES

This is the topic ... context for your argument. "

This is the Essen... Question for th... unit. How woul... answer this q... based on the te... the unit?

Now mark the... that identify ... what you are ... asked to prod...

Review these... you write an... when you fi... any needed...

160   Unit 2

WRITING TASK

Use the Mentor Text

Persuasive Language
Writers use different techniques to persuade readers. Using persuasive language is one technique. Persuasive language includes words with strong negative and positive connotations, which are the ideas and feelings attached to the words.

Terry Thompson didn't represent the typical responsible owner. He had a criminal record and animal abuse charges. What Thompson did was selfish and insane; we cannot regulate insanity.

The writer of "Let People Own Exotic Animals" uses words with strong negative connotations, like "selfish" and "insane," to make her point that typical exotic animal owners are not like Terry Thompson.

Apply What You've Learned Review your argument for words that you can replace with persuasive language. Consider whether the words you choose have positive or negative connotations.

Author's Craft
Writers often build interest and show the importance of their topic with well-chosen references to familiar stories and events. By citing examples that are relevant to their claims, writers find common ground with their readers—an important step in the process of persuasion.

But just as a 2007 raid on property owned by football star Michael Vick laid bare the little known and cruel world of dogfighting, a story that unfolded in a small Ohio city recently opened the public's eyes to the little known, distressing world of "exotic" pets.

The writer of "Wild Animals Aren't Pets" builds anticipation and foreshadows a similar sense of public outrage by referring to the 2007 Michael Vick dogfighting story.

© Houghton Mifflin Harcourt Publishing Company

Apply What You've Learned To help persuade your readers to agree with your claim, use the strategy of bringing up a well-known story that will influence their reaction to the evidence you cite.

Write an Argument   163

GRAMMAR STUDIO

The Subject and Predicate

A sentence is made up of two parts: the **subject** and the **predicate**. The **subject** tells whom or what the sentence is about. The **predicate** tells something about the subject. The **complete subject** consists of all the words needed to tell *whom* or *what* the sentence is about. The **complete predicate** consists of all the words that say something about the subject.

EXAMPLES

CS
Ten Lipizzaner stallions | jumped over the fence. | CP

CS
All of the clown's balloons | popped. | CP

FYI Because a subject and a verb are the essential parts of a sentence, they are called the **sentence base**.

WHY IT MATTERS

Vague or unclear subjects and predicates can rob your writing of meaning and interest. Consider the difference between the following sentences:

The dog sat down.

VS.

The enormous Saint Bernard sat in my lap.

The difference of a few words makes a big impact!

Your Turn!

Identifying Complete Subjects and Complete Predicates

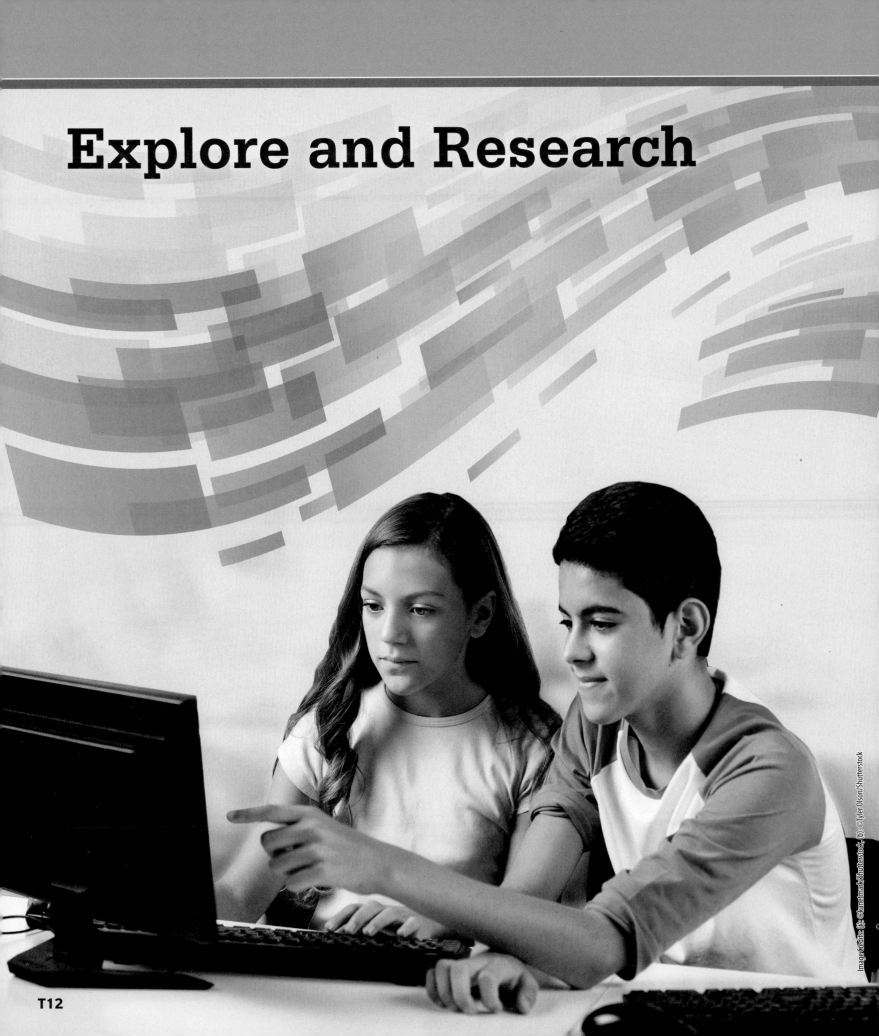

Explore and Research

Students who inquire...

- **Generate** questions
- **Plan** and revise
- **Synthesize** information
- **Cite** sources
- **Deliver** results

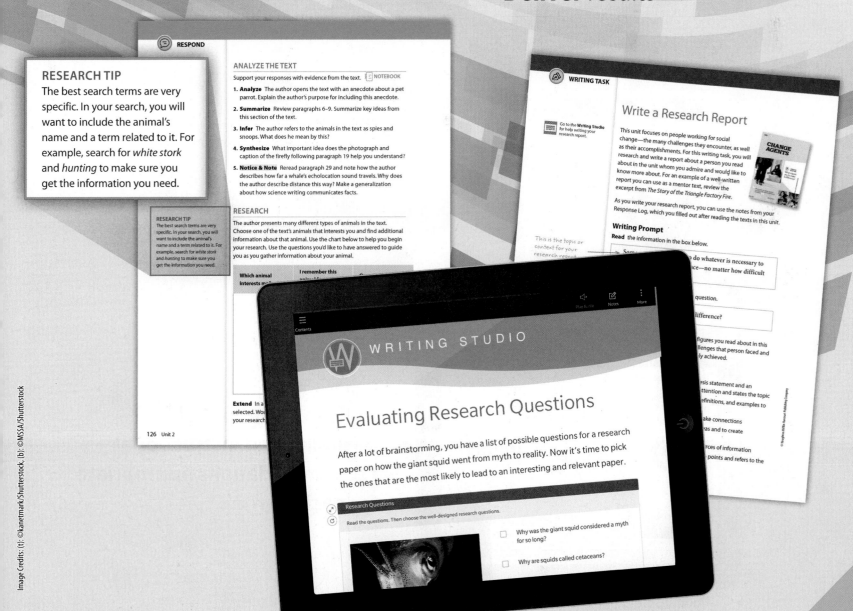

Maximize Growth through Data-Driven Differentiation and Assessment

Ongoing assessment and data reporting provide critical feedback loops to teachers and students, so that each experience encourages self-assessment and reflection, and drives positive learning outcomes for all students.

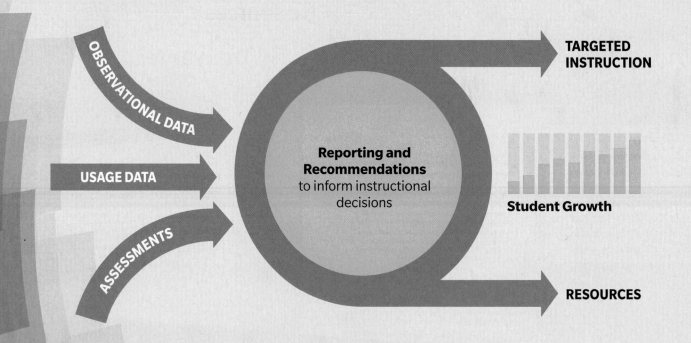

Actionable reports drive grouping and instructional recommendations appropriate for each learner.

Program Assessments

Adaptive Growth Measure

3 times per year

Adaptive Growth Measure allows teachers to gain an understanding of where students are on the learning continuum and identify students in need of intervention or enrichment.

Unit Assessments

6 times per year

Unit Assessments identify mastery of skills covered during the course of the unit across all literacy strands.

Ongoing Feedback from Daily Classroom Activities

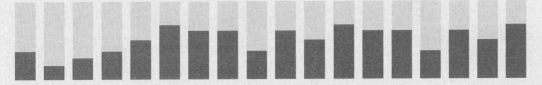

Formative Assessment data is collected across a variety of student activities to help teachers make informed instructional decisions based on data.

- Check Your Understanding
- Selection Tests
- Writing Tasks
- Independent Reading

- Usage Data
- Online Essay Scoring
- Teacher Observations
- Research Projects

Assessments

HMH Into Literature has a comprehensive suite of assessments to help you determine what your students already know and how they are progressing through the program lessons.

Diagnostic Assessment for Reading is an informal, criterion-referenced assessment designed to diagnose the specific reading comprehension skills that need attention.

Skills-based Diagnostic Assessments will help you quickly gauge a student's mastery of common, grade-level appropriate skills.

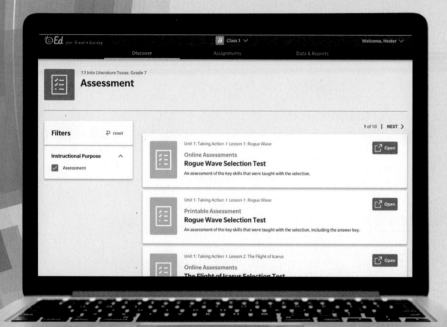

Every selection in the Into Literature program has a corresponding **Selection Test,** focusing on the skills taught in each lesson.
- Analyze & Apply
- Collaborate & Compare, and
- Independent Reading

A **Unit Test** assesses mastery of the skills taught in the entire Unit using new readings aligned with the Unit topic.

The **Diagnostic Screening Test** for Grammar, Usage, and Mechanics provides an assessment of strengths and weaknesses in the conventions of written English.

Each Module in the Grammar Studio has a **Diagnostic Assessment** and a **Summative Assessment,** for before and after instruction.

Foster a Learning Culture

As you encourage a culture of responsibility and collaboration, essential for students' success in the world of work, you will find learning activities that are social, active, and student owned.

Collaborate & Compare Designed to support individual accountability as well as team aptitude, this section requires students to read and annotate texts and compare their responses in small groups.

Peer Review is a critical part of students' creative process. Tools like Checklists for writing and listening and speaking tasks and the Revision Guide with questions, tips, and techniques offer practical support for peer interaction.

Learning Mindset notes and strategies in your Teacher's Edition are designed to help students acquire the attitude of perseverance through learning obstacles. Other resources like ongoing formative assessments, peer evaluation, and Reflect on the Unit questions encourage students to monitor their progress and develop metacognitive ability.

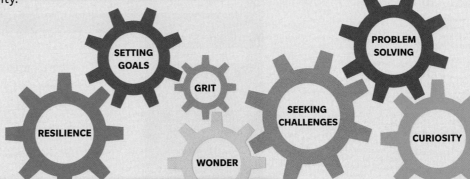

 **LEARNING MINDSET**

Seeking Challenges Explain that having a growth and learning mindset means taking risks. That involves trying new things and not being afraid to fail (or look silly) in front of friends. Emphasize that trying hard is important, but trying things that are hard is just as important. The brain needs to be stretched and challenged in much the same way as muscles do, and that's the way to think about difficult tasks, as challenges.

Build a Culture of Professional Growth

Embedded and on-going Professional Learning empowers you to develop high-impact learning experiences that provide all students with opportunities for reading and writing success.

Build agency with purposeful, embedded teacher support and high-impact strategies

- Notice & Note Strategies for Close Reading
- Classroom Videos
- On-Demand Professional Learning Modules

Grow Your Practice with Personalized Blended Professional Learning

- **Getting Started Course and Professional Learning Guide:** Learn the program components, pedagogy, and digital resources to successfully teach with *Into Literature*.

- **Follow-Up:** Choose from relevant instructional topics to create a personalized in-person or online Follow-Up experience to deepen program mastery and enhance teaching practices.

- **Coaching and Modeling:** Experience just-in-time support to ensure continuous professional learning that is student-centered and grounded in data.

- **askHMH:** Get on-demand access to program experts who will answer questions and provide personalized conferencing and digital demonstrations to support implementation.

- **Technical Services:** Plan, prepare, implement, and operate technology with ease.

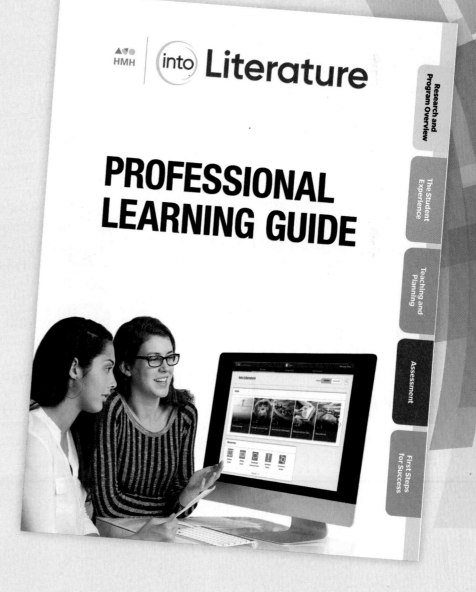

Annotated Student Edition Table of Contents

UNIT (1)

FINDING COURAGE

PAGE 1

Topical Focus
Each unit reflects a topic linking
selections, an Essential Question, a
quotation, and unit tasks for analysis,
discussion, synthesis, and response.

? **ESSENTIAL
QUESTION**

How do you
find courage in
the face of fear?

Essential Question
Posing thought-provoking ideas
for discussion and reflection
as students read, the Essential
Question stimulates analysis and
synthesis, leading to a richer
understanding of the unit's texts.

ANALYZE & APPLY

COLLABORATE & COMPARE

Additional Novel Connections

• **Wringer**
by Jerry Spinelli

• **Dragonwings**
by Laurence Yep

Key Learning Objectives

In abbreviated form, each unit's main instructional goals are listed for planning and quick reference.

Key Learning Objectives

• Analyze character and plot
• Analyze setting
• Analyze speaker
• Analyze refrain
• Cite evidence

• Analyze structure
• Analyze digital texts
• Make predictions
• Make inferences

 Visit the Interactive Student Edition for:

• Unit and Selection Videos
• Media Selections
• Selection Audio Recordings
• Enhanced Digital Instruction

© Houghton Mifflin Harcourt Publishing Company • Image Credits (t to b): ©Lightspring/Shutterstock; ©Photodisc/Getty Images; ©Barrett Hedges/Getty Images; ©Jeff Gross/Getty Images; ©Joseph Becker/Fotolia

UNIT ②
THROUGH AN ANIMAL'S EYES
PAGE 90

? ESSENTIAL QUESTION

What can you learn by seeing the world through an animal's eyes?

Analyze & Apply
This section of the Table of Contents groups a variety of selections for analysis, annotation, and application of the Notice & Note protocol, as well as standards instruction.

Collaborate & Compare
This section of the Table of Contents provides a comparative analysis of two selections linked by topic but different in genre, craft, or focus. Standards instruction and annotation are also applied.

FM8   Grade 6

Independent Reading

Interactive digital texts linked to the unit topic and in a wide range of genres and Lexile levels provide additional resources for students' independent reading, expanding student choice and experience.

Suggested Novel Connection

NOVEL
Black Beauty
by Anna Sewell

Additional Novel Connections

- **Old Yeller**
  by Fred Gipson

- **Julie of the Wolves**
  by Jean Craighead George

Key Learning Objectives
- Analyze point of view
- Analyze voice
- Infer theme
- Analyze text structure
- Determine key ideas
- Analyze imagery
- Analyze arguments

Online **Visit the Interactive Student Edition for:**
- Unit and Selection Videos
- Media Selections
- Selection Audio Recordings
- Enhanced Digital Instruction

Contents   FM9

UNIT ③

SURVIVING THE UNTHINKABLE
PAGE 170

? ***ESSENTIAL
QUESTION***

What does it take
to be a survivor?

Notice & Note Reading Model
Using a gradual release model to teach
the signposts referred to as Notice & Note,
the Reading Model describes two to three
signposts and illustrates them in a selection.

ANALYZE & APPLY

NOTICE & NOTE
READING MODEL

NOVEL
from **A Long Walk to Water** 174
by Linda Sue Park

DOCUMENTARY
Salva's Story 188
by POVRoseMedia

MEMOIR   MENTOR TEXT
Into the Lifeboat
from **Titanic Survivor** 192
by Violet Jessop

COLLABORATE & COMPARE

COMPARE
ACROSS GENRES

POEM
from **After the Hurricane** 206
by Rita Williams-Garcia

NOVEL
from **Ninth Ward** 220
by Jewell Parker Rhodes

Mentor Text
This selection exemplifies genre
characteristics and craft choices that
will be used in end-of-unit writing
tasks as models for students.

Additional Novel Connections

• **Life As We Knew It**
  by Susan Beth Pfeffer

• **The Clay Marble**
  by Minfong Ho

Key Learning Objectives
• Analyze setting
• Analyze character
• Analyze digital texts
• Explain author's purpose
• Analyze structure and meter
• Describe use of figurative language
• Analyze language

 Visit the Interactive Student Edition for:

• Unit and Selection Videos
• Media Selections
• Selection Audio Recordings
• Enhanced Digital Instruction

© Houghton Mifflin Harcourt Publishing Company • Image Credits (t to b): ©Lane Oatey/Corbis; ©Johan Dalstrom/Shutterstock; ©ewg3D/Getty Images; ©Corbis; ©S. Schwerdtfeger/Tierfotoagentur/Alamy; ©Doug Menuez/Photodisc/Getty Images

UNIT

DISCOVERING YOUR VOICE

PAGE 244

? **ESSENTIAL
QUESTION**

What are the ways
you can make yourself
heard?

Variety of Genres

Each unit is comprised of different kinds of
texts or genres. Essential characteristics of
each genre are identified and illustrated.
Students then apply those characteristics
to their own writing.

ANALYZE & APPLY

COLLABORATE & COMPARE

FM12   Grade 6

Tasks
Each unit concludes with one or two culminating tasks that demonstrate essential understandings, synthesizing ideas and text references in oral and written responses.

Additional Novel Connections

• **Beethoven In Paradise**
  by Barbara O'Connor

• **Amos Fortune, Free Man**
  by Elizabeth Yates

 © Houghton Mifflin Harcourt Publishing Company • Image Credits (t to b): ©Bundy Susan/EyeEm/Getty Images; ©Ondrej Prosicky/Shutterstock; ©Houghton Mifflin Harcourt; ©nienora/Shutterstock; ©Gina Easley/Stockimo/Alamy; ©PhotoAlto/Getty Images

Key Learning Objectives
• Analyze multimodal texts
• Analyze text structure
• Analyze purpose
• Make inferences
• Analyze figurative language
• Make connections
• Analyze rhetorical devices
• Identify audience

 Visit the Interactive Student Edition for:

• Unit and Selection Videos
• Media Selections
• Selection Audio Recordings
• Enhanced Digital Instruction

UNIT (5)
NEVER GIVE UP
PAGE 330

? ***ESSENTIAL
QUESTION***

What keeps people
from giving up?

ANALYZE & APPLY

COLLABORATE & COMPARE

INDEPENDENT READING 406

These selections can be accessed through the digital edition.

Suggested Novel Connection

 NOVEL
The Outsiders
by S. E. Hinton

> **Suggested Novel Connection**
> One extended text is recommended for its topical and thematic connection to other texts in the unit.

Additional Novel Connections

- **Across Five Aprils**
  by Irene Hunt

- **The Fighting Ground**
  by Avi

Key Learning Objectives

- Analyze text features
- Generate questions
- Analyze plot
- Analyze setting
- Analyze structure
- Make inferences about theme
- Analyze multimodal texts
- Determine key ideas

 Visit the Interactive Student Edition for:

- Unit and Selection Videos
- Media Selections
- Selection Audio Recordings
- Enhanced Digital Instruction

UNIT ⑥

HIDDEN TRUTHS

PAGE 418

? ESSENTIAL QUESTION

What hidden truths about people and the world are revealed in stories?

ANALYZE & APPLY

COLLABORATE & COMPARE

Additional Novel Connections

• **Black Ships Before**
by Rosemary Sutcliff

• **The Hobbit**
by J.R.R. Tolkien

Reflection
Students may pause and reflect on their process and understanding of the selections and the themes in each unit.

Key Learning Objectives
- Analyze informational text structures
- Make inferences about ideas
- Analyze character development in drama
- Analyze structure in poetry

- Make connections
- Analyze plot
- Identify point of view
- Infer theme
- Analyze purpose

Online Ed **Visit the Interactive Student Edition for:**

- Unit and Selection Videos
- Media Selections
- Selection Audio Recordings
- Enhanced Digital Instruction

© Houghton Mifflin Harcourt Publishing Company • Image Credits (t to b): ©SGV Photography/Moment/Getty Images; ©James Sparshatt/Media Bakery

SELECTIONS BY GENRE

HMH
Into Literature Dashboard

Easy to use and personalized for your learning.

Monitor your progress in the course.

Review your assignments and check your progress.

Quickly access content and search program resources.

Into Literature

View by **CONTENT** **STANDARDS**

Discover | Assignments | Data & Reports

Class 1 ⌄ | Welcome, Oliver ⌄

Units

Unit 1 — Finding Courage
Unit 2 — Through an Animal's Eyes
Unit 3 — Surviving the Unthinkable
Unit 4 — Discovering Your Voice
Unit 5 — Never Give Up

Resources

Reading Studio | Writing Studio | Speaking & Listening Studio | Grammar Studio | Vocabulary Studio

Show All ⌄

Explore Online to Experience the Power of HMH Into Literature

All in One Place

Readings and assignments are supported by a variety of resources to bring literature to life and give you the tools you need to succeed.

Supporting 21st Century Skills

Whether you're working alone or collaborating with others, it takes effort to analyze the complex texts and competing ideas that bombard us in this fast-paced world. What will help you succeed? Staying engaged and organized. The digital tools in this program will help you take charge of your learning.

Ignite Your Investigation

You learn best when you're engaged. The **Stream to Start** videos at the beginning of every unit are designed to spark your interest before you read. Get curious and start reading!

Learn How to Close Read

Close reading effectively is all about examining the details. See how it's done by watching the **Close Read Screencasts** in your eBook. Hear modeled conversations on targeted passages.

Bring the Meaning into Focus

Text in Focus videos dig deeper into complex texts by offering visual explanations for potential stumbling blocks.

Personalized Annotations

My Notes encourages you to take notes as you read and allows you to mark the text in your own customized way. You can easily access annotations to review later as you prepare for exams.

Interactive Graphic Organizers

Graphic organizers help you process, summarize, and keep track of your learning and prepare for end-of-unit writing tasks. **Word Networks** help you learn academic vocabulary, and **Response Logs** help you explore and deepen your understanding of the **Essential Question** in each unit.

No Wi-Fi? No problem!

With HMH *Into Literature,* you always have access: download when you're online and access what you need when you're offline. Work offline and then upload when you're back online.

Communicate "Raise a Hand" to ask or answer questions without having to be in the same room as your teacher.

Collaborate Collaborate with your teacher via chat and work with a classmate to improve your writing.

FM21

HMH

Into Literature

STUDIOS

All the help you need to be successful in your literature class is one click away with the Studios. These digital-only lessons are here to tap into the skills that you already use and help you sharpen those skills for the future.

WRITING STUDIO

Ways to Organize Reasons and Evidence

Every argument must include reasons and evidence to support a claim. There are several effective ways you can organize that support. Check out some of those ways here.

Read the following techniques that will help you achieve cohesion, or coherence, in your writing.

Order of Importance

Least to most important

Claim: Homewood must switch from a volunteer fire department to a full-time fire department.

- Reason 1: The town is growing and getting more calls during they day when volunteers are at their full-time jobs
- Reason 2: Full-time firefighters can train daily instead of once a month, giving them more time to improve firefighting skills.

Online Ed your brand in learning

Easy-to-find resources, organized in five separate STUDIOS. On demand and on ED!

Look for links in each lesson to take you to the appropriate Studio.

READING STUDIO

Go beyond the book with the Reading Studio. With over 100 full-length downloadable titles to choose from, find the right story to continue your journey.

WRITING STUDIO

Being able to write clearly and effectively is a skill that will help you throughout life. The Writing Studio will help you become an expert communicator—in print or online.

SPEAKING & LISTENING STUDIO

Communication is more than just writing. The Speaking & Listening Studio will help you become an effective speaker and a focused listener.

GRAMMAR STUDIO

Go beyond traditional worksheets with the Grammar Studio. These engaging, interactive lessons will sharpen your grammar skills.

VOCABULARY STUDIO

Learn the skills you need to expand your vocabulary. The interactive lessons in the Vocabulary Studio will grow your vocabulary to improve your reading.

An ABSOLUTELY, **POSITIVELY,** MUST READ
ESSAY in the FRONT of your Literature Book

YOUR TEACHER AGREES!

BY TWO PEOPLE YOU HAVE NEVER HEARD OF
Dr. Kylene Beers and Dr. Robert E. Probst

If you are reading this essay when we think you are, it's early in the school year. You have this big book in front of you and, for some reason, your teacher has asked you to read these pages by two people you've never met.

Let's begin by telling you something about us.

From Dr. Beers:

I've been a teacher all my adult life. I've worked with students at all grades and now I spend most of my time working with teachers, maybe even your teacher! I live in Texas and when I'm not on an airplane flying off to work in a school, I'm on my ranch, plowing a field. I like to read, cook, read, garden, read, spend time with my family and friends, and (did I mention?) read!

who are these people ? ? ?

From Dr. Probst:

I've also been a teacher all my adult life. When I first started teaching, I taught kids in middle school and high school, and then I spent most of my career teaching people how to be teachers. For many years now, Dr. Beers and I have written books together, books that are about teaching kids how to be better readers. I live in Florida and when I'm not in schools working with teachers and kids, I enjoy watching my grandkids play soccer and baseball and I love going out on my boat. And, like Dr. Beers, I love reading a great book, too.

So, we're teachers. And we're writers. Specifically, we write books for teachers, books teachers read so that they can help their students become better readers...

. . . and we're going to try to help you become a better reader this year.

We will because we both believe TWO things.

First, we've never met a kid who didn't want to get better at reading. Reading is important for almost everything you do, so doing it well is important.

Second, we believe that reading can change you. Reading something can open up your mind, your thinking, your ideas, your understanding of the world and all the people in it, so that you might choose to change yourself. Reading can help you change yourself.

We think too often it's easy to forget why reading is important. You can come to believe that you need to read better just so your grades will go up, or you need to read better so that you do well on a big state test. Those things are important—you bet—but they aren't as important as reading better so that you can become better. Yes, reading can help you change.

How would that happen—how can reading help you change yourself? Sometimes it is obvious. You read something about the importance of exercise and you start walking a little more.

Or, you read something about energy and the environment and you decide to make sure you always turn off the lights when you leave any room.

Other times, it might be less obvious. You might read *Wonder* and begin to think about what it really means to be a good friend. Maybe you walk over to that person sitting alone in the cafeteria and sit with him or her. Perhaps you'll read *Stella by Starlight* and that book helps you become someone who stands against racism. Or maybe it happens as you read *Mexican Whiteboy* and discover that who you are is more about what you are on the inside than what anyone ever sees on the outside. And when you realize that,

Note that Beers and Probst list some of the standard reasons students want to be better readers: improve grades and enhance standardized test performance. But they add that reading "can help you change yourself."

Ask students to use their consumable book's margins to complete a quick write answering this question:

How has reading led to personal change for you?

Encourage students to be specific.

Ask at least three to five students to share with the group.

FM25

perhaps it will give you the courage you need to be truer to yourself, to be the person you really want to be.

Reading gives us moments to think, and as we think we just might discover something about ourselves that we want to change. And that's why we say reading can help us change ourselves.

Finding Important Messages

It sure would be easy to find important messages in the things we read if the authors would just label them and then maybe give us a call.

The reality is, though, that would make the reading less interesting. And it would mean that every reader is supposed to find the same message. Not true! While the author has a message he or she wants to share, the reader—that's you!—has at least three jobs to do:

My Job

1 → **First**, enjoy what you are reading.

2 → **Second,** figure out the message the author wanted to share. Authors write for a reason (no, not to make a lot of money!), and part of that reason is to share something important. That's the author's message, and this year we'll be showing you some ways to really focus in on that.

3 → **Third,** you need to figure out the message that matters most to **YOU.** (YES, WE SAVED THE BEST FOR LAST!!!) Sometimes the author's message and what matters most to you will be the same; sometimes not. For instance, it's obvious that J.K. Rowling wrote the Harry Potter series to show us all the sustaining power of love.

From Dr. Beers:

" But when I read these books, what really touched my heart was the importance of standing up to our fears. "

From Dr. Probst:

" And what mattered most to me was the idea that one person, one small person, can make a huge difference in the world. I think that's a critically important point. "

Discuss with students the three "jobs" as readers that Beers and Probst suggest.

"Hello! I wanted to discuss the Important Message with you!"

Understanding the author's message requires you to do some work while you read, work that requires you to read the text closely. No. You don't need a magnifying glass. But you do need to learn how to notice some things in the text we call SIGNPOSTS.

A signpost is simply something the author says in the text that helps you understand how characters are changing, how conflicts are being resolved, and, ultimately, what theme—or lesson—the author is trying to convey.

You can also use signposts to help you figure out the author's purpose when you are reading nonfiction. If you can identify the author's purpose—why she or he wrote that particular piece of nonfiction—then you'll be better able to decide whether or not you agree, and whether you need more information.

We do want you thinking about signposts, but first, as you read, we want you to remember three letters: BHH.

B	Book	As you read, we want you to remember that you have to pay attention to what's in the book (or article).
H	Head	And, you need to think about what you are reading as you read—so you have to think about what's in your head.
H	Heart	And sometimes, maybe as you finish what you're reading, you'll ask yourself what you have taken to heart.

To think carefully about what's in the book and what's in your head, you need to become an alert reader, one who notices things. If you're reading fiction, for instance, you ought to pay attention to how characters act. When a character starts acting in a way you don't expect, something is up! That's as if the author has put up a blinking sign that says "Pay attention here!" Or, if you are reading nonfiction, and the author starts using a lot of numbers, that's the same as the author waving a huge flag that says "Slow down! Pay attention! I'm trying to show you something!"

How do I find the author's message?

So, as I read, I have to think about something called signposts?

Pay attention HERE!

Beers and Probst introduce the concept of **signposts,** which will be used throughout *Into Literature.* Ask students to underline this definition in their copy.

Ask students why the term *signpost,* which is used in other contexts, is also a good one for reading. ***Possible answer:*** *Writers give us direction, clues, and insight with their words just as drivers are given vital information with stop signs, yield signs, and school zone warnings.*

Ask students to bracket in their consumable book the reference to "BHH." Review each item. Provide an example and ask students for additional examples.

Example:

B I read an article in the local newspaper discussing five ways to get involved in my community. One suggestion was to begin volunteering.

H I thought about my personal interests: teaching, animals, and the environment.

H I decided to sign up for a volunteers' orientation at the local animal shelter.

FM27

Read aloud the four signposts listed here as examples. Explain that these are only four of the signposts they will be learning while using *Into Literature*. Refer students to the entire list of signposts on Student Edition page FM 29. Ask them to mark this page with a sticky note for easy reference.

Review the "keep reading" challenge. Ask students to discuss if this challenge is one they can accept.

Direct students to complete a three -minute quick write in the margin of their book responding to the quote:

"... reading is something that can help you become the person you most want to be."

Ask a few volunteers to share.

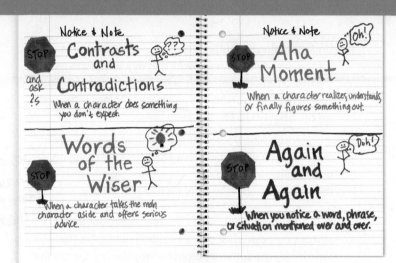

Don't worry about memorizing all the signposts. You'll learn them this year. Your teacher will probably have you make some notes—perhaps as the student above did.

Some of the things you'll read this year, you might not like. (OK—just being honest!) But most of the things we bet you will. What we hope you'll do, throughout this year, is keep reading.

Keep Reading

» Read every day.
» Read something hard.
» Read something easy.
» Read something you choose.
» Read what your teachers ask you to read.
» Read something that makes you laugh.
» And it's OK if sometimes what you read makes you cry.

One of us LOVES to read scary books while the other much prefers survival books, so don't worry if you like something your best friend doesn't. Read joke books and how-to books and love stories and mysteries and absolutely be sure you read about people who aren't like you. That's the best way to learn about the world around you, about other people, about other ways of thinking. The best way to become a more open person is to live for a while, in the pages of a book, the life of someone you are not.

We hope you have a great year. Stay alert for signposts that you'll be learning throughout this book.

And remember . . .

. . . reading is something that can help you become the person you most want to be.

NOTICE & NOTE SIGNPOSTS

Signpost	Definition	Anchor Question(s)
FICTION		
Contrasts and Contradictions	A sharp contrast between what we would expect and what we observe the character doing; behavior that contradicts previous behavior or well-established patterns	Why would the character act (feel) this way?
Aha Moment	A character's realization of something that shifts his actions or understanding of himself, others, or the world around him	How might this change things?
Tough Questions	Questions a character raises that reveal his or her inner struggles	What does this question make me wonder about?
Words of the Wiser	The advice or insight about life that a wiser character, who is usually older, offers to the main character	What is the life lesson, and how might this affect the character?
Again and Again	Events, images, or particular words that recur over a portion of the story	Why might the author bring this up again and again?
Memory Moment	A recollection by a character that interrupts the forward progress of the story	Why might this memory be important?
NONFICTION		
Contrasts and Contradictions	A sharp contrast between what we would expect and what we observe happening. A difference between two or more elements in the text.	What is the difference, and why does it matter?
Extreme or Absolute Language	Language that leaves no doubt about a situation or an event, allows no compromise, or seems to exaggerate or overstate a case.	Why did the author use this language?
Numbers and Stats	Specific quantities or comparisons to depict the amount, size, or scale. Or, the writer is vague and imprecise about numbers when we would expect more precision.	Why did the author use these numbers or amounts?
Quoted Words	Opinions or conclusions of someone who is an expert on the subject, or someone who might be a participant in or a witness to an event. Or, the author might cite other people to provide support for a point.	Why was this person quoted or cited, and what did this add?
Word Gaps	Vocabulary that is unfamiliar to the reader—for example, a word with multiple meanings, a rare or technical word, a discipline-specific word, or one with a far-removed antecedent.	Do I know this word from someplace else? Does it seem like technical talk for this topic? Can I find clues in the sentence to help me understand the word?

FM29

Read the chart on this page noting that it is divided into **Fiction** and **Nonfiction** signposts and includes a definition and an anchor question for each. An **anchor question** helps students identify the signposts as they read by "questioning" the text.

READING AND WRITING ACROSS GENRES

by Carol Jago

Reading is a first-class ticket around the world. Not only can you explore other lands and cultures, but you can also travel to the past and future. That journey is sometimes a wild ride. Other books can feel like comfort food, enveloping you in an imaginative landscape full of friends and good times. Making time for reading is making time for life.

Genre

One of the first things readers do when we pick up something to read is notice its genre. You might not think of it exactly in those terms, but consider how you approach a word problem in math class compared to how you read a science fiction story. Readers go to different kinds of text for different purposes. When you need to know how to do or make something, you want a reliable, trusted source of information. When you're in the mood to spend some time in a world of fantasy, you happily suspend your normal disbelief in dragons.

In every unit of *Into Literature,* you'll find a diverse mix of genres all connected by a common theme, allowing you to explore a topic from many different angles.

GENRE: INFORMATIONAL TEXT

GENRE: SHORT STORY

GENRE: HISTORICAL FICTION

GENRE: POETRY

Writer's Craft

Learning how writers use genre to inform, to explain, to entertain, or to surprise readers will help you better understand—as well as enjoy—your reading. Imitating how professional writers employ the tools of their craft—descriptive language, repetition, sensory images, sentence structure, and a variety of other features—will give you many ideas for making your own writing more lively.

Into Literature provides you with the tools you need to understand the elements of all the critical genres and advice on how to learn from professional texts to improve your own writing in those genres.

> **GENRE ELEMENTS: SHORT STORY**
> - is a work of short fiction that centers on a single idea and can be read in one sitting
> - usually includes one main conflict that involves the characters and keeps moving
> - includes the basic ele of fiction—plot, chara setting, and theme
> - may be based on real and historical events

> **GENRE ELEMENTS: INFORMATIONAL TEXT**
> - provides factual information
> - includes evidence to support ideas
> - contains text features
> - includes many forms, such as news articles and essays

> **GENRE ELEMENTS: HISTORICAL FICTION**
> - includes the basic elements of fiction: setting, character, plot, conflict, and theme
> - is set in the past and includes real places and real events of historical importance
> - is a type of realistic in which fictional cl behave like real pe use human abilities with life's challenge

> **GENRE ELEMENTS: POETRY**
> - may use figurative language, including personification
> - often includes imagery that appeals to the five senses
> - expresses a theme, or a "big idea" message about life

Reading with Independence

Finding a good book can sometimes be a challenge. Like every other reader, you have probably experienced "book desert" when nothing you pick up seems to have what you are looking for (not that it's easy to explain exactly what you are looking for, but whatever it is, "this" isn't it). If you find yourself in this kind of reading funk, bored by everything you pick up, give yourself permission to range more widely, exploring graphic novels, contemporary biographies, books of poetry, historical fiction. And remember that long doesn't necessarily mean boring. My favorite kind of book is one that I never want to end.

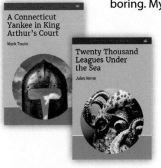

Take control over your own reading with *Into Literature's* Reader's Choice selections and the HMH Digital Library. And don't forget: your teacher, librarian, and friends can offer you many more suggestions.

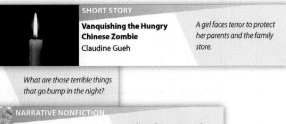

SHORT STORY
Vanquishing the Hungry Chinese Zombie
Claudine Gueh

A girl faces terror to protect her parents and the family store.

POEM
Horrors
Lewis Carroll

What are those terrible things that go bump in the night?

NARRATIVE NONFICTION
Running into Danger on an Alaskan Trail
Cinthia Ritchie

A long-distance runner has a terrifying encounter with a bear.

FM31

Direct students to read the paragraph under the heading "Writer's Craft." Ask students to write their own definition of writer's craft in the margin of *Into Literature*. Discuss.

Encourage students to find the Genre Elements feature with each selection in *Into Literature*.

Call students' attention to the **Reader's Choice** selections listed at the end of each unit and show students how to find the **HMH Digital Library** in the **Reading Studio.**

HMH | into **Literature**™

TEACHER'S EDITION

GRADE 6

Program Consultants:
Kylene Beers
Martha Hougen
Elena Izquierdo
Carol Jago
Erik Palmer
Robert E. Probst

Instructional Overview and Resources

		Instructional Focus	Online **Ed** Resources
	Unit Introduction **Finding Courage**	**Unit 1 Essential Question** **Unit 1 Academic Vocabulary**	**Stream to Start:** Finding Courage **Unit 1 Response Log**

ANALYZE & APPLY

	from The Breadwinner Novel Excerpt by Deborah Ellis **Lexile 590L** **NOTICE & NOTE** READING MODEL **Signposts** • Words of the Wiser • Aha Moment • Contrasts and Contradictions	**Reading** • Analyze How Character Develops Plot • Analyze Setting and Character **Writing:** Write a Letter **Speaking and Listening:** Give a Multimodal Presentation **Vocabulary:** Parts of Speech **Language Conventions:** Capitalization of Proper Nouns	🔊 **Audio** **Level-Up Tutorial:** Setting: Effect on Plot **Reading Studio:** Notice & Note **Writing Studio:** Writing Arguments: Formal Style **Speaking and Listening Studio:** Giving a Presentation **Grammar Studio:** Module 11: Lesson 2: Capitalizing Names of Persons and Places
	"Life Doesn't Frighten Me" Poem by Maya Angelou	**Reading** • Analyze Speaker • Analyze Refrain **Writing:** Write a Poem **Speaking and Listening:** Present a Poem	🔊 **Audio** **Reading Studio:** Notice & Note **Writing Studio:** Writing as a Process **Speaking and Listening Studio:** Giving a Presentation
	Mentor Text **"Fears and Phobias"** Article by kidshealth.org **Lexile 1080L**	**Reading** • Cite Evidence • Analyze Structure **Writing:** Write an Informative Essay **Speaking and Listening:** Discuss with a Small Group **Vocabulary:** Prefixes That Mean "Not" **Language Conventions:** Dashes	🔊 **Audio** **Video:** "Wired for Fear" **Text in Focus:** Previewing the Text **Close Read Screencasts:** Modeled Discussion **Reading Studio:** Notice & Note **Writing Studio:** Writing Informative Texts **Speaking and Listening Studio:** Participating in Collaborative Discussions **Vocabulary Studio:** Prefixes **Grammar Studio:** Modules 12 and 13: Punctuation
	"Wired for Fear" Video by The California Science Center	**Media:** Analyze Digital Text **Writing:** Write a Narrative **Speaking and Listening:** Produce a Podcast	**Writing Studio:** Writing Narratives **Speaking and Listening Studio:** Analyzing and Evaluating Presentations

SUGGESTED PACING: 30 DAYS

Unit Introduction	from The Breadwinner	Life Doesn't Frighten Me	Fears and Phobias	Wired for Fear
1	2 3 4 5 6	7 8 9	10 11 12 13 14	15 16

English Learner Support		Differentiated Instruction	Assessment
• Learn New Expressions • Learning Strategies			

English Learner Support		Differentiated Instruction	Assessment
• Text X-Ray • Track Story Elements • Use Cognates • Use Dialogue Tags • Confirm Understanding • Oral Assessment • Give a Multimodal Presentation • Review Vocabulary • Language Conventions		**When Students Struggle** • Discuss Setting and Plot	**Selection Test**
• Text X-Ray • Learning Strategies • Understand Slang		**When Students Struggle** • Make Connections **To Challenge Students** • Analyze Imagery and Line Length	**Selection Test**
• Text X-Ray • Understand Directionality • Use Cognates • Learning Strategies • Understand Language Structures • Understand Contrasts • Confirm Understanding • Oral Assessment	• Discuss with a Small Group • Vocabulary Strategy • Language Conventions	**When Students Struggle** • Compare and Contrast	**Selection Test**
• Text X-Ray • Analyze Digital Text • Understand Idioms	• Oral Assessment • Present a Podcast	**When Students Struggle** • Analyze Media	**Selection Test**

Embarrassed? Blame Your Brain / The Ravine

Independent Reading

End of Unit

17 > 18 > 19 > 20 > 21 > 22 > 23 > 24 > 25 > 26 > 27 > 28 > 29 > 30

UNIT 1 Continued

Instructional Focus

COLLABORATE & COMPARE

"Embarrassed? Blame Your Brain"
Informational Text by Jennifer Connor-Smith
Lexile 960L

Reading
• Make Predictions
• Analyze Organizational Patterns

Writing: Write an Advertisement

Speaking and Listening: Discuss with a Small Group

Vocabulary: Synonyms and Antonyms

Language Conventions: Commas

 Audio

Reading Studio: Notice & Note

Writing Studio: Writing Informative Texts

Speaking and Listening Studio: Participating in Collaborative Discussions

Vocabulary Studio: Synonyms and Antonyms

Grammar Studio: Module 12: Lesson 3: Using Commas Before Conjunctions Separating Independent Clauses

"The Ravine"
Short Story by Graham Salisbury
Lexile 680L

Reading
• Make Inferences
• Analyze Characters and Setting

Writing: Write a Compare and Contrast Essay

Speaking and Listening: Share and Discuss

Vocabulary: Using Context Clues

Language Conventions: Subordinating Conjunctions

 Audio

Text in Focus: Visualizing

Close Read Screencasts: Modeled Discussions

Reading Studio: Notice & Note

Writing Studio: Planning and Drafting

Speaking and Listening Studio: Participating in Collaborative Discussions

Vocabulary Studio: Context Clues

Grammar Studio: Module 3: Lesson 8: Conjunctions and Interjections

Collaborate and Compare

Reading: Collaborate to Synthesize

Speaking and Listening: Research and Share

 INDEPENDENT READING

The Independent Reading selections are only available in the eBook.

Go to the Reading Studio for more information on Notice & Note.

 "Horrors"
Poem by Lewis Carroll

 "Vanquishing the Hungry Chinese Zombie"
Short Story by Claudine Gueh
Lexile 760L

END OF UNIT

Writing Task: Informative Essay

Speaking and Listening Task: Present Information

Reflect on the Unit

Writing: Write an Informative Essay

Language Conventions: Compound and Complex Sentences

Speaking and Listening: Adapt an Informative Essay for Presentation

Unit 1 Response Log

Mentor Text: "Fears and Phobias"

Writing Studio: Writing a Informative Texts

Speaking and Listening Studio: Giving a Presentation

Grammar Studio: Module 1: The Sentence

English Learner Support	Differentiated Instruction	Online Ed Assessment
• Text X-Ray • Predicting • Use Cognates • Learning Strategies • Understand Language Structures • Organizational Patterns • Oral Assessment • Discuss with a Small Group • Vocabulary Strategy • Language Conventions	**When Students Struggle** • Make Predictions	**Selection Test**
• Text X-Ray • Use Prior Knowledge • Learning Strategies • Analyze Language • Improve Reading Fluency • Recognizing Sentence Patterns • Read Closely • Confirm Understanding • Understand Character Development • Oral Assessment • Language Conventions • Write a Compare and Contrast Essay • Using Context Clues	**When Students Struggle** • Analyze Character • Analyze Setting	**Selection Test**
• Ask Questions	**When Students Struggle** • Credible and Reliable Sources	
"Running into Danger on the Alaskan Trail" Narrative Nonfiction by Cinthia Ritchie **Lexile 860L**	"Facing Your Fears: Choking Under Pressure Is Every Athlete's Worst Nightmare" Informational Text by Dana Hudepohl **Lexile 870L**	**Selection Tests**
• Language X-ray • Understand Academic Language • Write a Group Essay • Use the Mentor Text • Use Synonyms • Use Connecting Words • Adapt the Essay	**For Struggling Writers** • Draft the Essay • Use Complex Sentences • Take Notes **To Challenge Students** • Conduct Research	**Unit Test**

Connect to the
ESSENTIAL QUESTION

Ask a volunteer to read aloud the Essential Question. Discuss how the images on the page relate to the question. Why might the man need to find courage to do what he is doing? What fear might this athlete need to overcome to find courage? Ask students to think of real-life situations that create fear and require courage.

■ English Learner Support

Learn New Expressions Make sure students understand the Essential Question. If necessary, explain the following idiomatic expressions:

- *To find courage* means "to be able to act bravely."
- *In the face of fear* means "when you feel scared."

Help students restate the question in simpler language: *How can you be brave when you feel scared?*

SUBSTANTIAL/MODERATE

DISCUSS THE QUOTATION

Tell students that Nelson Mandela (1918–2013) became president of South Africa in 1994 after spending nearly two decades in prison for his work fighting racial segregation, or apartheid, in his country. Ask students to read the quotation. Then discuss the two possible definitions of courage that Mandela mentions: the absence of fear (not feeling afraid) and the triumph over fear (feeling afraid but overcoming the fear). Ask students whether they agree with Mandela's conclusion, and have them support their opinions with reasons and examples.

FINDING COURAGE

ESSENTIAL QUESTION:

How do you find courage in the face of fear?

" I learned that courage was not the absence of fear, but the triumph over it. "

Nelson Mandela

Unit 1

⚙ LEARNING MINDSET

Growth Mindset Remind students that a growth mindset means believing you can get smarter by taking on challenges and pushing yourself. Encourage students to look at every selection as an opportunity to set higher goals and stretch past their comfort zone.

ACADEMIC VOCABULARY

Academic Vocabulary words are words you use to discuss and write about texts. In this unit, you will learn and practice using five words.

 ✓ evident ☐ factor ☐ indicate ☐ similar ☐ specific

Study the Word Network to learn more about the word **evident.**

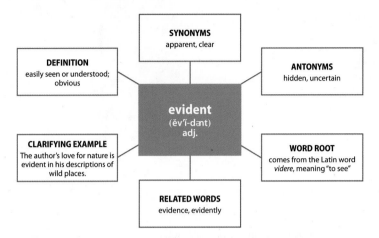

SYNONYMS
apparent, clear

DEFINITION
easily seen or understood; obvious

ANTONYMS
hidden, uncertain

evident
(ĕv´ĭ-dənt)
adj.

CLARIFYING EXAMPLE
The author's love for nature is evident in his descriptions of wild places.

WORD ROOT
comes from the Latin word *videre*, meaning "to see"

RELATED WORDS
evidence, evidently

Write and Discuss Discuss the completed Word Network with a partner, making sure to talk through all of the boxes until you both understand the word, its synonyms, antonyms, and related forms. Then, fill out Word Networks for the remaining four words. Use a dictionary or online resource to help you complete the activity.

 Go online to access the Word Networks.

RESPOND TO THE ESSENTIAL QUESTION

In this unit, you will explore how different people find courage in the face of many kinds of fear. As you read, you will revisit the **Essential Question** and gather your ideas about it in the **Response Log** that appears on page R1. At the end of the unit, you will write an **informational essay** about how people find the courage to face their fears. You will also give a presentation. Filling out the Response Log will help you prepare for these tasks.

UNIT 1 RESPONSE LOG

Use the Response Log to record your ideas about how each of the texts in Unit 1 relates to or comments on the **Essential Question.**

? **Essential Question:** How do you find courage in the face of fear?

from The Breadwinner	
Life Doesn't Frighten Me	
Fears and Phobias	
Wired for Fear	
Embarrassed? Blame Your Brain	
The Ravine	

 You can also go online to access the Response Log.

ACADEMIC VOCABULARY

As students complete Word Networks for the remaining four vocabulary words, encourage them to include all the categories shown in the completed network if possible, but point out that some words do not have clear synonyms or antonyms. Some words may also function as different parts of speech—for example, *factor* may be a noun or a verb.

evident (ĕv´ĭ-dənt) *adj.* Easily seen or understood; obvious. (Spanish cognate: *evídente*)

factor (făk´tər) *n.* Someone or something that has an effect on an event, a process, or a situation. (Spanish cognate: *factor*)

indicate (ĭn´dĭ-kāt´) *tr.v.* To point out, to serve as a sign or symbol of something. (Spanish cognate: *indicar*)

similar (sĭm´ə-lər) *adj.* Alike in appearance or nature, though not identical; having features that are the same. (Spanish cognate: *similar*)

specific (spĭ-sĭf´ĭk) *adj.* Clearly defined or identified. (Spanish cognate: *específico*)

RESPOND TO THE ESSENTIAL QUESTION

Direct students to the Unit 1 Response Log. Explain that students will use it to record ideas and details from the selections that help answer the Essential Question. When they work on the writing task at the end of the unit, their Response Logs will help them think about what they have read and make connections between texts.

ENGLISH LEARNER SUPPORT

Learning Strategies Use this strategy to help students learn how to take notes as they read or discuss a text.

- Before reading a selection, provide students with a graphic organizer they can use for notetaking, such as a story map, character chart, or main idea chart. Explain the purpose of each section of the organizer.
- Display a passage from the text, and ask students to take notes in the graphic organizer.

- Have students gather in small groups to compare and discuss their graphic organizers. Tell them that their task is to reach agreement about which notes are the most accurate, significant, and useful.
- Distribute a blank copy of the graphic organizer to each group, and have students complete it together with the notes they agreed upon. Have representatives from each group present their organizers to the class. **ALL LEVELS**

READING MODEL

from THE BREADWINNER

Novel Excerpt by Deborah Ellis

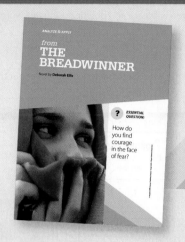

GENRE ELEMENTS
HISTORICAL FICTION

Tell students that **historical fiction** is realistic fiction that is set in the past and includes real places and real events of historical importance. Details about the way people lived in other times and cultures are included. Explain that **historical fiction** includes the basic elements of fiction—setting, character, plot, conflict, and theme. It is a type of realistic fiction, which means fictional characters behave like real people and use real human abilities. In this lesson, students will examine the elements of historical fiction as they read an excerpt from the novel *The Breadwinner*.

LEARNING OBJECTIVES

- Analyze how character develops plot.
- Analyze setting and character.
- Conduct research about humanitarian aid organizations.
- Write a letter to a humanitarian aid organization.
- Determine the parts of speech of words, and use the part of speech and context to help figure out a word's meaning.
- Give a multimodal presentation to accompany research.
- Use correct capitalization of proper nouns.
- **Language** Discuss the text using the key term *plot*.

TEXT COMPLEXITY

Quantitative Measures	**The Breadwinner**	Lexile: 590L
Qualitative Measures	**Ideas Presented** Much is explicit, but some implied meaning. Requires some inferential reasoning.	
	Structures Used Clear, chronological, conventional.	
	Language Used Mostly explicit, some figurative/allusive language or dialect/unconventional language.	
	Knowledge Required Some references to cultural and historical ideas and reliance on background knowledge.	

Online

RESOURCES

- Unit 1 Response Log
- Selection Audio
- Reading Studio: Notice & Note
- Level Up Tutorial:
  Setting: Effect on Plot
- Writing Studio: Writing Arguments
- Speaking and Listening Studio:
  Giving a Presentation
- Vocabulary Studio: Using Resources
- Grammar Studio: Module 11:
  Lesson 2: Capitalizing Names of
  Persons and Places
- *The Breadwinner* Selection Test

SUMMARIES

English

Eleven-year-old Parvana and her family are living in Kabul, the capital of Afghanistan, in the late 1990s. They live under the strict control of a group called the Taliban, which does not allow girls to go to school. Girls are not allowed to shop in stores, either. In order to get needed supplies, Parvana's family must cut her hair and dress her like a boy so she can go to the stores.

Spanish

Parvana tiene once años y vive con su familia en Kabul, la capital de Afganistán, a finales de la década de los noventa. Viven bajo el estricto control de un grupo llamado Talibán, que no permite que las niñas vayan a la escuela. A las niñas tampoco las aceptan dentro de tiendas o almacenes. Para poder obtener suministros, la familia de Parvana debe cortarle el cabello y vestirla como a un niño, para que la dejen entrar a las tiendas.

SMALL-GROUP OPTIONS

Have students work in small groups to read and discuss the selection.

Pinwheel Discussion

- Divide students into groups of six, with three students seated facing in, and three students seated facing out.
- Provide a question about the selection. Have students discuss the question with the student facing them for a designated amount of time, for example, 10 minutes.
- Tell students in the inner circle to remain stationary while the students in the outer circle rotate to their right. Provide students with a new discussion question.
- Continue to have students rotate until they have had a turn with all three students.

Three-Minute Review

- Pause at any time while reading or discussing the selection.
- Set a timer for three minutes, and have students work with a partner to reread a specific section of the text or answer a question.
- After three minutes, ask pairs to share what they noticed in their review. What new information did they learn?

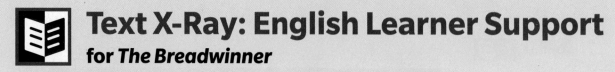

Text X-Ray: English Learner Support
for *The Breadwinner*

Use the Text X-Ray and the supports and scaffolds in the Teacher's Edition to help guide students at different proficiency levels through the selection.

INTRODUCE THE SELECTION
DISCUSS ELEMENTS OF FICTION

In this lesson, students will need to identify the elements of character, plot, and setting to analyze how the story relates to finding courage in the face of fear. Review how a *character* is a person or animal in a story, the *plot* of a story is the events that happen in it, and the *setting* of a story is the time and place where it happens. Have students discuss familiar stories using the following sentence frames:

- *In the story, the characters _____ .*
- *The plot of the story starts with _____ . At the end, _____.*
- *The setting of the story _____.*

CULTURAL REFERENCES

In *The Breadwinner*, Parvana and her family live in Afghanistan, so much of the culture may be unfamiliar to students. Review the following words or phrases:

- *Jalalabad* (paragraph 4): a city in eastern Afghanistan
- *Taliban* (paragraph 8): very strict political group waging war in Afghanistan
- *give in* (paragraph 11): agree to
- *sulk* (paragraph 36): cry and complain
- *hesitated* (paragraph 65): to pause for a minute because of fear

LISTENING

Understand Elements of Fiction

Remind students that they will need to identify the characters, setting, and plot in *The Breadwinner*. Tell them to be thinking about each element as they listen to you read. Before you begin to read the story, read aloud the Background section at the top of page 7.

Have students listen as you read aloud paragraphs 1–5. Use the following supports with students at varying proficiency levels:

- Have students listen as you summarize the passage, then nod if the summary is correct: *Parvana and her family live in Afghanistan. There are no boys or men left in her house, but girls cannot go to stores. Parvana's mom plans to dress her like a boy so she can get food for her family.* **SUBSTANTIAL**
- After students listen to the summary above, have them complete the following sentence frames to demonstrate listening comprehension: *Parvana's family wants to dress her like a _____. They are making her look like a boy because girls aren't allowed at the _____.* **MODERATE**
- After listening to you read, have pairs work together to restate the events in the summary. **LIGHT**

SPEAKING

Discuss Plot

Review the meaning of the word *plot*. Have students discuss the first event in the plot of this excerpt from *The Breadwinner*. Circulate around the room to make sure students are using the key term *plot* correctly.

Use the following supports with students at varying proficiency levels:

- Display and read aloud these sentences: *The plot is what happens in a story. The first event in the plot is Parvana's family telling her they will dress her like a boy.* Have students say the sentences aloud to you and then practice saying them to a partner. **SUBSTANTIAL**
- To help students express their ideas about plot, give them the following sentence frames: *The plot of a story is ____. The first event in the plot of this story is ____.* **MODERATE**
- Have student pairs discuss with each other the meaning of the word *plot* and what the first event in the plot of this story is. **LIGHT**

READING

Analyze Setting

Tell students that setting affects a character's feelings, thoughts, and behaviors. Remind them that the setting of this story is Kabul, Afghanistan, in the late 1990s.

Work with students to read paragraphs 42–44. Use the following supports with students at varying proficiency levels:

- Ask: *What are two things Parvana is not allowed to do in Afghanistan? How would she feel about that?* Accept single words or phrases. **SUBSTANTIAL**
- Guide students to identify the effect that living in Afghanistan has on Parvana. Supply sentence frames such as: *Parvana is not allowed to ____ or ____. She probably feels ____.* **MODERATE**
- Have student pairs work together to identify the effect that the setting might have on the characters. Supply sentence frames such as: *I think living in Afghanistan might make Parvana feel ____ and act ____. I think this because ____.* **LIGHT**

WRITING

Write a Letter

Work with students to read the writing assignment on page 17.

Use the following supports with students at varying proficiency levels:

- Work with students to craft a short letter together. Have students copy the letter in their notebooks. **SUBSTANTIAL**
- Provide a basic outline with the elements of a letter. Include sentence frames such as: *I am interested in ____. Please send me ____.* **MODERATE**
- Provide a sample letter with the elements of a letter clearly labeled. Give students a checklist to make sure they included all the required elements. **LIGHT**

Notice & Note

EXPLAIN THE SIGNPOSTS

Explain that **NOTICE & NOTE Signposts** are significant moments in the text that help readers understand and analyze works of fiction or nonfiction. Use the instruction on these pages to introduce students to the signposts **Words of the Wiser, Aha Moments,** and **Contrasts and Contradictions.** Then use the selection that follows to have students apply the signposts to a text.

For a full list of the fiction and nonfiction signposts, see p. 78.

▶ WORDS OF THE WISER

Explain that **Words of the Wiser** happens when a wise character in a story gives advice. Often this character is older than the person he or she is advising.

Read aloud the example passage and pause at the sentence "'As a boy, you'll be able to move in and out of the market, buy what we need, and no one will stop you,' Mother said." Model for students how to determine that the passage incudes Words of the Wiser. Point out that an older character, Mother, is talking to a younger character, Parvana. She is offering insight into the family's current situation and hinting at the **plot** of the story.

Tell students that when they spot Words of the Wiser, they should pause, mark it in their consumable texts, and ask the anchor question: *What's the lesson for the character?*

For more information on these and other signposts to Notice & Note, visit the **Reading Studio.**

When you read a scene between a main character and someone older or more experienced, pause to see if it's a **Words of the Wiser** signpost.

Anchor Question
When you notice this signpost, ask: What's the lesson for the character?

from THE BREADWINNER

You are about to read an excerpt from the novel *The Breadwinner*. In it, you will notice and note signposts that offer clues about the novel's setting and characters. Here are three key signposts to look for as you read this excerpt and other works of fiction.

▶ **Words of the Wiser** It can be easy to give advice, but much harder to take it. How do you feel when someone—especially someone older than you—makes a suggestion? Do you listen to the advice of the older or more experienced people in your life?

When a wise character in a work of fiction offers advice or a solution to a problem, it's worth listening. As a reader, paying attention to **Words of the Wiser** can:

- offer insight into the current dilemma or situation
- help you make predictions about what happens next
- reveal more about the main character
- hint at the theme or lesson of the story

In this example from *The Breadwinner*, a student has marked some Words of the Wiser spoken to a girl named Parvana:

1	They were going to turn her into a boy.
2	"As a boy, you'll be able to move in and out of the market, buy what we need, and no one will stop you," Mother said.
3	"It's a perfect solution," Mrs. Weera said.
4	"You'll be our cousin from Jalalabad," Nooria said, "come to stay with us while our father is away."

What solution to a problem is introduced?	To be able to shop in the market and buy things for her family, Parvana can pretend to be a boy.
Why do you think this advice is important to the story?	Even though it will be hard for Parvana to pretend to be a boy, she may learn some important lessons.

Aha Moment Have you ever looked in the mirror and been surprised at how totally different you look with a new hairstyle or new glasses? An **Aha Moment** is when you realize something that changes your understanding of yourself, others, or the world around you. In a story, Aha Moments allow characters the chance to reexamine themselves and their world. A character experiencing an **Aha Moment** may:

- change the way she feels about herself or others
- take a step toward solving a problem or reach a new understanding

Here's an example of a student finding and marking an Aha Moment in *The Breadwinner*:

> 7   "But no one will ask about you."
>
> 8   At these words, Parvana turned her head sharply to glare at her sister. If ever there was a time to say something mean, this was it, but she couldn't think of anything. <u>After all, what Nooria said was true.</u>

When you see a phrase like one of these, pause to see if it's an **Aha Moment:**

That's when I knew . . .

For the first time . . .

And just like that . . .

I suddenly realized . . .

Anchor Question
When you notice this signpost, ask: How might this change things?

What word(s) tell you something has changed?	"After all, what Nooria said was true."
What might this realization tell you about Parvana?	Parvana may be beginning to accept her family's plans for her.

Contrasts and Contradictions You probably pay close attention when a friend says or does something unexpected. If a character says or does something you haven't expected, you should pay attention, too. **Contrasts and Contradictions** like these can give you a deeper understanding of a character. If action and dialogue surprise you, take a minute to consider the meaning.

In this example, a student marked a Contrast and Contradiction:

> 5   Parvana stared at the three of them. It was as though they were speaking a foreign language, and <u>she didn't have a clue what they were saying.</u>

Anchor Question
When you notice this signpost, ask: Why did the character act or feel this way?

What contradiction is expressed here?	Even though Parvana speaks the same language as her family, she can't understand what they're telling her.
What does this moment tell us about Parvana?	Parvana cannot stand the thought of doing what they're asking.

WHEN STUDENTS STRUGGLE . . .

Use Strategies Visualizing is important in identifying signposts, especially Aha Moments. If students are struggling to notice signposts, have them use the Sketch to Stretch strategy to visualize what is happening in a text. Tell students to pick a confusing passage from the selection, reread it, and underline what they find confusing. Then, tell them to sketch what they see happening. Explain that it's acceptable to use stick figures. Finally, have students turn to a partner and share their drawings. To help students understand the importance of visualizing, have them consider how their sketches help them better understand the passage.

AHA MOMENT

Explain that **Aha Moments** almost always reveal a change in a **character**. Point out that some Aha Moments are not so sudden, but may be a more gradual realization over time.

Read aloud the example passage and pause at the underlined text, pointing out the words *After all*. These words signify that a character has come to a conclusion, and are significant because that character now understands something important. Ask students to consider what this moment might reveal about Parvana's life.

Tell students that when they spot an Aha Moment, they should pause, mark it in their consumable texts, and ask themselves the anchor question: *How might this change things?*

CONTRASTS AND CONTRADICTIONS

Explain to students that **Contrasts and Contradictions** occur when a character does something surprising. When a character does something unexpected, students should take a minute to consider what that action might mean for the **character** or **plot**.

Read aloud the example passage and pause at the underlined text. Explain to students that "she didn't have a clue what they were saying" is unexpected because the adults are speaking in a language Parvana understands. Ask students to consider what this thought tells us about Parvana.

Tell students that when they spot a Contrasts and Contradictions, they should pause, mark it in their consumable texts, and ask themselves the anchor question: *Why did the character act or feel this way?*

APPLY THE SIGNPOSTS

Have students use the selection that follows as a model text to apply the signposts. As students encounter signposts, prompt them to stop, reread, and ask themselves the anchor questions that will help them understand the story's themes and characters.

Tell students to look for these and other signposts as they read the selections in the unit.

? **Connect to the**
ESSENTIAL QUESTION

The Breadwinner is the story of a girl who is afraid when she must go to the market alone. She has to find courage so she can buy the supplies her family needs.

ANALYZE & APPLY

from
THE BREADWINNER

Novel by **Deborah Ellis**

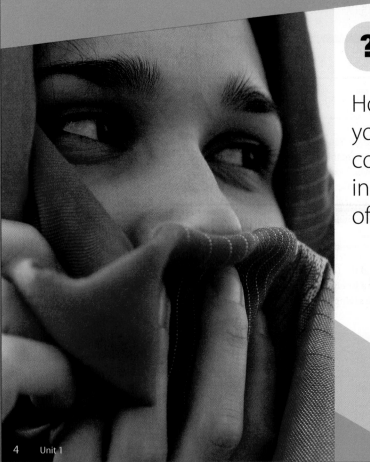

? **ESSENTIAL QUESTION:**

How do you find courage in the face of fear?

4   Unit 1

 LEARNING MINDSET

Setting Goals Remind students that setting goals for your learning helps you get the most out of the time you spend. Goals help focus your attention so you don't get distracted. Encourage students to set a goal for this reading selection. What do students want to learn? What intrigues them about this selection?

QUICK START

In a small group, discuss what you know about stories set in different cultures or time periods. How do those stories differ from stories about your own culture and times? What do those differences reveal?

ANALYZE HOW CHARACTER DEVELOPS PLOT

A fictional **character** is any person, animal, or imaginary creature who takes part in the action of a work of literature. Characters take part in a series of events that make up the **plot.** Both character and plot are essential to fiction because they work together to tell a good story. Here are some ways that character and plot interact:

- Authors use a character's personality and circumstances to help set the plot in motion.

- Characters respond to events of the plot in external ways (their own actions and their interactions with other characters) and internal ways (their inner thoughts and feelings).

- Characters' responses to events, in turn, shape the plot as it develops.

ANALYZE SETTING AND CHARACTER

Historical fiction is set in the past and uses cultural elements of a particular time and place to tell the story. The **setting,** or the time and place in which the action occurs, influences **character development,** or how characters change throughout the story. In *The Breadwinner,* the setting—Afghanistan during a time of harsh rule—influences how the characters develop.

As you read *The Breadwinner,* note how the characters respond to the cultural setting of Afghanistan, including its rules for how men and women should dress and behave. Use a chart like the one below.

Character	Features of Setting	Character's Response	My Ideas About the Character
Parvana			
Nooria			
Mother			

GENRE ELEMENTS: HISTORICAL FICTION

- includes the basic elements of fiction: setting, character, plot, conflict, and theme

- is set in the past and includes real places and real events of historical importance

- is a type of realistic fiction, in which fictional characters behave like real people and use human abilities to cope with life's challenges

QUICK START

Have students read the Quick Start question, and have them form groups to discuss what they know about stories set in other cultures or time periods. Then have them discuss how these stories are different from stories about their own culture and times, and what those differences reveal.

ANALYZE HOW CHARACTER DEVELOPS PLOT

Help students understand that the events in stories don't just happen, they are caused by other events, by character decisions, and by character reactions to events or other characters. Have students suggest ways in real life that people's decisions cause events to happen.

ANALYZE SETTING AND CHARACTER

Remind students that historical fiction is a story set in a different time. The time and place in which a story takes place is the setting. The setting can influence character development. Have students imagine living in the Wild West. How would the setting affect what actions people could take? Now have them imagine living in a science station in an isolated part of the Arctic. How would this affect what characters could do? Review the chart that students will have to complete as they analyze how the characters respond to the cultural setting of Afghanistan.

 ENGLISH LEARNER SUPPORT

Track Story Elements   Review with students the definitions of *characters*, *plot*, and *setting*. Display definitions of each. Discuss with students the setting, characters, and plot of a story they are familiar with. Provide students with a story map graphic organizer to track the characters, setting, and main events of the story. **MODERATE**

TEACH

CRITICAL VOCABULARY

Encourage students to read all the sentences before deciding which word best completes each one. Remind them to look for context clues that match the precise meaning of each word.

Answers:

1. *responsibility*
2. *fume*
3. *solution*
4. *stammer*

■ English Learner Support

Use Cognates Tell students that two of the Critical Vocabulary words have Spanish cognates: *responsibility/responsabilidad; solution/solución.* **ALL LEVELS**

LANGUAGE CONVENTIONS

Review the information about capitalization of proper nouns. Explain that the first example sentence uses proper nouns that are the names of people and places. The second example demonstrates that acronyms and names of organizations are proper nouns that need to be capitalized.

Display the sample sentences without capitalization, and ask students how removing the capital letters affects their comprehension. (*You can't tell that the sentences are talking about people, places, or specific organizations.*)

✎ ANNOTATION MODEL

Remind students of the information on how to annotate signposts on pages 2 and 3. As they read, they should make a note of a signpost and underline the words that help signify a signpost, then make a note of what the signpost might indicate. Review the example so they understand how to annotate. Remind them that in this selection they are looking for **Words of the Wiser, Aha Moments,** and **Contrasts and Contradictions**.

CRITICAL VOCABULARY

| solution | responsibility | stammer | fume |

To see how many Critical Vocabulary words you already know, use them to complete the sentences.

1. It was her _____ to walk the dog twice a day.

2. The insult made her _____ each time she remembered it.

3. Eating a healthy snack is a good _____ when you feel low on energy.

4. He had a tendency to _____ when he was speaking in front of large groups of people.

LANGUAGE CONVENTIONS

Capitalization of Proper Nouns A **common noun** is a general name for a person, place, thing, or idea. A **proper noun** names a specific person, place, thing, or idea. Proper nouns, including abbreviations (a shortened form of a word), acronyms (words whose letters stand for other words), initials, and organizations, should be capitalized.

"You'll be our cousin from Jalalabad," Nooria said.

She dreamed of working for the ICRC, the International Committee of the Red Cross, to help war refugees.

ANNOTATION MODEL   NOTICE & NOTE

As you read, notice and note signposts, including **Words of the Wiser, Aha Moments,** and **Contrasts and Contradictions.** Here is an example of how one reader responded to the beginning of *The Breadwinner.*

> 6 "If anybody asks about you, <u>we'll say that you have gone to stay with an aunt in Kunduz,</u>" Mother said.
>
> 7 "But no one will ask about you."
>
> 8 At these words, Parvana turned to glare at her sister.

That's odd. The mother wants everyone to lie about Parvana. Why? That contradicts what I think most parents would tell their children.

BACKGROUND

Deborah Ellis (b. 1960) wrote The Breadwinner after interviewing Afghan women and girls in a refugee camp in Pakistan. In this excerpt, 11-year-old Parvana lives with her family in Kabul, Afghanistan, in the 1990s. Parvana's family, like others, has suffered under harsh government rule. Parvana's father has been imprisoned and her older brother, Hossain, has been killed. With no men to help, Parvana's family must find a way to survive.

from
THE BREADWINNER
Novel by Deborah Ellis

SETTING A PURPOSE

As you read, pay attention to any changes in the way the main character, Parvana, perceives herself and her role within her family. Note details that help you understand her character, the setting, and the conflict she faces.

1 They were going to turn her into a boy.

2 "As a boy, you'll be able to move in and out of the market, buy what we need, and no one will stop you," Mother said.

3 "It's a perfect **solution**," Mrs. Weera said.

4 "You'll be our cousin from Jalalabad," Nooria said, "come to stay with us while our father is away."

5 Parvana stared at the three of them. It was as though they were speaking a foreign language, and she didn't have a clue what they were saying.

6 "If anybody asks about you, we'll say that you have gone to stay with an aunt in Kunduz,"[1] Mother said.

---
[1] **Kunduz** (koōn´dooz): the capital city of Kunduz Province in northern Afghanistan, situated north of Kabul.

Notice & Note

Use the side margins to notice and note signposts in the text.

solution
(sə-loō´shən) *n.* A *solution* is a way of handling a problem.

BACKGROUND

After students read the Background note, remind them that this is a work of historical fiction that happens in a different time and place. This story takes place in Kabul, the capital of Afghanistan, in the late 1990s. The people living in that time and place suffered under harsh leadership, which established rules restricting the behavior of women and girls. Girls were not allowed to go to school or to the store. In the story, Parvana and her family must figure out how to get food and supplies when her father has been imprisoned and her brother has been killed. With no men in the house, they decide to dress up Parvana as a boy so she can go to the stores.

SETTING A PURPOSE

Direct students to use the Setting a Purpose prompt to focus their reading.

For **listening support** for students at varying proficiency levels, see the **Text X-Ray** on page 2C.

CRITICAL VOCABULARY

solution: The author uses the word *solution* to indicate that the characters have figured out how to take care of a difficult situation.

ASK STUDENTS what problem the characters need to solve at this point in the story. (*how to get groceries when there are no men in the house and women and girls are not allowed in the market*)

TEACH

ANALYZE SETTING AND CHARACTER

Remind students that the story takes place in Kabul, Afgahnistan. At the time of this story, a group called the Taliban maintained strict rule over the region. (**Answer:** *These details indicate that the Taliban is strict and doesn't allow women and girls many freedoms. The setting may be dangerous, too, if people are fleeing to different parts of the country. These details about the setting might make the story's characters very afraid.*)

CONTRASTS AND CONTRADICTIONS

Guide students to underline the last two sentences of paragraph 11. Remind students that **Contrasts and Contradictions** are when a **character** thinks or acts in an unexpected way. (**Answer:** *Parvana cannot yet decide between two desires—the wish to relieve her mother's sadness and a desire to preserve her own identity.*)

ANALYZE HOW CHARACTER DEVELOPS PLOT

Discuss with students that a reaction is a response to an event. Ask them to describe what Parvana does in response to the suggestion she should disguise herself as a boy. (**Answer:** *Parvana's refusal to cut her hair and disguise herself as a boy helps build conflict in the plot. Her effort to get Nooria to disguise herself instead helps the reader learn that Nooria looks too mature to pass as a boy.*)

 For **speaking support** for students at varying proficiency levels, see the **Text X-Ray** on page 2D.

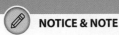 NOTICE & NOTE

ANALYZE SETTING AND CHARACTER

Annotate: Mark details in paragraph 8 that describe the cultural setting in which Parvana lives.

Infer: How might this setting affect the story's characters?

CONTRASTS AND CONTRADICTIONS

Notice & Note: What opposing thoughts does Parvana express in paragraph 11? Mark these details.

Draw Conclusions: Why is Parvana not ready to "give in"?

ANALYZE HOW CHARACTER DEVELOPS PLOT

Annotate: In paragraphs 12–16, mark Parvana's reaction to the idea that she should disguise herself as a boy.

Analyze: How might Parvana's reaction affect the plot?

8   Unit 1

---

7 "But no one will ask about you."

8 At these words, Parvana turned her head sharply to glare at her sister. If ever there was a time to say something mean, this was it, but she couldn't think of anything. After all, what Nooria said was true. None of her friends had seen her since the Taliban closed the schools. Her relatives were scattered to different parts of the country, even to different countries. There was no one to ask about her.

9 "You'll wear Hossain's clothes." Mother's voice caught, and for a moment it seemed as though she would cry, but she got control of herself again.

10 "They will be a bit big for you, but we can make some adjustments if we have to." She glanced over at Mrs. Weera. "Those clothes have been idle long enough. It's time they were put to use."

11 Parvana guessed Mrs. Weera and her mother had been talking long and hard while she was asleep. She was glad of that. Her mother already looked better. But that didn't mean she was ready to give in.

12 "It won't work," she said. "I won't look like a boy. I have long hair."

13 Nooria opened the cupboard door, took out the sewing kit and slowly opened it up. It looked to Parvana as if Nooria was having too much fun as she lifted out the scissors and snapped them open and shut a few times.

8   Unit 1

14 "You're not cutting my hair!" Parvana's hands flew up to her head.

15 "How else will you look like a boy?" Mother asked;

16 "Cut Nooria's hair! She's the oldest! It's her responsibility to look after me, not my **responsibility** to look after her!"

17 "No one would believe me to be a boy," Nooria said calmly, looking down at her body. Nooria being calm just made Parvana madder.

18 "I'll look like that soon," Parvana said.

19 "You wish."

20 "We'll deal with that when the time comes," Mother said quickly, heading off the fight she knew was coming. "Until then, we have no choice. Someone has to be able to go outside, and you are the one most likely to look like a boy."

21 Parvana thought about it. Her fingers reached up her back to see how long her hair had grown.

22 "It has to be your decision," Mrs. Weera said. "We can force you to cut off your hair, but you're still the one who has to go outside and act the part. We know this is a big thing we're asking, but I think you can do it. How about it?"

23 Parvana realized Mrs. Weera was right. They could hold her down and cut off her hair, but for anything more, they needed her cooperation. In the end, it really was her decision.

24 Somehow, knowing that made it easier to agree.

25 "All right," she said. "I'll do it."

26 "Well done," said Mrs. Weera. "That's the spirit."

27 Nooria snapped the scissors again. "I'll cut your hair," she said.

responsibility
(rĭ-spŏn´sə-bĭl´ĭ-tē) *n.* A *responsibility* is a duty, obligation, or burden.

WORDS OF THE WISER

Notice & Note: What insight does Mrs. Weera offer Parvana? Mark this detail.

Cite Evidence: How does Parvana come to the realization that Mrs. Weera is right?

 WORDS OF THE WISER

Remind students that the **Words of the Wiser** signpost occurs when a character gives advice to another character. Work with students to underline all of paragraph 23. Ask them to **cite evidence** that Parvana comes to the realization that Mrs. Weera is right. (***Answer:*** *They could hold her down and cut her hair, but for anything more they needed her cooperation.*)

EL ENGLISH LEARNER SUPPORT

Use Dialogue Tags It might be difficult for students to follow the quick back-and-forth of the dialogue in this section. Remind students to focus on the dialogue tags to help figure out who is speaking. These include "Mother said," "Parvana said," "Mother asked," and so on. Give other examples of dialogue tags found in the story, and have students make a list of the most commonly used words (*said, asked, responded,* etc).
MODERATE

CRITICAL VOCABULARY

responsibility: The author uses the word *responsibility* here to emphasize that Parvana is performing an unusual duty—taking care of her family—one that would usually fall to older members of the family to fulfill.

ASK STUDENTS why going to the market has to be Parvana's responsibility. (*Nooria is too old to pass as a boy.*)

TEACH

LANGUAGE CONVENTIONS

Explain that *Mother* is a proper noun when it takes the place of a specific person's name. In this case, *her mother* is not a proper noun, so it is not capitalized.

CONTRASTS AND CONTRADICTIONS

Discuss with students Parvana's context, or situation, due to the **setting** of the story. Have students note how the setting influences her contrasting feelings about her hair. (***Answer:*** *Parvana thinks that her hair was more important to her while it was still attached to her, but not very important after it was cut.*)

AHA MOMENT

Point out that this section is very focused on Parvana's **perspective** and gives readers a window into her inner thoughts and feelings. Discuss with students what Parvana's realization was, and how her realization changed the way she felt about her disguise. (***Answer:*** *Parvana realizes she has a nice face, and that makes her more comfortable with the way she looks. She may feel less resentment about appearing in public as a boy.*)

 For **reading support** for students at varying proficiency levels, see the **Text X-Ray** on page 2D.

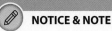

LANGUAGE CONVENTIONS
When the word *mother* is used as a proper noun to name a specific person it is capitalized throughout the excerpt. Explain why the word *mother's* is not capitalized in paragraph 34.

CONTRASTS AND CONTRADICTIONS

Notice & Note: What contrasting feelings does Parvana experience in paragraph 34? Mark each of her feelings.

Cause/Effect: What causes Parvana to change her feelings about her hair?

AHA MOMENT

Notice & Note: What is Parvana's realization in paragraph 40? Mark her realization.

Analyze: How might Parvana's realization change the way she feels about her disguise?

28 "I'll cut it," Mother said, taking the scissors away. "Let's do it now, Parvana. Thinking about it won't make it any easier."

29 Parvana and her mother went into the washroom where the cement floor would make it easier to clean up the cut-off hair. Mother took Hossain's clothes in with them.

30 "Do you want to watch?" Mother asked, nodding toward the mirror.

31 Parvana shook her head, then changed her mind. If this was the last she would see of her hair, then she wanted to see it for as long as she could.

32 Mother worked quickly. First she cut off a huge chunk in a straight line at her neck. She held it up for Parvana to see.

33 "I have a lovely piece of ribbon packed away," she said. "We'll tie this up with it, and you can keep it."

34 Parvana looked at the hair in her mother's hand. While it was on her head, it had seemed important. It didn't seem important any more.

35 "No, thanks," said Parvana. "Throw it away."

36 Her mother's lips tightened. "If you're going to sulk about it," she said, and she tossed the hair down to the floor.

37 As more and more hair fell away, Parvana began to feel like a different person. Her whole face showed. What was left of her hair was short and shaggy. It curled in a soft fringe around her ears. There were no long parts to fall into her eyes, to become tangled on a windy day, to take forever to dry when she got caught in the rain.

38 Her forehead seemed bigger. Her eyes seemed bigger, too, maybe because she was opening them so wide to be able to see everything. Her ears seemed to stick out from her head.

39 They look a little funny, Parvana thought, but a nice sort of funny.

40 I have a nice face, she decided.

41 Mother rubbed her hands brusquely[2] over Parvana's head to rub away any stray hairs.

42 "Change your clothes," she said. Then she left the washroom.

43 All alone, Parvana's hand crept up to the top of her head. Touching her hair gingerly[3] at first, she soon rubbed the palm of her hand all over her head. Her new hair felt both bristly and soft. It tickled the skin on her hand.

---

[2] **brusquely** (brŭsk´lē): abruptly or curtly.
[3] **gingerly** (jĭn´jər-lē): cautiously or carefully.

10 Unit 1

WHEN STUDENTS STRUGGLE . . .

Discuss Setting and Plot Review with students the setting of the story, both the time and the location. Discuss some of the rules Parvana and her family must follow. Then discuss how living in Afghanistan under harsh rule affects the plot of the story. Have students answer these questions: *Where is the story set? What challenge do the characters face? How do they respond to the challenge?* Remind students that the plot points they just described happened *because* of the particular setting in which the story's characters live.

For additional support, go to the **Reading Studio** and assign the following **Level Up tutorial: Setting: Effect on Plot**.

44   I like it, she thought, and she smiled.

45   She took off her own clothes and put on her brother's. Hossain's shalwar kameez[4] was pale green, both the loose shirt and the baggy trousers. The shirt hung down very low, and the trousers were too long, but by rolling them up at the waist, they were all right.

46   There was a pocket sewn into the left side of the shirt, near the chest. It was just big enough to hold money and maybe a few candies, if she ever had candies again. There was another pocket on the front. It was nice to have pockets. Her girl clothes didn't have any.

47   "Parvana, haven't you changed yet?"

48   Parvana stopped looking at herself in the mirror and joined her family.

49   The first face she saw was Maryam's. Her little sister looked as if she couldn't quite figure out who had walked into the room.

50   "It's me, Maryam," Parvana said.

51   "Parvana!" Maryam laughed as she recognized her.

52   "Hossain," her mother whispered.

53   "You look less ugly as a boy than you do as a girl," Nooria said quickly. If Mother started remembering Hossain, she'd just start crying again.

54   "You look fine," said Mrs. Weera.

55   "Put this on." Mother handed Parvana a cap. Parvana put it on her head. It was a white cap with beautiful embroidery all over it. Maybe she'd never wear her special red shalwar kameez again, but she had a new cap to take its place.

---
4 **shalwar kameez** (shäl´vär kə-mēz´): a type of long, loose shirt and pants, worn by both men and women.

ANALYZE HOW CHARACTER DEVELOPS PLOT

Annotate: In paragraph 53, circle what Nooria says in response to Parvana's disguise. Underline what Nooria is thinking.

Infer: What do you learn about Nooria here?

ANALYZE HOW CHARACTER DEVELOPS PLOT

Work with students to annotate paragraph 53. Remind students that an inference is not something that is stated in the text— it is something the reader figures out, or infers, based on clues from the text. (**Answer:** *We know that Nooria cares more about Mother's well-being than she does about Parvana's feelings. Nooria calls Parvana "less ugly" to distract Mother from feeling sad about Hossain.*)

EL ENGLISH LEARNER SUPPORT

Confirm Understanding Use the following supports with students at various proficiency levels:

- Display and read aloud these sentences: *Parvana has to cut her hair and dress like a boy so she can go to the market. She wears her dead brother's clothes, and her mother feels sad to see Parvana wearing them.* Have students echo read the sentences back to you. **SUBSTANTIAL**

- Have students complete the following sentence frames to confirm their understanding: *Parvana has to _____ in order to _____. Her mother sees her wearing her brother's clothes and feels _____.* **MODERATE**

- Have students answer the following questions in complete sentences: *Why does Parvana have to change her appearance? Why does her mother feel sad when she sees Parvana in her brother's clothes?* **LIGHT**

ANALYZE SETTING AND CHARACTER

Remind students that the cultural setting of a story—in this case, Afghanistan—can affect the way a character acts and feels. Have volunteers share the words they underlined. (**Answer:** *In Parvana's culture, there are very different expectations about what boys and girls can do or are allowed to do. She is used to wearing a chador that covers her hair and body, and when faced with the prospect of going out in public without it, she feels exposed to danger and feels tremendous panic.*)

NOTICE & NOTE

ANALYZE SETTING AND CHARACTER

Annotate: Mark the words in paragraphs 56–59 that refer to the story's cultural setting.

Synthesize: How do you explain the relationship between the cultural setting and Parvana's reaction in paragraph 59?

56 "Here's some money," her mother said. "Buy what you were not able to buy yesterday." She placed a pattu[5] around Parvana's shoulder. It was her father's. "Hurry back."

57 Parvana tucked the money into her new pocket. She slipped her feet into her sandals, then reached for her chador.[6]

58 "You won't be needing that," Nooria said.

59 Parvana had forgotten. Suddenly she was scared. Everyone would see her face! They would know she wasn't a boy!

60 She turned around to plead with her mother. "Don't make me do this!"

61 "You see?" Nooria said in her nastiest voice. "I told you she was too scared."

62 "It's easy to call someone else scared when you're safe inside your home all the time!" Parvana shot back. She spun around and went outside, slamming the door behind her.

---

[5] **pattu** (pə´tōō): a gray or brown woolen shawl worn by Afghan men and boys.

[6] **chador** (chä-dôr´): a cloth worn by women and girls to cover their hair and shoulders.

IMPROVE READING FLUENCY

Targeted Passage Have students work with partners to read paragraphs 55–62. First, use paragraph 55 to model reading with appropriate speed and expression. Then, have partners take turns reading aloud the remaining paragraphs. Encourage students to provide feedback and support for pronouncing difficult words. Remind students that when they are reading aloud for an audience, they should pace their reading so that listeners have time to understand the events of the story.

 Go to the **Reading Studio** for additional support in developing fluency.

63   Out on the street, she kept waiting for people to point at her and call her a fake. No one did. No one paid any attention to her at all. The more she was ignored, the more confident she felt.

64   When she had gone into the market with her father, she had kept silent and covered up her face as much as possible. She had tried her best to be invisible. Now, with her face open to the sunshine, she was invisible in another way. She was just one more boy on the street. She was nothing worth paying attention to.

65   When she came to the shop that sold tea, rice and other groceries, she hesitated for a slight moment, then walked boldly through the door. I'm a boy, she kept saying to herself. It gave her courage.

66   "What do you want?" the grocer asked.

67   "Some . . . some tea," Parvana **stammered** out.

68   "How much? What kind?" The grocer was gruff, but it was ordinary bad-mood gruff, not gruff out of anger that there was a girl in his shop.

ANALYZE HOW CHARACTER DEVELOPS PLOT

Annotate: Mark the words in paragraph 65 that show what Parvana is feeling or thinking.

Draw Conclusions: What does the author reveal about Parvana's character in this paragraph?

stammer
(stăm´ər) v. To *stammer* is to speak with involuntary pauses or repetitions.

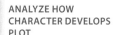

ANALYZE HOW CHARACTER DEVELOPS PLOT

Remind students that the way a character thinks or feels has an effect on their actions. A character's thoughts and feelings can be stated directly by the author or may be reflected in the character's actions. Discuss clues to how Parvana is thinking or feeling in paragraph 65, and have volunteers share and explain their annotations. (**Answer:** *Parvana has the strength to overcome her fears. She's coaching herself to gather enough courage to go into the shop.*)

CRITICAL VOCABULARY

stammer: The author repeats the word *some* in Parvana's dialogue here as a way to represent the stammer that signals how nervous she is about the situation of pretending to be a boy.

ASK STUDENTS what effect Parvana's stammer seems to have had on the grocer. (*It seems to have no effect. She is nervous that he will notice she isn't a boy, but he does not notice.*)

AHA MOMENT

Remind the students that an **Aha Moment** is when a character realizes something important. Remind students that an **Aha Moment** can often reveal something important about **character development**. Have students mark Parvana's sudden realization in paragraph 73. Have students share what they underlined. (**Answer:** *Parvana feels proud because she was able to deceive the man into thinking she was a boy. Parvana's pride means she has the confidence to continue to perform this important role for her family, so they have a better chance of surviving under tough circumstances.*)

WORDS OF THE WISER

Remind students that **Words of the Wiser** are pieces of advice that a wiser character gives to another character. That advice is often meant to help a character respond to events in the **plot** or make a decision that will push the plot forward. In this case, Nooria is the wise character. (**Possible Answer:** *Nooria is right—Parvana should keep her boy's disguise even inside the home so that everyone remains safe. The consequences are that Parvana may never quite feel like herself again, or not be able to relax. Mother will have to confront the distressing image of her son every time she looks at Parvana as a boy.*)

NOTICE & NOTE

69   Parvana pointed to the brand of tea they usually had at home. "Is that the cheapest?"

70   "This one is the cheapest." He showed her another one.

71   "I'll take the cheapest one. I also need five pounds of rice."

72   "Don't tell me. You want the cheapest kind. Big spender."

73   Parvana left the shop with rice and tea, feeling very proud of herself. "<u>I can do this!</u>" she whispered.

74   Onions were cheap at the vegetable stand. She bought a few.

75   "Look what I got!" Parvana exclaimed, as she burst through the door of her home. "I did it! I did the shopping, and nobody bothered me."

76   "Parvana!" Maryam ran to her and gave her a hug. Parvana hugged her back as best she could with her arms full of groceries.

77   Mother was back on the toshak,[7] facing the wall, her back to the room. Ali sat beside her, patting her and saying, "Ma-ma-ma," trying to get her attention.

78   Nooria took the groceries from Parvana and handed her the water bucket.

79   "As long as you've got your sandals on," she said.

80   "What's wrong with Mother now?"

81   "Shhh! Not so loud! Do you want her to hear you? She got upset after seeing you in Hossain's clothes. Can you blame her? Also, Mrs. Weera went home, and that's made her sad. Now, please go and get water."

82   "I got water yesterday!"

83   "I had a lot of cleaning to do. Ali was almost out of diapers. Would you rather wash diapers than fetch the water?"

84   Parvana fetched the water.

85   "Keep those clothes on," Nooria said when Parvana returned. "I've been thinking about this. <u>If you're going to be a boy outside, you should be a boy inside, too.</u> What if someone comes by?"

86   That made sense to Parvana. "What about Mother? Won't it upset her to see me in Hossain's clothes all the time?"

87   "She'll have to get used to it."

88   For the first time, Parvana noticed the tired lines on Nooria's face. She looked much older than seventeen. "I'll help you with supper," she offered.

89   "You? Help? All you'd do is get in my way."

AHA MOMENT

Notice & Note: What does Parvana suddenly realize in paragraph 73? Mark her realization.

Infer: How does Parvana feel about herself at this moment, and how might it affect her future and the future of her family?

WORDS OF THE WISER

Notice & Note: What advice does Nooria give Parvana in paragraphs 85–87? Mark Nooria's advice.

Evaluate: What do you think about Nooria's advice? What are the consequences for Parvana and Mother?

---

[7] **toshak** (tō´shŏk): a narrow mattress used in many Afghan homes instead of chairs or beds.

APPLYING ACADEMIC VOCABULARY

❏ evident   ❏ factor   ☑ indicate   ☑ similar   ❏ specific

Write and Discuss   Have students turn to a partner to discuss the following questions. Guide students to include the Academic Vocabulary words *indicate* and *similar* in their responses. Ask volunteers to share their responses with the class.

- When Parvana sees that Nooria looks older than seventeen, what does that **indicate** to her?

- What is Parvana's mother's reaction when she sees that Parvana looks **similar** to her deceased brother?

90   Parvana **fumed**. It was impossible to be nice to Nooria!

91   Mother got up for supper and made an effort to be cheerful. She complimented Parvana on her shopping success, but seemed to have a hard time looking at her.

92   Later that night, when they were all stretched out for sleep, Ali fussed a little.

93   "Go to sleep, Hossain," Parvana heard her mother say. "Go to sleep, my son."

 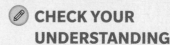

fume
(fyoom) *v.* To *fume* about something is to feel or show displeasure or resentment.

CHECK YOUR UNDERSTANDING

Answer these questions before moving on to the **Analyze the Text** section on the following page.

1 Which of the following sentences best shows the problem that Parvana's family is trying to solve?

  A There was no one to ask about Parvana.

  B Someone has to go to the market to buy food and supplies.

  C Hossain's clothes do not fit Parvana.

  D Mother misses her son Hossain.

2 In paragraphs 37–40, the writer describes Parvana's experience of the haircut in order to —

  F show how Nooria is envious of Parvana

  G describe a traumatic event

  H give directions on how to cut hair

  J show how Parvana's changing appearance is beginning to affect her outlook

3 Which one of the following ideas is true?

  A Parvana feels proud that she bought food at the market.

  B Mother is delighted that Parvana reminds her of Hossain.

  C The family forces Parvana to disguise herself as a boy.

  D Parvana treasures her long hair after Mother cuts it off.

The Breadwinner   15

CHECK YOUR UNDERSTANDING

Have students answer the questions independently.

Answers:

  1. *B*

  2. *J*

  3. *A*

If they answer any questions incorrectly, have them reread the text to confirm their understanding. Then they may proceed to ANALYZE THE TEXT on p. 16.

CRITICAL VOCABULARY

fume: The author uses *fume* here to depict the anger Parvana feels because of Nooria's reaction.

ASK STUDENTS why Parvana would especially fume at Nooria's comment. *(Parvana had just come to appreciate Nooria's sacrifices and had offered to do something nice for Nooria to show her appreciation, but Nooria just responded with an insult to Parvana.)*

 ENGLISH LEARNER SUPPORT

Oral Assessment Use the following questions to assess students' comprehension and speaking skills:

  1. What problem is Parvana's family trying to solve at the beginning of the story? *(Someone has to go to the market to buy food and supplies.)*

  2. Why does the writer describe Parvana's experience of the haircut? *(The author wants to show how Parvana's changing appearance affected her outlook.)*

  3. How does Parvana feel after she buys food at the market? *(Parvana feels proud after buying food at the market.)*

SUBSTANTIAL/MODERATE

ANALYZE THE TEXT

Possible answers:

1. **DOK 4**: *In paragraphs 64–72, the author describes Parvana's thoughts to show her fears about appearing in public as a boy. The author also shows readers what it's like to visit a shop in Kabul at that time. While Parvana shops, we learn more about her culture—the sorts of things her family eats and drinks—but also that she chooses the less expensive tea, reflecting her family's reduced income.*

2. **DOK 3:** *At the beginning of the excerpt, Parvana is reluctant to disguise herself as a boy and go to the market by herself. By the end, Parvana seems more mature. She's successfully gone shopping in the market while in disguise as a boy, and is even able to see that her sister, Nooria, looks tired and worn out. While Parvana matures in this excerpt, the plot advances, too. The family is fed, thanks to Parvana.*

3. **DOK 4:** *The author has effectively used the historical, wartime setting to show how Parvana and other characters respond to stresses such as repression, hunger, and loneliness. We see that Parvana accepts a challenge to feed her family—she becomes the breadwinner. We see how Mother is troubled by the memory of her deceased son.*

4. **DOK 2:** *In the last paragraphs of the excerpt, Mother refers to Ali, her baby son, by the name of her deceased son, Hossain. The author uses this moment to illustrate how Parvana's disguise as a boy reminds Mother of Hossain and to suggest that Mother may have a hard time dealing with her memories of Hossain as Parvana continues to disguise herself.*

5. **DOK 4**: *Parvana realizes that there are different ways to hide from the outside world. As a girl, she can cover herself with a chador and not be seen. Or as a boy, she can show her face but be indistinguishable in a crowd of many other faces. Now, with the freedom to blend in with a crowd of other boys, she can be more daring and take more risks to help her family.*

RESEARCH

Here are aid organizations students might research:

The nonprofit organization Canadian Women for Women in Afghanistan funds community schools, teachers, and libraries in Afghanistan. The international organizations Doctors Without Borders and International Committee of the Red Cross (ICRC) send doctors and nurses to give medical care to areas affected by war and disease.

Extend: *The Breadwinner* is a part of a four-book series that also includes *Parvana's Journey*, *Mud City*, and *My Name is Parvana*.

 RESPOND

ANALYZE THE TEXT

Support your responses with evidence from the text. ⬛ NOTEBOOK

1. **Analyze** What methods does the author use to describe elements of both culture and setting in paragraphs 64–72?

2. **Compare** Think about Parvana's character at the beginning of the excerpt (paragraphs 1–16) and near the end (paragraphs 85–88). What changes do you notice about Parvana over this time, and how do they affect the plot?

3. **Evaluate** How effectively has the author used setting to develop Parvana and other characters?

4. **Interpret** Review paragraphs 91–93 at the end of the excerpt. What does the author reveal about Mother, and how might this information affect the plot?

5. **Notice & Note** Review Parvana's observations about appearing in public in paragraphs 63–65. In your own words, describe what she realizes in this moment. How might this understanding help her in the future?

RESEARCH

RESEARCH TIP
Many well-known authors have their own websites. Visit Deborah Ellis's website to find out more about her and the humanitarian causes she supports.

Deborah Ellis, the author of *The Breadwinner*, has donated money from her book sales to help fund humanitarian efforts, including education projects for Afghan women and children. Research at least two aid organizations, which may include those shown below. Begin by generating questions that will guide your research. Record what you learn in the chart.

ORGANIZATION	RESEARCH QUESTION/ANSWER
Doctors Without Borders	Question: What does this group do? Answer: Sends doctors and nurses to provide medical care.
International Committee of the Red Cross (ICRC)	Question: What does this group do? Answer: Provides protection to victims of war.

Extend Deborah Ellis has written many books for young people. With a partner, find out about some of Ellis's other titles. Are there more books like *The Breadwinner*?

🛠 LEARNING MINDSET

Belonging Tell students that a belonging mindset means having confidence you have something to contribute to the learning community. Encourage students to bring their own previous experiences, insights, and questions to discussions about the reading selection. Emphasize the value of expressing and listening to diverse perspectives.

CREATE AND PRESENT

Write a Letter Compose a formal business letter to one of the aid organizations you researched, requesting more information about the organization's mission.

❏ Follow the structure of a formal letter by including the date and the organization's name and address before the salutation and body of the letter.

❏ Keep the tone of your writing formal. Request information in a courteous and respectful way. Include your name and address at the end of the letter.

❏ You may wish to send your letter via email. Check the organization's website for an email address.

Give a Multimodal Presentation Give a presentation that uses both text and visual elements to share what you learned about the organization with your class.

❏ Make sure your presentation is organized so that your audience can easily understand the information.

❏ Pay attention to your speaking rate, enunciation, and volume.

❏ Maintain eye contact with the audience. Use natural gestures while you speak. When you are finished, ask classmates if they have any questions about your presentation.

 RESPOND

 Go to **Writing Arguments: Formal Style** in the **Writing Studio** for more on formal style.

Go to **Giving a Presentation** in the **Speaking and Listening Studio** for help with giving a presentation.

RESPOND TO THE ESSENTIAL QUESTION

? How do you find courage in the face of fear?

Gather Information Review your annotations and notes on *The Breadwinner*. Then, add relevant details to your Response Log. As you determine which information to include, think about:

• the kinds of fears people face
• how people are willing to face fear to help those they love
• how people can overcome fear

At the end of the unit, use your notes to write an informational essay.

UNIT 1 RESPONSE LOG

? Essential Question: How do you find courage in the face of fear?

From *The Breadwinner*	
Life Doesn't Frighten Me	
Fears and Phobias	
Wired for Fear	
Embarrassed? Blame Your Brain	
The Ravine	

ACADEMIC VOCABULARY

As you write and discuss what you learned from the novel excerpt, be sure to use the Academic Vocabulary words. Check off each of the words that you use.

❏ **evident**
❏ **factor**
❏ **indicate**
❏ **similar**
❏ **specific**

CREATE AND PRESENT

Write a Letter Remind students that letters should be written using a formal tone and structure, including the date, organization name and address, salutation, body, closing, and the writer's name, school, and school address. Give examples of formal and informal language that might be used in a letter, such as "Hi. I'm wondering if you know" versus "I am writing to request." If possible, provide a model business letter for students.

 For **writing support** for students at varying proficiency levels, see the **Text X-Ray** on page 2D.

Give a Multimodal Presentation Presentations should include both text and visual elements that describe the mission of a humanitarian organization the student has researched. Presenters should maintain eye contact with the audience, speak loudly and clearly enough to be understood, and incorporate natural gestures.

RESPOND TO THE ESSENTIAL QUESTION

Allow time for students to add details from *The Breadwinner* to their Unit 1 Response Logs.

EL **ENGLISH LEARNER SUPPORT**

Give a Multimodal Presentation Provide students with an image related to a relief organization and three facts about the aid organization. Have students present the facts and refer to the image as they do so. Give them sentence frames to help them present. For example, *In this picture we see _____. _____ is helping _____.* Base sentence frames on the picture.
SUBSTANTIAL/MODERATE

CRITICAL VOCABULARY

Answers:

1. *b*

2. *a*

3. *a*

4. *a*

VOCABULARY STRATEGY:
Parts of Speech

Answers:

responsibility (noun), solution (noun), stammer (verb)

Dictionary definitions should closely resemble word definitions shown with the selection. Sentences will vary.

 RESPOND

WORD BANK
solution
responsibility
stammer
fume

 Go to the **Vocabulary Studio** for more on using resources.

CRITICAL VOCABULARY

Practice and Apply Mark the letter of the better answer to each question.

1. Which of the following is most likely to cause someone to **fume?**
   a. an act of kindness
   b. an insulting comment

2. Which of the following is an example of a **responsibility?**
   a. feeding a pet
   b. playing a game

3. Which of the following is likely to need a **solution?**
   a. a problem
   b. an airplane

4. Which of the following is an example of a **stammer?**
   a. speaking with repetitive sounds and pauses
   b. walking with uneven steps

VOCABULARY STRATEGY:
Parts of Speech

For a clear understanding of a word's meaning, determine the word's **part of speech,** or the function it performs in a sentence. Parts of speech and their dictionary abbreviations include noun (*n.*), pronoun (*pron.*), verb (*v.*), adjective (*adj.*), and adverb (*adv.*).

Review paragraphs 89–90 to see how the word *fume* is used in the selection. Parvana *fumed* after Nooria said something unkind. Here, the word's part of speech is a verb. If you look up *fume* in a dictionary, you will see that it can also be used as a noun, meaning "gas" or "smoke." For words with **multiple meanings,** such as *fume,* compare the word's usage in context to the various dictionary definitions and their corresponding parts of speech to determine the correct meaning.

Practice and Apply Work with a partner to determine the meanings of *responsibility, solution,* and *stammer* in *The Breadwinner.* Together, use a dictionary to determine each word's part of speech and its meaning. Finally, write original sentences for *fume, responsibility, solution,* and *stammer.*

EL **ENGLISH LEARNER SUPPORT**

Review Vocabulary Review vocabulary words with students in a small group before completing the vocabulary activities. Use several examples of each word, and have students draw a picture to represent each. **SUBSTANTIAL/MODERATE**

LANGUAGE CONVENTIONS:
Capitalization of Proper Nouns

Proper nouns name a specific person, place, thing, or idea. Proper nouns are capitalized to help distinguish them from common nouns, which serve as general names for people, places, things, or ideas. In *The Breadwinner* proper nouns are used in the following ways.

- To name specific people

    Parvana realized Mrs. Weera was right.

- To name specific places, such as cities

    "You'll be our cousin from Jalalabad," said Nooria, "come to stay with us while our father is away."

- To name a specific thing, in this case, the title of the novel

    The Breadwinner

Practice and Apply Write your own sentences using capitalized proper nouns, following the examples from *The Breadwinner*. Your sentences can be about how Parvana faces challenges or ways in which you or someone else found courage in the face of fear. When you have finished, share your sentences with a partner. Check each other's work to see whether proper nouns have been capitalized and common nouns have been written in lowercase letters.

> ! Go to the **Grammar Studio** for more on capitalization and proper nouns.

LANGUAGE CONVENTIONS:
Capitalization of Proper Nouns

Remind students that a proper noun names a specific person, place, thing, or idea. We capitalize proper nouns to distinguish them from common nouns, which serve as general names for people, places, things, or ideas. Ask for volunteers to give examples of each type of common noun and a corresponding proper noun. (For example, *city* is a common noun for a place, while *Los Angeles* is a proper noun for a specific place.)

Review the examples with students. Have students determine the proper noun and whether it refers to a specific person, place, thing, or idea.

- *Parvana (person); Mrs. Weera (person)*
- *Jalabad (place); Nooria (person)*
- *The Breadwinner (thing)*

Practice and Apply *Answers will vary. All proper nouns should be capitalized. All common nouns should be lowercase.*

© Houghton Mifflin Harcourt Publishing Company

 ENGLISH LEARNER SUPPORT

Language Conventions Remind native speakers of Spanish that many types of proper nouns are capitalized in English that are not capitalized in Spanish: days, months, nationalities, and languages are examples of proper nouns not capitalized in Spanish. Also, when writing titles, only the first word of the title is capitalized. Use the following supports with students at varying proficiency levels:

- Have students help you brainstorm a list of proper nouns that need to be capitalized. Display the list where students can refer to it. **SUBSTANTIAL**

- Have students copy and complete sentence frames for each type of proper noun. (For example: *My friend's name is___.*) **MODERATE**

- Ask students to write one sentence containing each of three types of proper noun: person, place, and thing. Review students' sentences to make sure they used proper capitalization. **LIGHT**

LIFE DOESN'T FRIGHTEN ME

Poem by Maya Angelou

GENRE ELEMENTS
POETRY

Tell students that **poetry** is a powerful way for people to express emotions, offering insights or new ways of thinking. It often uses rhyme, repetition, rhythm, and refrain to bring out a melodic quality. It may also use imagery, figurative language, and other literary techniques. This lesson explores the structure of a **lyric poem,** a form of poetry that is usually short and written in the first person, expressing a single speaker's personal ideas and feelings. Lyric poetry uses forms such as odes and sonnets and addresses topics ranging from complex ideas to everyday experiences.

LEARNING OBJECTIVES

- Use an understanding of structure to read and comprehend lyric poetry.
- Analyze word choices to identify a poem's speaker.
- Expand knowledge of literary genres and poetic forms.
- Analyze word choices to identify the tone and mood of a poem.
- Write a poem about fears.
- **Language**   Discuss the features of a poem using the term *speaker*.

TEXT COMPLEXITY

Quantitative Measures	Life Doesn't Frighten Me	Lexile: N/A
Qualitative Measures	**Ideas Presented** Single level of simple meaning.	
	Structures Used Regular stanzas with some liberties taken.	
	Language Used Some figurative language.	
	Knowledge Requires Experience includes unfamiliar aspects.	

RESOURCES

- Unit 1 Response Log
- 🔊 Selection Audio
- 📖 Reading Studio: Notice & Note
- **LEVELUP** Level Up Tutorial: Imagery
- Writing Studio: Writing as a Process
- 💬 Speaking and Listening Studio: Giving a Presentation
- ☑️ "Life Doesn't Frighten Me" Selection Test

SUMMARIES

English

The speaker of "Life Doesn't Frighten Me" lists and describes a great many things that frighten most people but that don't frighten him or her. The poem goes on to talk about reactions to potential dangers other than fear, and uses hyperbole to treat the theme with humor.

Spanish

La voz narrativa de "La vida no me asusta" hace una lista descriptiva de muchas cosas que asustan a casi todo el mundo, pero no le asustan a él o ella. El poema luego habla de las reacciones, distintas al miedo, que se pueden dar ante posibles peligros, y utiliza hipérboles que tratan el tema con humor.

 ## SMALL-GROUP OPTIONS

Have students work in small groups to read and discuss the selection.

Three-Minute Review

- Pause at any time during discussion of the poem.
- Direct students to work independently, and set the timer for three minutes.
- Students review the poem and their notes, and write questions they still have about it.
- After the three minutes are up, follow up with a short discussion of what students noticed during their review and what questions they still have.

Send a Problem

- Pose a question about the ideas or actions described in "Life Doesn't Frighten Me." Call on a student to respond.
- Wait up to 11 seconds.
- If the student does not have a response, the student must call on another student by name to answer the same question.
- The sending student repeats the question as he or she calls on another for assistance.
- The teacher monitors responses and can redirect or ask another question at any time.

Text X-Ray: English Learner Support
for "Life Doesn't Frighten Me"

Use the Text X-Ray and the supports and scaffolds in the Teacher's Edition to help guide students at different proficiency levels through the selection.

INTRODUCE THE SELECTION
DISCUSS FEARS

In this lesson, students will need to be able to discuss the theme of courage in the face of a variety of fears, real and imagined. Display a word web with "fears" in the middle. Ask volunteers to name things that people fear, from real dangers, such as fire, to imagined dangers, such as monsters in the closet. Elicit conversation about things that are real but pose no danger, such as most spiders and snakes.

Before analyzing the poem, facilitate comprehension by reading the poem aloud. Then read it a second time, pausing to ask students what ideas are brought out in each stanza.

Supply the following sentence frames:

- *Just like the speaker, I am not afraid of* _____.
- *Unlike the speaker, I am afraid of* _____.

CULTURAL REFERENCES

The following words or phrases may be unfamiliar to students:

- *Mother Goose* (line 7): fictional author of nursery rhymes and tales, some of which are quite frightening because the characters often face danger or undergo harm
- *boo* (line 13): a word often shouted by someone jumping out from a hiding place with the intent scaring another person
- *shoo* (line 14): leave because someone else frightens or drives you away
- *charm* (line 37): a small object that is supposed to protect a person or bring him or her good luck

LISTENING

Understand the Sounds of Poetry

Draw students' attention to the refrain in "Life Doesn't Frighten Me." Explain that a refrain is a phrase, line, or group of lines that is repeated throughout a poem. Note that a refrain is often the most memorable part of the poem.

Have students listen as you read aloud lines 1–12. Use the following supports with students at varying proficiency levels:

- Ask students to tell you a word that is repeated several times in the part of the poem they listened to. Then read just the refrain and ask whether the word they heard is in that sentence. **SUBSTANTIAL**
- Have students identify the refrain of the poem. Have them predict from the refrain what the poem will be about. **MODERATE**
- Pair students and have them take turns naming things people are afraid of that are not named in this excerpt. After each thing they name, have them repeat the refrain. **LIGHT**

SPEAKING

Discuss Speaker

Have students discuss the features of the poem using the key term *speaker*. Circulate around the room to make sure students are using the key term correctly.

Use the following supports with students at varying proficiency levels:

- To give students an understanding of the concept of speaker, ask students to pretend that they are someone else. Use these sentence frames: *I am _____ years old. I live in _____. I have _____ brothers.* **SUBSTANTIAL**
- In small groups, have students choose and speak in the voice of a character in one of the fiction or nonfiction selections they have read. Explain that this is what a poet does who writes in the voice of a created character. **MODERATE**
- Have students in small groups play vocal charades. Each student chooses a person in the public eye and speaks as that person. The other students may ask questions that the person who is "it" may answer with any information except a name. **LIGHT**

READING

Identify Refrain

Explain to students that poetry often involves repetition, including repeated letter sounds and rhythms. One form of repetition is the refrain, a repeated phrase, line, or stanza.

Work with students to read lines 28–32. Use the following supports with students at varying proficiency levels:

- Read lines 28–32. Emphasize the refrain. Ask students to raise a hand if they detect a difference. Explain that a refrain can have these small differences. **SUBSTANTIAL**
- Read lines 28–32. Have students point out the four appearances of the refrain. If necessary, help students understand that all the sentences that end with "frighten me at all" are variations on the refrain. **MODERATE**
- Have students read the entire poem and identify the refrain lines. Ask students to point out the words that are included in every variation of the refrain. **LIGHT**

WRITING

Write a Poem

Work with students to prepare them for writing a poem in the Create and Present section on page 27.

Use the following supports with students at varying proficiency levels:

- Review rhyming with students. Then give them these couplet frames and ask them to fill in the final word with either *bogs* or *light*: *I like dogs,/not slimy little _____. It's dark at night./ I turn on the _____.* **SUBSTANTIAL**
- Review rhyming with students. Then give them these couplet beginnings and ask them to write a second line: *I don't swim in lakes,/ _____. I would sure be cryin'/ _____.* **MODERATE**
- Review rhyming with students. Then have them write a couplet that follows the structure: *I like _____,/ not _____.* **LIGHT**

? Connect to the
ESSENTIAL QUESTION

As part of this unit's exploration of fear and courage, "Life Doesn't Frighten Me" expresses a bold and humorous fearlessness in the face of life's potential dangers.

LIFE DOESN'T FRIGHTEN ME

Poem by **Maya Angelou**

? **ESSENTIAL QUESTION:**

How do you find courage in the face of fear?

© Houghton Mifflin Harcourt Publishing Company • Image Credits: ©Mihai Blanaru/Shutterstock

LEARNING MINDSET

Growth Mindset Explain that students who look forward to the next challenge and have long-range plans for new challenges have the kind of mindset that leads to success. Encourage students to view difficulties they may encounter as opportunities to learn.

QUICK START

The poem you are about to read explores both real and imaginary fears that we all face as we grow up. Make notes about both real and imaginary fears that you have now or have had in the past. After you read the poem, you'll write your own poem about facing fear.

REAL FEARS	IMAGINARY FEARS

ANALYZE SPEAKER

"Life Doesn't Frighten Me" is a **lyric poem.** Lyric poetry is a form of poetry in which a single speaker expresses his or her personal ideas and feelings. Lyric poetry can take many forms and can address all types of topics, including complex ideas or everyday experiences.

The **speaker** in any type of poetry is the voice that "talks" to the reader. The speaker may be the poet or a fictional character. Lyric poems are usually written from a first-person perspective, using the pronoun *I* or *me*. However, use of first-person pronouns does not mean that the poet is the speaker. Clues in the title and individual lines can help you determine the speaker and identify his or her situation. As you read the lyric poem, use a chart like this to help you make inferences about the poem's speaker.

MY QUESTIONS	EVIDENCE FROM THE POEM
Who is speaking? How do I know?	
What ideas and feelings does the speaker communicate? Why?	

GENRE ELEMENTS: LYRIC POETRY

- usually short to convey emotional intensity
- usually written in first-person point of view to express the speaker's thoughts and feelings
- often uses repetition, refrain, and rhyme to create a melodic quality
- includes many forms, such as sonnets, odes, and elegies

QUICK START

When you introduce the Quick Start activity, be aware that fears may be among the most personal of emotions. Assure students that they do not need to talk about anything in their lives that might cause them embarrassment.

ANALYZE SPEAKER

The speaker in any type of poetry is the voice that "talks" to the reader, the "I" and "me" of the poem if the poem is in the first person. The way the speaker talks—the tone or attitude—is often a critical part of the poem. As students read "Life Doesn't Frighten Me," encourage them to look at word choices and think about what kind of person the speaker is, his or her tone, and whether he or she is telling the truth. Is the speaker really fearless? Is there any other reason someone would say they were not afraid? Is the speaker exaggerating for some reason? Why might that be?

 ENGLISH LEARNER SUPPORT

Learning Strategies Focus on how word choices can help create a sense of who the speaker of a poem is.

- Have students play "In Other Words." Give them these sentences, and ask whether the speaker of each sentence sounds like a kid, a teenager, or a teacher: *"Gaining knowledge can be an exciting process." "Learning can be fun." "Hey, school can be cool!"*
  SUBSTANTIAL/MODERATE
- Have students play a form of "In Other Words" in which they rephrase sentences in the voices of people of different ages and personalities: *"Learning can be fun!" "I like that music." "Go away! I don't need any help."* **LIGHT**

TEACH

ANALYZE REFRAIN

Explain that lyric poems were originally written to be sung; therefore, poems in that style often have a musical quality. Poets use sound devices like repetition and rhyme to create this quality.

- **Repetition** is a technique in which a sound, word, phrase, or entire line is repeated.

- A **rhyme scheme** is a pattern of end rhymes in a poem. A common rhyme scheme is a couplet, which is a rhymed pair of lines.

As students read "Life Doesn't Frighten Me," have them look for the refrain and note how it relates to the overall rhyme scheme of the poem.

 ANNOTATION MODEL

Remind students of the annotation ideas on page 22, which suggest marking important details that signal who the speaker is and how the poet uses a refrain, or repeated words. Point out that they may follow this suggestion or use their own system for marking up the selection in their write-in text. They may want to color-code their annotations by using highlighters. Their notes in the margin may include questions about ideas that are unclear or topics they want to learn more about.

 GET READY

ANALYZE REFRAIN

Poets use structure and poetic elements to create mood and reinforce meaning. Often a poet will repeat certain words, sounds, or even syllables in a poem. This device is called **repetition.** In many types of poetry, including lyric poems, poets use repetition to emphasize important ideas, to convey the speaker's attitude toward a subject or the audience, to reveal the author's purpose, and to give the poem a musical quality. One kind of repetition is **refrain**—a phrase, line, or set of phrases or lines repeated regularly throughout the poem at intervals, often at the end of a stanza.

Here is an example of a refrain from the narrative poem "Annabel Lee" by Edgar Allan Poe. Find the refrain and mark it.

> It was many and many a year ago,
>   In a kingdom by the sea,
> That a maiden there lived whom you may know
>   By the name of Annabel Lee…
>
> *I* was a child and *she* was a child,
>   In this kingdom by the sea,
> But we loved with a love that was more than love—
>   I and my Annabel Lee…

As you read the lyric poem "Life Doesn't Frighten Me," listen for the refrain, and think about how it conveys information about the speaker's voice and the poem's mood and message.

ANNOTATION MODEL   **NOTICE & NOTE**

As you read, note clues about the poem's speaker, and examine how the poet uses a refrain to convey a message. This model shows one reader's notes about the beginning of "Life Doesn't Frighten Me."

> Shadows on the wall
>
> Noises down the hall
>
> Life doesn't frighten (me) at all
>
> Bad dogs barking loud
>
> 5 Big ghosts in a cloud
>
> Life doesn't frighten me at all.

The poem uses the pronoun "me," but the speaker might not be the poet.

This line is repeated, so it must be a refrain.

© Houghton Mifflin Harcourt Publishing Company

22   Unit 1

BACKGROUND

Maya Angelou *(1928–2014) was born Marguerite Annie Johnson in St. Louis, Missouri. Though a childhood trauma led her to stop speaking for five and a half years, Angelou grew up to pursue a career as a singer and actor. She later turned to writing as her main form of expression, and in 1970, her best-selling autobiography* I Know Why the Caged Bird Sings *made her an international literary star. She is widely admired as a fearless and inspiring voice.*

LIFE DOESN'T FRIGHTEN ME

Poem by Maya Angelou

SETTING A PURPOSE

As you read, pay attention to the details that explain the nature of fear and how fear can affect everyday life, both physically and emotionally.

Shadows on the wall
Noises down the hall
Life doesn't frighten (me) at all
Bad dogs barking loud
5 Big ghosts in a cloud
Life doesn't frighten (me) at all.

Mean old Mother Goose
Lions on the loose
They don't frighten (me) at all
10 Dragons breathing flame
On (my) counterpane[1]
That doesn't frighten (me) at all.

---

[1] **counterpane:** a bedspread.

Notice & Note

Use the side margins to notice and note signposts in the text.

ANALYZE SPEAKER

Annotate: Circle words and phrases in lines 1–12 that give you clues about the identity of the speaker.

Infer: Who do you think the speaker is in this poem? Why?

Life Doesn't Frighten Me   23

BACKGROUND

After students have read the information about the author, explain that much of Angelou's poetry focuses on people's emotional responses to hardship and loss. Many critics believe that in order for her poems to be appreciated, they must be performed. Angelou frequently recited her poems to large crowds, and she was one of only two poets in history to have read a poem at a presidential inauguration. Her reading won a Grammy Award for Best Spoken Word.

SETTING A PURPOSE

Direct students to use the Setting a Purpose prompt to focus their reading. Remind them to write down questions as they read.

ANALYZE SPEAKER

Explain to students that a **lyric poem** is a poem that expresses the personal thoughts and feelings of a speaker. The **speaker** of a lyric poem can be the poet or an invented character who has had an experience that he or she is responding to. Have a student or students reread lines 1–12 aloud. Ask them to tell who they think the speaker is and why. (**Possible Answer:** *The speaker lists many things that often scare children and says that he or she is not afraid of them; the speaker may be a child.*)

 For **listening and speaking support** for students at varying proficiency levels, see the **Text X-Ray** on pages 20C and 20D.

WHEN STUDENTS STRUGGLE . . .

Make Connections Some students may struggle with the connection between the abstract concept of "Life" and the concrete images in the first stanzas of the poem. Explain to these students that the speaker is using "Life" to refer to all the things he or she experiences or imagines.

 For additional support, go to the **Reading Studio** and assign the following **Level Up tutorial: Imagery.**

ANALYZE REFRAIN

Ask students to look at the rhyme scheme of the poem and the line lengths. Point out how the refrain differs from the other lines because it doesn't rhyme with anything, and it is a longer line. Talk with students about the effect the refrain has because of these differences. (**Answer:** *The purpose of the repeated phrase, or refrain, is to emphasize an important theme in the poem, and to evoke the sense that the speaker is coaching him- or herself into having courage.*)

■ English Learner Support

Understand Slang Read lines 13 through 16 again. Ask students to identify any words that they are unsure of. Explain that *go* is a slang usage meaning "say." To "go boo" is to say the word *boo*. Students may not have encountered the word *shoo*. Model the meaning by making a shooing gesture while you say the word. Explain that when Angelou says that she makes them shoo, she means that she lets them know she doesn't want them around and they go away. Explain that "Way they run" is a slang way of saying "Away they run." **ALL LEVELS**

For **reading support** for students at varying proficiency levels, see the **Text X-Ray** on page 20D.

ANALYZE REFRAIN

Annotate: In lines 13–21, mark the phrase that is repeated in most of the stanzas.

Interpret: What is the purpose of the repeated phrase? What idea does it emphasize?

> I go boo
> Make them shoo
> 15 I make fun
> Way they run
> I won't cry
> So they fly
> I just smile
> 20 They go wild
> Life doesn't frighten me at all.
>
> Tough guys in a fight
> All alone at night
> Life doesn't frighten me at all.
>
> 25 Panthers in the park
> Strangers in the dark
> No, they don't frighten me at all.
>
> That new classroom where
> Boys all pull my hair
> 30 (Kissy little girls
> With their hair in curls)
> They don't frighten me at all.
>
> Don't show me frogs and snakes
> And listen for my scream,
> 35 If I'm afraid at all
> It's only in my dreams.

TO CHALLENGE STUDENTS

Analyze Imagery and Line Length Have students reread lines 22–27. Ask them to discuss how these lines differ from those immediately before and after them. What is different about the images and the ideas they represent? What is different about the language and form of the lines? (**Answer:** *The images are very real and are situations that could be quite dangerous. The lines are longer and the language more serious.*)

I've got a magic charm
That I keep up my sleeve,
I can walk the ocean floor
40 And never have to breathe.

Life doesn't frighten me at all
Not at all
Not at all
Life doesn't frighten me at all.

AGAIN AND AGAIN

Notice & Note: What lines are repeated in the last stanza? Mark the lines.

Interpret: Why do you think the speaker repeats those lines?

CHECK YOUR UNDERSTANDING

Answer these questions before moving on to the **Analyze the Text** section on the following page.

1 The speaker in the poem confronts fears by —

A screaming at scary things

B pulling classmates' hair

C smiling and making fun

D reading nursery rhymes

2 The lines "If I'm afraid at all / It's only in my dreams" emphasize that the speaker is —

F brave in the face of danger

G scared of waking up

H brave only when asleep

J tired and needs to rest

3 What is an important topic in the poem?

A Going to school every day

B Being afraid of animals

C Using your imagination

D Getting enough sleep

Life Doesn't Frighten Me   25

AGAIN AND AGAIN

Explain to students that, when they see **repetition** in a poem, it indicates that something is important. It's up to the reader to figure out what the importance is. In the last stanza of this poem, the refrain, which has been repeated many times before in the poem, is stated twice. And the phrase *Not at all* is also stated twice. Evidence in the poem indicates that the speaker is a child. Why would a child say again and again that he or she is not afraid at all? (**Answer:** *Sometimes people repeat things in order to convince themselves and the person to whom they are talking that something is true.*)

CHECK YOUR UNDERSTANDING

Have students answer the questions independently.

Answers:

1. C

2. F

3. C

If they answer any questions incorrectly, have them reread the text to confirm their understanding. Then they may proceed to ANALYZE THE TEXT on page 26.

ENGLISH LEARNER SUPPORT

Oral Assessment Use the following questions to assess students' comprehension and speaking skills.

1. How does the speaker face fears? (*The speaker smiles and makes fun of scary things.*)

2. The speaker says he or she is only afraid in dreams. Is the speaker brave or not brave when he or she is awake? (*brave*)

3. What is an important idea in this poem? (*using imagination*) **SUBSTANTIAL/MODERATE**

APPLY

ANALYZE THE TEXT

Possible answers:

1. **DOK 3:** *The speaker may be a highly imaginative and playful child. You can infer this because the speaker talks about childhood fears ("Big ghosts") and children's things, such as "Mother Goose." In lines 37–40, the speaker talks about the kind of imaginary things a child might believe in.*

2. **DOK 4:** *The scary things include "Big ghosts in a cloud" and "Dragons breathing flame." Possible real scary things could be "Noises down the hall" and "Bad dogs barking loud." All of them are things that young children might be afraid of and help emphasize that the speaker is young. They also point out that the speaker is no more afraid of the real things than the imagined things.*

3. **DOK 4:** *The shorter lines make the poem go faster and seem more exciting. They also make rhythm simpler and more singsong, like a nursery rhyme.*

4. **DOK 4:** *The speaker may be afraid of some things named in the poem, but uses the refrain to build his or her courage.*

5. **DOK 4:** *Listing all of the potentially scary things shows the reader how strong the speaker is; the speaker has many fears to face.*

RESEARCH

Suggest that students search reputable news archives to research their answers.

Extend Encourage students to use a compare and contrast graphic organizer to record their thoughts about these two poems.

RESPOND

ANALYZE THE TEXT

Support your responses with evidence from the text. NOTEBOOK

1. **Draw Conclusions** Review lines 1–9 and lines 37–40. What conclusions can you draw about the speaker's age and personality?

2. **Analyze** Reread lines 1–21. Which scary things are clearly imaginary? Which are possibly real? What effect does this variety of scary things create in the poem?

3. **Evaluate** Read aloud lines 1–24. Notice the change to shorter line lengths in the third stanza. What effect does this change have on your reading?

4. **Synthesize** Explain how the poet uses the refrain "Life doesn't frighten me at all" to help convey the meaning of the poem. Do you think the speaker of the poem is truly unafraid? Why or why not?

5. **Notice & Note** Review all the things that the speaker claims not to be afraid of. What is the effect of naming them?

RESEARCH TIP
When you conduct online research, evaluate the credibility of websites. Web addresses ending in .gov, .edu, or .org may be expertly reviewed more frequently, but you should always read critically. Look for an About section to help identify who created the website.

RESEARCH

With a partner, research the poem that Maya Angelou delivered at the 1993 presidential inauguration. Listen to or watch Angelou delivering the poem. Use what you learn to answer these questions.

QUESTION	ANSWER
Who was the new president inaugurated in 1993?	*Bill Clinton*
What poem did Maya Angelou recite at the inauguration?	*On the Pulse of Morning*
What award did Angelou win for her reading of the inaugural poem?	*a Grammy in the Spoken Word category*

Extend How is the poem Maya Angelou delivered at the 1993 presidential inauguration similar to "Life Doesn't Frighten Me"? Discuss with your partner what the two poems have in common.

CREATE AND PRESENT

Write a Poem Write a poem in which you employ a young speaker to express fears, both real and imaginary. Review your notes on the Quick Start activity before you begin.

- ❏ Decide if you want your poem to be humorous or serious.
- ❏ Choose examples of fears that create the most vivid picture in your mind or evoke the strongest feelings.
- ❏ Include a refrain to emphasize the meaning of the poem.

Present a Poem Different people can read the same poem aloud in very different ways. With a partner, prepare a choral reading of "Life Doesn't Frighten Me."

- ❏ Decide who will read which lines or stanzas of the poem.
- ❏ Practice reading the poem, adjusting the rhythm and pacing of your reading according to different line lengths in the poem.
- ❏ Make eye contact with your audience, and use facial expressions and natural gestures to convey the meaning of the poem.
- ❏ Practice your choral reading until you can present the poem smoothly. Then, read it aloud to a small group or the class.

RESPOND TO THE ESSENTIAL QUESTION

? How do you find courage in the face of fear?

Gather Information Review your annotations and notes on "Life Doesn't Frighten Me." Then, add relevant details to your Response Log. As you determine which information to include, think about:

- the difference between real and imaginary fears
- how the kinds of things you fear change as you grow up
- the best way to face fear

At the end of the unit, use your notes to write an informational essay.

RESPOND

Go to the **Writing Studio** for more on the writing process.

Go to the **Speaking and Listening Studio** for more on giving a presentation.

ACADEMIC VOCABULARY
As you write and discuss what you learned from the poem, be sure to use the Academic Vocabulary words. Check off each of the words that you use.

- ❏ evident
- ❏ factor
- ❏ indicate
- ❏ similar
- ❏ specific

CREATE AND PRESENT

Write a Poem Explain to students that beginning to write a poem can involve some thinking and planning. Suggest that they use some of these steps.

- Imagine a speaker. Think about your speaker's age, experience, and personality.
- Begin by saying a sentence aloud the way you think your speaker would say it. Then write that sentence.
- Get your thoughts and ideas down as quickly as they come to you.
- Revise your poem to make it more interesting or more fun.

For **writing support** for students at varying proficiency levels, see the **Text X-Ray** on page 20D.

Present a Poem Remind students that they should speak loudly enough to be heard at the back of the room, and that they can use variations in volume, as well as facial expressions and gestures, to communicate the emotions and ideas in the poem.

RESPOND TO THE ESSENTIAL QUESTION

Allow time for students to add details from "Life Doesn't Frighten Me" to their Unit 1 Response Logs.

MENTOR TEXT

FEARS AND PHOBIAS

Article by KIDSHEALTH.ORG

This article serves as a **mentor text**, a model for students to follow when they come to the Unit 1 Writing Task: Writing an Informational Essay.

GENRE ELEMENTS
INFORMATIONAL TEXT

Remind students that the purpose of **informational text** is to present facts and information. An **article** is a short informational text that focuses on a narrow topic. To help readers understand the topic, the article must be well organized. It may use text features such as headings, sidebars, and boldfaced type to guide the reader through different aspects of the topic. In this lesson, students will use text features to help them explore the topic of the article "Fears and Phobias."

LEARNING OBJECTIVES

- Cite evidence to support analysis of the text and use text features to navigate informational text.
- Conduct research about phobias.
- Write an informative essay about fears and phobias.
- Discuss information that can help someone overcome a fear.
- Use prefixes that mean "not" to define unfamiliar words.
- Analyze how writers use dashes.
- **Language** Discuss with a partner the features of the text using the key term *subheadings*.

TEXT COMPLEXITY

Quantitative Measures	Fears and Phobias	Lexile: 1080L
Qualitative Measures	**Ideas Presented** Mostly explicit, but moves to some implied meaning.	
	Structures Used Text features guide reading; ideas are generally sequential.	
	Language Used Mostly Tier II and III words; some technical words are used.	
	Knowledge Required Most of the text deals with common or easily imagined experiences.	

RESOURCES

- Unit 1 Response Log
- Selection Audio
- Previewing the Text
- Close Read Screencasts: Modeled Discussions
- Reading Studio: Notice & Note
- Level Up Tutorial: Reading for Details
- Writing Studio: Writing Informative Texts
- Speaking and Listening Studio: Participating in Collaborative Discussions
- Vocabulary Studio: Prefixes
- Grammar Studio: Modules 12 and 13: Punctuation
- "Fears and Phobias" Selection Test

SUMMARIES

English

Fear is a natural response to danger that has both physiological and emotional components. People are afraid of many things, some rational and some not. Children tend to fear situations that are unfamiliar, but outgrow these fears with support from adults. However, some fears develop into phobias, causing people to experience intense fear when faced with specific things or situations. Phobias can be overcome by gradually facing the object of fear, often with the support of a therapist.

Spanish

El miedo es una respuesta natural al peligro que tiene componentes fisiológicos y emocionales. La gente tiene miedo de muchas cosas, algunas racionales y otras no. Los niños tienden a temer situaciones que no son familiares, pero superan estos temores con el apoyo de los adultos. Sin embargo, algunos miedos se convierten en fobias, haciendo que la gente experimente un miedo intenso cuando se enfrentan con cosas o situaciones específicas. Las fobias se pueden superar enfrentando gradualmente el objeto del miedo, a menudo con el apoyo de un terapeuta.

SMALL-GROUP OPTIONS

Have students work in small groups to read and discuss the selection.

Jigsaw with Experts

- Divide the selection into six parts: the first two subheadings in the text are one part, and the remaining five subheadings are each one part.
- Have students count off, or assign each student a numbered section.
- After reading the text, have students form groups with other students who read the same section. Each expert group should discuss its section.
- Then, have students form new groups with a representative for each section. These groups should discuss all the sections and the selection as a whole.

Think-Pair-Share

- After students have read and analyzed "Fears and Phobias," pose this question: *What would be the most difficult part of overcoming a phobia?*
- Have students think about the question individually and take notes.
- Then, have pairs discuss their ideas about the question.
- Finally, ask pairs to share their responses with the class.

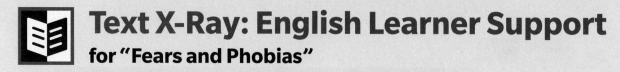

Text X-Ray: English Learner Support
for "Fears and Phobias"

Use the Text X-Ray and the supports and scaffolds in the Teacher's Edition to help guide students at different proficiency levels through the selection.

INTRODUCE THE SELECTION
DISCUSS EMOTIONS AND INSTINCTS

In this lesson, students will need to be able to discuss emotions and instincts. Read paragraph 2 with students, and point out the words *emotions* and *instincts*. Provide the following explanations:

- An emotion is a strong feeling, like love, anger, or fear.
- An instinct is a way of behaving or feeling that is not learned.

Explain to students that one or more emotions or feelings usually accompany an instinct. For example, when a person's instincts tell him or her to escape a situation, that person is usually feeling the emotion of fear. Have volunteers share instincts and the emotions that accompany them. Supply the following sentence frames:

- *_____ is an example of an emotion. _____ is an example of an instinct.*
- *When a person's instinct is to _____, that person is feeling _____.*

CULTURAL REFERENCES

The following words or phrases may be unfamiliar to students:

- *emotional reaction* (paragraph 8): the way someone responds to a feeling
- *public speaking* (paragraph 11): talking in front of a group of people
- *get used to* (paragraph 13): do more often
- *takeoff* (paragraph 13): when a plane leaves the ground and begins to go into the sky

LISTENING

Understand the Central Idea

Draw students' attention to the subheadings in the article. Explain that a subheading shows the beginning of a new section or topic. Direct students' attention to the heading on p. 17, "Fears People Have." Explain that the subheading of a section can help them figure out the main idea of the section.

Have students listen as you read aloud paragraphs 8–13. Use the following supports with students at varying proficiency levels:

- Tell students you will ask some questions about what they just heard. Model that they should give a thumbs up if the answer is yes, and a thumbs down for no. For example, ask: *Do people fear situations that make them feel safe? (No)* **SUBSTANTIAL**
- Have students identify the central idea of the excerpt. Ask: *How did the subheading help you identify the main idea?* **MODERATE**
- After listening to the excerpt read aloud, ask students to work in pairs to list details that support the central idea. **LIGHT**

SPEAKING

Discuss Text Features

Have students discuss the features of the text using the key term *subheading*. Circulate around the room to make sure students are using the key term correctly.

Use the following supports with students at varying proficiency levels:

- Display and read aloud this sentence: *The subheading "Fears People Have" tells me that this section of the article is about kinds of fear.* Have students say it aloud back to you and then practice saying it to a partner. **SUBSTANTIAL**
- To help students express their ideas about the subheadings in the article, display the following sentence frames: *Subheadings are one way the author _____. The subheading tells _____.* **MODERATE**
- Have students discuss with a partner how some of the subheadings can be rephrased as questions. (Point out that two of the subheadings are already questions.) How does rephrasing the subheadings into questions help them understand what the sections will be about? **LIGHT**

READING

Identify Central Idea

Tell students that authors of informational text provide evidence in the form of facts, examples, explanations, definitions, direct quotations, and other details to help readers understand the central idea, or most important idea.

Work with students to reread paragraphs 22–24. Use the following supports with students at varying proficiency levels:

- Explain that they can identify a central idea in these paragraphs, such as: *Phobias develop for different reasons.* Ask: *What is one reason a person might have a phobia?* Accept single words or phrases. **SUBSTANTIAL**
- Guide students to identify a central idea. Then, have students find evidence to support that idea. Supply sentence frames, such as: *According to the text, a phobia may be caused by _____.* **MODERATE**
- Have students identify a central idea in the text using this frame: *A central idea in these paragraphs is _____.* Then, ask students to identify and share two pieces of evidence to support this central idea. **LIGHT**

WRITING

Write an Informational Essay

Work with students to read the writing assignment on p. 39.

Use the following supports with students at varying proficiency levels:

- Work with students to create a Venn diagram comparing and contrasting fears and phobias. Help them identify words and phrases in the text to add to the diagram. Then use the details to write an informative paragraph on the board. Have students copy the paragraph in their notebooks. **SUBSTANTIAL**
- Provide sentence frames such as the following that students can use to craft their essays: *Fears and phobias are caused by _____. Fears are _____, but phobias are _____. When someone has a phobia, he or she _____. Fear is a good thing because _____.* **MODERATE**
- Remind students of the transitions they can use to compare and contrast, such as *both, similarly, in the same way, however, but, unlike,* and *on the other hand.* Have pairs find three places in their essays where they can use a transition. **LIGHT**

Connect to the
ESSENTIAL QUESTION

"Fears and Phobias" explains why people experience fear and, in some cases, develop specific phobias. The article then describes ways people can overcome phobias, gradually learning how to find courage in the face of fear.

MENTOR TEXT

At the end of the unit, students will be asked to write an informational essay. "Fears and Phobias" provides a model for how a writer can support ideas with facts and examples.

ANALYZE & APPLY

FEARS AND PHOBIAS

Informational Text by **kidshealth.org**

? ESSENTIAL QUESTION:

How do you find courage in the face of fear?

⚙ LEARNING MINDSET

Growth Mindset Remind students that a growth mindset means believing you can get smarter by taking on challenges and pushing yourself. Encourage students to look at every selection as an opportunity to set higher goals and stretch past their comfort zone.

QUICK START

The fear of heights is called *acrophobia*. How do you feel when you see a rollercoaster like the one on the previous page?

CITE EVIDENCE

To support analysis of any text that you read, you need to be able to **cite evidence,** or provide specific information from the text. Evidence can include details, facts, statistics, quotations, and examples.

❏ To gather support for an inference or conclusion, mark significant words and details throughout the text.

❏ To summarize the main idea and details, cite details from different sections of the text, in the correct order.

❏ To analyze how a text is organized, mark words that signal a pattern of organization, such as *because* or *as a result* for cause-and-effect organization.

ANALYZE STRUCTURE

Text features are design elements that highlight the organization and important details in an informational text.

GENRE ELEMENTS: INFORMATIONAL TEXT

• provides factual information

• includes evidence to support ideas

• contains text features

• includes many forms, such as news articles and essays

TEXT FEATURE	EXAMPLE
A **heading** or **subheading** indicates the beginning of a new topic or section.	**What Is Fear?** Fear is one of the most basic human emotions. It is programmed into the nervous system and works like an instinct. From the time we're infants. . . .
A **sidebar,** or **boxed feature,** contains information related to a main topic set in a box alongside or within an article.	*Some people find the rush of fear exciting. They might seek out the thrill of extreme sports and savor the scariest horror flicks. Others do not like the experience of feeling afraid or taking risks.*
Colored type is used to emphasize an important term or idea.	A tiny brain structure called the **amygdala** (pronounced: uh-mig-duh-luh) keeps track of experiences that trigger strong emotions.

You can use text features to get an idea of the topics in a text. They can also help you locate the controlling idea, or thesis statement, and its supporting evidence. As you read, you will note the author's use of text features.

QUICK START

Have students read the Quick Start question, and invite them to share their reactions to heights. Ask them to rate their fear of heights on a scale of 1 to 10. Call on students who are not very afraid of heights to name other things that are scarier. Then have the class brainstorm a list of specific responses to fear, including both emotional and physical sensations.

CITE EVIDENCE

Help students understand the terms and concepts related to citing evidence when discussing or analyzing an informational text. Discuss both the types of evidence (details, facts, statistics, quotations, examples) and the purposes for citing evidence (supporting an inference or conclusion, summarizing a text, analyzing text organization) mentioned on page 29. Then point out that all of these purposes and kinds of evidence can be used together when gathering information from an article.

ANALYZE STRUCTURE

Tell students that using text features will make it easier for them to understand important information in an article. Review the text features in the chart, and discuss which one might be most helpful in getting a general idea of what the text is about. Then ask students how each feature could help them locate a specific topic in the text.

Suggest that students use these questions to help them analyze and annotate text features:

• What text features does the text include?

• Which features help me preview and locate main ideas in the text?

• How does information under a particular heading fit into the whole text? What important ideas does it include?

 ENGLISH LEARNER SUPPORT

Understand Directionality Reinforce the directionality of English by reviewing how to read the Analyze Structure chart. Explain that each column heading applies to the text in all the rows beneath it. To read the chart, students should begin at the top left. The top row, left column introduces the first text feature—headings or subheadings. After reading this definition, students should track to the right to see the example of a heading. Then they should move on to the middle row, left column. Ask a volunteer to trace with a finger the order a reader would read the information in the chart. **SUBSTANTIAL**

TEACH

CRITICAL VOCABULARY

Encourage students to read all the sentences before deciding which word best completes each one. Remind them to look for context clues that match the precise meaning of each word.

Answers:

1. *trigger*

2. *Immaturity*

3. *activate*

4. *turbulence*

■ English Learner Support

Use Cognates Tell students that several of the Critical Vocabulary words have Spanish cognates: *activate/activar, turbulence/turbulencia, immaturity/inmadurez.*
ALL LEVELS

LANGUAGE CONVENTIONS

Review the information about dashes. Explain that the example sentence has dashes, but that if students were typing the sentence, they could substitute two hyphens (--) with no space before or after them.

Read aloud the example sentence, using appropriate pauses and emphasis to indicate the use of dashes. Then read it aloud again as though the dashes were not there. Discuss what the dashes add to the sentence. (*The dashes add emphasis to the phrase* and helpful, *drawing readers' attention to the idea that feeling afraid can be helpful.*)

ANNOTATION MODEL

Remind students of the annotation ideas in Cite Evidence on page 29, which suggest underlining important details and circling words that signal how the text is organized. Point out that they may follow this suggestion or use their own system for marking up the selection in their write-in text. They may want to color-code their annotations by using highlighters. Their notes in the margin may include questions about ideas that are unclear or topics they want to learn more about.

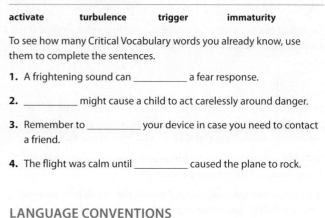

◎ GET READY

CRITICAL VOCABULARY

| activate | turbulence | trigger | immaturity |

To see how many Critical Vocabulary words you already know, use them to complete the sentences.

1. A frightening sound can _____ a fear response.

2. _____ might cause a child to act carelessly around danger.

3. Remember to _____ your device in case you need to contact a friend.

4. The flight was calm until _____ caused the plane to rock.

LANGUAGE CONVENTIONS

Dashes In this lesson, you will learn about the effective use of dashes in writing. Dashes are used to set off phrases that are added to sentences or that interrupt them:

Feeling afraid is very natural—and helpful—in some situations.

A dash is made with two unspaced hyphens. As you read "Fears and Phobias," note the author's use of dashes.

ANNOTATION MODEL   **NOTICE & NOTE**

As you read, note the author's use of text features to organize the article. You can also mark up evidence that supports your own ideas. In the model, you can see one reader's notes about "Fears and Phobias."

What Is Fear? ← ─────────────── subheading—introduces a new topic

2 Fear is <u>one of the most basic human emotions</u>. It is programmed into the nervous system and works like an instinct. From the time we're infants, <u>we are equipped with the survival instincts necessary to respond with fear when we sense danger or feel unsafe.</u>

important ideas about fear

3 Fear⌐helps protect us⌐. It makes us alert to danger and prepares us to deal with it. Feeling afraid is very natural—and helpful—in some situations. Fear can be⌐like a warning⌐, a signal that cautions us to be careful.

These details tell me fear can be helpful.

© Houghton Mifflin Harcourt Publishing Company

BACKGROUND

Most people experience fear now and then; fear is an ordinary part of life. Some fears may be overcome quickly; others may continue, in varying degrees, for a lifetime. Science explains why we experience fear and why sometimes our fears seem out of control. Whether it is a fear of spiders, a fear of the dark, or a fear of flying, using science to understand our responses to fear is the first step toward conquering it.

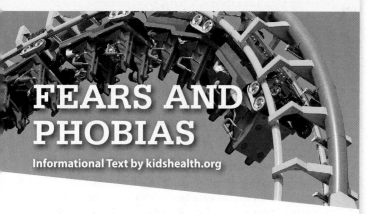

FEARS AND PHOBIAS

Informational Text by kidshealth.org

SETTING A PURPOSE

As you read, pay attention to the details that explain the nature of fear and how fear can affect everyday life, both physically and emotionally.

1   The roller coaster hesitates for a split second at the peak of its steep track after a long, slow climb. You know what's about to happen—and there's no way to avoid it now. It's time to hang onto the handrail, palms sweating, heart racing, and brace yourself for the wild ride down.

What Is Fear?

2   Fear is one of the most basic human emotions. It is programmed into the nervous system and works like an instinct. From the time we're infants, we are equipped with the survival instincts necessary to respond with fear when we sense danger or feel unsafe.

3   Fear helps protect us. It makes us alert to danger and prepares us to deal with it. Feeling afraid is very natural—

Notice & Note

Use the side margins to notice and note signposts in the text.

ANALYZE STRUCTURE

Annotate: Mark the first subheading in the article. Then, mark two details in paragraphs 2–4 that answer the question it asks.

Analyze: Does the writer suggest that fear is mostly helpful or unhelpful? Cite evidence in your answer.

BACKGROUND

After students read the Background note, explain that everyone experiences fear in different situations and in varying degrees. Science can help us understand the purposes fear has for the human body and human survival. The article identifies different types of fear and shows that understanding the fear response helps control it.

SETTING A PURPOSE

Direct students to use the Setting a Purpose prompt to focus their reading.

⏵ TEXT IN FOCUS

Previewing the Text   Have students view the **Text in Focus** video in their eBook to learn how to preview a nonfiction text. Then have students use **Text in Focus Practice PDF** to apply what they have learned.

✎ ANALYZE STRUCTURE

Remind students that the **subheadings** in informational texts often indicate the main topics or most important ideas. (**Answer:** *The writer suggests that fear is mostly helpful. It "helps protect us" from danger by acting "like a warning, a signal that cautions us to be careful."*)

📖   For **speaking support** for students at varying proficiency levels, see the **Text X-Ray** on page 28D.

🗨 ENGLISH LEARNER SUPPORT

Learning Strategies   Provide students with a main-idea-and-details organizer. Ask them to work individually to complete the organizer for the "What Is Fear?" section (paragraphs 2–4). Then have small groups compare their organizers, decide on the best main idea statements and most important details, and create a revised version that reflects their decisions. They may repeat this process for other subheadings throughout the article. **ALL LEVELS**

ENGLISH LEARNER SUPPORT

Understand Language Structures Have students locate the sentence in paragraph 5 with a phrase in parentheses. Explain that text in parentheses often explains the word or phrase that appears right before it. Ask students to discuss with partners how the text in parentheses is related to "physical action." *(The text in parentheses gives two examples of physical action, running and fighting, to help readers understand the author's meaning.)* **MODERATE**

 ANALYZE STRUCTURE

Remind students that a **boxed feature** contains extra information related to the topic of an article. This information is often set off in a box or colored space, near related text in the main article. **(Answer:** *The article has explained what fear is and how it works in the human body. The boxed feature is also about fear, but it explores different responses people may have to it—some people enjoy "the rush of fear," while others do not.)*

CRITICAL VOCABULARY

activate: When we feel danger, our brain starts a reaction that causes many changes in our bodies.

ASK STUDENTS what physical responses are activated by the signal from the nervous system. *(heart beats faster, blood pressure increases, skin sweats)*

trigger: The article explains that a reaction to danger can be caused instantly, but sometimes that cause is not dangerous at all.

ASK STUDENTS how the fear reaction is triggered and turned off by the brain within seconds. *(When the brain perceives no danger, it stops the reaction.)*

 NOTICE & NOTE

and helpful—in some situations. <u>Fear can be like a warning, a signal that cautions us to be careful.</u>

4   Like all emotions, fear can be mild, medium, or intense, depending on the situation and the person. A feeling of fear can be brief or it can last longer.

How Fear Works

5   When we sense danger, the brain reacts instantly, sending signals that **activate** the nervous system. This causes physical responses, such as a faster heartbeat, rapid breathing, and an increase in blood pressure. Blood pumps to muscle groups to prepare the body for physical action (such as running or fighting). Skin sweats to keep the body cool. Some people might notice sensations in the stomach, head, chest, legs, or hands. These physical sensations of fear can be mild or strong.

6   This response is known as "fight or flight" because that is exactly what the body is preparing itself to do: fight off the danger or run fast to get away. The body stays in this state of fight-flight until the brain receives an "all clear" message and turns off the response.

7   Sometimes fear is **triggered** by something that is startling or unexpected (like a loud noise), even if it's not actually dangerous. That's because the fear reaction is activated instantly—a few seconds faster than the thinking part of the brain can process or evaluate what's happening. As soon as the brain gets enough information to realize there's no danger ("Oh, it's just a balloon bursting—whew!"), it turns off the fear reaction. All this can happen in seconds.

Fear or Fun?

Some people find the rush of fear exciting. They might seek out the thrill of extreme sports and savor the scariest horror flicks. Others do not like the experience of feeling afraid or taking risks. During the scariest moments of a roller coaster ride one person might think, "I'll never get on this thing again—that is, if I make it out alive!" while another person thinks, "This is awesome! As soon as it's over, I'm getting back on!"

activate
(ăk´tə-vāt´) *v.* To *activate* something means to cause it to start working.

trigger
(trĭg´r) *v.* To *trigger* something means to cause it to begin.

ANALYZE STRUCTURE
Annotate: Mark the most important idea in the boxed feature "Fear or Fun?"

Connect: How does the information in this feature relate to what you have read so far?

© Houghton Mifflin Harcourt Publishing Company • Image Credits: ©Dmitry Burlakov/Shutterstock

Fears People Have

8 Fear is the word we use to describe our emotional reaction to something that seems dangerous. But the word "fear" is used in another way, too: to name something a person often feels afraid of.

9 People fear things or situations that make them feel unsafe or unsure. For instance, someone who isn't a strong swimmer might have a fear of deep water. In this case, the fear is helpful because it cautions the person to stay safe. Someone could overcome this fear by learning how to swim safely.

10 A fear can be healthy if it cautions a person to stay safe around something that could be dangerous. But sometimes a fear is unnecessary and causes more caution than the situation calls for.

11 Many people have a fear of public speaking. Whether it's giving a report in class, speaking at an assembly, or reciting lines in the school play, speaking in front of others is one of the most common fears people have.

12 People tend to avoid the situations or things they fear. But this doesn't help them overcome fear—in fact, it can be the reverse. Avoiding something scary reinforces a fear and keeps it strong.

13 People can overcome unnecessary fears by giving themselves the chance to learn about and gradually get used to the thing or situation they're afraid of. For example, people

NOTICE & NOTE

CITE EVIDENCE

Annotate: In paragraphs 8–13, mark an example of a healthy fear and an example of an unnecessary fear.

Compare: How are healthy fears different from unnecessary fears?

CITE EVIDENCE

Point out that this section compares helpful, healthy fears with unhealthy fears. The clue word *But* in paragraph 10 is a signal that the author has included a contrast. (**Answer:** *Healthy fears can keep a person safe from a dangerous situation, while unnecessary fears can keep people from experiencing new situations.*)

■ English Learner Support

Understand Contrasts Help students locate the words *helpful, healthy,* and *unnecessary* in the text, and make sure they understand the meanings. Then have students work in pairs to find examples of the two kinds of fear. **SUBSTANTIAL/MODERATE**

For **listening support** for students at varying proficiency levels, see the **Text X-Ray** on page 28C.

APPLYING ACADEMIC VOCABULARY

❏ **evident**   ❏ **factor**   ❏ **indicate**   ☑ **similar**   ☑ **specific**

Write and Discuss Have students turn to a partner to discuss the following questions. Guide students to include the Academic Vocabulary words *similar* and *specific* in their responses. Ask volunteers to share their responses with the class.

- Which fears that people have are **similar** to each other?
- How do **specific** fears and phobias affect different people in different ways?

TEACH

LANGUAGE CONVENTIONS

Review the three possible uses for dashes listed in the note. Explain that an interruption of thought would usually occur in a story—a character is thinking or speaking about one thing and is suddenly distracted or cut off by something else. Have them focus on the remaining two options as they analyze paragraph 14. **(Answer:** *The dash is used to emphasize the idea that certain fears are normal and natural for children. It makes sense that children would feel unsure and vulnerable because many of their experiences are new and unfamiliar.)*

CRITICAL VOCABULARY

turbulence: The author uses the word *turbulence* to describe a specific kind of sensation that may occur during flying. The phrase *It's just turbulence* might be frightening to someone who doesn't fly often.

ASK STUDENTS to discuss why an interruption in the flow of the wind makes turbulence terrifying. Have them consider what turbulence feels like to a passenger. (*A plane flying into a steady wind flies smoothly. If the plane bounces, as it does during turbulence, it may seem like the plane is no longer flying or that it is falling out of the sky.*)

34   Unit 1

NOTICE & NOTE

turbulence
(tûr′byə-ləns) *n.* In flying, *turbulence* is an interruption in the flow of wind that causes planes to rise, fall, or sway in a rough way.

LANGUAGE CONVENTIONS
Dashes can be used to show an interruption of thought, to include an additional detail, or to emphasize an idea. Explain how the writer uses a dash in paragraph 14.

who fly despite a fear of flying can become used to unfamiliar sensations like takeoff or **turbulence**. They learn what to expect and have a chance to watch what others do to relax and enjoy the flight. Gradually (and safely) facing fear helps someone overcome it.

Fears During Childhood

14 Certain fears are normal during childhood. That's because fear can be a natural reaction to feeling unsure and vulnerable—and much of what children experience is new and unfamiliar.

15   Young kids often have fears of the dark, being alone, strangers, and monsters or other scary imaginary creatures. School-aged kids might be afraid when it's stormy or at a first sleepover. As they grow and learn, with the support of adults, most kids are able to slowly conquer these fears and outgrow them.

16   Some kids are more sensitive to fears and may have a tough time overcoming them. When fears last beyond the expected age, it might be a sign that someone is overly fearful, worried, or anxious. People whose fears are too intense or last too long might need help and support to overcome them.

34   Unit 1

WHEN STUDENTS STRUGGLE . . .

Compare and Contrast Have individuals or partners use a chart to compare fears and phobias. Students may compare different aspects than the ones shown here.

	Fears	Phobias
What It Is	basic emotion, warning	intense fear, false alarm
What It Is Not	sign of weakness	sign of weakness

For additional support, go to the **Reading Studio** and assign the following [LEVEL] **Level Up tutorial: Reading for Details.**

Phobias

17 A phobia is an intense fear reaction to a particular thing or a situation. With a phobia, the fear is out of proportion to the potential danger. But to the person with the phobia, the danger feels real because the fear is so very strong.

18 Phobias cause people to worry about, dread, feel upset by, and avoid the things or situations they fear because the physical sensations of fear can be so intense. So having a phobia can interfere with normal activities. A person with a phobia of dogs might feel afraid to walk to school in case he or she sees a dog on the way. Someone with an elevator phobia might avoid a field trip if it involves going on an elevator.

19 A girl with a phobia of thunderstorms might be afraid to go to school if the weather forecast predicts a storm. She might feel terrible distress and fear when the sky turns cloudy. A guy with social phobia experiences intense fear of public speaking or interacting, and may be afraid to answer questions in class, give a report, or speak to classmates in the lunchroom.

20 It can be exhausting and upsetting to feel the intense fear that goes with having a phobia. It can be disappointing to miss out on opportunities because fear is holding you back. And it can be confusing and embarrassing to feel afraid of things that others seem to have no problem with.

21 Sometimes, people get teased about their fears. Even if the person doing the teasing doesn't mean to be unkind and unfair, teasing only makes the situation worse.

What Causes Phobias?

22 Some phobias develop when someone has a scary experience with a particular thing or situation. A tiny brain structure called the **amygdala** (pronounced: uh-mig-duh-luh) keeps track of experiences that trigger strong emotions. Once a certain thing or situation triggers a strong fear reaction, the amygdala warns the person by triggering a fear reaction every time he or she encounters (or even thinks about) that thing or situation.

23 Someone might develop a bee phobia after being stung during a particularly scary situation. For that person, looking at a photograph of a bee, seeing a bee from a distance, or even walking near flowers where there *could* be a bee can all trigger the phobia.

24 Sometimes, though, there may be no single event that causes a particular phobia. Some people may be more sensitive

CITE EVIDENCE

Annotate: In paragraph 17, mark the definition of *phobia*.

Connect: How might a phobia affect someone? Cite evidence from paragraphs 18–21 in your response.

> **WORD GAPS**

Notice & Note: Mark clues in paragraph 22 that help you understand the word in purple type.

Infer: Why does the author introduce the word *amygdala* in this section of the article?

CLOSE READ SCREENCAST

Modeled Discussion In their eBooks, have students view the Close Read Screencast, in which readers discuss and annotate paragraphs 22–23, an excerpt from the section under the heading "What Causes Phobias?"

As a class, view and discuss the video. Then have students pair up to do an independent close read of paragraphs 29–32. Students can record their answers on the Close Read Practice PDF.

 Close Read Practice PDF

 CITE EVIDENCE

Remind students that citing text evidence is a way to support a statement they make about the text. Encourage them to make a general statement about how a phobia can affect a person and then support the statement with an example from the text. (**Answer:** *A person with a phobia may feel unsafe in an everyday, safe situation. Seeing a dog or riding an elevator is usually safe, but a person with a phobia about dogs or elevators would be scared [paragraph 18].*)

 ENGLISH LEARNER SUPPORT

Confirm Understanding Use the following supports with students at varying proficiency levels:

• Write *amygdala* on the board, and draw lines to separate the syllables. Pronounce the word several times, with students repeating it after you. Then use simple drawings to illustrate the example about the bee phobia in paragraph 23. **SUBSTANTIAL**

• Have students pronounce *amygdala*, and help them understand what it means for this brain structure to "[keep] track of experiences that trigger strong emotions." Prompt them to state the steps in the development of the bee phobia using words like *first, then,* and *next.* **MODERATE**

• Ask students to pronounce *amygdala*, correcting them as needed. Then ask them to summarize in their own words the example of how a bee phobia could develop. **LIGHT**

For **reading support** for students at varying proficiency levels, see the **Text X-Ray** on page 28D.

> **WORD GAPS**

Explain to students that articles often include **technical terms,** whose meaning most readers would not know. When encountering a technical term, students should reread the paragraph or section to look for context clues. (*The amygdala is introduced in this section to explain the biological reason why some people develop phobias.*)

© Houghton Mifflin Harcourt Publishing Company

CITE EVIDENCE

Remind students that when they draw a conclusion based on what they have read, they must cite specific evidence from the text to support it. **(Answer:** *The strategy of approaching each fear from least to worst seems as though it would be effective. The text gives the example of a person with a dog phobia starting out by looking at a photo of a dog [paragraph 27]. Doing this with the support of a trained therapist could help the person learn that nothing bad will happen in this situation. Then the person's amygdala [paragraph 22] would no longer connect this experience with a fear response.)*

CRITICAL VOCABULARY

immaturity: The author uses the word *immaturity* to remind the reader not to think that a phobia is something only a child would have.

ASK STUDENTS to discuss what kinds of fear reactions might be the result of immaturity. *(A child might be frightened of a clown or a shadow because these are misunderstood or new and surprising; once he or she got older, that fear would probably go away.)*

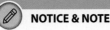

immaturity
(ĭm´ə-tyŏŏr´ĭ-tē) *n. Immaturity* is the state of not being fully developed or grown.

CITE EVIDENCE

Annotate: Mark details in paragraph 26 that explain how someone may overcome a phobia.

Interpret: Choose one of the strategies for overcoming fear discussed in paragraphs 27–32. Then, explain whether it seems effective, citing text evidence in your response.

to fears because of personality traits they are born with, certain genes[1] they've inherited, or situations they've experienced. People who have had strong childhood fears or anxiety may be more likely to have one or more phobias.

25   Having a phobia isn't a sign of weakness or **immaturity**. It's a response the brain has learned in an attempt to protect the person. It's as if the brain's alert system triggers a false alarm, generating intense fear that is out of proportion to the situation. Because the fear signal is so intense, the person is convinced the danger is greater than it actually is.

Overcoming Phobias

26   People can learn to overcome phobias by gradually facing their fears. This is not easy at first. It takes willingness and bravery. Sometimes people need the help of a therapist[2] to guide them through the process.

27   Overcoming a phobia usually starts with making a long list of the person's fears in least-to-worst order. For example, with a dog phobia, the list might start with the things the person is least afraid of, such as looking at a photo of a dog. It will then work all the way up to worst fears, such as standing next to someone who's petting a dog, petting a dog on a leash, and walking a dog.

28   Gradually, and with support, the person tries each fear situation on the list—one at a time, starting with the least fear. The person isn't forced to do anything and works on each fear until he or she feels comfortable, taking as long as needed.

29   A therapist could also show someone with a dog phobia how to approach, pet, and walk a dog, and help the person to try it, too. The person may expect terrible things to happen when near a dog. Talking about this can help, too. When people find that what they fear doesn't actually turn out to be true, it can be a great relief.

30   A therapist might also teach relaxation practices such as specific ways of breathing, muscle relaxation training, or soothing self-talk. These can help people feel comfortable and bold enough to face the fears on their list.

31   As somebody gets used to a feared object or situation, the brain adjusts how it responds and the phobia is overcome.

---

[1] **genes** (jēnz): the parts of cells that give a living thing its physical characteristics and make it grow and develop; a person's genes come from his or her parents and other blood relatives.

[2] **therapist** (thĕr´ə-pĭst): a person who is skilled in treating mental or physical illness.

IMPROVE READING FLUENCY

Targeted Passage Have students work with partners to read the section "Overcoming Phobias." First, use paragraph 26 to model how to read informational text. Have students follow along in their books as you read the text with appropriate phrasing and emphasis. Then, have partners take turns reading aloud each paragraph in the section. Encourage students to provide feedback and support for pronouncing multisyllabic words. Remind students that when they are reading aloud for an audience, they should pace their reading so the audience has time to understand difficult concepts.

 Go to the **Reading Studio** for additional support in developing fluency.

32   Often, the hardest part of overcoming a phobia is getting started. Once a person decides to go for it—and gets the right coaching and support—it can be surprising how quickly fear can melt away.

CHECK YOUR UNDERSTANDING

Answer these questions before moving on to the **Analyze the Text** section on the following page.

1 The author included the section "What Causes Phobias?" to —

  A express that it is important to overcome fears

  B explain that getting stung by a bee is dangerous

  C convince readers that there's nothing wrong with a phobia

  D describe what happens when people become afraid

2 In paragraph 27, the writer includes specific information on dog phobias to —

  F describe a physical reaction to fear

  G persuade readers to seek help for their fears

  H give a specific example of how a fear can be overcome

  J show that some fears can be unnecessary

3 Which idea is supported by information throughout the selection?

  A Adults enjoy the excitement that fear provides.

  B Fears can be overcome with help and support.

  C Phobias are the result of a single event.

  D Children are frightened by unfamiliar things.

Fears and Phobias   37

 CHECK YOUR UNDERSTANDING

Have students answer the questions independently.

Answers:

  1. *D*

  2. *H*

  3. *B*

If they answer any questions incorrectly, have them reread the text to confirm their understanding. Then they may proceed to ANALYZE THE TEXT on page 38.

EL ENGLISH LEARNER SUPPORT

Oral Assessment Use the following questions to assess students' comprehension and speaking skills:

  1. Why did the author include the section "What Causes Phobias?" *(The author included the section to describe what happens when people become afraid.)*

  2. Why did the writer include information on dog phobias in paragraph 27? *(The author included information on dog phobias to give a specific example of how a fear can be overcome.)*

  3. Which idea is supported by information throughout the selection? *(The idea that fears can be overcome with help and support is supported by information throughout the selection.)* **SUBSTANTIAL/MODERATE**

APPLY

ANALYZE THE TEXT

Possible answers:

1. **DOK 2:** *A sense of danger is a cause, and the effect is that our heart beats faster, we breathe more quickly, and our blood pressure increases. When the brain learns that a situation is not dangerous, it sends signals to turn off the fear reaction.*

2. **DOK 3:** *The text says that some phobias may arise from a "particularly scary situation," but that others may be related to personality traits or to genes a person has inherited.*

3. **DOK 3:** *The author says that it takes willingness and bravery to overcome a phobia. Therapy might include making a list of least-to-worst possible events and working through each one, or it might include relaxation techniques, such as breathing exercises. The author thinks that overcoming a phobia is worth the effort, because having one can be "exhausting and upsetting" and can cause people to "miss out on opportunities."*

4. **DOK 2:** *The sidebar explains that some people find fear exciting, while others do not like the experience. It helps the reader understand that two people might view experiences such as horror movies or roller-coaster rides differently; even though their physical reactions may be similar, their emotional reactions are not.*

5. **DOK 4:** *"Flight-fight" refers to the body's response to danger. Clues in the text that support this meaning are "fight off the danger or run fast to get away."*

RESEARCH

Remind students they should confirm any information they find by checking multiple websites and assessing the credibility of each one.

Connect Students may note that Oprah Winfrey faced her fear of balloons when her staff threw a birthday party for her and she had to step over and around all the balloons in the audience. Winston Churchill overcame his fear of public speaking by carefully writing and practicing his speeches over the course of many years. As for George Washington, it would have been difficult for him to face his fear of being buried alive while he was still living, and it appears that he held on to this fear until the end of his life.

 RESPOND

ANALYZE THE TEXT

Support your responses with evidence from the text. [≡] NOTEBOOK

1. **Cause/Effect** Examine paragraphs 5–7 and identify examples of cause-and-effect relationships.

2. **Cite Evidence** What causes phobias? Cite evidence from the text that explains where phobias come from.

3. **Draw Conclusions** Review paragraphs 26–32. What factors help people overcome phobias? Explain whether the author believes it is worthwhile to try to overcome phobias and why.

4. **Interpret** What additional information does the boxed feature provide? How does it add to your understanding of the article?

5. **Notice & Note** What does the term "fight-flight" refer to? How do the clues in paragraph 6 help you figure out the meaning of the term?

RESEARCH

RESEARCH TIP
The best search terms are very specific. Along with the well-known person's name, you will want to include a word such as *phobia* or *fear* to make sure you get the information you need.

Well-known people have not allowed phobias to prevent them from accomplishing great things. Research these well-known figures who have suffered from a phobia. Record what you learn in the chart.

WELL-KNOWN PEOPLE	PHOBIA
George Washington	*Washington feared being buried alive (taphophobia) and insisted his body not be buried for two days to make sure he was really dead.*
Oprah Winfrey	*Winfrey fears balloons (globophobia) because of the loud sound they make when they burst. She also fears chewing gum (chiclephobia).*
Winston Churchill	*As a young man, Churchill feared public speaking (glossophobia) because he stuttered.*

Connect In paragraph 26, the writer states that "People can learn to overcome phobias by gradually facing their fears." With a small group, and with this informational text in mind, discuss how these well-known people may or may not have overcome their fears.

⚙ LEARNING MINDSET

Belonging Ask students to share and celebrate a mistake they made while answering the Analyze the Text questions. Remind them that we all make mistakes and can learn from each other. You might say, "I make mistakes. Let's learn from each other." Then, model how to reflect on the mistake and learn from it.

CREATE AND PRESENT

Write an Informational Essay Write a three- to four-paragraph essay in which you compare and contrast fears and phobias.

- ❏ Introduce the topic and express your controlling idea on fears and phobias.
- ❏ Then, tell about similarities and differences between fears and phobias. Include details from the text to support your ideas. Use transitions as you move from point to point.
- ❏ In your final paragraph, state your conclusion.

Discuss with a Small Group Hold a small group discussion about whether the information in "Fears and Phobias" can help someone overcome a fear.

- ❏ As a group, review the text and decide which information is relevant to the discussion. Use the subheadings to help you locate information.
- ❏ Have group members take notes on ideas and details that relate to the topic.
- ❏ Together, review the ideas and suggest which ones can help someone overcome a fear. Listen respectfully to all ideas and identify points on which group members agree or disagree.

 Go to **Writing Informative Texts** in the **Writing Studio** for help writing an informational essay.

 Go to **Participating in Collaborative Discussions** in the **Speaking and Listening Studio** for help with having a group discussion.

RESPOND TO THE ESSENTIAL QUESTION

 How do you find courage in the face of fear?

Gather Information Review your annotations and notes on "Fears and Phobias." Then, add relevant details to your Response Log. As you determine which information to include, think about:

- the kinds of fears people face
- what happens to people when they face a specific fear
- how people can overcome a specific fear

At the end of the unit, use your notes to write an informational essay.

ACADEMIC VOCABULARY
As you write and discuss what you learned from the text, be sure to use the Academic Vocabulary words. Check off each of the words that you use.

- ❏ evident
- ❏ factor
- ❏ indicate
- ❏ similar
- ❏ specific

Fears and Phobias 39

APPLY

CREATE AND PRESENT

Write an Informational Essay Point out that the list on page 39 can serve as an outline for students' essays. Each item can be one paragraph, or they can have separate paragraphs for similarities and differences.

 For **writing support** for students at varying proficiency levels, see the **Text X-Ray** on page 28D.

Discuss with a Small Group Remind students that when they do not understand a comment made by another group member, they should ask questions to clarify meaning. The process of asking and answering questions can help everyone understand an issue more clearly and can lead to new ideas.

RESPOND TO THE ESSENTIAL QUESTION

Allow time for students to add details from "Fears and Phobias" to their Unit 1 Response Logs.

EL **ENGLISH LEARNER SUPPORT**

Discuss with a Small Group Restate the discussion prompt as a question: *How can information in "Fears and Phobias" help someone overcome a fear?* Allow students to work with partners to review the text for details that answer the question. Provide these sentence frames to help them formulate their ideas for the discussion: *The article says people can overcome a fear by gradually ___. The article says it can help to make a list of ___. After making the list, the person who is afraid can then ___.* **SUBSTANTIAL/MODERATE**

CRITICAL VOCABULARY

Answers:

1. *b. crying when you don't get your way; because someone who is more grown up would be able to explain something in a calm way*

2. *b. pressing the power button; because doing this starts a process in an electronic device*

3. *b. canoeing on a rushing river; because it involves roughness and unsteadiness*

4. *a. getting stung by a bee; because it may set off an allergic reaction*

VOCABULARY STRATEGY:
Prefixes That Mean "Not"

Answers:

1. *inconvenient: in-, not convenient*

2. *nonviolent: non-, not violent; peaceful*

3. *undemocratic: un-, not according to democratic principles*

4. *misquoted: mis-, incorrectly stated*

 RESPOND

WORD BANK
activate
trigger
turbulence
immaturity

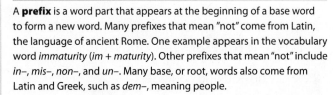 Go to the **Vocabulary Studio** for more on prefixes.

CRITICAL VOCABULARY

Practice and Apply Choose the better answer to each question. Then, explain your response.

1. Which of the following is an example of **immaturity?**

   a. explaining why you are upset | b. crying when you don't get your way

2. Which of the following is an example of **activate?**

   a. unplugging a computer | b. pressing the power button

3. Which canoe trip involves **turbulence?**

   a. canoeing on a calm lake | b. canoeing on a rushing river

4. Which of these is more likely to **trigger** an allergy?

   a. getting stung by a bee | b. reading about bees

VOCABULARY STRATEGY:
Prefixes That Mean "Not"

A **prefix** is a word part that appears at the beginning of a base word to form a new word. Many prefixes that mean "not" come from Latin, the language of ancient Rome. One example appears in the vocabulary word *immaturity* (*im + maturity*). Other prefixes that mean "not" include *in–, mis–, non–,* and *un–*. Many base, or root, words also come from Latin and Greek, such as *dem–,* meaning people.

Practice and Apply First, identify the prefix that means "not" in each boldface word. Then, state the meaning of the boldface word in your own words.

1. Not having Sunday hours at the library is **inconvenient** for people who work during the week.

   _____

2. A **nonviolent** protest would help the group avoid a confrontation.

   _____

3. Denying a citizen the right to vote is **undemocratic.**

   _____

4. The careless reporter **misquoted** the mayor's remarks.

   _____

 ENGLISH LEARNER SUPPORT

Vocabulary Strategy Give students additional practice in determining the meanings of unfamiliar words. Write the following words on the board: *incurable, impossible, mislead, nonsense, unknown.* Have pairs of students copy the words, underline the prefixes, and write definitions. Tell them to confirm their definitions by looking up each word in a dictionary.
ALL LEVELS

LANGUAGE CONVENTIONS:
Dashes

Writers use dashes to interrupt their thoughts abruptly or to emphasize important ideas. A stylistic choice—used in both literary and informational texts—dashes add variety and voice.

In "Fears and Phobias" dashes are used in the following ways:

• to set off emphatic and abrupt interruptions

> **Feeling afraid is very natural—and helpful—in some situations.**

• to mark sharp turns in thought

> **But this doesn't help them overcome fear—in fact, it can be the reverse.**

• to enclose added elements that give greater emphasis

> **Once a person decides to go for it—and gets the right coaching and support—it can be surprising how quickly fear can melt away.**

• to set off an expression that summarizes or illustrates a statement that precedes it

> **That's because the fear reaction is activated instantly—a few seconds faster than the thinking part of the brain can process or evaluate what's happening.**

Practice and Apply Write your own sentences with dashes using the examples from "Fears and Phobias" as models. Your sentences can be about your own fears and phobias or those of someone you know. When you have finished, share your sentences with a partner and compare your use of dashes.

> **!** Go to **Punctuation** in the **Grammar Studio** for more on punctuation.

LANGUAGE CONVENTIONS:
Dashes

Review the information about dashes with students. Explain that using dashes is called a stylistic choice because the author always has the option of using different punctuation. When students use dashes in their own writing, they should ask themselves whether the dashes do or do not help convey their ideas more clearly and effectively.

Illustrate the idea of stylistic choices by rewriting several of the example sentences with different punctuation and discussing the effect.

• *"Feeling afraid is very natural and helpful in some situations." (The idea that fear is helpful is no longer emphasized; readers might not realize it's important.)*

• *"Once a person decides to go for it, it can be surprising how quickly fear can melt away. The person will also need to get the right coaching and support." (The idea about getting coaching and support is out of sequence and feels tacked on; dashes allow this idea to appear in the same sentence while also being called out.)*

• *"That's because the fear reaction is activated instantly—a few seconds faster than the thinking part of the brain can process—or evaluate—what's happening." (Too many dashes make the sentence feel choppy and may confuse readers.)*

Practice and Apply Have partners discuss whether dashes are used correctly and effectively in their sentences. *(Students' sentences will vary.)*

🔲 ENGLISH LEARNER SUPPORT

Language Conventions Use the following supports with students at varying proficiency levels:

• Have students find other sentences in "Fears and Phobias" that use dashes and copy them in their notebooks. Make sure they recognize the difference between dashes and hyphens. **SUBSTANTIAL**

• Have students work with partners to write their original sentences with dashes. Then have them meet with another pair to compare their sentences. **MODERATE**

• Ask students to write one sentence modeled on each of the four examples from "Fears and Phobias." Then have them explain to partners why the dashes in each sentence perform the same function as in the corresponding example sentence. **LIGHT**

WIRED FOR FEAR

Video by The California Science Center

GENRE ELEMENTS
MEDIA

Remind students that the purpose of **media** is similar to the purpose of a piece of writing. A video that is informational, such as "Wired for Fear," shares some things in common with informational text. For example, it uses factual information to inform an audience about a particular topic. Like an informational text, videos may use graphic features, such as maps and photos, and will sometimes use text features, such as words that appear on screen. In this lesson, students will explore how elements of media convey information about fear in "Wired for Fear."

LEARNING OBJECTIVES

- Analyze the purpose of a video.
- Understand the visual and sound elements used in a video.
- Write a narrative based on personal experience.
- Write and present a podcast reviewing the video.
- Research stories that exhibit the physical reaction to fear.
- **Language** Discuss with a partner the purpose of the video, using the terms *visual* and *sound*.

TEXT COMPLEXITY

Quantitative Measures	Wired for Fear	Lexile: N/A
Qualitative Measures	**Ideas Presented** The video includes complex and scientific concepts.	
	Structure Used The video includes sophisticated graphics, essential to understanding the text; may also provide information not otherwise conveyed in the text.	
	Language Used The language has high levels of unfamiliar and technical language, including Tier III words having to do with the brain and nervous system.	
	Knowledge Required Background knowledge of the nervous system will aid understanding.	

Online **⦿ Ed**

RESOURCES

- Unit 1 Response Log
- Writing Studio: Writing Narratives
- 💬 Speaking and Listening Studio: Analyzing and Evaluating Presentations
- ✅ "Wired for Fear" Selection Test

SUMMARIES

English

When you sense something that might pose a danger, a message goes to the "threat center" of the brain—the amygdala. This causes the body to have a "freeze response." The amygdala also sends a message to the hypothalamus, which releases hormones that cause the fight or flight response. Using additional sensory information, the amygdala decides whether the danger is real or fake. Other parts of the brain create a memory of what happened.

Spanish

Cuando sientes que algo podría ser peligroso, sale un mensaje al "centro de amenazas" del cerebro, la amígdala. Esto causa en el cuerpo una "reacción de parálisis". La amígdala también manda un mensaje al hipotálamo, liberando hormonas que causan la reacción de lucha o huida. Utilizando información sensorial adicional, la amígdala decide si el peligro es real o falso. Otras partes del cerebro crean la memoria de qué sucedió.

SMALL-GROUP OPTIONS

Have students work in small groups to watch and discuss the video.

Sticky Note Peer Review

- Have students create their own graphic representations of the way the brain and body react to the fear stimulus.
- Students present their graphics to their small groups. Other students pay attention and write feedback on sticky notes. They record things they like, suggestions for improvement, and questions they have on separate sticky notes.
- Students share their sticky notes with the presenter.

Think-Pair-Share

- After students have watched and analyzed "Wired for Fear," ask: *Why do you think there are differences in what sparks a fear reaction in people? For example, some people find snakes frightening and others don't.*
- Have students think about the question individually and write brief notes of their ideas.
- Have pairs discuss their ideas about the question.
- Ask pairs to share their responses with the class. Discuss ways to find out more about this question.

Text X-Ray: English Learner Support
for "Wired for Fear"

Use Text X-Ray and the supports and scaffolds in the Teacher's Edition to help guide students at different proficiency levels through the selection.

INTRODUCE THE SELECTION
DISCUSS FEAR'S USES

In this lesson, students will learn about how the brain interprets information and decides when there is danger. This sense of nearby danger causes the feeling of fear. Introduce the topic by guiding a discussion of how fear is a useful feeling. Brainstorm words related to fear, such as *danger, afraid, hazard, scared, hurt, harm,* and *pain.* Then have students use the words to describe when they experience feelings of fear and how they act when they feel fear. Use frames to help students discuss:

- *I feel _____ when _____.*
- *When I am _____, I feel _____.*
- *Fear helps me _____.*

CULTURAL REFERENCES

The following words or phrases may be unfamiliar to students:

- *on the lookout:* staying alert; watching for
- *false alarm:* a message of danger when there was no real danger
- *orders a stand down:* instructs the body to stop reacting as if there was danger
- *spring into action:* act very quickly, without hesitation

LISTENING

Interpret Information

Point out that the video includes **subtitles,** or lines of text that show what the narrator is saying. Remind students that all the parts of a video support the creator's purpose.

Play the video once with the sound; then play it again without the sound. Ask students to discuss how the lack of sound affects their viewing of the film.

Use the following supports with students at varying proficiency levels:

- Have students complete sentence frames such as: *With the sound off, _____. With the sound on _____. I think the sound helped _____.* **SUBSTANTIAL**
- Have students identify the purpose of the text subtitles. Ask: *Why did the creator include these subtitles?* **MODERATE**
- Have student pairs work together to compare and contrast the experience of viewing the video with the sound off and the sound on. **LIGHT**

SPEAKING

Discuss Purpose

Have students discuss with a partner the purpose of the video, using the terms *visual* and *sound*. Circulate around the room to make sure students are using the key terms correctly.

Use the following supports for students at varying proficiency levels:

- Display and read aloud this sentence: *The visual and sound elements of the video give information about fear.* Have students repeat the sentence and practice saying it to a partner. **SUBSTANTIAL**
- To help students express their ideas about how visual and sound elements support the purpose of the video, display the following sentence frames: *The video uses visual elements to _____. The video uses sound to _____.* **MODERATE**
- Have student pairs work together to discuss how visual and sound elements support the purpose of the video. They should be prepared to share their answers with the group. **LIGHT**

READING

Summarize Main Ideas

Provide an overview of the video before students watch it. Work with students to summarize the main idea of each section.

Play each section and pause, allowing students to discuss its main idea: 0:00–1:08 explains how awareness of danger reaches the amygdala; 1:09–2:22 explains how the brain sends out an initial threat response; 2:23–3:03 tells what happens when the danger is confirmed or not confirmed; 3:04–4:05 explains how and why the brain creates a memory.

Use the following supports with students at varying proficiency levels:

- Use a short summary such as the one found on 42B. Write the sentences on separate index cards or slips of paper. Have students work with a partner to read the sentences aloud and choose the one(s) that summarize each part. **SUBSTANTIAL**
- Supply sentence frames to help students summarize, such as: *When I sense danger, a signal goes _____. My _____ sends messages to _____.* **MODERATE**
- Have students identify the main idea of each section by responding to questions: *What was this section mostly about? What parts of the brain did you learn about in this section of the video? How did this section help you understand how your brain is wired for fear.* **LIGHT**

WRITING

Write a Narrative

Work with students to read the writing assignment on p. 45.

Use the following supports with students at varying proficiency levels:

- Use questioning to guide students to tell their narrative orally, and help them rephrase their ideas using sequence words, such as *first, then, next, finally,* and *after.* **SUBSTANTIAL**
- Provide students with sentence frames to help them write their narrative, such as: *Once, I _____. First, _____. Then, _____. Next, _____. Finally, _____.* **MODERATE**
- Work with students to generate a list of transitional phrases and words that are useful for writing a narrative, such as *first, then, next, finally, before,* and *after.* Remind them to use these words to make the sequence of events in their narratives clear. **LIGHT**

Connect to the
ESSENTIAL QUESTION

"Wired for Fear" explains the human body's initial response when confronted with danger. Within seconds of perceiving a potential threat, the brain starts to prepare for "fight or flight." Once a person's body is on alert, he or she is ready to face fear with courage.

QUICK START

Have students form pairs to discuss the Quick Start prompt. Then invite pairs to share the physical reactions they discussed. List them on the board, and tell students that they will learn about the science behind some of these reactions.

ANALYZE DIGITAL TEXT

Have students read the information about digital text. Then review the video elements described in the charts. Ask them to think of examples of each element from videos or full-length movies they have seen.

Suggest that students use these questions to help them analyze visual and sound elements in the video:

- *Does the video use stills or animation? What purpose do they serve? How do they help me understand the topic?*
- *How does the music match the video's topic or content? What mood, or feeling, does the music help create?*
- *What does the narration add to the video?*

■ English Learner Support

Analyze Digital Text Clarify the meanings of *still, animation,* and *narration* by displaying examples of a still photograph, an animated sequence, and voice-over narration. Discuss each example, and tell students to watch for all three elements in "Wired for Fear."

SUBSTANTIAL/MODERATE

ANALYZE & APPLY

MEDIA
WIRED FOR FEAR

Video by the
California Science Center

? **ESSENTIAL QUESTION:**

How do you find courage in the face of fear?

QUICK START

Think about a time you were frightened or startled. Did your heart start racing? Did you start sweating? Describe to a partner what frightened you and how your body reacted to it.

ANALYZE DIGITAL TEXT

The **purpose,** or intent, of any video or digital text is usually to inform, entertain, persuade, or express the feelings or thoughts of the creator. To meet the purpose, the video's creator uses words as well as visual and sound elements to convey information.

GENRE ELEMENTS: MEDIA
- conveys a message
- targets a specific audience
- is created for a specific purpose
- includes TV broadcasts, videos, newspapers, magazines, and the Internet

Visual elements, or images, can help viewers understand **technical terms,** which are the words and phrases used in a particular profession or field of study.

STILLS	images that are motionless, such as illustrations or photographs
ANIMATION	images that appear to move and seem alive; created through drawings, computer graphics, or photographs

Sound elements include what you hear in a video:

MUSIC	sounds created by singing, playing instruments, or using computer-generated tones; creates a mood
NARRATION	the words as well as the expression and quality of voice used by the narrator

---

 ENGLISH LEARNER SUPPORT

Understand Idioms Discuss the title of the video. Explain that the word *wired* has both literal and figurative meanings. In the literal sense, it means "connected with wires," the way a house is wired for electricity. You might use a light switch or the power cord for a computer to demonstrate. Then tell students that *wired* can also mean "born with the ability to do something." For example, people are wired to learn languages. Similarly, people's brains are wired to respond to fear and protect them from danger. **ALL LEVELS**

BACKGROUND

"Fear is a full-body experience." This is how the website Goose Bumps! The Science of Fear introduces its topic "Fear and the Brain." This website includes a collection of videos, articles, and images about sensory information (what we see, hear, taste, smell, touch) that alerts us to what might be harmful to us. The section of the website titled "Wired for Fear" includes a video that provides an animated version of how the brain processes fear reactions.

SETTING A PURPOSE

As you view the animated video, consider how the information is presented. Notice how the video introduces and explains new terms and ideas using text, sound, and visuals. **NOTEBOOK**

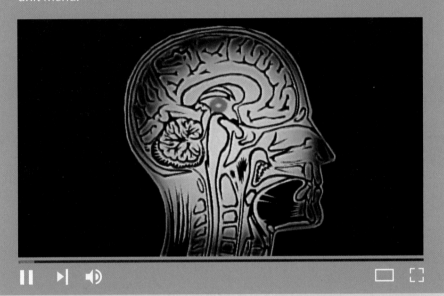

To view the video, log in online and select **"WIRED FOR FEAR"** from the unit menu.

As needed, pause the video to make notes about what impresses you or about ideas you might want to talk about later. Replay or rewind so that you can clarify anything you do not understand.

Center Foundation

BACKGROUND

After students read the Background note, ask them to consider the statement "Fear is a full-body experience." Does this description match their Quick Start discussion of fear responses? How might the brain be involved in reactions that take place elsewhere in the body, such as sweating?

SETTING A PURPOSE

Direct students to use the Setting a Purpose prompt to focus their viewing.

For **speaking, listening,** and **reading support** for students at varying proficiency levels, see the **Text X-Ray** activities on pages 42C and 42D.

WHEN STUDENTS STRUGGLE . . .

Analyze Media Have students view the video with partners. Suggest that they play the video once without stopping or taking notes, and then discuss what they learned and what was unclear. Then have them play the video a second time, pausing it at logical moments to review the segment they have just watched and jot down important ideas. To support note taking, you might provide them with a list of key terms that they can define as they view the media: *neurons, amygdala, sensory organs, thalamus, "short path," brain stem, freeze response, automatic expression of fear, hypothalamus, adrenaline, "fight or flight" response, "long path," visual cortex, hippocampus, prefrontal cortex.*

APPLY

ANALYZE MEDIA

Possible answers:

1. **DOK 2:** *The hiker is about to stumble upon something in his path; he is not sure whether it is a snake. The video shows how the hiker's body responds to (1) identify possible danger, (2) process the sensory information it receives, and (3) decide whether the danger is real.*

2. **DOK 2:** *We might freeze or change facial expression; heart rate, blood pressure, and sweating increase. The brain stem, facial muscles and nerves, the hypothalamus, and the hormones released by the hypothalamus all play a part in activating these responses.*

3. **DOK 4:** *The title helps you understand that the brain works in a way that is similar to wiring for lights and electricity. The lights help focus your attention on the area being discussed; the lighted railroad tracks use a familiar example of forward motion to help explain the motion of information along the pathways.*

4. **DOK 2:** *The music shifts to match the mood of each scene. Both music and narration help emphasize important ideas about how the amygdala works.*

5. **DOK 4:** *The video is an effective way to learn about the topic. Although the visual effects are not overly sophisticated, they help frame the important ideas in a way that helps viewers grasp them. The sound elements are appropriate; they emphasize ideas, but they are not too obvious.*

RESEARCH

Review the Research Tip with students. Point out that government websites and sites published by respected news organizations are other good sources for reliable facts.

Connect Remind students to review the visual and sound elements listed on page 42. Suggest that they consider all the elements they could use in their video and then decide which ones would be most effective in conveying their particular event. Point out that in a short video, a simpler presentation might have a greater impact than one with a lot of competing elements.

 RESPOND

ANALYZE MEDIA

Support your responses with evidence from the video. 📓 NOTEBOOK

1. **Summarize** Describe how the video explains what the hiker experiences.

2. **Cause/Effect** Review the sequence that uses the animated model. What are some ways our bodies respond when the amygdala senses danger? What parts of the brain activate these responses?

3. **Analyze** Explain the title "Wired for Fear." Why does the video use flashing lights and graphics that show movement in the animated model of how the brain processes potential danger?

4. **Interpret** Describe the music used in the video. In what ways does it support the purpose of the video?

5. **Critique** Think about the purpose of the video. Consider the techniques that are used to support the information presented. Do you think "Wired for Fear" is an effective informational video? Why or why not?

RESEARCH TIP
Information on the Internet is not always accurate; a search on a topic such as this one could result in some wildly exaggerated and undocumented stories. Be sure to use only reputable sources, such as *Scientific American*, *National Geographic*, or similar sources.

RESEARCH

As you've learned from the video, fear can have a dramatic impact on the body. In fact, there are many accounts of people performing superhuman feats of strength when faced with fear, such as lifting a car off someone after an accident. With a partner, do some research to find such a story and share it with the class.

EVENT	DETAIL

Connect Consider what you learned about using visual and sound elements in a video to achieve a specific purpose. What kind of video would you create to present the event you just researched? With your partner, sketch out the sound and visual elements you would include to convey the event.

EL ENGLISH LEARNER SUPPORT

Oral Assessment To gauge comprehension and speaking skills, conduct an informal assessment. Walk around the class, talking with students and asking these questions:

- What part of the brain organizes our response to fear? *(the amygdala)* **SUBSTANTIAL**
- What is the amygdala? *(It is a part of the brain that reacts to possible danger by creating a "fight or flight" response.)* **MODERATE**
- What happens when we see or hear something that might be dangerous? *(The amygdala starts a fear response. The body gets ready for "fight or flight." If the danger is not real, the body relaxes.)* **LIGHT**

CREATE AND PRESENT

Write a Narrative Write a story about a time you were frightened.

❏ Establish the situation by introducing the event. Where did it take place? Were other people there?

❏ Describe the sequence of events in a logical order.

❏ Include dialogue and vivid images to convey the experience.

❏ Review your story to add or clarify details of the event.

Produce a Podcast With a partner, create an audio recording for a podcast review of the video "Wired for Fear."

❏ Make notes about visual and sound elements in the video that made both positive and negative impressions.

❏ Explain how each element you have chosen clarifies the topic, using examples from the video. Present ideas for additional information that could have been included to improve the video, drawing on other videos or sources as needed.

❏ Create the recording of your review with a partner, using a conversational approach and clear enunciation. Share your podcast with a larger group.

RESPOND TO THE ESSENTIAL QUESTION

 How do you find courage in the face of fear?

Gather Information Review your annotations and notes on "Wired for Fear." Then, add relevant details to your Response Log. As you determine which information to include, think about why fear is a necessary emotion.

At the end of the unit, use your notes to write an informational essay.

UNIT 1
RESPONSE LOG

Go to **Writing Narratives** in the **Writing Studio** for more on writing a narrative.

Go to **Analyzing and Evaluating Presentations** in the **Speaking and Listening Studio** for help with reviewing a presentation.

ACADEMIC VOCABULARY
As you write and discuss what you learned from the video, be sure to use the Academic Vocabulary words. Check off each of the words that you use.

❏ **evident**

❏ **factor**

❏ **indicate**

❏ **similar**

❏ **specific**

CREATE AND PRESENT

Write a Narrative After students have drafted their narratives, encourage them to read their stories aloud, either to themselves or to a partner. This will help them identify any sections that are confusing or that need more detail. Remind them to use transitions to clarify the sequence of events, such as *while, then, suddenly,* and *finally.*

For **writing support** for students at varying proficiency levels, see the **Text X-Ray** on page 42D.

Produce a Podcast Have students form peer groups to critique each other's podcasts before presenting them to the class.

• Students should give concrete, specific ideas for how their peers might improve their podcasts.

• Pairs should review the suggestions and decide which ones to incorporate into their podcasts.

• Pairs may then record their podcasts again for posting on the Web.

RESPOND TO THE ESSENTIAL QUESTION

Allow time for students to add details from "Wired for Fear" to their Unit 1 Response Logs.

🔵 EL ENGLISH LEARNER SUPPORT

Present a Podcast Use these suggestions to support students as they critique the video and prepare a podcast:

• Have students work in pairs of different English facility to rewatch the video, noting one sound and one visual element that were effective. As needed, use sentence frames to help students explain their choices: _____ *worked well because* _____. *I think* _____ *could be added to make the video even better*. **SUBSTANTIAL/MODERATE**

• Have student pairs watch another informational video and find one visual or sound element that "Wired for Fear" does not have. Have them explain why this element could be added to "Wired for Fear" to make it stronger. **LIGHT**

EMBARRASSED? BLAME YOUR BRAIN

Informational Text by Jennifer Connor-Smith

GENRE ELEMENTS
INFORMATIONAL TEXT

Remind students that the purpose of **informational text** is to present facts and information. Informational text provides factual information and includes evidence to support ideas. Informational text often uses certain text features, including headings, graphics, chapters, sections, definitions, and graphs. Informational texts take many forms, such as news articles and essays. In this lesson, students will use text features to help them explore the processes of the human brain in "Embarrassed? Blame Your Brain."

LEARNING OBJECTIVES

- Use text features to make, correct, and confirm predictions.
- Identify organization and structure of informational text.
- Gather information from credible sources, then present the information using paraphrasing and appropriate source citation.
- Write and present an advertisement.
- Use synonyms and antonyms to better understand word meanings.
- Use commas after introductory elements.
- **Language** Discuss with a partner the organizational features of the text using the term *subheadings*.

TEXT COMPLEXITY

Quantitative Measures	Embarrassed? Blame Your Brain	Lexile: 960L
Qualitative Measures	**Ideas Presented** Much is explicit, but moves to some implied meaning.	
	Structure Used Text features, such as headings, guide reading.	
	Language Used Mostly Tier II and III words; some technical words are used.	
	Knowledge Required Most of the text deals with common or easily imagined experiences.	

RESOURCES

- Unit 1 Response Log
- Selection Audio
- Reading Studio: Notice & Note
- Level Up Tutorial: Making Predictions
- Writing Studio: Writing Informative Texts
- Speaking and Listening Studio: Collaborative Discussions
- Vocabulary Studio: Synonyms and Antonyms
- Grammar Studio: Module 12: Lesson 13: Using Commas
- "Embarrassed? Blame Your Brain"/ "The Ravine" Selection Test

SUMMARIES

English

Everyone gets embarrassed from time to time. Even if someone rarely felt embarrassed when they were very young, changes to the brain during the middle school years mean that they may feel more embarrassed than ever. In fact, the brain reacts the same way to embarrassment as it does to physical pain. What's worse, middle schoolers' brains haven't yet developed the ability to cope with embarrassment.

Spanish

Todo el mundo siente vergüenza de vez en cuando. Tal vez no te sentías avergonzado cuando eras pequeño, pero al llegar a los años de la escuela media, ocurren cambios en tu cerebro que te hacen sentir más avergonzado que nunca. De hecho, tu cerebro reacciona a la vergüenza de la misma manera que reacciona al dolor físico. Lo que es peor, el cerebro de los estudiantes de escuela media aún no ha desarrollado la capacidad de lidiar con la vergüenza. Así que si te sientes avergonzado, ¡culpa a tu cerebro!

SMALL-GROUP OPTIONS

Have students work in small groups to read and discuss the selection.

Three-Minute Review

- At any time during reading or discussion, pause and direct students to work in partnerships.
- Set a timer for three minutes.
- For three minutes, partners reread material and write clarifying questions.
- Bring the class together. Ask students what they noticed during their review. Have volunteers share their clarifying questions. Have a brief discussion with the class about any necessary clarifications.

Think-Pair-Share

- After students have read and analyzed "Embarrassed? Blame Your Brain," pose this question: *Why is it so hard to overcome feeling embarrassed?*
- Have students think about the question individually and write brief notes of their ideas.
- Then, have pairs discuss their ideas about the question.
- Finally, ask pairs to share their responses with the class.

Text X-Ray: English Learner Support
for "Embarrassed? Blame Your Brain"

Use the Text X-Ray and the supports and scaffolds in the Teacher's Edition to help guide students at different proficiency levels through the selection.

INTRODUCE THE SELECTION
DISCUSS EMBARRASSMENT AND REJECTION

In this lesson, students will need to be able to discuss feelings of embarrassment and rejection. Read paragraph 1 with students, and point out the word *embarrassment*. Then read paragraph 7 and point out the word *rejection*. Provide the following examples:

- *Embarrassment is when you feel silly or ashamed for something you or somebody else does.*
- *Rejection is when you feel like nobody wants you to be part of their group.*

Explain to students that feelings of embarrassment come from parts of the brain. Point out the diagram of the brain on page 50 to help clarify student understanding. Tell students that during middle school, their brains will feel more embarrassed and rejected than at other times in their lives. Have volunteers share examples of events that might make a person feel embarrassed or rejected. Supply the following sentence frames.

- *_____ might make a person feel embarrased.*
- *A person might feel rejected when _____.*

CULTURAL REFERENCES

The following words or phrases may be unfamiliar to students:

- *fitting in* (paragraph 3): being accepted by others and feeling like part of the group
- *tackle a challenge* (paragraph 4): try something hard
- *hurt feelings* (paragraph 5): feeling sad because of the way you are treated
- *broken hearted* (paragraph 5): very sad
- *tug-of-war* (paragraph 10): a game in which two sides pull a rope in opposite directions
- *potty break* (paragraph 14): a silly name for going to the bathroom

LISTENING

Understand the Central Idea

Remind students to pay attention to the subheadings in the article. Explain that a subheading shows the beginning of a new section or topic. Direct students' attention to the subheading on page 51, "Words Do Hurt Like Sticks and Stones." Remind students that they can use the subheading to help them figure out the central idea of the section.

Have students listen as you read aloud paragraphs 5–8. Use the following supports with students at varying proficiency levels:

- Have students indicate with a thumbs up or down whether this summary is accurate (it is not): *In the experiment, teenagers felt angry when nobody played the game with them; your brain reacts the same way when you feel left out as when you feel anger.* **SUBSTANTIAL**
- Have students agree or disagree with the summary above using sentence frames: The summary is ___. The students did not feel ____. They felt ____. **MODERATE**
- Have student pairs work together to summarize the central idea and details that support it from the text. Have them read aloud their summary to another pair and have the listening pair agree or disagree. **LIGHT**

SPEAKING

Discuss Organizational Patterns

Have students discuss the features of the text using the key term *subheading*. Circulate around the room to make sure students are using the key term correctly.

Use the following supports for students at varying proficiency levels:

- Display and read aloud this sentence: *The subheading "It's All in Your Head" tells me that this section of the text is about how the brain works.* Have students repeat the sentence and practice saying it to a partner. **SUBSTANTIAL**
- To help students express their ideas about subheadings, display the following sentence frames: *A subhead is a ____. This subheading "It's All in Your Head" tells me the section is about ____.* **MODERATE**
- Have student pairs work together to discuss the meaning of the subheading "It's All in Your Head." They should be prepared to share their answers with the group. **LIGHT**

READING

Connect Text and Diagram

Tell students that authors of informational texts provide text features like diagrams, subheadings, and boldface or italicized words to help readers understand the central idea of a text.

Point out the diagram under paragraph 4. Use the following supports with students at varying proficiency levels:

- Guide students to look at the diagram, and use simpler language to explain the information it shows. Summarize what the diagram shows, and have students repeat the summary after you: *A person's brain controls feelings, such as embarrassment.* **SUBSTANTIAL**
- Have students use sentence frames to summarize what the diagram shows, such as *The diagram shows how parts of ____ affect _____. The ____ causes _____. The _____ makes you feel _____.* **MODERATE**
- Have student pairs work together to discuss how the diagram fits into the section as a whole. **LIGHT**

WRITING

Write an Advertisement

Work with students to read the writing assignment on page 55.

Use the following supports with students at varying proficiency levels:

- Work with students to generate a list of ideas for how to overcome embarrassment. Work together to create a bulleted list of how their service would work. Have them copy this list. Provide support to help them write the initial slogan and call to action for their advertisements. **SUBSTANTIAL**
- Provide students with a sentence frame to help them write their initial slogan, such as: *Do you want to ____?* Then have them write a bulleted list under the heading "How We Help You Overcome Embarrassment." Finally, give them a sentence frame to write their final call to action, such as: *So, if you want to overcome embarrassment, just ____.* **MODERATE**
- Walk students through each step of the assignment. Make sure students understand the initial slogan, the bulleted list, and the call to action. Check student work on each component. **LIGHT**

Connect to the
ESSENTIAL QUESTION

"Embarrassed? Blame Your Brain" explains the way the brain responds to embarrassment and rejection. The text states that the ability to experience these emotions is heightened during the middle school years, while the brain's ability to cope with them is not yet developed. Following the text, tips are offered to help young people better respond when they feel embarrassed or rejected.

COMPARE THEME AND MAIN IDEA

Point out that "Embarrassed? Blame Your Brain" is an informational text, while "The Ravine" is a fictional story. Remind students that *theme* refers to the message an author wants to convey though fiction, poetry, or drama. An informational text's main idea is similar to a theme. Students will need to pay attention to ways the theme (or themes) of "The Ravine" connects to the main ideas of "Embarrassed?"

INFORMATIONAL TEXT

EMBARRASSED?
Blame Your Brain

by **Jennifer Connor-Smith**
pages 49–53

COMPARE THEME AND MAIN IDEA

As you read these texts, notice how their ideas relate to your own experiences, as well as how those ideas relate to the experiences of other young people. Then, look for ways that the ideas in the two texts relate to each other. After you read both selections, you will collaborate with a small group on a final project.

 ESSENTIAL QUESTION:

How do you find courage in the face of fear?

SHORT STORY

THE RAVINE

by **Graham Salisbury**
pages 61–71

46   Unit 1

Embarrassed?

QUICK START

Disappointing someone or feeling embarrassed won't cause physical pain or permanent damage, so why fear either one? With a group, discuss how fear of embarrassment can affect how we behave.

MAKE PREDICTIONS

You make **predictions,** reasonable guesses based on what you know from experience, all the time. Then, as you gain additional information, you either confirm that a prediction is correct or revise it if it happens to be wrong. You can also make and confirm predictions as you read.

Use the following aspects of informational texts to help you predict the topics, ideas, and evidence an author discusses.

- **Text Features:** Subheadings, boldfaced words, and graphics point out important ideas that you can use to make your predictions.
- **Text Structure:** The way a text is organized helps you take in new information and predict what the author will explain next.

ANALYZE ORGANIZATIONAL PATTERNS

To help you understand ideas that may be new to you, authors of informational texts organize facts and examples carefully. Here are some common organizational patterns.

ORGANIZATIONAL PATTERN	WHAT IT DOES
Definition	explains a topic or idea by identifying its key characteristics and/or distinguishing it from similar or related topics or ideas
Classification	organizes objects, ideas, or information into groups, or classes, based on common characteristics
Advantage and Disadvantage	evaluates a topic or proposal by analyzing both its positive and negative aspects

As you read "Embarrassed? Blame Your Brain," note how the author uses a variety of organizational patterns to help you better understand the text's topic and key ideas.

GENRE ELEMENTS: INFORMATIONAL TEXT

- provides factual information
- uses evidence to support ideas
- contains text features
- includes many forms, such as news articles and essays

QUICK START

Have students read the Quick Start question, and invite them to share their ideas on why we fear embarrassment and how fear of embarrassment can affect how we behave. Then have the class brainstorm a list of situations that might cause embarrassment.

MAKE PREDICTIONS

Help students understand that making predictions before and during reading is a way to better understand a text. Remind them to pause during reading to review their predictions and revise them if they were wrong. Point out the two elements on page 47 that can help students make predictions. Text features point out important ideas they can use to inform their predictions. Paying attention to the text structure, or how it is organized, makes predicting what the author might explain next easier.

ANALYZE ORGANIZATIONAL PATTERNS

Tell students that understanding the way an author has organized facts can help them better understand what they read. Review the chart of organizational patterns and their functions on page 47. Provide brief examples of each pattern. Discuss how each pattern could be useful in helping a reader comprehend a text.

Suggest that students use these questions to help them analyze and annotate organizational patterns:

- *What organizational patterns does the author use?*
- *What clues make an organizational pattern clear?*
- *What important ideas does that organizational pattern help a reader understand.*

Ⓔ ENGLISH LEARNER SUPPORT

Make Predictions Remind students that they can use text elements to help them predict. Review the terms *subheadings, boldfaced words,* and *graphics.* Have students identify examples of each in the selection. Have them complete sentence frames such as: *A subheading helps me predict _____; Words that are boldfaced can help me predict _____; Graphics help me predict _____.* **MODERATE**

TEACH

CRITICAL VOCABULARY

Encourage students to read all of the sentences before deciding which word best completes each one. Remind them to look for context clues that match the precise meaning of each word.

Answers:

1. *essential*

2. *amplify*

3. *generate*

4. *humiliation*

■ English Learner Support

Use Cognates Tell students that several of the Critical Vocabulary words have Spanish cognates: *essential/esencial; amplify/amplificar; generate/generar; humiliation/humillación.* **ALL LEVELS**

LANGUAGE CONVENTIONS

Review the information about commas used to set off an introductory word, phrase, or clause in a sentence.

Read aloud the example sentence, using an appropriate pause to indicate the use of a comma after the introductory phrase. Then read it again as though the comma weren't there. Discuss how the comma affects the sentence. (*The comma indicates that a reader should pause after "These days," to add emphasis to a particular time period. This emphasis helps indicate that a contrast is being drawn between these days and earlier times in a child's life.*)

✎ ANNOTATION MODEL

Remind students of the ideas in Make Predictions on page 47, which suggest using text features and structure to help predict what a section or text is about. Point out that they may use these suggestions as well as any other features that help them make predictions. They may want to highlight important ideas that help them make predictions. Their notes in the margin may include predictions or revisions to those predictions made during reading.

 GET READY

CRITICAL VOCABULARY

essential   amplify   generate   humiliation

To preview the Critical Vocabulary words, complete each of the following sentences with the correct vocabulary word.

1. It is necessary, or _____ , to bring water on a long hike.

2. Stereo speakers _____ music.

3. We used social media to _____ interest in our event.

4. No one likes to experience _____ or embarrassment.

LANGUAGE CONVENTIONS

Commas Among their other uses, **commas** help set off introductory words, phrases, or clauses in sentences. Read the sentence below. Notice the introductory element and the comma that follows it.

These days, you flood with embarrassment if your dad sings in front of your friends or you drop a tray in the cafeteria.

As you read, look for sentences with introductory elements and commas.

ANNOTATION MODEL

NOTICE & NOTE

Here is an example of how one reader made predictions while reading.

It's All in Your Head

3 Sometime during middle school, changes in <u>brain activity</u> transform how we see the world. Spending time with other kids becomes a top priority. Hormones power up the <u>brain's reward system</u>, making hanging out with friends more fun than ever before. (But) these changes come with a downside. Fitting in becomes essential. Threat-detection systems focus on what other people think and scan for any hints of disapproval. Hormones push the brain's shame and self-consciousness systems into overdrive.

> The subhead tells me that this section will talk about something imagined, or not real.

> My prediction is almost correct—the author is talking about how our brains affect what we experience.

> The author started out discussing advantages of hormones. The word "But" tells me that she'll now switch to explaining disadvantages.

48   Unit 1

BACKGROUND

We've all been in situations in which we've based a decision less on rational, logical thinking than on social pressure. Psychological research reveals that these snap decisions can have complex, confusing roots. In the following article, science writer and clinical psychologist **Jennifer Connor-Smith** *explains why teenagers naturally develop a strong and sometimes overwhelming fear of embarrassment.*

EMBARRASSED?
Blame Your Brain

Informational Text by Jennifer Connor-Smith

PREPARE TO COMPARE

As you read, make note of how fear of embarrassment can drive people's actions. This information will help you compare the ideas of this text with ideas in "The Ravine," which follows it.

1   Remember when you could pick your nose in public or run outside in your underpants without a second thought? These days, you flood with embarrassment if your dad sings in front of your friends or you drop a tray in the cafeteria.

2   What changed? Not the rules about nose picking or your father's singing voice, but your brain.

It's All in Your Head

3   Sometime during middle school, changes in brain activity transform how we see the world. Spending time with other kids becomes a top priority. Hormones[1] power up the brain's reward system, making hanging out with friends more fun

---

[1]   **hormones:** chemical messengers that travel through the blood.

© Houghton Mifflin Harcourt Publishing Company • Image Credits: ©Tom Grill/Corbis/Getty Images

Notice & Note

Use the side margins to notice and note signposts in the text.

MAKE PREDICTIONS
Annotate: Mark the subheading.

Predict: What do you think this section will be about?

BACKGROUND

After students read the Background note, explain that everybody makes decisions based on social pressure. Psychological research shows that the reason for this decision-making process is rooted in the brain and has developed in humans based on our ancestors' needs for survival. This text explains the processes that occur in the brain when we feel embarrassed or rejected and explains the positives and negatives to the brain's reactions.

PREPARE TO COMPARE

Direct students to use the Prepare to Compare prompt to focus their reading.

MAKE PREDICTIONS

Remind students that a subheading can help them predict what the section is about. It is often in a larger font size and may be a different color. (**Answer:** *The subheading indicates that feelings of embarrassment come from your head, or your brain.*)

For **speaking support** for students at varying proficiency levels, see the **Text X-Ray** on page 46D.

ⓔⓛ ENGLISH LEARNER SUPPORT

Use Learning Strategies   Help students make an idea web using the subhead "It's All in Your Head" as the center item. Have them list supporting details that relate to this subhead from paragraphs 3 and 4. Then have small groups compare their webs. They may repeat this process for other subheadings throughout the text. **ALL LEVELS**

ENGLISH LEARNER SUPPORT

Understand Language Structures Have students locate the sentence in paragraph 4 that contains a dash. Explain that this long dash, called an em-dash, helps emphasize part of a sentence. In this case, the em-dash introduces information that contrasts with the first part of the sentence.

Ask students to discuss with partners how the text after the em-dash emphasizes information that contrasts with the rest of the sentence. *(The text after the em-dash states that scientists don't just know about feeling embarrassed in middle school because of personal experience, they also know it from research studies.)*

MODERATE

For **reading support** for students at varying proficiency levels, see the **Text X-Ray** on page 46D.

essential
(ĭ-sĕn´shəl) *adj.* Something *essential* is so important that you can't do without it.

than ever before. But these changes come with a down side. Fitting in becomes **essential**. Threat-detection systems focus on what other people think and scan for any hints of disapproval. Hormones push the brain's shame and self-consciousness systems into overdrive.

4 Because of these brain changes, teens start reacting more strongly to social problems. Scientists don't know this *just* from surviving middle school—they have evidence from laboratory research. During a challenge like giving a speech, teens release

FEELINGS CENTRAL

A Quick Tour of Key Brain Regions Certain feelings and reactions take place in specific brain regions. Here are some regions associated with the emotional highs and lows of our social lives.

dACC The dorsal anterior cingulate cortex (dACC) and anterior insula comprise the brain's "Ow!" system that reacts to both physical and social pain.

Lateral Prefrontal Cortex Adults activate the lateral prefrontal cortex to help defend against hurt feelings. Something to look forward to?

Prefrontal Cortex

Anterior Insula

Septal Nuclei

Hypothalamus

Amygdala

Hippocampus

VTA

Limbic System The limbic system is where fight-or-flight reactions to stress or fear take place. Along with the ventral tegmental area (VTA), the limbic system is also involved in the brain's reward circuit.

CRITICAL VOCABULARY

essential: The changes in the brain that happen in middle school are essential, but not always comfortable.

ASK STUDENTS what changes happen in the brain that make fitting in feel essential in middle school. *(Hormones power up the brain's reward system when you hang out with other kids and push the brain's shame and self-consciousness system into overdrive.)*

more stress hormones and have higher blood pressure than kids or adults. Teens don't even have to tackle a challenge to feel stressed. Even being watched over a video monitor makes teens sweat more than adults.

Words Do Hurt Like Sticks and Stones

5 Why do we use pain words, like "hurt feelings" and "broken hearted," to talk about problems with other people? Maybe because our brains react to physical pain and social rejection in the same way. Psychologists explore this connection between physical and social pain by measuring brain activity while people play a computer game called Cyberball.

6 In Cyberball, research participants play a game of catch online with two other players. At least, that's what they believe is happening. In reality, the other "players" are fake, just part of the game's programming. The game starts fair, with the players programmed to share the ball with the research participant. Then, with no warning, the players start throwing the ball only to each other, leaving the research participant out completely.

7 No big surprise—teens in these Cyberball experiments feel sad and rejected. The surprising part? Rejection activates the same brain systems that physical pain triggers. Brain scans show that rejection fires up the "Ow!" part of our brain that makes pain upsetting. Without this pain-response system, we would recognize physical pain, but it wouldn't bother us. This physical pain system also responds to many kinds of social pain, like thinking about a breakup or being called boring.

8 Some people have especially reactive pain-response systems. A stronger "Ow!" brain response in the lab translates to people feeling more rejected, self-conscious, and sad in real life. Differences in pain-system reactivity may help explain why rejection hurts teenagers more than young kids. In Cyberball experiments comparing children to teens, teens activate brain systems related to pain and sadness more strongly.

Embarrassment Has an Unfair Advantage

9 Our thoughts and feelings depend on the balance between many different brain systems. Activity in one system can **amplify** or cancel out activity in another. Because our brains take more than two decades to develop, some brain systems come online sooner than others. Unfortunately, the systems that trigger embarrassment and fear of rejection fire up years before the systems that tame bad feelings.

ANALYZE ORGANIZATIONAL PATTERNS

Annotate: Mark the subhead.

Analyze: Which main organizational pattern is the author using? How can you tell?

LANGUAGE CONVENTIONS
Remember that a comma may be used to set off an introductory element in a sentence. In paragraph 8, mark an example of an introductory element and its comma.

amplify
(ăm´plə´fī) v. To *amplify* something is to make it stronger or more intense.

Embarrassed? Blame Your Brain   51

TEACH

ANALYZE ORGANIZATIONAL PATTERNS

Have students circle the subhead. Then have them refer back to the chart of Organizational Patterns on page 47 and determine which organizational pattern the author uses in this section and how they can tell the author is using this pattern. (**Answer:** *definition; you can tell because the author explains the idea that embarrassment and rejection provide pain reactions in the brain, and then provides evidence of this topic from a research experiment.*)

LANGUAGE CONVENTIONS

Help students locate the introductory element and comma in the sentence "In Cyberball experiments comparing children to teens, teens activate brain systems related to pain and sadness more strongly." Explain that the introductory phrase before the comma shows in what situation (experiments comparing two different groups) teens' brains responded more strongly.

For **listening support** for students at varying proficiency levels, see the **Text X-Ray** on page 46C.

APPLYING ACADEMIC VOCABULARY

❏ evident   ❏ factor   ☑ indicate   ☑ similar   ❏ specific

Write and Discuss Have students turn to a partner to discuss the following questions. Guide students to include the Academic Vocabulary words *indicate* and *similar* in their responses. Ask volunteers to share their responses with the class.

- What did brain scans **indicate** about the brain's reaction to rejection during the Cyberball experiment?
- What is **similar** about our reactions to physical pain and social rejection?

CRITICAL VOCABULARY

amplify: Brains often *amplify*, or increase the strength of, negative or embarrassing thoughts.

ASK STUDENTS what paragraph 9 says about which brain systems are amplified in middle schoolers. (*the systems that trigger embarrassment and fear of rejection*)

CONTRASTS AND CONTRADICTIONS

Explain to students that authors often use this signpost to make it easier for readers to compare and contrast two opposing things. (**Answer:** *The article includes both the positive and the negative effects to provide a balanced view of the fear so that the reader has enough information to make a fair judgement about it. The fear is good for us because it can help us behave better in a variety of situations.*)

✏ ANALYZE ORGANIZATIONAL PATTERNS

Have students circle the numbers of the two numbered steps. Note that numbered lists place items in a certain order, for a specific reason. (**Answer:** *The numbers indicate these are instructions to follow in order and also help separate the two separate steps from each other.*)

■ English Learner Support

Organizational Patterns Help students understand the use of a numbered list of instructions. Have partners work together to write a list of numbered instructions describing a simple activity (such as sharpening a pencil or getting a book off a shelf). Have partners trade with another partnership and practice following the instructions. **LIGHT**

CRITICAL VOCABULARY

generate: The adult brain has systems to fight embarrassing feelings and *generate* positive thoughts.

ASK STUDENTS what sorts of positive thoughts a brain might generate to soothe anxiety after an embarrassing situation. (**Possible answers:** *That's not a big deal; Nobody is laughing at you; It's going to be okay.*)

humiliation: When embarrassment is extreme, people often refer to their feelings of *humiliation*.

ASK STUDENTS to review what the text said about the benefits of humiliation. (*It makes you less selfish and nicer to other people.*)

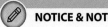
NOTICE & NOTE

generate
(jĕn´ə-rāt´) *v.* To *generate* is to create and develop something.

CONTRASTS AND CONTRADICTIONS

Notice & Note: In paragraphs 12–13, mark examples of the negative effects of a fear of rejection. Then, mark examples of its positive effects.

Analyze: Why does the article note both the positive and negative effects of a fear of rejection? Is that fear good for us? Why or why not?

humiliation
(hyōō-mĭl´ē-ā´shən) *n.* A feeling of *humiliation* is even more intense than a feeling of embarrassment.

ANALYZE ORGANIZATIONAL PATTERNS

Annotate: Mark the two steps listed in the boxed feature on this page and the next.

Analyze: How does numbering these steps help you better understand the text?

---

10 Imagine a tug-of-war with fear of rejection, the desire to fit in, and self-consciousness all pulling on the same side. With nothing pulling against them, they easily drag in all sorts of bad feelings. This imbalance means even small problems, like tripping in the hallway, can trigger a wave of embarrassment.

11 Brain scans reveal that adults unleash a powerful defender to pull the brain back into balance. Adult brains quickly fire up systems to soothe anxiety and **generate** positive thoughts. These systems help balance out concern about what other people think, so adults feel less hurt and embarrassed by rejection.

12 Wouldn't it be better if we could just turn off hurt feelings, embarrassment, and the desire to fit in? Probably not. Before modern society, people needed to belong to a group to survive. Without a group, people couldn't find enough food or protect themselves. Fear of rejection forced people to behave well enough for the community to keep them around.

13 Our lives don't depend on social acceptance anymore, but social pain is still helpful. Fear of rejection pulls on the right side in the tug-of-war against mean or selfish behavior. Shame punishes us for lying or cheating, even if we don't get caught. Social pain hurts, but it also makes us nicer. Brain scans show that teens with strong pain-response systems give more support to other kids.

14 Unfortunately, knowing the benefits of social pain won't save you from a flash of **humiliation** when your mom reminds you to take a "potty break" in front of your friends. But you can take comfort in reminding yourself that the pain makes you a better person. Maybe even one less likely to embarrass your own kids someday.

NEED HELP?

Your heart pounds, your face flames red, and your stomach feels like you've swallowed a live octopus. Meltdown mode doesn't come with an off switch—you need to hack your brain. Here are two steps you can take.

1. **Deactivate the alarm.** Your brain treats social slipups like a threat to survival, preparing your body to fight. You can't directly shut down this threat alert system, but you can trick your brain into doing it. Slow, deep breathing informs your brain the emergency has passed. Just relax your shoulders, fill your lungs completely, and exhale slowly. Your brain will respond by slowing your heart and reducing stress hormones.

WHEN STUDENTS STRUGGLE . . .

Make Predictions Have individuals or partners use a chart to list different text features that help them make predictions, an example of each, and what each helped students predict.

Feature	Example	What I Predict
subheading	It's All in Your Head	This will tell what happens in your brain when you get embarrassed.
graphic	brain diagram	I will learn about how the brain creates different emotions.

 For additional support, go to the **Reading Studio** and assign the following ▧ **Level Up tutorial: Making Predictions.**

2. **Disagree with yourself.** Stress floods your brain with negative thoughts. Imagining awful possibilities is your brain's attempt to protect you. The solution? Don't believe everything you think. If you wouldn't say it to a friend, find something more reasonable to say to yourself. In the moment, this boosts your mood. Over time, it rewires your brain. Brain cells forge new connections each time you talk back to negative thoughts. Eventually, realizing problems aren't so bad becomes automatic, just like riding a bike.

CHECK YOUR UNDERSTANDING

Answer these questions before moving on to the **Analyze the Text** section on the following page.

1 This article is mostly about —

  A situations that are embarrassing to teenagers

  B why teenagers are so sensitive to social pressure

  C how to avoid feeling embarrassed

  D the benefits of embarrassment

2 How does the author mainly support her ideas?

  F With references to other information sources

  G With experts' opinions

  H With funny anecdotes

  J With scientific evidence

3 What information does the section at the end of the article provide?

  A It tells who you should call if you need help.

  B It gives tips for handling the stress of embarrassment.

  C It defines important vocabulary words.

  D It summarizes the most important ideas in the article.

CHECK YOUR UNDERSTANDING

Have students answer the questions independently.

Answers:

  1. *B*

  2. *J*

  3. *B*

If they answer any questions incorrectly, have them reread the text to confirm their understanding. Then they may proceed to ANALYZE THE TEXT on page 54.

ENGLISH LEARNER SUPPORT

Oral Assessment Use the following questions to assess students' comprehension and speaking skills:

1. What is this article mostly about? (*This article is mostly about why teenagers are more sensitive to social pressure.*)

2. How does the author mainly support her ideas? (*The author mainly supports her ideas with scientific evidence.*)

3. What information does the sidebar at the end of the article provide? (*The sidebar provides tips for handling the stress of embarrassment.*)

SUBSTANTIAL/MODERATE

ANALYZE THE TEXT

Possible answers:

1. **DOK 2:** *Brain activity (hormones) changes in middle-school-age kids, causing them to exhibit more stress to social problems. Adults have learned how to alleviate the stress of these situations, making them less concerned about what people think.*

2. **DOK 4:** *Embarrassment and social pain help us become better people. I agree that some social pain might be good, but not an extreme amount.*

3. **DOK 2:** *The subheading makes it sound like the section will be about ways words can cause physical pain. Embarrassment can make our faces red, our hearts pound, and our stomachs churn—all physical effects that can be painful in varying degrees.*

4. **DOK 4:** *The text is about how parts of the brain influence our feelings. The graphic shows these parts and identifies how each one affects our feeling of embarrassment.*

5. **DOK 4:** *Paragraph 9 talks about a balance of systems in the brain, while paragraph 10 describes an uncontrolled "tug-of-war" of emotions in young peoples' brains. I know that tug-of-war is a game where two sides get pulled back and forth. Paragraph 11 describes how adults' brains are better able to balance out feelings of anxiety. I think the word anxiety describes that uneasy feeling of worrying and feeling out of balance in a situation. Someone might feel anxiety when he or she experiences a new, unfamiliar, or dangerous situation.*

RESEARCH

Remind students to use quotation marks any time they use the exact text from a source. It is important to do this both in a final research project and when taking notes. If they do not use quote marks in their notes, they may accidentally think their notes are paraphrased.

Connect As students share what they learned from their research, compile the main idea and most important facts into a list. Discuss whether any of the information was surprising or new.

RESPOND

ANALYZE THE TEXT

Support your responses with evidence from the text. NOTEBOOK

1. **Compare** Why is fear of embarrassment worse for teenagers than for younger children and adults, according to the article?

2. **Critique** Why does the author consider fear of embarrassment as at least somewhat positive? Do you agree with this view?

3. **Predict** Review the subheading "Words Do Hurt Like Sticks and Stones." What would you predict this section to be about? Summarize the section and explain whether your prediction was accurate.

4. **Analyze** Review the graphic on page 50. How does the text that accompanies the graphic help you predict what the graphic will show?

5. **Notice & Note** Reread paragraphs 9–11 and notice the word *anxiety*. Using clues from the text, provide your own definition of *anxiety* and give an example of when someone might experience it.

RESEARCH TIP
If you have a two-word search term, enclosing both words within quotation marks (for example, "Cyberball experiment") will help you target your search. The quotation marks around the term will find only examples that use both words together.

RESEARCH

Find out more about the Cyberball study the author discusses in the text. Keep track of your sources in a chart like the one shown. Remember to use quotation marks around text taken word-for-word from a source.

URL/SOURCE	PARAPHRASED OR QUOTED INFORMATION

Connect Share what you learned in a panel discussion or brief presentation. Provide the source for each piece of information you use.

CREATE AND DISCUSS

Write an Advertisement Use what you've learned from the selection to create an advertisement for a service that helps young people overcome their fear of embarrassment.

❑ Start with an attention-getting slogan or question.

❑ Then, include bulleted statements summarizing how your service works. Support your statements with text evidence.

❑ End with a call to action that encourages young people to hire you.

Discuss with a Small Group As you discuss how fear drives people's actions, take notes, ask for and discuss ideas from group members, and identify points of agreement and disagreement. Use ideas from your advertisements to inform your discussion. Discuss these ideas:

❑ Is there a difference between how you might respond to a genuine danger and how you might respond to the possibility of embarrassing yourself?

❑ What is going on in your brain when you're in a potentially embarrassing situation?

 RESPOND

 Go to the **Writing Studio** for more on writing informative texts.

 Go to the **Speaking and Listening Studio** for help with having a group discussion.

RESPOND TO THE ESSENTIAL QUESTION

? How do you find courage in the face of fear?

Gather Information Review your annotations and notes on "Embarrassed?" and highlight those that help answer the Essential Question. Then, add relevant details to your Response Log.

ACADEMIC VOCABULARY
As you write and discuss what you learned from the article, be sure to use the Academic Vocabulary words. Check off each of the words that you use.

❑ **evident**

❑ **factor**

❑ **indicate**

❑ **similar**

❑ **specific**

Embarrassed? Blame Your Brain 55

APPLY

CREATE AND DISCUSS

Write an Advertisement Point out that the list on page 55 should serve as a checklist so students can make sure they have included all components. Make sure students understand what is expected for each component.

For **writing support** for students at varying proficiency levels, see the **Text X-Ray** on page 46D.

Discuss with a Small Group Remind students that when they do not understand a comment made by another group member, they should ask questions to clarify meaning. The process of asking and answering questions can help everyone understand an issue more clearly and can lead to new ideas.

RESPOND TO THE ESSENTIAL QUESTION

Allow time for students to add details from "Embarrassed? Blame Your Brain" to their Unit 1 Response Logs.

ENGLISH LEARNER SUPPORT

Discuss with a Small Group Review the discussion questions with students and clarify any misunderstandings. Allow students to discuss with partners to review the text for details that answer the questions. Provide sentence frames to help them answer the questions: *I might respond to a genuine danger by _____, but I might respond to embarrassing myself by _____. When you are in an embarrassing situation, your brain _____.* **MODERATE**

Embarrassed? Blame Your Brain **55**

CRITICAL VOCABULARY

Answers:

1. **Possible answer:** *Feeding the cat is an essential part of my morning routine.*

2. **Possible answer:** *In the outdoors, there are no ceilings and walls for sound waves to bounce off, so a band needs to amplify their instruments to be heard.*

3. **Possible answer:** *I petition my friends via social media to generate ideas for the weekend party.*

4. **Possible answer:** *The humiliation of being ridiculed made me vow to never do that to someone else.*

VOCABULARY STRATEGY:
Synonyms/Antonyms

Possible answers:

Word	Synonym	Antonym
amplify	enlarge	reduce
essential	necessary	nonessential
generate	produce	destroy
humiliation	shame	praise

Practice and Apply

Answers:

1. reactive (paragraph 8: synonym) **Possible answer:** *responsive*

2. imbalance (paragraph 10: antonym) **Possible answer:** *equilibrium*

3. rewires (Need Help? section: synonym) **Possible answer:** *reconnects*

 RESPOND

WORD BANK

amplify	generate
essential	humiliation

 Go to **Synonyms and Antonyms** in the **Vocabulary Studio** for more on synonyms and antonyms.

CRITICAL VOCABULARY

Practice and Apply Answer each question using the Critical Vocabulary word in a complete sentence.

1. What is an **essential** part of your morning routine?
_____

2. Why would a band playing outdoors need to **amplify** their instruments? _____

3. What is a good way to **generate** ideas for a weekend activity?
_____

4. How does **humiliation** make someone feel?
_____

VOCABULARY STRATEGY:
Synonyms and Antonyms

A **synonym** has the same meaning as another word. An **antonym** has the opposite or nearly the opposite meaning of a word. For example, a synonym of *amplify* is *enlarge*; an antonym of *amplify* is *reduce*. Identifying synonyms and antonyms can help clarify and expand your understanding of a word.

Write a synonym and an antonym for each of the following words in the space provided. *Amplify* is used as an example. Use a print or online resource, if needed.

WORD	SYNONYM	ANTONYM
amplify	enlarge	reduce
essential		
generate		
humiliation		

Practice and Apply Write a sentence of your own, using a synonym or an antonym, for each of the following words used in the article.

1. reactive (paragraph 8: synonym)

2. imbalance (paragraph 10: antonym)

3. rewires (Need Help? section: synonym)

EL **ENGLISH LEARNER SUPPORT**

Vocabulary Strategy Give students additional practice identifying synonyms and antonyms. Have them come up with synonyms for the following words from the text: *transform* (paragraph 3); *monitor* (paragraph 4); *response* (paragraph 8); *desire* (paragraph 10).

Then have them determine antonyms for the following words: *disapproval* (paragraph 3); *rejected* (paragraph 8); *powerful* (paragraph 11); *likely* (paragraph 14).

LANGUAGE CONVENTIONS:
Commas after Introductory Elements

An **introductory element** is a clause, phrase, or word that sets the stage for the main idea of the sentence. **Commas** are used after an introductory element to help make the meaning clearer.

These examples from the article show how commas are used with the different types of introductory elements.

1. **Because of these brain changes, teens start reacting more strongly to social problems.** (introductory clause)

2. **In Cyberball, research participants play a game of catch online with two other players.** (introductory phrase)

3. **Unfortunately, the systems that trigger embarrassment and fear of rejection fire up years before the systems that tame bad feelings.** (introductory word)

Practice and Apply Write three or four sentences summarizing the article, using different types of introductory elements and commas.

 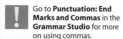

! Go to **Punctuation: End Marks and Commas** in the **Grammar Studio** for more on using commas.

LANGUAGE CONVENTIONS:
Commas After Introductory Elements

Review the information about commas after introductory elements with students. Emphasize that an introductory element is used at the beginning of the sentence to help establish a time, location, reason, or transition for the reader. Review the examples from the article and make sure students understand the difference between an introductory phrase and an introductory clause.

Read each of the sentences without pausing for the comma. Ask students how they feel the meaning of the sentence changes without the pause. Then have volunteers create sentences using each type of introductory element. Display the sentences for the whole group.

Practice and Apply Have partners work together to write three or four sentences summarizing the article, using different types of introductory elements.

Possible answers:

Because their brains are changing and developing, teens react more strongly to social problems. (introductory clause)

Although painful, hurt feelings and embarrassment are at the same time useful in helping us become better individuals. (introductory phrase)

Fortunately, teenagers can learn to use various techniques to manage embarrassment when it arises. (introductory word)

(EL) ENGLISH LEARNER SUPPORT

Language Conventions Use the following supports with students at varying proficiency levels:

- Have students find other sentences in the text that use commas with introductory elements and copy these sentences into their notebooks. **SUBSTANTIAL**

- Have students work with partners to write their own original sentences with commas after introductory elements. Encourage them to write one sentence using each type of introductory element. Then have them meet with another pair to compare their sentences. **MODERATE**

- Ask students to write one sentence modeled on each of the example sentences from the text. Then have them explain to partners why each original sentence uses the same type of introductory element as the example sentence. **LIGHT**

THE RAVINE

Short Story by Graham Salisbury

GENRE ELEMENTS
FICTION: SHORT STORY

Remind students that the purpose of fictional text is to provide stories that help us understand ourselves and the world. The **short story** often centers on one moment or event in life and is meant to be read in one sitting. Short stories contain the basic elements of setting, plot, conflict, theme, and character. In this lesson, students will focus on the theme of facing your fears and the elements of setting and character.

LEARNING OBJECTIVES

- Cite textual evidence; make inferences.
- Determine a theme or central idea.
- Describe story elements and structure.
- Determine the meaning of words and phrases from their context.
- Engage effectively in a range of collaborative discussions.
- Verify preliminary determination of the meaning of a word; consult reference materials.
- **Language** Identify and write simple and complex sentences.

TEXT COMPLEXITY

Quantitative Measures	The Ravine	Lexile: 680L
Qualitative Measures	**Ideas Presented** Much is explicit but moves to some implied meaning. Requires some inferential reasoning.	
	Structure Used Primarily explicit. Perhaps several points of view. May vary from simple chronological order. Largely conventional.	
	Language Used Mostly explicit. Some figurative or allusive language. Perhaps some dialect or other unconventional language.	
	Knowledge Required Requires no special knowledge. Situations and subjects familiar or easily envisioned.	

RESOURCES

- Unit 1 Response Log

- Selection Audio

- **Text in FOCUS** Text in Focus: Visualizing

- **Close Read** Close Read Screencasts: Modeled Discussions

- Reading Studio: Notice & Note

- **LEVEL UP** Making Inferences About Characters; Setting: Effect on Plot

- Writing Studio: Planning and Drafting

- Speaking and Listening Studio: in Collaborative Discussions

- Vocabulary Studio: Context Clues

- Grammar Studio: Module 3: Lesson 8: Conjunctions and Interjections

- "Embarrassed: Blame Your Brain"/ "The Ravine" Selection Test

SUMMARIES

English

In the short story, "The Ravine" by Graham Salisbury, a group of teens visit a setting where another young man died. A young man named Vinny struggles with his competing fears of death, embarrassment, and heights. He must face these fears and find his courage.

Spanish

En el cuento "El Barranco", de Graham Salisbury, un grupo de adolescentes visitan un sitio donde un joven ha muerto. Un joven llamado Vinny enfrenta con valentía sus miedos a la muerte, a la vergüenza y también a las alturas. Debe enfrentar estos miedos y hallar su valentía.

SMALL-GROUP OPTIONS

Have students work in small groups to read and discuss the selection.

Think-Pair-Share

- After students have read and analyzed "The Ravine," pose this question: *How would you handle it if you knew you had faced your greatest fear, but other people thought you had acted cowardly?*

- Have students think about the question individually and take notes.

- Then, have pairs discuss their ideas about the question.

- Finally, ask pairs to share their responses with the class.

Pinwheel Discussion

- After reading, place students in pinwheel configurations. Three students sit in the center facing out. Three more students arrange themselves to face each of the first three.

- The inner circle stays in place while the outer circle rotates to discuss these questions:

  1. *Is it courageous to do something risky you are not afraid to do? Why do you think so?*

  2. *Do you think Starlene and Joe-Boy felt the need to prove how brave they were? Why?*

  3. *If you do something you fear to prove to others you are courageous, is it still a courageous act?*

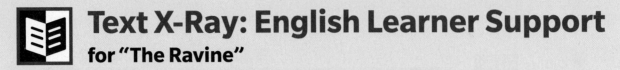

Text X-Ray: English Learner Support
for "The Ravine"

Use the Text X-Ray and the supports and scaffolds in the Teacher's Edition to help guide students at different proficiency levels through the selection.

INTRODUCE THE SELECTION
DISCUSS FEAR AND COURAGE

In this lesson, students will need to be able to discuss fear and courage. Read paragraph 1 with students, and point out the word *rumor* and the phrase *dead boy's body*. Explain that a rumor is information about someone that may or may not be true.

Discuss the fact that, while we all share some fears, different people are afraid of different things at different levels of intensity. For instance, one person may be more afraid of death than of being embarrassed. Remind students that what we fear—and how much we fear it—changes throughout our lives based on our knowledge and our experiences.

Ask students if they feel fear when watching a scary movie. Ask why some people may enjoy this feeling. Provide the following sentence frame: *Some people feel fear when watching a scary movie because ____.* (**Possible response:** *The feeling is exciting, but you know what you are watching is not real.*)

Ask students to define courage. (**Possible response:** *Facing your fears; Doing something that is right, even if you are afraid.*)

CULTURAL REFERENCES

There may be many words or phrases throughout the text that are unfamiliar to students. Use the following as examples and encourage students to ask about other English idioms or phrases they find as they read.

- *dropped down* (paragraph 1): walking down quickly
- *flat-out dangerous* (paragraph 2): there is no argument, it is very dangerous
- *cut it out* (paragraph 10): stop doing that

LISTENING

Understand Character

One way to understand what a character is like is to note what the character says or thinks, and what other characters say about or to him. Review that quotation marks signal when a character is speaking.

Have students listen as you read aloud paragraphs 5–8. Use the following supports with students at varying proficiency levels:

- Tell students you will ask questions about what they heard. They can respond with a thumb up for yes, and a thumb down for no. For example, *is Vinny teasing his friends?* (no) *Is Vinny being teased by his friends?* (yes) **SUBSTANTIAL**
- Read the following sentence frame and have students orally complete it: *People tease others because they want to ____.* **MODERATE**
- Have student pairs take turns describing how this scene might make Vinny feel rejected. **LIGHT**

SPEAKING

Make inferences

When you make an inference, you figure out something that the author has not explained or described in the text. To make an inference, use evidence from the text along with personal experience, or what you already know.

Use the following supports with students at varying proficiency levels:

- Ask students to give a thumbs up or down for statements of what makes a "good" friend. For example: *A good friend helps you become a better person. A good friend makes you feel afraid.* **SUBSTANTIAL**
- Have small groups discuss what happens when a good friend makes fun of a person's fears and concerns in front of others. **MODERATE**
- Have advanced pairs discuss how someone can hurt a friend's feelings, and whether a friend should forgive another when he or she has been embarrassed. **LIGHT**

READING

Understand Structure

Have students use graphic organizers to take notes on the characters and setting. This will help them see how characters and the setting connect to the plot.

Help students make a chart with two columns: "Character" and "Setting." Use the following supports with students at varying proficiency levels:

- Have students combine keywords in their own languages with the English translations, such as Character/*personaje*, Setting/*escenario*. **SUBSTANTIAL**
- As they read, have students add text examples that describe characters and setting to their charts. **MODERATE**
- As they read, have students list their ideas about characters, character relationships, and setting. Ask them to read their ideas to a partner. **LIGHT**

WRITING

Examine Sentence Types

Both informational texts and short stories use a variety of sentence types and patterns to help make meaning clear.

Use the following supports with students at varying proficiency levels:

- Help students find a simple sentence and a complex sentence in paragraphs 8–12, such as *Vinny scowled* and *Vinny moved to the edge of the trail, where the ravine. . . .* Help them identify each idea in the sentences. **SUBSTANTIAL**
- Ask pairs to work together to underline and list conjunctions in the first ten paragraphs. **MODERATE**
- Have partners list at least three interesting sentences from the story that have subordinating conjunctions. Ask students to share why these are interesting sentences. **LIGHT**

Connect to the
ESSENTIAL QUESTION

In "The Ravine," a teenage boy yearns for the courage to do something dangerous to impress his friends. Eventually, he discovers a different kind of courage.

COMPARE THEMES AND MAIN IDEAS

Remind students that the informational text "Embarrassed? Blame Your Brain" presented evidence that teens feel everything more intensely, including fear and especially the fear of embarrassment in front of peers. Now, in the short story "The Ravine," the main character is learning to face his fears. At the beginning of the story, Vinnie believes that courage is the ability to do dangerous things despite being afraid. As events in the story move forward, he learns that *true* courage is a lot more complicated.

ENGLISH LANGUAGE SUPPORT

Use Prior Knowledge Tell students that the word *courage* translates to *valor* in Spanish. *Valor* is also a word used in English to describe bold action or a brave person. In English, we say, "You are very brave," or "You are a person of valor." We don't always say, "You did a brave and courageous thing." Ask: *Do you think the way we use language makes us think courage is something we have or don't have, rather than something we do? Is courage something you are born with or something you can practice and improve?* **ALL LEVELS**

SHORT STORY
THE RAVINE

by **Graham Salisbury**
pages 61–71

COMPARE THEMES AND MAIN IDEAS

Now that you've read "Embarrassed? Blame Your Brain," read "The Ravine" and explore how this short story connects to some of the same ideas. As you read, notice how the ideas in both texts relate to your own experiences and how the ideas in the two texts relate to each other. After you have read both selections, you will collaborate with a small group on a final project that involves an analysis of both texts.

 ESSENTIAL QUESTION:

How do you find courage in the face of fear?

INFORMATIONAL TEXT
EMBARRASSED?
Blame Your Brain

by **Jennifer Connor-Smith**
pages 49–53

⚙️ LEARNING MINDSET

Setting Goals Remind students that setting goals is part of learning and that tracking progress on those goals can give them a sense of accomplishment. Encourage students to set a larger, long-term goal for this lesson, then break it down into smaller steps. Have them list these steps, then check them off as each is complete.

The Ravine

QUICK START

Sometimes it's difficult to do something you're afraid to do—just because you're embarrassed to let other people know you're afraid. List "smart" reasons to overcome a fear. Then list "silly" reasons. Discuss your reasons with a partner.

MAKE INFERENCES

An **inference** is a logical guess based on facts and one's own knowledge and experience. To support an inference, **cite evidence,** or provide examples from the text. Here is one way you might make an inference about Joe-Boy, a character in "The Ravine."

EVIDENCE FROM THE STORY	MY OWN KNOWLEDGE	INFERENCE
Joe-Boy is Vinny's "best friend." He teases Vinny for being afraid.	Sometimes friends tease each other in a friendly way, but Joe-Boy's teasing seems mean.	They may be friends, but Joe-Boy may be unkind—or even mean.

ANALYZE CHARACTERS AND SETTINGS

In realistic fiction, characters—like real people—have personalities and motivations and experience life-changing events. The **setting,** or the time and place in which the action occurs, often helps draw attention to the traits, motivations, and development of the characters.

- **Character traits** are the qualities shown by a character, such as physical traits (tall with brown eyes) or expressions of personality (kind or anxious).
- **Character motivations** are the reasons a character acts, feels, or thinks in a certain way.
- **Character development** is how a character changes over the course of a story.

As you read "The Ravine," note how the story's characters respond to events, the setting, and each other.

GENRE ELEMENTS: SHORT STORY

- includes the basic elements of fiction—setting, characters, plot, conflict, and theme
- may center on one particular moment or event
- can be read in one sitting

The Ravine   59

ENGLISH LEARNER SUPPORT

Learning Strategies Provide students with a two-column character chart before they begin reading the selection. Have them list a character name in the left-hand column and words or phrases from the text, or their own words, that help describe the character's traits and motivations in the right-hand column. **ALL LEVELS**

QUICK START

Have students read the Quick Start, and invite them to share their ideas on why we fear embarrassment, rejection, or judgment, and how fear can affect how we behave. Then have the group brainstorm a list of situations in which someone may feel embarrassed because of fear. After partners list their "smart" and "silly" reasons to overcome a fear, ask them to share their lists with the group.

MAKE INFERENCES

Explain that readers often have to figure out an idea in the text that an author has not fully described. Tell students that they can make an **inference,** or a logical guess based on facts and clues in the text and on their own knowledge and experience, to understand a story clearly. Review the inference on the chart on page 59. Ask students whether they think the inference makes sense based on what they understand about Joe-Boy's character.

Have students consider the following questions to help them make inferences:

- *What clues does the author give about characters and story events without directly stating information?*
- *What do I know about the character or type of person, setting, or situation?*
- *What can I guess from these clues and my own knowledge?*

ANALYZE CHARACTERS AND SETTINGS

Review the terms and concepts related to both character and setting. Explain that the characters and the setting are important story elements that an author usually identifies early in a story. The author quickly establishes who the main character or characters are and what the problem might be.

Have students read the first three paragraphs of the story and identify characters and setting. Ask who the main character is. (*The characters are Vinny, Joe-Boy, Mo, and Starlene; the setting is a jungle ravine; Vinny is the main character.*)

TEACH

CRITICAL VOCABULARY

Encourage students to read all of the sentences before deciding which word best completes each one. Remind them to look for context clues that match the precise meaning of each word.

Possible answers:

1. *cloudy*

2. *trickle*

3. *plunge*

4. *steep cliff*

LANGUAGE CONVENTIONS

Review the information about subordinating conjunctions used to connect ideas.

Read aloud the example sentence, emphasizing the word *because*. Then read it again normally. Discuss what the word *because* adds to the sentence. Point out to students that the subordinating conjunction joins two complete thoughts or ideas: the kids took their time and the reason why they did so. Point out that a subordinating conjunction introduces and connects additional information to the main clause.

✎ ANNOTATION MODEL

Remind students of the character categories in Analyze Characters and Setting on page 59. Review that they should look for and annotate details that help them understand character motivations and relationships in response to the setting. Point out that these details can be found in narrative and in dialogue.

CRITICAL VOCABULARY

| murky | rivulet | cascade | precipice |

To preview the Critical Vocabulary words, replace each boldfaced word with a different word or words that have the same meaning.

1. He dropped his watch into the (**murky**) _____ water and watched it disappear.

2. She hopped over a thin (**rivulet**) _____ of the stream.

3. The river's frightening (**cascade**) _____ into the canyon roared ahead of them.

4. When they arrived at the top, no one wanted to step any closer to the (**precipice**) _____ .

LANGUAGE CONVENTIONS

Subordinating Conjunctions In this lesson, you will learn about forming **complex sentences** by using **subordinating conjunctions,** which introduce adverb clauses, to connect ideas. As you read "The Ravine," watch for subordinating conjunctions, such as *because, if, since, until, when,* and *where,* and notice how they connect ideas.

Example:

        1st Idea   2nd Idea

They took their time (because) the hand and footholds were slimy with moss.

ANNOTATION MODEL   **NOTICE & NOTE**

As you read, note how each character responds to the setting and other characters. Consider what these responses tell you about the character's traits and motivations. You can also mark up evidence that supports your own ideas. In the model, you can see one reader's notes about a character's response to the setting in "The Ravine."

38 The fifteen-foot ledge was not the problem. 39 It was the one above it, the one you had to work up to, the big one, where you had to take a <u>deadly zigzag trail</u> that climbed up and away from the waterfall, then cut back and forth to a <u>foot-wide ledge</u> something more like <u>fifty feet up.</u> 40 <u>That was the problem.</u>	*Vinny's thoughts—his internal response to the setting—reveal something about him.* *He's afraid to climb to the higher ledge, "the problem." He also may not want his friends to know that he's afraid.*

BACKGROUND

Graham Salisbury (b. 1944) was born in Pennsylvania but grew up in Hawaii. His father was killed in World War II. Raised by a distant mother, Salisbury lacked guidance. His characters explore choices similar to those he faced—making and keeping friends and learning honesty and courage. Their struggles, like Salisbury's, also take place in a Hawaiian setting. Among his many writing awards are the Boston Globe/Horn Book award and a School Library Journal Best Book of the Year award.

THE RAVINE

Short Story by Graham Salisbury

PREPARE TO COMPARE

As you read, pay attention to Vinny's struggles with fear and his desire to please and impress his friends. Note details that help you understand what he's like, his motivations, and the conflict he faces.

1   When Vinny and three others dropped down into the ravine,[1] they entered a jungle thick with tangled trees and rumors of what might have happened to the dead boy's body.

2   The muddy trail was slick and, in places where it had fallen away, flat-out dangerous. The cool breeze that swept the Hawaiian hillside pastures above died early in the descent.

3   There were four of them—Vinny; his best friend, Joe-Boy; Mo, who was afraid of nothing; and Joe-Boy's *haole*[2] girlfriend, Starlene—all fifteen. It was a Tuesday in July, two weeks and a day after the boy had drowned. If, in fact, that's what had happened to him.

---

[1]   **ravine** (rə-vēn´): a deep, narrow valley made by running water.
[2]   **haole** (hou´lē): in Hawaii, a white person or non-native Hawaiian.

Notice & Note

Use the side margins to notice and note signposts in the text.

MAKE INFERENCES

Annotate: Mark details in paragraphs 1–3 that hint that this setting is frightening.

Infer: What might lead four teens to venture into a setting like this?

> Close Read

BACKGROUND

Have students read the information about the author. Explain that Salisbury's work focuses on the need to make choices in life and how young people struggle with this need wherever they may grow up. Making choices can be confusing and even frightening; Salisbury feels that as a writer he has a responsibility to explore these issues with readers through the authentic experiences and characters he creates.

PREPARE TO COMPARE

Direct students to use the Prepare to Compare prompt to focus their reading.

✎ MAKE INFERENCES

Have students review what they have marked and think about what has recently happened in this place. Have students connect these clues with what they know about the attitude many teens have about frightening places and events. (***Possible answers:*** *Curiosity, excitement, adventure, mystery*)

CLOSE READ SCREENCAST

Modeled Discussion   In their eBooks, have students view the Close Read Screencast, in which readers discuss and annotate paragraph 1–2, a key passage that introduces the setting and a central issue of the story.

As a class, view and discuss the video. Then have students pair up to do an independent close read of paragraphs 119–129. Students can record their answers on the Close Read Practice PDF.

 Close Read Practice PDF

ANALYZE CHARACTERS AND SETTINGS

Tell students to look for a speaker tag that shows them Vinny is talking. For dialogue that does not have a speaker tag, explain that Vinny and Joe-Boy are alternating comments. Point out that a reaction can also be a physical movement or a thought. To help students decide what they are learning about Vinny, have students think about how the words are said, or the tone of the dialogue. Ask them also to imagine how they would feel if a friend teased them in the same way. (**Possible answer:** *He is nervous or afraid to go down into the ravine. He doesn't want Joe-Boy to know he is afraid. He tells Joe-Boy to shut up when he teases him, and pleads with him to cut it out.*)

ENGLISH LEARNER SUPPORT

Analyze Language Explain to students that the characters often use informal English and sometimes dialect, a form of language spoken in a specific place by a particular group of people. Highlight *where you walking, Shaddup,* and *prob'ly.* Rewrite the words and phrase in standard English and read them aloud. Discuss the differences between the two versions. Then ask students to read aloud both versions of the dialogue. **MODERATE**

For **listening, speaking,** and **reading support** for students of varying proficiency levels, see the **Text X-Ray** on pages 58C and 58D.

▶ MEMORY MOMENT

Explain that a **Memory Moment** is a recollection by a character of an event that happened in the past. Memory Moments can often reveal important information about a **character**. (**Answer:** *The fact that the boy's body had never been found makes Vinny even more nervous and afraid.*)

 NOTICE & NOTE

ANALYZE CHARACTERS AND SETTINGS

Annotate: In paragraphs 5–12, mark each of Vinny's reactions to what Joe-Boy says.

Infer: What do Vinny's reactions tell you about him? What is he afraid to admit to Joe-Boy? How do you know?

MEMORY MOMENT ◀

Notice & Note: What does Vinny remember about events following the boy's disappearance? Mark details in paragraph 17 about the search for the missing boy.

Analyze: How might the memory of these details affect Vinny?

4   Vinny slipped, and dropped his towel in the mud. He picked it up and tried to brush it off, but instead smeared the mud spot around until the towel resembled something someone's dog had slept on. "Tst," he said.

5   Joe-Boy, hiking down just behind him, laughed. "Hey, Vinny, just think, that kid walked where you walking."

6   "Shuddup," Vinny said.

7   "You prob'ly stepping right where his foot was."

8   Vinny moved to the edge of the trail, where the ravine fell through a twisted jungle of gnarly trees and underbrush to the stream far below. He could see Starlene and Mo farther ahead, their heads bobbing as they walked, both almost down to the pond where the boy had died.

9   "Hey," Joe-Boy went on, "maybe you going be the one to find his body."

10   "You don't cut it out, Joe-Boy, I going . . . I going . . . "

11   "What, cry?"

12   Vinny scowled. Sometimes Joe-Boy was a big fat babooze.

13   They slid down the trail. Mud oozed between Vinny's toes. He grabbed at roots and branches to keep from falling. Mo and Starlene were out of sight now, the trail ahead having cut back.

14   Joe-Boy said, "You going jump in the water and go down and your hand going touch his face, stuck under the rocks. *Ha ha ha . . . a ha ha ha!*"

15   Vinny winced. He didn't want to be here. It was too soon, way too soon. Two weeks and one day.

16   He saw a footprint in the mud and stepped around it.

17   The dead boy had jumped and had never come back up. Four search and rescue divers hunted for two days straight and never found him. Not a trace. Gave Vinny the creeps. It didn't make sense. The pond wasn't that big.

18   He wondered why it didn't seem to bother anyone else. Maybe it did and they just didn't want to say.

19   Butchie was the kid's name. Only fourteen.

20   Fourteen.

21   Two weeks and one day ago he was walking down this trail. Now nobody could find him.

22   The jungle crushed in, reaching over the trail, and Vinny brushed leafy branches aside. The roar of the waterfall got louder, louder.

23   Starlene said it was the goddess that took him, the one that lives in the stone down by the road. She did that every now and then, Starlene said, took somebody when she got lonely. Took him and kept him. Vinny had heard that legend before, but he'd never believed in it.

IMPROVE READING FLUENCY

Targeted Passage Have students work with a partner to choral read the text and dialogue on pages 62–63, paragraphs 13–30. First, model by reading three paragraphs with a student and then stopping and providing feedback about the student's pronunciation and expression. Next, have student partners proceed with the reading, stopping every two or three paragraphs to review pronunciation and expression.

 Go to the **Reading Studio** for additional support in developing fluency.

24 Now he didn't know what he believed.

25 The body had to be stuck down there. But still, four divers and they couldn't find it?

26 Vinny decided he'd better believe in the legend. If he didn't, the goddess might get mad and send him bad luck. Or maybe take *him*, too.

27 *Stopstopstop! Don't think like that.*

28 "Come on," Joe-Boy said, nudging Vinny from behind. "Hurry it up."

29 Just then Starlene whooped, her voice bouncing around the walls of the ravine.

30 "Let's go," Joe-Boy said. "They there already."

31 Moments later, Vinny jumped up onto a large boulder at the edge of the pond. Starlene was swimming out in the brown water. It wasn't **murky** brown, but clean and clear to a depth of maybe three or four feet. Because of the waterfall you had to yell if you wanted to say something. The whole place smelled of mud and ginger and iron.

32 Starlene swam across to the waterfall on the far side of the pond and ducked under it, then climbed out and edged along the rock wall behind it, moving slowly, like a spider. Above, sun-sparkling stream water spilled over the lip of a one-hundred-foot drop.

NOTICE & NOTE 🖉

ANALYZE CHARACTERS AND SETTINGS

Annotate: Mark each of Vinny's thoughts in paragraphs 24–28.

Describe: What do his thoughts indicate about what he's like? How would you describe Vinny to a friend?

murky
(mur´kē) *adj.* Something *murky* is dark, obscure, and gloomy.

The Ravine   63

APPLYING ACADEMIC VOCABULARY

☑ **evident**   ☑ **factor**   ☐ **indicate**   ☐ **similar**   ☐ **specific**

Write and Discuss Have students turn to a partner to discuss the following questions. Guide students to include the Academic Vocabulary words *evident* and *factor* in their responses. Ask volunteers to share their responses with the class.

- What is **evident** about each character's traits and motivations? Remember to consider setting in your discussion.
- What **factors** affect the characters in the story?

🖉 **ANALYZE CHARACTERS AND SETTINGS**

Remind students that a character's thoughts can be described by the author and can also be indicated in italic type to show an internal dialogue.

Brainstorm with students a list of single words they could use to describe or tell about a character. Encourage them to think about how the character acts, and what he says and thinks. **(Answer:** *Vinny is impressionable and superstitious. Vinny is a nice kid. He's a deep thinker, and he doesn't like to cause trouble.)*

CRITICAL VOCABULARY

murky: The author uses the word *murky* to say what the water is not. The water is brown, but not dark or gloomy.

ASK STUDENTS to discuss what else they would describe as murky. **(Possible answer:** *a puddle in the dirt after a rain.)*

MAKE INFERENCES

Remind students that they learn more about a character through how that character responds to others and to story events. Have students recall how old Vinny and his friends are. Ask what other details they know about Vinny and how he feels about being there. Have them put this text evidence together with their own knowledge about how young people may feel about seeing others kissing. (**Answer:** *Vinny is shy and embarrassed to see his friends kissing.*)

ANALYZE CHARACTERS AND SETTINGS

Point out to students that Vinny is remembering the conversation his mother and dad had about the pond after the boy drowned. Tell students to look for the mother's words that show what she believes about the pond.

Ask students what Vinny's immediate reaction was to his mother telling him not to go to the pond. Then have them review and think about how she is influencing Vinny once he is at the pond. (**Answer:** *Vinny went to the pond because he did not want his friends to think he was afraid. But while he is there, he is constantly wondering what happened to the boy, if his body is still in the pond, and if the pond is haunted by the boy's spirit. So, what his mother said has greatly influenced him.*)

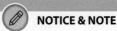 ### NOTICE & NOTE

33   Mo and Joe-Boy threw their towels onto the rocks and dove into the pond. Vinny watched, his muddy towel hooked around his neck. Reluctantly, he let it fall, then dove in after them.

34   The cold mountain water tasted tangy. Was it because the boy's body was down there decomposing?[3] He spit it out.

35   He followed Joe-Boy and Mo to the waterfall and ducked under it. They climbed up onto the rock ledge, just as Starlene had done, then spidered their way over to where you could climb to a small ledge about fifteen feet up. They took their time because the hand and footholds were slimy with moss.

36   Starlene jumped first. Her shriek echoed off the rocky cliff, then died in the dense green jungle.

37   Mo jumped, then Joe-Boy, then Vinny.

38   The fifteen-foot ledge was not the problem.

39   It was the one above it, the one you had to work up to, the big one, where you had to take a deadly zigzag trail that climbed up and away from the waterfall, then cut back and forth to a foot-wide ledge something more like fifty feet up.

40   That was the problem.

41   That was where the boy had jumped from.

42   Joe-Boy and Starlene swam out to the middle of the pond. Mo swam back under the waterfall and climbed once again to the fifteen-foot ledge.

43   <u>Vinny started to swim out toward Joe-Boy but stopped when he saw Starlene put her arms around him.</u> She kissed him. They sank under for a long time, then came back up, still kissing.

44   <u>Vinny turned away and swam back over to the other side of the pond, where he'd first gotten in.</u> His mother would kill him if she ever heard about where he'd come. After the boy drowned, or was taken by the goddess, or whatever happened to him, she said never to come to this pond again. Ever. It was off-limits. Permanently.

45   But not his dad. He said, "You fall off a horse, you get back on, right? Or else you going be scared of it all your life."

46   <u>His mother scoffed and waved him off. "Don't listen to him, Vinny, listen to me. Don't go there. That pond is haunted." Which had made his dad laugh.</u>

47   But Vinny promised he'd stay away.

MAKE INFERENCES

Annotate: Reread paragraphs 43–44, marking each of Vinny's responses to Joe-Boy and Starlene.

Infer: Why might Vinny respond as he does?

ANALYZE CHARACTERS AND SETTINGS

Annotate: In paragraphs 46–47, mark what Vinny's mother says about the setting of the pond.

Analyze: How might what Vinny's mother has said influence Vinny?

---

[3] **decomposing** (dē´kəm-pōz´ĭng): starting to decay and fall apart.

 ## ENGLISH LEARNER SUPPORT

Recognize Sentence Patterns Explain to students that authors vary the length, structure, and pattern of sentences, as well as use **repetition,** or repeated words or phrases, in their writing to appeal to reader interest, create emphasis, or to develop meaning. Have students read aloud paragraphs 37–41 to a partner, then point out specific instances of sentence variations and repetition that create interest and drama. Have students notice the rhythm of the short and long sentences and the repetition of words and phrases like *then, the problem, the one,* and *that was.* **MODERATE/LIGHT**

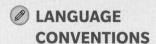

NOTICE & NOTE

48 But then Starlene and Joe-Boy said, "Come with us anyway. You let your mommy run your life, or what?" And Vinny said, "But what if I get caught?" And Joe-Boy said, "So?"

49 Vinny mashed his lips. He was so weak. Couldn't even say no. But if he'd said, "I can't go, my mother won't like it," they would have laughed him right off the island. No, he had to go. No choice.

50 So he'd come along, and so far it was fine. He'd even gone in the water. Everyone was happy. All he had to do now was wait it out and go home and hope his mother never heard about it.

51 When he looked up, Starlene was gone.

52 He glanced around the pond until he spotted her starting up the zigzag trail to the fifty-foot ledge. She was moving slowly, hanging on to roots and branches on the upside of the cliff. He couldn't believe she was going there. He wanted to yell, *Hey, Starlene, that's where he* died!

53 But she already knew that.

54 Mo jumped from the lower ledge, yelling, "Banzaiiii!" An explosion of coffee-colored water erupted when he hit.

55 Joe-Boy swam over to where Starlene had gotten out. He waved to Vinny, grinning like a fool, then followed Starlene up the zigzag trail.

56 Now Starlene was twenty-five, thirty feet up. Vinny watched her for a while, then lost sight of her when she slipped behind a wall of jungle that blocked his view. A few minutes later she popped back out, now almost at the top, where the trail ended, where there was nothing but mud and a few plants to grab on to if you slipped, plants that would rip right out of the ground, plants that wouldn't stop you if you fell, nothing but your screams between you and the rocks below.

57 Vinny's stomach tingled just watching her. He couldn't imagine what it must feel like to be up there, especially if you were afraid of heights, like he was. *She has no fear,* Vinny thought, *no fear at all. Pleasepleaseplease, Starlene. I don't want to see you die.*

58 Starlene crept forward, making her way to the end of the trail, where the small ledge was.

59 Joe-Boy popped out of the jungle behind her. He stopped, waiting for her to jump before going on.

60 Vinny held his breath.

LANGUAGE CONVENTIONS
Subordinating conjunctions are used to connect ideas in a complex sentence. Circle the word *until* in the first sentence of paragraph 52. What does the subordinating conjunction *until* suggest about Vinny's glance around the pond?

MAKE INFERENCES
Annotate: In paragraph 57, underline Vinny's descriptions of what Starlene is like. Then, circle the thoughts that show his worry.

Infer: How does Vinny feel about Starlene?

The Ravine 65

© Houghton Mifflin Harcourt Publishing Company

TEACH

LANGUAGE CONVENTIONS

Have students identify the two ideas that the subordinating conjunction connects. Ask them to think about what he does before the word *until* and what he does after. **(Answer:** *He was looking for Starlene, and then he spotted her and stopped looking.)*

MAKE INFERENCES

Remind students that italic type can signal internal responses to another character or event.

Have students first note what Vinny is feeling and then compare it to his thoughts about what Starlene is like. Ask them to consider how the setting is influencing his feelings about himself and Starlene, and how this helps them infer the feelings Vinny has that are not stated by the author. **(Answer:** *Vinny thinks Starlene is fearless. He has a crush on her.)*

 ## ENGLISH LEARNER SUPPORT

Read Closely Point out the words in italic type in paragraph 57. Explain that the slanted type is italic and using it is a way to call attention to certain words. Have students work with a partner to look through the selection to find italic type. Ask them to discuss why italic type is used. **(Answer:** *to voice Vinny's thoughts, to tell what other characters are feeling)* Have volunteers share what their groups conclude about the italic type.
ALL LEVELS

WHEN STUDENTS STRUGGLE . . .

Analyze Character To guide students' comprehension of character development throughout a story, have individuals or partners complete a character web for Vinny. Place "Vinny" in a central oval, then add words used to describe him in separate boxes around the center. Have students refer back to the beginning of the story as needed to create as complete a description of Vinny as possible.

For additional support, go to the **Reading Studio** and assign the following Level Up tutorials: **Character Traits, Making Inferences About Characters.**

ANALYZE CHARACTERS AND SETTINGS

Point out that the author is describing Starlene's external responses to the setting and to the other characters. Explain to students that they can learn about a character by how they act, as well as from their words and thoughts.

Encourage students to recall what Vinny thinks of Starlene and then to consider what they would think of someone who acted like she does in this situation. Ask them also to consider how her actions develop the plot. **(Answer:** *Starlene is a showoff, and seemingly disrespectful that a boy lost his life in that pond. Although Vinny thinks she is fearless, she may be masking her fear by showing off in front of the boys. He is right to think Starlene's actions are dangerous and disrespectful.)*

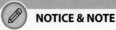

NOTICE & NOTE

61 Starlene, in her cutoff jeans and soaked T-shirt, stood perfectly still, her arms at her sides. Vinny suddenly felt like hugging her. Why, he couldn't tell. *Starlene, please.*

62 She reached behind her and took a wide leaf from a plant, then eased down and scooped up a finger of mud. She made a brown cross on her forehead, then wiped her muddy fingers on her jeans.

63 She waited.

64 Was she thinking about the dead boy?

65 She stuck the stem end of the leaf in her mouth, leaving the rest of it to hang out. When she jumped, the leaf would flap up and cover her nose and keep water from rushing into it. An old island trick.

66 She jumped.

67 Down, down.

68 Almost in slow motion, it seemed at first, then faster and faster. She fell feetfirst, arms flapping to keep balance so she wouldn't land on her back, or stomach, which would probably almost kill her.

69 Just before she hit, she crossed her arms over her chest and vanished within a small explosion of rusty water.

70 Vinny stood, not breathing at all, praying.

71 Ten seconds. Twenty, thirty . . .

72 She came back up, laughing.

ANALYZE CHARACTERS AND SETTINGS

Annotate: In paragraphs 61–69, mark each description of Starlene's actions.

Analyze: Based on her actions, how would you describe Starlene? How accurate is Vinny's view of her?

73   *She shouldn't make fun that way*, Vinny thought. It was dangerous, disrespectful. It was asking for it.

74   Vinny looked up when he heard Joe-Boy shout, "Hey, Vinny, watch how a man does it! Look!"

75   Joe-Boy scooped up some mud and drew a stroke of lightning across his chest. When he jumped, he threw himself out, face and body parallel to the pond, his arms and legs spread out. *He's crazy*, Vinny thought, *absolutely insane*. At the last second Joe-Boy folded into a ball and hit. *Ca-roomp!* He came up whooping and yelling, "*Wooo!* So *good!* Come on, Vinny, it's hot!"

76   Vinny faked a laugh. He waved, shouting, "Naah, the water's too cold!"

77   Now Mo was heading up the zigzag trail—Mo, who hardly ever said a word and would do anything anyone ever challenged him to do. *Come on, Mo, not you, too.*

78   Vinny knew then that he would have to jump.

79   Jump, or never live it down.

80   Mo jumped in the same way Joe-Boy had, man-style, splayed out in a suicide fall. He came up grinning.

81   Starlene and Joe-Boy turned toward Vinny.

82   Vinny got up and hiked around the edge of the pond, walking in the muddy shallows, looking at a school of small brown-backed fish near a ginger patch.

83   Maybe they'd forget about him.

84   Starlene torpedoed over, swimming underwater. Her body glittered in the small amount of sunlight that penetrated the trees around the rim of the ravine. When she came up, she broke the surface smoothly, gracefully, like a swan. Her blond hair sleeked back like river grass.

85   She smiled a sweet smile. "Joe-Boy says you're afraid to jump. I didn't believe him. He's wrong, right?"

86   Vinny said quickly, "Of course he's wrong. I just don't want to, that's all. The water's cold."

87   "Naah, it's nice."

88   Vinny looked away. On the other side of the pond Joe-Boy and Mo were on the cliff behind the waterfall.

89   "Joe-Boy says your mom told you not to come here. Is that true?"

90   Vinny nodded. "Yeah. Stupid, but she thinks it's haunted."

91   "She's right."

92   "What?"

93   "That boy didn't die, Vinny. The stone goddess took him. He's in a good place right now. He's her prince."

MAKE INFERENCES

Annotate: Circle Vinny's description of Mo in paragraphs 77–79.

Infer: Why might Vinny feel that he'll have to jump if Mo jumps? What would make him feel that he would "never live it down" if he doesn't jump?

ANALYZE CHARACTERS AND SETTINGS

Annotate: In paragraphs 85–96, mark what Starlene says to Vinny.

Analyze: What do Starlene's words say about her? What do Vinny's responses tell you about him?

The Ravine   67

MAKE INFERENCES

Have students look for a description that tells what Vinny is thinking about Mo. Ask students to recall how Vinny probably feels about jumping from the highest point. Then remind them of how Joe-Boy has been teasing Vinny. Have them use these details from the text, along with what they can guess about Vinny's reaction to what Mo does. (*Answer: Mo was quiet, like Vinny, and would do anything he was challenged to do regardless—probably because he was afraid of rejection. If Mo jumped and Vinny didn't, it would mean that Vinny was a bigger scaredy-cat than Mo.*)

ANALYZE CHARACTERS AND SETTINGS

Remind students to pay careful attention to the order in which characters speak, speaker tags, and the way characters address each other in the dialogue to clarify who is speaking. (*Answer: Starlene is attractive, athletic, charming, and likes to tease, even if she is not teasing now. Vinny has a crush on Starlene. He doesn't want her to think he is afraid to jump.*)

 ENGLISH LEARNER SUPPORT

Confirm Understanding   To help students describe what Vinny has been experiencing, discuss what he has been worrying about in his conversation with Starlene. Then have students work in pairs to reread paragraphs 85–96 and brainstorm words that describe Vinny. (**Possible answers:** *caring, worried, afraid, nervous, scared*) Have students use their words to write three sentences about why Vinny is worried. **MODERATE/LIGHT**

✏️ ANALYZE CHARACTERS AND SETTINGS

Remind students that setting includes all of the character's environment. Details about temperature, humidity, and natural features of the location all help paint a picture of the setting for readers to visualize. (**Answer:** *Vinny responds to the height of his position, the narrow trail, and the length of the drop with increasing fear and panic. The fact that he forces himself to continue shows his determination.*)

CRITICAL VOCABULARY

rivulet: The author uses the word *rivulets* to help explain why the trail is wet and muddy.

ASK STUDENTS to discuss how the word *rivulets* helps them picture the trail and the cliff more clearly. (*The use of the word* rivulets *shows how even a small stream of water can make the trail dangerous.*)

✏️ **NOTICE & NOTE**

94   Vinny scowled. He couldn't tell if Starlene was teasing him or if she really believed that. He said, "Yeah, prob'ly."

95   "Are you going to jump, or is Joe-Boy right?"

96   "Joe-Boy's an idiot. Sure I'm going to jump."

97   Starlene grinned, staring at Vinny a little too long. "He is an idiot, isn't he? But I love him."

98   "Yeah, well . . . "

99   "Go to it, big boy. I'll be watching."

100   Starlene sank down and swam out into the pond.

101   *Ca-ripes.*

102   Vinny ripped a hank[4] of white ginger from the ginger patch and smelled it, and prayed he'd still be alive after the sun went down.

103   He took his time climbing the zigzag trail. When he got to the part where the jungle hid him from view, he stopped and smelled the ginger again. So sweet and alive it made Vinny wish for all he was worth that he was climbing out of the ravine right now, heading home.

104   But of course, there was no way he could do that.

105   Not before jumping.

106   He tossed the ginger onto the muddy trail and continued on. He slipped once or twice, maybe three times. He didn't keep track. He was too numb now, too caught up in the insane thing he was about to do. He'd never been this far up the trail before. Once he'd tried to go all the way, but couldn't. It made him dizzy.

ANALYZE CHARACTERS AND SETTINGS

Annotate: In paragraphs 107–110, mark descriptions of the story's setting.

Infer: What do Vinny's responses to the setting tell you about him?

107   When he stepped out and the jungle opened into a huge bowl where he could look down, way, way down, he could see their three heads in the water, heads with arms moving slowly to keep them afloat, and a few bright rays of sunlight pouring down onto them, and when he saw this, his stomach fluttered and rose. Something sour came up and he spit it out.

108   It made him wobble to look down. He closed his eyes. His whole body trembled. The trail was no wider than the length of his foot. And it was wet and muddy from little rivulets of water that bled from the side of the cliff.

rivulet
(rĭv´yə-lĭt) *n.* A *rivulet* is a small brook or stream.

109   The next few steps were the hardest he'd ever taken in his life. He tried not to look down, but he couldn't help it. His gaze was drawn there. He struggled to push back an urge to fly, just jump off and fly. He could almost see himself spiraling down like a glider, or a bird, or a leaf.

---

[4] **hank** (hăngk): a coiled or looped bundle of something, such as rope or yarn.

WHEN STUDENTS STRUGGLE . . .

Analyze Setting Students may struggle with the idea that the text on pages 68–69, paragraphs 107–110, describes what Vinny is seeing, feeling, and thinking as he stands on the ledge. Guide students to read the definition of *precipice* on page 69. Draw a simple picture of a precipice on the board, and confirm that students understand that Vinny is standing on the edge of the precipice and thinking about jumping into the water. Have students reread the text. Ask them what Vinny decided.

 For additional support, go to the **Reading Studio** and assign the following ▣ **Level Up tutorial: Setting: Effect on Plot.**

110   His hands shook as if he were freezing. He wondered, *Had the dead boy felt this way?* Or had he felt brave, like Starlene or Joe-Boy, or Mo, who seemed to feel nothing.

111   Somebody from below shouted, but Vinny couldn't make it out over the waterfall, roaring down just feet beyond the ledge where he would soon be standing, **cascading** past so close its mist dampened the air he breathed.

112   *The dead boy had just come to the ravine to have fun,* Vinny thought. Just a regular kid like himself, come to swim and be with his friends, then go home and eat macaroni and cheese and watch TV, maybe play with his dog or wander around after dark.

113   But he'd done none of that.

114   Where was he?

115   Inch by inch Vinny made it to the ledge. He stood, swaying slightly, the tips of his toes one small movement from the **precipice**.

116   Far below, Joe-Boy waved his arm back and forth. It was dreamy to see—back and forth, back and forth. He looked so small down there. ▶ Text in FOCUS

117   For a moment Vinny's mind went blank, as if he were in some trance, some dream where he could so easily lean out and fall, and think or feel nothing.

118   A breeze picked up and moved the trees on the ridge-line, but not a breath of it reached the fifty-foot ledge.

119   Vinny thought he heard a voice, small and distant. Yes. Something inside him, a tiny voice pleading, *Don't do it. Walk away. Just turn and go and walk back down.*

120   " . . . I can't," Vinny whispered.

121   *You can, you can, you can. Walk back down.*

122   Vinny waited.

123   And waited.

124   Joe-Boy yelled, then Starlene, both of them waving.

125   Then something very strange happened.

126   Vinny felt at peace. Completely and totally calm and at peace. He had not made up his mind about jumping. But something else inside him had.

127   Thoughts and feelings swarmed, stinging him: *Jump! Jump! Jump! Jump!*

128   But deep inside, where the peace was, where his mind wasn't, he would not jump. He would walk back down.

cascade
(kăs-kād´) *v.* Something that can *cascade* will fall, pour, or rush in stages, like a waterfall over steep rocks.

precipice
(prĕs´ə-pĭs) *n.* A *precipice* is an overhanging or extremely steep area of rock.

ANALYZE CHARACTERS AND SETTINGS
Annotate: In paragraphs 119–130, underline each thought that encourages Vinny not to jump. Then, circle evidence of the feelings created by those thoughts.

Analyze: What fear is Vinny overcoming? What does this tell you about him?

The Ravine   69

WHEN STUDENTS STRUGGLE . . .

Analyze Character To help students locate and differentiate text that describes characters in this unit, ask them to do the following: (1) Highlight in yellow a character's thoughts or feelings. (2) Highlight in green a character's actions. (3) Highlight in blue a character's spoken words. (4) Review the highlights.

 For additional support, go to the **Reading Studio** and assign the following
LEVEL UP **Level Up tutorial: Methods of Characterization.**

✏ ANALYZE CHARACTERS AND SETTINGS

In paragraphs 119–128, remind students to look for internal thoughts signaled by italic type. Have them look for words that describe feelings. Explain to students that Vinny has experienced a sudden change at this point as evidenced by the sentence: *Then something very strange happened.* Have students recall what has worried and scared Vinny up to this point. Then have them compare those details to what has happened here. (**Answer:** *He is overcoming the fear of embarrassment and rejection. Vinny wants to belong to the group, but at the same time his better self is telling him he doesn't have to jump.*)

▶ Text in FOCUS   TEXT IN FOCUS

Visualizing Have students view the **Text in Focus** video in their eBook to learn how to use descriptive details to visualize the story's characters, setting, and events. Then have students use **Text in Focus Practice PDF** to apply what they have learned.

CRITICAL VOCABULARY

cascade: The author uses the word *cascading* to describe the power of the waterfall.

ASK STUDENTS to discuss how the word *cascading* works with other words in the paragraph to describe the waterfall. (*The word* cascading *tells about what Vinny sees; the word* roaring *tells what he hears; the words* its mist dampened the air he breathed *tell what he can feel on his body from the powerful waterfall.*)

precipice: The author uses the word *precipice* to describe the ledge where Vinny is standing.

ASK STUDENTS why they think the author chose to use the word *precipice* here rather than a word such as *edge* or *cliff*. (*The word* precipice *sounds more dangerous; it helps readers understand how the ledge overhangs the water and makes clear how Vinny feels as he stands there, looking down over the edge.*)

✎ MAKE INFERENCES

In paragraphs 132–133, have students look for descriptive words that tell what the characters are doing. Remind students that they only have Vinny's point of view, and that the author has not stated what Vinny knew about his friends' thoughts. Encourage them to use what they know about Vinny and their own understanding of what is happening. *(Answer: The group doesn't think of Vinny as an equal—they want to see him prove himself by jumping. They think Vinny is a scaredy-cat because he didn't jump.)*

▶ AHA MOMENT

Explain to students that an **Aha Moment** points to the moment when a **character** realizes that something has changed about himself, others, or the world around him. Remind them that Vinny has felt a sense of peace about his decision not to jump, and now realizes why that peace exists. Have them use what they know together with what they know about how Vinny felt before and after he decided not to jump to **infer** how Vinny has changed. *(Answer: Vinny realizes that although his friends will likely treat him differently now, he feels peace because he was true to himself, and this is more valuable than doing what others want to impress them. He feels that he made the right choice by not jumping.)*

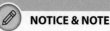

✎ NOTICE & NOTE

129   *No! No, no, no!*

130   Vinny eased down and fingered up some mud and made a cross on his chest, big and bold. He grabbed a leaf, stuck it in his mouth. *Be calm, be calm. Don't look down.*

131   After a long pause he spit the leaf out and rubbed the cross to a blur.

132   They walked out of the ravine in silence, Starlene, Joe-Boy, and Mo far ahead of him. They hadn't said a word since he'd come down off the trail. He knew what they were thinking. He knew, he knew, he knew.

133   At the same time the peace was still there. He had no idea what it was. But he prayed it wouldn't leave him now, prayed it wouldn't go away, would never go away, because in there, in that place where the peace was, it didn't matter what they thought.

134   Vinny emerged from the ravine into a brilliance that surprised him. Joe-Boy, Starlene, and Mo were now almost down to the road.

135   Vinny breathed deeply, and looked up and out over the island. He saw, from there, a land that rolled away like honey,

MAKE INFERENCES

Annotate: In paragraphs 132–133, mark words that indicate how the group leaves the ravine.

Infer: What does this suggest about the group and how they feel about Vinny?

AHA MOMENT

Notice & Note: What does Vinny suddenly realize in paragraph 133? Mark this detail.

Infer: What does this tell you about how Vinny feels about his choice?

🗨 ENGLISH LEARNER SUPPORT

Understand Character Development Review with students what they learned about Vinny's character before he decided not to jump, recalling words they used to describe him. (**Possible answers:** *nervous, scared, worried*) Then explain that the word *peace* means "a feeling of contentment," which is the opposite of how Vinny felt. Ask how this difference shows how Vinny's thinking about himself and his friends has changed. Have students work with a partner to discuss the last four paragraphs of the story, and how Vinny's **Aha Moment** has also changed how Vinny sees the world around him. **MODERATE/LIGHT**

easing down a descent of rich Kikuyu grass pasture-land, flowing from there over vast highlands of brown and green, then, finally, falling massively to the coast and flat blue sea. He'd never seen anything like it.

136   Had it always been here? This view of the island?

137   He stared and stared, then sat, taking it in.

138   He'd never seen anything so beautiful in all his life.

NOTICE & NOTE

CHECK YOUR UNDERSTANDING

Answer these questions before moving on to the **Analyze the Text** section on the following page.

1 Which of the following is not true?

   A Vinny's father encourages him to go back to the pond.

   B Starlene, Joe-Boy, and Mo jump from the fifty-foot ledge.

   C Butchie and Vinny had been close friends for many years.

   D Vinny tries to avoid jumping by claiming that the water is too cold.

2 Which of the following sentences shows that Starlene suspects that Vinny is afraid?

   F *"Are you going to jump, or is Joe-Boy right?"*

   G *"Come with us anyway. You let your mommy run your life, or what?"*

   H *Her shriek echoed off the rocky cliff, then died in the dense green jungle.*

   J *Starlene said it was the goddess that took him, the one that lives in the stone by the road.*

3 As the story concludes —

   A the four friends walk home together

   B readers know that the group found Butchie

   C Joe-Boy, Starlene, and Mo leave Vinny behind

   D Vinny feels embarrassed by his decision not to jump

CHECK YOUR UNDERSTANDING

Have students answer the questions independently

Answers:

   1. C

   2. F

   3. C

If they answer any questions incorrectly, have them reread the text to confirm their understanding. Then they may proceed to ANALYZE THE TEXT on page 72.

ENGLISH LEARNER SUPPORT

Oral Assessment   Use the following questions to assess students' comprehension and speaking skills.

   1. What do Vinny's thoughts about Butchie tell you in the beginning of the story? (*Vinny knows that the boy who drowned is named Butchie, but he does not know the boy.*)

   2. What has Joe-Boy been saying to Vinny about jumping? (*Joe-Boy has been teasing Vinny about being afraid to jump and being controlled by his mommy.*)

   3. Where are Joe-Boy, Starlene, and Mo when Vinny comes out of the ravine? (*They are almost down to the road; far ahead of Vinny.*) **SUBSTANTIAL/MODERATE**

ANALYZE THE TEXT

Possible answers:

1. **DOK 2:** *When the goddess that lives in the stone by the road feels lonely, she may take someone and keep him. Vinny had not believed the legend, but decides at the pond that he should in case the goddess returned the dead boy or took Vinnie, too. Thinking what that might mean for him makes Vinny nervous and worried.*

2. **DOK 3:** *The pond at the bottom of the ravine was surrounded by mud, rocks, and cliffs, and a steep waterfall cascaded into the pond. The water was cold. There was a rock ledge 15 feet above the pond. The zigzag trail is referred to as "deadly." The description of the pond and ravine indicate that the area is unsafe and mysterious.*

3. **DOK 2:** *Starlene's actions show that it was a ritual for her, a way, perhaps, of honoring the dead boy. Joe-Boy's ritual could mean he thinks of himself as a warrior or a hero. Mo imitates Joe-Boy's macho style, following the leader.*

4. **DOK 4:** *Vinny was uncomfortable about going to the ravine in the first place, and his discomfort only grows as the story unfolds. He also felt they were being disrespectful to the boy and perhaps the boy's family. When he decided not to jump, a great peace came over him. The fear of being ridiculed or ostracized from the group subsided. The experience helped Vinny be more comfortable with his true nature, a sign of becoming an adult.*

5. **DOK 4:** *Vinny suddenly realizes that Starlene is planning to jump from the cliff. It is a problem for Vinny because he doesn't think it is a good idea to jump from the same spot where the boy died.*

RESEARCH

Suggest that students find authentic sources by focusing their search on schools and cultural institutions (such as museums) that are based in Hawaii. Note that they should look for facts that both describe the activity and explain its meaning and value to the Hawaiian people.

Extend Have students begin by thinking about the things the activities they enjoy might tell other people about their own culture. Then have them consider, in a similar way, the relationship between Hawaiian sports and culture.

 RESPOND

ANALYZE THE TEXT

Support your responses with evidence from the text. 📓 NOTEBOOK

1. **Summarize** Review paragraphs 23–27. In your own words, summarize the legend about the goddess. Explain how this aspect of the story's cultural setting influences Vinny.

2. **Draw Conclusions** Review paragraphs 31–39. What are some examples of language the author uses to describe the setting? Why is the setting important to the story?

3. **Make Inferences** Before jumping, the characters perform certain rituals. Reread paragraphs 61–80 to review how they prepare to jump. What inferences can you make about the characters' feelings and their reasons for these rituals?

4. **Analyze** Consider Vinny's feelings and actions throughout the story. How is Vinny different by the end of the story? How is he the same?

5. **Notice & Note** What does Vinny suddenly realize in paragraphs 51–53? Why is this realization a problem for Vinny?

RESEARCH TIP
It's always easier to begin a research project by creating a research plan. First, identify exactly what you want to learn. Then, create a step-by-step plan to guide your research.

RESEARCH

Hawaii is known not only for its beautiful beaches, volcanoes, and waterfalls, but also for the culture of its people. Do some research to explore the history of a few sports played in Hawaii. Make sure your sources are reliable and credible, such as a respected university or an established media outlet.

SPORT	INFORMATION ABOUT THE SPORT AND ITS SIGNIFICANCE
lele kawa (diving)	*traditional Hawaiian sport of diving from a high cliff*
he'e nalu (surfing)	*surfing means to "slide on the waves"*
he'e hōlua (mountain surfing)	*sledding down a mountain, usually on lava rock, to worship Pele, the Goddess of the Volcano*
'o'o ihe (spear throwing)	*evolved from training young warriors to fight*

Extend Explain why each sport is significant to Hawaiian culture. What do these activities tell you about native Hawaiians?

 LEARNING MINDSET

Belonging Remind students that everyone in the classroom is part of a learning community. Everyone belongs, and everyone has something to contribute. When students come together in groups for discussions, encourage them to take advantage of the different perspectives and suggestions each person can offer that might help them understand the selection in a new way.

CREATE AND DISCUSS

Write a Compare and Contrast Essay Write a three- or four-paragraph essay in which you compare and contrast Vinny with one of the other characters in "The Ravine." Review your notes and annotations before you begin.

- ❑ Introduce your essay by describing the character traits of Vinny and the other character you have selected.
- ❑ Then, explain similarities and differences between the two characters. Include details from the text about the characters' actions and motivations to support your ideas.
- ❑ In your final paragraph, state your conclusion about the two characters.

Share and Discuss With a small group, discuss your opinions about Vinny's actions in "The Ravine." Can Vinny be characterized as a coward, a hero, or something else?

- ❑ Review the story with your group to identify the thoughts and actions that help you understand Vinny.
- ❑ Then, discuss Vinny's motivations and what those motivations reveal. As you discuss, listen closely, ask each other questions to help clarify ideas, and take notes.
- ❑ Finally, end your discussion by listing the conclusions of each member of your group.

RESPOND TO THE ESSENTIAL QUESTION

 How do you find courage in the face of fear?

Gather Information Review your annotations and notes on "The Ravine." Consider how Vinny found the courage to face a fear. Think about his actions, motivations, and traits as you respond. Then, add relevant details to your Response Log.

At the end of the unit, use your notes to write an informational essay.

RESPOND

Go to the **Writing Studio** for more on planning and drafting essays.

Go to the **Speaking** and **Listening Studio** for help with having a group discussion.

ACADEMIC VOCABULARY

As you write and discuss what you learned from "The Ravine," be sure to use the Academic Vocabulary words. Check off each of the words that you use.

- ❑ **evident**
- ❑ **factor**
- ❑ **indicate**
- ❑ **similar**
- ❑ **specific**

The Ravine   73

APPLY

CREATE AND DISCUSS

Write a Compare and Contrast Essay Point out that an essay with the purpose of comparing two characters would be an informational essay and should follow that structure. Then ask them to gather their writing resources. Have students include the list of Academic Vocabulary, and any notes on character—or graphic organizers on character—they have completed.

After students have individually drafted their essays, encourage them to read them aloud, either in pairs or in a small group. This will help them identify any sections that are confusing or need more detail. Have them help each other add subordinating conjunctions to help clarify meaning and make a mix of interesting sentences.

For **writing support** for students at varying proficiency levels, see the **Text X-Ray** on page 58D.

Share and Discuss Remind students that they have already discussed how the ways of defining courage may be more complicated than simply overcoming the fear to do dangerous things. As students discuss Vinnie's choices, point out that some people may be very brave in facing physical dangers but have to work harder to exercise the courage to speak up and disagree with someone else in a discussion. Encourage students to remember that for teens, this fear of embarrassment in a group discussion might be stronger than it would be for adults, and to be respectful of those differences.

RESPOND TO THE ESSENTIAL QUESTION

Allow time for students to add details from "The Ravine" to their Unit 1 Response Logs.

 ENGLISH LEARNER SUPPORT

Write a Compare and Contrast Essay Use these suggestions to support students' writing:

- Have students draw a Venn Diagram for their two characters and fill in the similarities and differences in their own language and in English, before beginning their essay. **SUBSTANTIAL**
- Have them outline the content of their paragraphs before they begin. **MODERATE**

- Ask students to make inferences about other ways the two characters might be alike and different. *Do you think Vinnie puts effort into his school work? Do you think he speaks up in class? What about the other character?* Explain the evidence and personal experiences that make you think your inferences might be true. Tell them they may add these educated guesses to their essays if they have evidence they can quote. Remind students to use Academic Vocabulary and subordinating conjunctions. **LIGHT**

CRITICAL VOCABULARY
Practice and Apply

Possible Answers:

1. *The word murky goes with cloudy and dark because these words can describe something that is difficult to see through. Sentence: The water was so murky you couldn't see the bottom.*

2. *The word precipice goes with edge because both words describe a place where the ground drops away. Sentence: Tara stood at the precipice and looked down into the deep canyon.*

3. *The word rivulet goes with trickle because both words describe small streams of something. Sentence: A rivulet of rainwater crossed the walkway, forming a large puddle beside it.*

4. *The word cascading goes with pouring because both words describe something flowing fast and powerfully. Sentence: The cascade of water fell with a powerful rush into a deep pool.*

VOCABULARY STRATEGY:
Context Clues

Practice and Apply

Possible Answers:

Word	Context Clues	My Guessed Definition	Dictionary Definition
winced	(paragraphs 14–15)	*frowned, making a face to show discomfort*	*to flinch, or startle, as in pain or distress, grimaced in anticipation of pain*
scoffed	(paragraphs 45–46)	*laughing or making a noise or face to show you think something is silly*	*showed or expressed scorn*
parallel	(paragraph 75)	*something is in line with something else, like two rails of a railroad track*	*relating to two planes that do not intersect*

RESPOND

WORD BANK

murky	cascade
rivulet	precipice

Go to the **Vocabulary Studio** for more on context clues.

CRITICAL VOCABULARY

Practice and Apply With a partner, discuss and write down an answer to each of the following questions. Then work together to write a sentence for each vocabulary word.

1. Which vocabulary word goes with *cloudy* and *dark?* Why?
   _____

2. Which vocabulary word goes with *edge?* Why?
   _____

3. Which vocabulary word goes with *trickle?* Why?
   _____

4. Which vocabulary word goes with *pouring?* Why?
   _____

VOCABULARY STRATEGY:
Context Clues

When you encounter an unfamiliar word, one way to figure out the meaning is to use **context clues,** or hints about meaning that may be found in the words, phrases, sentences, and paragraphs that surround that unknown word. Look at the following example from the text:

> **And it was wet and muddy from little rivulets of water that bled from the side of the cliff.**

To figure out the meaning of *rivulets*, look for clues in the surrounding words and ideas in the sentence. The sentence says that the rivulets of water "bled" from the cliff. This helps you imagine water flowing from the cliff in the same way that blood flows from a cut or scrape on your arm; the blood looks like a running stream. Combining this image with the word *little*, you can imagine that rivulets might be little streams. Then use a dictionary to confirm your guess: A rivulet is "a small brook or stream."

Practice and Apply Review "The Ravine" and find the following words. Look at the surrounding words and sentences for clues to each word's meaning. Fill out this chart.

WORD	LOCATION OF CONTEXT CLUES	MY GUESSED DEFINITION	DICTIONARY DEFINITION
winced	(paragraphs 14–15)		
scoffed	(paragraphs 45–46)		
parallel	(paragraph 75)		

ENGLISH LEARNER SUPPORT

USING CONTEXT CLUES Assist students in locating the sentences containing the words *winced, scoffed,* and *parallel.* Direct them to us their eBook annotation tools to: (1) Highlight each word. (2) Look for clues to the word's meaning in the surrounding words and sentences. (3) Underline clues you find. (4) Use your annotations to guess the word's meaning.

Help students look up the definitions in an online or print dictionary to complete their charts.
MODERATE/LIGHT

LANGUAGE CONVENTIONS:
Subordinating Conjunctions

A **simple sentence** expresses a single, complete thought: *They took their time. The hand and footholds were slimy with moss.* However, you can use connecting words and phrases called **subordinating conjunctions** to connect and clarify ideas, forming **complex sentences.** Complex sentences include answers to questions such as *How? Where? When? Why? For how long? How much? To what extent?* and *Under what condition?*

Why did Joe-Boy, Mo, and Vinny take their time?

They took their time (because) the hand and footholds were slimy with moss. (paragraph 35)

COMMON SUBORDINATING CONJUNCTIONS					
after	as long as	because	in order that	though	whenever
although	as much as	before	since	unless	where
as	as soon as	how	so that	until	wherever
as if	as though	if	than	when	while

The writer of "The Ravine" clarifies descriptions by creating complex sentences that answer questions such as these:
- Where? Where is the edge of the trail?

> **Vinny moved to the edge of the trail,** (where) **the ravine fell through a twisted jungle of gnarly trees and underbrush to the stream far below.** (paragraph 8)

- Under what condition? Under what condition would Vinny's mother get angry?

> **His mother would kill him** (if) **she ever heard about where he'd come.** (paragraph 44)

- When? When did the water erupt?

> **An explosion of coffee-colored water erupted** (when) **he hit.** (paragraph 54).

Practice and Apply Write three pairs of related simple sentences. Then, use a subordinating conjunction to connect the sentences in each pair. When you have finished, share your new complex sentences with a partner and work together to create a few more complex sentences.

RESPOND

 Go to **Conjunctions and Interjections** in the **Grammar Studio** for more on using subordinating conjunctions.

 © Houghton Mifflin Harcourt Publishing Company

The Ravine 75

APPLY

LANGUAGE CONVENTIONS:
Subordinating Conjunctions

Review the information about subordinating conjunctions with students. Explain that a subordinating conjunction can be used to join the complete thoughts in two simple sentences into a complex sentence that connects and clarifies ideas.

Point out the questions in the text, and explain that they will help students identify a subordinating conjunction to use when combining ideas in a complex sentence. Review the chart of Common Subordinating Conjunctions, and ask students to select a few and identify which question the conjunctions answer.

Practice and Apply If students have difficulty writing simple sentences, suggest that they look in the story or write their sentences about a part of the story. Have partners review each other's choice of conjunction in each complex sentence.

Possible Answers:

The girl loved swimming in the lake.

The trees came right up to the edge of the lake.

The girl loved swimming in the lake where the trees came right up to the edge.

The sky turns a deep purple.

A storm is coming.

The sky turns a deep purple when a storm is coming.

I will buy us a big container of ice cream.

The store closes at 7 p.m.

I will buy us a big container of ice cream if I arrive before the store closes at 7 p.m.

![EL] ENGLISH LEARNER SUPPORT

Language Conventions Use the following supports with students at varying proficiency levels:

- Have students orally say a simple sentence with one idea. Write that sentence. Then ask students to say another simple sentence related to the first. For example: *The family packed lunch. They wanted to go on a picnic.* Ask students to use the subordinating conjunction *because* to join the two sentences. **SUBSTANTIAL**

- Have students work with a partner to compose simple sentences that can be joined with a subordinating conjunction. Provide a list of subordinating conjunctions for students to use. **MODERATE**

- Read the following sentence aloud: *The trees came right up to the edge of the lake.* Have students notice that this sentence is still simple but has a more interesting idea than the sentence: *He likes soup.* Have students brainstorm interesting related sentences to combine with subordinating conjunctions. **LIGHT**

The Ravine **75**

COMPARE TEXTS

Collaborate to Synthesize Before groups work on the Venn diagram, emphasize that they are comparing not only what they learned from the two texts, but also how the information was presented in each genre. How did "Embarrassed?" inform readers about the fear of embarrassment? How did "The Ravine" convey some of the same ideas through Vinny's experiences? Note that reponses on the diagram will vary; a possible response is shown.

ANALYZE THE TEXTS

Possible answers:

1. **DOK 4:** *Vinny's character in "The Ravine" illustrates the teenage behavior discussed in the article "Embarrassed? Blame Your Brain." At the end of "The Ravine," Vinny displays a newfound ability to cope with his fears as an adult, as discussed in "Embarrassed? Blame Your Brain."*

2. **DOK 3:** *According to the article, as a teenager, Vinny should have strong feelings about wanting to fit in—which he does in the beginning of the story. He was afraid that if he didn't jump, he would be rejected by the others. Because of the intense peer pressure, it was surprising that he decided not to jump.*

3. **DOK 2:** *As Vinny stands at the top of the cliff deciding whether to jump, he argues with himself and tries to calm his thoughts. In the end, he is successful in calming himself, which enables him to make the decision not to jump. According to the article, adult brains are able to soothe anxiety and balance their negative feelings with positive thoughts. Vinny acted as an adult when he decided not jump.*

4. **DOK 4:** *Teenagers have a strong desire to fit in and be a part of group. Social rejection can cause tremendous anxiety and emotional distress in teenagers. They will often do risky things to gain acceptance from their peers.*

 RESPOND

Collaborate & Compare

EMBARRASSED?
Informational Text by
Jennifer Connor-Smith

THE RAVINE
Short Story by
Graham Salisbury

COMPARE TEXTS

When you compare two or more texts on the same topic, you **synthesize** the information, making connections and building your understanding of key ideas. It's often easy to synthesize information when the texts you're comparing are the same **genre,** or type of writing. However, you can often gain a more thorough understanding of a topic by comparing texts from different genres—like an informational text and a short story.

In a small group, complete the Venn diagram with similarities and differences in what you learned about responses to the fear of embarrassment in the two texts. Think about the themes and main ideas shared by the texts. One example is completed for you.

"Embarrassed?"   Both   "The Ravine"

fear of embarrassment can be overwhelming

ANALYZE THE TEXTS

Discuss these questions in your group.

1. **Connect** What similar ideas about fear of embarrassment do the article and the short story share? Cite evidence in your anwer.

2. **Contrast** What differences are there between the choice Vinny makes and what you would expect him to do, based on the article?

3. **Infer** Why does Vinny make the choice that he does? What is happening in his brain as he makes this choice, based on the article?

4. **Synthesize** What theme or message about how young people approach fear can you synthesize from the two texts? What theme or message do they share?

EL **ENGLISH LEARNER SUPPORT**

Ask Questions Use the following questions to help students compare the selections.

1. In the article, how do teenagers respond when they feel embarrassed? Does Vinny respond this way?

2. Were you surprised that Vinny didn't jump? Why was it surprising?

3. Why does Vinny decide not to jump? How would the author of the article explain what happens to him?
   MODERATE/LIGHT

RESEARCH AND SHARE

Now your group can continue exploring the main ideas in these texts by collaborating to present research in a panel discussion. Follow these steps:

1. **Develop Research Questions** In your group, brainstorm questions you'd like answered about young peoples' fear of embarrassment. Make sure that everyone contributes ideas to the list. Circle the most interesting questions. Then, assign each of the circled questions to group members for research. When those questions have been answered, your group will have gathered plenty of information to present in a panel discussion.

2. **Gather the Information** As you begin to research your individual question or questions from the list, check that your sources are reliable and credible.
   - A **reliable** source comes from an expert on the topic or someone with firsthand experience of the topic.
   - A **credible** source presents ideas fairly and accurately, avoiding bias (unfairly favoring one view), hyperbole (exaggeration), and stereotype (overgeneralizing a characteristic, such as saying that all teenagers are reckless).

RESPOND

RESEARCH TIP
To find strong sources, begin with the suggestions for Independent Reading at the end of this unit.

Take notes from two or more sources for each question, paraphrasing and summarizing key information that provides an answer. You can use this framework to synthesize what you learn:

My Question:	
Source 1 information:	Source 2 information:
Ideas the two sources share that answer my question:	

3. **Share What You Learn** Once research is complete, everyone in your group will have become an expert on a different aspect of the topic. Gather together and share what you have learned. Listen to what others have to say, ask questions to request and clarify information, and build on the ideas of others as you discuss the topic. Use your research notes to back up your views with text evidence.

Collaborate & Compare   77

RESEARCH AND SHARE

Explain that a panel discussion brings together a group of people who know something about a particular topic. During the discussion, each panel member contributes his or her unique knowledge and perspective on the topic.

1. **Develop Research Questions** As students develop questions, circulate among the groups and check that the questions are appropriate for the level of research you expect students to conduct. The questions should not be too broad or too involved.

   Point out that students' big question could serve as the title of their panel discussion. Encourage them to consider the question carefully to make sure it captures the main idea of all the other questions. They might write the big question on a sign to be displayed during their presentation.

2. **Gather the Information** Discuss the information about reliable and credible sources. Make sure all students understand the terms *bias, hyperbole,* and *stereotype* and why these characteristics make a source less credible. Point out the Research Tip and make sure students have access to the Independent Reading selections.

3. **Share What You Learn** Before students present their panel discussions, decide on the format. For example, one student might play the role of facilitator, posing questions and making sure everyone gets a turn to speak. The discussion might begin with each student making a statement about his or her research question, followed by a period of open discussion. Students in the audience might be invited to ask questions in a final segment.

WHEN STUDENTS STRUGGLE . . .

Credible and Reliable Sources Ask students to create a checklist with helpful examples to consult when they are checking sources: The first item for a reliable source might read: "My source is an expert on the topic" (Example: A sports journalist); "My source has a lot of personal experience with the topic" (Example: an Olympic diver). Then have students add checklist examples for a credible source and share with the class.

 For additional support, go to the **Reading Studio** and assign the following **Level Up tutorials: Evidence, Primary and Secondary Sources.**

READER'S CHOICE

Setting a Purpose Have students review their Unit 1 Response Log and think about what they've already learned about how people find courage to overcome fear. As they select their Independent Reading selections, encourage them to consider what more they want to know.

NOTICE & NOTE

Explain that some selections may contain multiple signposts; others may contain only one. Also explain that the same type of signpost can occur many times in the same text.

LEARNING MINDSET

Setting Goals Tell students that setting goals is an important part of having a learning mindset. Encourage students to set a goal for reading self-selected texts outside of class, for example, reading for a set time or a set number of pages a day. Consider setting up a class progress report for students to track their goals.

 INDEPENDENT READING

? ESSENTIAL QUESTION:

How do you find courage in the face of fear?

Reader's Choice

Setting a Purpose Select one or more of these options from your eBook to continue your exploration of the Essential Question.

- Read the descriptions to see which text grabs your interest.
- Think about which genres you enjoy reading.

Notice & Note

In this unit, you practiced noticing and noting three signposts: **Words of the Wiser, Aha Moment,** and **Contrasts and Contradictions.** As you read independently, these signposts and others will aid your understanding. Below are the anchor questions to ask when you read literature and nonfiction.

Reading Literature: Stories, Poems, and Plays		
Signpost	**Anchor Question**	**Lesson**
Contrasts and Contradictions	Why did the character act that way?	p. 3
Aha Moment	How might this change things?	p. 3
Tough Questions	What does this make me wonder about?	p. 172
Words of the Wiser	What's the lesson for the character?	p. 2
Again and Again	Why might the author keep bringing this up?	p. 92
Memory Moment	Why is this memory important?	p. 93

Reading Nonfiction: Essays, Articles, and Arguments		
Signpost	**Anchor Question(s)**	**Lesson**
Big Questions	What surprised me? What did the author think I already knew? What challenged, changed, or confirmed what I already knew?	p. 246 p. 420 p. 332
Contrasts and Contradictions	What is the difference, and why does it matter?	p. 247
Extreme or Absolute Language	Why did the author use this language?	p. 247
Numbers and Stats	Why did the author use these numbers or amounts?	p. 333
Quoted Words	Why was this person quoted or cited, and what did this add?	p. 333
Word Gaps	Do I know this word from someplace else? Does it seem like technical talk for this topic? Do clues in the sentence help me understand the word?	p. 421

 ENGLISH LEARNER SUPPORT

Develop Fluency Select a passage from a text that matches students' reading abilities. Read the passage aloud while students follow along silently.

- Echo read the passage by reading aloud one sentence and then having students repeat it. Then have the students read the passage silently several times. Check comprehension by asking yes/no questions.
  SUBSTANTIAL
- Have students read and then reread the passage silently. Ask students to time their reading to track improvements over time.   **MODERATE**

- Allow more fluent readers to select their own texts. Set a specific time for students to read silently (for example, 30 minutes). Check their comprehension by having them write a summary of what they've read.
  LIGHT

 Go to the **Reading Studio** for additional support in developing fluency.

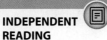

You can preview these texts in Unit 1 of your eBook.

Then, check off the text or texts that you select to read on your own.

POEM

Horrors

Lewis Carroll

What are those terrible things that go bump in the night?

SHORT STORY

Vanquishing the Hungry Chinese Zombie

Claudine Gueh

A girl faces terror to protect her parents and the family store.

NARRATIVE NONFICTION

Running into Danger on an Alaskan Trail

Cinthia Ritchie

A long-distance runner has a terrifying encounter with a bear.

INFORMATIONAL TEXT

Face Your Fears: Choking Under Pressure Is Every Athlete's Worst Nightmare

Dana Hudepohl

How do athletes handle fear and stress while dealing with the pressure to succeed at competitive sports?

Collaborate and Share   Find a partner to discuss what you learned from at least one of your independent readings.

- Give a brief synopsis or summary of the text.
- Describe any signposts that you noticed in the text and explain what they revealed to you.
- Describe what you most enjoyed or found most challenging about the text. Give specific examples.
- Decide whether you would recommend the text to others. Why or why not?

 Go to the **Reading Studio** for more resources on **Notice & Note**.

INDEPENDENT READING

MATCHING STUDENTS TO TEXTS

Use the following information to guide students in choosing their texts.

Horrors
  Genre: poem
  Overall Rating: Challenging

Vanquishing the Hungry Chinese Zombie   Lexile: 760L
  Genre: short story
  Overall Rating: Accessible

Running into Danger on the Alaskan Trail   Lexile: 860L
  Genre: narrative nonfiction
  Overall Rating: Challenging

Face Your Fears: Choking Under Pressure Is Every Athlete's Worst Nightmare   Lexile: 870L
  Genre: informational text
  Overall Rating: Accessible

Collaborate and Share To assess how well students read the selections, walk around the room and listen to their conversations. Encourage students to be focused and specific in their comments.

 for Assessment

- Independent Reading Selection Tests

 Encourage students to visit the **Reading Studio** to download a handy bookmark of **NOTICE & NOTE** signposts.

WHEN STUDENTS STRUGGLE . . .

Keep a Reading Log As students read their selected texts, have them keep a reading log for each selection to note signposts and their thoughts about them. Use their logs to assess how well they are noticing and reflecting on elements of the texts.

Reading Log for (title)		
Location	**Signpost I Noticed**	**My Notes about It**

UNIT (1) Tasks

- **WRITE AN INFORMATIONAL ESSAY**
- **GIVE A PRESENTATION**

MENTOR TEXT

FEARS AND PHOBIAS

Article by KIDSHEALTH.ORG

LEARNING OBJECTIVES

Writing Task

- Write an informational essay on a topic related to fear and how people respond to it.
- Use strategies to plan and organize information.
- Write an introduction that catches the reader's attention, states the topic, and includes a clear controlling idea or thesis statement.
- Support the main idea with evidence from sources.
- Connect related ideas effectively.
- End by summarizing ideas or drawing a conclusion.
- Revise drafts, incorporating feedback from peers.
- Use a rubric to evaluate writing.
- **Language** Use compound and complex sentences.

Speaking Task

- Present an informational essay to an audience.
- Adapt an informational essay for presentation.
- Use appropriate verbal and nonverbal techniques.
- Listen actively to a presentation.
- **Language** Share information using the sentence stem *I learned* _____.

Assign the Writing Task in *Ed.*

Online

RESOURCES

- Unit 1 Response Log
- Writing Studio: Writing Informative Texts
- Speaking and Listening Studio: Giving a Presentation
- Grammar Studio: Module 1: The Sentence

Language X-Ray: English Learner Support

Use the instruction below and the supports and scaffolds in the Teacher's Edition to help you guide students of different proficiency levels.

INTRODUCE THE WRITING TASK

Explain that an **informational essay** is a type of writing that presents or explains ideas and information about a topic. Point out that the word *informative* is related to the Spanish adjective *informativo*, which means "providing information." Make sure students understand that informational essays use facts, not personal experiences.

Remind students that the selections in this unit deal with how people respond to fear. Work with students to select a type of fear to write

about. Use sentence frames to help them articulate their ideas. For example: *A fear of _____ is very common in teenagers.*

Brainstorm words and phrases related to the topic and write them on the board. Then, have students work with a partner to write one sentence about the type of fear they chose. Tell students to use their sentences to begin their essays.

WRITING

Use Connecting Words

Tell students that one way to connect ideas in their essays is to combine two related sentences with a **connecting word**, such as *and, but, yet*, or *so* after a comma.

Use the following supports with students at varying proficiency levels:

- Provide students with a sample informational paragraph, and work with them to underline connecting words. Work with students to write sentences using connecting words. If necessary, have students dictate their sentences to you. **SUBSTANTIAL**
- Use sentence frames to help students practice using connecting words. For example: *Two common kinds of fear are fear of spiders _____ fear of heights.* **MODERATE**
- After students have completed their drafts, have them work with a partner to determine whether they have used connecting words carefully in their drafts. **LIGHT**

SPEAKING

Share Information

Tell students that one way to communicate the information in their essay is by using the sentence frame *I learned _____*. Pair students with a partner. Circulate around the room to make sure students are using the sentence frame correctly.

Use the following supports with students at varying proficiency levels:

- Work with students to complete the sentence stem by identifying a key idea in their essays. Have them practice saying the sentence aloud to a partner. **SUBSTANTIAL**
- Have students build on the sentence stem by adding two ideas from their essays. Allow them to present the information in the form of a conversation with a partner. **MODERATE**
- Have students build on the sentence stem by adding the following transitional words: *first, second*, and *finally*. Then, have students practice their presentations with a partner. **LIGHT**

WRITING

WRITE AN INFORMATIONAL ESSAY

Introduce students to the Writing Task by reading the introductory paragraph with them. Remind students to refer to the notes they recorded in the Unit 1 Response Log as they plan and draft their essays. The Response Log should contain ideas about fear from a variety of perspectives. Drawing on these different perspectives will make their own writing more interesting and well informed.

 For **writing support** for students at varying proficiency levels, see the **Language X-Ray** on page 80B.

USE THE MENTOR TEXT

Point out that student's informational essays will be similar to the informational article "Fears and Phobias" in that they will present facts and examples related to a topic. However, their essays will be shorter than the article and will focus on a more specific aspect of the topic of fear.

WRITING PROMPT

Review the prompt with students. Encourage them to ask questions about any part of the assignment that is unclear. Make sure they understand that the purpose of their essay is to answer the question using facts and examples from the texts they have read.

 WRITING TASK

Write an Informational Essay

Go to the **Writing Studio** for help writing an informational essay.

This unit focuses on fear and the ways it can shape and alter our lives. For this writing task, you will write an informational essay on a topic related to fear and how people respond to it. Review the article "Fears and Phobias" to see an example of a well-written informational selection that you can use as a mentor text.

As you write your essay, you can use the notes from your Response Log, which you filled out after reading each text in this unit.

Writing Prompt

Read the information in the box below.

This is the topic or context for your essay. →

> Fear can prevent you from achieving your goals, deciding something important, or fully enjoying your life.

Think carefully about the following question.

This is the essential question for the unit. How would you answer this question, based on the readings in this unit? →

> How do you find courage in the face of fear?

Now mark the words that identify exactly what you are being asked to produce. →

Write an essay explaining how people find the courage to face their fears.

Be sure to—

Review these points as you write and again when you finish. Make any needed changes.

- [ ] provide an introduction that catches the reader's attention, clearly states the topic, and includes a clear controlling idea or thesis statement
- [ ] support main ideas with evidence from sources
- [ ] organize information in a logical way
- [ ] connect related ideas effectively
- [ ] use appropriate word choice
- [ ] end by summarizing ideas or drawing an overall conclusion

80   Unit 1

 LEARNING MINDSET

Belonging Ask students to share and celebrate a mistake they made in the past. Remind students that we all make mistakes and can learn from each other. You might say, "I make mistakes. Let's learn from each other." Then, model how to reflect on the mistake and learn from it.

WRITING TASK

1 Plan

Before you start writing, plan your essay. First, choose a topic and appropriate genre. For this writing task, you already know that the topic relates to how people find the courage to face their fears, and you know that the genre is an informational essay. Next, identify your purpose and audience. Then, use a range of strategies to determine the ideas you'd like to include in your essay. These strategies may include discussing the topic with your classmates, doing some background reading, or thinking about how your own personal interests and experiences relate to the topic. Use the table below to assist you in planning your draft.

Go to **Writing Informative Texts: Developing a Topic** for help planning your essay.

Notice & Note
From Reading to Writing

As you plan your informational essay, apply what you've learned about signposts to your own writing. Remember that writers use common features, called signposts, to help convey their message to readers. Think about how you can incorporate **Quoted Words** into your essay.

Go to the **Reading Studio** for more resources on Notice & Note.

Informational Essay Planning Table	
Topic	How people find the courage to face fear
Genre	Informational essay
Purpose	
Audience	
Ideas from discussion with classmates	
Ideas from background reading	
Personal interests related to topic	

Background Reading Review the notes you took in your Response Log after reading the texts in this unit. Your notes will guide your review of the texts, and will help you carry out the background reading that will assist you as you formulate the key ideas of your essay.

Use the notes from your Response Log as you plan your essay.

1 PLAN

Allow time for students to discuss the topic with partners or in small groups and then to complete the planning table independently.

■ English Learner Support

Understand Academic Language Make sure students understand words and phrases used in the chart, such as *audience, purpose,* and *personal interests*. Work with students to fill in the blank sections, providing text that they can copy into their charts as needed.   **SUBSTANTIAL**

▶ NOTICE & NOTE

From Reading to Writing Remind students they can use Quoted Words to include the opinions or conclusions of someone who is an expert on the topic. Students can also use Quoted Words to provide support for a point they are trying to make. Remind students to format direct quotations correctly and to give credit to the source.

Background Reading As they plan their essays, remind students to refer to the notes they took in the Response Log. They may also review the selections to find additional facts and examples to support ideas they want to include in their writing.

TO CHALLENGE STUDENTS . . .

Conduct Research Challenge students to incorporate facts and examples from another text on the topic of overcoming fear. They may start by thinking of articles or stories they have already read that connect to the topic in some way. If they cannot think of an appropriate text, they may search online or at the library. Encourage them to add details from their chosen text to the Response Log and to think about how these details support the Essential Question.

WRITING

Organize Your Ideas Tell students that their outlines may have one main section for each paragraph of the essay. Provide the following sample based on the chart:

I. Introduction

II. Kinds of Fears

III. How People Respond to Fear

IV. How People Find Courage When Facing Fear

V. Conclusion

Then point out that they may also outline the body paragraphs by reading the chart from left to right, with one paragraph in each row. In this organizational pattern, each paragraph would introduce a specific kind of fear, describe how people respond to it, and explain how they can overcome it. By thinking about the details and examples they have gathered, students can select the best way to organize their essays.

2 DEVELOP A DRAFT

Remind students to follow their outlines as they draft their essays, but point out that they can still make changes to their writing plan during this stage. As they write, they may discover that they need a different example to support an idea, or that a particular detail really belongs in a different paragraph.

■ English Learner Support

Write a Group Essay Simplify the writing task and add direct support by working together to writing an informational paragraph that answers the Essential Question. Have students discuss their ideas before writing them down. **SUBSTANTIAL**

WRITING TASK

Go to **Writing Informative Texts: Organizing Ideas** for more help.

Organize Your Ideas Part of planning is organizing the ideas and information you have gathered. The process of organizing helps you decide on a logical order of information as you draft your essay. You can use the chart below to make an outline of the ideas you will cover. You can also use the chart to record the evidence that will support your ideas.

Main Topic: Finding Courage in the Face of Fear		
Kinds of fears people face	**How people respond to fear**	**How people find courage when facing fear**
Supporting Details	Supporting Details	Supporting Details

2 Develop a Draft

Once you have completed your planning activities, you will be ready to draft your informational essay. As you draft, refer to your graphic organizer and the outline you have created, as well as to any notes you took on the texts in the unit. Write an introduction, a main body of paragraphs that connect logically and reflect depth of thought, and then write a conclusion.

You might prefer to draft your essay online.

Using a word processor or online writing application makes it easier to make changes or move sentences around later when you are ready to revise your first draft.

WHEN STUDENTS STRUGGLE . . .

Draft the Essay Even when working from an outline, students may struggle to get started on their drafts. Encourage them to start with the section they feel most confident about—perhaps one of the body paragraphs. Once they have started the writing, they may find that their ideas flow more freely, even for the more difficult sections. Remind students that a first draft is not meant to be perfect. A first draft should be more about getting ideas written down on paper (or on the computer screen). Tell students that they will have time to revise and edit their writing later.

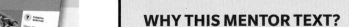

Use the Mentor Text

Author's Craft
Your introduction is your first chance to capture the reader's attention. In addition to your controlling idea or thesis statement, your introduction should include something that gets your reader interested in reading your essay. Note the way the writer captures the reader's attention in "Fears and Phobias."

> The roller coaster hesitates for a split second at the peak of its steep track after a long, slow climb. You know what's about to happen—and there's no way to avoid it now. It's time to hang onto the handrail, palms sweating, heart racing, and brace yourself for the wild ride down.

The writer uses a vivid description of riding a roller coaster to convey the fear that some people feel during this experience.

Apply What You've Learned To capture your reader's attention, you might include a surprising fact, a famous quotation, or a personal anecdote related to the topic.

Supporting Details
Supporting details are words, phrases, or sentences that tell more about a central idea. Notice how the author of "Fears and Phobias" uses the following example to support a key idea about one cause of phobias.

> Someone might develop a bee phobia after being stung during a particularly scary situation. For that person, looking at a photograph of a bee, seeing a bee from a distance, or even walking near flowers where there *could* be a bee can all trigger the phobia.

The author provides an example as a supporting detail to help explain how fright and pain can cause a phobia.

Apply What You've Learned The details you include in your own informational essay should be clearly related to your ideas about how people find courage to face fear. Some types of details you can use to support your ideas are facts, examples, and quotations.

Write an Informational Essay   83

WHY THIS MENTOR TEXT?
"Fears and Phobias" provides a good example of informational writing. Use the instruction below to help students use the mentor text as a model for writing engaging introductions and for integrating facts and details into their informational essays.

USE THE MENTOR TEXT

Author's Craft Ask a volunteer to read aloud the introduction from "Fears and Phobias." Discuss words and details that make this a vivid description of the experience of fear. Then invite students to offer examples of surprising facts, famous quotations, and personal anecdotes that could be used in an introduction. Discuss strategies that students might use to search for surprising facts and famous quotations online.

Supporting Details To help students understand how the example functions in the article, have them locate paragraph 23 in the text. Note that the context is the section called "What Causes Phobias?" and that the preceding paragraph talks about phobias in a general way: "Some phobias develop when someone has a scary experience with a particular thing or situation." A bee sting is one example of "a particular thing" that can trigger a phobia.

ENGLISH LEARNER SUPPORT

Use the Mentor Text Use the following supports with students at varying proficiency levels:

- Read the introduction aloud, using gestures to help students understand what is happening. Ask: *Is this exciting? Do you want to read more?* Allow students to answer with gestures or short descriptions. **SUBSTANTIAL**

- Read the introduction aloud, and invite students to ask about any words or phrases that are unclear. Ask students whether this text makes them want to read more, and why. **MODERATE**

- Ask students to read the introduction and identify words that add to the feeling of excitement. Then ask them to brainstorm other situations that could be used to introduce the topic of fear. **LIGHT**

WRITING

③ REVISE

Have students answer each question in the chart to determine how they can improve their drafts. Invite volunteers to model their revision techniques.

With a Partner Have students ask peer reviewers to evaluate their supporting evidence by answering the following questions:

- *Which pieces of evidence are unclear? Why?*
- *What questions do you have about my main points?*

Students should use the reviewer's feedback to add relevant facts, details, examples, or quotations that further develop their main points.

 WRITING TASK

③ Revise

 Go to **Writing Informative Texts: Precise Language and Vocabulary** for help revising your essay.

On Your Own Once you have written your draft, go back and look for ways to improve it. As you reread and revise it, think about whether you have achieved your purpose. The Revision Guide will help you focus on specific elements to make your writing stronger.

Revision Guide		
Ask Yourself	**Tips**	**Revision Techniques**
1. Does my introduction grab a reader's attention?	**Mark** the introduction.	**Add** an interesting fact, example, or quotation that illustrates the topic or central point.
2. Does my introduction clearly state the purpose?	**Mark** the controlling idea or thesis statement.	**Add** a sentence that clearly states your controlling idea.
3. Are my main ideas organized in a clear and logical way?	**Circle** each main idea. **Underline** transitions from one idea to the next.	**Reorder** ideas so that each one flows easily to the next. **Add** appropriate transitions to connect ideas and clarify the organization.
4. Do I support each main idea with evidence?	**Mark** each supporting fact, definition, example, or quotation.	**Add** facts, details, examples, or quotations to support ideas.
5. Do I use compound and complex sentences to make relationships between ideas clear?	**Mark** each compound and complex sentence.	**Combine** some simple sentences to form compound and complex sentences.
6. Does my conclusion support the topic?	**Mark** the conclusion.	**Add** a statement that summarizes the main ideas.

ACADEMIC VOCABULARY
As you conduct your **peer review,** be sure to use these words.

- ❑ evident
- ❑ factor
- ❑ indicate
- ❑ similar
- ❑ specific

With a Partner Once you and your partner have worked through the Revision Guide on your own, exchange papers and evaluate each other's drafts in a **peer review.** Focus on providing revision suggestions for at least three of the items mentioned in the chart. Explain why you think your partner's draft should be revised and what your specific suggestions are.

When receiving feedback from your partner, listen attentively and ask questions to make sure you fully understand the suggested revisions.

 ENGLISH LEARNER SUPPORT

Use Synonyms Explain that writers often connect ideas by referring back to a noun with a synonym. Have students identify the pair of synonyms in this passage:

People may experience different physical responses to fear, such as sweaty palms or sensations in the stomach. These reactions may range from mild to strong. (responses, reactions)

Encourage students to find opportunities to link ideas with synonyms in their essays.
LIGHT

④ Edit

Once you have addressed the organization, development, and flow of ideas in your essay, you can improve the finer points of your draft. Edit for the proper use of standard English conventions and make sure to correct any misspellings or grammatical errors.

Language Conventions

Compound and Complex Sentences Using too many simple sentences can make it difficult for readers to recognize how details are connected. You can clarify your ideas by including a variety of sentence structures in your writing.

> **!** Go to **Kinds of Sentences** in the **Grammar Studio** to learn more.

- A **compound sentence** consists of two or more independent clauses. The clauses in compound sentences are connected with commas or dashes and coordinating conjunctions (*and, but, or, nor, yet, for, so*).
- A **complex sentence** consists of one independent clause and at least one dependent clause. Many dependent clauses start with words such as *when, until, who, where, because,* and *so that*.

The chart contains examples of simple, compound, and complex sentences from "Fears and Phobias."

Sentence Type	Example
Simple Sentence	Fear is one of the most basic human emotions.
Compound Sentence	You know what's about to happen—and there's no way to avoid it now.
Complex Sentence	As they grow and learn, with the support of adults, most kids are able to slowly conquer these fears and outgrow them.

⑤ Publish

After you give your essay its finishing touches, choose a way to share it with your audience. Consider these options:

- Present your essay as a speech to the class.
- Post your essay as a blog on a classroom or school website.

④ EDIT

Suggest that students read their drafts aloud to assess how clearly and smoothly they have presented their ideas. If the text sounds choppy in places, or if the connection between certain ideas is unclear, they should consider combining simple sentences into compound or complex sentences.

LANGUAGE CONVENTIONS

Use Compound and Complex Sentences Review the information about compound and complex sentences with students. Then discuss the example sentences in the chart, asking students to identify the clauses in each one. To emphasize how combining sentences can improve writing, rewrite the compound and complex sentences as simple sentences and discuss the differences.

- *You know what's about to happen. There's no way to avoid it now. (This version sounds choppy.)*
- *They grow and learn, with the support of adults. Most kids are able to slowly conquer these fears and outgrow them. (The connection between the two ideas is less clear.)*

■ English Learner Support

Use Connecting Words Discuss the connecting words that can be used to combine sentences and encourage students to use these words as they edit their essays.
LIGHT

⑤ PUBLISH

Students can present their essays as blog posts on a school website. Encourage others to read the essays and write comments about them. The authors can then respond to the comments.

WHEN STUDENTS STRUGGLE . . .

Use Complex Sentences Some students may have difficulty analyzing the parts of the complex sentence in the chart. Ask them to circle all the verbs in the sentence: *grow, learn, are, conquer, outgrow.* Remind them that a clause may have more than one verb associated with its subject. Help them identify the subjects of the two clauses (*they, kids*), and point out the conjunction that signals a dependent clause (*As*). Clarify that "with the support of adults" is not a clause; it has no subject or verb. Instead, it is a phrase that describes how kids "grow and learn."

WRITING

USE THE SCORING GUIDE

Allow students time to read the scoring guide and ask questions about any words, phrases, or ideas that are unclear. Then have partners exchange final drafts of their informational essays. Ask them to score their partner's essay using the scoring guide. Each student should write a paragraph explaining the reasons for the score he or she awarded in each category.

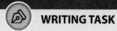 **WRITING TASK**

Use the scoring guide to evaluate your essay.

Writing Task Scoring Guide: Informational Essay		
Organization/Progression	**Development of Ideas**	**Use of Language and Language Conventions**
4 • The organization is effective and appropriate to the purpose. • All ideas are focused on the topic specified in the prompt. • Transitions clearly show the relationship among ideas.	• The introduction catches the reader's attention, clearly identifying the topic. • The essay contains a clear, concise, and well-defined controlling idea or thesis statement. • The topic is well developed with clear main ideas, supported by specific and well-chosen facts, details, examples, etc. • The conclusion effectively summarizes the information presented.	• Language and word choice is purposeful and precise. • A variety of simple, compound, and complex sentences is used to show how ideas are related. • Spelling, capitalization, and punctuation are correct. • Grammar, usage, and mechanics are correct. • Research sources are cited correctly.
3 • The organization is, for the most part, effective and appropriate to the purpose. • Most ideas are focused on the topic specified in the prompt. • A few more transitions are needed to show the relationship among ideas.	• The introduction could be more engaging. The topic is identified. • The essay contains a clear controlling idea or thesis statement. • The development of ideas is clear because the writer uses specific and appropriate facts, details, examples, and quotations. • The conclusion summarizes the information presented.	• Language is for the most part specific and clear. • Sentences vary somewhat in structure. • Some spelling, capitalization, and punctuation mistakes are present. • Some grammar and usage errors occur. • Research sources are cited with some formatting errors.
2 • The organization is evident but is not always appropriate to the purpose. • Only some ideas are focused on the topic specified in the prompt. • More transitions are needed to show the relationship among ideas.	• The introduction is only partly informative; the topic is unclear. • The controlling idea or thesis statement does not express a clear point. • The development of ideas is minimal. The writer uses facts, details, examples, etc., that are inappropriate or ineffective. • The conclusion is only partially effective.	• Language is often vague and general. • Compound and complex sentences are hardly used. • Spelling, capitalization, and punctuation are often incorrect but do not make reading difficult. • Grammar and usage errors are frequent, but ideas are still clear. • Only one or two research sources are cited, using incorrect format.
1 • The organization is not appropriate to the purpose. • Ideas are not focused on the topic specified in the prompt. • No transitions are used, making the essay difficult to understand.	• The introduction is missing or confusing. • The controlling idea or thesis statement is missing. • The development of ideas is weak. Supporting facts, details, examples, or quotations are unreliable, vague, or missing. • The conclusion is missing.	• Language is inappropriate for the text or is vague and confusing. • There is no sentence variety. • Many spelling, capitalization, and punctuation errors are present, making reading difficult. • Many grammatical and usage errors confuse the writer's ideas. • Research sources are not cited.

Give a Presentation

You will now adapt your informational essay for presentation to your classmates. You also will listen to their presentations, ask questions to better understand their ideas, and help them improve their work.

SPEAKING AND LISTENING TASK

Go to **Giving a Presentation** in the **Speaking and Listening Studio** to learn more.

1 Adapt Your Essay for Presentation

Review your informational essay, and use the chart below to guide you as you adapt your essay and create a script and presentation materials.

Presentation Planning Chart		
Title and Introduction	How will you revise your title and introduction to capture your listener's attention? Is there a more concise way to state your controlling idea or thesis?	
Audience	What information will your audience already know? What information can you exclude? What information should you add?	
Effective Language and Organization	Which parts of your essay should be simplified? Where can you add transitions such as *first, second,* and *finally*?	
Visuals	What images or graphics would help clarify ideas or add interest? What text should appear on screen?	

Give a Presentation   87

SPEAKING AND LISTENING

GIVE A PRESENTATION

Introduce students to the Speaking and Listening Task by discussing what makes reading an informational text different from hearing someone speak about the same topic. Point out that readers can adjust their reading rate when a text presents difficult or complicated information. They can also reread passages that they did not understand the first time. Have students consider what a speaker can do to make sure everyone in the audience understands the information.

1 ADAPT YOUR ESSAY FOR PRESENTATION

Have students read the questions in the chart. Then work with the class to list some general principles for presenting information orally. (**Examples:** *Use short sentences. Repeat important ideas. Use humor or interesting examples to keep the audience engaged.*) Point out that visuals, such as slides, can serve the same purpose as subheadings in a text. Students can use them to identify the main ideas of their presentations for the audience.

 For **speaking support** for students at varying proficiency levels, see the **Language X-Ray** on page 80B.

 ENGLISH LEARNER SUPPORT

Adapt the Essay Use the following supports with students at varying proficiency levels:

- Help students identify several key sentences in their essays. Then have them include the sentences in visuals that illustrate the ideas.   **SUBSTANTIAL**
- Review the questions in the chart to ensure students' understanding. Then have students work in pairs to apply the questions to their essays.   **MODERATE**
- Have students discuss the questions in the chart with partners before writing their answers independently.   **LIGHT**

SPEAKING AND LISTENING

2 PRACTICE WITH A PARTNER OR GROUP

Review the information and tips with the class, ensuring that all the terms and ideas are clear. Remind students that the purpose of practicing their presentations is to gain useful feedback from their peers. Emphasize that speaking before a group makes most people nervous, so everyone should be as supportive and helpful as possible.

3 DELIVER YOUR PRESENTATION

Set aside time for all students to give their presentations. When everyone has finished, ask students to share their thoughts on how their classmates' feedback helped them improve their performance.

 **SPEAKING AND LISTENING TASK**

As you work to improve your presentation, be sure to follow discussion rules:

❏ Listen closely to each other.
❏ Don't interrupt.
❏ Stay on topic.
❏ Ask relevant questions.
❏ Provide clear, thoughtful, and direct answers.

2 Practice with a Partner or Group

Once you've completed your draft, practice with a partner or group to improve both the presentation and your delivery.

Practice Effective Verbal Techniques

❏ **Enunciation** Replace words that you stumble over, and rearrange sentences so that your delivery is smooth.
❏ **Voice Modulation and Pitch** Use your voice to display enthusiasm and emphasis.
❏ **Speaking Rate** Speak slowly enough that listeners understand you. Pause now and then to let them consider important points.
❏ **Volume** Remember that listeners at the back of the room need to hear you.

Practice Effective Nonverbal Techniques

❏ **Eye Contact** Try to let your eyes rest on each member of the audience at least once.
❏ **Facial Expression** Smile, frown, or raise an eyebrow to show your feelings or to emphasize points.
❏ **Gestures** Stand tall and relaxed, and use natural gestures—shrugs, nods, or shakes of your head—to add meaning and interest to your presentation.

Provide and Consider Advice for Improvement

As a listener, pay close attention. Take notes about ways that presenters can improve their presentations and more effectively use verbal and nonverbal techniques. Paraphrase and summarize each presenter's key ideas and main points to confirm your understanding, and ask questions to clarify any confusing ideas.

As a presenter, listen closely to questions and consider ways to revise your presentation to make sure your points are clear and logically sequenced. Remember to ask for suggestions about how you might change onscreen text or images to make your presentation clearer and more interesting.

3 Deliver Your Presentation

Use the advice you received during practice to make final changes to your presentation. Then, using effective verbal and nonverbal techniques, present it to your classmates.

WHEN STUDENTS STRUGGLE . . .

Take Notes If students have difficulty taking notes during their classmates' presentations, divide the task between several students. One student may focus on the list of effective verbal techniques, checking off techniques that are used well and jotting down brief notes about ones that need improvement. Another student may do the same for the list of effective nonverbal techniques. A third one may listen for key ideas and write those down. This student may choose to listen with eyes closed to tune out distractions.

Reflect on the Unit

By completing your informational essay, you have created a writing product that pulls together and expresses your thoughts about the reading you have done in this unit. Now is a good time to reflect on what you have learned.

Reflect on the Essential Question

- How do you find courage in the face of fear? How has your answer to this question changed since you first considered it when you started this unit?

- What are some examples from the texts you've read that show how people find the courage to face their fears?

Reflect on Your Reading

- Which selections were the most interesting or surprising to you?

- From which selection did you learn the most about how people face their fears?

Reflect on the Writing Task

- What difficulties did you encounter while working on your informational essay? How might you avoid them next time?

- What parts of the essay were the easiest and hardest to write? Why?

Reflect on the Speaking and Listening Task

- What was the most significant change you made when you adapted your essay for oral presentation?

- How did you decide on which visuals to use? Which were effective?

- Public speaking is a common fear. How were your own feelings about public speaking affected by the knowledge you gained?

UNIT 1 SELECTIONS
- *The Breadwinner*
- "Life Doesn't Frighten Me"
- "Fears and Phobias"
- "Wired for Fear"
- "Embarrassed? Blame Your Brain"
- "The Ravine"

REFLECT ON THE UNIT

Have students reflect on the questions independently and write some notes in response to each one. Then have students meet with partners or in small groups to discuss their reflections. Circulate during these discussions to identify the questions that are generating the liveliest conversations. Wrap up with a whole-class discussion focused on these questions.

LEARNING MINDSET

Self Reflection Explain to students that an important part of developing a learning mindset is the ability to recognize strengths and weaknesses. As students reflect on the unit, encourage them to ask themselves these questions: *Did I ask questions if I needed help? Did I review my work for possible errors? Am I proud of the work I turned in?*

Instructional Overview and Resources

		Instructional Focus	Online Ed Resources
	**Unit Introduction** **Through an Animal's Eyes**	**Unit 2 Essential Question** **Unit 2 Academic Vocabulary**	**Stream to Start:** Through an Animal's Eyes **Unit 2 Response Log**

ANALYZE & APPLY

	from Pax Novel Excerpt by Sara Pennypacker Lexile 880L **NOTICE & NOTE** READING MODEL **Signposts** • Again and Again • Memory Moments • Contrasts and Contradictions	**Reading** • Analyze Point of View • Analyze Voice **Writing:** Write a Story **Speaking and Listening:** Create a Multimodel Presentation **Vocabulary:** Greek and Latin Roots **Language Conventions:** Complex Sentences	**Audio** **Reading Studio:** Notice & Note **Writing Studio:** Writing Narratives **Speaking and Listening Studio:** Using Media in a Presentation **Vocabulary Studio:** Understanding Word Origins **Grammar Studio:** Module 1: Lesson 10: Kinds of Sentences
	"Zoo" Science Fiction by Edward Hoch Lexile 1190L	**Reading** • Infer Multiple Themes • Analyze Point of View **Writing:** Create a Storyboard **Speaking and Listening:** Present and Discuss **Vocabulary:** Greek Roots **Language Conventions:** Verb Tenses	**Audio** **Reading Studio:** Notice & Note **Writing Studio:** Writing Narratives **Speaking and Listening Studio:** Collaborative Discussions **Vocabulary Studio:** Roots **Grammar Studio:** Module 7: Using Verbs Correctly
	from Animal Snoops: The Wondrous World of Wildlife Spies Informational Text by Peter Christie Lexile 1020L	**Reading** • Analyze Text Structure • Determine Key Ideas **Writing:** Write an Informational Essay **Speaking and Listening:** Discuss with a Small Group **Vocabulary:** Latin Roots **Language Conventions:** Capitalization	**Audio** **Reading Studio:** Notice & Note **Writing Studio:** Writing Informative Texts **Speaking and Listening Studio:** Participating in Collaborative Discussions **Vocabulary Studio:** Roots **Grammar Studio:** Module 11: Capital Letters

SUGGESTED PACING: 30 DAYS	Unit Introduction	Pax					Zoo				Animal Snoops				
	1	2	3	4	5	6	7	8	9	10	11	12	13	14	15

English Learner Support	Differentiated Instruction	Online Assessment
• Learn New Expressions • Learning Strategies		
• Text X-Ray • Understand Details • Use Cognates • Language Conventions • Understand Contrasts • Confirm Understanding • Oral Assessment • Write with Visuals • Vocabulary Strategy	**When Students Struggle** • Understand Point of View	**Selection Test**
• Text X-Ray • Understand Point of View • Use Cognates • Draw Vocabulary • Understand Point of View • Oral Assessment • Present and Discuss • Vocabulary Strategy • Verb Transfer Issues	**When Students Struggle** • Understand Theme	**Selection Test**
• Text X-Ray • Analyze Anecdotes • Use Cognates • Analyze Language • Determine Key Ideas • Language Conventions: Capitalization • Discuss with a Small Group • Write Sentences • Vocabulary Strategy	**When Students Struggle** • Analyze Text Features	**Selection Test**

Animal Wisdom / The Last Wolf 16 17 18 19

Wild Animals Aren't Pets / Let People Own Exotic Animals 20 21 22 23 24 25

Independent Reading 26 27

End of Unit 28 29 30

UNIT 2 Continued

		Instructional Focus	Online **Ed** Resources

COLLABORATE & COMPARE

"Animal Wisdom"
Poem by Nancy Wood

"The Last Wolf"
Poem by Mary TallMountain

Reading
• Analyze Personification and Imagery
• Paraphrase

Speaking and Listening: Discuss the Poems

Speaking and Listening: Present Imagery

🔊 **Audio**

Reading Studio: Notice & Note

Speaking and Listening Studio: Participating in Collaborative Discussions

Speaking and Listening Studio: Giving a Presentation

Collaborate and Compare

Reading: Compare Themes

Speaking and Listening: Compare and Present

Speaking and Listening Studio: Giving a Presentation

Mentor Text
"Wild Animals Aren't Pets"
Editorial by USA Today
Lexile 1170L

"Let People Own Exotic Animals"
Commentary by Zuzana Kukol
Lexile 1180L

Reading
• Identify Claims in Arguments
• Analyze Evidence

Writing: Write an Argument

Speaking and Listening: Create and Present a Public Service Announcement (PSA)

Vocabulary: Word Origin

Language Conventions: Words Spelled Correctly

🔊 **Audio**

Text in Focus: Comparing Arguments

Close Read Screencast: Modeled Discussion

Reading Studio: Notice & Note

Writing Studio: Writing Arguments

Speaking and Listening Studio: Giving a Presentation

Vocabulary Studio: Word Origins

Grammar Studio: Module 14: Spelling

Collaborate and Compare

Readinfg: Compare Arguments

Speaking and Listening: Hold a Debate

INDEPENDENT READING

The independent Reading selections are only available in the eBook.

📖 **Go to the Reading Studio for more information on Notice & Note.**

"The Caterpillar"
Poem by Robert Graves

"The Flying Cat"
Poem by Naomi Shihab Nye

END OF UNIT

Writing Task: Argument

Speaking and Listening Task: Present an Argument

Reflect on the Unit

Writing: Write an Argument

Language Conventions: Subject-Verb Agreement

Speaking and Listening: Adapt an Argumentative Essay for Presentation

Unit 2 Response Log

Writing Studio: Writing Arguments

Speaking and Listening Studio: Giving a Presentation

Grammar Studio: Module 6: Agreement

English Learner Support		Differentiated Instruction	Online Ed Assessment
• Text X-Ray • Reinforce Meaning • Learning Strategies • Oral Assessment			**Selection Test**
• Text X-Ray • Paraphrasing • Oral Assessment • Scaffold Answers		**When Students Struggle** • Paraphrase • Use Visual Aids	**Selection Test**
• Text X-Ray • Identify Cognates • Oral Assessment • Ask Questions		**When Students Struggle** • Examining Claims	**Selection Test**
• Text X-Ray • Identify Claims • Language Conventions • Words Spelled Correctly	• Oral Assessment • Vocabulary Strategy	**When Students Struggle** • Language Conventions • Research to Debate	**Selection Test**

"The Pod"
Short Story by Maureen Crane Wartski
Lexile 810L

"Tribute to the Dog"
Speech by George Graham Vest
Lexile 1170L

"Views on Zoos"
Arguments
Lexile 1190L

Selection Tests

English Learner Support	Differentiated Instruction	Online Ed Assessment
• Language X-Ray • Understand Academic Language • Use a Word Wall • Use the Mentor Text • Use Synonyms • Subject-Verb Agreement • Adapt the Essay	**When Students Struggle** • Draft the Essay • Identify Subjects and Verbs • Paraphrase Ideas **To Challenge Students** • Conduct Research	**Unit Test**

Connect to the
? ESSENTIAL QUESTION

Ask a volunteer to read aloud the Essential Question. Discuss how the images on page 90 relate to the question. Ask: *What do you think the chimpanzee is thinking about? What does the insect look like it is doing?* Ask students to think of how different animals view the world around them.

■ English Learner Support

Learn New Expressions Make sure students understand the Essential Question. If necessary, explain the following expressions:

- *Seeing the world* means "what someone thinks about the world."
- *Through an animal's eyes* means "from an animal's point of view."

Help students restate the question in simpler language: How do animals think about the world? **SUBSTANTIAL**

DISCUSS THE QUOTATION

Tell students that Jane Goodall (b. 1934) is considered to be the world's foremost expert on chimpanzees. She has spent more than 50 years observing chimpanzees in the wild and also advocates for conservation and animal welfare issues. Ask students to read the quotation. Then discuss why Jane Goodall would want to see the world through the eyes and mind of a chimpanzee. Discuss why Goodall mentions both the eyes and the mind. *How would they be similar? Different?* Ask students whether they share the same desire as Goodall, and have them explain their answers.

THROUGH AN ANIMAL'S EYES

? ESSENTIAL QUESTION:

What can you learn by seeing the world through an animal's eyes?

> " I have wished that I could . . . look out onto the world through the eyes, with the mind, of a chimpanzee. "
>
> Jane Goodall

90   Unit 2

⚙ LEARNING MINDSET

Curiosity Remind students that curiosity leads to learning. Encourage students to always be open to exploring new ideas, new books, and new skills. Urge them to consider how the things they learn while working at school can help them outside of the classroom in the real world. Note that reading is a great way to explore interests. Explain that whenever students are reading, they might find it helpful to keep in mind what they want to learn about and set themselves a purpose for reading and writing.

ACADEMIC VOCABULARY

Academic Vocabulary words are words you use when you discuss and write about texts. In this unit, you will learn and practice using five words.

☑ benefit ☐ distinct ☐ environment ☐ illustrate ☐ respond

Study the Word Network to learn more about the word **benefit.**

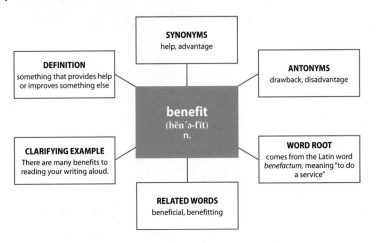

SYNONYMS
help, advantage

DEFINITION
something that provides help or improves something else

ANTONYMS
drawback, disadvantage

benefit
(bĕn´ə-fĭt)
n.

CLARIFYING EXAMPLE
There are many benefits to reading your writing aloud.

WORD ROOT
comes from the Latin word *benefactum,* meaning "to do a service"

RELATED WORDS
beneficial, benefitting

Write and Discuss Discuss the completed Word Network with a partner, making sure to talk through all of the boxes until you both understand the word, its synonyms, antonyms, and related forms. Then, fill out Word Networks for the remaining four words. Use a dictionary or online resource to help you complete the activity.

 Go online to access the Word Networks.

RESPOND TO THE ESSENTIAL QUESTION

In this unit, you will explore what can be learned by seeing the world through an animal's eyes. As you read, you will revisit the **Essential Question** and gather your ideas about it in the **Response Log** that appears on page R2. At the end of the unit, you will write an **argument** about what you can learn by seeing the world from an animal's perspective. You will also **present an argument.** Filling out the Response Log will help you prepare for these tasks.

 You can also go online to access the Response Log.

ACADEMIC VOCABULARY

As students complete Word Networks for the remaining four vocabulary words, encourage them to include all the categories shown in the completed network, if possible, but point out that some words do not have clear synonyms or antonyms. Some words may also function as different parts of speech—for example, *benefit* may be a noun or a verb.

benefit (bĕn' ə-fĭt) *n.* Something that provides help or improves something else. (Spanish cognate: *beneficio*)

distinct (dĭ-stĭngkt') *adj.* Clearly different from other things. (Spanish cognate: *distinto*)

environment (ĕn-vī'rən-mənt.) *n.* The natural world.

illustrate (ĭl'ə-strāt') *v.* To clarify by using examples or graphics. (Spanish cognate: *ilustrar*)

respond (rĭ-spŏnd') *v.* To reply; answer. (Spanish cognate: *responder*)

RESPOND TO THE ESSENTIAL QUESTION

Direct students to the Unit 2 Response Log. Explain that students will use it to record ideas and details from the selections that help answer the Essential Question. When they work on the writing task at the end of the unit, their Response Logs will help them think about what they have read and make connections between texts.

ENGLISH LEARNER SUPPORT

Learning Strategies Use this strategy to help students learn essential language and encourage collaborative discussion:

- Display the Essential Question.
- Tell students to examine the question and consider possible responses to it. Have students write answers to the question.
- Pair students and ask them to share their thoughts with their partners. Remind pairs to ask each other clarifying questions as they discuss their responses. When students finish, have them revise their written responses to reflect any changes to their ideas that may have arisen during discussion.
- Have students share their revised answers with the entire class. **ALL LEVELS**

READING MODEL

from PAX

Novel by Sara Pennypacker

GENRE ELEMENTS
NOVEL

Remind students that the purpose of a **novel** is to thoroughly develop and tell a story with plot and characters. The characters may be humans, animals, or fantasy beings. In addition to plot and characters, a novel includes a conflict, setting, and theme. A novel is longer than a short story or novella and is often organized in chapters.

LEARNING OBJECTIVES

- Analyze third-person point of view.
- Analyze how authors use details to develop voice.
- Research connections between people and their pets.
- Write a story about an animal using newly acquired vocabulary.
- Present a story using text and visuals.
- Use Latin roots to develop vocabulary.
- Analyze how writers use complex sentences.
- **Language** Discuss how to use words to describe images.

TEXT COMPLEXITY

Quantitative Measures	**Pax**	Lexile: 880L
Qualitative Measures	**Ideas Presented** Some ambiguity with a greater demand for inference.	
	Structures Used More complex point of view.	
	Language Used Mostly explicit with some figurative language.	
	Knowledge Required Requires no special knowledge.	

RESOURCES

- Unit 2 Response Log
- 🔊 Selection Audio
- 📖 Reading Studio: Notice & Note
- LEVEL UP Level Up Tutorial: Third-Person Point of View
- 📋 Writing Studio: Writing Narratives
- 💬 Speaking and Listening Studio: Using Media in a Presentation
- ⚛ Vocabulary Studio: Understanding Word Origins
- ❗ Grammar Studio: Module 1: Lesson 10: Kinds of Sentences
- ☑ *Pax* Selection Test

SUMMARIES

English

A boy and his pet fox get into a car driven by the boy's father. The boy is crying, and the fox draws closer to comfort him. The boy asks the father a question, but the response is a firm "No." After a while, the car stops, and the father puts the fox out of the car. Crying, the boy tosses the fox's favorite toy for him. As he fetches the toy, the fox notices the woods and the birds around him. As he runs back to the boy, the fox sees the car speed away, and he hears the boy call his name.

Spanish

Un niño y su zorro mascota entran en un auto conducido por el padre del niño. El niño está llorando y el zorro se le acerca para consolarlo. El niño le hace una pregunta a su padre, pero la respuesta es un firme "No". Después de un rato, el auto se detiene y el padre saca al zorro del auto. Llorando, el niño le lanza al zorro su juguete favorito. Mientras alcanza el juguete, el zorro nota el bosque y las aves a su alrededor. Mientras corre de regreso hacia el niño, el zorro ve cómo el auto se aleja y oye que el niño lo llama por su nombre.

SMALL-GROUP OPTIONS

Have students work in small groups to read and discuss the selection.

Reciprocal Teaching

- After students have read the excerpt from *Pax*, present the class with a list of generic question stems.
- Have students work individually to use the question stems to write three to five questions about the text.
- Group students into learning groups of up to three students.
- Each student offers two questions for discussion without duplicating other students' questions.
- Group reaches consensus on the answer to each question and finds text evidence to support it.

Think-Pair-Share

- After students have read and analyzed the excerpt from *Pax*, pose this question: *What are some ways the fox and the boy experience the world?*
- Have students think about the question individually and take notes.
- Then, have pairs discuss their ideas about the question.
- Finally, ask pairs to share their responses with the class.

Text X-Ray: English Learner Support
for *Pax*

Use the Text X-Ray and the supports and scaffolds in the Teacher's Edition to help guide students at different proficiency levels through the selection.

INTRODUCE THE SELECTION
DISCUSS DESCRIPTIVE DETAILS

In this lesson, students will need to be able to notice details to analyze point of view and voice. Read paragraph 1 with students, and point out the details of what the fox sees and feels. Provide the following explanations:

- Refer students to the picture of the fox on p. 97. Tell students that a fox is a wild animal that lives in the woods. A fox is larger than a house cat but smaller than a large dog.
- Pines are large evergreen trees that live in forests. Pine trees have scaly bark and needle-shaped leaves instead of flat leaves.
- Clover, wild garlic, and ferns are all plants that are native to forests.

Explain to students that the description tells what the fox senses and thinks. Everything is experienced through the fox's senses—from the fox's point of view. Have students preview the second photo in the selection and offer ideas about what the fox might see, hear, and smell in that environment.

CULTURAL REFERENCES

The following words and phrases may be unfamiliar to students:

- *baseball glove* (paragraph 2): a leather mitt that baseball players use to catch the ball
- *muzzle* (paragraph 3): an animal's snout
- *burled* (paragraph 17): covered with bumps
- *loped* (paragraph 19): ran easily

LISTENING

Understand Point of View

Tell students that point of view can be determined by looking at the pronouns used by the narrator of a story. Certain pronouns signal first-person point of view, while other pronouns signal third-person point of view.

Have students listen as you read aloud paragraph 6. Use the following supports with students at varying proficiency levels:

- Ask students to raise their hands every time they hear the pronouns *he* or *his*. Discuss with students how these pronouns signal that this paragraph is narrated from the third-person point of view of the fox. **SUBSTANTIAL**
- Have students raise their hands when they hear pronouns in this paragraph that signal the point of view from which it is narrated. Ask: *What is the point of view?* (*third person*) *What pronouns tell you this?* (*he, his*) **MODERATE**
- Have students complete the following sentence frame: *This paragraph is narrated from _____ point of view. The pronouns ___ and ___ refer to _____.* **LIGHT**

SPEAKING

Discuss Text Features

Have students describe the images in the text using descriptive words. Circulate around the room to make sure students are using descriptive words correctly.

Use the following supports with students at varying proficiency levels:

- Look at the picture of the fox on p. 97. Provide students with words such as *fuzzy, furry, smooth, orange, white, green, scared, happy,* and *silly,* and ask students to identify which words they would use to describe the fox. Have students complete the following sentence frame: *The fox is ___.* **SUBSTANTIAL**
- Pair students with a partner. Have students play a game with the images on pp. 97 and 100, taking turns with one student speaking the name of something he or she sees in the images and the other student pointing at what their partner sees. **MODERATE**
- Have students work with a partner to brainstorm words that could be used to describe the images on pp. 97 and 100. **LIGHT**

READING

Examine Voice

Tell students that authors use details to help develop the voice of a character. Remind students that voice conveys a character's personality or sensibility.

Work with students to read paragraphs 3–5 of the excerpt. Use the following supports with students at varying proficiency levels:

- Tell students that you will ask questions about what you just read aloud. For example, ask: *What does the fox notice about the boy? How is this different from how the boy usually acts?* **SUBSTANTIAL**
- Have students complete the following sentence frames: *The fox notices ____. The fox thinks that _____.* **MODERATE**
- Pair students. Have pairs work together to point out all the details that the fox notices. **LIGHT**

WRITING

Write a Story

Work with students to read the writing assignment on p. 103.

Use the following supports with students at varying proficiency levels:

- Work with students to create a graphic organizer for a narrative. Help them identify and plan the major elements of their story. **SUBSTANTIAL**
- Provide sentence frames to help students plan their stories: *The setting is _____. The characters are ____. The major events are _____.* **MODERATE**
- Remind students to use simple, compound, and complex sentences in their stories. Have students work in pairs to check for correct subject-verb agreement. **LIGHT**

Notice & Note
READING MODEL

EXPLAIN THE SIGNPOSTS

Explain that **NOTICE & NOTE Signposts** are significant moments in the text that help readers understand and analyze works of fiction and nonfiction. Use the instruction on these pages to introduce students to the signposts **Again and Again, Memory Moments,** and **Contrasts and Contradictions.** Then use the selection that follows to have students apply the signposts to a text.

For a full list of the fiction and nonfiction signposts, see p. 158.

▶ AGAIN AND AGAIN

Explain that **Again and Again** signposts are images, events, or particular words that recur throughout a story. A character might even do something like perform a similar action over and over at different moments during the story.

Read aloud the example paragraph, and pause at the phrase "By the vibrations, he learned." Point out to students that the fox is using his senses to gather information. Model for students how to note other instances of the fox using his senses to gather information. Point out that this repeated action provides important information about the **characters** and **point of view** of the story.

Tell students that when they spot an Again and Again, they should pause, mark it in their consumable texts, and ask the anchor question: *Why might the author keep bringing this up?*

For more information on these and other signposts to Notice & Note, visit the **Reading Studio.**

When you read and encounter repeated use of the following, pause to see whether it's an **Again and Again** signpost:

• an unusual word or phrase
• an image or symbol
• a behavior
• an action or event

Anchor Question
When you notice this signpost, ask: Why might the author keep bringing this up?

---

from PAX

You are about to read an excerpt from the novel *Pax*. In it, you will notice and note signposts that will give you clues about the novel's characters and themes. Here are three key signposts to look for as you read this excerpt and other works of fiction.

▶ **Again and Again** When you're reviewing for a test, you have a good reason for studying the same information again and again. In fiction, authors have a good reason for using repetition, too. Authors may repeat words and phrases again and again, as well as repeat images, actions, and events.

If you notice an author repeatedly using certain images, words, or actions in a work of fiction, pay attention. An **Again and Again** signpost may:

• suggest a theme or lesson of the text
• reveal an important symbol in the text
• explain a character's motivations or behaviors
• signal developments in a conflict and plot

In this example, a student underlined an instance of Again and Again.

> 1 <u>By the vibrations, he learned</u> also that the road had grown coarser. He stretched up from his boy's lap and <u>sniffed at threads of scent</u> leaking in through the window, <u>which told him</u> they were now traveling into woodlands.

What behavior is being repeated?	The character frequently uses his senses to get information.
Why is this repeated behavior important?	The use of senses and sensory information (sight, hearing, taste, smell, and touch) may reveal something about the character.

WHEN STUDENTS STRUGGLE . . .

Use KWL 2.0 Help students understand the text and apply signposts with KWL 2.0. This strategy transforms the imprecise question "What do I want to know?" into the more targeted query "What do I want to know about X?" Have students write what they know already about a text in one column. Then have them write a question in a second column identifying something more they want to know about an item from the first column. After they have read the text and figured out the answer to their question, have them write this answer in a third column and record any additional information they learned from reading in a fourth column.

Memory Moment Do you ever find yourself remembering important past events when you're experiencing new situations? Recalling a past event—whether it's happy, ordinary, or upsetting—can help you understand the past, and it can shape your response in the present.

When a fictional character pauses to remember a moment from the past, stop to think about the **Memory Moment.** A Memory Moment can:

- explain or provide insight into the current situation
- reveal something that's bothering or motivating a character
- hint at the theme or lesson of the text

Read this part of *Pax* to see a student's annotation of a Memory Moment.

> 3   The boy's anxiety surprised the fox. <u>The few times they had traveled in the car before,</u> the boy had been calm or even excited.

Anchor Question
When you notice this signpost, ask: Why is this memory important?

What moment is remembered here?	The boy felt calm on other car trips.
Why do you think this memory is important?	The memory of the boy's feelings contrasts with his feelings now. Something changed; something is bothering the boy.

Contrasts and Contradictions What if your best friend texted you every day and then one day suddenly didn't text you? You'd probably wonder what was going on: Is he mad at me? Is he not feeling well?

Sudden differences in fiction can grab your attention in the same way. **Contrasts and Contradictions** often help the reader better understand a character or the conflict of the story.

Here's an example of a student marking an instance of Contrasts and Contradictions.

When you see a phrase like any of those below, pause to see if it's a **Contrasts and Contradictions** signpost:

I don't know why I did it . . .

But this was different . . .

Even though . . .

> 3   The fox nudged his muzzle into the glove's webbing, <u>although he hated the leather smell.</u> His boy always laughed when he did this.

What contradiction is expressed here?	The fox is putting his nose near a smell that he hates.
Why do you think the fox is behaving this way?	The fox may be trying to get the boy to laugh. Maybe the fox is trying to help the boy feel happy again.

Notice & Note   93

MEMORY MOMENT

Explain that some **Memory Moments** are obvious. The character may say or think something like, "I remember when . . ." Other Memory Moments, like the one in the example passage, are more subtle.

Read aloud the example passage and pause at the phrase "The few times they." Model for students how to determine that the phrase is a signpost for a Memory Moment. Point out that this memory could be easy to miss, but it provides important information about the **characters**.

Tell students that when they spot a Memory Moment, they should pause, mark it in their consumable texts, and ask the anchor question: *Why is this memory important?*

CONTRASTS AND CONTRADICTIONS

Explain that **Contrasts and Contradictions** can give readers additional insight not only into a character, but also into the **conflict,** or problem, in a story. Read aloud the example passage and pause at the phrase "although he hated the leather smell." Model for students how to determine that the phrase is a signpost for a Contrast and Contradiction. Point out that the fox is putting his nose near a smell that he dislikes. Ask students to consider how this signpost may indicate something about the **characters**.

Tell students that when they spot a Contrast and Contradiction, they should pause, mark it in their consumable texts, and ask the anchor question: *Why would the character act or feel this way?*

APPLY THE SIGNPOSTS

Have students use the selection that follows as a model text to apply the signposts. As students encounter signposts, prompt them to stop, reread, and ask themselves the anchor questions that will help them understand the story's themes and characters.

Tell students to continue to look for these and other signposts as they read the other selections in the unit.

Connect to the
? ESSENTIAL QUESTION

Pax tells a story about the relationship between a pet fox and his owner, who is a young boy. Throughout the excerpt, the fox gives his impressions of what he sees, hears, and experiences in the world around him.

from
PAX

Novel by **Sara Pennypacker**

? ESSENTIAL QUESTION:

What can you learn by seeing the world through an animal's eyes?

94   Unit 2

LEARNING MINDSET

Effort Remind students that putting in effort is essential to having a learning mindset. In fact, effort is the key to growth and learning. Success is not handed to people. Instead, to accomplish great things, students must be prepared to put in some hard work. When students stumble on a reading or writing task, acknowledge the effort it takes to keep on going.

QUICK START

People can develop strong bonds with cats, dogs, and other pets. What bonds can we form with animals that are usually found in the wild? Discuss the topic with classmates.

ANALYZE POINT OF VIEW

Point of view is the vantage point, or perspective, from which a story is told. The author's choice of **narrator**—the voice that tells the story—depends on whose perspective the author wants to show. In a work told from the **first-person point of view,** the narrator is a character in the story. In a work told from the **third-person point of view,** the narrator is not a character in the story. Third-person narrators may be **omniscient,** knowing everything, or **limited,** knowing only certain aspects of the story. Use the diagram below as you read to help you determine which third-person point of view is used in *Pax.*

GENRE ELEMENTS: NOVEL

- includes the basic elements of fiction—plot, characters, conflict, setting, and theme
- is longer than a short story or novella and is often organized into chapters
- provides authors with the length to develop plot and characters (who may or may not be human) more thoroughly

Third-Person Limited Point of View

Narrator knows and describes the thoughts and feelings of just one character, usually the main character.

Narrator is an outside observer, not a character.

Narrator tells the story using third-person pronouns *she/he, her/him, they. I* and *we* are used only in dialogue.

Third-Person Omniscient Point of View

Narrator knows and describes the thoughts and feelings of all characters.

ANALYZE VOICE

Authors use key details and specific language to develop the **voice**—the unique personality or sensibility—of a character or a narrator.

- Voice helps readers "hear" a character's personality.
- Voice can reflect an attitude or way of seeing the world and can help set the **mood**—the feeling or atmosphere—of the work.
- Voice is developed through an author's choice of words and phrases, and may be revealed in thoughts, descriptions, and dialogue.

As you read, note specific details that help create the voice of the excerpt's main character.

ENGLISH LEARNER SUPPORT

Understand Details Reinforce the importance of details. Explain that details are information that an author provides about a character or scene. Tell students that details allow a reader to know more about a character. Have students describe themselves and the classroom using five details about each one. **MODERATE/LIGHT**

TEACH

QUICK START

Have students read the Quick Start question, and invite them to share instances they have heard of people forming bonds with animals found in the wild. Ask students how frequently they think this occurs and what dangers it may pose to both the human and the animal.

ANALYZE POINT OF VIEW

Explain that the author's choice of point of view controls how a story is told. Different narrators will be able to share different kinds of information about the things that happen in a story. For example:

- When the narrator is a person in the story telling the story from a first-person point of view, he or she can tell his or her own thoughts and feelings, but does not have access to the thoughts and feelings of the other characters. A **first-person narrator** is also limited to narrating only events at which he or she is present.
- Like a first-person narrator, a **third-person limited narrator** can also only report the thoughts and feelings of one character, but instead of portraying his or her own point of view, this third-person narrator stands outside of the story, telling about a character in the story, and might not be as emotionally invested in the action as a first-person narrator who is actually experiencing the story would be.
- A **third-person omniscient narrator**, on the other hand, can explore the minds and experiences of all the characters in a story. Point out that determining the point of view of a text can help you better understand the characters and events in the story.

ANALYZE VOICE

Review the bullet points in the chart and discuss how they might be helpful in determining a narrator or a character's voice. Point out that authors can use language in many ways to establish a particular voice. Does a character or narrator use simple and informal language or complex and flowery expressions? Does the character or narrator repeat certain terms or sayings? What reference points does the character or narrator use to describe the things in his or her world? Does the character or narrator speak often or instead spend a lot of time reflecting quietly on the things happening around him or her? As students read, ask them to note how the author uses specific details such as these to create the voice of the main character.

TEACH

CRITICAL VOCABULARY

Encourage students to read all the sentences before deciding which word best completes each one. Remind them to look for context clues that match the meaning of each word.

Answers:

1. *injury*
2. *anxiety*
3. *sensitive*
4. *displease*

■ English Learner Support

Use Cognates Tell students that several of the Critical Vocabulary words have Spanish cognates: *anxiety/ansiedad, sensitive/sensible.* **ALL LEVELS**

LANGUAGE CONVENTIONS

Review the information about complex sentences. Explain that the example sentence is made of a subordinate clause and an independent clause.

Read aloud the example sentence, pointing out the two clauses. Point out that the word *when* signals the subordinate clause.

✎ ANNOTATION MODEL

Students can review the Reading Model introduction if they have questions about any of the signposts. Suggest that they underline important phrases or circle key words that help them identify signposts. They may want to color-code their annotations by using a different color highlighter for each signpost. Point out that they may follow this suggestion or use their own system for marking up the selections in their write-in texts.

 GET READY

CRITICAL VOCABULARY

| sensitive | anxiety | injury | displease |

To see how many Critical Vocabulary words you already know, use them to complete the sentences below.

1. It takes a while for an _____ to heal.

2. _____ can cause a person to feel nervous about the future.

3. A cat has _____ whiskers that help it feel vibrations.

4. It may _____ your teacher if you forget to do your homework.

LANGUAGE CONVENTIONS

Complex Sentences Writers use different sentence structures to connect ideas. A **complex sentence** includes one independent clause and one or more subordinate clauses. An **independent clause** has both a subject and verb and can stand alone as a complete sentence. A **subordinate clause**—also called a dependent clause—has a subject and verb but cannot stand alone as a sentence. Subordinate clauses start with such words as *when, until, who, where, because,* and *so that.*

When I get a good night's sleep, I wake up feeling refreshed.

In the above complex sentence, *When I get a good night's sleep* is a subordinate clause. It cannot stand alone. *I wake up feeling refreshed* is an independent clause, or a complete sentence that can stand alone. Note the author's use of complex sentences as you read *Pax.*

ANNOTATION MODEL   **NOTICE & NOTE**

As you read, notice and note signposts, including **Again and Again, Memory Moments,** and **Contrasts and Contradictions.** The following example shows how one reader responded to the opening of *Pax.*

> 1 The fox felt the car slow before the boy did, as he felt everything first. Through the pads of his paws, along his spine, in the sensitive whiskers at his wrists. By the vibrations, he learned also that the road had grown coarser. He stretched up from his boy's lap and sniffed at threads of scent leaking in through the window, which told him they were now traveling into woodlands.

I see lots of description of what the fox senses here.

The narrator repeatedly describes what the fox senses through touch and smell.

BACKGROUND

Sara Pennypacker *(b. 1951) recalls feeling very shy as a child. She spent her time making art and reading and writing stories—activities she still enjoys as an adult. She is the author of many books, including the* Clementine *series and* Summer of the Gypsy Moths. *Honors for her books include a Golden Kite Award and a Christopher's Medal.*

from
PAX

Novel by Sara Pennypacker

SETTING A PURPOSE

As you read, pay attention to the ways in which the fox and the boy experience the world. Notice how the author uses sensory details to tell the story.

1 The fox felt the car slow before the boy did, as <u>he</u> felt everything first. Through the pads of <u>his</u> paws, along <u>his</u> spine, in the **sensitive** whiskers at <u>his</u> wrists. By the vibrations, he learned also that the road had grown coarser. He stretched up from <u>his</u> boy's lap and sniffed at threads of scent leaking in through the window, which told <u>him</u> they were now traveling into woodlands. The sharp odors of pine—wood, bark, cones, and needles—slivered through the air like blades, but beneath that, the fox recognized softer clover and wild garlic and ferns, and also a hundred things <u>he</u> had never encountered before but that smelled green and urgent.

2 The boy sensed something now, too. <u>He</u> pulled <u>his</u> pet back to <u>him</u> and gripped <u>his</u> baseball glove more tightly.

Notice & Note

Use the side margins to notice and note signposts in the text.

sensitive
(sĕn´sĭ-tĭv) *adj.* Something *sensitive* is able to perceive small differences or changes in the environment.

ANALYZE POINT OF VIEW
Annotate: Mark the pronouns that the narrator uses in paragraphs 1 and 2.

Interpret: In addition to telling you about thoughts and feelings, what do these pronouns tell you about the point of view used here?

Pax   97

 ## ENGLISH LEARNER SUPPORT

Identify Sensory Details Explain that sensory details refer to information about the world that can be gathered with the five senses: seeing, hearing, tasting, touching, and smelling. Have student pairs reread paragraph 1 and identify examples of details that relate to the senses, such as the vibrations relating to touching and the odors of pine relating to smelling. Invite students to discuss what these details tell them about the setting of the story (*woods*) and the point of view from which it is told (*the fox's*).

BACKGROUND

After students read the Background note, point out that Sara Pennypacker started writing stories as a child. Also note that her favorite childhood activities are activities she still enjoys as an adult. Then point out that she has won several awards for her work.

SETTING A PURPOSE

Direct students to use the Setting a Purpose prompt to focus their reading.

ANALYZE POINT OF VIEW

Tell students that **point of view** refers to the vantage point, or perspective, from which a story is told. Remind students that the pronouns an author uses gives clues that tell the point of view from which a story is narrated. Have students underline the pronouns the author uses in paragraphs 1 and 2. Then ask students what the pronouns, along with the thoughts and feelings described, tell you about the point of view used. (**Answer:** *These pronouns show that the excerpt is told in the third-person point of view. The narrator describes the thoughts and feelings of the fox (who we see is very sensitive to the boy's feelings), and so the point of view is limited third person.*)

 For **speaking support** for students at varying proficiency levels, see the **Text X-Ray** on page 92D.

CRITICAL VOCABULARY

sensitive: When the fox notices small differences in something, he is being sensitive.

ASK STUDENTS to explain how the word *sense* relates to the word *sensitive*. (*You use your senses to notice the small differences to which you are sensitive.*)

CONTRASTS AND CONTRADICTIONS

Explain to students that this signpost is often used to point out unexpected things that occur. In paragraph 5, have students identify and mark what the fox notices. Then have students answer the question to determine the purpose of the contrast. (**Answer:** *The boy's unexpected behavior is puzzling to the fox. The fox tries to remember past instances of the boy crying (Memory Moment) and cannot understand why the boy is now silently crying in the car.*)

 For **listening** and **reading support** for students at varying proficiency levels, see the **Text X-Ray** on pages 92C–92D.

AGAIN AND AGAIN

Explain to students that this signpost is often used to point out images, words, or events that occur repeatedly in a text. In paragraph 7, have students identify which of the five senses is repeatedly mentioned (*smell*) and underline the sensory details related to this sense. Then have students answer the question to determine the purpose of the repetition. (**Answer:** *A keen sense of smell is important to the fox, because that is how he experiences the world. The fox finds comfort in the smell of familiar things and hopes that the boy might be soothed by smelling the things in his suitcase, even though the fox admits the boy's sense of smell is much weaker than his own. As humans, we understand that the boy is so upset that he probably can't be soothed by a familiar scent.*)

CRITICAL VOCABULARY

anxiety: When the boy seems fearful and uncertain, he is experiencing anxiety.

ASK STUDENTS why the fox is trying to make the boy laugh. (*If the boy laughs, he will be calm instead of experiencing anxiety.*)

injury: If the boy had broken a bone or gotten a cut, he would have an injury.

ASK STUDENTS to explain why the fox is alarmed at the idea that the boy might have an injury. (*The fox cares for the boy, so he is upset by the idea that the boy might be hurt.*)

 NOTICE & NOTE

anxiety
(ăng-zī´ĭ-tē) *n.* Anxiety is a feeling of uneasiness, fear, or worry.

> **CONTRASTS AND CONTRADICTIONS**
>
> **Notice & Note:** What unexpected thing does the fox notice about the boy in paragraph 5? Mark what the fox notices.
>
> **Analyze:** How does this event affect the fox?

injury
(ĭn´jə-rē) *n.* An injury is damage or harm done to a person or a thing.

> **AGAIN AND AGAIN**
>
> **Notice & Note:** Which of the five senses is repeatedly mentioned in paragraph 7? Mark the sensory details.
>
> **Infer:** What do these references tell you about what is important to the fox and what is important to the boy?

3   The boy's **anxiety** surprised the fox. The few times they had traveled in the car before, the boy had been calm or even excited. The fox nudged his muzzle into the glove's webbing, although he hated the leather smell. His boy always laughed when he did this. He would close the glove around his pet's head, play-wrestling, and in this way the fox would distract him.

4   But today the boy lifted his pet and buried his face in the fox's white ruff, pressing hard.

5   It was then that the fox realized his boy was crying. He twisted around to study his face to be sure. Yes, crying—although without a sound, something the fox had never known him to do. The boy hadn't shed tears for a very long time, but the fox remembered: always before he had cried out, as if to demand that attention be paid to the curious occurrence of salty water streaming from his eyes.

6   The fox licked at the tears and then grew more confused. There was no scent of blood. He squirmed out of the boy's arms to inspect his human more carefully, alarmed that he could have failed to notice an **injury,** although his sense of smell was never wrong. No, no blood; not even the under-skin pooling of a bruise or the marrow leak of a cracked bone,[1] which had happened once.

7   The car pulled to the right, and the suitcase beside them shifted. By its scent, the fox knew it held the boy's clothing and the things from his room he handled most often: the photo he kept on top of his bureau and the items he hid in the bottom drawer. He pawed at a corner, hoping to pry the suitcase open enough for the boy's weak nose to smell these favored things and be comforted. But just then the car slowed again, this time to a rumbling crawl. The boy slumped forward, his head in his hands.

8   The fox's heartbeat climbed and the brushy hairs of his tail lifted. The charred[2] metal scent of the father's new clothing was burning his throat. He leaped to the window and scratched at it. Sometimes at home his boy would raise a similar glass wall if he did this. He always felt better when the glass wall was lifted.

9   Instead, the boy pulled him down onto his lap again and spoke to his father in a begging tone. The fox had learned the meaning of many human words, and he heard him use one

---

[1] **marrow leak of a cracked bone:** *marrow* is the thick, dark substance at the core of a bone, which is exposed when a bone is broken or cracked open.

[2] **charred** (chärd): burned or scorched.

 ENGLISH LEARNER SUPPORT

Understand Contrasts Help students locate the phrase "something the fox had never known him to do" in paragraph 5. Ask students to find the phrase "always before he had cried out" in the same paragraph. Have students explain how the boy's normal behavior has changed. **SUBSTANTIAL**

of them now: "NO." Often the "no" word was linked to one of the two names he knew: his own and his boy's. He listened carefully, but today it was just the "NO," pleaded to the father over and over.

10   The car juddered[3] to a full stop and tilted off to the right, a cloud of dust rising beyond the window. <u>The father reached over the seat again, and after saying something to his son in a soft voice that didn't match his hard lie-scent,[4] he grasped the fox by the scruff of the neck.</u>

11   His boy did not resist, so the fox did not resist. He hung limp and vulnerable[5] in the man's grasp, although he was now frightened enough to nip. He would not **displease** his humans today. The father opened the car door and strode over gravel and patchy weeds to the edge of a wood. The boy got out and followed.

12   The father set the fox down, and the fox bounded out of his reach. He locked his gaze on his two humans, surprised to notice that they were nearly the same height now. The boy had grown very tall recently.

13   The father pointed to the woods. The boy looked at his father for a long moment, his eyes streaming again. And then he dried his face with the neck of his T-shirt and nodded. He reached into his jeans pocket and withdrew an old plastic soldier, the fox's favorite toy.

14   The fox came to alert, ready for the familiar game. His boy would throw the toy, and he would track it down—a feat the boy always seemed to find remarkable. He would retrieve the toy and wait with it in his mouth until the boy found him and took it back to toss again.

15   And sure enough, the boy held the toy soldier aloft and then hurled it into the woods. <u>The fox's relief—they were only here to play the game!—made him careless. He streaked toward the woods without looking back at his humans.</u> If he had, he would have seen the boy wrench away from his father and cross his arms over his face, and he would have returned. <u>Whatever his boy needed—protection, distraction, affection—he would have offered.</u>

16   Instead, he set off after the toy. Finding it was slightly more difficult than usual, as there were so many other, fresher odors

---

[3] **juddered** (jŭd´ərd): to shake or vibrate rapidly.
[4] **lie-scent:** the smell that the fox detects of the father's insincerity.
[5] **vulnerable** (vŭl´nər-ə-bəl): open to harm.

ANALYZE POINT OF VIEW
Annotate: Mark the narrator's description of the father's words and actions in paragraph 10.

Evaluate: What effect on the reader does the third-person limited point of view have here?

displease
(dĭs-plēz´) v. To *displease* someone is to cause annoyance or irritation.

ANALYZE VOICE
Annotate: Mark the words in paragraph 15 that help show the fox's personality and attitude toward the boy.

Analyze: How do the author's word choices contribute to mood and voice?

ANALYZE POINT OF VIEW

Remind students that **point of view** refers to the vantage point, or perspective, from which a story is told. In paragraph 10, have students mark the narrator's description of the father's words and actions. Then have students answer the question to determine the effect of the third-person limited point of view. (**Answer:** *The use of limited third-person point of view describes the scene in the car from the fox's point of view. Because we are seeing the scene through the fox's eyes, we as readers feel as confused and troubled by the events as the fox. The fox knows the father is lying, but he is not sure what is going to happen.*)

ANALYZE VOICE

Remind students that **voice** refers to a character's personality or sensibilities. In paragraph 15, have students mark the words that show the fox's personality and attitude toward the boy. Then have students answer the question to determine how the author's word choice contributes to the mood and voice. (**Answer:** *The fox feels relieved when he concludes they are in the woods to play fetch. Because the narrator shows us the depth of the fox's devotion to the boy and does not reveal the inner thoughts and feelings of the boy, the reader feels compassion toward the fox, who is innocent and unsuspecting.*)

APPLYING ACADEMIC VOCABULARY

❑ **benefit**   ❑ **distinct**   ☑ **environment**   ❑ **illustrate**   ☑ **respond**

Write and Discuss Have students turn to a partner to discuss the following questions. Guide students to include the Academic Vocabulary words *environment* and *respond* in their answers.

- How does the fox use his senses to experience the **environment**?
- How does the fox **respond** to being outside?

CRITICAL VOCABULARY

displease: The fox can tell that the boy is upset and the father is lying about something, so he does not want to do anything to displease the humans or annoy them more.

ASK STUDENTS to explain how the word *displease* relates to *please*. Point out the prefix *dis-*. (*When you please someone, you make them happy, but when you displease them, you make them the opposite of happy.*)

ANALYZE VOICE

Remind students that **mood** refers to the feeling or atmosphere of a work. In paragraph 17, have students mark the words that help establish the mood. Then have students answer the question regarding how voice and mood have changed since paragraph 15. (**Answer:** *In paragraph 15, the mood is one of playfulness. By paragraph 17, the mood begins to feel ominous and despairing.*)

▶ MEMORY MOMENT

Explain to students that this signpost is used to point out recollections that a character has. In paragraph 20, have students mark what the fox recalls. Then have students answer the question to determine how this memory differs from other memories the fox has recalled and what it reveals about him. (**Answer:** *Most of the fox's memories relate to the boy, but this memory is about how the fox feels when he is locked up in his pen, wondering what it would be like to be free like the birds. It suggests that part of the fox longs for life in the wild, even though it would take him away from the boy.*)

EL ## ENGLISH LEARNER SUPPORT

Confirm Understanding Work through paragraph 20 with students, making sure students understand the vocabulary, especially *quivering*, *freedom*, and *mesmerized*. **SUBSTANTIAL**

 NOTICE & NOTE

ANALYZE VOICE

Annotate: Mark the words and details that help establish mood and voice in paragraph 17.

Compare: How have voice and mood changed since paragraph 15?

in the woods. But only slightly—after all, the scent of his boy was also on the toy. That scent he could find anywhere.

17   The toy soldier lay facedown at the burled root of a butternut tree, as if he had pitched himself there in despair. His rifle, its butt pressed tirelessly against his face, was buried to the hilt in leaf litter. The fox nudged the toy free, took it between his teeth, and rose on his haunches[6] to allow his boy to find him.

18   In the still woods, the only movements were bars of sunlight glinting like green glass through the leafy canopy. He stretched higher. There was no sign of his boy. A prickle of worry shivered up the fox's spine. He dropped the toy and barked. There was no response. He barked again, and again was answered by only silence. If this was a new game, he did not like it.

19   He picked up the toy soldier and began to retrace his trail. As he loped out of the woods, a jay streaked in above him, shrieking. The fox froze, torn.

MEMORY MOMENT

Notice & Note: What does the fox recall in paragraph 20? Mark this memory.

Compare: How does this memory differ from other moments the fox has recalled? What does this memory reveal about the fox?

20   His boy was waiting to play the game. But birds! Hours upon hours he had watched birds from his pen, quivering at the sight of them slicing the sky as recklessly as the lightning he often saw on summer evenings. The freedom of their flights always mesmerized[7] him.

---

[6] **haunches** (hôn´chĕz): the lower body and legs of an animal.
[7] **mesmerized** (mĕz´mə-rīzd): held fixed in attention as though hypnotized.

100   Unit 2

WHEN STUDENTS STRUGGLE . . .

Understand Point of View Remind students that a third-person limited point of view uses a narrator that is outside the story, but whose observations are limited to the thoughts and feelings of one character. Ask students to identify and list three places where the narration reveals thoughts or feelings that belong only to the fox.

 For additional support, go to the **Reading Studio** and assign the following **Level Up Tutorial: Third-Person Point of View.**

21 The jay called again, deeper in the forest now, but answered by a chorus of reply. For one more moment the fox hesitated, peering into the trees for another sight of the electric-blue wedge.

22 And then, behind him, he heard a car door slam shut, and then another. He bounded at full speed, heedless of the briars that tore at his cheeks. The car's engine roared to life, and the fox skidded to a stop at the edge of the road.

23 His boy rolled the window down and reached his arms out. <u>And as the car sped away in a pelting spray of gravel, the father cried out the boy's name, *"Peter!"*</u> And the boy cried out the only other name the fox knew.

24 *"Pax!"*

CHECK YOUR UNDERSTANDING

Answer these questions before moving on to the **Analyze the Text** section on the following page.

1 Which idea is not supported by information in the selection?

   A The fox likes and trusts the boy's father.

   B The fox and the boy share a close bond.

   C The fox is curious about the smells and sounds of nature.

   D The fox is confused by the boy's behavior.

2 Which of the following sentences suggests that the boy feels anxious?

   F *The fox felt the car slow before the boy did, as he felt everything first.*

   G *The boy sensed something now, too.*

   H *He pulled his pet back to him and gripped his baseball glove more tightly.*

   J *His boy did not resist, so the fox did not resist.*

3 What happens at the end of the selection?

   A The boy and the fox go home together.

   B The father takes the boy shopping for a dog.

   C The boy jumps out of the car and runs after the fox.

   D The fox is left at the edge of the road as the car speeds away.

LANGUAGE CONVENTIONS
Complex sentences combine subordinate clauses with independent clauses. Mark the word *as* in paragraph 23; then mark the independent clause and the subordinate clause. What does this complex sentence tell the reader about what is happening in this moment?

Pax 101

LANGUAGE CONVENTIONS

Review how complex sentences combine subordinate clauses with independent clauses. Remind students that an independent clause can stand on its own, while a subordinate clause cannot. In paragraph 23, have students mark *as*, the independent clause, and the subordinate clause. Ask students to describe what the complex sentence says about what is happening at that moment. (**Answer:** *The father is yelling the boy's name as he drives away.*)

CHECK YOUR UNDERSTANDING

Have students answer the questions independently.

Answers:

1. *A*

2. *H*

3. *D*

If they answer any questions incorrectly, have them reread the text to confirm their understanding. Then they may proceed to ANALYZE THE TEXT on page 102.

 ENGLISH LEARNER SUPPORT

Oral Assessment Use the following questions to assess students' comprehension and speaking skills:

1. How does the fox feel about the father? (*He is unsure of him and does not trust him.*)

2. How does the reader know that the boy feels anxious? (*The boy holds the fox and the baseball glove tightly.*)

3. How does the story end? (*The boy and his father leave the fox on the side of the road.*)

SUBSTANTIAL/MODERATE

APPLY

ANALYZE THE TEXT

Possible answers:

1. **DOK 4:** *The author uses details about the fox's use of his senses of touch ("he felt everything first. Through the pads of his paws, along his spine," etc.) and smell ("sniffed at the threads of scent" and "sharp odors of pine") to convey the idea that the fox "sees" using all his senses and that he is able to detect what humans tend to be unaware of.*

2. **DOK 3:** *Third-person limited, from the perspective of the fox. In the first paragraph, the focus is on the thoughts and perceptions of the fox. In paragraph 3, the narrator shows the fox recalling a game he plays with the boy and his baseball glove. Any sense we have of the boy's feelings comes mostly from the fox's perspective: "It was then that the fox realized his boy was crying." The author's purpose of using a limited third-person point of view is to show the world from an animal's vantage point and to make the reader feel what the animal feels.*

3. **DOK 2:** *The mood is anxious and expectant, as though we are waiting—with growing dread—for something bad to happen. The feeling of being trapped and waiting comes with the image of the car "pulled to the right," "slowed again, this time to a rumbling crawl," and "the boy slumped forward, his head in his hands." Next, "the fox's heartbeat climbed" and he smells the father's clothing "burning his throat." By the end of the passage the boy is "begging" his father, and the fox hears the word "NO."*

4. **DOK 2:** *"If this was a new game, he did not like it" indicates the fox's thoughts. He has definite opinions and is displeased and upset by his growing understanding that the boy is being forced to leave him in the woods.*

5. **DOK 4:** *There are two memories in paragraph 3: the memory of previous car rides, which were calm or exciting, and the memory of the game the fox and the boy would play with the boy's baseball glove. These memories suggest that they have a good, close relationship. The fox is loyal to the boy and puts the boy first in their friendship.*

RESEARCH

If students need a starting point to begin their research, suggest that they search for "working dogs for veterans," "police dog stories," or "emotional support animal."

Connect Students may have discovered stories in which dogs have been able to use their sense of smell to track criminals or find lost children. Ask students to consider the many ways that sense of smell can be used by animals to help humans.

 RESPOND

ANALYZE THE TEXT

Support your responses with evidence from the text. NOTEBOOK

1. **Evaluate** Review paragraph 1. What details does the author use to describe key ideas about the fox?

2. **Cite Evidence** Cite evidence from the text that indicates the narrator's point of view. What is the specific purpose or benefit of using this point of view in *Pax*?

3. **Summarize** Review paragraphs 7–9. What is the mood of this passage? Explain how the author's use of language contributes to the mood.

4. **Interpret** Review paragraph 18, especially the last sentence of the paragraph. How does point of view contribute to the character's voice?

5. **Notice & Note** Review paragraph 3. What do the fox's memories suggest about the relationship between the boy and the fox?

RESEARCH TIP
Consider searching for magazines or websites for children. Popular general-interest magazines, especially those for children, often include stories about pets and animals.

RESEARCH

What kinds of bonds do people have with their pets? Research at least two true stories that illustrate the special bond between humans and pets. If you'd like, you may include one story of your own pet or of the pets of people you know. Record what you learn in the chart.

PERSON AND PET	DETAILS ABOUT THEIR BOND

Connect In paragraph 16, the fox is certain he can fetch a toy that holds the boy's scent because "that scent he could find anywhere." With your classmates, discuss how an animal's sense of smell is important in the stories you have researched.

LEARNING MINDSET

Problem Solving If students get stuck when trying to respond to the Analyze the Text questions, help them by asking them to apply problem-solving strategies as they work through the questions. Encourage students to look at the question from a different angle or to try a different learning strategy.

CREATE AND PRESENT

Write a Story Write a fictional narrative from the point of view of an animal or an object.

- ❏ Think about what and how your character sees, hears, touches, smells, and tastes.
- ❏ Incorporate the elements of fiction: setting, character, plot, conflict, and theme.
- ❏ Include complex sentences, checking to make sure that you've used them correctly. If the subject of a sentence is singular, make sure that the verb is singular; if the subject is plural, make sure that the verb is plural.

Create a Multimodal Presentation Present your narrative, using both text and visual features.

- ❏ Keep the point of view you used in your narrative.
- ❏ Use images or video to help show your character's perspective.
- ❏ When you share your presentation with the class, communicate your ideas effectively by maintaining eye contact and speaking at an appropriate rate and volume.

 Go to **Writing Narratives** in the **Writing Studio** for more on writing a story, or narrative.

 Go to **Using Media in a Presentation** in the **Speaking and Listening Studio** for help with using media in presentations.

RESPOND TO THE ESSENTIAL QUESTION

 What can you learn by seeing the world through an animal's eyes?

Gather Information Review your annotations and notes on *Pax*. Then, add relevant details to your Response Log. As you decide which information to include, think about:

- how animals sense their surroundings
- how animals and people communicate
- what animals can teach humans

At the end of the unit, use your notes to write an argument.

**UNIT 2
RESPONSE LOG**

? Essential Question:
What can you learn by seeing the world through an animal's eyes?

from Pax	
Zoo	
from Animal Snoops: The Wondrous World of Wildlife Spies	
Animal Wisdom	
The Last Wolf	
Wild Animals Aren't Pets	
Let People Own Exotic Animals	

ACADEMIC VOCABULARY

As you write and discuss what you learned from the selection, be sure to use the Academic Vocabulary words. Check off each of the words that you use.

- ❏ **benefit**
- ❏ **distinct**
- ❏ **environment**
- ❏ **illustrate**
- ❏ **respond**

CREATE AND PRESENT

Write a Story Point out that students should consider how their character would interact with the world differently than another animal or object might. How would the character's size or ability to use certain senses affect what the character experiences or finds important to think about or act upon? In what setting would the character be found? What things would the character most likely do in this setting? The answers to these questions will direct how students can write most vividly from this character's point of view.

For **writing support** for students at varying proficiency levels, see the **Text X-Ray** on page 92D.

Create a Multimodal Presentation Emphasize that students should select visuals to include that best present the perspective of their chosen characters. How does this character view the world? Looking up at things? Looking down at other characters? Does their character move around a lot or is their character narrating the story from a stationary position? Which will convey the character's point of view best—a moving video or a series of still images? Encourage students to consider questions like these before putting their presentation together.

RESPOND TO THE ESSENTIAL QUESTION

Allow time for students to add details from *Pax* to their Unit 2 Response Logs.

ENGLISH LEARNER SUPPORT

Write with Visuals Allow students to use visuals when writing their narrative. Encourage students to find or draw images that communicate information about the point of view of their main character. Then provide students with frames to use to write about the visuals from their chosen point of view, such as *The _____ sees _____ when he _____ or I feel _____ as I _____ by the _____*. Ask students to write a sentence for each visual and then, for their multimodal presentation, to display their visuals and read their sentences in order to the class.

MODERATE

CRITICAL VOCABULARY

Possible answers:

1. upset; To be anxious is to feel worried.

2. insult; An insult would displease, or irritate, but a gift would bring pleasure.

3. doctor; A doctor treats injuries, such as broken bones or cuts.

4. yes; A sensitive scientific instrument, such as a barometer, is designed to detect small changes.

VOCABULARY STRATEGY:
Greek and Latin Roots

Possible answers:

1. A judge is someone who makes a decision about the law in a trial.

2. A jury is a group of people who make a decision about the law in a trial and determine guilt or innocence.

3. To justify means to prove something to be just, right, or necessary.

RESPOND

CRITICAL VOCABULARY

WORD BANK
sensitive
anxiety
injury
displease

Practice and Apply Use your understanding of the vocabulary words to answer each question.

1. Does someone experiencing **anxiety** feel happy or upset? Why?

   _____

2. Which is more likely to **displease** someone, a gift or an insult? Why?

   _____

3. If you had an **injury** would you need a doctor or a teacher? Why?

   _____

4. Can a **sensitive** scientific instrument detect small changes? Why?

   _____

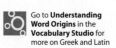 Go to **Understanding Word Origins** in the **Vocabulary Studio** for more on Greek and Latin roots.

VOCABULARY STRATEGY:
Greek and Latin Roots

A **root** is a word part that contains the core meaning of a word, so knowing its meaning can help you understand a word. Roots are often combined with word parts such as prefixes or suffixes to form words. Many English words contain roots and other word parts from older languages, including Greek and Latin. For example, the word *injury* contains the Latin root *jur* plus the prefix *in-*. The root *jur* or *jus* or *jud* means "justice" or "law," and the prefix *in-* means "not," so you can guess that *injury* sometimes means "unlawful physical or emotional harm."

Practice and Apply Find the word that contains the Latin root *jur* or *jus* or *jud* in each sentence. Use context clues and the root's meaning to write a definition of the word. Then use a dictionary to check your definition.

1. A judge was appointed to oversee the trial.

   _____

2. A jury of twelve people was chosen to decide guilt or innocence.

   _____

3. She had to justify to her mother that she needed a cell phone.

   _____

 ENGLISH LEARNER SUPPORT

Vocabulary Strategy Because the Spanish letter *j* is not pronounced like the English *j* used in words such as *judge* and *jury*, students may be confused by how to pronounce words that use the roots *jur* and *jus*. Provide students with additional practice with pronouncing the following words: *conjure, injure, justice, perjure*. Write the words on the board, and model how to say each one. Then have pairs of students practice reading the words aloud to one another, correcting each other's pronunciation of the words as necessary. **ALL LEVELS**

LANGUAGE CONVENTIONS:
Complex Sentences

Writers use **complex sentences** to connect related ideas and to make their writing flow more smoothly. Complex sentences can make your writing more expressive, as well as more formal.

As you practice writing complex sentences, make sure that you follow the rules of good grammar. Here are some mistakes to look out for.

• Comma splices (independent clauses joined by a comma alone)

Incorrect: The fox felt the car slow before the boy did, he felt everything first.

Correct: The fox felt the car slow before the boy did, as he felt everything first.

• Run-on sentences (two or more sentences written as though they were one)

Incorrect: The fox licked at the tears and then grew more confused there was no scent of blood.

Correct: The fox licked at the tears and then grew more confused. There was no scent of blood.

• Sentence fragments (a group of words that is only part of a sentence)

Incorrect: The boy slumped forward. His head in his hands.

Correct: The boy slumped forward, his head in his hands.

Practice and Apply Work independently to create your own complex sentences written from the point of view of the fox. Imagine what the fox experienced after the car drove away, and then describe it in your sentences. Share your sentences with a classmate, checking for use of complex sentences and correct grammar.

Go to **Complex Sentences** in the **Grammar Studio** for more on complex sentences.

LANGUAGE CONVENTIONS:
Complex Sentences

Review the information about complex sentences with students. Explain that complex sentences can connect ideas and make writing flow more smoothly. When writing complex sentences, students need to be sure to use correct construction and grammar.

Review the incorrect sentences with comma splices, run-on sentences, and sentence fragments and the corrected versions of each.

Practice and Apply Have students create complex sentences from the point of view of the fox. (*Students' sentences will vary.*)

ENGLISH LEARNER SUPPORT

Language Conventions Use the following supports with students at varying proficiency levels:

• Display complex sentences such as the following for students to practice reading and writing down: *The fox felt lonely, so he curled up at the bottom of a tree. The fox wrapped his tail around his body, as it was very cold in the forest.*   **SUBSTANTIAL**

• Have students work with a partner to write several complex sentences.
MODERATE

• Have students work in pairs to edit their stories. Challenge students to create at least three complex sentences in their stories.
LIGHT

ZOO

Science Fiction Short Story by Edward Hoch

GENRE ELEMENTS
SCIENCE FICTION

Remind students that **science fiction** is a category of fiction that combines scientific information and the author's imagination. It usually features technology and places that do not exist in the present time, and often takes place in the future. Science fiction short stories or novels may have a surprise ending, one that allows the author to make a statement about human nature or the human experience.

LEARNING OBJECTIVES

- Explain how to determine theme and describe the ways authors convey theme.
- Explain different points of view in literature.
- Conduct research about contemporary science fiction.
- Create and present a movie storyboard.
- Determine the meaning of unknown vocabulary words using Greek roots as a guide.
- Analyze proper usage and consistency of verb tense.
- **Language** Discuss the point of view of the text.

TEXT COMPLEXITY

Quantitative Measures	Zoo	Lexile: 1190L
Qualitative Measures	**Ideas Presented** Multiple levels, use of symbolism, irony, satire. Some ambiguity. Need for inference.	
	Structure Used Primarily explicit. Multiple points of view.	
	Language Used Mostly explicit, some figurative or allusive language. Some dialect.	
	Knowledge Requires Requires no special knowledge. Situations and subjects familiar or easily imagined.	

Online **Ed**

RESOURCES

- Unit 2 Response Log
- Selection Audio
- Reading Studio: Notice & Note
- Level Up Tutorial: Theme
- Writing Narratives
- Speaking and Listening Studio: Participating in Collaborative Discussions
- Vocabulary Studio: Roots
- Grammar Studio: Module 7: Using Verbs Correctly
- "Zoo" Selection Test

SUMMARIES

English

The residents of Chicago excitedly await the annual visit of Professor Hugo's Interplanetary Zoo, and this year turns out to be the most exciting yet. Professor Hugo delights Earthlings with the horse-spider people of Kaan. But after the zoo leaves Chicago and returns the horse-spiders back to Kaan, we learn that the real spectacle may not have been the horse-spiders after all.

Spanish

Los residentes de Chicago aguardan con emoción la visita anual del Zoológico Interplanetario del profesor Hugo, y este año ha resultado el más emocionante hasta el momento. El profesor Hugo deleita a los terrícolas con la gente caballo-araña de Kaan. Pero luego de que el zoológico se va de Chicago y los caballo-araña regresan a Kaan, aprendemos que el verdadero espectáculo tal vez no hayan sido los caballo-arañas después de todo.

SMALL-GROUP OPTIONS

Have students work in small groups to read and discuss the selection.

Pinwheel Discussion

- Have students sit in groups of eight with four students seated facing in and four students seated facing out.
- Ask questions, such as: *For what reasons do people visit zoos? Why might a traveling zoo be more interesting to visit than a zoo that stays in one place all of the time?* Have students in the inner circle remain stationary throughout the discussion.
- Ask students in the outer circle to move to their right after discussing each question.
- Control the discussion by providing a question for each rotation.

Send a Problem

- Pose a question to a student. Possible questions: *What are some good things that might happen to animals from living in a zoo? What are some downsides to living in a zoo?*
- Wait for up to 11 seconds.
- If the student does not have a response, have that student call on another student by name to answer the question.
- Tell the "sending" student to repeat the question and either answer or call on another student.
- Monitor responses and redirect or ask another question as appropriate.

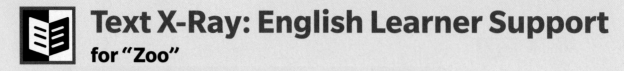

Text X-Ray: English Learner Support
for "Zoo"

Use the Text X-Ray and the supports and scaffolds in the Teacher's Edition to help guide students at different proficiency levels through the selection.

INTRODUCE THE SELECTION
DISCUSS ANIMAL EXHIBITS

In this lesson, students will need to be able to understand the concept of animal exhibits to appreciate the twist ending that reveals the perspective of the creatures in this story. Explain that a menagerie is a collection of wild animals displayed for people to view safely for fun. In the past, traveling menageries journeyed to different cities and charged residents to see exotic animals as a popular form of entertainment. Note that in "Zoo," the traveling animal exhibit exists in the future and includes creatures from other planets. Discuss why an organizer might set up a traveling menagerie and why people might prefer to visit such an exhibit instead of venturing into the wild themselves to see animals in their natural habitats. Invite students to describe how they expect the animals in a traveling menagerie might feel about being transported from place to place and exhibited in cages. Encourage students to keep these thoughts in mind as they read "Zoo."

CULTURAL REFERENCES

The following words and phrases may be unfamiliar to students:

- *annual* (paragraph 1): happening once a year
- *been treated to* (paragraph 3): given the gift of seeing
- *tongue* (paragraph 3): language
- *died down* (paragraph 4): slowly got quieter
- *filed by* (paragraph 6): walked by slowly in a straight line
- *offspring* (paragraph 9): children
- *garments* (paragraph 11): clothes

LISTENING

Identify Genre

Tell students that by listening for clues such as unfamiliar words or concepts, they can identify the genre of a text. Because this is a science fiction story, clues might include descriptions of things and places that do not exist in the world today.

Use the following supports with students at varying proficiency levels:

- Have students listen as you read pairs of sentences such as the following: *The great round ship settled slowly to Earth. The large truck drove into the city.* Ask students to give thumbs up when they hear the sentence that belongs in a science fiction story. **SUBSTANTIAL**

- Read paragraphs 1–3, and have students give a thumbs up when they hear a reference to an unfamiliar concept that signals this story is science fiction, such as *Interplanetary Zoo* or *men from Mars.* **MODERATE**

- Read paragraphs 1–3, and have student student pairs work together to identify what they have learned about the setting of this science fiction story. **LIGHT**

SPEAKING

Explore Vocabulary

Review how the vocabulary used in a science fiction story may be unfamiliar. Understanding how to pronounce and use such vocabulary can help students understand the story better.

Use the following supports with students at varying proficiency levels:

- Display the word *interplanetary*. Circle the word *planet* in it. Have students say *planet* and *interplanetary*. Then display the following sentence and have students say it aloud to you and then practice saying it to a partner: *The animals in the Interplanetary Zoo come from many planets.* **SUBSTANTIAL**
- Tell students to look at paragraphs 1–3. Display the following sentence frames. Have students practice completing them and saying them to a partner: *The _____ Zoo has creatures that come from many different _____. Three-legged creatures come from _____ and tall, thin men come from _____.* **MODERATE**
- Have student pairs discuss with each other the meaning of the word *interplanetary* and determine how it relates to the creatures described in paragraph 3. **LIGHT**

READING

Identify Point of View

Review the concepts of point of view, first person-point of view, third-person point of view, narrator, and omniscient.

Work with students to read paragraphs 8–12. Use the following supports with students at varying proficiency levels:

- Help students reread paragraph 9. Then write a summary for them to copy: *In this paragraph, the narrator tells the point of view of a she-creature. She welcomes her family home and asks about their trip.* **SUBSTANTIAL**
- Review how an omniscient narrator knows everything. Then supply sentence frames: *The point of view is _____. I can tell because _____. I can tell the narrator is omniscient because _____.* **MODERATE**
- Have student pairs work together to identify the point of view and support their answers. Ask: *Besides just the words used, how do these paragraphs let you know the story is told by a narrator and not a character in the story?* **LIGHT**

WRITING

Create a Storyboard

Work with students to read the writing assignment on p.113.

Use the following supports with students at varying proficiency levels:

- Work with students to craft a few sentences describing events in their storyboards together. They should copy these sentences into their notebooks and can use them as part of their presentations. **SUBSTANTIAL**
- Provide sentence frames for students to write about events in their storyboard, which they can later use in their presentation: *In this scene you can see _____. The characters are _____.* **MODERATE**
- Provide a few sample sentences to give students an idea of sentences they could write for their presentations. They should then use the models to write sentences about their own storyboard. **LIGHT**

"Zoo" is a science fiction story about a zoo in the future that includes animals from other planets. At the end of the story, the author describes life from the zoo animals' point of view, allowing readers to see the world through an animal's eyes.

ZOO

Science Fiction by **Edward Hoch**

? ESSENTIAL QUESTION:

What can you learn by seeing the world through an animal's eyes?

106 Unit 2

(⚙) **LEARNING MINDSET**

Seeking Challenges Remind students that having a growth mindset means taking risks and not being afraid to fail. This science fiction story may prove challenging because of some of its concepts and themes. Encourage students to think of difficult texts as a challenge that will lead to growth.

QUICK START

What do you think and feel when you see an animal at the zoo for the first time? What might the zoo experience be like for the animals themselves? Discuss your answers with classmates.

INFER MULTIPLE THEMES

A story's **theme** is its message about life or human nature. Stories often have multiple themes. For example, a story about a teenager who gets lost in the wilderness might include themes about the power of nature as well as the endurance of the human spirit.

Authors use narration, dialogue, details, characterization, and text structure to convey theme. Themes can be stated **explicitly** (in an outright way) or may be conveyed **implicitly** (indirectly) through repeated ideas, words, and imagery. As you read, use this chart to record evidence from the story that conveys theme. To **infer** the story's multiple themes, use your notes to help you make logical guesses based on evidence and your own knowledge and experience.

EVIDENCE FROM THE STORY	INFERENCE	POSSIBLE THEMES

GENRE ELEMENTS: SCIENCE FICTION

- combines scientific information and the author's imagination to create unexpected possibilities
- often makes a statement about human nature or the human experience
- is usually set in the future
- may have a surprise ending
- includes such forms as short stories and novels

ANALYZE POINT OF VIEW

Point of view refers to the perspective from which a story is told.

- In a story told from the **first-person point of view,** the narrator is a character in the story and uses first-person pronouns such as *I, me,* and *we.* The reader sees only what that character sees.

- In a story told from the **third-person point of view,** the narrator is not a character in the story and uses the pronouns *he, she,* and *they.* A third-person narrator who reveals what all the characters think and feel is said to be **omniscient.**

- As you read this story, note how its omniscient point of view affects the information you receive and helps convey the story's theme.

ENGLISH LEARNER SUPPORT

Recognize Point of View Display the definitions of *first-person point of view, third-person point of view, narrator,* and *omniscient.* Include examples of pronouns that might indicate first- or third-person point of view. Review the information in the display with students.

ALL LEVELS

TEACH

QUICK START

Have students read the Quick Start question, and invite them to share the thoughts and feelings they have had when seeing an animal at the zoo for the first time. Then ask them what living in a zoo might feel like for the animals.

INFER MULTIPLE THEMES

Help students understand that the theme is the author's message or lesson about life or human nature. Remind them that stories can have more than one theme. The story they are about to read is an example of a story with multiple themes.

Sometimes authors explicitly state the theme, as in the case of a moral of a story. More often, however, a reader has to infer the themes by looking for repeated ideas, words, and imagery. Students will need to infer the themes of "Zoo." They can fill in the chart as they read to help them look for evidence that helps them infer themes.

ANALYZE POINT OF VIEW

Review the definitions related to point of view. *First-person point of view* is when a story is told by a character in the story. *Third-person point of view* is when an outside narrator, who is not part of the story, tells the story. If that third-person narrator appears to be able to read a character's mind—that is, by saying what the character is thinking and feeling—the narrator is said to be *omniscient.*

Suggest that students use these questions to help them analyze and annotate point of view:

- From what point of view is this story written?
- What words give me clues about point of view?
- What else indicates the point of view?
- How does the point of view affect your interpretation of the story's themes?

TEACH

CRITICAL VOCABULARY

Encourage students to read all the sentences before deciding which word best completes each one. Remind them to look for context clues that match the precise definition of each word.

Answers:

1. *embrace*

2. *microphone*

3. *constantly*

4. *interplanetary*

■ English Learner Support

Use Cognates Tell students that some of the Critical Vocabulary words have Spanish cognates: *interplanetary/ interplanetario, constantly/constantemente, microphone/ micrófono.* **ALL LEVELS**

LANGUAGE CONVENTIONS

Review the information about verb tenses. Remind students that a verb in the present tense (such as *run, write,* or *is*) tells something that is happening now or ongoing. A verb in the past tense (such as *ran, wrote,* or *was*) tells something that happened in the past. Emphasize that writers need to be consistent with verb tenses—that is, they should not write a sentence that mixes verb tenses in a way that confuses the reader. (For example, *He drove to the store and eats apples.*)

Read the example sentence to illustrate how verb tense conveys information to the reader. Point out that both *died* and *continued* are past tense verbs, so a reader knows this sentence describes something that already happened. Remind students to pay attention to the author's use of verb tenses in "Zoo" to help them clarify when events occur.

✏ ANNOTATION MODEL

Remind students that they should annotate their student books when prompted. Point out that they may use their own system for marking up the selection in their write-in text in any way that helps their comprehension and analysis of the text. They may want to color-code their annotations by using highlighters. Their notes in the margin should indicate the generalization they can make about the author's use of verb tenses in each paragraph. They should also feel free to use the margin to make notes throughout the text about questions and ideas that are unclear or topics they want to learn more about.

 GET READY

CRITICAL VOCABULARY

| interplanetary | constantly | microphone | embrace |

To see how many Critical Vocabulary words you already know, use them to complete the sentences below.

1. The father wrapped his child in a warm _____ .

2. She used a _____ so that everyone could hear her speech.

3. The sounds of traffic _____ zooming by made sleep difficult.

4. Astronauts of the future may conduct _____ travel throughout the solar system.

LANGUAGE CONVENTIONS

Verb Tenses Notice the verbs in the following sentence from "Zoo." A **verb** expresses an action, condition, or a state of being. The **tense** of a verb shows the time of the action. The tenses of verbs and verb phrases describe present, past, and future events.

The crowd's noise died down and he continued.

Both *died* and *continued* are verb forms describing actions that have taken place in the past. They also help express the sequence of events. As you read "Zoo," notice how the author's use of verb tenses clarifies when events occur.

ANNOTATION MODEL   **NOTICE & NOTE**

As you read, note how the author's use of verb tense helps you understand when the action takes place. In the model, you can see one reader's notes about "Zoo."

1 The children <u>were</u> always good during the month of August, especially when it <u>began</u> to get near the twenty-third. It <u>was</u> on this day that Professor Hugo's Interplanetary Zoo <u>settled</u> down for its annual six-hour visit to the Chicago area.

> The verbs are in the past tense. These sentences describe events that have happened repeatedly in the past.

BACKGROUND

Edward Hoch *(1930–2008) is best known for his crime fiction and mysteries, having published more than 900 mystery stories. In this science fiction story, Hoch imagines a surprising, futuristic zoo. Throughout the history of zoos, most animals were exhibited in cages. However, zookeepers today have a greater understanding of animals' needs. Many modern zoo enclosures replicate animals' natural habitats, with the intent of making zoo animals healthier and more comfortable.*

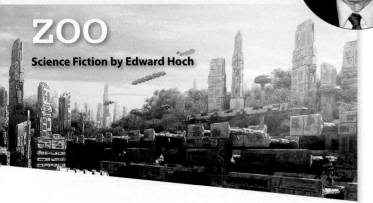

ZOO
Science Fiction by Edward Hoch

SETTING A PURPOSE
Read this short story to discover one writer's ideas about zoos of the future and the animals those zoos might display.

1   The children were always good during the month of August, especially when it began to get near the twenty-third. It was on this day that Professor Hugo's **Interplanetary** Zoo settled down for its annual six-hour visit to the Chicago area.

2   Before daybreak the crowds would form, long lines of children and adults both, each one clutching his or her dollar and waiting with wonderment to see what race of strange creatures the professor had brought this year.

3   In the past they had sometimes been treated to <u>three-legged creatures from Venus, or tall, thin men from Mars, or even snakelike horrors from somewhere more distant.</u> This year, as the great round ship settled slowly to Earth in the huge tri-city parking area just outside of Chicago, they watched with awe[1] as the sides slowly slid up to reveal

---

[1] **awe** (ô): a feeling of fear and wonder.

Notice & Note

Use the side margins to notice and note signposts in the text.

interplanetary
(ĭn´tər-plăn´ĭ-tĕr´ē) *adj.*
Interplanetary means existing or occurring between planets.

INFER MULTIPLE THEMES
Annotate: Mark the words and phrases used to describe the zoo animals in paragraph 3.

Analyze: What do the descriptions reveal about the humans' feelings toward the zoo animals?

Zoo   109

ENGLISH LEARNER SUPPORT

Draw Vocabulary   To visualize the sometimes strange characters and situations in this science fiction story, students must understand the meaning of vivid words and phrases, such as *three-legged* and *snakelike* (paragraph 3), *babbled* (paragraph 9), and *garments* (paragraph 11). Encourage students to copy unfamiliar words and then draw pictures to illustrate and help themselves remember the meaning of each one.   **SUBSTANTIAL/MODERATE**

BACKGROUND

After students read the Background note, point out the information about the history of zoos. The zoo in this story most closely resembles the "traveling menageries" of the 1700s and 1800s, in which exhibits consisting of caged animals would tour around the country and charge people at each stop to view the animals. As the Background note says, zoos of the past often forced animals to live in small cages, with little concern for the animals' comfort or welfare. Today's zoos create animal enclosures that resemble the animals' natural habitats and give them plenty of room to roam. We don't know exactly what the animals are thinking or feeling, but this story gives us a glimpse into their point of view.

SETTING A PURPOSE

Direct students to use the Setting a Purpose prompt to focus their reading.

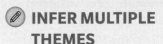 INFER MULTIPLE THEMES

Remind students that authors convey themes through words and details. Have them complete the annotation to help them begin to infer a theme about how people view different creatures. Ask for volunteers to share their annotations. Then pose the Analyze question. (***Answer:*** *The author's description and choice of words show that the humans view the alien creatures with fear and wonder, and as being totally different from human beings.*)

For **listening** and **speaking support** for students at varying proficiency levels, see the **Text X-Ray** on pages 106C–106D.

CRITICAL VOCABULARY

interplanetary: This story describes a zoo that in the past has displayed animals from other planets including Venus and Mars.

ASK STUDENTS what makes Professor Hugo's zoo an interplanetary zoo. *(It includes creatures from different planets, and it travels to different planets.)*

 LANGUAGE CONVENTIONS

Ask students to consider what it would be like to read a paragraph that jumped from tense to tense. Invite volunteers to share what verbs and verb phrases they marked in paragraph 5. Then with the class, discuss what different tenses they have identified, where the tenses appear, and work to see whether there is a consistent pattern. (**Answer:** *The writer consistently uses the past tense in his narration, because the action takes place in the past. However, he uses present tense to relate dialogue, because he is citing direct quotations.*)

✎ ANALYZE POINT OF VIEW

Review first-person and third-person point of view with students. Remind them that a story's point of view can be determined by looking at the pronouns the author uses. Have students mark the nouns and pronouns that help them determine point of view. (**Answer:** *The use of third-person pronouns indicates that the narrator is not a character in the story and that the story is told from third-person point of view.*)

■ English Learner Support

Understand Point of View Review how a pronoun is a word that takes the place of a noun. Then have students help you sort a list of pronouns into clues to first-person point of view and clues to third-person point of view. Ask them to find pronouns in the text and determine point of view with them. **SUBSTANTIAL/MODERATE**

CRITICAL VOCABULARY

constantly: The author uses the word *constantly* to show how the creature makes a noise that never stops.

ASK STUDENTS how they would feel listening to an animal that constantly chattered in a high-pitched voice. (**Possible answer:** *irritated, annoyed*)

microphone: Professor Hugo uses a microphone because he is a performer in a show in front of many people.

ASK STUDENTS why Professor Hugo would need a microphone. (*The crowd was so big that he needed to make his voice louder in order for everyone to hear him.*)

embrace: The she-creature moved to embrace her mate and child when they returned from their trip.

ASK STUDENTS Why do you think the she-creature hurried to embrace her mate and child? (*She was happy to see them, so she probably missed them while they were gone.*)

 NOTICE & NOTE

constantly
(kŏn´stənt-lē) *adv. Constantly* means something that is regularly occurring.

microphone
(mī´krə-fōn´) *n.* A *microphone* is an instrument that is often used to amplify the voice.

LANGUAGE CONVENTIONS
Writers use consistent **verb tenses** so that readers know when the action takes place. Mark the verbs and verb phrases used in paragraph 5. What generalization can you make about the use of verb tenses in this paragraph?

ANALYZE POINT OF VIEW
Annotate: Mark each noun and pronoun in paragraph 7.

Analyze: Is the narrator a character in the story? From what point of view is this story told? Explain.

embrace
(ĕm-brās´) *v.* To *embrace* someone is to hug or hold the person close.

---

the familiar barred cages. In them were <u>some wild breed of nightmare</u>—small, horselike animals <u>that moved with quick, jerking motions</u> and **constantly** chattered in a high-pitched tongue. The citizens of Earth clustered around as Professor Hugo's crew quickly collected the waiting dollars, and soon the good professor himself made an appearance, wearing his many-colored rainbow cape and top hat. "Peoples of Earth," he called into his **microphone**.

4   The crowd's noise died down and he continued. "Peoples of Earth, this year you see a real treat for your single dollar—the little-known horse-spider people of Kaan—brought to you across a million miles of space at great expense. Gather around, see them, study them, listen to them, tell your friends about them. But hurry! My ship can remain here only six hours!"

5   And the crowds slowly <u>filed</u> by, at once horrified and fascinated by these strange creatures that <u>looked</u> like horses but <u>ran</u> up the walls of their cages like spiders. "This <u>is</u> certainly worth a dollar," one man <u>remarked</u>, <u>hurrying</u> away. "I'm <u>going</u> home to get the wife."

6   All day long it went like that, until ten thousand people had filed by the barred cages set into the side of the spaceship. Then, as the six-hour limit ran out, Professor Hugo once more took the microphone in hand. "We must go now, but we will return next year on this date. And if you enjoyed our zoo this year, telephone your friends in other cities about it. We will land in New York tomorrow, and next week on to London, Paris, Rome, Hong Kong, and Tokyo. Then on to other worlds!"

7   <u>He</u> waved farewell to <u>them</u>, and as the ship rose from the ground, the <u>Earth peoples</u> agreed that this had been the very best Zoo yet. . . .

8   Some two months and three planets later, the silver ship of Professor Hugo settled at last onto the familiar jagged rocks of Kaan, and the odd horse-spider creatures filed quickly out of their cages. Professor Hugo was there to say a few parting words, and then they scurried[2] away in a hundred different directions, seeking their homes among the rocks.

9   In one house, the she-creature was happy to see the return of her mate and offspring.[3] She babbled a greeting in the strange tongue and hurried to **embrace** them. "It was a long time you were gone! Was it good?"

---

[2] **scurry** (skûr´ē): to run with light steps; scamper.
[3] **offspring** (ôf´sprĭng): a child or children.

APPLYING ACADEMIC VOCABULARY

☑ **benefit**   ☑ **distinct**   ☐ **environment**   ☐ **illustrate**   ☐ **respond**

Write and Discuss Have students turn to a partner to discuss these questions. Guide students to include the Academic Vocabulary words *benefit* and *distinct* in their responses. Ask volunteers to share their responses with the class.

- What **benefit** did the Earth people and the horse-spider people get from the zoo?
- What **distinct** features does each species have?

10 And the he-creature nodded. "The little one enjoyed it especially. We visited eight worlds and saw many things."

11 The little one ran up the wall of the cave. "On the place called Earth it was the best. The creatures there wear garments over their skins, and they walk on two legs."

12 "But isn't it dangerous?" asked the she-creature.

13 "No," her mate answered. "There are bars to protect us from them. We remain right in the ship. Next time you must come with us. It is well worth the nineteen commocs it costs."

14 And the little one nodded. "It was the very best Zoo ever. . . ."

 AGAIN AND AGAIN

Notice & Note: What phrase from earlier in the story is repeated in the final paragraph of the text? Who said it the first time? Who said it the second time? Mark each time the phrase is repeated.

Analyze: Why does the author repeat this sentence? How does the repetition help you understand one theme of the story?

CHECK YOUR UNDERSTANDING

Answer these questions before moving on to the **Analyze the Text** section on the following page.

1 In the first sentence of the story, the narrator tells us that *the children were always good during the month of August* to —

 A explain that they have a calendar similar to ours

 B let the reader know that children are the story's focus

 C build suspense as the reader wonders why the children are good

 D describe the importance of good and evil in the story

2 Which of the following excerpts from the story suggests that humans are a lot like other animals?

 F *"I'm going home to get the wife."*

 G *"But hurry! My ship can remain here only six hours!"*

 H *the Earth peoples agreed that this had been the very best Zoo yet. . . .*

 J *In one house, the she-creature was happy to see the return of her mate and offspring.*

3 What is an important theme in the selection?

 A People don't see themselves as others do.

 B Fear is good because it can keep you safe.

 C Professor Hugo is a brilliant man.

 D Everyone loves going to the zoo.

AGAIN & AGAIN

Review that the **Again and Again** signpost refers to something that is repeated. When something is repeated, students should pay attention because the author repeated it for a reason. In this case, the repetition of a phrase helps give clues that can help students infer theme. Ask students which phrase is repeated. *(very best zoo)* Who says it each time? *(the first time a human says it; the second time an alien child says it)* Have students answer the Analyze question. (**Answer:** *The author repeats this sentence to show that both humans and aliens believe they were the ones viewing the strange creatures on display. One theme of the story is that people view things different from them as strange and "alien." Another theme is that our differences may only be skin deep, whereas our thoughts and feelings are universal.*)

For **reading support** for students at varying proficiency levels, see the **Text X-Ray** on page 106D.

CHECK YOUR UNDERSTANDING

Have students answer the questions independently.

Answers:

 1. *C*

 2. *J*

 3. *A*

If they answer any questions incorrectly, have them reread the text to confirm their understanding. Then they may proceed to ANALYZE THE TEXT on page 112.

 ## ENGLISH LEARNER SUPPORT

Oral Assessment Use the following questions to assess students' comprehension and speaking skills.

 1. Why does the narrator tell us that the children were always good during the month of August? (*The author included this detail to build suspense about the reason why the children are so good at this time.*)

 2. Why does the author describe how the she-creature was happy to see the return of her mate and offspring? (*This information suggests that humans are a lot like other animals.*)

 3. What is one important theme in the selection? (*People don't see themselves as others do.*) **SUBSTANTIAL/MODERATE**

ANALYZE THE TEXT

Possible answers:

1. **DOK 2:** *Similarities: both Earth zoos and the Interplanetary Zoo charge admission; both have visitors staring at animals in awe or even fear. Differences: Earth zoos don't have creatures from other planets, nor do they travel from planet to planet. As a science fiction story, "Zoo" combines realistic elements with an imagined future to make a statement about human nature and how we perceive difference.*

2. **DOK 2:** *The Interplanetary Zoo animals are described as bizarre, frightening, and fascinating. Humans, likewise, are similarly perceived by the alien creatures.* **Possible themes:** *Humans are fascinated by the unknown. Humans and other animals share many characteristics. People do not see themselves as others see them.*

3. **DOK 3:** *The point of view is third person, and the narrator is omniscient. Clues: The pronoun I is not used, and the narrator is not a character in the story. The narrator is able to describe what all the characters see and feel.*

4. **DOK 3:** *The author uses repetition to create an element of humor and surprise: the reader finds out that the alien creatures' opinion of humans is similar to the humans' opinion of the alien creatures.*

5. **DOK 4:** *The author compares human and alien cultures by showing that both humans and aliens will pay money to be entertained by the strange or unusual (in this case, each other). The author may also be making a comment on human nature and Professor Hugo's ability to fool humans into paying money to be on display to the aliens.*

RESEARCH

Point out the tip about effective search terms. Additionally, remind students to confirm any information they find online by checking multiple websites and determining their credibility.

Extend Clarify that the phrase *human nature* refers to the feelings, traits, and behaviors that all humans are thought to naturally possess and carry out. Ask students for some examples of human nature. (**Examples:** *The ability to seek out love; the instinct to run away from danger; the need to care for one's young.*) Also review the lessons about human nature from "Zoo" before students determine what the other science fiction books reveal about human nature.

RESPOND

ANALYZE THE TEXT

Support your responses with evidence from the text.   NOTEBOOK

1. **Compare** How is Professor Hugo's Interplanetary Zoo like zoos that exist in our world? How does his zoo differ from ours? What do these similarities and differences help the author reveal?

2. **Infer** How does the author describe the animals in the Interplanetary Zoo? How do the zoo animals describe humans? How can you use these observations to make an inference about the story's themes?

3. **Evaluate** Review paragraphs 1–2 and 8–14. From which point of view is the story told? How do you know? Why do you think the author chose to tell the story this way?

4. **Draw Conclusions** Compare paragraphs 7 and 14. How does the author's use of repetition ("the very best Zoo yet"/"the best Zoo ever") affect the story?

5. **Notice & Note** Notice the author's repeated references to money, both in a familiar currency (dollars) and an unfamiliar currency ("commocs"). Why do you think the author mentions money more than once?

RESEARCH TIP
Choosing effective search terms will make your research more productive. Use specific words and phrases to pinpoint results. For example: *best new science fiction* or *science fiction reviews.*

RESEARCH

Investigate reviews of recent science fiction works (including novels, short stories, movies, or television) to identify several common messages revealed through science fiction. Record what you learn in the chart.

TITLE OF WORK	MESSAGE OR MESSAGES

Extend Works of science fiction typically present a theme, or message about life and human nature. What might the stories you researched have to say about human nature?

WHEN STUDENTS STRUGGLE . . .

Understand Theme To help students understand the story's theme, have students create a Venn diagram to illustrate repeated ideas. Label one circle "humans" and one circle "horse-spider people." Have students list similarities and differences between the two species and guide them to see how the repetition of ideas demonstrates how much the two species have in common.

 For additional support, go to the **Reading Studio** and assign the following **Level Up tutorial: Theme.**

CREATE AND PRESENT

Create a Storyboard Work in a small group to create a storyboard for a "Zoo" movie. Create futuristic illustrations of scenes and costumes suited to a science fiction story.

❏ Discuss ways to convert "Zoo" into a movie. Create a storyboard for the movie — a visual map that illustrates significant moments in each scene of the movie.

❏ Sketch set designs that highlight the interplanetary travels of Dr. Hugo. Be sure viewers will recognize that the movie is set in the future.

❏ Include sketches of costumes for different characters in the story.

Present and Discuss As a small group, present and discuss your storyboard with the class.

❏ Explain your group's storyboard to the class. Ask for questions from the class about your storyboard.

❏ Do your best to respond to questions and comments fully. Defend your group's decisions, but acknowledge suggestions for improvements.

❏ As a class, discuss and compare the strengths of each group's storyboard. Identify points of agreement and disagreement in your discussion.

RESPOND TO THE ESSENTIAL QUESTION

 What can you learn by seeing the world through an animal's eyes?

Gather Information Review your annotations and notes on "Zoo." Then, add relevant details to your Response Log. As you determine which information to include, think about:

- how people relate to animals
- how people relate to others
- how people are fascinated by or fearful of the unknown

At the end of the unit, use your notes to write an argument.

 Go to the **Writing Studio** for more on creating narratives.

 Go to the **Speaking and Listening Studio** for help with participating in a group discussion.

ACADEMIC VOCABULARY
As you write and discuss what you learned from the story, be sure to use the Academic Vocabulary words. Check off each of the words that you use.

❏ **benefit**

❏ **distinct**

❏ **environment**

❏ **illustrate**

❏ **respond**

CREATE AND PRESENT

Create a Storyboard Clarify the concept of a storyboard for students. You may want to show them some examples of storyboards, either created by other students or found online. Remind students to use the instructions on page 113 as a checklist to ensure they complete the assignment.

For **writing support** for students at varying proficiency levels, see the **Text X-Ray** on page 106D.

Present and Discuss Remind students to respectfully consider other group members' ideas. They should also rehearse their presentation several times and be prepared for constructive criticism from other students.

RESPOND TO THE ESSENTIAL QUESTION

Allow time for students to add details from "Zoo" to their Unit 2 Response Logs.

(EL) ENGLISH LEARNER SUPPORT

Present and Discuss Be sure to group students of different proficiency levels. Make sure beginning English learners are given linguistic support from their peers before giving the presentation and that they are assigned appropriate roles for their proficiency levels. Students should also be encouraged to practice their presentations several times to build confidence. **ALL LEVELS**

APPLY

CRITICAL VOCABULARY

Answers:

1. *a*

2. *b*

3. *a*

4. *b*

VOCABULARY STRATEGY:
Greek Roots

Answers:

1. **micromanaged; possible definition:** *oversaw or controlled small details*

2. **symphony; possible definition:** *a group of musicians*

3. **cacophony; possible definition:** *an unpleasant sound*

 RESPOND

CRITICAL VOCABULARY

Practice and Apply Circle the letter of the best answer to each question.

1. Which of the following is a **constantly** heard sound?
   a. the hum of an engine   b. the ring of a doorbell

2. Which of the following is most likely to **embrace?**
   a. a dog and a cat   b. a parent and a child

3. Which of the following is an example of **interplanetary** travel?
   a. travel among planets   b. travel on a planet

4. Which of the following is an example of a **microphone?**
   a. a device used to make phone calls   b. a device used to make the voice louder

VOCABULARY STRATEGY:
Greek Roots

 Go to the **Vocabulary Studio** for more on roots.

A **root** is a word part that contains the core meaning of a word. Many English words contain roots that come from older languages, such as Greek and Latin. Knowing the meaning of a word's root can help you determine the word's meaning.

For example, in *microphone,* the base word—a word part that by itself is also a word—is *phone*. The word *phone* comes from a Greek root meaning "sound." The prefix *micro-* comes from another Greek root meaning "small."

Practice and Apply Use your understanding of *micro* and *phone*, as well as context clues, to choose the word that best completes each sentence. Then write the meaning of each word under each sentence.

symphony   cacophony   micromanaged

1. He _____ the project by questioning every tiny detail.

   _____

2. Students in the school _____ made music together.

   _____

3. The blaring car horns created a _____.

   _____

ENGLISH LEARNER SUPPORT

Vocabulary Strategy Give students additional practice in distinguishing between two sounds used for the letter *c* in English. Write the following words on the board: *constantly*, *embrace*. Pronounce *constantly*, emphasizing the hard *c* sound, and have students repeat the word after you. Then pronounce *embrace,* emphasizing the soft *c* sound. Ask student pairs to practice pronouncing the two words, correcting each other as necessary. **ALL LEVELS**

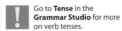

LANGUAGE CONVENTIONS:
Verb Tenses

A **verb** expresses an action, a condition, or a state of being. Helping verbs such as *is, could, has,* and *might* can be combined with verbs to form **verb phrases.** The **tense** of a verb shows the time of the action. The tenses of verbs and verb phrases allow you to describe present, past, and future events. Using verb tenses consistently and appropriately helps the reader understand when events in a story occur.

In "Zoo," verb tenses are used in the following ways.

• To narrate past events

> **In the past they had sometimes been treated to three legged creatures from Venus. . . .**

• To show that the action is consistently happening in the past

> **And the he-creature nodded. "The little one enjoyed it especially. We visited eight worlds and saw many things."**

• To make a distinction between past-tense narration and direct quotes spoken in the present tense

> **"This is certainly worth a dollar," one man remarked, hurrying away. "I'm going home to get the wife."**

Practice and Apply Write your own sentences using past and present verb tenses consistently to describe when action takes place. Your sentences can be about animals, or you can write your own imagined scene to add to "Zoo." When you have finished, share your sentences with a partner and compare your use of verb tenses.

> Go to **Tense** in the **Grammar Studio** for more on verb tenses.

LANGUAGE CONVENTIONS:
Verb Tenses

Review the information about verbs with students. Briefly review the definition of a verb and then discuss helping verbs and verb phrases.

Emphasize the importance of using the appropriate verb tense to indicate when an event happens—past, present, or future—as well as consistently using the same verb tenses when discussing an event.

Review the three example sentences:

• The first excerpt refers exclusively to events that happened in the past, so the usage of past-tense verbs *had* and *treated* is an example of consistently using verbs of the same tense.

• The second excerpt also describes events that happened in the past. These events happened several times in the past, but past-tense verbs are still used: *nodded, enjoyed, visited, saw.* Again, the author remains consistent by using all past-tense verbs to describe events in the past.

• The third excerpt mixes past and present tenses. The present-tense verbs take place inside of dialogue, because they are quotes that a character said in the present tense. However, because these quotes were said in the past, some past-tense verbs are used. This is an example of a time when it's okay to use different verb tenses in the same sentence, because they are referring to events that happened at different times.

Practice and Apply Have students write their own sentences using past and present verb tenses appropriately. When they are finished writing, they should turn to a partner and compare sentences and verb tenses used. Bring the whole group back together and invite volunteers to share their sentences, then ask students to determine the verb tenses used and whether the writer used verb tenses consistently and appropriately.

ENGLISH LEARNER SUPPORT

Verb Transfer Issues Speakers of Haitian Creole and Vietnamese may have difficulty identifying or writing past-tense verbs correctly. The verbs in their primary languages do not change form to express tense. As a result, speakers may produce incorrect sentences such as *He enjoy it yesterday* or *We visit eight worlds last year.* Review how adding the *-ed* ending to regular verbs will make past-tense verbs. Provide pairs with a list of regular verbs such as *enjoy, visit,* and *rain.* Demonstrate how to change each of these verbs into its past form and add these words to the list. Then invite pairs to practice using the past-tense verbs to make simple sentences that describe events that happened in the past. **ALL LEVELS**

from ANIMAL SNOOPS: THE WONDROUS WORLD OF WILDLIFE SPIES

Informational Text by Peter Christie

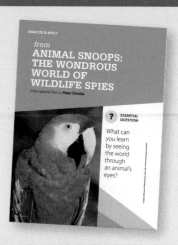

GENRE ELEMENTS
INFORMATIONAL TEXT

Remind students that the purpose of **informational text** is to present facts and information based on evidence. Informational texts include headings, subheadings, captions, and other text elements to organize information in a logical way. Scientific writing is one example of this kind of writing meant to make scientific topics easier to understand. *Animal Snoops: The Wondrous World of Wildlife Spies* focuses the author's use of anecdotes as an effective and engaging way to provide information.

LEARNING OBJECTIVES

- Analyze how anecdotes contribute to the structure of a text.
- Determine key ideas in a text.
- Conduct research about animals.
- Write an informative essay about animal communication.
- Discuss the behaviors of familiar animals with a small group.
- Use Latin roots.
- Use correct capitalization.
- **Language** Discuss the features of the text using the key terms *heading, subheading,* and *captions.*

TEXT COMPLEXITY

Quantitative Measures	Animal Snoops	Lexile: 1020L
Qualitative Measures	**Ideas Presented** Mostly explicit but moves beyond to some inferential meaning.	
	Structure Used Text features guide reading; ideas are generally sequential.	
	Language Used Mostly Tier II and III words; some technical words are used.	
	Knowledge Requires Some references to events or other texts. Begins to rely more on outside knowledge.	

RESOURCES

- Unit 2 Response Log
- Selection Audio
- Reading Studio: Notice & Note
- Level Up Tutorial: Reading Graphic Aids
- Writing Studio: Writing Informative Texts
- Speaking and Listening Studio: Participating in Collaborative Discussions
- Vocabulary Studio: Roots
- Grammar Studio: Module 11: Capital Letters
- *Animal Snoops: The Wondrous World of Wildlife Spies* Selection Test

SUMMARIES

English

Animal Snoops: The Wondrous World of Wildlife Spies adds the use of anecdote to make this informational text and scientific writing more engaging and easier to understand. The author looks at a number of different animals and the ways they snoop out information and communicate it in order to survive and thrive in nature.

Spanish

Fisgones animales: El maravilloso mundo de los detectives de la vida salvaje añade el uso de la anécdota para hacer de este texto informativo y de literatura científica algo más interesante y sencillo de entender. El autor observa a un número de animales distintos y las maneras en las que husmean información y la comunican para sobrevivir y prosperar en la naturaleza.

SMALL-GROUP OPTIONS

Have students work in small groups to read and discuss the selection.

Generating Inquiry

Write the following sentence stems on the board:

1. *An anecdote is _____.*

2. *Scientific writing is _____.*

3. *The words* snoops *and* spies *in the title make me think of _____.*

- Ask student groups to finish the sentences and to come to a consensus on the best answer. Invite groups to list all the questions that come up in their discussions or also finish the stem: *I am wondering _____.*

- Have students answer their questions as they read and add any more that arise.

Five-Minute Review

- Sit students in pairs and tell them they will be working together at the five-minute mark. Set a timer to begin silent reading.

- While students do sustained silent reading for five minutes, they should note interesting phrases that help them visualize what is happening. (Examples: *path home, narrow tunnel, ran briskly*) Tell them it does not matter if they understand what it means.

- At the five-minute mark, have students share their interesting phrases with their partner and review what they have read so far. Ask clarifying questions or have students ask and answer questions.

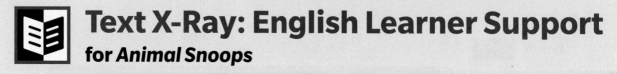

Text X-Ray: English Learner Support
for *Animal Snoops*

Use the Text X-Ray and the supports and scaffolds in the Teacher's Edition to help guide students at different proficiency levels through the selection.

INTRODUCE THE SELECTION
DISCUSS ANIMAL COMMUNICATION

In this lesson, students will learn how some animals benefit from "reading" and communicating messages in their environment. Tell students that to explain how these animals experience their world, the author includes several anecdotes, or short stories that are both entertaining and true. Then introduce important words relating to the kinds of animal communication discussed in this piece of science writing, such as *snoop, spy on, watch, pry into, warn, signal, listen in on, intercept,* and *broadcast.* Help students define these words and then work together to group them into two categories: words that tell how animals gather information and words that tell how and why animals communicate information. Then provide students with frames such as the following to practice using these words:

- *A snake might _____ a mouse it wants to eat.*
- *A mouse can _____ other mice that a snake is coming.*

CULTURAL REFERENCES

The following words and phrases may be unfamiliar to students:

- *crooks* (paragraph 2): slang for criminal
- *pipe up* (paragraph 2): slang for speaking up
- *private-eye* (paragraph 3): slang for private detective
- *a thing or two* (paragraph 3): slang for useful information

Point out to students that the author is using slang terms that come from spy and detective stories. Words like *nab, snoop,* or *foil* are good examples. Note that readers can use context clues or a dictionary to figure out what these expressions mean.

LISTENING

Understand the Central Idea

Draw students' attention to the title and the headings. Point out to students that each section begins with a heading and then an anecdote, which is a brief story that illustrates the point being made.

Have students listen as you read aloud paragraphs 6–8. Use the following supports with students at varying proficiency levels:

- Tell students that you will ask some questions about what they just heard. Model that they should give a thumbs up if the answer is yes, and a thumbs down for no. For example, ask: *Do animals take care not to let other animals hear them?* (*no*) **SUBSTANTIAL**
- Have students identify the central idea of the excerpt. Ask: *How did the title help you identify the main ideas?* **MODERATE**
- After listening to the excerpt read aloud, ask students to work in pairs to list details that support the central idea. **LIGHT**

SPEAKING

Discuss Text Features

Have students discuss the features of the text using the key terms *heading* and *subheading*. Circulate around the room to make sure students are using the terms correctly.

Use the following supports with students at varying proficiency levels:

- Display and read aloud these sentences: *A heading tells the main idea of a text. Subheadings tell what different parts of a text will talk about. An author can use subheadings to organize the ideas in a text.* Have students say each sentence aloud back to you and then practice saying them to a partner. **SUBSTANTIAL**
- To help students express their ideas about the subheadings in the article, display the following sentence frames: *Subheadings are one way the author can _____. Each subheading tells _____.* **MODERATE**
- Have students identify the heading and subheadings. Ask pairs to discuss how each subheading introduces a topic that will be discussed in the following section of text. **LIGHT**

READING

Identify Central Ideas

Tell students that authors of informational text provide evidence in the form of facts, anecdotes, examples, explanations, definitions, quotations, and other details to help readers understand the central idea, or most important idea.

Work with students to read paragraphs 17–19. Use the following supports with students at varying proficiency levels:

- Use guided questions to help students to identify a central idea in these paragraphs, such as *Snooping and spying can mean the difference between a full stomach and starvation.* Ask: *What is one reason a beetle flashing its light might mean another beetle lives or dies?* **SUBSTANTIAL**
- Guide students to identify a central idea. Then, have students find evidence to support that idea. Supply sentence frames, such as: *According to the anecdote, one type of firefly lights up because_____.* **MODERATE**
- Have students identify a central idea in the text using this frame: *A central idea in these paragraphs is _____.* Then, ask students to identify and share two pieces of evidence to support this central idea. **LIGHT**

WRITING

Write an Informational Essay

Work with students to read the writing assignment on p. 127 and plan each step carefully.

Use the following supports with students at varying proficiency levels:

- Work with a group of students who researched the same animal to make a list of facts they discovered. Then work together to write a group essay that they can copy. **SUBSTANTIAL**
- Provide sentence frames such as the following that students can use to craft their essays: *My animal _____ because _____. Another interesting thing my animal does is _____. Doing_____ helps my animal to _____.* **MODERATE**
- Remind students of the need to capitalize proper nouns and adjectives and to find out whether directional adjectives such as *North* or *northern* should be capitalized in specific instances. **LIGHT**

Connect to the
? ESSENTIAL QUESTION

Animal Snoops: The Wondrous World of Wildlife Spies is an example of science writing. It is an informational text that explains how animals use their senses to gather information and communicate it. Animals use that information to warn others and to find a mate, get food, and establish territory. By learning to see the world through their eyes, we learn more about our animal neighbors and how similar their worlds are to our own.

ANALYZE & APPLY

from

ANIMAL SNOOPS: THE WONDROUS WORLD OF WILDLIFE SPIES

Informational Text by **Peter Christie**

? ESSENTIAL QUESTION:

What can you learn by seeing the world through an animal's eyes?

116   Unit 2

LEARNING MINDSET

Perseverance Students may become frustrated when reading a lengthy or difficult text. As English learners or students who struggle with reading read *Animal Snoops: The Wondrous World of Wildlife Spies,* encourage them to have the patience and perseverance to keep reading and re-reading as necessary. Consider discussing how having the perseverance to keep trying can be very rewarding when it leads to the acquisition of new skills.

QUICK START

Have you ever had a sneaking suspicion that your family pet or the pet of someone you know has been spying on you or listening in on your conversations? Share your experience with the class.

ANALYZE TEXT STRUCTURE

An **anecdote** is a short account of an event that is usually intended to entertain or make a point. Authors use anecdotes to introduce or illustrate important ideas in a way that is easy to understand and remember. As you read the following informational text, note how the author uses anecdotes to structure and present his ideas. Think about how the anecdotes help explain those ideas in a humorous and entertaining way.

DETERMINE KEY IDEAS

To develop and deepen your understanding of what you read, you need to be able to determine key ideas and evaluate details of the text. A **key idea** is a very important idea about a topic in the text. As you read, write down key ideas of the text in the graphic organizer below. Include important details from the text that support each key idea.

KEY IDEA	SUPPORTING DETAILS

GENRE ELEMENTS: INFORMATIONAL TEXT

• provides factual information

• includes evidence to support ideas

• often contains text features

• includes many forms, such as news articles and essays

• includes science writing, which explains complex scientific topics in language that is easy to understand

QUICK START

Have students read the Quick Start question, and invite them to share their experiences. Students may describe a pet dog that understands spoken language and responds to such words as *walk*, *treat*, or *car*. Students may note that their pets are intelligent and listen to and understand much of what their owners are saying.

ANALYZE TEXT STRUCTURE

Help students understand the reasons why an author might use anecdotes—to make informational writing easier to understand and more interesting to read.

- Tell students that authors often use anecdotes to make a point or to provide information in an entertaining and/or memorable way.

- Have students identify what kind of evidence is given in paragraphs 1–5, tell what idea it introduces, and explain how it fits into the text's structure. (*This anecdote is a good introduction because the descriptive language, the crime, and the memorable parrot catch readers' attention.*)

DETERMINE KEY IDEAS

Tell students that one way to determine the key ideas of a text is to look at the details in one part of the text and consider what they have in common. For example, when reading the first few paragraphs of this text, the reader learns that Marshmallow the bird was able to eavesdrop on burglars and remember one thief's nickname. Taken together, these details support the key idea that pets such as birds are intelligent and listen to and imitate human speech. Suggest that as students read, they work to connect the details to figure out the key idea of each section of text.

 ENGLISH LEARNER SUPPORT

Analyze Anecdotes Explain that an anecdote is a story that is characterized by being short—focused on one main point rather than retelling a complicated series of events—and told for the specific purpose of illustrating an idea in a clear and entertaining way. Provide some examples, such as telling an anecdote about having trouble finding your shoes in a messy closet to illustrate the point that it is important to keep your room organized. Have students give a thumbs up if you are giving an example of an anecdote and a thumbs down if you are giving an example of a story. **ALL LEVELS**

TEACH

CRITICAL VOCABULARY

Encourage students to read all the sentences before deciding which word best completes each one. Remind them to look for context clues that match the meaning of each word.

Answers:

1. *eavesdrop*
2. *predator*
3. *stake*
4. *intercept*
5. *foil*

■ English Learner Support

Use Cognates Remind students to listen for similar words from their own languages when studying vocabulary—particularly if their languages are based in Greek, Latin, or Germanic languages. Spanish and Romanian are based in Latin. Tell students that several of the Critical Vocabulary words have Spanish cognates: *predator/depredador, stake/estaca, intercept/interceptar*. **ALL LEVELS**

LANGUAGE CONVENTIONS

Ask students to look for and list the following types of capitalized proper names from paragraphs 1–4 in the text. *(Memphis, Tennessee, Marshmallow, JJ, Bill Reilly)*

ANNOTATION MODEL

Clarify for students that in the example annotation on page 118, the reader has taken notes about the author's use of text features by marking a subheading and then underlining two types of information the author included in this portion of the text—a sound effect and an anecdote. The reader's annotations and notes help the reader see how these text features work together to organize and present this part of the text. Point out to students that they can follow their own system for marking up the selection in their write-in text. For example, they may want to color-code their annotations by using highlighters to distinguish between anecdotes and different types of text features used.

 GET READY

CRITICAL VOCABULARY

eavesdrop	foil	predator	stake	intercept

To see how many Critical Vocabulary words you already know, use them to complete the sentences.

1. A younger sibling might _____ on his older sibling's conversations.

2. A _____ such as the lion is a fierce hunter.

3. She knew what would be at _____ if she lost the important document.

4. The football player was able to _____ the pass; it was an incredible play.

5. The superhero attempted to _____ the villain's evil plan.

LANGUAGE CONVENTIONS

Capitalization Proper nouns name specific people, places, and things. Each word in a proper noun begins with a capital letter. **Proper adjectives** are formed from proper nouns. They are always capitalized and often end in the letters *n, an, ian, ese,* or *ish*. In the following sentence from *Animal Snoops*, note how the proper adjective is capitalized:

The tall grasses of the East African savannah surrounded him like a curtain. . . .

As you read *Animal Snoops*, note the capitalization of proper nouns and proper adjectives.

ANNOTATION MODEL   **NOTICE & NOTE**

As you read, note the author's use of text features and anecdotes to structure the text. In the model, you can see one reader's notes about *Animal Snoops*.

> <u>Deep Secrets Overheard</u>
>
> *Tick, tick, creak.*
> 27 In the eerie, deep-water gloom off the coast of Norway, an enormous sperm whale makes mysterious noises before it abruptly rakes its toothy mouth through a school of swimming squid.

The subheading introduces a new topic by using a sound effect, and it is followed by an anecdote about a whale.

118   Unit 2

BACKGROUND

Peter Christie *(b. 1962) loved exploring nature in the fields and streams of his native Canada as a child. As a freelance science author and editor, he enjoys writing for young people because they are naturally curious. Young people also love a good story, and for Christie, the best science writing is about telling a story. In his explorations of animal behavior and intelligence, Christie continues to find many stories to tell.*

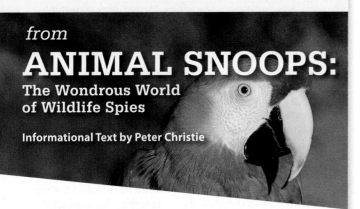

from
ANIMAL SNOOPS:
The Wondrous World of Wildlife Spies

Informational Text by Peter Christie

SETTING A PURPOSE

As you read, pay attention to the distinct ways animals snoop and spy on other animals in their environment, and note the reasons they do.

Presenting: The Bird-Brained Burglar Bust

1 The house in Memphis, Tennessee, sat empty: the coast was clear for a robbery. Quickly and secretively, the three young burglars checked the windows and doors and found a way in. They piled up computers, DVD players, and other electronic equipment.

2 The thieves talked as they worked, paying no attention to the parrot, nearly motionless in its cage. Only when the crooks were ready to make their getaway did the bird finally pipe up. "JJ," it said plainly. "JJ, JJ."

3 Marshmallow—a six-year-old green parrot—had been quietly **eavesdropping**. And the private-eye parrot had learned a thing or two, including the nickname of one of the robbers: JJ.

Notice & Note

Use the side margins to notice and note signposts in the text.

ANALYZE TEXT STRUCTURE
Annotate: Mark the subhead.

Predict: What do you think this section will discuss?

eavesdrop
(ēvz´drŏp´) *intr.v.* To *eavesdrop* is to listen secretly to others' private conversations.

Animal Snoops: The Wondrous World of Wildlife Spies   119

 ENGLISH LEARNER SUPPORT

Analyze Language   Review how informal language is used in everyday conversations with friends, while formal language is less personal speech that people use for business or school. Note that this author often uses informal language. Display paragraphs 1–3.

- Help students identify and define idiomatic or slang expressions. (*the coast was clear, make their getaway, pipe up*)
- Have pairs use context clues to define the informal expressions. (*coast was clear: "no one was around"; make their getaway: "escape without being detected"; pipe up: "speak"*)
SUBSTANTIAL/MODERATE

BACKGROUND

Have students read the information about the author. Tell students that Christie studied both science and writing in college. Note that writers are often advised to "write what they know." Christie uses what he knows about science to inform readers, in an entertaining and easy-to-understand way, about scientific topics.

SETTING A PURPOSE

Direct students to use the Setting a Purpose question to focus their reading. Remind students to write down questions that arise as they read.

✎ ANALYZE TEXT STRUCTURE

Remind students that subheadings provide information that can help readers figure out the main idea of the section of text that follows. After students have marked the subhead, work with them to identify the most important bits of information it conveys, such as the fact that it introduces a "bust," or an arrest, of some burglars. (**Answer:** *Students may predict that this section will discuss how a bird helped solve or prevent a burglary.*)

📖 For **speaking support** for students at varying proficiency levels, see the **Text X-Ray** on page 116D.

CRITICAL VOCABULARY

eavesdrop: The author is telling how a parrot was eavesdropping, or secretly listening to, the burglars.

ASK STUDENTS why they think the burglars were not paying attention to the parrot or aware that the bird was eavesdropping on them. (*People do not expect animals to pay attention to their conversations.*)

Animal Snoops: The Wondrous World of Wildlife Spies   **119**

TEACH

DETERMINE KEY IDEAS

Discuss ways that an author might include evidence to support a main idea, such as facts, details, or anecdotes. Once students have found a key idea at the end of paragraph 5, encourage students to read the descriptions in paragraphs 6–8 and look for examples of eavesdropping animals found in nature. After students have marked details, note that the author includes multiple examples, such as the gopher snakes and the female chickadees, to prove that this is common behavior and to illustrate a range of reasons why an animal might eavesdrop. (**Answer:** *Gopher snakes listen for noises made by kangaroo rats so they can find the rats and eat them, and female chickadees listen to males sing to choose a mate.*)

For **listening support** for students at varying proficiency levels, see the **Text X-Ray** on page 116C.

CRITICAL VOCABULARY

foil: The author uses the word *foil* to describe how the parrot's eavesdropping affected the human criminal's actions.

ASK STUDENTS why they think the author chose to use the word *foil* here rather than a word such as *stop* or *catch*. (*The word* foil *is a more descriptive word choice. Using it suggests the criminals were more than just stopped. They were frustrated in their plans because of a bird.*)

predator: This part of the text discusses how animals try to find out when predators are approaching.

ASK STUDENTS why they think an animal would want to know when a predator is coming near. (*The animal does not want to get eaten by the predator.*)

stake: The author compares the way animals spy on each other to a game with very high stakes, or valuable things that could be lost if the game is not won.

ASK STUDENTS to identify some of the stakes at play in the animal spy games. (*finding a mate, finding a home, staying alive*)

120 Unit 2

 NOTICE & NOTE

4   The burglars fled but soon realized that the parrot knew too much. "They were afraid the bird would stool[1] on them," said Billy Reilly, a local police officer. When the thieves returned to the crime scene to nab the bird, police captured them.

5   The Memphis crooks hadn't counted on Marshmallow's talents as an eavesdropper. Why would they? Few people imagine that animals can be highly skilled spies and snoops. Yet nature is filled with them.

6   More and more, scientists are discovering that creatures— from bugs to baboons—are experts at watching, listening, and prying into the lives of other animals. While Marshmallow's eavesdropping helped to **foil** human criminals, wild spies work for their own benefit. Spying can be the best or fastest way to find food or a mate, or get early warning of a **predator**.

7   Until recently, researchers preferred to think of communication between animals as similar to two people talking privately. But wildlife sounds and signals are often loud or bright enough that it is easy for others to listen in. It's like having conversations on social media that every one of your friends—and maybe some of your enemies—can read.

8   Animal messages are often detected by audiences that were not meant to get wind of[2] them. Hungry gopher snakes, for example, use foot-drumming signals between kangaroo rats to locate a snaky snack. Female chickadees listen in on singing contests of territorial[3] males when choosing a mate.

9   Biologists call it eavesdropping. It sounds sneaky, but it works well. And some animals are doubly sneaky, changing their behavior when they expect to be overheard. The animal communication network is far more complicated than researchers used to believe.

10   The **stakes** in wild spy games are high. Eavesdropping can determine whether animals mate, find a home, or enjoy a sneaky life instead of meeting sudden death. It can reveal whom they should trust and even affect the evolution of songs and signals.

DETERMINE KEY IDEAS
Annotate: Circle a key idea of the text in paragraph 5.
Cite Evidence: As you read, mark details in the text that support this idea.

foil
(foil) *v.* If you *foil* someone, you stop that person from being successful at something.

predator
(prĕd´ə-tər) *n.* A *predator* is an animal that survives by eating other animals.

stake
(stāk) *n.* A *stake* is something that can be gained or lost in a situation, such as money, food, or life.

---

[1] **stool:** a slang term meaning to tell on someone else, especially to spy on someone or to inform the police; to be a stool pigeon.
[2] **get wind of:** to learn of or find out about.
[3] **territorial** (tĕr´ĭ-tôr´ē-əl): displaying the behavior of defending a territory, or area, from other animals.

TEACH

11   Naturally clever secret agents learn things from snooping that help them survive and pass their genes to the next generation. It's one more tool that crafty creatures use to understand the world around them.

The Hungry Spy: Spying and Prying Predators

12   The path home was one the eastern chipmunk had traveled a hundred times before: under the ferns to the narrow tunnel into his burrow. The small animal ran briskly through the quiet Pennsylvania forest.

13   Suddenly, <u>a flash and a sting</u>. The startled chipmunk jumped. Dried leaves scattered. A sharp pain seared his haunches.[4] Scrambling away, he glimpsed the motionless length of a timber rattlesnake.

14   The ambush had succeeded. <u>The deadly serpent had lain coiled and still for many hours</u>, waiting. Even now, after striking, the snake was in no hurry. She would track down the chipmunk's lifeless body after her venom had done its work.

15   Patience is among the most practiced skills of a rattlesnake. Snooping is another. Before choosing an ambush site, timber <u>rattlesnakes study the habits of their prey.</u> Using their highly sensitive, flickering tongues, <u>the snakes use scent clues</u> to reveal the routines of rodents and other tasty animals.

_____
[4] **haunches** (hônch´əz): the hips, buttocks, and upper thighs of an animal.

DETERMINE KEY IDEAS
Annotate: Mark details in paragraphs 13–16 that describe how the snake hunts its prey.

Identify Patterns: How does the snake use its senses to hunt?

DETERMINE KEY IDEAS

Remind students that key ideas might include descriptions of actions or how things look. Point out that in this case, students should be on the lookout for words that provide information about the snake and its actions. (**Answer:** *The snake uses its sense of smell to follow and predict the habits of its prey.*)

▉ English Learner Support

Determine Key Ideas Ask students why they think the author chose to use the word *serpent* (Spanish: *serpiente*) instead of the word *snake* in paragraph 14. *(It sounds more dangerous and implies evil intent.)*
SUBSTANTIAL/MODERATE

APPLYING ACADEMIC VOCABULARY

☑ **benefit**   ☑ **environment**   ☐ **distinct**   ☐ **illustrate**   ☐ **respond**

Write and Discuss Have students turn to a partner to discuss the following questions. Guide students to use the Academic Vocabulary words *benefit* and *environment* in their response. Ask volunteers to share their responses with the class.

• How does spying or eavesdropping **benefit** each animal?

• What role does the **environment** of the animals mentioned in the text play in their spying?

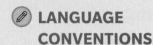

TEACH

✏ LANGUAGE CONVENTIONS

Review how proper nouns name specific people, places, and things, while proper adjectives are formed from proper nouns. Remind students that proper adjectives often end in the letters *n*, *an*, or *ian*. As students analyze paragraph 18, encourage them to look for capitalized words that name specific things. (*Proper noun: Photinus; Proper adjective: North American*)

✏ ANALYZE TEXT STRUCTURE

Discuss how authors might make up words to describe the sounds an animal makes. Once students have marked the sounds the frog makes, discuss how these sound effects convey the frog's repetitive song and then the sudden strike of a predator (a stork). (**Answer:** *This anecdote uses sound effects in a humorous and surprising way to show how a predator locates its prey by tracking the prey's sound.*)

For **reading support** for students at varying proficiency levels, see the **Text X-Ray** on page 116D.

CRITICAL VOCABULARY

intercept: The prefix *inter-* means "between" and *-cept* means "taken." Like the word *foil*, the word *intercept* recalls the human world of spies who might *intercept*, or take, a message being passed between enemy spies.

Have students read paragraph 17 aloud. Point out that this paragraph describes both spying and snooping.

ASK STUDENTS what these two activities are and the reason, or reasons, for them. (*One is spying on the movements of prey and one is snooping on their communication—for the purposes of both finding and eating them.*)

✏ NOTICE & NOTE

16 Their tongues are so remarkable that they also pry into the hunting habits of other rattlesnakes. Scenting the difference between a recently fed rattlesnake and a hungry one, they use the clues to hide where another snake has dined and the hunting is likely to be successful.

17 For many animals, snooping and spying can mean the difference between a full stomach and starvation. Some creatures, like the rattlesnake, spy on the habits of their prey. Others **intercept** private communication—and think of the signals as a call to supper.

18 *Photinus* fireflies, for instance, broadcast their mating messages with a light show. These plant-eating beetles flash luminescent[5] abdomens to wow potential mates on warm North American summer nights.

19 A bigger relative is named *Photuris*. They also blink biological tail lights during courtship, but are not always looking for a mate. These fireflies are predators that eat their smaller *Photinus* cousins. They spy on their blinking prey and follow the flashing beacon to a nighttime meal.

intercept
(ĭn´tər-sĕpt´) *v.* To *intercept* is to stop or interrupt something.

LANGUAGE CONVENTIONS
Proper nouns and proper adjectives should begin with a capital letter. Circle the proper noun and underline the proper adjectives in paragraph 18.

A flashing **Photinus** *firefly* looks good to his mate—but he looks delicious to his **Photuris** cousin!

ANALYZE TEXT STRUCTURE
Annotate: Mark the sound effects in paragraphs 20–22. What do these effects convey?

Evaluate: How does this anecdote use humor to help you understand the text's important ideas?

20 In the still-frigid early spring of northern Europe, a male moor frog begins his tuneless chorus: *Waug, waug, waug.*

21 Not minding that the ice has barely loosed its grip on the pond edge, the frog has emerged from wintering beneath marsh-bottom muck. He's all set to attract female moor frogs the moment they wake from chilly months of sleep.

---
[5] **luminescent** (lōō´mə-nĕs´ənt): brightly lit up.

🗨 ENGLISH LEARNER SUPPORT

Language Conventions: Capitalization Ask students to highlight the first letter of every sentence on page 122 that is capitalized in one color and all the other words that are capitalized in another color. Then have them discuss which capitalized words are proper names (*Photuris, Photinus, Europe*) and which ones are proper adjectives (*North American*). **SUBSTANTIAL/MODERATE**

Point out that in paragraph 20, the word *northern* is not capitalized because northern Europe is not considered a specific named place like West Virginia. Capitalizing some directional adjectives like "West Texas" is often debated, and newspapers and other publications decide which style to use. **LIGHT**

22 *Waug, waug, waug...* **WHAM!**

23 With a lightning strike, the long, lance-like bill of a white stork jabs through the marsh grass and snatches up the singing frog. In an instant, the tireless music-maker becomes the dinner of a spy.

24 White storks are master eavesdroppers. They rely on the songs of moor frogs to guide them when they're hunting. The birds are so skillful that they can stealthily follow frog sounds to within two or three strides of an unsuspecting singer.

25 Some spies can intercept signals sent by plants. Bright flowers invite bees and other animals to come for a meal of pollen or nectar (and to pollinate the plants at the same time). Scientists believe that the most symmetrical flowers—where each half mirrors the other like two sides of a face—help bees and birds recognize them as healthy, with top-quality pollen and nectar.

26 But crab spiders are deadly spies: they love to eat honeybees and know all about this flower-bee communication system. These sneaky spiders build their bee-trapping webs next to good-looking, symmetrical blooms that bees are more likely to visit.

DETERMINE KEY IDEAS
Annotate: Mark the definition of *symmetrical* in paragraph 25.

Summarize: Summarize how crab spiders use symmetrical flowers to hunt honeybees.

DETERMINE KEY IDEAS

Review how definitions are another way that authors of informational text provide readers with important information about a topic. Note how this author uses dashes to set the definition of *symmetrical* apart and make the definition easy for a reader to identify and comprehend. (**Answer:** *Honeybees prefer to visit symmetrical flowers because this indicates a healthy plant, and crab spiders build their webs next to symmetrical flowers to maximize the number of bees they catch.*)

WHEN STUDENTS STRUGGLE

Analyze Text Features Note that photographs and captions are other types of text features. Photographs provide visual information. Image or photo captions can provide new information or reinforce information in the text.

Ask students to reread paragraph 19 and explain why the photograph and caption fit into the section "The Hungry Spy: Spying and Prying Predators," telling how these elements help them better understand the text. (*The photograph shows a firefly that becomes a meal because a different kind of firefly—a predator—looks for the flashes of the smaller firefly and eats it.*) Have students caption the picture of the stork in a way that tells the reader how or why storks "eavesdrop."

 For additional support, go to the **Reading Studio** and assign the following [LEVEL] **Level Up tutorial: Reading Graphic Aids.**

NUMBERS AND STATS

To help students identify the animals being compared, suggest they scan the text for clue words related to size, such as *miniature*. (**Answer:** *The author uses a comparison to help the reader understand size instead of numbers because the text is an example of science writing, which uses simple language to convey scientific ideas. It is easier to understand the size of an unfamiliar animal when it is compared to an animal we know.*)

 ## DETERMINE KEY IDEAS

Review how the author has been using made-up words to recreate animal sounds. Assist students in searching this section of the text for another made-up descriptive word that sounds like the noises the bird makes. Note that the word *signal* acts as a clue to tell the reader that the author is about to explain how and why the birds use this noise. (**Answer:** *The dik-dik listens to the go-away bird because they share predators and the birds can spot these predators before the dik-dik can.*)

NOTICE & NOTE

Deep Secrets Overheard

Tick, tick, creak.

27 In the eerie, deep-water gloom off the coast of Norway, an enormous sperm whale makes mysterious noises before it abruptly rakes its toothy mouth through a school of swimming squid.

28 Scientists believe the whale is using echolocation[6]—in the same way bats use echoes of their ultrasonic[7] chirps to "see" in the dark. The whale's ticks and creaks help it zero in on prey.

29 But the sounds may also help distant sperm whales to find a good meal. The whales' echolocation sounds travel far, farther than the length of Manhattan Island. Sly sperm whales may eavesdrop to learn where another whale is hunting successfully, and drop by for lunch.

Live and Let Die: Spying and Prying to Stay Alive

30 The tiny antelope jerked his head up to listen.

31 He was a Gunther's dik-dik, a miniature antelope no larger than a Labrador dog. The tall grasses of the East African savannah[8] surrounded him like a curtain: he was well hidden from leopards and hyenas, but predators were also concealed from him. Through the chattering of birds and insects, the dik-dik recognized a familiar sound: *Gwaa, gwaa, gwaa.*

32 The insistent cry had an electric effect on the dik-dik. He leaped and bolted through the grass. The fleeing animal glimpsed the source of the sound—on a nearby tree sat a white-bellied go-away bird, sentinel of the savannah. Beyond it, barely visible above the grass, were the large black ears of a hunting wild dog.

33 Go-away birds are known for their noisy alarm call; the *gwaa* is thought by some to sound like a person shouting "g'away." These social birds feed together in chattering groups. A loud, urgent *gwaa* cry is <u>a signal to other go-away birds that an eagle, wild dog, or other predator has been spotted nearby</u>.

---

[6] **echolocation** (ĕk´ō-lō-kā´shən): a system used by some animals to locate objects around them; the animals produce high-pitched sounds and "listen" for the sounds to come back.

[7] **ultrasonic** (ŭl´trə-sŏn´ĭk): not able to be heard by humans; above the range of sound waves that humans can hear.

[8] **savannah** (sə-văn´ə): a flat grassland environment located in or near the tropics.

NUMBERS AND STATS

Notice & Note: Mark the two animals in paragraph 31 whose sizes are compared.

Infer: Why might the author use comparison to describe the size of the Gunther's dik-dik and not numbers, such as its weight?

DETERMINE KEY IDEAS

Annotate: In paragraph 33, circle the bird sound and underline its purpose.

Summarize: Review paragraph 33; then, explain why the dik-dik eavesdrops on the go-away bird.

IMPROVE READING FLUENCY

Targeted Passage Use paragraph 33 to model how to read informational text with proper pacing, intonation, and expression. Have students follow along in their books as you read this paragraph, showing how to read *gwaa* and "g'away" with correct emphasis and expression and how to pause briefly for the semicolon. Then reread the paragraph sentence by sentence, stopping after each sentence to allow students to echo read the sentence after you. Remind students that if they are reading text with odd words, such as the bird noises in this paragraph, they should slow down so their audience can understand what they are reading.

 Go to the **Reading Studio** for additional support in developing fluency.

34   Many of these dangerous hunters also eat dik-diks. The wary antelopes use every trick in the book to avoid becoming a meal—including eavesdropping on go-away bird communication. Unable to see far on the grassy savannah, dik-diks rely on the birds, which spot approaching predators from treetop lookouts.

35   For many animals, spying is a life-and-death business. Creatures that catch warning signals meant for others may stay one step ahead of enemies.

CHECK YOUR UNDERSTANDING

Answer these questions before moving on to the **Analyze the Text** section on the following page.

1 The author includes information about animal eavesdropping to —

   A explain that it is important to understand animal skills

   B inform readers about how this skill helps animals survive

   C convince readers that they should become animal scientists

   D give a funny example of how a parrot solved a crime

2 In paragraphs 20–24, the author includes an anecdote to —

   F show how eavesdropping provides an animal with prey

   G persuade readers to learn more about white storks

   H give a specific example of how animal sounds work

   J describe the mating rituals of moor frogs

3 Which idea is supported by information throughout the selection?

   A Animal eavesdropping is a real scientific term.

   B Animal sounds are for communication within the same species.

   C Animal spying is a fun game that only happens in the wild.

   D Animal snooping can determine life or death for animals.

CHECK YOUR UNDERSTANDING

Have students answer the questions independently.

Answers:

  1. *B*

  2. *F*

  3. *D*

If they answer any questions incorrectly, have them reread the text to confirm their understanding. Then they may proceed to ANALYZE THE TEXT on page 126.

 ## ENGLISH LEARNER SUPPORT

Oral Assessment   Use the following questions to assess students' comprehension and speaking skills.

  1. Why does the author tell about how animals can eavesdrop? (*So readers understand how this skill helps animals stay alive.*)

  2. The author tells an anecdote in paragraphs 20–24. Why did the author include this anecdote? (*It shows how an animal can use eavesdropping to find prey to eat.*)

  3. What is a big idea supported by the information in this text? (*Animal snooping can affect whether animals live or die.*)

  SUBSTANTIAL/MODERATE

ANALYZE THE TEXT

Possible answers:

1. **DOK 4:** *The author uses this engaging anecdote about a parrot repeating a name he heard to communicate that animals use their senses and skills to take note of their surroundings and to communicate effectively.*

2. **DOK 2:** *These paragraphs present key ideas of the text, including: animals "spy" to find food, to give warnings to other animals, or to find a mate. Scientists now realize animals interpret communication from species outside their own and that animal communication is more complex than scientists used to believe.*

3. **DOK 2:** *Like human spies and snoops who listen to what other people say and do and report about them, animals listen to or watch other animals and either take action or give warnings.*

4. **DOK 4:** *The photo shows what a Photinus firefly looks like. The caption reinforces the idea that the firefly's flashing light looks good to both a mate and a predator.*

5. **DOK 4:** *The author compares the distance a whale's echolocation sound travels to the length of Manhattan Island. The author describes distance and size through comparisons. Science writing communicates scientific facts through simple language; for example, by using familiar comparisons instead of numbers to express size.*

RESEARCH

Remind students they should answer the questions from their chart by assessing the credibility and reliability of each source they utilize. Note that good sources for finding information about animals might include encyclopedias, nonfiction books or magazines, and websites for zoos or universities.

Extend Students may find it helpful to use a two-column chart to compare and contrast the information they have researched with facts and details from *Animal Snoops*. If students in a group researched the same animal, suggest that they compare their results in more depth.

 RESPOND

ANALYZE THE TEXT

Support your responses with evidence from the text. ☰ NOTEBOOK

1. **Analyze** The author opens the text with an anecdote about a pet parrot. Explain the author's purpose for including this anecdote.

2. **Summarize** Review paragraphs 6–9. Summarize key ideas from this section of the text.

3. **Infer** The author refers to the animals in the text as spies and snoops. What does he mean by this?

4. **Synthesize** What important idea does the photograph and caption of the firefly following paragraph 19 help you understand?

5. **Notice & Note** Reread paragraph 29 and note how the author describes how far a whale's echolocation sound travels. Why does the author describe distance this way? Make a generalization about how science writing communicates facts.

RESEARCH TIP
The best search terms are very specific. In your search, you will want to include the animal's name and a term related to it. For example, search for *white stork* and *hunting* to make sure you get the information you need.

RESEARCH

The author presents many different types of animals in the text. Choose one of the text's animals that interests you and find additional information about that animal. Use the chart below to help you begin your research. Use the questions you'd like to have answered to guide you as you gather information about your animal.

Which animal interests me?	I remember this animal from the article because …	Questions I'd like to have answered …
green parrot	It was cool how the parrot learned the name of one of the crooks.	How many words can parrots learn to speak? Do they understand what they are saying? How do parrots communicate with one another in the wild?

Extend In a small group, share your research about the animal you selected. Work together to compare and contrast the information from your research with the information provided in *Animal Snoops*.

 LEARNING MINDSET

Curiosity Discuss the value of curiosity with your students. Explain that being curious is an important part of having a learning mindset because it is a first step toward taking on the challenges that come with learning new skills. Encourage students to think about the scientific curiosity that led to the discoveries of how and why animals snoop and spy. Then ask students to share what they are curious to learn more about. Point out that curiosity often leads to important interests and careers like becoming a science writer, nature photographer, or animal biologist.

CREATE AND DISCUSS

Write an Informational Essay Write a three- to four-paragraph essay about the animal you selected to research.

❏ Introduce the topic and end your first paragraph with a thesis statement, or a sentence that provides your controlling idea.

❏ Choose a way to organize your essay, such as gathering similar information into topic paragraphs. Include details from your research to support your ideas.

❏ Include transition words and phrases, such as *because, therefore,* and *for that reason,* to clarify ideas and to make connections among ideas.

❏ In your final paragraph, state your conclusion about your animal.

Discuss with a Small Group Work with a small group to discuss the behaviors of familiar animals, including pets and wildlife. What conclusions about animal intelligence can you draw based on the animal behaviors you have discussed? Use the following points to help you in discussion:

❏ Review the ideas together and ask questions of each other.

❏ Listen attentively to all ideas.

❏ Identify points of agreement and disagreement and discuss them respectfully.

RESPOND TO THE ESSENTIAL QUESTION

 What can you learn by seeing the world through an animal's eyes?

Gather Information Review your annotations and notes on *Animal Snoops*. Then, add relevant details to your Response Log. As you determine which information to include, think about:

- how animals pay close attention to their surroundings
- why animals observe their surroundings so closely
- what behaviors show animal intelligence

At the end of the unit, use your notes to write an argument.

 RESPOND

Go to the **Writing Studio** for help writing informational texts.

Go to the **Speaking and Listening Studio** for more on participating in discussions.

ACADEMIC VOCABULARY
As you write and discuss what you learned from the text, be sure to use the Academic Vocabulary words. Check off each of the words that you use.

❏ **benefit**

❏ **distinct**

❏ **environment**

❏ **illustrate**

❏ **respond**

CREATE AND DISCUSS

Write an Informational Essay Ask students to choose a topic related to the intelligence and behavior of animals. Point out that the list on page 127 can help students create an outline to make sure everything is included. Have students lay out main headings and subtopics before they begin writing.

For **writing support** for students at varying proficiency levels, see the **Text X-Ray** on page 116D.

Discuss with a Small Group Remind students that when they do not understand a comment made by another group member, they should ask questions to clarify meaning. The process of asking and answering questions can help everyone understand an issue more clearly and can lead to new ideas.

RESPOND TO THE ESSENTIAL QUESTION

Allow time for students to add details from *Animal Snoops: The Wondrous World of Wildlife Spies* to their Unit 2 Response Logs.

⊜ ENGLISH LEARNER SUPPORT

Discuss with a Small Group Allow students to work with partners to review the text for details. Provide these sentence frames to help them formulate their ideas for the discussion: *The article says animals snoop and spy because _____. One anecdote the author provided to demonstrate this was _____* **SUBSTANTIAL/MODERATE**

CRITICAL VOCABULARY

Possible answers:

1. **eavesdrop/listen;** *both are about using your ears to hear things; eavesdropping is about listening secretly.*

2. **stake/reward;** *both tell about something of value to someone; stakes can be won or lost, and imply a risky activity of some kind; a reward is something that is earned and is usually associated with something positive.*

3. **foil/intercept;** *both tell about ways to affect someone else's progress; foil means "to stop someone from being successful," while intercept simply means "to interrupt," but not necessarily to cause what is happening to stop.*

4. **predator/enemy;** *both tell about someone or something probably causing harm; a predator hunts another animal (prey) and eats it; an enemy may do different kinds of harm in different ways.*

VOCABULARY STRATEGY:
Latin Roots

Possible answers:

Words that end in -tory: *story, history, victory, dormitory, factory, oratory, respiratory, celebratory, circulatory, unsatisfactory, participatory, contradictory, introductory, explanatory, observatory, accusatory, auditory*

Words that end in -ory: *sensory, precursory, advisory, hickory, theory, savory, glory, ivory, memory, gory*

 RESPOND

WORD BANK
eavesdrop
foil
predator
stake
intercept

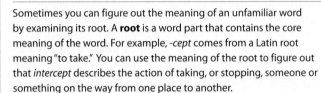 Go to the **Vocabulary Studio** for more on roots.

CRITICAL VOCABULARY

Practice and Apply Describe what is alike and different about the two words in each pair.

1. *eavesdrop* and *listen* _____

2. *stake* and *reward* _____

3. *foil* and *intercept* _____

4. *predator* and *enemy* _____

VOCABULARY STRATEGY:
Latin Roots

Sometimes you can figure out the meaning of an unfamiliar word by examining its root. A **root** is a word part that contains the core meaning of the word. For example, *-cept* comes from a Latin root meaning "to take." You can use the meaning of the root to figure out that *intercept* describes the action of taking, or stopping, someone or something on the way from one place to another.

Creating a word family is another way to use a Latin root to determine the meaning of an unfamiliar word. Thinking of other words that include the same root can help you recognize their related meanings and arrive at a meaning for an unfamiliar word. A word family that includes the same root as *intercept* would include words such as *reception, accept,* and *receptacle.*

Practice and Apply Think of words related to the word *predatory.* This word has a Latin root suffix, which comes at the end of the word. The suffixes *-tory* or *-ory* mean "relating to" or "having a place for." Fill in the word web with words that have these suffixes.

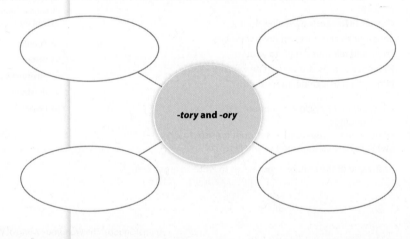

-tory and -ory

ENGLISH LEARNER SUPPORT

Vocabulary Strategy Speakers of languges such as Spanish, Vietnamese, Hmong, Cantonese, Haitian Creole, Korean, and Khmer may struggle to pronounce *r*-controlled vowels like *or* correctly. For example, Korean speakers may try to use the sound of the letter *l* for the sound of the letter *r*, and their pronunciation of the vowel sound *or* may sound more like *ir*. To help students practice correct pronunciation of this sound, have pairs of students copy words that end with *-tory* and *-ory* and circle the *or* in each word. Then have them take turns saying the *or* sound and pronouncing each word, correcting each other as necessary. **ALL LEVELS**

LANGUAGE CONVENTIONS:
Capitalization

Many proper adjectives describe cultural references or locations. The chart below shows two types of proper adjectives that require capitalization.

Go to the **Grammar Studio** for more on capitalization.

TYPE	EXAMPLES
cultural references	The Chinese dumplings were delicious. Erin is taking West African dance lessons.
location	We live close to the Canadian border. During our trip we visited many Midwestern cities.

Practice and Apply Mark the proper nouns and proper adjectives that should be capitalized in each sentence.

1. My sister and I love italian cooking.

2. Jamaica was formerly a british colony, a region ruled by the united kingdom, or uk.

3. The pacific northwest region of the united states has many national forests.

4. We visited the english countryside.

5. We enjoyed strolling through the quaint austrian village.

LANGUAGE CONVENTIONS:
Capitalization

Remind students that many proper nouns name specific places, such as *America, Florida,* and *France*. Proper adjectives are formed from proper nouns. Some proper adjectives are formed by adding an ending to the noun: *American, Floridian*. Other proper adjectives have a slightly different form than the noun from which they are formed, like *French*. Guide students to form phrases with proper adjectives based on your state, region, city, and so on (for example, *Midwestern city,* or *Californian*). Write the phrases and talk about the capitalization of the proper adjectives.

Answers:

1. *Italian*

2. *British, United Kingdom, UK*

3. *Pacific Northwest, United States*

4. *English*

5. *Austrian*

ENGLISH LEARNER SUPPORT

Write Sentences Work with students to review the capitalization rules for proper adjectives:

- Assist students in identifying the proper adjective in each Practice and Apply sentence. Have them rewrite each sentence correctly.

- Direct pairs of students to paragraphs 20 and 27 in the text. Ask them to write each sentence using a proper adjective. Remind them that the proper adjective will appear before the noun it modifies, not after it.

- After students complete the Practice and Apply, ask them to rewrite the sentences using proper nouns. Have pairs compare their sentences and discuss how the change affects the flow and sound of the sentence. **ALL LEVELS**

ANIMAL WISDOM
Poem by Nancy Wood

THE LAST WOLF
Poem by Mary TallMountain

GENRE ELEMENTS
POETRY

Remind students that **poetry** often uses short lines and sentence fragments to convey meaning, and point out that not all poems rhyme. Review the concept of figurative language, or language that has meaning beyond the literal definition of the words. Explain that one type of figurative language is personification, or assigning human characteristics to animals and objects. Note that poetry often includes imagery that appeals to all five senses, and emphasize that poems express a theme, or a "big idea" message about life.

LEARNING OBJECTIVES

- Analyze personification and imagery in poetry.
- Compare themes of two poems and present ideas to the class.
- Conduct research about wolves.
- Discuss poetry and create a poster depicting the imagery in the poems.
- **Language** Discuss with a partner the features of the poems using the key term *theme*.

TEXT COMPLEXITY

Quantitative Measures	Animal Wisdom	Lexile: N/A
	The Last Wolf	Lexile: N/A
Qualitative Measures	**Ideas Presented** Multiple levels. Use of symbolism, irony, satire, ambiguity.	
	Structures Used More complex. More deviation from chronological order.	
	Language Used Meanings are implied. More figurative and ironic language.	
	Knowledge Required Situations and subject are familiar or easily imagined.	

RESOURCES

- Unit 2 Response Log
- Selection Audio
- Reading Studio: Notice & Note
- Level Up Tutorial: Paraphrasing
- Speaking and Listening Studio: Participating in Collaborative Discussions
- Speaking and Listening Studio: Giving a Presentation
- "Animal Wisdom" / "The Last Wolf" Selection Test

SUMMARIES

English

"Animal Wisdom" and "The Last Wolf" are both poems about animals and nature. "Animal Wisdom" describes different animals first appearing on Earth—in each case, the animal comes to a realization about what Earth needs. "The Last Wolf" is told from the point of view of a person who meets and comes to an understanding with the last wolf in a ruined city. Although the poems are written from different perspectives, both allow a reader to see the world through animals' eyes.

Spanish

Los poemas "Sabiduría animal" y "El último lobo" son tanto acerca de los animales como acerca de la naturaleza. "Sabiduría Animal" describe la aparición de diferentes animales en la Tierra. Cada vez, el animal se da cuenta de lo que la Tierra necesita. "El último lobo" se cuenta a través del punto de vista de una persona que conoce y llega a un acuerdo con el último lobo de una ciudad en ruinas. Aunque los poemas son escritos desde distintas perspectivas, ambos permiten que el lector vea el mundo a través de los ojos de los animales.

SMALL-GROUP OPTIONS

Have students work in small groups to read and discuss the selections.

Think-Pair-Share

- After students have read both poems, pose a question to the class, such as: *How are the worlds of "Animal Wisdom" and "The Last Wolf" alike and different?*
- Students think about the question individually, making notes.
- Each student partners with another student to listen, discuss, and formulate a shared response.
- Call on a selected student from each pair to respond to the entire class.

Three-Minute Review

- During the discussion, pause and direct students to work with a partner.
- Set a timer for three minutes; and ask student pairs to work together to choose and reread one section of the poem. Pairs may find it useful to rewrite the section in prose, to make sure they understand exactly what is happening during this part of the poem.
- Once pairs have reviewed this section of the poem, have them write a clarifying question.
- Invite pairs to trade and answer questions, then present their answers to the class.

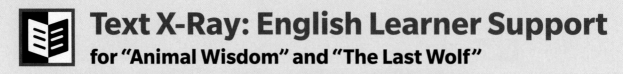

Text X-Ray: English Learner Support
for "Animal Wisdom" and "The Last Wolf"

Use the Text X-Ray and the supports and scaffolds in the Teacher's Edition to help guide students at different proficiency levels through the selection.

INTRODUCE THE SELECTION
DISCUSS SETTING

In this lesson, students will need to be able to identify the environments in which the animals in each poem live to comprehend what it is like to see these worlds through the eyes of these animals. Explain that the animals in "Animal Wisdom" are living in a world that is slowly changing and developing as water moves away from the land and mountains rise, while the animal in "The Last Wolf" lives in a ruined city.

Have students discuss the settings of the poems using these sentence frames:

- *In "Animal Wisdom," at first, Turtle leaves the _____ to live on _____. Then the water level lowers and more animals climb to _____. Next, _____ rise from heat.*
- *The wolf lives in a _____ city. The only other person who lives there is the _____.*

CULTURAL REFERENCES

The following words and phrases may be unfamiliar to students:

- *contentment* ("Animal Wisdom," line 5): feeling satisfied with life
- *slow-paced* ("Animal Wisdom," line 5): not rushing
- *devotion to place* ("Animal Wisdom," lines 10–11): staying true to a certain place
- *baying* ("The Last Wolf," line 3): making a sad howling sound
- *loping gait* ("The Last Wolf," line 12): slow walk
- *muzzle* ("The Last Wolf," line 23): the mouth and nose of an animal

LISTENING

Understand Personification

Clarify for students that personification is when animals or objects act like people. Give examples of personification, such as an elephant acting as a judge or food coming to life and talking. Invite students to provide their own examples of personification.

Have students listen as you read aloud "Animal Wisdom." Use the following supports with students at varying proficiency levels:

- Tell students to listen closely as you read aloud and to pay attention to what the poem says about each animal mentioned—particularly Turtle, Bear, and Eagle. Ask students to draw images that illustrate what they picture as they hear about each animal. **SUBSTANTIAL**

- Have students define personification. Ask: *What examples of personification do you see in this poem?* **MODERATE**

- Have student pairs work together to identify examples of personification in the poem. Invite pairs to share why they think each situation is an example of personification. **LIGHT**

SPEAKING

Discuss Theme

Review how the theme of a poem is an important lesson or idea from it. Tell students to look for important words and character's thoughts and actions that can help them determine the theme. Note that poems can have more than one theme, as the poems here do.

Use the following supports with students at varying proficiency levels:

- Have students practice saying sentences to a partner: *One theme of "Animal Wisdom" is that animals and people want the same things in life. One theme of "The Last Wolf" is that humans can destroy animals' homes.* **SUBSTANTIAL**
- To help students express their ideas about theme, display the following sentence frames: *The theme of a poem is _____ . One theme of "Animal Wisdom" is that animals and people _____. One theme of "The Last Wolf" is that people can _____ .* **MODERATE**
- Have student pairs discuss with each other the meaning of the word *theme* and determine one theme from each poem. **LIGHT**

READING

Examine Imagery

Review the concept of imagery. Remind students that imagery is language the author uses to help a reader imagine something. Usually the author wants the reader to imagine how something looks, tastes, feels, sounds, or smells.

Work with students to reread "The Last Wolf." Use the following supports with students at varying proficiency levels:

- Read a few lines from one section of "The Last Wolf" and have students draw what they visualize in their heads as you read. **SUBSTANTIAL**
- Guide students to identify examples of imagery from the poem. Supply sentence frames such as: *One example of imagery is _____. The author helps me imagine _____.* **MODERATE**
- Have student pairs work together to identify examples of imagery in the poem. Have them explain what each example helps them imagine. **LIGHT**

WRITING

Write a Summary

Work with students to summarize "Animal Wisdom" orally and to create a written summary of the poem.

Use the following supports with students at varying proficiency levels:

- Use questions to guide students to tell an oral summary of "Animal Wisdom." Prompt them to use words such as *first*, *then*, *next*, and *last* to organize their ideas as necessary. **SUBSTANTIAL**
- Provide sentence frames for students to use to write their summary, such as: *First, _____ lived _____. Turtle felt _____. Then some animals _____. Bear felt _____.* **MODERATE**
- Provide students with a list of transitional words to use when writing their summaries, such as *first*, *then*, *next*, *after a while*, and *finally*. Remind them to use these words and phrases to make the sequence of events in their summaries clear. **LIGHT**

Connect to the
ESSENTIAL QUESTION

Explain to students that they are going to read two poems that reflect on people's beliefs about people, animals, and nature. The authors of both poems imagine the thoughts and ideas of animals, allowing the reader to see the world through animals' eyes.

COMPARE THEMES

Remind students that a theme is the author's message or lesson to the reader. A story or poem can have more than one theme. As they read the poems, students should look for common themes between the two poems about life and human nature.

POEM

ANIMAL WISDOM

by **Nancy Wood**
pages 133–135

COMPARE THEMES

As you read, focus on discovering themes, or messages about life or human nature, that both poems share. What ideas are communicated by each poem? Which ideas do they have in common?

 ESSENTIAL QUESTION:

What can you learn by seeing the world through an animal's eyes?

POEM

THE LAST WOLF

by **Mary TallMountain**
pages 136–137

130   Unit 2

QUICK START

People and animals constantly interact with each other. Can you think of a time when you had an interaction in which an animal showed its intelligence? Think about why the interaction left an impression on you. Discuss your experience with your group.

ANALYZE PERSONIFICATION AND IMAGERY

Figurative language is language that has meaning beyond the literal meaning of the words. **Personification,** one type of figurative language, uses words to describe an object or animal as if it has human characteristics. Authors might use personification to emphasize an idea or create an emotional effect. For example, in "Animal Wisdom," a turtle is described as if it were human, talking the way a person would.

GENRE ELEMENTS: POETRY
- may use figurative language, including personification
- often includes imagery that appeals to the five senses
- expresses a theme, or a "big idea" message about life

"ANIMAL WISDOM" EXAMPLE	PERSONIFICATION
Turtle crawled up on land. He said: What's missing is the ability to find contentment in a slow-paced life.	The author uses personification to express an idea about what might be missing from the world.

Imagery is the use of words and phrases in a way that allows readers to experience, or imagine, how something looks, feels, sounds, smells, or tastes. To find imagery in a piece of writing, ask yourself, "What details help me experience what the author is describing? What sensory language helps me do that?" In "The Last Wolf," the author uses imagery to describe a wolf entering the city.

"THE LAST WOLF" EXAMPLE	IMAGERY
and I heard his baying echoes down the steep smashed warrens of Montgomery Street and past the few ruby-crowned highrises left standing	The sensory details in these lines help the reader imagine the sounds of the wolf and view what it sees.

As you read "Animal Wisdom" and "The Last Wolf," analyze the authors' use of imagery and personification to determine their specific reasons for using these techniques.

QUICK START

After students have had time to think about an interaction with an intelligent animal and discuss it with their partners, bring the class back together and invite volunteers to share. They should describe the interaction with the animal and what impression the interaction left on them.

ANALYZE PERSONIFICATION AND IMAGERY

Review with students the definitions of **figurative language** and personification. Discuss how an author could use personification to emphasize an idea or create an emotional effect. Review the example of personification from "Animal Wisdom," as well as the description of why the author chose to use that personification. Ask students for other examples of personification from books or movies with which they are familiar.

Read the paragraph about **imagery** with students. Emphasize that imagery is any language that helps a reader imagine how something looks, feels, sounds, smells, or tastes. Review the example of imagery from "The Last Wolf," as well as the information on why the author chose to use that imagery. Ask volunteers to share why they think it is important for authors to use imagery.

PARAPHRASE

Read the information about paraphrasing with students. Emphasize to students that paraphrasing is restating an author's ideas in the reader's words. Although a paraphrase conveys the same ideas as the author's original words and may be about the same length, paraphrasing does not mean copying the author's exact words. Tell students that when readers translate an author's ideas into their own words, this helps readers make sure they are comprehending what they read. Paraphrasing can be especially helpful when reading poetry, where the author may use a lot of figurative language or words that require readers to make their own inferences. Having to restate the author's language in a reader's own words ensures that the reader is understanding the poem.

 ANNOTATION MODEL

Remind students of the definitions of imagery and personification from page 131, and emphasize that they should mark examples of imagery and personification as they read the poems. Point out the example on page 132 in which *Turtle* and *said* are underlined, and the reader made a margin note about a turtle talking. Ask students what this annotation exemplifies (*personification*). Also point out the example paraphrasing, which can help students better understand difficult passages.

 GET READY

PARAPHRASE

Paraphrasing is restating text in your own words, which can help you **monitor comprehension** and ensure that you understand the text as you're reading. A paraphrase is written in simpler language and is about the same length as the original text, and an accurate paraphrase must keep the logical order and meaning of the original text. The chart below shows a paraphrase of a section of "The Last Wolf."

ORIGINAL TEXT	PARAPHRASE
he laid his long gray muzzle on the spare white spread and his eyes burned yellow his small dotted eyebrows quivered	The wolf put his head on the bed and stared with intense emotion.

Be sure your paraphrase accurately reflects the meaning of the original text, but avoid using the exact wording, or even the same sentence structure, of the text you are paraphrasing. If you do include exact words in your paraphrase, enclose those words in quotation marks.

ANNOTATION MODEL

NOTICE & NOTE

As you read, note examples of imagery and personification that move or surprise you. You can also paraphrase difficult passages in the side margin. In the model, you can see how one reader marked the first stanza of "Animal Wisdom" and made notes.

> At first, the wild creatures were too busy
> to explore their natural curiosity until
> <u>Turtle</u> crawled up on land. He <u>said</u>:
> What's missing is the ability
> 5 to find contentment in a slow-paced life.

A turtle talking! I wonder why?

Paraphrase: The animals did not take time to discover the world around them until turtle pointed it out to them.

WHEN STUDENTS STRUGGLE . . .

Paraphrase Have students make a two-column chart to help them note any words or phrases they don't understand. In the left column, they should write the word or phrase they don't understand, noting its line number. In the right column, they should write the definition of the word or phrase. Understanding the language of the poems will help them with paraphrasing.

 For additional support, go to the **Reading Studio** and assign the following [LEVEL UP] **Level Up tutorial: Paraphrasing.**

BACKGROUND

People and animals are in constant interaction with each other. It is not surprising, then, that animals have long been a favorite focus of poets and storytellers such as **Nancy Wood** *(1936–2013). In particular, Native American literature and culture express a strong reverence for animals and the land, air, and water they share with us. Nancy Wood was a poet, novelist, and photographer who lived in Colorado and New Mexico, where she was inspired by Native American culture and the wilderness.*

ANIMAL WISDOM

Poem by Nancy Wood

PREPARE TO COMPARE

As you read, note the ways the different animals in Wood's poem demonstrate their intelligence. Think about the speaker's view of nature and what it suggests about seeing the world through an animal's eyes.

At first, the wild creatures were too busy
to explore their natural curiosity until
Turtle crawled up on land. He said:
What's missing is the ability
5 to find contentment in a slow-paced life.

Notice & Note

Use the side margins to notice and note signposts in the text.

BACKGROUND

Have students read the background and the information about Nancy Wood. Explain that students are going to read two poems that reflect on people's beliefs about people, animals, and nature through the imagined thoughts and ideas of animals. The first poem focuses on the connections among animals, people, and nature.

PREPARE TO COMPARE

Direct students to use the Prepare to Compare prompt to focus their reading.

For **listening** and **writing support** for students at varying proficiency levels, see the **Text X-Ray** on pages 130C–130D.

ENGLISH LEARNER SUPPORT

Paraphrase the Poem Suggest that students pause after reading each stanza of the poem and write a note in the margin paraphrasing what they just read. You may have students work with partners for this activity so a more proficient English speaker can provide guidance to a less proficient English speaker. You can also work with students in small groups or with the whole class to assist with paraphrasing. **ALL LEVELS**

ANALYZE PERSONIFICATION

Have a volunteer remind classmates of the definition of personification. Make sure students know how to locate lines 6–11. Have them mark an example of personification, then ask volunteers to share what they marked. Ask the them to think about what has happened to the animals in the poem so far in these lines to help them answer the Infer question. **(Answer:** *Bear says that the world is missing both a commitment to where people and animals live and a search to find meaning in every day. Bear must believe that such commitment is important.)*

▶ AHA MOMENT

Remind students that an **Aha Moment** is when a character suddenly realizes a broader understanding about life. Have students mark Eagle's realization that begins in line 15. Use the Describe question to discuss the meaning of Eagle's realization. **(Answer:** *Eagle recognizes that solving conflicts with laughter will lessen the anger when there are problems between people and/or animals. This recognition will help others get along better.)*

ANALYZE IMAGERY

Have volunteers remind the class of the definition of imagery, making sure that the idea of imagery appealing to the senses is mentioned. Then have students mark two phrases in lines 23–34 that appeal to the senses and discuss the examples of imagery that they underlined. Have students look for additional examples of imagery about nature in lines 25–29 before answering the Interpret question. **(Answer:** *These images suggest that examples of natural beauty are all around us, and how some beautiful things last only a short time.)*

PARAPHRASE

Remind students that putting lines from a poem into one's own words can make it easier for a reader to understand the point a poet is making. **(Possible answer:** *When the people understood that they, too, were beautiful but fragile, they joined with the animals to protect Earth and all the beautiful, fragile things that depend on it.)*

 NOTICE & NOTE

ANALYZE PERSONIFICATION

Annotate: Mark an example of personification in lines 6–11.

Infer: What can you infer about the bear through the poet's use of personification?

AHA MOMENT

Notice & Note: What does Eagle realize about the animals? Mark what Eagle says.

Describe: What does Eagle recognize about disagreement? How might his recognition help others?

ANALYZE IMAGERY

Annotate: Mark two examples of imagery related to the natural world in lines 23–34.

Interpret: What ideas about nature does the poet convey through these images?

PARAPHRASE

Annotate: Mark the final thought expressed in the poem.

Interpret: Restate the final thought in your own words.

As the oceans receded, fish sprouted whiskers.
Certain animals grew four legs and were able
to roam from shore to shore. Bear stood
upright and looked around. He said:
10 What's missing is devotion
to place, to give meaning to passing time.

Mountains grew from fiery heat, while
above them soared birds, the greatest
of which was Eagle, to whom penetrating
15 vision was given. He said: What's missing
is laughter so that arguments
can be resolved without rancor.[1]

After darkness and light settled their
differences
20 and the creatures paired up,
people appeared in all the corners of
the world. They said: What's missing
is perception.[2] They began to notice
the beauty hidden
25 in an ordinary stone,
the short lives of snowflakes,
the perfection of bird wings, and
the way a butterfly speaks
through its fragility.[3] When they realized

30 they had something in common with animals,
people began saying the same things.
They defended the Earth together,
though it was the animals who insisted
on keeping their own names.

---

[1] **rancor** (răng´kər): long-lasting resentment or anger.
[2] **perception** (pər-sĕp´shən): the ability to understand something, usually through the senses; also insight, intuition.
[3] **fragility** (frə-jĭl´ĭ-tē): easily broken, damaged, or destroyed; frail.

CHECK YOUR UNDERSTANDING

Have students answer the questions independently.

Answers:

1. *D*

2. *J*

3. *A*

If they answer any questions incorrectly, have them reread the poem to confirm their understanding. Then they may proceed to the next poem.

CHECK YOUR UNDERSTANDING

Answer these questions about "Animal Wisdom" before moving on to the next poem.

1 The imagery in the poem suggests the animals are —

A silly

B angry

C tired

D curious

2 Which of the following is an example of personification?

F *above them soared birds*

G *animals were able to roam from shore to shore*

H *as the oceans receded*

J *darkness and light settled their differences*

3 An important message in "Animal Wisdom" is that —

A animals understand the earth

B people know more than animals

C eagles have excellent vision

D animals have many names

 ENGLISH LEARNER SUPPORT

Oral Assessment   Use the following questions to assess students' comprehension and speaking skills:

1. The poet uses imagery to describe Bear and Turtle. How are they similar? *(They are both curious and like to explore.)*

2. How does the poet use personification to talk about light and darkness? *(They poet says they "settled their differences.")*

3. What is a message in "Animal Wisdom" about how animals think about the earth? *(One message in "Animal Wisdom" is that animals understand Earth.)*   **SUBSTANTIAL/MODERATE**

BACKGROUND

Have students read the background and the information about Mary TallMountain. Discuss the idea that Mary TallMountain used poetry to try to reconnect with her lost home. Her poem "The Last Wolf," like "Animal Wisdom," reflects on beliefs about people and animals through the imagined thoughts and ideas of animals. "The Last Wolf" also conveys a perception about people's effects on the environment.

PREPARE TO COMPARE

Direct students to use the Prepare to Compare prompt to focus their reading.

 **PARAPHRASE**

Have students mark any unfamiliar words in lines 1–8, then look up the definitions of these words. Remind them that they can make notes of the definitions in their student books. Then have students complete the Interpret activity by writing a paraphrased version of lines 1–8 in their books. (**Answer:** *A wolf, alone, enters a city that has been destroyed. The wolf cries as it moves through the city, past the remains of tall buildings with unoccupied and unusable elevators and rooms.*)

■ English Learner Support

Paraphrasing Paraphrasing poetry can be a challenge to English learners. Before the whole class reads the poem, work with a small group to provide support for understanding unknown vocabulary and paraphrasing the poem. This would be a good time to review how to look up definitions as well. **SUBSTANTIAL/MODERATE**

 For **speaking** and **reading support** for students at varying proficiency levels, see the **Text X-Ray** on page 130D.

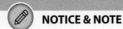 **NOTICE & NOTE**

BACKGROUND

Mary TallMountain *(1918–1994) was born in a small village along the Yukon River in Alaska. After her Athabaskan mother became seriously ill, TallMountain was adopted and taken away from her village. Living far from her family and home, TallMountain felt like an outsider. Many of her poems and stories reflect her struggles to reconnect with nature and her lost home. Her writing is highly praised as part of the renaissance of Native American literature during the last few decades of the 20th century.*

THE LAST WOLF

Poem by Mary TallMountain

Notice & Note

Use the side margins to notice and note signposts in the text.

PREPARE TO COMPARE

As you read, look for details and ideas that illustrate the speaker's perspective on wild animals and the environment.

the last wolf hurried toward me
through the ruined city
and I heard his baying echoes
down the steep smashed warrens[1]
5 of Montgomery Street and past
the few ruby-crowned highrises
left standing
their lighted elevators useless

passing the flickering red and green
10 of traffic signals
baying his way eastward
in the mystery of his wild loping gait
closer the sounds in the deadly night
through clutter and rubble of quiet blocks

PARAPHRASE

Annotate: Mark any unfamiliar words and phrases in lines 1–8. Use a dictionary to determine their meanings.

Interpret: Restate lines 1–8 in your own words. Remember to maintain the order and meaning of the original text.

---
[1] **warrens** (wôr´ənz): overcrowded living areas.

136 Unit 2

APPLYING ACADEMIC VOCABULARY

❑ **benefit**   ❑ **distant**   ☑ **environment**   ☑ **illustrate**   ❑ **respond**

Write and Discuss After reading both poems, have students turn to a partner and discuss the following questions. Guide students to include the Academic Vocabulary words *environment* and *illustrate*. Ask volunteers to share their responses with the class.

- What message does "The Last Wolf" give readers about the **environment**?
- What language does "Animal Wisdom" use to **illustrate** nature?

15 I heard his voice ascending[2] the hill
and at last his low whine as he came
floor by empty floor to the room
where I sat
in my narrow bed looking west, waiting
20 I heard him snuffle[3] at the door and
I watched
he trotted across the floor
he laid his long gray muzzle
on the spare white spread
25 and his eyes burned yellow
his small dotted eyebrows quivered

Yes, I said.
I know what they have done.

---

[2] ascending (ə-sĕn´dĭng): rising up.
[3] snuffle (snŭf´əl): sniff.

ANALYZE IMAGERY
Annotate: Mark striking examples of imagery used to describe the wolf in lines 15–26.

Infer: What does this use of imagery suggest about how the last wolf feels?

CHECK YOUR UNDERSTANDING

Answer these questions about "The Last Wolf" before moving on to the **Analyze the Texts** section.

1 In "The Last Wolf," what has happened to the city?

A Animals have attacked it.

B People have ruined it.

C A big storm has destroyed it.

D It is being rebuilt.

2 Which line in "The Last Wolf" appeals to the sense of sight?

F *and I heard his baying echoes*

G *in the mystery of his wild loping gait*

H *and at last his low whine as he came*

J *I heard him snuffle at the door and*

3 The line "their lighted elevators useless" emphasizes —

A the emptiness and ruin of the city

B the height of the buildings

C the size of the wolf

D the darkness of the city

TEACH

ANALYZE IMAGERY

Remind students to look for imagery that gives sensory details. Student annotations will vary. Ask volunteers to share their annotations before discussing the Infer question. (**Answer:** *The wolf seems upset. His eyes are burning and his eyebrows are quivering, probably with emotion.*)

CHECK YOUR UNDERSTANDING

Have students answer the questions independently.

Answers:

1. *B*

2. *G*

3. *A*

If they answer any questions incorrectly, have them reread the text to confirm their understanding. Then they may proceed to ANALYZE THE TEXTS on page 138.

ENGLISH LEARNER SUPPORT

Oral Assessment   Use the following questions to assess students' comprehension and speaking skills.

1. In "The Last Wolf," who has ruined the city? (*In "The Last Wolf," people have ruined the city.*)

2. What is a line in this poem that helps you imagine what the wolf looks like when he moves? (*The line "in the mystery of his wild loping gait" helps you imagine what the wolf looks like as he moves.*)

3. Does the line "their lighted elevators useless" tell about a part of the city that is working or not working? (*not working*)   **SUBSTANTIAL/MODERATE**

APPLY

ANALYZE THE TEXTS

Possible answers:

1. **DOK 3:** *The use of personification in lines 1–17 gives the perception that the animals are very in-tune to the world and their place in it. They are curious, asking questions and making assertions about their relationship with the world, such as Bear's statement, "What's missing is devotion/ to place, to give meaning to passing time" (lines 10–11).*

2. **DOK 2:** *People began to notice the lives and communication of animals and insects. People realized they are like animals and started looking after the world like the animals. The animals may have wanted to keep their own names to show they are not less than humans.*

3. **DOK 4:** *The imagery in lines 1–8 suggests a lonely or isolated mood because of the images of things abandoned and lonely sounds.*

4. **DOK 4:** *The poet creates a picture of the wolf as being intelligent, and the figurative language, mainly personification, supports that depiction. For example, the wolf is given a "voice" (line 15). This indicates that the wolf is "speaking" through his actions, which are filled with intent, such as his eyes that "burned yellow" (line 25).*

5. **DOK 4:** *The last two lines of "The Last Wolf" suggest the speaker communicates with the only wolf left and admits that humans destroyed the city and perhaps the world. This reveals a change in both the mind of the speaker and the reader because realization and acceptance of a new world/beginning is understood.*

RESEARCH

Point out the Research Tip about using other textbooks to find information. Make sure students know how to use an index or table of contents to search for information. Tell them that they can also use other reference books from the library to answer the questions. Online research is also an option, but remind them to verify facts on multiple sites and make sure those sites are reputable.

Connect Student responses should indicate that the poem emphasizes that humans have a responsibility to protect all areas of the environment for the good of animals and nature. When discussing other stories that feature wolves, students are likely to mention "Little Red Riding Hood" or *The Jungle Book*—stories where the wolves are personified and not behaving like real wolves the way the wolf in the poem does.

RESPOND

ANALYZE THE TEXTS

Support your responses with evidence from the texts. NOTEBOOK

1. **Cite Evidence** Reread lines 1–17 of "Animal Wisdom." How does the use of personification affect the way you perceive the animals? Cite text evidence in your response.

2. **Interpret** Paraphrase lines 29–34 of "Animal Wisdom." Why do you think the animals "insisted on keeping their own names"?

3. **Analyze** Reread lines 1–8 of "The Last Wolf." What mood or feeling does the imagery in these lines create?

4. **Evaluate** Reread lines 9–26 of "The Last Wolf." How does the poet's use of figurative language and details suggest that the wolf is intelligent? Is this use effective? Cite text evidence.

5. **Notice & Note** State in your own words the meaning of the last two lines of "The Last Wolf." How do these lines reflect a change in the speaker of the poem? How might the lines affect a reader?

RESEARCH

RESEARCH TIP
Consider using your textbooks from other subject areas as a source of information. For instance, you can search the index or table of contents of your science textbook to see whether it contains information about wolves.

The action of Mary TallMountain's poem takes place in a "ruined city," which is not a place one would expect to find a wolf. Do research and complete the chart below, providing details about wolves in your answers. Be sure to add your own questions and answers to the chart.

QUESTIONS	ANSWERS
What is a wolf's natural habitat? Where do wolves usually live?	tundra, forests, grasslands, or even deserts
What do wolves eat?	deer, rodents, birds, rabbits, and other small mammals
My own questions:	What is a wolf's lifespan? What color of fur do wolves usually have?

Connect In "The Last Wolf," the author presents the wolf outside its natural environment. What is TallMountain suggesting about humanity's relationship to the natural world? What other texts do you know that feature wolves, and how do those texts differ from "The Last Wolf"?

CREATE AND PRESENT

Discuss the Poems Hold a group discussion on how the different animals in the poems demonstrate their intelligence and what this suggests about each poet's view of wildlife.

❏ Discuss how the poets present the animals' intelligence in each poem. Support your ideas with details from the poems.

❏ Take notes about your ideas and other students' thoughts.

❏ As a group, identify points of agreement or disagreement, and then draw a conclusion on how each poet feels about wildlife.

Present Imagery With your group, create a poster on which you share your interpretation of key images from the poems.

❏ With your group, choose three images from the poems that struck you as especially memorable. Illustrate and display the examples of imagery on a board for your class to see.

❏ Indicate the sense to which each image appeals.

❏ Note the meaning conveyed by each image.

❏ Explain why the images you chose are memorable to you.

💬 Go to the **Speaking and Listening Studio** for more on holding a discussion.

RESPOND TO THE ESSENTIAL QUESTION

? What can you learn by seeing the world through an animal's eyes?

Gather Information Review your annotations and notes on "Animal Wisdom" and "The Last Wolf." Then, add relevant details to your Response Log. As you determine which information to include, think about:

• what the imagery suggests about the animals

• how animals and humans relate in the poems

• how the writers portray the animals in the poems

At the end of the unit, use your notes to write an argument.

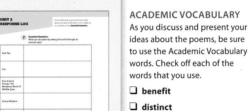

ACADEMIC VOCABULARY
As you discuss and present your ideas about the poems, be sure to use the Academic Vocabulary words. Check off each of the words that you use.

❏ **benefit**

❏ **distinct**

❏ **environment**

❏ **illustrate**

❏ **respond**

CREATE AND PRESENT

Discuss the Poems Remind students to use the checklist on page 139 to make sure they cover all topics of discussion. Tell them that all group members should take notes on the discussion, as well as write down their group's conclusion on how each poet feels about wildlife.

Present Imagery Remind students to work together to create an overall plan for their poster, then distribute the workload evenly to each group member. Students can help give each other feedback on their work.

RESPOND TO THE ESSENTIAL QUESTION

Allow time for students to add details from "Animal Wisdom" and "The Last Wolf" to their Unit 2 Response Logs.

COMPARE THEMES

Read the information about themes with students and emphasize that a poem does not usually state the theme directly. Instead, students have to infer the theme. Looking for key statements, significant events, or memorable images may help students infer the theme. Have student groups complete the chart on page 140. When groups finish, invite a representative from each group to share their group's answers.

ANALYZE THE TEXTS

Possible answers:

1. **DOK 2:** *Answers will vary, depending on the students' responses they discussed and wrote in their charts. However, some similar images are as follows: "Mountains grew from fiery heat" ("Animal Wisdom," line 12) is similar to the "few ruby-crowned highrises" in "The Last Wolf" (line 6). Different images are how animals roam from "shore to shore" in "Animal Wisdom," while one lone wolf moves through a "ruined city" in "The Last Wolf."*

2. **DOK 2:** *In "Animal Wisdom," humans learn from the animals and begin to relate to the world like the animals do: "they had something in common with animals, / people began saying the same things" (lines 31–32). In "The Last Wolf," humans have destroyed a city, and perhaps even more of the world, and the speaker communicates this realization with the last wolf, saying, "I know what they have done" (line 28). The texts' themes are similar in that they show human and animal relationships and communication, and both show humans learning from animals. However, "Animal Wisdom" expresses a more hopeful theme where humans learn to treat Earth well by relating to it as animals do, while "The Last Wolf" expresses a theme that acts more as a moral, communicating the hope that humans have learned their lesson and will not destroy Earth any more.*

3. **DOK 3:** *Answers will vary because of the students' opinions on which portrayal is more effective.*

4. **DOK 2:** *Humans can benefit from the wisdom of animals by noticing what is important to them, such as in "Animal Wisdom," the "slow-paced life" of turtles. This could teach humans that moving so fast through their days could cause them to miss important moments. Also, in "The Last Wolf," humans may learn to treat Earth better, so then we will not bring about its ruin.*

 RESPOND

Collaborate & Compare

ANIMAL WISDOM
Poem by Nancy Wood

THE LAST WOLF
Poem by Mary TallMountain

COMPARE THEMES

"Animal Wisdom" and "The Last Wolf" are poems about animals, nature, and human beings. Although the poems share similar topics, they may express different themes. A poem's **theme** is its "big picture" idea, or its message about life or human nature. When you ask what a poem means, you are asking about theme.

Poets do not generally state themes directly. It is up to you to **infer** a theme based on a poem's significant details. As you review the poems for details that hint at a theme, you might consider:

❏ key statements that the speaker or characters may make

❏ significant events that occur in the poem

❏ memorable images that describe the characters or setting

With your group, complete a chart with details from both poems.

	ANIMAL WISDOM	THE LAST WOLF
Key Statements		
Significant Events		
Memorable Images		

ANALYZE THE TEXTS

Discuss answers to these questions with your group.

1. **Compare** With your group, review the images that you cited in your chart. In what ways are the images similar? In what ways are they different? Explain.

2. **Infer** Both poems contain themes about the way humans relate to the natural world. Compare these themes. Cite text evidence in your discussion.

3. **Evaluate** In "Animal Wisdom," the animal characters speak as humans do. In "The Last Wolf," the wolf communicates without speaking. Discuss which portrayal you find more effective. Why?

4. **Interpret** Reflect on how human beings benefit from the wisdom of animals. Listen and learn from others in your group, and adjust your opinion, if needed.

EL ENGLISH LEARNER SUPPORT

Scaffold Answers Use the following sentence frames to help students complete the chart. Have them complete each frame for both poems.

• *A key statement, or important phrase, in "____" is ____.*

• *A significant, or important, event in "____" is when ____.*

• *A memorable image, or picture that stands out, in "____" is ____.*

Provide support to help students understand the terms and complete the sentence frames, because these concepts may be difficult for students to understand. **ALL LEVELS**

COMPARE AND PRESENT

Now your group can continue exploring the ideas in these texts by identifying and comparing their themes. Follow these steps:

1. **Decide on the most important details.** With your group, review your chart to identify the most important details from each poem. Identify points you agree on, and resolve disagreements through discussion, basing your decisions on evidence from the texts.

2. **Create theme statements.** State a theme for each poem, using complete sentences. Remember, it is up to you and your group to infer the themes based on details. You can use a chart like the one shown here to determine the theme each writer suggests.

Go to the **Speaking and Listening Studio** for help with giving a presentation.

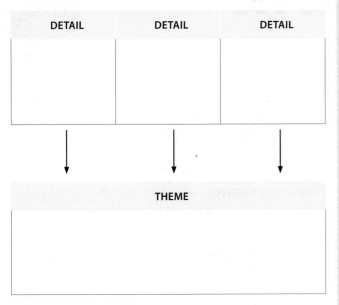

3. **Compare and contrast themes.** With your group, discuss similarities and differences in the themes of the poems. Listen actively to the members of your group, take notes, and ask the group to clarify any points you do not understand. Identify points of agreement or disagreement before you present your ideas.

4. **Present to the class.** Now it is time to present your ideas. State your conclusions about the themes of the poems. Discuss points of similarity and difference in themes. You may adapt the charts you created or use other visuals to help convey your ideas and information to the class.

Collaborate & Compare **141**

COMPARE AND PRESENT

1. **Decide on the most important details.** Key details in "Animal Wisdom":
   - Animals speak and make assertions about how the world should be, and though they suggest working with humans, they want to keep their names.
   - People realize they have much in common with animals and vow to protect Earth like the animals do.

   Key details in "The Last Wolf":
   - The last wolf enters a city ruined by humans.
   - Personification of the wolf suggests its communication with the speaker.
   - The speaker voices humans' destruction of the city.

2. **Create theme statements.** Possible theme statements:
   - Humans need to work to protect Earth.
   - Humans and animals share similarities and share a home.
   - Animals have more wisdom than humans at times because of their connection to Earth.
   - Animals communicate meaning about the world through their actions.

3. **Compare and contrast themes.** Remind students that they should compare and contrast the themes—that is, they should say how the themes are alike and how they are different. Remind all students in the group to take notes on the discussion. Also remind them that they need to resolve any differences of opinion and come to a group consensus before presenting their ideas.

4. **Present to the class.** Decide whether you want students to use the charts in their books or other visual aids for their presentations. Make sure to have materials available for other visual aids if you choose to let students create them. Remind students to practice their presentations several times before presenting to the class.

WHEN STUDENTS STRUGGLE . . .

Use Visual Aids If students are having trouble inferring theme from the poems, suggest that they draw pictures of their interpretations of each poem. Guide them to see that both poems refer to nature and the importance of animals. Their pictures of "Animal Wisdom" might help them see the theme that animals know a lot about Earth. Their pictures of "The Last Wolf" should help them see the theme that people need to work to protect the environment.

Collaborate & Compare **141**

WILD ANIMALS AREN'T PETS

Editorial by USA Today

LET PEOPLE OWN EXOTIC ANIMALS

Commentary by Zuzana Kukol

These articles serve as **mentor texts,** a model for students to follow when they come to the Unit 2 Writing Task: Write an Argument.

GENRE ELEMENTS
ARGUMENT

Explain to students an **argument** is a claim made by an author that is supported by reasons and evidence. Editorials and commentary are two examples of this kind of writing. In this lesson, students will learn to track and evaluate claims based on evidence, analyze persuasive and logical or emotional language, understand counterarguments, and compare two arguments on the same topic.

LEARNING OBJECTIVES

- Define and explain claims, evidence, arguments, fact, and opinion.
- Understand how authors support a claim.
- Write an argument taking a pro or con position.
- Compare and present by staging a debate in a formal register.
- Explain and use word origin to help with vocabulary meaning.
- Learn to spell commonly misspelled words.
- **Language** Demonstrate comprehension by summarizing a text.

TEXT COMPLEXITY

Quantitative Measures	Wild Animals Aren't Pets Lexile: 1170L Let People Own Exotic Animals Lexile: 1180L		
Qualitative Measures	**Ideas Presented** Multiple levels, use of irony and sarcasm. Most evidence is anecdotal.		
	Structure Used Primarily explicit. Largely conventional.		
	Language Used Mostly explicit, literal. Some Tier II and Tier III vocabulary.		
	Knowledge Requires Some references to events or other texts. Begins to rely more on outside knowledge.		

RESOURCES

- Unit 2 Response Log
- Selection Audio
- Comparing Arguments
- Close Read Screencasts: Modeled Discussions
- Reading Studio: Notice & Note
- Writing Studio: Writing Arguments
- Speaking and Listening Studio: Giving a Presentation
- Vocabulary Studio: Word Origins
- Grammar Studio: Module 14: Spelling
- "Wild Animals Aren't Pets"/"Let People Own Exotic Animals" Selection Test

SUMMARIES

English

"Wild Animals Aren't Pets" makes the claim that private ownership of wild animals endangers the health and safety of everyone and is cruel to the animals themselves. It promotes laws and regulations that will prevent or drastically limit this ownership. "Let People Own Exotic Animals" argues the opposite view, that as long as private owners are responsible, they should be allowed to own these animals with few regulations and no laws that limit or prohibit this ownership.

Spanish

En "Los animales salvajes no son mascotas" se afirma que la propiedad privada de animales salvajes pone en peligro la salud y seguridad de todos, y además es cruel para con los animales. El texto promueve leyes y regulaciones para impedir o reducir drásticamente este tipo de propiedad. En "Dejen que la gente tenga sus animales salvajes" se argumenta el punto de vista opuesto, que mientras los dueños sean responsables, deberían ser capaces de tenerlos con pocas regulaciones y sin leyes que limiten o prohíban su posesión.

SMALL-GROUP OPTIONS

Have students work in small groups to read and discuss the selection.

Think-Pair-Share

After students have read and analyzed "Wild Animals Aren't Pets" and "Let People Own Exotic Animals," pose this question: *What is the difference between a claim and a fact? Give examples.*

Model what it means to contribute a strong example by making a claim such as *Tigers are lions that mutated into tigers after swimming in a river.* Tell students this is a simple claim that can be researched and checked. A fact is something you can confirm as true. Some claims would require a lot of facts to confirm.

- Have students think about this question individually and take notes.
- Then, have pairs discuss their ideas about the question and share with the class.

Sticky Note Peer Review

Before they start reading, let students know there will be a peer review of notes and preparation materials. Before the debate, have them lay out their notes and materials on their desks.

In groups of 3, have students rotate counterclockwise twice, leaving sticky notes for the next student and then one more. The goal is to give constructive feedback to their peers. Allow time after the peer review for students to clean up or organize their notes and preparation materials or do more research and thinking.

Text X-Ray: English Learner Support
for "Wild Animals Aren't Pets" and "Let People Own Exotic Animals"

Use the Text X-Ray and the supports and scaffolds in the Teacher's Edition to help guide students at different proficiency levels through the selection.

INTRODUCE THE SELECTION
DISCUSS PETS AND EXOTIC ANIMALS

In this lesson, students will need to learn to see the world through the eyes of animals in order to make a strong argument for or against private ownership of wild or exotic animals. To do this, students will need to understand the difference between a domesticated pet and a wild animal. Provide students with terms such as the following to help them discuss these types of animals: *exotic, domestic, private, captive, responsibility*, and *caretaker*. Give them sentence frames such as the following to use to discuss each type of animal:

- An example of a _____ pet is a _____.
- An example of an _____ is a _____.
- It is a big _____ to be the owner of a _____.

CULTURAL REFERENCES

The following words and phrases may be unfamiliar to students:

"Wild Animals Aren't Pets"

- *laid bare* (paragraph 3): exposed
- *springing* (paragraph 4): slang for releasing from jail

"Let People Own Exotic Animals"

- *ban kids . . . ban humans* (paragraph 7): The author is using sarcasm to make a point about how silly it is to ban animals.

LISTENING

Summarize a Paragraph

Point out to students that if they listen carefully to a text, they can pay attention to its main points and include these ideas in a summary to show how well they listened.

Have students listen as you read aloud paragraph 3 in "Let People Own Exotic Pets." Use the following supports with students at varying proficiency levels:

- Tell students you will ask some questions about what they just heard. Model that they should give a thumbs up if the answer is yes, and a thumbs down for no. For example, ask: *Does the article claim that most exotic animals live in commerical places?* (yes) **SUBSTANTIAL**

- Have students write a list of three important points they heard in the paragraph you just read. If students need additional help, provide them with statements and ask them to identify which parts are true. For example, ask: *Are most of the exotic animals kept by people born in captivity or captured in the wild?* Ask students to write down each true statement as one of their points. **MODERATE**

- Have students identify several important points from the paragraph and then rewrite these points in summary form. **LIGHT**

SPEAKING

Ask for Assistance

Students will be able to read about and discuss a topic better if given pratice with asking for assistance when they encounter unfamiliar phrases.

Use the following supports with students at varying proficiency levels:

- Display the following request for assistance: *What does it mean to say something "serves as a backup"?* When the class reaches that point on page 149 when reading "Let People Own Exotic Animals," have students practice saying these words to ask for assistance, and ask volunteers to explain the meaning. **SUBSTANTIAL**

- As the class reads "Wild Animals Aren't Pets" and "Let People Own Exotic Animals," ask students to raise a hand if they encounter a phrase with a meaning that confuses them. Provide this frame for them to use to ask for assistance: *What does it mean to say ___?* Have volunteers explain the meaning of each phrase. **MODERATE**

- As the class reads the selections, have students raise their hands to ask for help to define confusing terms and phrases. Invite other students to explain the meanings. **LIGHT**

READING

Identify Facts and Opinions

Tell students that an author of an argument provides support for this claim in the form of facts and opinions. Explain that a fact can be proven true or false, while an opinion is what the author thinks about a subject.

Work with students to reread paragraph 2 in "Let People Own Exotic Animals." Use the following supports with students at varying proficiency levels:

- Write: *A fact can be checked to see if it is true or false.* Have students read this sentence. Then help students reread the sentence: *He had a criminal record and animal abuse charges.* Ask students to nod if this statement can be checked or shake their head no if it cannot be checked. **SUBSTANTIAL**

- Ask: *Which can be checked—a fact or an opinion?* (*fact*) Then read the fourth sentence in paragraph 2 and provide students with this frame to respond: *This is a _____ because _____.* Repeat with the first part of the fifth sentence. **MODERATE**

- Reread the following part of paragraph 2 and ask students to identify which is a fact and which is an opinion and explain how they can tell: *He had a criminal record and animal abuse charges. What Thompson did was selfish and insane.* **LIGHT**

WRITING

Write an Argument

Work with students to read the writing assignment on p. 153 and plan each step carefully.

Use the following supports with students at varying proficiency levels:

- Work with students to create an outline with a main claim and supporting claims. **SUBSTANTIAL**

- Provide sentence frames such as the following that students can use to craft their essays: *You should/should not keep a wild animal as a pet because_____. Another supporting claim is_____.* **MODERATE**

- Remind students of the need to check all spelling and to use Academic Vocabulary. Have pairs identify three places in their writing where they have included claims, supporting claims, and evidence. **LIGHT**

Connect to the
ESSENTIAL QUESTION

Both the editorial "Wild Animals Aren't Pets" and the commentary "Let People Own Exotic Animals" were written in response to an event involving wild animals released in Ohio. These selections cover the perspectives people, especially animal owners, might have on the issue of whether people should keep wild animals, but they also provide information that can be used to imagine the views animals might hold on this issue, if they could communicate.

COMPARE ARGUMENTS

Point out that while these selections take opposite viewpoints on the question of whether people should be able to keep wild animals as pets, they both contain strong arguments that are full of claims backed up with supporting evidence, such as facts and details. Encourage students to consider what kinds of evidence they find most convincing as they read these two selections and evaluate the argument presented by each.

MENTOR TEXTS

At the end of the unit, students will be asked to write an argument. "Wild Animals Aren't Pets" and "Let People Own Exotic Animals" provide models for how a writer can support arguments with facts and evidence.

ARGUMENT

WILD ANIMALS AREN'T PETS

by **USA TODAY**
pages 145–147

COMPARE ARGUMENTS

As you read, focus on the evidence used to support the claims in the arguments "Wild Animals Aren't Pets" and "Let People Own Exotic Animals." Think about which points in each selection make sense to you and which do not. Then, consider the strength of the evidence presented to support each point.

 ESSENTIAL QUESTION:

What can you learn by seeing the world through an animal's eyes?

ARGUMENT

LET PEOPLE OWN EXOTIC ANIMALS

by **Zuzana Kukol**
pages 148–151

142   Unit 2

 LEARNING MINDSET

Belonging   Remind students that everyone in the classroom is part of a learning community. When students team up with classmates to discuss the arguments in the selections or the arguments each student is making, encourage them to listen carefully to the different perspectives. This will help students expand their own understanding of the topic. Remind students often that the goal is not to have a fixed unshakable opinion at the end, but to learn to use and recognize facts and evidence, and to continue to be willing to grow and learn together as a community.

QUICK START

People everywhere have a fascination for wild, exotic animals. Do you think people should be allowed to keep these creatures as pets? Write down two reasons why or why not.

IDENTIFY CLAIMS IN ARGUMENTS

The selections "Wild Animals Aren't Pets" and "Let People Own Exotic Animals" present opposing arguments. A written **argument** expresses a position, or makes a claim about an issue or problem, and supports that position with reasons and evidence. The **claim,** or the writer's position, is often stated early in the argument, such as in the introductory paragraph or even in the title. A claim may be stated more than one time and in more than one way; often, a claim will be restated in the conclusion.

As you read the following texts, use a chart like the following to identify each argument's claim.

TITLE	CLAIM	LOCATION(S) IN THE TEXT
"Wild Animals Aren't Pets"		
"Let People Own Exotic Animals"		

ANALYZE EVIDENCE

Evidence is a specific piece of information that an author gives to support a claim. Evidence can include facts, quotations, examples, statistics, or even personal experiences. As you read each text, look for the specific types of evidence provided by the author.

To evaluate how convincing and accurate an author's evidence is, distinguish between **fact** and **opinion.** Facts are statements that can be proven, observed, or measured. Opinions are personal beliefs that may or may not be supported by facts. As you read each article, look for fact-based evidence and opinions.

GENRE ELEMENTS: ARGUMENT
- makes a claim or takes a position on an issue
- supports its claim with reasons and evidence (facts, statistics, quotations, and examples)
- presents counterarguments to address objections
- uses logic or emotion to persuade readers

QUICK START

Have students read the Quick Start question. Ask them to show thumbs up, down, or sideways to indicate their current opinion about owning wild animals or having them as pets. Holding their thumbs horizontally communicates "I am not sure" or "It depends." Ask students to commit to keeping an open mind even if they feel strongly about this topic before reading the selections.

IDENTIFY CLAIMS IN ARGUMENTS

Note that identifying the claim an author is making will focus a reader's attention and help him or her understand the reason why certain facts and details are included in a text. Keeping the claim in mind while reading the text will also help the reader evaluate the author's argument and decide whether the reader agrees with the author's point of view on an issue.

ANALYZE EVIDENCE

Tell students that the most difficult problem they will face when deciding what position to take on any kind of issue is the human tendency to decide first what the opinion is, then find facts to fit that opinion. Tell them that many adults are no better than students at this process.

Suggest that students use these questions to help them check the **evidence** they use in their own arguments:

- Did I look for evidence to prove my point or did I base my opinion on evidence?
- Did I check to see whether my evidence can be proven, observed (more than once), or measured?

WHEN STUDENTS STRUGGLE...

Identify Claims in Arguments Explain that an argument has a claim and reasons or evidence that support it. The first step is to identify the claim. Then readers can decide how well the evidence supports the claim. Tell students that they will read how two writers present different claims and evidence on the same topic. They will need to examine both arguments. After students have read the editorial, have them discuss the argument with a partner first by restating the claim in the title in their own words and then by identifying what kind of stronger laws the author thinks should be established and why.

© Houghton Mifflin Harcourt Publishing Company

TEACH

CRITICAL VOCABULARY

Encourage students to read all the sentences before deciding which word best completes each one. Remind them to look for context clues that match the meaning of each word.

Answers:

1. *regulate*
2. *exotic*
3. *dictate*
4. *exempt*

■ English Learner Support

Identify Cognates Have students read all the sentences aloud and look for cognates of the new words such as *regulate/regular, exotic/exotico, dictate/dictar,* as well as words that are similar, like *exempt* and the Spanish word *eximir*. **ALL LEVELS**

LANGUAGE CONVENTIONS:
Words Spelled Correctly

Remind students of familiar spelling errors they have already struggled with—and hopefully conquered—such as *your* versus *you're*. Tell students that in some cases, they will simply have to memorize the correct spelling and meanings of commonly misspelled or substituted words, such as *loose* and *lose*. In other cases, students can use the meanings of prefixes and suffixes to remember the differences, such as in the case of *accept* and *except*.

✐ ANNOTATION MODEL

Remind students that they can underline important details and circle words that signal how the text is organized. Point out that they may follow this suggestion or use their own system for marking up the selection in their write-in text. They may want to color-code their annotations by using highlighters or use sticky notes. Their notes in the margin may include questions about ideas that are unclear or topics they want to learn more about.

For these selections, take special note of the use of anecdotes, tone, and strong words that could trigger powerful emotions and quickly form opinions.

◎ **GET READY**

CRITICAL VOCABULARY

exotic   dictate   exempt   regulate

To preview the Critical Vocabulary words, replace the boldfaced word or words in parentheses with a vocabulary word with a similar meaning.

1. We want the city council to (**control**) _____ the amount of pollution that factories release into the air.
2. The (**unusual, foreign**) _____ plant looked like a creature from another planet.
3. Our leader's new orders (**command, require**) _____ what we should do next.
4. I was (**excused**) _____ from the test because I was sick.

LANGUAGE CONVENTIONS:
Words Spelled Correctly

To avoid confusion in your writing, it is important to use and spell words correctly. Many common words have similar spellings or sound alike but have different meanings. Here is an example from the text.

> **With animals running <u>loose</u> and darkness closing in, authorities arrived with no good choices to protect the public.**

The word *loose* is commonly misspelled as *lose*, which is a different word with a different meaning. *Lose* means "fail to win." If the writer had misspelled *loose* as *lose*, readers would have been confused and distracted. In this lesson, you will learn about other words that are commonly mistaken for each other and are often misspelled.

ANNOTATION MODEL   **NOTICE & NOTE**

As you read, note the author's use of emotion to convince readers to agree with the claim. In the model, you can see one reader's notes about the use of emotion at the beginning of "Wild Animals Aren't Pets."

2   Until recently, though, few people knew how easy it is to own a wild animal as a pet. Or how potentially (tragic)

3   But just as a 2007 raid on property owned by football star Michael Vick laid bare the little known and (cruel) world of dogfighting, a story that unfolded in a small Ohio city recently opened the public's eyes to the little known, (distressing) world of "exotic" pets.

strong words for negative emotions

BACKGROUND

Wild animals are animals that live in nature. They can be as rare as a snow leopard or as common as a tree squirrel. Although many states have laws that prohibit owning a wild animal, thousands of people in the United States keep animals, such as wolves, pythons, crocodiles, and bears, as pets. Some people want to make it illegal to have these kinds of pets. They argue that these animals pose a safety and health risk to people and the environment.

WILD ANIMALS AREN'T PETS

Argument by USA TODAY

PREPARE TO COMPARE

As you read, focus on the facts the author uses to support the claim.

1 In many states, anyone with a few hundred dollars and a yen[1] for the unusual can own a python, a black bear or a big cat as a "pet." For $8,000 a baby white tiger can be yours. Sometimes, wild animals are even offered free: "Siberian tigers looking for a good home," read an ad in the *Animal Finder's Guide.*

2 Until recently, though, few people knew how easy it is to own a wild animal as a pet. Or how potentially tragic.

3 But just as a 2007 raid on property owned by football star Michael Vick laid bare the little known and cruel world of dogfighting, a story that unfolded in a small Ohio city recently opened the public's eyes to the little known, distressing world of **"exotic"** pets. We're not suggesting that people who own these animals are cruel. Many surely love them. But public safety, common sense and compassion for animals all **dictate** the same conclusion: Wild animals are not pets. ▶ Close Read

---
[1] **yen** (yĕn): a strong desire or inclination.

Notice & Note

Use the side margins to notice and note signposts in the text.

IDENTIFY CLAIMS IN ARGUMENTS

Annotate: Mark the claim in the title.

Analyze: Do you think it's effective to state the claim in this location? Why or why not?

exotic
(ĭg-zŏt´ĭk) *adj.* Something that is *exotic* is from another part of the world.

dictate
(dĭk´tāt´) *v.* To *dictate* something is to require that it be done or decided.

Wild Animals Aren't Pets / Let People Own Exotic Animals 145

CLOSE READ SCREENCAST

Modeled Discussion In their eBook, have students view the Close Read Screencast, in which readers discuss and annotate paragraph 3, a key passage that includes the central claim of an argument.

As a class, view and discuss the video. Then have students pair up to do an independent close read of paragraph 10, which contains support for the author's argument. Students can record their answers on the Close Read Practice PDF.

 Close Read Practice PDF

BACKGROUND

Have students read the background information and briefly discuss their own knowledge, experience, or opinions about the issues.

"Wild Animals Aren't Pets" is an editorial that appeared in the newspaper *USA TODAY.* In the opinion and editorial sections of many newspapers, editorials are unsigned, meaning that they do not name the author. Unsigned editorials are usually written by a member of the newspaper's editorial board. Commentary, such as, "Let People Own Exotic Animals," is always signed so that readers know that the editorial reflects a particular person's point of view.

PREPARE TO COMPARE

Direct students to use the Prepare to Compare prompt to focus their reading.

▶ Text in FOCUS TEXT IN FOCUS

Comparing Arguments Have students view the **Text in Focus** video in their eBook to learn how to compare arguments. Then have students use **Text In Focus Practice PDF** to apply what they have learned.

IDENTIFY CLAIMS IN ARGUMENTS

Explain that an argument must have a claim, or the writer's position on the topic. Have students mark the title and evaluate if it is a strong claim. (**Answer:** *Stating the claim in the title immediately alerts the reader to what the piece is about. It sends a strong message.*)

CRITICAL VOCABULARY

exotic: This word does not mean *wild.* It refers to something we don't see every day. A squirrel is wild but is the opposite of exotic for us.

ASK STUDENTS what animals might be considered exotic to us. *(an ostrich; a tiger; any animal not seen often in your area)*

dictate: In this case, *dictate* means the conclusion is obvious.

ASK STUDENTS how they would put the last sentence of paragraph 3 into their own words.

TEACH

EXTREME OR ABSOLUTE LANGUAGE

Remind students that **extreme or absolute language** can evoke strong emotions. Have them read the paragraph and mark the examples of absolute language. Point out that these words describe the actions of the authorities and give clues to their emotions. Have students answer the question. (**Possible answer:** *The author wanted to show that the authorities had to do a terrible thing because the animal owner made a bad choice. The author wanted readers to sympathize with the authorities.*)

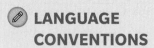 LANGUAGE CONVENTIONS

Write the following sentences on the board: *The brothers owned an alligator. "I'm* too *tired," said one of the* two *boys. "It's* to *hard to take care of him." "Yeah," said the brother, pointing* to *the alligator. He is getting* too *big!"* Point out the use of *two, too,* and *to.* Also point out that *too* sometimes means *also* and sometimes it means something is more than is wanted or needed, such as when something is *too much* or *too big* or *too many.*

✏ ANALYZE EVIDENCE

Note that the author includes this list of states to illustrate how many places do not have rules about keeping wild animals. Discuss how well this particular evidence strengthens the claim. (**Possible answer:** *The evidence does not logically support the author's claim; it suggests another claim: government should do more to regulate ownership.*)

CRITICAL VOCABULARY

exempt: When a new law or executive order is enacted, it does not immediately make what someone was doing illegal. If a citizen has been allowed to own wild animals in the past, they may be exempt, as in this case, so the law won't apply to them at all.

ASK STUDENTS if existing owners of wild animals should be exempt from new orders or laws. (*Answers will vary but use of the word* exempt *should be consistent and accurate.*)

146 Unit 2

 NOTICE & NOTE

EXTREME OR ABSOLUTE LANGUAGE

Notice & Note: What extreme or absolute language is used in paragraph 4? Mark the language used to describe the actions of the authorities.

Analyze: Why do you think the author chose these words?

LANGUAGE CONVENTIONS

Annotate: In paragraph 7, mark the word *too.*

Compare: What are two common misspellings of this word? What is the meaning of each of the three words?

ANALYZE EVIDENCE

Annotate: In paragraph 9, mark the states that do not have rules about keeping wild animals as pets.

Analyze: Does the evidence the author provides about state regulation support the claim? Explain.

exempt
(ĭg-zĕmpt´): *adj.* A person who is *exempt* is freed or excused from following a law or duty others must obey.

4   If that weren't already obvious, it became more so when collector Terry Thompson opened the cages on his Zanesville farm, springing dozens of lions, tigers, bears and other wild creatures before killing himself. With animals running loose and darkness closing in, authorities arrived with <u>no good choices to protect the public. They shot all but a handful of the animals</u> as the nation watched, transfixed[2] and horrified.

5   Owners of "exotic" animals claim they rarely maim or kill. But is the death rate really the point?

6   In 2009, a 2-year-old Florida girl was strangled by a 12-foot-long Burmese python, a family pet that had gotten out of its aquarium. That same year, a Connecticut woman was mauled and disfigured by a neighbor's pet chimp. Last year, a caretaker was mauled to death by a bear owned by a Cleveland collector. In Zanesville, it was the animals themselves, including 18 rare Bengal tigers, who became innocent victims.

7   Trade in these beautiful creatures thrives in the USA, where thousands are bred and sold through classified ads or at auctions centered in Indiana, Missouri and Tennessee. There's (too) little to stop it.

8   A 2003 federal law, which forbids the interstate transport of certain big cats, has stopped much of the trade on the Internet, according to the Humane Society of the U.S. But monkeys, baboons and other primates were left out, and measures to plug that hole have twice stalled in Congress.

9   Only collectors who exhibit animals need a federal license. Those, such as Thompson, who keep the animals as "pets" are left alone, unless states intervene.[3] And many do not. Eight—<u>Alabama, Idaho, Ohio, Nevada, North Carolina, South Carolina, West Virginia and Wisconsin</u>—have no rules, and in 13 others the laws are lax,[4] according to Born Free USA, which has lobbied for years for stronger laws.

10   After the Cleveland bear-mauling, then-Ohio Gov. Ted Strickland issued an emergency order to ban possession of wild animals. While it **exempted** current owners, Thompson might have been forced to give up his menagerie[5] because he had been cited for animal cruelty. We'll never know. Strickland's successor, John Kasich, let the order expire.

---
[2] **transfixed** (trăns-fĭkst´): motionless, as with terror, amazement, or other strong emotion.
[3] **intervene** (ĭn´tər-vēn´): to come between so as to block or change an action.
[4] **lax** (lăks): not rigorous, strict, or firm.
[5] **menagerie** (mə-năj´ə-rē): a collection of live wild animals, often kept for showing to the public.

146   Unit 2

WHEN STUDENTS STRUGGLE . . .

Examining Claims Provide students with practice identifying the main claim of "Wild Animals Aren't Pets" and the best evidence the author uses to support this claim. Reread the title, and invite students to restate the claim in their own words. Then go through the selection paragraph by paragraph and have students highlight each piece of supporting evidence. Suggest that they ask themselves whether each piece of evidence supports the claim in a logical way.

  For additional support, go to the **Reading Studio** and assign the following [LEVEL] **Level Up tutorial: Analyzing Arguments.**

Have students answer the questions independently.

Answers:

1. *B*

2. *H*

3. *A*

If they answer any questions incorrectly, have them reread the text to confirm their understanding. Then they may proceed to the commentary on page 148.

CHECK YOUR UNDERSTANDING

Answer these questions about "Wild Animals Aren't Pets" before moving on to the next selection.

1 What is the claim of the argument "Wild Animals Aren't Pets"?

   A Ownership of wild animals should be regulated.

   B Wild animals should not be kept as pets.

   C Owning a wild animal is not easy.

   D More needs to be done to prohibit the breeding of wild animals.

2 What point is supported by the author's evidence that wild animals in private ownership cause harm?

   F People who own wild animals are cruel.

   G Only wealthy people can afford to buy wild animals.

   H Ownership of wild animals can hurt the animals, humans, or both.

   J It is easy to own a wild animal.

3 Which sentence from the text suggests that the author will offer a counterargument to an opposing claim?

   A *Owners of "exotic" animals claim they rarely maim or kill.*

   B *Until recently, though, few people knew how easy it is to own a wild animal as a pet.*

   C *Only collectors who exhibit animals need a federal license.*

   D *We're not suggesting that people who own these animals are cruel.*

EL   ENGLISH LEARNER SUPPORT

Oral Assessment Use the following questions to assess students' comprehension and speaking skills:

1. Does the author argue that wild animals should or should not be pets? *(should not be pets)*

2. The author gives an example of people keeping wild animals as pets. The animals hurt people. What point does the author want to support? *(that wild animals can hurt people if they are kept as pets)*

3. What do owners of "exotic" animal argue? *(that "exotic" animals do not hurt or kill)*

   SUBSTANTIAL/MODERATE

IDENTIFY CLAIMS IN ARGUMENTS

Remind students that an argument expresses a position on an issue, and that an argument is made up of a claim, the writer's position on the topic, and support, which may include reasons and evidence. Have them read paragraph 2 and mark the claim. Then have them paraphrase the reasons that support the claim. (**Answer:** *The author's reasons include that most exotic animals born in captivity are cared for in well-regulated settings. They are also valuable in case a particular animal faces extinction.*)

■ English Learner Support

Identify Claims Read the title aloud and tell students that the claim is not in the title. In this case, the title is the action the claim supports. If the action is to let people own exotic pets, then the claim must logically state that having private individuals own wild or exotic pets is acceptable. Have students find the first sentence in the commentary that states that claim. (*paragraph 2: "Responsible private ownership of exotic animals should be legal if animal welfare is taken care of."*) Ask students to infer what the phrase *animal welfare* means. (*The animals will do well, or will be well taken care of.*) **LIGHT**

For **reading support** for students at varying proficiency levels, see the **Text X-Ray** on page 142D.

CRITICAL VOCABULARY

regulate: The word *regulate* refers to controlling or directing something so that it follows a set of rules or laws.

ASK STUDENTS to discuss what they think the author means when she states that "we cannot regulate insanity." (*There is no way anyone can control when, how, or if people become insane or unstable.*)

148 Unit 2

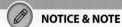

NOTICE & NOTE

BACKGROUND

Some people claim that private citizens have no business keeping wild and exotic animals as pets. Others disagree, claiming that with proper care, captivity is a safe place for animals. In 2012, in Zanesville, Ohio, Terry Thompson set free his collection of exotic animals. Most of them had to be killed on sight to protect nearby residents. In the aftermath of this tragedy, **Zuzana Kukol** *wrote this commentary, maintaining that private owners, through captive breeding, provide one of the most effective ways to save threatened species. "Tigers," Kukol has said, "are better than dogs. They don't bark."*

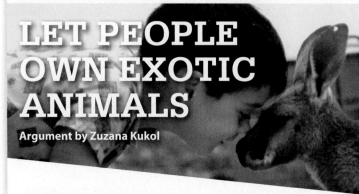

LET PEOPLE OWN EXOTIC ANIMALS

Argument by Zuzana Kukol

PREPARE TO COMPARE

As you read, look for ways the author supports her claim and addresses counterarguments. Do you agree with her claim? Why or why not?

Notice & Note

Use the side margins to notice and note signposts in the text.

1 The recent tragedy in Zanesville, Ohio brought back the question of whether private ownership of wild and exotic animals should be legal.

2 The simple answer is yes. Responsible private ownership of exotic animals should be legal if animal welfare is taken care of. Terry Thompson didn't represent the typical responsible owner. He had a criminal record and animal abuse charges. What Thompson did was selfish and insane; we cannot **regulate** insanity. [▶ Close Read]

IDENTIFY CLAIMS IN ARGUMENTS

Annotate: Mark the author's claim in the second paragraph.

Interpret: In your own words, give the reasons the author presents to support the claim.

regulate
(rĕg′yə-lāt′) *v.* If you *regulate* something, you control or direct it according to a rule, principle, or law.

148 Unit 2

CLOSE READ SCREENCAST

Modeled Discussion In their eBook, have students view the Close Read Screencast, in which readers discuss and annotate paragraph 2, a key passage that introduces the author's claim and presents reasons to support it.

As a class, view and discuss the video. Then have students pair up to do an independent close read of paragraph 4. Students can record their answers on the Close Read Practice PDF.

 Close Read Practice PDF

3   People keep exotic animals for commercial[1] reasons and as pets. Most exotic animals—such as big cats, bears or apes—are in commercial, federally inspected facilities. These animals are born in captivity, and not "stolen" from the wild. Captive breeding eliminates the pressure on wild populations, and also serves as a backup in case the animals go extinct.[2]

4   Dangers from exotic animals are low. On average in the United States, only 3.25 people per year are killed by captive big cats, snakes, elephants and bears. Most of these fatalities are owners, family members, friends and trainers voluntarily on the property where the animals were kept. Meanwhile, traffic accidents kill about 125 people per day.

ANALYZE EVIDENCE

Annotate: Mark the evidence the author provides to support her claim in paragraphs 4 and 5.

Compare: How are the two examples of evidence alike? How are they different?

[1] **commercial** (kə-mûr´shəl): of or relating to commerce or trade.
[2] **extinct** (ĭk-stĭngkt´): no longer existing or living.

Wild Animals Aren't Pets / Let People Own Exotic Animals   149

ANALYZE EVIDENCE

Tell students that authors often use a variety of methods of supporting an argument. Have them mark support provided by the author in paragraphs 4 and 5. Ask them how the two kinds of evidence are alike and different. (**Answer:** *Both kinds of evidence support the point. But paragraph 4 uses statistics, and paragraph 5 uses rhetorical questions and an appeal to reason.*)

For **listening** and **speaking support** for students at varying proficiency levels, see the **Text X-Ray** on pages 142C–142D.

LANGUAGE CONVENTIONS

Discuss how students may become confused when spelling the different tenses of a verb. While pronounced differently, often such tenses differ in spelling only by a letter or two. Once students have identified *chose* (the past tense of *choose*) as a common misspelling of *choose*, discuss how these two words are not homophones; they do not sound alike. They just look very similar. To help students remember how to spell *choose* correctly in the future, note that the double *oo* sound can be the sound in the words *foot* or *food*, but never has a long *o* sound.

■ English Learner Support

Language Conventions Have students practice correct spelling and pronunciation of different forms of a verb. Write *choose* and *chose* and have students copy these words on two cards. Then write the following sentence frames and have students practice completing them aloud, holding up the correct word each time:

• *Yesterday, I _____ to ride the bus home.*

• *She can _____ to wear either hat.*

• *What book will you _____ to read?*

• *Last summer, we _____ to go to the beach.*

SUBSTANTIAL/MODERATE

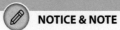

LANGUAGE CONVENTIONS
Annotate: Mark the word *choose* in paragraph 5.

Compare: What is a common misspelling of *choose*? What does each word mean?

5   If we have the freedom to <u>choose</u> what car to buy, where to live, or what domestic animal to have, <u>why shouldn't we have the same freedom to choose what species of wild or exotic animal to own and to love?</u>

6   Would the Ohio situation be any different if the animals were owned by a government and their caretaker released them? Is this really about private ownership, or is it about certain people's personal issues with exotics in captivity?

7   If society overreacts and bans exotics because of actions of a few deranged³ individuals, then we need to ban kids, as that is the only way to totally stop child abuse, and we need to ban humans, because that is the only way to stop murder. Silly, isn't it?

_____
³ **deranged** (dĭ-rānj′d): mentally unbalanced; insane.

IMPROVE READING FLUENCY

Targeted Passage Have students work with partners to read paragraphs 6–7. First, use paragraph 6 to model how to read with proper pacing, intonation, and expression. Point out how you raise your voice at the end of the paragraph when you reach the question mark. Then, have partners take turns reading aloud pargraphs 6 and 7, focusing on reading with proper expression when they reach question marks. Encourage students to provide feedback and support for using punctuation marks to read with correct expression.

  Go to the **Reading Studio** for additional support in developing fluency.

CHECK YOUR UNDERSTANDING

Have students answer the questions independently.

Answers:

1. *D*

2. *G*

3. *D*

If they answer any questions incorrectly, have them reread the text to confirm their understanding. Then they may proceed to ANALYZE THE TEXT on page 152.

CHECK YOUR UNDERSTANDING

Answer these questions before moving on to the **Analyze the Text** section on the following page.

1 What is the claim presented in the commentary "Let People Own Exotic Animals"?

   A Ownership of exotic animals should be regulated.

   B Exotic animals make good pets.

   C Captive breeding helps save wild populations.

   D Responsible private ownership of exotic pets should be permitted if the animals are properly cared for.

2 Which sentence or phrase from the text is a fact that supports the claim?

   F *We cannot regulate insanity.*

   G *On average in the United States, only 3.25 people per year are killed by captive big cats, snakes, elephants and bears.*

   H *Captive breeding eliminates the pressure on wild populations. . . .*

   J *Terry Thompson didn't represent the typical responsible owner.*

3 Which sentence or phrase from the text uses strong, emotional language to support the claim?

   A *Terry Thompson didn't represent the typical responsible owner.*

   B *Dangers from exotic animals are low.*

   C *People keep exotic animals for commercial reasons and as pets.*

   D *. . . why shouldn't we have the same freedom to choose what species or exotic animal to own and to love?*

 ENGLISH LEARNER SUPPORT

Oral Assessment Use the following questions to assess students' comprehension and speaking skills:

1. When does the author think people should be able to keep exotic animals as pets? *(If the animals are properly cared for.)*

2. The author says only a few people are killed by pet exotic animals each year. Why does the author tell the reader this information? *(To support the idea that people should be able to keep them as pets.)*

3. When does the author use emotional language to support a claim? *(why shouldn't we have the same freedom to choose what species or exotic animal to own and to love?)* **SUBSTANTIAL/MODERATE**

APPLY

ANALYZE THE TEXTS

Possible answers:

1. **DOK 2:** *Claim for "Wild Animals Aren't Pets" is in the title: Wild animals should not be pets. Claim for "Let People Own Exotic Pets" is in paragraph 2: "Responsible private ownership of exotic animals should be legal if animal welfare is taken care of." How they differ: "Wild Animals Aren't Pets" says wild animals should not be pets under any circumstances out of compassion for the animals and concern for public safety. "Let People Own Exotic Pets" says if people can be responsible in caring for wild animals, then it is okay to own them.*

2. **DOK 2:** *Most exotic animals are in facilities inspected by the government. Benefits: captive breeding helps support wild populations; may prevent extinction.*

3. **DOK 4:** *The writer cites the case of many wild animals that were killed by authorities because their owner set them loose before committing suicide. This evidence seems to support the writer's claim that owning wild animals can be dangerous, especially when an owner becomes unstable or is irresponsible.*

4. **DOK 4:** *In paragraph 4, the writer says that "dangers from exotic animals are low." She cites a statistic that says only about three people a year are killed by captive "big cats, snakes, elephants and bears." This evidence seems to support her claim that people should be able to own exotic animals, because certain wild animals kept in captivity pose little danger to humans.*

5. **DOK 4:** *Have students note the use of sarcasm in paragraph 7. Besides the use of the strong words deranged and silly, the writer's use of sarcasm is intended to trigger strong emotions against the argument in "Wild Animals Aren't Pets." Any thoughtful answer is acceptable.*

RESEARCH

As students research the pros and cons of owning a specific exotic pet, ask students to discuss whether the pros and cons listed by experts such as scientists who study animals, veterinarians, or private business owners such as circus owners would lend the most credibility to their ideas.

Connect Encourage students to review their research for details relating to how well exotic animals can be bred in captivity and consider whether enough animals are born and raised to truly offset the number of animals that die in the wild. Students might also consider which exotic animals are in danger of extinction.

ANALYZE THE TEXTS

Support your responses with evidence from the texts. 📓 NOTEBOOK

1. **Identify** What is the claim of each article and how do they differ?

2. **Summarize** Reread paragraph 3 in "Let People Own Exotic Animals." According to the writer, where are most exotic animals kept and what is the benefit of breeding them?

3. **Analyze** Reread paragraph 4 in "Wild Animals Aren't Pets." What specific evidence does the writer use to support the argument that people should not be allowed to own exotic animals? Explain how the evidence is or is not directly related to the claim.

4. **Analyze** Review paragraph 4 in "Let People Own Exotic Animals." What specific evidence does the writer use to support the argument that people should be allowed to own exotic animals? Explain how the evidence is or is not directly related to the claim.

5. **Notice & Note** Find examples of extreme or absolute language in "Wild Animals Aren't Pets" or "Let People Own Exotic Animals." Do you think the author's word choice exaggerates or overstates the author's points? Explain.

RESEARCH

RESEARCH TIP
The best search terms are very specific. Along with the animal's name, you will want to include terms such as *diet, protected species,* or *regulations.*

Investigate an exotic animal that you are interested in. What are the pros and cons of owning the animal as a pet? Generate questions about the needs of this animal. Then, gather information from a variety of sources and record what you learn in the chart.

EXOTIC ANIMAL: Lemur	
PROS OF OWNING AS A PET	**CONS OF OWNING AS A PET**
Cute and cuddly looking	They are illegal to own as pets.
Can be easily purchased	They can become aggressive.
At risk of going extinct	They climb and jump all over the place.
Can be trained	It is cruel to confine them.

Connect In "Let People Own Exotic Animals," the writer states, "Captive breeding eliminates the pressure on wild populations, and also serves as a backup in case the animals go extinct." With a small group, discuss whether your research uncovered any evidence to support this idea.

CREATE AND PRESENT

Write an Argument Take a position, pro or con, about owning the exotic animal you researched. Then, write a formal letter to a government official, supporting your position.

- ❏ Use appropriate vocabulary and a formal tone in your letter.
- ❏ Clearly state your argument's claim in the opening paragraph.
- ❏ In the next paragraphs, provide reasons and evidence that support your claim.
- ❏ In your final paragraph, state your conclusion about owning the exotic animal.

Create and Present a Public Service Announcement (PSA)
Take the argument you have developed about owning the exotic animal you investigated and create a PSA poster supporting your position.

- ❏ Present your PSA poster to your group. Make eye contact with your audience and use an appropriate speaking rate and volume.
- ❏ Ask group members to respond to your ideas by suggesting ways that you might improve your PSA.
- ❏ Work together to identify steps you might take to further educate people about your position. Listen closely and respectfully to all ideas.

RESPOND TO THE ESSENTIAL QUESTION

? What can you learn by seeing the world through an animal's eyes?

Gather Information Review your annotations and notes on "Wild Animals Aren't Pets" and "Let People Own Exotic Animals." Then, add relevant details to your Response Log. As you determine what points to include, think about the reasons people want to own exotic animals and the pros and cons of owning exotic animals.

At the end of the unit, you will use your notes to write an argument.

 Go to the **Writing Studio** for more on writing an argument.

 Go to the **Speaking and Listening Studio** for help giving a presentation.

ACADEMIC VOCABULARY
As you write and discuss what you learned from the texts, be sure to use the Academic Vocabulary words. Check off each of the words that you use.

- ❏ **benefit**
- ❏ **distinct**
- ❏ **environment**
- ❏ **illustrate**
- ❏ **respond**

APPLY

CREATE AND PRESENT

Write an Argument When students are deciding whether to take the pro or con position, encourage them to make a list of evidence they could use to support either position. Suggest that they brainstorm and consider the types of evidence they might use for support, such as statistics or expert opinions. Then, when they are researching, remind them to keep track of their research sources and experts so they can cite information from them.

Create and Present a Public Service Announcement (PSA) Remind students that a poster should present information concisely, with no more text than is necessary than to convey the main idea. It should also be visually appealing to catch a viewer's eye and, again, communicate ideas clearly. Caution students to make sure that any visuals dealing with the dangers of owning exotic animals are appropriate, not showing gory injuries or other violent subject matter.

For **writing support** for students at varying proficiency levels, see the **Text X-Ray** on page 142D.

RESPOND TO THE ESSENTIAL QUESTION

Allow time for students to add details from "Wild Animals Aren't Pets" and "Let People Own Exotic Animals" to their Unit 2 Response Logs.

APPLY

CRITICAL VOCABULARY

Answers:

1. *b*

2. *b*

3. *b*

4. *a*

VOCABULARY STRATEGY:
Word Origins

Answers:

dictate: *from Latin* dictare, *"to assert;" to command or say with authority*

exempt: *from Latin* exemptus, *"freed;" to be released from a duty or requirement*

exotic: *from Greek* exōtikos, *"foreign;" something from a foreign place*

regulate: *from Latin* regula, *"rule;" to control using rules*

RESPOND

WORD BANK

exotic	exempt
dictate	regulate

Go to **Understanding Word Origins** and **Using Reference Resources** the **Vocabulary Studio** for more on word origins and resources.

CRITICAL VOCABULARY

Practice and Apply Choose the correct response to each question.

1. Which of the following could be described as **exotic**?
   a. a pair of sneakers   **b.** a rare type of flower

2. Which of the following is something a school might **dictate**?
   a. students' hobbies   **b.** the length of recess

3. What might cause someone to be **exempt** from soccer practice?
   a. a previous absence   **b.** an injury

4. Which of the following might a government **regulate**?
   a. how fast people drive   **b.** what people eat for dinner

VOCABULARY STRATEGY:
Word Origins

Knowing the origin and historical development of a word, also known as its **etymology,** gives you a deeper understanding of the word. When you study a word's history and origin, you can find out when, where, and how the word came to be.

Practice and Apply Using print and online resources, look up each Critical Vocabulary word and complete the chart below. Use these resources to determine each word's syllabication and pronunciation, and then identify its etymology and current meaning.

WORD	SYLLABICATION / PRONUNCIATION	ETYMOLOGY / CURRENT MEANING
dictate		
exempt		
exotic		
regulate		

ENGLISH LEARNER SUPPORT

Vocabulary Strategy Help students understand the etymology of these words by encouraging them to mark up the words as they research and study them. For example, students might circle the root *dic* in *dictate* and make a list of other words that use this root, such as *dictator* or *dictionary*. **LIGHT**

LANGUAGE CONVENTIONS:
Words Spelled Correctly

Many common words with similar spellings and pronunciations are easily confused. Here are some examples.

advice/advise
lie/lay
passed/past
than/then
two/too/to
their/there/they're

Knowing which word is correct in a particular situation is critical for clear communication—as a writer and as a reader.

Practice and Apply Choose the word that correctly completes each sentence. You may use a dictionary if you'd like.

1. Gena did not (accept/except) Mindy's offer of a ride to school.

2. I will not discuss this any (farther/further) until I speak to my family.

3. A lawyer will (advice/advise) you of your rights.

4. The old bridge did not look like it could (bare/bear) the weight of the truck.

5. Russell slammed his foot on the (brake/break) to avoid hitting the ducks crossing the road in front of him.

6. The judge's ruling today will have a significant (affect/effect) on similar cases waiting to be heard.

7. Malia (passed/past) by the library on her way to the store.

8. We would rather see a movie (than/then) go to the park.

LANGUAGE CONVENTIONS:
Words Spelled Correctly

Practice and Apply Remind students to look for context clues in each sentence to help them figure out which word is the correct one to use in each situation.

Answers:

1. *accept*

2. *further*

3. *advise*

4. *bear*

5. *brake*

6. *effect*

7. *passed*

8. *than*

■ English Learner Support

Words Spelled Correctly Tell students that learning the meanings of commonly confused words can help students know which one to use and when to use it.

- Ask students to define the following words: *bear/bare* and *break/break* and create drawings or write sentences for each set. **SUBSTANTIAL**

- Have students add and compare the words *passed/past, than/then,* and *their/they're/there* and put them into sentences. **MODERATE**

- Ask students to define all of the previously mentioned words and add *accept/except, advice/advise,* and *affect/effect* and put them in sentences. **LIGHT**

WHEN STUDENTS STRUGGLE . . .

Language Conventions Ask students to make a word wall of commonly misspelled words with definitions and pictures. First, put five sets of words on index cards and fold them.

- Ask small groups to select a set of words and make a poster with their definitions.
- Then have groups exchange word sets and illustrate posters for the new word set.
- Use the words on the wall as "no excuses" words, meaning any writing a student turns in with one of those words misspelled will be handed back to be revised.

For additional support, go to the **Reading Studio** and assign the following [LEVEL UP] **Level Up tutorial: Spelling Words Often Confused.**

COMPARE ARGUMENTS

	"Wild Animals Aren't Pets"	"Let People Own Exotic Animals"
Claim	Wild animals should not be pets.	People can responsibly own exotic animals.
Evidence & Reasoning	Evidence: 2007 dogfighting raid, Zanesville incident Reasoning: for the public safety and compassion for animals	Evidence: only 3.25 people killed per year Reasoning: People can act responsibly towards exotic animals. Born in captivity, so not stealing from wild, backup to prevent extinction of species
Persuasive Language	Potentially tragic, cruel, distressing, compassion	Extinct, freedom to choose, silly
Why/ Why Not Convincing	Solid evidence: several examples	Not much strong evidence

ANALYZE THE TEXTS

Possible answers:

1. **DOK 2:** *The editorial claims that people should not own wild animals as pets. The commentary claims that people should be allowed to own wild animals as pets. Both writers present adequate evidence to support their claims.*

2. **DOK 3:** *Phrases such as "potentially tragic," "cruel world," "no good choices," "innocent victims," and "beautiful creatures" in the first selection suggest that the writer cares about wild animals and make the content seem reasoned. The phrases "selfish and insane," "cannot regulate insanity," and "why shouldn't we have the same freedom" show an impatient attitude and make the content in the second selection seem less logical and more emotional.*

3. **DOK 4:** *Opinions can strengthen an argument if they are founded on facts and add to the emotional appeal of the argument, but they can also weaken an argument if they seem to take the place of real facts and evidence.*

4. **DOK 4:** *Both editorials use strong evidence and persuasive language to support their claims. Students may find the first text more authoritative; it shows that accidents can happen, so better laws are needed.*

RESPOND

Collaborate & Compare

COMPARE ARGUMENTS

When you **compare and contrast** two arguments on the same issue, you analyze how each argument is presented. First, you trace and evaluate each argument: identify its claim, follow its support and reasoning, and decide whether it is convincing. Then, you determine how each author's viewpoint or attitude toward the issue differs.

WILD ANIMALS AREN'T PETS
Argument by USA TODAY

LET PEOPLE OWN EXOTIC ANIMALS
Argument by Zuzana Kukol

As a group, fill in the key points and evidence from both texts.

❏ Look at the evidence each writer provides as support—facts, reasons, examples, and statistics. Does the evidence support the claim in a logical way?

❏ Look for persuasive language—words with strong positive or negative connotations. Are the writers trying to be persuasive by appealing to your emotions, to your logic, or to both?

	WILD ANIMALS AREN'T PETS	LET PEOPLE OWN EXOTIC ANIMALS
Claim		
Evidence and Reasoning		
Persuasive Language		
Why/Why Not Convincing?		

ANALYZE THE TEXTS

Discuss these questions in your group.

1. **Compare** Compare each writer's claim and the kinds of evidence that support it. Does each author include enough evidence to support the claim?

2. **Evaluate** Examine each text and identify words that have a strong impact. For each text, tell whether the author's word choices are effective and why.

3. **Evaluate** Identify examples of the author's opinion in each text. Do these opinions strengthen or weaken the argument?

4. **Critique** Which argument seems more authoritative? Why?

ENGLISH LEARNER SUPPORT

Ask Questions Use the following questions to help students compare and contrast the arguments.

1. What are some examples of persuasive language that you find most moving? What are some examples of persuasive language that are too emotional or over the top to change your opinion?

2. What types of facts do you find most convincing? Why? **MODERATE/LIGHT**

RESEARCH AND DEBATE

Plan a **debate**—an organized exchange of opinions on an issue—about whether people should be permitted to sell exotic animals to private owners. Follow these steps to hold a fair, productive debate.

1. **Assign Roles** Select one person to be the **moderator,** who presents the topic and goals of the debate, keeps track of the time, and introduces and thanks the participants. Choose another person to be the **note taker,** who keeps track of points made during the debate.

2. **Form Two Teams** One team will argue the affirmative side of the issue (pro), and the other team will argue the negative side (con). Within your team, assign roles to each member.

   - ❏ One member of each team will introduce the team's claim and supporting evidence.
   - ❏ One member will respond to questions and opposing claims in an exchange with a member of the opposing team.
   - ❏ One member will present a strong closing argument.

3. **Research and Prepare Notes** Search the texts you've read as well as print and online sources for valid reasons and evidence to support your claim. Anticipate possible opposing claims and gather evidence to counter those claims.

4. **Hold the Debate** The moderator begins by stating the topic or issue and introducing the participants. The moderator tells participants whose turn it is to speak and how much time each speaker has.

SPEAKER	TASK	TIME
Affirmative Speaker 1	Present the claim and supporting evidence for the affirmative (pro) side of the argument.	5 minutes
Negative Speaker 1	Ask questions that will prompt the other team to address flaws in its argument.	3 minutes
Affirmative Speaker 2	Respond to the questions posed by the opposing team and counter any concerns.	3 minutes
Negative Speaker 2	Present the claim and supporting evidence for the negative (con) side of the argument.	5 minutes
Affirmative Speaker 2	Ask questions that will prompt the other team to address flaws in its argument.	3 minutes
Negative Speaker 1	Respond to the questions posed by the opposing team and counter any concerns.	3 minutes
Affirmative Speaker 3	Summarize the claim and evidence for the affirmative side and explain why your reasoning is more valid than that of the opposing team.	3 minutes
Negative Speaker 3	Summarize the claim and evidence for the negative side and explain why your reasoning is more valid than that of the opposing team.	3 minutes

EVALUATE DEBATE PERFORMANCE
Use this checklist to evaluate participants, including yourself.

- ❏ was well prepared with notes from research on topic
- ❏ presented claim and evidence effectively
- ❏ argued convincingly to support team's argument
- ❏ argued convincingly to rebut opposing team's argument
- ❏ used formal tone and appropriate vocabulary
- ❏ observed proper debate etiquette
- ❏ remained polite and did not interrupt
- ❏ presented a strong closing argument

RESEARCH AND DEBATE

Explain that a debate is a good way to explore the strengths of competing claims and counterclaims. Remind students to be polite and calm during the debate, not resorting to angry language or loud voices to try to make their points.

1. Assign Roles Be sure that students are clear about the responsibilities of their respective roles. Emphasize to the moderator that it is his or her task to keep the debate in order, not allowing debaters to yell over each other, interrupt one another, or take too long making each point.

2. Form Two Teams When students are assigning roles, suggest that they take a minute to consider the strengths of each student. Who is good at presenting a prepared statement and who is good at thinking on his or her feet and answering questions in the middle of an argument?

3. Research and Prepare Notes To make sure they have thought ahead to anticipate potential counterclaims, suggest that teams hold practice debates among their own members to test how well their arguments hold up.

4. Hold the Debate Remind participants to respect the moderator and listen to his or her instructions.

WHEN STUDENTS STRUGGLE...

Research to Debate Help students collaborate to complete the Research and Debate.

- First, write a focusing question frame on the board: *Should people be allowed to keep wild or exotic animals as pets?* Then, assign students randomly to opposing viewpoints.
- Have students work together to create a written outline of a sound argument for each position.
- Next, provide students with web diagrams. Have them discuss and identify reasons and evidence to support each contrasting opinion. Finally, have students use their organizers and appropriate technology to write their arguments, including counterarguments, and transfer them to index cards to use during the debate.

READER'S CHOICE

Setting a Purpose Have students review their Unit 2 Response Log and think about what they've already learned about seeing the world through an animal's eyes. As they select their Independent Reading selections, encourage them to consider what more they want to know.

NOTICE NOTE

Explain that some selections may contain multiple signposts; others may contain only one. And the same type of signpost can occur many times in the same text.

 LEARNING MINDSET

Curiosity Discuss the value of curiosity with your students. Explain that curiosity leads to learning new ideas and skills. Encourage students to think about the titles and accompanying photographs of the Independent Reading selections. Then ask students what questions they have about each selection.

 INDEPENDENT READING

 ESSENTIAL QUESTION:

What can you learn by seeing the world through an animal's eyes?

Reader's Choice

Setting a Purpose Select one or more of these options from your eBook to continue your exploration of the Essential Question.

- Read the descriptions to see which text grabs your interest.
- Think about which genres you enjoy reading.

Notice Note

In this unit, you practiced noticing and noting three signposts: **Again and Again, Memory Moment,** and **Contrasts and Contradictions.** As you read independently, these signposts and others will aid your understanding. Below are the anchor questions to ask when you read literature and nonfiction.

Reading Literature: Stories, Poems, and Plays		
Signpost	**Anchor Question**	**Lesson**
Contrasts and Contradictions	Why did the character act that way?	p. 3
Aha Moment	How might this change things?	p. 3
Tough Questions	What does this make me wonder about?	p. 172
Words of the Wiser	What's the lesson for the character?	p. 2
Again and Again	Why might the author keep bringing this up?	p. 92
Memory Moment	Why is this memory important?	p. 93

Reading Nonfiction: Essays, Articles, and Arguments		
Signpost	**Anchor Question(s)**	**Lesson**
Big Questions	What surprised me?	p. 246
	What did the author think I already knew?	p. 420
	What challenged, changed, or confirmed what I already knew?	p. 332
Contrasts and Contradictions	What is the difference, and why does it matter?	p. 247
Extreme or Absolute Language	Why did the author use this language?	p. 247
Numbers and Stats	Why did the author use these numbers or amounts?	p. 333
Quoted Words	Why was this person quoted or cited, and what did this add?	p. 333
Word Gaps	Do I know this word from someplace else?	p. 421
	Does it seem like technical talk for this topic?	
	Do clues in the sentence help me understand the word?	

 ENGLISH LEARNER SUPPORT

Develop Fluency Select a passage from a text that matches students' reading abilities.

- Echo read the passage by reading aloud one sentence and then having students repeat it back to you. Check their comprehension by asking yes/no questions about the passage. **SUBSTANTIAL**
- Pair students. Have students partner read, taking turns with each paragraph. Have pairs summarize what they have read. **MODERATE**

- Pair students. Allow more fluent pairs to select their own texts. Set a specific time for students to read silently. Then have each pair discuss what they read and share their summaries of the passage. **LIGHT**

 Go to the **Reading Studio** for additional support in developing fluency.

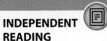

You can preview these texts in Unit 2 of your eBook.

Then, check off the text or texts that you select to read on your own.

POEM

The Caterpillar

Robert Graves

A poet sees the world through the eyes of a caterpillar.

POEM

The Flying Cat

Naomi Shihab Nye

What happens when a pet owner prepares to take her cat on a plane?

SHORT STORY

The Pod

Maureen Crane Wartski

A teenager recovering from a serious accident discovers empathy for a stranded animal.

SPEECH

Tribute to the Dog

George Graham Vest

A famous speech wins a case for a sheep farmer whose dog was shot and killed.

ARGUMENTS

Views on Zoos

What's your position on whether zoos should exist?

Collaborate and Share Get with a partner to discuss what you learned from at least one of your independent readings.

- Give a brief synopsis or summary of the text.
- Describe any signposts that you noticed in the text and explain what they revealed to you.
- Describe what you most enjoyed or found most challenging about the text. Give specific examples.
- Decide if you would recommend the text to others. Why or why not?

 Go to the **Reading Studio** for more resources on **Notice & Note**.

Independent Reading 159

INDEPENDENT READING

MATCHING STUDENTS TO TEXTS

Use the following information to guide students in using their texts.

The Caterpillar
Genre: poem
Overall Rating: Challenging

The Flying Cat
Genre: poem
Overall Rating: Accessible

The Pod   Lexile: 810L
Genre: short story
Overall Rating: Accessible

Tribute to the Dog   Lexile: 1130L
Genre: speech
Overall Rating: Challenging

Views on Zoos   Lexile: 1190L
Genre: arguments
Overall Rating: Challenging

Collaborate and Share To assess how well students read the selections, walk around the room and listen to their conversations. Encourage students to be focused and specific in their comments.

 Online **for Assessment**

- Independent Reading Selection Tests

 Encourage students to visit the **Reading Studio** to download a handy bookmark of **NOTICE & NOTE** signposts.

WHEN STUDENTS STRUGGLE . . .

Keep a Reading Log As students read their selected texts, have them keep a reading log for each selection to note signposts and their thoughts about them. Use their logs to assess how well they are noticing and reflecting on elements of the texts.

Reading Log for (title)		
Location	**Signpost I Noticed**	**My Notes about It**

UNIT ② Tasks

- **WRITE AN ARGUMENT**
- **PRESENT AN ARGUMENT**

MENTOR TEXTS

WILD ANIMALS AREN'T PETS

Editorial by USA TODAY

LET PEOPLE OWN EXOTIC ANIMALS

Commentary by ZUZANA KUKOL

LEARNING OBJECTIVES

Writing Task

- Write an argumentative essay about seeing the world from the perspective of an animal.
- Organize information with a purposeful structure.
- Develop a focused, structured draft.
- Provide an introduction that clearly states your claim.
- Support your claim with logical reasons and relevant text evidence.
- Use persuasive language.
- Address counterarguments.
- Conclude by effectively summarizing your claim.
- Revise drafts, incorporating feedback from peers.
- Edit drafts to incorporate transition words and phrases.
- Use a rubric to evaluate writing.
- **Language** Write about animals using correct subject-verb agreement.

Speaking Task

- Present an argument to an audience.
- Adapt an argumentative essay for presentation.
- Use appropriate tone, word choice, and visuals for your audience.
- Listen actively to a presentation.
- **Language** Share information using the sentence stem *I think ____*.

Assign the Writing Task in *Ed.*

 Online Ed

RESOURCES

- Unit 2 Response Log
- Writing Studio: Writing Arguments
- Speaking and Listening Studio: Giving a Presentation
- ! Grammar Studio: Module 6: Agreement

Language X-Ray: English Learner Support

Use the instruction below and the supports and scaffolds in the Teacher's Edition to help you guide students different proficiency levels.

INTRODUCE THE WRITING TASK

Explain that an **argument** is a type of writing that presents or explains an opinion about a topic. Point out that the word *argument* is related to the Spanish noun *argumento*, which means "a reason." Make sure students understand that argumentative essays give reasons to support a specific point of view.

Remind students that the selections in this unit address seeing the world through an animal's eyes. Work with students to select a topic to write about. Use sentence frames to help them articulate their ideas. For example: *I think that I can learn _____ by seeing the world from an animal's perspective*.

Brainstorm words and phrases related to the topic and write them on the board. Then, have students work with a partner to write one sentence about what they can learn by seeing the world from an animal's perspective. Tell students to use their sentences to begin their essays.

WRITING

Use Subject-Verb Agreement

Tell students that verbs must always agree with their subject in number. Singular subjects require singular verbs, while plural subjects require plural verbs.

Use the following supports with students at varying proficiency levels:

- Provide students with a sample informational paragraph and work with them to underline the subjects and verbs. Work with students to write sentences using correct subject-verb agreement. If necessary, have students dictate their sentences to you. **SUBSTANTIAL**
- Use sentence frames to help students practice subject-verb agreement. For example: *The woman _____ that animals have feelings*. **MODERATE**
- Have students work with a partner while writing their drafts, and ask them to check for subject-verb agreement. **LIGHT**

SPEAKING

Share Information

Tell students that one way to communicate the information in their essay is by using the sentence frame *I think _____* . Pair students with a partner. Circulate around the room to make sure students are using the sentence frame correctly.

Use the following supports with students at varying proficiency levels:

- Work with students to complete the sentence stem by identifying a key argument in their essays. Have them practice saying the sentence aloud to a partner. **SUBSTANTIAL**
- Have students build on the sentence stem by adding two pieces of text evidence from their essays. Allow them to present the information in the form of a conversation with a partner. **MODERATE**
- Have students build on the sentence stem by discussing three points that support their central idea. Then, have students practice their presentations with a partner. **LIGHT**

WRITING

WRITE AN ARGUMENT

Introduce students to the Writing Task by reading the introductory paragraph with them. Remind students to refer to the notes they recorded in the Unit 2 Response Log as they plan and draft their essays. The Response Log should contain ideas about seeing the world from the perspective of an animal. Drawing on these different ideas will make their own writing more interesting and well informed.

 For **writing support** for students at varying proficiency levels, see the **Language X-Ray** on page 160B.

USE THE MENTOR TEXTS

Point out that their argumentative essays will be similar to the arguments in "Wild Animals Aren't Pets" and "Let People Own Exotic Animals" in that they will present claims supported by logical reasons and relevant text evidence. However, their essays will be shorter than the articles and will only present one side of the topic.

WRITING PROMPT

Review the prompt with students. Encourage them to ask questions about any part of the assignment that is unclear. Make sure they understand that the purpose of their essay is to present a well-organized argument supported by reasons and evidence.

Write an Argument

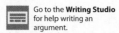 Go to the **Writing Studio** for help writing an argument.

This unit focuses on what we can learn by seeing the world through the eyes of animals. For this writing task, you will write an argumentative essay on a topic related to seeing the world from the perspective of an animal. For examples of arguments that you can use as mentor texts, review "Wild Animals Aren't Pets" and "Let People Own Exotic Animals."

As you write your argument, use the notes from your Response Log, which you filled out after reading the texts in this unit.

Writing Prompt

Read the information in the box below.

This is the topic or context for your argument.

> Considering a perspective other than your own can help you broaden your understanding of how the world works.

Think carefully about the following question.

This is the Essential Question for the unit. How would you answer this question, based on the texts in the unit?

> What can you learn by seeing the world through an animal's eyes?

Now mark the words that identify exactly what you are being asked to produce.

Write an argument defending your ideas about what you can learn by seeing the world from an animal's perspective.

Be sure to—

Review these points as you write and again when you finish. Make any needed changes.

- ❑ provide an introduction that clearly states your claim
- ❑ support your claim with logical reasons and relevant text evidence
- ❑ organize information with a purposeful structure
- ❑ use correct subject-verb agreement
- ❑ use persuasive language
- ❑ address counterarguments
- ❑ conclude by effectively summarizing your claim

160   Unit 2

 LEARNING MINDSET

Asking for Help   Ask students to ask peers and/or teachers for help. Explain that asking for help from others can help them get "unstuck" and move forward. Reinforce that asking for help does not equal failure. Rather, seeking help is a way of "trying smarter."

1 Plan

Before you start writing, plan your argument. Decide on a claim you will make about the topic. Your claim is the opinion, or stance, that you will take, support, and persuasively defend against counterarguments. In an argumentative essay, the claim is the thesis statement. First, write your claim. Then use the charts below to help you plan your argument. Next, consider how to effectively refute counterarguments.

My Claim: _____

_____

Reasons and Text Evidence
Reason: Evidence from text:
Reason: Evidence from text:
Reason: Evidence from text:

Opposing Claim	My Response

Background Reading Review the notes you have taken in your Response Log after reading the texts in this unit. These texts are the background reading that you will use to formulate the key ideas in your argument.

Go to **Writing Arguments: Building Effective Support** in the **Writing Studio** for help planning your argument.

Notice & Note

From Reading to Writing

As you plan your argument, apply what you've learned about signposts to your own writing. Remember that writers use common features, called signposts, to help convey their message to readers.

Think about how you can incorporate **Numbers and Stats** into your essay.

Use the notes from your Response Log as you plan your argument.

1 PLAN

Allow time for students to discuss the topic with partners or in small groups and then to complete the planning table independently.

■ English Learner Support

Understand Academic Language Make sure students understand words and phrases used in the chart, such as *claim, reasons,* and *text evidence.* Work with them to fill in the blank sections, providing text that they can copy into their charts as needed. **SUBSTANTIAL**

▶ NOTICE & NOTE

From Reading to Writing Remind students they can use **Numbers and Stats** to include statistics or present a comparison in order to support a point. Encourage students to make logical comparisons and double-check their research to make sure all numbers and statistics they include are accurate.

Background Reading As they plan their essays, remind students to refer to the notes they took in the Response Log. They may also review the selections to find additional text evidence to support ideas they want to include in their writing.

TO CHALLENGE STUDENTS . . .

Conduct Research Challenge students to incorporate facts and examples from well-known sources or scientists. They may start by thinking of sources or scientists they already know or have heard of that connect to the topic. If they cannot think of a source or scientist, they may search online or at the library. Encourage students to add evidence from the sources to support the argument they are making in their essay. Remind students to put any directly quoted information in quotation marks and to document their sources.

WRITING

Organize Your Ideas

Tell students that their outlines may have one main section for each paragraph of the essay. Provide the following sample based on the chart:

I. Introduction/Claim

II. First Reason and Evidence

III. Second Reason and Evidence

IV. Third Reason and Evidence

V. Counterarguments to Address

VI. Conclusion

Remind students that the claim should briefly mention the three reasons that support it. Each reason paragraph should build a logical argument that supports the claim with evidence. The counterargument paragraph should refute the main arguments opposing the claim. The conclusion should then briefly summarize the reasons and evidence without repeating what has already been said.

② DEVELOP A DRAFT

Remind students to follow their outlines as they draft their essays, but point out that they can still make changes to their writing plan during this stage. As they write, they may discover that they need different evidence to support a claim, or that a particular piece of evidence really belongs in a different paragraph.

■ English Learner Support

Use a Word Wall Allow students to use a word wall, dictionary, or other print resources when writing their essays. **MODERATE**

WRITING TASK

Go to **Writing Arguments: Creating a Coherent Argument** in the **Writing Studio** for help organizing your ideas.

Organize Your Ideas Part of planning is organizing the information you have gathered to draft your argument. How will you capture the reader's attention in your introduction? What is the best order to present your reasons? Which counterarguments will you refute? Use the chart below to make notes. An effective tactic is to lead and conclude with your strongest reasons and evidence; include one or two related reasons in between. Then, summarize your claim and reasons in a persuasive conclusion.

Organizing My Argument	
Introduction/Claim	
1st Reason and Evidence	
2nd Reason and Evidence	
3rd Reason and Evidence	
Counterarguments to Address	
Conclusion	

You might prefer to draft your essay online.

② Develop a Draft

Once you have completed your planning activities, you will be ready to begin drafting your argument. Refer to the planning work you did, as well as to any notes you took as you studied the texts in the unit. These will provide a kind of map for you to follow as you write. Using a word processor or online writing application makes it easier to make changes or move sentences around later, when you are ready to revise your first draft.

162   Unit 2

WHEN STUDENTS STRUGGLE . . .

Draft the Essay Remind students that a detailed outline will help make it easier to write their draft. Students can then put the notes from their outline into complete sentences to create the first draft of their essay. Remind students that a first draft is not meant to be perfect. At this stage, they are just getting their ideas down on paper (or on the computer screen). They will have time to revise and edit their writing later.

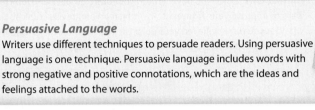

Use the Mentor Texts

Persuasive Language

Writers use different techniques to persuade readers. Using persuasive language is one technique. Persuasive language includes words with strong negative and positive connotations, which are the ideas and feelings attached to the words.

> Terry Thompson didn't represent the typical responsible owner. He had a criminal record and animal abuse charges. What Thompson did was selfish and insane; we cannot regulate insanity.

The writer of "Let People Own Exotic Animals" uses words with strong negative connotations, like "selfish" and "insane," to make her point that typical exotic animal owners are not like Terry Thompson.

Apply What You've Learned Review your argument for words that you can replace with persuasive language. Consider whether the words you choose have positive or negative connotations.

Author's Craft

Writers often build interest and show the importance of their topic with well-chosen references to familiar stories and events. By citing examples that are relevant to their claims, writers find common ground with their readers—an important step in the process of persuasion.

> But just as a 2007 raid on property owned by football star Michael Vick laid bare the little known and cruel world of dogfighting, a story that unfolded in a small Ohio city recently opened the public's eyes to the little known, distressing world of "exotic" pets.

The writer of "Wild Animals Aren't Pets" builds anticipation and foreshadows a similar sense of public outrage by referring to the 2007 Michael Vick dogfighting story.

Apply What You've Learned To help persuade your readers to agree with your claim, use the strategy of bringing up a well-known story that will influence their reaction to the evidence you cite.

Write an Argument 163

WHY THESE MENTOR TEXTS?

"Wild Animals Aren't Pets" and "Let People Own Exotic Animals" provide good examples of argumentative writing. Use the instruction below to help students use the mentor texts as a model for using persuasive language and for integrating relevant examples into their argumentative essays.

USE THE MENTOR TEXTS

Persuasive Language Ask a volunteer to read aloud the paragraph from "Let People Own Exotic Pets" on p. 163. Discuss which words have positive and negative connotations. Then invite students to offer examples of other words with positive and negative connotations that they could use in their essays.

Author's Craft To help students understand how examples can function in an essay, have them read the paragraph from "Wild Animals Aren't Pets" on p. 163. Point out that the author uses the example to create a common sense of outrage and find common ground with the reader. Once the reader and author find common ground, the reader is more likely to agree with the rest of the writer's argument.

 ENGLISH LEARNER SUPPORT

Use the Mentor Texts Use the following supports with students at varying proficiency levels:

- Write the opposite word pair *good* and *bad* on the board. Point out that the words are opposites. Use *good* and *bad* to explain the meaning of *positive* and *negative*. **SUBSTANTIAL**

- Have students work in small groups to read the mentor texts and identify words with positive and negative connotations. **MODERATE**

- Have students work in pairs to create word maps of words with positive and negative connotations. **LIGHT**

WRITING

③ REVISE

Have students answer each question in the chart to determine how they can improve their drafts. Invite volunteers to model their revision techniques.

With a Partner Have students ask peer reviewers to evaluate their supporting evidence by answering the following questions:

- How well does the evidence support the claims?
- What questions do you have about my claims?

Students should use the reviewer's feedback to add relevant facts, details, examples, and evidence that further support their claims.

 **WRITING TASK**

③ Revise

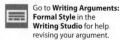 Go to **Writing Arguments: Formal Style** in the **Writing Studio** for help revising your argument.

On Your Own Once you have written your draft, go back and look for ways to improve your argument. As you reread and revise, think about whether you have achieved your purpose. The Revision Guide will help you focus on specific elements to make your writing stronger.

Revision Guide

Ask Yourself	Tips	Revision Techniques
1. Does my introduction create interest and clearly state a claim?	**Underline** the claim and **circle** the attention-getting opening.	**Add** a clear claim, and **add** a relevant attention-getting detail.
2. Are my reasons and evidence organized logically and linked with transitions?	**Underline** the reasons and text evidence. **Circle** transitional words and phrases.	**Reorder** reasons and evidence in a logical sequence, and **add** transitions to link reasons and evidence.
3. Are counterarguments expressed and addressed effectively?	**Mark** counterarguments and sentences that address or refute those views.	**Edit** sentences that refute a counterargument to clarify valid reasons.
4. Is there subject-verb agreement in my sentences?	**Underline** subjects and **circle** verbs.	**Replace** subjects and verbs that don't agree.
5. Do I use strong persuasive language?	**Mark** stated reasons and evidence.	**Add** persuasive language to emphasize points.
6. Does my conclusion summarize my claim?	**Mark** the conclusion.	**Add** a statement that summarizes the claim.

ACADEMIC VOCABULARY
As you conduct your **peer review,** be sure to use these words.

- ❏ benefit
- ❏ distinct
- ❏ environment
- ❏ illustrate
- ❏ respond

With a Partner Once you and your partner have worked through the Revision Guide on your own, exchange papers and evaluate each other's draft in a **peer review.** Focus on providing revision suggestions for at least three of the items mentioned in the chart. Explain why you think your partner's draft should be revised and what your specific suggestions are.

When receiving feedback from your partner, listen attentively and ask questions to make sure you fully understand the revision suggestions.

164   Unit 2

 ENGLISH LEARNER SUPPORT

Use Synonyms Explain that writers want to avoid using the same words repeatedly, even though they may often be referring to the same ideas. Have students read their essays and look for nouns, verbs, and adjectives that they use repeatedly. Then have students select the words that they use the most frequently and make a list of synonyms that they could use instead. Encourage students to revise their essays to incorporate the synonyms.
LIGHT

④ Edit

Once you have addressed the organization, development, and flow of ideas in your argument, you can work on improving the finer points of your draft. Edit for the proper use of standard English conventions and correct any misspellings or grammatical errors.

Language Conventions

Verb Tenses It's important to maintain consistency in verb tenses, both within a paragraph and across paragraphs. For example, if the beginning paragraph uses the present tense, the other paragraphs should, too.

Also, look for intervening phrases and clauses, and make sure that they do not affect subject-verb agreement in your sentences.

- An **intervening phrase** or **clause** is a group of words that comes between the subject and the verb.
- A singular subject should have a singular verb, and a plural subject should have a plural verb, even if there is an intervening phrase or clause between the subject and verb.

The chart contains examples of intervening phrases and clauses in sentences from "Wild Animals Aren't Pets."

> ! Go to **Subject-Verb Agreement** in the **Grammar Studio** to learn more.

Sentence	Intervening Phrase or Clause	Subject and Verb
A 2003 federal law, which forbids the interstate transport of certain big cats, has stopped much of the trade on the Internet, according to the Humane Society of the U.S.	which forbids the interstate transport of certain big cats	Subject: law [singular] Verb: has stopped [singular, present tense]
Only collectors who exhibit animals need a federal license.	who exhibit animals	Subject: collectors [plural] Verb: need [plural, present tense]

⑤ Publish

After you give your argument its finishing touches, choose a way to share it with your audience. Consider these options:

- Present your argument as a speech to the class.
- Post your argument as a blog on a classroom or school website.

④ EDIT

Suggest that students read their drafts aloud to assess how clearly and smoothly they have presented their ideas. If the text sounds disjointed, students should check that they have consistently used the same verb tense throughout their essay.

LANGUAGE CONVENTIONS

Verb Tenses Review the information about verb tenses with students. Then discuss the example sentences in the chart. Ask students to rewrite each sentence without the intervening phrase or clause. Read the revised sentences aloud so students can see and hear how the subject and verb agree. Have students look for intervening clauses in their essays. For each one, have students confirm that the subject and verb agree and that the verb uses the correct tense.

⑤ PUBLISH

Form small groups of students with arguments of varying opinions. Have students read each other's essays and then write a paragraph commenting on each essay. Remind students that their comments should address the content of the claims and evidence, not personally attack the writer or his/her opinion.

WHEN STUDENTS STRUGGLE...

Identify Subjects and Verbs Some students may have difficulty identifying the subjects and verbs in sentences. Remind students that a subject is what the sentence is discussing and the verb tells what the subject does. Allow students to use one color to circle the subjects in their sentences and another color to underline the verbs. Some students may benefit from working with a partner or adult helper to identify the subjects and verbs in their sentences.

WRITING

USE THE SCORING GUIDE

Have students read the scoring guide and ask questions about any words, phrases, or ideas that are unclear. Put students in groups of three. Then have students take turns reading the final drafts of their group members' argumentative essays. Ask them to score the essays using the scoring guide. Each student should write a paragraph explaining the reasons for the score he or she awarded in each category.

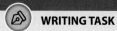 **WRITING TASK**

Use the scoring guide to evaluate your argument.

Writing Task Scoring Guide: Argument		
Organization/Progression	**Development of Ideas**	**Use of Language and Conventions**
4 • The introduction is highly engaging and clearly states a claim. • Reasons and evidence are well organized and persuasive. • The claim is well supported and summarized in the conclusion.	• Counterarguments are addressed and well refuted. • Coherence occurs within and across the paragraphs. • Transitions clearly show the relationship between ideas.	• Language and word choice are purposeful and persuasive. • Verb tenses are used consistently and appropriately. • Spelling, punctuation, grammar, usage, and mechanics are correct.
3 • The introduction is engaging and states a claim. • Reasons and evidence are organized and somewhat persuasive. • The claim is supported and summarized in the conclusion.	• Counterarguments are addressed and refuted. • Coherence occurs within and across most paragraphs. • Transitions show the relationship between ideas.	• Language and word choice are often purposeful and persuasive. • Most verb tenses are used consistently and correctly. • Some mistakes occur in spelling, punctuation, grammar, usage, or mechanics.
2 • The introduction has a topic but no clearly stated claim. • Reasons and evidence are disorganized and not persuasive. • The claim is not well supported or not addressed in the conclusion.	• Counterarguments are not addressed logically. • There is little coherence within and across paragraphs. • Transitions are ineffective or confusing.	• Language is often vague and too general. • Verb tenses are not always used consistently or correctly. • Spelling, punctuation, grammar, usage, and mechanics are often incorrect.
1 • The introduction does not include a claim. • Reasons and evidence are disorganized or missing. • The claim is not supported and the conclusion is missing.	• Counterarguments are not addressed. • The argument is incoherent. • Transitions are nonexistent or are unclear.	• Language is inappropriate for an argument. • Verb tenses are incorrect. • Language is vague and confusing. • Many errors occur in spelling, punctuation, grammar, mechanics, and usage.

Present an Argument

You will now adapt your argument to create a video presentation for your classmates. You will also listen to their presentations, ask questions to better understand their ideas, and help them improve their work.

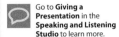

SPEAKING AND LISTENING TASK

Go to **Giving a Presentation** in the **Speaking and Listening Studio** to learn more.

① Adapt Your Argument for Presentation

Use the chart below to guide you as you create a script for a video "news editorial" based on your argument, with you as the speaker.

Presentation Planning Chart		
Title and Introduction	• How will you revise your title and introduction to capture the listener's attention? • Is there a way to state your claim aloud that is more engaging for video?	
Audience	• Who is your audience? What do you want them to understand? • Are your tone, word choices, and visual elements or graphics appropriate for persuading this audience?	
Effective Language and Organization	• Is your script logically organized? Is it interesting to listen to? Should parts be rearranged or excluded? • Where can you add evidence, persuasive language, or interesting examples to strengthen your argument? • Do you address a counterargument?	
Visuals	• What type of media or visual elements will you use? • What type of audio elements will you use? What text will appear on screen?	

Present an Argument 167

PRESENT AN ARGUMENT

Introduce students to the Speaking and Listening Task by discussing what makes an argument essay or speech different from an informational one. Point out that the reason for presenting an argument is to persuade the listener to agree with you. Thus, it is important to use persuasive language and a tone that will appeal to the audience. Have students consider how a speaker may need to adapt his or her language and tone to appeal to different audiences.

① ADAPT YOUR ESSAY FOR PRESENTATION

Have students read the questions in the chart. Then work with the class to list some general principles for adapting information for a script. (Examples: Use words that will appeal to the audience. Use examples the audience identifies with.) Point out that visuals, such as slides, can serve the same purpose as subheadings in a text. Students can use them to identify the reasons in their presentations for the audience.

For **speaking support** for students at varying proficiency levels, see the **Language X-Ray** on page 160B.

ENGLISH LEARNER SUPPORT

Adapt the Essay Use the following supports with students at varying proficiency levels:

- Help students identify several key sentences in their essays. Then have them identify visuals that illustrate these ideas. **SUBSTANTIAL**
- Review the questions in the chart to ensure students' understanding. Then have students work in pairs to apply the questions to their scripts. **MODERATE**
- Have students discuss the questions in the chart with partners before writing their scripts independently. **LIGHT**

SPEAKING AND LISTENING

② PRACTICE WITH A PARTNER OR GROUP

Review the information and tips with the class, ensuring that all the terms and ideas are clear. Remind students that the purpose of practicing their presentations is to gain useful feedback from their peers. Emphasize that speaking before a group makes most people nervous, and that everyone should be as supportive and helpful as possible.

③ DELIVER YOUR PRESENTATION

Set aside time for all students to give their presentations. When everyone has finished, ask students to share their thoughts on how their classmates' feedback helped them improve their performance.

 **SPEAKING AND LISTENING TASK**

As you work on improving your presentations, be sure to follow discussion rules:

- ❑ Listen closely to each other.
- ❑ Don't interrupt.
- ❑ Stay on topic.
- ❑ Ask only helpful, relevant questions.
- ❑ Provide clear, thoughtful, and direct responses.

② Practice with a Partner or Group

Once you've completed a first draft of your video script, practice with a partner or group to gather feedback and make improvements. Consider both verbal and nonverbal techniques while practicing your presentation and creating a draft recording.

Practice Your Presentation

- ❑ Begin with an attention-grabbing statement. Then, clearly state your argument's claim.
- ❑ Don't just read the script. Speak with enthusiasm and conviction.
- ❑ Replace words that you stumble over and rearrange sentences so that your delivery is smooth.
- ❑ Use your voice effectively, varying your pitch and tone. Pause now and then to let the audience consider important points.
- ❑ Avoid using slang. Use formal language that shows the importance of your topic and vocabulary that is persuasive.
- ❑ Look directly at the camera frequently to give the impression that you are directly addressing individuals in your audience.
- ❑ Use gestures and facial expressions to emphasize ideas and express emotion. Smile, frown, or raise an eyebrow to show your feelings or emphasize a point. Stay calm and relaxed.

Provide and Consider Advice for Improvement

As a listener, pay close attention. Take notes about ways that presenters can improve their presentations. Paraphrase each presenter's key ideas and main points to confirm your understanding, and ask questions to clarify any confusing ideas.

As a presenter, listen closely to questions and consider ways to revise your presentation to make sure your points are clear and logically sequenced. Remember to ask for suggestions about how you might change onscreen text, images, or audio to make your presentation more interesting and persuasive.

③ Deliver Your Presentation

Use the advice you received to make changes. Then, record a final version, and show it to your classmates.

WHEN STUDENTS STRUGGLE . . .

Paraphrase Ideas If students have difficulty paraphrasing the ideas in a presentation, have students only listen while the student is speaking. Tell students to listen for only the main claim made in the presentation. After each presentation, allow a few minutes for students to write a sentence or two summarizing the claim of the presentation.

Reflect on the Unit

By completing your argument, you have created a writing product that pulls together and expresses your thoughts about the reading you have done in this unit. Now is a good time to reflect on what you have learned.

Reflect on the Essential Question

- What can you learn by seeing the world through an animal's eyes? How has your answer to this question changed since you first considered it?

- What are some examples from the texts you've read that show what you can learn by seeing the world through an animal's eyes?

Reflect on Your Reading

- Which selections presented viewpoints with which you agreed or disagreed?

- If you were to recommend one selection to a friend, which would it be? Why?

Reflect on the Writing Task

- What was challenging about writing your argument? Based on your experience, how might you change the way you plan and organize your work the next time you write an essay?

- What were the hardest and easiest parts of writing a claim?

- What improvements did you make during revision? Why did you make them?

Reflect on the Speaking and Listening Task

- What changes did you make to adapt your essay to a video news editorial?

- What was challenging about video production? What did you enjoy about it?

UNIT 2 SELECTIONS
- *Pax*
- "Zoo"
- *Animal Snoops: The Wondrous World of Wildlife Spies*
- "Animal Wisdom"
- "The Last Wolf"
- "Wild Animals Aren't Pets"
- "Let People Own Exotic Animals"

REFLECT ON THE UNIT

Have students reflect on the questions independently and write some notes in response to each one. Then have students meet with partners or in small groups to discuss their reflections. Circulate during these discussions to identify the questions that are generating the liveliest conversations. Wrap up with a whole-class discussion focused on these questions.

 LEARNING MINDSET

Problem Solving Remind students that there are many different ways to solve problems. Sometimes it helps to change strategies, while at other times it is beneficial to ask for help. Everyone solves problems in his or her own way. Remind students that everyone runs into problems when learning something new. Every problem solved makes you smarter.

UNIT (3)

Instructional Overview and Resources

		Instructional Focus	**Online Resources**
	**Unit Introduction** **Surviving the Unthinkable**	Unit 3 Essential Question Unit 3 Academic Vocabulary	**Stream to Start:** Surviving the Unthinkable **Unit 3 Response Log**

ANALYZE & APPLY

	from *A Long Walk to Water* Novel by Linda Sue Park Lexile 560L **NOTICE & NOTE** READING MODEL **Signposts** • Tough Questions • Again and Again • Aha Moment	**Reading** • Analyze Setting and Character • Monitor Comprehension **Writing:** Write an Informational Essay **Speaking and Listening:** Discuss with a Small Group **Vocabulary:** Vocabulary Resources **Language Conventions:** Prepositions and Prepositional Phrases	🔊 **Audio** **Reading Studio:** Notice & Note **Level-Up Tutorial:** Making Inferences **Writing Studio:** Writing Informative Texts **Speaking and Listening Studio:** Participating in Collaborative Discussions **Vocabulary Studio:** Vocabulary Resources **Grammar Studio:** Module 3: Lesson 6: The Preposition, Lesson 7: Prepositional Phrases
	Salva's Story Documentary by POVRoseMedia	**Reading** • Analyze Characteristics of Digital Text **Writing:** Write a Summary **Speaking and Listening:** Analyze and Evaluate the Video	**Writing Studio:** Summarizing, Paraphrasing, and Quoting **Speaking and Listening Studio:** Participating in Collaborative Discussions
	Mentor Text **"Into the Lifeboat" from *Titanic Survivor*** Memoir by Violet Jessop Lexile 950L	**Reading** • Explain Author's Purpose & Message • Create Mental Images **Writing:** Write a Friendly Letter **Speaking and Listening:** Create a Multimedia Presentation **Vocabulary:** Context Clues **Language Conventions:** Commas	🔊 **Audio** **Text in Focus:** Analyzing Comparisons and Contrasts **Reading Studio:** Notice & Note **Level-Up Tutorial:** Author's Purpose **Writing Studio:** Task, Purpose, and Audience **Speaking and Listening Studio:** Using Media in a Presentation **Vocabulary Studio:** Context Clues **Grammar Studio:** Module 12: Lesson 2–5: Using Commas Correctly

SUGGESTED PACING: **30 DAYS**	Unit Introduction	A Long Walk to Water					Salva's Story		Into the Lifeboat *from* Titanic Survivor						
	1	2	3	4	5	6	7	8	9	10	11	12	13	14	15	16

English Learner Support	Differentiated Instruction	Online Ed Assessment
• Use Word Parts • Use Learning Strategies		

English Learner Support	Differentiated Instruction	Assessment
• Text X-Ray • Use Cognates • Use Visual Supports • Use Visual Support • Oral Assessment • Discuss with a Small Group • Vocabulary Strategy • Language Conventions	**When Students Struggle** • Focus on the Character • Monitor Comprehension **To Challenge Students** • Identify Mood	Selection Test
• Text X-Ray • Use Prereading Supports • Use Support to Enhance Understanding • Oral Assessment	**When Students Struggle** • Analyze Media	Selection Test
• Text X-Ray • Use Cognates • Demonstrate Comprehension • Explain Author's Message • Oral Assessment • Support Language Transfer • Support Language Transfer	**When Students Struggle** • Explain Author's Message • Language Conventions: Commas	Selection Test

from **After the Hurricane**/*from* **Ninth Ward**   **Independent Reading**   **End of Unit**

17 | 18 | 19 | 20 | 21 | 22 | 23 | 24 | 25 | 26 | 27 | 28 | 29 | 30

UNIT 3 Continued

Instructional Focus

COLLABORATE & COMPARE

from "After the Hurricane"
Poem by Rita Williams-Garcia

Reading
• Analyze the Effects of Structure and Meter
• Describe an Author's Use of Figurative Language

Writing: Write a Poem

Speaking and Listening: Poetry Jam

🔊 **Audio**

Close Read Screencasts: Modeled Discussions

Reading Studio: Notice & Note

Level-Up Tutorial: Narrative Poetry

Writing Studio: Writing Narratives

Speaking and Listening Studio: Participating in Collaborative Discussions

from Ninth Ward
Novel by Jewell Parker Rhodes
Lexile 570L

Reading
• Analyze Historical and Cultural Setting
• Analyze Author's Use of Language

Writing: Write Live Posts

Speaking and Listening: Create a Poster

Vocabulary: Use Context Clues

Language Conventions: Pronouns

🔊 **Audio**

Reading Studio: Notice & Note

Level-Up Tutorial: Setting and Mood

Writing Studio: The Language of Narrative

Speaking and Listening Studio: Giving a Presentation

Vocabulary Studio: Using Context Clues

Grammar Studio: Module 2: Lesson 2: Pronouns

Collaborate and Compare

Reading: Compare Texts

Speaking and Listening: Research and Share

The independent Reading selections are only available in the eBook.

 Go to the Reading Studio for more information on **Notice & Note.**

"Watcher: After Katrina, 2005"
Poem by Natasha D. Trethewey

"The Day I Didn't Go to the Pool"
Short Story by Leslie J. Wyatt
Lexile 790L

END OF UNIT

Writing Task: Nonfiction Narrative

Reflect on the Unit

Writing: Write a Nonfiction Narrative

Language Conventions: Consistent Verb Tense

Unit 3 Response Log

Reading Studio: Notice & Note

Writing Studio: Writing Narratives

Grammar Studio: Module 7: Using Verbs Correctly

English Learner Support	Differentiated Instruction	Online **Ed** Assessment
• Text X-Ray • Understand Structure • Understand Repetition • Enhance Understanding • Provide Visual Support • Learn Language Structures • Oral Assessment • Speak Lines of Poetry	**To Challenge Students** • Analyze Speaker **When Students Struggle** • Genre Reformulation	**Selection Test**
• Text X-Ray • Use Word Families • Demonstrate Comprehension • Understand Aha Moments • Oral Assessment • Use Context Clues • Language Conventions	**When Students Struggle** • Analyze Author's Use of Language	**Selection Test**
• Expand Reading Skills • Present Your Guidelines		

"Tuesday of the Other June" Short Story by Norma Fox Mazer **Lexile 570L**	"In the Event of Moon Disaster" Speech by Bill Safire **Lexile 900L**	"Ready: Preparing Your Pets for Emergencies Makes Sense" Informational Text **Lexile 1070L**	**Selection Tests**

English Learner Support	Differentiated Instruction	Assessment
• Language X-Ray • Understand Academic Language • Use the Mentor Text • Use Signal Words • Use Consistent Verb Tense	**When Students Struggle** • Draft the Narrative • Identify Verbs **To Challenge Students** • Create a Multimedia Presentation	**Unit Test**

SURVIVING THE UNTHINKABLE

ESSENTIAL QUESTION:

What does it take to be a survivor?

? Connect to the *ESSENTIAL QUESTION*

Ask a volunteer to read aloud the Essential Question. Discuss with students how that question might apply to their own lives. Are there certain character traits that help people survive? Courage? Intelligence? Kindness? Loyalty?

■ English Learner Support

Use Word Parts Point out to students that the name of this unit is "Surviving the Unthinkable." Focus on the word *unthinkable,* and show students how they can guess the meaning of the word by looking at its parts.

un–think–able

The base word is *think*, and students should be familiar with that word. Explain that the suffix *-able* means "able to do or able to be done." So *thinkable* means "able to be thought about." But *un-* is a negative prefix. So *unthinkable* means "not able to be thought about." In other words, the unit is about surviving things that are so terrible they can't even be thought about or imagined. **ALL LEVELS**

DISCUSS THE QUOTATION

Robert Fulghum is a best-selling author and a Unitarian Universalist minister. He has also been a cowboy, an artist, and a teacher of painting and drawing. His first book, a collection of essays called *All I Really Need To Know I Learned in Kindergarten*, made the *New York Times* best-seller list and stayed there for two years. The title essay proposed the theory that the world would be a better place if people followed the rules about kindness and sharing that they were taught in kindergarten. The quotation is from that book and refers to all living beings, not just people.

Through every kind of disaster and setback and catastrophe. We are survivors. 〞

Robert Fulghum

170   Unit 3

⚙ LEARNING MINDSET

Setting Goals Explain that having a growth and learning mindset means setting goals. That involves setting goals to try new things and not being afraid to set goals that you might, at first, fail to achieve. Emphasize that trying hard is important, but setting goals to try and achieve things that are hard is just as important. The brain needs to be stretched and challenged in much the same way as the muscles need to be challenged. So set goals that challenge you to stretch to achieve new things.

ACADEMIC VOCABULARY

Academic Vocabulary words are words you use when you discuss and write about texts. In this unit, you will practice and learn five words.

☑ circumstance ☐ constraint ☐ impact ☐ injure ☐ significant

Study the Word Network to learn more about the word **circumstance**.

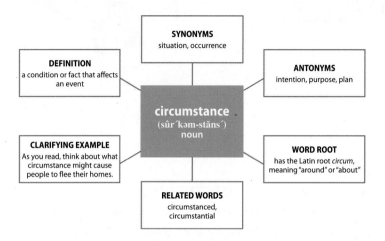

Write and Discuss Discuss the completed Word Network with a partner, making sure to talk through all of the boxes until you both understand the word, its synonyms, antonyms, and related forms. Then, fill out Word Networks for the remaining four words. Use a dictionary or online resource to help you complete the activity.

 Go online to access the Word Networks.

RESPOND TO THE ESSENTIAL QUESTION

In this unit, you will read about people who overcome great obstacles to survive truly difficult situations. As you read, you will revisit the **Essential Question** and gather your ideas about it in the **Response Log** that appears on page R3. At the end of the unit, you will have the opportunity to write your own **nonfiction narrative** about an event in your life or the life of someone you know that shows what it takes to be a survivor. Filling out the Response Log will help you prepare for this writing task.

 You can also go online to access the Response Log.

ACADEMIC VOCABULARY

As students complete Word Networks for the remaining four vocabulary words, encourage them to include all the categories shown in the completed network if possible, but point out that some words do not have clear synonyms or antonyms. Some words may also function as different parts of speech—for example, *impact* may be a noun or a verb.

circumstance (sûr´kəm-stăns´) *n.* A condition, or set of conditions, that affects an event.

constraint (kən-strānt´) *n.* Limitation.

impact (ĭm´păkt´) *n.* An influence or effect. (Spanish cognate: *impacto*)

injure (ĭn´jər) *tr. v.* To harm or cause damage to.

significant (sĭg-nĭf´ĭ-kənt) *adj.* Important. (Spanish cognate: *significativo*)

RESPOND TO THE ESSENTIAL QUESTION

Direct students to the Unit 3 Response Log. Explain that students will use it to record ideas and details from the selections that help answer the Essential Question. When they work on the writing task at the end of the unit, their Response Logs will help them think about what they have read and make connections between texts.

ENGLISH LEARNER SUPPORT

Use Learning Strategies As students read the selections in this unit, help them focus on a character and the traits that character reveals:

- Have students create a cluster diagram with the name of the character in the center. As they read, have them make notes in the diagram of things they learn about the character.
- Suggest that students fill in the diagram with things the character says or thinks, details about the character's life and appearance, and anything else students find important.

- Explain to students that characters may change from the beginning of a story to the end. They should not go back and change the notes in their diagram if the character changes. They should make a new note and draw a line to link it to the earlier note about the character.
- At the end of the story, have students compare their diagrams with a partner and use them to begin a conversation. **ALL LEVELS**

READING MODEL

from A LONG WALK TO WATER

Novel by Linda Sue Park

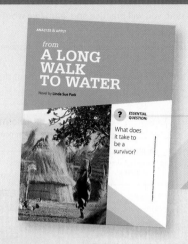

GENRE ELEMENTS
NOVEL

Remind students that the purpose of a **novel** is to entertain, inspire, and, sometimes, to inform. A novel is a long work of fiction. Like a short story, a novel is essentially the product of a writer's imagination, but a **historical novel** is based on actual events and people. Because a novel is much longer than a short story, a novelist can develop a wider range of characters and a more complex plot. Point out that this selection is an excerpt from a novel and focuses on only one part of the plot of the novel as a whole.

LEARNING OBJECTIVES

- Monitor comprehension of text and make adjustments.
- Analyze the characters and setting of a novel excerpt.
- Research the organization Water for South Sudan.
- Write an informative essay about setting and character.
- Use both print and digital vocabulary resources.
- Understand and use prepositional phrases.
- Understand and use subject/verb agreement.
- Discuss in a group character traits of a survivor.
- **Language** Discuss with a partner challenges faced by Salva using the term *setting*.

TEXT COMPLEXITY

Quantitative Measures	A Long Walk to Water	Lexile: 560L
Qualitative Measures	**Ideas Presented** Much is explicit, but some inferential reasoning required.	
	Structure Used Clear, chronological, conventional.	
	Language Used Explicit, literal, contemporary, familiar language.	
	Knowledge Required Cultural, historical references may make heavier demands.	

RESOURCES

- Unit 3 Response Log
- Selection Audio
- Reading Studio: Notice & Note
- Level Up Tutorial: Making Inferences
- Writing Studio: Writing Informative Texts
- Speaking and Listening Studio: Participating in Collaborative Discussions
- Vocabulary Studio: Vocabulary Resources
- Grammar Studio: Module 3: Lesson 6: The Preposition, Lesson 7: Prepositional Phrases
- A Long Walk to Water Selection Test

SUMMARIES

English

When his village in southern Sudan is bombed, Salva escapes, first running and then walking. He joins up with others who are fleeing the war between government and rebel forces, and they encounter a group of rebels. The rebels force men and teenaged boys to join them, and eleven-year-old Salva is left with the women and children. They spend the night in a barn, but when Salva wakes up, he is alone. He has been left behind.

Spanish

Cuando su aldea en Sudán del Sur es bombardeada, Salva escapa, primero corriendo y luego caminando. Se junta con otros que huyen de la guerra entre el gobierno y las fuerzas rebeldes, y encuentran un grupo de rebeldes. Los rebeldes obligan a los hombres y a los adolescentes a unírseles y a Salva, que tiene once años, lo dejan con una mujer y sus hijos. Pasan la noche en un establo, pero cuando Salva despierta, está solo. Lo han dejado atrás.

SMALL-GROUP OPTIONS

Have students work in small groups to read and discuss the selection.

Numbered Heads Together

- Form groups of four students and then number off 1 – 2 – 3 – 4 within the group.
- Ask students, *What do you think is the most difficult thing for Salva to deal with as he tries to survive?*
- Have students discuss their responses in their groups.
- Call a number from 1 to 4. That "numbered" student will then respond for the group.
- If you like, groups may adopt names, such as "Wildcats," to identify their groups. You will then call on Wildcat number 4.

Send a Problem

- Pose a question about the ideas or actions described in *A Long Walk to Water*. Call on a student to respond.
- Wait up to 11 seconds.
- If the student does not have a response, the student must call on another student by name to answer the same question.
- The sending student repeats the question as he or she calls on another for assistance.
- Monitor responses and can redirect or ask another question at any time.

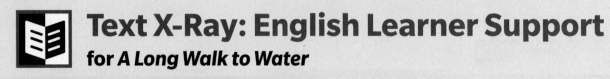

Text X-Ray: English Learner Support
for *A Long Walk to Water*

Use the Text X-Ray and the supports and scaffolds in the Teacher's Edition to help guide students at different proficiency levels through the selection.

INTRODUCE THE SELECTION
DISCUSS TOUGH QUESTIONS

In this lesson, students will need to be able to discuss the tough questions that a survivor faces. Preview by reading paragraph 7 with students and point out the questions Salva asks himself. Provide a basic definition of survival, obstacles to survival, and survival skills.

- *Survival* means staying alive even when there are dangers facing you.
- *Obstacles* to survival are the things that get in the way of your survival—the problems you face.
- *Survival skills* are what you know and what you are able to do to help you survive.

Have students discuss how the questions Salva asks himself relate to his survival.

CULTURAL REFERENCES

The following words and phrases may be unfamiliar to students:

- *the school village* (paragraph 6): the small town where Salva's school was located
- *too dark to see the path* (paragraph 8): the area where Salva is walking consists mainly of grasslands, with dirt paths and roads
- *rebel camp* (paragraph 18): a place where the soldiers fighting against the government live and hold prisoners temporarily

LISTENING

Understand Descriptive Language

Draw students' attention to the descriptive language that the author uses to bring color and life to the story of Salva's journey. Use vocal expression to help communicate the meanings of descriptive and figurative phrases in the text.

Have students listen as you read aloud paragraph 2. Use the following supports with students at varying proficiency levels:

- Make correct and incorrect statements about the paragraph, and have students agree or disagree with a thumbs up or down. For example: *A bomb made the "Boom!" that starts this story.* (*true*) *The loud "BOOM" made Salva feel safe.* (*false*) **SUBSTANTIAL**
- Have students follow along as you read aloud, and mark with a pencil or highlighter words they find vivid and descriptive. Have students share what they marked. **MODERATE**
- Have pairs of students work together to mark the descriptive details in the paragraph, then use their markings to take turns reading the paragraph expressively. **LIGHT**

SPEAKING

Discuss the Setting

Draw students' attention to the setting of the novel, in terms of both place and point in history. Using the term *setting*, discuss how it affects the main character's survival challenges.

Use the following supports with students at varying proficiency levels. Encourage students to use the term *setting* in their responses.

- Tell students that you will ask questions about the setting of the story. Provide these sentence frames: *Salva lives in _____. This setting is dangerous because _____.* **SUBSTANTIAL**
- Have students identify the setting of the story. Ask: *Where is Salva? What is happening that makes this a dangerous setting? (South Sudan, civil war)* **MODERATE**
- Pair students to discuss the challenges of the setting of the story. Ask: *What aspects of the setting make Salva's survival more difficult? (The setting is hot and isolated, with risks from wild animals. The civil war presents dangers from the warring forces.)* **LIGHT**

READING

Analyze a Character

Draw students' attention to the character of Salva and how the author helps us understand what kind of person he is through description, dialogue, and Salva's actions.

Work with students to read paragraphs 19–30. Use the following supports with students at varying proficiency levels:

- Tell students to read for details the author gives about Salva's family. Ask: *Is Salva's family important in the village? Who was the village named for? (yes, Salva's grandfather)* **SUBSTANTIAL**
- Pair students to find details about Salva and his family. Use sentence frames to help students share these with a partner: *Salva is _____ years old. His family is _____ in the village.* **MODERATE**
- Pair students to find two pieces of information about Salva and his family. Have them share these details with a partner. *(For example: Salva is eleven and the son of an important family in his village).* **LIGHT**

WRITING

Write an Informational Essay

Introduce the writing assignment on page 185. Explain to students the importance of writing clear, grammatically correct sentences to state and support their thesis in an informational essay.

Use the following supports with students at varying proficiency levels:

- Work with students to fill in a cause-and-effect diagram about the setting of the story and Salva's character and personality. Then write a thesis statement based on the diagram and have students copy it in their notebooks. **SUBSTANTIAL**
- Have groups of students discuss the setting of the story and how it affected Salva's ability to survive. Then ask them to complete this thesis statement. *Salva's background helped prepare him to _____. (survive, be a survivor, meet challenges)* **MODERATE**
- Have pairs of students discuss the setting of the story and how it affected Salva's ability to survive. Then ask each student to write a thesis statement. Pairs should trade statements and make suggestions for improvement. **LIGHT**

EXPLAIN THE SIGNPOSTS

Explain that **NOTICE & NOTE Signposts** are significant moments in the text that help readers understand and analyze works of fiction or nonfiction. Use the instruction on these pages to introduce students to the signposts **Tough Questions, Again and Again,** and **Aha Moment.** Then use the selection that follows to have students apply the signposts to a text.

For a full list of the fiction and nonfiction signposts, see p. 234.

For a full list of the fiction and nonfiction signposts, see p. 234.

▶ TOUGH QUESTIONS

Explain that **Tough Questions** are among the signposts that students may encounter when reading fiction. These are questions that a character raises when she is dealing with an **internal conflict.** Sometimes they are clearly phrased as questions, and sometimes they are sentences that express confusion or lack of understanding. "I couldn't image how I could . . ." might be a Tough Question.

In this excerpt from *A Long Walk to Water*, the main character asks himself questions that refer both to his internal conflict and to the **external conflict** between himself and his circumstances. In both cases, the questions express his feelings of loss and confusion.

Tell students that when they spot a Tough Question, they should pause, mark it in their consumable texts, and ask the anchor question: *What does this make me wonder about?*

READING MODEL

  For more information on these and other signposts to Notice & Note, visit the **Reading Studio.**

When you read and encounter an expression of doubt like these, pause to see if it's a **Tough Questions** signpost:

I couldn't understand how this happened . . .

I couldn't imagine why she . . .

It was so confusing . . .

from A LONG WALK TO WATER

You are about to read an excerpt from the novel *A Long Walk to Water*. In the excerpt, you will notice and note signposts that give you clues about the novel's characters and themes. Here are three key signposts to look for as you read this excerpt and other works of fiction.

▶ **Tough Questions** *Why didn't I stick up for my friend? Why did I pass up that opportunity? Whom should I turn to for advice?* Sometimes the most difficult questions we ask ourselves have answers that are hard for us to accept. In a work of fiction, a setting or set of extreme circumstances may force a character to ask Tough Questions.

When a character expresses doubt and confusion about an issue, it's usually for a good reason. Paying attention to **Tough Questions** can:

- reveal a character's internal conflict
- offer insight into the theme of the work
- help you, the reader, think about the answers to the questions
- show how the author develops the character

Here's an example of a student finding and marking a pair of Tough Questions asked by Salva Dut, the main character in *A Long Walk to Water*:

Anchor Question
When you notice this signpost, ask: What does this make me wonder about?

> 16   Some of the rebels then joined the back of the line; now the villagers were surrounded.
>
> 17   *What are they going to do to us? Where is my family?*

What Tough Questions are asked?	What are they going to do to us? Where is my family?
What doubt or confusion do the questions convey?	Salva feels confused about what the rebels may want, and he has doubts about his own safety.

Again and Again When an author repeats words, images, or events throughout a literary work, he or she is calling attention to elements important to understanding the text. **Again and Again** signposts can help the reader understand plot, setting, symbolism, theme, character development, and conflict.

When you notice a recurring word, phrase, image, or event, think about what it means. In this part of *A Long Walk to Water*, a student has underlined an example of Again and Again:

> 5   He ran until he could not run anymore. Then he walked. For hours, until the sun was nearly gone from the sky.
>
> 6   Other people were walking, too.

Anchor Question
When you notice this signpost, ask: Why might the author keep bringing this up?

What words or images are used repeatedly?	The text repeats words and images related to running and walking.
Why do you think the author repeats these words and images?	The repetition shows something about Salva's character; he runs until he's exhausted, so he begins walking for hours. He refuses to give up.

Aha Moment During certain points in a work of fiction, a character may come to a sudden realization that changes his understanding of himself, others, and the world around him.

A character experiencing an **Aha Moment** may:

- suddenly understand something
- discover a way to solve a problem
- reach a broader understanding about life

Aha Moments help further the plot and help develop characters. In this example, an Aha Moment is underlined:

When you see a phrase like one of these, pause to see if it's an **Aha Moment**:

That's when I knew . . .

Finally, I understood . . .

Everything was clear . . .

I realized . . .

All of a sudden . . .

> 3   In the smoke and dust, he couldn't see the school building anymore. He tripped and almost fell. No more looking back; it slowed him down.

Anchor Question
When you notice this signpost, ask: How might this change things?

What realization does Salva have?	He can't look back any more. Looking back slows him down and may cost him his life.
What might this realization reveal about Salva's character?	Salva may have to give up his old life. He may be facing a dramatic change in his life, testing his character.

Notice & Note   **173**

WHEN STUDENTS STRUGGLE . . .

Focus on the Character If students struggle with recognizing an Aha Moment, suggest that they focus on the main character, ignoring for the moment everything else in the story. An Aha Moment always involves something that a character in the story realizes—usually the main character. Have students look at what the character is like at the beginning of the story and watch his or her thoughts and feelings for a change.

AGAIN AND AGAIN

Point out that, sometimes, events, images, or even particular words appear more than once—or **Again and Again**— in a short story or part of a novel. When this **repetition** happens, the author is usually trying to bring a certain element of the story to the reader's attention.

The example here is one where certain words are repeated in the space of a few sentences. The same things happens again in paragraphs 22–30 with the words *gun* and *barrel*, reinforcing the danger the soldiers represent and the fear Salva experiences.

Tell students that when they spot an Again and Again, they should pause, mark it in their consumable text, and ask themselves the anchor question: *Why might the author keep bringing this up?*

AHA MOMENT

Explain that **Aha Moments** almost always reveal a change in a character. A **dynamic character**, one who undergoes important changes as the plot unfolds, has at least one such moment in a story.

Read aloud the example passage and pause at the underlined text. These words show that Salva has come to a realization that will guide him through the rest of his journey. Ask students to consider how important this moment may be and what it refers to beyond the simple act of running.

Explain to students that, when they spot an Aha Moment, they should pause, mark it in their consumable texts, and ask themselves the anchor question: *How might this change things?*

APPLY THE SIGNPOSTS

Have students use the selection that follows as a model text to apply the signposts. As students encounter signposts, prompt them to stop, reread, and ask themselves the anchor questions that will help them understand the story's themes and characters.

Tell students to continue to look for these and other signposts as they read the other selections in the unit.

Connect to the
ESSENTIAL QUESTION

This excerpt from the novel *A Long Walk to Water* looks at one survivor of a country at war, the challenges he faces, and the kind of person he will need to be to meet those challenges.

ANALYZE & APPLY

from
A LONG WALK TO WATER

Novel by **Linda Sue Park**

ESSENTIAL QUESTION:

What does it take to be a survivor?

LEARNING MINDSET

Curiosity   Reinforce that being curious is the beginning of the learning process. Curious learners are constantly wondering about what they read and experience. They ask questions and are open to new ideas and trying new things. Suggest that students think about how schoolwork can help outside of class. Explain that they can use reading to explore interests. Ask, *What do you want to learn about?* Encourage them to set a purpose for themselves in reading and writing.

QUICK START

How would you feel if you had to leave your home, family, and community without any warning? What might you miss the most? Discuss your thoughts with a partner.

ANALYZE SETTING AND CHARACTER

A **character** is a person, animal, or imaginary creature who takes part in the action of a work of literature. In realistic fiction, characters—like real people—have personalities and motivations; they experience life-changing events. The **setting,** or the time and place in which the action occurs, influences the development of the characters. Elements of setting include geographic location, historical period, season, time of day, and culture.

- To understand historical setting, find the setting's geographic location on a map, and read to learn about the time period.

- To analyze character, annotate and compare passages that describe the character's thoughts or actions at the beginning, middle, and end of the work.

- To understand how setting affects character, note how characters respond to historical and cultural events.

MONITOR COMPREHENSION

Readers sometimes finish a section of text without fully understanding it. Perhaps your attention drifted while reading, or you hurried through a key passage too quickly. When you **monitor comprehension,** you use different strategies to check your understanding as you read. If you are confused after reading a passage, use any of the techniques below to help you understand the text.

MONITORING STRATEGY	BENEFIT
Question	Develop and ask questions as you read to clarify understanding.
Connect	Use background knowledge to connect with the text, including any background information provided with the selection.
Reread	Reread passages you don't understand—even out loud or extra slowly—to aid comprehension.
Annotate	Mark specific words that will help you understand plot, conflict, character development, and other elements of fiction.

GENRE ELEMENTS: HISTORICAL FICTION

- has the basic features of fiction, including plot, characters, conflict, setting, and theme
- is set in the past and includes real places and real events of historical importance
- may be based on actual people who lived during the work's historical and cultural setting and who dealt with the setting's challenges in remarkable ways

A Long Walk to Water   175

QUICK START

If students have trouble imagining a situation in which they might have to leave their home and family, suggest a natural disaster—flooding, for example—in which they are separated from the rest of their family and taken to a temporary shelter.

ANALYZE SETTING AND CHARACTER

Help students think about the character of Salva by suggesting they take notes about his traits, asking themselves these questions.

- How old is Salva?
- What does he usually do?
- How does Salva react to events?
- What emotions does Salva experience?

Help students think about the setting of the story by discussing what South Sudan is like. Help students answer these questions:

- Is Salva in a city or in the countryside?
- What kind of land is in South Sudan, where Salva is?
- Is it hot or cold, wet or dry in the area?
- What is happening in the area that causes Salva's flight?

MONITOR COMPREHENSION

Explain to students that good readers monitor comprehension all the time, even when they don't realize they're doing it. The more students practice monitoring strategies, the more natural they will become.

TEACH

CRITICAL VOCABULARY

Encourage students to think carefully about the meaning of each vocabulary word before completing the sentence. Remind them to include context clues that reveal the meaning of each word.

Possible answers:

1. *there was an earthquake*

2. *they're not comfortable in water*

3. *it hears a cat*

4. *heavy packs full of water and food*

5. *try to get it back on course*

■ English Learner Support

Use Cognates These Critical Vocabulary words have Spanish cognates: *hesitate/hesitar, collapse/colapso.*
ALL LEVELS

LANGUAGE CONVENTIONS

Review the information about prepositions and prepositional phrases. Emphasize the relational nature of prepositions by holding an object and asking questions about how it relates to other objects in the room. Point out prepositions in the answers.

ANNOTATION MODEL

Remind students of the annotation ideas in Notice & Note on pages 172 and 173, which suggest underlining important details and circling words that signal how the text is organized. Point out that they may follow this suggestion or use their own system for marking up the selection in their write-in text. They may want to color-code their annotations by using highlighters. Their notes in the margin may include questions about ideas that are unclear or topics they want to learn more about.

CRITICAL VOCABULARY

veer   hesitate   collapse   scurry   shoulder

See which Critical Vocabulary words you already know. Complete each sentence in a way that shows the meaning of the vocabulary word.

1. A building might **collapse** if _____.

2. Someone might **hesitate** to join a swim team because _____.

3. A mouse may **scurry** when _____.

4. When hiking, travelers might **shoulder** _____.

5. If you were riding a bicycle that began to **veer,** you might _____.

LANGUAGE CONVENTIONS

Prepositions and Prepositional Phrases A **preposition** is a word that relates one word to another word. The words *around, at, by, for, from, in, of, over, to, under,* and *with* are examples of prepositions. Prepositions are useful for expressing where, when, and how words and ideas relate to one another.

> Salva hestitated <u>for</u> a moment.
> Salva took a few steps <u>toward</u> the men.

A **prepositional phrase** consists of a preposition, its object, and any modifiers of the object.

> The soldier was holding the gun <u>with only one hand.</u>

As you read, look for prepositions and prepositional phrases.

ANNOTATION MODEL   **NOTICE & NOTE**

As you read, notice and note signposts, including **Tough Questions, Again and Again,** and **Aha Moments.** In the model, you can see how one reader responds to *A Long Walk to Water.*

1   *BOOM!*

2   Salva turned and looked. Behind him, <u>a huge black cloud of smoke rose. Flames darted out of its base.</u> Overhead, <u>a jet plane veered</u> away like a sleek evil bird.

3   In the <u>smoke and dust,</u> he couldn't see the school building anymore.

Where is the sound coming from?

Repeated images describe an explosion. The details are related to violence, and the jet suggests that this may be a wartime bombing.

BACKGROUND

Linda Sue Park (b. 1960) *has written several books for young people.*
A Long Walk to Water is historical fiction based on the story of Salva
Dut, who fled his home in Sudan in 1985 during a civil war. He,
like many boys, was separated from his family. Eventually,
he found refuge in the United States and later returned
to what is now the country of South Sudan. To aid the
people of his homeland, he formed an organization
that drills wells, which provide clean water.

from
A LONG WALK TO WATER

Novel by Linda Sue Park

SETTING A PURPOSE

War and violence can lead to anxiety, panic, and confusion. As you
read, consider how the main character, Salva, is affected by the
wartime setting.

1 **B**^{OOM!}

2   Salva turned and looked. Behind him, a huge black cloud of smoke rose. Flames darted out of its base. Overhead, a jet plane **veered** away like a sleek evil bird.

3   In the smoke and dust, he couldn't see the school building anymore. He tripped and almost fell. No more looking back; it slowed him down.

4   Salva lowered his head and ran.

5   He ran until he could not run anymore. Then he walked. For hours, until the sun was nearly gone from the sky.

6   Other people were walking, too. There were so many of them that they couldn't all be from the school village; they must have come from the whole area.

Notice & Note

Use the side margins to notice and note signposts in the text.

veer
(vîr) *v.* Something that can *veer* will swerve, or suddenly change course or direction.

A Long Walk to Water   **177**

ENGLISH LEARNER SUPPORT

Use Visual Supports Point out to students that paragraphs 1–4 use vivid descriptions to create the setting of the story. Have students look at the photos included in the selection, and point out details of setting. Show students additional photos of a cloud of smoke, fire, and a jet plane to help them visualize the beginning of the selection. **SUBSTANTIAL/MODERATE**

BACKGROUND

The main character of this story lives in an area of Africa that is mainly clay plains. The year is divided into wet and dry. When the rain is falling, the plains are grasslands, dotted with trees and providing food and water for animals. During the dry season, the grass dries up, along with streams and ponds, and life becomes very hard.

SETTING A PURPOSE

Direct students to use the Setting a Purpose prompt to focus their reading.

For **listening and speaking support** for students at varying proficiency levels, see the **Text X-Rays** on pages 172C and 172D.

CRITICAL VOCABULARY

veer: The plane turned very suddenly before flying away.

ASK STUDENTS why turning suddenly made the plane look like a bird. *(When birds fly, they swoop and turn, and move very quickly and easily.)*

A Long Walk to Water   **177**

TOUGH QUESTIONS

Remind students that the conflict in a story can be between the protagonist and some outside force, or it can be within the person himself. In that case, it is called **internal conflict**. Encourage them to look at Salva's fears and worries to understand what his internal conflicts are. (**Answer:** *Salva is struggling with his uncertainty about the future and the feeling of being alone in the world.*)

 NOTICE & NOTE

TOUGH QUESTIONS

Notice & Note: In paragraph 7, Salva seems concerned and confused. Mark the questions Salva asks.

Analyze: What do Salva's questions tell you about his internal conflict?

7   As Salva walked, the same thoughts kept going through his head in rhythm with his steps. *Where are we going? Where is my family? When will I see them again?*

8   The people stopped walking when it grew too dark to see the path. At first, everyone stood around uncertainly, speaking in tense whispers or silent with fear.

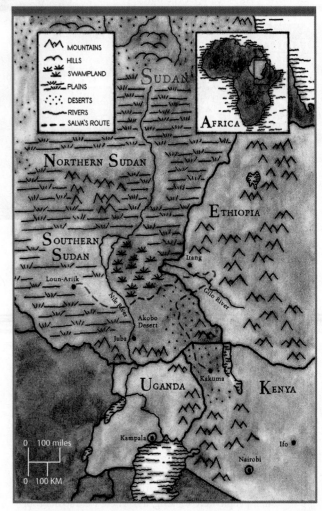

Map of Sudan, 1985

APPLYING ACADEMIC VOCABULARY

☑ circumstance   ☐ constraint   ☑ impact   ☐ injure   ☑ significant

Write and Discuss Have students turn to a partner to discuss the following questions. Guide students to include the Academic Vocabulary words *circumstance*, *impact*, and *significant* in their responses. Ask volunteers to share their responses with the class.

- What **circumstance** causes Salva to run from his village?
- What **impact** does being alone and lost have on Salva?
- How **significant** to Salva is seeing people from his village?

9 Then some of the men gathered and talked for a few moments. One of them called out, "Villages—group yourselves by villages. You will find someone you know."

10 Salva wandered around until he heard the words "Loun-Ariik! The village of Loun-Ariik, here!"

11 Relief flooded through him. That was his village! He hurried toward the sound of the voice.

12 A dozen or so people stood in a loose group at the side of the road. Salva scanned their faces. There was no one from his family. He recognized a few people—a woman with a baby, two men, a teenage girl—but no one he knew well. Still, it was comforting to see them.

13 They spent the night right there by the road, the men taking shifts to keep watch.[1] The next morning, they began walking again. Salva stayed in the midst of the crowd with the other villagers from Loun-Ariik.

14 In the early afternoon, he saw a large group of soldiers up ahead.

---

[1] **taking shifts to keep watch:** the men take turns watching for dangerous wild animals, including lions, as well as dangerous people, such as fighters with weapons.

ANALYZE SETTING AND CHARACTER

Annotate: Circle the words in paragraphs 9–11 related to setting, and underline words that describe Salva's thoughts and actions.

Connect: Think about how it might feel to be lost. How does Salva's reaction to the setting help you understand his character?

LANGUAGE CONVENTIONS

In paragraph 13, circle the prepositions and underline the prepositional phrases in the sentence that begins, "Salva stayed. . . ." How do these prepositions and prepositional phrases help you understand what is happening?

A Long Walk to Water   179

ANALYZE SETTING AND CHARACTER

Explain to students that the setting of a story can be described in terms of its relationship to the characters. In that sense, the place where Salva is walking is not just a road through a grassland. It is a place that is not his home. It is strange and unfamiliar. At this point in the story, it is also a dark place because it is night. How would most eleven-year-olds feel in this setting? How does Salva feel? (**Answer:** *Most young people would feel uncertain and frightened. That is how Salva feels until he is somewhat comforted by familiar faces.*)

LANGUAGE CONVENTIONS

Remind students that prepositional phrases describe relationships. In this paragraph, they describe the relationship between the travelers and the road and then between Salva and the other travelers. What was the relationship between Salva and the others when they set out in the morning? (**Answer:** *He stays in the middle of the crowd, not on the edges, and he stays with the people from his village.*)

APPLYING ACADEMIC VOCABULARY

☐ circumstance ☑ constraint ☐ impact ☑ injure ☐ significant

Write and Discuss Have students turn to a partner to discuss the following questions. Guide students to include the Academic Vocabulary words *constraint* and *injure* in their responses. Ask volunteers to share their responses with the class.

• What **constraint** made Salva hesitate to go with the children?

• What happened when the soldiers **injured** the man who protested?

AGAIN AND AGAIN

Remind students that an example of **Again and Again** indicates an important bit of information that the author is choosing to emphasize or draw the reader's attention to. In this case, the author uses **repetition** of a question to give the reader a glimpse into Salva's thoughts to help the reader get to know this character better. (**Answer:** *Salva has already asked the question "Where is my family?" The author is continuing to provide a window into Salva's internal struggle. The repetition in this new situation shows that Salva is a little in denial, however, because he has enough evidence to begin to deduce the answers to these questions.*)

 For **reading support** for students at varying proficiency levels, see the **Text X-Ray** on page 172D.

CRITICAL VOCABULARY

hesitate: Salva hesitates, or stops for a moment, to think.

ASK STUDENTS why Salva hesitates. (*He is unsure what to do.*)

collapse: Salva is so afraid he almost collapses, or falls.

ASK STUDENTS what keeps Salva from collapsing. (*He thinks about seeing his family again.*)

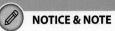 **NOTICE & NOTE**

15   Word passed through the crowd: "It's the rebels." The rebels—those who were fighting against the government.[2]

16   Salva passed several rebel soldiers waiting by the side of the road. Each of them held a big gun. Their guns were not pointed at the crowd, but even so, the soldiers seemed fierce and watchful. Some of the rebels then joined the back of the line; now the villagers were surrounded.

17   *What are they going to do to us? Where is my family?*

18   Late in the day, the villagers arrived at the rebel camp. The soldiers ordered them to separate into two groups—men in one group, women and children and the elderly in the other. Teenage boys, it seemed, were considered men, for boys who looked to be only a few years older than Salva were joining the men's group.

19   Salva **hesitated** for a moment. He was only eleven, but he was the son of an important family. He was Salva Mawien Dut Ariik, from the village named for his grandfather. His father always told him to act like a man—to follow the example of his older brothers and, in turn, set a good example for Kuol.[3]

20   Salva took a few steps toward the men.

21   "Hey!"

22   A soldier approached Salva and raised his gun.

23   Salva froze. All he could see was the gun's huge barrel, black and gleaming, as it moved toward his face.

24   The end of the barrel touched his chin.

25   Salva felt his knees turn to water. He closed his eyes.

26   *If I die now, I will never see my family again.*

27   Somehow, this thought strengthened him enough to keep him from **collapsing** in terror.

28   He took a deep breath and opened his eyes.

29   The soldier was holding the gun with only one hand. He was not *aiming* it; he was using it to lift Salva's chin so he could get a better look at his face.

30   "Over there," the soldier said. He moved the gun and pointed it toward the group of women and children.

AGAIN AND AGAIN

Notice & Note: In paragraph 17, mark each question. Which question has Salva asked before?

Evaluate: Why does the author repeat Salva's question? Is it reasonable for Salva to ask this at this point of the novel? Why?

hesitate
(hĕz´ĭ-tāt´) v. To *hesitate* is to pause or wait in uncertainty.

collapse
(kə-lăps´) v. When something is said to *collapse*, it falls down.

---

[2] **those who were fighting against the government:** in Sudan's civil war, government soldiers fought against opposition groups who wanted to seize control of territory and take over the Sudanese government.
[3] **Kuol:** Salva's younger brother.

WHEN STUDENTS STRUGGLE . . .

Monitor Comprehension In paragraph 39, Salva is awake, trying to fall asleep. In paragraph 40, he is waking up. Without explicitly stating it, the author expects the reader to understand that, in between, the night has passed and Salva has slept through it. Explain to students that this is something they need to **infer**.

 For additional support, go to the **Reading Studio** and assign the following [LEVEL] **Level Up tutorial: Making Inferences.**

31   "You are not a man yet. Don't be in such a hurry!" He laughed and clapped Salva on the shoulder.

32   Salva **scurried** over to the women's side.

33   The next morning, the rebels moved on from the camp. The village men were forced to carry supplies: guns and mortars, shells, radio equipment.[4] Salva watched as one man protested that he did not want to go with the rebels. A soldier hit him in the face with the butt of a gun.[5] The man fell to the ground, bleeding.

34   After that, no one objected. The men **shouldered** the heavy equipment and left the camp.

scurry

(skûr´ē) v. Something that can *scurry* will run with quick, light steps.

MONITOR COMPREHENSION

Annotate: Mark the words in paragraph 33 related to war and violence.

Analyze: Use background knowledge and information provided in the footnotes to help you understand the setting. How would you describe the setting to a friend?

shoulder

(shōl´dər) v. To *shoulder* something is to carry it on one's shoulders.

[4] **guns and mortars, shells, radio equipment:** mortars are large, portable weapons that fire explosive bombs, called *shells;* radio equipment is used to communicate, often in remote areas.

[5] **butt of a gun:** the thicker end of a gun, which is held in the hand, or in the case of a rifle, held up against the shoulder while firing.

A Long Walk to Water   181

ENGLISH LEARNER SUPPORT

Use Visual Support Focus on the word *clapped* in paragraph 31. Ask a volunteer to demonstrate the familiar meaning of the word by clapping their hands. Then explain that clapping can mean making a similar motion with one hand against another object or person. **SUBSTANTIAL**

MONITOR COMPREHENSION

Discuss with students the military terms in paragraph 33 and what kind of mood they create. Ask students what effect these terms have on your sense of Salva's situation. (**Answer:** *The setting is a camp where the village men are being forced to participate in military activities. The details related to war and violence help in understanding the danger inherent in the selection's setting. The rebels are forcing men to fight for them; they may injure or kill people who refuse to join them.*

CRITICAL VOCABULARY

scurry: Salva moves quickly, like a small animal.

ASK STUDENTS whether this is a bold movement. *(no)*

shoulder: The men carry the equipment on their shoulders.

ASK STUDENTS whether this is a difficult job. *(yes)*

AHA MOMENT

Remind students that an **Aha Moment** is a character's realization of something that shifts his actions or understanding of himself, others, or the world around him. In the ending of this excerpt, beginning with paragraph 40, Salva realizes that he has been left alone. This is a very important shift in his situation. He now has nothing and no one to depend on except himself if he is going to survive. Have students answer the question about why the others may have left. (**Answer:** *The others may have thought that it would be too hard to try to provide for one more person.*)

■ English Learner Support

Develop Vocabulary Explain to students that certain "cue words" indicate that the author is going to tell the reader what a character is thinking or feeling. Write the cue words *think, feel, realize, sense,* and *understand* on the board for students to refer to. Read aloud the words. Then have students focus on paragraph 40 and circle the cue word that signals the **Aha Moment**. *(feel)* **MODERATE**

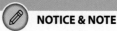

NOTICE & NOTE

35 Everyone else began walking again. They went in the opposite direction from the rebels, for wherever the rebels went, there was sure to be fighting.

36 Salva stayed with the group from Loun-Ariik. It was smaller now, without the men. And except for the infant, Salva was the only child.

37 That evening they found a barn in which to spend the night. Salva tossed restlessly in the itchy hay.

38 *Where are we going? Where is my family? When will I see them again?*

39 It took him a long time to fall asleep.

40 Even before he was fully awake, Salva could feel that something was wrong. He lay very still with his eyes closed, trying to sense what it might be.

41 Finally, he sat up and opened his eyes.

42 No one else was in the barn.

43 Salva stood so quickly that for a moment he felt dizzy. He rushed to the door and looked out.

44 Nobody. Nothing.

45 They had left him.

46 He was alone.

AHA MOMENT

Notice & Note: What has Salva realized in paragraphs 40–46? Mark the words that show what he suddenly realizes.

Draw Conclusions: Why might Salva's fellow villagers have done this?

TO CHALLENGE STUDENTS . . .

Identify Mood Explain that authors select specific words to create a mood, or the emotion the reader feels while reading. Ask students to find words and phrases on the last page of the selection that create a strong feeling, such as "only child" and "Nothing." Have them discuss with a partner the mood, or feeling, these words create.

CHECK YOUR UNDERSTANDING

Have students answer the questions independently.

Answers:

1. *A*

2. *H*

3. *A*

If they answer any questions incorrectly, have them reread the text to confirm their understanding. Then they may proceed to ANALYZE THE TEXT on page 184.

CHECK YOUR UNDERSTANDING

Answer these questions before moving on to the **Analyze the Text** section on the following page.

1 Which of the following is not true about the selection?

  A Salva is a rebel who battles the Sudanese government.

  B The setting is Sudan during a civil war in 1985.

  C Salva is fleeing from wartime violence.

  D Many people have left their villages.

2 In paragraph 4, Salva "lowered his head and ran" because —

  F he was late and he had to get home

  G it was beginning to thunderstorm

  H he heard and saw what seemed to be an explosion

  J he heard that a famous storyteller was coming to his village

3 When Salva awakens at the end of the selection he —

  A realizes he is abandoned and alone

  B discovers the other villagers have taken his food

  C realizes that his fear and confusion were part of a dream

  D smells breakfast cooking

EL ENGLISH LEARNER SUPPORT

Oral Assessment Use the following questions to assess students' comprehension and speaking skills:

1. Is Salva fighting the government or running away from war? (*He is running away from war.*)

2. Read paragraph 4. Why did Salva run? (*He thought he saw and heard an explosion.*)

3. At the end of the selection, Salva wakes up. What does he think when he wakes up? (*He thinks he is alone.*) **SUBSTANTIAL/MODERATE**

APPLY

ANALYZE THE TEXT

Possible answers:

1. **DOK 2:** *The background information said that the author based the novel on a true story about a boy and his country's civil war. This helped me understand that the BOOM! in the first paragraph is probably a bomb and that Salva must flee to save his life.*

2. **DOK 4:** *Details about setting include evening, barn, and itchy hay. In the darkness, on an uncomfortable bed of hay, the unfamiliar setting probably makes Salva miss his family even more and not want to be alone.*

3. **DOK 3:** *Salva may have felt humiliated after the rebel told him, "You are not a man yet." But after Salva sees a man beaten for not wanting to go with the rebels, Salva may feel relieved.*

4. **DOK 2:** *Why does Salva feel that something is wrong? Why was no one else in the barn? Who was in the barn the night before? Have the villagers abandoned him for good, or are they just outside? How will Salva survive on his own?*

5. **DOK 4:** *Salva realizes that looking back "slowed him down." He may have to focus more on the future if he wants to survive in such difficult circumstances.*

RESEARCH

Suggest that students begin with websites connected to the organization Water for South Sudan and to the author of the book to help them with their research.

Connect Encourage students to identify and make a list of moments in the text that provide them with insight into challenges Salva Dut faced while trying to survive during his journey. Point out that knowing about times when Salva struggled to meet his needs will help them understand better why improving the lives of other people was important to Salva once he was grown.

 RESPOND

ANALYZE THE TEXT

Support your responses with evidence from the text. **NOTEBOOK**

1. **Interpret** How does the background information that precedes the selection help you understand what is happening in the selection's opening scene (paragraphs 1–4)?

2. **Evaluate** Review paragraphs 37–39. Identify details that describe the setting. How might Salva's surroundings affect his thoughts and actions?

3. **Draw Conclusions** Review paragraphs 31–34. What might Salva have felt after he went to the women's side? How might Salva's feelings have changed after witnessing what happened to the man who did not want to go with the rebels? Explain.

4. **Predict** Review paragraph 40 to the end of the excerpt. What questions can you ask to monitor your comprehension and help you predict what will happen next?

5. **Notice & Note** Review paragraphs 3–4. What does the phrase *No more looking back* mean? How might this realization affect Salva as the novel continues?

RESEARCH TIP
Reputable websites often link to other reliable sites offering more information on the subject. Following links such as these can offer more in-depth information and insights.

RESEARCH

A Long Walk to Water is based on the true story of a Sudanese boy named Salva Dut. As an adult, Dut founded the organization Water for South Sudan which drills wells to supply water to the people of his homeland. Use multiple sources to conduct your own research on Water for South Sudan. Use the chart to record what the organization does, how it raises money, what challenges it faces, and how well it has succeeded.

WATER FOR SOUTH SUDAN	
Research Question	**Answer/Source**
	Answers will vary.

Connect Salva Dut's difficult journey inspired him to work to improve and transform the lives of others. With a small group, discuss any moments in *A Long Walk to Water* that help you understand the real-life Salva Dut who you learned about in your research.

 LEARNING MINDSET

Try Again Explain that making mistakes is how we learn. Reassure students that the classroom is a "risk-free" zone where making mistakes is encouraged. Have students share mistakes they have made and what they learned from them.

CREATE AND DISCUSS

Write an Informational Essay Write an essay explaining how the setting of *A Long Walk to Water* shapes Salva's experience and character.

❏ Review the selection's background information, graphics, and footnotes about Sudan.

❏ Review annotations you made during reading that relate to setting and character, and find a cause-and-effect relationship between the novel's setting and Salva's character.

❏ As you write, use prepositions and prepositional phrases to help express relationships between ideas.

❏ Make sure your essay is guided by a thesis statement or a clear controlling idea, and be sure to support your thesis with explicit and implicit evidence from the text.

Discuss with a Small Group Have a discussion about the challenges Salva faces and what character traits would be required to meet these challenges.

❏ As a group, review the text and make a list of each challenge. Review the ending and make predictions about the challenges Salva may face later.

❏ Have group members volunteer character traits, such as independence, perseverance, or kindness, that would be helpful in meeting each challenge.

❏ Draw upon personal experience and ideas in other texts to inform your thinking and responses.

RESPOND TO THE ESSENTIAL QUESTION

 What does it take to be a survivor?

Gather Information Review your annotations and notes on *A Long Walk to Water*. Then, add relevant details to your Response Log. As you determine which information to include, think about:

• the significant challenges Salva faces
• how characters respond to the setting
• what Salva must do to survive

At the end of the unit, use your notes to write a nonfiction narrative.

 Go to the **Writing Studio** for more on writing informative texts.

Go to the **Speaking and Listening Studio** for help with having a group discussion.

GROUP WORK CHECKLIST
Follow these guidelines when working in groups:

❏ Listen actively.

❏ Ask specific questions.

❏ Respond respectfully.

❏ Consider all ideas.

❏ Take notes about important points.

❏ Adjust your responses as new evidence is discovered.

ACADEMIC VOCABULARY
As you write and discuss what you learned from the selection, be sure to use the Academic Vocabulary words. Check off each of the words that you use.

❏ **circumstance**
❏ **constraint**
❏ **impact**
❏ **injure**
❏ **significant**

CREATE AND DISCUSS

Write an Informational Essay Point out to students that they need to organize their ideas in an informational essay in a logical way that clearly develops the thesis. The organizational structure they choose could be **chronology**, **cause and effect**, or **main idea and details**. The important thing is that the organization supports the thesis.

Remind students that, to help make the organization clear to the reader, they should use transition words such as *then*, *because*, and *as a result*.

 For **writing support** for students at varying proficiency levels, see the **Text X-Ray** on page 172D.

Discuss with a Small Group Remind students they should listen respectfully to points made by other group members. When responding to those points, they might refer to them, indicating that they have heard and understood.

RESPOND TO THE ESSENTIAL QUESTION

Allow time for students to add details from *A Long Walk to Water* to their Unit 3 Response Logs.

ENGLISH LEARNER SUPPORT

Discuss with a Small Group Restate the discussion prompt as a question: *What challenges does Salva face, and what character traits would be required to meet those challenges?* Allow students to work with partners to review the text for details that answer the question. Provide these sentence frames to help them formulate their ideas for the discussion: *The country is fighting a _____. Salva's village has been _____. Salva has lost _____. Salva will need to be _____.*
SUBSTANTIAL/MODERATE

CRITICAL VOCABULARY

Answers:

1. *a*

2. *a*

3. *b*

4. *a*

5. *a*

VOCABULARY STRATEGY:
Vocabulary Resources

Answers:

1. *noun, verb (transitive, intransitive)*

2. Shouldered *is used as a transitive verb, in the past tense.*

3. *They each have two syllables.*

4. *Possible answer: origin: Middle English* shulder *and Old English* sculdor; *meaning: to carry or place on a shoulder*

 RESPOND

WORD BANK
veer
hesitate
collapse
scurry
shoulder

 Go to the **Vocabulary Studio** for more on vocabulary resources.

CRITICAL VOCABULARY

Practice and Apply Choose the letter of the better answer to each question.

1. Which of the following is an example of **collapse?**

   a. a falling tower   **b.** a stack of paper

2. Which of the following would cause most people to **hesitate?**

   a. skydiving   **b.** knitting

3. Which of the following is an example of **scurry?**

   a. a brown bear sitting down   **b.** a running squirrel

4. Which of the following would someone **shoulder?**

   a. a heavy package   **b.** a baseball

5. Which of the following is an example of **veer?**

   a. a car quickly changing direction   **b.** a thin coat of paint

VOCABULARY STRATEGY:
Vocabulary Resources

A print or online dictionary is a useful tool for determining the meaning of a word. Many words have multiple meanings, and some words can be used as different parts of speech. A dictionary includes every meaning of a word, as well as its syllabication (how it breaks into syllables), pronunciation, part of speech, and word origin.

Practice and Apply Look up *shouldered* in a dictionary by searching for its base word, *shoulder,* and then answer the questions.

1. What parts of speech are listed for *shoulder?*

   _____

2. Review the use of *shouldered* in paragraph 34. According to its context and suffix and the dictionary, what part of speech is *shouldered?*

   _____

3. How many syllables do *shoulder* and *shouldered* have?

   _____

4. What is the word origin and dictionary meaning of *shoulder* as it is used in the selection?

   _____

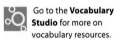 **ENGLISH LANGUAGE LEARNERS**

Vocabulary Strategy Give students additional practice in determining the meanings of unfamiliar words using resources. Have pairs of students find three unfamiliar words in the selection, and use a print or online dictionary to find the definition. If there are multiple definitions, have them go back to the selection to see how the word is used—its part of speech and context. **LIGHT**

LANGUAGE CONVENTIONS:
Prepositions and Prepositional Phrases

Writers use **prepositions** and **prepositional phrases** to express where, when, and how words and ideas are related. When inserting prepositional phrases between a subject and a verb, be sure to correctly identify the subject and verb so that they agree. If the sentence has a singular subject, it should have a singular verb. If the sentence has a plural subject, it should have a plural verb.

In the following sentence, *the villagers* is the subject, and *in the text* is a prepositional phrase. The subject is plural, so the verb must also be plural.

<u>**The villagers**</u> in the text seems/seem frightened.

The verb *to be* presents special problems in agreement. This verb does not follow the usual patterns. Study the sentence below to determine which form of *to be* is correct. First identify the subject of the sentence, and then mark the correct verb.

Each of the students is/are required to attend.

Each is the subject of the sentence, while *of the students* is a prepositional phrase that modifies *each*. Because *each* is singular, use *is*, the singular form of the verb *to be*.

Practice and Apply Write your own sentences about Salva's response when he discovers that he has been left alone. Use prepositions and prepositional phrases. When you have finished writing, compare your use of prepositions and prepositional phrases with a partner. Check your partner's work for subject-verb agreement.

Go to the **Grammar Studio** for more on prepositions and prepositional phrases.

LANGUAGE CONVENTIONS:
Prepositions and Prepositional Phrases

Review with your students the basics of subject-verb agreement.

- The subject and verb of a sentence or clause must agree in number.
- A singular subject requires a singular verb.
- A plural subject requires a plural verb.

Example: The cat sits in the window all day.

Cat is a singular subject. *Sits* is a singular verb. When the subject and the verb are close together, this is easy to see.

However, the question of what verb to use can seem more difficult if the subject and verb are separated by one of more prepositional phrases.

Example: The cat with the green eyes and gray stripes sits in the window all day.

In this case, it is important to determine the subject and the verb in the sentence and ignore the prepositional phrases when determining what form of the verb is correct.

Practice and Apply Students' sentences should accurately reflect the text, include prepositional phrases, and maintain subject-verb agreement. As partners check and compare sentences, have them identify the subject, the verb, and the preposition in each sentence and then discuss how the information in the prepositional phrase relates to the rest of the sentence.

ENGLISH LEARNER SUPPORT

Language Conventions Use the following supports with students at varying proficiency levels:

1. Write this sentence: *The boy plays ball.* Point out that regular nouns add an *s* to become plural and, in the present tense, regular verbs take away an *s* to form the plural. Have a volunteer "move the *s*" to make the subject and verb plural: *The boys play ball.*
   SUBSTANTIAL/MODERATE

2. Write this sentence: *Each of the forty students in the room need/needs a pencil.* Have a volunteer cross out or erase the prepositional phrases in the sentence and then choose the correct form of the verb. Explain to students that, if they have any doubts about subject/verb agreement when they are writing, they can simply remove all the words and phrases between the subject and the verb. It will then be easy to see whether they agree in number.
   LIGHT

MEDIA
SALVA'S STORY
Documentary by POVRoseMedia

GENRE ELEMENTS
DOCUMENTARY

Review that a **documentary** is an informational video or film created to showcase an important person, place, cause, or event. Factual information about the subject may be presented through primary sources, voice-over narration, footage or reenactments of actual events, and animated graphics. In this lesson, students will see Salva Dut explain why he started Water for South Sudan, Inc., to bring clean water to his people.

LEARNING OBJECTIVES

- Analyze characteristics of digital texts.
- Analyze use of print and graphic features to achieve purposes.
- Write a summary of events in a video.
- Evaluate and rate video features.
- Generate research questions from a variety of sources.
- Discuss the effectiveness of the video's elements.
- **Language** Discuss the video using the terms *animated* and *voice-over*.

TEXT COMPLEXITY

Quantitative Measures	Salva's Story	Lexile: N/A
Qualitative Measures	**Ideas Presented** Much is explicit. Requires some inferential reasoning.	
	Structure Used Varies from simple chronological order. Graphics clarify points.	
	Language Used Mostly explicit. Some words may need to be clarified.	
	Knowledge Required Experiences less familiar. References may make heavier demands.	

Online Ed

RESOURCES

- Unit 3 Response Log

- Writing Studio: Using Textual Evidence: Summarizing, Paraphrasing, and Quoting

- Speaking and Listening Studio: Participating in Collaborative Discussions

- ✓ "Salva's Story" Selection Test

SUMMARIES

English

Salva Dut was one of the 12,000 Lost Boys who survived the 1,800 mile walk to refugee camps during the Sudanese civil war in 1985. In 1996, Salva was one of 3,800 boys resettled in the United States. He became a U.S. citizen and attended college. He learned his dad was still alive, but sick from waterborne disease. Salva returned to South Sudan to help his father. He then founded Water for South Sudan, Inc., to drill wells for his people. Since then, Salva has earned several awards for service.

Spanish

Salva Dut fue uno de los 12.000 Niños Perdidos que sobrevivió la caminata de 1.800 millas a los campos de refugiados en la Guerra Civil Sudanesa en 1985. En 1996, Salva fue uno de los 1.800 niños reubicados en los Estados Unidos. Se convirtió en ciudadano americano y estudió en la universidad. Se enteró de que su padre estaba vivo pero enfermo, debido a una enfermedad transmitida por el agua. Salva regresó a Sudán del Sur para ayudar a su padre. Luego fundó la compañía Agua Para Sudán del Sur Inc. para taladrar pozos para su gente. Desde entonces, Salva ha ganado premios por sus servicios.

 ## SMALL-GROUP OPTIONS

Have students work in small groups to read and discuss the selection.

Double-Entry Journal

- For taking notes during the video, have students divide their paper into two columns to record "Quotes" on the left and "My Notes" on the right.

- Have students pause the video to note an important or confusing quote from the voice-over narration or from Salva Dut. Then students should write their own interpretations, summaries, or questions about each quote.

- Have students share and discuss their notes with a partner.

Think-Pair-Share

- After students have watched and analyzed "Salva's Story," ask: *How do you think Salva's work has impacted the lives of people in South Sudan?*

- Have students think about the question individually and write brief notes of their ideas.

- Have pairs discuss their ideas about the question.

- Ask pairs to share their responses with the class. Discuss ways to find out more about this question.

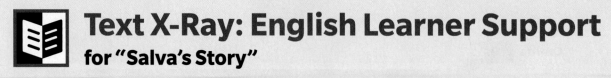

Text X-Ray: English Learner Support
for "Salva's Story"

Use the Text X-Ray and the supports and scaffolds in the Teacher's Edition to help guide students at different proficiency levels through the selection.

INTRODUCE THE SELECTION
DISCUSS SALVA'S STORY

In this lesson, students will hear and see Salva Dut's story. As one of the Lost Boys of Sudan, he survived the difficult journey, found a new life, and returned to help his family and the people of South Sudan. Introduce words related to Salva's story, such as *refugees, survive, separated, displaced,* and *civil war.* Guide a discussion of what students expect to see and hear in the documentary, and how this might be different from reading a text about Salva. Use frames to help students with their discussions:

- *A documentary may show families _____ because of a civil war.*
- *A text can _____, but a video can _____ what life for Salva was like.*

CULTURAL REFERENCES

The following words and phrases may be unfamiliar to students:

- *clinic*: a place where people get medical help
- *the bush:* a large area of vegetation that is not used for farming
- *nonprofit*: done to help or support people and not to make money
- *U.N.:* United Nations; an international organization that works for world peace and security
- *waterborne*: spread or carried by water

LISTENING

Listen for Key Ideas

Preview the video:

- 0:00–0:20 introduces Salva at his former village in South Sudan
- 0:21–1:31 tells about the Lost Boys
- 1:32–2:09 Salva speaks about his life in the United States
- 2:10–3:51 Salva tells about finding his father and starting Water for South Sudan

Share the basic video summary shown. Then play each section, pausing to discuss important ideas. Use the following supports with students at varying proficiency levels:

- Provide brief statements of important ideas from each section (and some that are not accurate), and ask students to give a thumbs up or down to show whether the statement is accurate. **SUBSTANTIAL**
- Have students identify important ideas using sentence frames, such as: *Salva helped start Water for South Sudan because _____. Salva's life in the U.S. was _____.* **MODERATE**
- Pair students to discuss the key ideas they heard discussed in each section of the video. **LIGHT**

SPEAKING

Discuss Purpose

Have students discuss with a partner the purpose of using an animated map with voice-over narration in the video. Circulate to make sure students are using the terms *animated* and *voice-over* correctly.

Use the following supports with students at varying proficiency levels:

- Display and read aloud this sentence: *The voice-over narration tells what happened to the Lost Boys.* Have students repeat the sentence and practice saying it to a partner. **SUBSTANTIAL**
- Have pairs discuss the purpose of the map and voice-over. Then have pairs complete the following sentence frame orally: *The video uses an animated map and voice-over narration to _____.* **MODERATE**
- Have student pairs discuss how animation and voice-over narration work together to support the purpose of the map. Ask them to share their answers with the group. **LIGHT**

READING

Use Subtitles

Point out that the video includes **subtitles,** or text that highlights the most important ideas the narrator says. Subtitles also give the viewer additional information, such as identifying a person.

Play the video from the beginning to the end of the animated map sequence with sound. Then play the segment again without sound. Ask students how the subtitles supported their understanding. Use the following supports with students at varying proficiency levels:

- Have students list words they do not recognize as they watch the subtitles. Clarify the words and their meanings, then play the segment again with the subtitles. **SUBSTANTIAL**
- Have students complete sentence frames, such as: *I knew who Salva Dut was because _____. I could/could not understand the map without sound because _____.* **MODERATE**
- Have students identify the purpose of the text subtitles on the map. Ask: *Why did the filmmaker include these subtitles?* **LIGHT**

WRITING

Write a Summary

Work with students to read the writing assignment on p. 191.

Use the following supports with students at varying proficiency levels:

- Use questioning to guide students to tell their summary orally, and help them rephrase their ideas using sequence words such as *first, then, next, finally,* and *after.* **SUBSTANTIAL**
- Provide students with sentence frames to help them write their summary, such as: *Salva had to leave _____ because _____. _____, he moved to the United States. _____, he moved back to South Sudan. He started _____.* **MODERATE**
- Work with students to generate a list of transitional phrases and words that will help them write a chronological summary, such as *first, then, next, finally, at last, during, since, as soon as,* and *after.* Provide a sequence graphic organizer to help them put events in order using the sequence words. **LIGHT**

Connect to the
ESSENTIAL QUESTION

"Salva's Story" documents Salva Dut's dangerous journey to refugee camps during the Sudanese civil war and his eventual resettlement in the United States. His experience leads him back to South Sudan to find his father and help his people.

QUICK START

Have students form pairs to discuss the Quick Start prompt. Then invite pairs to share their ideas for returning to a place of great suffering.

ANALYZE CHARACTERISTICS OF DIGITAL TEXT

Have students read the information about a documentary, a form of digital text. Then review the documentary features and elements described in the chart and in the list in the left margin.

Suggest that students use these questions to help them analyze the graphic and sound features in the video:

- Does the video use animated graphics and voice-over narration? How do they help me understand Salva's story?
- How does the footage help bring Salva's experience to life?
- What does the recording of Salva's talk to an audience add to the video?

 For **listening, speaking, and reading support** for students at varying proficiency levels, see the **Text X-Ray** on pages 188C and 188D.

MEDIA

SALVA'S STORY

Documentary by
POVRoseMedia

? ESSENTIAL QUESTION:

What does it take to be a survivor?

QUICK START

Why might someone choose to return to a place where he or she had once undergone great suffering? Discuss your ideas with a partner.

ANALYZE CHARACTERISTICS OF DIGITAL TEXT

GENRE ELEMENTS: DOCUMENTARY

- highlights a person, place, event, or cause
- targets a specific audience
- is created for a specific purpose
- includes TV broadcasts, videos, newspapers, magazines, and the Internet

A **documentary** is a nonfiction film or video that tells about important people, historic places, or significant events. A documentary's purpose is often to inform or explain. Filmmakers gather information about a topic and present the material in an engaging way. They do this by incorporating some of the following features in their work.

FEATURE OF A DOCUMENTARY	HOW THE FEATURE MIGHT BE USED
animated graphics, such as maps and charts	to provide visual support for complex ideas
voice-over narration, or the voice of an unseen speaker	to summarize key scenes or events; to provide background information
primary sources, such as recordings from an event	to show real-life experiences and historical details
footage, such as reenactments or film clips	to bring a topic to life

---

EL ENGLISH LEARNER SUPPORT

Use Prereading Supports Discuss with students that the video title explains that this documentary is about a person and it will tell about that person's life. Give students a KWL graphic organizer to begin before they watch the video. Students can write what they know about Salva Dut from the Background note for *A Long Walk to Water* and from the novel excerpt based on his difficult journey. They may ask questions about what was happening when the excerpt ended, or what happened next. Tell students to keep this information in mind as they view and listen to the video, then revisit the KWL chart after watching to complete it.

MODERATE/LIGHT

BACKGROUND

During a long and brutal civil war in Sudan, thousands of children fled on foot to neighboring countries. Along the way, many died. Salva Dut was one of the children, called the Lost Boys, who survived. For almost six years, he lived in a refugee camp with nearly 100,000 other refugees. In 1996, he became one of the first Lost Boys to resettle in the United States. Dut founded the organization Water for South Sudan. The group drills wells and provides clean water to villages in South Sudan. The book A Long Walk to Water *is based on Salva Dut's life story.*

SETTING A PURPOSE

As you view the short documentary, consider how the information about Salva Dut is presented. Notice how different features help to engage the viewer. **NOTEBOOK**

To view the video, log in and select *Salva's Story* from the unit menu.

As needed, pause the video to make notes about what impresses you or ideas you might want to talk about later. Replay or rewind so that you can clarify anything you do not understand.

TEACH

BACKGROUND

After students read the Background note, ask them to relate the description of the company Water for South Sudan, Inc., to the title of the book based on Salva Dut's story. Ask: *How does this connection help you understand Salva's suffering as a Lost Boy and why he returned to South Sudan?*

SETTING A PURPOSE

Direct students to use the Setting a Purpose prompt to focus their viewing and listening.

ENGLISH LEARNER SUPPORT

Use Support to Enhance Understanding Clarify the meanings of *animated, voice-over, primary,* and *footage.* Provide examples or describe an example that illustrates each term. Encourage students to watch and listen for each example in "Salva's Story."
SUBSTANTIAL/MODERATE

WHEN STUDENTS STRUGGLE . . .

Analyze Media Have students view the video with partners. Suggest they view the video the first time without pausing or taking notes. Invite them to discuss what part of Salva's story each part showed. Then have them view the video a second time and pause after each segment. Encourage them to take notes on each part. Suggest they use a two-column chart for notes, with segments identified by time-stamp in the left column and notes about each segment in the right column.

ANALYZE THE TEXT

Possible answers:

1. **DOK 2:** *The voice-over narration provides historical background information about Sudan's civil war and the hardships faced by the Lost Boys.*

2. **DOK 4:** *The map was effective because it showed how far the Lost Boys traveled. Additionally, the inset of footage gave an idea of what happened on the journey and at the end, and the voice-over described how hard it was for the Lost Boys to survive.*

3. **DOK 4:** *The footage helps the viewer develop an emotional connection to Salva.*

4. **DOK 2:** *The clips help the viewer imagine what it must have been like for the Lost Boys to travel through the extreme desert and to feel hunger and desperation.*

5. **DOK 4:** *Visiting his father made Salva realize that he needed to be proactive and help people in South Sudan who are without clean water, a basic necessity for life.*

RESEARCH

Review the Research Tip with students. Remind students to check the sites they visit to make sure they are established organizations that support the information they are looking for.

Extend Ask students what the video would be like if it had included the information they gathered to answer their research question. Discuss whether this would improve the documentary. Then have them review the features on page 188 and decide which techniques they would use to incorporate the new information into the existing documentary.

 RESPOND

ANALYZE MEDIA

Support your responses with evidence from the video. 📓 NOTEBOOK

1. **Summarize** Describe the purpose of the voice-over narration in *Salva's Story*.

2. **Critique** Think about the purpose of the map of Sudan, Ethiopia, and Kenya. Do you think the graphic was effective? Why or why not?

3. **Analyze** Review the scenes that show Salva Dut in his former village. What effect is achieved by showing footage of him in that environment?

4. **Interpret** Why do you think the filmmakers chose to use footage depicting people walking through a desert and children clamoring for food?

5. **Connect** Why did Dut tell the filmmakers the story of visiting his father when he was ill? How did that experience shape decisions Dut made afterward?

RESEARCH

RESEARCH TIP
When you research a specific group of people, consider visiting sites of established organizations that support or represent that group. The International Rescue Committee and UNICEF are two organizations that work with the Lost Boys of Sudan.

The video provides a brief explanation about who the Lost Boys of Sudan are and what they experienced. Consider other information you would like to know about the Lost Boys. Identify one research question that you would like to have answered, and then use reputable sources to find the answer. Use more than one source.

RESEARCH QUESTION	NOTES AND SOURCES
Answers will vary.	

Extend Consider what you learned in your research. Would *Salva's Story* be improved if it included this information? Why or why not? If you were one of the filmmakers, which features or techniques might you use to incorporate the information?

EL **ENGLISH LEARNER SUPPORT**

Oral Assessment To gauge comprehension and speaking skills, conduct an informal assessment. Walk around the class, talking with students and asking these questions:

- *How many years passed before Salva returned to South Sudan?* (*19 years*)
  SUBSTANTIAL

- *What is the purpose of Water for South Sudan?* (*to bring clean water to villages*)
  MODERATE

- *How does Water for South Sudan accomplish its purpose?* (*It provides water by drilling wells.*) **LIGHT**

CREATE AND PRESENT

Write a Summary Write a summary of the main events described in *Salva's Story*.

❏ Review *Salva's Story* and take notes on the events described in the video. Make sure to jot down dates when they are provided.

❏ If necessary, review the video several times to make sure your notes are accurate.

❏ Create a simple timeline to help you organize the main events in chronological order—the order in which they occurred.

❏ Write your summary using your own words. To create a concise summary, only include the main events described in the video.

❏ Refer to the timeline you created as you write.

Analyze and Evaluate the Video With a small group, closely examine the effectiveness of the features in *Salva's Story*.

❏ As a group, make a chart listing the features used in the video, such as voice-over narration and footage.

❏ Review the video on your own. Then, using a rating system from 1 to 5, score the effectiveness of each feature.

❏ Gather as a group again and discuss your evaluations. Share the reasons for the scores that you gave. Consider group members' positions that are different from your own, and adjust your scores as appropriate.

RESPOND TO THE ESSENTIAL QUESTION

 What does it take to be a survivor?

Gather Information Review your notes on *Salva's Story*. Then, add relevant details to your Response Log. As you determine which information to include, think about what it takes to be a survivor.

At the end of the unit, use your notes to write a nonfiction narrative.

© Houghton Mifflin Harcourt Publishing Company

 Go to the **Writing Studio: Summarizing, Paraphrasing, and Quoting** in the **Writing Studio** for more on writing a summary.

Go to **Participating in Collaborative Discussions** in the **Speaking and Listening Studio** for help with having a small group discussion.

GROUP WORK CHECKLIST

❏ Listen actively.

❏ Ask specific questions.

❏ Respond respectfully.

❏ Consider group members' suggestions.

❏ Take notes about important points.

❏ Use the Academic Vocabulary words in your discussion.

  ❏ circumstance

  ❏ constraint

  ❏ impact

  ❏ injure

  ❏ significant

CREATE AND PRESENT

Write a Summary After students have drafted their summaries, encourage them to check their writing to make sure the events they noted are in sequence. Then have them read aloud their summaries to a partner. Encourage partners to point out sections that are confusing or need to be rearranged. Remind them to check for time-order transitions that help to connect events.

 For **writing support** for students at varying proficiency levels, see the **Text X-Ray** on page 188D.

Analyze and Evaluate the Video Have students form groups to evaluate the effectiveness of features in the documentary.

• Remind students to check the list of features on page 188 to help them create their charts.

• Have groups make sure that each member has their own chart to review the video.

• Suggest that they use 1 as the lowest rating for a feature and 5 for the highest. Have the group decide what each number should represent.

• As students rate the video, suggest they note their reasons for each rating to use in their follow-up discussion.

RESPOND TO THE ESSENTIAL QUESTION

Allow time for students to add details from "Salva's Story" to their Unit 3 Response Logs.

MENTOR TEXT

INTO THE LIFEBOAT *from* TITANIC SURVIVOR

Memoir by Violet Jessop

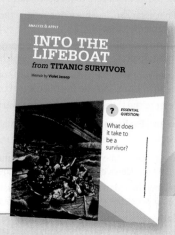

This memoir serves as a **mentor text,** a model for students to follow when they come to the Unit 3 Writing Task: Write a Nonfiction Narrative.

GENRE ELEMENTS
MEMOIR

Remind students that the purpose of a **memoir** is to tell a true story that presents insights into the impact of events on people's lives. It is a form of narrative nonfiction known as autobiographical writing. Autobiographical writing includes the writer's personal observations and is almost always told in the first person using an informal tone.

LEARNING OBJECTIVES

- Create mental imagery through strong word choice and sensory description.
- Use context clues to increase understanding of vocabulary.
- Develop and modify a research plan.
- Write using an informal register or voice
- Create a multimedia presentation.
- Analyze how writers use commas.
- **Language** Discuss imagery using vivid words.

TEXT COMPLEXITY

Quantitative Measures	"Into the Lifeboat" from *Titanic Survivor*	Lexile: 950
Qualitative Measures	**Ideas Presented:** Much is explicit but moves to some implied meaning. Requires some inferential reasoning.	
	Structure Used: Primarily explicit. Largely conventional.	
	Language Used: Mostly explicit. Some figurative or allusive language. A few references are mildly archaic.	
	Knowledge Required: References to historical events. Situations mostly familiar or easily envisioned	

RESOURCES

- Unit 3 Response Log

- 🔊 Selection Audio

- 📺 **Text in FOCUS** Analyzing Comparisons and Contrasts

- 📖 Reading Studio: Notice & Note

- **LEVEL UP** Level Up Tutorials: Author's Perspective

- 💬 Speaking and Listening Studio: Giving a Presentation; Using Media in a Presentation

- ⚙️ Vocabulary Studio: Context Clues

- ❗ Grammar Studio: Module 12: Lesson 2–5: Using Commas Correctly

- ✅ "Into the Lifeboat" Selection Test

SUMMARIES

English

Violet Jessop served as a stewardess aboard the *Titanic* when it hit an iceberg in the North Atlantic. Jessop describes the confusion as the crew tries to get passengers into the lifeboats. Some lifeboats are lowered into the ocean with very few people; others are lowered with too many. As Jessop is boarding a lifeboat, a crew member tosses a baby to her. As the lifeboat rows away, Jessop comforts the baby and counts the decks of the ship. Each time she looks back, she realizes that one fewer deck is above the water. Finally, the *Titanic* sinks into the ocean, taking many people with her.

Spanish

Violet Jessop trabajaba como camarera abordo del *Titanic* cuando el barco chocó contra un iceberg en el Atlántico Norte. Jessop describe la confusión reinante cuando la tripulación intenta hacer subir a los pasajeros a los botes salvavidas: algunos botes se echan al agua con muy pocas personas; otros, con demasiadas personas. Cuando Jessop está abordando uno de los botes, un miembro de la tripulación le avienta un bebé. A medida que el bote se aleja, Jessop consuela al bebé y cuenta la cantidad de cubiertas del barco. Cada vez que se voltea a mirar, se da cuenta de que hay una cubierta menos sobre el nivel del agua. El *Titanic* termina naufragando, llevándose la vida de muchísimas personas.

 ## SMALL-GROUP OPTIONS

Have students work in small groups to read and discuss the selection.

Think-Pair-Share

Organize the class into six small discussion groups. Two groups will have the same question. Have those with questions 2 and 3 check with other groups so they do not duplicate topics and answers. When all the groups have finished, let them take turns presenting their answers to the class.

1. What are all the reasons, or purposes, Violet Jessop might have had for writing about the *Titanic*?

2. What very strong mental imagery stayed in your mind and why?

3. What is a good example from this text of understanding new vocabulary because of the context?

Three Before Me

As students plan their writing assignment from page 203, let them know that when they finish their second draft of the letter, they will:

1. Ask three students to check the letter and to suggest edits, then initial the draft to say they checked for comma use, vivid vocabulary, correct spelling, and an informal tone.

2. Students will then create a third draft of the letter, incorporating any needed edits, and then turn in both copies to the teacher.

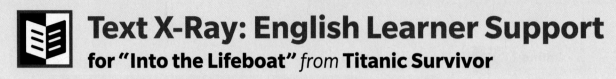

Text X-Ray: English Learner Support
for "Into the Lifeboat" *from* **Titanic Survivor**

Use the Text X-Ray and the supports and scaffolds in the Teacher's Edition to help guide students at different proficiency levels through the selection.

INTRODUCE THE SELECTION
DISCUSS SURVIVAL

In this lesson, students will need to be able to understand the experience of a disaster survivor and why a survivor might want to tell their story.

Survival often takes a combination of luck and skill. Violet Jessop survived partially because she was a woman (women and children were evacuated first) and she was in a lifeboat. Her story helps memorialize that day and those who did not survive. She may have felt compelled to tell her story because so many did not live to do so.

Have students discuss the traits a person might need to survive, and why such a person might want to tell the story. Use sentence frames to guide the discussion:

- *A person needs to be _____ to survive.*
- *A survivor may want to share their story because _____.*

CULTURAL REFERENCES

The following words and phrases may be unfamiliar to students:

- *Shining example for backwards souls* (paragraph 7): This phrase is sarcastic. The "backward souls" are those who did not do as they were asked to do.
- *terrible plight* (paragraph 12): These words are often used together in English to mean a dangerous and difficult situation, in this case not speaking English during a disaster when all the directions are being given in English.

LISTENING

Listen for Details

Tell students that reading a memoir means you are seeing the event from one person's point of view. Details about what is happening come through that person's eyes and ears.

Have students listen as you read aloud paragraphs 25–27. Have students listen for important details related to what is happening. Use the following supports with students at varying proficiency levels:

- Summarize an important detail from the excerpt, and have students repeat it after you: *Violet Jessop counts the decks she sees. This tells her how many are still above water.* **SUBSTANTIAL**
- Have students identify important details about what is happening. Ask: *Did the ship go down right away? What is happening to the ship during these three paragraphs?* (*The ship is filling with water and getting lower and lower in the water.*) **MODERATE**
- Pair students and have them summarize to each other orally what is happening in this section. **LIGHT**

SPEAKING

Discuss Imagery

Draw students' attention to the strong word choices and sensory images that Violet Jessop used in the first two pages of her memoir.

After reading the first two pages, pause and have students discuss the most memorable images. Use the following supports with students at varying proficiency levels: **SUBSTANTIAL**

- Tell students to close their eyes and visualize what they have read. Have them offer one-word descriptions of what they see in their mind's eye. **MODERATE**
- Have students say aloud words and phrases that describe what was left behind. Ask: *What did Jessop see as she went to get something to keep her warm?* (*people milling around, some people working, jewelry and silver slippers*) **LIGHT**
- Pair students to discuss the images that they found most memorable. Use sentence frames if needed: *I thought that _____ was interesting. The details I remember are _____.*

READING

Analyze Character Reactions

Descriptions of how different people reacted to the emergency create a sense of chaos and disbelief.

Work with students to analyze character reactions in paragraphs 13–14. Read the paragraphs together. Use the following supports with students at varying proficiency levels:

- Tell students that different people reacted in different ways to the emergency. Make statements and have students agree or disagree. For example: *Jessop was worried some people would not understand the directions.* (*true*) *People were calm and orderly.* (*false*) **SUBSTANTIAL**
- Have students point to words that show people were reacting with panic and fear. (*rapidly, dashed, throwing, hurled*) **MODERATE**
- Have students identify the action and conflict in the excerpt. Ask: *What were different individuals and groups doing?* (*throwing things off the ship, running around, trying to get in lifeboats.*) **LIGHT**

WRITING

Write a Letter

Draw students' attention to the letter assignment on page 203. Review the use of commas in a letter.

Use the following supports with students at varying proficiency levels:

- Give students a sample letter with commas after the greeting and closing. Have them use this as a model for using commas in their letters. **SUBSTANTIAL**
- Provide a model letter as above, but make sure to use one sentence with a subordinate clause separated by a comma. Have students use this as a model for their own letters. **MODERATE**
- Have students write their letters, then work with a partner to combine two simple sentences using a comma. **LIGHT**

INTO THE LIFEBOAT
from TITANIC SURVIVOR

Memoir by **Violet Jessop**

Connect to the
ESSENTIAL QUESTION

What does it take to be a survivor? When the *Titanic*—a British luxury passenger ship—left the port in England on April 10, 1912, and headed for New York City, there were 2,208 people aboard. Records show 1,503 died when the ship sank in the North Atlantic on April 12. Who physically survived, and why did they survive? "Into the Lifeboat" from *Titanic Survivor* is a memoir, a nonfiction narrative account, that gives some of these answers.

MENTOR TEXT

At the end of the unit, students will be asked to write a nonfiction narrative. "Into the Lifeboat" provides a model for how a writer uses specific details, thoughtful word choice, and clear imagery as well as well-placed commas to create an interesting and informative narrative.

ESSENTIAL QUESTION:

What does it take to be a survivor?

LEARNING MINDSET

Seeking Challenges Remind students that seeking out challenges is essential to learning, and that sometimes a challenge might be something you don't want to do, rather than something that is hard to do. In fact, overcoming challenges is key to developing skills and intelligence. Reassure students that making mistakes is part of the learning process. By taking risks and trying different strategies, students will find that challenges result in learning and personal growth.

QUICK START

What do you know about the *Titanic?* Where did you get your information about the ship? Discuss your answers with a partner.

EXPLAIN AUTHOR'S PURPOSE AND MESSAGE

To explain the **author's purpose,** begin by asking why the author wrote the text. In the case of a memoir, the genre offers clues to the author's purpose. Memoirs are first-person accounts of historical events or moments in a person's life that are especially meaningful. The purpose is to recreate a moment in the author's own experience and enable the reader to understand that moment's significance.

The **author's message** is what the author wants you to take away—an insight, a personal connection, a deeper understanding. To explain the author's message within a text, think about the following:

- What does the author want the reader to feel?
- What main idea or theme is the author presenting?

To see if your ideas about the author's purpose and message are on the right track, find evidence in the text. Text evidence supports your ideas and refines your understanding of the author's purpose and message.

CREATE MENTAL IMAGES

Authors choose words that create mental images to establish a text's setting, action, and characters. Vivid descriptions help readers "see" pictures in their minds. Creating mental images as you read will help you understand the author's purpose and message as well as identify the evidence to support your ideas. Look at the examples below.

DESCRIPTIVE LANGUAGE	MENTAL IMAGE
A tiny breeze, the first we had felt on this calm night, blew an icy blast across my face....	The words *breeze* and *calm* are opposites of *icy blast,* creating tension and a sense of sudden danger.
...as the ship seemed to right herself like a hurt animal with a broken back.	Similes are a kind of comparison. This simile compares the ship to an injured animal. Readers can imagine a creature, too injured to survive, that nevertheless fights to live.

GENRE ELEMENTS: MEMOIR

- is a form of autobiographical writing
- includes the writer's personal experiences and observations of significant events or people
- often has an informal or intimate tone
- presents insights into the impact of historical events on people's lives

Into the Lifeboat   193

QUICK START

Have students read the Quick Start questions. Ask them to show thumbs up if they are already familiar with the story of the *Titanic.* Ask them whether they have seen any documentaries or movies about the sinking of this ship and what they remember about those. Ask them what sounds, images, or feelings stayed in their minds. Then allow time for students to respond to the prompt and discuss with partners.

EXPLAIN AUTHOR'S PURPOSE AND MESSAGE

Why does anyone write a story about an event in their own lives? Why write about disaster? Ask students to brainstorm reasons and list them on the board.

Potential answers:

- to express feelings about events
- to explain what happened
- to examine the role the writer played in the event
- to memorialize someone who may have died in the event
- to criticize the way things were handled
- to serve as an eyewitness
- to tell an interesting true story

Tell students that identifying the reasons an author writes a memoir will help them understand the main ideas of a text.

CREATE MENTAL IMAGES

After students study and discuss the chart on page 193, have them think of a simple event like a violent rain or snowstorm and write a one-sentence description using vivid images and similes. Ask a few students to share these with the class.

TEACH

CRITICAL VOCABULARY

Encourage students to read all the sentences before deciding which word best completes each one. Remind them to look for context clues that match the meaning of each word.

Answers:

1. *a*
2. *a*
3. *b*
4. *a*
5. *a*
6. *b*

■ English Learner Support

Use Cognates Tell students that several of the Critical Vocabulary words have Spanish cognates: *illuminate/ iluminar, facinate/fascinan, agonizing/agonizante*. Have students use their knowledge of the definitions of these words to compare each word's definition to that of its cognate. **ALL LEVELS**

LANGUAGE CONVENTIONS

Review the information about commas. Explain that one of the best ways to learn about how commas make meaning clearer is to read a sentence aloud and pause slightly when there is a comma. Ask students to mark all the commas on the first two pages. To help students begin to analyze when to use commas, ask them to use a different color pencil or highlighter for commas after introductory elements like "True," in paragraph 1 or "Out on deck," in paragraph 5.

✎ ANNOTATION MODEL

Remind students they can underline important sentences and phrases and circle words that are significant. Point out that they may follow this suggestion or use their own system for marking up the selection in their write-in text.

They may want to color-code their annotations by using highlighters or use sticky notes. For these selections, take special note of the use of imagery in the narrative. In this case imagery refers to sights, but also sounds, smells, and touch. Have them note strong word choices (e.g. *briskly* versus *quickly*) and comma use.

CRITICAL VOCABULARY

reluctance	illuminate	unrestrainedly
reassure	fascinate	agonizing

See which Critical Vocabulary words you know by choosing the better answer.

1. If you do something with **reluctance,** you are _____.
   a. unwilling   b. excited

2. If you are _____, you want someone to **reassure** you.
   a. unsure   b. confident

3. When street lights **illuminate** a highway, they _____ the road.
   a. hide   b. brighten

4. If books **fascinate** you, they _____ you.
   a. interest   b. bore

5. If a person behaves **unrestrainedly,** he or she acts _____.
   a. without control   b. with interest

6. If you are **agonizing** about a test, you are _____ about it.
   a. really confident   b. extremely worried

LANGUAGE CONVENTIONS

Commas In this lesson, you will learn about the correct use of commas in complex sentences, transitions, and introductory elements. Commas set dependent clauses and phrases off so that a reader can quickly grasp a sentence's meaning. The following example from the text shows comma use in a complex sentence:

Fascinated, my eyes never left the ship, as if by looking I could keep her afloat.

As you read the selection, note the author's use of commas.

ANNOTATION MODEL   **NOTICE & NOTE**

As you read, note the author's word choices and imagery. In the model, you can see one reader's notes about mental images.

1 You could almost imagine this a scene of busily curious people with not very much to do. True, there were officers and men briskly getting lifeboats ready to lower, their tense faces strangely in contrast to the well ordered groups wandering about.

> These words give me a mental image of people trying not to panic.

BACKGROUND

Violet Jessop *(1887–1971) was a stewardess on board the Titanic for its first and only voyage in 1912. Because of its state-of-the-art construction, the luxurious Titanic was considered practically unsinkable—so it didn't carry enough lifeboats for all of its passengers. When the ship sank, Jessop, along with most of the women and children, was rescued on one of the lifeboats. Despite surviving two other disasters aboard ships, she continued to work aboard them until 1950.*

INTO THE LIFEBOAT

from **Titanic Survivor**

Memoir by Violet Jessop

SETTING A PURPOSE

As you read, note the author's word choice and use of imagery. Be aware of the mental images they create in your mind. Think about how these images enrich the experience of reading this selection.

1   You could almost imagine this a scene of busily curious people with not very much to do. True, there were officers and men briskly getting lifeboats ready to lower, their tense faces strangely in contrast to the well ordered groups wandering about. I felt chilly without a coat, so I went down again for something to cover my shoulders and picked up a silk eiderdown[1] from the first open cabin I came to. How strange it was to pass all those rooms lit up so brilliantly, their doors open and contents lying around in disorder. Jewels sparkled on dressing tables and a pair of silver slippers were lying just where they had been kicked off.

---

[1] **silk eiderdown** (sĭlk ī'dər-doun'): a quilt stuffed with the down, or feathers, of the eider duck; this luxurious item would have been considered inappropriate for a stewardess to wear while at work.

Notice & Note

Use the side margins to notice and note signposts in the text.

Into the Lifeboat   195

BACKGROUND

Violet Jessop was born in Ireland and lived in Britain so she could find work. Her mother had been a stewardess on ocean liners, and, even though she was afraid of ships, Violet began to do the same work. She was serving aboard the *Olympic* when it collided with the HMS *Hawke* in 1911 and was serving as a nurse for the Red Cross aboard the *Britannic* when it sank in 1916. She survived both disasters. In between the *Olympic* and the *Britannic*, Violet took a job aboard the ship she believed would be the safest of all the ships at sea, the *Titanic*.

SETTING A PURPOSE

Direct students to use the Setting a Purpose prompt to focus their reading.

 ENGLISH LEARNER SUPPORT

Demonstrate Comprehension   Tell students you will be reading the first two sentences of paragraph 1 aloud without pausing for punctuation. Ask them to avoid looking at the text but simply listen for places that it sounds as though there should be a pause. Then ask students to look at the text, circling periods and commas. Read the text again, pausing at commas and periods, as students follow along. Have students compare the two readings. Then have students choral read the paragraphs.

MODERATE/LIGHT

CONTRASTS AND CONTRADICTIONS

Remind students that they should look out for surprising contrasts in narratives. Point out that Jessop uses vivid **imagery** to show a contrast between the band playing music while people were crowding the deck and getting into the lifeboats. (**Answer:** *The purpose could be to show that people were in shock and denial. It seemed to be a slow-motion disaster, and people did not always act like it was really happening.*)

EXPLAIN AUTHOR'S PURPOSE

Remind students that authors don't choose details randomly; they include details that are relevant to a narrative. Students should ask themselves, "Why is this detail relevant?" (**Possible answer:** *This is an important point for the author to present early in the text because it sets the scene for who may or may not survive the sinking ship.*)

CRITICAL VOCABULARY

reluctance: This word means that someone does not want to do something, so they are holding back.

ASK STUDENTS why they think passengers were so reluctant to get on the lifeboats. To base their answers on the text, they may reread paragraph 5.

reassure: Sometimes people look for reasons to believe something and are reassured even if the reason is not a good one.

ASK STUDENTS why seeing the lights in the distance reassured passengers even though the lights could have been anything.

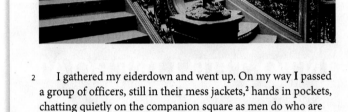

CONTRASTS AND CONTRADICTIONS

Notice & Note: What surprises Jessop in paragraph 3? Mark something unexpected.

Infer: What could be Jessop's purpose for including this observation?

EXPLAIN AUTHOR'S PURPOSE

Annotate: Reread paragraphs 4–5. Mark who was allowed to get into the lifeboats first.

Evaluate: Why would this be an important point for the author to present early in the text?

reluctance
(rĭ-lŭk´təns) *n.* Showing *reluctance* to do something means you are unwilling.

reassure
(rē´ə-sho͝or´) *v.* To *reassure* someone is to give comfort or confidence to that person.

---

2   I gathered my eiderdown and went up. On my way I passed a group of officers, still in their mess jackets,[2] hands in pockets, chatting quietly on the companion square as men do who are waiting for something. They smiled at me and I waved back.

3   As I turned I ran into Jock, the bandleader and his crowd with their instruments. "Funny, they must be going to play," thought I, and at this late hour! Jock smiled in passing, looking rather pale for him, remarking, "Just going to give them a tune to cheer things up a bit," and passed on. Presently the strains of the band reached me faintly as I stood on deck watching a young woman excitedly remonstrating[3] with an embarrassed young officer. He wanted her to get into the lifeboat he was trying to fill but she refused to go without her father.

4   "He must wait," responded the officer, "till the decks are cleared of women and children."

5   Out on deck, the first arguments started over who would and who wouldn't go into the boats which appeared to be suspended miles above the yawning blackness below.

6   Nobody was anxious to move; *Titanic* seemed so steady. To justify their **reluctance**, some pointed to a light on the horizon: another ship's lights![4] People were **reassured**, content to bide their time.[5]

---

[2] **mess jacket:** a man's short, close-fitting jacket worn by the military or as part of a uniform for officers, waiters, etc.

[3] **remonstrating** (rĭ-mŏn´strāt´ĭng): to say or plead in protest or objection.

[4] **another ship's lights:** two ships were nearby, the *Carpathia* and the *Californian*; the *Carpathia* was more than 50 miles away, and the *Californian* was about 20 miles away.

[5] **bide their time:** to wait in a patient way for further developments.

7   One boat was already being lowered with very few people in it. When this was pointed out as a shining example for backward souls by the officer near me, he got a rather alarming response as the crowd surged forward to embark. The boat was lowered very full, almost too full this time; and so on. Always, some held back in need of coaxing while a few were too eager.

8   A steward stood waiting with his back to the bulkhead,[6] hands in his pockets. It struck me forcibly as the first time I had ever seen a steward stand thus amid a group of distinguished guests.

9   A woman standing near me gave an approving glance as John Jacob Astor handed his wife into a boat, waving encouragingly to her as he stepped back into an ever-increasing crowd of men.

10   Ann Turnbull,[7] still silent and unmoved, dragged a little behind me. I suggested we keep together and we stood awhile to watch. There was nothing else we could do. Dimly I heard a shot.

11   Glancing forward I caught my breath as a white rocket shot up,[8] then another. Distress rockets! They went very high with great noise. The lights on the horizon seemed to come nearer. That cheered up the group about us, who had slowly started to fill a boat. Young officers urged them to greater speed, showing unlimited patience, I thought. Another rocket went up into the night.

12   A few women near me started to cry loudly when they realized a parting had to take place, their husbands standing silently by. They were Poles[9] and could not understand a word of English. Surely a terrible plight, to be among a crowd in such a situation and not be able to understand anything that is being said.

13   Boats were now being lowered more rapidly and a crowd of foreigners was brought up by a steward from the third class. They dashed eagerly as one man over to a boat, almost more than the officer could control. But he regained order and managed to get the boat away. It descended slowly, uncertainly

---

[6] **bulkhead:** a supporting barrier or wall dividing a ship into compartments that prevents leaks and fires.
[7] **Ann Turnbull:** another stewardess aboard the *Titanic* and a friend to Jessop.
[8] **a white rocket shot up:** a large Roman candle that indicated a ship's identity and condition to other ships; at the time, it was a way to communicate over long distances.
[9] **Poles:** people from Poland.

© Houghton Mifflin Harcourt Publishing Company

NOTICE & NOTE

CONTRASTS AND CONTRADICTIONS

Notice & Note: In paragraph 7, mark people's contrasting reactions to getting into the lifeboats.

Cause/Effect: What caused these different responses to leaving the *Titanic*?

LANGUAGE CONVENTIONS
Annotate: In paragraphs 10–12, mark commas that set off introductory elements at the beginning of sentences.

CREATE MENTAL IMAGES
Annotate: Mark the author's word choices in paragraph 11 that create mental images.

Connect: How do these images help develop the scene and show the author's feelings about the situation?

Into the Lifeboat   197

TEACH

CONTRASTS AND CONTRADICTIONS

Remind students that a narrative moves forward because of a series of events, often causes and their effects, and characters' reactions to those events develop **characters** and propel the **plot**. (***Possible answer:*** *People may have been reluctant to get on lifeboats because they did not want to leave their male family members, were afraid, or thought other help would come. Some may have not believed the* Titanic *was going to sink. In contrast, others panicked, realizing the ship was sinking, and pushed others out of the way to save themselves.*)

LANGUAGE CONVENTIONS

After students have marked commas that set off introductory elements, discuss how the introductory elements affect the meaning and structure of the sentence.

CREATE MENTAL IMAGES

Remind students that vivid adjectives and precise verbs help create memorable images that appeal to the reader's senses. (***Possible answer:*** *The word choices to describe the rockets going "high" and with "great noise" give the sense that the author feels hopeful they will be saved.*)

TEXT IN FOCUS

Analyzing Comparisons and Contrasts Have students view the **Text in Focus** video in their eBook to learn how to analyze comparisons and contrasts. Then have students use the **Text in Focus Practice PDF** to apply what they have learned.

APPLYING ACADEMIC VOCABULARY

☑ **circumstance**   ☐ **constraint**   ☐ **impact**   ☐ **injure**   ☑ **significant**

Write and Discuss Have students turn to a partner to discuss the following questions. Guide students to include the Academic Vocabulary words *circumstance* and *significant* in their responses. Ask volunteers to share their responses with the class.

- What were the **circumstances** the author found herself in?
- Why do you think this disaster is considered a **significant** one?

EXPLAIN AUTHOR'S MESSAGE

Have students read paragraphs 19–23 and note details they find jarring or particularly vivid. Have them discuss how Jessop is feeling as she receives and holds the "forgotten baby." (**Possible answer:** *The author wants the reader to understand why it felt like a dream and not like a disaster, so she tells us each moment to moment detail to show us that everyone was in shock and seemed to be sleepwalking. Someone might throw or catch a baby in a dream. Yet if you stop and think about what is really happening, it is frightening.*)

■ English Learner Support

Explain Author's Message Explain that authors choose details carefully to help readers understand a situation and how characters feel about the situation. Point out the phrase "prepared to throw it" in the first sentence of paragraph 19. Make sure students understand that "it" is a baby. Ask students why the author included this detail. (**Possible answer:** *This detail makes the situation seem confusing and dangerous. Under normal circumstances no one would think of throwing a baby.*) **SUBSTANTIAL/MODERATE**

For **reading support** for students at varying proficiency levels, see the **Text X-Ray** on page 192D.

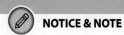 **NOTICE & NOTE**

at first, now one end up and then the other; the falls were new and difficult to handle.[10] Some men nearby were throwing things over the side—deck chairs, rafts or any wooden thing lying nearby.

14 Suddenly, the crowd of people beside me parted. A man dashed to the ship's side, and before anyone could stop him, hurled himself into the descending boat. There was a murmur of amazement and disapproval.

15 I turned to say something to Ann. Looking along the length of the ship, I noticed the forward part of her was lower now, much lower! For a fraction of a second, my heart stood still, as is often the case when faith, hitherto unshaken faith, gets its first setback.

16 One of the mailmen from our sorting office joined us. His work was finished, he remarked unemotionally. "The mail is floating up to F-deck with the water," he told us.

17 I tried not to hear what he said, not wanting to believe what he accepted so stoically.[11] Instead, I listened to the faint sounds of music from Jock's men. They were playing *Nearer My God to Thee*.[12]

18 My arm was suddenly jerked and I turned to see young Mason who had been busy filling a boat. His face looked weary and tired, but he gave a bright smile as he ordered my group into the boat, calling out "Good luck!" as we stepped in, helped by his willing, guiding hand. I nearly fell over the tackle and oars[13] as I tried to assist Ann in beside me. She was suffering with her feet, I could see, and found her lifebelt got in the way of moving freely.

EXPLAIN AUTHOR'S MESSAGE

Annotate: Mark details in paragraphs 19–23 related to the baby Jessop holds in the lifeboat.

Explain: What message is conveyed through the use of details about the baby?

19 Before I could do anything, young Mason hailed me and held up something, calling as he prepared to throw it, "Look after this, will you?" and I reached out to receive somebody's forgotten baby in my arms.

20 It started to whimper as I pressed it to me, the hard cork surface of the lifebelt being anything but a comfort, poor mite. The boat was full now, full of people with dull, inquiring faces. I spoke to one woman but she shook her head, not understanding a word I said.

---

[10] **the falls were new and difficult to handle:** lifeboat "falls" are the ropes and blocks used with a crane to lower the boat.

[11] **stoically** (stō ´ĭk-əl-lē): enduring pain and hardship without showing feelings or complaining.

[12] **playing *Nearer My God to Thee*:** a 19th-century Christian hymn popularly believed to have been played as the *Titanic* sank.

[13] **tackle and oars:** lifeboat equipment and paddles.

198 Unit 3

WHEN STUDENTS STRUGGLE . . .

Explain Author's Message Have students reread paragraphs 16 and 17 and discuss which words and events remind the reader of one of the author's main messages: that in spite of evidence, many people did not act as though the ship was sinking. (*"unemotionally," "I tried not to hear," musicians were playing*)

 For additional support, go to the **Reading Studio** and assign the following [LEVEL] **Level Up Tutorial: Author's Perspective**

WHITE STAR LINE

21   Groaning, the boat descended a fearful distance into that inky blackness beneath, intensified as the lights fell on it occasionally.

22   "Surely it is all a dream," I thought as I looked up the side of the ship, beautifully **illuminated**, each deck alive with lights; the dynamos were on the top deck.[14] I tried to make myself believe it could not be true, all this. I even noticed a few people leaning over the rail, watching in an unconcerned manner; perhaps they too were persuading themselves it was a bad dream!

23   We touched the water with a terrific thud, a bone-cracking thud which started the baby crying in earnest. Somebody in the forepart ordered oars out and we slowly pulled away from

illuminate
(ĭ-lōō´mə-nāt´) v. To *illuminate* means to brighten or give light.

---

[14] **the dynamos were on the top deck:** dynamos were electric generators on the ship; their location helps explain why the lights remained on.

Into the Lifeboat   199

CRITICAL VOCABULARY

illuminate: This sentence suggests that the ship was beautiful when it was lit up. We know it had carved wood paneling painted white in first class rooms. The light and shadows of those curves, when illuminated, would have been beautiful.

ASK STUDENTS to think about times when they might want to use the word *illuminated* to describe something beautiful when lit. *(Students may talk about churches, city streets, homes during the winter holidays, or candlelight.)*

CREATE MENTAL IMAGES

Review common types of figurative language with students—metaphor, simile, personification—before they mark the text. Have them identify the type of figurative language used. (**Possible answer:** *The phrase "like a knife" helps the reader feel the sharp cold. The smokestacks that fall "like a cardboard model" creates an image of a toy, making the reader feel what the writer felt: that it was all very unreal. Comparing the ship to an "animal with a broken back" creates an image of death coming slowly to something that was alive.*)

For **listening** and **speaking support** for students at varying proficiency levels, see the **Text X-Ray** on pages 192C and 192D.

CRITICAL VOCABULARY

fascinate: The word *fascinated* is a much stronger word than *interested*. In this case, it would mean that the author could not look away.

ASK STUDENTS to reread paragraph 24 and think about why the author was so fascinated with watching the Titanic sink. (*She did not want to believe it was sinking or so many were dying. She needed the evidence of her own eyes to believe it.*)

unrestrainedly: Have students reread the sentence with the word *unrestrainedly* in it. The author could have said that some women began to *sob*, but didn't.

ASK STUDENTS why the author chose the words she did. (*It is a very solemn and serious moment, so her language is serious. The women in the boat were realizing that their fathers, husbands, sons, and those who refused to leave, or did not have a boat to get into, were dying right at that moment.*)

NOTICE & NOTE

the side of the ship. I noticed one of the few men in the boat rowing; he was a fireman who had evidently just come up from the stokehold,[15] his face still black with coal dust and eyes red-rimmed, wearing only a thin singlet[16] to protect him from the icy cold.

fascinate
(făs´ə-nāt´) *v.* To *fascinate* someone means to capture the interest or attention of that person.

24   **Fascinated,** my eyes never left the ship, as if by looking I could keep her afloat. I reflected that but four days ago I had wished to see her from afar, to be able to admire her under way; now there she was, my *Titanic*, magnificent queen of the ocean, a perfection of man's handiwork, her splendid lines outlined against the night, every light twinkling.

25   I started unconsciously to count the decks by the rows of lights. One, two, three, four, five, six; then again—one, two, three, four, five. I stopped. Surely I had miscounted. I went over them again more carefully, hushing the whimpering baby meanwhile.

26   No, I had made no mistake. There were only five decks now; then I started all over again—only four now. She was getting lower in the water, I could not any longer deny it.

unrestrainedly
(ŭn´rĭ-strā´nĭd-lē) *adv.* Doing something *unrestrainedly* means doing it without control.

27   As if all could read my mind, the women in the boat started to weep, some silently, some **unrestrainedly.** I closed my eyes and prayed, prayed for one and all but dared not think of anyone in particular. I dared not visualize those people I had just left, warm and alive as I was. I tried to busy myself with the baby, but could not refrain from looking up again. Only three decks now, and still not a list to one side or the other.[17]

28   Desperately, I turned to where that other ship's lights shone on the horizon; surely they should be getting nearer by now. It was such a long, long time since we had first seen their comforting glow. They should be with us by now, taking off those patient waiting people over there. But no, she did not seem nearer, in fact, she seemed further away. Strange!

CREATE MENTAL IMAGES
Annotate: Mark the figurative language in paragraph 29.

Infer: Discuss the mental images invoked by this language.

29   A tiny breeze, the first we had felt on this calm night, blew an icy blast across my face; it felt like a knife in its penetrating coldness. I sat paralyzed with cold and misery, as I watched *Titanic* give a lurch forward. One of the huge funnels toppled off[18] like a cardboard model, falling into the sea with a fearful roar. A few cries came to us across the water, then silence, as the ship seemed to right herself like a hurt animal with a

---
15 **stokehold:** the area or compartment into which a ship's furnaces or boilers open.
16 **thin singlet:** a sleeveless, tight-fitting undershirt or athletic shirt.
17 **not a list to one side or the other:** no tilt of the ship.
18 **One of the huge funnels toppled off:** a smokestack fell off.

IMPROVE READING FLUENCY

Targeted Passage   Read paragraph 28 aloud, then have students work in pairs to list all the words and phrases that help create strong mental images and feelings. Then have them practice reading the paragraph to a partner, using expression to emphasize important details.

Go to the **Reading Studio** for additional support in developing fluency.

broken back. She settled for a few minutes, but one more deck of lighted ports disappeared. Then she went down by the head with a thundering roar of underwater explosions, our proud ship, our beautiful *Titanic* gone to her doom.

30   One awful moment of empty, misty blackness enveloped us in its loneliness, then an unforgettable, **agonizing** cry went up from 1500 despairing throats, a long wail and then silence and our tiny craft tossing about at the mercy of the ice field.

agonizing
(ăg´ə-nīz´ĭng) *adj.* To be in an *agonizing* state means to feel great mental suffering and worry.

CHECK YOUR UNDERSTANDING

Answer these questions before moving on to the **Analyze the Text** section on the following page.

1 The author wrote this text to —

   A express her opinion about a time in history

   B explain exactly why the *Titanic* sank

   C inform readers about how she survived the *Titanic*

   D describe what daily life was like for her on the *Titanic*

2 The author includes information about what others were doing before she got on the lifeboat in order to —

   F describe how everyone was worried about their clothes

   G show how many didn't realize the ship would sink

   H give a specific example of how to get on a lifeboat

   J entertain readers with interesting facts

3 Why does the author describe how she counted the rows of deck lights when she was in the lifeboat?

   A To show how she realized that the ship was truly sinking

   B To prove that she was right in a conversation with another passenger

   C To show that she wanted to soothe the baby she was holding

   D To explain that the deck lights were on as a signal for help

Into the Lifeboat 201

TEACH

CHECK YOUR UNDERSTANDING

Have students answer the questions independently.

Answers:

1. C

2. G

3. A

If they answer any questions incorrectly, have them reread the text to confirm their understanding. Then they may proceed to ANALYZE THE TEXT on page 202.

CRITICAL VOCABULARY

agonizing: The author says an agonizing cry, or wail, came from 1,500 people who were dying. They surely felt both emotional pain and physical pain right before they died, but hearing this cry would also create a feeling of mental suffering in the survivors.

ASK STUDENTS whether they think the author—in paragraph 30—meant those who were dying were in agony, or that hearing the dying caused agony in listeners. *(Either or both answers would be correct with thoughtful reasoning.)*

 ENGLISH LEARNER SUPPORT

Oral Assessment Use the following questions to assess students' comprehension and speaking skills:

1. Why did the author write this memoir? *(to inform readers how she survived the disaster)*

2. Why did the author talk so much about how people felt about getting on the lifeboats? *(to show how many did not take action because they didn't realize the ship would sink)*

3. The author described counting rows of deck lights on the *Titanic* as they rowed away. Why did she count the rows? *(to show that every few minutes there were fewer rows, which meant the ship was sinking)*

SUBSTANTIAL/MODERATE

APPLY

ANALYZE THE TEXT

Possible answers:

1. **DOK 4:** *The image is of someone interrupted in a task; he didn't have time to grab something warm to wear. His eyes are red-rimmed because he may have had coal dust in them, but he might also be tearing up from the sudden change from working in the heat to being in the cold night.*

2. **DOK 2:** *Both "yawning blackness below" and "that inky blackness beneath" emphasize that the passengers must descend into a terrifying unknown space.*

3. **DOK 4:** *The author notes people observing the lifeboat exit with an "unconcerned manner," so she wants to show how others were unable to take in the seriousness of the situation, or were in shock.*

4. **DOK 3:** *The author admires the crew members who helped the passengers without showing their own fear or frustration. She says that the young officers showed "unlimited patience" in paragraph 11.*

5. **DOK 4:** *The author uses metaphor to describe the Titanic, calling the ship the "magnificent queen of the ocean." The author conveys how it seemed impossible and unreal that such a new, well-made, and large ship could be destroyed.*

RESEARCH

Have students evaluate the reliability and credibility of the sites they query.

Example: Charlotte Appleton has a link to her death notice in the *New York Times*. Tell students that while almost anyone the right age could make this claim, *Times* obituaries are fact-checked against passenger lists and other sources. Tell students to look for links to reliable sites at the end of these articles to learn more.

Connect After students have discussed the survivors in a small group and looked for similarities in their experiences, have them share their results with the class.

 RESPOND

ANALYZE THE TEXT

Support your responses with evidence from the text. NOTEBOOK

1. **Analyze** What mental image does the author's choice of words create in the passage "... his face still black with coal dust and eyes red-rimmed, wearing only a thin singlet to protect him from the icy cold" (paragraph 23)?

2. **Compare** Compare the author's use of the phrase "yawning blackness below" in paragraph 5 with her reference to "that inky blackness beneath" in paragraph 21. What does the author convey about the characters' feelings by returning to this image?

3. **Evaluate** Consider the author's purpose in paragraph 22. Does she communicate that purpose effectively? Cite evidence to support your claim.

4. **Draw Conclusions** Which characters in the text does the author admire? Cite evidence to support your claim.

5. **Notice & Note** How do the author's thoughts and observations about the *Titanic* in paragraph 24 help readers understand the author's purpose? Cite evidence to support your claim.

RESEARCH TIP
The best search terms are very specific. Think about your topic and come up with key words or phrases. For example, a key phrase could be "names of *Titanic* survivors." Using quotation marks around your search phrase often yields more targeted results.

RESEARCH

Look up *Titanic* survivors other than author Violet Jessop, and choose one to investigate. First, use the chart below to make a list of survivors. Then, choose one person to research further, using multiple sources. What happened to that person at the time of the ship's sinking? What happened afterward?

SURVIVOR'S NAME	AGE, GENDER	NOTES
Answers will vary.		

Connect With a small group, discuss the survivor you researched. Then, learn about the survivors others researched. Are there any similarities in the way these survivors described their experiences? Synthesize the information you have uncovered in your research.

⚙ LEARNING MINDSET

Try Again Tell students that getting things wrong is part of the learning process. If they never take a risk—only staying in their comfort zone—they will never challenge themselves. Reassure students they should not be embarrassed when they get an answer wrong. Trying again is the follow-up to making errors. If they miss the mark, have them to go back to the text and reread until they find the information they need. Trying again will help them master the material.

APPLY

CREATE AND PRESENT

Write a Friendly Letter Write a letter to a friend describing a crowded or disorganized situation that you've seen or experienced recently. It could be at a sports event, in the cafeteria, on the bus, or another place. Follow the instructions and format below to compose your letter.

- ❏ Use the letter conventions, such as a date at the top, a greeting, and a closing, that are appropriate for a letter to a friend.
- ❏ Write in the informal, familiar tone you would use with a friend.
- ❏ Help the reader imagine what it was like to be at the scene by using vivid descriptions to create mental images.
- ❏ When revising, check for correct use of commas.

CREATE A MULTIMEDIA PRESENTATION

Gather video clips and images to create a short multimedia presentation about Violet Jessop. Decide whether you want your presentation to be a video or a slideshow. Follow these steps:

- ❏ Review Jessop's story and decide which parts you want to focus on in your presentation.
- ❏ Search for images and video that you can use.
- ❏ Develop a clear narrative by making connections between the different media sources you've chosen.
- ❏ Revise drafts before deciding on a final sequence.
- ❏ Practice your presentation in order to express your ideas effectively.

 Go to **Task, Purpose, and Audience** in the **Writing Studio** for more on tone and style.

Go to **Using Media in a Presentation** in the **Speaking and Listening Studio** for help creating a multimedia presentation.

REVIEW PRESENTATIONS
Evaluate yourself and your classmates using this checklist.
- ❏ makes eye contact
- ❏ speaks at an appropriate rate and volume
- ❏ enunciates clearly
- ❏ uses natural gestures

RESPOND TO THE ESSENTIAL QUESTION

? What does it take to be a survivor?

Gather Information Review your annotations and notes on "Into the Lifeboat." Add relevant details to your Response Log. Think about the author's:

- detailed observations
- experience as a survivor
- contribution to understanding what it takes to be a survivor

At the end of the unit, use your notes to write a nonfiction narrative.

ACADEMIC VOCABULARY
As you write and discuss what you learned from the memoir, be sure to use the Academic Vocabulary words. Check off each of the words that you use.
- ❏ circumstance
- ❏ constraint
- ❏ impact
- ❏ injure
- ❏ significant

CREATE AND PRESENT

Write a Friendly Letter Ask students to write a first draft of the letter following the main directions in the prompt. Their focus is on using a conversational style and vivid language. Tell them if a vague word like *nice* is all they can think of when they write the first draft, they should underline it and come back later to find a better, more descriptive word to use. Share with students that it will help them to choose one particular friend to keep in mind when they write.

For **writing support** for students at varying proficiency levels, see the **Text X-Ray** on page 192D.

CREATE A MULTIMEDIA PRESENTATION

Tell students to use the checklist steps to create their presentations. They should take each checklist item as something to do, and do well, before moving on to the next step. For instance, they can begin by working in pairs to review each page of the story and write down what parts of the story, or section, they will use. They should plan to dedicate 1 slide per section or 20–60 seconds, depending on the medium they choose to use. Remind students that if they are making a video, they will still need to do the same historical research to be sure of accuracy.

RESPOND TO THE ESSENTIAL QUESTION

Allow time for students to add details from "Into the Lifeboat" from *Titanic Survivor* to their Unit 3 Response Logs.

CRITICAL VOCABULARY

Encourage students to read all the sentences before deciding which word best completes each one. Remind them to look for context clues that match the meaning of each word.

Answers:

1. *agonizing*
2. *fascinate*
3. *unrestrainedly*
4. *illuminated*
5. *reluctance*
6. *reassure*

VOCABULARY STRATEGY:
Context Clues

Answers:

1. *hailed:* Context Clues: "Before I could do anything" and "calling as he prepared to throw it"; Definition: to call out to get the attention of; to greet

2. *whimper:* Context Clues: The baby is whimpering after it is tossed in the air. It is being pressed against an uncomfortable "hard cork surface." The author calls it "poor mite."; Definition: to cry or sob with soft sounds that start and stop

WORD BANK
reluctance
reassure
illuminate
fascinate
unrestrainedly
agonizing

Go to the **Vocabulary Studio** for more on context clues.

CRITICAL VOCABULARY

Practice and Apply Fill in the blank with the correct Critical Vocabulary word from the Word Bank.

1. The sound of crying from the sinking ship was _____ to hear.

2. Volcanoes and tsunamis _____ me.

3. _____ , she splashed paint all over the canvas.

4. The lights _____ the football field for the night game.

5. With _____ , he turned in his incomplete test.

6. The coach takes time to _____ players before a game.

VOCABULARY STRATEGY: Context Clues

To figure out what an unfamiliar word in a text means, look for **context clues.** Context clues are words or phrases that provide hints about the meaning of a word that you don't know. The following are two types of context clues: analogies and definitions.

UNFAMILIAR WORD	CONTEXT CLUE	TYPE OF CLUE	POSSIBLE MEANING
Like a bear cub losing sight of its mother, Laura was **reluctant** to part with her rescuer.	like a bear cub about to lose sight of its mother	analogy—a pair of items that are related in some way	resisting or not wanting something to happen
He felt **confounded,** or bewildered, when he learned that the ship had sunk.	bewildered	definition—words in the text define the unfamiliar word	greatly confused

Once you think you understand a new term, confirm your definition by checking a dictionary.

Practice and Apply Locate the following words in the selection: *hailed* (paragraph 19) and *whimper* (paragraph 20). Mark context clues, and then write definitions for the words. Use a dictionary to check your definitions.

ENGLISH LEARNER SUPPORT

Support Language Transfer As students work through the vocabulary activities, emphasize pronunciation of any new words encountered. Note that students with language backgrounds in Hmong, Cantonese, Korean, and Haitian Creole may struggle with /r/ as in *rabbit*, so the Critical Vocabulary words *reluctance, reassure,* and *unrestrainedly* may need more practice.

ALL LEVELS

LANGUAGE CONVENTIONS: Commas

Commas help communicate and clarify ideas by grouping words together to form units of meaning in a sentence.

In "Into the Lifeboat" commas are used in the following ways:

• to set off dependent clauses (groups of words that contain a verb and its subject but cannot stand alone) in complex sentences

> **A few women near me started to cry loudly when they realized a parting had to take place, their husbands standing silently by.**

• to set off transitions that link different words and phrases

> **Fascinated, my eyes never left the ship, as if by looking I could keep her afloat.**

• to set off introductory elements

> **Instead, I listened to the faint sounds of music from Jock's men.**

Using commas or other punctuation incorrectly causes confusion and misunderstanding. For example, comma splices incorrectly connect two independent clauses without a conjunction, such as *and* or *but*.

Incorrect: She agonized over leaving the ship, she eventually did go.
Correct: She agonized over leaving the ship, but she eventually did go.

In a run-on sentence, punctuation might be missing altogether.

Incorrect: The steward did not smile he served the musicians.
Correct: The steward did not smile. He served the musicians.

Practice and Apply Write your own sentences about the selection, using commas. Use the examples from "Into the Lifeboat" as models. When you have finished, share your sentences with a partner and explain each comma you used. Then, work together to identify places that a comma might make a sentence clearer. Revise your sentences as needed for clarity.

 Go to **Punctuation: End Marks and Commas** in the **Grammar Studio** for more on using commas correctly.

LANGUAGE CONVENTIONS: Commas

Photocopy a page from the text and cut up the paragraphs. Assign paragraphs to small groups. Ask groups to choose a sentence and evaluate it to decide the reason, or reasons, for the comma use.

- Dependent clause
- Set off transitions
- Set off introductory elements

Once students have come to a consensus, ask them to write the sentence on the board and explain.

Practice and Apply Ask students to choose the sentence their group evaluated, or one they saw successfully explained on the board, and use it as a model for their own sentences.

Students who finish early may check each other's work and challenge themselves to use a full paragraph from the text as a model for writing a paragraph about an event or disaster in their own lives, using commas.

ENGLISH LEARNER SUPPORT

Support Language Transfer As students look for dependent clauses in the selection, be aware that Vietnamese-speaking students may omit relative pronouns such as *who, that,* and *which,* because these are not required in Vietnamese. Hmong students may be used to using the same relative pronoun for personal (*who*) and inanimate (*that*) objects. Take the opportunity to have students practice using relative clauses if students identify them during the activity.

ALL LEVELS

WHEN STUDENTS STRUGGLE . . .

Language Conventions: Commas Have students reread paragraphs 29 and 30 aloud, pausing when there are commas and stopping at periods. Then have them use different pencil or highlighter colors (or use symbols above sentences if they have highlighted for a different reason) for commas that set off introductory elements, dependent clauses, and the transitions that link different words and phrases. Have them work in small groups to confirm and explain their choices.

from **AFTER THE HURRICANE**

Poem by Rita Williams-Garcia

GENRE ELEMENTS
FREE VERSE POETRY

Students will be familiar with poetry, but emphasize that **free verse poetry** is a special kind of poetry that doesn't have any sort of structure. That means it doesn't have regular patterns of rhyme, rhythm, or line length. It often sounds like ordinary speech. The lines vary in length in order to call attention to important words and ideas. Free verse poetry includes some of the poetic devices that students have already seen, such as alliteration, figurative language, imagery, and rhythm.

LEARNING OBJECTIVES

- Analyze the effects of structure and meter in poetry.
- Describe an author's use of figurative language.
- Conduct research and present findings on a recent disaster and the people who responded to it.
- Write an original poem about a life experience.
- Present an original poem in a poetry jam.
- **Language** Discuss the poem with a partner using the term *repetition*.

TEXT COMPLEXITY

Quantitative Measures	After the Hurricane	Lexile: N/A
Qualitative Measures	**Ideas Presented** Multiple levels. Symbolism, irony, satire. Some ambiguity. Greater demand for inference.	
	Structure Used More complex. More deviation from chronological or sequential order.	
	Language Used Meanings are implied. More figurative or ironic language. More inference is demanded.	
	Knowledge Required Requires no special knowledge. Situations and subject familiar or easily envisioned.	

Online **Ed**

RESOURCES

- Unit 3 Response Log

- Selection Audio

- Close Read Screencasts: Modeled Discussions

- Reading Studio: Notice & Note

- Level Up Tutorial: Narrative Poetry

- Writing Studio: Writing Narratives

- Speaking and Listening Studio: Participating in Collaborative Discussions

- ✓ "After the Hurricane"/Ninth Ward Selection Test

SUMMARIES

English

"After the Hurricane" is a free verse poem recounting the struggle in New Orleans after Hurricane Katrina in 2005. It is told from the perspective of Frederika, or "Freddie," who is trapped with her family and friends in New Orleans without adequate food or water. Freddie and her friends from the school band search for food and water for their families, vowing to never give up and showing what it really takes to be a survivor.

Spanish

"Después del huracán" es un poema en verso libre que recuenta la lucha en Nueva Orleans después del Huracán Katrina en 2005. Se cuenta desde la perspectiva de Frederika, o "Freddie", quien está atrapada con su familia y amigos en Nueva Orleans sin suficiente comida ni agua. Freddie y sus amigos de la banda escolar buscan comida y agua para sus familias, jurando nunca rendirse y mostrando qué se necesita para ser un superviviente.

👥 SMALL-GROUP OPTIONS

Have students work in small groups to read and discuss the selection.

Pinwheel Discussion

- Have students sit in groups of eight with four students seated facing in and four students seated facing out.

- Ask questions, such as: *How is life after the hurricane and flooding different from life before the disaster? How do the members of the Brass Crew support each other as they work to survive?* Have students in the inner circle remain stationary throughout the discussion.

- Ask students in the outer circle to move to their right after discussing each question.

- Control the discussion by providing a question for each rotation.

Double-Entry Journal

- Have students use a notebook or journal for recording Double-Entry Journal notes.

- Model how to divide each page down the middle by drawing a line from top to bottom. The heading on the left side of the page is "Quotes from the Text," and the heading on the right side is "My Notes."

- Ask students to record text passages in the left column that offer vivid details about life after the hurricane.

- Have students write their reactions (including interpretations and questions) in the right column, opposite the quoted material.

Text X-Ray: English Learner Support
for "After the Hurricane"

Use the Text X-Ray and the supports and scaffolds in the Teacher's Edition to help guide students at different proficiency levels through the selection.

INTRODUCE THE SELECTION
DISCUSS HISTORICAL EVENTS

In this lesson, students will need to be able to reference the events of Hurricane Katrina as they analyze free verse poetry. Provide the following explanations, reviewing any definitions as needed:

- In August 2005, Hurricane Katrina hit New Orleans, Louisiana, causing flooding.
- About 2,000 people died, and thousands were left homeless.
- Many people were unable to get out of New Orleans for several days. They had to stay in the city among the floodwaters, without enough food or water.
- They stayed in the Superdome football stadium, until a giant hole formed in the roof.

You may want to use the photographs in the poem to help students visualize some of the concepts. Then discuss the events of Hurricane Katrina using the following sentence frames:

- *After Hurricane Katrina, people needed _____. They also needed _____.*
- *The events of Hurricane Katrina were terrible, because _____.*

CULTURAL REFERENCES

The following words and phrases may be unfamiliar to students:

- *Special Effects* (line 9): visual illusions created by computers and cameras
- *Red Cross* (line 44): an international organization that provides help to disaster victims
- *diorama* (line 87): a miniature scene created to show something important that happened
- *Beauxmart* (line 166): a grocery store in New Orleans (actually called BreauxMart)
- *looters* (line 183): people who break into a store and steal items after a disaster
- *Big Empty* (line 203): a turn on the phrase the *Big Easy*, which is New Orleans's nickname

LISTENING

Compare Form and Free Verse

Tell students that some poems have a specific form. The lines are about the same length. The poem is set up so every line or every other line rhymes. Explain that free verse poetry doesn't have lines that are the same length, and it often doesn't rhyme. It's written like somebody would speak.

Have students compare "After the Hurricane" with a poem written in a regular meter and rhyme scheme, such as Robert Frost's "Stopping by Woods on a Snowy Evening." Have students listen as you read the rhyming poem, then lines 1–15 from "After the Hurricane." Use the following supports with students at varying proficiency levels:

- Ask yes/no questions, such as: *Did the poem have rhyming words? Did the poem have a regular rhythm, or beat?* **SUBSTANTIAL**
- Have students complete sentence frames to compare the way the poems sound: *_____ has a regular rhythm, or beat. _____ does not have rhyming words.* **MODERATE**
- Have students discuss with a partner how the two poems sound different, using the terms *rhythm* and *rhyme*. **LIGHT**

SPEAKING

Discuss Repetition

Discuss the poem's use of repeated words and lines using the term *repetition*. Explain to students that repetition in a poem is when a poet uses the same words, phrases, or lines over and over.

Discuss the use of repetition in lines 40–53. Use the following supports with students at varying proficiency levels:

- Have students find the words "The world is here" three times in these lines. Have them repeat this explanation after you: *The speaker repeats "The world is here." The repetition means this is an important idea in the poem.* **SUBSTANTIAL**
- Have students complete the following sentence frames in their discussion: *The speaker repeats _____. The repetition shows _____.* **MODERATE**
- Have pairs discuss why the speaker repeats "The world is here." Ask: *What or who is "the world"?* (*people watching on television; news people, police, and relief groups*) *Why does the speaker use repetition in this section?* (*to emphasize how many people are there*) **LIGHT**

READING

Analyze Structure

Review the concept of *structure*. Structure in a poem can include sentence length, rhythm, and repetition. The poet uses specific structures to draw the readers' attention to a specific point.

Work with students to reread lines 136–161. Use the following supports with students at varying proficiency levels:

- Have students look at line length and say whether the lines are mostly the same length or mostly different lengths. (*mostly the same*) Explain that the regular, short lines are meant to seem like marching. Demonstrate walking or marching as you read the lines. **SUBSTANTIAL**
- Guide students to describe line length. Use sentence frames to guide responses: *The lines in this part are mostly _____ length. There are many short _____.* Have students march as you read aloud the lines. **MODERATE**
- Have student pairs explain how the lines in this section compare to each other in length and how this reflects a marching band. **LIGHT**

WRITING

Write a Poem

Work with students to read the writing assignment on p. 219. Explain that a narrative poem is a poem that tells a story and is often narrated from the point of view of a character who plays a part in the story.

Use the following supports with students at varying proficiency levels:

- Help students brainstorm a word bank of descriptive words to describe an event they experienced or witnessed. Encourage students to incorporate one or two words or phrases from their first language into their poems. **SUBSTANTIAL**
- Suggest that students use a question-and-answer structure for part or all of their poems. Have them look at questions and answers in the selection for ideas. **MODERATE**
- Give students several poems that are simpler and shorter than this selection to use as models for their own poems. **LIGHT**

Connect to the
ESSENTIAL QUESTION

"After the Hurricane" is a free verse poem that tells the story of a young person and her friends trying to survive in New Orleans after Hurricane Katrina. The group will stop at nothing to get food and water for their families, demonstrating what it takes to be a survivor.

COMPARE ACROSS GENRES

Explain that the authors of "After the Hurricane" and *Ninth Ward* use different genres to explore the same historical event—the aftermath of Hurricane Katrina. As students read, have them look for similarities and differences in the way each author uses language and text structure to describe the events.

COLLABORATE & COMPARE

POEM

from

AFTER THE HURRICANE

by **Rita Williams-Garcia**
pages 209–217

COMPARE ACROSS GENRES

As you read, notice how both texts tell about young peoples' experiences with the same natural disaster, Hurricane Katrina. Look for ideas in the two texts that are similar or related. After you read both selections, you will collaborate with a small group on a final project.

 ESSENTIAL QUESTION:

What does it take to be a survivor?

NOVEL

from

NINTH WARD

by **Jewell Parker Rhodes**
pages 223–227

206   Unit 3

from **After the Hurricane**

QUICK START

Read the title of the poem. What do you predict it will be about?

ANALYZE THE EFFECTS OF STRUCTURE AND METER

A poem's **form,** or **structure,** is the way its words and lines are arranged on a page. Some forms are also defined by poetic devices, such as rhyme, repetition, and rhythm. Many traditional forms of poetry use regular patterns of stressed and unstressed syllables to establish a regular rhythm, or **meter.** Paying attention to a poem's structure and meter can help you determine a poem's meaning, message, and theme.

Free verse is a form of poetry with no regular patterns of line length, rhyme, or rhythm. In free verse, poets use poetic devices such as repetition, word choice, catalogs (lists of related words and ideas), and alliteration (the repetition of consonant sounds at the beginning of words) to create rhythm and express ideas. Although free verse does not have a set structure, you can understand the organization of a free verse poem by analyzing its basic structural elements.

GENRE ELEMENTS: FREE VERSE POETRY

- lacks regular patterns of rhyme, rhythm, or line length
- captures the sounds and rhythms of ordinary speech
- varies line length to call attention to words and ideas
- includes poetic devices— alliteration, figurative language, imagery, and rhythm

STRUCTURAL ELEMENT	DEFINITION
line	any text appearing on one line—a sentence, a phrase, or a single word
line break	the place where a line of poetry ends; may be used to add emphasis to certain words and phrases
stanza	a group of two or more lines that form a unit in a poem to express related ideas— as a paragraph functions in prose

To analyze free verse, pay attention to line breaks and groupings of lines, and note the effects these choices have on the sound and feel of the poem. Ask and answer these questions as you read.
- What ideas are expressed in particular lines and stanzas, and in the entire poem?
- How does the use of free verse support the poem's ideas?
- What rhythms are created by repetition or line lengths?
- How do poetic devices work to create structure and organization?
- How do poetic devices contribute to the poem's message or theme?

QUICK START

Have students think about their predictions, then discuss them with a partner. After partner discussion, bring the class back together and have volunteers share predictions. You may want to note the predictions on a chart and display it in the classroom.

ANALYZE THE EFFECTS OF STRUCTURE AND METER

Review the first paragraph of this section about structure and meter in traditional poems. You may want to share some examples of traditional poems, emphasizing that line lengths are similar and there is a rhyming pattern. You may also want to demonstrate meter by having students clap at stressed and unstressed syllables.

Next, read the second paragraph about how free verse poetry does not have any regular structure like traditional poetry. Instead, free verse relies on repetition, word choice, catalogs, and alliteration to express ideas. Discuss the definitions of each of these terms.

The table shows some of the structural elements that free verse poetry uses. Emphasize to students that the "free" in free verse comes from the fact that the author feels free to vary lines, line breaks, and stanzas in order to drive home a message. Students should pay attention to line breaks and stanzas in a free verse poem, and note how the poet's choice to use that particular structure contributes to the message and feel of the poem. Review with students the bulleted list of questions they should ask themselves while reading in order to better understand the poem's message.

EL ENGLISH LEARNER SUPPORT

Understand Structure Explain the poetry terms *line* and *stanza*. Help students see the varying structure of line lengths and line breaks by having them draw a small vertical line at the end of each line in a passage, then connect those lines to create a zigzag or stair-step pattern. Provide statements that students can flag as true or false with a thumbs up or down, such as: *A stanza is made up of lines of poetry. A line is made up of stanzas of poetry.* More advanced students may work in pairs to circle stanzas and compare the different sizes of each using the words *longer, shorter, more, fewer.* **SUBSTANTIAL/MODERATE**

DESCRIBE AN AUTHOR'S USE OF FIGURATIVE LANGUAGE

Ask students what they know about figurative language. Many will already know that figurative language is language that communicates meanings beyond the literal meaning of the words. Review three types of figurative language and provide an example of each:

- **Personification** is a type of figurative language in which animals, objects, or ideas are given human qualities. For example, *She couldn't sleep the night before her vacation because excitement kept shaking her and screaming in her ear.*

- **Simile** is a comparison using the connecting words *like* or *as* to compare two things that people might not usually associate with each other. For example, *That morning the fog rolled in, thick as pea soup.*

- **Metaphor** is a comparison between two things, which does not use the connecting word *like* or *as*. For example, *The storm was a symphony of sounds playing together.* Make sure to review the concept of **extended metaphor**—when a metaphor continues for a greater length and in different ways. For example, *I like to think life is like the river that flows outside my window. Most days it is calm, gently flowing the way it usually does. Sometimes it grows overwhelmed and fierce as it rages angrily in waves and currents. Other times it is too empty to flow at all. It often encounters obstacles, and it learns to flow around them. The river has to adapt.*

Review the bulleted list of questions students can use to determine figurative language as they read. Emphasize that poets choose figurative language to convey a specific idea, lesson, or meaning, and readers must figure out what the poet is trying to say.

✏ ANNOTATION MODEL

Remind students that they should annotate their student books when prompted. They are free to mark up their books in any way that helps their comprehension and analysis of the text. The example on this page uses underlining, but they are free to use their own system for marking up the selection in their write-in texts. They may want to color-code their annotation by using highlighters. Their notes in the margin may include questions about ideas that are unclear or topics they want to learn more about. You may wish to review the example on this page that models paraphrasing of the first part of the poem, because doing so will help students understand the extended metaphor at the poem's beginning.

 GET READY

DESCRIBE AN AUTHOR'S USE OF FIGURATIVE LANGUAGE

Figurative language is language that communicates meanings beyond the literal meanings of words. Authors use figurative language to create effects, to emphasize ideas, and to evoke emotions. Personification, simile, and metaphor are types of figurative language.

Personification is a type of figurative language in which an animal, object, or idea is given human qualities. A **simile** uses the words *like* or *as* to make a comparison between two essentially unlike things. A **metaphor** compares two unlike things without using *like* or *as*. An **extended metaphor** compares two unlike things at length and in several ways.

To identify and analyze figurative language in a poem, ask:
- Does the poet portray animals, objects, or ideas with human characteristics? Why? What is the effect of the personification?
- Does the poet use simile or metaphor to make comparisons? What things are being compared? What message or emotion is the poet trying to convey through the comparison?
- How might the poet's use of figurative language connect to the theme or message of the poem?

ANNOTATION MODEL

NOTICE & NOTE

As you read, note elements of free verse and examples of figurative language. Mark evidence that suggests theme, plus any words that make you pause to think. Here are one reader's notes about "After the Hurricane."

this could be a disaster movie with

helicopters whipping up sky overhead,

Special Effects brought in to create Lake George

10   and not the great Mississippi

meeting Lake Ponchartrain.

The disaster movie metaphor gives me a strong image of the scene. The helicopters and special effects make an extended metaphor. I should look up Lake George.

There are 3 references to water. I wonder if they are hints about the theme.

208   Unit 3

BACKGROUND

Rita Williams-Garcia *(b. 1957) draws on her own experiences to write about issues that urban teenagers face today. The following poem focuses on one young person's experience with Hurricane Katrina. On August 29, 2005, Hurricane Katrina ripped through the Gulf Coast, causing massive damage along the coast. In the city of New Orleans, thousands of people were left homeless, almost 2,000 people lost their lives, and hundreds more were missing. Years later, parts of the city have still not been rebuilt.*

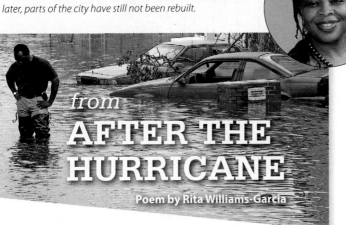

from

AFTER THE HURRICANE

Poem by Rita Williams-Garcia

PREPARE TO COMPARE

As you read, pay attention to the events that take place and how the speaker reacts to them. These observations will help you compare the poem with the selection that follows.

If toilets flushed,
if babies slept,
if faucets ran,
old bodies didn't die in the sun,
5   if none of it were real,
if we weren't in it,
this could be a disaster movie with
helicopters whipping up sky overhead,
Special Effects brought in to create Lake George
10   and not the great Mississippi
      meeting Lake Pontchartrain.
Out-of-work waiters would pose as policemen,
locals as extras paid in box lunches.
For set design, dump raw sewage, trash everywhere,
15 news trucks, patrol cars, army tanks, Humvees.

(b) ©Ethan Miller/Getty Images

Notice & Note

Use the side margins to notice and note signposts in the text.

ANALYZE THE EFFECTS OF STRUCTURE AND METER
Annotate: Mark the use of repetition in lines 1–6.

Identify Patterns: How does repetition and line length affect the poem's rhythm?

BACKGROUND

Have students read the background and information about the author. Explain that the loss and devastation caused by Hurricane Katrina was enormous. Thousands of residents of the city of New Orleans evacuated, leaving homes, jobs, and businesses behind, and in many cases separating their families. Thousands of others had no transportation or could not afford to travel. Tell students that the poem captures the struggles and emotions of people who did not evacuate and were then trapped in a city without power, water, or food.

PREPARE TO COMPARE

Direct students to use the Prepare to Compare prompt to focus their reading.

ANALYZE THE EFFECTS OF STRUCTURE AND METER

Have students complete the annotation instructions and share what they marked. Many will say they marked the repetition of the word *if*. Point out that repetition influences structure and rhythm, but also creates mood and tone. *If* suggests the speaker is wishing things could be otherwise. (**Possible answer:** *The effect of the repetition and line length is to create a regular rhythm with a fast pace that takes the reader quickly into the poem. The use of if phrases in the next stanza helps to recall the rhythm once again.*)

For **listening support** for students at varying proficiency levels, see the **Text X-Ray** on page 206C.

AGAIN AND AGAIN

Remind students that the **Again and Again** signpost refers to the author's **repetition** of the same word or idea. Authors use this repetition to convey a certain message or **theme.** Ask volunteers to share what they marked. Then discuss the question. (**Possible answer:** *The frequent repetition of the word* water *shows that water is important to the speaker and the people she's interacting with.*)

■ English Learner Support

Understand Repetition Help students understand the meaning of *repetition*. Demonstrate repeated words or phrases by repeating back to students what they say to you, or by repeating the same sentence over and over. Then demonstrate repeated rhythms by tapping out a rhythm with a pencil and having students repeat it several times. Explain that poems use repeated words and repeated rhythms. Find additional examples in the text. **SUBSTANTIAL/MODERATE**

 For **speaking support** for students at varying proficiency levels, see the **Text X-Ray** on page 206D.

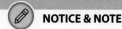 **NOTICE & NOTE**

If none of it were real,
if we weren't in it,
this could be a big-budget disaster flick
King, Jasper, and I'd rent
20 after band practice
like we did last Tuesday watching *Titanic* on Grandmama's sofa.
That Jasper could *laaaugh* at all the actors drowning
while the band played—*glub, glub, glub*—to the death.

25 But this ain't that. We're waist high in it.
Camera crews bark, "Big Mike! Get this, over here!"
"Roll tape."
"Got that?"
"Good God!"
30 "Shut it down."
This ain't hardly no picture.
We're not on location.
We're herded. Domed in,
feels like for good
35 unless you caught a bus like Ma
or Jasper's family (save Jasper).
I still want to smash a camera,
break a lens, make them stop shooting.
But King says, "No, Freddie. Gotta show it.
40 Who'd believe it without film?"

AGAIN AND AGAIN

Notice & Note: Why is water so significant to the speaker? Mark words used to describe water in lines 41–65.

Infer: What does the repetition of *water* and the way it is described tell you about its importance to the speaker?

Still no running water, no food, no power, no help. [Close Read]
The world is here but no one's coming.
The Guard[1] is here with rifles pointed.
The Red Cross got their tables set up.
45 Weathermen, anchors,[2] reporters, meteorologists,
a fleet of black Homeland SUVs.
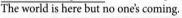
The world is here
but where is the water? The food? The power?
The way to Ma or Jasper's people.
50 They just herd us, split us, film us, guard us.

---

[1] **The Guard:** the National Guard of the United States, units of reserve soldiers that are controlled by each state. The National Guard responds to both the federal (national) and state governments for a variety of emergencies, both in this country and abroad.

[2] **anchors** (ăng´kərs): people who organize and read the news on media newscasts (television, radio, online); they work with a team that includes reporters and camera operators to report the news.

CLOSE READ SCREENCAST

Modeled Discussion In their eBooks, have students view the Close Read Screencast, in which readers discuss and annotate lines 41–53, a description of the desperate situation at the Superdome.

As a class, view and discuss the video. Then have students pair up to do an independent close read of lines 174–183. Students can record their answers on the Close Read Practice PDF.

 Close Read Practice PDF

No one said feed us. No one brought water.
The world is here but no one's coming.
Helicopters overhead beat up on our skies.

* * *

Miracle One.
55 King noses around the news guys,
   runs back to Jasper and me.
   "There's water trucks held up on the highway.
   Gallons, girl! Water by the gallons.
   Fresh drinking water.
60 Clean shower water.
   See that, Freddie. The water company loves us.
   Somebody thought to send us water."
   Even with our trumpets drowned, King's chest swells.
   He booms, "Brass Crew, are you with me?
65 Let's get outta here, bring back some water."

   How can I leave TK and Grandmama?
   How can I leave, and be happy to leave?
   Watch me. Just watch me
   high step on outta here
70 for the water I say I'll bring back.
   Honest to God, I heard "Brass Crew" and was gone.
   I heard *Elbows up,*
   natural breath!
   That was enough.
75 How can I leave, and be happy to leave?
   Easy. As needing to breathe new air.

   King's got a First Trumpet stride. Jasper walks.
   I lick the salt off my bare arms,
   turn to look back at the people
80 held up by canes, hugging strollers, collapsible
   black and newly colored people,
   women with shirts for head wraps.
   Salt dries my tongue.
   I turn my eyes from them and walk.
85 I don't have to tell myself
   it's not a school project for Ms. LeBlanc,

DESCRIBE AN AUTHOR'S USE OF FIGURATIVE LANGUAGE

Annotate: In lines 60–65, mark the use of personification.

Interpret: Why did the poet use personification here?

▶ **TOUGH QUESTIONS**

Notice & Note: What are the questions asked by the speaker in lines 66–76? Mark the repeated questions.

Draw Conclusions: What conflict is revealed by these questions and their answers?

DESCRIBE AN AUTHOR'S USE OF FIGURATIVE LANGUAGE

Annotate: Mark the words making comparisons to "Freddie's Diorama" in lines 85–101.

Evaluate: What is the effect of the speaker saying that all of these images are "not a school project"?

After the Hurricane 211

DESCRIBE AN AUTHOR'S USE OF FIGURATIVE LANGUAGE

Remind students that personification means talking about inanimate objects as if they are people. This type of figurative language can tug at the reader's emotions, because the inanimate objects take on needs, desires, and feelings. (**Possible answer:** *Suggesting that the water company "loves" shows that the speaker feels there are still people out there, working to help. Saying the trumpets "drowned" makes the loss of them more full of grief than saying they were washed away or buried.*)

▶ TOUGH QUESTIONS

Remind students that the **Tough Questions** signpost is when a character pauses to ask herself or others a tough question. Repetition of a tough question suggests an **internal conflict** in the mind of the speaker—some question that cannot be resolved or answered. (**Possible answer:** *The questions reveal the speaker's mixed feelings about getting out of a terrible place and leaving her family behind.*)

DESCRIBE AN AUTHOR'S USE OF FIGURATIVE LANGUAGE

Tell students that Freddie's comparison of real life to a school diorama is an example of an extended metaphor. A metaphor always compares mostly unlike things to bring out one particular similarity. Have students discuss what is being compared and the purpose of the comparison. (**Answer:** *The author uses "Freddie's Diorama" as a metaphor for the aftermath of Katrina. By saying that it is not like a diorama, the reader is able to see an aerial image of a diorama and compare it to that of Katrina. We are taken from a school project—a diorama—to imagining disaster scenes in far parts of the world, and then brought back startlingly to the United States and Katrina.*)

ENGLISH LEARNER SUPPORT

Understand Figurative Language To help English learners understand the meanings intended by the use of figurative language, introduce a simple simile, such as "the water is like glass." Use scaffolding to help students understand the simile:

Tell students this does not mean the water is glass, but that it looks clear and smooth the way a window is clear and smooth. Confirm understanding by asking: *Is water hard like glass?* (*no*) *Can it be clear like glass?* (*yes*) **SUBSTANTIAL/MODERATE**

Review that water and glass are different materials, and explain that the simile shows one way they are similar. Have pairs make up similes of their own. **LIGHT**

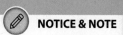
NOTICE & NOTE

ANALYZE THE EFFECTS OF STRUCTURE AND METER

Review the meaning of *catalogs* as a literary device. Explain that a catalog is a list of repeated words or items that can affect the pace of the poem. A catalog may feel steady, like a drum beat or funeral march, or it may give a poem a sense of acceleration—ideas and experiences tumbling ever faster towards an end point. Reading a poem aloud often gives readers a better sense of the effect of a catalog. (**Answer:** *The words in the list refer to members of the community who have been devastated by Katrina. The catalog has the effect of a chant, becoming hypnotic as you read through the many people who have been stranded by loss. It's a place in the poem to pause, and then gain momentum until reaching the end of the catalog. The few lines afterward help the reader understand what the catalog means and what these people have in common.)*

ANALYZE THE EFFECTS OF STRUCTURE AND METER

Annotate: Catalogs, or lists of related words, give structure and rhythm to free verse. Mark the catalog in lines 102–114.

Analyze: Identify how the words in the list are related. What effect does this catalog have on the poem's structure and meter? What effect does it have on the poem's meaning?

"The Colored Peoples of Freddie's Diorama."[3]
Green pasted just so, around the huts just so.
The despair just right.
90 It's not my social studies diorama
depicting "Over There," across the Atlantic,
the Pacific. Bodies of water.
Way, way over there.
The refugees of the mudslides,
95 refugees of the tsunami,
refugees of Rwanda.
No. It is US. In state. In country.
Drowned but not separated by
bodies of water or by spoken language.
100 The despair is just right, no translation needed.
We are not the refugees in my social studies diorama.
We are 11th graders,
a broken brass line,
old homeowners, grandmamas, head chefs, street

---

[3] **diorama** (dī´ə-răm´ə): a three-dimensional scene in which models of people, animals, or other objects are arranged in natural poses against a painted background.

APPLYING ACADEMIC VOCABULARY

☑ circumstance   ☑ constraint   ☐ impact   ☐ injure   ☑ significant

Write and Discuss Have students turn to a partner to discuss the following questions. Guide students to include the Academic Vocabulary words *circumstance, constraint,* and *significant* in their responses. Ask volunteers to share their responses with the class.

- What **circumstance** do the people in this poem find themselves in?
- What sort of **constraints** prevent them from getting what they need?
- Why is water so **significant** in this part of the poem?

105 performers, a saxophonist mourning the loss of his Selmer
    horn of 43 years and wife of 38 years. We are aunties,
    dry cleaners, cops' daughters, deacons, cement mixers,
    auto mechanics, trombonists without trombones, quartets
    scattered, communion servers, stranded freshmen, old
110 nuns, X-ray technicians, bread bakers, curators,[4] diabetics,
    shrimpers,[5] dishwashers, seamstresses, brides-to-be, new
    daddies, taxi drivers, principals, Cub Scouts crying, car
    dealers, other dealers, hairstylists, too many babies, too
    many of us to count.
115 Still wearing what we had on when it hit.
    When we fled,
    or were wheeled, piggybacked, airlifted, carried off.
    Citizens herded.
    We are Ms. LeBlanc, social studies teacher, a rag wrapped
120 around her head,
    And Principal Canelle. He missed that last bus.

                    * * *

    Minor Miracle.
    We walk past the Guard.
    You'd think they'd see us
125 marching on outta here.
    You'd think they'd stop us. Keep us domed.
    But we're on the march, a broken brass line.
    King, Jasper, and me, Fredericka.
    King needs to lead; I need to leave.
130 Been following his lead since
    band camp. Junior band. Senior band.
    Box formations, flying diamonds, complicated transitions.
    Jasper sticks close. A horn player, a laugher. Not a talker.
    See anything to laugh about?
135 Jasper sticks close. Stays quiet. Maybe a nod.

    Keeping step I would ask myself,
    Aren't you ashamed? No.
    Of band pride? No.
    You band geek. So.
140 Aren't you ashamed? No.
    You want to parade? So.
    Raise your trumpet? So.

---

[4] **curators** (kyŏŏ-rā´tərz): people who manage and oversee; most often describes those who manage a museum and its collection of art.

[5] **shrimpers** (shrĭmp´ərz): people who catch shrimp—small edible sea animals with a semihard outer shell.

DESCRIBE AN AUTHOR'S USE OF FIGURATIVE LANGUAGE

Annotate: Mark the language in lines 123–133 that compares the speaker and her friends to part of a school band.

Analyze: How does the speaker use the metaphor of a school band to develop an idea?

DESCRIBE AN AUTHOR'S USE OF FIGURATIVE LANGUAGE

Tell students this part of the poem uses another extended metaphor, a metaphor that compares Freddie and her friends to part of a school band. Make sure to clarify any unknown terms, such as *box formations, flying diamonds, complicated transitions.* (These are all terms for formations that marching bands do, some of which are challenging.) (**Answer:** *The speaker uses the metaphor of a school band to show that Freddie and her friends have a history in school band and have developed relationships as band members. The strength and relationship they developed is going to help them leave the shelter and find water for their families.*)

■ English Learner Support

Provide Visual Support Show students pictures and videos of marching bands performing various formations. Discuss how the band members would need to work together and persevere through challenges in order to master such elaborate shows. **SUBSTANTIAL**

For **reading support** for students at varying proficiency levels, see the **Text X-Ray** on page 206D.

TO CHALLENGE STUDENTS . . .

Analyze Speaker Have students research videos of marching bands performing various formations. Have students discuss with a partner how traits developed by working together on difficult shows helps Freddie and her friends face the challenge of the hurricane's effects. *(Being in a band together for so long and working through challenges has helped Freddie and her friends learn to work together and face challenges, two skills they need to help their families after the hurricane.)* Have students make a connection with their own lives by writing for ten minutes about how an activity they do now (band, sports, scouts) helps them develop traits and skills they could use to help others.

ANALYZE THE EFFECTS OF STRUCTURE AND METER

Remind students that poets often use repetition of certain words and phrases to emphasize important ideas or feelings. They should look for the phrase that is repeated throughout these lines. (**Answer:** *The speaker says "Aren't you ashamed? No." several times, indicating her confidence that what she is doing is right. The frequent line breaks and fast, clipped meter give the effect of an argument, which makes the speaker sound very determined in her beliefs.*)

EL ## ENGLISH LEARNER SUPPORT

Learn Language Structures Point out to students that the poet uses a series of questions and answers in lines 136–161. Read the stanza to students, identifying the questions and answers. Point out that the repetition of "No" makes the speaker sound confident. Ask students to describe how the speaker feels in this section. (*She is proud and confident that she can leave the shelter and help find water for their families.*)

LIGHT

ANALYZE THE EFFECTS OF STRUCTURE AND METER

Annotate: Read lines 136–161 aloud and mark repeated words and phrases.

Analyze: How do elements of structure and meter—including line breaks, repetition, and rhythm—help convey the speaker's feelings at this point in the poem?

Aren't you ashamed? No.
To praise Saint Louis?
145 "Oh, when the saints go marching in?"
Aren't you ashamed? No.
Of strutting krewe[6]
On Mardi Gras? The Fourth of July?
These very streets
150 Purple and gold, bop
Stars and Stripes, bop
Aren't you ashamed?
To shake and boogie?
Aren't you ashamed?
155 To enjoy your march,
while Grandmama suffers
and no milk for TK?
Tell the truth. Aren't you ashamed?
No. I'm not ashamed.
160 I step high, elbows up.
Band pride.

King asks, "Freddie, what you thinking?"
I say, "I'm not thinking, King."
But I'm dried out on the inside.
165 Hungry talks LOUD, you know.
"Let's try the Beauxmart. The Food Circle. Something."

King knows better. He doesn't say.
Still, we go and find (no surprise)
the Beauxmart's been hit. Stripped. Smashed.
170 Forget about Food Circle and every corner grocery.
Nothing left but rotten milk,
glass shards.[7] Loose shopping carts.
Jasper sighs. Grabs a cart.

Stomach won't shut up.
175 Talking. Knotting. Cramping. I whine,
"Let's go to Doolie's."
Again, King knows better. Still, we go,
almost passed right by. Didn't see it until
Jasper points. King sighs.

---

[6] **krewe** (krōo): any of several groups of people who organize and participate in the annual Mardi Gras carnival in New Orleans.
[7] **shards** (shärdz): small pieces of something that has been broken.

AHA MOMENT

Review with students that an **Aha Moment** is when a character realizes something important. Such a realization might mark a mental or emotional turning point for the character or speaker, or the resolution of an **internal conflict**. (*Answer: This passage describes a loss of innocence for the speaker. Sean Doolie, who was always generous to the community, especially to the band, has turned on the community and will shoot the looters. She realizes that nothing will be the same, that she will have to be wary of people she thought she could trust.*)

180 Check out the D in Doolie's, blown clear off.
The outside boarded up, chained up, locked.
Black and red spray-painted:
LOOTERS WILL BE SHOT.
I can't believe it.
185 Doolie who buys block tickets to home games
Doolie who sponsors our team bus
Band instruments, uniforms (all underwater),
Chicken bucket championships. The band eats half-price.
My eyes say, *Freddie, believe the spray paint:*
190 *Big Sean Doolie will shoot the looters.*
Yeah. Big Sean Doolie.
Believe.

King (First Trumpet) was right,
he doesn't make me (Second) like I'm second.
195 A simple, "Come on, Brass. Let's get this water."
I follow King. Jasper pushes the cart.
First, Second, Third. No bop step,
high step, no feather head shake,
no shimmy[8] front, boogie back.
200 Just walk.

---

[8] **shimmy** (shĭm´ē): to do the shimmy, a dance involving rapid shaking of the body.

AHA MOMENT

Notice & Note: What does the speaker realize in lines 184–192? Mark the words that indicate that the speaker's view of her world is changing.

Cite Evidence: What evidence in the stanza shows the speaker has come to realize something? Why is this realization important?

ANALYZE THE EFFECTS OF STRUCTURE AND METER

Discuss with students the idea that in this section of the poem, the speaker sees yet another helicopter she knows won't help them. Ask students to look for repeated phrases and examples of alliteration that convey the speaker's feelings. (**Answer:** *The repetition of the word* Another *suggests the speaker is weary of more and more helicopters that aren't going to help them. The repetition of the initial sound in the alliterative phrase "heavy heat" makes the heat feel even more oppressive. The speaker repeats the phrase "Big Empty" twice, a play on New Orleans's nickname The Big Easy, to emphasize that the atmosphere is empty of hope.*)

NOTICE & NOTE

ANALYZE THE EFFECTS OF STRUCTURE AND METER

Annotate: In lines 201–208, mark repeated phrases and examples of alliteration.

Draw Conclusions: How do these elements help convey the speaker's feelings?

"Hear that?"
Another helicopter overhead.
Another chopper stirring up the Big Empty.
Wide blades good for nothing but whirling up
205 heavy heat, heavy stink on empty streets
full of ghosts and mosquitoes.
Swat all you want. Look around.
Nothing here but us in Big Empty.

WHEN STUDENTS STRUGGLE . . .

Genre Reformulation Students who struggle to comprehend the story being told by this poem may benefit from rewriting the poem as prose that tells a story. Begin by creating an idea web with "After the Hurricane" at the center, and have students offer ideas to go in the spokes. Then have students work with partners to write the narrative told in "After the Hurricane." (You may also want to work as a whole group and create a group narrative that students can copy.) If students need extra help, supply sentence frames that they can complete.

For additional support, go to the **Reading Studio** and assign the following [LEVEL] **Level Up tutorial: Narrative Poetry.**

CHECK YOUR UNDERSTANDING

Answer these questions before moving on to the **Analyze the Text** section on the following page.

1 In lines 5–7, the speaker in the poem says *if none of it were real* to —

A express that the hurricane never happened, and that it is as fictional as a disaster movie

B express a dislike for disaster movies

C express that the disaster is very real, but she wishes it was fictional, like a disaster movie

D suggest that the story of the hurricane would never make a good disaster movie

2 In lines 136–146, the speaker's questions and answers show that —

F she is writing a journal entry to remember her experience

G she dislikes the experiences she has had in the school band

H she will stay inside the shelter because it is the right thing to do

J despite her doubts, she is determined to leave the shelter because it is the right thing to do

3 Which idea expresses how the speaker feels by the end of the excerpt?

A She feels relieved that the helicopter is there to help them.

B She feels dismayed and stranded in the devastation.

C She is happy that they will soon find some water.

D She has come to love the sound of the helicopters.

After the Hurricane   217

CHECK YOUR UNDERSTANDING

Have students answer the questions independently.

Answers:

1. C

2. J

3. B

If they answer any questions incorrectly, have them reread the text to confirm their understanding. Then they may proceed to ANALYZE THE TEXT on page 218.

(EL) ENGLISH LEARNER SUPPORT

Oral Assessment Use the following questions to assess students' comprehension and speaking skills:

1. Read lines 5–7. What does the speaker compare reality to? (*She compares reality to a disaster movie.*)

2. Why does Freddie leave TK and Grandmama to march away with the Brass Crew? (*She is going to get water from water trucks.*)

3. What words could describe the speaker's feelings in lines 201–208? (*sad and hopeless*) **SUBSTANTIAL/MODERATE**

APPLY

ANALYZE THE TEXT

Possible answers:

1. **DOK 2:** *In line 50 ("herd us, split us, film us, guard us") the poet uses repetition to establish a rhythm, but also uses imagery to suggest that the hurricane's refugees are being treated like cattle rather than human beings. With no food or water, plus the image of helicopters that "beat up our skies," the words suggest the outside world is assaulting them rather than assisting them.*

2. **DOK 2:** *The use of "how can I leave" and "be happy to leave" emphasize the speaker's mixed feelings about getting out of a terrible place and leaving her family behind, and point to a theme of making difficult choices to live one's life.*

3. **DOK 4:** *The short sentences give the poem a fast pace. The lines ending in questions and answers make it sound like a conversation.*

4. **DOK 3:** *A stomach that "won't shut up" by "Talking. Knotting. Cramping" is an example of personification. The author may be trying to express that the speaker's hunger is alive, persistent, and in need of attention.*

5. **DOK 4:** *The poem refers to water ("if toilets flushed"; "if faucets ran") from the beginning, and frequently mentions large bodies of water, such as Lake George, the Mississippi River, and Lake Ponchartrain, and then later the Atlantic and Pacific Oceans. It also talks about the need for fresh water. Setting up a contrast between the need for fresh water despite being surrounded by water shows the irony of their situation.*

RESEARCH

Review the point that the speaker in the poem criticizes the response of those who are supposed to help them, reflecting many people's belief that the response to Hurricane Katrina was insufficient and slow. Students will now look at the way people responded after other recent disasters. You may want to give them some suggestions of disasters they can research. Point out the research tip about using news clips for research. Help students locate these clips online if they ~~a~~re struggling to find them.

~~Co~~nnect If no one in the class is willing or able to share ~~pers~~onal experiences, have them read a news article about a ~~natur~~al disaster and use it to inform a discussion comparing ~~th~~em with a more journalistic account.

 RESPOND

ANALYZE THE TEXT

Support your responses with evidence from the text. 📖 NOTEBOOK

1. **Summarize** How does the poet use figurative language in lines 50–53 to convey meaning or ideas?

2. **Infer** Identify examples of repetition in lines 66–76. How might the poet's use of repetition point to a theme in the poem?

3. **Analyze** Reread lines 155–166 aloud. How do elements of free verse contribute to the pace and rhythm of the poem?

4. **Draw Conclusions** Identify the examples of figurative language in lines 174–175. What idea might the poet be trying to express by using this figurative language?

5. **Notice & Note** Identify ways in which water is mentioned throughout the poem. What ideas are conveyed by water images in the poem?

RESEARCH

RESEARCH TIP
Reviewing video clips and news reports that followed the disaster your group selects may help you identify organizations involved in relief efforts.

"After the Hurricane" describes the speaker's experience following Hurricane Katrina, revealing how a group of students responds to the disaster. The poem's speaker criticizes some of the responses of others—including the media and aid organizations—to the disaster.

In a small group, choose and research a more recent natural disaster to identify volunteers, professionals, and organizations that responded to that disaster. Generate questions about the responders, such as *What did they do? Who did they help? How effective were they?* Then, conduct research to answer your questions.

RESPONDER	QUESTION	ANSWER
Answers will vary		

Connect How does the experience of the poem's speaker compare to any disasters experienced by members of your group, class, or someone you know or have heard about? With your group, discuss ways in which the poem does or does not reflect personal experiences.

⚙️ **LEARNING MINDSET**

Curiosity Remind students that curiosity leads to learning. Being curious about new ideas and new topics opens up paths into learning about the world from new perspectives. Asking questions is something a curious reader does. Encourage students to ask questions about the poem they have read. What do they wonder about? How did the poem change the way they think about natural disasters?

CREATE AND PRESENT

Write a Poem Using "After the Hurricane" as a model, write a narrative poem describing an event that you have experienced or witnessed. Your poem can be about a disaster, an important milestone or achievement, or another experience that made an impression on you.

❏ Write a quick sketch or description of your experience.

❏ Use everyday speech to expand your description of the experience into a poem.

❏ Vary the length and grouping of your lines to change the rhythm and meter of your poem.

❏ Incorporate elements of free verse in your poem, such as catalogs, alliteration, and repetition.

❏ Include poetic devices, such as simile, metaphor, and extended metaphor.

Poetry Jam A poetry jam is a way to share poetry in an informal atmosphere. Hold a poetry jam to present your poem to a small group or to the entire class.

❏ Maintain eye contact as much as possible when presenting.

❏ Speak clearly, at a rate and volume that allows everyone to hear you. Speak at a pace that emphasizes the rhythm of your poem.

❏ Use an appropriate stance and gestures while speaking.

❏ Listen actively to each presenter and ask questions to help clarify understanding. Offer constructive advice where helpful.

RESPOND TO THE ESSENTIAL QUESTION

 ? What does it take to be a survivor?

Gather Information Review your annotations and notes on the poem. Then, add relevant details to your Response Log. As you determine which information to include, think about the needs of the people in the poem and how they responded to obstacles and challenges.

At the end of the unit, use your notes to write a nonfiction narrative.

 Go to the **Writing Studio** for more on writing narratives.

Go to the **Speaking and Listening Studio** for help with having a group discussion.

ACADEMIC VOCABULARY
As you write and discuss what you learned about "After the Hurricane," be sure to use the Academic Vocabulary words. Check off the words that you use.

❏ **circumstance**

❏ **constraint**

❏ **impact**

❏ **injure**

❏ **significant**

CREATE AND PRESENT

Write a Poem Tell students to first think of an important life event. Remind them that the assignment says they do not have to write about a disaster, although they can if they would like to. Other life events they can write about are important milestones, achievements, or experiences that made an impression on them. Emphasize to students that they need to pick a topic first, then write a quick sketch of the event. Review the checklist on page 219 so students understand all the elements of poetry they need to include in their poems. Remind students that this is a free verse poem that should sound like everyday speech.

For **writing support** for students at varying proficiency levels, see the **Text X-Ray** on page 206D.

Poetry Jam You may want to show students online videos of poetry jams so they become familiar with the concept. Review the checklist for presenting poems, emphasizing what students should and should not do when speaking in public. You may want to model some examples of inappropriate presentations (for example, staring down at the floor while talking) and have students discuss why your presentation was ineffective or uninteresting. Tell students they need to practice their presentations several times before the poetry jam.

RESPOND TO THE ESSENTIAL QUESTION

Allow time for students to add details from "After the Hurricane" to their Unit 3 Response Logs.

 ENGLISH LEARNER SUPPORT

Speak Lines of Poetry Some English learners may feel uncomfortable speaking in front of a group. Work with a group of students to present one poem that they divide up into different speaking parts. Help each student with pronunciation of his or her part. Guide students to echo read their part after you, practicing several times before presenting.

COLLABORATE & COMPARE

from **NINTH WARD**

Historical Fiction by Jewell Parker Rhodes

GENRE ELEMENTS
HISTORICAL FICTION

Remind students that **historical fiction** is a category of fiction that combines actual places and events from the past with imaginative elements of fiction found in short stories and novels. Historical fiction is usually focused on a significant event or moment. Setting is the most important element of this genre. Characters, plot, and conflict may involve a mix of real and fictional events. All characters behave in realistic ways and speak in dialogue that reflects the thoughts and knowledge of people in the historical situation.

LEARNING OBJECTIVES

- Analyze historical and cultural setting of the text.
- Analyze the author's use of language to develop mood and theme.
- Conduct research about the history of the Ninth Ward in New Orleans before and after Hurricane Katrina.
- Write posts based on events during Hurricane Katrina.
- Determine the meaning of unfamiliar words using context clues.
- Create and present a poster about fortitude.
- Use pronouns correctly.
- **Language** Discuss and identify pronouns in a text.

TEXT COMPLEXITY

Quantitative Measures	Ninth Ward	Lexile: 570L
Qualitative Measures	**Ideas Presented** Mostly explicit; requires some inferential reasoning.	
	Structure Used Clear, chronological, largely conventional.	
	Language Used Mostly explicit; some figurative or allusive language, some dialect.	
	Knowledge Required Situation easily envisioned; some references to other texts.	

Online **Ed**

RESOURCES

- Unit 3 Response Log

- Selection Audio

- Reading Studio: Notice & Note

- Level Up Tutorial: Setting and Mood

- Writing Studio:
  The Language of Narratives

- Speaking and Listening Studio:
  Giving a Presentation

- Vocabulary Studio: Using Context
  Clues

- Grammar Studio: Module 2: Lesson
  2: Pronouns

- "After the Hurricane"/*Ninth Ward*
  Selection Test

SUMMARIES

English

Two children, Lanesha and TaShon, and a dog named Spot are sitting on a rooftop in the Ninth Ward after Hurricane Katrina. They see devastation brought by the hurricane and flooding. The children are disappointed when a rescue helicopter appears, but fails to stop for them. As night turns to day, Lanesha begins to worry that they may not be rescued.

Spanish

Dos niños, Lanesha y TaShon, y un perro llamado Spot están sentados en un techo en el Noveno Distrito después del Huracán Katrina. Ven la devastación causada por el huracán y la inundación. Los niños se sienten defraudados cuando un helicóptero de rescate aparece, pero no se detiene por ellos. Mientras la noche se hace día, Lanesha empieza a preocuparse de que puede que no los rescaten.

SMALL-GROUP OPTIONS

Have students work in small groups to read and discuss the selection.

Numbered Heads Together

- Ask students to form into groups of four and then number off 1 – 2 – 3 – 4 within the group.

- Pose a higher-order discussion question to the group or class, such as: *What aspects of the friendship between Lanesha and TaShon make it more or less likely that they will survive their situation?*

- Have students discuss their responses in their groups.

- Call out a number from 1 to 4. That "numbered" student then responds for the group.

Think-Pair-Share

- Pose a question to the class, such as: *What are some of the worst threats that Lanesha and TaShon face together?*

- Have students think about the question individually, making notes.

- Tell each student to partner with another student to listen, discuss, and formulate a shared response.

- After they have created a response, ask student pairs to work with another pair to reach consensus before responding.

- Call on a selected student to respond to the entire class.

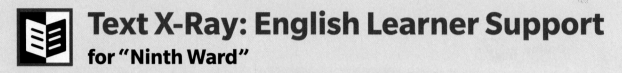

Text X-Ray: English Learner Support
for "Ninth Ward"

Use the Text X-Ray and the supports and scaffolds in the Teacher's Edition to help guide students at different proficiency levels through the selection.

INTRODUCE THE SELECTION
DISCUSS SURVIVING SEVERE WEATHER

This text is historical fiction, and its blend of real and imaginary may be difficult for some English learners to comprehend. Begin by discussing real-life historical events that involve severe weather, such as hurricanes, tornadoes, blizzards, and earthquakes. Explain that severe weather events often provide challenges to residents living in the affected area. Ask students to discuss personal experiences with severe weather events.

Help students understand that writers of historical fiction are careful to use specific and accurate details about the setting and events involved. Be sure to emphasize that in historical fiction, characters, their responses, and dialogue are imaginary. Stress that writers of historical fiction often base these genre elements on real-life experiences.

CULTURAL REFERENCES

The following words and phrases may be unfamiliar to students:

- Spot is the name of the dog stranded on the roof with Lanesha and TaShon
- *scoot* (paragraph 8): to move closer to someone
- *"big bird wings"* (paragraph 12): the rotating blades on the helicopter
- *copter man* (paragraph 13): the pilot flying the helicopter
- *"touched them with a hot iron"* (paragraph 20): a simile describing the way her sunburn feels

LISTENING

Listen for Main Events

Work with students on separating important events from less-important details.

Have students listen as you read aloud paragraphs 9–12. Use the following supports with students at varying proficiency levels:

- Give students two summaries of the section, including one that includes insignificant details. Have students choose the summary that tells the main, more important events. **SUBSTANTIAL**
- Use sentence frames to help students identify the main event in this section: *In this section, Lanesha and TaShon see____. Lanesha and TaShon are disappointed that____.* **MODERATE**
- Have students work together to identify the main events in this section, as well as two details that describe the main events. **LIGHT**

SPEAKING

Discuss Pronouns

Tell students that understanding which pronouns refer to which people or things will help them better understand what is happening in a story. Have students use the term *pronoun* to discuss pronoun usage in *Ninth Ward*.

Have students listen as you read aloud paragraphs 4–14. Use the following supports with students at varying proficiency levels:

- Tell students that you will ask questions about what you just read aloud. For example, ask: *Which person does the pronoun* I *refer to in paragraph 4?* (Lanesha) *Which person does the pronoun* he *refer to in paragraph 5?* (TaShon) **SUBSTANTIAL**
- Have students identify the pronouns used in paragraph 8. Ask: *Whose arms does* our *refer to in paragraph 8?* (Lanesha's and TaShon's arms) **MODERATE**
- Pair students and have them identify pronouns in paragraphs 11–12 that refer to the helicopter. Ask: *Which pronouns refer to the helicopter in paragraphs 11–12?* (*it, its*) **LIGHT**

READING

Analyze Mood

Explain that the mood of a story is the feeling it evokes. Students can ask themselves "What feelings does this section of the story create?" "What feelings do the characters feel?"

Analyze the mood of paragraphs 1–6 of the selection. Read the paragraphs as students follow along. Use the following supports with students at varying proficiency levels:

- List words from the paragraphs on the board—words that evoke mood and those that don't—and have students read them aloud with you. Then work with them to think of synonyms and antonyms for these words. **SUBSTANTIAL**
- Ask: *Which words help you understand how TaShon feels?* (*The words "head buried in Spot's fur," "crying full out," and "sobbing" show that TaShon is very upset.*) **MODERATE**
- Point out the mood shifts to a more hopeful one in paragraphs 3–6. Ask: *Which words does the author use to show Lanesha and TaShon are hopeful?* (*fortitude, endure*) **LIGHT**

WRITING

Write a Live Post

Work with students to read the writing assignment on page 229. Discuss the length of text allowed on different social platforms and the role of photos and other images.

Use the following supports with students at varying proficiency levels:

- Have students choose a photo or image to post, along with one word that describes the image. **SUBSTANTIAL**
- Provide sentence frames such as the following to help students craft their posts: _____ *and* I *are* _____. *Please try to help us by* _____. **MODERATE**
- Ask students to post a photo of a moment from the story—for example, the helicopter overhead —and write a caption to go with the picture. **LIGHT**

Connect to the
ESSENTIAL QUESTION

In this excerpt from *Ninth Ward,* Lanesha, a twelve-year old girl, and her young neighbor TaShon find the fortitude to survive the immediate aftereffects of Hurricane Katrina, which hit New Orleans in 2005.

COMPARE ACROSS GENRES

Point out that *Ninth Ward* is a work of historical fiction that is set during the same event described in the poem, "After the Hurricane." How might the characters in the historical fiction be alike or different from the speaker in the poem? How might the authors of these selections use language similarly and differently to describe the setting and the characters' experiences?

COLLABORATE & COMPARE

NOVEL

from
NINTH WARD

by **Jewell Parker Rhodes**
pages 223–227

COMPARE ACROSS GENRES

Now that you've read "After the Hurricane," read an excerpt from *Ninth Ward* to see how this work of historical fiction tells another story of survival related to Hurricane Katrina. As you read, think about how the author uses setting and language to describe the narrator's experience. After you read, you will collaborate with a small group on a final project.

 ESSENTIAL QUESTION:

What does
it take.to
be a survivor?

POEM

from
AFTER THE HURRICANE

by **Rita Williams-Garcia**
pages 209–217

220   Unit 3

from **Ninth Ward**

QUICK START

What do you say to yourself when the going gets tough? What if you had to coach a friend or a sibling through a difficult time? Write three encouraging things you would say.

ANALYZE HISTORICAL AND CULTURAL SETTING

The **setting** of a work of literature is the time and place of the action. In historical fiction, the time period and culture play a significant role in both plot and characterization. This selection's setting is one area of New Orleans during the aftermath of Hurricane Katrina. As the text's fictional characters respond to the setting, the author reveals the characters' important qualities and values.

• Setting can influence characters' values, beliefs, and emotions.
• Setting can affect how characters act and interact with others.
• Characters develop as they respond to historical and cultural elements throughout the story. Their response may suggest the story's theme.

ANALYZE AUTHOR'S USE OF LANGUAGE

Mood is the feeling or atmosphere that a writer creates for the reader. Descriptive words, imagery, and figurative language all influence the mood of a work. *Ninth Ward* is a first-person narrative, so the mood created by the narrator's voice can reveal something about the main character. As you read, note how language helps create the mood of the text, and what the mood reveals about the text's characters and theme. Use a chart like the one below.

GENRE ELEMENTS: HISTORICAL FICTION

• is set in the past
• includes real places and real events of historical importance
• can be a short story or a novel
• has the basic features of realistic fiction, including plot, characters, conflict, setting, and theme

TEXT	MOOD	MY IDEAS ABOUT CHARACTER AND THEME
TaShon lifts his head and wipes his eyes. He looks far-off.	expectant	TaShon is someone who takes time to think before speaking.

QUICK START

Have students share some of the things people say to help them or others get through difficult situations. Discuss how what they say might change based on the type of difficulty being faced. Have students brainstorm expressions of encouragement they might use.

ANALYZE HISTORICAL AND CULTURAL SETTING

Help students distinguish between historical setting and cultural setting. *Historical setting* refers to the time period and actual events that occur. *Cultural setting* refers to the traditions and values that shape the beliefs of characters and affect their behavior and decision making. Review each of the bulleted statements in light of these two types of setting. Ask: *Which type of setting do you think will be most significant in* Ninth Ward? *How might the two types of setting be intertwined?*

ANALYZE AUTHOR'S USE OF LANGUAGE

Review key elements—for example, word choice, imagery, and figurative language—that students can use when evaluating an author's use of language. Ask: *How might each element affect the development of mood and character? How might the choice of a narrator or speaker used in a text affect the author's choice of words and literary devices?*

TEACH

CRITICAL VOCABULARY

Encourage students to read all the sentences before deciding which word best completes each one. Remind them to look for context clues that match the meaning of each word.

Answers:

1. *fortitude*

2. *focus*

3. *angular*

4. *horizon*

5. *endure*

■ English Learner Support

Use Word Families Tell students that several Critical Vocabulary words can be used to build other words with related meanings. Discuss new words that are formed with a base word and suffix, such as: *endure/endurance, horizon/ horizontal.* **ALL LEVELS**

LANGUAGE CONVENTIONS

Review the information about personal pronouns and indefinite pronouns. Emphasize the idea that a pronoun stands in place of a noun—a word that names a person, place or thing—or another pronoun.

Write the subject and object forms of personal pronouns on the board. Have students practice using them in complete sentences such as, "*Lanesha* showed courage by *her* actions." Encourage students to identify the noun that each personal pronoun refers to.

Then read aloud the model sentence with an indefinite pronoun. Ask students to practice using and identifying other indefinite pronouns in sentences—for example, "*Someone* yelled for help."

ANNOTATION MODEL

Remind students to use the skills listed on page 221 of the lesson when making annotations that involve setting and the use of language to create mood. Review annotation tools such as underlining, circling, and highlighting. Suggest that marginal notes may include comments or questions about ideas that are unclear.

 GET READY

CRITICAL VOCABULARY

fortitude   endure   horizon   angular   focus

To see how many Critical Vocabulary words you already know, use them to complete the sentences.

1. Happy memories gave them _____ to survive the challenge.

2. The performer had to_____ his attention to walk on the tightrope.

3. Sharp, straight lines meet to create a/an _____ pattern.

4. The setting sun slipped beneath the _____ .

5. He could not _____ walking against the icy cold wind.

LANGUAGE CONVENTIONS

Pronouns A **pronoun** is a word that takes the place of a noun or another pronoun. **Personal pronouns,** such as *I, me, he, she, we, us, you,* and *it,* refer to the person making a statement, the person(s) being addressed, or the person(s) or thing(s) the statement is about.

The helicopter doesn't seem to see us. It keeps flying.

The personal pronoun *us* refers to the narrator, Lanesha, and her neighbor TaShon. *It* refers to an object, the helicopter. As you read, notice the author's use of pronouns.

ANNOTATION MODEL **NOTICE & NOTE**

As you read, note words the author uses to indicate setting. Notice the effect of the author's use of language on the mood and characterization, and how mood may indicate theme. You can also mark evidence that supports your own ideas. In the model, you can see one reader's notes about *Ninth Ward.*

1 No land. <u>Only sky</u> and <u>dirty water.</u> 2 TaShon has his head buried in Spot's fur. He's crying full-out—sobbing <u>like the world has ended</u> and <u>Noah hasn't landed his ark.</u>	Sounds bleak. I wonder where they are. More details about water, and also sadness. Maybe they are stranded or surrounded by water.

BACKGROUND

Jewell Parker Rhodes *(b. 1954) loved to read and write as a child. Ninth Ward is her first published book for young people. The Ninth Ward is one of seventeen wards, or administrative districts, in New Orleans. The largest and easternmost ward, the Ninth Ward is divided by a shipping channel and another waterway. When Hurricane Katrina struck New Orleans in 2005, the Ninth Ward received the greatest damage. Many residents lost their lives and homes in the hurricane.*

from

NINTH WARD

Novel by Jewell Parker Rhodes

PREPARE TO COMPARE

As you read, pay attention to the selection's mood and setting. Note how characters respond to events. Think about how these elements may help you recognize the selection's theme, or message.

1 No land. Only sky and dirty water.

2   TaShon has his head buried in Spot's fur. He's crying full-out—sobbing like the world has ended and Noah hasn't landed his ark.[1]

3   I want to sit and cry, too. But it's almost dawn, and I think when there's light, someone will surely find us. I also think, still dark, I've got to make sure TaShon doesn't fall off the roof into the water.

---

[1] **Noah hasn't landed his ark:** in the biblical flood story, Noah builds an ark, or large boat, to save his family and animals of every kind from a flood.

> **Notice & Note**
>
> Use the side margins to notice and note signposts in the text.
>
> ---
>
> **ANALYZE HISTORICAL AND CULTURAL SETTING**
>
> **Annotate:** Mark words in paragraphs 1–3 that show the setting.
>
> **Identify:** Which elements tell you about the place and time? Are there any elements that tell you about the cultural setting?

TEACH

BACKGROUND

Have students read the Background note. Explain that more than a decade after Hurricane Katrina hit, parts of the Ninth Ward are still living with the devastating effects of the storm. In some neighborhoods, there are blocks of severely damaged and abandoned homes and streets strewn with garbage and overgrown vegetation. Other properties have become infested with snakes and rodents and covered with toxic mold, resulting in ongoing safety and health hazards. In contrast to the Ninth Ward, other wards have largely recovered with federal and state aid.

PREPARE TO COMPARE

Direct students to use the Prepare to Compare prompt to focus their reading on historical and cultural setting and on characterization.

ANALYZE HISTORICAL AND CULTURAL SETTING

Review the distinction between historical and cultural setting discussed on page 221. (**Answer:** *References to "No land" and "Only sky and dirty water," as well as "[Noah's] ark" describe the historical setting, indicating that there has been a monumental flood. The children are sitting on a roof with floodwaters below. Morning is breaking on the day after Katrina.*)

> For **speaking and reading support** for students at varying proficiency levels, see the **Text X-Ray** on page 220C.

ANALYZE AUTHOR'S USE OF LANGUAGE

Discuss how the author's use of language contributes to the mood of a selection. Remind students that repeated words and phrases often are important. (**Answer:** *The atmosphere is tense but also one of determination and strength.*)

LANGUAGE CONVENTIONS

Review the antecedents to which the personal pronouns refer. (**Answer:** *The pronoun* me *refers to the speaker, Lanesha. The pronoun* our *refers to Lanesha and TaShon.*)

For **listening support** for students at varying proficiency levels, see the **Text X-Ray** on page 220C.

CRITICAL VOCABULARY

fortitude: TaShon knows he needs fortitude to face the difficult situation at hand.

ASK STUDENTS to name some examples of different types of fortitude a person may need in a difficult situation. *(Physical fortitude or strength; emotional fortitude not to give up or show fear; moral fortitude to act justly and do the right thing.)*

endure: When we *endure,* we have the strength not give up, just like Lanesha and TaShon.

ASK STUDENTS to name some other phrases are that might be used to explain the meaning of *endure. (never say never, grin and bear it, stick it out)*

horizon: When we look out in the distance like Lanesha does, we can see where Earth meets the sky.

ASK STUDENTS to name another horizon that people may experience. *(Earth and ocean, Earth and outer space)*

angular: When something is angular, it has at least two sides that meet to form a sharp corner, or angle, like the rooftops in the story.

ASK STUDENTS what type of geometric shape the rooftops resemble. *(a triangle)* What type of geometric shape does the side of a house resemble? *(a rectangle)*

 NOTICE & NOTE

fortitude
(fôr′tĭ-tōōd) *n.* To have *fortitude* is to show strength of mind and face difficulty with courage.

endure
(ĕn-dŏŏr′) *v.* To *endure* is to carry on despite difficulty or suffering.

ANALYZE AUTHOR'S USE OF LANGUAGE

Annotate: Mark the words in paragraph 8 that help establish the mood of this scene.

Analyze: How would you describe the mood here?

LANGUAGE CONVENTIONS

Mark the pronouns in the first sentence of paragraph 12. Who are the pronouns referring to?

horizon
(hə-rī′zən) *n.* The *horizon* is the intersection of the earth and sky.

angular
(ăng′gyə-lər) *adj.* Something that is *angular,* such as a peaked roof, has two sides that form an angle.

---

4   I feel tired, sad. Even though I expect to see her as a ghost, I know I'll still miss the flesh and blood Mama Ya-Ya.[2] The warm hands. Her making breakfast. And me resting my head upon her shoulder. I'll miss talking to her. Listening to her stories.

5   TaShon lifts his head and wipes his eyes. He looks far-off. For a minute, I think he's going to be his quiet old self, and pretend to disappear. Then, he says softly, "**Fortitude**."

6   "Strength to **endure**."

7   "That's right. We're going to show fortitude."

8   TaShon and I scoot closer, our arms and legs touching. I put my arms around him; he puts his arms around me. Neither of us moves. I know we are both thinking, murmuring in our minds, over and over again, "Fortitude. Fortitude. Fortitude."

9   Sunrise. As far as my eye can see, there is water.

10   The Mississippi is brown, filled with leaves, branches, and pieces of folks' lives. I see a plastic three-wheeler tangled in algae. I see a picture frame with a gap-toothed boy smiling in black and white. I see a red car, a Ford, floating.

11   Overhead, I hear a helicopter. It sounds like a lawn mower in the sky.

12   Me and TaShon start yelling, waving our hands. "Here, over here." The helicopter doesn't seem to see us. It keeps flying south. Its big bird wings circling and the roar of its engine getting softer.

13   TaShon is cursing now. I haven't the heart to say, "Watch your mouth." I'm positive the 'copter man saw us. How come he didn't stop? Lift us in the air with rope?

14   I start trembling and look around my neighborhood. The **horizon** is like none I've seen before. Just tips of houses. Tops or halves of trees. Lampposts hacked off by water. Rooftops—some flat, some **angular**—most, empty.

15   Far left, I see a man and woman sitting on a roof, their feet in the water. Two blocks east, I see what I think is an entire family. Five, six people, all different sizes, waving white sheets.[3] I hear them screaming, calling for help.

16   Where are the others? At the Superdome? Safe in Baton Rouge?[4]

---

[2] **Mama Ya-Ya:** Lanesha's elderly caretaker who has died during the water's rise.
[3] **waving white sheets:** in wartime, soldiers wave white flags to signal their willingness to surrender to the enemy.
[4] **At the Superdome? Safe in Baton Rouge?:** the Superdome is the name of the stadium in New Orleans that sheltered Katrina refugees. Baton Rouge is Louisiana's capital, and the city to which thousands of New Orleans residents fled to escape Hurricane Katrina.

 ENGLISH LEARNER SUPPORT

Demonstrate Comprehension   Have students identify examples of repetition in sentence structure that appear in paragraph 10.

Ask students to discuss with partners how the repetition of "I see" helps build drama about the setting and emphasize the narrator's mood. *(The repetition creates drama by presenting a list of specific examples of devastation and by enhancing the sense of concern the characters are experiencing because of these unusual sights.)* **MODERATE/LIGHT**

17   TaShon says softly, "At least we made it out of the attic, didn't we, Lanesha?"

18   I look at TaShon. I should've known better. Should've known that there was more to see about TaShon than he ever let show. He's a butterfly, too.

19   "Yes, we did," I say. "We made it out."

20 No one is coming. All day and all night, we waited. Spot panted, slept. TaShon swatted at mosquitoes and his feet turned itchy red after he left them in the water to cool off. We are both sunburned. Funny, I didn't think black folks sunburned. But all day in the sun, no shade, has made me and TaShon red faced. My cheeks and shoulders hurt like someone touched them with a hot iron.

21   I keep **focused** on the horizon. Above it, I search for helicopters. Below it, I search for signs of my neighbors.

22   I used to think the Mississippi was beautiful. Not anymore. Up close, it is filled with garbage; clothes and furniture, ugly catfish and eels.

23   My lips are cracked. I'm hungry. Thirsty. Tired. I tell TaShon a hundred different Bible stories—all about hope. I tell him about Moses, David and Goliath, and Noah's ark.[5] "Someone's coming," I insist. "People know we're here." But I feel Spot, if he could talk, would say, "That's a lie;" then blink his big brown eyes.

24 The moon is high. TaShon is feverish and asleep. His legs, up to his knees, are bright red. His face is peeling.

25   I haven't seen any ghosts either. Are they scared?

26   I murmur, "Mama Ya-Ya, help me. Momma, help me." But the night doesn't answer. Nothing shimmers. There's no message from another world.

27 Day two since the flood. Day three since the hurricane.

28   No one has come to our rescue. There's no TV. No radio. No news from anywhere. The family that has been hollering for help is quiet now.

29   I can't make the Mississippi disappear. I can't make food and water appear. But we're going to go stir-crazy, get more and more miserable.

30   I press my head to my hand. I feel dizzy.

---

[5] **Moses, David and Goliath, and Noah's ark:** in a set of stories from the Bible, Moses is directed by God to lead the Israelites out of Egypt; David is a boy who killed Goliath, a giant warrior; and Noah's ark is the large boat Noah built to save his family and animals from a flood.

AHA MOMENT

Notice & Note: What does Lanesha realize about TaShon in paragraphs 16–19? Mark the words that show Lanesha is realizing something about TaShon's character.

Interpret: What does Lanesha mean when she compares TaShon to a butterfly?

focus
(fō´kəs) v. When you *focus* on something, you keep attention fixed on it.

ANALYZE AUTHOR'S USE OF LANGUAGE

Annotate: Mark the words in paragraph 23 that help show mood.

Infer: What does the mood suggest about the kind of person the narrator is?

AHA MOMENT

Explain that an **Aha Moment** signals that a character has come to realize, or fully understand, the significance of someone or something. Aha Moments most often relate to an important insight, a change in **plot**, and the development of **character** or **mood**. Then have the students answer the question to determine the significance of the moment when Lanesha realizes that TaShon is "a butterfly, too." (**Answer:** *By "butterfly," the author could mean that TaShon's beauty and strength are not revealed immediately, just as a butterfly begins as a caterpillar and only reveals its shape and true colors when it has undergone change.*)

■ English Learner Support

Understand Aha Moments Help students brainstorm a list of other words that might be used to indicate an **Aha Moment**—for example, *surprise, startle, amaze,* and *astonish.* Then have students work in pairs to create summary sentences about the Aha Moment in the selection using these synonyms. (**Possible answers:** *Lanesha was surprised by her friend's strength in the face of danger. TaShon was astonished by his friend's bravery and determination to stay safe.*) **LIGHT**

ANALYZE AUTHOR'S USE OF LANGUAGE

Point out that paragraph 23 gives vivid details about Lanesha's physical distress and her actions in spite of that distress to help the reader understand how she feels. (**Answer:** *Lanesha has fortitude and is determined that she and her friend will survive. She is clearheaded enough to realize she and TaShon are in danger, caring enough to comfort her friend, but also realistic enough to be concerned.*)

APPLYING ACADEMIC VOCABULARY

☑ **circumstance**   ☐ **constraint**   ☐ **impact**   ☐ **injure**   ☑ **significant**

Write and Discuss Have students turn to a partner to discuss the following questions. Guide students to include the Academic Vocabulary words *circumstance* and *significant* in their responses. Ask volunteers to share their responses with the class.

- What **circumstances** created the situation that Lanesha and TaShon are in?
- Why is Lanesha's insight about TaShon being a butterfly **significant**?

CRITICAL VOCABULARY

focus: Lanesha, like other survivors on the rooftops, kept her eyes focused on the horizon.

ASK STUDENTS to explain why Lanesha would look to the horizon and not the sky above the roof. (*Lanesha is looking for helicopters to arrive and take TaShon and her to a safe place. If helicopters were in the sky overhead, Lanesha would have already seen them.*)

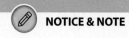

ANALYZE HISTORICAL AND CULTURAL SETTING

Remind students that they can use vivid descriptive details provided by the author to picture the setting in their heads and understand better how their surroundings affect how the characters act. (**Answer:** *The roof on which TaShon and Lanesha are standing is slippery, and the house next door is mostly covered by water. A rowboat has gotten caught between the two houses. It will be hard to reach the boat because it is out of reach and its rope seems to be underwater, but Lanesha appears to be planning to figure out how to get it unstuck.*)

NOTICE & NOTE

ANALYZE HISTORICAL AND CULTURAL SETTING

Annotate: Mark the details in paragraphs 34–40 that help describe the scene.

Predict: What do these details reveal about the challenges Lanesha and TaShon now face?

31   TaShon's itching, rubbing his left foot against his right leg. "Look. A rowboat."

32   I exhale. "Mr. Henri's! He liked catfish. He always gave some to Mama Ya-Ya."

33   TaShon's eyes are bright.

34   I move to the left—careful not to slip in the water, my feet angling on the roof. It's slippery. Water is in my tennis shoes. The shingles are slick with oil and gunk.

35   I can barely see the house next door. Most of it is covered with water. But a rowboat is floating, caught between our two houses and a bigger willow tree that kept it from floating down the street. It is maybe six, seven feet away. It's south, *perpendicular* to both our houses. "A sharp right angle." If it'd been parallel, it might've floated out—at least on the north side. But the angle kept it safe.

36   "Do you think we can reach it?" asks TaShon. "The boat?"

37   I squint. The boat's rope must be floating deep, loose inside the water.

38   My arms aren't long enough to push the boat free and I'm not sure I can doggy-paddle to it.

39   "The angle's all wrong."

40   Well, right and wrong, I think. Right, 'cause being perpendicular, it didn't get swept away in the storm. Wrong, 'cause being perpendicular, it needs to be unstuck.

41   I see TaShon's shoulders sagging. Giving up.

42   How can I rescue a rowboat?

43   EVERYTHING IS MATH. Think, Lanesha.

44   I look about. There are all kinds of pieces of wood, trees floating in the water. I see a long, thin trunk floating.

45   "TaShon. We've got to catch that tree." It looks like a young willow. Just a few years old.

46   I'm sure my hands can fit around its trunk. With effort, I can hold it like a stick.

47   I lie down on my stomach, shouting, "Come on, come on!" like a lunatic to the tree. It bobs left, then right. Then turns sideways.

48   "We've got to grab it, TaShon!"

49   TaShon lies beside me on his stomach, too. We flap our hands in the water, trying to make it draw near. Trying to create another current in the muddy tide.

50   "It's coming," hollers TaShon. "It's coming."

51   "Brace yourself." Though the tree is moving slow, it'll be heavy. "Don't fall! Don't fall in."

WHEN STUDENTS STRUGGLE . . .

Analyze Author's Use of Language Have students record specific examples of the author's use of language to describe setting and mood.

- Examples of setting: "No land. Only sky and dirty water." and "The Mississippi is brown, filled with leaves, branches, and pieces of folks' lives."

- Examples of mood: "Me and TaShon start yelling, waving our hands." and "I start trembling and look around my neighborhood."

For additional support, go to the **Reading Studio** and assign the following **Level Up tutorial: Setting and Mood.**

52   I stretch my arms wide, clawing at the water, trying to move the trunk closer. I strain, feeling the pull in my shoulders. Water is lapping, almost to my chin.

53   I clutch bark. A piece cracks away in my hand.

54   "Get it, get it," TaShon screams. His arms are too short. The trunk is floating by.

55   I inch my body further, my hips and legs still touching the roof. Inhaling, I plunge forward. My arms are around the tree.

CHECK YOUR UNDERSTANDING

Answer these questions before moving on to the **Analyze the Text** section on the following page.

1 Which sentence from the text suggests that Lanesha and TaShon want to be rescued?

   A *The horizon is like none I've seen before.*

   B *I see a red car, a Ford, floating.*

   C *I think when there's light, someone will surely find us.*

   D *"Yes, we did," I say. "We made it out."*

2 In paragraph 2, the narrator says, "Noah hasn't landed his ark" to —

   F introduce another character in the story

   G show that the story is set in the time of the Bible

   H show that TaShon enjoys Bible stories

   J show that the land has been covered by floodwater

3 Which idea is supported by information at the conclusion of the selection?

   A Lanesha has faith that Spot will help them escape.

   B Lanesha is determined to save them.

   C Lanesha no longer enjoys telling Bible stories.

   D Lanesha is very certain that they will be rescued.

CHECK YOUR UNDERSTANDING

Have students answer the questions independently.

Answers:

1. *C*

2. *J*

3. *B*

If students answer any questions incorrectly, have them reread the text to confirm their understanding. Then they may proceed to ANALYZE THE TEXT on page 228.

 ENGLISH LEARNER SUPPORT

Oral Assessment Use the following questions to assess students' comprehension and speaking skills:

1. How can you tell that Lanesha and TaShon want to be rescued? *(The sentence, "I think when there's light, someone will surely find us," suggests that Lanesha and TaShon want to be rescued.)*

2. In paragraph 2, the author mentions Noah's ark. What does this tell you about the land around the characters? *(The land has been covered by floodwater.)*

3. How does Lanesha feel about being rescued at the end of the selection? *(Lanesha has doubts that they will ever be rescued.)*
    SUBSTANTIAL/MODERATE

ANALYZE THE TEXT

Possible answers:

1. **DOK 4:** *The setting is the flooded neighborhood ("No land. Only sky and water."), where Lanesha and her neighbor TaShon live. The historical setting is after a real natural disaster. The characters react to the setting in different ways. TaShon is "sobbing like the world has ended." Lanesha would like to cry, too, but she is older so she has to make sure "TaShon doesn't fall off the roof into the water."*

2. **DOK 3:** *As Lanesha and TaShon "scoot" closer together and hug on the rooftop, the author indicates that they are very still and intent on survival. Their repeated "murmuring" thoughts of "fortitude" suggest a theme of inner strength being essential to survival.*

3. **DOK 2:** *The scene opens with the word, Sunrise, which acts like a curtain pulled back to reveal the devastated neighborhood. Evidence includes items floating in the "brown water,"—a tricycle, a picture of a boy, and a red Ford. The neighborhood seems family-oriented.*

4. **DOK 2:** *In paragraph 3, Lanesha thinks "someone will surely find us," but in paragraph 12 she is angry because she is "positive the 'copter man saw us" and wonders, "How come he didn't stop?" She has changed from being innocently hopeful to being more concerned and worldly.*

5. **DOK 4:** *At the beginning of the story, Lanesha seems hopeful about being rescued. She believes that fortitude will help her and TaShon survive. She tells Bible stories to keep TaShon's spirits up, even as hers are sinking.*

RESEARCH

Encourage students to confirm any information they find by checking multiple sources and assessing the credibility of each. Federal, state, and local resources are generally reliable sources of such data.

Connect *Answers will vary. Encourage students to check with local and state historical societies.*

 RESPOND

ANALYZE THE TEXT

Support your responses with evidence from the text. 📓 NOTEBOOK

1. **Analyze** Reread paragraphs 1–3 and note details about setting and character traits. How is the historical setting related to the characters?

2. **Draw Conclusions** Review the author's use of language in paragraph 8. How do mood and characterization suggest the text's theme?

3. **Summarize** Review paragraphs 9–11. How does the text help you understand the novel's cultural setting?

4. **Compare** Review paragraphs 3 and 13. How would you compare the narrator's attitude in the two passages? Explain how Lanesha's character has changed over time.

5. **Notice & Note** Review paragraphs 36–48. What does Lanesha realize about their situation? Explain how Lanesha uses this realization to help TaShon overcome his sense of hopelessness.

RESEARCH TIP
Use the search words "image of _____" to find photographs of an event. Type "map of _____" to help you understand the geography of an area. Try the search words "history of Ninth Ward" to find websites about the Ninth Ward. Evaluate your search results by looking for information about the organization that runs the site.

RESEARCH

The city of New Orleans is divided into areas called "wards." The Ninth Ward suffered badly from Hurricane Katrina. Investigate the history of the Ninth Ward, from the time before Hurricane Katrina to the present. Use a chart like the one shown to record relevant information from reliable sources.

NINTH WARD	
FACT	**SOURCE**
Sources will vary.	

Connect Is there information online about the history of your own city or neighborhood? Many areas have local historical societies that also maintain websites. Go online to find information about your community's history.

CREATE AND PRESENT

Write Live Posts What would the narrator of *Ninth Ward* have posted on social media if she had had a smartphone? Imagine you are Lanesha, looking out from her rooftop describing the setting surrounding her. Write a sequence of social media posts from Lanesha's point of view, directed at a friend far away.

❏ Use what you know about the character of Lanesha, including her voice, personality traits, and relationship to TaShon, to describe what she sees, thinks, and feels.

❏ Follow spelling and grammar conventions.

❏ Make sure you use pronouns correctly. Check to see if they agree with the nouns to which they refer.

Create a Poster In the beginning of the selection, the characters reflect on the importance of fortitude. In a small group, work together to write your own definition of *fortitude*. Then, gather images from magazines or the Internet, or make your own drawings, to represent fortitude. Design your poster around the images you have selected. Present your poster to the class and explain the images you chose. When listening to other groups' presentations, take notes and ask questions respectfully.

RESPOND TO THE ESSENTIAL QUESTION

 What does it take to be a survivor?

Gather Information Review your annotations and notes on *Ninth Ward* and highlight those that help answer the Essential Question. Then, add relevant details to your Response Log.

At the end of the unit, use your notes to write a nonfiction narrative.

 Go to **The Language of Narrative** in the **Writing Studio** for more on descriptive writing.

Go to **Giving a Presentation: Delivering Your Presentation** in the **Speaking and Listening Studio** for help presenting your ideas.

PRESENTATION CHECKLIST

❏ **Maintain eye contact.**

❏ **Speak at a natural rate.**

❏ **Be loud and clear.**

❏ **Point to different parts of your poster as you speak.**

ACADEMIC VOCABULARY

As you write and discuss what you learned from the selections, be sure to use the Academic Vocabulary words. Check off each of the words that you use.

❏ **circumstance**

❏ **constraint**

❏ **impact**

❏ **injure**

❏ **significant**

APPLY

CREATE AND PRESENT

Write Live Posts Remind students that social media posts are usually brief. Encourage students to follow the sequence of events in the text as they post. For example, a post about the helicopter arriving but not picking up Lanesha and TaShon would come before a post about other people waving white sheets and yelling from rooftops.

For **writing support** for students at varying proficiency levels, see the **Tex X-Ray** on page 220D.

Create a Poster Remind students that they can search for images by using phrases such as "Images of People and Hurricanes," "Images of People in Earthquakes," "Images of People in Dangerous Waters," etc. Encourage students to look for images of individuals and groups of people working together to survive. Be sure students write a brief definition of fortitude for their poster or labels for some of the images they use.

RESPOND TO THE ESSENTIAL QUESTION

Allow time for students to add details from *Ninth Ward* to their Unit 3 Response Logs.

CRITICAL VOCABULARY

Answers:

1. *horizon; you can watch the sun set at the horizon*

2. *fortitude; to have fortitude means to have strength of mind*

3. *endure; to endure means to last long enough to get through a difficulty*

4. *focus; when you focus on something, you concentrate on it*

5. *angular; something angular is pointed, like the peak of a roof*

VOCABULARY STRATEGY:
Context Clues

Answers:

• *fortitude: "Strength to endure." "That's right. We going to show fortitude." / true grit / courage in face of adversity*

• *endure : "Strength" / live through / ability to carry on despite difficulties*

• *angular: "Rooftops—some flat, some angular" / has an angle like a triangle / pointed*

 RESPOND

CRITICAL VOCABULARY

WORD BANK
fortitude
endure
horizon
angular
focus

Practice and Apply Explain which vocabulary word is most closely related to another word you know.

1. Which vocabulary word goes with *sunset?* Why?

2. Which vocabulary word goes with *strength?* Why?

3. Which vocabulary word goes with *lasting?* Why?

4. Which vocabulary word goes with *concentrate?* Why?

5. Which vocabulary word goes with *pointed?* Why?

VOCABULARY STRATEGY: Context Clues

Go to the **Vocabulary Studio** for more on context clues.

Context clues are the words and phrases surrounding a word that provide hints about its meaning. Sometimes, you may find a context clue in the same sentence as an unfamiliar word. The whole sentence can also be a good clue. In *Ninth Ward,* the meaning of *horizon* is suggested by its context.

I keep focused on the horizon. Above it, I search for helicopters. Below it, I search for signs of my neighbors.

If you didn't know what *horizon* means, the words "above it" and "below it" are clues. Reread the whole paragraph for another context clue: above the horizon she looks for helicopters (in the sky); below it, she looks for people (on the ground or in the water). Together these hints can help you guess that *horizon* is "the place where the earth and sky meet." Confirm your guess by checking a print or online dictionary.

Practice and Apply Find context clues for each of the following words and guess the word's meaning. Then, check your definition.

WORD	CONTEXT CLUES	GUESSED DEFINITION	DEFINITION
fortitude (paragraph 5)			
endure (paragraph 6)			
angular (paragraph 14)			

 ## ENGLISH LEARNER SUPPORT

Use Context Clues Give students additional practice opportunities to determine meaning based on context clues. Read the following model sentences aloud.

• TaShon **swatted** at mosquitoes that flew around his face.

• The **helicopter**, with its large circling blades, roared overhead and flew right by us.

Have pairs of students determine the meaning of the underlined word based on context clues. Ask students to write a clear definition of each word and use it correctly in an original sentence. **MODERATE**

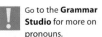
LANGUAGE CONVENTIONS:
Pronouns

Pronouns are words used in place of a noun or another pronoun.

In *Ninth Ward,* the author uses both **personal pronouns** (including *I, me, my, we, us, our, you, yours, she, he, it, they, them,* and *theirs*) and **indefinite pronouns** (including *both, all, most, many, anyone, everybody, several,* and *none*).

In *Ninth Ward,* personal pronouns are used in the following ways:
- To refer to a person making a statement

    My lips are cracked. I'm hungry.

- To refer to the person being addressed

    TaShon has his head buried in Spot's fur. He's crying full out.

- To refer to the people the statement is about

    TaShon says softly, "At least we made it out of the attic, didn't we, Lanesha?"

The selection also uses **indefinite pronouns** to refer to one or more persons or things not specifically mentioned.

> **But it's almost dawn, and I think when there's light, someone will surely find us.**

Someone refers to the unknown people that Lanesha hopes will rescue them.

Practice and Apply Write your own sentences with personal and indefinite pronouns, using the examples from *Ninth Ward* as models. Your sentences can be about your own survival under difficult circumstances or about another topic. When you have finished, share your sentences with a partner and compare your use of pronouns.

> **!** Go to the **Grammar Studio** for more on pronouns.

LANGUAGE CONVENTIONS:
Pronouns

Review the information about pronouns. Explain that the main purpose of pronouns is to avoid the repetition of words and to make connections between sentence elements easier to understand. Emphasize that different pronouns are used depending on whether the noun or pronoun referred to is a subject, an object, or shows possession and ownership.

Review each of the listed uses of a pronoun and its related model sentence. As you move through a discussion of the examples, have volunteers identify each pronoun and its antecedent, or the word it is standing in for.

Practice and Apply Have partners discuss whether pronouns are used correctly and effectively in their sentences. *(Students' sentences will vary.)*

ENGLISH LEARNER SUPPORT

Language Conventions Use the following supports with students of varying proficiency levels:

- Have students find pronouns used in *Ninth Ward* and list the words in their notebooks. Have them practice reading aloud the words. **SUBSTANTIAL**

- Have students identify sentences in *Ninth Ward* that use pronouns, read the sentences aloud, and identify who or what each one refers to. **MODERATE**

- Have students write one original sentence modeled after each of the four different uses for pronouns presented as examples on page 231. Then have students read their sentences aloud and ask a partner to explain how each pronoun is being used. **LIGHT**

COMPARE TEXTS

Before groups of students work on completing the table, emphasize that they are comparing the themes of the two selections along with the ways the two genres present these themes. Review the difference between explicitly stated themes and implicitly stated themes. How does "After the Hurricane" express its theme? How does *Ninth Ward* express its theme? In what way are the themes of the two texts alike or different?

ANALYZE THE TEXTS

Possible answers:

1. **DOK 1:** *Both the poem's speaker and the novel's narrator are hopeful that they will be helped. In the poem, the speaker hopes that water will be delivered. In the novel, the narrator hopes that she will be rescued from her rooftop.*

2. **DOK 2:** *In the poem, the speaker has been evacuated, so she has the freedom to leave the shelter and search for water with her band mates. She can respond to her difficulties with physical action. In the novel, the narrator is trapped with her neighbor and dog on a roof, awaiting rescue. They lack physical freedom and a means of escape. Instead, they look inward for the "fortitude" to get them through their ordeals.*

3. **DOK 2:** *The helicopters in the poem are treated as the outside world watching but doing little to help. In the novel, the helicopter seen by the characters is a sign of hope, but then a symbol of dashed hopes, because it does not drop a rope to rescue the children. The overall idea is that the world isn't even watching them—but that the world has forgotten them, or passed them by.*

4. **DOK 3:** *To be a survivor, you must draw upon an inner strength to endure, and you must also lean on those closest to you—whether they are your band mates, relatives, or friends. You can hope for help from the outside world, but that does not guarantee that you will get it.*

RESPOND

Collaborate & Compare

from AFTER THE
HURRICANE
Poem by
Rita Williams-Garcia

from NINTH WARD
Novel by
Jewell Parker Rhodes

COMPARE TEXTS

"After the Hurricane" and *Ninth Ward* use different **genres,** or types of writing, to explore the effects of Hurricane Katrina on residents of New Orleans. Even though the works are about a similar topic, they may express different themes. **Theme** is a message about life or human nature. Comparing texts from different genres—like poetry and historical fiction—can give you a deeper understanding of the topic.

Often, writers do not state themes directly. Instead, readers must **infer** themes based on information from the text and their own knowledge. This information may include key statements, significant events, and memorable images or symbols.

With your group, complete the chart by citing text evidence from the selections.

	"AFTER THE HURRICANE"	*NINTH WARD*
Key Statements	The world is here but no one's coming. (l.42)	I'm positive copter man saw us. How come he didn't stop? (par. 12)
Significant Events	Big Sean Doolie will shoot the looters. (l.190)	"someone's coming," I insist. "People know we're here." (par. 21)
Memorable Images	helicopters whipping up sky overhead. (l.8)	Overhead I hear a helicopter. It sounds like a lawn mower in the a lawn mower in the sky. (par. 10)

ANALYZE THE TEXTS

Discuss these questions in your group.

1. **Identify** How are the speaker in "After the Hurricane" and the narrator in *Ninth Ward* similar?

2. **Compare** How are the circumstances faced by the poem's speaker and the novel's narrator different? How are their responses to their circumstances different?

3. **Infer** Think about the image of helicopters in both selections. What ideas does this image suggest in each selection?

4. **Draw Conclusions** What have you learned from these selections about what it takes to be a survivor?

 ENGLISH LEARNER SUPPORT

Expand Reading Skills Have students create a Venn diagram to compare the selections. Use these questions to guide discussion as students decide how to fill in the Venn diagram:

1. How is the experience of the poem's speaker like the experience of the novel's narrator?

2. How do the speaker in the poem and the narrator in the novel respond to the appearance of a helicopter overhead?

3. How are the ending of the poem and the ending of historical novel different?

   MODERATE/LIGHT

RESEARCH AND SHARE

Continue exploring the ideas in the texts by developing your own guidelines for how an organization can provide help in a natural disaster. Follow these steps:

1. **Develop a Question** In your group, brainstorm questions about how government and volunteer organizations help victims of natural disasters. Make sure that everyone contributes ideas to the list. Circle the most interesting questions, and then decide which group member or members will research each question.

2. **Gather Information** As you begin to research your assigned question, avoid plagiarism by properly citing your sources.

   ❏ **Plagiarism** is the unauthorized use of someone else's words or ideas. Plagiarism is not honest.

   ❏ You can avoid plagiarism by including a proper **citation** for each source you use.

   ❏ To **cite print or digital sources,** include author, title, and publication information, according to the style guide your teacher prefers.

As you take notes on your research, be sure to record information about your sources. Take notes from two or more sources, paraphrasing and summarizing key information that answers your question.

MY QUESTION:

Source 1 Information:	Source 2 Information:
Citation:	Citation:

Ideas from the sources that answer my question:

---

3. **Develop and Share Instructions** Share and discuss your research with your group. Use everyone's research to help develop a set of guidelines that describe how an organization can help victims of a natural disaster. Present your guidelines to the class, and include your citations.

When using a search engine for Internet research, don't automatically click on the first result that comes up. Sometimes, the topmost results are paid ads. Make sure the search result doesn't say "Ad" before the link. Read the summaries for each result, determine which ones are best for your search, and choose two or three to click on.

GROUP WORK CHECKLIST

❏ Contribute your own ideas.
❏ Consider the ideas of others.
❏ Ask clarifying questions.
❏ Take notes as necessary.
❏ When presenting, maintain eye contact.
❏ Speak at a natural rate.
❏ Be loud and clear.
❏ Gesture naturally.

RESEARCH AND SHARE

Explain that making a group presentation involves collaboration and careful planning. In addition to activities required as part of the planning and development phase, it is important to practice making a presentation in order to identify areas requiring improvement. Remind students that listening carefully and being respectful of the contributions of others are essential to the preparation of a good presentation.

1. **Develop a Question** Circulate among groups and provide guidance to help students determine whether their questions are appropriate for the level of research they are expected to do. Remind students that their questions should not be too broad or too complex.

   Review the chart in the text and explain the importance of keeping track of sources, including avoiding plagiarism and assessing accuracy.

2. **Gather Information** Remind students about the importance of identifying reliable and credible sources. Explain that sites ending in *.gov* or *.edu* tend to present reliable information, whereas those with a tag ending in *.com* may include biased information. Point out the research tip, which warns against using sites labeled as "Ads."

3. **Develop and Share Instructions** Review the checklist for making presentations in the margin. Encourage students to prepare a poster or handout of the guidelines they developed to share with others.

ENGLISH LEARNER SUPPORT

Present Your Guidelines Students requiring support giving a presentation can benefit greatly by practicing their parts. Have students work with a partner to practice speaking skills:

- Students prepare notes of their part that they can read from.
- Students should take turns rehearsing their part in front of a small group, using a strong, clear voice and eye contact.
- Group members can give feedback on what needs improvement.

   MODERATE/LIGHT

READER'S CHOICE

Setting a Purpose Have students review their Unit 3 Response Log and think about what they've already learned about what it takes to be a survivor. As they select their Independent Reading selections, encourage them to consider what more they want to know.

 NOTICE & NOTE

Explain that some selections may contain multiple signposts; others may contain only one. And the same type of signpost can occur many times in the same text.

 LEARNING MINDSET

Planning Discuss the importance of planning with your students. Remind students that planning is essential to completing work efficiently and exceptionally. Explain that planning will help students learn discipline, which will help them in the future. Encourage students to create a plan for completing an assignment, including mapping out the steps.

 INDEPENDENT READING

? ESSENTIAL QUESTION:

What does it take to be a survivor?

Reader's Choice

Setting a Purpose Select one or more of these options from your eBook to continue your exploration of the Essential Question.

- Read the descriptions to see which text grabs your interest.
- Think about which genres you enjoy reading.

Notice & Note

In this unit, you practiced noticing and noting three signposts: **Tough Questions, Again and Again,** and **Aha Moment.** As you read independently, these signposts and others will aid your understanding. Below are the anchor questions to ask when you read literature and nonfiction.

Reading Literature: Stories, Poems, and Plays		
Signpost	**Anchor Question**	**Lesson**
Contrasts and Contradictions	Why did the character act that way?	p. 3
Aha Moment	How might this change things?	p. 3
Tough Questions	What does this make me wonder about?	p. 172
Words of the Wiser	What's the lesson for the character?	p. 2
Again and Again	Why might the author keep bringing this up?	p. 92
Memory Moment	Why is this memory important?	p. 93

Reading Nonfiction: Essays, Articles, and Arguments		
Signpost	**Anchor Question(s)**	**Lesson**
Big Questions	What surprised me? What did the author think I already knew? What challenged, changed, or confirmed what I already knew?	p. 246 p. 420 p. 332
Contrasts and Contradictions	What is the difference, and why does it matter?	p. 247
Extreme or Absolute Language	Why did the author use this language?	p. 247
Numbers and Stats	Why did the author use these numbers or amounts?	p. 333
Quoted Words	Why was this person quoted or cited, and what did this add?	p. 333
Word Gaps	Do I know this word from someplace else? Does it seem like technical talk for this topic? Do clues in the sentence help me understand the word?	p. 421

 ENGLISH LEARNER SUPPORT

Develop Fluency Select a passage from a text that matches students' reading abilities. Pair students with a peer on a similar reading level:

- Have students read one to two pages of the passage silently. Then have students echo read the passage, switching who reads first and second each paragraph. **SUBSTANTIAL**
- Have students look through the text together, looking for words with which they are unfamiliar. Then, have students partner read, taking turns with each page. **MODERATE**

- Allow more fluent pairs to select their own texts. Set a specific time for students to read silently (for example, 15 minutes). Then have each pair discuss what they read. **LIGHT**

 Go to the **Reading Studio** for additional support in developing fluency.

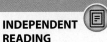

You can preview these texts in Unit 3 of your eBook.
Then, check off the text or texts that you select to read on your own.

POEM

**Watcher:
After Katrina, 2005**
Natasha D. Trethewey

In the weeks following a devastating hurricane, what might you observe?

SHORT STORY

The Day I Didn't Go to the Pool
Leslie J. Wyatt

An older brother must think fast in order to save his siblings.

SHORT STORY

Tuesday of the Other June
Norma Fox Mazer

Relentless bullying affects all aspects of a girl's life.

SPEECH

In Event of Moon Disaster
Bill Safire

What speech would the president have given if the first moon landing had ended in disaster?

INFORMATIONAL TEXT

Ready: Preparing Your Pets for Emergencies Makes Sense
Ready.gov

A practical guide prepares pet owners for an emergency.

Collaborate and Share   Find a partner to discuss what you learned from at least one of your independent readings.

- Give a brief synopsis or summary of the text.
- Describe any signposts that you noticed in the text and explain what they revealed to you.
- Describe what you most enjoyed or found most challenging about the text. Give specific examples.
- Decide if you would recommend the text to others. Why or why not?

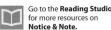 Go to the **Reading Studio** for more resources on **Notice & Note.**

INDEPENDENT READING

MATCHING STUDENTS TO TEXTS

Use the following information to guide students in using their texts.

Watcher: After Katrina, 2005
Genre: poem
Overall Rating: Challenging

The Day I Didn't Go to the Pool   Lexile: 790L
Genre: short story
Overall Rating: Accessible

Tuesday of the Other June   Lexile: 770L
Genre: short story
Overall Rating: Accessible

In Event of Moon Disaster   Lexile: 900L
Genre: speech
Overall Rating: Challenging

Ready: Preparing Your Pets for Emergencies Makes Sense   Lexile: 1070L
Genre: informational text
Overall Rating: Challenging

Collaborate and Share   To assess how well students read the selections, walk around the room and listen to their conversations. Encourage students to be focused and specific in their comments.

 Online **for Assessment**

- Independent Reading Selection Tests

 Encourage students to visit the **Reading Studio** to download a handy bookmark of **NOTICE & NOTE** signposts.

WHEN STUDENTS STRUGGLE . . .

Keep a Reading Log As students read their selected texts, have them keep a reading log for each selection to note signposts and their thoughts about them. Use their logs to assess how well they are noticing and reflecting on elements of the texts.

Reading Log for (title)		
Location	**Signpost I Noticed**	**My Notes About It**

UNIT ③ Task

• **WRITE A NONFICTION NARRATIVE**

LEARNING OBJECTIVES

Writing Task

- Write a nonfiction narrative about someone who shows what it is to be a survivor.
- Establish a situation that introduces real people, places, and events, using specific details and strong imagery.
- Organize an event sequence that unfolds naturally and logically.
- Include elements such as setting, pacing, conflict, and dialogue.
- Use precise words and sensory language, and maintain a consistent style and tone.
- Develop a mood.
- Provide a conclusion that follows from and reflects on events.
- Develop a focused, structured draft.
- Revise and edit drafts, incorporating feedback from peers.
- Use a rubric to evaluate writing.
- **Language** Use appropriate verb tenses.

Assign the Writing Task in **Ed.**

Online **Ed**

RESOURCES

- Unit 3 Response Log
- Writing Studio: Writing Narratives
- Grammar Studio: Module 7: Using Verbs Correctly

Language X-Ray: English Learner Support

Use the instruction below and the supports and scaffolds in the Teacher's Edition to help you guide students at different proficiency levels.

INTRODUCE THE WRITING TASK

Explain that **narrative nonfiction** is a type of writing that presents true events in the form of a story. Point out that the word *narrative* is related to the Spanish adjective *narrativo*, which means "a story." Make sure students understand that narrative nonfiction contains a setting, characters, events, and a mood.

Remind students that the selections in this unit address what it takes to be a survivor. Work with students to select a topic to write about.

Encourage students to write about themselves or someone they know. Use sentence frames to help them articulate their ideas. For example: _____ *is a survivor because* _____.

Brainstorm words and phrases related to the topic and write them on the board. Then, have students work with a partner to write one sentence about what it takes to be a survivor. Tell students to use their sentences to begin their essays.

WRITING

Use Verb Tenses

Tell students that verb tenses indicate when events occur. Verb tenses should remain consistent throughout a text.

Use the following supports with students at varying proficiency levels:

- Provide students sample sentences containing different verb tenses. Have students underline the verb in each sentence. Work with students to write sentences using different verb tenses. If necessary, have students dictate their sentences to you. **SUBSTANTIAL**
- Have students select five to ten common verbs. Write the past, present, and future tenses of each verb. **MODERATE**
- Allow students to work with a partner when writing their drafts, and have students check for correct and consistent verb tenses. **LIGHT**

WRITING

Use Precise Words and Sensory Vocabulary

Tell students that precise words and sensory vocabulary allow them to more clearly communicate their messages.

Use the following supports with students at varying proficiency levels:

- Review the five senses with students. Work with students to create a list of precise words and sensory vocabulary to use in their writing. **SUBSTANTIAL**
- Have students select three sentences in their drafts. Have students revise the sentences to incorporate precise words and sensory vocabulary. **MODERATE**
- Allow students to work with a partner when writing their drafts to revise for precise words and sensory vocabulary. **LIGHT**

WRITING

WRITE A NONFICTION NARRATIVE

Introduce students to the Writing Task by reading the introductory paragraph with them. Remind students to refer to the notes they recorded in the Unit 3 Response Log as they plan and draft their narratives. The Response Log should contain ideas about what it takes to be a survivor. Drawing on these different ideas will make their own writing more interesting and well-informed.

 For **writing support** for students at varying proficiency levels, see the **Language X-Ray** on page 236B.

USE THE MENTOR TEXT

Point out that their nonfiction narratives will be similar to the memoir excerpt "Into the Lifeboat" in that they will tell a true story that contains a setting, character, events, and a mood. However, their narratives will be about themselves or someone they know.

WRITING PROMPT

Review the prompt with students. Encourage them to ask questions about any part of the assignment that is unclear. Make sure they understand that the purpose of their narrative is to tell a true story about a person who is a survivor.

 WRITING TASK

Write a Nonfiction Narrative

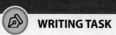 Go to the **Writing Studio** for help writing narratives.

This unit focuses on what it takes to be a survivor. For this writing task, you will write a nonfiction narrative about the qualities of a survivor, about what it takes to survive a disaster or a difficult event. For an example of a nonfiction narrative you can use as a mentor text, review the memoir "Into the Lifeboat."

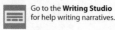

As you write your nonfiction narrative, you can use the notes from your Response Log, which you filled out after reading each text in this unit.

Writing Prompt

Read the information in the box below.

> *This is the topic or context for your nonfiction narrative.*

> The instinct to survive is powerful: you do what you must in order to stay alive, and you help others do the same.

Think carefully about the following question.

> *This is the unit's Essential Question. How would you answer this question, based on the texts in this unit?*

> What does it take to be a survivor?

Write a nonfiction narrative or memoir about what it took for you or someone you know to survive a disaster or difficult event.

> *Now mark the words that identify exactly what you are being asked to produce.*

Be sure to—

> *Review these points as you write and again when you finish. Make any needed changes.*

❏ establish a situation that introduces real people, places, and events, using specific details and strong imagery

❏ organize an event sequence that unfolds naturally and logically

❏ include elements such as setting, pacing, conflict, and dialogue

❏ use precise words and sensory language, and maintain a consistent style and tone

❏ develop a mood

❏ provide a conclusion that follows from and reflects on the events

236   Unit 3

LEARNING MINDSET

Seeking Challenges Remind students that having the willingness to take on challenges is essential to having a learning mindset. In fact, overcoming challenges is key to developing skills and intelligence. Assure students that they are not expected to be perfect and that making mistakes is part of the learning process. By taking risks and trying different strategies, students can learn to overcome challenges.

① Plan

Before you start writing, plan your nonfiction narrative. First, decide which experience you are going to write about. Next, choose your narrator, who can be someone in the narrative or an observer. Then consider whether using sources such as news articles, emails, and texts will add interest and credibility to your narrative. Finally, think about setting and mood. Where and when will your narrative take place? What mood would you like to establish? Take notes in the chart below to help you plan your nonfiction narrative.

Nonfiction Narrative Planning Chart	
Subject of my narrative	
Narrator and point of view	
Main event and characters	
Setting	
Mood	
Sources of information	
Conclusion reflecting on the event	

Background Reading Review the notes you have taken in your Response Log after reading the texts in this unit. These texts are the background reading that will help you formulate the key ideas that will inform your narrative.

Go to **Writing Narratives: Introduction** for help planning your narrative.

Notice & Note
From Reading to Writing

As you plan your nonfiction narrative, apply what you've learned about signposts to your own writing. Remember that writers use common features, called signposts, to help convey their message to readers. Think about how you can incorporate **Contrasts and Contradictions** into your narrative.

Go to the **Reading Studio** for more resources on Notice & Note.

Use the notes from your Response Log as you plan your nonfiction narrative.

① PLAN

Allow time for students to discuss the topic with partners or in small groups and then to complete the planning table independently.

■ English Learner Support

Understand Academic Language Make sure students understand words and phrases used in the chart, such as *narrator, characters, setting,* and *mood.* Work with students to fill in the blank sections, providing text that they can copy into their charts as needed. **SUBSTANTIAL**

▶ NOTICE & NOTE

From Reading to Writing Remind students they can use **Contrasts and Contradictions** to include moments where people behave in unexpected ways. These shocking reactions that contradict usual patterns of behavior can highlight the drama and danger contained in an experience. Remind students to use vivid descriptive words and interesting dialogue to present such contrasts and contradictions.

Background Reading As they plan their narratives, remind students to refer to the notes they took in the Response Log. They may also review the selections to find additional text evidence to support ideas they want to include in their writing.

TO CHALLENGE STUDENTS . . .

Create a Multimedia Presentation Challenge students to present their narrative as a multimedia presentation. Encourage them to include elements such as photographs, voice-over narration, animation, and clips from reenactments and news reports.

WRITING

Organize Your Ideas Tell students that their outlines should contain three main events for their narratives. Provide the following sample based on the chart:

I. Introduction

II. Main Event 1

III. Main Event 2

IV. Main Event 3

V. Conclusion

Remind students that the narrative should be told chronologically in a logical order. Just as in all narratives, students' writing should include pacing, setting, conflict, and dialogue. The conclusion should follow from and reflect on the events.

② DEVELOP A DRAFT

Remind students to follow their outlines as they draft their narratives, but point out that they can still make changes to their writing plan during this stage. As they write, they may discover that they need different details, or that they need to insert a different event in the narrative.

■ English Learner Support

Use a Group Narrative Allow students to work together in pairs or in a small group to write a narrative together.

MODERATE

 **WRITING TASK**

 Go to **Writing Narratives: Narrative Structure** for help organizing your ideas.

Organize Your Ideas Planning includes organizing your ideas in an order that will help your reader understand your narrative. In a nonfiction narrative, the story is often told in chronological order, or the sequence in which the events took place. Use a graphic organizer like the one below to organize your narrative's events in chronological order.

EVENTS IN MY NARRATIVE

② Develop a Draft

 You might prefer to draft your narrative online.

Once you have completed your planning activities, you will be ready to begin drafting your narrative. Refer to the planning chart and graphic organizer you have created, as well as to any notes you took as you studied the texts in the unit. These will provide a kind of map for you to follow as you write. Using a word processor or online writing application makes it easier to make changes or move sentences around later when you are ready to revise your first draft.

WHEN STUDENTS STRUGGLE . . .

Draft the Narrative Remind students that a detailed outline will help make it easier to write their narratives. Students can then put the notes from their outlines into complete sentences to create the first drafts of their narratives. Remind students that a first draft is not meant to be perfect. At this stage, they are just getting their ideas down on paper (or on the computer screen). They will have time to revise and edit their writing later.

Use the Mentor Text

Setting and Mood

Using descriptive language and sensory details can help establish the setting and mood of your narrative. Specific details, thoughtful word choice, and clear imagery will help your reader form mental images of the events and characters you write about, giving the reader a deeper sense of the experience.

> How strange it was to pass all those rooms lit up so brilliantly, their doors open and contents lying around in disorder. Jewels sparkled on dressing tables and a pair of silver slippers were lying just where they had been kicked off.

The author uses vivid imagery to establish the luxurious setting and a dreamlike mood. The glamorous scene contrasts with the unfolding tragedy and shows that people had left everything behind.

Apply What You've Learned Review your narrative and find scenes that you can enhance using descriptive and sensory language. Identify places in your narrative where you can add more detail.

Sequence

Describing events in chronological order pulls readers into the story as if they were experiencing it along with the narrator. Words signaling time, such as *first, then, next, at last,* and *finally,* mark the sequence. The pace at which events unfold—anywhere from slow and dreamy to fast and furious—helps set the tone.

> I started unconsciously to count the decks by the rows of lights. One, two, three, four, five, six; then again—one, two, three, four, five. I stopped. Surely I had miscounted. I went over them again more carefully, hushing the whimpering baby meanwhile.
> No, I had made no mistake. There were only five decks now; then I started all over again—only four now. She was getting lower in the water, I could not any longer deny it.

The author relates the order of events chronologically—and the steady, solemn pace reflects the tragic sinking of the majestic ship, deck by deck, right before her eyes.

Apply What You've Learned Events in your narrative should be told in the order they occurred to reveal how the experience took place in real life. Review your narrative and look for ways to make the sequence clear.

Write a Nonfiction Narrative **239**

WHY THIS MENTOR TEXT?

"Into the Lifeboat" provides a good example of a nonfiction narrative. Use the instruction below to help students use the mentor text as a model for using descriptive language and sensory details to create a setting and mood and describing events in chronological order in their nonfiction narratives.

USE THE MENTOR TEXT

Setting and Mood Ask a volunteer to read aloud the top paragraph from "Into the Lifeboat" on p. 239. Discuss which words contain vivid imagery and sensory details. Then invite students to offer examples of other words with vivid imagery and sensory details that they could use in their narratives.

Sequence To help students understand how to show chronological order in a narrative, have them read the bottom paragraph from "Into the Lifeboat" on p. 239. Point out that the author uses steady, consistent pacing to show the chronological order of events. Remind students that pacing can vary based on the story and the mood they want to convey. Also, remind students that signal words also help a reader understand the chronological order of a text.

 ENGLISH LEARNER SUPPORT

Use the Mentor Text Use the following supports with students at varying proficiency levels:

- Write the words *good, wonderful,* and *exceptional* on the board. Discuss with students how the different words provide a different level of description. Work with students to think of vivid vocabulary to use in their narratives. **SUBSTANTIAL**

- Have students work in pairs to come up with vivid vocabulary and sensory details to describe everyday objects such as a book, a car, shoes, and a shirt. **MODERATE**

- Remind students that synonyms are words with similar meanings. Have students work in pairs to come up with vivid synonyms for commonly used adjectives such as *good, bright, old,* and *new.* **LIGHT**

WRITING

③ REVISE

Have students answer each question in the chart to determine how they can improve their drafts. Invite volunteers to model their revision techniques.

With a Partner Have students ask peer reviewers to evaluate their use of sensory language by answering the following questions:

- How well do the descriptions help you "see" the characters?
- How well does the vocabulary help you understand the events?

Students should use the reviewer's feedback to add details, dialogue, and phrases that describe the characters and events.

WRITING TASK

Go to **The Language of Narrative** in the **Writing Studio** for help revising your narrative.

③ Revise

On Your Own Once you have written your draft, go back and look for ways to improve your nonfiction narrative. As you reread and revise, think about whether you have achieved your purpose of fully capturing the experience of a survivor. The Revision Guide will help you focus on specific elements to make your writing stronger.

Revision Guide		
Ask Yourself	**Tips**	**Revision Techniques**
1. Do I use narrative elements such as setting, conflict, and dialogue?	**Mark** details that show when and where the experience happened.	**Add** details about setting and conflict. Include dialogue.
2. Do I maintain a clear and consistent point of view?	**Mark** pronouns such as *I*, *my*, *he*, and *she*.	**Change** pronouns that cause a shift in the point of view.
3. Do I tell events in chronological order?	**Mark** words that show time order.	**Connect** events with words and phrases that show the order in time.
4. Do I use sensory language to develop events and characters?	**Mark** words and phrases that appeal to the senses.	**Add** words and phrases that describe sights, sounds, and feelings.
5. Do I use verbs and verb phrases to tell when events occurred?	**Mark** verbs and verb phrases.	**Add** verbs and verb phrases that describe when the action takes place, keeping verb tense consistent.
6. Does my conclusion reflect on the event?	**Mark** the conclusion.	**Add** a sentence that reflects on the event.

ACADEMIC VOCABULARY
As you conduct your **peer review**, be sure to use these words.

- ❏ circumstance
- ❏ constraint
- ❏ impact
- ❏ injure
- ❏ significant

With a Partner Once you and your partner have worked through the Revision Guide on your own, exchange papers and evaluate each other's draft in a **peer review**. Focus on providing revision suggestions for at least three of the items in the chart. Explain why you think your partner's draft should be revised and what your specific suggestions are.

When receiving feedback from your partner, listen attentively and ask questions to make sure you fully understand the revision suggestions.

© Houghton Mifflin Harcourt Publishing Company

 ENGLISH LEARNER SUPPORT

Use Signal Words Explain that writers frequently use signal words to show the order of events in a narrative. Have students read their narratives and look for words that signal a time relationship. Then have students add words and phrases to signal chronological order, as needed. **LIGHT**

4 Edit

Once you have addressed the organization, development, and flow of ideas in your narrative, you can improve the finer points of your draft. Edit for the proper use of standard English conventions and correct any misspellings or grammatical errors.

Language Conventions

Consistent Verb Tense A **verb** expresses an action, a condition, or state of being. Helping verbs such as *is*, *could*, *has*, and *might* can be combined with verbs to form **verb phrases.** For example, adding the helping verb *was* to the verb *run* makes the verb phrase *was running*. The **tense** of a verb or verb phrase shows the time of action: present, past, or future. Keeping the verb tense consistent is important, but there are instances in which prepositions or prepositional phrases can "interrupt" or affect a verb tense. In the excerpt below, the verb tense remains consistently past tense (yellow highlight), except for in the dialogue, which is in future tense (blue highlight).

> **As I turned I ran into Jock, the bandleader and his crowd with their instruments. "Funny, they must be going to play," thought I. . . .**

Look at the examples in the chart below.

> Go to the **Grammar Studio** to learn more about using verbs.

Verb or Phrase	Verb Tense	Example Sentence
Verbs: was, seemed	past	Nobody **was** anxious to move; *Titanic* **seemed** so steady.
Verb Phrase: could keep	past	Fascinated, my eyes never left the ship, as if by looking I **could keep** her afloat.
Interrupting Prepositional Phrase	past and present	Violet Jessop climbed awkwardly into the lifeboat and, **in an act that demonstrates the desperate nature of the moment,** reached up to catch a bundle that turned out to be a baby.

5 Publish

After you give your nonfiction narrative its finishing touches, choose a way to share it with your audience. Consider these options:

- Present your nonfiction narrative as a speech to the class.
- Post your nonfiction narrative as a blog on a classroom or school website.

WHEN STUDENTS STRUGGLE . . .

Identify Verbs Some students may have difficulty identifying the verbs and verb phrases in sentences. Remind students that a verb tells the action that is occurring in each sentence. Allow students to highlight the verbs and verb phrases in their narrative. Some students may benefit from working with a partner or adult helper to identify the verbs and verb phrases in their sentences.

4 EDIT

Suggest that students read their drafts aloud to assess how well they used consistent verb tenses. Remind students that they should use the same tense throughout their narrative.

LANGUAGE CONVENTIONS

Consistent Verb Tense Review the information about verb tense with students. Then discuss the example sentences in the chart, asking students to identify the verbs in each example. To emphasize the importance of consistent verb agreement, write a brief paragraph on the board using inconsistent verb tenses. Read the paragraph aloud so students can see and hear the difference. Have students carefully edit their narratives to use a consistent verb tense.

■ English Learner Support

Consistent Verb Tense First, confirm that students understand that *consistent* means "to stay the same." Next, have students work in pairs to locate the verbs and verb phrases in their essays. Have students work together to check that their sentences use a consistent verb tense. **MODERATE**

5 PUBLISH

Place students in small groups. Have students read the narrative of each person in their group, making notes about what each narrative says about survival. After students have read all the narratives, have students discuss what each narrative says about what it takes to be a survivor.

WRITING

USE THE SCORING GUIDE

Have students read the scoring guide and ask questions about any words, phrases, or ideas that are unclear. Put students in groups of three. Assign one student to score the development of ideas, one to score the organization and progression, and one to score the use of language and conventions. Ask them to score the assigned portion of each narrative using the scoring guide. Each student should write a paragraph explaining the reasons for the score he or she awarded in each category.

 **WRITING TASK**

Use the scoring guide to evaluate your nonfiction narrative.

	Writing Task Scoring Guide: Nonfiction Narrative		
	Organization/Progression	**Development of Ideas**	**Use of Language and Conventions**
4	• The organization is effective and logical; events are organized chronologically. • The introduction identifies the subject and creates a strong impression. • Transitions clearly connect events. • Pacing skillfully builds anticipation. • The conclusion reflects on the significance of the experience and leaves the reader with new insight.	• Background information helps to explain events. • Descriptions effectively establish the setting and set the mood. • Use of dialogue and conflict create a strong sense of the characters. • The narrative depicts what it takes to be a survivor.	• Point of view, style, and tone are consistent and effective. • Sensory language and details vividly reveal characters, places, and events. • Sentences are varied and have a rhythmic flow. • Tense in verbs and verb phrases are used correctly and clarify the sequence of events. • Spelling, grammar, usage, and mechanics are correct.
3	• The organization is generally logical; the sequence of events is confusing in a few places. • The introduction identifies the subject. • More transitions would make the sequence of events clearer. • Pacing is somewhat effective. • The conclusion reflects on the experience.	• Background information mostly helps to explain events. • Descriptions mostly establish the setting and set the mood. • Use of dialogue and conflict mostly help to develop the characters. • The narrative mostly addresses the topic of what it takes to be a survivor.	• Point of view, style, and tone are occasionally inconsistent. • Some sensory language is used to reveal characters, places, and events. • Sentences are somewhat varied. • Some errors in the use of tense in verbs and verb phrases occur. • Some spelling, grammar, usage, and mechanics errors occur.
2	• The organization is confusing; missing or extraneous events are distracting. • The introduction briefly mentions the subject. • Few transitions are used throughout. • Pacing is choppy and ineffective. • The conclusion only hints at the significance of the experience.	• More background is needed throughout. • More descriptions are needed to establish the setting and set the mood. • Inadequate use of dialogue and conflict contribute to weak character development. • The narrative vaguely indicates what it might take to be a survivor.	• Point of view, style, and tone are inconsistent. • Sensory language and details are lacking. • Sentences hardly vary; fragments or run-on sentences are present. • The use of tense in verbs and verb phrases is inconsistent. • Multiple spelling, grammar, usage, or mechanics errors occur.
1	• There is no evident organization or sequence of events. • The introduction does not identify the subject. • There is no evident pacing of events. • Transitions are not used, making the narrative difficult to understand. • There is no conclusion.	• Necessary background is missing. • Descriptions needed to establish the setting and set the mood are lacking. • Character development is lacking. • The narrative does not provide a sense of what it takes to be a survivor.	• Point of view, style, and tone are never established. • Sensory language is not used. • Sentences do not vary; several fragments and run-on sentences are present. • Incorrect use of tense in verbs and verb phrases makes the sequence of events confusing. • Spelling, grammar, usage, or mechanics errors create confusion.

Reflect on the Unit

By completing your nonfiction narrative, you have created a writing product that pulls together and expresses your thoughts about the reading you have done in this unit. Now is a good time to reflect on what you have learned.

Reflect on the Essential Question

- What do you think it takes to be a survivor? How has your answer to this question changed since you first considered it when you started this unit?

- What are some examples from the texts you've read that show how people survived a catastrophic event?

Reflect on Your Reading

- Which selections gave you the strongest sense of what it would be like to experience a particular disaster?

- From which selection did you learn the most about what it takes to be a survivor?

Reflect on the Writing Task

- What did you learn about yourself or others as you wrote about what it takes to be a survivor?

- Which writing skills did you strengthen as you drafted and edited your narrative?

UNIT 3 SELECTIONS
- *A Long Walk to Water*
- *Salva's Story*
- "Into the Lifeboat" from *Titanic Survivor*
- "After the Hurricane"
- *Ninth Ward*

REFLECT ON THE UNIT

Have students reflect on the questions independently and write some notes in response to each one. Then have students meet with partners or in small groups to discuss their reflections. Circulate during these discussions to identify the questions that are generating the liveliest conversations. Wrap up with a whole-class discussion focused on these questions.

LEARNING MINDSET

Self-Reflection Explain to students that an important part of developing a learning mindset is the ability to recognize strengths and weaknesses. As students reflect on the unit, encourage them to ask themselves these questions: *Did I ask questions if I needed help? Did I review my work for possible errors? Am I proud of the work I turned in?*

Instructional Overview and Resources

		Instructional Focus	Online Ed Resources
	Unit Instruction **Discovering Your Voice**	**Unit 4 Essential Question** **Unit 4 Academic Vocabulary**	**Stream to Start:** Discovering Your Voice **Unit 4 Response Log**

ANALYZE & APPLY

	from _Selfie: The Changing Face of Self-Portraits_ Multimodal Text by Susie Brooks Lexile 1000L **NOTICE & NOTE** READING MODEL **Signposts** • Big Questions • Extreme or Absolute Language • Contrasts and Contradictions	**Reading** • Analyze Multimodal Texts • Analyze Print and Graphic Features **Writing:** Summarize Key Ideas **Speaking and Listening:** Critique with a Small Group **Vocabulary:** Context Clues **Language Conventions:** Commas After Introductory Elements	**Audio** **Reading Studio:** Notice & Note **Writing Studio:** Using Textual Evidence **Speaking and Listening Studio:** Participating in Collaborative Discussions **Vocabulary Studio:** Context Clues **Grammar Studio:** Module 12: Lesson 4: Using Commas Correctly
	from _Brown Girl Dreaming_ Memoir in Verse by Jacqueline Woodson	**Reading** • Analyze Text Structure and Purpose • Make Connections **Writing:** Describe a Connection **Speaking and Listening:** Compose and Present a Biographical Poem	**Audio** **Reading Studio:** Notice & Note **Level Up Tutorial:** Narrative Poetry **Writing Studio:** Writing Informative Texts **Speaking and Listening Studio:** Giving a Presentation
	"What's So Funny, Mr. Scieszka?" Humor by Jon Scieszka Lexile 710L	**Reading** • Make Inferences About Author's Purpose and Message • Analyze Author's Use of Language **Writing:** Analyze Author's Purpose and Message **Speaking and Listening:** Explain the Steps for Telling a Joke **Vocabulary:** Resources **Language Conventions:** Pronouns	**Audio** **Reading Studio:** Notice & Note **Level Up Tutorial:** Summarizing **Writing Studio:** Writing Informative Texts **Speaking and Listening Studio:** Participating in Collaborative Discussions **Vocabulary Studio:** Using Reference Resources **Grammar Studio:** Module 8: Using Pronouns Correctly

SUGGESTED PACING: 30 DAYS	Unit Introduction	_from_ Selfie: The Changing Face of Self-Portraits	_from_ Brown Girl Dreaming	What's So Funny, Mr. Scieszka?		A Voice
	1	2　3　4　5　6	7　8　9	10　11　12　13　14		15　16

English Learner Support	Differentiated Instruction	Online Ed Assessment
• Discuss Figurative Language • Possible Sentences		

English Learner Support	Differentiated Instruction	Assessment
• Text X-Ray • Use Visual Support • Use Cognates • Use Graphic Organizers • Recognize Base Words • Practice Pronunciation • Oral Assessment • Discuss with a Small Group • Recognize Consonant Blends • Write Sentence Patterns	**When Students Struggle** • Focus on Figurative Language • Sequence Events **To Challenge Students** • Extend the Analysis	**Selection Test**
• Text X-Ray • Produce Different Sounds • Understand Directionality • Use Context Clues • Oral Assessment • Write a Biographical Poem	**When Students Struggle** • Analyze Text Structure **To Challenge Students** • Analyze a Social Issue	**Selection Test**
• Text X-Ray • Use Visual Support • Use Cognates • Use Prereading Supports • Summarize Events • Oral Assessment • Use Recordings to Self-Correct • Practice Pronunciation • Write with Pronouns	**When Students Struggle** • Somebody-Wanted-But-So Grid	**Selection Test**

Words Like Freedom	Better Than Words: Say It with a Selfie	OMG, Not *Another* Selfie!		Independent Reading	End of Unit
17 > 18 > 19	20 > 21 > 22	23 > 24 > 25		26 > 27	28 > 29 > 30

PLAN

	Instructional Focus	Online **Ed** Resources

COLLABORATE & COMPARE

"A Voice"
Poem by Pat Mora

Reading
• Analyze Figurative Language
• Make Inferences

Writing: Characterize the Speaker

Speaking and Listening: Discuss and Analyze Figurative Language

 Audio

Text in Focus: Interpreting Figurative Language

Reading Studio: Notice & Note

Level Up Tutorial: Figurative Language

Writing Studio: Writing Informative Texts

Speaking and Listening Studio: Participating in Collaborative Discussions

"Words Like Freedom"
Poem by Langston Hughes

Collaborate and Compare

Reading: Make Connections to Speakers

Speaking and Listening: Discuss Connections to Speakers

 Audio

Speaking and Listening Studio: Participating in Collaborative Discussions

Level Up Tutorial: Elements of Poetry

"Better Than Words: Say It with a Selfie"
Argument by Gloria Chang
Lexile 1050L

Reading
• Analyze Rhetorical Devices
• Identify an Argument's Audience

Writing: Compose an Argument

Speaking and Listening: Create and Present "The Perfect Selfie"

Vocabulary: Context Clues

Language Conventions: Commonly Confused Words

 **Audio**

Close Read Screencasts: Modeled Discussions

Reading Studio: Notice & Note

Level Up Tutorial: Making Predictions

Writing Studio: Writing an Argument

Speaking and Listening Studio: Giving a Presentation

Vocabulary Studio: Using Context Clues

Grammar Studio: Module 14: Spelling

MENTOR TEXT

"OMG, Not *Another* Selfie!"
Argument by Shermakaye Bass
Lexile 1070L

Collaborate and Compare

Reading: Compare and Evaluate Arguments

Online **Ed** INDEPENDENT READING

The Independent Reading selections are only available in the eBook.

 Go to the Reading Studio for more information on Notice & Note.

"I Was a Skinny Tomboy Kid"
Poem by Luz Villanueva

"Words Are Birds"
Poem by Francisco X. Alarcón

END OF UNIT

Writing Task: Multimodal Argument	**Writing:** Create a Multimodal Argument	**Unit 4 Response Log**
	Language Conventions: Pronouns	**Mentor Text:** "OMG, Not *Another* Selfie!"
Reflect on the Unit		**Writing Studio:** Writing Arguments
		Reading Studio: Notice & Note
		Grammar Studio: Module 8: Using Pronouns Correctly

English Learner Support	Differentiated Instruction	Online Ed Assessment
• Text X-Ray • Use Supportive Charts • Draw Ideas and Concepts • Oral Assessment	**When Students Struggle** • Genre Reformulation	**Selection Test**
• Oral Assessment • Discuss and Analyze Figurative Language		**Selection Test**
• Share Information	**When Students Struggle** • Venn Diagram	
• Text X-Ray • Use Academic Language • Explore Word Families • Learn New Language Structures • Demonstrate Comprehension • Oral Assessment	**When Students Struggle** • Make Predictions	**Selection Test**

• Confirm Understanding
• Use Contractions
• Understand Language Structures
• Oral Assessment
  • Compare Texts
  • Create and Present
  • Practice Pronunciation
  • Use Commonly Confused Words
		Selection Test

• Express Opinions		

"Eleven"
Short Story by Sandra Cisneros
Lexile 1090L

"On Dragonwings"
Short Story by Lucy D. Ford
Lexile 620L

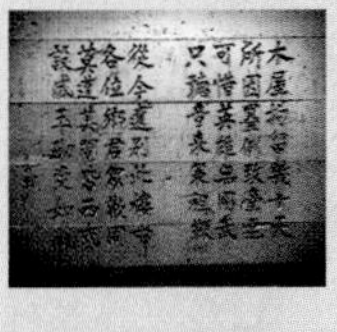

"Carved on the Walls"
Informational Text by Judy Yung
Lexile 1060L

Selection Test

English Learner Support	Differentiated Instruction	Assessment
• Language X-Ray • Understand Academic Language • Use a Word Wall • Use the Mentor Text • Write Captions • Check Pronoun-Antecedent Agreement	**When Students Struggle** • Draft the Argument • Identify Pronouns and Antecedents **To Challenge Students** • Conduct Research	**Unit Test**

DISCOVERING YOUR VOICE

? Connect to the ESSENTIAL QUESTION

Ask a volunteer to read aloud the Essential Question. Discuss how the images on page 244 relate to the question. Ask what students do now to make themselves heard. Do they use social networking? Do they make art? Do they belong to organizations that work for things they believe in? What are ways they would like to make their voices heard in the future?

■ English Learner Support

Discuss Figurative Language Explain to students that "discovering your voice" is an example of figurative language. Discuss the meaning of this phrase.

- *Voice* means "the expression of thoughts, feelings, and opinions."
- *Discovering* means "looking for possibilities and opportunities."
- "Discovering your voice" means "finding ways to express your thoughts, feelings, and opinions."
  ALL LEVELS

DISCUSS THE QUOTATION

Jacqueline Woodson, the author of the quotation, is an award-winning author of books for young people. Although she is probably best known for *Miracle's Boys*, which won the Coretta Scott King Award in 2001, it was *Brown Girl Dreaming* that won the National Book Award for Young People's Literature in 2014. Her own description of coming to know that she wanted to write makes it clear that Woodson always had a strong voice and a need to make it heard. She writes about issues that many people find controversial, including race, class, and gender, and young people are drawn to her honesty and willingness to deal realistically with life.

? ESSENTIAL QUESTION:

What are the ways you can make yourself heard?

 When I speak, the words come pouring out of me. 🙶🙶

Jacqueline Woodson

⚙ LEARNING MINDSET

Effort Remind students that effort is necessary for growth and that hard work leads to success. Remember to praise students for effort, not for being "smart." Offer feedback: "I noticed you put a lot of effort into your reading/writing today. When you stumbled on [something] you stopped, took a breath, and kept going."

ACADEMIC VOCABULARY

Academic Vocabulary words are words you use when you discuss and write about texts. In this unit, you will practice and learn five words.

☑ **appropriate**   ☐ **authority**   ☐ **consequence**   ☐ **element**   ☐ **justify**

Study the Word Network to learn more about the word **appropriate**.

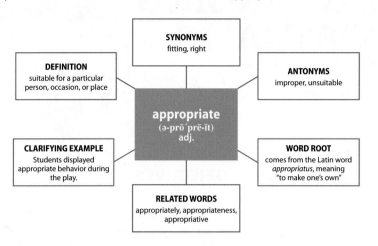

SYNONYMS
fitting, right

DEFINITION
suitable for a particular person, occasion, or place

ANTONYMS
improper, unsuitable

appropriate
(ə-prō´prē-ĭt)
adj.

CLARIFYING EXAMPLE
Students displayed appropriate behavior during the play.

WORD ROOT
comes from the Latin word *appropriatus*, meaning "to make one's own"

RELATED WORDS
appropriately, appropriateness, appropriative

Write and Discuss Discuss the completed Word Network with a partner, making sure to talk through all of the boxes until you both understand the word, its synonyms, antonyms, and related forms. Then, fill out Word Networks for the remaining four words. Use a dictionary or online resource to help you complete the activity.

 Go online to access the Word Networks.

RESPOND TO THE ESSENTIAL QUESTION

In this unit, you will read about the different ways that people find their voices and express their ideas. As you read, you will revisit the **Essential Question** and gather your ideas about it in the **Response Log** that appears on page R4. At the end of the unit, you will have the opportunity to create a **multimodal argument** about your favorite way to express yourself. You will gather graphics and images that help support your argument. Filling out the **Response Log** will help you prepare for this task.

 You can also go online to access the Response Log.

UNIT 4
RESPONSE LOG

Essential Question:
What are the ways you can make yourself heard?

from Selfie: The Changing Face of Self-Portraits

from Brown Girl Dreaming

What's So Funny, Mr. Scieszka?

A Voice

Words Like Freedom

Better Than Words: Say it with a Selfie

OMG, Not Another Selfie!

R4 Response Log

ACADEMIC VOCABULARY

As students complete Word Networks for the remaining four vocabulary words, encourage them to include all the categories shown in the completed network if possible, but point out that some words do not have clear synonyms or antonyms.

appropriate (ə-prō´prē-ĭt) *adj.* suitable for a particular person, occasion, or place

authority (ə-thôr´ĭ-tē) *n.* a trusted source of information (Spanish cognate: *autoridad*)

consequence (kŏn´sĭ-kwĕns´) *n.* the result of something that happened earlier; effect (Spanish cognate: *consecuencia*)

element (ĕl´ə-mənt) *n.* a part of a whole that can be discovered through analysis (Spanish cognate: *elemento*)

justify (jŭs´tə-fī´) *v.* to defend as right or reasonable (Spanish cognate: *justificar*)

RESPOND TO THE ESSENTIAL QUESTION

Direct students to the Unit 4 Response Log. Explain that students will use it to record ideas and details from the selections that help answer the Essential Question. When they work on the writing task at the end of the unit, their Response Logs will help them think about what they have read and make connections between texts.

 ENGLISH LEARNER SUPPORT

Use Topic-Related Vocabulary Help students think about the content of the text before they read it. Use this strategy with selections in this unit.

- Choose 4 topic-related vocabulary words from the selection that you think students know. Choose words that communicate an important idea. (For "Selfies": *selfie, artist, paint, mirror*). Give students this sentence to complete: *Before phone cameras, a _____ could _____ a picture of himself or herself using a _____.* **SUBSTANTIAL/MODERATE**

- Choose 8 to 14 topic-related vocabulary words from the selection that you think students know. Be sure to tell students that the words are from a nonfiction selection. Have pairs of students write 4 or 5 sentences using 3 to 5 of these words in each sentence. Ask volunteers to share some of their sentences with the class. Then have the class discuss what they think the selection will be about. **LIGHT**

READING MODEL

from SELFIE: THE CHANGING FACE OF SELF-PORTRAITS

Multimodal Text by Susie Brooks

GENRE ELEMENTS
MULTIMODAL TEXT

Remind students that the purpose of **multimodal text** is to present facts and information. A multimodal text uses more than one mode, or form, of communication. The modes might include image, music, gesture, or voice. The text can be print or digital. It can even be live performance. This excerpt from the book *Selfie: The Changing Face of Self-Portraits* uses written words and images to present a clear explanation of the development of painted self-portraits.

LEARNING OBJECTIVES

- Analyze a multimodal text.
- Analyze a variety of print and graphic features.
- Research the life and work of an artist.
- Infer word meanings using context clues.
- Use commas to clarify meaning.
- Write a summary.
- Discuss headings and graphic features of a text.
- **Language** Discuss the author's analysis with a partner using the terms *seem* and *express*.

TEXT COMPLEXITY

Quantitative Measures	*from Selfie: The Changing Face of Self-Portraits*	Lexile: 1000
Qualitative Measures	**Ideas Presented** Much is explicit, but inference and interpretation are necessary.	
	Structures Used Conventional text structure, complicated by interaction between text and images.	
	Language Used Explicit, literal, contemporary, familiar language. Some more difficult vocabulary.	
	Knowledge Required Relies to a small extent on knowledge of context of Western art.	

RESOURCES

- Unit 4 Response Log
- Selection Audio
- Reading Studio: Notice & Note
- Writing Studio:
  Using Textual Evidence
- Speaking and Listening Studio:
  Participating in Collaborative
  Discussions
- Vocabulary Studio:
  Context Clues
- Grammar Studio: Module 12:
  Lesson 4: Using Commas Correctly
- *Selfie: The Changing Face of Self-Portraits* Selection Test

SUMMARIES

English

In this excerpt from *Selfie: The Changing Face of Self-Portraits*, art historian Susie Brooks looks at how artists of the past painted their "selfies," or self-portraits. From Albrecht Dürer in the 15th century to Vincent Van Gogh in the 19th century, these artists revealed much of themselves in a way that resonates with selfie-takers today.

Spanish

En este pasaje de *Selfi: La cara cambiante de los autorretratos*, la historiadora del arte Susie Brooks mira cómo los artistas del pasado pintaban sus "selfis", o autorretratos. Desde Abrecht Dürer, en el siglo XV, hasta Vincent Van Gogh, en el siglo XIX, estos artistas revelan mucho de sí mismos de una manera que resuena con los tomadores de autofotos de hoy en día.

SMALL-GROUP OPTIONS

Have students work in small groups to read and discuss the selection.

Reciprocal Teaching

- Have students read the selection. Present them with a list of generic question stems, such as: *What was the main _____? Which one of the _____? How important was _____?*
- Have each student write three to five questions about the selection, using the stems.
- Put students in groups of three and ask each student to offer at least two questions for group discussion without duplicating another student's questions.
- Tell the groups to reach a consensus on the answer to each question and find text evidence to support it.

Jigsaw with Experts

- Divide the selection into six parts: the introduction and conclusion forming one part and the other five focusing on one artist each.
- Assign each student to a reading section and have them read and take notes on the selection.
- Have the "experts" on each section form a group to talk about their section.
- Have students form new groups that include a representative for each section of the divided reading.
- Ask students to discuss each section and then the whole piece.

Text X-Ray: English Learner Support
for *Selfie: The Changing Face of Self-Portraits*

Use the Text X-Ray and the supports and scaffolds in the Teacher's Edition to help guide students at different proficiency levels through the selection.

INTRODUCE THE SELECTION
DISCUSS DISCOVERING SELF-EXPRESSION

In this lesson, students will need to be able to discuss discovering their own voice. It will be important for them to think about how they express themselves. They will also read about and discuss what others have done or do today to express themselves. Draw a brainstorming graphic organizer. Work with students to come up with aspects of themselves that they might try to express to others. These things might include:

- emotions (sadness, happiness, loneliness, anger, pride)
- needs (food, water, shelter, love, friendship)
- thoughts (ideas, worries, hopes, questions)
- opinions (about sports, politics, fashion, school)

Ask students what they might do to express some of these emotions, needs, thoughts, and opinions. Supply the following sentence frame:

- *I could _____ to express _____.*

CULTURAL REFERENCES

The following words and phrases may be unfamiliar to students:

- *commissioned* (paragraph 2): hired an artist to create a specific work of art, such as a portrait
- *higher social status* (paragraph 7): more respect and power
- *Japanese print* (paragraph 19): a print is a work of art that is made by cutting a picture into a block, usually using blades or acid, and then putting ink on the block to make many copies. Japanese print methods were far ahead of European print methods in the 19th century and were much admired by European artists.

LISTENING

Examine Images and Captions

Draw students' attention to images in the multimodal text. Explain that there is a lot of information in an image if you look closely and think carefully about what you see. Then point out the captions and explain that an author uses this feature to provide additional information about an image.

Use the following supports with students at varying proficiency levels:

- Have students listen as you talk about the Dürer self-portrait. Tell students that you will ask questions about what you see in the painting. They should give a thumbs up for yes and a thumbs down for no. For example, ask: *I see a striped hat. Do you? I see a window. Do you? I see mountains through the window. Do you?* **SUBSTANTIAL**

- Have students listen and follow directions as you ask them to mark different kinds of information in various captions. For example, ask: *Find Rembrandt's first self-portrait. Circle the year when he painted it. Mark an X on the year when he was born. Underline the year he died. Look at the other self-portrait on this page. Circle the other person shown in this portrait. Underline her name.* **MODERATE**

- Read aloud various captions. Have students take notes that summarize the information they have learned from listening to each one. **LIGHT**

SPEAKING

Discuss an Analysis

Draw students' attention to one of the paintings reproduced in the selection and to the author's comments on it. Provide students with words that will help them analyze and make inferences about the paintings.

Read paragraphs 10–11 while you look at the Rembrandt self-portrait. Use the following supports with students at varying proficiency levels:

- Provide students with a list of words the author uses in her analysis: *sad, calm, dignified*. Have students use the words to complete the following frame: *The author thinks Rembrandt seems _____.* **SUBSTANTIAL**
- Have partners use the words *seems* and *express/expresses* to analyze the self-portrait. Provide them with frames such as: *The author says Rembrandt _____. I think Rembrandt _____. Rembrandt expresses _____ by _____.* **MODERATE**
- Have students comment on the Rembrandt portrait, using the words *seem* and *express*. Ask: *The author says Rembrandt looks sad, calm, and dignified. How would you describe him?* (**Possible answer:** *He seems almost angry. His eyes express a lot.*) **LIGHT**

READING

Read for Details

Tell students that the details that an author includes can help them understand better the topic that the author is explaining. Looking for details as they read will help them comprehend a text better.

Work with students to read paragraph 19. Use the following supports with students at varying proficiency levels:

- Read only the first sentence of paragraph 19. Tell students that you will ask questions about what they just read. For example, ask: *What kind of brushstrokes did van Gogh use?* **SUBSTANTIAL**
- Provide students with sentence frames to use to explain the details they can identify in this paragraph: *Van Gogh used ___, ____ brushstrokes. He painted pictures by _____. He liked Japanese art because _____.* **MODERATE**
- Pair students. Have pairs work together to point out all the details the author includes to tell about van Gogh's brushstrokes, painting style, and artistic influences. **LIGHT**

WRITING

Write a Summary of Key Ideas

Work with students to choose the most important ideas in the selection in preparation for writing a summary. Review the terms *key ideas*, *details*, and *evidence*. Remind students that they need evidence to support their ideas.

Use the following supports with students at varying proficiency levels:

- Give students practice spelling the terms *key ideas*, *details*, and *evidence*. Write the terms on the board. Have students copy them on sticky notes. Then have students put the sticky notes next to places in the text where they see examples of each. **SUBSTANTIAL**
- Provide students with a two-column graphic organizer. Have pairs of students work together to identify three key ideas and copy them in the first column. Then ask them to find and record in the second column at least two pieces of evidence for each idea. **MODERATE**
- Have students complete a two-column graphic organizer to help them record and organize the key ideas and evidence they locate. Have students write a few sentences using each key idea and its supporting evidence. **LIGHT**

EXPLAIN THE SIGNPOSTS

Explain that **NOTICE & NOTE Signposts** are significant moments in the text that help readers understand and analyze works of fiction or nonfiction. Use the instruction on these pages to introduce students to the signposts **Big Questions**, **Extreme or Absolute Language**, and **Contrasts and Contradictions**. Then use the selection that follows to have students apply the signposts to a text.

For a full list of the fiction and nonfiction signposts, see p. 320.

BIG QUESTIONS

Explain that students need to ask themselves **Big Questions** whenever they read nonfiction. These questions concern what the reader knows, what surprises the reader, and how the text confirms or changes what the reader knows.

Point out that, when the author surprises the reader, it's a signal to pay close attention. The author may be challenging the reader's **bias**. Or making a **claim** that will need to be supported. Or just trying to get the reader's attention.

When Susie Brooks mentions that Vincent van Gogh cut off part of his ear, she will be surprising a great many readers and supporting in advance her claim that some of the artists who created these self-portraits were "a bit bonkers."

Tell students that when they spot a Big Question, they should pause, mark it in their consumable texts, and ask themselves: *What surprised me? What is the author's purpose in including this detail?*

Notice & Note

from SELFIE: THE CHANGING FACE OF SELF-PORTRAITS

You are about to read an excerpt from the multimodal text *Selfie: The Changing Face of Self-Portraits*. In it, you will notice and note signposts that give you clues about the text's main idea and the author's purpose. Here are three key signposts to look for as you read this text and other works of nonfiction.

📖 For more information on these and other signposts to Notice & Note, visit the **Reading Studio**.

When you are surprised by something you read, pause and ask yourself if you should apply the **Big Questions** strategy. Then, do the following:

Identify words or phrases that surprised you.

Ask yourself why the author included this surprising element.

Continue to look for and clarify surprising information as you read.

Big Questions Have you ever read something that suddenly made you pause to catch your breath—or maybe even laugh out loud? Sometimes an author will include a startling observation, an unusual fact, or an unexpected phrase that makes you sit up and take notice. If you're reading a text and experience a moment of astonishment, then it's a good idea to pause and ask yourself what was so surprising about it. Asking **Big Questions** such as **What surprised you?** can clarify information that you did not already know and lead you to ask and answer more questions as you read.

Read this part of *Selfie: The Changing Face of Self-Portraits* to see a student's annotation of a Big Question:

> 4   Take Vincent van Gogh, who cut off a piece of his ear, but still thought it would make a nice picture.

What surprised you?	I didn't know Vincent van Gogh cut off a piece of his ear! It surprised me that he did this and then painted a picture of himself afterwards.
What is the author's purpose in including this detail?	The text is about self-portraits, and this would be an example of a very unusual self-portrait. Why would he paint something like that?

Extreme or Absolute Language Have you ever caught yourself exaggerating when you tell a friend a story? The story itself may be true, but the details may be overstated for the sake of effect. **Hyperbole** is a figure of speech in which the truth is exaggerated for emphasis or humorous effect. In nonfiction, writers sometimes use hyperbole and other types of extreme or absolute language to make a point.

Extreme or Absolute Language includes words that indicate certainty (*all, none, everyone, no one, always, never, totally*) without supporting evidence, as well as statements that appear exaggerated or express a rigid position.

Here is an example of a student finding and marking instances of Extreme or Absolute Language:

> 3   . . . but most of all they let us look right inside the minds of the brilliant (and sometimes a bit bonkers) people who created them.

When you read a phrase like these, pause to see if it's an **Extreme or Absolute Language** signpost:

We must all agree . . .

Everyone knows . . .

Nothing in the universe . . .

You will never believe . . .

Anchor Question
When you notice this signpost, ask: Why did the author use this language?

What is extreme or absolute about this language?	Use of hyperbole: self-portraits don't literally show us the inside of a person's mind. Bonkers is a slang word meaning "crazy," which seems extreme or exaggerated.
What might be the author's purpose in using this language?	The author may be using exaggeration and humor to help explain and emphasize the point about what self-portraits reveal.

Contrasts and Contradictions The writer of this selection compares artists of the past to the selfie-snapping smart-phone users of today. In this example, a student underlined a **Contrast and Contradiction.**

> 1   They never saw a smartphone, or the Internet, and most of them couldn't even tell you what a camera was. But they did all know about selfies!

Anchor Question
When you notice this signpost, ask: What is the difference, and why does it matter?

What contrast or contradiction is shown here?	People in the past didn't have Internet, smart phones, or even cameras. But they did have selfies, like we do today.
Why did the author include this contrast or contradiction?	The contrast shows that while technology may have changed over time, what people actually do with technology has not.

EXTREME OR ABSOLUTE LANGUAGE

Explain to students that **Extreme or Absolute Language** is language that leaves no doubt about a situation or an event, allows no compromise, or seems to exaggerate or overstate a case. In some cases, as with **hyperbole**, the exaggeration is obvious and used for effect. In other words, it is a kind of **figurative language** and is not intended to be taken literally. In other cases, Extreme or Absolute Language can be a sign that the author's claim needs to be investigated.

Tell students that when they spot Extreme or Absolute Language, they should pause, mark it in their consumable texts, and ask themselves the anchor question: *Why did the author use this language?*

CONTRASTS AND CONTRADICTIONS

Explain to students that **Contrasts and Contradictions** occur when the author points out a difference between two people, things, or situations. Often, the point of this kind of contrast is to help the reader understand something unfamiliar in terms of its difference from something familiar.

Tell students that when they spot a Contrast and Contradiction, they should pause, mark it in their consumable texts, and ask themselves the anchor question: *What is the difference, and why does it matter?*

APPLY THE SIGNPOSTS

Have students use the selection that follows as a model text to apply the signposts. As students encounter signposts, prompt them to stop, reread, and ask themselves the anchor questions that will help them understand the main points that the author is making and how the author uses various print and graphic features to present these points.

Tell students to continue to look for these and other signposts as they read the other selections in the unit.

WHEN STUDENTS STRUGGLE . . .

Focus on the Figurative Language If students struggle with recognizing **hyperbole**, review the basics of figurative language. Explain that figurative language communicates meaning beyond the literal meanings of the words. Give students these examples: "Sue is as fast as Maria is." and "Sue is as fast as the wind." Ask students whether each of these statements is actually true and which is a way of expressing that Sue is very fast.

Connect to the
ESSENTIAL QUESTION

This excerpt from *Selfie: The Changing Face of Self-Portraits* deals with a kind of voice, or form of self-expression, that can still speak clearly after half a millennium. The author looks at the self-portraits of five artists and talks about what each artist used the portrait to communicate.

from
SELFIE:
THE CHANGING FACE OF SELF-PORTRAITS

Multimodal Text by **Susie Brooks**

ESSENTIAL QUESTION:

What are the ways you can make yourself heard?

248   Unit 4

LEARNING MINDSET

Seeking Challenges Explain that having a growth and learning mindset means taking risks. That involves trying new things and not being afraid to fail (or look silly) in front of friends. Emphasize that trying hard is important, but trying things that are hard is just as important. The brain needs to be stretched and challenged in much the same way as muscles do, and that's the way to think about difficult tasks, as challenges.

QUICK START

Some of the world's most famous "selfies" have been displayed in art museums around the world. What do you think it would take for one of your own selfies to be exhibited in a museum? Discuss your response with the class.

ANALYZE MULTIMODAL TEXTS

The multimodal selection you are about to read conveys ideas through text and visual details. To find the key ideas in this multimodal text, follow these steps:

- Identify the specific topic of each paragraph or section.
- Examine all the details the author provides, including details found in text, illustrations, images, and graphic features.
- Reread the text after studying the artwork, synthesizing information from both. This will reinforce key ideas the author is trying to convey.

ANALYZE PRINT AND GRAPHIC FEATURES

Print features are elements of text design, such as boldface type, headings, captions, and fonts. **Graphic features** are visual elements that help call attention to information, such as charts, diagrams, graphs, photographs, maps, and art. Together, print and graphic features present information, create interest, and guide readers through a text. You can **skim**—quickly read or view—these features before a close reading to help you **predict** what the text will be about and set a purpose for reading. As you read, note how print and graphic features help convey information. These features can also help you quickly locate topics or ideas after reading.

> **GENRE ELEMENTS: MULTIMODAL INFORMATIONAL TEXT**
> - provides factual information
> - includes evidence to support ideas
> - uses more than one mode of communication: text, art, sound, video, and so on
> - includes many forms, such as picture books, websites, and digital media

PRINT FEATURES	GRAPHIC FEATURES
A **heading** or **subheading** indicates the beginning of a new topic or section. New sections may begin with a **drop cap,** or a large capital letter at the beginning of a paragraph.	**Color effects,** such as highlighted text, doodles, and colored backgrounds, can organize and call attention to information.
A **caption** contains information about an image or illustration.	A box, speech balloon, or other shape may be used to display information about an image or to call attention to additional information.

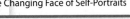

QUICK START

To further explore the idea of selfies, ask volunteers to show the class a selfie they particularly like. Screen the selfies before you show them to the class to make sure that no inappropriate content is displayed.

ANALYZE MULTIMODAL TEXTS

Explain to students that a multimodal text is not just a written word text with illustrations. The graphic elements and written text are equal in importance. Reading this excerpt from *Selfie: The Changing Face of Self-Portraits* without the images would not make sense. And while looking at the portraits without the text would be interesting, this experience would not communicate the message of the selection as a whole. It is the combination of text and imagery that makes this multimodal text effective.

ANALYZE PRINT AND GRAPHIC FEATURES

One of the most important print features in this multimodal text is the use of captions. The captions serve several important purposes.

- Captions provide specific information about images that might interrupt the flow of the text narrative if it was included there.
- Captions identify images so that the reader will be able to connect them to the text.
- In some cases, a caption provides enough information so readers may do further research about the image, going beyond the information that is available in the text.

ENGLISH LEARNER SUPPORT

Use Visual Support Help students understand the text by connecting it directly to the imagery. When the text makes a statement about the person in one of the images, model the adjectives used. For example, "Dürer looks haughty and confident." Walk across the room looking haughty and confident. Ask for volunteers to act out some of the descriptions once they are familiar with the adjectives. Explain to students that once they understand what the author is saying about an image, they may agree or disagree.

SUBSTANTIAL/MODERATE

TEACH

CRITICAL VOCABULARY

Encourage students to read all the sentences before deciding which word best completes each one. Remind them to look for context clues that match the precise meaning of each word.

Answers:

1. *span*
2. *portrait*
3. *reflection*
4. *etch*

■ English Learner Support

Use Cognates Tell students that the Critical Vocabulary word *reflection* has a Spanish cognate: *reflexión*.
ALL LEVELS

LANGUAGE CONVENTIONS

Explain that adverbial phrases usually come right after the verb, and there is no comma between the phrase and the verb. When one of those phrases is at the beginning of a sentence, it is separated from the rest of the sentence with a comma in most cases.

✎ ANNOTATION MODEL

Students can review the Reading Model introduction on pages 246–247 if they have questions about any of the signposts. Suggest that they underline important phrases or circle key words that help them identify signposts. They may want to color-code their annotations by using a different color highlighter for each signpost. Point out that they may follow this suggestion or use their own system for marking up the selections in their write-in texts.

 GET READY

CRITICAL VOCABULARY

portrait	etch	reflection	span

To see how many Critical Vocabulary words you already know, use them to complete the sentences.

1. Their trip around the world will _____ at least six months.

2. A _____ of the president is in the hall.

3. His _____ in the mirror smiled back at him.

4. In art class, we learned how to _____ drawings into wood.

LANGUAGE CONVENTIONS

Commas can clarify the meaning of sentences by separating certain words, phrases, or clauses. In this lesson, you will learn how to use commas to set off introductory elements. An **introductory element** is a word, phrase, or dependent clause that appears at the beginning of a sentence.

By the end of his life, Rembrandt was an expert in capturing character.

In the sentence above, a comma separates the introductory phrase *By the end of his life* from the independent clause that completes the sentence. The comma makes the sentence easier to understand.

ANNOTATION MODEL   NOTICE & NOTE

As you read, notice and note signposts, including **Big Questions, Extreme or Absolute Language,** and **Contrasts and Contradictions.** In the model shown, you can see how one reader responded to the opening of *Selfie: The Changing Face of Self-Portraits*.

1   You can probably do it with your eyes closed: point your phone camera at your face; press the shutter button and bingo—a selfie! But next time you smile/hug a celebrity and post the pic, spare a thought for Rembrandt van Rijn and Vincent van Gogh, among others.

> Why would I take a picture of myself with my eyes closed?
>
> These are exaggerations, but they grabbed my attention!

BACKGROUND

Does it surprise you to learn that selfies actually have a long history in art? Children's author and art historian **Susie Brooks** *explains how even before the invention of photography, the Internet, and the smart phone, people throughout history have longed to put their best face forward and share their images with the world.*

from
SELFIE:
THE CHANGING FACE OF SELF-PORTRAITS

Multimodal Text by Susie Brooks

SETTING A PURPOSE

As you read, pay attention to how the multimodal elements of the text, including images, and print and graphic features, work together to convey topics and key ideas.

All By Your Selfie

1 You can probably do it with your eyes closed: point your phone camera at your face; press the shutter button and bingo—a selfie! But next time you smile/hug a celebrity and post the pic, spare a thought for Rembrandt van Rijn and Vincent van Gogh, among others. They never saw a smartphone, or the Internet, and most of them couldn't even tell you what a camera was. But they did all know about selfies!

2 Back in the old days, selfies were more commonly known as self-portraits. Before photography was invented, people who wanted pictures of themselves (and could afford it) commissioned artists to paint their **portraits.** If you were

---

NOTICE & NOTE

Notice & Note

Use the side margins to notice and note signposts in the text.

LANGUAGE CONVENTIONS

In paragraph 2, how are commas used to set off introductory elements? What effect do the commas have on the sentences?

portrait

(pôr´trĭt) *n.* A *portrait* is a person's likeness, especially one showing the face, which may be painted, photographed, or otherwise represented.

Selfie: The Changing Face of Self-Portraits   251

ENGLISH LEARNER SUPPORT

Use Graphic Organizers Provide students with a two-column graphic organizer.

- Have students write the names of two artists in the left column and draw two pictures in the right column, each showing one thing they learned about that artist. **SUBSTANTIAL**

- Have students write the names of two artists in the left column and then write a few words or phrases in the right column to tell what they learned about each artist. **MODERATE**

- Have students write the names of three artists in the left column and write a sentence telling about each artist in the right column. **LIGHT**

TEACH

BACKGROUND

Explain to students that in addition to painting separate self-portraits, artists have often put themselves into paintings of other subjects. Sometimes they did this to save money because models had to be paid. Sometimes they did it just for fun. The filmmaker Alfred Hitchcock did a similar thing when he appeared in the background of a scene in almost every one of his movies.

SETTING A PURPOSE

Direct students to use the Setting a Purpose prompt to focus their reading.

LANGUAGE CONVENTIONS

Review how authors set off introductory words, phrases, and dependent clauses with commas. Then ask students to read the following sentence: *Much of the time traveling is very difficult.*

Discuss with students why a comma after the word *time* would help clarify this sentence. (**Answer:** *Without the comma, the sentence could be about time traveling. With it, the sentence is about regular traveling.*) Then discuss with students how the commas after the words *days* in the first sentence and *invented* in the second sentence of paragraph 2 make the meaning of these sentences clearer.

CRITICAL VOCABULARY

portrait: When someone creates a portrait, they are trying to show something about a person.

ASK STUDENTS how today's selfies are different from old-fashioned self-portraits. How were portraits created before photography? (*Today, anyone can snap a selfie of themselves with a camera. In the past, people had to be good at painting to make a portrait of themselves or request that an artist make a portrait of them.*)

Selfie: The Changing Face of Self-Portraits   **251**

ENGLISH LEARNER SUPPORT

Recognize Base Words Explain that students can get help in determining the meaning of a word by looking for a base word within it that may be more familiar. Have pairs of students work together to identify the base words in *reflection* and *expressive (reflection/reflect, expressive/express)*, define these base words, and then use this information to define *reflection* and *expressive*. **LIGHT**

ANALYZE PRINT AND GRAPHIC FEATURES

Remind students that a caption often supplies information about an image that is not provided in the text. (**Answer:** *Captions use a different font from other print features. They are found near the art. They offer specific information. Some captions also offer comments about the image itself.*)

For **listening support** for students at varying proficiency levels, see the **Text X-Ray** on page 246C.

CRITICAL VOCABULARY

etch: The author explains that etching is one of the ways Rembrandt used to make an image of himself.

ASK STUDENTS to discuss how etching compares to methods they have seen artists today use to make drawings.

reflection: The author says that Rembrandt painted and etched his reflection—or what he saw in the mirror.

ASK STUDENTS why they think there were more self-portraits after mirrors became common and cheap. *(It would be hard to paint a self-portrait if you didn't have a mirror right in front of you to show you your face.)*

 NOTICE & NOTE

etch
(ĕch) *v.* To *etch* is to cut or carve a drawing into a surface such as wood or metal.

reflection
(rĭ-flĕk´shən) *n.* A *reflection* is an image shown back, as from a mirror.

ANALYZE PRINT AND GRAPHIC FEATURES
Annotate: Mark information included in the caption for the Dürer painting.

Compare: How can you distinguish the caption from other print features, such as headings? What is the purpose of the caption?

an artist it was even easier—you just looked in the mirror and painted what you saw!

3   Self-portraits can often tell us about the clothing of a particular time, about art material and styles, and how old or rich or handsome the artist was or is—but most of all they let us look right inside the minds of the brilliant (and sometimes a bit bonkers) people who created them.

4   Take Vincent van Gogh, who cut off a piece of his ear, but still thought it would make a nice picture. Rembrandt drew, painted and **etched** his own **reflection** so many times we can see almost every stage of his life!

Albrecht Dürer

5   Dürer looks haughty[1] and confident, with a stiff but elegant pose. His clothing is expensive, extravagant and Italian in style.

Born: 1471 in Germany
Died: 1528, aged 56

Self-Portrait, 1500

---

[1] **haughty** (hô´tē): scornfully proud or arrogant.

6   We all want to look good in a selfie—and 500 years ago it was the same. Albrecht Dürer dressed up in fancy clothes for this self-portrait, announcing to the world that he was rich and grand.

7   Dürer was 26 when he painted this and already a leading artist, best known for his woodcut prints. On a trip to Italy, he noticed that great artists had a higher social status than they did at home in Germany. Dürer wanted to be treated like that too! After Dürer's death, admirers cut locks of his hair to remember him by. You can still see some at the Academy of Fine Arts in Vienna, Austria.

Rembrandt van Rijn ✔

8   Rembrandt was the biggest selfie maker of his time, creating nearly 100 self-portraits that **spanned** 40 years of his life. They track his changing appearance, as well as his developing painting style.

9   Rembrandt pictured himself in all sorts of poses, outfits and moods. As a young man, he often appeared in fine clothing, perhaps in the style of the rich people whose portraits he painted. Sometimes his scenes were theatrical, like the one he painted at the age of 29 with his wife Saskia sitting on his knee.

NOTICE & NOTE 🖉

ANALYZE PRINT AND GRAPHIC FEATURES
Annotate: Mark the print and graphic features on this page, such as headings, captions, and images. Then, predict what this section will be about.

Analyze: How does each feature help organize and present the information in an effective way?

span
(spăn) *v.* To *span* is to extend over a period of time.

Born: 1606 in the Netherlands ✔
Died: 1669, aged 63

Self-Portrait as a Young Man, 1634

Self-Portrait with Saskia, 1636 ✔

APPLYING ACADEMIC VOCABULARY

❑ **appropriate**   ☑ **authority**   ❑ **consequence**   ☑ **element**   ❑ **justify**

Write and Discuss Have students turn to a partner to discuss the following questions. Guide students to include the Academic Vocabulary words *authority* and *element* in their responses. Ask volunteers to share their responses with the class.

- Does being an art historian make the author an **authority** on self-portraits?
- In terms of color, what are the main **elements** of Rembrandt's self-portraits?

🖉 ANALYZE PRINT AND GRAPHIC FEATURES

Have students identify what information the subheading on the page gives about the text that follows. Then review how each caption relates to the image it describes. (**Answer:** *Instead of letting all of the text run together, subheadings divide the text into smaller sections—this next section will focus on the artist named in the subheading. Captions provide information such as biographical dates and the name of a painting in a quick and concise way.*)

CRITICAL VOCABULARY

span: The self-portraits were not done all at once. They were done over the course of his life.

ASK STUDENTS how a person today could see what they have looked like at different points over the course of their life. (*They could look at family snapshots and pictures they have posted on social networks.*)

CONTRASTS AND CONTRADICTIONS

Encourage students to look back at the portraits that show Rembrandt as a younger man and to consider what adjectives would best describe how he looks in each painting. (**Answer:** *Rembrandt looks young, attractive, and merry in the other portraits, while here he does look calmer and more old and wrinkly. It suprises me that he looks so serious here, but I would choose to take a picture of myself that didn't show me looking at my best if, like this portrait, it showed something real about my character and personality.*)

NOTICE & NOTE

CONTRASTS AND CONTRADICTIONS

Notice & Note: Do you agree with the author's description of Rembrandt's last self-portrait? Mark the description and study the image to see if you agree.

Connect: How does Rembrandt's final "selfie" surprise you? Would you choose to take a picture of yourself that didn't show you looking your best? Why or why not?

10   By the end of his life, Rembrandt was an expert at capturing character. He stripped away all the fancy dress and showed us simply Rembrandt the person. <u>In his last self-portrait aged 63, he seems sad yet calm and dignified. We see him inside and out, with every lump, sag and wrinkle on display.</u>

11   When experts examined his painting under X-ray, they discovered that the artist had made some changes. Originally his hat was much bigger and all white, and his hands had held a paintbrush. Rembrandt painted over this detail, bringing all our attention back to his face.

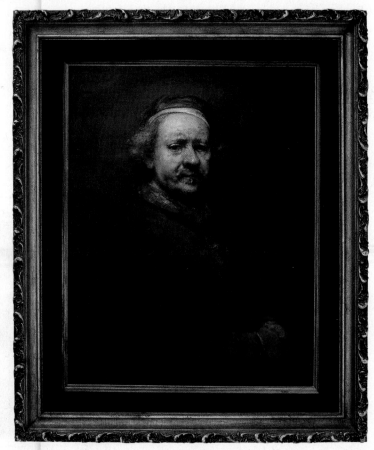

Self-Portrait at the Age of 63, 1669

WHEN STUDENTS STRUGGLE . . .

Sequence Events In paragraph 10, the author describes the final appearance of Rembrandt's last self-portrait. In paragraph 11, the author describes the changes experts discovered that Rembrandt made to the portrait after he first painted it. Help students avoid confusion by asking them to list the sequence of events chronologically so they can follow exactly what happened: 1) Rembrandt painted a version of the painting with a larger hat and paintbrush. 2) Rembrandt made the hat smaller and erased the paintbrush. 3) The finished portrait focuses the viewer's attention on Rembrandt's wrinkled, mature face. 4) Modern experts studied the painting and discovered how Rembrandt changed it over time.

Born: 1755 in France
Died: 1842, aged 86

Self-Portrait in a Straw Hat, 1782

Elizabeth Vigée Le Brun

12 This lady looks pretty in her straw hat and pink dress. She has a gentle smile and a friendly and welcoming gaze. Vigée Le Brun wanted people to like her in this selfie—and they did.

13 In the 18th century, female artists had to work hard to be taken seriously. Traditionally, painting was something that women did mostly as a hobby. Vigée Le Brun was extremely talented and she also sold her skills well. Self-portraits like this one were a way to attract attention and win people's hearts.

14 Elizabeth looks natural and relaxed in the painting. She seems comfortable with her palette and brushes, but they aren't the focus of the scene.

ANALYZE MULTIMODAL TEXTS

Annotate: In paragraphs 12–14, mark the descriptions of the painting.

Summarize: Use details in the text to explain how Vigée Le Brun used her self-portraits to help promote her work.

ANALYZE MULTIMODAL TEXTS

Remind students that the author is describing the portrait they are looking at, and they can make up their own minds about it. (**Answer:** *She made herself look very likeable so that people would want to have her paint them.*)

■ English Learner Support

Practice Pronunciation If students are unfamiliar with the word *gaze*, explain that it refers to the way Le Brun is looking out from the painting. Then pronounce slowly the sounds that make up this word, emphasizing the hard *g* sound, the long *a* sound, and the *z* sound. Have students repeat each sound after you and then repeat the word *gaze* several times until they are proficient at pronouncing it and its component sounds. Then point out the word *aged* in the caption and repeat this process, again emphasizing the long *a* sound, and this time noting the different pronunciation of *g*. Once more have students repeat the word several times after you until they have mastered the pronunciation.

SUBSTANTIAL

For **speaking support** for students at varying proficiency levels, see the **Text X-Ray** on page 246D.

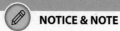
Joseph Ducreux

CONTRASTS AND CONTRADICTIONS

Explain to students that, when an artist shows you something that strongly contradicts what you might expect to see, that contradicting element is usually important.

(**Answer:** *Ducreux is being silly in the portrait by pretending to be caught yawning. None of the other artists look silly in their self-portraits. In fact, usually self-portaits show people posing seriously so they look their best. However, many people act silly in selfies today. Ducreux might be revealing that he has a sense of humor, which is an important thing to know about him if you are thinking about hiring him to do a portrait of you.*)

CONTRASTS AND CONTRADICTIONS

Notice & Note: How does Ducreux's painting contrast with other self-portraits you have learned about? Mark how the author describes Ducreux's self-portrait.

Infer: What might the artist wish to reveal about himself in this portrait?

15 These days, funny faces in selfies are nothing unusual, but in the 1700s people tended to be more straight-faced.[2] Most self-portraits avoided any strong feeling of being happy, cross or tired. It was different for the artists on these pages, though!

16 Joseph Ducreux found traditional portraiture[3] too prim and proper. Instead, he tried to capture the personalities of everyone he painted. In this self-portrait, he caught himself in the middle of a yawn. There's nothing shy or self-conscious about it—he pushes out his belly and opens his mouth wide, in a way that makes us want to yawn too.

Born: 1735 in France
Died: 1802, aged 67

Self-Portrait, Yawning, 1783

---
[2] **straight-faced:** showing no sign of emotion.
[3] **portraiture** (pôr´trĭ-chŏŏr´): the practice of creating portraits.

APPLYING ACADEMIC VOCABULARY

☑ **appropriate** ☐ **authority** ☐ **consequence** ☐ **element** ☑ **justify**

Write and Discuss Have students turn to a partner to discuss the following questions. Guide students to include the Academic Vocabulary words *appropriate* and *justify* in their responses. Ask volunteers to share their responses with the class.

- What might people say about whether Ducreux's pose is **appropriate** for a portrait?
- How would you **justify** the pose to someone who thought it wasn't proper?

Born: 1853 in Netherlands
Died: 1890, aged 37

Self-Portrait with Bandaged Ear, 1889

Vincent van Gogh

17 You might take a selfie when something unusual happens to you. Van Gogh made this one after he cut a piece from his ear following an argument with his friend and fellow artist, Gauguin.

18 Can you see the bandage on the side of van Gogh's head? The unlucky ear was actually the left one, but he was looking in a mirror when he painted this. Rather than hiding his injury, he made it the focus of the picture. His face looks as if he's lost in thought.

19 Notice how van Gogh used big, thick brushstrokes. They bring out the different textures of his clothes, fur cap, bandage and bony face. Sometimes he squeezed paint straight from the tube onto the canvas, and it would take weeks and weeks to dry! Behind the artist we can see a Japanese print. Van Gogh was fascinated by Japanese art. He loved its bold outlines, flat colours and shapes, and did his best to use them in his own work.

20 When he painted this selfie, van Gogh was mentally ill. After cutting the chunk off his ear, he gave it to a woman as a "gift." He was taken into a hospital and a few months later checked into an asylum.

ANALYZE PRINT AND GRAPHIC FEATURES

Annotate: Mark the graphic features used in the Vincent Van Gogh section.

Summarize: What effect do the graphic features have on the presentation of the author's ideas?

BIG QUESTIONS

Notice & Note: Mark the words in paragraph 20 that may come as a surprise to many readers.

Draw Conclusions: Why might the author have included this detail?

ANALYZE PRINT AND GRAPHIC FEATURES

Remind students that graphic features are important when comprehending meaning because they present information in a visual way. Graphic features such as charts or images both support text and may contain additional details not mentioned in the main text. (**Answer:** *The graphic feature of an image of van Gogh's self-portrait supports the author's ideas by showing the reader exactly what the author is talking about when claiming that van Gogh made his bandaged ear the focus of his self-portrait and by allowing the reader to see for his or herself the big, thick brushstrokes that the author describes van Gogh as using. The informal frame drawn around this self-portrait adds visual interest to the page.*)

BIG QUESTIONS

Remind students that surprises often suggest important points in the text. Paragraph 20 contains a very surprising fact, and this fact suggests something important about van Gogh. (**Answer:** *The author might wish to give readers deeper insight into van Gogh's troubled life.*)

For **reading support** for students at varying proficiency levels, see the **Text X-Ray** on page 246D.

EXTREME OR ABSOLUTE LANGUAGE

Remind students that writers may use extreme or absolute language to catch the reader's attention, and that **hyperbole** is a form of figurative language, not intended to be taken seriously. (**Answer:** *Selfies aren't really "everywhere," and every person is not actually able to take a selfie at every single instant, but these exaggerations suggest in a humorous way that selfies are very popular in U.S. culture and in other cultures around the world.*)

NOTICE & NOTE

Selfies Today

21 Selfies today are everywhere! With digital cameras and smartphones, anyone can snap themselves in an instant and share the picture with their friends or the world. Celebrities are doing it. Politicians are doing it. Will the selfie craze ever end?

22 2013 was the year that "#selfie" took off. More than 17 million people were posting a selfie on social media every week. In 2014, the word "selfie" made it into the Oxford Dictionary and was approved for the board game Scrabble! Technologies such as front-facing cameras, selfie sticks and hand-gesture sensors have made selfie-snapping easier than ever before.

23 In 2013, Pope Francis went viral in the first "Papal selfie," taken with young fans at the Vatican.

24 When you post a selfie, you're displaying a view of yourself that you want other people to see. When artists make self-portraits, it's the same! So next time you pose, remember you have something in common with every famous face in this book!

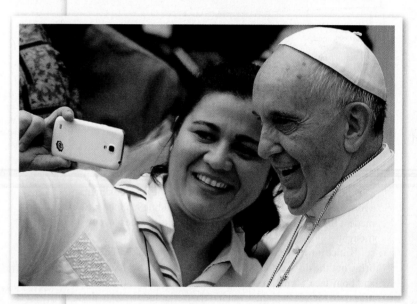

Selfie with Pope Francis

TO CHALLENGE STUDENTS . . .

Extend the Analysis   Show students several other great self-portraits. Possibilities include Norman Rockwell, *Triple Self-Portrait*; Frida Kahlo, *Self-portrait with Bonito Parrot and Butterfly*; Gustave Courbet, *The Desperate Man*; Georgia O'Keeffe, *Self-Portrait*. Ask students to choose a painting and write an analysis of it, using Brooks's analyses as their model. Then have them research the artist's life and see whether that makes their analysis of the painting different.

CHECK YOUR UNDERSTANDING

Answer these questions before moving on to the **Analyze the Text** section on the following page.

1 The author included the section "All By Your Selfie" to —

A teach the reader how to take a selfie

B introduce the reader to the selection's topic

C discuss female artists who made self-portraits

D show that selfies are unique to modern times

2 In the section on artist Elizabeth Vigée Le Brun, the author includes a portrait by the artist to show that she —

F considered painting just a hobby

G made copies of her work for admirers

H lived long ago

J used self portraits to attract attention

3 Which idea is not supported by information throughout the selection?

A Selfies and self-portraits have a lot in common.

B Self-portraits offer information about the past.

C Only wealthy, famous artists could create self-portraits.

D Self-portraits can express personality and feeling.

CHECK YOUR UNDERSTANDING

Have students answer the questions independently.

Answers:

1. *B*

2. *J*

3. *C*

If they answer any questions incorrectly, have them reread the text to confirm their understanding. Then they may proceed to ANALYZE THE TEXT on page 260.

EL ENGLISH LEARNER SUPPORT

Oral Assessment Use the following questions to assess students' comprehension and speaking skills.

1. Is a selfie a picture you take of yourself or of someone else? *(yourself)*

2. Who painted self-portraits so people would see them and hire this artist to paint them—Rembrandt or Elizabeth Vigée Le Brun? *(Le Brun)*

3. This selection supports the idea that selfies and self-portraits have a lot in common—yes or no? *(yes)*

SUBSTANTIAL/MODERATE

ANALYZE THE TEXT

Possible answers:

1. **DOK 2:** *His painting grew more realistic, focusing more on the character of a person rather than external props and fun details.*

2. **DOK 4:** *She introduces the images and talks about what the painter was probably trying to accomplish with each one. She then refers the reader to the images themselves, pointing out some things, but letting the images speak for themselves.*

3. **DOK 3:** *The author argues that selfies are taken to display a view of yourself that you want others to see. A selfie taken with the pope allows a person to present to other people a picture showing this important meeting.*

4. **DOK 3:** *The headings use boldface type and color effects to gain the reader's attention; they organize ideas by artist and include key ideas. The graphics catch the reader's attention with wooden frames that surround some of the portraits; the portraits provide helpful visual information about the work of each artist.*

5. **DOK 4:** *The author contrasts commissioned portraits to self-portraits by saying self-portraits were "even easier." She says you just looked in the mirror and painted what you saw! This contradicts what readers might expect about painting a good self-portrait.*

RESEARCH

Remind students to keep track of the sources of their information so they can give proper credit and show that their sources are reliable.

Extend A modern photographer such as Cindy Sherman uses a camera to capture different images of herself.

RESPOND

ANALYZE THE TEXT

Support your responses with evidence from the text. NOTEBOOK

1. **Summarize** Review the last two paragraphs of the section about Rembrandt. How did Rembrandt evolve as a portrait painter over time, and how is it apparent in his final self-portrait?

2. **Analyze** In the section about Vincent van Gogh, how does the author use writing and visual modes of communication to communicate key ideas?

3. **Draw Conclusions** Review the section "Selfies Today," and note the selfie of Pope Francis. How does this selfie support the author's ideas about selfies and self-portraits?

4. **Critique** Review the way headings and graphics are presented throughout the selection. How effectively do the print and graphic features of the selection contribute to its overall structure?

5. **Notice & Note** Identify an idea in the text that surprised you. What about the idea was surprising?

RESEARCH TIP
When you conduct research online, make sure that your sources are reliable. For biographical information on artists, consider using art museum websites or a trusted online encyclopedia.

RESEARCH

With a partner, research one of the artists mentioned in the text. Use more than one source, and guide your research with *who, what, where, when, how,* and *why* questions, like those below.

QUESTIONS	ANSWERS
Who was this artist, and when did he or she live?	
What was the artist's style and medium?	
Where did the artist work?	
How was his/her artwork viewed during his/her lifetime?	
Why is this artist remembered today?	

Extend Identify an artist alive today who is known for creating self-portraits. Share images of the artist's work with the class.

 LEARNING MINDSET

Asking for Help Explain to students that asking for help is a sign of strength, not weakness. It is a sign that you are open and ready to learn. Encourage students to ask peers/teachers/parents for help. Explain that asking for help from others can help students get "unstuck" and move forward. Reinforce that asking for help does not equal failure. Rather, seeking help is a way of "trying smarter."

CREATE AND DISCUSS

Summarize Key Ideas Write a summary of the key ideas in the selection. Use evidence from the text and the images to support the ideas you identify. Your summary should:

❏ Clearly state the key ideas presented in the selection.

❏ Support the ideas with evidence from the text, including print and graphic features.

❏ Use commas correctly, especially after introductory elements.

Critique with a Small Group Review the selection's headings and other graphic features. Discuss the purpose and effectiveness of each element. Then create new graphic features for the selection.

❏ As you review, have a group member create a list of the selection's graphic features.

❏ As you discuss the selection's features, analyze the strengths and weaknesses of each.

❏ Work together to create new heading designs and add other graphic features to help organize the selection.

 Go to **Using Textual Evidence: Summarizing, Paraphrasing, and Quoting** in the **Writing Studio** for more on using textual evidence in a summary.

 Go to **Participating in Collaborative Discussions** in the **Speaking and Listening Studio** for help with having a group discussion.

RESPOND TO THE ESSENTIAL QUESTION

 What are the ways you can make yourself heard?

Gather Information Review your annotations and notes on *Selfie: The Changing Face of Self-Portraits*. Then, add relevant details to your Response Log. As you determine which information to include, think about the ways that people express themselves and how self-expression communicates ideas about the individual.

At the end of the unit, use your notes to write a multimodal argument.

ACADEMIC VOCABULARY

As you write about and discuss what you learned from the selection, be sure to use the Academic Vocabulary words. Check off each of the words that you use.

❏ appropriate

❏ authority

❏ consequence

❏ element

❏ justify

CREATE AND DISCUSS

Summarize Key ideas Remind students that summaries should cover only the most important ideas in a selection. Smaller points should be left out of a summary. Have students go over their written summaries in their revision process to make sure that they have omitted anything that is not key to understanding what the selection is about.

For **writing support** for students at varying proficiency levels, see the **Text X-Ray** on page 246D.

Critique with a Small Group Remind students that group work demands cooperation and respect. It is important to value the contributions of all members of the group.

RESPOND TO THE ESSENTIAL QUESTION

Allow time for students to add details from *Selfie: The Changing Face of Self-Portraits* to their Unit 4 Response Logs.

 ENGLISH LEARNER SUPPORT

Discuss with a Small Group Restate the discussion prompt as a question: *What are the purposes of the heading designs and other graphic features? How effective are they?* Allow students to work with partners to review the text for details that answer the question. Provide these sentence frames to help them formulate their ideas for the discussion: *The purpose of the heading designs is to ___. The author includes the images in order to___. The effect of the images is ___.* **MODERATE**

CRITICAL VOCABULARY

Answers:

1. *using a sharp tool to scratch a design on a thin sheet of metal.*

2. *the image of a person, especially his or her face.*

3. *another car following behind.*

4. *12 months.*

VOCABULARY STRATEGY:
Context Clues

Answers:

Students' may define commissioned as "to hire." The dictionary definition is "to order something to be made." Students' partner discussions will vary.

 RESPOND

WORD BANK
portrait
etch
reflection
span

 Go to the **Vocabulary Studio** for more on context clues.

CRITICAL VOCABULARY

Practice and Apply Complete each sentence in a way that shows the meaning of the Critical Vocabulary word.

1. The art teacher showed the class how to **etch** by

_____

2. A **portrait** is a type of painting that shows

_____

3. The **reflection** in the car's rear-view mirror showed

_____

4. The **span** of one year is equal to _____.

VOCABULARY STRATEGY:
Context Clues

When you come across an unfamiliar word in your reading, one way to determine its meaning is to use **context clues.** Context clues are hints about the meaning of an unknown word that may be found in the words, phrases, sentences, and paragraphs that surround that unknown word. Sometimes you can find a definition of an unknown word within the text. At other times, you can use surrounding words and phrases to infer the meaning of that word. Look at the following example:

> **Before photography was invented, people who wanted pictures of themselves (and could afford it) commissioned artists to paint their portraits. If you were an artist it was even easier—you just looked in the mirror and painted what you saw!**

If the meaning of *portraits* is unclear, look for clues to its meaning nearby. Notice how the sentence that follows *portraits* hints at the word's meaning. It says that artists who wanted to paint their own portraits "just looked in the mirror and painted" what they saw. This clue allows you to infer that *portrait* means "the painted likeness of a person's face."

Practice and Apply Working with a partner, use context clues to determine the meaning of *commissioned* in the previous example. Write a definition for the word. Finally, look up *commission* in a print or an online dictionary. Compare your definition to the dictionary definition. Discuss the similarities and differences with your partner.

262   Unit 4

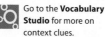 **ENGLISH LEARNER SUPPORT**

Recognize Consonant Blends Have students practice pronouncing common consonant blends in English words. Vietnamese, Hmong, Cantonese, and Korean speakers may struggle particularly to pronounce such blends. Display the vocabulary words *portrait, reflection,* and *span.* Review that a consonant blend is a group of consonant sounds that are pronounced together. Have students help you locate and circle the consonant blends *tr, fl,* and *sp* in these words. Model how to pronounce each blend, and have students repeat it after you. Then repeat each blend and the word in which it appears, and have students repeat those after you. Finish by having pairs of students practice pronouncing other words that use these blends.
ALL LEVELS

LANGUAGE CONVENTIONS:
Commas After Introductory Elements

An **introductory element** is a word, phrase, or dependent clause used to begin a sentence. A **phrase** is a group of related words that does not contain a subject and a predicate but functions in a sentence as a single part of speech. A **dependent clause** is a group of words containing a subject and predicate, but it cannot stand alone as a sentence. These introductory elements modify and clarify the ideas they precede. Writers place commas after introductory elements to make their sentences easier to understand.

Go to **Punctuation: End Marks and Commas** in the **Grammar Studio** for more on using commas.

In *Selfie: The Changing Face of Self-Portraits,* commas are used in the following ways:

- to set off an introductory word

    Instead, he tried to capture the personalities of everyone he painted.

- to set off an introductory phrase

    On a trip to Italy, he noticed that great artists had a higher social status than they did at home in Germany.

- to set off a dependent clause used as an introductory element

    When he painted this selfie, van Gogh was mentally ill.

Practice and Apply Write your own sentences with commas that set off introductory words, phrases, and dependent clauses. Your sentences can express your observations about the self-portraits shown in the selection, or they can be about your own experiences with selfies. When you have finished, share your sentences with a partner and compare your use of commas.

LANGUAGE CONVENTIONS:
Commas After Introductory Elements

Remind students that correct punctuation can make a complicated sentence clearer, and that adding clauses is a way for a writer to develop an idea by providing additional material that fleshes out the main topic. Without such punctuation, all the words in a sentence will run together and make it difficult for readers to follow an author's train of thought.

Use sentences such as the following to explore the various ways an author can use commas to make writing clearer and more effective. Ask students to identify in each case what is being set apart by a comma or commas.

- Actually, people today can take selfies and paint self-portraits. (*The comma sets off the introductory word Actually.*)
- On the wall, paintings of many sizes hung in a row. (*The comma sets off an introductory phrase to make the meaning of the whole sentence clearer.*)
- While he was painting my portrait, I found it hard not to sneeze. (*The comma sets off a clause that explains when the main action is taking place.*)

Practice and Apply

(*Answers will vary.*)

Have partners discuss how they used the commas in their sentences, identifying what introductory words, phrases, or dependent clauses they have set off and explaining why they chose to set these elements off.

 ENGLISH LEARNER SUPPORT

Write Sentence Patterns Use the following supports with students at varying proficiency levels:

- Have students find other sentences in the excerpt from *Selfie* that have introductory words, phrases, or clauses and copy them in their notebooks. Make sure they recognize and copy the comma at the end of each element. **SUBSTANTIAL**

- Have students work with partners to write their original sentences with introductory elements. Then have them meet with another pair to compare their sentences. **MODERATE**

- Ask students to write one sentence modeled on each of the three examples from *Selfie*. Then have them explain to partners why the comma in each sentence performs the same function as in the corresponding example sentence. **LIGHT**

from BROWN GIRL DREAMING

Memoir in Verse by Jacqueline Woodson

GENRE ELEMENTS
MEMOIR IN VERSE

Review with students that a memoir is a personal narrative. It is told from the writer's perspective in a first-person point of view and includes personal experiences and observations. Add that a **memoir** written in **verse** tells the author's story in a series of poems that convey feelings about a topic or experience.

LEARNING OBJECTIVES

- Analyze how text structure contributes to the author's purpose.
- Make connections to personal experiences and ideas in other texts.
- Conduct research using multiple sources.
- Write a formal letter or email.
- Write and present a biographical poem.
- Pose and answer questions about classmates' work.
- **Language** Discuss with a partner the structure of the text, using the term *memoir*.

TEXT COMPLEXITY

Quantitative Measures	from *Brown Girl Dreaming*	Lexile: N/A
Qualitative Measures	**Ideas Presented** Some implied meaning; requires inferential reasoning.	
	Structure Used Complex; deviates some from chronological order.	
	Language Used Figurative language with a variety of sentence structures.	
	Knowledge Required Situations and subjects easily envisioned.	

RESOURCES

- Unit 4 Response Log

- Selection Audio

- Reading Studio: Notice & Note

- Level Up Tutorial: Narrative Poetry

-  Writing Studio: Formal Style

- Speaking and Listening Studio: Giving a Presentation

- *Brown Girl Dreaming* Selection Test

SUMMARIES

English

The author remembers in verse her school experiences, how difficult it was to write the stories that flowed so easily when spoken, how her hesitation to write a *q* resulted in her nickname, Jackie, and what it was like to be closely compared to her older sister, who was always so brilliant. She relates her determination to read the books she chose, her excitement at finding a book that featured brown children like her, and her family's disbelief when she declared she wanted to be a writer.

Spanish

La autora revela a través de versos sus experiencias en la escuela; lo difícil que era escribir las historias que fluían tan fácilmente cuando las contaba; y cómo su vacilación al escribir una q resultó en su sobrenombre, Jackie. Además, habla de su determinación para leer los libros que escogía, su emoción al encontrar un libro en que figurasen niños marrones como ella, y la incredulidad de su familia cuando declaró que quería ser escritora.

SMALL-GROUP OPTIONS

Have students work in small groups to read and discuss the selection.

Numbered Heads Together

- After students have read the poems, have them form groups of four. Ask groups to number themselves 1 to 4.

- Pose the following question: *Why did the author reject all the ways the teacher wanted her to read a book?*

- Have groups discuss their responses.

- Call out a number and a group if there is more than one group. Ask the student with that number to tell how the group answered the question.

Jigsaw with Experts

- Have students count off from 1 to 6. Students with the same number will form a group.

- Assign one of Woodson's poems to each group. Each group reads and takes notes on their assigned poem.

- Encourage the groups to discuss what they have read.

- Have students form new groups that include one representative from each group.

- Invite the new groups to share their ideas about the poems.

Text X-Ray: English Learner Support
for *Brown Girl Dreaming*

Use the Text X-Ray and the supports and scaffolds in the Teacher's Edition to help guide students at different proficiency levels through the selection.

INTRODUCE THE SELECTION
DISCUSS SELF-EXPRESSION

In this lesson, students will learn about the challenges a person might face when struggling to be able to express his or her true self to others. Introduce the subject by noting that until a person has discovered his or her voice, he or she will find it difficult to tell others about his or her feelings, ideas, and opinions. Supply students with words relating to self-expression, such as *communicate, confidence, confident, nervous, connection,* and *connect.* Use frames to help students discuss:

- *When you are _____, it is difficult to _____ your ideas to other people.*
- *It is easier to _____ an opinion when you feel a _____ to someone or something.*

CULTURAL REFERENCES

The following references may need to be explained:

- In the 1970s, students sat at individual desks arranged in rows.
- *fly into the air* (lines 42–43): her arm would not literally fly into the air; instead, she would raise it quickly so the teacher would call on her first
- *do hair* (line 123): means to be a hairdresser or stylist in a hair salon

LISTENING

Understand Informal Tone

Prepare students to understand the informal tone used in these poems, which creates a sense of listening to a friend who is telling her thoughts. Note that an informal tone often includes short sentences, contractions, and slang language.

Use the following supports with students at varying proficiency levels:

- Read lines 1–7. Repeat in an informal tone: "Then just starts going on and on." Then say in a formal tone: *Then begins to speak for a very long time.* Model each sentence again, and then have students repeat after you and give thumbs up when they read in an informal tone. **SUBSTANTIAL**
- Read lines 1–7. Repeat in an informal tone: "Then just starts going on and on." Then say in a formal tone: *Then begins to speak for a very long time.* Ask students to repeat each sentence, copying your tones, identify which example contains an informal tone, and explain how they know. **MODERATE**
- After listening to lines 1–7 read aloud in a informal tone, ask partners to work together to list three reasons why they know that these lines should not be read in a formal tone. **LIGHT**

SPEAKING

Discuss Text Structure and Purpose

Have students discuss the structure of a memoir and how poems can be used as part of a memoir. Circulate around the room to make sure students use the term *memoir* correctly.

Use the following supports with students at varying proficiency levels:

- Display and read aloud this sentence: *In a memoir, an author remembers important events from his or her past.* Have students repeat the sentence and practice saying it to a partner. **SUBSTANTIAL**
- Provide students with sentence frames to discuss the structure of a memoir. *In a memoir, an author tells about _____. Each poem in this memoir describes a different _____.* **MODERATE**
- Pair students to read the poem "when i tell my family." Have student pairs use the term *memoir* to discuss what the author is remembering in this poem. **LIGHT**

READING

Use Inferential Skills

Tell students that using inferential skills such as drawing conclusions will help them understand the meaning of a text they are reading. Remind them to pay attention to details that will help them figure out things the author does not actually explain.

Work with students to read and draw conclusions about the poem "the other woodson." Use the following supports with students at varying proficiency levels:

- Reread lines 33–36. Ask: *What do people think Woodson and her sister are?* Accept single words or phrases. **SUBSTANTIAL**
- Have students complete the following sentence frames. *Woodson's sister is _____. Therefore, teachers think Woodson is _____, too. When teachers ask questions, Woodson _____. Therefore, teachers begin to _____.* **MODERATE**
- Pair students to identify what happens in the poem. Ask: *Why do the teachers compare Woodson and her sister? Why do the teachers stop calling on Woodson when they figure out she isn't like her sister?* **LIGHT**

WRITING

Write a Biographical Poem

Work with students to prepare them to write a biographical poem in the Create and Present section on page 275. Clarify that unlike a formal poem, a free verse poem does not have to rhyme or follow a specific pattern.

Use the following supports with students at varying proficiency levels:

- Ask students to draw pictures of important events from their past. Then help them write one or two word labels to add to the pictures. **SUBSTANTIAL**
- Provide sentence frames to help students plan which details to include in their biographical poems. *The big event was _____. First, _____. Then, _____. Next, _____. I felt _____.* **MODERATE**
- Review how Woodson uses italics to include spoken dialogue in her biographical poems and emphasize that the way she writes is the way students might speak to their friends. Then have one partner act out an important moment from his or her life while the other partner writes down phrases and dialogue the student can use to write part of a poem about this moment. **LIGHT**

Connect to the
ESSENTIAL QUESTION

In her memoir *Brown Girl Dreaming*, Jacqueline Woodson expresses how teachers and family did not hear her when she said she wanted to be a writer, that she was not like her older sister, and that she wanted to read books in her own way. The selected poems show how Woodson began to find her voice through writing and the discovery of books with characters who looked like her.

from

BROWN GIRL DREAMING

Memoir in Verse by **Jacqueline Woodson**

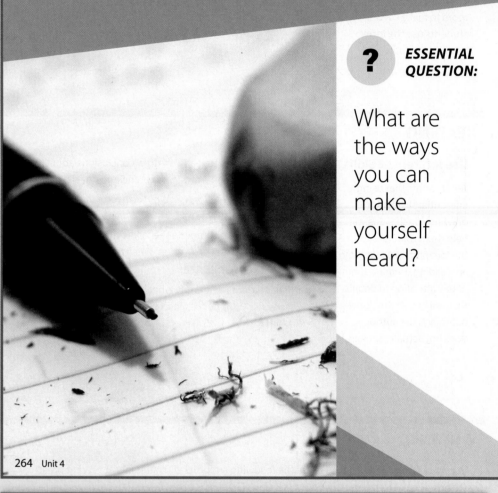

? ESSENTIAL QUESTION:

What are the ways you can make yourself heard?

LEARNING MINDSET

Questioning Reinforce for students that asking questions keeps a person open to new ideas and trying new things. Encourage students to always feel comfortable asking questions. Note that being able to ask questions can help students when they get stuck: they can always question how they arrived at an answer and ask themselves, "Can I try this a different way?" Motivate students to continue to ask questions by complimenting them on the questions they do ask and mentioning to them how asking questions shows curiosity and leads to learning new things.

QUICK START

Look at the titles of the poems in this selection. What do you think you will learn about the author and her life? Share your thoughts with the class.

ANALYZE TEXT STRUCTURE AND PURPOSE

Poems, rather than chapters, create the **structure** for *Brown Girl Dreaming*, Jacqueline Woodson's memoir in verse. The word *memoir* comes from French, meaning "memory." Memoirs are written from the first-person point of view, detailing a writer's observations about significant events and people in the writer's life. Memoirs also may inform readers about historical events and their effects on the writer. While most memoirs are written in prose, Jacqueline Woodson structured her memoir as verse. Her poems contain all of the elements of a memoir.

Why might Woodson have used this particular style to write her memoir? As you read the excerpt from *Brown Girl Dreaming*, take notes on the elements of memoir and consider how they connect to the **author's purpose**—the main reason for writing the text.

ELEMENTS OF A MEMOIR	AUTHOR'S PURPOSE

GENRE ELEMENTS: MEMOIR IN VERSE

- is a personal narrative told from first-person point of view
- includes the writer's own experiences and observations of significant events or people
- has an informal or even intimate tone
- presents insights into the impact of historical events on people's lives, particularly the writer's
- tells the story through a series of poems

TEACH

QUICK START

Have students read the Quick Start question. Invite them to share their impressions of the poem titles and their ideas for what they may learn about the author and her life.

ANALYZE TEXT STRUCTURE AND PURPOSE

Help students understand the structural elements of a memoir and identify how Woodson's memoir departs from the traditional structure because it is written in verse. Point out that the poems in Woodson's memoir are written in free verse and contain poetic elements such as line breaks, repetition, and rhythm. As students read the poems, have them note examples of the author's informal tone, her first-person point of view, and the experiences and observations she has chosen for her poems.

 ENGLISH LEARNER SUPPORT

Produce Different Sounds Help students master the pronunciation of the term *memoir*. Point out that because *memoir* comes from French, it is pronounced the way French people would say this word. Model the pronunciation of *memoir,* and have students repeat the word after you. Then model how to pronounce the English word *memory,* and have students repeat it after you. As needed, continue the practice by pointing first to one and then the other word, having students pronounce each word in turn. **SUBSTANTIAL**

TEACH

MAKE CONNECTIONS

Review with students the meaning of making connections between an author's observations and experiences to their own lives, current ideas in society, and other texts they have read. Encourage students to pay attention to their own memories that the author's experiences relate to. Remind them that the author is recalling her own memories of long ago when she was a student. Have students compare what school was like for the author with their own experiences with school today.

ANNOTATION MODEL

Remind students of the annotation ideas noted in the model for identifying the structure of a memoir and the author's purpose. Point out that the reader has underlined parts of the text as clues to structure and purpose. Explain to students that they may decide to use underlining or some other system for marking the text. For example, they may want to circle words or phrases or use a highlighter. Add that their marginal notes can also include questions about the text or notes on anything that is confusing.

MAKE CONNECTIONS

The full text of *Brown Girl Dreaming* presents events from Woodson's life along with her family's stories, drawing on a history from periods of enslavement to the civil rights era to Woodson's childhood in the 1970s. Her approach allows readers to connect their personal experiences to hers, as well as to connect her ideas to society and other texts. As you read, use a web diagram like the one below to organize your connections between *Brown Girl Dreaming* and your own experiences and ideas, and between the memoir and other texts.

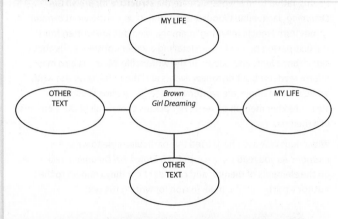

ANNOTATION MODEL   **NOTICE & NOTE**

As you read, note clues that reveal the author's purpose and examine how she uses text structure to convey a message. This model shows one reader's notes from the beginning of the excerpt from *Brown Girl Dreaming*.

writing #1

It's easier to make up stories

than it is to write them down. When I speak,

the words come pouring out of me. <u>The story</u>

<u>wakes up and walks all over the room. Sits in a chair,</u>

5 <u>crosses one leg over the other, says,</u>

<u>*Let me introduce myself.*</u> Then just starts going on and on.

> Does #1 mean it's the first poem about writing? Maybe there will be more poems about writing later.
>
> She personifies "story," as if it's a close friend talking to her. It feels very personal.

BACKGROUND

Jacqueline Woodson *(b. 1963), who had difficulty reading when she was young, has written more than 30 books. She wrote* Brown Girl Dreaming *to learn about her family and to discover what led her to become a writer. She says her memoir is a series of poems "because memories come to people in small bursts."* Brown Girl Dreaming *won the National Book Award in 2014, and Woodson was named National Ambassador for Young People's Literature for 2018–2019.*

from

BROWN GIRL DREAMING

Memoir in Verse by Jacqueline Woodson

SETTING A PURPOSE

As you read, notice how Woodson uses elements of poetry, including repetition, line breaks, and imagery, to describe events.

writing #1

It's easier to make up stories
than it is to write them down. When I speak,
the words come pouring out of me. The story
wakes up and walks all over the room. Sits in a chair,
5 crosses one leg over the other, says,
Let me introduce myself. Then just starts going on and on.
But as I bend over my composition notebook,
only my name
comes quickly. Each letter, neatly printed
10 between the pale blue lines. Then white
space and air and me wondering, *How do I
spell introduce?* Trying again and again
until there is nothing but pink
bits of eraser and a hole now.
15 where a story should be.

Use the side margins to notice and note signposts in the text.

ANALYZE TEXT STRUCTURE AND PURPOSE
Annotate: Mark the result of the author not being able to spell *introduce.*

Infer: What might this reveal about the author's purpose?

BACKGROUND

After students read the Background note, point out that the author had difficulty reading when she was young and that she wrote *Brown Girl Dreaming* to trace the process she followed to become a writer. Explain to students that when Woodson was a student, the experience of going to school was both similar to and yet different from their experience of school. For example, point out that African American children did not have many models of characters in literature that looked like them or had similar experiences.

SETTING A PURPOSE

Direct students to use the Setting a Purpose prompt to focus their reading.

 ANALYZE TEXT STRUCTURE AND PURPOSE

Have students annotate lines 12–15. Remind them that an inference is a logical conclusion based on evidence. Then have them answer the question by inferring the author's purpose. (**Possible answer:** *This result reveals the author's struggle with writing, and yet, her dream is to be a writer. One of the reasons she writes the memoir is to show her path to becoming a writer and to show the value of stories. The "hole" in the paper, "where a story should be," reveals that a story can always be made up and presented to the world; all it takes is imagination.*)

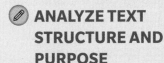 For **listening and speaking support** for students at varying proficiency levels, see the **Text X-Ray** on pages 264C and 264D.

 ENGLISH LEARNER SUPPORT

Understand Directionality Reinforce the directionality of English by reviewing how to read the Background note and the lines of a poem. For the Background note, remind students to begin at the top left of the text, read across the first line to the right, and then move down to the left side of the next line of text. Then guide students through reading the poem "writing #1." Note that even though the lines are different lengths, students should still read them the same way they read the Background note. Suggest that students trace the words with a finger if that helps them keep track of where they should be reading. **SUBSTANTIAL**

TEACH

▶ MEMORY MOMENT

Point out that this signpost is often used to explain a speaker's or narrator's motivation for doing or not doing something. After students mark and identify the author's motivation in lines 24–25, have them state why this memory is important and if the author is able to "make herself heard." (**Answer:** *This memory is important to the author's motivation because as the verse continues, readers learn she does not want to be called "Jackie," but she lies and agrees with the teacher so that she will not have to admit and explain her difficulty with writing the "q" in "Jacqueline." This memory must motivate her in some way because she does become a very successful writer.*)

■ English Learner Support

Use Context Clues Ask students to locate the word *cursive* in the text. To help them understand the meaning of the word *cursive* and the difference between print and cursive writing, remind them that they can look for context clues in the surrounding text. Work with students to locate the phrase "connect it to *c* and *u*." Discuss with students how cursive is a type of writing where the letters are run together and the writer never lifts his or her hand while writing a word. Clarify with students that Woodson has no difficulty with printing her name, but that writing in cursive was hard for her to do. Have students identify which letter in cursive writing was a problem for Woodson, pointing out as necessary a context clue that helps them know this—the phrase "I am scared of that cursive *q*."
SUBSTANTIAL/MODERATE

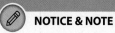

MEMORY MOMENT

Notice & Note: What does the author remember writing on the board? Mark what she writes and then mark why she writes it.

Analyze: Why might this memory be important to the author? Is she able to "make herself heard"?

late autumn

Ms. Moskowitz calls us one by one and says,
Come up to the board and write your name.
When it's my turn, I walk down the aisle from
my seat in the back, write *Jacqueline Woodson*—
20 the way I've done a hundred times, turn back
toward my seat, proud as anything
of my name in white letters on the dusty blackboard.
But Ms. Moskowitz stops me, says,
In cursive too, please. But the *q* in Jacqueline is too hard
25 so I write *Jackie Woodson* for the first time. Struggle
only a *little* bit with the *k*.

Is that what you want us to call you?

I want to say, *No, my name is Jacqueline*
but I am scared of that cursive *q*, know
30 I may never be able to connect it to *c* and *u*
so I nod even though
I am lying.

268 Unit 4

APPLYING ACADEMIC VOCABULARY

❑ **appropriate**   ❑ **authority**   ☑ **consequence**   ❑ **element**   ☑ **justify**

Write and Discuss Have students discuss with a partner the following questions. Guide students to include the Academic Vocabulary words *consequence* and *justify* in their responses. Call on volunteers to share their responses with the class.

- What is a **consequence** of not speaking up?
- How does the author **justify** writing *Jackie* instead of *Jacqueline*?

268   Unit 4

the other woodson

Even though so many people think my sister and I
are twins,

35 I am the other Woodson, following behind her each year
into the same classroom she had the year before. Each
teacher smiles when they call my name. *Woodson,* they
say. *You must be Odella's sister.* Then they nod
slowly, over and over again, call me Odella. Say,
40 *I'm sorry! You look so much like her and she is SO brilliant!*
then wait for my brilliance to light up
the classroom. Wait for my arm to fly into
the air with every answer. Wait for my pencil
to move quickly through the too-easy math problems
45 on the mimeographed sheet.[1] Wait for me to stand
before class, easily reading words even high school
students stumble over. And they keep waiting.
And waiting
and waiting
50 and waiting

until one day, they walk into the classroom,
almost call me Odel—then stop

remember that I am the other Woodson

and begin searching for brilliance

55 at another desk.

MAKE CONNECTIONS
Annotate: Mark comparisons other people make about the author and her sister.

Connect: Have you ever been compared to someone else? How did it make you feel?

 MAKE CONNECTIONS

Remind students that a comparison is how two things are alike, while a contrast is how two things are different. Encourage students to connect the comparison the teachers made between Woodson and her sister with how Jacqueline demonstrated to the teachers how she contrasted with her sister, or was quite different from her, instead. Then have students recall and consider their feelings during a time when they were compared to someone else. (*Answers will vary.*)

For **reading support** for students at varying proficiency levels, see the **Text X-Ray** on page 264D.

IMPROVE READING FLUENCY

Targeted Passage Have students work with partners to read lines 33–50. First, use lines 33–38 to model how to read a prose poem with unusual line breaks. Have students follow along as you read with appropriate phrasing. Point out that breaking the line at the word *nod* allows the reader to pause and then start the next line with the word *slowly*. Then have partners take turns reading aloud the section. Encourage students to provide feedback and support.

 Go to the **Reading Studio** for additional support in developing fluency.

MEMORY MOMENT

After students mark and identify the answer to the question, have them review the most important details associated with this memory.

(**Answer:** *Even though there are parts of this memory that may be difficult for the author, such as recalling how people tell her to "Read faster," there is also the part of the memory that explains how stories stay with her; as she says, the story becomes "a part of me." This contributes to the development of her writing because she realizes how important stories can become to someone, where the characters are very real, and the story itself is a part of another person. This may have added to her desire to write her own stories.*)

NOTICE & NOTE

reading

I am not my sister.
Words from the books curl around each other
make little sense
until
60 I read them again
and again, the story
settling into memory. *Too slow*
the teacher says.
Read faster.
65 *Too babyish,* the teacher says.
Read older.
But I don't want to read faster or older or
any way else that might
make the story disappear too quickly from where it's settling
70 inside my brain,
slowly becoming
a part of me.
A story I will remember
long after I've read it for the second, third,
75 tenth, hundredth time.

MEMORY MOMENT

Notice & Note: Why does the author reread books? Mark the memory the narrator describes.

Infer: Why might this memory be important to the development of the author's writing?

WHEN STUDENTS STRUGGLE . . .

Analyze Text Structure Have students note where a sentence begins and ends to understand sentences that stretch across line breaks. Students can use a chart like this.

Poem	Sentence
Words from the books curl around each other / make little sense / until / I read them again / and again, the story / settling into memory.	Words from the books curl around each other make little sense until I read them again and again, the story settling into memory.

For additional support, go to the **Reading Studio** and assign the following [LEVEL] **Level Up tutorial: Narrative Poetry.**

stevie and me

Every Monday, my mother takes us
to the library around the corner. We are allowed
to take out seven books each. On those days,
no one complains
80 that <u>all I want are picture books.</u>

Those days, no one tells me to read faster
to read harder books
to read like Dell.

No one is there to say, *Not that book,*
85 when I stop in front of the small paperback
with a brown boy on the cover.
Stevie.

I read:
One day my momma told me,
90 *"You know you're gonna have*
a little friend come stay with you."
And I said, "Who is it?"

If someone had been fussing with me
to read like my sister, I might have missed
95 the picture book filled with brown people, more
brown people than I'd ever seen
in a book before.

The little boy's name was Steven but
his mother kept calling him Stevie.
100 *My name is Robert but my momma don't*
call me Robertie.

If someone had taken
that book out of my hand
said, *You're too old for this*
105 maybe
I'd never have believed
that someone who looked like me
could be in the pages of the book
that someone who looked like me
110 had a story.

ANALYZE TEXT STRUCTURE AND PURPOSE

Annotate: Mark the type of library books the author likes.

Analyze: How might the books relate to the author's purpose for writing about this memory?

ANALYZE TEXT STRUCTURE AND PURPOSE

Remind students that the author has a reason or purpose for the memories she chose to include in her memoir. Explain that at this point, readers will be seeing what the selected memories have in common: they all relate to the author's formation as a writer. After students mark line 80, have them answer the question about the author's purpose for including this memory about library books. Then discuss how the structure the author uses to tell about her discovery adds to her purpose. (**Answer:** *The poem title "stevie and me" is important because it shows a connection between a character and the author, suggesting how she feels very close to this character, as if they are friends. This shows the value the author places on books and the stories within them, suggesting she thinks that stories have powerful messages and places in the world. With this said, it is important to the author that stories have people of color as characters and communicate their stories to the world.*)

TO CHALLENGE STUDENTS . . .

Analyze a Social Issue Remind students of the time frame during which Woodson would have been visiting a library and checking out children's books to take home. Then review lines 106–110, in which the author restates why the book *Stevie* was so important to her. Ask students to consider what the author's amazement at finding someone who looked like her in a book tells them about the prevalence of diverse characters at the time when she was in school. Have partners work together to determine how this prevalence has changed, which may include interviewing the school media specialist or librarian.

MAKE CONNECTIONS

Review with students that readers often make connections between their own experiences and the memories an author relates or the situations in which characters in a text are involved. Ask students to think about times in their own lives when they may have shared a plan or a goal and were not taken seriously by an adult. Have them also think of characters in other texts who experienced something similar. Remind students to record these connections on their web diagram. Then, after they mark the italicized phrases of what the adults say, have students answer the question by explaining how connections they made compare to Woodson's memory. (**Answer:** *Answers will vary. Students may note that an adult responded to their announcement of a goal in much the same way that Woodson's family responded to her, by considering her plan to be a childish hobby.*)

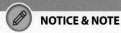 **NOTICE & NOTE**

MAKE CONNECTIONS

Annotate: Mark the italicized phrases.

Connect: How do these messages compare to ones you have heard from adults in your life? Recall another text in which a character was given conflicting messages about adult life. How does it compare to Woodson's memory?

when i tell my family

When I tell my family
I want to be a writer, they smile and say,
We see you in the backyard with your writing.
They say,
115 *We hear you making up all those stories.*
And,
We used to write poems.
And,
It's a good hobby, we see how quiet it keeps you.
120 They say,
But maybe you should be a teacher,
a lawyer,
do hair . . .

I'll think about it, I say.

125 And maybe all of us know

this is just another one of my
stories.

272   Unit 4

TEACH

 CHECK YOUR UNDERSTANDING

Have students answer the questions independently.

Answers:

1. *B*

2. *F*

3. *D*

If they answer any questions incorrectly, have them reread the text to confirm their understanding. Then they may proceed to ANALYZE THE TEXT on page 274.

CHECK YOUR UNDERSTANDING

Answer these questions before moving on to the **Analyze the Text** section on the following page.

1 The poems reveal that as a child the author struggled with —

A listening to her mother

B reading and writing

C going on family outings

D playing and practicing sports

2 The book *Stevie* is important to the author because —

F it has people of color in it

G it is the first library book she checks out

H it has a character in it who is a writer

J it is the first book she can read

3 Which phrase best fits the author's description of her older sister?

A Helpful and kind

B Competitive and ambitious

C Protective and watchful

D Intelligent and studious

 ENGLISH LEARNER SUPPORT

Oral Assessment Use the following questions to assess students' comprehension and speaking skills:

1. As a child, the author found it hard to _____ and _____. (*read, write*)

2. The book *Stevie* was important to the author because it had _____ in it. (*people of color*)

3. The author's older sister was very _____. (*smart*) **SUBSTANTIAL/MODERATE**

APPLY

ANALYZE THE TEXT

Possible answers:

1. **DOK 4:** *Selected lines and text connections will vary.*

2. **DOK 3:** *The titles all point to a significant moment or an important person in the author's life. Crafting the titles in this way shows that the author's purpose for writing the memoir was to track the difficulties she had finding her own voice and the moments when she began to discover that voice.*

3. **DOK 4:** *The author italicizes words to show what other people say to her, what she replies, thoughts she had at the moment, and to emphasize an action. For example, in "reading," she quotes what the teacher said about the author's choice of books—"too babyish" and "read older." In "writing #1," she italicizes what she imagined a story would say to her, and a thought she had about spelling when she was trying to write on paper.*

4. **DOK 2:** *The author states that it is much easier to tell a story than to write it. She imagines a story walking around, sitting in a chair, and introducing itself. She remembers not being able to write a story on paper and worrying about spelling. The first two lines state how she feels about writing versus telling and set a personal tone by saying "When I speak. . . ."*

5. **DOK 4:** *The author is trying to say that she gave her family an answer that she had no intention of doing and then reflects that she and her family probably knew this already and considered her answer to be made up. She included it to show how determined she was to be a writer, no matter what anyone said.*

RESEARCH

Remind students to look for the author's own website first for answers to the questions. Then have them search for publisher biographies and interviews. Students may work with a partner.

Connect Have partners share their own questions about Woodson, then compare the information they found in their research. Encourage them to discuss whether any of their questions were answered in their research.

ANALYZE THE TEXT

Support your responses with evidence from the text. NOTEBOOK

1. **Connect** Choose a few lines from the selection that connect to another text you have read. What is the connection? Explain.

2. **Draw Conclusions** Review the titles of the verses in this excerpt. What do the titles have in common? How do you think this feature relates to the author's overall purpose in writing the memoir?

3. **Analyze** Review the italicized words throughout the selection. Why do you think the author italicized these words? Cite evidence in your answer.

4. **Summarize** Review and summarize the first poem, "writing #1." How do the first two lines provide structure and meaning?

5. **Notice & Note** Review lines 124–127. What do you think the author is trying to say here? Why did she include this memory?

RESEARCH TIP
You can research authors online. Authors often host their own websites with information on their lives, their books, and their writing process. Publishers may post interviews, video clips, and photos.

RESEARCH

Use multiple sources to research and answer questions about the author Jacqueline Woodson. Ask your own questions about Woodson and her work, and then find the answers.

QUESTION	ANSWER
What helped Woodson most as she learned to write?	Reading picture books helped her because the visuals helped her understand the story without reading all of the words.
How did "lying" influence her writing?	She told lies up until fifth grade. Then she wrote a story that was well received by a teacher, and this made her realize "lies" could be put in stories.
What did her teachers think of her writing?	They didn't always believe that she actually wrote the story or poem herself.
What are some fun facts about Woodson?	• She can only write in her notebook sideways. • Fall is her favorite season. • She can double-dutch.
My question(s):	Answers will vary.

Connect Consider what you've learned about Jacqueline Woodson in your research. Discuss the information you've discovered with a partner. Does the information you learned clarify any questions you had about *Brown Girl Dreaming*?

 LEARNING MINDSET

Asking for Help Encourage students to feel comfortable asking peers, teachers, or parents for help when they encounter a challenge. Explain that asking for help from others can help students get "unstuck" and move forward. Reinforce that asking for help does not equal failure. Rather, seeking help is a way of "trying smarter."

CREATE AND PRESENT

Describe a Connection Write a brief, formal letter or email to Jacqueline Woodson. Describe a meaningful connection you found between your life and an aspect or event in her memoir.

- ❏ Include the date and the name of the person your letter is for.
- ❏ Write the body of your letter, describing the connection.
- ❏ What aspects or events in the selection moved you or brought meaning to your life? Provide details about your life that will help Woodson understand the connection.
- ❏ Remember to sign your letter.

Compose and Present a Biographical Poem Choose an event that affected your life. Write a free verse or formal poem about that event.

- ❏ Choose an event to write about and the poetic form that best conveys your experience, either free verse or formal. Write your poem.
- ❏ Practice reading your poem aloud and present it to a small group or to the class.
- ❏ Make eye contact with your audience and use pacing, tone, and voice to help convey your poem's meaning.
- ❏ Answer questions about your poem, and ask questions about the purpose and message of the poems of other students.

 Go to **Writing Informative Texts: Formal Style** in the **Writing Studio** for more on styles of writing.

 Go to **Giving a Presentation: Delivering Your Presentation** in the **Speaking and Listening Studio** for more on presenting your work.

RESPOND TO THE ESSENTIAL QUESTION

? What are the ways you can make yourself heard?

Gather Information Review your annotations and notes from *Brown Girl Dreaming*. Then, add relevant details to your Response Log. As you determine what information to include, think about:

- how the author expresses herself
- how verse can be used to express oneself
- what kinds of things are important to express

At the end of the unit, use your notes to create a multimodal argument.

UNIT 4 RESPONSE LOG

? Essential Question:
What are the ways you can make yourself heard?

from Selfie: The Changing Face of Self-Portraits	
from Brown Girl Dreaming	
What's So Funny, Ms. Scieszka?	
A Voice	
Words Like Freedom	
Better Than Words: Say It with a Selfie	
OMG, Not Another Selfie!	

ACADEMIC VOCABULARY
As you write and discuss what you learned from the poems, be sure to use the Academic Vocabulary words. Check off each of the words that you use.

- ❏ **appropriate**
- ❏ **authority**
- ❏ **consequence**
- ❏ **element**
- ❏ **justify**

CREATE AND PRESENT

Describe a Connection Remind students that a formal letter or email has a particular structure and language that they will need to follow and use. Point out that they should be respectful and clear in what they write.

Compose and Present a Biographical Poem Point out to students that they have choices in format for composing their poem. Remind them to practice reading their poem aloud several times before presenting it.

For **writing support** for students at varying proficiency levels, see the **Text X-Ray** on page 264D.

RESPOND TO THE ESSENTIAL QUESTION

Allow time for students to add details from *Brown Girl Dreaming* to their Unit 4 Response Logs.

EL ENGLISH LEARNER SUPPORT

Write a Biographical Poem Support students' writing by providing them with strategies that will help them compose their biographical poems. Remind them to narrate their experience from a first-person point of view and provide them with a list of first-person pronouns to use: *I, me, my, we, us, our*. To help them write with an informal tone and include details, suggest that they begin by drawing a picture of the event and telling a partner about it, having the partner write down words and phrases the poet could use then to write the poem.

MODERATE

WHAT'S SO FUNNY, MR. SCIESZKA?

Humor by Jon Scieszka

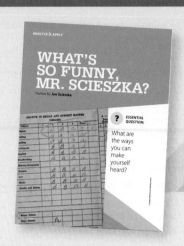

GENRE ELEMENTS
HUMOR

Most students will be familiar with the term *humor*, but they may not know that **humor** is a specific genre. The purpose of a humorous work is to make the reader laugh; so the author will use amusing descriptions. Often the author will exaggerate for the purpose of comedy. Other devices found frequently in humor writing are comic irony, double meanings, and witty dialogue.

LEARNING OBJECTIVES

- Make inferences about author's purpose and message.
- Analyze author's use of language.
- Research popular humorists.
- Write an essay analyzing the author's purpose and message.
- Give and follow instructions for telling a joke.
- Use resources to determine word meaning.
- Use pronouns correctly.
- **Language** Discuss the selection with a partner using the term *author's purpose*.

TEXT COMPLEXITY

Quantitative Measures	What's So Funny, Mr. Scieszka?	Lexile: 710L
Qualitative Measures	**Ideas Presented** Simple, single meaning, literal, explicit, and direct.	
	Structure Used Clear, chronological, conventional.	
	Language Used Explicit, literal, contemporary language.	
	Knowledge Required Requires no special knowledge. Situations and subject familiar or easily envisioned.	

Online Ed

RESOURCES

- Unit 4 Response Log
- Selection Audio
- Reading Studio: Notice & Note
- Level Up Tutorial: Summarizing
- Writing Studio: Writing Informative Texts
- Speaking and Listening Studio: Participating in Collaborative Discussions
- Vocabulary Studio: Using Reference Resources
- Grammar Studio: Module 8: Using Pronouns Correctly
- "What's So Funny, Mr. Scieszka?" Selection Test

SUMMARIES

English

"What's So Funny, Mr. Scieszka?" is a true story recounting a childhood experience of author Jon Scieszka. Scieszka gets in trouble for laughing during religion class at school, and the teacher asks him if he would like to share his joke with the class. Scieszka is faced with a choice: keep quiet and stay out of trouble, or tell the joke and make himself heard. He chooses to tell the joke, setting himself on a lifelong path of trying to make people laugh.

Spanish

"¿Qué es tan divertido, Sr. Scieszka?" es una historia verdadera que recuenta una experiencia de la infancia del autor, Jon Scieszka. Jon se mete en problemas por reírse durante la clase de religión en la escuela y el profesor le pregunta que si le gustaría compartir el chiste con la clase. Jon se enfrenta a una elección: callar y evitar problemas, o contar el chiste y hacerse oír. Escoge contar el chiste, poniéndose en un camino de toda la vida para hacer reír a la gente.

SMALL-GROUP OPTIONS

Have students work in small groups to read and discuss the selection.

Think-Pair-Share

- Pose a question to the class, such as: *How can the choices a person makes as a child—like Scieszka's choice to tell the joke—affect how that person ends up behaving as a grown-up?*
- Request that students think about the question individually, making notes.
- Organize students in pairs and ask partners to listen, discuss, and formulate a shared response.
- Call on each individual or a selected student from each pair to respond to the entire class.

Three Before Me

- Have each student prepare and edit a piece of writing to bring it to final form, such as the analysis students write about Scieszka's purpose for writing this humorous story.
- Instruct each student to ask three other students to edit his or her writing before turning it in. Explain that editors should read for one kind of error at a time or edit the entire paper.
- Explain that each student writer is responsible for evaluating editing suggestions and making appropriate edits to his or her writing before turning it in.

Text X-Ray: English Learner Support
for "What's So Funny, Mr. Scieszka?"

Use the Text X-Ray and the supports and scaffolds in the Teacher's Edition to help guide students at different proficiency levels through the selection.

INTRODUCE THE SELECTION
DISCUSS HUMOROUS WRITING

In this lesson, students will read a humorous story about the author as a child. Tell students that the author's purpose in humorous writing is to make a reader laugh. Some humorous stories are true, like this one, and others are fictional. Even when the story is true, the author may use techniques to retell it in a funny way. Identify and define terms related to humorous writing: *exaggeration, funny descriptions, funny dialogue.* Provide students with the following sentence frames to help them discuss the concepts:

- *"This bus ride is taking forever!" is an example of _____.*
- *Telling in a silly way how something looks is an example of a _____.*

CULTURAL REFERENCES

The following words and phrases may be unfamiliar to students:

- *Sister Margaret Mary* (paragraph 3): The author attended a religious school, where some teachers were nuns. Sister Margaret Mary was his religion class teacher. *Sister* is a term used to address a nun.
- *train wreck* (paragraph 14): a disastrous situation
- *punch line* (paragraph 23): the funny part at the end of the joke
- *"his face rings a bell"* (paragraph 24): the phrase "rings a bell" refers to something that makes a person remember something. This is a double-meaning phrase because in this joke, the man actually uses his face to ring a bell.

LISTENING

Understand Author's Use of Language

To understand why authors choose certain words to create a mood or voice for their writing, students must first understand the words and phrases themselves. Work with students to decipher humorous images from this story.

Have students listen as you read aloud paragraphs 1–3 from "What's So Funny, Mr. Scieszka?" Use the following supports with students at varying proficiency levels:

- Tell students you will ask questions about what they just read. They can answer each question with single words or phrases: *Whose voice flies across the room? (Sister Margaret Mary's) Can a voice really fly? (no)* **SUBSTANTIAL**
- Have students complete the following sentence frames: *It feels like Sister Margaret Mary's voice flew across the room because the voice moves _____. The author feels nailed to his seat by her voice because _____.* **MODERATE**
- Have student pairs work together to describe the image the author is creating with these phrases and to explain what is really happening. **LIGHT**

SPEAKING

Discuss Author's Purpose

Tell students that the author's purpose is the reason the author wrote the text. Have students discuss the features of the text using the term *author's purpose*. Circulate around the room to make sure students are using the term correctly.

Use the following supports with students at varying proficiency levels:

- Have students complete the following sentence frames: *Author's purpose means why an author _____ a story. In this story, the author's purpose is to tell about an important _____ that he made.* **SUBSTANTIAL**
- Have students complete the following sentence frames in their discussion: *The author's purpose in this story is _____. One example of how the author achieves this purpose is _____.* **MODERATE**
- Have student pairs discuss with each other the meaning of the term *author's purpose* and identify the author's purpose in this particular story. Have pairs look together for examples of at least two ways the author tried to achieve his purpose. **LIGHT**

READING

Understand Humorous Language

Provide students with two-column graphic organizers to use to take notes about examples of humorous language they find while they are reading.

Use the following supports with students at varying proficiency levels:

- Have students reread paragraph 14. Ask them to find, circle, and read aloud the phrases "eyes pop open" and "train wreck." **SUBSTANTIAL**
- Have students reread paragraphs 12–18 and note in the first column examples of the author exaggerating how Sister's eyes look. Provide a sentence frame for them to complete in the second column: *The author describes her eyes as popping open wide because _____.* **MODERATE**
- Have students reread paragraphs 12–18 and copy examples of humorous language in the first column of their chart. Ask partners to label each example as exaggeration, humorous description, and so on. **LIGHT**

WRITING

Write an Essay

Work with students to read the writing assignment on page 285.

Use the following supports with students at varying proficiency levels:

- Write a list of important terms and phrases on the board, such as *author's purpose, mood, voice,* and *dialogue.* Have students write the terms down, drawing a picture for each to help them remember its meaning. **SUBSTANTIAL**
- Provide students with sentence frames to use to organize their essays: *I think the author wrote this story because _____. One reason I think this is because _____. Another reason I think this is that _____.* **MODERATE**
- Have students review their ideas and identify which are supporting details and which relate to a main idea about why the author wrote this story. Then have students write their main idea as the thesis statement for their essay. **LIGHT**

? Connect to the
ESSENTIAL QUESTION

In "What's So Funny, Mr. Scieszka?" the author tells a true story about a time in his childhood when he was faced with an important choice: keep silent in class and stay out of trouble, or tell a joke and make himself heard. He chose to make himself heard, and his career as a comedy writer was born.

WHAT'S SO FUNNY, MR. SCIESZKA?

Humor by **Jon Scieszka**

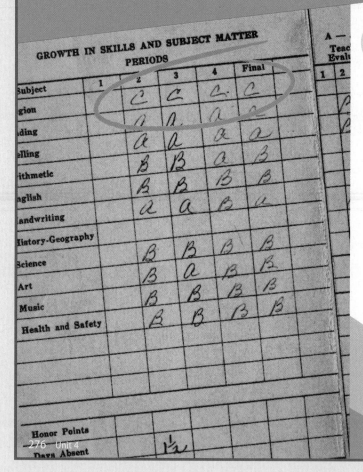

? ESSENTIAL QUESTION:

What are the ways you can make yourself heard?

QUICK START

Have you ever had to make an on-the-spot choice that could change your life forever? Think of a big choice you made and how it has changed your life. Write down your thoughts.

MAKE INFERENCES ABOUT AUTHOR'S PURPOSE AND MESSAGE

An **author's purpose** is the main reason for writing the text. The purpose may be to inform, entertain, persuade, or express thoughts and feelings. Most writers do not state a purpose directly, but suggest it through the information they present and the text's tone and structure. Structural elements include how sentences and paragraphs are organized, as well as how the text presents ideas or describes events.

An **author's message** is the main idea of a particular work. Often, the author doesn't explicitly state a message. Readers must **infer** or discover that message as they read.

To make an inference about an author's purpose and message, make a logical guess based on facts and clues in the text, combined with your own knowledge and experience. Support your inference with evidence from the text, and confirm or revise your inference as you read.

Here is an inference, based on evidence from the text, about the message of "What's So Funny, Mr. Sciezska?"

INFERENCE ABOUT THE MESSAGE	EVIDENCE FROM THE TEXT
At times you are faced with making a choice that can alter the course of your life.	That day I reached a life-choice fork in the road. I saw two life paths laid out clearly before me.

GENRE ELEMENTS: HUMOR
- may include exaggeration
- often uses double meanings
- relies on amusing descriptions
- may incorporate comic irony
- often includes witty or funny dialogue

ANALYZE AUTHOR'S USE OF LANGUAGE

Writers use descriptive words, imagery, and figurative language to create a feeling, or **mood.** A mood might be tense, creepy, or peaceful, for example. Writers also use language to create **voice,** or the distinct personality readers hear as they read a text.

- To analyze how the author uses language to create mood, mark figurative language, imagery, and word choices, noting their effects.
- To determine voice, mark significant words that capture personality.

QUICK START

Have students read the Quick Start question and write down their thoughts. Invite students to share their examples of life-changing choices.

MAKE INFERENCES ABOUT AUTHOR'S PURPOSE AND MESSAGE

Review the first paragraph about author's purpose with students. Emphasize that authors usually do not state their purpose directly—rather, students have to infer the author's purpose. Have students suggest different texts they have read that exemplify the different author's purposes of informing, entertaining, persuading, or expressing thoughts and feelings. Ask students for examples of how each purpose might affect the text structure of that piece of writing. Then ask students what the author's purpose would be in a humorous piece such as the one they are about to read. Review the Genre Elements list for some ideas on how humor writing affects the structure and ideas of the piece.

Review the paragraph about an author's message. Students should be familiar with the author's message from their study of theme. A message is the most important idea an author is trying to convey, and, like author's purpose, it usually has to be inferred by the reader. Encourage students to make personal connections to the message as they read. Have students read the paragraph about inferences, and review with them the table that shows an example inference.

ANALYZE AUTHOR'S USE OF LANGUAGE

Ask students what the mood of humor writing might be. Review the definitions of *imagery* and *figurative language*, since students will be looking for these language devices as they read. Also discuss students' predictions of what the voice of a humorous text might be. Tell them that they will be looking for descriptive language the author uses to achieve this voice.

ENGLISH LEARNER SUPPORT

Use Visual Support Students may be unfamiliar with the type of classroom atmosphere that Scieszka refers to in this story. Look for pictures online that show Catholic schools in the 1960s. Point out that students had to wear uniforms and sit in very straight rows, both of which created a very serious classroom atmosphere. Visualizing Scieszka's strict classroom atmosphere will help readers understand what a huge risk he was taking by standing up to tell a joke in the classroom. To assess understanding, have students act out sitting neatly in rows and pantomiming only speaking when called upon by a teacher. **SUBSTANTIAL**

TEACH

CRITICAL VOCABULARY

Encourage students to read all the sentences before deciding which word best completes each one. Remind them to look for context clues that match the precise meaning of each word.

Answers:

1. *pause*

2. *apology*

3. *terror*

4. *history*

■ English Learner Support

Use Cognates Tell students that some of the Critical Vocabulary words have Spanish cognates: *history/historia, terror/terror, pause/pausa.* **ALL LEVELS**

LANGUAGE CONVENTIONS:
Pronouns

Have students read the information about pronouns. Write two example sentences on the board, and have students determine the pronoun and antecedent for each. (Examples: Elena was tired, so she took a nap; The students in Room 15 worked hard on their history projects.) Next, review the idea of singular and plural pronouns. Work with students to brainstorm lists of each type.

ANNOTATION MODEL

Clarify for students that in the example annotation on p. 278, the reader has underlined an example of figurative language that helps the reader figure out what kind of mood the author wants to establish for this part of the story. The note the reader has written on the side explains that the reader thinks this mood is a tense one. Point out to students that they can follow their own system for marking up the selection in their write-in text. For example, they may want to color-code their annotations by using highlighters to distinguish between descriptive words, figurative language, and imagery.

 GET READY

CRITICAL VOCABULARY

apology	history	terror	pause

To see how many Critical Vocabulary words you already know, use them to complete the sentences.

1. _____ between key points when speaking to an audience.

2. The newspaper issued a/an _____ for printing misinformation.

3. The soldier recounted the _____ of the frightening battle.

4. Do you have records of your family's _____?

LANGUAGE CONVENTIONS

Pronouns A pronoun is a word used in place of a noun or another pronoun, such as *he*, *she*, or *it*. The word or word group to which a pronoun refers is its **antecedent**. If an antecedent is singular, use a singular pronoun. If an antecedent is plural, use a plural pronoun.

> **My friend and back-row pal, Tim K. had just told me the funniest joke I had ever heard. The fact that he had told it while Sister Mary Margaret was droning on . . . only made it funnier.**

The singular pronoun *it* relates to the singular noun *joke*. The singular pronoun *he* refers to the singular *Tim K.*

> **Sister Mary Margaret's eyes were wider than I had ever seen them.**

The plural pronoun *them* relates to the plural antecedent *eyes*.

As you read the text, notice the pronouns and antecedents.

ANNOTATION MODEL   NOTICE & NOTE

As you read, mark descriptive words, figurative language, and imagery to understand mood and voice. In the model, you can see how one reader responded to a passage in "What's So Funny, Mr. Scieszka?"

1 The <u>voice flew across the room and nailed me to the back of my seat.</u>

2 "What's so funny, Mr. Scieszka?"

3 The voice belonged to Sister Margaret Mary. And it had just flown across our fifth-grade religion class at St. Luke's Elementary School to find me in what I had thought was the safety of the back row.

This figurative language makes me feel the harshness of Sister Margaret Mary's voice. The mood seems tense.

BACKGROUND

Jon Scieszka (b. 1954) grew up in Flint, Michigan, with five brothers, who provided plenty of material for writing funny stories. Scieszka's The Stinky Cheese Man and Other Fairly Stupid Tales won a Caldecott Honor medal. In 2008, the Library of Congress appointed Scieszka the first Ambassador for Young People's Literature. "What's So Funny, Mr. Scieszka?" is from Knucklehead, a humorous memoir about his rambunctious childhood.

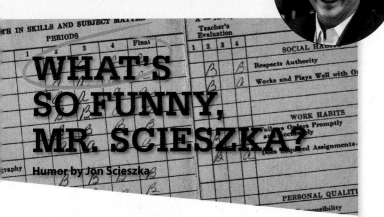

WHAT'S SO FUNNY, MR. SCIESZKA?

Humor by Jon Scieszka

SETTING A PURPOSE

Humor can be an effective way to make your voice heard. In this story, the author uses humor to describe a choice he made as a child that had life-changing consequences. The choice is between playing it safe or taking a leap and making himself heard.

1 The voice flew across the room and nailed me to the back of my seat.

2 "What's so funny, Mr. Scieszka?"

3 The voice belonged to Sister Margaret Mary.[1] And it had just flown across our fifth-grade religion class at St. Luke's Elementary School to find me in what I had thought was the safety of the back row.

4 "What's so funny?" I repeated, trying desperately to stop laughing.

5 I knew the correct answer to this question was, "Nothing, Sister."

6 "I'm sorry, Sister," was also a very good reply.

---

[1] **Sister Margaret Mary:** the nun teaching religion class; Sister is the form of address for a nun.

Notice & Note

Use the side margins to notice and note signposts in the text.

ANALYZE AUTHOR'S USE OF LANGUAGE

Annotate: Reread paragraphs 1–3. Mark examples of descriptive words and imagery.

Infer: How does this language create the mood and voice of the story?

BACKGROUND

After students read the Background note, emphasize to them that the story they are about to read is part of a humorous memoir about the author's childhood. That is, the author is telling a true story about something that really happened to him when he was a child. Tell students that the story is about a time when the author faced an important decision and chose to make himself heard. His decision led him on a path of dedicating his life to humor. Students can see from the list of his other books that he certainly has made a career of writing humor stories.

SETTING A PURPOSE

Direct students to use the Setting a Purpose prompt to focus their reading.

ANALYZE AUTHOR'S USE OF LANGUAGE

Have students mark examples of descriptive words and imagery. Invite volunteers to share what they marked and to explain the meaning of these annotations. Note how different details work together and build upon one another to form a full picture of the scene. Then pose the question. (**Answer:** *The image of a voice flying across the room and nailing somebody to their chair is graphic and funny. It establishes a humorous mood. You can imagine yourself put on the spot by your teacher. The voice is funny; you get the idea the voice is a young mischievous boy.*)

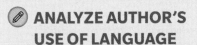 For **listening support** for students at varying proficiency levels, see the **Text X-Ray** on page 276C.

ENGLISH LEARNER SUPPORT

Use Prereading Supports Use sketching to prepare students ahead of time to comprehend the imagery used in this story. Preview the imagery by reading examples, such as paragraph 1, with students before they read the entire story. Clarify the details of what is happening in each image, and have students draw simple sketches to remind themselves of what the author is communicating with each image. Encourage students to add to their drawings as the story continues. **SUBSTANTIAL/MODERATE**

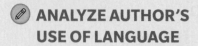

ANALYZE AUTHOR'S USE OF LANGUAGE

Review how extreme language or exaggeration states something in an over-the-top way, making a claim that is so big it would never be true in real life. Once students have marked instances of this type of language, discuss the question. (**Answer:** *The exaggeration establishes a humorous mood and prepares the reader to accept that the joke will be very funny.*)

▶ TOUGH QUESTIONS

Remind students that the **Tough Questions** signpost is a point in a story where a character must ask him or herself a difficult question, one whose answer might change the course of the rest of his or her life. Have students underline and share the two life paths that the main character must choose from. Discuss the question. (**Answer:** *Not telling the joke would be easier, but wouldn't express Scieszka's personality. Telling the joke would let him experience what it feels like to make people laugh and point him toward becoming a humor writer.*)

▶ AHA MOMENT

Help students recall that an **Aha Moment** is when a character makes an important realization. Ask students to mark and share Mr. Scieszka's important realization in paragraphs 11 and 12. Discuss the question about why this is a crucial moment for him. (**Answer:** *He knew his choice would have important consequences.*)

 For **reading support** for students at varying proficiency levels, see the **Text X-Ray** on page 276D.

CRITICAL VOCABULARY

apology: Scieszka realizes that if he makes an apology, he won't get in big trouble, but he also won't have the fun of telling the joke and making the class laugh.

ASK STUDENTS whether they think Mr. Scieszka should choose an apology or choose to continue with the joke, and why. (*Answers will vary.*)

 NOTICE & NOTE

ANALYZE AUTHOR'S USE OF LANGUAGE

Annotate: Read paragraphs 7–8. Mark instances of extreme language or exaggeration.

Infer: Why do you think the author uses extreme language and exaggeration?

TOUGH QUESTIONS

Notice & Note: How does the author describe the two life paths he sees before him? Mark the author's two choices in paragraph 10.

Evaluate: What do you think the long-term consequences of each choice might be?

AHA MOMENT

Notice & Note: Mark the author's realization in paragraphs 11–12.

Infer: Why is this a crucial moment for him?

apology
(ə-pŏl´ə-jē) *n.* An *apology* is an expression of regret or a request for forgiveness.

7 And nine times out of ten, ninety-nine times out of a hundred, I would have used one of those answers. But that day in fifth-grade religion class, something happened. That day I reached a life-choice fork in the road.[2]

8 My friend and back-row pal, Tim K. had just told me the funniest joke I had ever heard. The fact that he had told it while Sister Margaret Mary was droning on about our future place in heaven or hell only made it funnier.

9 Now I was called out.

10 I saw two life paths laid out clearly before me. Down the one path of the quick **apology** lay a good grade for religion class, a spot in heaven, maybe even sainthood if things worked out later in life. Down the other path lay the chance of a very big laugh . . . though mixed with punishment, maybe a note to my parents, quite possibly one mad God and forever in hell.

11 A good grade in religion class is always a good thing in Catholic school. I knew that. But I also knew this was a really funny joke. I was torn between going for the A and heaven, and

---
[2] **fork in the road:** a metaphor referring to a moment in life when you have to make a big choice.

APPLYING ACADEMIC VOCABULARY

☑ **appropriate** ☐ **authority** ☐ **consequence** ☐ **element** ☑ **justify**

Write and Discuss Have students turn to a partner to discuss the following questions. Guide students to include the Academic Vocabulary words *appropriate* and *justify* in their responses. Ask volunteers to share their responses with the class.

- Was Mr. Scieszka's choice **appropriate**?
- Did Mr. Scieszka's discovery of his life's path **justify** his interrupting class?

going for the laugh with a chance of hell. Both were right in front of me.

12   So when Sister Margaret Mary asked her next question, "Would you like to share it with the rest of the class?" I chose my life's path.

13   2 "Well, there's this guy who wants to be a bell ringer,"[3] I begin. "But he doesn't have any arms."

14   3 Sister Margaret Mary's eyes pop open wider than I have ever seen them. The whole class turns to look at me and the train wreck about to happen. Even my pal Tim K. is shaking his head. Nobody in the **history** of St. Luke's Elementary School has ever chosen to "share it with the rest of the class." But I feel it. I have to do it. It is my path.

15   4 "The priest who is looking for a good bell ringer says, 'You can't ring the bells. You don't have any arms.' "

16   The faces of my fellow fifth-graders are looking a bit wavy and blurry. " 'I don't need arms,' says the bell-ringing guy. 'Watch this.' And he runs up the bell tower and starts bouncing his face off the bells and making beautiful music."

17   Half of the class laughs. I'm not sure if it's out of nervousness or pity. But it's a lot of laughs.

18   Sister Margaret Mary's eyes open impossibly wider.

19   5 Light floods the classroom. I can't really see anybody now. I can only feel the punch line building. I head toward the light.

20   6 "So the bell-ringing guy goes to finish his song with one last smack of his face, but this time he misses the bell and falls right out of the tower. He lands on the ground and is knocked out. A whole crowd gathers around him."

21   7 The whole fifth-grade religion class has gathered around me. It is a feeling of unbelievable power mixed with **terror** for a low-profile[4] fifth-grader like myself.

22   " 'Who is this guy?' the villagers ask."

23   8 I feel the whole world **pause** for just a single beat, like it always does before a good punch line.

---

[3] **bell ringer:** a person who rings the bells of a church or tower, usually by pulling on a rope.
[4] **low profile:** subdued or modest behavior to avoid attracting attention.

MAKE INFERENCES ABOUT AUTHOR'S PURPOSE AND MESSAGE

Annotate: Reread paragraphs 12–23. Mark the sequence of events as they occur in chronological order.

Infer: How do you think the way the text is structured supports the author's main purpose for writing the text?

history
(hĭsʹtə-rē) *n.* History is a chronological record of events of a person or institution.

ANALYZE AUTHOR'S USE OF LANGUAGE

Annotate: Reread paragraphs 14–21. Mark descriptive words and imagery that create a distinct mood.

Infer: What do you think Scieszka is feeling as he tells the joke? What do you think Sister Margaret Mary and the class are feeling?

terror
(tĕrʹər) *n.* Terror is extreme fear of something.

pause
(pôz) *v.* To pause is to hesitate or suspend action.

MAKE INFERENCES ABOUT AUTHOR'S PURPOSE AND MESSAGE

Review that chronological order means the order in which events happen. Once students number the events, discuss the question. (**Answer:** *The author uses the same structure you would use telling a joke, which is what he is doing in the text, but at the same time he is describing a life choice that helped him ultimately become a humor writer.*)

ANALYZE AUTHOR'S USE OF LANGUAGE

Explain that often an author will develop an image by adding details to heighten suspense and slowly form a complete picture. For example, Scieszka describes how his vision starts to get blurry in paragraph 16 and then, in paragraph 19, describes how light floods the classroom (from his perspective) and he heads toward this light. Discuss what this image might mean, then have students answer the question. (**Answer:** *Mr. Scieszka is feeling a bit shaky at first, but he gains a sense of empowerment as he nears the punchline of the joke. Sister Margaret Mary is horrified. The class at first thought he was making a mistake, but as he tells the joke, they get drawn in, waiting for the punchline.*)

CRITICAL VOCABULARY

history: The author refers to the school's history to emphasize that nothing like this has happened before.

ASK STUDENTS if Mr. Scieszka actually knows that nobody in the history of the school has ever chosen to share a joke with the class. (*No, he is just exaggerating to be funny.*)

terror: The author feels terror when all of the class is listening to him tell the joke.

ASK STUDENTS why Mr. Scieszka felt terror. (*He usually behaved and did not attract this much attention.*)

pause: The author feels everything stop for a moment as everyone is waiting to hear him tell the end of the joke.

ASK STUDENTS what Mr. Scieszka might be feeling during this pause. (*He might feel afraid that nobody will laugh at his joke, but powerful because he has the attention of the whole class.*)

IMPROVE READING FLUENCY

Targeted Passage Have students work with partners to read paragraphs 13–24 on pages 281 and 282. First, use the first three paragraphs to model how to read humorous text. Have students follow along in their books as you read the text with appropriate phrasing and emphasis. Then, have partners take turns reading aloud paragraphs 13–24. Encourage students to provide feedback and support for pronouncing multisyllabic words. Remind students that when they are reading aloud for an audience, they should pace their reading so the audience has time to understand difficult concepts.

 Go to the **Reading Studio** for additional support in developing fluency.

 ## MAKE INFERENCES ABOUT AUTHOR'S PURPOSE AND MESSAGE

Note that the concepts that relate to the author's message have been mentioned earlier in the story, such as wanting to get a laugh and finding a lifelong path. Then have students share their ideas by answering the question. (**Answer:** *Don't be afraid to follow your instincts when making a choice—it can set you on the right path in life.*)

 For **speaking support** for students at varying proficiency levels, see the **Text X-Ray** on page 276D.

LANGUAGE CONVENTIONS

Have students mark the pronouns in paragraph 25. Have students share the pronouns that they marked and identify the antecedent for each one. (**Answer:** *All instances of the pronoun* it *relate to "the laugh."*)

(EL) ENGLISH LEARNER SUPPORT

Summarize Events To help students summarize the events of the story, give them the following sentence frames to complete:

- *Mr. Scieszka is in _____ and he gets in trouble for _____.*
- *The teacher asks him if he wants to _____.*
- *Mr. Scieszka decides to _____.*
- *The rest of the class _____ and Mr. Scieszka realizes that he likes making people _____.* **MODERATE**

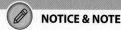 ✏ **NOTICE & NOTE**

MAKE INFERENCES ABOUT AUTHOR'S PURPOSE AND MESSAGE
Annotate: Reread the last paragraph. Mark words or phrases that help identify the author's message.

Infer: What is the author's message in this story?

LANGUAGE CONVENTIONS
It is used several times in paragraph 25. Mark each instance of the pronoun *it*, and indicate the antecedent for each one.

24 9 " 'I don't know his name,' says the priest. 'But his face rings a bell.' "

25 10 I don't remember the grade I got in fifth-grade religion class. But I do remember the laugh I got. It was huge. It was the whole class (except Sister Margaret Mary). It was out-of-control hysterical. It was glorious. And it set me on my lifelong path of answering that classic question, "What's so funny, Mr. Scieszka?"

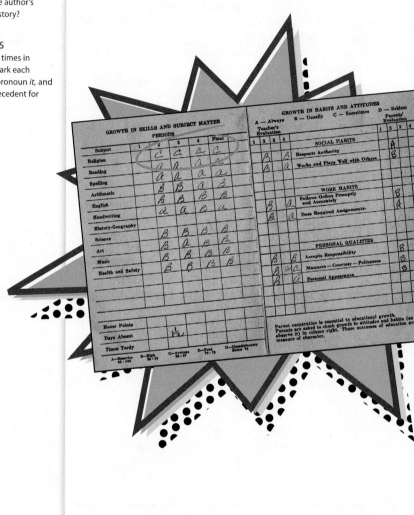

WHEN STUDENTS STRUGGLE . . .

Somebody-Wanted-But-So Grid To help students summarize the story, have them fill out a Somebody-Wanted-But-So grid. Have students write a 2–3 sentence summary of the story.

Somebody	Wanted	But	So
Mr. Scieszka	to tell a joke	his teacher got mad and asked if he wanted to share the joke with the rest of the class	he chose to tell the joke anyway, got a huge laugh, and learned he wanted to make people laugh for the rest of their lives.

 For additional support, go to the **Reading Studio** and assign the following 🔼 **Level Up tutorial: Summarizing.**

CHECK YOUR UNDERSTANDING

Answer these questions before moving on to the **Analyze the Text** section on the following page.

1. The author's purpose for writing this humorous narrative is most likely to —

   A make people tell jokes

   B describe a life-changing moment in his life

   C explain why he didn't get a good grade in religion class

   D describe what it's like to go to Catholic school

2. In what way does the structure of the text contribute to its effectiveness?

   F It builds momentum to keep the reader engaged until the end.

   G The sequence of events takes the reader into the past.

   H The structure tells the reader that this is a kind of memoir.

   J The structure supports the purpose of the article.

3. Which sentence from the text best relates to the message of the story?

   A *I knew the correct answer to this question was, "Nothing, Sister."*

   B *That day I reached a life-choice fork in the road.*

   C *A good grade in religion class is always a good thing in Catholic school.*

   D *The whole class turns to look at me and the train wreck about to happen.*

✏ CHECK YOUR UNDERSTANDING

Have students answer the questions independently.

Answers:

1. *B*

2. *F*

3. *B*

If they answer any questions incorrectly, have them reread the text to confirm their understanding. Then they may proceed to ANALYZE THE TEXT on page 284.

🔵 ENGLISH LEARNER SUPPORT

Oral Assessment Use the following questions to assess students' comprehension and speaking skills:

1. What was the author's purpose? (*The author's purpose was to tell about a life-changing moment in his life.*)

2. Does this story get more or less exciting as it moves toward the end? (*It gets more exciting.*)

3. Which sentence best tells the message of the story? (*That day I reached a life-choice fork in the road.*) **SUBSTANTIAL/MODERATE**

APPLY

ANALYZE THE TEXT

Possible answers:

1. **DOK 3:** *The voice is of someone who is thoughtful and weighs the pros and cons of different actions. He describes what would happen if he went down each path. It is also the voice of a risk-taker. He's willing to risk getting in trouble. The voice is of someone who really wants to make people laugh. Letting everyone in on the joke is more important to him than playing it safe: "But I also knew this was a really funny joke."*

2. **DOK 4:** *The author's purpose is to share an experience in his life that may inspire others and make them laugh: "That day I reached a life-choice fork in the road"; "And it set me on my lifelong path of answering that classic question, 'What's so funny, Mr. Scieszka?'" The structure of the text builds like telling a joke—it keeps you engaged because you want to hear the punch line.*

3. **DOK 3:** *Mr. Scieszka was feeling nervous to the point that his vision was blurry: "The faces of my fellow fifth-graders are looking a bit wavy and blurry." He also felt compelled to tell the joke—he couldn't help himself: "Light floods the classroom. I can't really see anybody now. I can only feel the punch line building. I head toward the light."*

4. **DOK 3:** *No, the author is someone who tries to stay unnoticed. He sits at the back of the class and often answers in a way that keeps him out of trouble. Near the end of the story he says he is a "low-profile fifth-grader."*

5. **DOK 4:** *The first sentence is an example of extreme language that creates a strong image: "The voice flew across the room and nailed me to the back of my seat." It sets the mood by putting you on high alert—a reaction most people have when they are caught doing something they should not be doing. The extreme language and exaggeration creates a mood of suspense. The exaggerated language makes the story funny.*

RESEARCH

If necessary, give students some suggestions of humorists to research. Jerry Seinfeld, Jim Gaffigan, Ellen DeGeneres, and Mike Birbiglia are child-friendly stand-up comedians. Students may want to research a humorous children's author, such as Jeff Kinney, Mo Willems, or Barbara Park.

Extend Students might want to begin their research at John Scieszka's official website, jsworldwide.com.

 RESPOND

ANALYZE THE TEXT

Support your responses with evidence from the text. 📓 NOTEBOOK

1. **Evaluate** Review paragraphs 10–14. How would you describe the voice of the narrator? Cite evidence from the text to support your description.

2. **Analyze** How does the text structure contribute to the author's purpose? Support your reasoning with evidence from the text.

3. **Evaluate** Review paragraphs 13–23. What was Mr. Scieszka feeling as he repeated the joke in front of the class? Cite examples of the language the author uses to convey his experience.

4. **Draw Conclusions** Is the author usually someone who seeks attention or who likes to perform? Cite evidence from the text to support your answer.

5. **Notice & Note** Find examples of extreme or absolute language in "What's So Funny, Mr. Scieszka?" Explain how this language contributes to the mood and voice of the story.

RESEARCH

RESEARCH TIP
The best search terms are very specific. Along with the humorist's name, include the books, TV shows, or movies with which he or she is associated.

Conduct research into your favorite childhood humorist. Identify what inspired that person to become a humorist, and why that person considers humor important. What does your research reveal about his or her purpose? Record what you learn in the chart.

NAME OF HUMORIST: Jerry Seinfeld	
Inspiration for Becoming a Humorist	He was inspired by his father, who was funny.
Why Humor Is Important	Making people laugh makes the world "a tiny bit better."
Humorist's Purpose	He makes funny observations about everyday life.

Extend Conduct research on Jon Scieszka, the author of "What's So Funny, Mr. Scieszka?" Find out more about what inspired him to become a humorist and why he thinks humor is important. What else has he written or produced? Share the results of your research with a partner.

⚙️ **LEARNING MINDSET**

Belonging Ask students to share and celebrate a mistake they made while answering the Analyze the Text questions. Remind students that we all make mistakes and can learn from each other. You might say, "I make mistakes. Let's learn from each other." Then, model how to reflect on the mistake and learn from it.

CREATE AND PRESENT

Analyze Author's Purpose and Message Review your notes and annotations from the reading. Then, write a three- to four-paragraph analysis of Scieszka's purpose. Why does he tell this story? What is his purpose and message? Follow these steps:

❏ Include a controlling idea or thesis about the author's purpose.

❏ Provide text evidence to support your ideas.

❏ Make pronouns clearly identify and agree with their antecedents.

Explain the Steps for Telling a Joke Discuss with a small group what you know about how to deliver a silly joke to someone much younger than you.

❏ Select a joke that is appropriate for a younger audience. Remember to consider suggestions from all group members.

❏ Outline the steps for telling the joke successfully to a younger audience. Include how you say the joke, what facial expressions and gestures to use, what tone of voice to use, when to pause, and how often to make eye contact.

❏ Deliver your joke to the class, following the steps in your outline. After you tell the joke, explain the steps in your outline.

 RESPOND

 Go to **Writing Informative Texts** in the **Writing Studio** for more on writing an analysis.

Go to **Participating in Collaborative Discussions** in the **Speaking and Listening Studio** for help with having a group discussion.

RESPOND TO THE ESSENTIAL QUESTION

 What are the ways you can make yourself heard?

Gather Information Review your annotations and notes on "What's So Funny, Mr. Scieszka?" Then, add relevant details to your Response Log. As you determine which information to include, think about:

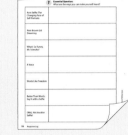

• the kinds of choices people make in life
• what happens when people must make quick decisions
• how humor can help people cope with challenging situations

At the end of the unit, use your notes to write a multimodal argument.

ACADEMIC VOCABULARY

As you discuss what you learned from the text, be sure to use the Academic Vocabulary words. Check off each of the words that you use.

❏ **appropriate**

❏ **authority**

❏ **consequence**

❏ **element**

❏ **justify**

CREATE AND PRESENT

Analyze Author's Purpose and Message Point out that students should outline their essays before writing, starting first with a thesis statement. Then they should list evidence for their thesis. Remind them that pronouns should agree with their antecedents—that is, nobody should be guessing what or who *it* or *she* refers to.

 For **writing support** for students at varying proficiency levels, see the **Text X-Ray** on page 276D.

Explain the Steps for Telling a Joke Remind student groups that everybody in the group must agree on the joke being told, and that the joke must be appropriate for a younger child. Tell students that everyone in the group needs to agree on the steps and write them down in their outlines. Have students practice telling their jokes before presenting them to the class.

RESPOND TO THE ESSENTIAL QUESTION

Allow time for students to add details from "What's So Funny, Mr. Scieszka?" to their Unit 4 Response Logs.

 ENGLISH LEARNER SUPPORT

Use Recordings to Self-Correct Encourage students to record themselves telling the joke and explaining the steps of the outline. Then have students play the recording back with a partner who will help them listen for places to clarify and correct their pronunciation or any mistakes in word choice. Once students have received feedback from their partner, have them record and listen to themselves again, working to incorporate the feedback and give a more polished and correct presentation. **MODERATE**

APPLY

CRITICAL VOCABULARY

Answers:

1. *terror—terror is an expression of extreme fright. They waited in terror as the hurricane raged outside their building.*

2. *pause—to pause is to wait a moment before going forward with something. I paused the movie by pushing a button on the remote.*

3. *history—History is a record of the past. The man's history was full of good deeds.*

4. *apology—an apology is an expression of regret. He accepted her apology for telling a lie.*

VOCABULARY STRATEGY:
Resources

Answers:

Word	Origin/ Meaning	Greek or Latin Root	Related Words from Same Root
apology	a thoughtful reply or response (as a defending speech in court)	from Greek *apologiā, apo-* (off) + *logo* (speech)	apologist apologize apological
history	an account of one's inquiries	from Greek *historia,* a learning or inquiry from *histōr* learned man	historic historical historian
terror	great fear, dread, panic, cause for alarm	from Latin *terror, terrēre*	terrorist terrorize terrible
pause	interruption, stopping, or ceasing	from Latin *pausa* from Greek *pausis*	pausing paused

 RESPOND

CRITICAL VOCABULARY

WORD BANK
apology
history
terror
pause

Practice and Apply With a partner, discuss and write down an answer to each of the following questions. Then work together to write a sentence for each vocabulary word.

1. Which vocabulary word goes with *fright?* Why?

2. Which vocabulary word goes with *wait?* Why?

3. Which vocabulary word goes with *the past?* Why?

4. Which vocabulary word goes with *regret?* Why?

VOCABULARY STRATEGY:
Resources

Go to **Using Reference Resources** in the **Vocabulary Studio** for more on how to determine origins and sources of meanings.

You can often determine the meaning of an unfamiliar word by examining its root. A **root** is a word part that contains the core meaning of the word. For example, *tech* comes from a Greek root that can mean "art," "skill," or "craft." You can find this root in the word *technician;* you can use the root to figure out that *technician* refers to someone who has a specific skill.

Practice and Apply Using dictionaries and online resources, determine the origin and source of meaning for each Critical Vocabulary word. Then build related words from each word, emphasizing the role of the Greek or Latin root.

WORD	ORIGIN/MEANING	ROOT	RELATED WORDS FROM SAME ROOT
apology	a thoughtful reply or response (as a defending speech in court)	from *apologiā* apo- (off) + logo (speech)	apologist apologize apologetic
history			
terror			
pause			

ENGLISH LEARNER SUPPORT

Practice Pronunciation Spanish, Vietnamese, Hmong, and Haitian Creole speakers may struggle to pronounce the sound the letters *au* make in *pause.* Pair more proficient speakers with struggling partners and have the more proficient speaker model how to pronounce first just the sound and then the word: *au, pause.* Ask the struggling partner to repeat the sound and word until he or she has mastered the pronunciation of the sound and word. To extend the practice, have the proficient speaker model how to pronounce other words such as *pausing, paused,* and *pauses,* with the struggling student again repeating each word until he or she has mastered its pronunciation. **ALL LEVELS**

LANGUAGE CONVENTIONS: Pronouns

A **pronoun** is a word used in place of a noun or another pronoun. The word or group that the pronoun refers to is its **antecedent.**

Personal, indefinite, and relative pronouns are three common types of pronouns. **Personal pronouns** may replace nouns representing people. **Indefinite pronouns** refer to one or more persons or things not specifically mentioned and usually have no antecedents. **Relative pronouns** relate, or connect, adjective clauses to the words they modify in sentences. Look at these examples:

PERSONAL	INDEFINITE	RELATIVE
I, you, we, they, me, ours, she, it, my, us	another, anybody, both, all, none, most, no one	who, which, that, whose, whom
Maria is tall; she is taller than I am.	No one is taking the bus today.	The author, who wrote my favorite book, will speak here next week.

Pronoun-Antecedent Agreement To make sure a personal pronoun agrees with its antecedent, ask yourself: "Which noun is this pronoun replacing?" Read the following two sentences. Which one is correct?

• The little girl fed the cat; she was kind to animals.

• The little girl fed the cat; they were kind to animals.

The first sentence is correct. The noun being replaced is *girl.* The personal pronoun *she* agrees with the antecedent because it is singular and feminine. In the second sentence, *they* is plural and does not agree with the antecedent.

Practice and Apply Write two humorous sentences for each type of pronoun—personal, indefinite, and relative. Don't use the same pronoun twice.

! Go to the **Grammar Studio** for more on pronouns.

LANGUAGE CONVENTIONS:
Pronouns

Review the information about pronouns. Make sure students understand the concept of *antecedents* and the idea that antecedents and pronouns should agree. Further, emphasize that students should make sure that antecedents are clear when they use pronouns in their writing. For example, in the sentence *After putting the hat with the scarf, Mrs. Johnson lost it,* it is unclear what antecedent the pronoun *it* refers to—the hat or the scarf. A clearer sentence would be: *Mrs. Johnson lost the hat after she put it with the scarf.*

Practice and Apply Have students write humorous sentences for the Practice and Apply activity. Remind them not to use the same pronoun twice. Invite volunteers to share their sentences. Suggest that students write their sentences on a Pronoun Poster to display in the classroom.

 ENGLISH LEARNER SUPPORT

Write with Pronouns Hmong, Spanish, and Vietnamese speakers are used to a language in which speakers mention a topic and then make a comment on it, which may lead them incorrectly to use both a noun and a pronoun at the same time. Use the following supports with students at varying proficiency levels.

• Write an incorrect sentence: *The joke it is very funny.* Have students use the Language Conventions chart to help them identify the pronoun—*it.* Cover up *The joke,* and have students read the sentence. Then cover up

the pronoun, and have students read the sentence again. Emphasize that the pronoun is taking the place of the noun. **SUBSTANTIAL**

• Write an incorrect sentence: *The joke it is very funny.* Have students identify the pronoun and explain what part of the sentence should be crossed out because the pronoun is actually replacing it. **MODERATE**

• Have students work with partners to edit incorrect sentences such as *The joke it is very funny.* Suggest students circle the pronoun and cross out the part of the sentence it is replacing. **LIGHT**

A VOICE
Poem by Pat Mora

WORDS LIKE FREEDOM
Poem by Langston Hughes

GENRE ELEMENTS
POETRY

Remind students that the function of **poetry** is to rouse emotion in the reader. The poet achieves this purpose through the use of sound devices, imagery, and figurative language—such as simile, metaphor, and personification—to express ideas and feelings. Many poems also use rhyme and rhythm to add a musical quality to the language. Poets also arrange words and lines in different ways to produce their intended effect and get their message across.

LEARNING OBJECTIVES

- Analyze figurative language in poetry.
- Make inferences based on tone and speaker.
- Research the Harlem Renaissance.
- Write an essay based on inferences drawn from speaker and tone.
- Discuss and analyze figurative language.
- Make inferences and use evidence to describe speakers.
- **Language** Discuss with a partner the features of the text using the key term *figurative language*.

TEXT COMPLEXITY

Quantitative Measures	A Voice	Lexile: N/A	Words Like Freedom	Lexile: N/A
Qualitative Measure	**Ideas Presented** In both poems, much is explicit but there are multiple levels of meaning.			
	Structure Used Both poems use traditional poetic structure.			
	Language Used Both poems use figurative language; more inference is demanded.			
	Knowledge Required The situation and ideas in both poems may be unfamiliar to some students.			

RESOURCES

Online *Ed*

- Unit 4 Response Log
- 🔊 Selection Audio
- **Text in FOCUS** Interpreting Figurative Language
- 📖 Reading Studio: Notice & Note
- **LEVEL UP** Level Up Tutorials: Figurative Language; Elements of Poetry
- Writing Studio: Writing Informative Texts
- 💬 Speaking and Listening Studio: Participating in Collaborative Discussions
- ✅ "A Voice"/"Words Like Freedom" Selection Test

SUMMARIES

English

In "A Voice," the speaker tells the story of her mother, a daughter of Mexican immigrants, trying to make her voice heard despite her fear.

In "Words Like Freedom," the poet voices his thoughts and feelings about the concepts of freedom and liberty from his perspective as an African American.

Spanish

En "Una voz", la voz poética cuenta la historia de su madre, hija de inmigrantes mexicanos, que intenta hacer escuchar su voz a pesar del miedo.

En "Palabras como libertad", la voz poética expresa sus pensamientos y sentimientos acerca del concepto de la libertad desde la perspectiva de un afroamericano

 ## SMALL-GROUP OPTIONS

Have students work in small groups to read and discuss the selections.

Poetry Jigsaw

- Divide students into small groups or pairs, and assign each a stanza of one of the poems.
- Students should discuss and take notes on the stanza's use of sound devices, imagery, simile, metaphor, and personification.
- Students should also discuss the rhythm of their stanza and the effect of line length on the stanza's tone.
- Each group should create and present a visual aid sharing their group's ideas, as well as the meaning of their assigned stanza.

Think-Pair-Share

- Pause at any point during the reading and pose a question to students that requires higher-order thinking.
- First have students think about the answer to the question on their own, and jot down a few notes.
- Then have students work with partners to share their ideas.
- Finally, have pairs share their ideas with the class.
- You may wish to have students note ideas on a poster that can be displayed in the classroom.

Text X-Ray: English Learner Support
for "A Voice" and "Words Like Freedom"

Use the Text X-Ray and the supports and scaffolds in the Teacher's Edition to help guide students at different proficiency levels through the selection.

INTRODUCE THE SELECTION
DISCUSS POETIC DEVICES

In this lesson, students will need to be able to analyze two poems in order to examine how people make their voices heard. To help English learners comprehend the poetic language necessary to understand and explain the theme, review the following terms and their definitions: *imagery* (the use of descriptive language to create pictures that appeal to the senses), *figurative language* (language that means something other than the literal definition of the words), *simile* (a comparison of two unlike things using *like* or *as*), *metaphor* (a comparison of two things that are basically unlike), and *personification* (giving an object, idea, or animal human qualities). Have students think of themselves as poets and brainstorm and discuss writing situations when they might use each of these types of poetic language.

CULTURAL REFERENCES

The following words and phrases may be unfamiliar to students:

- *flatbed truck* ("A Voice," line 10): a large truck with a back, or "bed," that is open—it does not have a roof or sides; in the poem, the speaker says her grandfather came to America on a truck like this.
- *state capitol* ("A Voice," line 26): a building where the state government meets
- *heartstrings* ("Words Like Freedom," line 3): a noun that refers to a person's deepest feelings or emotions
- *Liberty* ("Words Like Freedom," line 5): another word for *freedom*

LISTENING

Understand Characters

Help students explore the feelings and motivations of a character in a poem by having them listen to a passage and demonstrate comprehension. Review that the speaker of the poem is telling about how her mother felt as she is standing on a stage to give a speech.

Have students listen as you read aloud lines 1–10 from "A Voice." Use the following supports with students at varying proficiency levels:

- Tell students that you will ask questions about what you just read aloud. For example, ask: *Does the speaker's mother feel afraid when she gives her speech?* (yes) **SUBSTANTIAL**
- Have students demonstrate listening comprehension by completing the following sentence frames: *The speaker's mother is giving _____. (a speech) She feels afraid because she does not _____ as well as _____. (speak English; the other students)* **MODERATE**
- Ask students: *What is happening in this passage? (The mother is giving a speech.) Why does she feel so nervous? (She doesn't speak English as well as her classmates.)* **LIGHT**

SPEAKING

Discuss Figurative Language

Before discussion, review the term *figurative language* as well as examples of figurative language: *simile, metaphor,* and *personification.* During discussion, circulate around the room to make sure students are using the terms correctly.

Use the following supports with students at varying proficiency levels:

- Write the following sentences on the board, and help students practice reading them aloud several times: *A simile compares two things using* like *or* as. *The simile "he walked slow as a hot river" compares the way a man walks to the way a hot river moves.* **SUBSTANTIAL**
- Have students complete the sentence frames: *A simile compares two things using _____ or _____. The simile "he walked slow as a hot river" compares _____ with _____.* Repeat for *metaphor* and *personification,* using similar sentence frames and examples of these types of figurative language from the poems. **MODERATE**
- Pair students to discuss the definitions of *figurative language, simile, metaphor,* and *personification.* **LIGHT**

READING

Make Inferences

Remind students that an inference is not something that is stated in the text, but something a reader has to figure out based on clues. Students should pay close attention to word choice and events in order to make inferences.

Work with students to read lines 25–39 in "A Voice." Use the following supports with students at varying proficiency levels:

- Have students echo-read lines 34–36. Ask: *Who did the mother teach to speak up?* (her children) **SUBSTANTIAL**
- Have students complete the sentence frames to practice using clues to make inferences: *When the speaker's mother was supposed to give a speech, she _____. The speaker's mother finally made her voice heard when her children _____.* **MODERATE**
- Have partners infer what happened when the mother was asked to give a speech and how the mother's voice was finally heard. Ask them to identify three text clues that helped them. **LIGHT**

WRITING

Write an Informational Essay

Work with students to read the writing assignment on page 297. Then provide students with a graphic organizer with three small boxes to record details about their speaker and one large box for their main idea.

Use the following supports with students at varying proficiency levels:

- Provide students with a list of terms that can be used to describe poetry, such as *tone, speaker,* and *characterize.* Have partners take turns reading each word aloud and spelling it correctly. **SUBSTANTIAL**
- Help students use the details from the three smaller graphic organizer boxes to craft a thesis statement to put in the large box. Provide students with the following sentence frame: *In the poem _____, the speaker is _____.* Then help them write a paragraph that includes their ideas. **MODERATE**
- Pair students to write a paragraph together. They should start by filling in the graphic organizer with evidence and then using this evidence to write a clear thesis that you approve. Then have them create an essay together based on their notes. **LIGHT**

Connect to the
ESSENTIAL QUESTION

The two poems in this lesson explore how people make themselves heard. The first poem, "A Voice," is about a woman struggling to make herself heard because of a language barrier. In the second poem, "Words Like Freedom," the author uses poetry to make his message about injustice heard.

COMPARE POEMS

Point out that both "A Voice" and "Words Like Freedom" feature first-person speakers expressing their thoughts and feelings about subjects that are personally important to them. Ask students to pay attention to the details and word choices that reveal the different personalities of the speakers and the varying ways the authors use figurative language to express ideas. What does each speaker care most about? What is similar about what both speakers value?

POEM
A VOICE
by **Pat Mora**
pages 291–293

COMPARE POEMS

As you read, notice the use of figurative language and identify details that help you understand each poem's speaker and tone. After you read both poems, you will collaborate with a small group on a final project.

ESSENTIAL QUESTION:

What are the ways you can make yourself heard?

POEM
WORDS LIKE FREEDOM
by **Langston Hughes**
pages 294–295

288   Unit 4

 LEARNING MINDSET

Seeking Challenges Remind students that having the willingness to take on challenges is essential to having a learning mindset. In fact, overcoming challenges is key to developing skills and intelligence. Assure students that they are not expected to be perfect and that making mistakes is part of the learning process. This lesson will present new challenges in terms of making inferences and analyzing poetry. Remind students to see the challenges as opportunities for growth as learners and point out that by taking risks and trying new strategies, students can learn to overcome challenges.

QUICK START

Make a list of what you think about when you hear the words *freedom* and *liberty*. Discuss your list with classmates.

ANALYZE FIGURATIVE LANGUAGE

Poets use **figurative language,** such as simile and metaphor, to express ideas in an imaginative way. A **simile** is a comparison of two unlike things using the words *like* or *as*. A **metaphor** is a comparison of two unlike things that have some qualities in common, but a metaphor does not use *like* or *as*. The poem "A Voice" opens with a simile:

> **Even the <u>lights on the stage</u> unrelenting as <u>the</u> <u>desert sun</u> couldn't hide the other students . . .**

The simile compares the stage lights to a desert sun, emphasizing how unforgiving and severe the lights seem. When analyzing simile and metaphor, ask yourself: What two things is the poet comparing? Why? What feelings and attitudes does the simile or metaphor help explain?

Personification is a type of figurative language in which an object, animal, or idea is given human qualities. Poets use personification to emphasize an idea or to create an emotional effect. The poem "Words Like Freedom" contains personification:

> **On my heartstrings <u>freedom</u> <u>sings</u>**

Here, the poet gives the abstract idea of freedom the human ability to sing. When analyzing personification, ask yourself: What nonhuman things are given human qualities? Why? What is the effect of the personification?

As you read "A Voice" and "Words Like Freedom," use a chart like the following to analyze each poet's use of figurative language.

EXAMPLE	TYPE OF FIGURATIVE LANGUAGE	WHAT IS THE POET TELLING ME?
Their eyes were pinpricks	metaphor	Their stares were painful.

GENRE ELEMENTS: POETRY

- uses sound devices, imagery, and figurative language, such as simile, metaphor, and personification, to express ideas and emotions
- includes rhyme or rhythm to emphasize the musical quality of language
- arranges words and lines in different ways to produce an effect

A Voice / Words Like Freedom **289**

QUICK START

Have students read the Quick Start prompt and write down what they think about when they hear the words *freedom* and *liberty.* Have students discuss their lists with classmates, and ask students whether they think liberty and freedom are the same or two separate concepts.

ANALYZE FIGURATIVE LANGUAGE

Remind students that figurative language is language that means something besides the literal, or dictionary, meaning of the words. Figurative language is an important feature of poetry, and students will need to analyze figurative language in order to comprehend the two poems in this lesson.

After reading the information about figurative language, ask volunteers to clarify the difference between *similes* and *metaphors*. Then ask students to share original examples of each. Write down the examples, and have students clarify the two (or more) items being compared. Remind students that knowing what is being compared is key to understanding similes and metaphors.

Next, ask students to state the definition of *personification* in their own words. Emphasize that while stories with talking animals are the most obvious examples of personification, often it is non-living objects that are given human qualities. Such is the case in the example given in the student book, in which the concept of freedom is given the ability to sing. Invite students to share their own examples of personification, encouraging them to use ideas, concepts, or objects in their comparisons.

 ENGLISH LEARNER SUPPORT

Use Supportive Charts Create a three-column chart titled "Figurative Language," with columns headed "Simile," "Metaphor," and "Personification." Write a brief definition of each term as part of the heading. Work with students to find examples of similes, metaphors, and personification from the poems and write them on index cards. Have students sort the cards and tape them under the correct heading. Then have students underline the two items being compared and explain what the comparison means. **MODERATE**

MAKE INFERENCES

Remind students that an inference is not stated directly in the text. An inference is a conclusion that the reader must draw from different clues in the text. Sometimes a reader has to infer that an event happened by using other events as clues. For example, if a poem starts at a funeral and a character says he is going to miss his grandfather, the reader can infer that the character's grandfather just died. Inferring events like this is easier than making inferences based on trickier concepts like imagery, word choice, and tone. Students will need to make these more challenging types of inferences while reading the poems in this lesson. Review the checklist so students feel more comfortable with the concepts they'll need to look for in order to make inferences from the poems.

ANNOTATION MODEL

Clarify for students that in the example annotation on page 290, the reader underlined figurative language that helped give a clue to an inference. The reader does not yet know why the poet used this simile, so he or she notes a question in the margin. Point out to students that they may follow this suggested format for annotation, or use their own system for marking up the selection in their write-in text. They may want to color-code their annotations by using highlighters. Their notes in the margin may include questions about ideas that are unclear or topics they want to learn more about.

 GET READY

MAKE INFERENCES

When you make an **inference** about a literary work, you use evidence from the text and your own knowledge and experience to make a logical guess. Readers can identify and put together clues, such as a poet's choice of words and images, to make inferences about a poem.

The **tone** of a literary work expresses the writer's voice and attitude toward his or her subject, helping to communicate **mood.** Words such as *angry*, *playful*, or *mocking* can be used to describe different tones. Writers establish tone through images and descriptions. Tone is very closely linked to the **speaker** in a poem. The speaker is the voice that "talks" to the reader.

Read these lines from "A Voice":

> **In your house that smelled like**
> **rose powder, you spoke Spanish formal . . .**

These lines provide a clue about the home of the person in the poem. From this, readers can infer that the poem's speaker has a deep understanding of this person's home life. The speaker's tone can be described here as *understanding* or *intimate*. The following checklist will help you make inferences about speaker and tone:

- ❏ Identify the topic of the poem.
- ❏ Pay attention to images and descriptions. Are they serious, silly, happy, or sad?
- ❏ Decide how the speaker feels about the topic. Does he or she feel happy, sad, proud, or angry?

ANNOTATION MODEL

NOTICE & NOTE

As you read, note inferences about the poem and the speaker of the poem. In the model, you can see one reader's notes about the first stanza of "A Voice."

1 <u>Even the lights on the stage unrelenting</u> <u>as the desert sun</u> couldn't hide the other students, their eyes also unrelenting,	*Interesting! The speaker compares lights on a stage to the desert sun. I wonder why.*

BACKGROUND

Pat Mora *(b. 1942) was born in El Paso, Texas, to a Mexican-American family that spoke both English and Spanish. Mora grew up speaking both languages, and today she writes in English and in Spanish. When not writing, Mora spends much of her time encouraging children of all languages to read books. In 1996, she founded a holiday called "El día de los niños/El día de los libros," or "Children's Day/Book Day."*

A VOICE
by Pat Mora

PREPARE TO COMPARE

As you read, note how figurative language and tone help you understand the special relationship between the poem's speaker and her Mexican-American mother.

1   Even the lights on the stage unrelenting[1]
     as the desert sun couldn't hide the other
     students, their eyes also unrelenting,
     <u>students who spoke English every night</u>

5   as they ate their meat, potatoes, gravy.
     <u>Not you.</u> In your house that smelled like
     rose powder, <u>you spoke Spanish formal</u>
     as your father, the judge without a courtroom

     in the country he floated to in the dark
10   on a flatbed truck. He walked slow
     as a hot river down the narrow hall
     of your house. You never dared to race past him,

---

1   **unrelenting** (ŭn´rĭ-lĕn´tĭng): steady and persistent; continuing on without stopping.

Notice & Note

Use the side margins to notice and note signposts in the text.

MAKE INFERENCES

Annotate: In lines 1–8, mark the differences between the students who spoke English and the person in the poem referred to as "you."

Compare: What does this comparison tell you about the speaker of the poem and her subject, "you"?

BACKGROUND

Have students read the Background note. Point out that the poet, Pat Mora, was born into a Mexican American family like the speaker of the poem. It is not clear whether Mora is telling her own mother's story in the poem, but the speaker tells a story about her mother that could easily be about Mora's own mother. In the poem, the speaker says her mother grew up in a house where only Spanish was spoken, so she didn't feel comfortable with her English skills and was afraid to speak in front of a large group.

PREPARE TO COMPARE

Direct students to use the Prepare to Compare prompt to focus their reading.

 MAKE INFERENCES

Tell students their annotations will help them make an inference about the character's background and why she feels and behaves the way she does. (**Answer:** *These comparisons show that the speaker sees her mother—referred to as "you" here—as different and apart from other students. Readers learn from the words "Not you" that the speaker's mother spoke formal Spanish at home and ate foods different from the "meat, potatoes, gravy" that other children ate. Students may infer that the speaker's mother and her family have immigrated to the United States from a Spanish-speaking country.*)

 For **listening** and **speaking support** for students at varying proficiency levels, see the **Text X-Ray** on pages 288C and 288D.

ENGLISH LEARNER SUPPORT

Draw Ideas and Concepts   Help English learners visualize the events in the poem. After reading each line out loud, pause to have students draw an image from the line. Have them write one English word or phrase next to each image. By adding something from each line, they will create a drawing representing the poem.   **SUBSTANTIAL/MODERATE**

MAKE INFERENCES

Have students annotate lines 13–16 to help them make an inference about the speaker's mother's background. (*Answer: The speaker seems proud of her mother, who easily and defiantly learned English. The speaker's mother seems smart and spirited—she learns English even though she is not allowed to speak it at home, and she speaks English "to fight with the neighbors.")*

TEXT IN FOCUS

Interpreting Figurative Language Have students view the **Text in Focus** video in their eBook to learn how to interpret figurative language in a poem. Then have students use the **Text in Focus Practice PDF** to apply what they have learned.

▶ MEMORY MOMENT

Remind students that a **Memory Moment** is when a character recalls or shares a memory that explains the present moment. (*Answer: During her experience at the state capitol, the speaker's mother felt out of place and she wanted to hide from "those strange faces" that were different from her and her family. This memory explains why the mother taught her children to speak up.)*

ANALYZE FIGURATIVE LANGUAGE

Remind students to look at what is being compared in order to interpret the meaning. (*Answer: The metaphor "Their eyes were pinpricks" emphasizes feeling scared and judged by the audience. The simile "felt your breath stick in your throat / like an ice-cube" describes the feeling of choking. These both show nervousness and anxiety.)*

 For **reading support** for students at varying proficiency levels, see the **Text X-Ray** on page 288D.

NOTICE & NOTE

MAKE INFERENCES

Annotate: In lines 13–16, mark how the speaker describes her subject's ability to learn English and how English is viewed in her home.

Evaluate: How does this description help you understand the speaker's tone?

MEMORY MOMENT

Notice & Note: What does the memory in lines 25–29 reveal? Mark the speaker's memory.

Infer: What does this memory help explain about the present moment?

ANALYZE FIGURATIVE LANGUAGE

Annotate: Mark the figurative language in lines 30–34.

Interpret: How do these comparisons express the emotions of the poem's subject?

---

to say, "Please move," in the language
you learned effortlessly, as you learned to run,
15 the language forbidden at home, though your mother
said you learned it to fight with the neighbors.

You liked winning with words. You liked
writing speeches about patriotism and democracy.
You liked all the faces looking at you, all those eyes.
20 "How did I do it?" you ask me now. "How did I do it

when my parents didn't understand?"
The family story says your voice is the voice
of an aunt in Mexico, spunky[2] as a peacock.
Family stories sing of what lives in the blood.

25 You told me only once about the time you went
to the state capitol, your family proud as if
you'd been named governor. But when you looked
around, the only Mexican in the auditorium,

you wanted to hide from those strange faces.
30 Their eyes were pinpricks,[3] and you faked
hoarseness. You, who are never at a loss
for words, felt your breath stick in your throat

like an ice-cube. "I can't," you whispered.
"I can't." Yet you did. Not that day but years later.
35 You taught the four of us to speak up.
This is America, Mom. The undo-able is done

in the next generation.[4] Your breath moves
through the family like the wind
39 moves through the trees.

---

[2] **spunky** (spŭng´kē): spirited, plucky; having energy and courage.
[3] **pinpricks** (pĭn´prĭkz´): small wounds or punctures made by, or as if by, a pin.
[4] **generation** (jĕn´ə-rā´shən): people at the same stage of descent from a common ancestor; grandparents, parents, and children represent three different generations.

WHEN STUDENTS STRUGGLE . . .

Genre Reformulation If students are struggling to comprehend the poem, work with them to rewrite the poem as a prose paragraph. Make sure they mention that the speaker is referring to her mother.

 For additional support, go to the **Reading Studio** and assign the following **Level Up Tutorial: Figurative Language.**

CHECK YOUR UNDERSTANDING

Answer these questions about "A Voice" before moving on to the next poem.

1 What language did the speaker's mother primarily use at home?

  A Spanish

  B English

  C an unknown language

  D an ancient language

2 Which of the following is an example of a simile?

  F *their eyes also unrelenting*

  G *He walked slow / as a hot river*

  H *country he floated to in the dark*

  J *You liked writing speeches*

3 "A Voice" makes the statement that —

  A learning a new language is difficult

  B family stories should only be spoken in native languages

  C people should memorize family stories

  D family stories communicate a family's history

CHECK YOUR UNDERSTANDING

Have students answer the questions independently.

Answers:

  1. *A*

  2. *G*

  3. *D*

If they answer any questions incorrectly, have them reread the text to confirm their understanding. Then they may proceed to the next poem on page 294.

EL ENGLISH LEARNER SUPPORT

Oral Assessment Use the following questions to assess students' comprehension and speaking skills:

  1. What language did the speaker's mother speak at home? (*The speaker's mother spoke Spanish at home.*)

  2. What does the speaker compare her father to in lines 10–11? (*She compares her father walking down the hall to a "hot river."*)

  3. "A Voice" helps you understand that a family's stories can tell you about the family's _____. (*past*)
  SUBSTANTIAL/MODERATE

BACKGROUND

Have students read the Background note. Explain to students that during the Harlem Renaissance, the new, growing African-American middle class also began advocating for racial equality. New York City became the epicenter of this movement. Three of the largest civil rights groups established their headquarters there, helping establish a sense of community for African Americans around the country.

PREPARE TO COMPARE

Direct students to use the Prepare to Compare prompt to focus their reading.

✎ ANALYZE FIGURATIVE LANGUAGE

Ask volunteers to identify the type of figurative language used in line 3. Students should be able to identify the language as personification. As needed, clarify for students that this is an example of an idea being given human qualities. (**Answer:** *The personification of freedom as a singer creates a joyful, emotional feeling.*)

✎ MAKE INFERENCES

Have students share how they think the tone changes from the first to the second stanza, and what this tells them about the speaker's feelings. (**Answer:** *In the first stanza, the speaker has a joyful tone, celebrating the meaning of freedom. In the second stanza, his tone changes to sadness. I think he is remembering all the people who have suffered fighting for liberty, and the costs of liberty seem very high to him. He may also be thinking about how people must fight for liberty again and again; it is a battle that never seems completely won.*)

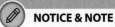 **NOTICE & NOTE**

BACKGROUND

Langston Hughes *(1902–1967) began writing poetry as a child, but he didn't gain fame until he met a famous poet in a restaurant where Hughes was working. Hughes left several of his poems at the poet's table; the poet was impressed and helped introduce Hughes to a wider audience. Hughes became one of the most important voices in the Harlem Renaissance. Much of his work focuses on the experiences of his fellow African Americans who lived around him in Harlem.*

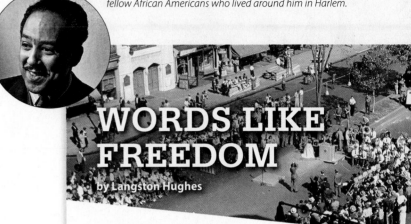

WORDS LIKE FREEDOM
by Langston Hughes

Notice & Note

Use the side margins to notice and note signposts in the text.

PREPARE TO COMPARE

As you read, note the poet's use of figurative language and identify details that help you make inferences about the speaker and that speaker's tone.

There are words like *Freedom*
Sweet and wonderful to say.
On my heartstrings freedom sings
All day everyday.

5 There are words like *Liberty*
That almost make me cry.
If you had known what I know
You would know why.

ANALYZE FIGURATIVE LANGUAGE

Annotate: Mark the figurative language the speaker uses to describe freedom in line 3.

Analyze: What emotional effect does this figurative language create?

MAKE INFERENCES

Annotate: In line 6, mark the speaker's reaction to the word *liberty*.

Compare: How has the tone changed from the first to the second stanza? What does this change tell you about the speaker's feelings?

CHECK YOUR UNDERSTANDING

Answer these questions about "Words Like Freedom" before moving on to the **Analyze the Texts** section on the following page.

1 In "Words Like Freedom," which two feelings are expressed?

A courage and wonder

B happiness and pride

C sadness and frustration

D joy and sadness

2 Which line in "Words Like Freedom" suggests the speaker has experienced hardships?

F *All day everyday.*

G *There are words like* Liberty

H *If you had known what I know*

I *Sweet and wonderful to say.*

3 In the poem, the words *freedom* and *liberty* are italicized and capitalized to emphasize —

A the importance of these ideals

B the fact that they are proper nouns

C their place in the U.S. Constitution

D how often they are misunderstood

CHECK YOUR UNDERSTANDING

Have students answer the questions independently.

Answers:

1. *D*

2. *H*

3. *A*

If they answer any questions incorrectly, have them reread the text to confirm their understanding. Then they may proceed to ANALYZE THE TEXT on page 296.

 ENGLISH LEARNER SUPPORT

Oral Assessment   Use the following questions to assess students' comprehension and speaking skills:

1. What are two feelings that the poet in "Words Like Freedom" feels? (*Joy and sadness are two feelings that the poet in "Words Like Freedom" feels.*)

2. Which line in "Words Like Freedom" makes you think the speaker has faced hard times? (*The line "If you had known what I know" makes me think the speaker has faced hard times.*)

3. The poet writes the words *freedom* and *liberty* in italics. He starts them with a capital letter. Why does he treat these words differently than other words? (*The words are treated differently to show how important they are.*)
SUBSTANTIAL/MODERATE

ANALYZE THE TEXTS

Possible answers:

1. **DOK 2:** *The simile is "He walked slow / as a hot river down the narrow hall / of your house." The words "You never dared to race past him" help the reader infer that the speaker's mother has a sense of fear and respect for her father.*

2. **DOK 2:** *The speaker is proud of her mother and describes her mother as intelligent and brave. "You liked winning with words" (line 17) shows the deep understanding the speaker has for her mother.*

3. **DOK 4:** *The personification of "freedom sings" indicates that the speaker feels great love for and personal connection with freedom. The personification sets a tone of joyful love.*

4. **DOK 4:** *The tone of "Words Like Freedom" shifts from joyful love to sorrow. The poet shifts the tone of the poem to show how important freedom is and how great the price he and other African Americans have paid for their freedom.*

5. **DOK 4:** *The speaker's mother looks back on her childhood and wonders how she was capable of achieving so much on her own: "How did I do it / when my parents didn't understand?" The speaker's mother remembers the conflict between herself and her parents, and she finds it hard to acknowledge her own strength in meeting life's challenges.*

RESEARCH

Remind students that they have to research one artist from each art form: literature, painting, and music. If students struggle to find artists to research, you may want to provide a list of possible artists.

Extend Give students enough time to create quality presentations. Have them write down what they are going to say about the ideas their artist's work conveys.

RESPOND

ANALYZE THE TEXTS

Support your responses with evidence from the texts. NOTEBOOK

1. **Infer** Reread lines 7–14 of "A Voice," in which the speaker describes her grandfather. What is the simile in these lines? What inferences can you make about the relationship between the speaker's mother and her father?

2. **Interpret** Reread lines 17–18 of "A Voice." What do the lines tell you about the speaker's view of her mother and the overall tone of the poem? What word would you use to describe the mood?

3. **Analyze** Identify the figurative language in line 3 of "Words Like Freedom." What tone is expressed through this use of figurative language?

4. **Analyze** Describe how and why the tone changes through "Words Like Freedom." How would you describe the poem's mood?

5. **Notice & Note** Reread lines 20–24 of "A Voice." How does the speaker's memory about the family story connect to lines 35–39?

RESEARCH

RESEARCH TIP
General search terms such as "Harlem Renaissance artists" will bring up many artists to choose from. To find information on a specific artist, search using the artist's name.

The Harlem Renaissance was a movement in the 1920s and 1930s centered in Harlem in New York. African American poets, writers, artists, and musicians gathered in Harlem to create art and press for civil rights. Research three artists active during the Harlem Renaissance. Write a short description of the type of art they created and the message they wanted to express through their art.

ARTISTS OF THE HARLEM RENAISSANCE		
NAME	**ART FORM**	**DESCRIPTION/MESSAGE**
Zora Neale Hurston	literature	Wrote fiction, autobiography, and researched and adapted African-American folklore; wrote in black vernacular for her acclaimed novel Their Eyes Were Watching God.
Aaron Douglas	painting	Created murals and paintings about freedom of blacks in Africa, slavery in the United States, and liberation after the Civil War; illustrated covers for African-American publications.
Billie Holiday, Chick Webb, Louie Armstrong	music	Brought different social classes together in jazz clubs; music has elements of blues and gospel and includes brass and/or string instruments.

Extend Pick one individual you researched and share your favorite example of his or her artwork, music, or writing with a small group. Discuss the ideas the work conveys.

CREATE AND PRESENT

Characterize the Speaker Write a brief informational essay describing the speaker of one or both poems. Cite evidence from the poem or poems to support your description.

❏ Review what you've learned about tone and speaker.

❏ Develop a clear controlling idea or thesis statement.

❏ Make inferences about the speaker(s) based on textual evidence and your own experiences.

Discuss and Analyze Figurative Language With a group, use the checklist below to discuss and analyze figurative language in the poems.

❏ Review and share your notes and annotations.

❏ Identify each use of figurative language in "A Voice" and "Words Like Freedom."

❏ Identify what is being compared or given human characteristics, and analyze the effect of the figurative language.

❏ Explain what the figurative language suggests about each poem's speaker and ideas.

RESPOND TO THE ESSENTIAL QUESTION

 What are the ways you can make yourself heard?

Gather Information Review your annotations and notes on "A Voice" and "Words Like Freedom." Then, add relevant details to your Response Log. As you determine which information to include, think about:

- Why it is important to speak out
- How tone expresses feelings and attitudes about certain subjects
- How poetry can bring out strong emotions in readers

At the end of the unit, you will use your notes to write a multimodal argument.

 RESPOND

Go to the **Writing Studio** for more on writing informational texts.

Go to the **Speaking and Listening Studio** for help with having a group discussion.

ACADEMIC VOCABULARY
As you write and discuss what you learned from the poems, be sure to use the Academic Vocabulary words. Check off each of the words that you use.

❏ **appropriate**

❏ **authority**

❏ **consequence**

❏ **element**

❏ **justify**

CREATE AND PRESENT

Characterize the Speaker Before students write their essays, review with them who the speaker was in both poems. You should also review the tone of the poems. Remind students to make sure they have completed all components on the assignment checklist before turning in work.

For **writing support** for students at varying proficiency levels, see the **Text X-Ray** on page 288D.

Discuss and Analyze Figurative Language Remind students to take turns speaking and sharing ideas, and to be respectful of others' ideas.

RESPOND TO THE ESSENTIAL QUESTION

Allow time for students to add details from "A Voice" and "Words Like Freedom" to their Unit 4 Response Logs.

EL **ENGLISH LEARNER SUPPORT**

Discuss and Analyze Figurative Language Support students in a demonstration of their understanding of figurative language. Help students identify an example of figurative language in each poem, such as a simile in "A Voice" (lines 22–23) and personification in "Words like Freedom" (line 3). Students should circle what is being compared or given human characteristics. Have them create a pictorial representation for each use of figurative language. After students have finished, ask them to use single words or simple phrases to answer the questions, *How did the speaker feel? What was the poem about?*
MODERATE

MAKE CONNECTIONS TO SPEAKERS

Clarify with students who the speaker was in each poem. Remind them that when filling out the chart, the answers for the **Topic or Subject of the Poem** and the **Tone of the Poem** will not be obvious. Students will have to analyze figurative language and word choice to make inferences. Remind them to allow each member of the group to contribute.

ANALYZE THE TEXTS

Possible answers:

1. **DOK 3:** *A poet might choose to express different tones within the same poem to show his or her different, or even contradictory, feelings toward his or her subject matter.*

2. **DOK 4:** *Based on the background information provided with the selections, students may conclude that the speakers of each poem share the identity of the poet. Both poems may be autobiographical and express the experiences of Pat Mora and Langston Hughes. Emphasize to students that we can't know for sure whether the poet is really the speaker of the poem.*

3. **DOK 3:** *The poems share similar topics of life in the United States as a minority and how ideas of freedom and liberty affect these groups.*

4. **DOK 2:** *Both speakers suggest themes of exclusion, or being an outsider in the United States. In "A Voice," for example, the speaker describes how her mother felt uncertain and uncomfortable when she was the only Mexican American at the state capitol. In "Words Like Freedom," the speaker almost cries in response to the word liberty, indicating sadness, frustration, or conflicting emotions about what this word means to an African American.*

 RESPOND

Collaborate & Compare

A VOICE
Poem by Pat Mora

WORDS LIKE FREEDOM
Poem by Langston Hughes

MAKE CONNECTIONS TO SPEAKERS

The **speaker** in a poem is the voice that "talks" to the reader, similar to the narrator in fiction. The speaker of a poem may be the poet or a fictional character. You can use details in the text to draw conclusions about the speaker of a poem. As you review the poems to compare the speakers of "A Voice" and "Words Like Freedom," consider the following:

- who the speaker of the poem is

- how figurative language and word choice help you determine the tone(s) of the poem

- how tone helps you understand the attitude of the speaker or the poet toward the subject

With your group, complete the chart.

	SPEAKER	TOPIC OR SUBJECT OF THE POEM	TONE OF THE POEM
A Voice	A woman who is speaking to her Mexican-American mother	Immigration; Life in a Mexican-American family. Speaking Out; Ideas of "patriotism and democracy"	Proud Happy Understanding
Words Like Freedom	An African-American person	Ideas of freedom and liberty and the African-American experience	Joyful Sad

ANALYZE THE TEXTS

Discuss these questions in your group.

1. **Evaluate** Why might a poet choose to convey multiple tones within the same poem? Explain.

2. **Synthesize** Is the speaker in each poem the same person as the poet? Explain.

3. **Compare** Do these poems share the same topic or subject matter? Explain your reasoning.

4. **Infer** Based on your analysis of the poems' speakers, what themes, or messages about life, are the speakers trying to convey? Cite text evidence in your discussion.

 ENGLISH LEARNER SUPPORT

Share Information Support English learners in sharing information in a cooperative interaction where small groups work together to complete frames to help them compare the speakers. Remind groups to share what they know with the group to complete each frame.

- In "A Voice," the speaker is ___ who thinks ___.
- In "Words Like Freedom," the speaker is ___ who thinks ___.
- The tone of "A Voice" tells you the speaker feels ___ of her mother.
- The tone of "Words Like Freedom" tells you the speaker feels ___ about freedom.

MODERATE

DISCUSS CONNECTIONS TO SPEAKERS

Compare the poems' speakers and discuss your own reactions and connections to the speakers. Follow these steps.

1. **Discuss and identify similarities.** With your group, review your work and identify the speakers' shared thoughts or attitudes. Find points you agree on, and resolve disagreements through discussion based on evidence from the poems.

2. **Record the similarities.** Fill in the chart below to record similarities, and provide evidence from the poems.

3. **Connect.** Make connections and discuss how your thoughts, experiences, and attitudes are similar to and different from the thoughts, experiences, and attitudes of the speakers in the poems.

SPEAKERS' SIMILARITIES	EVIDENCE FROM THE POEMS	HOW I AM SIMILAR AND DIFFERENT
Sample answer: Both value the freedoms and liberties that we are allowed as Americans	*The speaker in "A Voice" is proud of her mother's strong voice and her love of "winning with words." In "Words Like Freedom," the speaker is filled with joy at the idea of "freedom."*	*Student answers will vary.*

RESPOND

 Go to the **Speaking and Listening Studio** for help with group discussions.

GROUP WORK CHECKLIST
- ☐ Listen actively.
- ☐ Ask specific questions.
- ☐ Respond respectfully.
- ☐ Consider group members' suggestions.
- ☐ Take notes about important points.

DISCUSS CONNECTIONS TO SPEAKERS

Reinforce with students that in this activity they will be making inferences and citing evidence, then making connections between the poems and their own lives.

Provide the following guidelines to help group work run smoothly:

- Allow all students in the group to share their ideas about the speakers' shared thoughts or attitudes. One group member should take notes on each person's responses, so there is a record of everyone's ideas. Students need to pick three ideas from this record to put in the "Speakers' Similarities" column. If multiple students shared the same idea, that idea is an obvious choice for the chart. If group members can't agree on what to put in the chart, encourage students to come to an agreement based on the preferences of the majority. They may also be able to synthesize multiple ideas into one entry on the chart.

- Next, students should all look for evidence from the poem and share it with the group. Everyone in the group should agree on the same entries for the "Evidence from the Poems" column.

- Students can record entries in the "How I Am Similar and Different" column individually, and then come back together as a group to take turns sharing their answers.

WHEN STUDENTS STRUGGLE...

Venn Diagram If students are struggling to compare the poems, work with them to create a group Venn diagram on a poster. Label one circle "A Voice" and the other "Words Like Freedom." Review with students different aspects of the poems, such as speaker, tone, subject, and message. Have volunteers suggest answers and discuss whether they are common to both poems or different. Encourage students to use evidence from the text to support their answers.

 For additional support, go to the **Reading Studio** and assign the following **Level Up Tutorial: Elements of Poetry.**

MENTOR TEXT

BETTER THAN WORDS/ OMG, NOT *ANOTHER* SELFIE!

Arguments by Gloria Chang and Shermakaye Bass

The argument "OMG, Not *Another* Selfie!" serves as a **mentor text**, a model for students to follow when they come to the Unit 4 Writing Task: Create a Multimodal Argument.

GENRE ELEMENTS
ARGUMENT

An **argument** is a form of persuasive writing in which a writer makes a claim, or states a position on a central idea, he or she wants the audience to agree with. A claim expresses the writer's position on a problem or issue. The strength of an argument relies on the reasons and evidence used to prove the claim. A successful argument:

- contains an engaging introduction that establishes the claim
- supports key points with reasons and relevant evidence from reliable sources
- uses language that effectively conveys ideas and interest
- concludes by forcefully summing up the claim.

LEARNING OBJECTIVES

- Analyze the the structure of an argument and the use of rhetorical devices.
- Identify the intended audience of an argument.
- Conduct research about photographic self-portraits.
- Write an argument about cell phone usage.
- Discuss the "perfect selfie."
- Determine the meaning of unfamiliar words using context clues.
- Distinguish between commonly confused words.
- **Language** Discuss arguments with a partner using the term *audience*.

TEXT COMPLEXITY

Quantitative Measures	**Better Than Words**	Lexile: 1050	**OMG, Not *Another* Selfie!**	Lexile: 1070
Qualitative Measures	**Ideas Presented** Mostly explicit; some abstract, require inferential reasoning.			
	Structure Used Conventional argument with claim, evidence, and conclusion; subheadings.			
	Language Used Mostly explicit, complex language; some rhetorical devices and logical fallacies.			
	Knowledge Required Familiarity with technology.			

Online

RESOURCES

- Unit 4 Response Log

- Selection Audio

- Close Read Screencasts: Modeled Discussions

- Reading Studio: Notice & Note

- Level Up Tutorial: Making Predictions

- Writing Studio: Writing an Argument

- Speaking and Listening Studio: Giving a Presentation

- Vocabulary Studio: Using Context Clues

- Grammar Studio: Module 14: Spelling

- ☑ "Better Than Words" / "OMG, Not Another Selfie!" Selection Test

SUMMARIES

English

In "Better Than Words: Say It with a Selfie," the author argues that selfies have positive effects including helping the user engage in self-discovery and self-expression, as well as improve self-confidence.

In "OMG, Not Another Selfie!" the author claims that selfies are self-indulgent and that the practice of taking such pictures can cause emotional problems.

Spanish

En "Mejor que palabras: Dilo con un selfi", el autor argumenta que los selfis tienen efectos positivos, como por ejemplo, que sirven para ejercer el autoconocimiento y la autoexpresión, así como para mejorar la autoestima.

En "¡OMG, no otro selfi!", el autor afirma que los selfis son autoindulgentes y que su práctica puede causar problemas emocionales.

👥 SMALL-GROUP OPTIONS

Have students work in small groups to read and discuss the selection.

PINWHEEL DISCUSSION

- Organize students into groups of eight.
- Have four students sit in a circle facing out. Have the other four students form a circle around the inner circle and sit facing in.
- Ask a question about selfies, such as: *Why do people send selfies?*
- Have students in the inner circle remain in the same spot throughout the discussion.
- Have students in the other circle move to their right after discussion of each question.
- Ask a new question for each rotation.

SEND A PROBELM

- Pose a question about the selection, and call on a student. Possible questions: *What is the main point of disagreement between the two selections? What was the most persuasive point of each argument?*
- Wait up to 11 seconds. If the student does not have a response, have that student repeat the question and call on another student by name to answer the same question.
- Monitor responses and redirect or ask another question as appropriate.

Text X-Ray: English Learner Support

for "Better Than Words: Say It with a Selfie" and "OMG, Not *Another* Selfie!"

Use the Text X-Ray and the supports and scaffolds in the Teacher's Edition to help guide students at different proficiency levels through the selections.

INTRODUCE THE SELECTIONS
DISCUSS SELFIES AND SOCIAL MEDIA

Tell students that to express something is to demonstrate or show it, and explain that *self-expression* is the act of showing other people things about your "self"—such as your feelings, thoughts, ideas, and overall personality. Point out the relationship between the words *selfie* and *self-expression,* and discuss how a selfie is a photograph a person takes to show something about him or herself to other people. Note that selfies are now one of the most common forms of self-expression, especially because they can be electronically shared with others so easily through texting and the Internet. A selfie lets a person control how they want the world to see them, so many people spend a lot of time photographing themselves in certain ways.

Ask students to discuss personal experiences with self-expression and selfies, using frames such as: *A selfie lets me express _____. I only share selfies that _____. I can tell _____ about someone from a selfie. Self-expression is important because _____.*

CULTURAL REFERENCES

The following words and phrases may be unfamiliar to students:

- *social media platforms* ("Better Than," paragraph 1): technologies that use the Internet to let people share images, videos, text, and sounds
- *self-portrait* ("Better Than," paragraph 2): a portrait painting of an artist made by the artist
- *OMG* (title): short for "Oh my god," used as an expression of surprise, especially on social media
- *craze* ("OMG," paragraph 2): a very popular thing to do

LISTENING

Understand Repetition

Review the definition of *repetition*. Explain that knowing what this rhetorical device is and being able to identify when an author is using it can help students better understand arguments.

Have students listen as you read aloud the first sentence from paragraph 6 from "OMG." Use the following supports with students at varying proficiency levels:

- Before you read, ask students to listen for certain words that will be repeated over and over: *reposting, re-snapping,* and *on*. Then reread the sentence and ask students to raise a hand every time they hear one of these words. Ask: *What device is the author using here?* (repetition) **SUBSTANTIAL**
- Ask students to identify the words that are repeated over and over. (*reposting, re-snapping, on*) Provide students with a frame to complete to identify the point the author is making with this use of repetition: *When people are reposting and re-snapping pictures on and on, they start to feel ____.* **MODERATE**
- Ask pairs to identify an example of repetition in this sentence and then describe the point the author is making with this repetition. **LIGHT**

SPEAKING

Discuss an Audience

Review how the audience for an argument is the person or group of people to whom an author is writing. Note that the reader can use clues to figure out who this audience is. Remind students to use the term *audience*.

Use the following supports with students at varying proficiency levels:

- Define the term *audience* orally and read aloud this article title: "The Dangers of the Selfie and How You Can Help Your Kids." Ask: *Are parents the audience for this essay?* **SUBSTANTIAL**
- Read aloud this article title: "The Dangers of the Selfie and How You Can Help Your Kids." To help students express their thoughts about the audience for this article, display the following sentence frames: *The article says it will tell _____ how to help _____. The audience for this article is _____.* **MODERATE**
- Ask pairs to discuss who the audience is for an article titled, "The Dangers of the Selfie and How You Can Help Your Kids," and what clues in the title help them figure that out. **LIGHT**

READING

Identify Evidence

Explain that the author of an argument can provide many different types of evidence in support of his or her claim, including facts, examples, personal stories, scientific studies, and quotations from experts.

Use the following supports with students at varying proficiency levels:

- List and define words that show bad effects, such as *hurt feelings, rejected,* and *nobody.* Then have students read paragraph 10 from "OMG" and locate and circle these words. **SUBSTANTIAL**
- Tell students to identify an example of one type of evidence found in "Better Than Words." Provide a sentence frame for students to use to describe this evidence: *In paragraph _____, the writer says, "_____."* **MODERATE**
- Have students work in small groups to create a chart or graphic organizer that shows the different types of evidence used in the two arguments and provides examples of each type. **LIGHT**

WRITING

Write an Argument

Work with students to read the writing assignment on page 315. Discuss key elements of an argument, including a claim, evidence, rhetorical devices, and a conclusion.

Use the following supports with students at varying proficiency levels:

- Provide a frame sentence for students to copy and complete: *Cell phones _____ be allowed in movie theaters.* **SUBSTANTIAL**
- Have students organize their argument by writing their claim at the top of a page and then working with a partner to think up and write down three supporting statements. **MODERATE**
- Ask students to identify rhetorical devices they might use in their arguments. Have students create a two-column chart with "parallelism," "repetition," and "hyperbole" in column 1. Encourage students to come up with examples of each type of device they might use. **LIGHT**

Connect to the
ESSENTIAL QUESTION

In this text, the author argues that selfies are a new and important means of self-expression, creativity, and social connection.

COMPARE ARGUMENTS

Point out that "Better Than Words: Say It with a Selfie" and "OMG, Not *Another* Selfie!" are both arguments in which the authors present conclusions about the importance or insignificance of taking and sending "selfies." As you read, think about the following questions: What claims do the authors make? What evidence do they present in support of their claims? How are the rhetorical devices the two authors use to develop their arguments alike and different? What audience is each author trying to reach?

MENTOR TEXT

At the end of the unit, students will be asked to write a multimodal argument. "OMG, Not *Another* Selfie!" provides a model for how a writer uses a clear claim with strong, supporting evidence to present a compelling argument.

ARGUMENT

BETTER THAN WORDS:
SAY IT WITH A SELFIE

by **Gloria Chang**
pages 303–307

COMPARE ARGUMENTS

As you read the arguments, focus on the reasons and evidence used to support the claims. Think about which points seem convincing to you and which do not; then, consider why.

 ### ESSENTIAL QUESTION:

What are the ways you can make yourself heard?

ARGUMENT

OMG, NOT *ANOTHER* SELFIE!

by **Shermakaye Bass**
pages 308–313

QUICK START

Why do people take selfies? Do they take them for good reasons? For bad reasons? Write down two good reasons for taking a selfie; then, write down two bad reasons.

ANALYZE RHETORICAL DEVICES

In arguments, writers use **rhetorical devices,** or techniques for convincing readers to agree with a claim. These include **parallelism** (repeating similar grammatical structures), **hyperbole** (exaggerating the truth for effect), and **repetition** (repeating a word, phrase, or line).

During an analysis, you may suspect that something is wrong with an argument. This may be because the argument contains faulty reasoning or a **logical fallacy,** an error in logic. As you read, distinguish between rhetorical devices used for effect and fallacies. Recognizing fallacies will help you explain why an argument is unconvincing.

Analyzing a writer's argument will help you draw conclusions about the writer's reliability, credibility, and bias (the side of the argument the writer favors). Look for these and other types of misleading techniques:

> **GENRE ELEMENTS:**
> **ARGUMENT**
> • states a position or makes a claim about a topic
> • includes evidence—facts, statistics, quotations, examples, or personal experience—to support the position
> • uses logic or emotion, as well as rhetorical devices, to persuade readers

FALLACY	DEFINITION	EXAMPLE
Personal attack or name-calling (*ad hominem*)	An attempt to discredit an idea by attacking the character of a person or group associated with the idea	Only immature people like Frank enjoy video games.
Overgeneralization, or sweeping generalization	A generalization that is too broad; uses words such as *all, everyone, every time, no one,* and *none*	They make bad choices all the time.
Stereotyping	Broad statements about people based on gender, age, ethnicity, race, or other qualities	Boys are better at sports than girls.

IDENTIFY AN ARGUMENT'S AUDIENCE

How a writer presents and supports an argument depends on the intended audience of readers. For example, some audiences may be persuaded by statistics and factual evidence. Other audiences may respond more strongly to evidence that focuses on personal experience. Analyze types of evidence to help you identify the intended audience. As you read, ask yourself: To whom might this type of evidence appeal? To students? Teachers? Parents? Others?

© Houghton Mifflin Harcourt Publishing Company

QUICK START

When students have completed the task, have them share some of the positive and negative reasons why people take and share selfies. Conclude the discussion by taking a vote to determine the overall opinion of the class. Is the class opinion overwhelmingly positive or negative? Is the class opinion divided?

ANALYZE RHETORICAL DEVICES

Help students distinguish between the different types of rhetorical devices a writer uses to persuade the audience. Provide and discuss examples of each device. Explain that a sound argument presents valid reasons and examples to support the claim the author is making. Discuss each fallacy presented in the chart along with its accompanying example. Have students explain the effect that each type of fallacy has on the overall argument. Ask if they can think of another example of each type of fallacy.

IDENTIFY AN ARGUMENT'S AUDIENCE

Discuss how the audience for an argument might affect an author's choice of examples or supporting details. For example, if you are trying to persuade an audience about the benefits of playing video games, what kinds of evidence might be used for an audience of teenagers? What kinds of evidence might be used for an audience of parents of teenagers? How might sources of the evidence used in an argument affect the way the audience evaluates it?

EL ENGLISH LEARNER SUPPORT

Use Academic Language Write the terms *parallelism, hyperbole,* and *repetition* on the board, and review their definitions and pronunciations. Read aloud and have students repeat the following examples. Ask students to identify the type of rhetorical device each represents.

- Tyrol was always busy <u>at school</u>, <u>at work</u>, and <u>at home</u>. (*parallelism*)
- I have <u>a million things to do</u> today. (*hyperbole*)
- He is the <u>wrong</u> person, for the <u>wrong</u> job, at the <u>wrong</u> time. (*repetition*)

Finish by inviting students in mixed proficiency groups to come up with and write down an original example of each rhetorical device.   **ALL LEVELS**

CRITICAL VOCABULARY

Encourage students to read all the sentences before deciding which word best completes each one. Remind them to consider the context of each word as it is used.

Answers:

1. *celebrity*
2. *eternity*
3. *passion*
4. *narcissist*
5. *indulgent*
6. *intimacy*
7. *saturated*

■ English Learner Support

Explore Word Families Tell students that several Critical Vocabulary words can be used to build other words with related meanings. Discuss new words that are formed with a base word and suffix, such as: *passion/passionate/ passionately, celebrate/ celebration/celebrity.*

ALL LEVELS

LANGUAGE CONVENTIONS

Review the information about commonly confused words. Emphasize the importance of learning the difference between these words in order to use the correct word and spelling in writing.

Read aloud the model sentence from "Better Than Words: Say It with a Selfie." Encourage students to replace the confusing word with the complete phrase from which the contraction is formed. Explain that this will help them identify which is the correct word to use.

🖉 ANNOTATION MODEL

Remind students to look for the rhetorical devices listed on page 301 of the lesson when making annotations in their texts. Review annotation tools such as underlining, circling, and highlighting. Point out that students could use different colors or markings to indicate the use of various rhetorical devices and then write comments in the margin to note how persuasive they find each one. Emphasize that marginal notes often also include comments or questions about important ideas expressed in the text.

 GET READY

CRITICAL VOCABULARY

saturated   indulgent   narcissist   intimacy
passion   eternity   celebrity

To preview the words, replace the boldfaced word(s) in parentheses with a vocabulary word that has a similar meaning.

1. The Olympic athlete is a/an (**star**) _____ .

2. It took a/an (**long time**) _____ for the bus to arrive.

3. She has a/an (**enormous enthusiasm**) _____ for skiing.

4. I don't know a single (**self-obsessed person**) _____.

5. Eating candy all the time is (**excessively permissive**) _____.

6. Good friends often share a/an (**closeness**) _____ .

7. The ground was (**drenched**) _____ with rain.

LANGUAGE CONVENTIONS

Many common words have similar spellings or sound the same but have different meanings. Watch out for **commonly confused words.** Here is an example from "Better Than Words: Say It with a Selfie":

<u>It's</u> easy to create a self-portrait with a smart phone and <u>its</u> filters.

The word *its* is commonly misspelled as *it's*. *It's* is the contraction for "it is" or "it has." The word *its* is the possessive form of the pronoun *it*. In this lesson, you will learn about other commonly confused words.

ANNOTATION MODEL

NOTICE & NOTE

As you read, note ways in which the writer tries to persuade the reader. In the model, you can see one reader's notes about hyperbole in "Better Than Words: Say It with a Selfie."

> 1 Everyone everywhere owns and uses a smart phone, and, with at least a million different social platforms available, you'd have to live in a cave not to take part in and appreciate this form of communication.

Examples of hyperbole, or exaggeration. Not everyone owns and uses a smart phone. There aren't really one million social platforms.

302   Unit 4

BACKGROUND

Today, people of all ages—young and old—use smart phones. Children grow up sending photos and making video calls to grandparents. Students use phones to carry out research for school and to connect with friends, and, though the word selfie *only entered our vocabulary in the early 2000s, people know all about them. With the rise in popularity, people have developed strong opinions about selfies. As you read this writer's argument, consider your own opinion.*

BETTER THAN WORDS:
Say It with a Selfie

Argument by Gloria Chang

PREPARE TO COMPARE

As you read, identify the writer's claim and the evidence she uses to support that claim. Pay attention to how the writer's persuasive techniques affect your thoughts about selfies. Who do you think her audience is?

1   In our digital age, the selfie is the best way to <u>express oneself</u>, <u>empower oneself</u>, and even <u>surround oneself</u> with friends. Everyone everywhere owns and uses a smart phone, and, with at least a million different social media platforms available, you'd have to live in a cave not to take part in and appreciate this form of communication. Sure, there are critics who say that selfies are taken only by narcissists[1] craving attention, but those critics really do live in caves— and they certainly have no friends.

---

[1] **narcissists** (när´sĭ-sĭstz): people who are preoccupied with their looks. From the Greek myth of Narcissus, a young man who fell in love with his own reflection in a pool of water.

Better Than Words: Say It with a Selfie / OMG, Not *Another* Selfie!   303

NOTICE & NOTE

Notice & Note

Use the side margins to notice and note signposts in the text.

ANALYZE RHETORICAL DEVICES

Annotate: Mark an example of repetition in paragraph 1.

Connect: What is the purpose of this repetition? What effect does the use of this rhetorical device have on you as a reader?

TEACH

BACKGROUND

Have students read the Background note. Explain that the use of the term *selfie* predates popular social media sites. such as Facebook and Instagram. Teens and young adults were the first to popularize selfies, and the term entered into everyday English by 2012. *Selfie* was declared the new word of the year by the *Oxford English Dictionary* in 2013.

PREPARE TO COMPARE

Read the Prepare to Compare prompt. Direct students to focus their reading on determining the author's persuasive techniques and audience for this text.

ANALYZE RHETORICAL DEVICES

Review the distinction between *repetition* and *parallelism*. Explain that repetition involves the use of the same exact word(s), whereas parallelism refers to the repetition of similar grammatical structures. (**Answer:** *The use of parallelism makes the sentence sound forceful and convincing.*)

(EL) ENGLISH LEARNER SUPPORT

Learn New Language Structures   Focus on how repetition is often used to provide emphasis and connect related ideas. Read the opening sentence of paragraph 1, and tell students to listen closely for repeated words. Then ask students the following questions:

- *Which word is repeated in this sentence?*
- *Which words come before* oneself *in each phrase?*
- *Does this repetition catch the reader's interest—yes or no?*   **SUBSTANTIAL/MODERATE**

EXTREME OR ABSOLUTE LANGUAGE

Discuss how the writer's use of such strong language reveals her bias toward photographers. (**Answer:** *The writer uses phrases such as "don't care," "only," and "don't know" to discredit professional photographers. Her argument is that a person can take the best photographs of himself or herself.*)

ENGLISH LEARNER SUPPORT

Demonstrate Comprehension Have students demonstrate comprehension of the text by identifying and discussing analogies. Explain to students that an analogy is a comparison between two unlike things. Have small groups of students reread paragraph 5 silently. Then ask them to discuss as a group what the analogy in this paragraph might be. After the group discussion, have students express to partners their opinion about the analogy in this paragraph.

LIGHT

CRITICAL VOCABULARY

saturated: The author emphasizes how important social media is to people today by describing our society as saturated with it.

ASK STUDENTS to name some examples of social media that saturate people's lives today. (*messaging apps, websites*)

passion: Someone who loves a hobby might make that hobby their passion.

ASK STUDENTS why someone might want to take selfies of a passion. (*Showing people your passion tells them what you are interested in and expresses part of your personality.*)

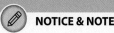

NOTICE & NOTE

saturated
(săch´ə-rāt´əd) *adj.* Something that is *saturated* is filled until it is unable to hold or contain more.

passion
(păsh´ən) *n. Passion* means boundless enthusiasm.

EXTREME OR ABSOLUTE LANGUAGE

Notice & Note: Why do you think the writer uses extreme or absolute language to describe photographers and their work? Mark extreme or absolute language used in paragraph 4.

Analyze: What bias does this language reveal?

Selfies are about art and about life.

2 In a society **saturated,** stuffed to the brim, with social media, selfies are an artistic form of self-expression. Humans, since the beginning of time, have used self-portraits to express themselves. From ancient Egypt to the early Greeks to famous painters such as Rembrandt and Van Gogh,[2] people have expressed themselves artistically through self-portraits.

3   The only difference between the artists of old and modern selfie-takers is that technology now allows anyone and everyone to be an artist, and a "self-portrait" is now called a "selfie." It's easy to create a "self-portrait" with a smart phone and its filters. You don't need to know how to draw or paint when you have a cell phone!

Selfies are about self discovery.

4 Selfies allow people to show different parts of themselves. Maybe it's their artistic side, maybe it's their silly side, or maybe it's to show an interest or **passion,** such as a love of certain foods. Whatever that side may be, by showing the selfie-taker's interests, selfies become more real than any boring photographer's work. Photographers don't care if they show who you truly are in those boring photos; they're interested only in making sure you are in focus. They don't know what you are like. How can they? None of us even know ourselves until we experiment with different views, explore different interests, and discover the things that influence us.

5   In this way, selfies—unlike past self-portraits that weren't taken on handy mobile devices—allow us an easier and better way to find out who we are. Just like trying on different clothes to find what works best for our personalities, taking selfies is an excellent way to test how we look and feel in certain outfits, poses, and places. Our own reactions to these pictures, along with the reactions of friends and strangers, help us figure out what works for us as unique individuals.

Selfies are about self-expression.

6 Taking a selfie is like saying to the world, "this is me, right now, right here!" And a selfie does a better job of communicating this who, when, and where than spoken or written words can. After all, the human brain, as science shows, is hard-wired to

---

[2] **Rembrandt and Van Gogh:** Rembrandt van Rijn (rĕm´ brănt´ văn rīn´) (1606–1669) and Vincent van Gogh (văn gō´) (1853–1890) were Dutch painters known for their self-portraits.

recognize faces. In other words, we naturally recognize things and people visually. The <u>effect</u> is more immediate. The objects, people, and background in a selfie can show what a selfie-taker likes, hates, admires, or aspires to.[3] The taker's attitude will naturally <u>affect</u> his or her facial expressions. As they say, a picture is worth a thousand words.

7   Even museums and art galleries know that selfies can be an artistic means of self-expression. They encourage visitors to take selfies with works of art to share as art. One gallery in London even held an international selfie competition for people to submit the most artistic selfies.

8   But don't just trust the artists and everyone who takes selfies. Trust science. O<u>ne scientist who studied the motivation for taking selfies found that we take selfies as a form of self-expression, not to be narcissistic.</u> So don't assume that you're a narcissist; don't assume that it's all about you.

Selfies are about self-confidence.

9   Selfies empower us because they fulfill our need for validation from friends, family, and the rest of the world. If you don't believe it, try it. Science has shown, once again, that taking selfies makes you more confident, especially kids. We all know it. Some people are not allowed to say positive things about themselves because other people will say that they are full of themselves. But a selfie is a photo, so it's acceptable for those people to show what they're proud of.

10   Sure, people may get fixated on selfies being about physical things, but that doesn't mean the selfie has to be about how someone looks. Everything in a selfie can tell you about a person. For example, a selfie can show that someone may be the next celebrity chef because that person always posts selfies of himself or herself cooking and eating at different places in the world.

11   Selfies also empower us because they make us happy. In two studies, researchers discovered that people who took selfies and people who didn't both thought pictures taken by themselves (those are selfies!) made them more attractive and likable. If you like photos of yourself, taking them boosts your confidence. In another study, scientists had college students take selfies and share them. This made them more confident and comfortable with their smiling faces. It may not even be possible to take too many selfies.

[3] **aspires to:** strives toward, wants to be like.

© Houghton Mifflin Harcourt Publishing Company

NOTICE & NOTE

LANGUAGE CONVENTIONS
Annotate: Mark the words *effect* and *affect* in paragraph 6.

Identify: Explain each word's part of speech and meaning.

IDENTIFY AN ARGUMENT'S AUDIENCE
Annotate: Mark the evidence or support the writer provides in paragraph 8 to support her claim.

Draw Conclusions: Who do you think the writer's audience is?

TEACH

LANGUAGE CONVENTIONS

Effect and *affect* are commonly confused words in writing. In addition to their similar spellings and pronunciations, both words can be used as nouns or verbs. Explain to students that in most cases, *affect* is used as a verb and *effect* as a noun. (**Answer:** Effect *is a noun that means "the result of something." Affect* is a verb that means "to influence or produce a change.")

IDENTIFY AN ARGUMENT'S AUDIENCE

Remind students that the strength of evidence to support a claim depends on the intended audience. Some audiences respond better to personal or emotional evidence, whereas others may respond better to scientific and other objective evidence. (**Possible answer:** *The audience is made of people who think taking selfies is a harmful practice. The writer also may think that her audience is made of those who are impressed or swayed by mentioning a scientific study, but she does not think that facts or statistics from the study may be useful to her reader. Her audience does not have a strong scientific background.*)

 For **speaking support** for students at varying proficiency levels, see the **Text X-Ray** on page 300D.

APPLYING ACADEMIC VOCABULARY

☑ **appropriate**   ☐ **authority**   ☐ **consequence**   ☐ **element**   ☑ **justify**

Write and Discuss   Have students turn to a partner to discuss the following questions. Guide students to include the Academic Vocabulary words *appropriate* and *justify* in their responses. Ask volunteers to share their responses with the class.

- Is it **appropriate** to send a selfie to people you don't know?
- Does the ease of sending a selfie **justify** sending so many of them?

ANALYZE RHETORICAL DEVICES

Explain that the language and type of evidence an author uses affects the reader's view of the writer's credibility. Writers who resort to logical fallacies in support of their claim often lessen their credibility. (**Answer:** *Stereotypical statements, such as people who are shy or lack confidence hate confident people, and name-calling, such as "cavemen," makes the writer's argument weaker. The writer does not effectively consider the counterargument here; she resorts to name-calling and stereotyping.*)

IDENTIFY AN ARGUMENT'S AUDIENCE

Note that rather than citing specific scientific facts and data, the author is relying on anecdotal testimony from people. (**Possible answer:** *The author reports details about how teens describe their experiences with sharing selfies on social networks. Such evidence would most appeal to teens and to people who are very interested in using social networks to connect with other people.*)

 NOTICE & NOTE

ANALYZE RHETORICAL DEVICES

Annotate: Mark examples of stereotyping and name-calling in paragraph 12.

Draw Conclusions: How do these examples affect the writer's credibility?

IDENTIFY AN ARGUMENT'S AUDIENCE

Annotate: Mark evidence the writer uses to support her claim in paragraph 14.

Analyze: Who might this type of evidence appeal to? Who is the intended audience of the argument?

12   In short, taking and sharing selfies boosts both self-confidence and self-esteem. People who say otherwise are like cavemen. They're probably people who've never taken selfies, so they probably don't have any self-confidence whatsoever. They probably hate people who do have self-confidence.

Selfies are about making connections.

13   The best part of taking selfies is that they're a great way to connect with friends or even make new friends. Since we all have smart phones and social media is everywhere and here to stay, we stay in touch with friends by taking selfies. It's like sending a letter in past times. But selfies are faster and are sent with a phone instead of a horse. By taking and sharing a selfie, you can share what you are thinking, feeling, or doing with your friends. Social media is made for others to give feedback so friends can tell you what they are thinking, feeling, or doing. They can do this by sending their favorite emoticons[4] or posting comments or sending a selfie of themselves back to you.

14   Selfies are all about online social networks and social networks lead to better relationships. Teens especially say they have more positive experiences than negative ones when using social media. Selfies may have been around for only about a dozen years, but they're today's way to connect with other people.

Selfies are about making memories.

15   Selfies also help us create special memories. By posing with friends or at special events or places, we create snapshots that we can look back on with fond feelings. Obviously, taking selfies helps create memories because people naturally take selfies when something is happening right there close to them. They also take selfies when visiting places they like or think are funny or strange or interesting.

---

[4] **emoticons:** emojis, or icons used to express an emotion in text messages or online.

WHEN STUDENTS STRUGGLE . . .

Make Predictions Remind students that they can use text elements, such as subheadings, to help them predict what the writer's focus will be in a section of the argument.

Have students identify and read aloud the subheadings used in this argument. Discuss the following questions:

• What do you think will be the main idea of the text under this subheading?

• In what way are the subheadings similar?

 For additional support, go to the **Reading Studio** and assign the following **LEVEL** **Level Up tutorial: Making Predictions.**

16   There are even "relfies," where couples take photos of themselves. Did you know that couples who take and show more relfies are more satisfied with and committed to their relationships than people who don't? And there are "groupies," selfies that include the selfie-taker and friends or family or even celebrities. They make the best memories since they include people we want to remember.

Selfies really are better than words.

17   Whether by ourselves, or with our favorite things, places, or people, selfies obviously say it better than words.

18   They express who we are and what matters most to us.

CHECK YOUR UNDERSTANDING

Answer these questions before moving on to the next selection.

1   What is the primary claim the writer makes about the role of selfies today?

   A People who take selfies are healthier than people who don't.

   B Photographers don't know how to take good selfies.

   C Selfies are the most effective tool for expressing ourselves.

   D Everyone needs a cell phone to survive.

2   What point is the writer trying to make by saying that anyone who doesn't take or appreciate selfies must live in a cave?

   F People who don't take selfies are likely to be alone.

   G Anyone who does not like selfies is isolated from society and living in the past.

   H People who don't take selfies don't have cellular service.

   J The only way to have friends today is to take and share selfies.

3   How does the writer mainly support her ideas?

   A with direct quotations from other informational sources

   B with experts' opinions

   C with anecdotes and personal experience

   D with statistics from scientific studies

© Houghton Mifflin Harcourt Publishing Company

CHECK YOUR UNDERSTANDING

Have students answer the questions independently.

Answers:

1. C

2. G

3. C

If they answer any questions incorrectly, have them reread the text to confirm their understanding. Then they may proceed to the next selection on page 308.

ENGLISH LEARNER SUPPORT

Oral Assessment   Use the following questions to assess students' comprehension and speaking skills:

1. The author believes that selfies are the _____ way to show people important things about yourself. *(best)*

2. The author says that people who don't take selfies "live in caves." Does she mean that these people are very in touch with the world or living in the past? *(living in the past)*

3. Does the author support her ideas more with scientific facts and statistics or more with examples from everyday life? *(examples from everyday life)* **SUBSTANTIAL/MODERATE**

BACKGROUND

Selfies are now so commonplace that billions of them have been posted. These include pictures of daily and special events such as meals, concerts, parties, and births. By 2003, even astronauts while in space began taking selfies. A recent study projects that a teen today will post more than 25,000 selfies during the course of a lifetime and spend an hour or more a week sending or responding to selfies.

PREPARE TO COMPARE

Read the Prepare to Compare prompt. If necessary, review the meaning of the terms involving rhetorical devices and logical fallacies introduced on page 301.

CRITICAL VOCABULARY

indulgent: When someone readily permits another person to do something, he or she is being indulgent.

ASK STUDENTS to name other words that might be used to explain the meaning of *indulgent.* (*easy-going, lenient, permissive*)

NOTICE & NOTE

BACKGROUND

Most people have friends or family members who love to post their pictures of meals, sporting events, vacations, outfits, and pets to social media. Sometimes we may wonder if some of our friends spend every waking hour on their phones. Is there such a thing as sharing too many photos? The author of this argument takes a stand.

OMG, NOT ANOTHER SELFIE!

Argument by Shermakaye Bass

Notice & Note

Use the side margins to notice and note signposts in the text.

indulgent
(ĭn-dŭl´jənt) *adj. Indulgent* means excessively permissive. *Self-indulgent* is when one is overly permissive with oneself. The pun *selfie-indulgent* means that a person indulges in taking many selfies.

PREPARE TO COMPARE

As you read, pay attention to the rhetorical devices the writer uses to enhance her argument and persuade her audience. Can you identify any logical fallacies or faulty reasoning?

1 "Hey, guys—look! Look at me! Here I am on summer vacation at the beach. Oh, and here I am with my bestie at the soccer game! And check this out: Me doing duck face. And, oh, here I am with this morning's . . . pancakes."

2 Those lines might have been spoken by any one of us who's caught up in the selfie craze these days. Social media sites are filled with the selfie-**indulgent,** people who've given in to the desire to be seen. But do people really want to see what you had for breakfast? And do you really want to see how much "fun" other people are having? Especially if their lives seem so much cooler than yours?

3 The answer is probably "no," yet most of us do look at our friends' selfies, and most of us do post selfies ourselves. In fact, one search engine giant has found that almost 24 billion selfies were uploaded through its online photo application in 2015.

IMPROVE READING FLUENCY

Targeted Passage Have students work with partners to read the selection. First, use paragraphs 1 and 2 to model how to read an argument. Have students follow along as you read the text with appropriate phrasing and emphasis. Then have partners take turns reading each paragraph. Encourage students to provide feedback and support for pronouncing difficult words. Remind students that when they are reading aloud for an audience, the goal is to give the audience time to understand difficult concepts.

 Go to the **Reading Studio** for additional support in developing fluency.

That number doesn't even include those uploaded to popular social media sites.

4　　We take selfies without even thinking. We strike a favorite pose. We click. We tap a couple of times. We share. This allows the rest of the world to see us as we'd like to be seen; however, it's not as we usually look in person.

5　　One problem with this selfie mania is that once you've posted a picture of yourself you can't take it back, even if you decide that it's not quite your best shot. It's out there. For as many years as there are stars in the sky or grains of sand in the Sahara.[1] For all of **eternity.**

6　　The only cure for a bad selfie is to take another one and post *it,* but you know what happens next: this reposting and re-snapping and reposting and re-snapping and reposting can go on and on and on, creating a cycle of frustration and wounded confidence! That cycle, inspired by the desire to control and "improve" our own images can lead to some serious psychological trouble, especially for young people. Selfies can be downright bad for us—bad for our self esteem and body image, bad for our productivity and our schoolwork, even bad for our friendships. If we're too selfie obsessed, we start to look as foolishly self-centered and shallow as poor old Narcissus[2] as he sat there falling madly in love with his own reflection. And no one wants to sit in the school cafeteria with a known **narcissist,** anyway, right? After all, <u>selfie takers are *so* in love with themselves!</u>

7　　The truth is that taking selfies may seem harmless and fun, but more and more research shows that this fad can confuse a person's sense of identity, and it may even fiddle with his or her sense of reality. We might start to think that we look better than we actually do. That wouldn't be so terrible. But we also might start comparing ourselves to others too often. We might start believing negative things like, "I'll never be as cute as my best friend," or "I'll never be as popular as the new kid," or "I'll never have that much fun. Ever."

8　　On the other hand, we may continue to think that "if I can just make myself look good enough and cool enough, I'll get more 'likes,' which means I'll get more friends. Then people will like me for real. Then, one day I'll become a real

---

[1] **grains of sand in the Sahara:** the Sahara is a desert in Africa that covers an area the size of the United States.

[2] **Narcissus** (när-sĭs´əs): in Greek mythology, Narcissus was a young man who fell in love with his own reflection in a pool of water.

eternity
(ĭ-tûr´nĭ-tē) *n. Eternity* refers to infinite time, without beginning or end.

ANALYZE RHETORICAL DEVICES
Annotate: Mark the overgeneralization about people who take selfies in the last sentence of paragraph 6.

Evaluate: How does the writer's use of this rhetorical device affect her credibility?

narcissist
(när´sĭ-sĭst´) *n.* A person who is preoccupied with his or her looks is a *narcissist.*

ANALYZE RHETORICAL DEVICES

Emphasize that an overgeneralization is a logical fallacy in which the writer draws a conclusion that is too broad or is unsupported by sufficient evidence to be accurate. Discuss how words such as *all, everyone, no one,* and *none* provide clues that signal overgeneralizations. (**Answer:** *Students may point out that not all people who take selfies are narcissists as the writer claims. The use of this overgeneralization calls into question the credibility of the writer.*)

For **listening support** for students at varying proficiency levels, see the **Text X-Ray** on page 300C.

CRITICAL VOCABULARY

eternity: When someone talks about eternity, they are referring to an endless amount of time.

ASK STUDENTS what other words might be used to explain the meaning of *eternity.* (*forever, never-ending, limitless*)

narcissist: If someone is a narcissist, he or she is only concerned with himself or herself and how he or she looks.

ASK STUDENTS which words might be used to explain the meaning of *narcissist.* (*egotist, swellhead, braggart*)

CLOSE READ SCREENCAST

Modeled Discussion　In their eBooks, have students view the Close Read Screencast, in which readers discuss and annotate paragraph 5 and the first sentence of paragraph 6, a key point in the argument.

As a class, view and discuss the video. Then have students pair up to do an independent close read of paragraph 17. Students can record their answers on the Close Read Practice PDF.

 Close Read Practice PDF

LANGUAGE CONVENTIONS

Emphasize that many English words have more than one meaning. Explain that the context in which the word is used helps determine the intended meaning of the word. (**Answer:** *In this sentence,* sense *means "a feeling that something is the case." It is often confused with* cents.)

ENGLISH LEARNER SUPPORT

Confirm Understanding Use the following supports with students at various proficiency levels:

- Write *sure-fire* and *self-esteem* on the board, define them, and circle the hyphen in each. Point out that English words are sometimes joined together by hyphens. Pronounce each word several times and have students repeat it after you. **SUBSTANTIAL**

- Direct students to point to and pronounce *sure-fire* and *self-esteem* in paragraph 10. Explain that some hyphenated words may appear before a noun they describe. Add that other hyphenated words are so commonly linked together that they are always hyphenated. Have students identify which of these words is an example of the first type of hyphenated word and which of these words is an example of the second kind. **MODERATE**

- Challenge students to locate and pronounce two words with hyphens in paragraph 10. Correct students as needed. Then ask them to summarize in their own words the point the author is making about selfies with these two words. **LIGHT**

For **reading support** for students at varying proficiency levels, see the **Text X-Ray** on page 300D.

CRITICAL VOCABULARY

celebrity: A person who is famous is a celebrity.

ASK STUDENTS what other words might be used to explain the meaning of *celebrity*. (*superstar, big shot, VIP*)

NOTICE & NOTE

celebrity
(sə-lĕb′rĭ-tē) *n.* A *celebrity* is a famous person.

LANGUAGE CONVENTIONS
Annotate: Mark the word *sense* in paragraph 11.

Summarize: Explain the meaning of the word. What word is it commonly confused with?

celebrity." However, selfies can put distance between us and the people we care about; they can sometimes create jealousy and competition. That's certainly no way to become a star.

9   Selfies can even have the opposite effect of what we'd hoped. Recent studies show that the selfie process not only has become oddly addictive and dangerous, but it can even set up the selfie-taker for ridicule. Some people will spend hours taking photos of themselves, trying for that perfect shot, and still wind up disappointed. Their thinking is that if they can just find the right "capture," they'll be popular, pretty—a somebody.

10   Of course, this is not true. Therefore, when we take certain actions (posting selfie after selfie) expecting certain results (fame and friendship) and then don't get those results, we get hurt feelings instead. We feel rejected, as if we don't matter. And that's a sure-fire formula for low self-esteem: "I posted this picture of myself and nobody has liked it," we think, "so I must be a nobody."

11   "One of the reasons kids take selfies is to post those pictures online. And the purpose of posting online often is to get 'likes,'" affirms author and former teacher Katie Schumacher, who launched the "Don't Press Send Campaign" in 2013. "If you post something and get a lot of 'likes,' it reinforces the feeling of importance and the <u>sense</u> of approval from others," Mrs. Schumacher says in a 2016 *ParentCo* story, "The Dangers of the Selfie and How You Can Help Your Kids."

ENGLISH LEARNER SUPPORT

Use Contractions Review how contractions are formed by combining two words, taking out some letters and replacing them with an apostrophe. Then have students read paragraph 9 and identify two examples of contractions.

- Which two words are combined to make the contraction *we'd*? (*we had*)

- Which two words are combined to make the contraction *they'll*? (*they will*)

Have students practice using these contractions in sentences.

12 "The 'like' is the reward. But if you don't get enough 'likes,' you will keep trying to get a better picture from a different angle or with someone more popular," Mrs. Schumacher says.

13 On top of hunting for "likes," young people often take selfies hoping to impress or catch the attention of someone in particular. Maybe it's someone they have a crush on or someone who's bullied them. Maybe they want that person to have a better opinion of them. If that someone doesn't notice the post or makes a negative comment, then the selfie-taker can feel worse than if he or she had never posted at all!

14 Dr. Allison Chase, a psychologist and behavior specialist in Austin, Texas, also has weighed in. "This is particularly challenging for kids and teens, as they are trying to figure out who they are and what their identity is." In that 2016 *ParentCo* article, Dr. Chase warns about getting caught in the trap of worrying too much about appearances and approval.

15 She warns against believing that posting and sharing and liking creates actual friendship and **intimacy**. As Dr. Chase says, we "create the illusion of feeling more connected and more 'liked' in a way that is controllable and oftentimes, staged. The end result is a competitive environment with increased self-focus, less true connection and, more often than not, increased self-criticism."

16 That, as you now know, can lead to more selfie sessions and even deeper disappointment. We begin to think that if we could only catch that perfect angle, or frame the picture to disguise our braces or acne or big nose, we'd be more popular. But, seeing all these selfies of cool kids in cool places with cool parents and friends, we wonder, "How can I possibly compete?"

17 Still, all dangers aside, the selfie has grown to be as much a part of our culture as the Declaration of Independence or our Constitution.[3] And the person who invented the selfie stick—Wayne Fromm, who patented a version in 2005—is probably pretty rich by now. But believe it or not, the term "selfie" wasn't even used until 2002, when the word first entered our vocabulary, according to Merriam-Webster's Dictionary. Now, more than 15 years later, we've turned it into a verb ("I'm going to selfie on my new kick-scooter!"). And in 2013, a national news agency reported that the Oxford Dictionaries had chosen "selfie" as its Word of the Year, claiming that the use of the word had grown by 17,000 percent between 2012 and 2013!

---

[3] **Declaration of Independence or our Constitution:** foundational documents of the United States.

NOTICE & NOTE

IDENTIFY AN ARGUMENT'S AUDIENCE

Annotate: Mark the name and professional background of the person quoted in paragraph 14. Underline the quotation from this person and its source.

Draw Conclusions: How does the quote help you understand who the audience is? How does the use of this quotation affect the credibility of the writer?

intimacy
(ĭn′tə-mə-sē) *n. Intimacy* means close friendship and familiarity.

TEACH

IDENTIFY AN ARGUMENT'S AUDIENCE

Discuss the importance of evidence in supporting a writer's claim and in evaluating credibility. Explain that evidence may also reveal the audience to whom an argument is directed. (**Answer:** *The writer uses evidence from an expert in psychology and human behavior to support her claim that selfies can be damaging. Her citation of an expert shows that she thinks her audience will be more likely to believe her claim when it is supported by words from an expert. The source, ParentCo, shows that the quotation appeared in a publication geared toward parents. Therefore, the writer's audience is most likely adults—parents or teachers. The quotation from an expert makes the writer seem more credible.*)

CRITICAL VOCABULARY

intimacy: When someone talks about intimacy, they are usually referring to a closeness between friends.

ASK STUDENTS to name other words that might be used to explain the meaning of *intimacy*. (*affection, familiarity*)

ANALYZE RHETORICAL DEVICES

Remind students that repeating a word or phrase calls attention to it. Repetition is a clue that readers should stop and figure out what the author is trying to convey by using the repeated phrase or word. **(Answer:** *By repeating the phrase "we think," the author is pointing out that we are not always correct, so even if we think selfies give us a way to show our best selves, we could actually be wrong about this. Through repetition, the author conveys doubt about the good selfies do.)*

NOTICE & NOTE

ANALYZE RHETORICAL DEVICES

Annotate: In paragraph 19, mark repeated phrases.

Respond: What effect does the writer achieve by repeating these phrases?

18 Wow.

19 Don't let all the hoopla fool you, though. The reality—the "real" reality—is that spending too much time taking our own pictures or focusing on how we look or spending too much time on other people's selfies can be more harmful than helpful to our tender egos. Selfies are carefully posed and selected images that present us at our best (<u>we think</u>). They're images that literally put our best face forward (<u>we think!</u>). But that's not actually so.

20 Selfies don't represent reality, and they certainly don't represent who we truly are.

CHECK YOUR UNDERSTANDING

Have students answer the questions independently.

Answers:

1. *A*

2. *J*

3. *B*

If they answer any questions incorrectly, have them reread the text to confirm their understanding. Then they may proceed to ANALYZE THE TEXT on p. 314.

CHECK YOUR UNDERSTANDING

Answer these questions before moving on to the **Analyze the Texts** section on the following page.

1 What is the writer's position on selfies?

A Taking too many selfies can be bad for a person's self-esteem.

B If you take enough selfies, your self-esteem will eventually improve.

C People who take selfies can only be friends with other people who take selfies.

D People who take lots of selfies are the best photographers.

2 Which group is most likely the writer's intended audience?

F Narcissists

G Shy people

H Psychologists

J Parents and their children

3 The writer mainly supports her claim with —

A funny stories and personal experiences

B experts' opinions

C interviews with celebrities

D scientific data and charts

 ENGLISH LEARNER SUPPORT

Oral Assessment Use the following questions to assess students' comprehension and speaking skills:

1. Does the writer think it can hurt people to take too many selfies? *(yes)*

2. Who is the writer's audience? *(parents and their children)*

3. What evidence does the author use to support her claim? *(experts' opinions)* **SUBSTANTIAL/MODERATE**

ANALYZE THE TEXTS

Possible answers:

1. **DOK 4:** *In "Better Than Words: Say It with a Selfie," the writer uses parallelism to structure sentence headings. This is a strong way to structure her argument and shows all the positive ways selfies can help us.*

2. **DOK 4:** *In "OMG, Not Another Selfie!" the writer says, "Social media sites are filled with the selfie-indulgent, people who've given in to the desire to be seen." This is a stereotype about people who use social media. The writer's use of stereotype indicates that she doesn't actually understand the wide range of people using social media. This undermines her credibility.*

3. **DOK 3:** *In "Better Than Words" the writer refers to "two studies." In "OMG, Not Another Selfie!" the writer cites Dr. Allison Chase, a psychologist in Austin, Texas, who is quoted from a 2016 ParentCo. article. The writer of "OMG" gives the name of the expert, her profession, and the source. This is more credible evidence than that offered by the author of "Better Than Words" because it is more complete and readers can look up the article.*

4. **DOK 4:** *The writer uses sweeping generalizations, "we all have smart phones" and "social media is everywhere and here to stay, to explain why we "stay in touch with friends by taking selfies." This use of generalizations reveals a flaw in the writer's logic: it may sound as if she provides a logical explanation for why we use selfies to stay in touch, but that explanation is fallacious. Her assertion is illogical.*

5. **DOK 4:** *In "Better Than Words," the writer says, "Everything in a selfie can tell you about a person." The writer is trying to support the idea that selfies are good for self-expression and self-discovery.*

RESEARCH

Remind students to use reputable sources for their research. They may find good information at museum or university websites or pages that cover the history of photography.

Connect Suggest that students use a two-column chart to record the details they research about historical self portraits. Use the chart to compare this information with the reasons why people take selfies today.

 RESPOND

ANALYZE THE TEXTS

Support your responses with evidence from the text. ▤ NOTEBOOK

1. **Evaluate** Find an instance of parallelism in either argument and evaluate its impact on the argument. Does the use of this rhetorical device make the argument stronger? Explain.

2. **Critique** Find an example of stereotyping in either argument. Explain how stereotyping affects the writer's credibility and the effectiveness of her argument.

3. **Compare** Reread paragraph 11 in "Better Than Words: Say It with a Selfie" and paragraph 11 in "OMG, Not *Another* Selfie!" Both writers use experts to back up their claims. What specific evidence does each writer use to support her argument? Explain which writer's evidence you think is more persuasive and credible and why.

4. **Analyze** Review paragraph 13 in "Better Than Words: Say It with a Selfie." Find an example of a logical fallacy and explain how it shows an error in the writer's logic.

5. **Notice & Note** Find and then list an example of extreme or absolute language in either argument. Why do you think the writer chose these words?

RESEARCH TIP
Before researching, consider the best search terms to use. For general information, try "photography and history." Try "early selfies" to find out about early self-portrait photography.

RESEARCH

Conduct research into the first use of photography to take self-portraits. Use multiple sources to investigate early photographers, types of cameras, and technical breakthroughs. Then fill in the chart.

QUESTION	ANSWER
Who is credited with taking the first self-portrait with a camera?	*Robert Comelius in 1839*
What early portable camera led to self-portraiture becoming widespread?	*Kodak Brownie Box*
What technical breakthrough in the 1880s made it easier to create self-portraits?	*self-timer*
When and in what country did the term *selfie* originate?	*Australia*

Connect Consider what you learned about early pioneers in self-portraiture. Why did people first take self-portraits? Compare the reasons to what motivates people to take selfies today. Discuss your answers with a small group.

EL ## ENGLISH LEARNER SUPPORT

Compare Texts Use the following supports to help students compare the selections.

- Help students locate and copy words and phrases from each selection that describe that author's view on selfies. Assist students in reading each group of words/phrases and deciding whether they present a positive or negative view of selfies. **SUBSTANTIAL**

- Provide students with sentence frames to use to make comparisons: *The author _____ selfies because _____. The author does not _____ selfies because he/she thinks _____.* **MODERATE**

- Have partners discuss with one another ways the selections are alike and different. **LIGHT**

CREATE AND PRESENT

Compose an Argument Take a position—pro or con—about whether the use of cell phones should be permitted in movie theaters or at the dinner table, and write a three- or four-paragraph argument.

❏ Select an audience likely to disagree with your claim.

❏ Clearly state your claim in the opening paragraph. Use vocabulary appropriate to your audience.

❏ Use at least one rhetorical device to enhance your argument and help persuade your audience.

❏ Provide evidence that supports your claim and use sound reasoning that appeals to your audience. Do not use faulty reasoning or include logical fallacies.

❏ In your final paragraph, state your conclusion.

❏ Check your spelling to ensure that you have correctly used any confusing words, such as *its/it's*, *affect/effect*, and *their/there/they're*.

 Go to the **Writing Studio** for more on writing an argument.

Create and Present "The Perfect Selfie" In a small group, discuss how to explain the "perfect selfie" to someone who has never taken one and doesn't want to. Work with your group to identify the qualities that make a perfect selfie. Then write a short speech explaining the perfect selfie to your audience.

❏ Discuss what to include in your speech to persuade a person who doesn't want to take a selfie that there might be some benefit to taking one.

❏ Anticipate your audience's opposing viewpoint and identify evidence to help overcome your audience's objections.

❏ Listen closely and respectfully to all speakers in your group.

Go to the **Speaking and Listening Studio** for help with creating and presenting a speech.

RESPOND TO THE ESSENTIAL QUESTION

? What are the ways you can make yourself heard?

Gather Information Review your annotations and notes on the selections. Then, add relevant details to your Response Log. As you determine what points to include, think about the pros and cons of selfies as a form of self-expression. At the end of the unit, you will use your notes to create a multimodal argument.

ACADEMIC VOCABULARY

As you write and discuss what you learned from the selections, be sure to use the Academic Vocabulary words. Check off the words that you use.

❏ **appropriate**

❏ **authority**

❏ **consequence**

❏ **element**

❏ **justify**

CREATE AND PRESENT

Compose an Argument Point out that the list on page 315 can serve as a checklist for writing a successful argument. Emphasize that to be successful, an argument must clearly state a claim in its introductory paragraph, provide evidence in support of that claim in the body paragraphs, and state a conclusion about the claim at the end of the argument. Remind students that they must keep their audience in mind as they compose all parts of their argument.

 For **writing support** for students at varying proficiency levels, see the **Text X-Ray** on page 300D.

Create and Present "The Perfect Selfie" Remind students to follow guidelines about conducting a small-group discussion. Note that when a student does not understand a comment made by another group member, he or she should ask questions to clarify meaning. Emphasize that during a discussion, students should speak and listen respectfully to other students.

RESPOND TO THE ESSENTIAL QUESTION

Allow time for students to add details from the texts to their Unit 4 Response Logs.

EL **ENGLISH LEARNER SUPPORT**

Create and Present Help students prepare for their small group discussion. Restate the discussion prompt as a question: *What is a perfect selfie?* Have students work with partners to identify details in the texts that help them answer the question and provide them with a word web graphic organizer to record and organize the information they locate. Provide these sentence frames to help them shape their argument: *One important quality of the perfect selfie is ___. Another important quality is ___ because ___.* **MODERATE**

© Houghton Mifflin Harcourt Publishing Company

APPLY

CRITICAL VOCABULARY

Answers:

1. *a*
2. *a*
3. *a*
4. *b*
5. *b*
6. *b*
7. *b*

VOCABULARY STRATEGY:
Context Clues

Sample answers:

1. **Word:** *rejected*

2. **Context Clue:** *We feel rejected, as if we don't matter.*

3. **My Guessed Definition:** Rejected *means "feeling unimportant."*

4. **Dictionary Definition:** *unacceptable in society*

 RESPOND

Go to the **Vocabulary Studio** for more on context clues.

WORD BANK

saturate	narcissist
passion	celebrity
indulgent	intimacy
eternity	

CRITICAL VOCABULARY

Practice and Apply Use what you know about the vocabulary words to answer these questions.

1. Which of the following is an example of **indulgent?**
   a. eating three desserts **b.** eating one dessert

2. Which of these is more likely to be **saturated?**
   a. a sponge **b.** a waterproof jacket

3. Which of the following is the better example of **intimacy?**
   a. a close friendship **b.** a new acquaintance

4. Which of the following is an example of **passion?**
   a. quiet laughter **b.** a strong emotion

5. Which of the following is an example of a **narcissist?**
   a. someone who loves flowers **b.** someone who loves only himself

6. Which of the following is most similar to **eternity?**
   a. the future **b.** forever

7. Which of the following is an example of a **celebrity?**
   a. a favorite teacher **b.** a TV star

VOCABULARY STRATEGY:
Context Clues

When you encounter an unfamiliar word, one way to figure out its meaning is to use **context clues,** or hints about meaning found in the text surrounding the unfamiliar word. Here is an example:

> **There are critics who say that selfies are taken only by narcissists[1] craving attention.**

To figure out the meaning of *narcissists,* note the words *craving attention* that appear after the unfamiliar word. These words hint that narcissists are people who crave attention. Also note that the word is footnoted. A footnote gives information about an unfamiliar word. Here, the footnote reads "people who are preoccupied with their looks. From the Greek myth of Narcissus, a young man who fell in love with his own reflection in a pool of water." This confirms that a *narcissist* is someone obsessed with his or her appearance.

Practice and Apply Find an unfamiliar word in each of the texts. Look at the surrounding text for clues to help you determine each word's meaning. Check your guesses in a dictionary.

 ENGLISH LEARNER SUPPORT

Practice Pronunciation Vietnamese and Hmong speakers may struggle to pronounce the soft sound of *c*. Model how to pronounce the soft *c* sound and have students repeat after you. Then write *narcissist, celebrity,* and *intimacy.* Circle the letter *c* in each word. Point to each letter *c*, pronounce soft *c*, and have students repeat the sound after you. Then point to the letter *c*, say the soft *c* sound, and then point to and pronounce the entire word. Again, have students repeat after you. Finally, invite pairs to practice saying the words to each other, correcting each other's pronunciation of soft *c* when necessary.   **SUBSTANTIAL/MODERATE**

LANGUAGE CONVENTIONS:
Commonly Confused Words

The main reason for writing is to communicate ideas with others. Therefore, to avoid creating confusion, it is extremely important for writers to use and spell words correctly. Many common English words, such as *its* and *it's,* are spelled similarly but have different meanings. Remember that *it's* is the contraction of "it is" or "it has," and the word *its* is the possessive form of the pronoun *it*. Other commonly confused words include *effect/affect, there/their/they're,* and *to/two/too.* Study how these words are used correctly in the selections.

The <u>effect</u> is more immediate. (noun)

The taker's attitude will naturally <u>affect</u> his or her facial expressions. (verb)

People naturally take selfies when something is happening right <u>there</u> close to them. (adverb describing location)

This made them more confident and comfortable with <u>their</u> smiling faces. (adjective, possessive form of *they*)

<u>They're</u> probably people who've never taken selfies. (contraction of "they are")

In <u>two</u> studies, researchers discovered that people who took selfies. . . . (the number 2)

It may not even be possible <u>to</u> take <u>too</u> many selfies. (part of verb *to take;* adverb meaning "more than enough" or "very")

Practice and Apply Choose the word that correctly completes each sentence.

1. My mom comes in to say goodnight when (its/it's) bedtime.

2. Jerome decided not to use the black-and-white (affect/effect) on his photograph.

3. (There/Their/They're) all obsessed with playing the latest computer game.

4. Andrea was (to/two/too) tired to wake up when her alarm rang.

5. My cousins gave me a ride (to/two/too) (there/their/they're) house.

6. What time will you be (there/their/they're)?

7. How much you study may (affect/effect) your grade on the test.

> ! Go to **A Glossary of Usage** in the **Grammar Studio** for more on commonly confused words.

LANGUAGE CONVENTIONS:
Commonly Confused Words

Emphasize the importance of learning to distinguish between commonly confused words. Write confusing words on the board:

- *effect/affect*
- *there, their, they're*
- *two, too, to*

Discuss the meaning and function of each word. Then review each of the model sentences. As you move through a discussion of the examples, have volunteers identify each commonly confused word.

Practice and Apply Have partners discuss their choices. Remind them one way to check their responses is to replace commonly confused words with complete phrases that represent contractions, for example, *they are* for *their* and *they're* and *you are* for *your* and *you're.*

1. *it's*

2. *effect*

3. *They're*

4. *too*

5. *to, their*

6. *there*

7. *affect*

 ENGLISH LEARNER SUPPORT

Use Commonly Confused Words Use the following supports with students of varying proficiency levels:

- Have students write sets of commonly confused words on index cards. Then write sets of sentence frames on the board that use these words, and have pairs practice working together to place the correct word in the correct sentence. **SUBSTANTIAL**

- Have students copy sets of commonly confused words. Then ask pairs to write sentences that use each word correctly. **MODERATE**

- After students have written sets of sentences that use commonly confused words, have them explain the meaning of the words or contractions. **LIGHT**

COMPARE AND EVALUATE ARGUMENTS

Before groups of students work on completing the table, emphasize that they are comparing two arguments. Review the meaning of the terms *claim, evidence, source,* and *logical fallacy.* Discuss the difference between explicitly stated claims and implicitly stated claims. In what way are the claims of the two texts alike or different?

ANALYZE THE TEXTS

Possible answers:

1. **DOK 3:** *The audience for "Better Than Words: Say It with a Selfie" seems to be mostly teens and young adults who have not begun taking and posting selfies. Phrases such as "Taking a selfie is like saying to the world, 'this is me, right now, right here!'" and calling critics "cavemen" support this idea. In "OMG, Not Another Selfie!" the audience is most likely parents, teachers, and other adults. Phrases such as "One of the reasons kids take selfies" and quoting from an article entitled "The Dangers of the Selfie and How You Can Help Your Kids" support this idea.*

2. **DOK 4:** *In "Better Than Words," the author argues that selfies are about self-discovery and self-expression. In "OMG, Not Another Selfie!" the author claims that selfies are about bringing attention to oneself so you feel better.*

3. **DOK 4:** *"OMG, Not Another Selfie!" provides the strongest evidence because it summarizes real studies and quotes named professionals.*

4. **DOK 3:** *"Better Than Words" uses hyperbole the most effectively, including references to critics as "cavemen" and the fact that "they probably hate people who do have self-confidence." In "OMG, Not Another Selfie!" the author uses repetition and parallelism the most effectively. Examples include: "We take selfies without even thinking. We strike a favorite pose. We click. We tap a couple of times. We share." "Maybe it's someone they have a crush on or someone who's bullied them. Maybe they want that person to have a better opinion of them."*

 RESPOND

Collaborate & Compare

BETTER THAN WORDS: SAY IT WITH A SELFIE
Argument by Gloria Chang

OMG, NOT *ANOTHER* SELFIE!
Argument by Shermakaye Bass

COMPARE AND EVALUATE ARGUMENTS

When you **compare and evaluate** two arguments on the same topic, you analyze how each argument is presented and decide how effective each argument is. First, determine the claim of each argument. Then, examine the strength of the evidence and the sources cited. Does the evidence effectively support the claim? Finally, identify flaws in the argument, including examples of logical fallacies. How do these flaws weaken the argument?

As a group, complete a chart like the one below. As you discuss, ask questions to help clarify group members' positions. Notice points on which you agree and disagree. Then, reach a group consensus about which text you think presents its argument more effectively.

	"BETTER THAN WORDS: SAY IT WITH A SELFIE"	**"OMG, NOT *ANOTHER* SELFIE!"**
Claim	*Selfies are the best way to express oneself.*	*Selfies are overused and can actually cause psychological or emotional damage.*
Evidence and Support	*Mostly anecdotal evidence; some references to science but no sources cited*	*quote from Dr. Allison Chase, information from ParentCo article, and reference sources*
Sources	*No specific sources cited*	*Katie Schunacher, Don't Press Send campaign of 2013; ParentCo articles*
Flaws in the Argument	*Hyperbole; Loaded language/ name-calling; stereotype; emotional appeal*	*Stereotype; emotional appeal*

ANALYZE THE TEXTS

Discuss these questions in your group.

1. **Compare** Do you think the two writers are addressing the same audience? How do you know?

2. **Synthesize** Both texts offer explanations about why people take selfies. Explain what each writer states is the purpose of the selfie.

3. **Critique** Which argument do you think provides the strongest evidence to support its claim? Explain.

4. **Evaluate** Which rhetorical device does each argument use most effectively? Explain.

RESEARCH AND DISCUSS

How have cell phones changed since they were first invented? With your group, briefly discuss how cell phones have changed since you—or your parents or grandparents—first began using them. Then, research developments and advancements in cell phone technology.

1. **Develop Questions** What would you like to know about the history of cell phones? As a group, brainstorm questions you would like to research. Then, decide who in your group is going to research which questions.

2. **Gather Information** As you research, make sure your sources are reliable and credible. Take notes from two or more sources, paraphrasing and summarizing key information to avoid plagiarism (the unauthorized use of someone else's words), and keep track of your sources. Use the checklist in the margin to help you identify information to include for each source. Cite those sources, following the format your teacher prefers.

3. **Share What You Learn** As a group, discuss your research. Listen closely to what others say, ask questions to request and clarify information, and build on the ideas of others as you examine the history of cell phones. Use your research notes to back up your ideas with text evidence.

4. **Prepare a Presentation** Use the information you gathered with your group to create an informational presentation that describes major events in the history of the cell phone. Consider using a sequence chart like the one below to help you organize important events in the development of the cell phone.

History of the Cell Phone

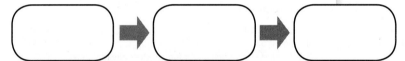

5. **Practice and Share Your Presentation** Decide who in your group will be responsible for sharing the different parts of your presentation with the class. Make sure all members participate. Practice your presentation and identify areas that need improvement. Finally, deliver your presentation to the class. As you present, make sure to make eye contact with the class, speak at a comfortable rate, enunciate clearly, and use natural gestures.

TRACKING SOURCES
- ❏ Author(s) name
- ❏ Article title
- ❏ Source or publisher
- ❏ Name of site
- ❏ Publication date

GROUP WORK CHECKLIST
- ❏ Listen actively.
- ❏ Ask specific questions.
- ❏ Respond respectfully.
- ❏ Consider group members' suggestions.
- ❏ Take notes about important points.

RESEARCH AND DISCUSS

Emphasize that making a group presentation involves collaboration and careful planning. In addition to activities required as part of the preparation phase, it is important to practice making a presentation. Remind students that listening carefully and being respectful of the contributions of others are essential to making a good presentation.

1. **Develop Questions** As students develop questions, circulate among groups and check that the questions are appropriate to the goal. Remind students that their questions should be specific and not too broad.

2. **Gather Information** Review the list in the margin about keeping track of sources. Remind students about the importance of identifying reliable and credible sources.

3. **Share What You Learn** Review the items in the checklist for group work that appears in the margin. Have students discuss each item and explain its significance.

4. **Prepare a Presentation** Discuss other visuals such as timelines and photographs that can be used to enhance the group's presentation. Remind students of the importance of assigning different roles to group members in the final stages of preparation.

5. **Practice and Share Your Presentation** Emphasize the importance of practicing a presentation to make sure it part is properly timed and effectively communicated. Encourage class discussion of outstanding questions after each presentation.

 ENGLISH LEARNER SUPPORT

Express Opinions Students requiring support for how best to express their opinions as part of a presentation can benefit greatly by practicing their presentations ahead of time. Prepare students to present their ideas by providing them with an outline they can fill in to map out the points they will cover and encouraging them to draw or research visual aids to include. Then pair students and have them practice giving their presentations to each other. Partners should correct pronunciation and misused words, as well as offering feedback for how to offer a more polished presentation to an audience. **MODERATE**

INDECENT READING

READER'S CHOICE

Setting a Purpose Have students review their Unit 4 Response Log and think about what they've already learned about ways you can make yourself heard. As students select their Independent Reading selections, encourage them to consider what more they want to know.

NOTICE NOTE

Explain that some selections may contain multiple signposts; others may contain only one. The same type of signpost can occur many times in the same text.

 LEARNING MINDSET

Persistence Encourage students to not give up when something is challenging. Remind students that challenges are part of learning. Explain that effort is the key to growth. Model positive self-talk, such as, "I know I can do this if I keep at it."

 **INDEPENDENT READING**

 ESSENTIAL QUESTION:

What are the ways you can make yourself heard?

Reader's Choice

Setting a Purpose Select one or more of these options from your eBook to continue your exploration of the Essential Question.

- Read the descriptions to see which text grabs your interest.
- Think about which genres you enjoy reading.

Notice & Note

In this unit, you practiced asking **Big Questions** and noticing and noting two signposts: **Extreme or Absolute Language** and **Contrasts and Contradictions.** As you read independently, these signposts and others will aid your understanding. Below are the anchor questions to ask when you read literature and nonfiction.

Reading Literature: Stories, Poems, and Plays		
Signpost	**Anchor Question**	**Lesson**
Contrasts and Contradictions	Why did the character act that way?	p. 3
Aha Moment	How might this change things?	p. 3
Tough Questions	What does this make me wonder about?	p. 172
Words of the Wiser	What's the lesson for the character?	p. 2
Again and Again	Why might the author keep bringing this up?	p. 92
Memory Moment	Why is this memory important?	p. 93

Reading Nonfiction: Essays, Articles, and Arguments		
Signpost	**Anchor Question(s)**	**Lesson**
Big Questions	What surprised me? What did the author think I already knew? What challenged, changed, or confirmed what I already knew?	p. 246 p. 420 p. 332
Contrasts and Contradictions	What is the difference, and why does it matter?	p. 247
Extreme or Absolute Language	Why did the author use this language?	p. 247
Numbers and Stats	Why did the author use these numbers or amounts?	p. 333
Quoted Words	Why was this person quoted or cited, and what did this add?	p. 333
Word Gaps	Do I know this word from someplace else? Does it seem like technical talk for this topic? Do clues in the sentence help me understand the word?	p. 421

 ENGLISH LEARNER SUPPORT

Develop Fluency Select a passage from a text that matches students' reading abilities. Read the passage aloud while students follow along silently.

- Echo read the passage by reading aloud one sentence and then having students repeat the sentence back to you. Then have the students read the passage silently several times. Check their comprehension by asking yes/no questions about the passage. **SUBSTANTIAL**
- Have students read and then reread the passage silently. Ask students to time their reading to track improvements over time. **MODERATE**

- Allow more fluent readers to select their own texts. Set a specific time for students to read silently (for example, 15 minutes). Check their comprehension by having them write a summary of what they read. **LIGHT**

Go to the **Reading Studio** for additional support in developing fluency.

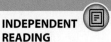

You can preview these texts in Unit 4 of your eBook.
Then, check off the text or texts that you select to read on your own.

POEM

I Was a Skinny Tomboy Kid
Alma Luz Villanueva

As a tomboy grows up, her self-perception shifts.

POEM

Words are Birds
Francisco X. Alarcón

A poet imagines words having the qualities and characteristics of birds.

SHORT STORY

Eleven
Sandra Cisneros

Can you be eleven but still feel ten, eight, or even two years old?

SHORT STORY

On Dragonwings
Lucy D. Ford

If you saw dragons in the night sky, would your life change?

INFORMATIONAL TEXT

Carved on the Walls
Judy Yung

A discovery on the walls of an immigration detainment center reveals a painful history.

Collaborate and Share   Find a partner to discuss what you learned from at least one of your independent readings.

- Give a brief synopsis or summary of the text.
- Describe any signposts that you noticed in the text and explain what they revealed to you.
- Describe what you most enjoyed or found most challenging about the text. Give specific examples.
- Decide if you would recommend the text to others. Why or why not?

 Go to the **Reading Studio** for more resources on **Notice & Note**.

INDEPENDENT READING

MATCHING STUDENTS TO TEXTS

Use the following information to guide students in using their texts.

I Was a Skinny Tomboy Kid
   Genre: poem
   Overall Rating: Challenging

Words Are Birds
   Genre: poem
   Overall Rating: Challenging

Eleven   Lexile: 1090L
   Genre: short story
   Overall Rating: Accessible

On Dragonwings   Lexile: 620L
   Genre: short story
   Overall Rating: Accessible

Carved on the Walls   Lexile: 1060L
   Genre: informational text
   Overall Rating: Challenging

Collaborate and Share   To assess how well students read the selections, walk around the room and listen to their conversations. Encourage students to be focused and specific in their comments.

Online **for Assessment**

- Independent Reading Selection Tests

 Encourage students to visit the **Reading Studio** to download a handy bookmark of **NOTICE & NOTE** signposts.

WHEN STUDENTS STRUGGLE . . .

Keep a Reading Log As students read their selected texts, have them keep a reading log for each selection to note signposts and their thoughts about them. Use their logs to assess how well they are noticing and reflecting on elements of the texts.

Reading Log for (title)		
Location	**Signpost I Noticed**	**My Notes about It**

UNIT ④ Task

- **CREATE A MULTIMODAL ARGUMENT**

MENTOR TEXT

OMG, NOT *ANOTHER* SELFIE!

Argument by
Shermakaye Bass

LEARNING OBJECTIVES

Writing Task

- Create a multimodal argument explaining why a specific medium is effective.
- State your argument's claim in the introduction.
- Support your claim with text evidence, sound reasoning, and relevant graphics or images.
- Organize information with a purposeful structure.
- Use words and a tone appropriate for your audience.
- Use appropriate rhetorical devices.
- Conclude by effectively summarizing the claim.
- Develop a focused, structured draft.
- Revise and edit drafts, incorporating feedback from peers.
- Use a rubric to evaluate writing.
- **Language** Use correct pronoun-antecedent agreement in writing.

Assign the Writing Task in *Ed.*

RESOURCES

- Unit 4 Response Log
- Reading Studio: Notice & Note
- Writing Studio: Writing Arguments
- ! Grammar Studio: Module 8: Using Pronouns Correctly

Language X-Ray: English Learner Support

Use the instruction below and the supports and scaffolds in the Teacher's Edition to help you guide students at different proficiency levels.

INTRODUCE THE WRITING TASK

Explain that a **multimodal argument** is a type of writing that allows you to use graphics and images to support your ideas. Point out that the word *argument* is related to the Spanish noun *argumento*, which means "a reason." Make sure students understand that a multimodal argument includes text evidence, images, and reasons to support a claim.

Remind students that the selections in this unit address ways you can make yourself heard. Work with students to select a topic to write about.

Encourage students to write about a form of self-expression they know well. Use sentence frames to help them articulate their ideas. For example: *I think ___ is the best form of self-expression because ____.*

Brainstorm words and phrases related to the topic, and write them on the board. Then, have students work with a partner to write one sentence about an effective form of self-expression. Tell students to use their sentences to begin their essays.

WRITING

Use Pronoun Agreements

Tell students that pronouns should always agree with the noun they replace. The word a pronoun refers to is its antecedent.

Use the following supports with students at varying proficiency levels:

- Provide students sample sentences containing different nouns and pronouns. Have students draw an arrow between each pronoun and its antecedent. **SUBSTANTIAL**
- Allow students to use a pronoun chart when writing their drafts. **MODERATE**
- After students have completed their drafts, have them work with a partner to check for correct pronoun agreement. **LIGHT**

WRITING

Use Words and Tone Appropriate for an Audience

Tell students that the audience is who an essay is intended for. The audience may be an informal group of peers or a more formal group of adults.

Review the potential types of audiences with students. Help students determine the audience for their multimodal argument. Use the following supports with students at varying proficiency levels:

- Review the terms *informal, formal, tone,* and *audience*. Have partners take turns naming one of these terms while the other writes it down to practice spelling it correctly. **SUBSTANTIAL**
- Have students select three sentences in their drafts. Have students revise the sentences to strengthen their choice of vocabulary. **MODERATE**
- Allow students to work with a partner when writing their drafts and focus on using vocabulary and tone appropriate for their audience. **LIGHT**

CREATE A MULTIMODAL ARGUMENT

Introduce students to the Writing Task by reading the introductory paragraph on page 322 with them. Remind students to refer to the notes they recorded in the Unit 4 Response Log as they plan and draft their arguments. The Response Log should contain ideas about ways to find your voice. Drawing on these different ideas will make their own writing more interesting and well- informed.

 For **writing support** for students at varying proficiency levels, see the **Language X-Ray** on page 322B.

USE THE MENTOR TEXT

Point out that their multimodal arguments will be similar to the argument "OMG, Not *Another* Selfie!" in that it uses rhetorical devices to construct an argument. However, their arguments will be shorter than the mentor text.

WRITING PROMPT

Review the prompt with students. Encourage them to ask questions about any part of the assignment that is unclear. Make sure they understand that the purpose of their argument is to use text evidence, reasoning, and graphics or images to convince the reader of their point of view.

 WRITING TASK

Create a Multimodal Argument

 Go to the **Writing Studio** for help writing your argument.

This unit focuses on the different ways people express themselves. Whether it's fine art, graphic design, photography, video, poetry, or comedy, there are many ways to make your unique voice heard. Select your favorite mode of self-expression, and write an argument explaining why that medium is effective. Include graphics or images to support your ideas. For an example of an engaging argument, review "OMG, Not *Another* Selfie!"

As you create your multimodal argument, use the notes from your Response Log, which you filled out after reading the texts in this unit.

Writing Prompt

Read the information in the box below.

This is the topic or context for your essay.

> There are many creative options for discovering your voice and making yourself heard.

Think carefully about the following question.

Based on the texts you read in this unit, how would you answer this question?

> What are the ways you can make yourself heard?

Write an argument explaining why your favorite type of self-expression is effective. Include images or graphics to support your ideas.

Now mark the words that identify exactly what you are being asked to produce.

Be sure to—

Review these points as you write and again when you finish. Make any needed changes.

- ❏ clearly state the argument's claim in your introduction
- ❏ support your claim with text evidence, sound reasoning, and relevant graphics or images
- ❏ organize information with a purposeful structure
- ❏ use words and a tone appropriate for your audience
- ❏ use appropriate rhetorical devices
- ❏ use correct pronoun-antecedent agreement
- ❏ conclude by effectively summarizing the claim

322   Unit 4

 ## LEARNING MINDSET

Belonging Remind students that they are all valuable members of the class and should support each other as learners. Encourage students to ask for help from a friend or teacher if they are struggling with the planning or drafting of their multimodal arguments.

① Plan

Use the charts below to help you plan your argument. A strong argument states a clear claim and supports it with sound reasons and evidence. Who is your audience and what do these readers already know about your topic? What graphics and images will you use to support your claim? Think about images that represent your favorite type of self-expression. For example, if you're writing about photography, choose favorite photographs that express the power of the medium. Be creative and selective with your choices.

Claim	
Audience	
Evidence and Reasoning	

Graphics and Images	How They Support the Argument

Background Reading Review the notes you have taken in your Response Log after reading the texts in this unit. These texts provide background reading that will help you formulate the key ideas you will include in your argument.

Go to **Writing Arguments: What is a Claim?** for help planning your argument.

Notice & Note
From Reading to Writing

As you plan your multimodal argument, apply what you've learned about signposts to your own work. Remember that writers use common features, called signposts, to help convey their message to readers.

Think about how you can incorporate **Quoted Words** into your argument.

Go to the **Reading Studio** for more resources on Notice & Note.

Use the notes from your **Response Log** as you plan your multimodal argument.

Create a Multimodal Argument 323

① PLAN

Allow time for students to discuss the topic with partners or in small groups and then to complete the planning table independently.

■ English Learner Support

Understand Academic Language Make sure students understand words and phrases used in the chart, such as *claim*, *audience*, *evidence*, and *reasoning*. **SUBSTANTIAL**

▶ NOTICE & NOTE
From Reading to Writing

Remind students they can use **Quoted Words** to include the opinions or conclusions of someone who is an expert on the topic of their argument. Students can also use Quoted Words to support a claim they are trying to make. Remind students to format direct quotations correctly and to give credit to the source.

Background Reading As they plan their multimodal arguments, remind students to refer to the notes they took in the Response Log. They may also review the selections to find additional text evidence to support ideas they want to include in their writing.

TO CHALLENGE STUDENTS . . .

Conduct Research Challenge students to incorporate examples from well-known sources or artists. Students may start by thinking of sources or artists they have already read or heard of that connect to the topic. If they cannot think of a source or artist, they may search online or at the library. Encourage students to add evidence from the sources to support the argument they are making. Remind students to put any directly quoted information in quotation marks and to document their sources.

WRITING

Organize Your Ideas Tell students that their outlines may have one main section for each paragraph of the essay. Provide the following sample based on the chart:

I. Introduction/ Claim

II. First Reason and Evidence

III. Second Reason and Evidence

IV. Third Reason and Evidence

V. Conclusion

Remind students that the claim should briefly mention the three reasons that support it. Each paragraph should build a logical argument that supports the claim with evidence. Tell students that all images and graphics should include captions that explain how they relate to the claim. The conclusion should then briefly summarize the reasons and evidence without repeating what has already been said.

❷ DEVELOP A DRAFT

Remind students to follow their outlines as they draft their essays, but point out that they can still make changes to their writing plan during this stage. As they write, they may discover that they need different evidence to support a claim, or that a particular piece of evidence works more effectively in a different paragraph.

■ English Learner Support

Use a Word Wall Help students create a word wall with significant words from the unit. Allow students to use the word wall, a dictionary, and other print resources when writing their essays. **MODERATE**

 WRITING TASK

 Go to **Writing Arguments: Building Effective Support** for help organizing your ideas.

Organize Your Ideas After you have gathered reasons, text evidence, and images to support your claim, organize the information. This will help you draft your argument. How will you capture the reader's attention in your introduction? What is your strongest evidence? Where will you insert images that support your argument? What information is important to include in the captions? How will you summarize your claim in a persuasive conclusion? Use the chart below to make notes about the elements of your multimodal argument.

Organizing My Multimodal Argument	
Introduction and claim	
Reason/Evidence	
Reason/Evidence	
Reason/Evidence	
Images and graphics with captions	
Conclusion	

❷ Develop a Draft

 You might prefer to draft your argument online.

Once you have completed your planning activities, you will be ready to begin drafting your argument. Refer to your charts and the outline you have created, as well as to any notes you took as you studied the texts in the unit. These will provide a kind of map for you to follow as you write. Using a word processor or online writing application makes it easier to make changes or move sentences around later when you are ready to revise your first draft.

WHEN STUDENTS STRUGGLE . . .

Draft the Argument Remind students that a detailed outline will help make it easier to write their multimodal argument. Students can then put the notes from their outline into complete sentences to create the first draft of their argument. Remind students that a first draft is not meant to be perfect. At this stage, they are just getting their ideas down on paper (or on the computer screen). They will have time to revise and edit their writing later.

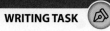

Use the Mentor Text

Audience

Authors consider their **audience** when they decide what words and tone to use. For example, a formal **tone** may be appropriate in an essay addressing government leaders, but it wouldn't be the best choice in an essay addressing teens. Note the way the author of "OMG, Not *Another* Selfie!" uses specific language to "speak" to her audience.

> "Hey, guys — look! Look at me! Here I am on summer vacation at the beach. Oh, and here I am with my bestie at the soccer game! And check this out: me doing duck face. And, oh, here I am with this morning's . . . pancakes."

The author uses a conversational tone and words like "bestie," "guys," and "check this out" to appeal to an audience of young people.

Apply What You've Learned Think about phrases and expressions that are appropriate for your audience. Use terms that will make your audience feel as if you are speaking directly to them.

Rhetorical Devices

Rhetorical devices are techniques writers use to enhance their arguments and communicate more effectively. They include parallelism, emotional appeals, and repetition. Notice how the author of "OMG, Not *Another* Selfie!" uses repetition and parallelism in the following passage.

> We take selfies without even thinking. We strike a favorite pose. We click. We tap a couple of times. We share.

The author repeats "we" in a series of short, parallel sentences. The rhetorical devices stress the idea that taking selfies is something that people do with little thought or consideration.

Apply What You've Learned Consider using repetition to emphasize one of your points. Experiment with repeating a word or phrase to capture the reader's attention and strengthen your argument.

Create a Multimodal Argument 325

WHY THIS MENTOR TEXT?

"OMG, Not *Another* Selfie!" provides an excellent example of an argument. Use the instruction below to help students use the mentor text as a model for using rhetorical devices and considering their audience when creating a multimodal argument.

USE THE MENTOR TEXT

Audience Ask a volunteer to read aloud the top paragraph from "OMG, Not *Another* Selfie!" on p. 325. Discuss how the author uses vocabulary and a conversational tone to appeal to her audience. Then invite students to discuss who the audience will be for their multimodal argument and how to use vocabulary and tone to appeal to that audience.

Rhetorical Devices To help students understand how to use rhetorical devices in a multimodal argument, have them read the bottom paragraph from "OMG, Not *Another* Selfie!" on p. 325. Point out that the author uses repetition and parallelism to make her point. Remind students that emotional appeal is another effective rhetorical device to use in an argument.

 ENGLISH LEARNER SUPPORT

Use the Mentor Text Use the following supports with students at varying proficiency levels:

- Write the word *audience* on the board. Tell students that an audience is the person or group who views, listens to, or reads a work. Help students think of different types of audiences. **SUBSTANTIAL**

- Have students work in pairs to read the mentor text and identify the rhetorical devices used in the argument. **MODERATE**

- Have students work in small groups or pairs to construct examples of rhetorical devices they can use in their arguments. **LIGHT**

WRITING

③ REVISE

On Your Own Have students answer each question in the chart to determine how they can improve their drafts. Invite volunteers to model their revision techniques.

With a Partner Have students ask peer reviewers to evaluate their use of rhetorical devices by answering the following questions:

- How well do the rhetorical devices strengthen the argument?
- Can persuasive language be added to the rhetorical devices to make them even stronger?

Students should use the reviewer's feedback to add relevant examples, evidence, and graphics that further support the claims.

 **WRITING TASK**

③ Revise

 Go to **Writing Arguments: Creating a Coherent Argument** for help revising your argument.

On Your Own Once you have written your draft, go back and look for ways to improve your multimodal argument. As you reread and revise, think about whether you have achieved your purpose. The Revision Guide will help you focus on specific elements to make your writing stronger.

Revision Guide		
Ask Yourself	**Tips**	**Revision Techniques**
1. Does my introduction create interest and clearly state a claim?	**Underline** the claim and **circle** the attention-getting opening.	**Add** a clear claim, and **add** a relevant, attention-getting detail.
2. Are my reasons and evidence organized logically?	**Mark** the reasons and evidence.	**Reorder** reasons and evidence in a logical sequence.
3. Do my images and graphics support my claim?	**Mark** images and graphics.	**Revise** captions to clarify the connection between the claim and the images and graphics.
4. Is there pronoun-antecedent agreement in my sentences?	**Underline** pronouns and **circle** antecedents.	**Replace** pronouns and antecedents that don't agree.
5. How well have I used persuasive language and rhetorical devices?	**Mark** persuasive language and rhetorical devices.	**Add** persuasive language or strengthen a rhetorical device to emphasize a point.
6. Does my conclusion summarize my claim?	**Mark** the conclusion.	**Add** a statement that summarizes the claim.

ACADEMIC VOCABULARY
As you conduct your **peer review**, be sure to use these words.

- ❑ appropriate
- ❑ authority
- ❑ consequence
- ❑ element
- ❑ justify

With a Partner Once you and your partner have worked through the Revision Guide on your own, exchange papers and evaluate each other's draft in a **peer review.** Focus on providing revision suggestions for at least three of the items mentioned in the chart. Explain why you think your partner's draft should be revised and what your specific suggestions are.

When receiving feedback from your partner, listen attentively and ask questions to make sure you fully understand the revision suggestions.

 ENGLISH LEARNER SUPPORT

Write Captions Explain that images and graphics often use captions to demonstrate how they connect to the text. Have students read their captions for each image or graphic. Then have students revise the captions to clarify the connection between the images, graphics, and claim. **LIGHT**

④ Edit

Once you have addressed the organization, development, and flow of ideas in your argument, improve the finer points of your draft. Edit for the proper use of standard English conventions and correct any misspellings or grammatical errors.

WRITING TASK

Go to the **Grammar Studio** to learn more about pronouns.

Language Conventions

A **pronoun** is a word that is used in place of a noun or another pronoun. The word that the pronoun refers to is its **antecedent**. Pronouns should always agree in number with their antecedents.

To make sure a pronoun agrees with its antecedent, ask yourself, "Which noun is this pronoun replacing?"

In the sentence below, the pronoun "them" replaces the noun "phones."

   Please turn your *phones* off, and keep *them* off during the movie.

As you edit, stay aware of personal, indefinite, and relative pronouns.

- **Personal pronouns** express person or thing, number, gender, and case. Singular examples include *I, you, she, he, it;* plural examples are *we, you,* and *they.*

- **Indefinite pronouns** refer to one or more persons or things not specifically mentioned. They usually have no antecedents. Indefinite pronouns include: *another, anybody, no one, neither, both, many, none, more, most, some, any.*

- **Relative pronouns** relate, or connect, adjective clauses to the words they modify in sentences. They include *who, whom, which, what,* and *that.*

In the chart below, pronouns are underlined and antecedents are circled.

PRONOUN TYPE	EXAMPLE
Personal	Selfies don't represent reality, and they don't capture people realistically, either.
Indefinite	And no one wants to sit in the school cafeteria with a known narcissist, right?
Relative	And the person who invented the selfie stick—Wayne Fromm, who patented his selfie stick in 2005—is probably pretty rich by now.

⑤ Publish

Finalize your argument and choose a way to share it with your audience. Consider these options:

- Post your argument as a blog on a classroom or school website.
- Publish your essay in the school newsletter.

WHEN STUDENTS STRUGGLE . . .

Identify Pronouns and Antecedents Some students may have difficulty identifying the pronouns and their antecedents in sentences. Remind students that a pronoun takes the place of a noun, its antecedent, and that the pronouns and their antecedents should always agree in number. Allow students to use one color to circle the pronouns in their sentences and another color to circle the antecedents. Some students may benefit from working with a partner or adult helper to identify the pronouns and antecedents in their sentences.

④ EDIT

Suggest that students read their drafts aloud to assess how well they used pronouns. Remind students that pronouns should always agree in number with their antecedents.

LANGUAGE CONVENTIONS

Pronouns Review the information about pronouns with students. Then discuss the example sentences in the chart, asking students to identify the pronouns in each one. To emphasize the importance of pronoun–antecedent agreement, write a brief paragraph on the board using pronouns and antecedents that do not agree. Read the paragraph aloud so students can see and hear the difference. Have students carefully edit their multimodal arguments to use consistent pronoun-antecedent agreement.

■ English Learner Support

Check Pronoun-Antecedent Agreement Have students work in pairs to locate the pronouns and their antecedents in their arguments. Have students work together to check that each pronoun agrees with its antecedent. **MODERATE**

⑤ PUBLISH

Form small groups of students whose arguments promote different forms of self-expression. Have students read each other's arguments and then write a paragraph commenting on each one. Remind students that their comments should address the content of the claims and evidence, not personally attack the writer or his/her opinion.

WRITING

USE THE SCORING GUIDE

Have students read the scoring guide and ask questions about any words, phrases, or ideas that are unclear. Put students in groups of three. Then have students take turns reading the final drafts of their group members' multimodal arguments. Ask them to score the arguments using the scoring guide. Each student should write a paragraph explaining the reasons for the score he or she awarded the argument in each category.

 **WRITING TASK**

Use the scoring guide to evaluate your essay.

Writing Task Scoring Guide: Multimodal Argument		
Organization/Progression	**Development of Ideas**	**Use of Language and Conventions**
4 • The reasons, evidence, images, and graphics are organized logically and consistently to persuasive effect. • Coherence occurs within and across the paragraphs.	• The introduction skillfully pulls the reader in; the writer clearly states a claim about the topic. • The claim is convincingly supported by logical reasons, relevant text evidence, and appropriate images and graphics. • The conclusion effectively summarizes the claim.	• Language and word choice is purposeful and persuasive. • Pronouns are used correctly. • Spelling, capitalization, and punctuation are correct. • Grammar, usage, and mechanics are correct.
3 • The organization of reasons, evidence, images, and graphics is confusing in a few places. • Coherence occurs within and across most paragraphs.	• The introduction is somewhat engaging; the writer states a claim about the topic. • Most reasons, evidence, and images and graphics support the claim. • The conclusion restates the claim.	• Language and word choice is often purposeful and persuasive. • Pronouns are used correctly in most instances. • Some spelling, capitalization, and punctuation mistakes are present. • Some grammar and usage errors occur.
2 • The organization of reasons, evidence, images, and graphics is confusing in many places. • There is little coherence within and across paragraphs.	• The introduction is incomplete; the writer identifies a topic, but the claim is not clearly stated. • The reasons, evidence, and images and graphics are not always logical or relevant. • The conclusion includes an incomplete summary of the claim.	• Language is often vague and unpersuasive. • Pronouns are often incorrectly used. • Spelling, capitalization, and punctuation are often incorrect but do not make reading difficult. • Grammar and usage errors make the writing difficult to understand in some places.
1 • The organization is not logical; reasons, evidence, images, and graphics are presented randomly. • A lack of coherence within and across paragraphs makes the argument difficult to understand.	• The introduction does not include a claim. • Supporting reasons, evidence, images, and graphics are missing. • The conclusion is missing.	• Language is inappropriate for the text. • Language is vague and confusing. • Pronouns are used incorrectly most of the time. • Many spelling, capitalization, and punctuation errors are present. • Many grammatical and usage errors confuse the writer's ideas.

Reflect on the Unit

By completing your multimodal argument, you have created a writing product that pulls together and expresses your thoughts about the reading you have done in this unit. Now is a good time to reflect on what you have learned.

Reflect on the Essential Question

- What are the ways you can make yourself heard? How has your answer to this question changed since you first considered it when you started this unit?

- From the texts you've read, what are some examples of ways to make yourself heard?

Reflect on Your Reading

- Which selections were the most interesting or surprising to you?

- From which selection did you learn the most about how people make their voices heard?

Reflect on the Writing Task

- What difficulties did you encounter while working on your multimodal argument? How might you avoid them next time?

- Which image or graphic do you think adds the most value to your argument? Why do you think so?

- What improvements did you make to your argument as you were revising?

LEARNING MINDSET

Try Again   Tell students that sometimes they may think they know the answer to a question, but then find out they were incorrect. Encourage students to go back to the text and reread until they figure it out.

REFLECT ON THE UNIT

Have students reflect on the questions independently and write some notes in response to each one. Then have students meet with partners or in small groups to discuss their reflections. Circulate during these discussions to identify the questions that are generating the liveliest conversations. Wrap up with a whole-class discussion focused on these questions.

Instructional Overview and Resources

	Instructional Focus	Online **Ed** Resources
Unit Instruction **Never Give Up**	Unit 5 Essential Question Unit 5 Academic Vocabulary	**Stream to Start:** Never Give Up **Unit 5 Response Log**

ANALYZE & APPLY

"A Schoolgirl's Diary"
from *I Am Malala*
Memoir by Malala Yousafzai
with Patricia McCormick
Lexile 820L

> **NOTICE & NOTE** READING MODEL
> **Signposts**
> • Big Questions
> • Numbers and Stats
> • Quoted Words

Reading
• Analyze Characteristics and Features of Informational Texts
• Generate Questions

Writing: Write a Formal Letter

Speaking and Listening: Discuss with a Small Group

Vocabulary: Greek and Latin Roots

Language Conventions: Capitalization

🔊 **Audio**

Reading Studio: Notice & Note

Level Up Tutorial: Setting: Effect on Plot

Level Up Tutorial: Setting a Purpose for Reading

Writing Studio: Writing Arguments

Speaking and Listening Studio: Participating in Collaborative Discussions

Vocabulary Studio: Analyzing Word Structure

Grammar Studio: Module 11: Capital Letters

"The First Day of School"
Short Story by R.V. Cassill
Lexile 780L

Reading
• Analyze Elements of Plot
• Analyze Influence of Setting on Plot and Character

Writing: Write an Analytical Essay

Speaking and Listening: Compare and Contrast with a Small Group

Vocabulary: Thesaurus

Language Conventions: Sentence Patterns

🔊 **Audio**

Close Read Screencasts: Modeled Discussions

Reading Studio: Notice & Note

Level Up Tutorial: Plot Stages

Writing Studio: Writing Informative Texts

Speaking and Listening Studio: Participating in Collaborative Discussions

Vocabulary Studio: Using Resources

Grammar Studio: Module 1: Lesson 10: Kinds of Sentences

"Speech to the Young:
Speech to the Progress-
Toward"
Poem by Gwendolyn Brooks

Reading
• Analyze the Effects of Meter and Structural Elements
• Make Inferences About Theme and Author's Purpose

Writing: Write a Short Poem

Speaking and Listening: Record Your Poem

🔊 **Audio**

Reading Studio: Notice & Note

Level Up Tutorial: Theme

Writing Studio: Writing as a Process

Speaking and Listening Studio: Producing and Publishing with Technology

---

	Unit Introduction	A Schoolgirl's Diary *from I Am Malala*							The First Day of School						Speech to the Young
SUGGESTED PACING: **30 DAYS**	1	2	3	4	5	6	7	8	9	10	11	12	13	14	15 16

English Learner Support	Differentiated Instruction	Online Ed Assessment
• Discuss Feelings • Practice Academic Vocabulary		

English Learner Support	Differentiated Instruction	Assessment
• Text X-Ray • Explore Synonyms • Understand Text Features • Use Cognates • Capitalize Correctly in Writing • Use Questioning as a Pre-Reading Strategy • Ask Big Questions • Answer Big Questions • Make a Timeline • Edit for Capitalization • Oral Assessment • Discuss with a Small Group • Develop Vocabulary	**When Students Struggle** • Use a Graphic Organizer • Use a Graphic Organizer • Analyze Characteristics and Features • Ask Big Questions	**Selection Test**
• Text X-Ray • Decode and Understand Segregation • Use Cognates • Develop Vocabulary • Recognize Informal Language • Ask Questions for Comprehension • Oral Assessment • Compare and Contrast with a Small Group • Internalize Language • Write Sentences	**When Students Struggle** • Use the Plot Diagram	**Selection Test**
• Text X-Ray • Distinguish Consonant Sounds • Learn Letter Sounds • Oral Assessment		**Selection Test**

from **Into the Air**/*from* **The Wright Brothers**

Independent Reading **End of Unit**

17 · 18 · 19 · 20 · 21 · 22 · 23 · 24 · 25 · 26 · 27 · 28 · 29 · 30

UNIT 5 Continued

| | **Instructional Focus** | **Resources** |

COLLABORATE & COMPARE

from *Into the Air*
Graphic Biography by Robert Burleigh
Lexile 760L

Reading
• Analyze Characteristics of Multimodal Texts
• Determine Key Ideas in Multimodal Texts
Writing: Write a Summary

Speaking and Listening: Discuss with a Small Group

Vocabulary: Affixes

Language Conventions: Adverbs and Adverb Clauses

 Audio

Reading Studio: Notice & Note

Level Up Tutorial: Main Idea and Details

Writing Studio: Using Textual Evidence

Speaking and Listening Studio: Participating in Collaborative Discussions

Vocabulary Studio: Roots, Base Words, and Affixes

Grammar Studio: Module 3: Lesson 5: The Adverb

MENTOR TEXT

from *The Wright Brothers: How They Invented the Airplane*
Biography by Russell Freedman
Lexile 1100L

Reading
• Analyze Characteristics of Informational Texts
• Determine Key Ideas
Writing: Write a Summary

Speaking and Listening: Hold a Small Group Discussion

Vocabulary: Resources

Language Conventions: Commas and Sentence Types

 Audio

Text in Focus: Understanding Technical Language

Reading Studio: Notice & Note

Level Up Tutorial: Using Transitions

Writing Studio: Using Textual Evidence

Speaking and Listening Studio: Participating in Collaborative Discussions

Vocabulary Studio: Using Resources

Grammar Studio: Module 12: Lessons 2–5: Using Commas Correctly

---

Collaborate and Compare

Reading: Infer and Synthesize Key Ideas Within and Across Texts

Speaking and Listening: Compare Key Ideas

 INDEPENDENT READING

The Independent Reading selections are only available in the eBook.

 Go to the Reading Studio for more information on Notice & Note.

"Paul Revere's Ride"
Poem by Henry Wadsworth Longfellow

"The Road Not Taken"
Poem by Robert Frost

END OF UNIT

Writing Task: Biographical Report

Reflect on the Unit

Writing: Write a Biographical Report

Language Conventions: Adverbs and Conjunctive Adjectives

Speaking and Listening: Produce and Present a Podcast

Unit 5 Response Log

Mentor Text: from *The Wright Brothers: How They Invented the Airplane*

Writing Studio: Conducting Research; Using Textual Evidence

Speaking and Listening Studio: Using Media in a Presentation

Grammar Studio: Module 3: Lesson 5: The Adverb

English Learner Support		Differentiated Instruction	Online **Ed** Assessment
• Text X-Ray • Develop Vocabulary with Visual Supports • Use Cognates • Monitor Understanding • Discuss Multimodal Text • Speak Using Adverbs • Decode Compound Words • Oral Assessment • Internalize Language • Write Basic Vocabulary		**When Students Struggle** • Idea Web • Using a Graphic Organizer **To Challenge Students** • Write Descriptively	**Selection Test**
• Text X-Ray • Internalize Language • Practice Vocabulary • Listen for Details About Time • Internalize and Confirm Understanding • Understand Important Details • Practice Using Units of Measure	• Identify Transitions • Oral Assessment • Hold a Small Group Discussion • Use Resources • Use Commas	**When Students Struggle** • Transitions and Commas **To Challenge Students** • Problems and Solutions	**Selection Test**
• Ask Questions		**When Students Struggle** • Make a Presentation	

Damon and Pythias
Drama by Fan Kissen

"Education First" from "Malala's Speech to the United Nations"
Speech by Malala Yousafzai
Lexile 870L

Selection Tests

• Language X-Ray • Understand Academic Language • Use a Word Wall • Use the Mentor Text • Use Transitional Words • Use Adverbs • Adapt the Essay		**When Students Struggle** • Draft the Report • Identify Adverbs • Provide Feedback **To Challenge Students** • Conduct Additional Research	**Unit Test**

NEVER GIVE UP

? Connect to the ESSENTIAL QUESTION

Ask a volunteer to read aloud the Essential Question. Discuss how the image on page 330 relates to the question. Why was a sunrise used as a symbol for refusing to give up? Ask students to think of times they or people they know have faced major problems and pushed through to keep getting up each day, even when it may have felt impossible. Point out that by sharing our thoughts and experiences in writing, we help each other resist the urge to give up.

■ English Learner Support

Discuss Feelings Ask students to discuss a time when they lay down to sleep feeling unhappy about having to face something the next day that felt too big to handle. Ask: *Who or what keeps you going?* Pantomime for beginners the process of going to bed unhappy and waking up determined. **ALL LEVELS**

DISCUSS THE QUOTATION

Explain that this quotation is from "Speech to the Young" by poet Gwendolyn Brooks. Encourage students to look up the poem. Born in Kansas in 1917, Brooks was a poet and teacher and the first African American to win the Pulitzer Prize. She was also the first African American woman to serve as a poetry consultant to the Library of Congress.

After the line from her poem quoted here, she goes on to say that we should not live for the battles we win, but for the battles we fight—although she expresses this thought in a more poetic way. Point out to students the theme: "Never Give Up." It is not about one instance of achievement—winning or getting the prize. It is about the value of individual determination. It is about the principle of determination, not the outcome.

? ESSENTIAL QUESTION:

What keeps people from giving up?

> " Even if you are not ready for day / it cannot always be night. "
>
> Gwendolyn Brooks

330   Unit 5

⚙ LEARNING MINDSET

Plan Remind students to set a plan for completing their work. Encourage students to create a plan for reading and completing all of the tasks for every selection in this unit. Encourage them to stick to their plans as they complete their work, but remind them that it is okay to revise their plans as circumstances change.

ACADEMIC VOCABULARY

Academic Vocabulary words are words you use when you discuss and write about texts. In this unit you will practice and learn five words.

☑ achieve   ☐ individual   ☐ instance   ☐ outcome   ☐ principle

Study the Word Network to learn more about the word **achieve.**

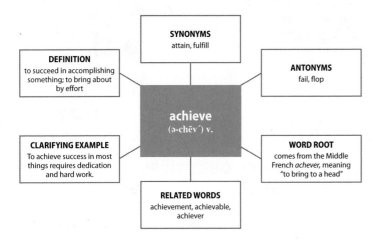

Write and Discuss Discuss the completed Word Network with a partner, making sure to talk through all of the boxes until you both understand the word, its synonyms, antonyms, and related forms. Then, fill out Word Networks for the remaining four words. Use a dictionary or online resource to help you complete the activity.

  Go online to access the Word Networks.

RESPOND TO THE ESSENTIAL QUESTION

In this unit, you will read about the different ways people succeed and thrive in the face of adversity or difficulties. As you read, you will revisit the **Essential Question** and gather your ideas about it in the **Response Log** that appears on page R5. At the end of the unit, you will have the opportunity to write a **biographical report**. The report will be based on your research on a well-known person who refused to give up. Filling out the Response Log will help you prepare for this writing task.

  You can also go online to access the Response Log.

ACADEMIC VOCABULARY

As students complete Word Networks for the remaining four vocabulary words, encourage them to include all the categories shown in the completed network if possible, but point out that some words do not have clear synonyms or antonyms. Some words may also function as different parts of speech—for example, *individual* may be a noun or an adjective.

achieve (ə-chēv´) *v.* To succeed in accomplishing something; to bring about by effort

individual (ĭn´də-vĭj´ŏŏ-əl) *adj.* Of or relating to an individual, especially a single human: individual consciousness (Spanish cognate: *individual*)

instance (ĭn´stəns) *n.* An example that is cited to prove or illustrate a point; one time something happened

outcome (out´kŭm´) *n.* An end result; a consequence

principle (prĭn´sə-pəl) *n.* A basic truth, law, or assumption; a rule or standard; a basic quality or element (Spanish cognate: *principio*)

RESPOND TO THE ESSENTIAL QUESTION

Direct students to the Unit 5 Response Log. Explain that students will use it to record ideas and details from the selections that help answer the Essential Question. When they work on the writing task at the end of the unit, their Response Logs will help them think about what they have read and make connections between texts.

 ENGLISH LEARNER SUPPORT

Practice Academic Vocabulary Write the following on the board: *Never Give Up: This theme is not about what you can* ***achieve*** *by winning or getting the prize. It is about the value of* ***individual*** *determination. It is about the* ***principle***, *not the* ***outcome***.

Ask students to work together in three small, mixed-ability groups to examine the meaning of this statement. Ask beginners to practice pronouncing the words and using references to translate the ones that do not have cognates.

- Ask the first group to take the first sentence of the statement. Have the next group take the second sentence of the statement. And have the last group take the last sentence of the statement.
- Provide the groups the definitions from Teacher's Edition page 331 and encourage them to use what they know about the theme from page 330 to craft their own version of this statement in their own words and languages. **ALL LEVELS**

READING MODEL

A SCHOOLGIRL'S DIARY
from I AM MALALA

Memoir by Malala Yousafzai with Patricia McCormick

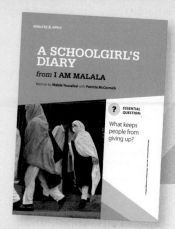

GENRE ELEMENTS
MEMOIR/AUTOBIOGRAPHY

While a biography tells the story of someone else's life, both **memoir** and **autobiography** involve a person telling his or her own story. An autobiography will often focus on the facts of an entire life, rather than on inner thoughts. A memoir focuses on a few important stories and has a more informal conversational tone. It includes people and events that have been very important to the writer's life and have helped him or her achieve a deeper understanding of his or her role in the world.

LEARNING OBJECTIVES

- Analyze characteristics and features of informational text.
- Generate questions to guide reading.
- Generate questions and key words to guide research.
- Discuss in a small group the importance of going to school.
- Use Greek and Latin roots to understand vocabulary.
- Understand correct capitalization of proper nouns.
- **Language** Discuss with a partner the purpose of features of informational text using the key term *prologue*.

TEXT COMPLEXITY

Quantitative Measures	A Schoolgirl's Diary *from* I Am Malala	Lexile: 820L
Qualitative Measures	**Ideas Presented** Much is explicit, but moves to some implied meaning. Requires some inferential reasoning.	
	Structure Used Primarily explicit. Varies from simple chronological order. Supports with prologue and subheadings.	
	Language Used Explicit, contemporary. Some culturally and regional specific language.	
	Knowledge Required Some references to other events. Relies on some background knowledge.	

Online

RESOURCES

- Unit 5 Response Log

- Selection Audio

- Reading Studio: Notice & Note

- Level Up Tutorials: Setting: Effect on Plot; Setting a Purpose for Reading

- Writing Studio: Writing Arguments

- Speaking and Listening Studio: Participating in a Collaborative Discussion

- Vocabulary Studio: Analyzing Word Structure

- Grammar Studio: Module 11: Capital Letters

- "A Schoolgirl's Diary" from *I Am Malala* Selection Test

SUMMARIES

English

Malala Yousafzai was a teenage girl in Mingora, Pakistan, in 2012. The local Taliban had forbidden girls to attend school, but Malala and a few of the other girls continued to attend. Malala agreed to keep a diary for the British Broadcasting Corporation (BBC) so the rest of the world would know what was happening to girls under Taliban rule. In October, a man boarded the school bus and shot Malala. She survived to write a memoir and win the Nobel Peace Prize for her support of education for girls. This is a selection from that memoir.

Spanish

Malala Yousafzai era una joven adolescente en Mingora, Pakistán en 2012. El grupo local del Talibán les había prohibido a las niñas asistir a la escuela, pero Malala y otras niñas continuaron asistiendo. Malala accedió a mantener un diario con la Corporación de Radiodifusión Británica (BBC) para que el resto del mundo supiera qué les pasaba a las niñas bajo el dominio del Talibán. En octubre, un hombre abordó el autobús escolar y le disparó a Malala. Ella sobrevivió para escribir una autobiografía y ganar el Premio Nobel de la Paz por su apoyo a la educación de niñas. Esto es una selección de esa autobiografía.

SMALL-GROUP OPTIONS

Have students work in small groups to read and discuss the selection.

Numbered Heads Together

This will help students get ready to generate questions based on text. Before the class reads the text, put students into groups of four and ask students to number themselves 1–4.

- Ask the class a question such as: Why would anyone want to create an edict that forbids any other group of people from attending school?

- Students discuss their theories in each group and come up with additional questions, such as "What is an edict?" Ask them to record their questions for later activities. They may also look up words.

- Call out a number and ask those with that number in each group to summarize their discussion and give details about their questions.

Activating Academic Vocabulary

Post the Academic Vocabulary words *achieve, individual, outcome, instance,* and *principle* on the board.

- Tell students to use at least one of these words in all discussions about the first selection. You may choose to make a game of this, such as giving points for every correct usage. Do not take away points for incorrect usage so that you will not discourage risk-taking.

- Allow students to use references, but focus on modeling use of the words in context. Ask: *Malala and her family seemed to live their lives based on some important* principles. *What do you think a few of them might be? Do you live your life based on any* principle *or* principles?

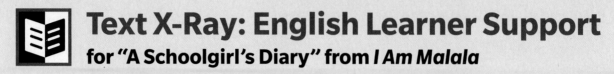

Text X-Ray: English Learner Support
for "A Schoolgirl's Diary" from *I Am Malala*

Use the Text X-Ray and the supports and scaffolds in the Teacher's Edition to help guide students at different proficiency levels through the selection.

INTRODUCE THE SELECTION
DISCUSS PERSISTENCE

In this lesson, students will need to be able to understand the idea of persistence in the face of fear. Define *persistence* as "not giving up." The Essential Question is: What keeps people from giving up? The author of this selection, Malala Yousafzai, had to face many obstacles to get an education and resist the Taliban. Ask students to discuss what makes a person fight to overcome obstacles instead of giving up. Use these questions and sentence frames to facilitate the discussion:

- *What real or imaginary stories include a character who shows persistence? The character _____ shows persistence when _____.*
- *When have you or someone you know shown persistence? _____ showed persistence when _____. _____ did not give up when _____.*

CULTURAL REFERENCES

The following words and phrases may be unfamiliar to students:

- *human rights* (paragraph 1): These are rights everyone has no matter where they live, such as physical safety.
- *mosque* (paragraph 3): The building used for Muslim worship is called a mosque in English. In Arabic, the word is *masgid*.
- *Pashtun* (paragraph 4): An ethnic group that live mainly in Afghanistan and Pakistan.

Point out to students that there are many references included in footnotes to explain things they may not understand in the text. Tell students to take the time to read the footnotes as well as the main text. Remind them to be willing to ask questions.

LISTENING

Understand the Author's Purpose

Draw students' attention to the background description and the first paragraph. Explain that the author's main purpose is often revealed right at the beginning of a text.

Have students listen as you read aloud the background information and paragraph 1 (the dedication). Use the following supports with students at varying proficiency levels:

- Tell students that you will ask questions, and they can indicate yes or no with thumbs up or down. For example, ask: *Is the author talking about sports?* (*no*) *Is the author talking about religion?* (*no*) *Is the author talking about education or schools?* (*yes*) **SUBSTANTIAL**
- Have students identify the words in the introduction that reveal the author's purpose. Ask: *What words in the text tell you what Yousafzai wanted to support or promote by telling her story?* ("no access to education," "fought for their basic human rights and education") **MODERATE**
- Pair students to circle and discuss the words and phrases in the excerpts that reveal that the author's purpose is to reach people worldwide. Ask: *How do you know the author's purpose is to help more than just Pakistani girls?* ("to those children all over the world . . . to those teachers . . . anyone who has fought for their basic human rights and education") **LIGHT**

SPEAKING

Discuss Text Features

Have students discuss the features of the text using the key term *prologue*. Circulate around the room to make sure students are using the term correctly.

Use the following supports with students at varying proficiency levels:

- Display and read aloud this sentence with students echo reading: *The prologue is also sometimes called the preface or the introduction.* Have students practice saying the sentence to each other. **SUBSTANTIAL**
- Have students skim through the prologue of the selection. Note that the prologue is in two parts: Part 2 begins after paragraph 9. Ask students to identify why there is a line between the parts of the prologue. (*Part 1 of the prologue is about her home and family; Part 2 is about going to school.*) **MODERATE**
- Pair students to discuss the purpose of Part 1 of the prologue. Ask: *What does the author want you to know about her life before she tells you her story?* (*The prologue shows that Malala's home life is not so different from that of other teens around the world.*) **LIGHT**

READING

Analyze Visuals

Draw students' attention to the photographs and the map. Point out that they should use visuals as a prereading strategy because they can learn a lot by skimming these features first.

Work with students to study the five photographs and one map. Use the following supports with students at varying proficiency levels:

- Tell students that you will ask questions about the photographs and map, and they can indicate yes or no with thumbs up or down. For example, ask: *Is the author talking about America?* (*no*) *Is the author talking about boys?* (*no*) *Girls?* (*yes*) *Is the author talking about Pakistan?* (*yes*) **SUBSTANTIAL**
- Have students identify Malala's central problem. Ask: *Why do all the photographs show girls at school?* (*In her area, the Taliban said Muslim girls were not allowed to attend school.*) **MODERATE**
- Point out the photograph on page 344. Pair students to identify what they can tell about present-day Malala from this photograph. (*confident, happy, willing to take charge of things*) **LIGHT**

WRITING

Write a Letter

Guide students to use formal language for the letter-writing assignment on page 349.

Before beginning the writing assignment, discuss student opinions in a group. Write down words and phrases that come up in discussion on the board so students can spell them correctly in their letters. Model formal language. Use the following supports with students at varying proficiency levels:

- Provide a model business letter, and work with students to create text for the letter by using simple text frames, such as: *In my opinion, the BBC _____. I think this because _____.* **SUBSTANTIAL**
- Provide a model business letter for students to use as a template, and allow students to work in small groups with native speakers or advanced language learners to write the letter. **MODERATE**
- Provide a model business letter for students to use as a template, and have students work with a partner to write the letter using the words and phrases on the board. **LIGHT**

EXPLAIN THE SIGNPOSTS

Explain that **NOTICE & NOTE Signposts** are significant moments in the text that help readers understand and analyze works of fiction or nonfiction. Use the instruction on these pages to introduce students to the signposts **Big Questions, Numbers and Stats,** and **Quoted Words**. Then use the selection that follows to have students apply the signposts to a text.

For a full list of the fiction and nonfiction signposts, see page 406.

BIG QUESTIONS

Write the following **Big Questions** on the board:

- What surprised me?
- What challenged, changed, or confirmed what I already knew?

Explain that the first question for students to ask is what surprises them about a text. Note that asking that question will help them **generate questions** of their own.

Point out that sometimes readers overlook smaller surprises. Model this by reading aloud paragraphs 1–3 of the selection. In the beginning, stop and share your thoughts as surprises occur to you. Possible responses to the text include:

I was a bit surprised that Malala's teenage life as a Muslim in Pakistan was so much like the lives of teens in the United States. I live in the suburbs, but a neighbor has chickens and a rooster. I hear the rooster every day. I also pretend I don't hear him and snuggle down in bed, forcing a family member to wake me up.

In some ways these things in the text *confirm what* I knew, like the call to prayer, but in other ways they *challenge* the visualization I had in my mind of what the lives of teens in Pakistan are like. I will *change* what I visualize now.

Tell students to pause from time to time as they read to ask themselves a Big Question and write an answer, explanation, or additional question in their consumable texts.

READING MODEL

A SCHOOLGIRL'S DIARY *from*
I AM MALALA

For more information on these and other signposts to Notice & Note, visit the **Reading Studio.**

You are about to read an excerpt from the autobiographical memoir *I Am Malala*. In it, you will notice and note signposts that will give you clues about the writer's thoughts and feelings, important events in the writer's life, and her purpose for writing. Here are three key signposts to look for as you read this selection and other works of nonfiction.

Big Questions When you are reading something that confirms what you already know, you might find yourself nodding your head as you read, as if to say, "Yes, I know exactly what that's like." At other times, writing casts a light on something that is totally unfamiliar—challenging our assumptions, surprising us, or changing our beliefs.

As you compare what you're reading to your own experiences, take a moment and reflect on the ideas the author is presenting. Ask yourself **Big Questions** such as the following:

- What confirms what I already know?
- What challenges what I already know?
- What changes what I already know?

Read this paragraph from *I Am Malala* and notice how a student annotated text associated with two Big Questions.

> 47   I had never written a diary before and didn't know how to begin, so the BBC correspondent said he would help me. He had to call me on my mother's phone because, even though we had a computer, there were frequent power cuts and few places in Mingora with Internet access.

What confirms something that you may already know?	It can be difficult to start a new writing project, especially when you've never tried that writing form.
What challenges or changes something you may have known?	I know that not everyone has their own computer, but I didn't know that some places in the world have frequent power cuts or no Internet access at all.

Numbers and Stats When an author writes that he walked five miles to the closest market, readers learn about more than just the distance. The author may be explaining the setting (perhaps it's rural), economic conditions (poverty may prevent the construction of roads), or personality (perhaps he's stubborn). When an author provides **Numbers and Stats,** think about why this information is included. In this example, a student marked a few Numbers and Stats.

> 13   We piled inside, <u>twenty girls</u> and <u>two teachers</u> crammed into the <u>three rows of benches</u> stretching down the length of the *dyna*.

Anchor Question
When you notice this signpost, ask: Why did the author use these numbers or amounts?

How are numbers or statistics used here?	They show how many people have to fit into the vehicle and how much seating is available.
Why do you think the author included numbers here?	The numbers emphasize how crowded it is; the author may be showing that the school is poor.

Quoted Words In autobiography and memoir, authors may use quotations to express the personal perspective of friends or family members, or to highlight the words of other significant persons in the author's life. When you encounter **Quoted Words,** ask yourself how the words may support the author's point of view and purpose. In this example, a student marked an instance of Quoted Words.

> 25   <u>"After the fifteenth of January, no girl, whether big or little, shall go to school. Otherwise, you know what we can do. And the parents and the school principal will be responsible."</u>
>
> 26   That was the news that came over Radio Mullah in late December 2008. . . .

Anchor Question
When you notice this signpost, ask: Why was this person quoted or cited and what did this add?

Who said the quoted words and what do they mean?	The words came from a radio station. They mean that no girls can go to school, and they hint that something bad will happen if they do go.
Why did the author include the quoted words?	Using quoted words adds credibility to the author's description; the threat sounds very real.

WHEN STUDENTS STRUGGLE

Use a Graphic Organizer Have students who need more structure for studying Quoted Words create a graphic organizer such as the one below. Model how to use it. Walk around the class checking that struggling students are using it for every page.

Paragraph #	Quoted words that have an impact	Source of quoted words	Why did the author include these quoted words?

Allow students to compare their graphic organizers after a few pages of silent reading.

NUMBERS AND STATS

Explain to students that **Numbers and Stats** provide the reader with valuable information about what is happening in a text. The information can come in many forms. An author might talk about money or percentages or make simple comparisons. If an author mentions that 9 out of 10 people own and ride a bicycle in a certain city, the reader would know much more about that city than just those numbers. Numbers help readers draw conclusions, identify details, make comparisons, and understand the author's purpose. Tell students to look for words such as *many, most,* and *some* to identify ideas that have numbers or number comparisons.

Ask students what they could infer about a city where 90% of citizens ride bicycles. Then ask follow-up questions, such as: *Is this city more likely to be a warm or a cold place? Are there a lot of elderly people in the city?*

Tell students that when they spot an example of Numbers and Stats, they should pause, mark it in their consumable texts, and ask themselves the anchor question: *Why did the author use these numbers or amounts?*

QUOTED WORDS

Explain that noticing **Quoted Words** helps readers compare points of view, understand relationships and ideas, and separate facts from opinions. Because the author chooses which words to quote, these words also help the reader understand the author's point of view. Quoted words from an expert may serve as evidence. In the example on Student Edition page 333, the person Malala is quoting was very dangerous to her. Point out that Malala may have wanted the reader to experience what she experienced. Hearing his actual words has a much stronger impact than Malala simply stating that going to school was dangerous for her and the other girls.

Tell students that when they spot an example of Quoted Words, they should pause, mark it in their consumable texts, and ask themselves the anchor question: *Why was this person quoted or cited, and what did this add?*

APPLY THE SIGNPOSTS

Have students use the selection that follows as a model text to apply the signposts. As students encounter signposts, prompt them to stop, reread, and ask themselves the questions that will help them understand the main themes and author's purpose.

Tell students to continue to look for these and other signposts as they read the other selections in the unit.

ANALYZE & APPLY

? Connect to the
ESSENTIAL QUESTION

"A Schoolgirl's Diary" from *I Am Malala* helps explain why some people stand up for what they want, never giving up on their rights.

In examining what made Malala refuse to give up, students will gain insight into some of the principles that keep many people from giving up when faced with injustice.

A SCHOOLGIRL'S DIARY

from **I AM MALALA**

Memoir by **Malala Yousafzai** with **Patricia McCormick**

? *ESSENTIAL QUESTION:*

What keeps people from giving up?

334   Unit 5

ENGLISH LEARNER SUPPORT

Explore Synonyms A synonym for the word *grit* is the word *resolve*, which has a Spanish cognate: *resolver*. This means to be strong and determined. Ask students to discuss how knowing the meaning of *resolver* can help them understand the meaning of *grit*.
ALL LEVELS

LEARNING MINDSET

Grit Define the concept of grit for students. Discuss the idea that it is important to persevere in order to reach goals even though it can be very difficult, particularly when a person's principles and beliefs are challenged. As they read the text, have students pay attention to how the author of this memoir shows grit in staying focused on her goals in the face of events and threats that she cannot control.

QUICK START

Which right do you value the most? Freedom of thought or expression? Access to education? How would you react if you were told suddenly that this right was being taken away because of who you are? Share your thoughts with the class.

ANALYZE CHARACTERISTICS AND FEATURES OF INFORMATIONAL TEXTS

The following selection is an excerpt from the book *I Am Malala*, which is a **memoir**, or a form of autobiography in which a writer shares his or her personal experiences and observations. A memoir shows how the writer remembers his or her own life and may focus on a specific period in the writer's life.

As you read the selection, pay attention to characteristics and features this selection shares with other informational texts.

- A **prologue,** or preface, is an introduction that helps provide readers with background information about the text. It may describe the text's setting or an important event, or the writer may use the prologue to tell readers why he or she decided to write the memoir.

- A **map** is a graphic feature that shows where events in the text take place.

- A **controlling idea** is the main point the author wants to convey in the writing. In a memoir, the controlling idea may be tied to the author's purpose for writing the work.

GENRE ELEMENTS: MEMOIR

- told in the first-person point of view from the writer's own perspective
- includes descriptions of people and events that have influenced the writer
- expresses the writer's personal thoughts and feelings, often using an informal or intimate tone

GENERATE QUESTIONS

Readers improve their understanding of a text when they generate, or produce, questions before, during, and after they read. As you read the selection, monitor your comprehension and deepen your understanding of the text by asking *who, what, when, where, why,* and *how* questions.

GENERATE QUESTIONS	TRY THIS
Set a purpose **before** reading. By asking yourself what you expect to learn from the text, you'll be ready to find the answers as you read.	Preview the text by scanning background information, headings, maps, etc. **Ask:** Why am I reading this text? What do I know about the subject already? What am I going to learn?
Monitor comprehension **during** reading. Ask questions as you read, pause to reread, and confirm your understanding.	Reread words, sentences, and paragraphs as needed to clarify understanding. **Ask:** Why did the author add this detail? What idea does the author want to share?
Identify or confirm the controlling idea **after** reading. The questions you ask yourself will help you understand the work as a whole.	Take time to think about what you just read. Review the key ideas. **Ask:** Did I learn what I thought I would? What was the author's purpose in writing?

A Schoolgirl's Diary *from* I Am Malala   335

QUICK START

Ask students to read the Quick Start question and invite them to share their responses with the class. Point out that sometimes a group may want to protect their authority to deny other groups rights that go against an opposing set of beliefs. Ask: *Should everyone have all rights, or does society or government have the right to limit some rights? Who decides?*

ANALYZE CHARACTERISTICS AND FEATURES OF INFORMATIONAL TEXT

Help students understand the terms and concepts related to the feature of an informational text known as the *preface*. Point out that *prologue* is the term often used for this feature in storytelling, and that because this selection is both informational and a story, either term can be used.

Point out that the Notice & Note activities in students' consumable text, such as **Quoted Words,** will help them define the author's controlling idea and purpose. Also point out that maps, captions, and footnotes will help them understand the context of the memoir, both in terms of culture and of geography.

GENERATE QUESTIONS

After students read the introduction for this section, have them read aloud the examples in the table. Ask: *What do you do to generate questions before reading the text? What do you do during reading? What can you do after reading the text?*

 ENGLISH LEARNER SUPPORT

Understand Text Features   Explain that texts sometimes have a section that comes before the main text. This may be called a preface or a prologue. Write *prologue = preface*. Point out that the word *prologue* has a Spanish cognate of *prologo* and means "introduction." The Spanish cognate for *preface* is *prefacio* and comes from the Latin word *praefatio,* which means "to say before." Discuss the purpose of a preface or prologue and the type of information it might contain.   **ALL LEVELS**

TEACH

CRITICAL VOCABULARY

Encourage students to read all the sentences before deciding which word best completes each one. Remind them to look for context clues that match the meaning of each word.

Answers:

1. *debate*
2. *anonymous*
3. *defy*
4. *pseudonym*
5. *edict*

■ English Learner Support

Use Cognates Tell students that several of the Critical Vocabulary words have Spanish cognates: *debate/debate, anonymous/anonimo, pseudonym/seudónimo, edict/edicto.* Also have them note the similar words *defy/desafiar.*

ALL LEVELS

LANGUAGE CONVENTIONS

Capitalization Review the information about capitalization. Read aloud the sentence in the first paragraph that defines a proper noun, and ask students to provide examples from the selection. (*Malala Yousafzai, Taliban, Pakistan*)

ANNOTATION MODEL

Students can review the Reading Model introduction on pages 332–333 if they have questions about any of the signposts. Suggest that they underline important phrases or circle key words that help them identify signposts. They may want to color-code their annotations by using a different color highlighter for each signpost. Point out that they may follow this suggestion or use their own system for marking up the selection in their write-in texts.

 GET READY

CRITICAL VOCABULARY

| debate | edict | defy | pseudonym | anonymous |

To see how many Critical Vocabulary words you already know, use them to complete the sentences.

1. The class held a/an _____ to address the issue's pros and cons.

2. I gave a/an _____ donation to keep my identity secret.

3. It is natural for toddlers to _____ their parents.

4. The spy used a/an _____ instead of her real name.

5. The commander gave a/an _____ describing the new rules.

LANGUAGE CONVENTIONS

Capitalization In this lesson, you will learn about the capitalization of proper nouns. A **proper noun** names a specific person, place, thing, or idea.

Haji Baba Road was a jumble of brightly colored rickshaws, women in flowing robes, men on scooters. . . .

As a proper noun, *Haji Baba Road* is capitalized because it names a specific place and thing. As you read the selection, notice how the author uses capitalization to distinguish proper nouns.

ANNOTATION MODEL

NOTICE & NOTE

As you read, notice and note signposts, including **Big Questions, Numbers and Stats,** and **Quoted Words.** Here is an example of how one reader responded to the opening paragraphs of the selection.

> 2 It was the most ordinary of days. I was fifteen, in grade nine, and I'd stayed up far too late the night before, studying for an exam.
>
> 3 I'd already heard the rooster crow at dawn but had fallen back to sleep. I'd heard the morning call to prayer from the mosque nearby but managed to hide under my quilt. And I'd pretended not to hear my father come to wake me.

I stay up late a lot, too. I also pretend to be asleep!

I know about morning prayers, but I've never heard a "call." I wonder where she lives.

 ENGLISH LEARNER SUPPORT

Capitalize Correctly in Writing Provide students with a graphic organizer to capture and categorize words from the text that begin with capital letters. Demonstrate by writing *Malala is from Pakistan* on the board. Underline the capital letters to show students, then copy the words to your chart.

Name	Place Name	Other
Malala	*Pakistan*	

SUBSTANTIAL/MODERATE

BACKGROUND

*In 2007, an extreme militant group took control of the area of Pakistan where **Malala Yousafzai's** (b. 1997) family lived. The group banned girls from attending school. Yousafzai publicly supported girls' education, and in 2012 she was attacked. Her family moved to England, where she continued to advocate for girls' rights. In 2014 she became the youngest recipient of the Nobel Peace Prize. This selection is from the Young Readers Edition of her memoir,* I Am Malala, *published in 2014.*

A SCHOOLGIRL'S DIARY

from I AM MALALA

Memoir by Malala Yousafzai with **Patricia McCormick**

SETTING A PURPOSE

As you read, pay attention to the details the author includes to convey ideas about her life at home, at school, and in her community. Use these details to help you answer these questions: What kind of person is Malala? What is most important to her?

DEDICATION

1 To those children all over the world who have no access to education, to those teachers who bravely continue teaching, and to anyone who has fought for their basic human rights and education.

PROLOGUE

2 It was the most ordinary of days. I was fifteen, in grade nine, and I'd stayed up far too late the night before, studying for an exam.

3 I'd already heard the rooster crow at dawn but had fallen back to sleep. I'd heard the morning call to prayer from the mosque nearby but managed to hide under my quilt. And I'd pretended not to hear my father come to wake me.

Notice & Note

Use the side margins to notice and note signposts in the text.

ANALYZE CHARACTERISTICS AND FEATURES OF INFORMATIONAL TEXTS

Annotate: Mark details in paragraphs 2–3 that help set the scene of the prologue.

Identify: What does this background information reveal about the author?

BACKGROUND

After students read the Background note, explain that sometimes people are tempted to give up when they are challenged. Reading memoirs and autobiographical stories about people who have not given up can provide inspiration to persevere when faced with difficult situations. Note that Malala did not give up on her dream of going to school despite being attacked and losing her home and country. While she was lucky she did not die, she also had to persist in her rehabilitation and in writing her story after being threatened. Suggest students research her Nobel Peace Prize speech.

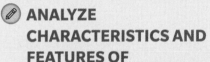 For **listening support** for students at varying proficiency levels, see the **Text X-Ray** on page 332C.

SETTING A PURPOSE

Direct students to use the Setting a Purpose prompt to focus their reading.

ANALYZE CHARACTERISTICS AND FEATURES OF INFORMATIONAL TEXTS

Remind students that the details mentioned in a prologue often give a reader a sense of time and place, as well as information about the people in the story. Guide students to note where this prologue begins and how it ends. (**Answer**: *The information shows she is a typical teenager who goes to school and stays up late to study, but also suggests she lives in a more rural area where Islam is the main religion.*)

 For **speaking and reading support** for students at varying proficiency levels, see the **Text X-Rays** on page 332D.

WHEN STUDENTS STRUGGLE...

Analyze Characteristics and Features Point out to students that a prologue is used to help the reader understand the setting and the scene before telling the story. Before reading the first three paragraphs aloud, ask students to pay close attention to description. After reading, ask students: *What did you see or hear in your mind as I read?*

TEACH

QUOTED WORDS

Point out that in the **Quoted Words**, the nickname *pisho*, meaning "kitten," sounds like it's a term of endearment. (**Answer**: *By calling Malala "pisho" while reminding her that she's late for school, Malala's mother is saying she cares about Malala and is looking out for her interests. She cares about her daughter and her daughter's education.*)

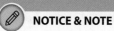

NOTICE & NOTE

QUOTED WORDS

Notice & Note: What can you tell from the author's use of quoted words? Mark the quoted words in paragraph 4.

Draw Conclusions: What do these words suggest about Malala's relationship to her mother?

4   Then my mother came and gently shook my shoulder. "Wake up, *pisho*," she said, calling me *kitten* in Pashto, the language of the Pashtun people. "It's seven thirty and you're late for school!"

5   I had an exam on Pakistani studies. So I said a quick prayer to God. *If it is your will, may I please come in first?* I whispered. *Oh, and thank you for all my success so far!*

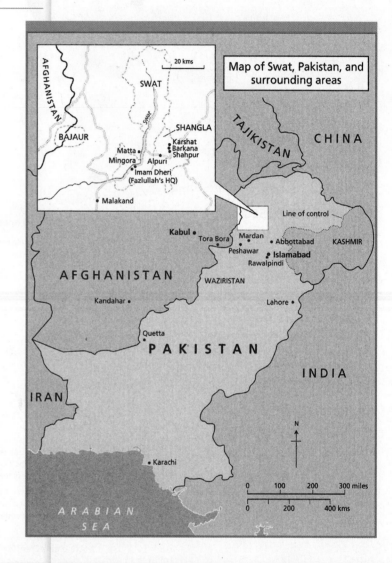

Map of Swat, Pakistan, and surrounding areas

APPLYING ACADEMIC VOCABULARY

☑ **achieve**   ☑ **individual**   ☐ **outcome**   ☐ **instance**   ☐ **principle**

Write and Discuss Have students turn to a partner to discuss the following questions. Guide students to include the Academic Vocabulary words *achieve* and *individual* in their responses. Ask volunteers to share their responses with the class.

- What does Malala's family think she might **achieve** in her life? Why might this be so?

- Do you think the right to an education is important for every **individual**?

6   I gulped down a bit of fried egg and chapati[1] with my tea. My youngest brother, Atal, was in an especially cheeky mood that morning. He was complaining about all the attention I'd received for speaking out about girls getting the same education as boys, and my father teased him a little at the breakfast table.

7   "When Malala is prime minister[2] someday, you can be her secretary," he said.

8   Atal, the little clown in the family, pretended to be cross. "No!" he cried. "She will be *my* secretary!"

9   All this banter nearly made me late, and I raced out the door, my half-eaten breakfast still on the table. I ran down the lane just in time to see the school bus crammed with other girls on their way to school. <u>I jumped in that Tuesday morning and never looked back at my home.</u>

———————

10   The ride to school was quick, just five minutes up the road and along the river. I arrived on time, and exam day passed as it always did. The chaos of Mingora city surrounded us with its honking horns and factory noises while we worked silently, bent over our papers in hushed concentration. By day's end I was tired but happy; I knew I'd done well on my test.

11   "Let's stay on for the second trip," said Moniba, my best friend. "That way we can chat a little longer." We always liked to stay on for the late pickup.

12   When our bus was called, we ran down the steps. As usual, Moniba and the other girls covered their heads and faces before we stepped outside the gate and got into the waiting *dyna*,[3] the white truck that was our Khushal School "bus." And, as usual, our driver was ready with a magic trick to amuse us. That day, he made a pebble disappear. No matter how hard we tried, we couldn't figure out his secret.

---

[1] **chapati** (chə-pä´tē): a flat, circular bread common in Pakistan and northern India.
[2] **prime minister:** in Pakistan, the prime minister is the head of government.
[3] **dyna** (dĭn´ə): a small, bus-like truck with a roof, sides, an open back, and benches for seats.

GENERATE QUESTIONS

Annotate: In paragraph 9, mark details that lead you to pause and ask questions.

Draw Conclusions: What questions can you ask at this point in the text? Look for the answers as you continue to read.

 GENERATE QUESTIONS

Students may have inferred that Malala will be attacked and never go back to her house, but they may have missed several key points in the events depicted in the memoir. Tell students that stopping to ask questions at key moments will help them be ready for the next part of a story. (**Possible answers:** *"Why does she never look back at her home? Does this mean she never returns home? What will happen to her at school? Is she just anxious to get to school and take the test?"*

 For **speaking support** for students at varying proficiency levels, see the **Text X-Ray** on page 332D.

 ENGLISH LEARNER SUPPORT

Use Questioning as a Pre-Reading Strategy Put students in pairs, and ask them to make and discuss a list of questions. Ask students: *What do you want to know about Malala and her town?* Post the lists in the room and cross off questions as they are answered by the text or through other sources in the unit. **MODERATE/LIGHT**

BIG QUESTIONS

Have students **visualize** the scene being described, and discuss how it either aligns with or challenges their expectations. Have them name details that seem surprising. (**Possible answer**: *How are these details similar and different from a typical street scene in my town? How are these details surprising or different than I expected? The author probably included this information to give the reader an idea of what it was like where she lived, and that what she saw on that day was very ordinary to her.*)

■ English Learner Support

Ask Big Questions Read aloud paragraphs 13 and 14, and either draw or have a volunteer draw the scene being described—a street, a school bus with benches, shops with their signs, and so on. Have students point to parts of the drawing that are surprising, and guide them to ask questions about the scene. **MODERATE/LIGHT**

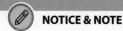

NOTICE & NOTE

BIG QUESTIONS

Notice & Note: Mark the words in paragraph 14 that challenge, change, or confirm what you already know.

Analyze: What questions can you ask yourself about this passage? Why did the author include this information?

13   We piled inside, twenty girls and two teachers crammed into the three rows of benches stretching down the length of the *dyna*. It was hot and sticky, and there were no windows, just a yellowed plastic sheet that flapped against the side as we bounced along Mingora's crowded rush-hour streets.

14   Haji Baba Road was a jumble of brightly colored rickshaws,[4] women in flowing robes, men on scooters, honking and zigzagging through the traffic. We passed a shopkeeper butchering chickens. A boy selling ice-cream cones. A billboard for Dr. Humayun's Hair Transplant Institute. Moniba and I were deep in conversation. I had many friends, but she was the friend of my heart, the one with whom I shared everything. That day, when we were talking about who would get the highest marks[5] this term, one of the other girls started a song, and the rest of us joined in.

15   Just after we passed the Little Giants snack factory and the bend in the road not more than three minutes from my house, the van slowed to a halt. It was oddly quiet outside.

16   "It's so calm today," I said to Moniba. "Where are all the people?"

17   I don't remember anything after that, but here's the story that's been told to me:

18   Two young men in white robes stepped in front of our truck.

19   "Is this the Khushal School bus?" one of them asked.

20   The driver laughed. The name of the school was painted in black letters on the side.

21   The other young man jumped onto the tailboard and leaned into the back, where we were all sitting.

22   "Who is Malala?" he asked.

23   No one said a word, but a few girls looked in my direction. He raised his arm and pointed at me. Some of the girls screamed, and I squeezed Moniba's hand.

24   Who is Malala? I am Malala, and this is my story.

---

[4] **rickshaws** (rĭk´shôz): in Pakistan, a small motorized vehicle that carries passengers.
[5] **marks:** school grades.

WHEN STUDENTS STRUGGLE . . .

Ask Big Questions Have student partners review the text about Big Questions on page 332. Then have them work to share, evaluate, and revise any Big Questions that they have recorded in their write-in text. Remind them to ask and answer questions that have been developed up to this point in the text.

    For additional support, go to the **Reading Studio** and assign the following 🔲 **Level Up Tutorial: Setting a Purpose for Reading.**

My friends keep a chair in class for me (far right) at the Khushal School.

A Schoolgirl's Diary

25 "After the fifteenth of January, no girl, whether big or little, shall go to school. Otherwise, you know what we can do. And the parents and the school principal will be responsible."

26 That was the news that came over Radio Mullah[6] in late December 2008. At first, I thought it was just one of his crazy pronouncements. It was the twenty-first century! How could one man stop more than fifty thousand girls from going to school?

27 I am a hopeful person—my friends may say too hopeful, maybe even a little crazy. But I simply did not believe that this man could stop us. School was our right.

28 We **debated** his **edict** in class. "Who will stop him?" the other girls said. "The Taliban[7] have already blown up hundreds of schools, and no one has done anything."

29 "We will," I said. "We will call on our government to come and end this madness."

30 "The government?" one girl said. "The government can't even shut down Fazlullah's radio station!"[8]

debate
(dĭ-bāt´) v. To *debate* is to discuss opposing points or ideas.

edict
(ē´dĭkt´) n. An *edict* is a command or pronouncement enforced as law.

---

[6] **Radio Mullah:** the on-air name for radio broadcaster Maulana Fazlullah, who spread his radical beliefs that girls should not go to school and encouraged violence.

[7] **Taliban** (tăl´ə-băn´): a group of militant Islamic fundamentalists. The name comes from *Talib*, which means "religious student."

[8] **Fazlullah's radio station:** Maulana Fazlullah, the voice of Radio Mullah (see footnote 6). Fazlullah became head of the Taliban in Pakistan.

A Schoolgirl's Diary *from* I Am Malala   341

ENGLISH LEARNER SUPPORT

Answer Big Questions Have students meet in small groups to discuss the following questions. Ask: *What surprised you when you came to America, or to this state? If you were born here or you don't remember, have your parents or grandparents ever told you what surprised them? What confirmed what you already knew?* Then read aloud paragraphs 25–30 and ask: *What surprised you? What challenged what you thought you already knew about the Middle East or Pakistan? What other questions do you have now?*
MODERATE/LIGHT

CRITICAL VOCABULARY

debate: The students were debating whether a radio personality would be able to enforce his edict, or whether the Pakistani federal government would protect their rights and stop him.

ASK STUDENTS to have a debate similar to the one Malala had with her friends and classmates. Ask students to *debate* whether a radio personality could eventually have the same power in the United States to issue edicts regarding who could get an education. Why or why not?

edict: Remind students that one of the causes of the American revolution was the issuing of edicts, or commands, by the British Crown.

ASK STUDENTS why the word *edict* might be used in paragraph 28, not the word *law* or *rules*. (**Answer**: *Laws in the United States are determined by legislatures. The word* edict *is usually reserved for rules decided by kings and dictators alone.*)

NUMBERS AND STATS

Point out that the numbers increase **suspense** by giving the impression that time is running out. The girls are trying to make the most of the little time they have left in school, because after January 14, they will not be able to go to school. (**Answer:** *Understanding the way the girls feel about school and how much they value it helps readers understand why Malala takes action later.*)

CRITICAL VOCABULARY

defy: Malala says in paragraph 34 that girls do not resist the edicts of their fathers and other males in her area of the world. Point out that Malala's father supported Malala in her desire to get an education and become a doctor.

ASK STUDENTS how difficult it might have been for Malala if her father had not supported her education. Would she have been able to defy him? The discussion should bring more clarity to understanding the word *defy*. Students should understand that to defy someone is a brave act with consequences, not simply a refusal to come in from the rain.

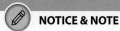

NOTICE & NOTE

31 The debate went round and round. I didn't give in. But even to me, my argument sounded a bit thin.

32 One by one, girls stopped coming to school. Their fathers forbade them. Their brothers forbade them.

33 <u>Within days</u> we had gone from <u>twenty-seven girls in our grade to ten.</u>

34 I was sad and frustrated—but I also understood. In our culture, girls do not **defy** the males in their families. And I realized that the fathers and brothers and uncles who made my friends stay home were doing so out of concern for their safety. It was hard not to feel a bit depressed sometimes, not to feel as though the families who kept their girls at home were simply surrendering to Fazlullah. But whenever I'd catch myself giving in to a feeling of defeat, I'd have one of my talks with God. *Help us appreciate the school days that are left to us, God, and give us the courage to fight even harder for more.*

---

defy
(dĭ-fī′) *v.* To *defy* someone is to oppose or refuse to cooperate with that person.

NUMBERS AND STATS

Notice & Note: Why does Malala include numbers and dates in paragraphs 33 and 35? Mark where numbers are used.

Infer: What is the importance of understanding these details?

35 School had been due to end the first week of January for our usual winter break, so my father decided to postpone the holiday. <u>We would remain in classes through 14 January.</u> That way we could <u>squeeze in every minute</u> left to us. And the <u>ten remaining girls in my class</u> lingered in the courtyard <u>every day</u> after school in case these were our <u>last chances</u> to be together.

36 At home in the evenings I wondered what I would do with my life if I couldn't go to school. One of the girls at school had gotten married off before Fazlullah's edict. She was twelve. I knew my parents wouldn't do that to me, but I wondered, what *would* I do? Spend the rest of my life indoors, out of sight, with no TV to watch and no books to read? How would I complete my studies and become a doctor, which was my greatest hope at the time? I played with my shoebox dolls and thought: *The Taliban want to turn the girls of Pakistan into identical, lifeless dolls.*

37 While we girls savored the days until January 15, Fazlullah struck again and again. The previous year had been hard, but the days of January 2009 were among the darkest of our lives. Every morning, someone arrived at school with a story about another killing, sometimes two, sometimes three a night. Fazlullah's men killed a woman in Mingora because they said she was "doing *fahashi*," or being indecent, because she was a

---

ENGLISH LEARNER SUPPORT

Make a Timeline To help students gain a deeper understanding of how Numbers and Stats are used in this section of the text, ask them to form small groups and create a timeline for paragraphs 31–37, using tape on the wall and index cards for different numbers and stats. They may find this difficult because of phrases such as "one by one" in paragraph 32. Have them check and double check their work.

MODERATE/LIGHT

dancer. And they killed a man in the valley because he refused to wear his pants short the way the Taliban did. And now, we would be forbidden from going to school.

38   One afternoon I heard my father on the phone. "All the teachers have refused," he said. "They are too afraid. But I will see what I can do." He hung up and rushed out of the house.

39   A friend who worked at the BBC, the powerful British Broadcasting Corporation network, had asked him to find someone from the school to write a diary about life under the Taliban for its Urdu[9] website—a teacher or an older student. All the teachers had said no, but Maryam's younger sister Ayesha, one of the older girls, had agreed.

40   The next day, we had a visitor: Ayesha's father. He would not allow his daughter to tell her story. "It's too risky," he said.

41   My father didn't argue with him. The Taliban were cruel; but even *they* wouldn't hurt a child, he wanted to say. But he respected Ayesha's father's decision and prepared to call the BBC with the bad news.

42   I was only eleven, but I said, "Why not me?" I knew he'd wanted someone older, not a child.

43   I looked at my father's hopeful—nervous—face. He had been so brave for speaking out. It was one thing to talk to national and local media, but this diary might be read by people outside Pakistan. It was the BBC, after all. My father had always stood by me. Could I stand by him? I knew without even thinking that I could. I would do anything to be able to continue going to school. But first we went to my mother.

44   If she was afraid, I wouldn't do it. Because if I didn't have her support, it would be like speaking with only half my heart.

45   But my mother agreed. She gave us her answer with a verse from the Holy Quran.[10] "Falsehood has to die," she said. "And truth has to come forward." God would protect me, she said, because my mission was a good one.

46   Many people in Swat[11] saw danger everywhere they looked. But our family didn't look at life that way. We saw possibility. And we felt a responsibility to stand up for our homeland. My father and I are the starry-eyed ones. "Things have to get better," we always say. My mother is our rock. While our heads are in the sky, her feet are on the ground. But we all believed

ANALYZE CHARACTERISTICS AND FEATURES OF INFORMATIONAL TEXTS

Annotate: In paragraph 45, mark the term that is footnoted.

Analyze: How does the footnote help you understand the reason that Malala's mother agrees to the decision?

---

[9] **Urdu** (ûr´dōō): Pakistan's national language.
[10] **Quran** (kə-rän´): the sacred book of the religion of Islam, also spelled Koran.
[11] **Swat:** the Swat Valley of northwest Pakistan and the town of Mingora is where the memoir's narrative takes place.

ANALYZE CHARACTERISTICS AND FEATURES OF INFORMATIONAL TEXTS

Make sure students know that a small number near a word indicates there is a footnote that helps explain the word. (**Answer**: *The footnote explains that the Quran is the holy book of Islam, like the Christian Bible or the Hebrew Scriptures of Judaism. Malala's mother quotes the Quran in support of her daughter. Readers may infer that Malala's mother is a religious and moral person.*)

LANGUAGE CONVENTIONS

Review that proper nouns that name specific people, places, and things are capitalized. (**Answer**: *Capitalization is used for the abbreviation of a specific organization [BBC], a specific place [Mingora], and a specific thing [Internet].*)

■ English Learner Support

Edit for Capitalization Have students work in pairs to practice capitalization. Have each partner copy a sentence with capitalized words from the text, leaving out the capitalization. Then have them switch papers and correct the capitalization, referring to the chart they began on page 336. Give students a chance to add additional information to the charts, including capitalizing abbreviations. **SUBSTANTIAL/MODERATE**

For **reading support** for students at varying proficiency levels, see the **Text X-ray** on page 332D.

CRITICAL VOCABULARY

pseudonym: Malala's father gives her a pseudonym, or different name, to hide her true identity as the writer of the diary.

ASK STUDENTS why they think Malala's father chose the pseudonym for her that he did. (**Possible answer:** *Her pseudonym was the name of a heroine in a folk story. Her father chose it because Malala was acting like a hero to the girls.*)

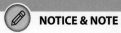

Students outside during a science fair at the Khushal School.

LANGUAGE CONVENTIONS
Proper nouns are capitalized, as are their abbreviations. Explain how each instance of capitalization is used in paragraph 47.

pseudonym
(sōōd´n-ĭm´) *n.* A *pseudonym* is a fictitious name, particularly a pen name.

in hope. "Speaking up is the only way things will get better," she said.

47   I had never written a diary before and didn't know how to begin, so the BBC correspondent said he would help me. He had to call me on my mother's phone because, even though we had a computer, there were frequent power cuts and few places in Mingora with Internet access. The first time he called, he told me he was using his wife's phone because his own phone had been bugged[12] by the intelligence services.

48   He suggested that I use a fake name so the Taliban wouldn't know who was writing the diary. I didn't want to change my name, but he was worried about my safety. That is why he chose a **pseudonym** for me: Gul Makai, which means "cornflower" and is the name of a heroine in a Pashtun folk story.

49   My first diary entry appeared on 3 January 2009, about two weeks before Fazlullah's deadline. The title was "I Am Afraid." I wrote about how hard it was to study or to sleep at night with the constant sounds of fighting in the hills outside town. And I

---

[12]**bugged:** equipped with a concealed listening device to overhear private conversations.

344   Unit 5

described how I walked to school each morning, looking over my shoulder for fear I'd see a Talib following me.

50   I was writing from the privacy of my bedroom, using a secret identity, but thanks to the Internet, the story of what was happening in Swat was there for the whole world to see. It was as if God had at long last granted my wish for that magic pencil.

51   In my next entry, I wrote about how school was the center of my life and about how proud I was to walk the streets of Mingora in my school uniform.

52   As exciting as it was to be Gul Makai, it was hard not to tell anyone—especially at school. The diary of this **anonymous** Pakistani schoolgirl was all anyone talked about. One girl even printed it out and showed it to my father.

53   "It's very good," he said with a knowing smile.

———————

54   With the threat of school closing quickly becoming a reality, I appreciated going even more. In the days leading up to the last one, it was decided that wearing our uniforms was too dangerous, so we were told to dress in our everyday clothes. I decided I wasn't going to cower in fear of Fazlullah's wrath. I would obey the instruction about the uniform, but that day I chose my brightest pink *shalwar kamiz*.[13]

55   As soon as I left the house, I thought for a second about turning back. We'd heard stories of people throwing acid in the faces of girls in Afghanistan. It hadn't happened here yet, but with everything that *had* happened, it didn't seem impossible. But somehow my feet carried me forward, all the way to school.

56   What a peculiar place Mingora had become. Gunfire and cannons as background noise. Hardly any people in the streets. (And if you did see anyone, you couldn't help but think, *This person could be a terrorist.*) And a girl in a pink *shalwar kamiz* sneaking off to school.

———————

[13] **shalwar kamiz** (shäl´vär kə-mēz´): a type of long, loose shirt and pants, worn by both men and women.

anonymous

(ə-nŏn´ə-məs) *adj.* Someone who is *anonymous* has an undisclosed or unknown name.

ANALYZE CHARACTERISTICS AND FEATURES OF INFORMATIONAL TEXTS

Annotate: Underline words in paragraph 54 that convey facts. Circle words that convey thoughts and feelings.

Synthesize: How does the author use facts, thoughts, and feelings to convey an idea in the paragraph? What is that idea?

ANALYZE CHARACTERISTICS AND FEATURES OF INFORMATIONAL TEXTS

Remind students that authors can use the thoughts and feelings of a character or real-life person in a text to convey important information about the main point of the text. Here, Malala's response to the threat and the prohibition against wearing her uniform help the reader gain a deeper understanding of who she is. (***Possible answer:*** *By presenting facts ["told to dress in our everyday clothes"] and the thoughts or feelings in reaction to the facts ["I wasn't going to cower in fear"], the author shows Malala's bravery. Her thoughts, feelings, and actions show she will find a way to express herself and her ideals, no matter what the circumstances.*)

CRITICAL VOCABULARY

anonymous: Malala thought she was anonymous and protected, but secrets are hard to keep.

ASK STUDENTS what tells the reader that Malala did not want to be anonymous. (***Answer****: In paragraph 52, Malala says everyone is talking about the diary of a Pakistani schoolgirl, which she says she thought was "exciting." In paragraph 50, Malala says it "was as if God had at long last granted my wish for that magic pencil." In paragraph 52, she says, "it was hard not to tell anyone—especially at school." Students may also mention her choice of wearing bright pink clothing when she could not wear the uniform.*)

IMPROVE READING FLUENCY

Targeted Passage Have students work with partners to read paragraphs 50–56. First, read the paragraphs aloud. Have students follow along in their books as you read the text with appropriate phrasing and emphasis. Then, have partners take turns reading aloud the paragraphs. Encourage students to provide feedback and support for pronouncing difficult words. Remind students that when they are reading aloud for an audience, they should pace their reading and pause for punctuation, so the listeners have time to understand each sentence.

 Go to the **Reading Studio** for additional support in developing fluency.

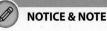

GENERATE QUESTIONS

This excerpt ends on a note of suspense, with the reader unsure what exactly will happen next. Point out that some people have been able to guess Malala's identity, and from what students have already read in the excerpt, they should be able to form some idea about the consequences she might face next in her life. Generating questions can help them focus this knowledge to predict what might happen next. (**Possible questions:** *What does this mean for Malala's safety? Who is the man from the* New York Times? *Why did the author single out the reporter from the* New York Times? **Possible answers:** *I predict that the added attention will put Malala in further danger. Perhaps her family will suffer as well. Maybe the attention of the* New York Times *will expose Malala.*)

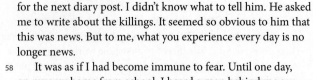

57   The BBC correspondent asked for more news from Swat for the next diary post. I didn't know what to tell him. He asked me to write about the killings. It seemed so obvious to him that this was news. But to me, what you experience every day is no longer news.

58   It was as if I had become immune to fear. Until one day, on my way home from school, I heard a man behind me say, "I will kill you." My heart stopped, but somehow my feet kept going. I quickened my pace until I was far ahead of him. I ran home, shut the door, and, after a few seconds, peeked out at him. There he was, oblivious to me, shouting at someone on his phone.

59   I laughed a bit at myself. "Malala," I told myself, "there are real things to be afraid of. You don't need to imagine danger where there is none."

60   The real worry, it seemed to me, was being found out. And, of course, it was Moniba who was first to guess the identity of Gul Makai. "I read a diary in the newspaper," she told me one day at recess, "and the story sounded like our story, what happens in our school. It's you, isn't it?" she said.

61   I could not lie, not to Moniba. But when I confessed, she became more angry than ever. "How can you say you're my best friend when you're keeping such an important secret from me?" She turned on her heel and left. And yet I knew, as angry as she was, she wouldn't reveal my secret.

62   It was my father who did that. By accident, of course. He was telling a reporter how terrifying it was for children just to walk to and from school. His own daughter, he said, thought a man on his phone had threatened to kill her. Just about everyone recognized the story from the diary, and <u>by April, my days as Gul Makai, the secret diarist, would be over.</u>

63   But the diary had done its job. <u>Now a number of reporters were following the story</u> of Fazlullah's attempt to shut down the girls' schools of Pakistan, <u>including a man from the *New York Times*.</u>

GENERATE QUESTIONS
Annotate: Mark any words in paragraphs 62 and 63 that lead you to ask questions.

Predict: What questions do you have at the end of the excerpt? Based on what you have read, what do you predict will happen to Malala next?

CHECK YOUR UNDERSTANDING

Have students answer the questions independently.

Answers:

1. *D*

2. *G*

3. *B*

If they answer any questions incorrectly, have them reread the text to confirm their understanding. Then they may proceed to ANALYZE THE TEXT on page 348.

CHECK YOUR UNDERSTANDING

Answer these questions before moving on to the **Analyze the Text** section on the following page.

1 Which of the following expresses Malala's ideas about the importance of education?

  A *I'd already heard the rooster crow at dawn but had fallen back asleep.*

  B *I had an exam on Pakistani studies.*

  C *"After the fifteenth of January, no girl, whether big or little, shall go to school."*

  D *How would I complete my studies and become a doctor, which was my greatest hope at the time?*

2 The author wrote her diary entries under a false name mainly because —

  F she feared that her father would punish her if she used her real name

  G she feared that the Taliban would punish her for speaking out

  H she was too modest to use her real name

  J she did not want her friends to be envious of her

3 Which of the following is not true?

  A Malala's father wanted her to go to school.

  B Malala and her best friend, Moniba, wrote the diary entries.

  C Education is very important to Malala.

  D Malala is a spiritual person who says prayers regularly.

ENGLISH LEARNER SUPPORT

Oral Assessment Use the following questions to assess students' comprehension and speaking skills.

1. How does the reader know that Malala wants more education? (*She said she wanted to become a doctor.*)

2. Why did Malala use a false name? (*She was in danger because she was going to school and speaking out against the Taliban leader.*)

3. True or false—Moniba helped to write the diary entries. (*False*)
    SUBSTANTIAL/MODERATE

ANALYZE THE TEXT

Possible answers:

1. **DOK 4:** *What does an ordinary day look like for 15-year-old Malala—going to school and spending time with her friend, Moniba? The author wants to show that Malala and Moniba are close friends. The author also wants the reader to know that fateful events can happen on ordinary days.*

2. **DOK 2:** *In the prologue, the man on the dyna "raised his arm and pointed" at Malala, but the author doesn't say exactly what happened next. I could ask: What did this man do to Malala? In paragraph 55, we learn that some girls in Afghanistan had been attacked by people who threw acid in their faces. I can predict that the man in the bus hurt Malala in some way.*

3. **DOK 4:** *The title,* I Am Malala, *tells the reader that the work is a memoir about a person named Malala, while the last three paragraphs of the prologue give the reader a much deeper understanding of how significant that statement is. Ending the prologue with this statement is a powerful and effective way to introduce the reader to who Malala is and what she values.*

4. **DOK 3:** *Using a familiar tone, the author describes moments that are personal—an argument with her best friend—and how they relate to significant life events, such as the unveiling of her identity as a diarist, Fazlullah's attempts to stop the education of girls, and the publicity from the New York Times. These elements show the risks Malala was taking and how important it was to her that girls receive an education.*

5. **DOK 4:** *A man walking behind Malala says, "I will kill you." By showing that her first reaction is to assume he is talking to and about her, the author communicates the kind of fear and anxiety she is living with. When she quotes her own thoughts, we understand she is a person who does not normally give in to fear; instead, she is brave and determined.*

RESEARCH

Remind students they should assess the credibility and reliability of any sites they use to answer their questions.

Extend As students identify the stories, remind them to explain why they think each one is newsworthy.

 RESPOND

ANALYZE THE TEXT

Support your responses with evidence from the text. 📓 NOTEBOOK

1. **Analyze** Review paragraph 2 and paragraphs 10–11. What question can you ask about Malala's life that is answered in paragraphs 10–11? Why do you think the author includes these details? What is her purpose?

2. **Predict** Review paragraphs 23 and 55. What question might you ask when you read paragraph 23? Using information from paragraph 55, what prediction can you make about what happened to Malala on the bus?

3. **Evaluate** Review the title of the memoir and paragraphs 22–24. How has the author used the statement "I am Malala" to communicate an idea? Is it an effective way to communicate her idea?

4. **Cite Evidence** Review paragraphs 61–63. How does the author use characteristics common to a memoir to convey key ideas?

5. **Notice & Note** What quoted words does the author use in paragraphs 58–59? How do these quotations help you understand Malala's character and her purpose for writing?

RESEARCH TIP
Malala Yousafzai has won several important awards. Check sites of organizations that have honored her work to find biographical information you can use in your research.

RESEARCH

When the selection ends, the reader does not know what happens to Malala Yousafzai, her family, and her friends. Generate questions you can use to research how her life unfolds after this excerpt ends. Use the book *I Am Malala* or other sources to answer your questions. Record your findings in a table like this one.

RESEARCH QUESTION	ANSWER AND SOURCE
Students' responses will vary.	

Extend In paragraph 57, the author writes, "But to me, what you experience every day is no longer news." Using a print or online newspaper, find stories on topics that may be everyday experiences for some people, but seem newsworthy to you. Discuss your findings in a small group.

 LEARNING MINDSET

Questioning Remind students that when you are curious, you naturally ask questions. You may ask them aloud or in your own mind and write those questions in your notes. You may ask questions of yourself, like: *What would you do in the same circumstances as Malala?* Encourage students to ask questions with genuine curiosity, and point out that this is the best way to take control of their own learning.

CREATE AND DISCUSS

Write a Formal Letter Should the British Broadcasting Corporation (BBC) have asked Malala, or any student, to report on news under dangerous conditions, such as those faced by Pakistani schoolchildren? Compose a business letter that reflects your opinion on the topic, addressed to a news organization. Be sure to capitalize proper nouns. Include these features:

- ❏ **Heading:** your name and address at the top of the page
- ❏ **Date:** the date of your letter
- ❏ **Address:** the name and address of the person and company who will receive your letter
- ❏ **Salutation:** a greeting, such as *To Whom It May Concern*, or, if you are writing to a specific person, *Dear Mr./Ms.* _____; end the greeting with a colon.
- ❏ **Body:** Include an introduction, then state your point, and finish with a concluding sentence or two. Keep your communication brief, polite, and clear. Be sure to capitalize proper nouns.
- ❏ **Closing and Signature:** *Sincerely,* followed by a space for your signature, and then your full name

Discuss with a Small Group Freewrite in response to this question: What would you do with your time if you couldn't go to school? Share your response with a small group. Discuss whether you would be happy or satisfied not going to school and what you think the long-term consequences would be.

 Go to **Writing Arguments: Formal Style** in the **Writing Studio** for more on writing in a formal style.

 Go to **Participating in Collaborative Discussions** in the **Speaking and Listening Studio** for help with having a group discussion.

GROUP WORK CHECKLIST
- ❏ **Listen actively.**
- ❏ **Ask specific questions.**
- ❏ **Respond respectfully.**
- ❏ **Consider group members' suggestions.**
- ❏ **Take notes about important points.**

RESPOND TO THE ESSENTIAL QUESTION

 ? What keeps people from giving up?

Gather Information Review your annotations and notes on the selection. Then, add relevant details to your Response Log. As you determine which information to include, think about what Malala values and how others can learn from her example.

At the end of the unit, use your notes to write a biographical report.

ACADEMIC VOCABULARY
As you write and discuss what you learned from the selection, be sure to use the Academic Vocabulary words. Check off each of the words that you use.

- ❏ **achieve**
- ❏ **individual**
- ❏ **instance**
- ❏ **outcome**
- ❏ **principle**

CREATE AND DISCUSS

Write a Formal Letter Remind students that when writing a formal letter, they should not just make sure to include all the necessary parts—heading, proper salutation, closing signature, and so on. They should also use a polite tone and avoid the use of slang, sentence fragments, or informal language. Suggest that students imagine they are writing this letter to a teacher or other authority figure to guarantee that they maintain an appropriate tone, or attitude.

📖 For **writing support** for students at varying proficiency levels, see the **Text X-Ray** on page 332D.

Discuss with a Small Group Remind students they should listen respectfully to ideas presented by other group members. When responding to those ideas, they might refer to them, indicating that they have heard and understood and can relate what other people have said to their own contributions.

RESPOND TO THE ESSENTIAL QUESTION

Allow time for students to add details from "A Schoolgirl's Diary" from *I Am Malala* to their Unit 5 Response Logs.

 ENGLISH LEARNER SUPPORT

Discuss with a Small Group Read the discussion prompt aloud and clarify any confusion that students have about the question. Allow students to work with partners to share personal experiences and brainstorm ideas to answer the question. Provide these sentence frames to help them formulate their ideas for the discussion: *Some things I like to do are ___. Some things I do at school are___. If I were not at school, I would still like to ___.*

SUBSTANTIAL/MODERATE

CRITICAL VOCABULARY

Possible answers:

1. *I know the author of an article is anonymous when I don't see an author's name anywhere before or after the article, or if the byline reads, "Anonymous."*

2. *I like to debate because it's interesting to talk about the pros and cons of a topic.*

3. *I might defy an edict telling me what books I can or cannot read or what rights I have. I don't like edicts that restrict my freedom.*

4. *If I had a pen name or some sort of pseudonym, it would be fun to create a name that's a version of the name I have. That way people could try to guess who I really am.*

VOCABULARY STRATEGY:
Greek and Latin Roots

Possible Answers:

anonymous: The word *anonymous* comes from a Greek word, *anōnumos*, which means "nameless." The prefix *an-* means "without"; the root *onuma* means "name." Adding together the prefix and root translates to "without name."

debate: The word *debate* comes from Middle English *debaten* and Old French *debatre*. The prefix *de-* has Latin origins and means "make the opposite of" or "reverse," while *bate* comes from the Old French *battre* meaning "to beat."

defy: This word is from an Old French word meaning "to challenge or provoke." The Latin word *disfidāre* is similar, and it means "to refuse."

edict: This word comes from the Latin *ēdictum, ēdīcere* meaning "to declare."

RESPOND

WORD BANK
debate
edict
defy
pseudonym
anonymous

Go to **Analyzing Word Structure** in the **Vocabulary Studio** for more on Greek and Latin roots.

CRITICAL VOCABULARY

Practice and Apply Use what you know about the Critical Vocabulary words to answer these questions.

1. How would you know that an article was written by an **anonymous** author?

_____

2. Do you like to **debate?** Why or why not?

_____

3. What kind of **edict** might you **defy?** Why?

_____

4. If you wanted to use a **pseudonym,** what would you choose? Why?

_____

VOCABULARY STRATEGY:
Greek and Latin Roots

Many English words contain Greek or Latin roots. A **root** is a word part that contains the core meaning of the word. Knowing the origin and meaning of roots and affixes can help you determine the meaning of an unfamiliar word.

Remember that a **prefix** is an affix that appears at the beginning of a word and a **suffix** is an affix that appears at the end of a word. For example, the word *pseudonym* contains the Greek prefix *pseudo-,* meaning "false," and *nym,* which comes from a Greek root meaning "name."

Use an online or print dictionary to check the meaning and origins of words, word roots, and affixes. Your dictionary may also have a section about word roots, which will offer additional information on meaning.

Practice and Apply Work in small groups to determine the origin and meaning of the word parts in *anonymous, debate, defy,* and *edict.* Use a dictionary to look up entire words as well as roots, prefixes, and affixes.

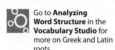

ENGLISH LEARNER SUPPORT

Develop Vocabulary Have students create "Root Trees" in their notebooks. A root tree is a picture of a tree with roots. Demonstrate how to put an Academic or Critical Vocabulary word at the top, a cognate or translation in the middle, and a root at the bottom using the Latin root *aqua* (water, *aquarium*). They can make additional trees for *multi-* and *circum-*.

SUBSTANTIAL/MODERATE

Ask students to create a root tree to find words that share the Greek root *graph*. Have them write the root at the bottom of the tree, add the translation, and add words that use the root to the branches. Repeat with other common Greek roots, such as *bio, poly,* and *gram*.

LIGHT

LANGUAGE CONVENTIONS:
Capitalization

Writers capitalize proper nouns to distinguish them from common nouns. Recall that a **proper noun** names a particular person, place, thing, or idea; a **common noun** is a general name for a person, place, thing, or idea. Proper nouns include languages, cities, ethnicities, school names, brands, titles, organizations and their abbreviations, initials that stand for someone's name, and acronyms (words formed by combining the initial letters of a series of words). In the selection, capitalization is used in the following ways.

> Go to the **Grammar Studio** for more on capitalization.

CATEGORY OF PROPER NOUN	EXAMPLE
Names of schools	the Khushal School bus
Titles used before a name, names of people, and names of businesses	Dr. Humayun's Hair Transplant Institute
Organizations and their acronyms	British Broadcasting Corporation BBC
Countries	Pakistan
Ethnicities	Pashtun
Languages	Urdu, Pashto
Titles of books, chapters, published works, and newspapers	Quran "A Schoolgirl's Diary" "I Am Afraid" New York Times
Days of the week, months of the year	Tuesday October

Practice and Apply Write your own sentences with proper nouns, using the examples from *I Am Malala* as models. Your sentences can be about Malala Yousafzai or your own experiences with challenges and persistence. When you have finished, share your sentences with a partner and compare your work.

LANGUAGE CONVENTIONS:
Capitalization

Review the rules for capitalization by asking students to cover the left side of the table with a card or piece of paper and look at the example. Have students take turns testing each other in pairs, asking: *What is the rule? For example, look at "the Khushal School bus." What is the rule? (The name of the school is capitalized, but the words the and bus are not part of the name so they are not capitalized.)*

Practice and Apply Answers will vary. Tell students to make sure they can explain why capitalization is used in their sentences. Ask a few of the students to present their partner's sentence to the class and explain the rule.

THE FIRST DAY OF SCHOOL

Short Story by R.V. Cassill

GENRE ELEMENTS
SHORT STORY

Remind students that a **short story** is a fictional story that can be read in one sitting. It usually includes one main conflict and centers on a single idea. A short story includes the basic elements of fiction, such as plot, characters, setting, and theme. Although short stories are fictional, some are based on real people or historical events.

LEARNING OBJECTIVES

- Analyze plot, as well as how setting influences plot and character.
- Generate and research questions about a historical setting.
- Write an informational essay on the influence of setting on character in the selection.
- Discuss comparisons and contrasts between students' lives and the lives of characters.
- Use a thesaurus effectively.
- Practice writing sentences with varying sentence patterns.
- **Language** Discuss features of the text using the key term *plot*.

TEXT COMPLEXITY

Quantitative Measures	The First Day of School	Lexile: 780L
Qualitative Measures	**Ideas Presented** Much is explicit, but moves to some implied meaning.	
	Structure Used Primarily explicit, but may vary from simple chronological order.	
	Language Used Mostly explicit, some dialect or other unconventional language.	
	Knowledge Required Some references to events. Begins to rely more on outside knowledge.	

RESOURCES

- Unit 5 Response Log
- 🔊 Selection Audio
- ▶ Close Read Close Read Screencasts: Modeled Discussions
- 📖 Reading Studio: Notice & Note
- LEVEL UP Level Up Tutorial: Plot Stages
- 📃 Writing Studio: Writing Informative Texts
- 💬 Speaking and Listening Studio: Participating in Collaborative Discussions
- 🔬 Vocabulary Studio: Using Resources
- ❗ Grammar Studio: Module 1: Lesson 10: Kinds of Sentences
- ☑ "The First Day of School" Selection Test

SUMMARIES

English

The year is 1958, and John Hawkins and his sister Audrey are two of the very few African American students preparing to attend a previously all-white local high school. Tensions are high in their town as protesters gather around the school and the National Guard is brought in to keep order. John says he will only go to school if Audrey doesn't, but when Audrey tells him of the sacrifices their family has made for them to go to the school, John decides neither of them should give up on going to the new school.

Spanish

El año es 1958 y John Hawkins y su hermana, Audrey, son dos de los pocos estudiantes afroamericanos preparándose para ingresar a una escuela secundaria local que antes era únicamente para gente blanca. La tensión es alta en el pueblo mientras la gente se reúne alrededor de la escuela para protestar. La Guardia Nacional es llamada para mantener el orden. John dice que él solo asistirá a la escuela si Audrey no asiste, pero cuando Audrey le cuenta de los sacrificios que su familia ha hecho para que ambos puedan asistir a la escuela, John decide que ninguno de los dos debería renunciar a asistir a la nueva escuela.

SMALL-GROUP OPTIONS

Have students work in small groups to read and discuss the selection.

Pinwheel Discussion

- Divide students into groups of six, with three students seated facing in, and three students seated facing out.
- Provide a question about the selection. Have each student discuss the question with the student facing them for a designated amount of time, for example, 10 minutes.
- Tell students in the inner circle to remain stationary while the students in the outer circle rotate to their right. Provide students with a new discussion question.
- Continue to have students rotate until they have gone full circle.

Three-Minute Review

- Pause at any time while reading or discussing the selection.
- Set a timer for three minutes, and have students work with a partner to reread a specific section of the text or answer a question.
- After three minutes, ask pairs to share what they noticed in their review. What new information did they learn?

Text X-Ray: English Learner Support
for "The First Day of School"

Use the Text X-Ray and the supports and scaffolds in the Teacher's Edition to help guide students at different proficiency levels through the selection.

INTRODUCE THE SELECTION
DISCUSS SCHOOL DESEGREGATION

Use the following activity to help students understand the concepts of school segregation and desegregation:

- Write the following terms on the board: *segregation, desegregation,* and *integration*.
- Have students repeat each word three times.
- Discuss the definitions of each term, using pictorial support as needed.
- Explain that many schools in the South in the 1950s and 1960s used segregation and then changed their policies by practicing integration, or desegregation. Use visual aids to help students understand that *segregation* and *desegregation* are antonyms, and that *desegregation* and *integration* are synonyms.
- Have students complete the following sentence frame for each of the three terms: *An example of _____ is when _____.*

CULTURAL REFERENCES

The following words and phrases may be unfamiliar to students:

- *mine* (paragraph 15): an underground area where workers pick out resources, such as coal
- *a quarter past eight* (paragraph 17): fifteen minutes past eight o'clock
- *National Guard* (paragraph 22): a part of the military that responds to disasters in the United States
- *condition* (paragraph 29): a situation that must be met before a person agrees to do something
- *"laid him off on account of us"* (paragraph 33): the father got fired because the boss was mad that his children were going to the all-white school

LISTENING

Understand Historical Setting

Draw students' attention to the fact that setting includes the time when a story takes place. The setting affects the way characters act and feel. Remind them that this story's setting is 1958 in the southern United States, where many white people are upset about school integration.

Have students listen as you read aloud paragraphs 22–23. Use the following supports with students at varying proficiency levels:

- Make the following statements, and have students answer with a thumbs-up for yes and a thumbs-down for no: *This story takes place now. John and Audrey are going to be among the first black students to attend an all-white high school. Some people in the town are mad about black students going to the high school.* **SUBSTANTIAL**
- Have students complete these sentence frames: *John and Audrey are going to be among the first _____ to _____. Some people in the town are angry because _____.* **MODERATE**
- Have students demonstrate listening comprehension by answering the following questions: *What are John and Audrey about to do? What is happening in town?* **LIGHT**

SPEAKING

Discuss Elements of Plot

Refer students to the plot diagram on page 353. Discuss each element, using a familiar story to illustrate the elements. Then have students discuss the plot of "The First Day of School." Circulate to make sure students are using the word *plot* correctly.

Work with a group of students to determine each element of plot. Write the terms *rising action, climax, falling action,* and *resolution* on the board. Use the following supports with students at varying proficiency levels:

- Tell a simple story and use stick-figure drawings or online pictures to illustrate each plot element. Place the pictures next to the name of the plot element. Then mention events from the story, and have students point to the picture and plot element that corresponds to that event. **SUBSTANTIAL**
- Discuss each plot element with students. Then have students complete sentence frames such as: *Rising action is when* _____. **MODERATE**
- Have student pairs discuss examples from the story for each plot element. Then have them summarize the story's plot. **LIGHT**

READING

Discuss the Effects of Setting on Plot and Character

Review with students that the setting of the story is the American South in 1958, when schools were just being desegregated. Point out that this setting affects the conflict of the story and the way the characters respond to it.

Work with students to read paragraphs 31–36. Use the following supports with students at varying proficiency levels:

- Write the words *setting, plot,* and *character* on the board. Write definitions for each word. Have students read each word and definition chorally. Provide pictorial support for each definition. **SUBSTANTIAL**
- Display and discuss the definitions for the terms *setting, plot,* and *character*. Have students discuss each term using sentence frames such as: *The setting of this story is* ____. **MODERATE**
- Have student pairs answer the questions: *How does this setting affect John's feelings about Audrey going to school? Why does Audrey tell John they have to go to school?* **LIGHT**

WRITING

Write an Analytical Essay

Draw students' attention to the writing assignment on page 363.

Use the following supports with students at varying proficiency levels:

- Work with students to create an idea web about the effects of setting on characters. Accept single words or short phrases to include in the web. Provide support for writing a group essay, and have students copy it. They should illustrate the essay to demonstrate comprehension of the concepts. **SUBSTANTIAL**
- Give students a sentence frame to write a controlling idea: *John feels* ____ *about going to school.* Provide additional sentence frames to help students explain how the setting affects John and to explain how John's response to events in his past affects his actions in the present. Help students write a concluding statement for their essays. **MODERATE**
- Have student pairs use the first four checkboxes of the assignment to create an outline for their essays. Remind them to use the words *setting* and *character* in their outlines and writing. Conference with pairs about their ideas and needed revisions. Have students create first drafts that you review. **LIGHT**

Connect to the
ESSENTIAL QUESTION

"The First Day of School" tells the story of John and Audrey Hawkins, a brother and sister who are among the few African American students who will attend a previously all-white high school in the fall of 1958. John knows many white people in town are angry about school desegregation and that their protests are likely to turn violent and require intervention from the National Guard. John is afraid to go to school, and he's especially afraid for Audrey. When he asks Audrey to skip school, she tells him that their father has been fired because Audrey and John will be going to the all-white high school. Audrey's description of their father's sacrifice convinces John that neither he nor Audrey should give up in their effort to integrate the school.

THE FIRST DAY OF SCHOOL

Short Story by **R. V. CASSILL**

ESSENTIAL QUESTION:

What keeps people from giving up?

QUICK START

How much do you know about the historical practice of segregation in U.S. public schools? List three facts about segregation and three questions you have about it.

ANALYZE ELEMENTS OF PLOT

The series of events in a work of fiction is called the **plot.** The plot usually centers on a conflict, or struggle, faced by the main character. Most plots have the following five stages: exposition, rising action, climax, falling action, and resolution:

Climax is the point of greatest tension in the work. Here, the conflict is resolved and the outcome becomes clear.

Rising action introduces or develops the conflict. Events occur that make the conflict get more complicated and build toward the climax.

Falling action is the stage in which the story begins to draw to a close. Events show the results of the important decision or action that happened at the climax.

Exposition provides background information and introduces the setting, characters, and sometimes the conflict.

Resolution is the final outcome of the story.

Sometimes authors use **nonlinear elements,** including flashbacks, to provide a better understanding of a character or of the plot's action. A **flashback** is an interruption of the plot that presents events that took place at an earlier time. As you read, consider what a flashback reveals about the characters and how it fits into the story's structure.

ANALYZE INFLUENCE OF SETTING ON PLOT AND CHARACTER

In "The First Day of School," the characters are fictional, but the historical events described are not. As you read, note how the story's historical and cultural setting influences its characters and plot development. Read the background information and look for clues about the time and place of the story as you read. Ask yourself, how does the setting help create and reveal the conflicts of the plot?

GENRE ELEMENTS: SHORT STORY

• is a work of short fiction that centers on a single idea and can be read in one sitting

• usually includes one main conflict that involves the characters and keeps the story moving

• includes the basic elements of fiction—plot, character, setting, and theme

• may be based on real people and historical events

The First Day of School **353**

TEACH

QUICK START

Have students read the Quick Start prompt and write down facts they know and questions they have about school desegregation. If students get stuck, you may want to refer them to the Background note for more information or jog their memories about famous school desegregation cases they may have learned about (e.g., Ruby Bridges or the Little Rock Nine). Have students share their ideas and questions. You may want to write these ideas down and display them on a poster in the room throughout the lesson.

ANALYZE ELEMENTS OF PLOT

Review the definition of the word *plot* with students. Tell them that many stories' plots follow the diagram shown on page 353. Together with students, pick a familiar story to use as an example when exploring plot elements. Draw the plot diagram on the board and write each of the plot elements. Ask volunteers to share the details of each plot element from your chosen example story, and add these details to your diagram.

Draw special attention to the section about flashbacks. Explain that "The First Day of School" contains a flashback that helps explain a character's feelings in the present.

ANALYZE INFLUENCE OF SETTING ON PLOT AND CHARACTER

Tell students to ask themselves these questions as they read:

• What is the historical and cultural setting?

• How does this setting affect the characters?

• What effect does this setting have on the plot?

 For **speaking support** for students at varying proficiency levels, see the **Text X-Ray** on page 352D.

ENGLISH LEARNER SUPPORT

Decode and Understand Segregation Write *segregation* on the board, and help students decode by segmenting the syllables. Give a simple definition. Then write the following sentences on the board and have students repeat them after you: *There were different schools for black students and white students. In 1954 the Supreme Court said schools must include everyone. A lot of people were mad about black and white students going to school together. In many schools there was yelling and fighting outside the school when black students tried to attend.*
SUBSTANTIAL

TEACH

CRITICAL VOCABULARY

Encourage students to read all the sentences before deciding which word best completes each one. Remind them to look for context clues that match the meaning of each word.

Answers:

1. *stealthily*

2. *linger*

3. *serene*

4. *resentment*

5. *lament*

6. *poised*

■ English Learner Support

Use Cognates Tell students that some of the Critical Vocabulary words have Spanish cognates: *lament/lamentar, resentment/resentimiento, serene/serena.*
ALL LEVELS

LANGUAGE CONVENTIONS

Review examples of each type of sentence with students. Have volunteers provide original examples of each type of sentence. Point out that if a writer is joining two clauses that could each be a sentence by themselves, the writer uses a comma and the word *and.* Demonstrate for students what a series of non-varied sentences sounds like, and ask them to explain why it's important for writers to vary their sentence patterns. (Using only simple sentences sounds dull. Using only compound or complex sentences makes it difficult for a reader to keep track of everything you are saying. You must use different types of sentences to serve different purposes.)

ANNOTATION MODEL

Remind students of the annotation ideas on page 353. Point out the example annotation on this page and tell students they are free to use the annotation style of the model or come up with their own system for annotations.

 GET READY

CRITICAL VOCABULARY

resentment   lament   stealthily   linger   serene   poised

Use the Critical Vocabulary words to complete the sentences.

1. The cat crept _____ through the bushes, stalking a bird.

2. I decided to _____ in bed for a few minutes of extra sleep.

3. In the portrait, the woman looked relaxed and _____ .

4. I feel _____ when my sister gets to stay up later than me.

5. I will _____ going to the movies if you can't come too!

6. He appeared _____ and confident in front of the class.

LANGUAGE CONVENTIONS

Sentence patterns include simple, compound, complex, and compound-complex sentences. The following is an example of a compound sentence from "The First Day of School."

He heard the tap of heels on the stairs, and his sister came down into the kitchen.

A comma is used to separate the two independent clauses joined by the coordinating conjunction *and.* As you read the selection, pay attention to the variety of sentence patterns and how commas are used in each.

ANNOTATION MODEL   **NOTICE & NOTE**

As you read, note the stages of plot and instances of flashback. You can also mark details that help you understand the setting of the story. In the model, you can see one reader's notes about "The First Day of School."

13   He heard the tap of heels on the stairs, and his sister came down into the kitchen. <u>She looked fresh and cool in her white dress.</u> Her lids looked heavy. She must have slept all right—and for this John felt both envy and a faint **resentment**. <u>He had not really slept since midnight.</u> The heavy traffic in town, the long wail of horns as somebody raced in on the U.S. highway holding the horn button down, and the restless murmur, like the sound of a celebration down in the courthouse square, had kept him awake after that.

This description of getting ready for school shows that this day seems different.

This is the start of a flashback. The setting is tense and unsettled.

BACKGROUND

In 1954, the United States Supreme Court ruled that segregation in public schools (the practice of having "separate but equal" schools for whites and blacks) was unconstitutional. This decision meant that schools had to begin integrating students at all levels. Schoolchildren, particularly in the southern United States, prepared to face the anger, hatred, and often violence of those who opposed this policy. In 1958, in the midst of this difficult time, **R. V. Cassill** *(1919–2002) wrote this story.*

THE FIRST DAY OF SCHOOL

Short Story by R. V. Cassill

SETTING A PURPOSE

As you read, pay close attention to details about the setting and the clues that indicate what is significant about this first day of school.

1 Thirteen bubbles floated in the milk. Their pearl transparent hemispheres[1] gleamed like souvenirs of the summer days just past, rich with blue reflections of the sky and of shadowy greens. John Hawkins jabbed the bubble closest to him with his spoon, and it disappeared without a ripple. On the white surface there was no mark of where it had been.

2 "Stop tooling[2] that oatmeal and eat it," his mother said. She glanced meaningfully at the <u>clock on the varnished</u> cupboard. She nodded a heavy, emphatic affirmation[3] that now the clock was boss. <u>Summer was over,</u> when

---

[1] **hemispheres** (hĕm´ ĭ-sfîrz´): halves of a sphere, which is a three-dimensional circular, or ball, shape.

[2] **tooling** (tōō´lĭng): working with something, as with a tool such as a spoon.

[3] **affirmation** (ăf´ər-mā´shən): positive, strong support of the truth of something.

NOTICE & NOTE

Notice & Note

Use the side margins to notice and note signposts in the text.

ANALYZE INFLUENCE OF SETTING ON PLOT AND CHARACTER

Annotate: In paragraph 2, mark details of setting.

Analyze: What does the setting reveal about this stage of the plot?

The First Day of School 355

BACKGROUND

Have students read the Background and information about the author. Tell students that the 1954 Supreme Court ruling is known as *Brown v. Board of Education.* In spite of the ruling, many school districts in the South resisted. In 1957 in Little Rock, Arkansas, a mob of white people and hundreds of armed guardsmen prevented the nine chosen black students from entering Central High School for weeks. Finally, President Eisenhower had to authorize federal troops to escort the students safely into the school. A detail of those troops remained at the school for the entire year to ensure the students' safety.

SETTING A PURPOSE

Direct students to use the Setting a Purpose prompt to focus their reading.

ANALYZE INFLUENCE OF SETTING ON PLOT AND CHARACTER

Remind students that setting includes more than just place; it also includes time. In this story, the time in history will be important, but in paragraph 2 students should focus on annotating details about the time of day and season. This early point in the story is a good time to start a discussion on how setting affects plot and character from the beginning. (**Answer:** *These details about setting affect the rising action of the plot: we see the character of the mother and the setting of the family's home. The beginning of the school year contrasts with the ease of summer. Students may note the introduction of the conflict: John Hawkins and his family seem tense for some reason other than this day being the first day of school.*)

ENGLISH LEARNER SUPPORT

Develop Vocabulary Point out that the beginning of this story includes words students see often (such as *the, like, just, eat, where, when*). Reinforce these words by writing them on the board and reading them aloud as students echo you. Then point out that there are also many words that are less common. (*jabbed, ripple, emphatic*) Have students point out words that are unfamiliar and work together to define them. Remind students to use resources such as a thesaurus to find simpler synonyms for unfamiliar words. **MODERATE**

TEACH

ANALYZE ELEMENTS OF PLOT

Tell students the details they mark are part of the exposition: the characters have been introduced, and the reader is just learning early details about the conflict. (**Answer:** *The conflict is just hinted at here in the exposition: John is reluctant to go to school and face the day. He may be afraid for his sister, too, but we don't know exactly why yet.*)

LANGUAGE CONVENTIONS

Review with students the types of sentences and the purposes of commas. (**Answer:** *The author uses a variety of sentence patterns here, including compound sentences, "He heard the tap of heels on the stairs, and his sister came down into the kitchen," and compound-complex sentences, "The heavy traffic in town, the long wail of horns as somebody raced in on the U.S. highway holding the horn button down, and the restless murmur, like the sound of a celebration down in the courthouse square, had kept him awake after that." Commas help clarify ideas and allow for pauses. The varying sentence patterns contribute to the flow and tempo of this section of flashback.*)

CRITICAL VOCABULARY

resentment: John felt envy and anger at his sister because she slept all night and he couldn't sleep.

ASK STUDENTS why John would resent Audrey for sleeping. (**Possible answer**: *John was mad that he was kept awake by the horns and sirens so that he felt tired, but she didn't.*)

356 Unit 5

 NOTICE & NOTE

ANALYZE ELEMENTS OF PLOT
Annotate: In paragraphs 3–12, mark the details that show you John is worried and upset about something.

Analyze: What is the conflict that is introduced here? What stage of the plot is this?

LANGUAGE CONVENTIONS
Authors vary their sentence patterns to make their writing smooth, clear, and interesting to read. Explain the effect of the author's use of varying sentence patterns and commas in paragraph 13.

resentment
(rĭ-zĕnt′mənt) *n.* If you feel *resentment*, you feel anger or irritation.

the gracious oncoming of <u>morning light</u> and the stir of <u>early breezes</u> promised that time was a luxury.

3   "Audrey's not even down yet," he said.

4   "Audrey'll be down."

5   "You think she's taking longer to dress because she wants to look nice today?"

6   "She likes to look *neat*."

7   "<u>What I was thinking,</u>" he said slowly, "<u>was that maybe she didn't feel like going today. Didn't feel *exactly* like it.</u>"

8   "Of course she'll go."

9   "<u>I meant she might not want to go until tomorrow, maybe. Until we see what happens.</u>"

10   "Nothing's going to happen," his mother said.

11   "<u>I know there isn't. But what if it did?</u>" Again John swirled the tip of his spoon in the milk. It was like writing on a surface that would keep no mark.

12   "Eat and be quiet. Audrey's coming, so let's stop this here kind of talk."

13   He heard the tap of heels on the stairs, and his sister came down into the kitchen. She looked fresh and cool in her white dress. Her lids looked heavy. She must have slept all right—and for this John felt both envy and a faint **resentment**. He had not really slept since midnight. The heavy traffic in town, the long wail of horns as somebody raced in on the U.S. highway holding the horn button down, and the restless murmur, like the sound of a celebration down in the courthouse square, had kept him awake after that. Each time a car had passed their house his breath had gone tight and sluggish. It was better to stay awake and ready, he had told himself, than to be caught asleep.

14   "Daddy gone?" Audrey asked softly as she took her place across the table from her brother.

15   "He's been gone an hour," their mother answered. "*You* know what time he has to be at the mine."

16   "She means, did he go to work today?" John said. His voice had risen impatiently. He met his mother's stout[4] gaze in a staring contest, trying to make her admit by at least some flicker of expression that today was different from any other day. "I thought he might be down at Reverend Specker's," John said. "Cal's father and Vonnie's and some of the others are going to be there to wait and see."

17   Maybe his mother smiled then. If so, the smile was so faint that he could not be sure. "You know your father isn't much of a hand for waiting," she said. "Eat. It's a quarter past eight."

---

[4] **stout** (stout): bold, brave, determined.

356   Unit 5

 ENGLISH LEARNER SUPPORT

Recognize Informal Language Point out that the conversation between family members shows examples of informal language, such as Audrey's question "Daddy gone?" rather than the formal "Is Daddy gone?" and the idiom "isn't much of a hand for waiting," which means "isn't very good at waiting." Challenge students to find other examples of informal language in the dialogue, and discuss how it makes the characters more realistic.
LIGHT

18   As he spooned the warm oatmeal into his mouth he heard the rain crow calling again from the trees beyond the railroad embankment. He had heard it since the first light came before dawn, and he had thought, Maybe the bird knows it's going to rain, after all. He hoped it would. *They won't come out in the rain,* he had thought. Not so many of them, at least. He could wear a raincoat. A raincoat might help him feel more protected on the walk to school. It would be a sort of disguise, at least.

19   But since dawn the sun had lain across the green Kentucky trees and the roofs of town like a clean, hard fire. The sky was as clear as fresh-washed window glass. The rain crow was wrong about the weather. And still, John thought, its **lamenting,** repeated call must mean something.

lament
(lə-mĕnt´) *v.* If you *lament*, you are wailing or crying as a way of expressing grief.

20   His mother and Audrey were talking about the groceries she was to bring when she came home from school at lunch time. A five-pound bag of sugar, a fresh pineapple, a pound of butter . . .

21   "Listen!" John said. Downtown the sound of a siren had begun. A volley of automobile horns broke around it as if they meant to drown it out. "*Listen* to them."

22   "It's only the National Guard, I expect," his mother said calmly. "They came in early this morning before light. And it may be some foolish kids honking at them, the way they would. Audrey, if Henry doesn't have a good-looking roast, why then let it go, and I'll walk out to Weaver's this afternoon and get one there. I wanted to have something a little bit special for our dinner tonight."

23   So . . . John thought . . . she wasn't asleep last night either. Someone had come **stealthily** to the house to bring his parents word about the National Guard. That meant they knew about the others who had come into town, too. Maybe all through the night there had been a swift passage of messengers through the neighborhood and a whispering of information that his mother meant to keep from him. Your folks told you, he reflected bitterly, that nothing is better than knowing. Knowing whatever there is in this world to be known. That was why you had to be one of the half dozen kids out of some nine hundred colored of school age who were going today to start classes at Joseph P. Gilmore High instead of Webster. Knowing and learning the truth were worth so much they said—and then left it to the hooting rain crow to tell you that things were worse than everybody had hoped.

stealthily
(stĕl´thə-lē) *adv.* To do something *stealthily* means doing it quietly and secretly so no one notices.

ANALYZE INFLUENCE OF SETTING ON PLOT AND CHARACTER
Annotate: Mark details in paragraph 23 that help you better understand the setting of the story.

Analyze: How does the cultural and historical setting of the story affect John and lead to the conflict?

CLOSE READ SCREENCAST

Modeled Discussion In their eBooks, have students read the Close Read Screencast, in which readers discuss and annotate paragraph 18.

As a class, view and discuss the video. Then have students pair up to do an independent close read of paragraph 26. Students can record their answers on the Close Read Practice PDF.

 Close Read Practice PDF

TEACH

ANALYZE INFLUENCE OF SETTING ON PLOT AND CHARACTER

Tell students to look for details that describe the historical setting. Point out that these details will help students understand the climax of the plot. (**Answer:** *The National Guard is coming to help the children attend school without a problem. We learn the crux of John's conflict: he and his sister are among a few African Americans who are attending a white school after desegregation, and he is worried for his and his sister's safety.*)

For **listening support** for students at varying proficiency levels, see the **Text X-Ray** on page 352C.

CRITICAL VOCABULARY

lament: John thought the crow's sad wailing must be a warning of something bad about to happen.

ASK STUDENTS what the crow's usual lamenting meant, and what John thinks it means on that morning. (**Possible answer:** *Usually the crow's lamenting means it's going to rain. Today John thinks that because the weather is nice, the crow's lamenting must be a warning of danger at his new school.*)

stealthily: An unnamed person came quietly and secretly in the middle of the night to warn John's parents about the National Guard.

ASK STUDENTS why the person came stealthily. (**Possible answer:** *to avoid the angry citizens*)

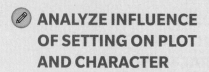

ANALYZE INFLUENCE OF SETTING ON PLOT AND CHARACTER

Tell students that this is an example of historical setting influencing characters' actions and plot. If not for the particular historical situation, the children probably wouldn't need a complicated plan for many adults to walk with them to school. (**Answer:** *Prominent adults in the community, such as religious leaders, are accompanying them to protect the children from desegregation protestors.*)

CRITICAL VOCABULARY

linger: Audrey's mom seemed to pause as she felt Audrey's dress, like she didn't want to let go.

ASK STUDENTS why Audrey's mom's hands would linger on Audrey's shoulders. (**Possible answer:** *Audrey's mom is terrified that Audrey and John will get hurt going to school, so she wants to hug her daughter for just a little longer.*)

NOTICE & NOTE

ANALYZE INFLUENCE OF SETTING ON PLOT AND CHARACTER

Annotate: In paragraph 25, mark details about who will walk to school with John and his sister.

Draw Conclusions: Why is it necessary that the children are walked to school by adults?

linger
(lĭng´gər) *v.* To *linger* means to leave slowly and reluctantly, not wanting to go.

24   Something had gone wrong, bad enough wrong so the National Guard had to be called out.

25   "It's eight twenty-five," his mother said. "Did you get that snap sewed on right, Audrey?" As her experienced fingers examined the shoulder of Audrey's dress they **lingered** a moment in an involuntary, sheltering caress. "It's all arranged," she told her children, "how you'll walk down to the Baptist Church and meet the others there. You know there'll be <u>Reverend Chader, Reverend Smith, and Mr. Hall to go with you. It may be that the white ministers will go with you, or they may be waiting at school.</u> We don't know. But now you be sure, don't you go farther than the Baptist Church alone." Carefully she lifted her hand clear of Audrey's shoulder. John thought, Why doesn't she hug her if that's what she wants to do?

26   He pushed away from the table and went out on the front porch. The dazzling sunlight lay shadowless on the street that swept down toward the Baptist Church at the edge of the colored section. The street seemed awfully long this morning, the way it had looked when he was little. A chicken was

---

WHEN STUDENTS STRUGGLE . . .

Use the Plot Diagram The plot diagram on page 353 lends itself to helping struggling students comprehend the events of the story. Just as young students are told to summarize a story by saying what happened at the beginning, middle, and end, older students can be asked what events make up the exposition, rising action, climax, falling action, and resolution. Draw the diagram on the board, and have students tell you which events belong on each part of the diagram.

 For additional support, go to the **Reading Studio** and assign the following LEVEL UP **Level Up tutorial: Plot Stages.**

clucking contentedly behind their neighbor's house, feeling the warmth, settling itself into the sun-warmed dust. Lucky chicken.

27   He blinked at the sun's glare on the concrete steps leading down from the porch. <u>He remembered something else from the time he was little.</u> Once he had kicked Audrey's doll buggy down these same steps. He had done it out of meanness—for some silly reason he had been mad at her. But as soon as the buggy had started to bump down, he had understood how terrible it was not to be able to run after it and stop it. It had gathered speed at each step and when it hit the sidewalk it had spilled over. Audrey's doll had smashed into sharp little pieces on the sidewalk below. His mother had come out of the house to find him crying harder than Audrey. "Now you know that when something gets out of your hands it is in the Devil's hands," his mother had explained to him. Did she expect him to forget—now—that that was always the way things went to smash when they got out of hand? (Again he heard the siren and the hooting,) mocking horns from the center of town. Didn't his mother think *they* could get out of hand?

28   He closed his eyes and seemed to see something like a doll buggy bump down long steps like those at Joseph P. Gilmore High, and it seemed to him that it was not a doll that was riding down to be smashed.

29   He made up his mind then. He would go today, because he had said he would. Therefore he had to. But he wouldn't go unless Audrey stayed home. That was going to be his condition. His bargaining looked perfect. He would trade them one for one.

30   His mother and Audrey came together onto the porch. His mother said, "My stars, I forgot to give you the money for the groceries." She let the screen door bang as she went swiftly back into the house.

31   As soon as they were alone, he took Audrey's bare arm in his hand and pinched hard. "You gotta stay home," he whispered. "Don't you know there's thousands of people down there? Didn't you hear them coming in all night long? You slept, didn't you? All right. You can hear them now. Tell her you're sick. She won't expect you to go if you're sick. I'll knock you down, I'll smash you if you don't tell her that." He bared his teeth and twisted his nails into the skin of her arm. "Hear them horns," he hissed.

32   He forced her halfway to her knees with the strength of his fear and rage. They swayed there, locked for a minute. Her knee

---

NOTICE & NOTE

ANALYZE ELEMENTS OF PLOT

Annotate: In paragraph 27, underline the words that show a flashback is beginning. Circle the words that signal the flashback has ended.

Analyze: How does the flashback help you understand John's character?

The First Day of School   359

TEACH

✎ ANALYZE ELEMENTS OF PLOT

Remind students that a flashback is a memory from a character's past. It is a special plot element that doesn't belong on the plot diagram. Flashbacks help readers understand the reasons behind a character's personality or actions. (**Answer:** *Readers find out that John is self-aware and caring; his anger is caused by worry and tension. This flashback takes readers out of the present action to show something about John; it moves the story forward by helping readers understand John's actions.*)

■ English Learner Support

Ask Questions for Comprehension   Help students demonstrate understanding of the flashback by asking them yes/no questions such as: *Is the story of the doll a flashback from when John and Audrey were young?* Have students ask questions about the flashback to clarify their understanding. Discuss each question until it has been sufficiently clarified. **SUBSTANTIAL**

📖   For **reading support** for students at varying proficiency levels, see the **Text X-Ray** on page 352D.

IMPROVE READING FLUENCY

Targeted Passage   Have students work with partners to read paragraphs 32 and 33. First, use paragraph 32 to model how to read text with appropriate speed and phrasing. Remind students to pause for commas and to read at a speed appropriate for a tension-filled moment in the story. Then, have partners take turns reading aloud the paragraphs. Encourage students to provide feedback and support for any challenging multisyllabic words, and to encourage each other to read with appropriate speed and phrasing.

   Go to the **Reading Studio** for additional support in developing fluency.

© Houghton Mifflin Harcourt Publishing Company

The First Day of School   **359**

TEACH

AHA MOMENT

Remind students that the **Aha Moment** signpost is a moment when a character realizes or finally understands something. When you encounter an **Aha Moment,** you should ask yourself, "How might this change things?" You should look for a big change in **character** or **plot** following an **Aha Moment**. (*Answer: In response to John's anger and fierceness, Audrey reveals her own strength. Readers may infer that she has overheard her parents talk or perhaps that she simply better understands what was said than John does. Readers may also infer that Audrey has not shared information with him out of a desire to protect him or shield him from unpleasantness.*)

 ## ANALYZE ELEMENTS OF PLOT

Refer students to the plot diagram on page 353 and remind them that the resolution is the outcome of the story. (*Answer: The resolution of the story is John's acceptance of going to school with Audrey and facing whatever dangers are in front of them. Their mother acts as though this is just another normal school day, and this is supported in her everyday actions and her words, "Behave yourselves." Though she must have a great deal of internal conflict and worry, John's mother does not show these feelings to her children. This closes the story and shows the family's strength and determination in the face of a challenging setting.*)

📖 For **speaking support** for students at varying proficiency levels, see the **Text X-Ray** on page 352D.

CRITICAL VOCABULARY

serene: Audrey was standing calmly next to John when their mother came out to the porch.

ASK STUDENTS why Audrey would be serene during such a frightening situation. (*Audrey knows she has to go to school because of the sacrifices her parents have made, so she puts on a brave, serene face and accepts the situation.*)

poised: Audrey's voice is calm and assured when she speaks to her mother.

ASK STUDENTS why Audrey is so poised when she tells her mother she is too old for ice cream. (*She knows her mother is afraid, so she reassures her by using her tone of voice and her words to communicate to her mother that she and John are no longer scared little children.*)

360 Unit 5

 ## NOTICE & NOTE

Notice & Note: What new information does Audrey provide in paragraph 33? Mark the new information.

Analyze: What does John learn about his sister and his family? How does this information help you better understand Audrey's character and her relationship to her brother?

---

serene
(sə-rēn´) *adj.* If you are *serene,* you are calm and unflustered.

poised
(poizd) *adj.* To be poised means to be calm and assured, showing balanced feeling and action.

ANALYZE ELEMENTS OF PLOT

Annotate: Mark details in paragraphs 40–44 that contribute to the resolution of the story.

Summarize: What is the resolution, or final outcome, of the story?

360 Unit 5

---

dropped to the porch floor. She lowered her eyes. He thought he had won.

33 But she was saying something and in spite of himself he listened to her almost whispered refusal. "Don't you know anything? <u>Don't you know it's harder for them than us? Don't you know Daddy didn't go to the mine this morning? They laid him off on account of us.</u> They told him not to come if we went to school."

34 Uncertainly he relaxed his grip. "How do you know all that?"

35 "I listen," she said. Her eyes lit with a sudden spark that seemed to come from their absolute brown depths. "But I don't let on all I know the way you do. I'm not a . . ." Her last word sunk so low that he could not exactly hear it. But if his ear missed it, his understanding caught it. He knew she had said "coward."

36 He let her get up then. She was standing beside him, **serene** and prim when their mother came out on the porch again.

37 "Here, child," their mother said to Audrey, counting the dollar bills into her hand. "There's six, and I guess it will be all right if you have some left if you and Brother get yourselves a cone to lick on the way home."

38 John was not looking at his sister then. He was already turning to face the shadowless street, but he heard the unmistakable **poised** amusement of her voice when she said, "Ma, don't you know we're a little too old for that?"

39 "Yes, you are," their mother said. "Seems I had forgotten that."

40 <u>They were too old to take each other's hand, either, as they went down the steps of their home and into the street.</u> As they turned to the right, facing the sun, they heard the chattering of a tank's tread on the pavement by the school. A voice too distant to be understood bawled a military command. There were horns again and a crescendo[5] of boos.

41 Behind them they heard their mother call something. It was lost in the general racket.

42 "What?" John called back to her. "What?"

43 She had followed them out as far as the sidewalk, but not past the gate. As they hesitated to listen, she put her hands to either side of her mouth and called to them the words she had so often used when she let them go away from home.

44 <u>"Behave yourselves," she said.</u>

---

[5] **crescendo** (krə-shĕn´dō): a slow, gradual increase in volume, intensity, or force.

APPLYING ACADEMIC VOCABULARY

☑ achieve ☐ individual ☐ instance ☐ outcome ☑ principle

Write and Discuss Have students turn to a partner to discuss the following questions. Guide students to include the Academic Vocabulary words *achieve* and *principle* in their responses. Ask volunteers to share their responses with the class.

- What will John, Audrey, and the other black students **achieve** by going to school?
- What **principle** did John's parents share with him?

CHECK YOUR UNDERSTANDING

Answer these questions before moving on to the **Analyze the Text** section on the following page.

1 John Hawkins is upset with his mother because —

   A she acts as if this morning is like any other day

   B she gives grocery money to his sister and not to him

   C she makes him eat his breakfast even though he is ill

   D she doesn't take his father to work

2 The author includes details about the National Guard to —

   F describe the work that they do

   G add tension to the situation and complicate the plot

   H give a side detail that doesn't add much to plot

   J describe the characters in vivid details

3 Why does John tell his sister to pretend to be sick?

   A He likes to tell his little sister what to do.

   B He believes she is ill and pretending to be well.

   C He knows that is what his mother really wants.

   D He does not want either of them to face danger at school.

CHECK YOUR UNDERSTANDING

Have students answer the questions independently.

Answers:

1. *A*

2. *G*

3. *D*

If they answer any questions incorrectly, have them reread the text to confirm their understanding. Then they may proceed to ANALYZE THE TEXT on page 362.

ENGLISH LEARNER SUPPORT

Oral Assessment Use the following questions to assess students' comprehension and speaking skills:

1. Is John Hawkins upset because his mother acts worried or because she acts like today is like any other day? *(like any other day)*

2. John's parents find out that the National Guard is in the town. Does this knowledge make the situation seem more serious or less serious? *(more serious)*

3. John thinks going to school will be _____ for him and his sister. *(dangerous)*

   SUBSTANTIAL/MODERATE

APPLY

ANALYZE THE TEXT

Possible answers:

1. **DOK 1:** *John hears "the long wail of horns" and a "restless murmur, like the sound of a celebration down in the courthouse square". These details are indicative of the tension surrounding the issue of school desegregation in the American South in the 1950s. Details about the church and its leaders who will accompany the children to school show a cultural setting in which religion is important to the community. As the children leave for school, they hear "a tank's tread . . . a military command . . . horns," and "a crescendo of boos." The setting is frightening and threatening.*

2. **DOK 2:** *Several details about setting in these paragraphs contribute to the conflict in the story. John hears "the rain crow calling again." On this day, John hopes the rain will come, causing fewer people to be at school to harass the black students. Yet the day is clear—"the sun had lain across the green Kentucky trees and the roofs of town like a clean, hard fire." This setting detail confirms that the story is set in the South, and the fine weather adds to the conflict because more protesters will come out to jeer at or threaten the students.*

3. **DOK 4:** *John remembers his feeling of powerlessness when he was unable to stop the buggy. His mother's words from that event are important now, too, because John feels powerless again. But the memory pushes John to action, perhaps to feel less powerless; he decides he will go to school, but only if Audrey stays home; he wants to protect her now.*

4. **DOK 2:** *The climax of the story is when John and Audrey have their confrontation on the porch. John acts aggressively to frighten his sister into staying home. Audrey reveals that she knows that their father was laid off of work because his children are attending a white school.*

5. **DOK 4:** *John realizes that his sister views him as a coward because everyone else in the family is willing to make sacrifices to have the children attend a desegregated school. After acknowledging that everyone in his family is acting bravely in the face of danger, John decides to go to school willingly with his sister, and his conflict is resolved.*

RESEARCH

To refresh students' memories about the Little Rock Nine, reread the Background information on page 355.

Extend After their research, ask students to share why they think the Little Rock Nine were chosen to win Congressional Gold Medals.

362 Unit 5

 RESPOND

ANALYZE THE TEXT

Support your responses with evidence from the text. 🗒 NOTEBOOK

1. **Identify** What are three details in the story that help you understand the text's historical and cultural setting?

2. **Infer** Reread paragraphs 18–19. How does the setting reveal, contribute to, and create conflict in the story?

3. **Analyze** Reread paragraphs 27–29. What is the connection between what John remembers and what is happening in the story now? Describe what you learn about John and how the flashback moves the plot of the story forward.

4. **Interpret** What is the climax of the story? Explain.

5. **Notice & Note** Review paragraphs 33–36. Summarize what John realizes about other members of his family. How does this help him resolve his own internal conflict?

RESEARCH

RESEARCH TIP
To begin online research about the historical and cultural setting of the story, use "Little Rock Nine" or "*Brown v. Board of Education*" as your search terms.

The short story "The First Day of School" is based on events surrounding the 1954 Supreme Court ruling known as *Brown v. Board of Education* and the actions of a group of students in Little Rock, Arkansas, known as the Little Rock Nine. In a small group, brainstorm several questions about the historical and cultural setting of the story. After your discussion, work individually to research and answer one or more of your questions. Use the chart below to take notes.

QUESTION	ANSWER

Extend In 1999, the Little Rock Nine were honored with Congressional Gold Medals. Research why this award is given and who other recipients are. Share your findings with the class.

CREATE AND DISCOVER

Write an Analytical Essay Write a one-page essay that explains John's feelings and actions on the morning of his first day of school. Focus on how the historical setting of the story motivates him. Include the following in your essay:

❏ Introduce a controlling idea about how John feels about going to school on this day.

❏ Discuss how the historical and cultural setting of the story affects John.

❏ Show how John's response to events in his past affects his actions in the present.

❏ Sum up your ideas with a concluding statement.

❏ Remember to use transitions to connect ideas, vary your sentence patterns, and punctuate your sentences correctly.

Compare and Contrast with a Small Group Have a discussion about the story's historical context, based on your research and the setting of the text. Compare and contrast that context with your own experiences on a typical first day of school. Use the following approaches to help with the discussion:

❏ Encourage everyone to participate and listen actively.

❏ Take notes.

❏ Respectfully consider other viewpoints.

❏ Identify points of agreement and disagreement.

 Go to **Writing Informative Texts** in the **Writing Studio** for more on developing a topic and organizing ideas.

Go to **Participating in Collaborative Discussions: Speaking Constructively** in the **Speaking and Listening Studio** for help with having a group discussion.

RESPOND TO THE ESSENTIAL QUESTION

 What keeps people from giving up?

Gather Information Review your annotations and notes on "The First Day of School." Then, add relevant details to your Response Log. As you determine which information to include, think about:

• the kinds of hardships people face

• what keeps people going during hard times

• how this story is an example of not giving up

At the end of the unit, use your notes to write a biographical report.

UNIT 5 RESPONSE LOG

Essential Question: What keeps people from giving up?

A Schoolgirl's Diary from I Am Malala
The First Day of School
Speech to the Young Speech to the Progress-Toward
Here into the Air
from The Wright Brothers: How They Invented the Airplane

ACADEMIC VOCABULARY
As you write and discuss what you learned from the short story, be sure to use the Academic Vocabulary words. Check off each of the words that you use.

❏ **achieve**

❏ **individual**

❏ **instance**

❏ **outcome**

❏ **principle**

CREATE AND DISCOVER

Write an Analytical Essay Remind students that they can use the first four checkboxes on the assignment to help them write an outline. Each item can be one paragraph. The final checkbox is a reminder about skills students should demonstrate in their essays.

For **writing support** for students at varying proficiency levels, see the **Text X-Ray** on page 352D.

Compare and Contrast with a Small Group Remind students that they should begin with a discussion of the story's historical context. They should then each be given a chance to share their own experiences on the first day of school, and compare and contrast them with John's. Remind them that *compare and contrast* means to find similarities and differences. Even though students never had to start school among angry, violent protesters, they might agree that the first day of school is still anxiety-producing for everyone. Some students might relate to the idea of feeling different or not knowing anybody on the first day of school.

RESPOND TO THE ESSENTIAL QUESTION

Allow time for students to add details from "The First Day of School" to their Unit 5 Response Logs.

ENGLISH LEARNER SUPPORT

Compare and Contrast with a Small Group Give students the following sentence frames to help them participate in the compare/contrast discussion about John's first day of school:

• *On John's first day of school, he felt scared because ___. On my first day of school, I felt ___ because ___.*

• *One thing John and I have in common is that on the first day of school, we both ___.*
MODERATE

APPLY

CRITICAL VOCABULARY

Answers:

1. A serene sky would indicate sunny weather; the word means "calm," "unruffled"; there would be no storm clouds.

2. You are likely to linger at the end of a school dance because it was fun and you don't want it to end.

3. The person would be calm; the word means "composed," "in balance."

4. You can tell if a teammate is lamenting the score because he or she is expressing disappointment, regret, or sadness.

5. Resentment feels like you are jealous of someone and are upset that they have something that you do not have.

6. An animal that moves stealthily would be quiet and would try to make as little noise as possible.

VOCABULARY STRATEGY:
Thesaurus

Possible answers:

Word	Synonym	Sentence
resentment	animosity	My opponent scowled after I beat him; I could sense his *animosity*.
lament	wail	The *wail* of the distant train whistle made me homesick.
stealthily	furtively	The thief moved *furtively* through the shadows.
linger	dawdle	We *dawdled* on the way home, not wanting such a great day to end.

 RESPOND

CRITICAL VOCABULARY

WORD BANK
resentment
lament
stealthily
linger
serene
poised

Practice and Apply Answer these questions.

1. Does a **serene** sky indicate stormy or sunny weather? Explain.

2. Why are you likely to **linger** at the end of a school dance?

3. Does a **poised** person appear calm or appear nervous? Explain.

4. How can you tell if a teammate is **lamenting** the score?

5. Describe what **resentment** feels like.

6. Describe the behavior of an animal that moves **stealthily.**

VOCABULARY STRATEGY: Thesaurus

 Go to the **Vocabulary Studio** for more on using resources.

A **thesaurus** is a reference book of synonyms, or words that have nearly the same meaning. As with a dictionary, words are listed alphabetically. Each word has a list of synonyms and often a list of antonyms, or words with opposite meanings, as well. To use an online thesaurus:

- Look for the search box and type in your word.
- Click on the onscreen icon, such as a magnifying glass, and the thesaurus will display the word's meaning and synonyms.
- You also may be able to click an icon to hear a pronunciation.

Practice and Apply Use a thesaurus to select a synonym for each vocabulary word. Then use the synonym in a sentence that shows its meaning, as in the example below for *resentment*.

WORD	SYNONYM	SENTENCE
resentment	animosity	My opponent scowled after I beat him; I could sense his *animosity*.
lament		
stealthily		
linger		

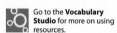 **ENGLISH LEARNER SUPPORT**

Internalize Language Give students additional practice using a thesaurus by having them look up simple words like *good, nice, fun, say, friend, big,* and *small*. Have them write three synonyms for each word. This activity will give them extra thesaurus practice and help them expand and internalize their English vocabularies. **ALL LEVELS**

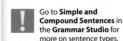
LANGUAGE CONVENTIONS:
Sentence Patterns

Authors use a variety of sentence patterns to make their writing smooth, clear, and interesting to read. Review the sentence patterns and examples from "The First Day of School" in the chart. Note how commas are used to separate clauses and make the sentences easier to read.

! Go to **Simple and Compound Sentences** in the **Grammar Studio** for more on sentence types.

SENTENCE PATTERN	DESCRIPTION AND EXAMPLE
Simple	one independent clause **She looked fresh and cool in her white dress.**
Compound	two or more independent clauses joined with a coordinating conjunction, such as *and, or, but, not, yet, so* **He heard the tap of heels on the stairs, and his sister came down into the kitchen.**
Complex	one independent clause and one or more subordinate, or dependent, clauses **Summer was over, when the gracious oncoming of morning light and the stir of early breezes promised that time was a luxury.**
Compound-Complex	two or more independent clauses and one or more subordinate clauses **It had gathered speed at each step and when it hit the sidewalk it had spilled over.**

Practice and Apply Change the sentence pattern of each sentence or group of sentences. First, identify the original pattern used in each sentence. Then revise, using a different sentence pattern.

1. John hadn't slept very well the night before because the sounds of car horns and loud voices kept him awake.

   _____

2. Audrey came down the stairs. She acted prim. The dress she had chosen looked fresh and cool.

   _____

3. Their mother came onto the porch. She called to them. She followed them down the street.

   _____

LANGUAGE CONVENTIONS:
Sentence Patterns

Review the information about sentence patterns with students. Ask volunteers to share ideas for why it is important to vary sentence patterns in their writing.

Review each type of sentence. Clarify for students the difference between independent clauses and subordinate/dependent clauses. An independent clause is a group of words that could make up a complete sentence on their own. In the example of the compound sentence in the table, "He heard the tap of heels on the stairs" and "his sister came down into the kitchen" could both be sentences on their own, so they are independent clauses. Stress that *subordinate clause* and *dependent clause* have the same meaning—that is, a grouping of words that doesn't make a complete sentence. In the compound-complex example sentence, "As John ate his oatmeal" is a subordinate/dependent clause.

Practice and Apply

Possible Answers:

1. *complex, changed to simple: John hadn't slept very well. The sounds of car horns and loud voices kept waking him up.*

2. *simple, changed to compound: Audrey came primly down the stairs, and the dress she had chosen looked fresh and cool.*

3. *simple, changed to compound-complex: Their mother called to them as she came onto the porch, and then she followed them down the street.*

 ENGLISH LEARNER SUPPORT

Write Sentences Use the following supports with students at varying proficiency levels:

- Write examples of simple, compound, complex, and compound-complex sentences without commas, modeled after the ones on page 365. Have students read each sentence aloud. Work together to add commas where they are needed. **SUBSTANTIAL**

- Have student partners work together to write an original example of each type of sentence. **MODERATE**

- Have students write an example of each type of sentence, leaving out commas. Have them switch sentences with a partner to add commas and identify sentence types. **LIGHT**

SPEECH TO THE YOUNG: SPEECH TO THE PROGRESS-TOWARD

Poem by Gwendolyn Brooks

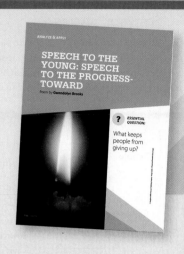

GENRE ELEMENTS
POETRY

Remind students that one purpose of **poetry** is to convey the poet's feelings about a topic or experience. A free verse poem does not follow a specific rhyming pattern or metrical form. It does, however, use other elements of poetry, such as line breaks, repetition, rhythm, and alliteration.

LEARNING OBJECTIVES

- Analyze the effects of meter and structural elements.
- Make inferences about theme and author's purpose.
- Research poet Gwendolyn Brooks.
- Write a poem or inspirational speech.
- Record a poem or presentation as a podcast.
- **Language** Discuss elements of a poem using the terms *meter*, *alliteration*, and *repetition*.

TEXT COMPLEXITY

Quantitative Measures	Speech to the Young: Speech to the Progress-Toward	Lexile: N/A
Qualitative Measures	**Ideas Presented** Multiple levels of meaning with abstract ideas.	
	Structure Used Deviates from chronological or sequential.	
	Language Used Figurative language with complex sentence structures.	
	Knowledge Required Explores complex ideas.	

RESOURCES

- Unit 5 Response Log
- Selection Audio
- Reading Studio: Notice & Note
- Level Up Tutorial: Theme
- Writing Studio: Writing as a Process
- Speaking and Listening Studio: Producing and Publishing with Technology
- "Speech to the Young: Speech to the Progress-Toward" Selection Test

SUMMARIES

English

The poet exhorts the reader to ignore the naysayers and keep pushing forward. Justice will prevail in the end. Live for the experience of personal growth and for fighting for what is right.

Spanish

El poeta exhorta al lector a que ignore a los negativistas y a seguir adelante. La justicia prevalecerá al final. Vive por la experiencia del crecimiento personal y para luchar por lo que es justo.

SMALL-GROUP OPTIONS

Have students work in small groups to read and discuss the selection.

Think-Pair-Share

- After students have read and analyzed the poem, pose this question: *What are your thoughts about the poem's message?*
- Have students think about the question individually and take notes.
- Then, have pairs discuss their ideas about the question.
- Finally, ask pairs to share their responses with the class.

Jigsaw with Experts

- Divide the poem into four groups of three lines.
- Assign each student a group of three lines.
- Put students into groups of four.
- After students have read the poem, have students meet with other students who are assigned the same section. Have students discuss what they think the lines mean.
- Students will then return to their original group to discuss the poem as a whole.

Text X-Ray: English Learner Support
for "Speech to the Young: Speech to the Progress-Toward"

Use the Text X-Ray and the supports and scaffolds in the Teacher's Edition to help guide students at different proficiency levels through the selection.

INTRODUCE THE SELECTION

DISCUSS UNCONVENTIONAL VOCABULARY

Explain to students that the poet uses unconventional vocabulary throughout the poem. Read line 2 with students, and point out the word *down-keepers*. Provide the following explanations:

• *Down-keepers* is not a word you will find in a dictionary. It is a word that the poet created to convey her point.

• Explain to students the expressions "to keep someone down" and "won't be down for long."

• Help students see how the word *down-keepers* relates to these expressions.

Point out the words *sun-slappers* (line 3), *self-soilers* (line 4), and *harmony-hushers* (line 5). Ask students what strategies they could use to figure out the meanings of the words. Work with students to figure out the meaning of the words.

CULTURAL REFERENCES

The following words and phrases may be unfamiliar to students:

• *"cannot always be night"* (line 7): cannot always be bad

• *home-run* (line 9): to round all the bases on one play in a baseball or softball game

---

LISTENING

Understand Meter

Tell students that poems often have *meter*—a rhythm or beat that moves a poem along. Poems do not have to have meter, but many poems do.

Have students listen as you read the poem aloud several times. Use the following supports with students at varying proficiency levels:

• Have students either clap or snap when you read a word with emphasis. **SUBSTANTIAL**

• Have students tell what they noticed most about the poem's rhythm. Use sentence frames, such as: *I noticed the poem's rhythm____.* **MODERATE**

• Put students in pairs. Have students work together to find stressed words and syllables in a few lines of the poem. **LIGHT**

SPEAKING

Discuss Structural Elements

Have students describe the structural elements, such as line length and repetition. Circulate around the room to make sure students are using the terms *meter*, *alliteration*, and *repetition* correctly.

Use the following supports with students at varying proficiency levels:

- Read lines 10–12 aloud. Have students circle repeated words. Read the lines again having students echo read each line. **SUBSTANTIAL**
- Pair students with a partner. Have students discuss the effect of the repetition of the word *live*. **MODERATE**
- Pair students with a partner. Have students discuss the effect of the alliteration of *harmony-hushers* and *hard home-run*. **LIGHT**

READING

Infer Theme

Tell students that readers often have to make inferences about the theme of a poem. Remind them that making an inference involves using what you already know and text evidence to draw a conclusion.

Work with students to read and infer the theme of the poem. Use the following supports with students at varying proficiency levels:

- Help students infer the theme of the poem. Ask questions, such as: *Does the poet think that people should give up easily? Does the poem say that people should keep trying until they succeed?* **SUBSTANTIAL**
- Have students complete the following sentence frames: *The poet believes ____. The theme of the poem is _____.* **MODERATE**
- Pair students. Ask students to explain in their own words what the poem is about. **LIGHT**

WRITING

Write a Poem

Work with students to read the writing assignment on p. 373.

Use the following supports with students at varying proficiency levels:

- Put students with a partner to co-write their poem. Review *theme* with students. Discuss possible themes with students and have them select a theme for their poem. **SUBSTANTIAL**
- Provide sentence frames to help students plan their poems: *The theme is _____. The points of advice are ____.* **MODERATE**
- Allow students to incorporate only two to three poetic elements in their poems, if working individually. Have students working in pairs to incorporate all of the poetic elements. **LIGHT**

Connect to the
ESSENTIAL QUESTION

"Speech to the Young: Speech to the Progress-Toward" explains what keeps people from giving up. The poem exhorts the reader to keep moving forward despite people who try to keep them down.

SPEECH TO THE YOUNG: SPEECH TO THE PROGRESS-TOWARD

Poem by **Gwendolyn Brooks**

ESSENTIAL QUESTION:

What keeps people from giving up?

LEARNING MINDSET

Grit Review the definition of *grit* with students. Focus on the idea that persevering despite challenges is a key element of reaching goals. In other words, hard work leads to success. Encourage students to adopt flexible thinking patterns. Tell them that flexible people see opportunities, not problems. In addition to noticing when students provide a correct answer or successfully complete an activity, make a habit of rewarding students for effort.

QUICK START

What kind of advice have you been given by the adults in your life? Have you found this advice helpful or not? Explain your thoughts to a partner.

ANALYZE THE EFFECTS OF METER AND STRUCTURAL ELEMENTS

"Speech to the Young: Speech to the Progress-Toward" is a **free verse poem,** which means that it does not follow a specific rhyming pattern or metrical form. It does use other elements of poetry to convey meaning and ideas, including:

❏ **Line breaks** and different line lengths to create effects and emphasis

❏ **Repetition,** or repeated sounds, words, phrases, or lines, to reinforce meaning and create an appealing rhythm, emphasis, or sense of unity

❏ **Rhythm,** or the pattern of stressed and unstressed syllables in a line, to bring out the musical quality of language, create mood, and emphasize ideas

❏ **Alliteration,** or the repetition of the consonant sounds at the beginning of words, to contribute to and create rhythm in a poem

As you read the poem, use a chart like this to help you analyze what the poetic elements reveal.

POETIC ELEMENT	EXAMPLE IN POEM	EFFECT
Line break		
Repetition		
Rhythm		
Alliteration		

GENRE ELEMENTS: POETRY

• may include rhyme, rhythm, and meter

• features line breaks and the use of white space for effects and meaning

• may use repetition and rhyme to create a melodic quality

• often contains figurative language and literary devices such as alliteration, consonance, and assonance

---

QUICK START

Have students read the Quick Start question, and invite them to share advice they have been given by adults. Ask students whether and how they found the advice helpful.

ANALYZE THE EFFECTS OF METER AND STRUCTURAL ELEMENTS

Help students understand the terms and concepts related to the structural elements of poetry. Tell students that even though the poem is free verse, it does contain structural elements of poetry. Discuss line breaks, repetition, rhythm, and alliteration and how they can be used in a poem. Give simple examples of each structural element to illustrate them. For example:

• Write a familiar poem, song, or nursery rhyme without line breaks, then show a version with line breaks.

• Repeat a phrase several times as the beginning of a string of sentences, such as "I wish I could _____." Emphasize the repetition.

• Clap to the rhythm of a simple song or poem that has a strong rhythm. Have students find the stressed syllables in a line of dialogue from a story. Note that some poems have a rhythm that is regular and some have a rhythm that is more like regular speech.

• Write letters on the board, and have students think of alliterative phrases that use the letter.

 ENGLISH LEARNER SUPPORT

Distinguish Consonant Sounds Remind students that alliteration is the repetition of consonant sounds. Say aloud examples of alliteration ("bouncing baby boy" and "she sells seashells") as well as nonexamples. Have students identify the examples with alliteration and the consonant sound used in each. **MODERATE**

MAKE INFERENCES ABOUT THEME AND AUTHOR'S PURPOSE

Review the meanings of *theme* and *inference*. Tell students that the theme and purpose of a poem can sometimes be inferred from the structural elements in a poem. Discuss the sample graphic organizer on the Student Edition page, which illustrates how an inference can be based on and supported by a poem's structural elements. Remind students that they will need to make inferences to complete the "Effect" column in the graphic organizer on page 367.

ANNOTATION MODEL

Remind students of the annotation ideas regarding the poem's theme and author's purpose, which suggest noting clues about the poem's theme and author's purpose. Point out that they use their own system for marking up the selection in their write-in text. They may want to color code their annotations by using highlighters. Their notes in the margin may include questions about ideas that are unclear or that they want to explore further.

 GET READY

MAKE INFERENCES ABOUT THEME AND AUTHOR'S PURPOSE

Poets use structure and poetic elements to create mood and communicate meaning and themes. A **theme** is a message about life or human nature that a writer shares with readers. Often, especially with shorter poems, the metrical and structural elements express theme and purpose indirectly. Many times readers must **infer,** or form a logical opinion, about what the writer's message may be. When making inferences, readers need to support their ideas with evidence from the text and use personal experience or knowledge to inform their inferences.

Using a graphic organizer like the one below can help guide your thoughts when making inferences about the theme and the author's purpose.

> Theme:
>
> Author's Purpose:

> Structural or Metrical Elements:

> Other Evidence:

ANNOTATION MODEL   **NOTICE & NOTE**

As you read, note clues about the poem's theme and author's purpose, and examine how the poet uses poetic elements to convey a message. This model shows one reader's notes about the beginning of "Speech to the Young: Speech to the Progress-Toward."

> Say to them,
>
> say to the down-keepers,
>
> the sun-slappers,
>
> the self-soilers,
>
> 5 the harmony-hushers,
>
> "Even if you are not ready for day
>
> It cannot always be night."

The poet uses "er" words to describe people who put down or criticize other people or other people's ideas.

BACKGROUND

Gwendolyn Brooks *(1917–2000) published more than twenty books of poetry and several books of prose. Her writing portrays African Americans in daily life and relies on a number of poetic devices and forms. In 1950, for her book of poetry* Annie Allen, *she became the first African American to win a Pulitzer Prize. The longtime Chicago resident became Poet Laureate of Illinois in 1968. In 1985, she became the first African American woman to become Poet Laureate of the United States.*

SPEECH TO THE YOUNG: SPEECH TO THE PROGRESS-TOWARD

Poem by Gwendolyn Brooks

SETTING A PURPOSE

As you read, pay attention to repeated words and sounds and think about how they add to the meaning of the poem. Note the effect of Brooks' use of line breaks and line length to create rhythm and emphasis.

Say to them,
say to the down-keepers,
the sun-slappers,
the self-soilers,
5 the harmony-hushers,
 <u>"Even if you are not ready for day
 it cannot always be night."</u>

Notice & Note

Use the side margins to notice and note signposts in the text.

MAKE INFERENCES ABOUT THEME AND AUTHOR'S PURPOSE

Annotate: Mark the quotation in the poem.

Infer: Why do you think these lines are in quotes, and what is the meaning of these lines?

TEACH

BACKGROUND

After students read the background note, point out that the poet typically wrote about the everyday experience of African Americans in urban settings. Also note that the poet won numerous awards and was the first African American woman to be named Poet Laureate of the United States.

SETTING A PURPOSE

Direct students to use the Setting a Purpose prompt to focus their reading.

For **listening support** for students at varying proficiency levels, see the **Text X-Ray** on page 366C.

MAKE INFERENCES ABOUT THEME AND AUTHOR'S PURPOSE

Remind students that an **inference** is a logical conclusion based on what readers already know, combined with text evidence. The text evidence is the underlined quote. Students need to think about what they know about quotations to infer why the words are quoted in the poem. **(Answer:** *These lines could be quoted to emphasize that the speaker is older than the "young" the poem is directed to, and the speaker wants to show she or he said these words. The lines mean that even if a person does not want to face the events that happen in life, there is no choice but to face them and make decisions.)*

 ENGLISH LEARNER SUPPORT

Learn Letter Sounds Tell students this poem has many examples of alliteration, or the repetition of the same consonant sound at the beginning of several words near each other in the poem. Write *sun-slappers, self-soilers,* and *harmony-hushers* on the board, and guide students to identify the beginning letter and sound of each word. Underline these letters as students say them aloud. Then have them decode the words by blending the sounds slowly. Finally, say the words as you point to each in turn, and have students repeat them.

SUBSTANTIAL

TEACH

 **ANALYZE THE EFFECTS
OF METER AND
STRUCTURAL ELEMENTS**

Remind students that *advice* refers to something that someone tells you to try to provide help. Have them read the lines aloud to better determine the rhythmic qualities of the poem. Ask them to listen for stressed syllables. (**Answer:** *These lines speak directly to the young and repeat the phrase "live not for" and the word "live." This contributes to the rhythm of the poem because it gives a chant quality due to repetition and some internal and end rhyme. The rhythm of the poem suggests a heartbeat quality, and the last lines mirror this rhythm with repetitions and beats.*)

For **reading and speaking support** for students at varying proficiency levels, see the **Text X-Ray** on page 366D.

▶ **WORDS OF THE WISER**

Remind students that this signpost is often used to point out advice. The speaker of this poem is giving advice to "the young." (**Answer:** *Life is not always about winning things, and success can be measured in many ways, not just the "battles won." Also, line 11 expresses the idea of living in the present, living for every day, not just for some future date — "the-end-of-the-song."*)

 NOTICE & NOTE

ANALYZE THE EFFECTS OF METER AND STRUCTURAL ELEMENTS

Annotate: Mark lines in the poem that give direct advice.

Analyze: How do these lines contribute to the rhythm of the poem?

WORDS OF THE WISER

Notice & Note: What words of the wiser are being communicated to readers? Mark repeated and rhyming words in lines 10–13.

Draw Conclusions: What message does Brooks express in these last lines of the poem?

You will be right.
For that is the hard home-run.

10 Live not for battles won.
Live not for the-end-of-the-song.
Live in the along.

WHEN STUDENTS STRUGGLE . . .

Theme Remind students a theme is a message about life or human nature. To find theme, readers consider what lesson can be learned from a text. Point out that this poem is made up of advice, so the lesson is what the speaker wants to teach the reader. Help students determine the theme of the poem by asking, "What does this speaker want to teach?"

 For additional support, go to the **Reading Studio** and assign the following [LEVEL] **Level Up tutorial: Theme.**

 **CHECK YOUR UNDERSTANDING**

Have students answer the questions independently.

Answers

1. *D*

2. *G*

3. *A*

If they answer any questions incorrectly, have them reread the text to confirm their understanding. Then they may proceed to ANALYZE THE TEXT on p. 372.

CHECK YOUR UNDERSTANDING

Answer these questions before moving on to the **Analyze the Text** section on the following page.

1 The speaker in the poem is talking to —

A her country

B her family

C newborns

D young people

2 The repetition of the word *Live* in the second stanza emphasizes the author's message about —

F being brave in the face of danger

G being present and aware during one's life

H being awake during the day, not at night

J being ready for the next competition

3 Which phrase describes the poem's message?

A advice from the speaker

B correction for the reader

C sadness from the speaker

D insulting for the reader

EL **ENGLISH LEARNER SUPPORT**

Oral Assessment Use the following questions to assess students' comprehension and speaking skills:

1. Who is the speaker talking to? *(young people)*

2. Look at the second stanza. The author repeats the word *live*. What message does this send? *(to be present and aware during one's life)*

3. What is the poem's message? *(Live your life and keep going even if others try to bring you down.)* **SUBSTANTIAL/MODERATE**

ANALYZE THE TEXT

Possible answers:

1. **DOK 2:** *To soil something means to dirty or spoil it in some way, so an inference could be that this type of person does something to ruin himself or herself; in addition, since the speaker is telling young people to say something to this type of person, one may infer that the "self-soilers" may also encourage others to soil something for someone else.*

2. **DOK 4:** *Lines 5 and 9 repeat the "h" sound at the beginnings of words: "harmony-hushers" (line 5) and "hard home-run" (line 9). This creates a choppy effect, very much like the "h" sound itself, and in turn, creates a halting, stopping rhythm. This effect mirrors what the speaker is telling the young: make others who put you down stop doing it.*

3. **DOK 3:** *Strength of self is a theme expressed in the poem. The speaker has strength of voice, telling the young what to say and who to say it to, and the speaker passes this confidence on to the young. The line "You will be right" (line 8) conveys this theme. The repetition of the word Live (lines 10–12) promotes this theme and communicates the importance of a life lived to its fullest. She is also conveying the importance of relying on oneself, not listening to the naysayers.*

4. **DOK 4:** *The use of the word speech twice in the title draws attention to the purpose—giving advice to a listener who is younger than the speaker. The poem, much shorter than a real speech and a rather short poem, suggests that speeches, especially advice to the youth, do not need to be lengthy to be effective. Being succinct and direct may work better in order to get points across to a younger audience.*

5. **DOK 4:** *The speaker conveys the message that the young should stay away from people who do not encourage them, for example, the "down-keepers" (line 2). The lesson centers on living life following your own path and not for a "win," or as the poem says, "for battles won" (line 10). Advice to be hopeful comes through in lines 6–7: "'Even if you are not ready for day/ it cannot always be night.'"*

RESEARCH

Encourage students to add 2–3 key life events, 2–3 key career events, and 2–3 details about the importance of Brooks's poetry. Students may work with a partner or small group.

Extend Students may wish to begin reading more of Brooks' poetry by searching for an Illinois government website related to her time as Illinois Poet Laureate.

 RESPOND

ANALYZE THE TEXT

Support your responses with evidence from the text. NOTEBOOK

1. **Infer** What conclusions can you draw about the meaning of the phrase "self-soilers" in line 4?

2. **Analyze** Reread lines 5-9. Where are there instances of alliteration in those lines? What emphasis does this poetic device create?

3. **Cite Evidence** What theme is the author conveying through this poem? How does she express this theme? Cite evidence to support your inference.

4. **Synthesize** Explain the author's purpose in using the word "speech" twice in the long title, yet making the poem itself very brief.

5. **Notice & Note** What lesson or message is the speaker conveying, and what is meant by the phrase "progress-toward" in the title? Cite evidence to support your response.

RESEARCH TIP
When you conduct online research, evaluate the credibility of websites. Web addresses ending in .gov, .edu, or .org may be reviewed more frequently, but always read critically. Look for an About section to help identify who created the website.

RESEARCH

Research the life and career of poet Gwendolyn Brooks. Use the graphic organizer below to guide your research.

KEY LIFE EVENTS	KEY CAREER EVENTS	IMPORTANCE OF HER POETRY
Students' responses will vary.		

Extend Find another poem by Gwendolyn Brooks. With your partner, discuss the effects that rhythm, line breaks, and other devices create.

 LEARNING MINDSET

Questioning Reinforce that asking questions is about being open to new ideas and trying new things. Encourage students to feel comfortable asking questions. When students get stuck, invite them to question whether they could arrive at the answer a different way. Compliment students' questions and mention how asking questions shows curiosity and leads to learning.

CREATE AND PRESENT

Write a Short Poem Write a short poem in the spirit of "Speech to the Young: Speech to the Progress-Toward." Craft your own inspirational "speech" to a student, relative, or friend who is younger than you are.

- ❏ Choose a theme and message that you want to communicate.
- ❏ Choose points of advice and think of creative ways to express them.
- ❏ Include poetic elements, such as alliteration, repetition, rhythm, rhyme, and thoughtful line breaks.

Record Your Poem Record your poem to present to your class as a video or audio podcast.

- ❏ Practice reading the poem, adjusting the rhythm of your reading according to different line lengths in the poem.
- ❏ Practice your reading until you can present the poem as if you were in front of an audience. Rehearse making eye contact and using natural facial expressions and gestures, speaking clearly, and using proper pacing and volume to help convey the meaning of your poem.
- ❏ Record your poem.

 Go to the **Writing Studio** for more on the writing process.

 Go to **Producing and Publishing with Technology: Writing for the Internet** in the **Speaking and Listening Studio** for more on online writing and podcasts.

RESPOND TO THE ESSENTIAL QUESTION

? What keeps people from giving up?

Gather Information Review your annotations and notes on "Speech to the Young: Speech to the Progress-Toward." Then, add relevant details to your Response Log. As you determine which information to include, think about:

- how the poet conveys her purpose
- how poetic devices and elements influence theme in a poem
- how advice can help us make choices

At the end of the unit, use your notes to write a biographical report.

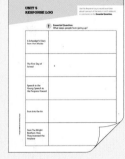

ACADEMIC VOCABULARY
As you write and discuss what you learned from the poem, be sure to use the Academic Vocabulary words. Check off each of the words that you use.

- ❏ **achieve**
- ❏ **individual**
- ❏ **instance**
- ❏ **outcome**
- ❏ **principle**

CREATE AND PRESENT

Write a Short Poem Point out to students that their poems need to have a theme and several points of advice. Encourage them to write the advice in prose before revising it to include poetic elements.

For **writing support** for students at varying proficiency levels, see the **Text X-Ray** on page 366D.

Record Your Poem Remind students that they will need to practice reading their poem several times, using expression as they read. Look online for recordings and have them listen to poets read their own poems, such as Gwendolyn Brooks and Billy Collins. After students have settled on a presentation, have them record their poem.

RESPOND TO THE ESSENTIAL QUESTION

Allow time for students to add details from "Speech to the Young: Speech to the Progress-Toward" to their Unit 5 Response Logs.

from **INTO THE AIR**

Graphic Biography Written by Robert Burleigh and Illustrated by Bill Wylie

GENRE ELEMENTS
GRAPHIC BIOGRAPHY

Tell students that a **graphic biography** uses both illustrations and text to tell a person's life story. Biographies are usually written in the third-person point of view, and include facts and descriptions of events, people, and experiences that shaped the subject's life. Biographies might tell more than one person's life story.

LEARNING OBJECTIVES

- Analyze characteristics and determine key ideas in multimodal texts.
- Conduct research about early advances in flight.
- Write a summary of the selection's content.
- Discuss the functions of elements of multimodal text.
- Use knowledge of affixes to determine a word's meaning.
- Identify and use adverbs and adverb clauses.
- **Language** Discuss with a partner the features of the text using the key term *multimodal*.

TEXT COMPLEXITY

Quantitative Measures	*from* Into the Air	Lexile: 760L
Qualitative Measures	**Ideas Presented** Simple, single meaning. Literal, explicit, and direct.	
	Structure Used Primarily explicit and conventional. May vary from simple chronological order.	
	Language Used Mostly explicit, some figurative language used.	
	Knowledge Required Some reference to events or other texts.	

RESOURCES

- Unit 5 Response Log

- Selection Audio

- Level Up Tutorial: Reading Studio: Notice & Note

- Main Idea and Supporting Details

- Writing Studio: Using Textual Evidence

- Speaking and Listening Studio: Participating in Collaborative Discussions

- Vocabulary Studio: Roots, Base Words, and Affixes

- Grammar Studio: Module 3: Lesson 5: The Adverb

- *Into the Air* Selection Test

SUMMARIES

English

In 1901, Brothers Orville and Wilbur Wright encounter setback after setback attempting to get their experimental glider off the ground. Discouraged but not defeated, the brothers never give up on their dream of flight. After much experimentation, adjustment, and construction, the Wright brothers finally solve their design problems and achieve their goal of a successful takeoff at Kitty Hawk in the fall of 1902.

Spanish

En 1901, los hermanos Orville y Wilbur Wright encontraron una gran cantidad de contratiempos al intentar elevar su planeador experimental. Desanimados, pero no derrotados, los hermanos nunca desecharon su sueño de volar. Luego de muchos ajustes, experimentos y construcciones, los hermanos Wright finalmente resolvieron los problemas de diseño y alcanzaron su meta de despegar exitosamente durante el otoño de 1902 en Kitty Hawk.

 ## SMALL-GROUP OPTIONS

Have students work in small groups to read and discuss the selection.

Think-Pair-Share

- After students have read the excerpt from *Into the Air*, pose this question: *Why do you think the Wright brothers never gave up on their dreams of flight?*
- Have students think about the question individually and write down a few notes.
- Then have pairs discuss their ideas about the question.
- Finally, ask pairs to share their responses with the class.

Three-Minute Review

- Pause at any time while reading or discussing the selection.
- Set a timer for three minutes, and have students work with a partner to reread a specific section of the text or answer a question.
- After three minutes, ask pairs to share what they noticed in their review. Ask: *What new information did you learn?* Have partners share their responses with the class.

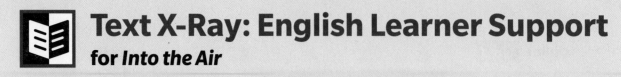

Text X-Ray: English Learner Support
for *Into the Air*

Use the Text X-Ray and the supports and scaffolds in the Teacher's Edition to help guide students at different proficiency levels through the selection.

INTRODUCE THE SELECTION
DISCUSS CREATIVITY AND PERSISTENCE

Tell students that Orville and Wilbur Wright never gave up on their dreams of flying. They studied, experimented, and rebuilt until one day, in 1902, they got their glider to fly. The Wright brothers will always be known as the first people to fly an airplane. They used creativity and science to solve problems and come up with new ideas. They persisted until they found success.

Have students discuss people who are creative or show persistence, or times they showed creativity or persistence, using the terms *creative, creativity, persist,* and *persistence.* Use frames as needed:

- *An example of creativity is _____.*
- *People who are creative _____.*
- *When people persist, they _____.*
- *Someone who has persistence is _____.*

CULTURAL REFERENCES

The following words and phrases may be unfamiliar to students:

- *campsite* (page 378): an area where people set up tents while camping
- *charm* (page 383): success (the saying is "third time's a charm," but the Wright brothers wonder whether their third year of flying will be a charm)
- *admit defeat* (page 383): to say you are unsuccessful

LISTENING

Understand the Afterword

Tell students that an afterword is a note at the end of a story that tells what happens to the characters after the action of the story has concluded. This section lends itself best to practicing listening comprehension because graphic novels are difficult to read aloud.

Have students listen as you read aloud paragraphs 1–3 of the afterword. Use the following supports with students at varying proficiency levels:

- Ask the following questions and have students answer with a thumbs-up or thumbs-down: *Did the Wright brothers keep working on airplanes after their first flight? Was the government interested in the Wright brothers' work right away? Did both Wright brothers live to see the "age of flight"?* **SUBSTANTIAL**
- Have students complete these sentence frames: *After their first flight, the Wright brothers worked on _____. The _____ was not interested in the Wright brothers' work at first. Wilbur died before he could see _____.* **MODERATE**
- Have students demonstrate listening comprehension by answering the following questions: *What did the Wright brothers do after their first flight? How did the rest of the world feel about the Wright brothers' work?* **LIGHT**

SPEAKING

Discuss Multimodal Text

Tell students that a **multimodal** text is a text that uses two or more ways to share information. This text uses pictures and words. Circulate as students discuss the excerpt from *Into the Air*, making sure they use the word *multimodal* correctly.

Use the following supports with students at varying proficiency levels:

- Write the following on the board and have students echo read it after you: *This text is multimodal because it uses more than one way to give information. It uses pictures and words.* **SUBSTANTIAL**
- Have students work in pairs to discuss the text structure using the following sentence frames: *A multimodal text is a text that uses _____. This text uses _____ and _____ to teach about the Wright brothers.* **MODERATE**
- Pair students to discuss the following questions. *What is a multimodal text? What features make this a multimodal text? What do you learn from the words? What do you learn from the pictures?* **LIGHT**

READING

Read Multimodal Text

Draw students' attention to the first full spread of the text on pp. 378 and 379. Remind students that the excerpt from *Into the Air* is a multimodal text—that is, it uses more than one way to give information.

Work with students to read pages 378 and 379. Use the following supports with students at varying proficiency levels:

- Tell students they will practice learning about key ideas from the text and pictures. Simply state pieces of information from the pages, and have students identify where you found the information—"picture," "text," or "picture and text." **SUBSTANTIAL**
- Have students complete the sentence frame: *The key idea is the Wright brothers want to _____ but _____.* Then have them point to the different features of multimodal text and explain how each supports the key idea. **MODERATE**
- Pair students, and have them determine the key idea of this spread. Ask them to point out the features of multimodal text and say how each provides supporting evidence for their key idea. **LIGHT**

WRITING

Write a Summary

Draw students' attention to the writing assignment on p. 387.

Use the following supports with students at varying proficiency levels:

- Allow students to use pictorial representation to summarize the story. Encourage them to also use single words, short phrases, or simple sentences to describe each drawing. **SUBSTANTIAL**
- Give students the following sentence frame to write their key idea: *The Wright brothers never gave up on their dream to _____ and finally they _____.* Then, have students write three sentences supporting their key idea using the following sentence frame: *A detail from the story that shows they never gave up is _____.* If students feel capable, they can add additional sentences to elaborate on their details. **MODERATE**
- Have student pairs work together to write a key idea sentence and outline supporting evidence. Both partners should use the outline to write their own summaries. **LIGHT**

? Connect to the
ESSENTIAL QUESTION

Orville and Wilbur Wright were born before the invention of airplanes, but they dreamed their whole lives of flying a plane of their own. Even though their first planes couldn't get off the ground, they never gave up on their dreams to fly. They worked hard—experimenting, building, researching, and rebuilding—until they finally flew a plane in 1903. They became known as the first people to fly an airplane. What kept them from never giving up?

COMPARE PRESENTATIONS

Note that both *Into the Air* and *The Wright Brothers: How They Invented the Airplane* are biographies, or texts that present important events from the life of a significant person (or, in this case, two people). To prepare students to be able to compare these two selections, suggest that they consider how the key events included by each author in these biographies are similar. Do the authors include key dates? Descriptions of the same moments in the subjects' lives? Once students have identified what material is covered by both texts, they will be ready to compare the ways in which the authors present this information to readers.

GRAPHIC BIOGRAPHY

from
INTO THE AIR

by **Robert Burleigh**
illustrated by **Bill Wylie**
pages 377–385

COMPARE PRESENTATIONS

As you read each selection, look for the key ideas each author wants the reader to understand about similar events. Notice the ways in which elements of each genre are used to present those ideas. After you read both selections, you will collaborate with a small group on a final project.

 ESSENTIAL QUESTION:

What keeps people from giving up?

BIOGRAPHY

from
THE WRIGHT BROTHERS:
HOW THEY INVENTED THE AIRPLANE

by **Russell Freedman**
pages 393–399

374   Unit 5

 LEARNING MINDSET

Grit Tell students that having grit means having a "never give up" spirit. Those with a growth mindset demonstrate grit by taking on challenges and persevering even when they want to give up. Remind students to have an attitude of grit during this lesson.

from **Into the Air**

QUICK START

Have you ever built something or assembled a complicated toy from a kit? Would you rather do it alone, or with a partner? Share your thoughts with the class.

ANALYZE CHARACTERISTICS OF MULTIMODAL TEXTS

Multimodal texts present information through multiple modes, or ways of expression. The graphic biography you are about to read uses both written text and comic-book style illustrations to tell a biographical story. These print and graphic features work together to organize information, deliver ideas, and guide readers through the text. Look for these features as you read:

MULTIMODAL FEATURE	DESCRIPTION
caption	a text box that provides narration; text may be set in all capital letters
speech balloon	a balloon-shaped graphic with a pointer containing dialogue—what a character says aloud
thought bubble	a cloud-shaped graphic that tells what a character is thinking
image panel	an illustration, often set within a border or frame

DETERMINE KEY IDEAS IN MULTIMODAL TEXTS

In a graphic biography, details in print and graphic features convey the text's **key ideas,** or important points. You can use key ideas to make inferences about a text's **controlling idea,** or thesis statement. Look for a summary of key ideas in the **afterword,** a section sometimes found at the end of a text that offers more information about the biographical subject. To find key ideas in a graphic biography:

- Examine details in each print feature.
- Study illustrations that accompany the text; then, reread the text.
- Use details from the text and illustrations to make inferences about key ideas.

GENRE ELEMENTS: GRAPHIC BIOGRAPHY

- uses illustrations and text to present information
- includes the basic elements of biography—a true account of someone's life—as told by another person; usually written from a third-person point of view
- includes facts and descriptions of events, people, and experiences that shape subjects' lives.

Into the Air   375

QUICK START

Have students read the Quick Start prompt. If students have trouble thinking of examples of something they built or assembled, you may want to list an example of a project they completed for school. Ask students to share their ideas about whether they would rather build something alone or with a partner. Explain that the Wright brothers were successful because they worked together and were able to share ideas and information.

ANALYZE CHARACTERISTICS OF MULTIMODAL TEXTS

Review the characteristics of multimodal texts. Tell students that there are many modes of delivering information, and ask students to give examples of different modes. (Some examples are words, graphics, music, speech, and acting.) A multimodal text uses more than one mode—in this case, illustration and text. Discuss with students why they think using two modes is more helpful to deliver information than using just one. Then review the features in the table and have students find an example of each in the text.

DETERMINE KEY IDEAS IN MULTIMODAL TEXTS

Remind students that a multimodal text—in this case, a graphic biography—has a key idea (or main idea) just like any other text. Ask students how each mode can help them determine the key idea. Suggest that they use these questions to help them determine key ideas:

- What pictorial elements do I see recurring in the text?
- What is the written text mostly about?

ENGLISH LEARNER SUPPORT

Develop Vocabulary with Visual Supports Before reading, preteach the topic by showing students pictures of the Wright brothers and their airplane. Have them look through the graphic biography before reading and use single words or simple phrases to convey what they see in the pictures. Write some of these on the board, and use the listed words to have students work on pronouncing consonant clusters *fl* and *pl* in topic-related words like *fly*, *plane*, and *flight*. **SUBSTANTIAL**

TEACH

CRITICAL VOCABULARY

Encourage students to read all the sentences before deciding which word best completes each one. Remind them to look for context clues that match the meaning of each word.

Answers:

1. *defeat*
2. *Prepare*
3. *discourage*
4. *incorrect*
5. *Preserve*
6. *demonstration*

■ English Learner Support

Use Cognates Tell students that some of the Critical Vocabulary words have Spanish cognates: *demonstration/ demonstración, incorrect/incorrecto, prepare/preparer, preserve/preserver.* **ALL LEVELS**

LANGUAGE CONVENTIONS

Review the information about adverbs and adverb clauses. Remind students that adverbs can describe verbs, adjectives, or other adverbs. An adverb describes how, when, or why something is done. An adverb clause is a group of words that function the same way as an adverb. Give the following example sentence, and have students identify the adverb clause: *She stayed up all night long.* (*all night long*)

ANNOTATION MODEL

Point out the example annotation and tell students they are free to use the annotation style of the model, or come up with their own system for annotations. For example, they may want to color-code their annotations using highlighters or different color pens.

CRITICAL VOCABULARY

discourage	incorrect	prepare
defeat	preserve	demonstration

To see how many Critical Vocabulary words you already know, use them to complete the sentences.

1. We were able to _____ our opponents by six points.

2. _____ for your road trip by planning a route.

3. Don't let a few minor setbacks _____ you.

4. After finishing a test, check for any _____ answers.

5. _____ a long-term friendship by being a good listener.

6. We watched a cooking _____ on using spices correctly.

LANGUAGE CONVENTIONS: Adverbs and Adverb Clauses

Adverbs modify, or describe, verbs, adjectives, or other adverbs. Adverbs are often formed by adding the suffix *-ly* to an adjective. For example: *slow + -ly = slowly*. An **adverb clause** is a subordinate clause that functions as an adverb. Adverb clauses answer questions of *When? Where? How? Why? How often? How long? Under what condition? To what extent?* or *How much?*

> <u>**As the fan blows air through the tunnel,**</u> **the brothers <u>carefully</u> note how each kind of wing works.**

The adverb clause describes when the brothers make notes; the adverb describes how they make notes.

ANNOTATION MODEL

NOTICE & NOTE

As you read, note how multimodal text features communicate key ideas. You can also mark up evidence that supports your own ideas. In the model, you can see one reader's notes about *Into the Air*.

Day after difficult day, <u>discouraged but not defeated</u>, the Wrights carry the damaged glider back to the campsite, repair it, and <u>try again</u>.	*I see ideas about facing challenges without giving up, about trying again and again. These details tell me that the Wrights refused to give up.*

376 Unit 5

BACKGROUND

*As boys, brothers Orville and Wilbur Wright were fascinated by flight. In the late 1800s, they honed their mechanical skills at their bicycle sales and repair shop in Ohio, and later studied the work of Otto Lilienthal, who had built a glider with bat-like wings. The following excerpt, by author **Robert Burleigh** and illustrator **Bill Wylie**, begins in 1901, as the Wrights try to build a glider for longer flights—an important step toward powered flight.*

from INTO THE AIR

Graphic Biography by Robert Burleigh
illustrated by Bill Wylie

PREPARE TO COMPARE

As you read, note how the Wright brothers are able to pursue their dreams despite difficult challenges. This information will help you compare Into the Air with the biography of the Wright brothers that follows.

Notice & Note

Use the side margins to notice and note signposts in the text.

BACKGROUND

Have students read the Background note. Remind them that people dreamed of flight for a long time, but nobody successfully flew an airplane until the Wright brothers' flight in 1903. Getting an aircraft to fly is very complicated, and students will see in the text that the Wright brothers worked for years researching, collecting data, building, rebuilding, and experimenting before successfully flying a plane.

PREPARE TO COMPARE

Direct students to use the Prepare to Compare prompt to focus their reading.

▶ NOTICE & NOTE

Remind students of the prompt to indicate signposts in the margin. This lesson asks students to look for the **Big Questions** signpost, but students may also notice other signposts such as **Aha Moments** and **Again and Again** in this story.

WHEN STUDENTS STRUGGLE . . .

Using a Graphic Organizer Give students a main-idea-and-details organizer. Work with them to complete the organizer for the first three pages of the graphic biography. They can use single words, simple phrases, or drawings in their organizers. You may want to have them complete additional graphic organizers for different sections of the text.

📖 For additional support, go to the **Reading Studio** and assign the following 🔼 **Level Up tutorial: Main Idea and Supporting Details.**

TEACH

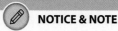
✏️ ANALYZE CHARACTERISTICS OF MULTIMODAL TEXTS

Remind students that the different print features—captions, speech balloons, and thought bubbles—perform different functions. The different features allow a graphic text to include narration, dialogue, and inner thoughts just like any other story would. (**Answer:** *The caption box performs the job of the narrator, here from a third-person perspective. It describes the action pictured in the background illustration on this page. The speech balloon shows Wilbur's dialogue. Here he is trying to encourage his brother to keep pushing on. The thought bubble shows what Orville is thinking but not saying to his brother, Wilbur.*)

discourage
(dĭ-skûr′ĭj) *v.* To *discourage* is to take away hope or confidence.

defeat
(dĭ-fēt′) *v.* To *defeat* a person or his or her efforts is to prevent his or her success.

ANALYZE CHARACTERISTICS OF MULTIMODAL TEXTS

Annotate: Mark the print features on this page.

Identify: Name the types of print features and explain the purpose of each.

¹ **glider:** an aircraft that relies on gravity and air currents, rather than an engine, for flight; early experiments in glider flight were essential to developing motorized aircraft.

CRITICAL VOCABULARY

discourage: The Wright brothers have lost hope and confidence.

ASK STUDENTS why the Wright brothers feel discouraged. (**Answer:** *They can't get their glider off the ground.*)

defeat: Even though the Wright brothers are discouraged, they have not allowed failure to win out.

ASK STUDENTS why the Wright brothers are discouraged but not defeated. (**Answer:** *They refuse to give up on their dream of flying, no matter how challenging it is.*)

378   Unit 5

² **Lilienthal's air-pressure tables:** a set of calculations produced by German aviation pioneer Otto Lilienthal used in the design of aircraft wings.

© Houghton Mifflin Harcourt Publishing Company

NOTICE & NOTE

incorrect
(ĭn´kə-rĕkt´) *adj.* Something *incorrect* is faulty or wrong.

DETERMINE KEY IDEAS IN MULTIMODAL TEXTS
Annotate: Mark details in the text and illustrations that express any doubts the brothers share.

Infer: How do these details work together to express an idea?

Into the Air   379

APPLYING ACADEMIC VOCABULARY

☐ **achieve**   ☑ **individual**   ☐ **instance**   ☑ **outcome**   ☐ **principle**

Write and Discuss Have students turn to a partner to discuss the following questions. Guide students to include the Academic Vocabulary words *individual* and *outcome* in their responses. Ask volunteers to share their responses with the class.

- Does working together give the Wright brothers an advantage over somebody working as an **individual**?
- What has been the **outcome** of the Wright brothers' flight experiments so far?

TEACH

✎ DETERMINE KEY IDEAS IN MULTIMODAL TEXTS

Remind students that they need to use both modes— illustration and text—to help them determine key ideas in this text. (***Answer:*** *The doubt expressed in "Can our data be incorrect?" is reflected in the illustration of Wilbur's furrowed brow and doubt-filled eyes and in Orville's hunched posture. Then Wilbur says, "Yes, but could those tables be wrong?" as he and his brother look out at their glider. The text and the illustrations work together to show the brothers' doubts.*)

■ English Learner Support

Monitor Understanding Have students demonstrate understanding of key ideas. Read the first three paragraphs aloud, then ask them to answer the following *yes/no* questions: *Have the Wright brothers built an airplane that can fly yet? Do the pictures show them looking happy? Do they think they made a mistake?* **SUBSTANTIAL**

For **reading support** for students at varying proficiency levels, see the **Text X-Ray** on page 374D.

CRITICAL VOCABULARY

incorrect: Wilbur wonders whether the data they collected was wrong.

ASK STUDENTS who created the data tables that Wilbur and Orville think might be incorrect. (***Answer:*** *German aviation pioneer Otto Lilienthal created data tables about the airplane wings he designed.*)

Into the Air   **379**

ANALYZE CHARACTERISTICS OF MULTIMODAL TEXTS

Tell students that a background picture shows a larger scene, while an inset picture shows a smaller detail from the background picture. It is the reader's job to figure out how the pictures are related and what information they convey. (**Answer:** *The background illustration gives us the big picture, which is supported by the caption box, that the brothers are traveling in the summer of 1901. The inset illustration shows the details of what's going on inside the train: the brothers share doubts about their ability to solve the puzzle of flight.*)

■ English Learner Support

Discuss Multimodal Text Give students the following sentence frames to help them discuss the characteristics of multimodal text and the information they convey: *The Wright brothers are on a ___. I can tell because ___. The Wright brothers feel discouraged because ___. I can tell because ___.*
MODERATE

For **speaking support** for students at varying proficiency levels, see the **Text X-Ray** on page 374D.

 NOTICE & NOTE

ANALYZE CHARACTERISTICS OF MULTIMODAL TEXTS

Annotate: Study the two illustration panels on this page. Mark the background illustration and the inset illustration.

Compare: How do the illustrations work together and on their own to tell this part of the story?

---

[3] **hit rock bottom:** to reach the most bleak and hopeless moment.

WHEN STUDENTS STRUGGLE . . .

Idea Web Work with struggling students to determine a key idea from the text, such as: *The Wright brothers never gave up on their dream to fly until they finally built an airplane that got off the ground.* Write this idea in the center of an idea web. Ask students to give supporting details for this main idea, using evidence from both text and graphics. Write those details in the spokes of your web.

 For additional support, go to the **Reading Studio** and assign the following **Level Up tutorial: Main Idea and Supporting Details.**

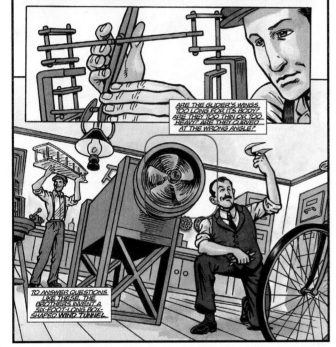

DETERMINE KEY IDEAS IN MULTIMODAL TEXTS

Annotate: Mark the print and graphic details on this page that refer to asking and answering questions.

Draw Conclusions: What inferences can you make from these details?

🖉 **DETERMINE KEY IDEAS IN MULTIMODAL TEXTS**

Remind students that an inference is an idea or conclusion that the reader makes using evidence in the text. The reader of a graphic biography makes inferences based on details or clues in both the text and the illustrations. (***Answer:*** *Asking and answering questions is how the brothers work through their problems and meet challenges. They continually test assumptions to find new ways to solve problems.*)

TO CHALLENGE STUDENTS . . .

Write Descriptively   Challenge students to write vivid descriptions of panels of the graphic biography. Have them choose any three panels to describe. Descriptions should tell what is happening in the panel, focusing on the main idea shown and the most important details. Encourage them to keep the descriptions brief but vivid.

LANGUAGE CONVENTIONS

Remind students that an adverb is a word that describes a verb, adjective, or another adverb. It tells how, when, where, or why something is done. Many adverbs end in -*ly*. An adverb clause is a group of words that functions as an adverb, but here students are looking for a single-word adverb. (**Answer:** *The word* carefully *helps describe how the Wright brothers' notes were taken.*)

■ English Learner Support

Speak Using Adverbs Give students practice speaking using adverbs. Write: *When they were boys, the Wright brothers happily dreamed about flying.* Have students read the sentence aloud. Ask: *How did the Wright brothers dream?* (happily) *What is the adverb?* (happily) Write: *The brothers patiently gathered data from the wind tunnel for many weeks.* Have students read the sentence aloud. Ask: *How did the brothers gather data?* (patiently) *What is the adverb?* (patiently) **LIGHT**

LANGUAGE CONVENTIONS

Adverbs modify verbs, adjectives, or other adverbs. Mark the adverb in the caption that begins "As the fan blows." What does this adverb reveal about how the brothers work?

preserve
(prĭ-zûrv´) *v.* To *preserve* something is to keep it or save it.

CRITICAL VOCABULARY

preserve: Orville says the data was being kept safe until they could discover it.

ASK STUDENTS why Orville says the data was being preserved. (**Possible answer:** *He means that the information was waiting to be discovered, and they needed to put in the time and effort to discover it.*)

ANALYZE CHARACTERISTICS OF MULTIMODAL TEXTS

Annotate: Mark the details that help describe the brothers' new glider design.

Analyze: How do the print and graphic features work together to help you understand the design?

prepare
(prĭ-pâr´) v. To *prepare* is to get ready for an event or an occasion.

 ANALYZE CHARACTERISTICS OF MULTIMODAL TEXTS

Remind students that in a multimodal text, at least two communication modes work together to convey information. Discuss with students whether just a picture or just text would help them understand the Wright brothers' new wing design. Then ask them to explain how the print and graphic features work together to help them understand the design. (**Answer:** *The illustration clearly shows the design of the new tail, making the design much easier to understand and visualize.*)

For **speaking support** for students at varying proficiency levels, see the **Text X-Ray** on page 374D.

ENGLISH LEARNER SUPPORT

Spell Double Consonants Explain that some words have a double consonant pattern in the middle. Writers need to know how to spell these words to understand where the dividing point is between syllables.

Have students write the following words and circle the double consonants in each: *butter, follow, battle,* and *happen.* Then have them practice writing the words in sentences.
SUBSTANTIAL/MODERATE

Have students fill in the missing double consonants in each word: bu ___ er, fo ___ ow, ba ___ le, ha ___ en. Then have them divide each word into syllables (*but/ter, fol/low, bat/tle, hap/pen*).
LIGHT

CRITICAL VOCABULARY

prepare: The Wright brothers did a lot of work to get ready to try their glider again at Kitty Hawk.

ASK STUDENTS what the Wright brothers did to prepare. (**Answer:** *They collected data and used it to change the weight, shape, and angles of the wings. They added a new kind of tail and made new wing covers.*)

BIG QUESTIONS

The **Big Questions** signpost asks students to answer the question of how the author and illustrator taught readers new information about a well-known topic. To answer this question, they have to think about what they already knew about the Wright brothers and what they learned from the **graphic biography**. *(Answers will vary. New information may include the ways the brothers solved the puzzle of how to design the glider, such as the problem of controlling the machine in the air, or how frequently they had to test and retest their assumptions and designs.)*

■ English Learner Support

Decode Compound Words Draw attention to the word *Afterward* and point out that it is made up of two shorter words: *after* and *word*. Write the word, drawing a line between its two parts. Have students read the word aloud. Discuss how the meanings of the two words combine to create the meaning of *afterword*. **ALL LEVELS**

 For **listening support** for students at varying proficiency levels, see the **Text X-Ray** on page 374C.

BIG QUESTIONS

Notice & Note: Mark the places in the text that confirm what you may have already known about the Wright brothers.

Analyze: How did the writer reveal new information while discussing known facts?

VICTORY! BACK AT KITTY HAWK IN THE FALL OF 1902, THE WRIGHTS SOLVE THE PROBLEM OF CONTROLLING THEIR GLIDING MACHINE.

AN EXCITED NEIGHBOR HELPS AT TIMES WITH THE TAKEOFF, AND THE BROTHERS MAKE MANY SUCCESSFUL FLIGHTS—AT LAST!

I NEVER THOUGHT I'D SEE THE DAY!

YOU HAVEN'T SEEN ANYTHING YET, MY FRIEND.

AFTERWORD

1 The Wright brothers' story did not end at Kitty Hawk. As the brothers well knew, there was more work to be done on the airplane. Some of the problems still to be resolved included making the takeoff simpler, learning to execute complete turns in the air, and designing the plane so that the pilot could fly sitting up. In 1904 and 1905, the brothers used an empty pasture near their home in Dayton for many additional experiments and tests.

IMPROVE READING FLUENCY

Targeted Passage Have students work with partners to read the Afterword. Use the first paragraph to model how to read text with appropriate speed and phrasing. Remind students to pause for commas, and to make sure they read at an appropriate speed for the listener to understand the facts. Then have partners take turns reading aloud the paragraphs. Encourage students to provide feedback and support for any challenging multisyllabic words and to encourage each other to read with appropriate speed and phrasing.

 Go to the **Reading Studio** for additional support in developing fluency.

2   Meanwhile, only slowly did people in the United States and abroad become aware of the Wright brothers and the importance of their invention. For several years, the American government showed no interest in the Wrights' flying machine. Finally, in 1908, the brothers were able to convince the government that flight was possible and useful. During the same year, Wilbur went to Europe and gave a series of flying **demonstrations** that made him and Orville instant celebrities.

3   Wilbur died of an illness in 1912. But Orville, who died in 1948, lived to see "the age of flight" expand in ways that he and his brother never foresaw. Today there is a sixty-foot high monument to the Wright brothers at Kill Devil Hills, North Carolina. But perhaps the real monuments to the vision, courage, and dedication of Wilbur and Orville Wright are the airplanes you see above you, flying back and forth across the country, every day.

demonstration
(děm´ən-strā´shən) *n.* A *demonstration* is a presentation meant to show how something works.

CHECK YOUR UNDERSTANDING

Answer these questions before moving on to the **Analyze the Text** section on the following page.

1 The selection includes illustrations of the Wright brothers' experiments to —

  A show that testing ideas was important to their work

  B make us think the Wright brothers were intelligent

  C show how they were always doubting themselves

  D help describe outdated technology

2 The Wright brothers invented a box-shaped wind tunnel to —

  F earn money by selling it to other inventors

  G answer their questions about wing design

  H use as a model for a much larger tunnel they would build later

  J use in a flight demonstration

3 Which of the following is not true about *Into the Air*?

  A The brothers did not like to give up.

  B The brothers were always successful.

  C The brothers sometimes felt discouraged.

  D The brothers asked and answered questions to develop their ideas.

CHECK YOUR UNDERSTANDING

Have students answer the questions independently.

Answers:

1. *A*

2. *G*

3. *B*

If they answer any questions incorrectly, have them reread the text to confirm their understanding. Then they may proceed to ANALYZE THE TEXT on page 386.

CRITICAL VOCABULARY

demonstration: Wilbur Wright did many presentations in Europe to show how their plane worked.

ASK STUDENTS whether they think the Wright brothers did a lot of demonstrations in the United States after their first flight. Why or why not? (**Possible answer:** *They probably didn't do a lot of demonstrations in the United States after their first flight because the text says people were slow to get excited about flight, and the U.S. government wasn't interested in their work at all.*)

ENGLISH LEARNER SUPPORT

Oral Assessment Use the following questions to assess students' comprehension and speaking skills:

  1. The author includes pictures of the Wright brothers' experiments. Was testing ideas important or not important to their work? *(important)*

  2. What did the Wright brothers invent to test wing design? *(The Wright brothers invented a box-shaped wind tunnel.)*

  3. True or False? The Wright brothers were always successful. *(False; it is not true that the brothers were always successful.)* **SUBSTANTIAL/MODERATE**

APPLY

ANALYZE THE TEXT

Possible answers:

1. **DOK 2:** *The print and graphic features—including captions, a speech balloon, and a thought bubble, as well as the panel illustration—indicate that the brothers are having trouble with their glider design and that they are "discouraged but not defeated."*

2. **DOK 4:** *The caption narrates the story in third-person perspective. It helps describe the setting and the action in the illustration, and indicates that the type of discussion shown in the illustration recurs night after night.*

3. **DOK 2:** *The speech balloons show the brothers' conversation at a time when they're feeling particularly discouraged. The author may have included this conversation to show how the brothers faced disappointment with humor by saying "Maybe we should start calling ourselves the **Wrong** brothers."*

4. **DOK 2:** *The first three pages show the brothers looking grim, determined, and sometimes discouraged. The last three pages show the brothers' faces looking a little more hopeful, sometimes smiling, indicating a more hopeful mood. The last page has a full-page panel showing the glider flying successfully. The vantage point of the viewer/reader, the faces of the observers, and the flying birds surrounding the glider all help create a joyful, exciting mood.*

5. **DOK 4:** *Answers will vary.*

RESEARCH

Remind students that the Wright brothers' aircraft did not have a motor. Adding motors, along with all the other features that led to today's modern aircraft, was the job of other flight pioneers. Point out the Research Tip if students are having trouble thinking of other flight pioneers.

Connect *Make sure students give effective presentations by having them prepare ahead of time. Have them write down what they are going to say, and possibly create visual aids.*

ANALYZE THE TEXT

Support your responses with evidence from the text. 📓 NOTEBOOK

1. **Summarize** Review the print and graphic features on the first page of the selection. What do these elements tell you about the Wright brothers at this point in the story?

2. **Evaluate** Review the caption that begins, "Late into the nights" on the second page of the selection. What is the caption's purpose, and how effectively does it communicate an idea?

3. **Infer** Review the speech balloons appearing in the train illustration on the third page of the selection. What might be the author's purpose in including this dialogue?

4. **Compare** Review the illustrations in the last three pages of the selection; then, compare them to the illustrations on the first three pages. How do the illustrations convey a change in mood?

5. **Notice & Note** Reread the afterword. How does the information presented in the afterword challenge, change, or confirm what you knew about the Wright brothers before reading this selection?

RESEARCH TIP
Follow links from reliable web sites about the Wright brothers to other sites that provide information about later pioneers of flight, such as Louis Bleriot, Charles Lindbergh, Harriet Quimby, and Amelia Earhart.

RESEARCH

At the end of this excerpt, the Wright brothers have yet to achieve their ultimate goal of powered flight (motor-driven aircraft). One of the Wright brothers' biggest achievements was to inspire other people to make flight discoveries. Investigate advances in flight that followed the work of the Wright brothers. Who made these advances? Why were they important? Record what you learn in the chart.

FLIGHT PIONEERS	ACHIEVEMENTS AND THEIR IMPORTANCE
Answers will vary.	

Connect Choose one of the aviation pioneers you learned about in your research. Share what you've learned with a small group.

⚙️ LEARNING MINDSET

Questioning Remind students that people don't grow as learners by having all the answers—they grow by asking questions. Learners with a growth mindset ask specific questions, and ask questions about their own thinking. Their questions should challenge the text, the task, and the teacher.

CREATE AND DISCUSS

Write a Summary Write a three- to four-paragraph objective summary of *Into the Air*.

- ❏ Use your own words to paraphrase the selection's print and graphic content.
- ❏ Use your annotations and analysis of the selection to make inferences about the selection's main or controlling idea, or thesis statement.
- ❏ Include details and evidence that support the controlling idea.
- ❏ Use adverbs and adverbial clauses in your summary.

Discuss with a Small Group With a group, discuss the purpose of each type of print and graphic feature in the selection, including captions, speech balloons, thought bubbles, and illustrations.

- ❏ Review the table of print and graphic features.
- ❏ Discuss how each element contributes to your understanding of the historical and biographical information in the selection.
- ❏ Check off each item on the table after it has been discussed.
- ❏ Take notes on your discussion; then, compare your notes with those of other members in the group.
- ❏ Participate actively: listen closely, pose and answer questions, and ask others for their opinions.

RESPOND TO THE ESSENTIAL QUESTION

 What keeps people from giving up?

Gather Information Review your annotations and notes on *Into the Air*. Then, add relevant details to your Response Log. As you determine which information to include, consider how people solve problems and think about failure and success.

At the end of the unit, use your notes to write a biographical report.

© Houghton Mifflin Harcourt Publishing Company

Go to **Using Textual Evidence: Summarizing, Paraphrasing, and Quoting** in the **Writing Studio** for more on summarizing and paraphrasing texts.

Go to **Participating in Collaborative Discussions** in the **Speaking and Listening Studio** for help with having a group discussion.

ACADEMIC VOCABULARY
As you write and discuss what you learned from the article, be sure to use the Academic Vocabulary words. Check off each of the words that you use.

- ❏ **achieve**
- ❏ **individual**
- ❏ **instance**
- ❏ **outcome**
- ❏ **principle**

CREATE AND DISCUSS

Write a Summary Remind students that a summary doesn't tell every detail that happens in a text, but it does give the most important ideas. Students should also make sure their summaries are written in their own words, not copied from the text. Have them begin by making some notes in which they paraphrase the events of the story. If they do want to include exact words from the text, they need to use quotation marks and cite the source of their quotes. Then they should use these notes to write a sentence about the selection's main idea. They should look for details and evidence that support the main idea, using examples from both the text and the graphics. Then they should use their main idea and supporting details to write an organized summary of the passage. Remind them to use adverbs and adverbial clauses in their writing.

For **writing support** for students at varying proficiency levels, see the **Text X-Ray** on page 374D.

Discuss with a Small Group Remind students that they need to use the table of print and graphic features on page 375 as a checklist during their discussion. Tell them they also need paper to take notes.

RESPOND TO THE ESSENTIAL QUESTION

Allow time for students to add details from *Into the Air* to their Unit 5 Response Logs.

CRITICAL VOCABULARY

Possible answers:

1. *checking the air pressure in the tires*

2. *look for the right answer*

3. *we could see how it worked*

4. *it continues to rain*

5. *chewing on shoes*

6. *people could continue to enjoy it*

VOCABULARY STRATEGY:

Affixes

Answers:

• **discouraged:** *dis-: deprived of; -ed: changes verb to past tense*

• **defeated:** *-ed: changes verb to past tense*

• **incorrect:** *in-: not*

• **preserved:** *pre-: before; -ed: changes verb to past tense*

• **preparing:** *pre-: before; -ing: changes verb to present tense*

• **demonstrations:** *-ation: action or process; -s: change to plural*

 RESPOND

WORD BANK
discourage
defeat
incorrect
preserve
prepare
demonstration

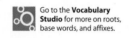 Go to the **Vocabulary Studio** for more on roots, base words, and affixes.

CRITICAL VOCABULARY

Practice and Apply Complete each sentence in a way that shows the meaning of the Vocabulary word.

1. You might **prepare** for a bicycle ride by _____.

2. If your answer is **incorrect**, return to the text and _____.

3. He gave a **demonstration** of his new invention so _____.

4. The weather might **defeat** the campers if _____.

5. She tried to **discourage** the puppy from _____.

6. The museum worked to **preserve** the artwork so that _____.

VOCABULARY STRATEGY:

Affixes

Adding an **affix**—a prefix or a suffix—to a base word forms a new word. A **prefix** appears at the beginning of a base or root word to form a new word. A **suffix** is added to the end of a base or root word to form a new word. Knowing the meaning of common affixes can help you determine the meaning of some unfamiliar words.

PREFIX	MEANING	SUFFIX	EFFECT OR MEANING
dis-	"deprive of"	-d, -ed, -ing	to change verb tense
in-	"not"	-s, -es	to change the number of a noun
pre-	"earlier, before"	-ation	"action, or process"

Practice and Apply Use the chart above to determine the meaning of the prefix and/or affix in each of the following words: *discouraged, defeated, incorrect, preserved, preparing, demonstrations.* With a partner, write a definition for each word and determine its part of speech. Check your work in a dictionary.

 ENGLISH LEARNER SUPPORT

Internalize Language Give students practice with affixes to help them internalize new language by having them write down the following words: *disease, incomplete, angered, preparation, predicting.* Work with students to underline prefixes and circle suffixes. Have students suggest possible meanings for the words, then use a dictionary to confirm their definitions. **MODERATE/LIGHT**

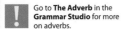
LANGUAGE CONVENTIONS:
Adverbs and Adverb Clauses

Recall that **adverbs** can modify verbs, adjectives, or other adverbs. Writers use adverbs and adverb clauses to tell more about the time, manner, place, or cause of an event. A **conjunctive adverb** is an adverb that is used to connect ideas. Here are a few examples of conjunctive adverbs:

however	meanwhile	nonetheless
therefore	moreover	then
finally	furthermore	otherwise

Here is an example of the conjunctive adverb *meanwhile* as used in *Into the Air*:

> **Meanwhile**, only slowly did people in the United States and abroad become aware of the Wright brothers. . . .

Notice how the conjunctive adverb *meanwhile* introduces the main clause and that a comma is used to separate the conjunctive adverb from the rest of the sentence. Note also how the adverb *slowly* modifies the verb phrase *did become*.

Practice and Apply Write your own sentences using the examples from *Into the Air* as models. Your sentences can be about what kept the Wright brothers from giving up, or they can include your own advice on how to persist in the face of challenges. When you have finished, share your sentences with a partner and compare your use of adverbs, adverb clauses, and conjunctive adverbs.

> Go to **The Adverb** in the **Grammar Studio** for more on adverbs.

LANGUAGE CONVENTIONS:
Adverbs and Adverb Clauses

Review the information on adverbs and adverb clauses with students. Briefly review that an adverb describes a verb, adjective, or another adverb. An adverb explains how, why, when, or where something happens. Adverbs can be one word, and often that word ends in *-ly* (*happily, quickly, angrily*).

Conjunctive adverbs are a more complicated concept. Explain to students that conjunctive adverbs are adverbs used to connect ideas. Students may be familiar with many of the conjunctive adverbs as transition words they use in their writing.

Adverb clauses are also a complicated concept. They function just as single-word adverbs do—by explaining how, why, when, or where something happens—but they are groups of words rather than single words.

Write the following sentences on the board:

- *The girls walked slowly to the train station.* (**Answer:** *slowly; adverb*)
- *The fireworks started when the sun went down.* (**Answer:** *when the sun went down: adverb clause*)
- *Finally, she got to meet her new puppy.* (**Answer:** *Finally; conjunctive adverb*)

Have students determine the adverb or adverb clause and underline it. Ask them to explain what question the adverb or adverb clause answers. Then have them classify each sentence as having an adverb, conjunctive adverb, or adverb clause.

Practice and Apply After students have completed and shared their sentences, have them write one of their sentences on a sentence strip. Have students attach their strips to the board under the appropriate heading: "Adverb," "Conjunctive Adverb," or "Adverb Clause."

ENGLISH LEARNER SUPPORT

Write Basic Vocabulary Use the following supports with students at varying proficiency levels:

- Write *however, finally, therefore,* and *then* on the board, and read them aloud as students say them after you. Then have students write the words on index cards. Have them work in pairs to practice spelling the words. **SUBSTANTIAL**

- Give students sentence frames to complete with conjunctive adverbs from the list on page 389, for example: *It was after dark when they ___ reached home. I like apples. ___ I like apple juice.* **MODERATE**
- Have pairs use the conjunctive adverbs on page 389 to write their own sentences about what they learned. **LIGHT**

MENTOR TEXT

from THE WRIGHT BROTHERS: HOW THEY INVENTED THE AIRPLANE

Biography by Russell Freedman

> This excerpt serves as a **mentor text,** a model for students to follow when they come to the Unit 5 Writing Task: Write a Biographical Report.

GENRE ELEMENTS
BIOGRAPHY

Remind students that a **biography** is a type of informational text intended to present facts and information about a person or persons. A traditional biography includes mostly text, along with some photographs, that tell a true-life story about the subject's life. Biographies are usually written in third-person point of view, but they often include direct quotations from the subject, based on speeches, letters, and books. A main focus of a biography is to provide facts and descriptions of key events that shaped the subject's life.

LEARNING OBJECTIVES

- Analyze characteristics and structural elements of texts.
- Determine key ideas in informational texts.
- Conduct research about the Wright brothers using resources.
- Work with a group to a give a presentation.
- Write a summary of a section of informational text.
- Use resources to determine meanings of new words.
- Use commas correctly in sentences.
- **Language** Discuss the selection using the term *evidence*.

TEXT COMPLEXITY

Quantitative Measures	from *The Wright Brothers: How They Invented the Airplane*	Lexile: 1100
Qualitative Measures	**Ideas Presented** Mostly explicit; requires some inferential reasoning.	
	Structure Used Conventional with chronological sequence of events.	
	Language Used Mostly explicit; some technical words are used.	
	Knowledge Required Mostly casual knowledge of technology, but complex ideas discussed.	

Online Ed

RESOURCES

- Unit 5 Response Log

- 🔊 Selection Audio

- ▶ Text in FOCUS Understanding Technical Language

- 📖 Reading Studio: Notice & Note

- LEVEL UP Level Up Tutorial: Using Transitions

- ▬ Writing Studio: Using Textual Evidence

- 💬 Speaking and Listening Studio: Participating in Collaborative Discussions

- 🔵 Vocabulary Studio: Using Resources

- ❗ Grammar Studio: Module 12: Lesson 2–5: Using Commas Correctly

- ✓ *The Wright Brothers* Selection Test

SUMMARIES

English

The Wright Brothers: How They Invented the Airplane presents a traditional biographical sketch of the period between 1901 and 1902, when the brothers sought to overcome numerous technical problems with their earlier gliders. During this period, the Wright brothers repeatedly demonstrate their determination and creativity as they seek to realize their dream of human flight.

Spanish

Los hermanos Wright: Cómo inventaron el avión presenta un estilo biográfico tradicional del período entre 1901 y 1902, cuando los hermanos buscaban solventar los numerosos problemas técnicos de sus primeros planeadores. Durante este período, los hermanos Wright demostraron repetidamente su determinación y creatividad mientras buscaban cumplir su sueño del vuelo humano.

SMALL-GROUP OPTIONS

Have students work in small groups to read and discuss the selection.

Generating Inquiry

Write the following sentence stems on the board before students enter the room for this lesson.

1. *A traditional biography is _____.*

2. *A graphic biography is _____.*

3. *The biggest obstacle the Wright brothers faced was _____.*

4. *I am curious to find out more about _____.*

Have groups discuss their responses and use their discussion as the basis for further inquiry about the topic of the selections.

Five-Minute Paired Reading

Have pairs of students work together to complete this activity. Explain that they will be reading the same section of the text for five minutes. Tell students to note language that helps them visualize what is happening. (*Examples: wind tunnel, moveable tail rudder, wing warp.*) Explain that it does not matter if they completely understand the text, especially its technical aspects. At the five-minute mark, have students share their understanding, explaining key ideas and pointing out sections of the text they found difficult. Work with students to clarify any questions they have.

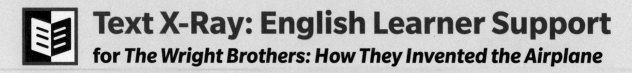

Text X-Ray: English Learner Support
for *The Wright Brothers: How They Invented the Airplane*

Use the Text X-Ray and the supports and scaffolds in the Teacher's Edition to help guide students at different proficiency levels through the selection.

INTRODUCE THE SELECTION
DISCUSS BIOGRAPHIES

Tell students this selection is a biography, a type of informational text that presents facts and details about a subject's life. The goal of a biography is to explain the subject's actions, intentions, and motivations as the subject deals with important issues and events in his or her life.

Break the word *biography* into two parts, writing each on the board as you explain that *bio-* is a Greek prefix meaning "life," and *graph* is a Greek root meaning "write." So a *biography* is a written text about someone's life.

Have students use this understanding to discuss the biography they are about to read. Lead the discussion by asking questions such as: *Whose life is this biography about? What do you think you will learn in this biography? Who would you like to read a biography about?*

CULTURAL REFERENCES

The following words and phrases may be unfamiliar to students:

- *Otto Lilienthal* (paragraph 2): a German inventor who popularized the study and development of gliders throughout Europe
- *Outer Banks* (paragraph 13): 200-mile long string of barrier islands along the coast of Virginia and North Carolina

LISTENING

Listen for Organizational Patterns

Chronological order is a common organizational pattern used in informational texts. Dates and sequence words are clues that an author is using chronological order as a structure.

Read aloud paragraphs 7–9. Use the following supports with students at varying proficiency levels:

- Ask questions about the sequence of events, and have students give one-word answers. For example: *Did the brothers feel confident before or after their tests were completed?* (after) *Did they test the wings before or after they attached them to the balances?* (after) **SUBSTANTIAL**
- Have students complete sentence frames to put several of the events in these paragraphs in order: *First, _____. After that, _____. Then, _____.* **MODERATE**
- Assign students one of the paragraphs, and have them work in pairs to put the events in that paragraph in order using the words *first, next, then,* and *finally.* **LIGHT**

SPEAKING

Discuss Evidence

Remind students that authors support their main ideas with supporting details and evidence. Discuss a main idea using the key term *evidence*.

Display and read aloud this sentence from paragraph 5: *The experiments that Wilbur and Orville had carried out with their latest glider in 1901 were far from encouraging.* Have students look for evidence to support this statement in paragraphs 2–4. Use the following supports at varying proficiency levels:

- Say these sentences, and have students repeat after you: *The author uses evidence to support the main idea. The failure of their glider is evidence. The evidence supports the idea that the experiments were not encouraging.* **SUBSTANTIAL**
- To help students discuss the evidence that supports this main idea, display the following sentence frame: *The detail ___ is evidence that shows the experiments were not encouraging.* **MODERATE**
- Have students explain how the problems discussed in paragraphs 2–4 are evidence that supports the main idea that the experiements were not encouraging. **LIGHT**

READING

Identify Key Ideas

Remind students that key ideas are supported by details. Not every detail is equally important. Give students practice distinguishing key ideas from details.

Read paragraph 9 with students. Use the following supports with students at varying proficiency levels:

- Ask questions about the details of the paragraph. For example: *The text says they jotted down data. Is that an important detail?* (no) *The text says they replaced other people's calculations with their own. Is that an important detail?* (yes) **SUBSTANTIAL**
- Ask students: *Which sentence from the paragraph best expresses its key idea?* (*When their lab tests were finally completed, they felt confident that they could calculate in advance the performance of an aircraft's wings with far greater accuracy than had ever before been possible.*) **MODERATE**
- Have students work together in pairs to identify a key idea and an important detail in the paragraph. **LIGHT**

WRITING

Write a Summary

Work with students to read the writing assignment on page 401.

Provide guidance for students as they summarize paragraphs 1–4. Use the following supports with students at varying proficiency levels:

- Provide the sentences of a simple summary, and have students put the sentences in the correct order. For example: *The Wright brothers returned to Kitty Hawk in 1901 to test their new glider. Their experiments did not go as they hoped. They were sad and confused when they went back to Dayton. Wilbur predicted they would not succeed in flying.* **SUBSTANTIAL**
- Provide an outline of frame sentences for students to use. For example: *The Wright brothers returned to Kitty Hawk in 1901 to test their new _____. Their experiments ____ as they hoped. They were _____ when they went back to Dayton.* **MODERATE**
- Have students work in pairs to complete a sequence graphic organizer to guide their summary writing. Have them work with a partner to ensure that they use a variety of sentence types in their summaries. **LIGHT**

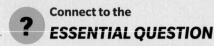

? Connect to the
ESSENTIAL QUESTION

In this text, the author describes how Wilbur and Orville Wright improved the design of their glider and successfully flew it during their 1903 experiments at Kitty Hawk.

MENTOR TEXT

The Wright Brothers: How They Invented the Airplane provides a model for how a writer uses factual information about a well-known historical figure drawn from primary and secondary sources to create an interesting and informative report about this person's life and significance.

COMPARE PRESENTATIONS

Point out that *Into the Air* is a graphic biography consisting of images and mostly imagined dialogue about the work of Wilbur and Orville Wright. In contrast, *The Wright Brothers: How They Invented the Airplane* is a traditional biography comprised of a detailed text enhanced with some photographs. Explain that this selection covers the same time period in the Wright Brothers' lives as *Into the Air*.

BIOGRAPHY

from
THE WRIGHT BROTHERS:
HOW THEY INVENTED THE AIRPLANE

by **Russell Freedman**
pages 393–399

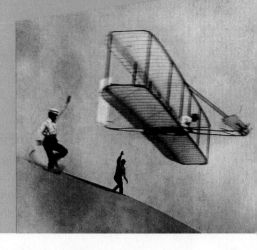

COMPARE PRESENTATIONS

Now that you have read *Into the Air*, read *The Wright Brothers: How They Invented the Airplane* to see how this selection presents some of the same ideas as it describes similar events. As you read, think about your own experiences with problem solving and persevering. After you are finished, you will collaborate with a small group on a final project analyzing the two texts.

 ESSENTIAL QUESTION:

What keeps people from giving up?

GRAPHIC BIOGRAPHY

from
INTO THE AIR

by **Robert Burleigh**
illustrated by **Bill Wylie**
pages 377–385

 LEARNING MINDSET

Grit *The Wright Brothers: How They Invented the Airplane* is a lengthy and detailed text. As they read the excerpt, encourage students to write notes in their text about how the Wright Brothers exhibited grit, or perseverance, in their quest to fly. Remind students that sticking with a book, a class, or another activity even when it is difficult or challenging will help them reach their goals. Grit means thinking hard, solving problems, and putting in the effort to keep making progress toward their goals.

from **The Wright Brothers**

QUICK START

Would you like to build and test your own flying machine? Why or why not? Discuss your answers with a partner.

ANALYZE CHARACTERISTICS OF INFORMATIONAL TEXTS

Informational texts present facts, events, and ideas in an organized way so that they make sense to the reader. Recognizing a **pattern of organization**—the way ideas and information are arranged in a nonfiction text—will help you better understand the information. As you read, note examples of organizational patterns listed below.

GENRE ELEMENTS: BIOGRAPHY

- uses text and sometimes photographs or illustrations to tell a true-life story about a person or group of people
- usually written in third-person but may include direct quotations, including the words of the subject or subjects
- includes facts and descriptions of events, people, and experiences that shaped the subject or subjects

ORGANIZATIONAL PATTERNS	
definition	defines new terms or technical language within the text
classification	sorts ideas into groups and then describes characteristics
chronological order	relates information in time-order sequence
cause and effect	explains a cause-and-effect relationship
advantage and disadvantage	presents the pros and cons of an issue to clarify ideas
key idea and supporting details	establishes a key idea and supports it with details as evidence

DETERMINE KEY IDEAS

Key ideas are important ideas the author wants readers to understand. As you read, look for the text's main idea, as well as key ideas in each paragraph. Sometimes these ideas are not stated directly, but are implied, or suggested by details. As you read, determine key ideas by following these steps:

- Identify the topic of each paragraph or section.
- Note details, including descriptions, facts, and quotations.
- Ask yourself what key idea the details convey about the topic.

QUICK START

When students have completed the task, have them share some of their ideas for flying machines. Conclude the discussion by taking a vote to determine which ideas the class finds most interesting and why.

ANALYZE CHARACTERISTICS OF INFORMATIONAL TEXTS

Explain that writers of informational texts use one or more organizational patterns when presenting their facts and ideas. Discuss each of the organizational patterns described in the table. Encourage students to make connections between the organizational patterns and definitions by providing brief examples. For example, suggest that if a writer wants to discuss the reasons for global warming, he or she might use a cause-and-effect organizational pattern. Ask: *What is a topic for which a writer might use advantages and disadvantages as an organizational pattern?* Continue with similar questions for some of the other patterns listed in the table.

DETERMINE KEY IDEAS

Discuss the difference between the main idea of an entire informational text and the key idea of a paragraph or section. Remind students that both the main idea of the text and the key ideas in each paragraph may be directly stated or implied. Ask: *What are the key supporting details in this text? What are these details mainly about?* Stress the idea that students should look for the main idea of the text as they read, not after they have finished it.

 ENGLISH LEARNER SUPPORT

Internalize Language Read aloud the name of each organizational pattern and its definition. Have students work in small groups to come up with a graphic representation of each organizational pattern. Show an example for the pattern "Definition": pizza = crust + sauce + cheese. Allow beginning proficiencies to use pictures as needed (happy face/sad face for advantages/disadvantages) and write any words they include in their home language. Have students present their representations by naming the organizational pattern.
ALL LEVELS

TEACH

CRITICAL VOCABULARY

Encourage students to read all the sentences before deciding which word best completes each one. Remind them to consider the context clues that the other words provide.

Answers:

1. *calculate*

2. *experiment*

3. *apparatus*

4. *prediction*

5. *accurate*

■ English Learner Support

Practice Vocabulary Have advanced students work with small groups to find which word can be both a noun and a verb. Have them write two sentences using the word each way. **LIGHT**

LANGUAGE CONVENTIONS

Commas Review the information about the use of commas in transitions. Explain that transitions help connect details and ideas in a sentence.

Read aloud the model sentence and have students repeat the transitional phrase. Note that a comma is used after the transition to set it off. Write other transitions on the board: *because, first of all, however, therefore, for that reason.* Model the use of each transition in a sentence and then have students repeat it.

ANNOTATION MODEL

Remind students to keep in mind the information about organizational patterns listed on page 391 of the lesson when making annotations. Encourage students to include comments or questions about any patterns of organization and key ideas they notice. Remind students that they can underline, circle, or highlight examples directly in the text.

 GET READY

CRITICAL VOCABULARY

experiment   prediction   accurate   calculate   apparatus

To see how many Critical Vocabulary words you already know, use them to complete the sentences.

1. We should _____ how long it will take us to drive 500 miles.

2. We conducted the _____ in our new laboratory.

3. A wheelchair is a/an _____ that increases a person's mobility.

4. Make a/an _____ about what will happen in the story.

5. She took careful and _____ measurements.

LANGUAGE CONVENTIONS

Commas help clarify the meaning of sentences by separating certain words or phrases. Commas also set off transitions. **Transitions** such as *because* and *for that reason* clarify relationships between ideas.

To begin with, they were very cautious.

In the above example, "to begin with" links ideas about time with how the Wright brothers acted—with caution. As you read the text, note the author's use of commas after transitions.

ANNOTATION MODEL

NOTICE & NOTE

As you read, note the organizational patterns that are used to present key ideas and structure the text. You can also mark up evidence that supports your own ideas. In the model, you can see one reader's notes about the beginning of *The Wright Brothers:*

1   The brothers <u>returned</u> to Kitty Hawk on <u>July 10, 1901. This year</u> they wanted to be closer to their launching site at Kill Devil Hills, so they loaded their camping equipment, glider parts, and some lumber into a beach cart, drove it 4 miles south, and set up camp a few hundred feet from the bottom of Big Hill.

> Details about time tell me that the Wright Brothers have been to Kitty Hawk before.

BACKGROUND

Russell Freedman (b. 1929) specializes in nonfiction storytelling, especially biographies. He has written numerous works for young people, including Freedom Walkers: The Story of the Montgomery Bus Boycott and Becoming Ben Franklin: How a Candle-Maker's Son Helped Light the Flame of Liberty. He won a Newbery Medal—a prize seldom given for nonfiction—for his 1988 biography of Abraham Lincoln, Lincoln: A Photobiography.

from
THE WRIGHT BROTHERS:
HOW THEY INVENTED THE AIRPLANE
Biography by Russell Freedman

PREPARE TO COMPARE

As you read, note times when the Wright brothers could have given up on their dream, but did not. Look for details that show how they worked together to overcome obstacles.

1   The brothers returned to Kitty Hawk on July 10, 1901. This year they wanted to be closer to their launching site[1] at Kill Devil Hills, so they loaded their camping equipment, glider parts, and some lumber into a beach cart, drove it 4 miles south, and set up camp a few hundred feet from the bottom of Big Hill. Again they lived in a tent, but they also put up a large wooden shed to use as a workshop and hangar[2] for the new glider. This year they would share their camp with visitors. Their friend Octave Chanute and two associates joined the Wrights for a few days to observe their **experiments** and to test a new glider that Chanute had recently designed.

---

[1] **site:** the place or setting where something happens.
[2] **hangar:** a shelter for storing aircraft.

The Wright Brothers: How They Invented the Airplane   393

Notice & Note

Use the side margins to notice and note signposts in the text.

ANALYZE CHARACTERISTICS OF INFORMATIONAL TEXTS

Annotate: Mark any references to chronology, or the sequence in which events occur, in paragraph 1.

Analyze: How do references to time help you understand the text?

experiment
(ĭk-spĕr´ə-mənt) *n.* An *experiment* is a test to determine if an idea is true or to see if a device works.

BACKGROUND

Have students read the Background note. Remind students that the Wright brothers had to overcome many technical problems before they could control their glider. Even more complicated problems arose as they began work on a heavier-than-air, motor-driven aircraft. After their successes, Wilbur took over business details until his death in May 1912. Orville lived until January 1948, having seen the dream of human flight transformed into an global industry. His one regret was that airplanes had been become an essential part of warfare.

PREPARE TO COMPARE

Read the Prepare to Compare prompt. Direct students to focus their reading on identifying instances of how the Wright brothers worked together to overcome obstacles.

✎ ANALYZE CHARACTERISTICS OF INFORMATIONAL TEXTS

Review the importance of chronology, or sequence of events, in tracking the flow of events in a biography or in an informational text that explains the development of a new technology over time. (**Answer:** *Phrases such as "on July 10, 1901," "this year," and "again" indicate chronological order. The chronological organizational pattern helps readers understand the order of events. This section discusses what changes the brothers made and how this year's efforts were like previous ones. Chronology helps the reader understand that this is not the first experiment at Kitty Hawk.*)

■ English Learner Support

Listen for Details About Time   Read aloud the first paragraph, and have students raise their hands when they hear a reference to time (*July, 10, 1901, this year, for a few days*.) Ask simple questions to make sure students understand when the story takes place and how long Chanute stayed with them. **SUBSTANTIAL**

TO CHALLENGE STUDENTS . . .

Problems and Solutions   The author of this text uses the problems faced by the Wright brothers to show some of their characteristics. These characteristics allowed them to make important scientific discoveries. As a challenge to students, have them note these problems as they read, along with the way the brothers reacted to and handled each one. At the end of the selection, have them write a short explanation of how the many problems faced by the brothers reveal important character traits.

ANALYZE CHARACTERISTICS OF INFORMATIONAL TEXTS

Remind students that one important organizational pattern involves explaining a cause-and-effect relationship between events and ideas. Discuss how the Wright brothers responded to learning that the previously published data was unreliable. (**Answer:** *The doubt raised by using existing, inaccurate scientific data caused the Wright brothers to rely entirely on their own investigations.*)

For **speaking support** for students at varying proficiency levels, see the **Text X-Ray** on page 390D.

CRITICAL VOCABULARY

prediction: Wilbur made a prediction, or guess about what would happen in the future, about whether humans would achieve flight.

ASK STUDENTS why Wilbur shared his prediction in a later writing. (**Answer:** *to show it was wrong*)

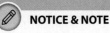 **NOTICE & NOTE**

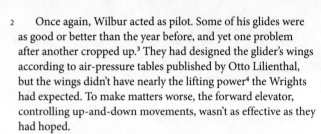

2   Once again, Wilbur acted as pilot. Some of his glides were as good or better than the year before, and yet one problem after another cropped up.[3] They had designed the glider's wings according to air-pressure tables published by Otto Lilienthal, but the wings didn't have nearly the lifting power[4] the Wrights had expected. To make matters worse, the forward elevator, controlling up-and-down movements, wasn't as effective as they had hoped.

3   Puzzled and dejected, they closed their camp at the end of August, sooner than they had planned, and went back to Dayton.

4   "We doubted that we would ever resume our experiments," Wilbur wrote later. "When we looked at the time and money which we had expended, and considered the progress made and the distance yet to go, we considered our experiments a failure. At this time I made the **prediction** that man would sometime fly, but that it would not be in our lifetime."

5   The experiments that Wilbur and Orville had carried out with their latest glider in 1901 were far from encouraging. Reflecting on their problems, Wilbur observed: "We saw that the calculations upon which all flying machines had been based were unreliable,[5] and that all were simply groping in the dark.[6]

prediction
(prĭ-dĭk´shən) *n.* When someone makes a *prediction*, they make a guess about something that has not yet happened.

ANALYZE CHARACTERISTICS OF INFORMATIONAL TEXTS

Annotate: Mark the words in paragraph 5 that refer to the disadvantages of the existing data.

Cause and Effect: What decision did the Wright brothers make about data, and why did they make it?

---

[3] **cropped up:** happened suddenly or unexpectedly.
[4] **lifting power:** the force that holds the glider in the air; most of the lift is produced by airflow over the wings.
[5] **calculations . . . unreliable:** a reference to the data in the air-pressure tables produced by German aviation pioneer Otto Lilienthal. The Wrights had used this data to design the wings of their glider.
[6] **groping in the dark:** looking for answers without much guidance.

 ENGLISH LEARNER SUPPORT

Internalize and Confirm Understanding   Have students confirm and internalize their understanding of new words using body language.

- Act out the meaning of the words *puzzled* and *dejected* (from paragraph 3) using body language, including facial expressions, body movement, and other gestures. Say the words, and have students repeat them. Then say the words as students act them out. **SUBSTANTIAL/MODERATE**

- Have students work in pairs to figure out a way to act out the words *puzzled* and *dejected* (from paragraph 3). **LIGHT**

Having set out with absolute faith in the existing scientific data, we were driven to doubt one thing after another, till finally, after two years of experiment, we cast it all aside, and decided to rely entirely on our own investigations."

6   In the gaslit workroom[7] behind their bicycle shop, Wilbur and Orville began to compile their own data. They wanted to test different types of wing surfaces and obtain **accurate** air-pressure tables. To do this, they built a wind tunnel—a wooden box 6 feet long with a glass viewing window on top and a fan at one end. It wasn't the world's first wind tunnel, but it would be the first to yield valuable results for the construction of a practical airplane.

7   The materials needed to make model wings, or *airfoils*, and the tools to shape them were right at hand. Using tin shears, hammers, files, and a soldering iron, the brothers fashioned as many as two hundred miniature wings out of tin, galvanized iron, steel, solder, and wax. They made wings that were thick or thin, curved or flat, wings with rounded tips and pointed tips, slender wings and stubby wings. They attached these experimental airfoils to balances made of bicycle spokes and old hacksaw blades. Then they tested the wings in their wind tunnel to see how they behaved in a moving airstream.

8   For several weeks they were absorbed in painstaking and systematic lab work—testing, measuring, and **calculating** as they tried to unlock the secrets of an aircraft wing. The work was tedious. It was repetitious. Yet they would look back on that winter as a time of great excitement, when each new day promised discoveries waiting to be made. "Wilbur and I could hardly wait for morning to come," Orville declared, "to get at something that interested us. *That's* happiness." Text in FOCUS

9   The Wrights knew that they were exploring uncharted territory with their wind-tunnel tests. Each new bit of data jotted down in their notebooks added to their understanding of how an airfoil works. Gradually they replaced the calculations of others with facts and figures of their own. Their doubts vanished, and their faith in themselves grew. When their lab tests were finally completed, they felt confident that they could calculate in advance the performance of an aircraft's wings with far greater accuracy than had ever before been possible.

---

[7] **gaslit workroom:** indoor lighting came from gas-fueled lamps, which were dimmer than the electric lights used today.

accurate
(ăk´yər-ĭt) *adj.* Something *accurate* is correct.

DETERMINE KEY IDEAS
Annotate: Mark the key idea of paragraph 8.

Analyze: How do details found in the paragraph support this key idea?

calculate
(kăl´kyə-lāt´) *v.* To *calculate* is to figure out an answer by using math.

DETERMINE KEY IDEAS

Remind students that the key ideas of an informational text are related to the topic, and authors add details to support the key ideas. Emphasize that not all key ideas are explicitly stated. Stress the importance of looking for surrounding details that support a key idea. (**Answer:** *The details in this paragraph show that the work was very hard and tedious. But the brothers' reaction to the work is not one of boredom or disappointment. They are excited by the work, even though it is hard.*)

■ English Learner Support

Understand Important Details To help students find details that support the key idea, read aloud paragraph 8, and have them listen for details that describe what was special or unique about these winter weeks. Ask: *What details show the work was hard? What details show how the brothers felt about the work?* Guide students to see that the key idea supported by these details is that the work was hard, but the brothers were excited about it.

ALL LEVELS

For **listening and reading support** for students at varying proficiency levels, see the **Text X-Ray** on pages 390C and 390D.

Text in FOCUS TEXT IN FOCUS

Understanding Technical Language Have students view the **Text in Focus** video in their eBooks to learn how to understand technical language. Then have students use **Text in Focus Practice PDF** to apply what they have learned.

APPLYING ACADEMIC VOCABULARY

❏ **achieve**   ❏ **individual**   ❏ **principle**   ☑ **instance**   ❏ **outcome**

Write and Discuss Have students turn to a partner to discuss the following question. Guide students to include the Academic Vocabulary word *instance* in their responses. Ask volunteers to share their responses with the class.

• How did each new **instance** of success affect the Wright brothers?

CRITICAL VOCABULARY

accurate: If facts or details are correct, they are accurate.

ASK STUDENTS why accurate data was important for the Wright brothers. (**Answer:** *They needed accurate data to make sure their airplane would fly safely.*)

calculate: If you are calculating to solve to a problem, you are using math to figure out the answer.

ASK STUDENTS how the Wright brothers made their calculations. (**Answer:** *They made them by hand, without a computer or calculator.*)

TEACH

NUMBERS AND STATS

Remind students that authors use **details** to support their **key ideas.** Sometimes these details are statistics, measurements, and other numerical data. Use a tape measure to show students the length and width of the aircraft wings (32 ft long, 5 ft wide) and tail (6 ft high) as described in paragraph 10. Have students make comparisons about a human's weight and the aircraft's weight. (**Answer:** *The numbers are used as specific, detailed evidence to support the paragraph's key idea: "... they designed their biggest glider yet"*)

■ English Learner Support

Practice Using Units of Measure Students requiring English support may be unfamiliar with English standard units of measure. Write these equivalent measures: *1 centimeter = 0.39 inch; 1 meter = 3.3 feet; 1 kilogram = 2.2 pounds.* Review these units with students.
ALL LEVELS

CRITICAL VOCABULARY

apparatus: When you use an apparatus of some kind, you are using a piece of equipment.

ASK STUDENTS to give an example of an apparatus from a hobby or sport they enjoy. (**Sample answer:** *I use a weight-training apparatus to build strength for volleyball.*)

396 Unit 5

NUMBERS AND STATS

Notice & Note: What does the numeric information in paragraph 10 reveal? Mark the places where the author provides numeric information.

Draw Conclusions: What is the purpose of including these numbers?

apparatus
(ăpʹə-rătʹəs) *n.* An *apparatus* is a piece of equipment.

10 Armed with this new knowledge, they designed their biggest glider yet. Its wings, longer and narrower than before, measured 32 feet from tip to tip and 5 feet from front to rear. For the first time, the new glider had a tail—two 6-foot-high vertical fins, designed to help stabilize the machine during turns. The hip cradle[8] developed the year before to control wing warping[9] was retained. The craft weighed just under 120 pounds.

11 With growing anticipation, Wilbur and Orville prepared for their 1902 trip to the Outer Banks. "They really ought to get away for a while," Katharine wrote to her father. "Will is thin and nervous and so is Orv. They will be all right when they get down in the sand where the salt breezes blow. . . . They think that life at Kitty Hawk cures all ills, you know.

12 "The flying machine is in process of making now. Will spins the sewing machine around by the hour while Orv squats around marking the places to sew [the cotton wing covering]. There is no place in the house to live but I'll be lonesome enough by this time next week and wish I could have some of their racket around."

13 The brothers reached the Outer Banks at the end of August with their trunks, baggage, and crates carrying the glider parts.

14 By the middle of September they had assembled their new glider and were ready to try it out. This year they took turns in the pilot's position, giving Orville a chance to fly for the first time. To begin with, they were very cautious. They would launch the machine from the slope on Big Hill and glide only a short distance as they practiced working the controls. Steering to the right or left was accomplished by warping the wings, with the glider always turning toward the lower wing. Up-and-down movements were controlled by the forward elevator.

15 In a few days they made dozens of short but successful test glides. At this point, things looked more promising than ever. The only mishap occurred one afternoon when Orville was at the controls. That evening he recorded the incident in his diary:

16 "I was sailing along smoothly without any trouble . . . when I noticed that one wing was getting a little too high and that the machine was slowly sliding off in the opposite direction. . . . The next thing I knew was that the wing was very high in the air, a great deal higher than before, and I thought I must have worked the twisting **apparatus** the wrong

---

[8] **hip cradle:** a device that allowed the pilot to lie down and use hip movement to control the rudder and wings.
[9] **wing warping:** the Wright Brothers' discovery of how they could twist the ends of the wings in order to balance and control the aircraft.

396 Unit 5

WHEN STUDENTS STRUGGLE . . .

Transitions and Commas Have students read paragraph 10 and identify two examples of introductory phrases set off with a comma.

- "Armed with this new knowledge, they designed their biggest glider yet."
- "For the first time, the new glider had a tail."

Model reading these sentences aloud so students can hear the slight pause after the introductory phrases. Discuss how commas signal pauses or separations in sentences.

 For additional support, go to the **Reading Studio** and assign the following ▣LEVEL UP **Level Up tutorial: Using Transitions.**

LANGUAGE CONVENTIONS

Remind students how authors use commas to mark off introductory phrases. (**Answer:** *It is easier to understand these sentences with the addition of the commas. Without the commas, the words run together, making it harder to follow the action described by the author in each sentence.*)

way. Thinking of nothing else . . . I threw the wingtips to their greatest angle. By this time I found suddenly that I was making a descent backwards toward the low wing, from a height of 25 or 30 feet. . . . The result was a heap of flying machine, cloth and sticks in a heap, with me in the center without a bruise or scratch. The experiments thereupon suddenly came to a close till repairs can be made. In spite of this sad catastrophe we are tonight in a hilarious mood as a result of the encouraging performance of the machine."

17   A few days' labor made the glider as good as new. It wasn't seriously damaged again during hundreds of test glides, and it repeatedly withstood rough landings at full speed. Wilbur and Orville became more and more confident. "Our new machine is a very great improvement over anything we had built before and over anything anyone has built," Wilbur told his father. "Everything is so much more satisfactory that we now believe that the flying problem is really nearing its solution."

18   And yet the solution was not yet quite at hand. As they continued their test flights a baffling new problem arose. On most flights the glider performed almost perfectly. But every so often—in about one flight out of fifty—it would spin out of control as the pilot tried to level off after a turn.

LANGUAGE CONVENTIONS

Writers use commas to make the meaning of their sentences clear. Mark the commas in the second and third sentences in paragraph 18. Then, read the sentences aloud, pausing after each comma. Finally, read the sentences without the pauses. Which is easier to understand? Why?

IMPROVE READING FLUENCY

Targeted Passage Have students work with partners as they read paragraphs 17 and 18. Model how to read an informational text. Have students follow along as you read the passage with appropriate phrasing and emphasis. Then have partners take turns reading each paragraph. Encourage students to provide support to others, and assist them in pronouncing difficult words. Remind students that when reading aloud, the goal is to give the audience time to understand difficult ideas and complex sentence structures.

    Go to the **Reading Studio** for additional support in developing fluency.

TEACH

DETERMINE KEY IDEAS

Remind students that the key idea of a paragraph sometimes appears in the first or last sentence. Note that in this example, the first sentence provides a general sense of the key idea and the last sentence provides a key idea with specific details. Emphasize that it is important to look for the key idea as you are reading a text, not just after you have read it. (**Answer:** *Orville figured out why the glider was spinning out of control and devised a solution. Details that support this key idea: "During some turns . . . pressure was built up on the tail, throwing the glider off balance and into a spin"; "The cure was to make the tail movable—like a ship's rudder or a bird's tail"*)

QUOTED WORDS

Discuss the value of direct **quotations** in an informational text. Ask: *Where might this quotation have come from?* (**Answer:** *From a direct source such as a diary, autobiography, or letter written by Wilbur Wright.*) Have students speculate about the purpose of including this quotation. (**Answer:** *A direct quotation from Wilbur Wright is valuable evidence supporting the author's statement about the brothers' success with a new tail design: "From then on, there were no more problems." Review with students how quotations are used throughout the selection as supporting evidence.*)

 NOTICE & NOTE

DETERMINE KEY IDEAS
Annotate: Mark the words in paragraph 19 that suggest the key idea of the paragraph.

Summarize: Use your own words to restate the key idea of paragraph 19. How do details support this idea?

QUOTED WORDS

Notice & Note: What does the quotation in paragraph 21 reveal? Mark the quotation.

Analyze: What was likely the author's purpose for including this quotation?

19 Lying in bed one sleepless night, Orville figured out what the problem was. The fixed tail worked perfectly well most of the time. During some turns, however—when the airspeed was low and the pilot failed to level off soon enough—pressure was built up on the tail, throwing the glider off balance and into a spin. That's just what happened to Orville the day of his accident. The cure was to make the tail movable—like a ship's rudder or a bird's tail.

20 The next morning at breakfast, Orville told Wilbur about his idea. After thinking it over for a few minutes, Wilbur agreed. Then he offered an idea of his own. Why not connect the new movable tail to the wing-warping wires? This would allow the pilot to twist the wings and turn the tail at the same time, simply by shifting his hips. With the wings and tail coordinated, the glider would always make a smooth banked turn.

21 They removed the original tail and installed a movable single-vaned tail[10] 5 feet high. From then on, there were no more problems. The movable tail rudder finally gave the Wright brothers complete control of their glider. "With this improvement our serious troubles ended," wrote Wilbur, "and thereafter we devoted ourselves to the work of gaining skill by continued practice."

---
[10]**single-vaned tail:** the one-piece plate that extends from the back end of the aircraft for stability and control.

EL ENGLISH LEARNER SUPPORT

Identify Transitions Discuss the importance of transitions in connecting ideas, including clarifying the sequence of events. Have students work in pairs to highlight transitions in paragraphs 19–21 that indicate time order. In paragraph 19: "one sleepless night," "During some turns"; in paragraph 20: "the next morning at breakfast"; in Paragraph 21: "From then on." **MODERATE**

22   Wilbur and Orville made hundreds of perfectly controlled glides in 1902. They proved that their laboratory tests were accurate. The next step was to build a powered airplane. "Before leaving camp," Orville wrote, "we were already at work on the general design of a new machine which we proposed to propel with a motor."

CHECK YOUR UNDERSTANDING

Answer these questions before moving on to the **Analyze the Text** section on the following page.

1 What is the main subject of this biography?

  A All early aviators

  B Aviation pioneers Orville and Wilbur Wright

  C The entire Wright family

  D The correct way to design a motor-powered airplane

2 How does the author mainly support his ideas?

  F With facts, quotations, and historical information

  G With historians' and engineers' opinions

  H With illustrations, photographs, and tables

  J With references to websites

3 Which idea is supported by information throughout the selection?

  A The Wright brothers were more interested in bicycles than airplanes.

  B The Wright brothers did not believe in building on the work of other pioneers.

  C The Wright brothers used science and creativity to solve the puzzle of flight.

  D The Wright brothers relied mostly on inspiration to solve the puzzle of flight.

CHECK YOUR UNDERSTANDING

Have students answer the questions independently.

Answers:

1. *B*

2. *F*

3. *C*

If they answer any questions incorrectly, have them reread the text to confirm their understanding. Then they may proceed to ANALYZE THE TEXT on page 400.

The Wright Brothers: How They Invented the Airplane   399

ENGLISH LEARNER SUPPORT

Oral Assessment Use the following questions to assess students' comprehension and speaking skills:

1. Who is the subject of this biography? (*Orville and Wilbur Wright*)

2. How does the author support his ideas? (*facts, quotations, and historical information*)

3. How did the Wright brothers solve the puzzle of flight? (*They used science and creativity. They kept trying.*) **SUBSTANTIAL/MODERATE**

ANALYZE THE TEXT

Possible answers:

1. **DOK 4:** *Wind tunnel is defined as "a wooden box 6 feet long with a glass viewing window on top and a fan at one end." The definition clarifies what the structure looks like.*

2. **DOK 2:** *The wind tunnel allowed the brothers to experiment and gather their own data on wing designs. As they collected data, "their faith in themselves grew," and they could continue to build on their success.*

3. **DOK 2:** *This paragraph uses the Key Idea and Details pattern. By reading about the problem, the reader can think about how it might be solved and better understand the solution.*

4. **DOK 3:** *Details: "The next morning at breakfast, Orville told Wilbur about his idea" suggests that sharing information was important to their work process. Wilbur "thinking it over for a few minutes" agreed and "offered an idea of his own." This shows that they actively listened to one another and built on each other's ideas. Key idea: Cooperation and collaboration was important to their success.*

5. **DOK 4:** *The author uses direct quotations from the Wright brothers to support the text's key ideas. Using direct quotations helps the reader understand the frustrations the brothers felt as well as their successes.*

RESEARCH

Point out the suggestions for research that appear in the margin.

Extend Students should note that Lilienthal legitimized attempts at heavier-than-air flight through his gliders and inspired other inventors, such as the Wright brothers.

RESPOND

ANALYZE THE TEXT

Support your responses with evidence from the text. 📓 NOTEBOOK

1. **Analyze** Review paragraph 6. How does the author define *wind tunnel*? How does the description of a wind tunnel affect your understanding of the text?

2. **Cause and Effect** Review paragraph 9. What effect did the wind tunnel tests have on the Wright brothers and their work?

3. **Identify Patterns** Review paragraph 18. What pattern of organization is used to structure the paragraph's information? How does the organization add to your understanding of the selection?

4. **Cite Evidence** Review paragraphs 19–21. What details does the author provide about how the brothers work together? What key idea do these details suggest?

5. **Notice & Note** Review the use of direct quotations throughout the selection. How do the quotations help you understand the key ideas in the selection?

RESEARCH TIP
Specific search terms will give you the best results. If you want to find out more about the Wrights' test flights, try *Wright brothers Kitty Hawk*. If you want to learn what the Wright brothers were working on at a specific time, add the year to your search words. For example, *Wright brothers Kitty Hawk 1903*.

RESEARCH

At the end of this excerpt, the Wrights plan to use what they have learned about creating a successful glider to build a motorized airplane. Work individually to investigate what steps the Wrights took toward achieving their final goal of powered flight. Note the successes and failures they experienced along the way. Use multiple sources, and record what you learn in the following table.

AIRCRAFT DESIGN CHANGES	RESULTS
Flight controls	*Used an anemometer to measure wind speed and a stopwatch to measure time.*
Propellers	*Created forward thrust so the aircraft could move forward.*
Transmission	*Chain and sprocket transmission allowed the transfer of power from the engine to the propellers.*

Extend The selection mentions the work of German flight pioneer Otto Lilienthal. Research Lilienthal's life and achievements to find out how his work inspired others to make advances in flight.

LEARNING MINDSET

Questioning Explain to students that having questions about the reading is not a problem—it is a gift! Having questions means they are actively thinking about the text and wondering about the information. Sometimes readers ask questions when they are confused or stuck in a text. Tell students not to be shy about asking questions. They are a path to learning. If students seem reluctant to ask questions aloud, have them write them on sticky notes. Invite the class to answer them (without naming the questioner.)

CREATE AND DISCUSS

Write a Summary Review paragraphs 13–22; then, write a three-paragraph summary of that section.

- ❑ State key ideas and supporting details found in the section.
- ❑ Paraphrase ideas by stating them in your own words.
- ❑ Use transitions and introductory elements.
- ❑ Use Critical Vocabulary words when appropriate.

Hold a Small Group Discussion Have a group discussion to determine a possible central or main idea for the selection.

- ❑ Remind group members that you are not looking for a topic. Instead, you are looking for a message that is central to the text.
- ❑ Provide support for your ideas by citing text evidence.
- ❑ Review the ideas together. Listen closely and actively to each other.
- ❑ Ask questions to clarify points. Respond appropriately.

RESPOND TO THE ESSENTIAL QUESTION

? What keeps people from giving up?

Gather Information Review your annotations and notes on *The Wright Brothers: How They Invented the Airplane*. Then, add relevant details to your Response Log. As you determine which information to include, think about how the Wright brothers faced challenges and how readers might follow their example.

At the end of the unit, use your notes to write a biographical report.

Go to **Using Textual Evidence: Summarizing, Paraphrasing, and Quoting** in the **Writing Studio** for more on summarizing and paraphrasing.

Go to **Participating in Collaborative Discussions: Listening and Responding** in the **Speaking and Listening Studio** for help with having a group discussion.

ACADEMIC VOCABULARY
As you write and discuss what you learned from the selection, be sure to use the Academic Vocabulary words. Check off the words that you use.

- ❑ **achieve**
- ❑ **individual**
- ❑ **instance**
- ❑ **outcome**
- ❑ **principle**

CREATE AND DISCUSS

Write a Summary Remind students that the list on page 401 can be used as a set of steps to follow when writing a summary. Emphasize that a good summary is objective and gives answers to basic questions such as: *What are the key ideas of the text? What are the supporting details? What major pieces of evidence does the writer offer?* Stress that a summary is expressed in the summary writer's own words.

For **writing support** for students at varying proficiency levels, see the **Text X-Ray** on page 390D.

Hold a Small Group Discussion Remind students of the distinction between the topic of informative text and its message. Explain that the topic is subject of the text, whereas the message is the main idea that the writer wants to persuade his audience to accept. Stress that when holding a small group discussion, it is important to encourage everyone to contribute and to treat all group members respectfully.

RESPOND TO THE ESSENTIAL QUESTION

Allow time for students to add details from *The Wright Brothers: How They Invented the Airplane* to their Unit 5 Response Logs.

ENGLISH LEARNER SUPPORT

Hold a Small Group Discussion Remind students that a central idea is supported by the details of a text. Use the following sentence frames to assist students in participating in the discussion:

- *I think this text is mostly about _____.*
- *The central idea is _____.*
- *A detail that supports this main idea is _____.*
- *I disagree because _____.*
- *I agree because _____.* **SUBSTANTIAL/MODERATE**

APPLY

CRITICAL VOCABULARY

Possible answers:

1. *You must be **accurate** when you **calculate** how much water to bring on a trip through the desert because there are limited sources of water there and it is very hot.*

2. *A scale is an **apparatus** used to measure weight or mass.*

3. *One purpose of an **experiment** is to test a hypothesis.*

4. *If you make a **prediction** before taking a risk, you can assess the outcome of the action and decide whether the risk is worth taking.*

VOCABULARY STRATEGY:
Resources

1. **air pressure:** *in flight, the force of air flowing over the aircraft's wings*

2. **forward elevator:** *a movable horizontal surface in front of the wings to control up-and-down movements of the aircraft*

3. **airfoil:** *the shape of airplane wings*

RESPOND

Go to the **Vocabulary Studio** for more on using resources.

CRITICAL VOCABULARY

Practice and Apply Use what you know about the Vocabulary words to answer these questions.

1. Why is it important to be **accurate** when you **calculate** how much water to bring on a trip through the desert?

2. What type of **apparatus** could be used to measure weight?

3. What is one possible purpose of an **experiment?**

4. Why is it useful to make a **prediction** before taking a risk?

VOCABULARY STRATEGY:
Resources

In *The Wright Brothers: How They Invented the Airplane,* the author uses technical and scientific language to describe how the Wrights developed their glider. Sometimes, writers provide definitions or context clues to help readers determine the meaning of technical terms. But if you need more help to understand a technical term or subject in your reading, turn to online and print resources for additional information.

A **standard dictionary** will tell you a word's definitions, pronunciation, syllabication, parts of speech, history, and origin. A **specialized dictionary** focuses on terms related to a particular field of study or work. An **encyclopedia** includes facts and background information on many subjects. Finally, many professional and technical organizations host websites that may be useful in defining terminology.

Practice and Apply Use context clues in the selection, as well as online and print resources, to define these terms: *air pressure* (paragraphs 2 and 6), *forward elevator* (paragraphs 2 and 14), and *airfoil* (paragraphs 7 and 9). Cite the resources you used to write your definition. Share your definitions with a classmate and compare results.

EL ENGLISH LEARNER SUPPORT

Use Resources Have students work in small groups and use resources such as dictionaries, encyclopedias, and online websites to locate information about two terms used in the selection: *soldering iron* and *galvanized iron*. Have students answer the following questions:

- What is a soldering iron?

- What is galvanized iron?

- How is *iron* used differently in these terms?

- What additional questions do you have about the terms?
  MODERATE/LIGHT

LANGUAGE CONVENTIONS:
Commas and Sentence Types

As you have learned, writers use commas to make the meaning of their sentences clear. In addition to setting off introductory elements and transition words, commas are used in a variety of sentence types. Commas are useful in **compound sentences,** or sentences that consist of two or more independent clauses. They are also needed to clarify **complex sentences,** sentences that combine an independent clause with one or more dependent clauses.

The selection uses commas in the following ways:

- To separate independent clauses in a compound sentence

  Their doubts vanished, and their faith in themselves grew.

- To separate a dependent clause from an independent clause in a complex sentence

  When their lab tests were finally completed, they felt confident that they could calculate in advance the performance of an aircraft's wings with far greater accuracy than had ever before been possible.

- To set off a transitional phrase that clarifies sequence

  At this point, things looked more promising than ever.

Practice and Apply Write your own sentences with commas, using the examples from the selection as models. Your sentences can be about how your own work habits are similar to or different from those of the Wright brothers, or your sentences may be about some other topic related to the Wright brothers. When you have finished, share your sentences with a partner and compare your use of commas.

Go to **Commas with Compound Sentences** in the **Grammar Studio** for more on commas and sentence types.

LANGUAGE CONVENTIONS:
Commas and Sentence Types

Review the two types of sentences—compound and complex—mentioned in the introductory paragraph. Emphasize that in a sentence with two independent clauses connected by a conjunction such as *and, or,* and *but*, a writer must use a comma before the conjunction. Clarify the difference between a compound sentence and a sentence with a compound subject or predicate, neither of which take commas. Stress that each independent clause of a compound sentence has its own subject and predicate.

He was excited by the result, but his brother was quiet. (compound sentence)

Orville and his brother worked together to overcome problems. (compound subject)

The brothers took every lesson as a learning experience and worked even harder than before. (compound predicate)

Discuss each example on page 403, and have students identify the use of the comma it models.

Practice and Apply Encourage students to identify other examples of comma use in the selection and record them in their journals. *(Students' sentences will vary.)*

 ENGLISH LEARNER SUPPORT

Use Commas Have students work in small groups to complete and share their original sentences using commas.

- Have students focus on writing compound sentences and sentences with transitional phrases, using frames such as: *The Wright brothers _____, but I _____. After school, I _____.* **SUBSTANTIAL/MODERATE**
- Give students simpler models to use for each type of comma use, so they can pattern their own sentences in the same way. For example: *They worked hard, and they found success. When they had problems, they kept working. After a long time, they finally achieved flight.* **LIGHT**

© Houghton Mifflin Harcourt Publishing Company

INFER AND SYNTHESIZE KEY IDEAS WITHIN AND ACROSS TEXTS

Before groups of students work on completing the table, emphasize that they are comparing the key ideas of two selections that cover the same basic events. Note that their goal is to determine one key idea the texts share. Discuss the difference between a guess and an inference, noting that the latter is a logical guess based on evidence and sound reasoning.

ANALYZE THE TEXTS

Possible answers:

1. **DOK 2:** *The graphic biography uses speech balloons for dialogue between the brothers, but the dialogue is probably not direct quotations. The traditional biography uses direct quotations from the brothers' writing.*

2. **DOK 2:** *The captions and especially the illustrations in the graphic biography—such as the facial close-ups or the boots digging into the sand—show how frustrated, yet committed, the brothers are. The traditional biography relies on direct quotes to show how the brothers felt about their work: "We doubted that we would ever resume our experiments." Both texts show that despite these frustrations, the brothers persisted in their work. The brothers were determined and committed to their work, which was very important to them.*

3. **DOK 4:** *Both genres present facts, but the traditional biography contains more text and more facts. Key ideas about difficulties the brothers faced were delivered equally well, though the traditional biography provides more textual evidence. The graphic biography effectively conveys mood and emotion through illustrations. The documentary photos in The Wright Brothers show the actual aircrafts and workroom.*

4. **DOK 4:** *Together, both sources presented the idea that when you come up against a difficult problem, you don't have to give up on it. Rather, you can look at it from another angle and try again. It helps to have a partner as committed as you are to solving the problem.*

RESPOND

from **INTO THE AIR**
Graphic Biography
by Robert Burleigh
illustrated by Bill Wylie

from **THE WRIGHT BROTHERS: HOW THEY INVENTED THE AIRPLANE**
Biography
by Russell Freedman

Collaborate & Compare

INFER AND SYNTHESIZE KEY IDEAS WITHIN AND ACROSS TEXTS

The two selections you have read focus on some of the same events in the lives of Wilbur and Orville Wright. You will now review and compare the **key ideas** you have found in these texts and **synthesize** the information to determine a key idea that the two texts share.

In this task, you will need to make inferences to determine the messages that the authors have not stated outright. An **inference** is a logical guess based on facts and your own knowledge and experience. Evidence from the text should support an inference.

In a small group, complete a chart like the one below. Analyze each scene or event listed in the first column, and infer the key ideas in each selection.

Scene/Event	Key Ideas from *Into the Air*	Key Ideas from *The Wright Brothers*
Summer 1901	The brothers think the data may be incorrect. They are discouraged.	The glider does not work. The brothers are discouraged.
Wind Tunnel Experiments	The brothers use the data from their own wind tunnel to redesign the glider.	The brothers use their own wind tunnel data for experiments. They become more confident.
Fall 1902	The brothers make successful flights. They are encouraged to continue.	The new glider works well. They are ready to build a motorized aircraft.

ANALYZE THE TEXTS

Discuss these questions in your group.

1. **Compare** Think about the Wright brothers' quotations and dialogue in each text. How are these words presented in each biography? Describe similarities and differences.

2. **Infer** What do the frustrations experienced by the brothers in the summer of 1901 say about what they were like and what was important to them? Use evidence to explain your response.

3. **Evaluate** Between the two selections, which is more effective in communicating facts? Ideas? Moods and emotions? Explain.

4. **Synthesize** What have you learned from these sources about the importance of trying hard and not giving up?

ENGLISH LEARNER SUPPORT

Ask Questions Use the following questions and sentence frames to help students compare key ideas within and across the texts:

- *What is a key idea of* Into the Air? *A key idea is _____ .*
- *What is a similar key idea of* The Wright Brothers: How They Invented the Airplane? *A similar key idea is _____ .*
- *What do these key ideas have in common? Both ideas are about _____ .*
  MODERATE/LIGHT

COMPARE KEY IDEAS

Now, your group can continue exploring the ideas in these texts by collaborating on a presentation to give to your class. Follow these steps:

1. **Gather Information** In your group, review and then list the key events that appear in both texts.

2. **Discuss** Examine the similarities and differences in how each event is presented in the texts. Ask:
   - ❏ How do the authors use **text** to describe this event?
     - ❏ Between the two selections, how is the text similar?
     - ❏ Between the two selections, how is the text different?

   - ❏ How do the authors use **images** to describe this event?
     - ❏ Between the two selections, how are the images similar?
     - ❏ Between the two selections, how are the images different?

   - ❏ What is the **key idea** of this event, as presented in each selection?
     - ❏ Between the two selections, how are the ideas similar?
     - ❏ Between the two selections, how are the ideas different?

As you discuss, remember to listen to what others say, to ask questions to request and clarify information, and to build on the ideas of others. Use the chart below to take notes. As a group, determine what you think is the main idea shared by the two selections.

Scene/Event:	
Similarities:	Differences:
Key Idea:	Key Idea:

3. **Share What You Learn** Now you can share your group's findings with the rest of the class. Begin by stating what your group thinks is the main idea expressed by the two selections. Use your notes to remember important points to talk about. Speak clearly and loudly enough for others to hear. Remember to invite the class to ask questions. Answer questions respectfully.

COMPARE KEY IDEAS

Remind students that making a group presentation involves careful planning and collaboration among group members.

1. **Gather Information** Remind students to use their Response Logs and selection annotations as they identify events that appear in both texts. Encourage students to assign roles for group members before they begin work—for example, one pair of students might identify an event in *Into the Air*, and another pair might look for a reference to it in *The Wright Brothers: How They Invented the Airplane*.

2. **Discuss** Point out the questions related to text, graphics, and key ideas on page 405. Remind students that listening carefully, asking clarifying questions, and being respectful of the ideas of others are essential to a good group discussion.

3. **Share What You Learn** Guide students to come to a consensus about what they believe is the main idea expressed by the two selections. If unanimous agreement cannot be reached, suggest that group members take a vote. Emphasize the importance of making notes or an outline for the group's presentation, collecting graphics, and practicing before the actual presentation. Encourage class discussion of outstanding questions after each presentation.

WHEN STUDENTS STRUGGLE . . .

Make a Presentation Students requiring support can benefit greatly by practicing their parts in advance of a presentation. Remind students to:

- use notes, a brief outline, and visual aids to remember key points
- assign roles for different group members before practicing
- practice making the presentation and, if possible, record it
- discuss ways to improve the presentation based on practice sessions

READER'S CHOICE

Setting a Purpose Have students review their Unit 5 Response Log and think about what they've already learned about what keeps people from giving up. As students select their Independent Reading selections, encourage them to consider what more they want to know.

NOTICE NOTE

Explain that some selections may contain multiple signposts; others may contain only one. Remind students that the same type of signpost can occur many times in the same text.

 LEARNING MINDSET

Seeking Challenges Remind students that having the willingness to seek and take on challenges is essential to having a learning mindset. In fact, overcoming challenges is key to developing skills and intelligence. Assure students that they are not expected to be perfect and that making mistakes is part of the learning process. By taking risks and trying different strategies, students can learn to overcome challenges.

 INDEPENDENT READING

? ESSENTIAL QUESTION:

What keeps people from giving up?

Reader's Choice

Setting a Purpose Select one or more of these options from your eBook to continue your exploration of the Essential Question.

- Read the descriptions to see which text grabs your interest.
- Think about which genres you enjoy reading.

Notice & Note

In this unit, you practiced asking **Big Questions** and noting two signposts: **Numbers and Stats** and **Quoted Words**. As you read independently, these signposts and others will aid your understanding. Below are the anchor questions to ask when you read literature and nonfiction.

Reading Literature: Stories, Poems, and Plays		
Signpost	**Anchor Question**	**Lesson**
Contrasts and Contradictions	Why did the character act that way?	p. 3
Aha Moment	How might this change things?	p. 3
Tough Questions	What does this make me wonder about?	p. 172
Words of the Wiser	What's the lesson for the character?	p. 2
Again and Again	Why might the author keep bringing this up?	p. 92
Memory Moment	Why is this memory important?	p. 93

Reading Nonfiction: Essays, Articles, and Arguments		
Signpost	**Anchor Question(s)**	**Lesson**
Big Questions	What surprised me?	p. 246
	What did the author think I already knew?	p. 420
	What challenged, changed, or confirmed what I already knew?	p. 332
Contrasts and Contradictions	What is the difference, and why does it matter?	p. 247
Extreme or Absolute Language	Why did the author use this language?	p. 247
Numbers and Stats	Why did the author use these numbers or amounts?	p. 333
Quoted Words	Why was this person quoted or cited, and what did this add?	p. 333
Word Gaps	Do I know this word from someplace else?	p. 421
	Does it seem like technical talk for this topic?	
	Do clues in the sentence help me understand the word?	

 ENGLISH LEARNER SUPPORT

Develop Fluency Select a passage from a text that matches students' reading abilities. Pair students with a peer on a similar reading level.

- Have students look through the text together and discuss what they think it will be about. Then have students partner read, taking turns with each paragraph or stanza. **SUBSTANTIAL**
- Have students look through the text together, looking for words with which they are unfamiliar. Then have students partner read, taking turns with each page. **MODERATE**

- Allow more fluent pairs to select their own texts. Set a specific time for students to read silently (for example, 15 minutes). Then have each pair discuss what they read. **LIGHT**

Go to the **Reading Studio** for additional support in developing fluency.

You can preview these texts in Unit 5 of your eBook.

Then, check off the text or texts that you select to read on your own.

POEM

Paul Revere's Ride

Henry Wadsworth Longfellow

Paul Revere gallops through villages all night, alerting settlers of the coming attack by the British.

POEM

The Road Not Taken

Robert Frost

How do you choose between two unknowns?

DRAMA

Damon and Pythias

dramatized by Fan Kissen

In prison, Damon waits for his best friend to return to face the consequences.

SPEECH

Education First
from **Malala's Speech to the United Nations**

Malala Yousafzai

A near fatal gunshot wound makes Malala even more committed to speaking up for change.

Collaborate and Share   With a partner discuss what you learned from at least one of your independent readings.

- Give a brief synopsis or summary of the text.

- Describe any signposts that you noticed in the text and explain what they revealed to you.

- Describe what you most enjoyed or found most challenging about the text. Give specific examples.

- Decide if you would recommend the text to others. Why or why not?

 Go to the **Reading Studio** for more resources on **Notice & Note.**

INDEPENDENT READING

MATCHING STUDENTS TO TEXTS

Use the following information to guide students in using their texts.

Paul Revere's Ride
   Genre: poem
   Overall Rating: Challenging

The Road Not Taken
   Genre: poem
   Overall Rating: Challenging

Damon and Pythias
   Genre: drama
   Overall Rating: Accessible

Education First
from **Malala's Speech to the United Nations**   Lexile: 870L
   Genre: speech
   Overall Rating: Accessible

Collaborate and Share   To assess how well students read the selections, circulate throughout the room and listen to their conversations. Encourage students to be focused and specific in their comments.

Online
 Ed   **for Assessment**

- Independent Reading Selection Tests

Encourage students to visit the **Reading Studio** to download a handy bookmark of **NOTICE & NOTE** signposts.

WHEN STUDENTS STRUGGLE . . .

Keep a Reading Log   As students read their selected texts, have them keep a reading log for each selection to note signposts and their thoughts about them. Use their logs to assess how well they are noticing and reflecting on elements of the texts.

Reading Log for (title)		
Location	**Signposts I Noticed**	**My Notes about It**

UNIT 5 Tasks

- **WRITE A BIOGRAPHICAL REPORT**
- **PRODUCE AND PRESENT A PODCAST**

MENTOR TEXT

THE WRIGHT BROTHERS: HOW THEY INVENTED THE AIRPLANE

Biography by RUSSELL FREEDMAN

LEARNING OBJECTIVES

Writing Task

- Write an introduction that has a thesis statement.
- Use primary and secondary research sources.
- Cite and use materials ethically.
- Organize information in a logical way.
- Connect related ideas effectively.
- Use appropriate word choice, voice, and tone.
- Conclude by summarizing or drawing a conclusion.
- Revise drafts, incorporating feedback from peers.
- Edit drafts to incorporate transitions.
- Use a rubric to evaluate writing.
- **Language** Use conjunctive adverbs to show relationships.

Speaking and Listening Task

- Create a podcast for an audience.
- Use appropriate tone, word choice, and organization strategy for your audience.
- Listen actively to a presentation.

Assign the Writing Task in *Ed.*

Online

RESOURCES

- Unit 5 Response Log
- Reading Studio: Notice & Note
- Writing Studio: Conducting Research; Using Textual Evidence
- Speaking and Listening Studio: Using Media in a Presentation
- Grammar Studio : Module 3: Lesson 5: The Adverb

Language X-Ray: English Learner Support

Use the instruction below and the supports and scaffolds in the Teacher's Edition to help you guide students at different proficiency levels.

INTRODUCE THE WRITING TASK

Explain that a **biographical report** is a type of writing that presents facts and information about a specific person. Point out that the word *biography* is related to the Spanish noun *biografía* which means "a true story about a person." Make sure students understand that biographical reports are based on information learned during research about a well-known person.

Remind students that the selections in this unit address what keeps people from giving up. Work with students to select a person who

does not give up to write about. Use sentence frames to help them articulate their ideas. For example: _____ *is a well-known person in history because _____.*

Brainstorm words and phrases related to the topic, and write them on the board. Then, have students work with a partner to write one sentence about why the person they are writing about did not give up. Tell students to use their sentences to begin their reports.

WRITING

Use Adverbs

Tell students that adverbs describe verbs, adjectives, and other adverbs. Adverbs often answer the questions *when*, *where*, and *how*. Conjunctive adverbs are adverbs that connect ideas, such as *also*, *however*, *next*.

Use the following supports with students at varying proficiency levels:

- Provide students with a sample informational paragraph, and work with them to underline the adverbs. Work with students to write sentences using adverbs. **SUBSTANTIAL**
- Use sentence frames to help students practice using adverbs. For example: *The woman walked _____. The man spoke _____.* **MODERATE**
- Allow students to work with a partner when writing their drafts, and have students work together to add adverbs to their writing. **LIGHT**

SPEAKING

Share Information

Tell students that one way to communicate the information in their biographical report is by using the sentence frame _____ *is important because_____.* Pair each student with a partner. Circulate around the room to make sure students are using the sentence frame correctly.

Use the following supports with students at varying proficiency levels:

- Work with students to complete the sentence frame. Have them practice saying the sentence aloud to a partner. **SUBSTANTIAL**
- Have students build on the sentence frame by adding two pieces of information from their reports. Have student pairs practice presenting their podcasts. **MODERATE**
- Have students build on the sentence frame by discussing three points that support their central idea. Then, have students practice their podcasts with a partner. **LIGHT**

WRITING

WRITE A BIOGRAPHICAL REPORT

Introduce students to the Writing Task by reading the introductory paragraph with them. Remind students to refer to the notes they recorded in the Unit 5 Response Log as they plan and draft their biographical reports. The Response Log should contain ideas about what keeps people from giving up from a variety of perspectives. Drawing on these different perspectives will make their own writing more interesting and well informed.

 For **writing support** for students at varying proficiency levels, see the **Language X-Ray** on page 408B.

USE THE MENTOR TEXT

Point out that their biographical reports will be similar to the excerpt from *The Wright Brothers: How They Invented the Airplane* in that they will present factual information about a person in history who did not give up when faced with challenges. However, their reports will be shorter than the excerpt and will draw from fewer sources.

WRITING PROMPT

Review the prompt with students. Encourage them to ask questions about any part of the assignment that is unclear. Make sure they understand that the purpose of their report is to present a well-organized report based on cited research.

Write a Biographical Report

 Go to **Conducting Research** in the **Writing Studio** for help researching and writing a report.

This unit focuses on what makes people persist, or keep trying, despite struggle and hardship. For this writing task, you will research and write a biographical report explaining why a well-known person from history refused to give up when faced with a crisis or difficult problem to solve. For an example of a well-written biography, review the mentor text from *The Wright Brothers: How They Invented the Airplane*.

As you write your report, use the notes from your Response Log, which you filled out after reading the texts in this unit.

Writing Prompt

Read the information in the box below.

This is the topic or context for your report.

> The human spirit is capable of profound resilience and a powerful drive to never give up in the face of adversity.

Think carefully about the following question.

This is the Essential Question for the unit. How would you answer this question, based on the texts in this unit?

> What keeps people from giving up?

Now mark the words that identify exactly what you are being asked to produce.

Write a biographical report explaining why a well-known person from history refused to give up.

Be sure to—

Review these points as you write and again when you finish. Make any needed changes.

- ☐ write an engaging introduction that clearly states the topic and highlights a controlling idea or thesis statement
- ☐ use primary and secondary sources in your research
- ☐ avoid plagiarism; cite and use source materials ethically
- ☐ organize information in a logical way
- ☐ connect related ideas effectively
- ☐ use appropriate word choice and a formal voice and tone
- ☐ end by summarizing ideas or drawing an overall conclusion

---

 LEARNING MINDSET

Try Again Tell students that sometimes they may think they know the answer to a question, but then find out they got it incorrect. Encourage students to go back to the text and reread until they figure it out.

① Plan

Before you start writing, plan your biographical report. Which well-known historical person will you write about? Follow these preliminary steps and use a table like the one below to keep research notes.

❏ Think of questions you have about this person, related to the topic of never giving up; focus your research on answering these questions.

❏ Conduct research, using primary and secondary sources. Keep track of where you get your information so that you can cite it correctly.

Research Notes
Questions I have about this person:
Source: title; author; page number; date; url, if source is online
Notes:
Source: title; author; page number; date; url, if source is online
Notes:
Source: title; author; page number; date; url, if source is online
Notes:

List your sources at the end of the report or cite them in footnotes, using the style your teacher prefers. If you quote directly from a source, cite it in the report and use quotation marks. Otherwise, put information in your own words, paraphrasing to avoid plagiarism.

Background Reading Review the notes you took in your Response Log after reading the texts in this unit. These texts are the background reading that will help you formulate the key ideas you will include in your biographical report.

Go to **Conducting Research: Introduction** for help planning your research.

PRIMARY SOURCES
- letters and diaries
- autobiographies
- eyewitness accounts

SECONDARY SOURCES
- biographies
- news articles
- textbooks
- encyclopedias

Notice & Note

From Reading to Writing

As you plan your report, apply what you've learned about signposts to your own writing. Remember that writers use common features, called signposts, to help convey their message to readers. Think about how you can incorporate **Numbers and Stats** into your report.

Go to the **Reading Studio** for more resources on **Notice & Note.**

Use the notes from your **Response Log** as you plan your report.

---

① PLAN

Allow time for students to discuss the subject of their biographies with partners or in small groups and then to complete the research notes table independently.

■ English Learner Support

Understand Academic Language Make sure students understand words and phrases used in the chart, such as *source, title, author,* and *url*. Work with them to find the pertinent information in their research sources, and copy the information into the chart. **SUBSTANTIAL**

▶ NOTICE & NOTE

From Reading to Writing Explain to students that **Numbers and Stats** are often used to add precision. Encourage students to use numerical data to quantify specific information about the subject of their biographical report.

Background Reading As they plan their reports, remind students to refer to the notes they took in the Response Log. They may also review the selections to find additional examples of biographical texts.

TO CHALLENGE STUDENTS . . .

Conduct Additional Research Challenge students to incorporate more than three sources of information into their report. Encourage students to look for primary documents related to their historical figure, as well as high-quality secondary sources. Remind students to put any directly quoted information in quotation marks and to document their sources.

WRITING

Organize Your Ideas Tell students that their outlines may have one main section for each paragraph of the report. Provide the following sample based on the chart:

I.   Introduction

II. Childhood and Early Life

III. Main Events and Struggles

IV. Accomplishments

V.   Conclusion

Remind students that the introduction should include their thesis statement or central idea. Each supporting paragraph should build a logical argument that supports the thesis with evidence. The conclusion should then briefly summarize the ideas or draw an overall conclusion based on the information presented in the report.

② DEVELOP A DRAFT

Remind students to follow their outlines as they draft their reports, but point out that they can still make changes to their writing plan during this stage. As they write, they may discover that they need different information to support the thesis, or that a particular piece of information really belongs in a different paragraph.

■ English Learner Support

Use a Word Wall Allow students to use a word wall, dictionary, or other print resources when writing their reports. **MODERATE**

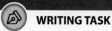 **WRITING TASK**

 Go to the **Using Textual Evidence: Writing an Outline** in the **Writing Studio** for help organizing your ideas.

Organize Your Ideas The next step in planning is to create an outline. The outline helps you organize the information you have collected and prepares you for writing your rough draft. Since you are writing a biographical report, organize your notes chronologically—the order in which events took place. Use the table below to help you plan your draft.

Biographical Report Outline	
Purpose of report; audience	
Introduction: background on subject and controlling idea or thesis	
Childhood and early life related to controlling idea or thesis	
Main events, struggles	
Accomplishments and ideas from background reading	
Conclusion	

② Develop a Draft

You might prefer to draft your biographical report online.

Once you have completed your planning activities, you will be ready to write the rough draft of your biographical report. Refer to your research notes and the outline you have created, as well as to any notes you took as you studied the texts in the unit. These will provide a kind of map for you to follow as you write. Using a word processor or online writing application makes it easier to make changes or move sentences around later when you are ready to revise your first draft.

WHEN STUDENTS STRUGGLE...

Draft the Report Remind students that a detailed outline will make it easier to write their drafts. Students can then use the notes from their outline to write complete sentences and create the first drafts of their reports. Remind students that a first draft is not meant to be perfect. At this stage, they are just getting their ideas down on paper (or on the computer screen). They will have time to revise and edit their writing later.

Use the Mentor Text

Author's Craft

Authors use descriptive language and details to chronicle the steps leading up to a major accomplishment, including struggles and obstacles faced along the way. This method is an effective way to communicate what it means to never give up and to achieve something important or overcome a crisis.

> Using tin shears, hammers, files, and a soldering iron, the brothers fashioned as many as two hundred miniature wings out of tin, galvanized iron, steel, solder, and wax.

Specific details create a vivid sense of how the Wright brothers struggled to find the right design.

Apply What You've Learned To hold your reader's attention, use descriptive details to communicate how the subject of your report overcame obstacles on the way to achieving success.

Primary and Secondary Sources

Writers of biographies and other nonfiction texts depend on reliable primary, or firsthand, and secondary, or secondhand, sources for their information. Readers have confidence that the text is accurate when writers cite their sources. Readers also refer to these sources if they want more information about a topic or if they want proof that a source is dependable.

> With growing anticipation, Wilbur and Orville prepared for their 1902 trip to the Outer Banks. "They really ought to get away for a while," Katharine wrote to her father.

The writer paraphrases, or puts in his own words, information in the first sentence. He quotes a letter, which is a primary source, in the second sentence.

Apply What You've Learned. When you copy text from a source exactly as it's written, put it in quotes. Otherwise, readers will think you wrote it yourself, and that is plagiarism. Most of the time you will restate information and put it in your own words. Whether you are quoting directly or paraphrasing, cite and list your sources according to the style your teacher prefers.

WHY THIS MENTOR TEXT?

The excerpt from Russell Freedman's *The Wright Brothers: How They Invented the Airplane* provides good examples of using descriptive language and details, along with primary and secondary sources. Use the instruction below to help students use the mentor text as a model for using descriptive language and for integrating relevant primary and secondary sources into their biographical reports.

USE THE MENTOR TEXT

Author's Craft Ask a volunteer to read aloud the top paragraph from *The Wright Brothers: How They Invented the Airplane*. Discuss which descriptive details the author uses to show how the Wright brothers overcame a challenge. Then invite students to write some examples of descriptive details that they could use in their biographical reports.

Primary and Secondary Sources To help students understand how primary and secondary sources can enhance their report, have them read the bottom paragraph from *The Wright Brothers: How They Invented the Airplane*. Point out that the author combines information from both primary and secondary sources to show the Wright brothers going to the Outer Banks of North Carolina. Invite students to examine their primary and secondary sources to see how they can be used in their biographical reports.

ENGLISH LEARNER SUPPORT

Use the Mentor Text Use the following supports with students at varying proficiency levels:

- Write the words *primary* and *secondary* on the board. Explain to students that *primary* means "first" and *secondary* means "second." Use these definitions to explain the difference in primary and secondary sources to students. **SUBSTANTIAL**

- Have students work in pairs to reread the mentor text and identify descriptive words and details the author uses. **MODERATE**

- Have students work in small groups or pairs to create word maps of descriptive words and phrases to use in their reports. **LIGHT**

WRITING

 3 REVISE

Have students answer each question in the chart to determine how they can improve their drafts. Invite volunteers to model their revision techniques.

With a Partner Have students ask peer reviewers to evaluate their descriptive details and relevant facts by answering the following questions:

- How well do the facts support the thesis?
- How well do the descriptive details help the reader see what is occurring?

Students should use the reviewer's feedback to add relevant facts and descriptive details that support their thesis.

 **WRITING TASK**

3 Revise

 Go to **Using Textual Evidence: Attribution** in the **Writing Studio** the for help with citing sources.

On Your Own Once you have written your draft, go back and look for ways to improve your biographical report. As you reread and revise, think about whether you have achieved your purpose. The Revision Guide focuses on specific elements to make your writing stronger.

Revision Guide		
Ask Yourself	**Tips**	**Revision Techniques**
1. Does my introduction describe the subject's background?	**Mark** the introduction.	**Add** an interesting fact, example, or quotation that describes the subject's background.
2. Do I use descriptive details and relevant, interesting facts?	**Mark** each descriptive detail and fact.	**Replace** words and phrases with more vivid details and interesting facts.
3. Are events arranged in chronological order?	**Mark** each event.	**Reorder** events if necessary.
4. Do I use transitions between ideas effectively so that events are connected?	**Mark** transitional words and phrases.	**Include** appropriate transitional words to smooth and clarify the flow of information.
5. Do I cite sources correctly and use source materials ethically?	**Mark** facts, examples, and quotations.	**Add** academic citations according to your teacher's preference, indicating the source for each piece of information.
6. Does my conclusion convey how never giving up was the key to the subject's accomplishments?	**Mark** the conclusion.	**Add** a reflection on why never giving up was pivotal to the subject's success.

ACADEMIC VOCABULARY
As you conduct your **peer review,** be sure to use these words.

- ❏ achieve
- ❏ individual
- ❏ instance
- ❏ outcome
- ❏ principle

With a Partner Once you and your partner have worked through the Revision Guide on your own, exchange papers and evaluate each other's draft in a **peer review.** Focus on providing revision suggestions for at least three of the items mentioned in the chart. Explain why you think your partner's draft should be revised and what your specific suggestions are.

When receiving feedback from your partner, listen attentively and ask questions to make sure you fully understand the revision suggestions.

 ENGLISH LEARNER SUPPORT

Use Transitional Words Explain that writers use transitional words and phrases to smooth the flow of a report. Have students read their reports and look for transitional words and phrases. Encourage students to revise their reports to incorporate more transitional words and phrases. **LIGHT**

4 Edit

Once you have addressed the organization, development, and flow of ideas in your draft, you are ready to improve its finer points. Edit for the proper use of standard English conventions and correct any misspellings or grammatical errors. Ensure that the tone of your report is formal.

Language Conventions

Adverbs describe verbs, adjectives, and other adverbs by telling *where, when, how,* or *to what extent*. Examples of adverbs include *very, now,* and *slowly*.

Conjunctive adverbs often connect two independent clauses to show that the second clause relates to the first. They can also be used in a single clause (sentence). *Conjunctive* means joining or connecting. Examples of conjunctive adverbs include *consequently, finally, then, furthermore, however,* and *nevertheless*. Punctuation sets conjunctive adverbs off: a semicolon before and a comma after when connecting two independent clauses, and a comma before and after when used within a single clause. Here are some examples:

- **Single clause:** The manager, **however,** maintains that he kept his promise to stay within the budget.
- **Two independent clauses:** The pepperoni pizza was the best I've ever had; **nevertheless,** I like plain cheese pizza even more.

Writers use adverbs and conjunctive adverbs to add variety and nuance, or shades of meaning, to their sentences.

The chart shows examples from *The Wright Brothers: How They Invented the Airplane*.

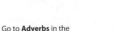 Go to **Adverbs** in the **Grammar Studio** to learn more about adverbs.

	Example
Adverb	<u>Gradually</u> they replaced the calculations of others with their own.
Conjunctive Adverb	"With this improvement our serious troubles ended . . . <u>thereafter,</u> we devoted ourselves to the work of gaining skill by continued practice."

5 Publish

After you have given your biographical report its finishing touches, choose a way to share it with your audience. Options include presenting your report as a speech to the class, or posting it as a blog on a classroom or school website.

WHEN STUDENTS STRUGGLE . . .

Identify Adverbs   Some students may have difficulty identifying the adverbs in sentences. Remind students that an adverb describes a verb, adjective, or other adverb. Allow students to use a highlighter to highlight the adverbs in their report. Some students may benefit from working with a partner or adult helper to identify the adverbs in their report.

4 EDIT

Suggest that students read their drafts aloud to assess how clearly and smoothly they have presented their ideas. If the text sounds disjointed, students should check that they have consistently used transitional words and phrases throughout their report.

LANGUAGE CONVENTIONS

Adverbs and Conjunctive Adverbs   Review the information about adverbs and conjunctive adverbs with students. Then discuss the example sentences in the chart, asking students to identify the adverbs and conjunctive adverbs in each one. To emphasize the importance of adverbs, rewrite the sentences without any adverbs. Read the sentences aloud so students can see and hear the difference. Have students look for adverbs in their reports and add adverbs and conjunctive adverbs where needed.

■ English Learner Support

Use Adverbs   Have students work in pairs to locate the adverbs and conjunctive adverbs in their reports. Have students work together to check that adverbs are used correctly and to add more adverbs to their reports as needed. **MODERATE**

5 PUBLISH

Have students publish their reports on the classroom blog. Additionally, you may want to consider hosting a parent night at which students dress as their historical figure and tell parents about him or her.

WRITING

USE THE SCORING GUIDE

Have students read the scoring guide and ask questions about any words, phrases, or ideas that are unclear. Put students in groups of three. Then have students take turns reading the final drafts of their group members' biographical reports. Ask them to score the reports using the scoring guide. Each student should write a paragraph explaining the reasons for the score he or she awarded in each category.

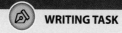 **WRITING TASK**

Use the scoring guide to evaluate your biographical report.

Writing Task Scoring Guide: Biographical Report		
Organization/Progression	**Development of Ideas**	**Use of Language and Conventions**
4 • The organization is smooth, effective and logical; events are organized chronologically. • All ideas are focused on the topic specified in the prompt. • Background information helps identify an individual and explain events. • Transitions logically connect events in sequence. • All research sources are cited correctly.	• The introduction catches the reader's attention and clearly identifies the historical figure/subject. • The report contains a clear, concise, and well-defined thesis statement or controlling idea. • The events are supported by specific and well-chosen facts, details, quotations, etc. • The conclusion reflects on the significance of never giving up as a key factor in the historical figure's accomplishments.	• Tone is appropriately formal. • Descriptive language and varied sentence structures make the report appealing and interesting. • Spelling, grammar, usage, and mechanics are correct. • Adverbs and conjunctive adverbs are used correctly and effectively.
3 • The organization is appropriate to the purpose; events are organized chronologically. • Most ideas are focused on the topic specified in the prompt. • More background information would help identify the individual and explain events. • A few more transitions are needed to logically connect events. • Most research sources are cited correctly.	• The introduction could be more engaging. The historical figure/subject is identified. • The report contains a clear thesis statement or controlling idea. • The events are supported by facts, details, quotations, etc. • The conclusion indicates the role of never giving up in the historical figure's accomplishments.	• Tone is usually appropriate and formal. • Language is usually descriptive and there is some variation in sentence structure. • Spelling, grammar, usage, and mechanics are mostly correct. • Adverbs and conjunctive adverbs are correctly used most of the time.
2 • The organization is confusing; missing or extraneous events are distracting. • Only some ideas are focused on the topic specified in the prompt. • Not enough background information is given to explain events. • More transitions are needed to logically connect events. • Not all research sources are cited.	• The introduction is not engaging and does not provide a clear picture of the historical figure. • The thesis statement or controlling idea is unclear. • The events are not well supported by facts, details, quotations, etc. • The conclusion is only partially effective.	• Tone is inconsistent and sometimes too casual. • Language is not descriptive and sentence structure lacks variation. • Spelling, grammar, usage, and mechanics are not always correct. • Adverbs and conjunctive adverbs are not always used correctly.
1 • Events are out of sequence and disorganized. • Ideas are not focused on the topic specified in the prompt. • Background information is nonexistent. • No transitions are used, making the report difficult to understand. • Research sources are not cited.	• The introduction is confusing. • The thesis statement or controlling idea is missing. • Supporting facts, details, examples, or quotations are unreliable, vague, or missing. • The conclusion does not connect never giving up to the historical person's accomplishments.	• Tone is inappropriate and too casual. • Language is vague and confusing. • Many spelling, capitalization, and punctuation errors are present. • Many grammatical and usage errors confuse the writer's ideas. • Adverbs and conjunctive adverbs are misused or missing.

Produce and Present a Podcast

You will now turn your biographical report into an audio podcast to present to your classmates. You will also listen to their podcasts, ask questions, and help them make improvements.

 Go to the **Speaking and Listening Studio: Using Media in a Presentation** for help planning and crafting your podcast.

1 Develop a Script

First, craft a script from your biographical report. You want to make the same points, but your script will be shorter than your report, so choose facts and details that will be interesting to hear, rather than read.

2 Plan Your Podcast

Use the planning chart below to write a script based on your biographical report and to record an engaging audio podcast.

Podcast Planning Chart		
Write a Script	How will you write your script to appeal to listeners? How will you repurpose the report to sound natural and convincing when you read your script aloud?	
Audience	In a spoken medium, you reach your audience in a more personal way than in a report. How will you connect with your listeners?	
Effective Language and Organization	Which parts of your report can be simplified for your podcast? How should the descriptions change for reading aloud and creating impressions through your voice?	
Practice and Revise	Do you sound natural and knowledgeable? Practice reading your script aloud; revise until you are satisfied with how it sounds.	

PRODUCE AND PRESENT A PODCAST

Introduce students to the Speaking and Listening Task by listening to excerpts from some podcasts. Point out that a podcast requires the speaker to draw the listener into the story. Thus, it is important to use descriptive language and a tone that will appeal to the audience. Have students consider how they may need to adapt their biographical reports to appeal to a listener.

1 DEVELOP A SCRIPT

Have students read the questions in the chart. Then work with the class to list some general principles for adapting a report for a podcast. (**Examples:** *Use words that will appeal to the audience. Use an expressive tone of voice.*)

2 PLAN YOUR PODCAST

Point out that aurally engaging the audience will be the key to an interesting podcast. Unlike videos, podcasts rely solely on what the audience can hear.

For **speaking support** for students at varying proficiency levels, see the **Language X-Ray** on page 408B.

EL ENGLISH LEARNER SUPPORT

Adapt the Essay Use the following supports with students at varying proficiency levels:

- Help students identify several key sentences in their reports. Then have them include the sentences in their podcast scripts. **SUBSTANTIAL**
- Review the questions in the chart to ensure students' understanding. Then have students work in pairs to apply the questions to their reports. **MODERATE**
- Have students discuss the questions in the chart with partners before writing their answers independently. **LIGHT**

SPEAKING AND LISTENING

③ PRACTICE WITH A PARTNER OR GROUP

Review the information and tips with the class, ensuring that all the terms and ideas are clear. Remind students that the purpose of practicing their podcasts is to gain useful feedback from their peers. Emphasize that speaking before a group makes most people nervous, so everyone should be as supportive and helpful as possible.

④ RECORD AND PRESENT YOUR PODCAST

Set aside time for all students to record their podcasts. When everyone has finished, create a center for students to listen to their classmates' podcasts, and ask students to share their thoughts on how their classmates' feedback helped them improve their performance.

 **SPEAKING AND LISTENING TASK**

As you work to improve your podcast, follow discussion rules:

- ❏ listen closely to each other
- ❏ don't interrupt
- ❏ stay on topic
- ❏ ask only helpful, relevant questions
- ❏ provide only clear, thoughtful, and direct answers

③ Practice with a Partner or Group

Once you've completed a satisfactory draft of your script, practice it aloud with a partner or group to improve it. Consider the following points to create an engaging podcast.

Effective Script-Writing Techniques

- ❏ **Outline** Create an outline to help you organize the events and key information in your script.
- ❏ **Spoken Word** A script is different from a report or essay in that it is spoken aloud. Keep your sentences conversational, as if you are talking to a friend, using appropriate language.
- ❏ **Transitions** Remember to use transitional words such as *first, next, consequently,* and *finally,* to make your script flow naturally between ideas and events.
- ❏ **Tell a Story** A good script tells a story that entertains and engages your audience.

Effective Verbal Techniques

- ❏ **Enunciation** Replace words that you stumble over, and rearrange sentences so that your delivery is smooth.
- ❏ **Voice Modulation and Pitch** Use your voice to display enthusiasm and emphasis.
- ❏ **Speaking Rate** Speak slowly enough that listeners understand you. Pause now and then to let them consider important points.
- ❏ **Volume** Remember to maintain a volume that is loud enough for listeners to hear every word easily.

Provide and Consider Advice for Improvement

As a listener, pay close attention. Take notes about ways that presenters can improve their scripts and more effectively use verbal techniques. Paraphrase and summarize each presenter's key ideas and main points to confirm your understanding, and ask questions to clarify any confusing ideas.

As a presenter, listen closely to questions and consider ways to revise your script to make sure your points are clear and logically sequenced. Remember to ask for suggestions about how you might change your script to make your podcast clearer and more interesting.

④ Record and Present Your Podcast

Use the advice you received during practice and record your podcast. Then, play your finished podcast for your classmates.

WHEN STUDENTS STRUGGLE . . .

Provide Feedback If students have difficulty providing feedback, provide some sentence frames for students to use as starters. For example: *My favorite part of the podcast was _____. I had trouble understanding _____. I learned that _____.*

Reflect on the Unit

By completing your biographical report, you have created a writing product that pulls together and expresses your thoughts about the reading you have done in this unit. Now is a good time to reflect on what you have learned.

Reflect on the Essential Question

- How did the people you read about in this unit shed light on why people don't give up? What did they have in common, and how are they different in the way they handled adversity and crisis?

- What are some examples from the texts you've read that show what keeps people from giving up?

Reflect on Your Reading

- Of the people you read about in this unit, who inspired you the most, and why?

- Consider one of the texts you read. If you had been in the situation described in the text, would you have persisted or would you have given up? Explain your answer.

Reflect on the Writing Task

- How did you choose a person from history to write about?

- What was your strategy for conveying this person's story as effectively as possible?

- What was challenging about using primary and secondary sources?

Reflect on the Speaking and Listening Task

- What did you change about your report to turn it into a script?

- What qualities do the best podcasts share?

UNIT 5 SELECTIONS
- "A Schoolgirl's Diary" from *I Am Malala*
- "The First Day of School"
- "Speech to the Young: Speech to the Progress-Toward"
- *Into the Air*
- *The Wright Brothers: How They Invented the Airplane*

REFLECT ON THE UNIT

Have students reflect on the questions independently and write some notes in response to each one. Then have students meet with partners or in small groups to discuss their reflections. Circulate during these discussions to identify the questions that are generating the liveliest conversations. Wrap up with a whole-class discussion focused on these questions.

LEARNING MINDSET

Questioning   Reinforce that asking questions is about being open to new ideas and trying new things. Encourage students to always feel comfortable asking questions. When students get stuck, encourage them to question how they arrived at their answer and consider whether they can try a different way. Compliment students' questions and mention how asking questions shows curiosity and leads to learning new things.

UNIT 6

Instructional Overview and Resources

	Instructional Focus	Resources
Unit Instruction **Hidden Truths**	Unit 6 Essential Question Unit 6 Academic Vocabulary	**Stream to Start:** Hidden Truths **Unit 6 Response Log**

ANALYZE & APPLY

from *Storytelling*
Book Introduction by Josepha Sherman
Lexile 1050L

NOTICE & NOTE READING MODEL

Signposts
• Big Questions
• Word Gaps
• Quoted Words

Reading
• Analyze Characteristics of Informational Texts
• Make Inferences About Key Ideas

Writing: Write a Speech

Speaking and Listening: Discuss with a Small Group

Vocabulary: Context Clues

Language Conventions: Complex Sentences

 Audio

Reading Studio: Notice & Note

Level Up Tutorial: Prose Forms

Writing Studio: Using Textual Evidence

Speaking and Listening Studio: Participating in Collaborative Discussions

Vocabulary Studio: Context Clues

Grammar Studio: Module 1, Lesson 10: Sentence Types

The Prince and the Pauper
by Mark Twain
dramatized by Joellen Bland

Reading
• Analyze How Playwrights Develop Characters
• Create Mental Images to Deepen Understanding

Writing: Write a Character Study

Speaking and Listening: Dramatic Reading

Vocabulary: Resources

Language Conventions: Prepositions and Prepositional Phrases

 Audio

Text in Focus: Reading Stage Directions

Close Read Screencast: Modeled Discussion

Reading Studio: Notice & Note

Level Up Tutorial: Elements of Drama

Writing Studio: Using Textual Evidence

Speaking and Listening Studio: Giving a Presentation

Vocabulary Studio: Resources

Grammar Studio: Module 3: Lessons 6–7: The Preposition

COLLABORATE & COMPARE

"Archetype"
Poem by Margarita Engle

"Fairy-Tale Logic"
Poem by A.E. Stallings

Reading
• Analyze the Effect of Meter and Structural Elements in Poems
• Make Connections

Writing: Paraphrase Lines in a Poem

Speaking and Listening: Have a Group Discussion

Audio

Reading Studio: Notice & Note

Level Up Tutorial: Myths, Legends, and Tales

Writing Studio: Using Textual Evidence

Speaking and Listening Studio: Collaborative Discussion

SUGGESTED PACING:
30 DAYS

Unit Introduction	*from* Storytelling	The Prince and the Pauper	Archetype/Fairy-Tale Logic
1	2 3 4 5	6 7 8 9 10 11	12 13 14 15 16

English Learner Support		Differentiated Instruction	Online Ed Assessment
• Learn New Expressions • Use Learning Strategies			
• Text X-Ray • Understand Text Evidence • Use Cognates • Understand Cause and Effect • Understand Context Clues	• Confirm Understanding • Oral Assessment • Discuss with a Small Group • Vocabulary Strategy • Language Conventions	**When Students Struggle** • Use Strategies • Visualize	**Selection Test**
• Text X-Ray • Introduce the Cast of Characters • Use Cognates • Understand Plot • Recognize Dialogue • Practice Prepositions • Act It Out • Use Pictorial Support • Support Comprehension	• Pantomime Actions • Make a Storyboard • Support Comprehension • Acquire Vocabulary • Support Comprehension • Oral Assessment • Stage a Dramatic Reading • Use Resources • Practice with Prepositional Phrases	**When Students Struggle** • Sketch to Stretch	**Selection Test**
• Text X-Ray • Explore Rhythm • Make Connections • Oral Assessment		**When Students Struggle** • Make Connections	**Selection Tests**
• Analyze Meter and Structure • Oral Assessment • Use Cognates			

The Boatman's Flute / The Mouse Bride **Independent Reading** **End of Unit**

17 18 19 20 21 22 23 24 25   26 27   28 29 30

UNIT 6 Continued

Instructional Focus

COLLABORATE & COMPARE

Collaborate and Compare	**Reading:** Infer Themes Within and Across Texts **Speaking and Listening:** Compare Themes	**Speaking and Listening Studio:** Collaborative Discussion
"The Boatman's Flute" Folktale retold by Sherry Garland Lexile 1050L	**Reading** • Analyze Plot • Identify Point of View **Writing:** A Different Point of View **Speaking and Listening:** Share Your Writing **Vocabulary:** Word Structure **Language Conventions:** Quotation Marks	🔊 **Audio** **Reading Studio:** Notice & Note **Writing Studio:** Writing Narratives **Speaking and Listening Studio:** Giving a Presentation **Vocabulary Studio:** Analyzing Word Structure **Grammar Studio:** Module 13, Lessons 1–2: Using Quotation Marks
MENTOR TEXT **"The Mouse Bride"** Folktale retold by Heather Forest Lexile 780L	**Reading** • Infer Theme • Analyze Purpose and Text Structure **Writing:** Write an Analytical Essay **Speaking and Listening:** Present and Discuss **Vocabulary:** Context Clues **Language Conventions:** Adjectives and Adverbs	🔊 **Audio** **Reading Studio:** Notice & Note **Writing Studio:** Using Textual Evidence **Speaking and Listening Studio:** Collaborative Discussion **Vocabulary Studio:** Context Clues **Grammar Studio:** Module 2, Lesson 3: Adjectives; Module 3, Lesson 5: Adverbs
Collaborate and Compare	**Reading:** Compare Themes **Speaking and Listening:** Compare and Present	

Online **Ed** INDEPENDENT READING

The independent Reading selections are only available in the eBook. 📖 Go to the Reading Studio for more information on Notice & Note.	"The Golden Serpent" Fable retold by Walter Dean Myers Lexile 470L	"Echo and Narcissus " Folktale retold by Lancelyn Green Lexile 1100L

END OF UNIT

Writing Task: Short Story **Reflect on the Unit**	**Writing:** Write a Short Story **Language Conventions:** Style, Word Choice, and Sentence Variety	**Unit 6 Response Log** **Mentor Texts:** "The Mouse Bride" **Writing Studio:** Writing Narratives **Reading Studio:** Notice & Note **Grammar Studio:** Module 1, Lesson 10: Kinds of Sentences

English Learner Support		Differentiated Instruction	Online Ed Assessment
• Practice Plurals		**When Students Struggle** • Infer Themes Within and Across Texts	
• Text X-Ray • Analyze Plot • Use Cognates • Analyze Plot • Identify Point of View	• Understand Dialogue • Use Graphic Organizers • Oral Assessment • Use Critical Vocabulary • Use Quotation Marks	**When Students Struggle** • Focus on Figurative Language	**Selection Test**
• Text X-Ray • Read Charts • Use Cognates • Establish Time and Place • Read Dialogue • Use Adverbs	• Practice Using Time Idioms • Use Noun Phrases with Modifiers • Oral Assessment • Use Context Clues • Use Adjectives and Adverbs	**When Students Struggle** • Time Phrases and Transitions	**Selection Test**
• Ask Questions • Prepare a Presentation			
"The Fisherman and the Chamberlain" Folktale retold by Jane Yolen **Lexile 620L**		"Urban Legends, Suburban Myths" Informational Text by Robert T. Carroll **Lexile 1060L**	**Selection Tests**
• Language X-Ray • Understand Academic Language • Use a Word Wall	• Use the Mentor Text • Use Vivid Vocabulary • Use Pronouns	**When Students Struggle** • Draft the Short Story • Identify Tone **To Challenge Students** • Explore Narrative Perspectives	**Unit Test**

Connect to the
ESSENTIAL QUESTION

Ask a volunteer to read aloud the Essential Question. Discuss how the images on page 418 relate to the question. What do you think the doorway and the light symbolize? How are the dancers portraying a hidden truth? Ask students to think about what hidden truths about people and the world are revealed in stories.

■ English Learner Support

Learn New Expressions Make sure students understand the Essential Question. If necessary, explain the following expressions:

- *Hidden truth* means "something that is true but not obviously seen or observed."
- *Revealed* means "to make known."

Help students restate the question in simpler language: How and what can we learn about our world through stories? **SUBSTANTIAL**

DISCUSS THE QUOTATION

Tell students that Harold Goddard (1878–1950) was a well-known college English professor. Dr. Goddard specialized in the works of Shakespeare. Ask students to read the quotation. Then discuss why Harold Goddard believes that stories are more powerful than battles. Discuss how stories can be powerful. Ask students whether they agree with Goddard, and have them explain their answers.

HIDDEN TRUTHS

 ESSENTIAL QUESTION:

What hidden truths about people and the world are revealed in stories?

> " The destiny of the world is determined less by battles that are lost and won than by the stories it loves and believes in. "
>
> Harold Goddard

418   Unit 6

⚙ LEARNING MINDSET

Growth Mindset Remind students that a growth mindset means believing you can get smarter by taking on challenges and pushing yourself. Encourage students to look at every selection as an opportunity to set higher goals and stretch past their comfort zone.

ACADEMIC VOCABULARY

Academic Vocabulary words are words you use when you discuss and write about texts. In this unit you will practice and learn five words.

☑ emphasize ☐ occur ☐ period ☐ relevant ☐ tradition

Study the Word Network to learn more about the word **emphasize**.

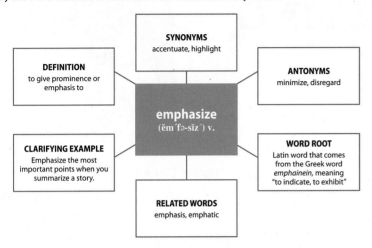

SYNONYMS
accentuate, highlight

DEFINITION
to give prominence or emphasis to

ANTONYMS
minimize, disregard

emphasize
(ĕm´fə-sīz´) v.

CLARIFYING EXAMPLE
Emphasize the most important points when you summarize a story.

WORD ROOT
Latin word that comes from the Greek word *emphainein*, meaning "to indicate, to exhibit"

RELATED WORDS
emphasis, emphatic

Write and Discuss Discuss the completed Word Network with a partner, making sure to talk through all of the boxes until you both understand the word, its synonyms, antonyms, and related forms. Then, fill out Word Networks for the remaining four words. Use a dictionary or online resource to help you complete the activity.

 Go online to access the Word Networks.

RESPOND TO THE ESSENTIAL QUESTION

In this unit, you will read stories about behaviors and traits common in people the world over. As you read, you will revisit the **Essential Question** and gather your ideas about it in the **Response Log** that appears on page R6. At the end of the unit, you will have the opportunity to write a **short story** or **folktale** that communicates a message about life or human nature. Filling out the Response Log will help you prepare for this writing task.

 You can also go online to access the Response Log.

UNIT 6
RESPONSE LOG

Essential Question:
What hidden truths about people and the world are revealed in stories?

from Storytelling	
The Prince and the Pauper	
Archetype	
Fairy-tale Logic	
The Boatman's Flute	
The Mouse Bride	

ACADEMIC VOCABULARY

As students complete Word Networks for the remaining four vocabulary words, encourage them to include all the categories shown in the completed network, if possible, but point out that some words do not have clear synonyms or antonyms. Some words may also function as different parts of speech—for example, *period* may be a noun or an adjective.

emphasize (ĕm´fə-sīz´) *v.* To give prominence or emphasis to

occur (ə-kûr´) *intr. v.* To take place (Spanish cognate: *ocurrir*)

period (pîr´ē-əd) *n.* An interval of time characterized by a specific condition, culture, or event (Spanish cognate: *periodo*)

relevant (rĕl´ə-vənt) *adj.* Having a bearing on or a connection with the matter at hand (Spanish cognate: *relevante*)

tradition (trə-dĭsh´ən) *n.* A set of beliefs or customs that have been handed down for generations (Spanish cognate: *tradición*)

RESPOND TO THE ESSENTIAL QUESTION

Direct students to the Unit 6 Response Log. Explain that students will use it to record ideas and details from the selections that help answer the Essential Question. When they work on the writing task at the end of the unit, their Response Logs will help them think about what they have read and make connections between texts.

 ENGLISH LEARNER SUPPORT

Learning Strategies Use this strategy to help students learn essential language and encourage collaborative discussion:

- Display the Essential Question.
- Tell students to examine the question and consider possible responses to it. Ask students to write answers to the question.
- Pair students and ask them to share their thoughts with their partners. Remind pairs to ask each other clarifying questions as they discuss

their responses. When students finish, have them revise their written responses to reflect any changes to their ideas that may have arisen during discussion.

- Have students share their revised answers with the entire class.
  MODERATE/LIGHT

READING MODEL

from **STORYTELLING**

Book Introduction by Josepha Sherman

GENRE ELEMENTS
BOOK INTRODUCTION

Remind students that a **book introduction** always precedes the main text. Its function is to introduce readers to the author's ideas and the purpose of the text. Just as in other informational texts, a book introduction includes key ideas from the text that are supported by evidence.

LEARNING OBJECTIVES

- Analyze the characteristics and structures of informational text.
- Make inferences about key ideas.
- Research guidelines for expressive storytelling.
- Write a speech about the importance of storytelling.
- Engage in a group discussion about the selection's key ideas.
- Use context clues to determine the meaning of unknown words.
- **Language** With a partner, tell a story based on an image.

TEXT COMPLEXITY

Quantitative Measures	*from* **Storytelling**		Lexile: 1050L
Qualitative Measures	**Ideas Presented** Much is explicit, but moves to some implied meaning.		
	Structures Used Largely conventional with some variations.		
	Language Used Some inference is demanded.		
	Knowledge Required Some complexity of theme.		

RESOURCES

- Unit 6 Response Log

- Selection Audio

- Reading Studio: Notice & Note

- Level Up Tutorial: Prose Forms

- Writing Studio: Using Textual Evidence

- Speaking and Listening Studio: Participating in Collaborative Discussions

- Vocabulary Studio: Context Clues

- Grammar Studio: Module 1: Lesson 10: Sentence Types

- "Storytelling" Selection Test

SUMMARIES

English

Telling and listening to stories is a universal experience across all cultures and time periods. The process of telling stories creates a bonding experience for the storyteller and the audience. Families and communities often connect their history with stories they told and heard. Stories can be used for educational purposes, to pass on traditions, and to encourage empathy and emotional growth in the listener.

Spanish

Contar y escuchar historias es una experiencia universal que se extiende a través de culturas y épocas. El proceso de contar historias crea una experiencia de unión entre el narrador y el público. Familias y comunidades conectan su historia con otras historias que han contado y escuchado. Las historias pueden servir para educar, para pasar tradiciones y para estimular la empatía y el crecimiento emocional del oyente.

SMALL-GROUP OPTIONS

Have students work in small groups to read and discuss the selection.

Reciprocal Teaching

- After students have read *Storytelling,* present the class with a list of generic question stems.

- Have students work individually to use the question stems to write three to five questions about the text.

- Group students into learning groups of up to three students.

- Each student offers two questions for discussion without duplicating other students' questions.

- The group reaches consensus on the answer to each question and finds text evidence to support it.

Think-Pair-Share

- After students have read and analyzed *Storytelling,* pose this question: *How can telling stories unlock hidden truths about the world and the human experience?*

- Have students think about the question individually and take notes.

- Then, have pairs discuss their ideas about the question.

- Finally, ask pairs to share their responses with the class.

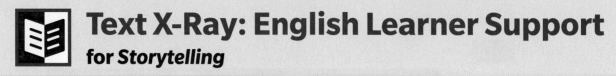

Text X-Ray: English Learner Support
for *Storytelling*

Use the Text X-Ray and the supports and scaffolds in the Teacher's Edition to help guide students at different proficiency levels through the selection.

INTRODUCE THE SELECTION
DISCUSS INFORMATIONAL TEXT

In this lesson, students will need to be able to discuss the characteristics of **informational text**. Read paragraph 3 with students and point out the supporting details for the paragraph's main idea. Provide the following explanations:

- Tell students that in this paragraph the main idea is expressed in the first sentence. Sometimes the main idea will be in a later sentence, and sometimes the main idea will have to be inferred.
- Discuss how the supporting details all support the main idea.

Explain to students that the supporting details talk about people who tell and listen to stories, places where stories are told, and types of stories told. Point out that all of these details present storytelling as a universal human experience.

CULTURAL REFERENCES

The following words and phrases may be unfamiliar to students:

- *opera* (paragraph 3): a theater performance in which the story is told through vocal music
- *campfire tales* (paragraph 3): stories told around a campfire at night; often spooky stories
- *moral* (paragraph 6): a lesson
- *catch-phrases* (paragraph 7): brief sayings familiar to a group of people

LISTENING

Listen to Stories

Tell students that storytelling usually involves listening to a story that someone tells aloud. It may also involve watching a performance of a story in the form of a play, movie, or television show.

Have students listen as you read aloud paragraph 3. Use the following supports with students at varying proficiency levels:

- Ask the following questions and have students respond with a thumbs up for yes and a thumbs down for no: *Are stories told by members of a family? Are stories sometimes told in the business world? Do storytellers always insist, "It is not true!"?* **SUBSTANTIAL**
- Have students complete the following sentence frames: *Professional storytellers might tell stories at _____ or _____. Some mediums that use stories are _____ or _____. Storytellers always insist _____!* **MODERATE**
- Have students demonstrate listening comprehension by answering the following questions: *Where do professional storytellers tell stories? Who are some people who tell stories? What forms of media use stories to tell tales?* **LIGHT**

SPEAKING

Tell a Story

Invite students to create a story based on the image on p. 426 of the selection. Circulate around the room to make sure students are using the image as the basis for their story.

Use the following supports with students at varying proficiency levels:

- Direct students to look at the image. Display and read aloud these sentences: *Some dancers leaped high in the air. Some dancers kneeled on the ground. They all liked to dance.* Have students say them aloud to you and practice saying them to each other. **SUBSTANTIAL**
- Have pairs use these sentence frames to create a story based on the image: *Some dancers _____. Other dancers _____. All of the dancers _____.* **MODERATE**
- Put students in pairs. Have students work together to create a story based on the image. **LIGHT**

READING

Identify Main Idea and Details

Tell students that authors use supporting details to support the key idea of a text. Remind students that the key idea may be clearly stated or may need to be inferred.

Work with students to read paragraph 6. Use the following supports with students at varying proficiency levels:

- Have students find and read aloud the words *moral, greedy,* and *chief.* Explain that a moral is a lesson taught by a story, and ask students to consider who this storyteller wants to teach a lesson to. Provide students with a sentence frame to use for their answer: *He wants the chief to stop being so _____.* **SUBSTANTIAL**
- Have students complete the following sentence frames: *The main idea is _____. Two supporting details are _____.* **MODERATE**
- Put students in pairs. Have students work together to identify the main idea and three supporting details. **LIGHT**

WRITING

Write a Speech

Work with students to read the writing assignment on p. 431.

Use the following supports with students at varying proficiency levels:

- Have partners give each other spelling tests on the Critical Vocabulary words. **SUBSTANTIAL**
- Provide sentence frames to help students plan their speeches: *The key idea of the selection is _____. Storytelling is important because _____.* **MODERATE**
- Remind students to use complex sentences in their speeches. Have students work in pairs to check for correct use of subordinating and correlative conjunctions. **LIGHT**

EXPLAIN THE SIGNPOSTS

Explain that **NOTICE & NOTE Signposts** are significant moments in the text that help readers understand and analyze works of fiction or nonfiction. Use the instruction on these pages to introduce students to the signposts **Big Questions**, **Word Gaps**, and **Quoted Words**. Then use the selection that follows to have students apply the signposts to a text.

For a full list of the fiction and nonfiction signposts, see p. 502.

BIG QUESTIONS

Explain that **Big Questions** encourage more critical reading. By asking yourself what the author thinks you already know, you can clarify the point the author is trying to make.

Read aloud the example paragraph, and look at the first sentence, "The pull of the story is universal." Point out to students that this sentence is confusing. Model for students how to note instances of what the author thinks the reader already knows and what surprises them. Point out that the repeated use of this skill provides an opportunity to critically ask questions about what you read.

Tell students that when they spot Big Questions, they should pause, mark the question in their consumable texts, and ask the anchor questions: *What surprised me? What did the author think I already knew? What challenged, changed, or confirmed what I already knew?*

READING MODEL

 For more information on these and other signposts to Notice & Note, visit the **Reading Studio.**

from STORYTELLING

You are about to read the introduction to the nonfiction book *Storytelling*. As you read, you will notice and note signposts that will give you clues about the author's ideas and purpose for writing. Here are three key signposts to look for as you read this introduction and other works of nonfiction.

Whenever you read nonfiction, remember to ask yourself these **Big Questions:**

What did the author think I already knew?

What challenged, changed, or confirmed what I already knew?

What surprised me?

Big Questions Have you ever walked into the classroom while your teacher was in the middle of explaining a lesson? Maybe what he or she said mostly made sense, but you probably didn't understand everything. Sometimes you can get that same feeling while you're reading. Even when you've read every word, you may get the feeling that you've missed something.

If you feel lost or confused while reading, it's time to stop and ask yourself, **What did the author think I already knew?** By asking yourself this Big Question, you can clarify the point the author is trying to make and decide what to look for as you continue reading. In this example, a student underlined challenging phrases in *Storytelling*:

> 2   The pull of the story is universal. There is no known culture without some form of storytelling, and the craving to know "what comes next" has been felt by every human being, regardless of age, gender, culture, or century.

Which words or phrases are confusing?	The pull of the story is universal. the craving to know "what comes next"
What did the author think I already knew?	The author thought I already knew what "the pull of the story" means and that I've felt a strong desire to know what comes next in a story.

Word Gaps It doesn't matter how old you are or how strong a reader you are—authors sometimes use words and phrases that you don't understand. When you come across **Word Gaps,** or words that are unfamiliar to you, pause to clarify their meaning. Ask:

- Do I know this word from someplace else? Does the word have another meaning that is familiar to me?
- Does the word seem like technical talk related to this topic or like special vocabulary used when writing about this topic?
- Can I find clues in the context to help me understand the word?

By taking the time to fill in those gaps, you will gain a deeper understanding of the text. Here, a student annotated a Word Gap:

> 4   Every conversation is <u>rife</u> with information-packed stories of what the teller has been doing recently.

Anchor Question
When you notice this signpost, ask: Do context clues in the sentence help me understand the word?

What is the unfamiliar word?	rife
Do context clues in the sentence help me understand the word?	The clue "information-packed" makes me think the word "rife" may mean "a lot of something" or "abundant." I'll check a dictionary to find out if I'm right.

Quoted Words Have you noticed that nonfiction authors sometimes quote or paraphrase the words of experts on a topic? Quotations from authorities help support the author's ideas. If you spot quotation marks or someone's name, title, and credentials (information about their area of study or professional background), pause to consider this evidence. **Quoted Words** often direct readers to important ideas. This example shows a student's annotation of Quoted Words:

> 6   The <u>Liberian storyteller</u> <u>Won-Ldy Paye related how</u> Anansi spider stories have been used to <u>"say without saying"</u> in front of a chief.

Anchor Question
When you notice this signpost, ask: Why was this person quoted or cited and what does this add?

What clues tell you that someone has been quoted or cited?	Name and credentials (Liberian storyteller Won-Ldy Paye), plus quotation marks
Why was this person quoted?	She must have knowledge about the topic.

WHEN STUDENTS STRUGGLE . . .

Use Strategies Syntax Surgery is a strategy that helps students clarify confusions that may occur while they are reading. When teaching this strategy, encourage students to underline or circle any parts of a text that confuse them. Then draw arrows to any words or phrases that help them figure out the confusing portions of the text. Also encourage students to write notes in the margins about why they are confused by the text or how they figure it out.

WORD GAPS

Explain that **Word Gaps** address vocabulary that is unfamiliar to the reader.

Read aloud the example passage and pause at the word *rife*. Model for students how to find context clues that help you figure out the meaning of the word.

Tell students that when they spot a Word Gap, they should pause, mark it in their consumable texts, and ask the anchor question: *Do context clues in the sentence help me understand the word?*

QUOTED WORDS

Explain that **Quoted Words** provide the opinions or conclusions of someone who is an expert on a subject, or someone who might be a participant in or a witness to an event.

Read aloud the example passage, and pause at the phrase "say without saying." Model for students how to determine that the phrase is a quote. Point out that quotation marks, an author's name, and credentials indicate a quote.

Tell students that when they spot Quoted Words, they should pause, mark the words in their consumable texts, and ask the anchor question: *Why was this person quoted or cited and what does this add?*

APPLY THE SIGNPOSTS

Have students use the selection that follows as a model text to apply the signposts. As students encounter signposts, prompt them to stop, reread, and ask themselves the anchor questions that will help them understand the text.

Tell students to continue to look for these and other signposts as they read the other selections in the unit.

Connect to the
ESSENTIAL QUESTION

The introduction of *Storytelling* relates how telling and listening to stories is a universal experience. Throughout the text, the author emphasizes how humans use stories as cultural and bonding experiences.

from
STORYTELLING

Book Introduction by **Josepha Sherman**

? ESSENTIAL QUESTION:

What hidden truths about people and the world are revealed in stories?

© Houghton Mifflin Harcourt Publishing Company • Image Credits: ©vandyke/Shutterstock

422 Unit 6

⚙ LEARNING MINDSET

Planning Remind students that planning is essential to completing work efficiently and exceptionally. Encourage students to make a plan for completing an assignment, including mapping out the steps. Explain that planning will help students learn discipline, which will help them in the future.

QUICK START

Imagine you wanted to persuade someone to read a book that you really enjoyed. What might you say to introduce the book and explain its importance? Discuss your ideas with the class.

ANALYZE CHARACTERISTICS OF INFORMATIONAL TEXTS

Nonfiction writers organize and present facts and ideas in a variety of ways. Recognizing **structural elements** and **organizational patterns** will help deepen your understanding of a work and its controlling idea.

The selection you are about to read is the introduction to a book about storytelling. An **introduction** is a feature that provides background information about the text's subject, often offering the writer's point of view on that subject. As you read the introduction, look for the ways that the author presents and organizes information.

ORGANIZATIONAL PATTERN	DESCRIPTION
Definition/Description	states, explains, and describes new terms or ideas
Cause and Effect	explains a cause-and-effect relationship between events and ideas
Classification	presents information by topic or type of idea
Key Ideas and Supporting Details	establishes ideas and supports them with evidence

MAKE INFERENCES ABOUT KEY IDEAS

Key ideas are important ideas that an author wants readers to understand. Authors may state these ideas **explicitly,** or directly. However, some ideas are stated **implicitly,** or indirectly. In such cases, readers must make inferences about implied ideas. An **inference** is a logical guess based on evidence from the text as well as prior knowledge. Making inferences about key ideas will help you identify and understand an author's **controlling idea**—the main point of the text.

As you read, look for explicit and implicit ideas. Use text evidence and your knowledge of the structure of the text, as well as your personal knowledge, to make inferences about the author's key ideas.

GENRE ELEMENTS: BOOK INTRODUCTION

- appears before the main text
- introduces readers to the author's ideas and the purpose of the main text
- includes ideas and supporting evidence

QUICK START

Have students read the Quick Start question, and invite them to share how they would try to persuade someone to read a book that they enjoyed. Ask students how they would introduce the book and explain its importance.

ANALYZE CHARACTERISTICS OF INFORMATIONAL TEXTS

Help students understand the terms and concepts related to the characteristics and structures of informational text. Discuss the organizational strategies of definition/description, cause and effect, classification, and key ideas and supporting details. Point out that determining the structure of an informational text deepens students' understanding of the text's controlling idea.

MAKE INFERENCES ABOUT KEY IDEAS

Tell students that key ideas are the main or most important ideas an author wants a reader to know. Remind students that sometimes key ideas are clearly stated, and sometimes the key ideas must be inferred. As students read, ask them to look for ideas that are stated directly or indirectly, as well as the evidence used to support the text's controlling idea.

 ENGLISH LEARNER SUPPORT

Understand Text Evidence   Reinforce the importance of text evidence. Explain that text evidence provides necessary support for inferences. Tell students that making inferences helps them better understand a text. Have students look for text evidence to support the main idea of each paragraph. **MODERATE**

TEACH

CRITICAL VOCABULARY

Encourage students to read all the sentences before deciding which word best completes each one. Remind them to look for context clues that match the precise meaning of each word.

Answers:

1. *Universal*

2. *Invariably; adversity*

3. *integral*

4. *chastise; nurture*

5. *trance*

■ English Learner Support

Use Cognates Tell students that two of the Critical Vocabulary words have Spanish cognates: *nurture/nutrir, trance/trance.* **ALL LEVELS**

LANGUAGE CONVENTIONS

Review the information about complex sentences. Explain that the example sentence is made of an independent and a dependent clause.

Read aloud the example sentence, pointing out the two clauses. Point out that the word *where* signals the dependent clause.

ANNOTATION MODEL

Students can review the Reading Model introduction if they have questions about any of the signposts. Suggest that they underline important phrases or circle key words that help them identify signposts. They may want to color-code their annotations by using a different color highlighter for each signpost. Point out that they may follow this suggestion or use their own system for marking up the selections in their write-in texts.

⊚ **GET READY**

CRITICAL VOCABULARY

universal	invariably	nurture	adversity
integral	trance	chastise	

To see how many Critical Vocabulary words you already know, use them to complete the sentences.

1. _____ experiences are those shared by all humanity.

2. _____ , most of us face stress and _____.

3. Weekly practice is a/an _____ part of the team's training.

4. A coach may _____ a team for laziness and _____ the team with encouragement.

5. The dance seemed to put the audience into a/an _____.

LANGUAGE CONVENTIONS

Complex Sentences In a **complex sentence**, an independent clause is combined with one or more dependent clauses. An **independent clause** expresses a complete thought and can stand alone. A **dependent clause** cannot stand alone. In the complex sentence below, the dependent clause is "where remarkable things happen."

The teller takes the listener to distant places where remarkable things happen.

As you read the selection, look for the ways in which the author uses complex sentences to combine ideas.

ANNOTATION MODEL   **NOTICE & NOTE**

As you read, notice and note the signposts **Big Questions, Word Gaps,** and **Quoted Words**. Here is an example of how one reader responded to unfamiliar ideas in the selection:

> 2   Once a story has begun, there is something deep within the human <u>psyche</u> that must hear what will happen next. <u>The pull of the story is universal.</u> There is no known culture without some form of storytelling, and <u>the craving to know "what comes next" has been felt by every human being</u>, regardless of age, gender, culture, or century.

What is the psyche? What is the "pull of the story"? What does the author think I already know?

BACKGROUND

Author and folklore expert **Josepha Sherman** *(1946–2012) became interested in folktales at an early age. She loved to compare and retell folktales from around the world. Her works include* Trickster Tales: Forty Folk Stories from Around the World *and* The Shining Falcon, *which is based on Russian folklore and was awarded the 1990 Compton Cook Award for best fantasy fiction. The excerpt you are about to read is from the introduction to an encyclopedia of mythology and folklore that Sherman edited.*

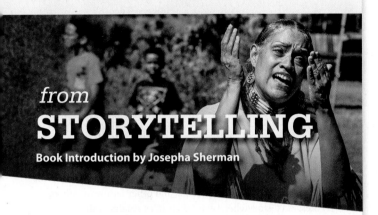

from
STORYTELLING
Book Introduction by Josepha Sherman

SETTING A PURPOSE

As you read, study the organizational patterns in the text as well as the details about the importance of storytelling to understand why the author wrote this introduction.

Once Upon a Time . . .

1   . . . there was a story. Story openings take a number of forms: "once there was," "once there was not," "once, in the long ago days," and many others. But no matter what shape the opening words take, the result is always the same— listeners are hooked.

2   Once a story has begun, there is something deep within the human psyche[1] that must hear what will happen next. The pull of the story is **universal**. There is no known culture without some form of storytelling, and the craving[2] to know "what comes next" has been felt by every human being, regardless of age, gender, culture, or century.

---

[1] **psyche** (sī´kē): the spirit or soul.
[2] **craving** (krā´vĭng): an overwhelming urge or desire.

NOTICE & NOTE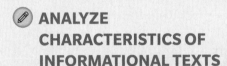

Notice & Note

Use the side margins to notice and note signposts in the text.

ANALYZE
CHARACTERISTICS OF
INFORMATIONAL TEXTS
Annotate: Mark cause-and-effect words in paragraphs 1–2.

Summarize: What idea is the author sharing here?

LANGUAGE CONVENTIONS
Complex sentences combine dependent and independent clauses to clarify ideas. Explain how the writer uses a complex sentence to connect ideas in paragraph 2.

universal
(yoo´nə-vûr´-səl) *adj.* Something that is *universal* affects every member of a group.

Storytelling   425

ENGLISH LEARNER SUPPORT

Understand Cause and Effect Help students locate the word *result* in paragraph 1. Explain that this word has the same meaning as the word *effect*. Then point out and read aloud "what comes next" in paragraph 2, and have students repeat it after you. Explain that this—what comes next—is what the readers of a text want to know.   **SUBSTANTIAL**

BACKGROUND

After students read the Background note, point out that the author became interested in stories as a child and is particularly interested in comparing folktales across cultures. Remind students that this text is an introduction to an encyclopedia of mythology and folklore.

SETTING A PURPOSE

Direct students to use the Setting a Purpose prompt to focus their reading.

ANALYZE CHARACTERISTICS OF INFORMATIONAL TEXTS

Remind students that a **cause-and-effect organizational pattern** explains a cause-and-effect relationship between the events and ideas discussed in the text. In paragraphs 1–2, have students mark the cause-and-effect words. Then have students answer the question to determine what idea the author is sharing. (**Answer:** *Stories cause, or compel, people to listen.*)

LANGUAGE CONVENTIONS

Review how **complex sentences** use **subordinating conjunctions** to join dependent and independent clauses. Remind students that an independent clause can stand on its own, while a dependent clause cannot. Ask students to explain how the author uses a complex sentence to connect the ideas in paragraph 2. (**Answer:** *"Once a story has begun, there is something deep within the human psyche that must hear what will happen next." In this sentence, "once" acts as a subordinating conjunction to join a dependent clause, "once a story has begun," with an independent clause, "there is something deep within the human psyche that must hear what will happen next."*)

CRITICAL VOCABULARY

universal: When something is experienced by most people, it is universal.

ASK STUDENTS to explain how the pull of a story is universal. (*Most people are interested in and enjoy stories.*)

ENGLISH LEARNER SUPPORT

Understand Context Clues Remind students that context clues are words in or around an unknown word that help them figure out the meaning of the unknown word. Help students locate the words *rife* and *information-packed* in paragraph 4, and explain that *information-packed* is a context clue for *rife*, because something that is *rife with information* contains a lot of information. Have students work in pairs to locate context clues for other unknown words. **MODERATE**

WORD GAPS

Explain to students that this signpost is often used to point out unknown words. In paragraphs 4 and 5, have students identify and mark any unknown words or phrases. Then have students think about what questions they can ask themselves to figure out the meaning of the unknown words. Also have students think about why the author chose to use these words. (**Possible Answer:** *To find the meaning of* rehash, *I can look for context clues earlier the sentence—I see* retell. *I think I have heard the word* rehash *before, and* retell *makes me think it has a similar meaning—"to go over something or tell it again." Maybe the author wanted to vary her word choice, so she chose another word with a similar meaning so as not to repeat herself.*)

 For **listening and speaking support** for students at varying proficiency levels, see the **Text X-Ray** on pages 420C and 420D.

CRITICAL VOCABULARY

integral: If something is integral, it is a necessary part of something.

ASK STUDENTS why stories are integral to movies and film. (*Movies show stories as a visual medium.*)

invariably: Something that invariably occurs will always happen over and over.

ASK STUDENTS what it means that the storyteller invariably says, "It's true!" (*That means that this is a common response when telling an urban legend.*)

---

integral
(ĭn-tĕ´grəl) *adj.* Something that is *integral* is necessary or essential for completeness.

invariably
(ĭn-vâr´ē-ə-blē) *adv.* Something that happens *invariably* occurs again and again or constantly.

WORD GAPS

Notice & Note: Mark any Word Gaps in paragraphs 4 and 5.

Analyze: What questions can you ask yourself to understand the meaning of the words? Why do you think the author chose to use these words?

3   Storytelling is present in many aspects of human life. Stories are told by grandparents, parents, and other family members. Professional storytellers share their tales at fairs, festivals, schools, libraries, and other sites. Stories are **integral** to the mediums of television, film, opera, and theater, and storytelling sessions sometimes take place in the business world at special meetings. Campfire tales are meant to make campers shiver. And urban legends, contemporary folktales that usually are attributed to a "friend of a friend," are told and retold. No matter how unlikely the tale may be, the teller **invariably** insists, "It's *true!*"

Why Tell Stories?

4   The real question may be how can one *not* tell stories? Every conversation is rife[3] with information-packed stories of what the teller has been doing recently. People share stories they have heard from others, retell stories they have read, and even rehash things they have seen on television. Anyone who chooses to formalize this sharing takes on the role of the "storyteller."

5   The most wonderful gift of story is the bonding of a group. Held close under the spell of a story, the group breathes as one. The shared experience softens the edges between

---
[3] **rife** (rīf): prevalent or in widespread use.

individuals and brings everyone closer in the warmth of the moment. Together, the members of the group enter a "story **trance**." Storytellers benefit, in turn, as they experience the heartwarming feeling of holding the audience's attention and **nurturing** the group by sharing a beloved tale.

6   Many stories also serve the community in a broader sense. All societies use stories to pass on <u>group values</u>. <u>Wrapped in the sweet pill of an entertaining story, a moral goes down easily.</u> Stories also can be useful tools that allow individuals to **chastise** or expose negative behaviors without overtly speaking the truth. The Liberian storyteller Won-Ldy Paye related how <u>Anansi spider stories</u> have been used to "say without saying" in front of a chief. If the chief has behaved in a greedy manner, the storyteller shows Anansi in this incorrect behavior. Everyone knows whom the storyteller is talking about. The chief hears, and he knows, too.

7   <u>Many families draw "catch-phrases" from their favorite stories, with which they can quickly refer to a story in the course of their daily lives.</u> A phrase, such as "It don't take long to look at a horseshoe,"[4] can bring family members back to the original story, as well as remind them of the moral of the tale.

8   Communities and families also may wrap their history in stories in order to remember details of events long past. A moment in time can be preserved by creating a story and telling it a few times. The story format bundles the facts into a neatly tied packet that is more readily stored and retrieved[5] than a number of separate details.

9   Stories also help to broaden awareness of other cultures. The folktale genre, in particular, reflects many traditions and helps to familiarize people with world cultures.

10   Stories also can be used for educational purposes. Stories can help to develop a child's literary sensibilities, and listening to tales impresses a sense of story structure into a child's mind. Stories aid in stretching vocabulary, and children who are able to tell stories often gain advanced verbal ability and an increased sense of self-worth.

---

[4] **"It don't take long to look at a horseshoe":** In an old story, a blacksmith warns a boy not to touch a hot metal horseshoe. The boy picks up the horseshoe, then quickly drops it in surprise and pain. When the blacksmith asks if the boy burned himself, the boy quickly says, "No, it just don't take me long to look at a horseshoe."

[5] **retrieve** (rĭ-trēv´): to get back or regain possession of something.

---

trance
(trăns) *n.* When someone is in a *trance*, he or she is in a daze or daydreaming.

BIG QUESTIONS

Notice & Note: What does the author expect readers to know in paragraph 6? Mark what you're expected to know.

Analyze: Why do you think the author expects you to know this? Where could you get more information?

nurture
(nûr´chər) *v.* To *nurture* is to provide love, affection, nourishment, or something else necessary for development.

chastise
(chăs,tīz´) *v.* To *chastise* is to punish or criticize.

MAKE INFERENCES ABOUT KEY IDEAS

Annotate: Mark the ideas that are stated explicitly, or directly, in paragraph 7.

Infer: How can you use stated ideas and any other information in the paragraph to make an inference about why families use catch phrases?

BIG QUESTIONS

Explain to students that this signpost is often used to encourage critical thinking about the text. In paragraph 6, have students mark what the author expects the reader to know. Then have students answer the questions to determine why the author expects the reader to know this and where they could get more information about it. (**Answer:** *The author expects readers to know about Anansi the spider, perhaps because stories about Anansi are well-known folktales. The fact that the author quotes a storyteller from the African country of Liberia provides a clue that Anansi is from African folktales.*)

 MAKE INFERENCES ABOUT KEY IDEAS

Remind students that an **inference** is a logical guess based on evidence from the text, as well as prior knowledge. In paragraph 7, have students mark ideas that are explicitly stated. Then have students answer the question to see how they can use these stated ideas to infer why families use catch phrases. (**Answer:** *Families might use catch phrases from familiar stories, such as the one about the boy and the horseshoe, to remind themselves about important life lessons.*)

For **reading support** for students at varying proficiency levels, see the **Text X-Ray** on page 420D.

CRITICAL VOCABULARY

trance: People in a trance are focused on thinking about or imagining something in their mind, instead of paying attention to the world around them.

ASK STUDENTS to explain what a "story trance" may look like. (*People are only paying attention to the story and nothing else.*)

nurture: When a mother cares for a child, she is nurturing her.

ASK STUDENTS to explain how a storyteller nurtures a group. (*The storyteller creates a shared enjoyable experience with the group listening to the story.*)

chastise: People chastise others to stop bad behavior and encourage good behavior.

ASK STUDENTS to give an example of being chastised. (*A parent might chastise a child for breaking a rule.*)

APPLYING ACADEMIC VOCABULARY

☐ **emphasize**   ☑ **occur**   ☐ **period**   ☐ **relevant**   ☑ **tradition**

Write and Discuss Have students turn to a partner to discuss the following questions. Guide students to include the Academic Vocabulary words *occur* and *tradition* in their answers.

• In what situations might storytelling **occur**?

• How does telling stories incorporate a culture's **traditions**?

QUOTED WORDS

Explain to students that this signpost is often used to point out information that is cited by an authority on a subject. In paragraph 11, have students mark the words that show that an expert has been cited. Then have students answer the question to determine how the expert's words or ideas support the ideas of Josepha Sherman. (**Answer:** *Sherman states that storytelling provides children with "growth opportunities." She paraphrases the ideas of this expert in child psychology to support her claim: "stories are important to children because battling difficulties through story can help them face real-life problems.")*

■ English Learner Support

Confirm Understanding Using simple language, summarize paragraph 11 with students, making sure students understand any difficult vocabulary. **SUBSTANTIAL**

✎ MAKE INFERENCES ABOUT KEY IDEAS

Remind students that an **inference** is a logical guess based on evidence from the text as well as prior knowledge. In paragraph 12, have students mark details that describe how stories affect imagination. Then have students answer the question to infer the meaning of the final sentence. (**Answer:** *The author means that when we are exposed to stories, we become more imaginative and creative people.*)

CRITICAL VOCABULARY

adversity: When someone deals with challenges or problems in life, they face adversity.

ASK STUDENTS how stories can show someone triumphing over adversity. (*Stories show examples of people doing well when things go wrong.*)

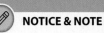

✎ NOTICE & NOTE

QUOTED WORDS

Notice & Note: What words in paragraph 11 tell you that an expert has been cited? Mark the words.

Cite Evidence: How do the expert's words or ideas support the ideas of author Josepha Sherman?

adversity
(ăd-vûr´sĭ-tē) *n. Adversity* is misfortune or hardship.

MAKE INFERENCES ABOUT KEY IDEAS

Annotate: Mark details in paragraphs 11–12 that describe how stories affect the imagination.

Infer: Use these details to infer the meaning of the final sentence.

11   Storytelling provides other growth opportunities, as stories help listeners to see through another's eyes and to share the protagonist's[6] feelings of anger, fear, or love—all from a safe place. The Austrian-born American writer and child psychologist Bruno Bettelheim explained that stories are important to children because battling difficulties through story can help them face real-life troubles. Stories provide role models who show us how to face demons and overcome **adversity**.

12   Perhaps best of all, stories stretch the imagination. The teller takes the listener to distant places where remarkable things happen. And once stretched, an imagination stays stretched.

---

[6] **protagonist** (prō-tăg´ĭ-nĭst): the leading character in a work of fiction, such as a novel or play.

WHEN STUDENTS STRUGGLE . . .

Visualize Help students understand what is occurring in the text by encouraging them to visualize what is being described.

Ask students what it means for a story to stretch the imagination. Have students describe examples of using their imaginations.

  For additional support, go to the **Reading Studio** and assign the following **LEVEL** **Level Up tutorial: Prose Forms.**

CHECK YOUR UNDERSTANDING

Answer these questions before moving on to the **Analyze the Text** section on the following page.

1 The author included the section "Why Tell Stories?" to —

A tell readers her favorite story about a blacksmith

B explain the benefits and rewards of storytelling

C persuade readers to become writers

D tell readers about the spider Anansi

2 In paragraph 3, the author mentions that stories are told by parents and professionals and in theaters and over campfires as a way to —

F explain that there are three kinds of storytelling

G persuade readers to see more movies

H provide examples of how storytelling is part of everyone's life

J describe where stories are told

3 Which idea is not supported by information in the selection?

A Storytelling was more popular in the past.

B Storytelling is part of being human.

C Storytelling is an important educational tool.

D Anyone can be a storyteller.

✏ CHECK YOUR UNDERSTANDING

Have students answer the questions independently.

Answers:

1. *B*

2. *H*

3. *A*

If they answer any questions incorrectly, have them reread the text to confirm their understanding. Then they may proceed to ANALYZE THE TEXT on page 430.

🗨 ENGLISH LEARNER SUPPORT

Oral Assessment Use the following questions to assess students' comprehension and speaking skills:

1. Does listening to a story make people feel closer? *(Yes, it brings a group closer together.)*

2. Where are some stories told? *(in theaters and over campfires)*

3. Were stories more popular in the past? *(no)*
   SUBSTANTIAL/MODERATE

APPLY

ANALYZE THE TEXT

Possible answers:

1. **DOK 3:** *Key idea: storytelling is part of everyday life. Supporting evidence: "grandparents, parents, and other family members" tell stories, as do professional storytellers at "fairs, festivals, schools," etc. Stories are used to entertain in "television, film, opera" and so on. The ideas are structured by stating the key idea first, then offering details as supporting evidence.*

2. **DOK 2:** *Based on the heading, the author's purpose for this section is to describe benefits of storytelling. The author will probably discuss ways in which storytelling positively impacts people's lives. Details in paragraphs 4–10 confirm this prediction.*

3. **DOK 4:** *The heading "Why Tell Stories?" lets the reader know that the information in paragraphs 4–10 will answer this question. In paragraph 8, the author uses description and imagery to talk about how stories convey family and community history. In paragraphs 9–10, the author explicitly states key ideas in the topic sentences, followed by supporting details to convey that stories tell us about other cultures and that they are important educational tools.*

4. **DOK 2:** *Storytelling is important because it shapes how humans learn and interact with one another in ways that are instinctive and long lasting.*

5. **DOK 4:** *The expert, an African storyteller, says that Anansi stories could be used to tell a chief to correct his bad behavior, in a way that would not shame the chief in front of his people. This example supports the author's idea that "the sweet pill of an entertaining story" helps a moral to "[go] down easily."*

RESEARCH

If students need a starting point to begin their research, suggest that they look at a website for professional storytellers.

Extend Encourage students to use a chart or other graphic organizer to help them compare and contrast the different opening lines.

ANALYZE THE TEXT

Support your responses with evidence from the text. NOTEBOOK

1. **Cite Evidence** Review paragraph 3. What key idea is presented in the paragraph? Cite evidence from the paragraph that supports the idea. How does the author organize the information in this paragraph?

2. **Predict** Reread the heading before paragraph 4. Based on the heading, what would you predict about the author's purpose for that section of the introduction? What ideas would you expect the author to discuss? Is your prediction correct?

3. **Evaluate** Review paragraphs 4–10. Identify how the author structures ideas in the text. Does the author effectively present and organize her ideas? Explain.

4. **Interpret** Use your annotations and what you've learned from the selection to determine the author's controlling idea in the introduction to *Storytelling*.

5. **Notice & Note** Review the quoted words in paragraph 6. How do the words and ideas of the expert add to the author's ideas about storytelling?

RESEARCH TIP

Begin your research by exploring the website of one of the many organizations of professional storytellers. If your teacher approves, consider working in a small group to develop and send questions about storytelling to a children's storyteller. Ask your teacher or a librarian for help.

RESEARCH

Professional storytellers know how to create and tell captivating stories. Investigate the rules or guidelines they follow for how to tell stories to children and young people. Record what you learn in the chart.

GUIDELINE	DETAILS
Answers will vary.	

Extend In the first paragraph of this selection, the author includes examples of how stories begin, such as "Once upon a time." In a small group, find multiple folktales online or in the library. Make your own list that shows how these stories begin. Find at least five different examples of opening lines. Then compare them to those provided in the selection. Discuss your findings with the group.

LEARNING MINDSET

Problem Solving If students get stuck when trying to respond to the Analyze the Text questions, help them by asking them to apply problem-solving strategies as they work through the questions. Encourage students to look at a question from a different angle or to try a different learning strategy.

CREATE AND DISCUSS

Write a Speech Summarize the selection's key ideas and use your summary to write a three-paragraph speech about the importance of storytelling.

- ❏ Draw upon ideas stated explicitly and implicitly in the selection. Be alert to details that will help you identify these key ideas.
- ❏ Paraphrase the author's key ideas by restating them in your own words. Make sure that you cite both the author and selection in your speech.
- ❏ Include complex sentences in your writing.

Discuss with a Small Group Work in a small group to discuss the selection's key ideas. Begin by sharing your speeches from the writing activity. Use your speeches to compile one list of key ideas.

- ❏ Work together to agree upon the list of ideas.
- ❏ Make sure the ideas are supported by evidence in the text. Refer to the selection to discuss how ideas are supported explicitly or implicitly.
- ❏ Make sure every group member participates fully. Listen closely and respectfully to all ideas.

RESPOND TO THE ESSENTIAL QUESTION

? What hidden truths about people and the world are revealed in stories?

Gather Information Review your annotations and notes on the selection. Then, add relevant details to your Response Log. As you determine which information to include, think about how and why people tell stories and the importance of stories in your own life.

At the end of the unit, use your notes to write a short story or folktale.

RESPOND

Go to **Using Textual Evidence: Summarizing, Paraphrasing, and Quoting** in the **Writing Studio** for more on summarizing and paraphrasing.

 Go to **Participating in Collaborative Discussions** in the **Speaking and Listening Studio** for help with having a group discussion.

ACADEMIC VOCABULARY
As you write and discuss what you learned from the selection, be sure to use the Academic Vocabulary words. Check off each of the words that you use.

- ❏ **emphasize**
- ❏ **occur**
- ❏ **period**
- ❏ **relevant**
- ❏ **tradition**

© Houghton Mifflin Harcourt Publishing Company

APPLY

CREATE AND DISCUSS

Write a Speech Point out to students that their speeches need to cite the author, her key ideas, and supporting details used in the text. Remind students to use complex sentences.

 For **writing support** for students at varying proficiency levels, see the **Text X-Ray** on page 420D.

Discuss with a Small Group Remind students that they will use their speeches as a starting point for the discussion. Tell students that their discussion will create one list of key ideas about why storytelling is important and that these ideas must be supported by text evidence.

RESPOND TO THE ESSENTIAL QUESTION

Allow time for students to add details from *Storytelling* to their Unit 6 Response Logs.

 ENGLISH LEARNER SUPPORT

Discuss with a Small Group Help students all participate in the discussion and develop confidence in their ability to contribute to the team by assigning a specific role to each group member, such as reader, recorder, evidence locator, and moderator. **MODERATE**

Storytelling   431

Storytelling   **431**

CRITICAL VOCABULARY

Possible Answers:

1. *Because so many things can go wrong each day, I do think that everyone **invariably** faces some kind of **adversity**.*

2. *I would **chastise** my brother for borrowing my stuff without asking.*

3. *Stories are **integral** to books and movies because the function of both books and movies is to tell stories.*

4. *I would **nurture** a new pet by giving it food, attention, and a comfortable place to live.*

5. *A person in a **trance** might have a distant or blank expression.*

6. *Something **universal** is experienced by everyone in a group.*

VOCABULARY STRATEGY:
Context Clues

Answers:

- **trance:** *"under the spell of a story"; "members of the group enter a 'story trance'"; These clues suggest that trance means "a state of separation from one's physical surroundings."*

- **chastise:** *"pass on group values"; "expose negative behaviors without overtly speaking the truth"; "If the chief has behaved in a greedy manner, the storyteller shows Anansi in this incorrect behavior." These clues suggest that chastise means "to criticize or reprimand."*

 RESPOND

WORD BANK
universal
integral
invariably
trance
nurture
chastise
adversity

CRITICAL VOCABULARY

Practice and Apply Use your understanding of the Critical Vocabulary words to answer the questions.

1. Do you think everyone **invariably** faces **adversity?** Explain.

   _____

2. Would you ever **chastise** a friend or sibling? Explain.

   _____

3. Are stories **integral** to movies? Explain.

   _____

4. How would you **nurture** a new pet?

   _____

5. If you saw a person in a **trance,** what might he or she look like?

   _____

6. Name a **universal** idea, behavior, or experience. Explain.

   _____

 Go to the **Vocabulary Studio** for more on context clues.

VOCABULARY STRATEGY:
Context Clues

The **context** of a word is the words, sentences, and paragraphs that surround the word. Context can give you important clues about a word's meaning. Context clues include definitions, analogies or comparisons, and examples. Take a look at the following passage:

> **The pull of the story is <u>universal</u>. There is no known culture without some form of storytelling, and the craving to know "what comes next" has been felt by every human being, regardless of age, gender, culture, or century.**

The surrounding words "no known culture without" and "felt by every human being" provide clues to the meaning of *universal*. You can use the context clues to figure out that *universal* means "applying to every member of a group."

Practice and Apply Identify context clues that help explain the meaning of the words *trance* (paragraph 5) and *chastise* (paragraph 6). Record the context clues and explain how they hint at the meaning of each word.

(EL) ENGLISH LEARNER SUPPORT

Vocabulary Strategy Give students additional practice in using context clues to determine the meaning of unknown words. Write the following word on the board: *overtly*. Have pairs of students read paragraph 6 to look for context clues to help determine the meaning of this word. Have students confirm their definitions by looking up this word in a dictionary.

MODERATE/LIGHT

LANGUAGE CONVENTIONS:
Complex Sentences

If you used only simple sentences in your writing, it would be hard for your readers to understand how your ideas connect to one another. Writers use **complex sentences** to help clarify and connect their ideas. Using complex sentences correctly will add sentence variety and improve the flow and coherence of your writing.

Writers use **subordinating conjunctions**—including *if, although, after, as, before, because, once, since, when,* and *unless*—to introduce dependent clauses. The following example from *Storytelling* shows a dependent clause beginning with the subordinating conjunction *if:*

> <u>If the chief has behaved in a greedy manner</u>, the storyteller shows Anansi in this incorrect behavior.

Writers also connect ideas within sentences by using **correlative conjunctions,** or paired conjunctions that join words or word groups. Correlative conjunctions include *both/and, either/or,* and *neither/nor.* In the following example, paired conjunctions appear in the independent clause of a complex sentence:

> <u>Neither</u> children <u>nor</u> adults will attend, if the tickets are unaffordable.

Practice and Apply Write your own complex sentences using the above examples as models. Use at least one pair of correlative conjunctions in your sentences. Write about the ideas explored in the selection or the importance of stories in your own life. When you have finished, compare your sentences with a partner's.

RESPOND

Go to **Simple and Compound Sentences** in the **Grammar Studio** for more on types of sentences.

LANGUAGE CONVENTIONS:
Complex Sentences

Review the information about complex sentences with students. Explain that complex sentences can help clarify and connect their ideas. When writing complex sentences, students need to be sure to use subordinating and correlative conjunctions to connect the clauses.

Review the examples of complex sentences using subordinating and correlative conjunctions.

Practice and Apply Have students create complex sentences and include at least one pair of correlative conjunctions in their sentences. Students' sentences will vary.

ENGLISH LEARNER SUPPORT

Language Conventions Use the following supports with students at varying proficiency levels:

- Have students find complex sentences in *Storytelling* and copy them in their notebooks. **SUBSTANTIAL**
- Have students work with partners to write a complex sentence using a pair of correlative conjunctions and a sentence using a subordinating conjunction. **MODERATE**
- Have students work in pairs to edit their sentences. Challenge students to create at least four complex sentences with correlative and subordinating conjunctions. **LIGHT**

THE PRINCE AND THE PAUPER

by Mark Twain, dramatized by
Joellen Bland

GENRE ELEMENTS
DRAMA

Remind students that a **drama** is a play. Therefore, the text of the drama is written in the form of a script. The beginning of the script will usually list the cast of characters. Dramas are divided into acts and scenes. An act is a larger section of the story, which may contain many scenes. Each time there is a change in time or setting, there is a new scene. A drama's story is told through dialogue, or what the characters say. Stage direction, written in italics and in parentheses, tells what the characters do. Stage direction is an important part of the storytelling, but it is never spoken out loud.

LEARNING OBJECTIVES

- Analyze how playwrights develop characters.
- Create mental images to deepen understanding.
- Research the life of a real-life character depicted in the play.
- Write a character sketch.
- Perform a dramatic reading.
- Use a variety of resources to define vocabulary terms.
- Identify and use preposition and prepositional phrases.
- **Language** Discuss with a partner the features of the text using the key term *characters*.

TEXT COMPLEXITY

Quantitative Measures	The Prince and the Pauper	Lexile: N/A
Qualitative Measures	**Ideas Presented** Much is explicit, but moves to some implied meaning; requires inferential reasoning.	
	Structures Used Primarily explicit and largely conventional.	
	Language Used Mostly explicit, some dialect or other unconventional language.	
	Knowledge Required Begins to rely more on outside knowledge.	

RESOURCES

- Unit 6 Response Log

- Selection Audio

- Reading Stage Directions

- Close Read Screencasts: Modeled Discussions

- Reading Studio: Notice & Note

- Level Up tutorial: Elements of Drama

- Writing Studio: Using Textual Evidence

- Speaking and Listening Studio: Giving a Presentation

- Vocabulary Studio: Using Resources

- Grammar Studio: Module 3: Lessons 6–7: The Preposition

- "The Prince and the Pauper" Selection Test

SUMMARIES

English

The year is 1547, and young Prince Edward VI is overwhelmed by his royal obligations as he prepares to become king after his ailing father dies. Meanwhile, a young pauper named Tom Canty is miserable in his life of starvation and abuse. When Tom visits the palace one day, he and the prince decide to switch clothing and live each other's lives for a day. However, they find it difficult to convince anybody of their true identities. The way others treat the two boys reveals many hidden truths about people.

Spanish

El año es 1547 y el joven príncipe, Eduardo VI, se siente abrumado por sus obligaciones reales mientras se prepara para convertirse en rey luego de la muerte de su padre enfermo. Mientras tanto, un joven mendigo llamado Tom Canty lleva una vida deprimente, llena de abusos y hambruna. Cuando Tom visita el palacio un día, él y el príncipe deciden cambiar de ropa y vivir la vida del otro por un día. Sin embargo, encuentran difícil convencer a los demás de sus identidades verdaderas. La manera en que los otros tratan a los dos niños revela muchas verdades ocultas acerca de la gente.

SMALL-GROUP OPTIONS

Have students work in small groups to read and discuss the selection.

Readers' Theater

- Divide the class into groups, and assign each group a portion of the script to perform.

- Tell students to designate roles for each group member, either randomly or based on volunteers. Some scenes may require a student to play multiple characters.

- Have students rehearse their scenes several times, including acting out the stage directions. Emphasize that students do not have to memorize their scripts.

- If you prefer, students may create or bring simple props and scenery.

- Have groups present their scenes to the class.

Reciprocal Teaching

- Present students with a list of generic question stems.

- Have students use the stems to independently write three to five questions about the text. They do not have to be able to answer the questions.

- Put students in groups of three. Each student should ask at least two questions to the group, without duplicating another student's questions.

- The group should reach consensus on how to answer the question and find text evidence to support their answers.

Text X-Ray: English Learner Support
for *The Prince and the Pauper*

INTRODUCE THE SELECTION
DISCUSS FEATURES OF DRAMA

In this lesson, students will discuss the events that unfold in a play. Helping them understand the features of drama will facilitate their ability to understand and discuss the plot events as they unfold.

Create a classroom poster defining each of the features of drama, such as *script*, *cast of characters*, *acts*, *scenes*, *dialogue*, and *stage direction*. Include a pictorial representation or example of each. Review the poster with students, and display it in the classroom.

Give students the following sentence frames to help them discuss the play:

- *In Scene _____, the most important event is _____.*
- *I know that _____ happened because the stage direction says _____.*
- *The dialogue _____ shows that the character _____ is _____.*

CULTURAL REFERENCES

The following words and phrases may be unfamiliar to students:

- *Westminster Palace* (paragraph 2): the castle where kings and queens of England used to live
- *merciful* (paragraph 39): kind and understanding
- *pauper* (paragraph 47): a poor person
- *banquet* (paragraph 60): a fancy dinner
- *mad* (paragraph 63): crazy
- *mount the throne* (paragraph 63): become king
- *imposter* (paragraph 65): somebody who pretends to be someone they are not
- *inn* (paragraph 94): a hotel
- *constable* (paragraph 121): police officer
- *Justice* (paragraph 128): judge

LISTENING

Understand Initial Plot Events

Tell students you will read aloud several paragraphs from the beginning of the play. Then they will answer questions about what you read to demonstrate their comprehension of early plot events.

Have students listen as you read aloud paragraphs 10–32. Use the following supports with students at varying proficiency levels:

- Ask the following yes/no questions: *Is Tom Canty a rich person?* (no) *Do Tom and Prince Edward switch clothes?* (yes) *Are they planning to live each other's lives for a day?* (yes) **SUBSTANTIAL**
- Have students complete the following sentence frames: *Tom Canty is _____. Tom and Prince Edward decide to _____. Their plan is to _____.* **MODERATE**
- Have students answer the following questions: *Who is Tom Canty?* (a pauper) *What do Tom and Prince Edward decide to do?* (switch clothes) *What do they plan to do?* (switch places for a day) **LIGHT**

SPEAKING

Discuss Characters

Many of the annotations in this selection ask students to analyze how playwrights develop characters. Have students discuss character development. Circulate to make sure students are using the word *characters* correctly in their discussions.

Use the following supports with students at varying proficiency levels:

- Write the following sentences on the board and have students echo read them: *A character is a person in a story. In a play, we learn about characters by looking at their actions and words. Learning more about a character is called* character development. **SUBSTANTIAL**

- Have students use the following sentence frames to discuss character development: *A character is _____. A playwright is _____. A playwright teaches us about characters through _____ and _____. Learning about characters is called _____.* **MODERATE**

- Ask students to answer the following questions in their discussions: *What is a character? What is a playwright? How does a playwright develop characters?* **LIGHT**

READING

Make Mental Images

Help students practice forming mental images, or pictures they imagine in their minds while reading, for scenes without illustration.

Work with students to read paragraphs 1–3. Use the following supports with students at varying proficiency levels:

- Work with students to highlight words that help them form a mental image. Read the words aloud as they draw a picture of the scene described. **SUBSTANTIAL**

- Have student pairs highlight words that help them form a mental image. Then have them draw the image. **MODERATE**

- Have students draw a picture of the mental image they formed after reading the paragraphs. Have them label each part of the drawing using words from the text. **LIGHT**

WRITING

Write a Character Study

Draw students' attention to the writing assignment on page 455.

Use the following supports with students at varying proficiency levels:

- Work with a group of students and select a character to study. Create an idea web on the board, and have students use single words or simple phrases to describe the character. Use the web to write a paragraph together and have students copy it in their notebooks. **SUBSTANTIAL**

- Work with students to create an idea web about a character, having students use text evidence to suggest ideas about the character. Then have students work in pairs to use the web to write a paragraph about the character. **MODERATE**

- Have student pairs create idea webs together about a character, using text evidence. Then have each student use the web to write his or her own paragraph. **LIGHT**

? **Connect to the**
ESSENTIAL QUESTION

In this selection, a prince and a pauper decide to switch clothes and pretend to be each other for a day. Both of them quickly learn that people treat them differently because of their clothes. The prince finds that many people are cruel to him when they think he is a pauper. The pauper, on the other hand, discovers that he cannot convince people that he is not the real prince as long as he is wearing the prince's royal clothing. With their disguised identities, both are able to learn hidden truths about people and the world.

THE PRINCE AND THE PAUPER

by **Mark Twain**
dramatized by **Joellen Bland**

? ESSENTIAL QUESTION:

What hidden truths about people and the world are revealed in stories?

434   Unit 6

 LEARNING MINDSET

Persistence Remind students that they will grow as learners if they have a "stick to it" attitude and don't give up on challenging tasks. This can develop stamina, which allows them to finish the most difficult tasks. Tell them persistence is key to not quitting before an assignment is complete.

QUICK START

A drama, or play, is a story performed by actors on stage, often in front of a live audience. Many dramas are also filmed. What do you think makes a drama worth reading or watching? Discuss your ideas with your group.

ANALYZE HOW PLAYWRIGHTS DEVELOP CHARACTERS

The person who writes a play, the **playwright,** uses stage directions and dialogue to develop the play's characters. **Stage directions** are instructions in the script to the actors, director, and stage crew. Stage directions might suggest scenery, lighting, sound effects, and ways for actors to move and speak. These instructions are often set in italics within parentheses in the script.

Stage directions help reveal character by:

- explaining how a character delivers, or says, his or her lines
- describing the gestures and movement of a character
- noting how characters respond to each other and to events

Dialogue is the conversation between two or more characters. Through dialogue, characters:

- express their thoughts, feelings, and motivations
- respond and react to other characters and events in the play

As you read, look for ways the playwright uses stage directions and dialogue to develop characters.

CREATE MENTAL IMAGES TO DEEPEN UNDERSTANDING

As you read a play, pause often to use stage directions and dialogue to help you visualize, or **create mental images,** of how the characters act and interact. Creating mental images can help you deepen your understanding of the text and make connections to your own experiences. Consider reading aloud, **adjusting fluency,** or how quickly you read, to suit the purposes of dialogue and stage directions.

ELEMENT	PURPOSE	EXAMPLE
Stage directions	describe the setting and characters' actions	*He seizes* Prince, *but* Miles *strikes him with flat of his sword.*
Dialogue	helps readers imagine what the characters think and feel	**Tom.** Oh there is no hope for me now. They will hang me for certain!

GENRE ELEMENTS: DRAMA

- includes a script, or the text of the play
- contains a list of all the characters, called the cast of characters
- is divided into large sections called acts and smaller sections called scenes
- in a one-act play, each episode of the plot is presented as one scene
- tells a story through dialogue, the spoken words of characters
- includes stage directions that give instructions about performing the drama

The Prince and the Pauper   435

QUICK START

Have students read the Quick Start prompt. Ask them to share any experiences they have had watching, reading, or acting in plays. Have them share how they think reading a play is different from reading a more traditional story. Then have them form groups to discuss what makes a play worth reading or watching.

ANALYZE HOW PLAYWRIGHTS DEVELOP CHARACTERS

Remind students that in a traditional story, an author can develop a character by describing that character's thoughts and feelings. A playwright—or the author of a play—has to reveal details about a character through staging and dialogue. Review the information about staging and dialogue with students. Ask volunteers to share what is revealed about Tom in the dialogue example at the bottom of the page.

CREATE MENTAL IMAGES TO DEEPEN UNDERSTANDING

Tell students that although there are illustrations in this play, not every scene is illustrated. They will have to imagine some of the scenes in their minds, just as they have done with many other stories. Tell students to ask themselves the following questions to help them create mental images as they read:

- What details of the scene are described in the stage directions?
- How do I think the characters look and act based on both the stage direction and their dialogue?

Ask partners to draw a picture of what they imagine based on the stage directions example at the bottom of the page and share their drawings with the class.

 ENGLISH LEARNER SUPPORT

Introduce the Cast of Characters Provide prereading support by displaying brief descriptions of each of the characters: Edward is the prince who is soon to become king; Tom Canty is a poor boy who lives in the kingdom; Lord Hertford and Lord St. John are two royals who care for the prince; King Henry is Edward's father, who is very sick; Miles Hendon is a returning soldier; John Canty is Tom's cruel father; Hugo is John's friend and a thief; Sir Hugh Hendon is Miles' dishonest brother who stole his wife. Also define the terms *herald, justice, constable, jailer, pages, lords, ladies,* and *villagers.* **ALL LEVELS**

TEACH

CRITICAL VOCABULARY

Encourage students to read all the sentences before deciding which word best completes each one. Remind them to look for context clues that match the meaning of each word.

Answers:

1. *wistfully*

2. *perplexed*

3. *jest*

4. *rueful*

5. *anxiously*

6. *discreetly*

■ English Learner Support

Use Cognates Tell students that some of the Critical Vocabulary words have Spanish cognates: *anxiously/ansiosamente, discreetly/discretemente, perplexed/perplejo.*
ALL LEVELS

LANGUAGE CONVENTIONS

Emphasize that a preposition's purpose is to relate a noun or pronoun to the rest of the sentence. Provide example sentences using the prepositions in the chart and discuss how each preposition connects a noun or pronoun to the sentence. Review that a prepositional phrase consists of two or more words: the preposition and a noun or pronoun. Ask students to create original sentences containing prepositional phrases, and have partners identify the prepositional phrases in the sentences.

✎ ANNOTATION MODEL

Remind students that they will practice developing mental images. Some of their annotations will focus on analyzing the language the playwright uses to help the reader develop these images. The sample annotation shows how a reader took notes in the margin about mental images. Remind students they are free to use whatever system of annotation is most useful to them.

CRITICAL VOCABULARY

wistfully   anxiously   discreetly   rueful   jest   perplexed

To preview the Critical Vocabulary words, choose the best word to complete each sentence.

1. She _____ imagined having fun swimming in the pool.

2. I was _____ when my best friend didn't reply to my message.

3. The actors _____ with each other to make us laugh.

4. The boy was _____ after he was caught cheating.

5. The class waited _____ for the results of the final exam.

6. Not wanting to disturb the class, he whispered _____.

LANGUAGE CONVENTIONS

Prepositions and Prepositional Phrases A **preposition** shows the relationship of a noun or pronoun to another word. Commonly used prepositions include *at, by, for, from, in, of, on, to,* and *with.* A **prepositional phrase** consists of a preposition, its object, and any modifiers of the object. A prepositional phrase functions as an adverb or an adjective because it modifies, or describes, a verb or a noun. As you read the play, note the playwright's use of prepositions and prepositional phrases.

ANNOTATION MODEL   NOTICE & NOTE

As you read, note how stage directions and dialogue can help you create mental images. In the model, you can see how one student marked stage directions and made notes about mental images.

2   **Setting:** *Westminster Palace, England. Gates leading to courtyard are at right. Slightly to the left, off courtyard and inside gates, interior of palace anteroom is visible. There is a couch with a rich robe draped on it, screen at rear, bellcord, mirror, chairs, and a table with bowl of nuts, and a large golden seal on it. Piece of armor hangs on one wall. Exits are rear and downstage.*

> Italics show that this is a stage direction.
>
> The details help me picture the setting—a fancy room in a palace.

BACKGROUND

Mark Twain (1835–1910) is one of America's most beloved writers. Born Samuel Clemens, he adopted his pen name when he began his writing career. He is well known for his novels The Adventures of Tom Sawyer and Adventures of Huckleberry Finn. Twain's The Prince and the Pauper concerns Prince Edward, King Henry VIII's son, who became king in 1547 at the age of nine. This adaptation is by **Joellen Bland,** who has been writing scripted versions of classic stories for more than 30 years.

THE PRINCE AND THE PAUPER

by Mark Twain
dramatized by Joellen Bland

SETTING A PURPOSE

As you read, pay attention to how the stage directions and dialogue help you understand the play's characters and visualize the play's setting and action.

Notice & Note

Use the side margins to notice and note signposts in the text.

CHARACTERS

Edward, Prince of Wales	Justice
Tom Canty, the Pauper	Constable
Lord Hertford	Jailer
Lord St. John	Sir Hugh Hendon
King Henry VIII	Two Prisoners
Herald	Two Guards
Miles Hendon	Three Pages
John Canty, Tom's father	Lords and Ladies
Hugo, a young thief	Villagers
Two Women	

The Prince and the Pauper   437

BACKGROUND

Have students read the background information about the author. Explain that even today, Mark Twain is one of America's most famous writers because of his style and humor. Through some of his writing, Twain reveals his ideas about society, about rich and poor, and about how people should treat each other.

SETTING A PURPOSE

Direct students to use the Setting a Purpose prompt to focus their reading.

▶ Text in FOCUS   TEXT IN FOCUS

Reading Stage Directions   Have students view the **Text in Focus** video in their eBook to learn how to use stage directions to better understand the play's characters, setting, and action. Then have students use **Text in Focus Practice PDF** to apply what they have learned.

▶ NOTICE & NOTE

Remind students of the prompt to indicate signposts in the margin. This lesson asks students to look for the **Aha Moment** signpost, which indicates when a character realizes something very important.

EL ENGLISH LEARNER SUPPORT

Understand Plot   To help students understand the play's plot and provide practice speaking in English, write the following sentences on the board:

- Prince Edward is about to become the King after his father dies.
- Tom Canty is a poor boy with a hard life.
- Prince Edward and Tom switch clothes.
- People think Tom is the prince.
- People think Edward is a poor boy.

Have students repeat each sentence twice chorally, then twice to a partner. **SUBSTANTIAL**

LANGUAGE CONVENTIONS

Remind students that a preposition's purpose is to relate a noun or pronoun to the rest of the sentence. Review that a prepositional phrase consists of two or more words: the preposition and a noun or pronoun. Refer students back to page 436 if they are having trouble understanding which words and phrases to mark.

ENGLISH LEARNER SUPPORT

Recognize Dialogue Tell students that *dialogue* means the words the characters actually say. Have them point to a boldfaced word. Tell students that boldfaced words are characters' names, which aren't spoken aloud. Then have students point to italicized words. Tell them that italicized words are stage directions and they are not spoken aloud either. Work with students to highlight the dialogue in paragraphs 4–6, and have three volunteers read the dialogue aloud.
MODERATE

ANALYZE HOW PLAYWRIGHTS DEVELOP CHARACTERS

Review that playwrights must reveal details about characters through the characters' dialogue and actions. A reader must infer certain details about a character by analyzing what that character says and does. (**Answer:** *The prince is a curious person and wants to know all about Tom. He is sensitive because he is shocked that Tom's father beats him. And he is observant: he notices that Tom speaks well and has "an easy grace," which is unexpected in a boy of Tom's circumstances.*)

 For **listening, speaking, and reading support** for students at varying proficiency levels, see the **Text X-Ray** on pages 434C and 434D.

 NOTICE & NOTE

LANGUAGE CONVENTIONS
The setting's description includes several prepositional phrases that add details. Mark the prepositions and prepositional phrases.

Scene 1

1 **Time:** *1547.*

2 **Setting:** *Westminster Palace, England. Gates leading to courtyard are at right. Slightly to the left, off courtyard and inside gates, interior of palace anteroom[1] is visible. There is a couch with a rich robe draped on it, screen at rear, bellcord, mirror, chairs, and a table with bowl of nuts, and a large golden seal on it. Piece of armor hangs on one wall. Exits are rear and downstage.*

3 **At Curtain Rise:** *Two Guards—one at right, one at left—stand in front of gates, and several Villagers hover nearby, straining to see into courtyard where Prince may be seen through fence, playing. Two Women enter right.*

4 **1st Woman.** I have walked all morning just to have a glimpse of Westminster Palace.

5 **2nd Woman.** Maybe if we can get near enough to the gates, we can have a glimpse of the young Prince. (*Tom Canty, dirty and ragged, comes out of crowd and steps close to gates.*)

6 **Tom.** I have always dreamed of seeing a real Prince! (*Excited, he presses his nose against gates.*)

7 **1st Guard.** Mind your manners, you young beggar! (*Seizes Tom by collar and sends him sprawling into crowd.* Villagers *laugh, as Tom slowly gets to his feet.*)

8 **Prince** (*rushing to gates*). How dare you treat a poor subject of the King in such a manner! Open the gates and let him in! (*As Villagers see Prince, they take off their hats and bow low.*)

9 **Villagers** (*shouting together*). Long live the Prince of Wales! (Guards *open gates and Tom slowly passes through, as if in a dream.*)

10 **Prince** (*to Tom*). You look tired, and you have been treated cruelly. I am Edward, Prince of Wales. What is your name?

11 **Tom** (*looking around in awe*). Tom Canty, Your Highness.

12 **Prince.** Come into the palace with me, Tom. (*Prince leads Tom into anteroom. Villagers pantomime[2] conversation, and all but a few exit.*) Where do you live, Tom?

13 **Tom.** In the city, Your Highness, in Offal Court.

14 **Prince.** Offal Court?[3] That is an odd name. Do you have parents?

ANALYZE HOW PLAYWRIGHTS DEVELOP CHARACTERS
Annotate: Mark the dialogue in paragraphs 12–18.

Analyze: What does this conversation reveal about the character of the Prince?

---

[1] **anteroom** (ăn´tē-rōōm´): an outer room that leads to another room and is often used as a waiting room.
[2] **pantomime** (păn´tə-mīm´): to communicate by gestures and facial expressions.
[3] **Offal Court:** a place very poor people lived, named after the waste products from butchering animals.

438   Unit 6

15 **Tom.** Yes, Your Highness.

16 **Prince.** How does your father treat you?

17 **Tom.** If it please you, Your Highness, when I am not able to beg a penny for our supper, he treats me to beatings.

18 **Prince** (*shocked*). What! Beatings? My father is not a calm man, but he does not beat me. (*looks at* Tom *thoughtfully*) You speak well and have an easy grace. Have you been schooled?

19 **Tom.** Very little, Your Highness. A good priest who shares our house in Offal Court has taught me from his books.

20 **Prince.** Do you have a pleasant life in Offal Court?

21 **Tom.** Pleasant enough, Your Highness, save when I am hungry. We have Punch and Judy shows,[4] and sometimes we lads have fights in the street.

22 **Prince** (*eagerly*). I should like that. Tell me more.

23 **Tom.** In summer, we run races and swim in the river, and we love to wallow in the mud.

24 **Prince** (*sighing, wistfully*). If I could wear your clothes and play in the mud just once, with no one to forbid me, I think I could give up the crown!

25 **Tom** (*shaking his head*). And if I could wear your fine clothes just once, Your Highness . . .

wistfully
(wĭst´fəl-ē) *adv.* When you think of something *wistfully*, you do so with sadness and longing.

_____
[4] **Punch and Judy shows:** famous puppet show originating in 16th-century Italy, featuring Mr. Punch and his wife, Judy, who are always fighting.

The Prince and the Pauper 439

APPLYING ACADEMIC VOCABULARY

☐ emphasize   ☑ occur   ☑ period   ☐ relevant   ☐ tradition

Write and Discuss Have students turn to a partner to discuss the following questions. Guide students to include the Academic Vocabulary words *occur* and *period* in their responses. Ask volunteers to share their responses with the class.

- What is surprising about the events that **occur** after the guards push Tom down at the gate?
- What details about the time **period** of this story have you learned?

CRITICAL VOCABULARY

wistfully: The prince sighs with sad longing.

ASK STUDENTS why the prince would sigh wistfully when thinking about Tom's life. (*The prince sometimes wishes he could lead a normal life and play like a normal kid.*)

ANALYZE HOW PLAYWRIGHTS DEVELOP CHARACTERS

Tell students that in this scene, the playwright uses words and actions that help further develop the character of the prince. (**Answer:** *The prince is caring; when he sees the bruise, he speaks "angrily" and says that the guard was "shameful and cruel." The prince is a person of action and wants to set things right immediately. The prince is also used to giving orders. Though he is being friendly and taking care of Tom, he says, "I command you!"*)

EL ENGLISH LEARNER SUPPORT

Act it Out To help students understand the key plot point in which Tom and Edward switch clothes, have two students act out this event, using a simple costume piece such as a jacket. Give one student a name tag that says "Tom" and the student wearing the jacket or hoodie a name tag that says "Prince Edward." Then have the student wearing the jacket or hoodie give it to the other student. To demonstrate the confusion that the other characters in the play are experiencing, point to Tom's nametag and say, "Hello, Prince." Have other students greet Tom as the prince as well. Then say, "You're just a dirty pauper!" to the prince and have several students repeat those words to the prince.
SUBSTANTIAL

CRITICAL VOCABULARY

anxiously: When he first leaves the palace, Tom looks around with dread.

ASK STUDENTS why Tom is feeling anxious. (*He cannot find the Prince.*)

 NOTICE & NOTE

ANALYZE HOW PLAYWRIGHTS DEVELOP CHARACTERS

Annotate: Reread paragraphs 30–32. Mark words and phrases that help you understand the Prince's character.

Draw Conclusions: What do you learn about the Prince through his words and actions in these paragraphs?

anxiously
(ăngk´shəs-lē) *adv.* To think of something *anxiously* means that you dread it.

26 **Prince.** Would you like that? Come, then. We shall change places. You can take off your rags and put on my clothes—and I will put on yours. (*He leads* Tom *behind screen, and they return shortly, each wearing the other's clothes.*) Let's look at ourselves in this mirror. (*leads* Tom *to mirror*)

27 **Tom.** Oh, Your Highness, it is not proper for me to wear such clothes.

28 **Prince** (*excitedly, as he looks in mirror*). Heavens, do you not see it? We look like brothers! We have the same features and bearing.[5] If we went about together, dressed alike, there is no one who could say which is the Prince of Wales and which is Tom Canty!

29 **Tom** (*drawing back and rubbing his hand*). Your Highness, I am frightened. . . .

30 **Prince.** Do not worry. (*seeing* Tom *rub his hand*) Is that a bruise on your hand?

31 **Tom.** Yes, but it is a slight thing, Your Highness.

32 **Prince** (*angrily*). It was shameful and cruel of that guard to strike you. Do not stir a step until I come back. I command you! (*He picks up golden Seal of England[6] and carefully puts it into piece of armor. He then dashes out to gates.*) Open! Unbar the gates at once! (*2nd Guard opens gates, and as* Prince *runs out, in rags,* 1st Guard *seizes him, boxes him on the ear, and knocks him to the ground.*)

33 **1st Guard.** Take that, you little beggar, for the trouble you have made for me with the Prince. (Villagers *roar with laughter.*)

34 **Prince** (*picking himself up, turning on* Guard *furiously*). I am Prince of Wales! You shall hang for laying your hand on me!

35 **1st Guard** (*presenting arms; mockingly*). I salute Your Gracious Highness! (*Then, angrily,* 1st Guard *shoves* Prince *roughly aside.*) Be off, you mad bag of rags! (Prince *is surrounded by* Villagers, *who hustle him off.*)

36 **Villagers** (*ad lib,[7] as they exit, shouting*). Make way for His Royal Highness! Make way for the Prince of Wales! Hail to the Prince! (*etc.*)

37 **Tom** (*admiring himself in mirror*). If only the boys in Offal Court could see me! They will not believe me when I tell them about this. (*looks around* **anxiously**) But where is the Prince? (*Looks cautiously into courtyard. Two* Guards *immediately snap*

---

[5] **features and bearing:** parts of the face and ways of standing or walking.
[6] **Seal of England:** a device used to stamp a special design, usually a picture of the ruler, onto a document, thus indicating that it has royal approval.
[7] **ad lib:** talk together about what is going on, but without an actual script.

CLOSE READ SCREENCAST

Modeled Discussion In their eBook, have students view the Close Read Screencast, in which readers discuss and annotate paragraphs 34–36 (a passage in which Edward is mistaken for a beggar) and 114–119 (a passage in which Edward is with thieves).

As a class, view and discuss the videos. Then have students pair up to do an independent close read of paragraphs 188–191. Students can record their answers on the Close Read Practice PDF.

 Close Read Practice PDF

to attention and salute. *He quickly ducks back into anteroom as* Lords Hertford *and* St. John *enter at rear.*)

38 **Hertford** (*going toward* Tom, *then stopping and bowing low*). My Lord, you look distressed. What is wrong?

39 **Tom** (*trembling*). Oh, I beg of you, be merciful. I am no Prince, but poor Tom Canty of Offal Court. Please let me see the Prince, and he will give my rags back to me and let me go unhurt. (*kneeling*) Please, be merciful and spare me!

40 **Hertford** (*puzzled and disturbed*). Your Highness, on your knees? To me? (*bows quickly, then, aside to* St. John) The Prince has gone mad! We must inform the King. (*to* Tom) A moment, your Highness. (Hertford *and* St. John *exit rear.*)

41 **Tom.** Oh, there is no hope for me now. They will hang me for certain! (Hertford *and* St. John *re-enter, supporting* King. Tom *watches in awe as they help him to couch, where he sinks down wearily.*)

42 **King** (*beckoning* Tom *close to him*). Now, my son, Edward, my prince. What is this? Do you mean to deceive me, the King, your father, who loves you and treats you so kindly?

43 **Tom** (*dropping to his knees*). You are the King? Then I have no hope!

44 **King** (*stunned*). My child, you are not well. Do not break your father's old heart. Say you know me.

45 **Tom.** Yes, you are my lord the King, whom God preserve.

46 **King.** True, that is right. Now, you will not deny that you are Prince of Wales, as they say you did just a while ago?

47 **Tom.** I beg you, Your Grace, believe me. I am the lowest of your subjects, being born a pauper, and it is by a great mistake that I am here. I am too young to die. Oh, please, spare me, sire!

48 **King** (*amazed*). Die? Do not talk so, my child. You shall not die.

49 **Tom** (*gratefully*). God save you, my king! And now, may I go?

50 **King.** Go? Where would you go?

51 **Tom.** Back to the alley where I was born and bred to misery.

52 **King.** My poor child, rest your head here. (*He holds* Tom's *head and pats his shoulder, then turns to* Hertford *and* St. John.) Alas, I am old and ill, and my son is mad. But this shall pass. Mad or sane, he is my heir and shall rule England. Tomorrow he shall be installed and confirmed in his princely dignity! Bring the Great Seal!

CREATE MENTAL IMAGES
Annotate: Reread paragraphs 39–40. Mark phrases that help you visualize the characters and the play's action.

Analyze: Why do you think Tom is "trembling"? Why is Hertford "puzzled and disturbed"?

ANALYZE HOW PLAYWRIGHTS DEVELOP CHARACTERS
Annotate: Reread paragraphs 43–47. Mark words and phrases that provide information about Tom's character.

Infer: How do you think Tom feels in the presence of the King? Why does he think he is going to die?

CREATE MENTAL IMAGES

Before students annotate, ask them to explain what Hertford, St. John, and the King think. Also ask them what the stage directions reveal about the King and what they predict might happen to the King next. (**Answer:** *Tom is afraid because he knows Hertford will not understand that the prince switched clothes with Tom on purpose. Hertford is "puzzled and disturbed" because he is seeing Tom as the prince and doesn't understand why the boy is acting like a beggar. This scene established the switching of the identities that affects events to come.*)

■ English Learner Support

Use Pictorial Support Help students create a mental image by illustrating the scene using simple drawings. Make sure you include Tom dressed as the prince, looking afraid, and the other characters addressing him as the prince. Depict the king as sickly and close to death.   **SUBSTANTIAL**

ANALYZE HOW PLAYWRIGHTS DEVELOP CHARACTERS

Understanding that Tom and Edward never intended to deceive anyone is important to getting an insight into their characters. Ask leading questions to make sure students know that both boys are honest about their identities, yet nobody believes them. (**Answer:** *Tom is in awe of the king. Tom drops to his knees and speaks very respectfully to the king. However, he is also very nervous in the presence of the king. Tom thinks he will be punished for pretending to be the prince.*)

WHEN STUDENTS STRUGGLE . . .

Sketch to Stretch The emphasis on mental images during this selection provides an excellent opportunity to use a Sketch to Stretch activity for struggling readers. Work with students to underline any text they find confusing. Have them attempt to sketch out what that text is about. They should label their drawings with words from the text. Have them turn to a partner and share their drawing.

For additional support, go to the **Reading Studio** and assign the following **Level Up tutorial: Elements of Drama.**

TEACH

 CREATE MENTAL
IMAGES

Clarify for students that *pages* are servants. Ask a volunteer to remind the class how they can determine that text is stage direction and not dialogue. **(Answer:** *The pages stop Tom from doing things and do them for him, which looks comical. The repeated phrase "does it for him" in the stage directions emphasizes the humor of these actions. Tom's comment, "I wonder that you do not try to breathe for me also!" is humorous, though he might say it in frustration. These interactions show that Tom is tired but is still very much himself and not the prince.)*

 ANALYZE HOW
PLAYWRIGHTS
DEVELOP CHARACTERS

Ask a volunteer to briefly paraphrase Hertford's thinking so the class is clear about the meaning of this important piece of dialogue. **(Answer:** *Hertford thinks that anyone who would pretend to be the prince and succeed in fooling the king and court would never then admit that he was an imposter. But we know that Tom never meant to impersonate the prince in the first place. All he wanted to do was try on the prince's clothes for a moment. Tom does not have royal aspirations. He is honest and also terrified of punishment.)*

CREATE MENTAL IMAGES
Annotate: Reread paragraphs 60–61. Mark stage directions and visualize the action.

Infer: How do the Pages' actions and Tom's reaction to them create humor in this scene?

ANALYZE HOW PLAYWRIGHTS DEVELOP CHARACTERS
Annotate: In paragraph 65, mark Hertford's lines in which he explains how a real impostor would act.

Analyze: Why does Hertford reason that the "Prince" cannot be an impostor? What do we know about Tom to prove that Hertford is wrong?

---

53 **Hertford** (*bowing low*). Please, Your Majesty, you took the Great Seal from the Chancellor two days ago to give to His Highness the Prince.

54 **King.** So I did. (*to* Tom) My child, tell me, where is the Great Seal?

55 **Tom** (*trembling*). Indeed, my lord, I do not know.

56 **King.** Ah, your affliction[8] hangs heavily upon you. 'Tis no matter. You will remember later. Listen, carefully! (*gently, but firmly*) I command you to hide your affliction in all ways that be within your power. You shall deny to no one that you are the true prince, and if your memory should fail you upon any occasion of state, you shall be advised by your uncle, the Lord Hertford.

57 **Tom** (*resigned*). The King has spoken. The King shall be obeyed.

58 **King.** And now, my child, I go to rest. (*He stands weakly, and* Hertford *leads him off, rear.*)

59 **Tom** (*wearily, to* St. John). May it please your lordship to let me rest now?

60 **St. John.** So it please Your Highness, it is for you to command and us to obey. But it is wise that you rest, for this evening you must attend the Lord Mayor's banquet in your honor. (*He pulls bellcord, and* Three Pages *enter and kneel before* Tom.)

61 **Tom.** Banquet? (*Terrified, he sits on couch and reaches for cup of water, but* 1st Page *instantly seizes cup, drops on one knee, and serves it to him.* Tom *starts to take off his boots, but* 2nd Page *stops him and does it for him. He tries to remove his cape and gloves, and* 3rd Page *does it for him.*) I wonder that you do not try to breathe for me also! (*Lies down cautiously.* Pages *cover him with robe, then back away and exit.*)

62 **St. John** (*to* Hertford, *as he enters*). Plainly, what do you think?

63 **Hertford.** Plainly, this. The King is near death, my nephew the Prince of Wales is clearly mad and will mount the throne mad. God protect England, for she will need it!

64 **St. John.** Does it not seem strange that madness could so change his manner from what it used to be? It troubles me, his saying he is not the Prince.

65 **Hertford.** Peace, my lord! If he were an impostor and called himself Prince, that would be natural. But was there ever an impostor, who being called Prince by the King and court, denied it? Never! This is the true Prince gone mad. And tonight

---

[8] **affliction** (ə-flĭk′shən): a condition that causes pain and suffering.

all London shall honor him. (*Hertford and* St. John *exit. Tom sits up, looks around helplessly, then gets up.*)

66 **Tom.** I should have thought to order something to eat. (*sees bowl of nuts on table*) Ah! Here are some nuts! (*looks around, sees Great Seal in armor, takes it out, looks at it curiously*) This will make a good nutcracker. (*He takes bowl of nuts, sits on couch and begins to crack nuts with Great Seal and eat them, as curtain falls.*)

Scene 2

67 **Time:** *Later that night.*

68 **Setting**: *A street in London, near Offal Court. Played before the curtain.*

69 **At Curtain Rise:** Prince *limps in, dirty and tousled. He looks around wearily. Several* Villagers *pass by, pushing against him.*

70 **Prince.** I have never seen this poor section of London. I must be near Offal Court. If I can only find it before I drop! (John Canty *steps out of crowd, seizes* Prince *roughly.*)

71 **Canty.** Out at this time of night, and I warrant you haven't brought a farthing[9] home! If that is the case and I do not break all the bones in your miserable body, then I am not John Canty!

72 **Prince** (*eagerly*). Oh, are you his father?

73 **Canty.** *His* father? I am *your* father, and—

74 **Prince.** Take me to the palace at once, and your son will be returned to you. The King, my father, will make you rich beyond your wildest dreams. Oh, save me, for I am indeed the Prince of Wales.

75 **Canty** (*staring in amazement*). Gone stark mad! But mad or not, I'll soon find where the soft places lie in your bones. Come home! (*starts to drag* Prince *off*)

76 **Prince** (*struggling*). Let me go! I am the Prince of Wales, and the King shall have your life for this!

77 **Canty** (*angrily*). I'll take no more of your madness! (*raises stick to strike, but* Prince *struggles free and runs off, and* Canty *runs after him*)

Scene 3

78 **Setting:** *Same as Scene 1, with addition of dining table, set with dishes and goblets, on raised platform. Throne-like chair is at head of table.*

---

[9] **farthing** (fär´thĭng): a former British coin worth one-fourth of a British penny.

CREATE MENTAL IMAGES

Annotate: Mark information about the setting of Scene 2.

Analyze: Describe how this setting differs from the setting of Scene 1. What does the difference reveal?

EL ENGLISH LEARNER SUPPORT

Support Comprehension The hidden Great Seal will become important later in the play, so make sure students are clear on what has happened. Use drawings to help students understand that Prince Edward hid the Great Seal in a suit of armor before he left the palace. Then show Tom, unaware of the significance of the Great Seal, using it as a nutcracker. Have students complete the following sentence frames to demonstrate understanding: *The Prince hid the _____ in a _____. Tom used the _____ to _____.*

SUBSTANTIAL/MODERATE

✏ CREATE MENTAL IMAGES

Review with students where Scene 1 was set. Remind students that the word *offal* means "the parts of an animal that are inedible." It can also be a synonym for *garbage*. By giving the name Offal Court to Tom's home region, the playwright is trying to emphasize that Tom comes from really awful circumstances. **(Answer:** *Scene 1 starts at the palace, which is beautiful and lavish. Scene 2 starts on the street in Offal Court, a dirty part of town.*)

ENGLISH LEARNER SUPPORT

Pantomime Actions The King's death is another important plot point. Have volunteers pantomime paragraphs 79–87, in which guests are seated at the banquet and the herald announces the King's death. Have one student play Tom, and ask the other students look to Tom and say, "The King is dead. Long live the King! Long live Edward, King of England!" Have a student play the role of the prince knocking on the door, begging to be let in. Emphasize to students that the King has died, so the prince will become king. Everybody thinks Tom is the prince, so he is about to become king. The prince is very upset that he can't even get into the palace. **SUBSTANTIAL**

CRITICAL VOCABULARY

discreetly: Hertford speaks to Tom, who he thinks is the Prince, using self-restraint.

ASK STUDENTS why Hertford would speak discreetly. (*He thinks Tom is the prince, and finds his question strange. He is trying to show self-restraint and not speak in a tone that suggests he thinks the prince has gone crazy.*)

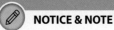

NOTICE & NOTE

discreetly
(dĭ-skrĕt´-lē) *adv.* To act *discreetly* means to act with self-restraint; attracting little notice.

79 **At Curtain Rise:** *A banquet is in progress.* Tom, *in royal robes, sits at head of table, with* Hertford *at his right and* St. John *at his left.* Lords *and* Ladies *sit around table eating and talking softly.*

80 **Tom** (*to* Hertford). What is this, my Lord? (*holds up a plate*)

81 **Hertford.** Lettuce and turnips, Your Highness.

82 **Tom.** Lettuce and turnips? I have never seen them before. Am I to eat them?

83 **Hertford** (*discreetly*). Yes, Your Highness, if you so desire. (Tom *begins to eat food with his fingers. Fanfare of trumpets is heard, and* Herald *enters, carrying scroll. All turn to look.*)

84 **Herald** (*reading from scroll*). His Majesty, King Henry VIII, is dead! The King is dead! (*All rise and turn to* Tom, *who sits, stunned.*)

85 **All** (*together*). The King is dead. Long live the King! Long live Edward, King of England! (*All bow to* Tom. Herald *bows and exits.*)

86 **Hertford** (*to* Tom). Your Majesty, we must call the council. Come, St. John. (Hertford *and* St. John *lead* Tom *off at rear.* Lords *and* Ladies *follow, talking among themselves. At gates, down right,* Villagers *enter and mill about.* Prince *enters right, pounds on gates and shouts.*)

87 **Prince.** Open the gates! I am the Prince of Wales! Open, I say! And though I am friendless with no one to help me, I will not be driven from my ground.

88 Miles Hendon (*entering through crowd*). <u>Though you be Prince or not, you are indeed a gallant lad and not friendless. Here I stand to prove it, and you might have a worse friend than Miles Hendon.</u>

89 1st Villager. Tis another prince in disguise. Take the lad and dunk him in the pond! (*He seizes* Prince, *but* <u>Miles *strikes him with flat of his sword.* Crowd, *now angry, presses forward threateningly, when fanfare of trumpets is heard offstage.* Herald, *carrying scroll, enters up left at gates.*)</u>

90 Herald. Make way for the King's messenger! (*reading from scroll*) His Majesty, King Henry VIII, is dead! The King is dead! (*He exits right, repeating message, and* Villagers *stand in stunned silence.*)

91 Prince (*stunned*). The King is dead!

92 1st Villager (*shouting*). Long live Edward, King of England!

93 Villagers (*together*). Long live the King! (*shouting, ad lib*) Long live King Edward! Heaven protect Edward, King of England! (*etc.*)

94 Miles (*taking* Prince *by the arm*). Come, lad, before the crowd remembers us. I have a room at the inn, and you can stay there. (*He hurries off with stunned* Prince. Tom, *led by* Hertford, *enters courtyard up rear.* Villagers *see them.*)

95 Villagers (*together*). Long live the King! (*They fall to their knees as curtains close.*)

Scene 4

96 Setting: Miles' *room at the inn. At right is table set with dishes and bowls of food, a chair at each side. At left is bed, with table and chair next to it, and a window. Candle is on table.*

97 At Curtain Rise: Miles *and* Prince *approach table.*

98 Miles. I have had a hot supper prepared. I'll bet you're hungry, lad.

99 Prince. Yes, I am. It's kind of you to let me stay with you, Miles. I am truly Edward, King of England, and you shall not go unrewarded. (*sits at table*)

100 Miles (*to himself*). <u>First he called himself Prince, and now he is King. Well, I will humor him.</u> (*starts to sit*)

101 Prince (*angrily*). Stop! Would you sit in the presence of the King?

102 Miles (*surprised, standing up quickly*). <u>I beg your pardon, Your Majesty. I was not thinking.</u> (*Stares uncertainly at* Prince, *who sits at table, expectantly.* Miles *starts to uncover dishes of food, serves* Prince *and fills glasses.*)

ANALYZE HOW PLAYWRIGHTS DEVELOP CHARACTERS

Annotate: In paragraphs 88–89, mark words and phrases that help you understand the character of Miles Hendon.

Analyze: Do you think that Miles Hendon is an important character? Why or why not?

AHA MOMENT

Notice & Note: What is Miles's opinion of the Prince? In paragraphs 100–102, mark Miles's thoughts.

Infer: Describe how Miles treats the Prince. Have his feelings changed? If so, how?

TEACH

ANALYZE HOW PLAYWRIGHTS DEVELOP CHARACTERS

Tell students that Miles Hendon is just being introduced, so the playwright is just starting to develop his character. Discuss students' initial impressions of Miles, and their predictions for how he might be important later. (**Answer:** *Miles offers friendship to the prince, and he protects him from the villager who grabs him. He will probably be important because he is a good, caring person, and the prince needs a friend right now.*)

AHA MOMENT

Remind students that an **Aha Moment** is when a character comes to an important realization. Here Miles has an Aha Moment about how he should treat the person claiming to be the new king. (**Answer:** *At first Miles is casual; he takes care of the prince the way a kindly grown-up would care for a child. However, when the prince speaks "angrily" as Miles "starts to sit," Miles stands up quickly and says, "I beg your pardon, Your Majesty." He then begins serving the prince his dinner; he decides he must "humor" the prince and go along with his claim that he is king.*)

ENGLISH LEARNER SUPPORT

Derive Meaning from Environmental Print Explain to students that environmental print includes words associated with things they use and places they go every day, including brand logos, traffic signs, and classroom labels.

Point out a sign, such as a label on a bookshelf, or a poster, such as classroom rules or the daily schedule, and read it aloud to students. Discuss how the print elements help readers identify specific items or information. Then have students work in small groups to find and write a list of these and other examples in the classroom, such as logos on computers and textbooks, your name plate, or even an exit sign, and discuss what each example identifies or describes.

ALL LEVELS

TEACH

✏ ANALYZE HOW PLAYWRIGHTS DEVELOP CHARACTERS

Point out the footnote so students are clear on the definition of a *baronet*. Ask volunteers to restate Miles's backstory. **(Answer:** *The prince has a strong sense of right and wrong and is outraged that Miles has been so badly treated. He also believes in repaying good deeds with more good deeds, because he wants to reward Miles for saving him "from injury and possible death.")*

■ English Learner Support

Make a Storyboard   Help students to understand Miles's backstory. Write the following sentences on the board:

Miles was the son of an important man.

Miles's father made him leave home 7 years ago.

Miles fought in the war and was taken prisoner.

Miles was in prison for 7 years.

Now Miles is free and he has returned home.

Have students read the sentences chorally, then copy each one, leaving room for a drawing. Have students draw simple pictures to illustrate each sentence. Have them write "Miles's Story" at the top of their papers.   **SUBSTANTIAL**

CRITICAL VOCABULARY

rueful: Miles looks sadly at his uneaten dinner.

ASK STUDENTS why Miles has a rueful look as he stands up. *(He isn't going to be able to eat his own supper because the prince asked him to watch over him as he sleeps.)*

ANALYZE HOW PLAYWRIGHTS DEVELOP CHARACTERS

Annotate: Reread paragraphs 104–109. Mark the Prince's response to Miles's story.

Analyze: What does the Prince's response to Miles's story reveal about him?

rueful
(rōō´fəl) *adj.* To be *rueful* is to show sorrow or regret.

103 **Prince.** Miles, you have a gallant way about you. Are you nobly born?

104 **Miles.** My father is a baronet,[10] Your Majesty.

105 **Prince.** Then you must also be a baronet.

106 **Miles** (*shaking his head*). My father banished me from home seven years ago, so I fought in the wars. I was taken prisoner, and I have spent the past seven years in prison. Now I am free, and I am returning home.

107 **Prince.** You have been shamefully wronged! But I will make things right for you. You have saved me from injury and possible death. Name your reward and if it be within the compass of my royal power, it is yours.

108 **Miles** (*pausing briefly, then dropping to his knee*). Since Your Majesty is pleased to hold my simple duty worthy of reward, I ask that I and my successors[11] may hold the privilege of sitting in the presence of the King.

109 **Prince** (*taking Miles' sword, tapping him lightly on each shoulder*). Rise and seat yourself. (*returns sword to Miles, then rises and goes over to bed*)

110 **Miles** (*rising*). He should have been born a king. He plays the part to a marvel! If I had not thought of this favor, I might have had to stand for weeks. (*sits down and begins to eat*)

111 **Prince.** Sir Miles, you will stand guard while I sleep? (*lies down and instantly falls asleep*)

112 **Miles.** Yes, Your Majesty. (*With a **rueful** look at his uneaten supper, he stands up.*) Poor little chap. I suppose his mind has been disordered with ill usage. (*covers Prince with his cape*) Well, I will be his friend and watch over him. (*Blows out candle, then yawns, sits on chair next to bed, and falls asleep. John Canty and Hugo appear at window, peer around room, then enter cautiously through window. They lift the sleeping Prince, staring nervously at Miles.*)

113 **Canty** (*in loud whisper*). I swore the day he was born he would be a thief and a beggar, and I won't lose him now. Lead the way to the camp Hugo! (*Canty and Hugo carry Prince off right, as Miles sleeps on and curtain falls.*)

Scene 5

114 **Time:** *Two weeks later.*

---

[10] **baronet** (băr´ə-nĭt): a rank of honor in Britain, below a baron and above a knight.
[11] **successors** (sək-sĕs´ərz): those, in sequence or line of succession, who have a right to property, to hold title or rank, or to hold the throne one after the other.

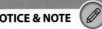

115 **Setting:** *Country village street.*

116 **Before Curtain Rise:** Villagers *walk about.* Canty, Hugo, *and* Prince *enter.*

117 **Canty.** I will go in this direction. Hugo, keep my mad son with you, and see that he doesn't escape again! (*exits*)

118 **Hugo** (*seizing* Prince *by the arm*). He won't escape! I'll see that he earns his bread today, or else!

119 **Prince** (*pulling away*). I will not beg with you, and I will not steal! I have suffered enough in this miserable company of thieves!

120 **Hugo.** You shall suffer more if you do not do as I tell you! (*raises clenched fist at* Prince) Refuse if you dare! (Woman *enters, carrying wrapped bundle in a basket on her arm.*) Wait here until I come back. (Hugo *sneaks along after* Woman, *then snatches her bundle, runs back to* Prince, *and thrusts it into his arms.*) Run after me and call, "Stop, thief!" But be sure you lead her astray! (*Runs off.* Prince *throws down bundle in disgust.*)

121 **Woman.** Help! Thief! Stop, thief! (*rushes at* Prince *and seizes him, just as several* Villagers *enter*) You little thief! What do you mean by robbing a poor woman? Somebody bring the constable! (Miles *enters and watches.*)

122 **1st Villager** (*grabbing* Prince). I'll teach him a lesson, the little villain!

123 **Prince** (*struggling*). Take your hands off me! I did not rob this woman!

124 **Miles** (*stepping out of crowd and pushing man back with the flat of his sword*). Let us proceed gently, my friends. This is a matter for the law.

125 **Prince** (*springing to* Miles' *side*). You have come just in time, Sir Miles. Carve this rabble to rags!

126 **Miles.** Speak softly. Trust in me and all shall go well.

127 **Constable** (*entering and reaching for* Prince). Come along, young rascal!

128 **Miles.** Gently, good friend. He shall go peaceably to the Justice.

129 **Prince.** I will not go before a Justice! I did not do this thing!

130 **Miles** (*taking him aside*). Sire, will you reject the laws of the realm, yet demand that your subjects respect them?

131 **Prince** (*calmer*). You are right, Sir Miles. Whatever the King requires a subject to suffer under the law, he will suffer himself while he holds the station of a subject. (Constable *leads them off right.* Villagers *follow. Curtain.*)

ANALYZE HOW PLAYWRIGHTS DEVELOP CHARACTERS

Annotate: Reread paragraphs 120-131. Mark words and phrases that show the behavior of both the Prince and Miles.

Evaluate: How does their behavior fit with what you know about them?

✏ ANALYZE HOW PLAYWRIGHTS DEVELOP CHARACTERS

Ask students to recap what they already know about Miles and the prince. Lead them to suggest that Miles is kind and helpful and had a hard life in prison. The prince, while kind, doesn't have any experience living in the real world and believes people should be giving him special treatment just because he is the prince. (**Answer:** *Without Miles, the prince was getting into deeper and deeper trouble. He wants Miles to behave as a servant or knight and "Carve this rabble to rags!" for him. With the calm advice of Miles, however, the prince finally goes along with "Whatever the King requires." Miles continues to play along with the prince by addressing him as "Sire," even though there is no evidence that Miles thinks he is anything other than an ordinary poor boy.*)

ANALYZE HOW PLAYWRIGHTS DEVELOP CHARACTERS

Discuss with students what hidden truths have been revealed about the woman and the constable during this brief exchange. **(Answer:** *The value of the stolen property determines the level of punishment of the thief. The woman doesn't want the boy to hang, so the Justice allows her to change the pig's value so the boy's punishment is not so severe. The constable is looking for some cheap food. The woman has stated in court that the pig is worth eight pence, though it is worth much more; the constable takes advantage of this, knowing that she can't make him pay more because he will tell the Justice, and the boy will hang.)*

■ English Learner Support

Support Comprehension Explain to students that *shillings* and *pence* were kinds of money used in England at the time this story is set. They are like *dollars* and *cents*.

Check that students understand what is happening in this scene by having them complete the following sentence frames:

- The woman and the constable think the prince _____.

- The woman tells the Justice that _____ is worth three shillings and eight pence.

- The Justice says that _____ will hang for stealing something that expensive.

- The woman doesn't want the boy to _____, so she says her pig is worth eight pence.

- The greedy constable tells the woman he will _____.
  MODERATE

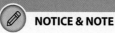
NOTICE & NOTE

ANALYZE HOW PLAYWRIGHTS DEVELOP CHARACTERS

Annotate: Reread paragraphs 134–147. Mark passages in the text that reveal the characters of the Woman and the Constable.

Analyze: Why does the Woman change the valué of her pig to eight pence? Why does the Constable do what he does?

Scene 6

132 **Setting:** *Office of the Justice. A high bench is at center.*

133 **At Curtain Rise:** *Justice sits behind bench.* Constable *enters with* Miles *and* Prince, *followed by* Villagers. Woman *carries wrapped bundle.*

134 **Constable** (*to* Justice). A young thief, your worship, is accused of stealing a dressed pig from this poor woman.

135 **Justice** (*looking down at* Prince, *then* Woman). My good woman, are you absolutely certain this lad stole your pig?

136 **Woman.** It was none other than he, your worship.

137 **Justice.** Are there no witnesses to the contrary? (*All shake their heads.*) Then the lad stands convicted. (*to* Woman) What do you hold this property to be worth?

138 **Woman.** Three shillings and eight pence, your worship.

139 **Justice** (*leaning down to* Woman). Good woman, do you know that when one steals a thing above the value of thirteen pence, the law says he shall hang for it?

140 **Woman** (*upset*). Oh, what have I done? I would not hang the poor boy for the whole world! Save me from this, your worship. What can I do?

141 **Justice** (*gravely*). You may revise the value, since it is not yet written in the record.

142 **Woman.** Then call the pig eight pence, your worship.

143 **Justice.** So be it. You may take your property and go. (Woman *starts off, and is followed by* Constable. Miles *follows them cautiously down right.*)

144 **Constable** (*stopping* Woman). Good woman, I will buy your pig from you. (*takes coins from pocket*) Here is eight pence.

145 **Woman.** Eight pence! It cost me three shillings and eight pence!

146 **Constable.** Indeed! Then come back before his worship and answer for this. The lad must hang!

147 **Woman.** No! No! Say no more. Give me the eight pence and hold your peace. (Constable *hands her coins and takes pig.* Woman *exits, angrily.* Miles *returns to bench.*)

148 **Justice.** The boy is sentenced to a fortnight[12] in the common jail. Take him away, Constable! (Justice *exits.* Prince *gives* Miles *a nervous glance.*)

---
[12] **fortnight:** 14 days; two weeks.

149 **Miles** (*following* Constable). Good sir, turn your back a moment and let the poor lad escape. He is innocent.

150 **Constable** (*outraged*). What? You say this to me? Sir, I arrest you in—

151 **Miles.** Do not be so hasty! (*slyly*) The pig you have purchased for eight pence may cost you your neck, man.

152 **Constable** (*laughing nervously*). Ah, but I was merely **jesting** with the woman, sir.

153 **Miles.** Would the Justice think it a jest?

154 **Constable.** Good sir! The Justice has no more sympathy with a jest than a dead corpse! (*perplexed*) Very well, I will turn my back and see nothing! But go quickly! (*exits*)

155 **Miles** (*to* Prince). Come, my liege.[13] We are free to go. And that band of thieves shall not set hands on you again, I swear it!

156 **Prince** (*wearily*). Can you believe, Sir Miles, that in the last fortnight, I, the King of England, have escaped from thieves and begged for food on the road? I have slept in a barn with a calf! I have washed dishes in a peasant's kitchen, and narrowly escaped death. And not once in all my wanderings did I see a courier[14] searching for me! Is it no matter for commotion and distress that the head of state is gone?

157 **Miles** (*sadly, aside*). Still busy with his pathetic dream. (*to* Prince) It is strange indeed, my liege. But come, I will take you to my father's home in Kent. We are not far away. There you may rest in a house with seventy rooms! Come, I am all impatience to be home again! (*They exit,* Miles *in cheerful spirits,* Prince *looking puzzled, as curtains close.*)

Scene 7

158 **Setting:** *Village jail. Bare stage, with barred window on one wall.*

159 **At Curtain Rise:** Two Prisoners, *in chains, are onstage.* Jailer *shoves* Miles *and* Prince, *in chains, onstage. They struggle and protest.*

160 **Miles.** But I tell you, I am Miles Hendon! My brother, Sir Hugh, has stolen my bride and my estate!

161 **Jailer.** Be silent! Impostor! Sir Hugh will see that you pay well for claiming to be his dead brother and for assaulting him in his own house! (*exits*)

---

[13] **my liege** (lēj): my lord.
[14] **courier** (kŏŏr´ē-ər): messenger.

ANALYZE HOW PLAYWRIGHTS DEVELOP CHARACTERS

Annotate: In paragraphs 149–157, mark how Miles gets the best of the Constable.

Infer: What does this reveal about Miles?

jest
(jĕst) *v.* To *jest* means to make playful remarks.

perplexed
(pər-plĕkst´) *adj.* When you are *perplexed,* you are puzzled.

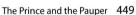 **ANALYZE HOW PLAYWRIGHTS DEVELOP CHARACTERS**

Discuss with students what this interaction reveals about Miles. Have them think about what they already know about Miles and what new information about him is revealed during this exchange. **(Answer:** *Miles cleverly threatens to turn the constable in to the justice for cheating the woman out of her pig. This shows a cunning side of Miles we haven't seen before. The constable allows the prince to escape with Miles, advancing the plot.)*

CRITICAL VOCABULARY

jest: The constable says he was just joking when he offered to buy the pig for eight pence.

ASK STUDENTS why the constable says he was jesting. *(Miles says the justice will hang the constable for ripping off the woman, so the constable pretends he was just kidding.)*

perplexed: The constable is puzzled as to why he is being asked to let the boy run away.

ASK STUDENTS why the constable might be perplexed. *(He thinks the boy is guilty and doesn't understand why he should be allowed to escape.)*

© Houghton Mifflin Harcourt Publishing Company

TEACH

AHA MOMENT

Tell students that in this **Aha Moment** signpost, the prince is coming to an important realization. This realization comes after he finally learns how hard people's lives are outside the palace. (**Answer:** *The prince shows sympathy with the plight of Miles and the other prisoners, even though they have, technically, committed crimes; he has learned that "Kings should go to school to learn their own laws and be merciful."*)

■ ENGLISH LEARNER SUPPORT

Acquire Vocabulary During the **Aha Moment**, the prince learns that kings should be merciful. The word *merciful* is repeated throughout the play, and the idea of granting mercy is an important theme of the story. Help students understand the meaning of *merciful*. Write *merciful* on the board and its definition "full of kindness." Then have them copy the word and its definition in their notebooks. Have them copy the sentence that uses the term in the play: "Kings should go to school to learn their own laws and be merciful." Have students illustrate the sentence. Discuss other ways a person could be merciful using the following sentence frames:

- *A person could be merciful to an animal by _____.*

- *The owner of a store might be merciful to a hungry thief by _____.* **MODERATE**

AHA MOMENT

Notice & Note: Reread paragraphs 163–165. Mark the Prince's response to the prisoners' stories.

Draw Conclusions: What lesson does the Prince learn in prison?

162 **Miles** (*sitting, with head in hands*). Oh, my dear Edith . . . now wife to my brother Hugh, against her will, and my poor father . . . dead!

163 **1st Prisoner.** At least you have your life, sir. I am sentenced to be hanged for killing a deer in the King's park.

164 **2nd Prisoner.** And I must hang for stealing a yard of cloth to dress my children.

165 **Prince** (*moved; to* Prisoners). <u>When I mount my throne, you shall all be free. And the laws that have dishonored you shall be swept from the books.</u> (*turning away*) <u>Kings should go to school to learn their own laws and be merciful.</u>

166 **1st Prisoner.** What does the lad mean? I have heard that the King is mad, but merciful.

167 **2nd Prisoner.** He is to be crowned at Westminster tomorrow.

168 **Prince** (*violently*). King? What King, good sir?

169 **1st Prisoner.** Why, we have only one, his most sacred majesty, King Edward the Sixth.

170 **2nd Prisoner.** And whether he be mad or not, his praises are on all men's lips. He has saved many innocent lives, and now he means to destroy the cruelest laws that oppress the people.

171 **Prince** (*turning away, shaking his head*). How can this be? Surely it is not that little beggar boy! (Sir Hugh *enters with* Jailer.)

172 **Sir Hugh.** Seize the impostor!

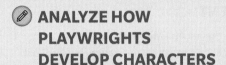

173 **Miles** (*as Jailer pulls him to his feet*). Hugh, this has gone far enough!

174 **Sir Hugh.** You will sit in the public stocks for two hours, and the boy would join you if he were not so young. See to it, jailer, and after two hours, you may release them. Meanwhile, I ride to London for the coronation![15] (*Sir Hugh* exits *and* Miles *is hustled out by* Jailer.)

175 **Prince.** Coronation! What does he mean? There can be no coronation without me! (*curtain falls*)

Scene 8

176 **Time:** *Coronation Day.*

177 **Setting:** *Outside gates of Westminster Abbey, played before curtain. Painted screen or flat at rear represents Abbey. Throne is in center. Bench is near it.*

178 **At Curtain Rise:** Lords *and* Ladies *crowd Abbey. Outside gates,* Guards *drive back cheering* Villagers, *among them* Miles.

179 **Miles** (*distraught*). I've lost him! Poor little chap! He has been swallowed up in the crowd! (*Fanfare of trumpets is heard, then silence.* Hertford, St. John, Lords *and* Ladies *enter slowly, in a procession, followed by* Pages, *one of whom carries crown on a small cushion.* Tom *follows procession, looking about nervously. Suddenly,* Prince, *in rags, steps out from crowd, his hand raised.*)

180 **Prince.** I forbid you to set the crown of England upon that head. I am the King!

181 **Hertford.** Seize the little vagabond!

182 **Tom.** I forbid it! He is the King! (*kneels before* Prince) Oh, my lord the King, let poor Tom Canty be the first to say, "Put on your crown and enter into your own right again." (Hertford *and several* Lords *look closely at both boys.*)

183 **Hertford.** This is strange indeed. (*to* Tom) By your favor, sir, I wish to ask certain questions of this lad.

184 **Prince.** I will answer truly whatever you may ask, my lord.

185 **Hertford.** But if you have been well trained, you may answer my questions as well as our lord the King. I need a definite proof. (*thinks a moment*) Ah! Where lies the Great Seal of England? It has been missing for weeks, and only the true Prince of Wales can say where it lies.

---

[15]**coronation** (kôr´ə-nā´shən): the act of crowning someone king or queen. In England, coronations usually take place at a large church in London called Westminster Abbey.

ANALYZE HOW PLAYWRIGHTS DEVELOP CHARACTERS

Annotate: Reread paragraphs 180–184. Mark key words and phrases that reveal the Prince's and Tom's behavior.

Analyze: Is their behavior consistent with how they've behaved before? Explain.

ANALYZE HOW PLAYWRIGHTS DEVELOP CHARACTERS

Tell students that a Coronation Day is the day a ceremony is held to crown a new king or queen. Everybody still thinks Tom is the prince, so he is about to be crowned king. It is Tom and the prince's last chance to convince people of their true identities, and fortunately in this scene their behavior finally causes people to question the mix-up. (**Answer:** *The prince and Tom work together to try to sort out the identity switch. The prince interrupts the royal procession and identifies himself as the king. This is the "I'm used to being waited on" prince that we have seen glimpses of in the past. Tom immediately kneels, in keeping with his role as a subject of the king, a regular, humble citizen who has no desire to continue in this false role as royal heir. Both are continuing to act, as best they can, as their real selves, which has been true all along. Their behavior has pointed out how easily people are swayed by appearances and how unfair this can be. Their behavior, now that they are seen together, is finally forcing others to question their own mistaken ideas and work toward sorting out the identity issue together.*)

AHA MOMENT

Remind students that an **Aha Moment** signpost is a moment when a character comes to a great realization, but also that this realization has a significant effect on the plot. Here the prince's realization is the key to resolving the plot. (**Answer:** *No one has been able to find the royal seal; only the "true Prince of Wales can say where it lies." Tom helps the prince remember where he put it before he "rushed out of the palace wearing [Tom's] rags." When it is found where the prince says it will be, everyone believes that he is Edward, Prince of Wales, and now King of England.*)

■ English Learner Support

Support Comprehension This is the point in the play where the Great Seal becomes significant again. Use pictures to illustrate the prince retrieving the Great Seal, Miles looking embarrassed, and all the people shouting and bowing at the prince when they realize his true identity. Have students complete the following sentence frames to demonstrate understanding: *The prince got the Great Seal out of the _____. Everyone knew only the prince would know where the _____ was. Therefore, when the prince finds the seal, everyone realizes _____.* **SUBSTANTIAL/MODERATE**

CREATE MENTAL IMAGES

Tell students that reading the stage direction helps give them a clear mental image of Miles when he realizes the boy he was befriending was actually the prince. This mental image gives a clue to Miles's feelings and the reason behind his words. (**Answer:** *Miles is stunned. He really thought he was helping an unfortunate, misguided boy. He asks for a bag to cover his head because he is embarrassed to have been so informal and casual with the king.*)

✎ NOTICE & NOTE

186 **Tom.** Wait! Was the seal round and thick, with letters engraved on it? (Hertford *nods.*) I know where it is, but it was not I who put it there. The rightful King shall tell you. (*to* Prince) Think, my King, it was the very last thing you did that day before you rushed out of the palace wearing my rags.

187 **Prince** (*pausing*). I recall how we exchanged clothes, but have no recollection[16] of hiding the Great Seal.

188 **Tom** (*eagerly*). Remember when you saw the bruise on my hand, you ran to the door, but first you hid this thing you call the Seal.

189 **Prince** (*suddenly*). Ah! I remember! (*to* St. John) Go, my good St. John, and you shall find the Great Seal in the armor that hangs on the wall in my chamber. (St. John *hesitates, but at a nod from* Tom, *hurries off.*)

190 **Tom** (*pleased*). Right, my King! Now the scepter[17] of England is yours again. (St. John *returns in a moment with* Great Seal.)

191 **All** (*shouting*). Long live Edward, King of England! (Tom *takes off his cape and throws it over* Prince's *rags. Trumpet fanfare is heard.* St. John *takes crown and places it on* Prince. *All kneel.*)

192 **Hertford.** Let the small impostor be flung into the Tower!

193 **Prince** (*firmly*). I will not have it so. But for him, I would not have my crown. (*to* Tom) My poor boy, how was it that you could remember where I hid the Seal, when I could not?

194 **Tom** (*embarrassed*). I did not know what it was, my King, and I used it to . . . to crack nuts. (*All laugh, and* Tom *steps back.* Miles *steps forward, staring in amazement.*)

195 **Miles.** Is he really the King? Is he indeed the sovereign of England, and not the poor and friendless Tom o' Bedlam[18] I thought he was? (*He sinks down on bench.*) I wish I had a bag to hide my head in!

196 **1st Guard** (*rushing up to him*). Stand up, you mannerless clown! How dare you sit in the presence of the King!

197 **Prince.** Do not touch him! He is my trusty servant, Miles Hendon, who saved me from shame and possible death. For his service, he owns the right to sit in my presence.

AHA MOMENT

Notice & Note: What do Tom and the Prince remember about the royal seal? In paragraphs 186–189, mark their memories.

Analyze: Why is the royal seal so important here?

CREATE MENTAL IMAGES

Annotate: Reread paragraph 195. Mark the stage direction.

Evaluate: How does the stage direction help you visualize how Miles reacts to the knowledge that the "mad" boy he has been helping really is the King?

---

[16] **recollection** (rĕk´ə-lĕk´shən): a memory or recalling to mind of something that happened before.

[17] **scepter** (sĕp´tər): a staff held by a king or queen as an emblem of authority.

[18] **Tom o' Bedlam:** an insane person, such as someone hospitalized at St. Mary of Bethlehem Hospital, or Bedlam Hospital, in London.

IMPROVE READING FLUENCY

Targeted Passage Have students work with partners to read the parts of the prince and Tom in paragraphs 186–190. Use the first paragraph to model how to read dramatic text with appropriate emotion and phrasing. Remind students to pause for commas and to make sure they read at an appropriate speed for the listener to understand what is being said. Then, have partners work together to read aloud the two characters' lines in the paragraphs. Encourage students to provide feedback and support for any challenging multisyllabic words and to encourage each other to read with appropriate speed and phrasing.

  Go to the **Reading Studio** for additional support in developing fluency.

198 **Miles** (*bowing, then kneeling*). Your Majesty!

199 **Prince.** Rise, Sir Miles. I command that Sir Hugh Hendon, who sits within this hall, be seized and put under lock and key until I have need of him. (*beckons to* Tom) From what I have heard, Tom Canty, you have governed the realm with royal gentleness and mercy in my absence. Henceforth, you shall hold the honorable title of King's Ward! (Tom *kneels and kisses* Prince's *hand.*) And because I have suffered with the poorest of my subjects and felt the cruel force of unjust laws, I pledge myself to a reign of mercy for all! (*All bow low, then rise.*)

200 **All** (*shouting*). Long live the King! Long live Edward, King of England! (*curtain*)

CHECK YOUR UNDERSTANDING

Answer these questions before moving on to the **Analyze the Text** section on the following page.

1 Why don't people realize that the Prince and Tom Canty are wearing each other's clothes?

 A People think the boys are wearing costumes in a play.

 B People do realize it, but they are afraid to say anything.

 C The Prince and Tom look and move like each other.

 D The Prince often dresses in the clothes of a commoner.

2 In paragraph 32, the Prince hides the royal seal in a piece of armor. How is this significant to the plot of the play?

 F It indicates that the royal seal has no meaning.

 G The armor keeps the seal shiny.

 H The Prince is able to prove his identity because he knew where the seal was hidden.

 J He wanted to hide the seal from his father.

3 What happens to Miles and the Prince when they arrive at the home of Miles's father?

 A They are greeted with open arms.

 B They are politely turned away.

 C A huge banquet is thrown in their honor.

 D They are put in chains and thrown in jail.

The Prince and the Pauper   453

TEACH

CHECK YOUR UNDERSTANDING

Have students answer the questions independently.

Answers:

 1. C

 2. H

 3. D

If they answer any questions incorrectly, have them reread the text to confirm their understanding. Then they may proceed to ANALYZE THE TEXT on page 454.

ENGLISH LEARNER SUPPORT

Oral Assessment   Use the following questions to assess students' comprehension and speaking skills:

1. Why don't people realize that the prince and Tom Canty are wearing each other's clothes? (*The people don't realize that the prince and Tom Canty are wearing each other's clothes because the prince and Tom look and move like each other.*)

2. The prince hides the royal seal in a piece of armor. Why is this important? (*It is important because later the Prince is able to prove his identity by knowing where the seal was hidden.*)

3. Miles and the prince go to the home of Miles's father. What happens to them there? (*Miles and the prince are put in chains and thrown in jail.*)

 SUBSTANTIAL/MODERATE

APPLY

ANALYZE THE TEXT

Possible answers:

1. **DOK 2:** *The prince and Tom change into each other's clothes, and the prince exclaims that they look like brothers. He hides the Great Seal of England in a piece of armor and goes to reprimand the guard for striking Tom. The guard, not recognizing the prince, knocks him to the ground. The prince tries to reprimand the guard, but he mocks him and makes him leave because he thinks he is the beggar.*

2. **DOK 3:** *No. Tom is anxious and afraid because he is sure Hertford will recognize him as an impostor. One piece of evidence is from Scene 1, paragraph 39: "Tom (trembling). Oh, I beg of you, be merciful. I am no Prince . . . and he will give my rags back to me and let me go unhurt. (kneeling) Please, be merciful and spare me!" Again, he drops to his knees in the presence of the king and asks to be spared (paragraphs 43–47). Even when the king assures Tom that he will not die, Tom says, "God save you, my king! And now, may I go?" (paragraph 49).*

3. **DOK 3:** *Miles is a kind, just man. Even though Miles thinks the prince is "mad," he takes him to his room at the inn and feeds and shelters him. He protects the prince from the crowd on the street who want to throw him in the pond. He continues to help and protect the prince throughout the play, even though he thinks he is deluded.*

4. **DOK 2:** *The stage direction tells us where the play takes place in each scene. For example, in scene 1 it says that the scene takes place in Westminster Palace. It gives descriptive details of the room. Stage direction also describes the action of the characters and deepens the reader's understanding by creating mental images. For example, in paragraph 6 Tom "presses his nose against gates" to get a glimpse of the prince.*

5. **DOK 4:** *The prince learns what it is like to be treated as a common person, a pauper, and a prisoner. He learns the importance of knowing the laws and being a merciful ruler. The prince learned in prison that Tom would have made a good king because he was kind and just. Tom was also honest and did not want to continue to act as king once the prince returned.*

RESEARCH

Point out the Research Tip about using specific search terms. Also make sure students understand the Roman numeral nomenclature used in the characters' names.

Connect Have groups create a visual aid, such as a Venn Diagram, to share their comparisons and contrasts with the class.

454 Unit 6

 RESPOND

ANALYZE THE TEXT

Support your responses with evidence from the text. ▤ NOTEBOOK

1. **Summarize** Review paragraphs 24–34. Summarize the events leading up to the Prince being thrown out of his own palace.

2. **Cite Evidence** Do you think Tom Canty is comfortable in his new role as the Prince? Cite evidence in the dialogue and stage directions that explains why or why not.

3. **Draw Conclusions** Review Scene 4. Based on the way Miles acts toward the Prince, what type of person do you think he is? Describe some of his character traits.

4. **Interpret** What types of information do the stage directions provide in the play? Give some examples. How do your examples help you visualize the action, guide you to adjust fluency (how quickly you read), and add to your understanding of the play?

5. **Notice & Note** How does the Prince's character change because of his experiences outside the palace? What is revealed about Tom Canty in his role as the Prince?

RESEARCH TIP
The best search terms are very specific. Along with the name *King Edward VI*, you will want to include a word such as *biography* or *childhood* to make sure you get the information you need.

RESEARCH

Prince Edward became king as a young boy, after the death of his father, King Henry VIII, in 1547. Research King Edward VI and what is known about his childhood. Use the chart below to record your results.

KING EDWARD VI: IMPORTANT CHILDHOOD EVENTS AND PEOPLE	
EVENT/PERSON	**DETAILS**
Birth	*October 12, 1537 Westminster Abbey, London, England*
Henry VIII Tudor and Jane Seymour	*Parents; King and Queen of England*
Mary and Elizabeth	*Edward's half-sisters; he was closer to Elizabeth who was only four years older.*

Connect With a small group, discuss what you learned about King Edward VI. Contrast the facts of Edward's childhood with the play's characterization of him.

454 Unit 6

 LEARNING MINDSET

Problem Solving Remind students that when students with a growth mindset encounter problems, they find resources to solve those problems instead of giving up. Ask volunteers to share examples of problems they solved during the lesson.

CREATE AND PRESENT

Write a Character Study Write a brief essay in which you describe and analyze one of the major characters in *The Prince and the Pauper*. Choose Edward, Tom Canty, Miles Hendon, or John Canty.

- ❑ Think about the character's traits, and describe how the playwright develops the character throughout the play.
- ❑ Use evidence from both the dialogue and stage directions in the play to support your analysis.
- ❑ Revise and edit your draft, using prepositions and prepositional phrases correctly.

Dramatic Reading With a small group, rehearse and perform a portion of the play. Then, watch another group perform a portion of the play.

- ❑ Decide who in your group will play each character.
- ❑ As you rehearse, adjust your delivery according to the intention and purpose of the lines you are reading, taking into account stage directions and what you know about the character.
- ❑ Invite suggestions from group members and consider them carefully. Take notes about how to deliver your lines.
- ❑ When you perform, remember to make eye contact, speak clearly and loudly, and pronounce words correctly.
- ❑ When you watch others perform, contrast the performance with what you "see" and "hear" when you read the text on your own.
- ❑ Record or take a video of your dramatic readings.

Go to **Using Textual Evidence** in the **Writing Studio** for more on using textual evidence.

Go to **Giving a Presentation: Delivering Your Presentation** in the **Speaking and Listening Studio** for help delivering your lines.

RESPOND TO THE ESSENTIAL QUESTION

? What hidden truths about people and the world are revealed in stories?

Gather Information Review your annotations and notes on the play. Then, add relevant details to your Response Log. Consider what makes a person hide true feelings and how a person's behavior can reveal character.

At the end of the unit, use your notes to write a short story or folktale.

ACADEMIC VOCABULARY
As you write and discuss what you learned from the play, be sure to use the Academic Vocabulary words. Check off each of the words that you use.

- ❑ **emphasize**
- ❑ **occur**
- ❑ **period**
- ❑ **relevant**
- ❑ **tradition**

CREATE AND PRESENT

Write a Character Study Tell students to write down the name of their chosen character and create an outline in which they list a few notes about that character's traits. They should leave room between notes and then use that space to write down text evidence (stage direction and dialogue) for each character trait. They can use this outline to write their character sketches, citing the text evidence to explain how the character is developed. Remind them that when they edit their first drafts, they should pay special attention to their use of prepositions and prepositional phrases.

For **writing support** for students at varying proficiency levels, see the **Text X-Ray** on page 434D.

Dramatic Reading Divide the play into sections for groups to perform. Remind students that they may have to play more than one character if their section has a lot of characters in it. They may want to use nametags to indicate which character they are playing.

Tell students that they do not need to memorize their lines, but they do need to rehearse their portion of the script many times so the dialogue comes easily to them. Their goal is to read the lines with appropriate emotion, and other students in their group should offer feedback as to how a character should be played.

RESPOND TO THE ESSENTIAL QUESTION

Allow time for students to add details from *The Prince and the Pauper* to their Unit 6 Response Logs.

EL **ENGLISH LEARNER SUPPORT**

Stage a Dramatic Reading Make sure to assign each English learner a role appropriate to his or her proficiency and comfort level. Find time to conference with students individually to ensure they understand what is happening in their assigned scene and dialogue. Have them practice their lines with you to gain confidence before they rehearse with their groups. With proper support, a dramatic reading provides an excellent opportunity to practice and learn spoken vocabulary.   **ALL LEVELS**

CRITICAL VOCABULARY

Answers:

1. *You wish you were there, because you are not happy with your current situation or because you have wonderful memories of a time you spent there and you wish you could go back.*

2. *He is feeling pressed for time because he is looking at his watch with a worried expression. He is probably late for an appointment.*

3. *She is trying to respect your privacy because information about your health is private, and as a doctor, she is bound by laws to protect your privacy.*

4. *You should comfort your friend because she is sad or regretting something.*

5. *Your brother is trying to make a joke because jesting is good-natured teasing.*

6. *I am finding the problem hard to solve because I am puzzled by it.*

VOCABULARY STRATEGY:
Resources

Word	Synonym	Antonym	Sentence with Synonym
wistfully	longingly	happily	*Ruth dreamed longingly of her chilhood home.*
anxiously	nervously	confidently	*Alex waited nervously for his turn to speak.*
discreetly	tactfully	indiscreetly	*The lawyer acted tactfully on behalf of his client.*
rueful	sorrowful	cheerful	*Buddy gave the coach a sorrowful look as he walked off the field.*
jest	tease	comfort	*Joe likes to tease or make fun of his friend.*
perplexed	confused	untroubled	*She was confused by the complicated directions.*

💬 **RESPOND**

WORD BANK
wistfully
anxiously
discreetly
rueful
jest
perplexed

CRITICAL VOCABULARY

Practice and Apply Answer each question. Explain your response.

1. If you gaze **wistfully** at a picture of a sunny tropical island, does it mean you wish to be there or are you glad you are not? Why?

_____

2. If someone looks **anxiously** at his watch, is he feeling pressed for time or relieved by the time? Why?

_____

3. When a doctor asks to speak to you **discreetly,** is she trying to respect your privacy or to speak openly? Why?

_____

4. If your friend is feeling **rueful,** should you congratulate or comfort your friend? Why?

_____

5. If you and your sibling **jest** at the dinner table, are you making a joke or trying to start an argument? Why?

_____

6. If you are **perplexed** by an algebra problem, are you finding it hard to solve or does the solution come easily to you? Why?

_____

 Go to the **Vocabulary Studio** for more on using resources.

VOCABULARY STRATEGY: Resources

You can use a print or online dictionary and a thesaurus to identify synonyms and antonyms of vocabulary words. Using these resources to identify synonyms and antonyms of words can help you better understand the meaning and usage of unfamiliar words.

Practice and Apply Use a dictionary and a thesaurus to find a synonym and an antonym for each of these vocabulary words: *wistfully, anxiously, discreetly, rueful, jest,* and *perplexed*. For each vocabulary word, write your own sentence using the word. Then, replace the vocabulary word with a synonym to make sure that the sentence still has the same meaning. Be sure that the synonym is the same part of speech as the word it replaces.

EL **ENGLISH LEARNER SUPPORT**

Use Resources Give students an opportunity to expand their vocabularies by using a dictionary and thesaurus. Have student partners work together to use these resources to make a synonym/antonym table for the following words: *enjoyable, mean, grin, yelled, giant, miniature, jog, beautiful, simple, glum.* **MODERATE**

LANGUAGE CONVENTIONS:
Prepositions and Prepositional Phrases

A **preposition** is a word that relates one word to another word. Prepositions include *at, by, for, from, in, of, on, to,* and *with*. A **prepositional phrase** includes a preposition and a noun—the object of the preposition. A prepositional phrase modifies or relates to another word in a sentence, telling *which one, where, why,* or *to what extent*. In writing, prepositional phrases are used to add detail and create imagery.

Here are some examples from *The Prince and the Pauper*.

> The boy is sentenced <u>to a fortnight</u> <u>in the common jail</u>.

The prepositional phrase "to a fortnight" describes to what extent the boy will be sentenced, and "in the common jail" describes where he will be sentenced.

Notice the importance of these prepositions and prepositional phrases in the stage directions at the opening of Scene 4.

> Miles' room <u>at the inn</u>. <u>At right</u> is table set <u>with dishes and bowls</u> <u>of food</u>, a chair <u>at each side</u>. <u>At left</u> is bed, <u>with table and chair</u> <u>next to it</u>, and a window. Candle is <u>on table</u>.

The prepositional phrases add details that help readers visualize the scene.

Practice and Apply Think of a scene from your everyday life; for example, walking your dog, going to school, or eating dinner with your family. Write stage directions and dialogue for your scene using prepositions and prepositional phrases. Use sentences from *The Prince and the Pauper* as a model.

> Go to the **Grammar Studio** for more on prepositions and prepositional phrases.

LANGUAGE CONVENTIONS:
Prepositions and Prepositional Phrases

Review the information on prepositions and prepositional phrases with students. Remind them that a preposition is a part of speech whose purpose is to relate a noun or pronoun to the rest of the sentence. Give two example sentences and have volunteers identify the prepositions in each. (**Examples:** *Mr. Lopez went to the store. I ate my pie with ice cream.*)

Review that a prepositional phrase consists of two or more words: the preposition and a noun or pronoun. Provide a few written sentences and ask volunteers to underline the prepositional phrases. (**Examples:** *She studied for the test with great intensity. The boy walked his dog around the block. She watched the fireworks at the park.*)

Practice and Apply Before students create their own scripts using prepositions and prepositional phrases, model one of your own to refresh students' memories about the proper formatting of stage direction and dialogue. For example:

Teacher *(to students).* You should write your name on your paper. Work quickly to complete the assignment. Then you will share your answers with a partner.

 ENGLISH LEARNER SUPPORT

Practice with Prepositional Phrases Create sentence strips containing prepositional phrases such as *on a bicycle, with her grandma, from the beach, across the street,* and *at the movies*. Have pairs of students draw a sentence strip from a bowl and work together to write a sentence using the prepositional phrase on their strip. **MODERATE**

ARCHETYPE
Poem by Margarita Engle

FAIRY-TALE LOGIC
Poem by A. E. Stallings

GENRE ELEMENTS
POETRY

Poetry is a form of storytelling that may include rhythm, rhyme, and meter. Poems also include breaks in sentence structure leaving white space. This is used to create effects and to focus on meaning and emotion. Poetry uses figurative language and language devices to make it more expressive and interesting, and to make it easier to remember. Devices include alliteration, consonance, and assonance.

LEARNING OBJECTIVES

- Understand the difference between sonnets and free verse.
- Analyze the effect of meter and form on poetic expression.
- Make personal and thematic connections to stories and poetry.
- Discuss, paraphrase, infer, and compare themes and meaning within and across texts.
- Research other authors and make connections.
- Analyze and discuss how writers use allusion, rhyme, rhythm, alliteration, and repetition to express meaning.
- **Language** Discuss with a partner types of characters found in different kinds of stories, using the key term *archetype*.

TEXT COMPLEXITY

Quantitative Measures	Archetype, Fairy-tale Logic	Lexile: N/A
Qualitative Measures	**Ideas Presented** Much is explicit; some ambiguity and allusion; requires some inferential reasoning.	
	Structures Used Primarily explicit; some complex phrasing.	
	Language Used Meanings are implied, but support is offered; more allusive and figurative language.	
	Knowledge Required Cultural and historical references make heavier demands; refers to texts and ideas that may be beyond student's experience.	

RESOURCES

- Unit 6 Response Log
- Selection Audio
- Reading Studio: Notice & Note
- Level Up tutorial: Myths, Legends, and Tales
- Writing Studio: Using Textual Evidence
- Speaking and Listening Studio: Participating in Collaborative Discussions
- "Archetype"/"Fairy-tale Logic" Selection Test

SUMMARIES

English

Most children grow up being told the fantastical stories known as fairy tales.

In the poem "Archetype," the author suggests that we are drawn to certain stories because they reveal something deeply personal. In "Fairy-tale Logic," the author both celebrates and makes fun of how fairy tales are often about people in truly impossible situations being given impossible tasks and somehow overcoming them.

Spanish

La mayoría de los niños crece escuchando historias fantásticas conocidas como cuentos de hadas.

En el poema "Arquetipo", el autor sugiere que nos atraen ciertas historias porque éstas revelan algo profundamente personal. En "Lógica de los cuentos de hadas", el autor celebra y se burla de cómo los cuentos de hadas usualmente tratan de personas en situaciones verdaderamente imposibles a las que le son dadas misiones verdaderamente imposibles y, de alguna manera, son capaces de superarlas.

SMALL-GROUP OPTIONS

Have students work in small groups to read and discuss the selection.

Genre Reformulation in Small Groups

- Ask the students who liked "Archetype" best to raise their hands. Form these students into small groups of three to five students. Do the same with "Fairy-tale Logic."
- Ask each group to choose any two to four stanzas from the poem and reformulate them from poetry into an expository speech, dialogue from a play, essay, or memoir using paragraph structure and full, rather than fragmented, sentences.
- Tell all students to start with the idea of the theme and the author's purpose. What did she want to tell the reader? Give students a lot of leeway to reformulate the genre in their own way. Ask volunteers to share with the class.

Paraphrase Passport

- Have pairs look together at the first stanza of the same poem: "Archetype" or "Fairy-tale Logic."
- Have Partner A read the first stanza aloud while Partner B reads silently. Partner B may coach Partner A, if needed, for pronunciation. Model how they should give a slight pause at the line break and pause for punctuation.
- Ask Partner B to paraphrase the stanza that Partner A read: *I think that means/says ____.*
- Have students alternate roles as they go through the rest of the stanzas. In a class discussion, ask: *What meaning was made clearer to you through this process?*

Text X-Ray: English Learner Support
for "Archetype" and "Fairy-tale Logic"

Use the Text X-Ray and the supports and scaffolds in the Teacher's Edition to help guide students at different proficiency levels through the selection.

INTRODUCE THE SELECTION
DISCUSS WHAT WE CAN LEARN FROM STORIES

Some stories teach us about humanity or human nature. Both poems included in this selection address the essential question by suggesting we can learn a lot about ourselves from fairy tales.

Read the titles of each poem aloud, and ask students to wonder about each title. Write their questions on the board. Examples: *What does the word* archetype *mean? How do archetypes relate to fairy tales? Why is the word* Logic *in the title? Is using the word* logic *supposed to be funny or ironic?* Then have students discuss possible answers as a class.

CULTURAL REFERENCES

The following words and phrases may be unfamiliar to students:

- *All the fuss* ("Archetype" line 5): many people talking about something

- *Fight magic with magic* ("Fairy-tale Logic" line 9): This is a common English expression that means you have to match whatever weapon someone might bring against you.

- *beck* ("Fairy-tale Logic" line 12): This is taken from the expression, "beck and call," meaning the ants would have to do whatever you beckoned or called upon them to do.

- In both poems, there are many complex allusions to different fairy tales. Students may or may not know these references. Point out to students that dragons show up in tales from many different places all over the world, so they will not have to understand exactly what the allusion is to understand the point being made.

LISTENING

Understand Sounds and Elements of English Poetry

Translations of poetry are difficult because words may not rhyme or create the same rhythm in a different language. Provide students with practice developing their ear to hear rhyming words in poems.

Have students look at the text and listen as you read aloud "Fairy-tale Logic" lines 9–14. Emphasize the end consonants. Use the following supports with students at varying proficiency levels:

- Ask: *Which words rhyme?* (*The word* rhyme *in Spanish is* rima; *in Arabic it is* quafia; *in Ukranian/ Russian* ryfma/rifma; *in Korean/Chinese:* Un/Yun.) Have students repeat the words aloud then answer with thumbs up or down: *Do* believe *and* cloak *rhyme?* (*no*) Cloak/done? (*no*) Cloak/joke? (*yes*) Believe/sleeve? (*yes*) **SUBSTANTIAL**

- Ask one student in a pair to read this stanza aloud, while the partner listens and then identifies the rhyming words. Have partners switch roles and repeat the activity. **MODERATE**

- Pair students to read lines 11–12 aloud while listening for and emphasizing the /k/ sound. Ask students to identify the other word in the stanza that has that sound. (*magic*) **LIGHT**

SPEAKING

Discuss Archetypes

Draw students' attention to the fact that archetypes are found in all types of stories and genres, not just poems. Tell students that gods and other magical beings are often considered archetypes in stories because they are a simplified type, not a complicated individual.

Explain that the word *archetype* (Spanish cognate *arquetipo*) means an original model or type that other similar things are patterned after. Use the following supports with students at varying proficiency levels:

- Write a few names of various fairy-tale characters, gods, and magical beings from comics, movies, and books on the board. Have students brainstorm other names in small groups, come up and add to the list, and practice pronouncing their names in standard American English. **SUBSTANTIAL**
- Have students identify a favorite archetypal character and discuss in small groups why they admire him or her. Provide them with discussion frames: *I like _____ because _____. This type of character always _____. That makes me feel _____.* **MODERATE**
- Pair students to discuss the title of the poem: "Archetype." Ask: *Why is this poem called "Archetype" and not "The Nightingale"? (The author wants the reader to think of their own archetype.)* **LIGHT**

READING

Analyze Details

Point out allusions to specific and nonspecific fairy tales in each of the selection poems. Tell students that both authors make specific choices of what to include and what to leave out. Looking at the details included can help them understand the poems better.

Use the following supports with students at varying proficiency levels:

- Help students read lines 7–11 of "Archetype." List on the board the words used to refer to details from Hansel and Gretel's story: *serial killer, ovens, absent parents, famine, crumbs.* Explain their meanings and have students say "The details include . . ." and read each word after you. **SUBSTANTIAL**
- Have students read lines 7–11 of "Archetype." Ask: *What words does the author use to provide details about the story of Hansel and Gretel? (serial killer, ovens, absent parents, famine, crumbs) What do these details make you think of their story? (These details show that it is a sad, violent story.)* **MODERATE**
- Have students reread "Archetype" and identify the words the author uses to provide details about the story of Hansel and Gretel and "The Nightingale." Invite students to explain how these sets of words and the details provided for each story differ. **LIGHT**

WRITING

Paraphrase Lines

Explain to students that paraphrasing is a way to rewrite a text in one's own words. Point out that they can paraphrase a poem in sentences, without using the same rhymes and rhythms, but they must include the most important ideas.

Use the following supports with students at varying proficiency levels:

- Reread the first line of "Fairy-tale Logic." Discuss the meanings of *full, impossible,* and *tasks*. Provide students with a sentence frame to complete to write a paraphrase of this line: *Fairy tales tell about _____ things.* **SUBSTANTIAL**
- Have pairs reread the first and eighth line of "Fairy-tale Logic" and discuss what they think these lines mean. Provide pairs with a sentence frame to use in their written paraphrase: *In fairy tales, people ask _____.* **MODERATE**
- Ask pairs to read lines 1–8 of "Fairy-tale Logic" and work together to identify the most important ideas. Then have pairs write a one- or two-sentence paraphrase of this section. **LIGHT**

Connect to the
? ESSENTIAL QUESTION

The free verse poem "Archetype" by Margarita Engle expresses the idea that the act of choosing a favorite fairy tale reveals a lot about who each of us is deep down and the roles we might play in the world. The fact that the poem is free verse and has its own unique structure fits the idea that each person relates to stories in their own way.

The more structured sonnet "Fairy-tale Logic" by A. E. Stallings expresses the idea that fairy tales teach us not only who we are and what our roles may be, but how to act in the world—that we can accomplish the impossible, if we set our minds to the steps of the tasks we are handed, no matter how impossible they seem.

COMPARE POEMS

Point out that both of these selections are poems that take fairy tales as their subject matter and address themes of how stories can affect how people act. However, they do so using rhythm and rhyme differently. As students read, they can keep these differences in mind, while also looking for similarities in the allusions and references the poets make to other fairy tales and stories. Why might each poet connect her poem to these other tales? What can these references help the reader understand about the point each poet is making about the influence of stories on people?

POEM

ARCHETYPE

by **Margarita Engle**
pages 461–463

COMPARE POEMS

As you read, look for details that will help you identify themes—messages about life and the human experience. To identify themes and state them will require that you make inferences, or logical guesses based on text evidence and what you already know. After you read both poems, you will collaborate with a small group on a final project.

 ESSENTIAL QUESTION:

What hidden truths about people and the world are revealed in stories?

POEM

FAIRY-TALE LOGIC

by **A. E. Stallings**
pages 464–465

458   Unit 6

QUICK START

Choose a favorite fairy tale, myth, or other traditional story that interests you. What message does this story have about life or the human experience? Discuss the story and its theme with your group.

ANALYZE THE EFFECTS OF METER AND STRUCTURAL ELEMENTS IN POEMS

A poem's **form,** or structure, is the way its words and lines are arranged on a page. During the writing process, poets often choose a particular form because it helps shape and express their ideas. In this way, a poem's meaning becomes closely tied to its form. Examining a poem's structure will help you discover its meaning.

"Archetype" is in **free verse,** a poetic form that has no regular patterns of line length, rhyme, or rhythm. To analyze free verse, pay attention to how line lengths and line breaks affect meaning. Note how ideas are arranged into **stanzas,** or groups of lines that form a unit.

"Fairy-tale Logic" is written in a traditional form called a **sonnet.** Sonnets generally include 14 lines with **end rhymes,** or rhyming words at the ends of lines. Sonnet structure is also established by **meter** —a pattern of stressed and unstressed syllables that create a regular rhythm.

Many poetic forms, including sonnets and free verse, use devices such as **internal rhyme** (rhymes within lines) and **alliteration** (repetition of consonant sounds at the beginnings of words) to establish rhythm and draw attention to words and ideas. Repeated sounds within words can also establish rhythm and create emphasis. As you read, pause to ask yourself, "What repeated sounds do I hear? Where are these sounds in the line?" The answers will help you identify end rhyme, internal rhyme, and alliteration. Then ask, "Why has the author created this emphasis? What does the author want me to notice or realize?"

GENRE ELEMENTS: POETRY

- may include rhyme, rhythm, and meter
- includes line breaks and white space for effects and meaning
- may use repetition and rhyme to create a melodic quality
- often includes figurative language and a variety of poetic devices

EXAMPLE	RHYME OR REPEATED SOUND AND ALLITERATION	IMPORTANCE
I never understood all the fuss/ about princesses poisoned/ or rescued from dragons. ("Archetype" lines 5–7)	• understood / *fuss* / princesses / rescued = repeated *s* sounds	The *p* sounds make it sound as if the speaker is spitting the words out in disdain.
	• princesses / poisoned / dragons = repeated *z* sounds	The repeated *s* and *z* sounds hiss, sounding angry.
	• *princesses poisoned* = repeated initial consonant sounds	

Archetype / Fairy-tale Logic   459

TEACH

QUICK START

As a warm up to the Quick Start assignment, ask students to brainstorm all the fairy tales, myths, and other often-told stories they can think of, and write the titles on the board before forming groups. Tell students they can choose from these stories or share another traditional story in their groups.

ANALYZE THE EFFECTS OF METER AND STRUCTURAL ELEMENTS IN POEMS

Share with students that poetry, like fairy tales, was originally transmitted orally. Poets, storytellers, and singers went from village to village spreading traditional stories and telling new ones. This was true in regions throughout the world. Like children's movies and cartoons today, they contained messages and universal themes for both children and adults because the whole village would gather around to listen.

Point out that rhythms, rhyming, and the sounds of words were ways of making stories fun and interesting to listen to, but also made them easier to memorize and share.

Tell students it will be important to read these poems aloud— on their own or in groups—to hear the metered rhythms and different structural elements, and to make sure each poem is understood fully.

Ask: *What are the elements to look for today?*

- sonnets and free verse
- end rhymes and internal rhymes
- line breaks and meter
- alliteration and repetition

 ENGLISH LEARNER SUPPORT

Explore Rhythm Help students understand meter, and sonnets versus free verse. Together with students, clap out the first four lines of "Archetype," saying the syllables. Ask students to listen closely for accents. Then, clap out the first three lines of "Fairy-tale Logic," again saying the syllables. Discuss what students have observed about the rhythm of each poem, leading students to see that "Fairy-tale Logic" has more definite rhythm and rhyme.
SUBSTANTIAL/MODERATE

TEACH

MAKE CONNECTIONS

Write the word *allusions* (Spanish cognates: *allusion/allusion, allude/aludir*) on the board. Begin to point out to students when speakers allude to something (or make allusions to something) in regular conversation. Ask students to read each poem and start filling out their tables individually. Remind them to look at footnotes as well as the text to find these allusions. After they have finished, have students share what they have found with the class.

Point out to students that many people share Western cultural traditions—like many childhood stories, the Bible, Roman and Greek myths, and authors like Shakespeare or Cervantes—but also have different modern, cultural knowledge. When you allude to those things, it might not be clear to everyone. Point out that sharing culture means being as well educated as you can so you will understand the allusions being made.

✏ ANNOTATION MODEL

Remind students of the structural elements to look for from the Analyze the Effects of Meter and Structural Elements in Poems directions on page 459. Point out that they may follow this suggestion or use their own system for marking up the selection in their write-in text. They may want to color-code their annotations by using highlighters. If they are looking for three different things, have them use brackets around words, as well as underlining and highlighting. Their notes in the margin may include questions about ideas that are unclear or topics they want to learn more about.

 GET READY

MAKE CONNECTIONS

The poems "Fairy-tale Logic" and "Archetype" include allusions to myths, fairy tales, popular works, and biblical stories. An **allusion** is a reference to a famous person, place, event, or work of literature. Poets and authors use allusions to connect the ideas of their works to the ideas in these references. Readers can then use their own knowledge of the references to make connections to the text, creating a deeper understanding of the text's complex ideas.

Use the chart below to help you use your own understanding of allusions to make connections. One example has been done for you.

POEM	ALLUSION	TEXT CONNECTION	PERSONAL CONNECTION
"Fairy-tale Logic"	The language of snakes, perhaps, an invisible cloak. . . .	J. K. Rowling's character, Harry Potter, can speak to snakes and has a cloak of invisibility.	I've read the books and know that Harry uses his abilities to overcome certain challenges.

ANNOTATION MODEL

NOTICE & NOTE ✏

As you read, take notes on meter and other structural elements, text connections, and evidence that support your own ideas. This model shows one reader's notes about the beginning of "Archetype."

1 Is it true that nothing reveals
   <u>more</u> about a person's secret <u>heart</u>
   than the adult memory of a <u>favorite</u>
   <u>childhood fairy tale</u>?

The lines are breaking in the middle of a thought, which makes me want to keep reading. The words that end each line seem important, too.
I wonder if the rest of the poem will answer this question?

© Houghton Mifflin Harcourt Publishing Company

WHEN STUDENTS STRUGGLE . . .

Make Connections Have small groups discuss how they use allusions in their own conversations that adults might not "get." Students might understand allusions to Japanese myths and legends used in Japanese anime or to the worlds of popular video games. Have them record in a graphic organizer the allusions to myth, legend, and fairy or folk tales they hear and see throughout a day or week. Ask them to notice and note allusions in the animated movies they watch and share these with the class. Ask: *Is this a Western culture allusion, such as an allusion to the Bible or a Greek myth, or is it more familiar to a certain country, region, or generation?*

 For additional support, go to the **Reading Studio** and assign the following **Level Up** tutorial: Myths, Legends, and Tales.

BACKGROUND

Margarita Engle *(b. 1951) is an award-winning Cuban American writer. She was named the Poetry Foundation's Young People's Poet Laureate for the 2017-2019 term. She has published several children's books, novels, and young adult novels in verse. Many of her books are inspired by her Cuban American heritage and focus on history and life in Cuba. Among her many award-winning books are* The Surrender Tree: Poems of Cuba's Struggle for Freedom *(2008), and her verse memoir,* Enchanted Air.

ARCHETYPE[1]

by Margarita Engle

PREPARE TO COMPARE

As you read, pay attention to the different stories and fairy tales mentioned in the poem. Think about how the author uses these allusions, or references to famous works, to share her ideas.

1 Is it true that nothing reveals
 more about a person's <u>secret heart</u>
 than the adult memory of a favorite
 childhood fairy tale?

5 I never understood all the fuss
 about princesses poisoned
 or rescued from dragons.
 Hansel and Gretel seemed like a recitation[2]
 of the sorrowful evening news
10 a serial killer, the ovens, absent parents
 a famine, crumbs . . .

---

[1] **archetype** (är´kĭ-tīp´): model after which things are patterned; ideal type.
[2] **recitation** (rĕs´ĭ-tā´shən): a public presentation of memorized material.

Notice & Note

Use the side margins to notice and note signposts in the text.

MAKE CONNECTIONS

Annotate: In stanza 1, mark the phrase that refers to something hidden.

Connect: What is the author asking the reader to reflect on?

BACKGROUND

After students read the Background note, explain that everyone experiences a story differently. This poem encourages us to look deeply at the stories we love in order to understand what makes us love that story more than another. Tell students this is one reason teachers ask students to read so many stories: not everyone will love and learn from each story equally, and it helps in communication because students will understand more cultural allusions.

PREPARE TO COMPARE

Direct students to use the Prepare to Compare prompt to focus their reading.

MAKE CONNECTIONS

Engle points out that stories other children loved—about princesses, dragons and scary situations—didn't interest her much. Yet, she remembers them and understands allusions to them. (**Answer:** *First, the author poses a question about how fairy tales affect us. By sharing her feelings about certain fairy tales, she invites the reader to reflect on how such stories affect them.*)

For **reading support** for students at varying proficiency levels, see the **Text X-Ray** on page 458D.

ENGLISH LEARNER SUPPORT

Make Connections Ask students to discuss the stories alluded to in each text and included on their charts from page 460. Ask students who do know these stories to share them with those who do not.

Students from Eastern cultures may not know some or any of these stories. Ask those students to think about stories they loved and stories with impossible tasks from their own cultures to discuss with their groups. **MODERATE/LIGHT**

TEACH

ANALYZE THE EFFECTS OF METER AND STRUCTURAL ELEMENTS IN POEMS

Remind students that reading aloud may help them analyze the effects of alliteration. Encourage students to read the lines aloud and listen for repeated sounds. Then, they should consider how the sounds relate to what the poem is talking about in this part. (**Answer:** *The repetition of the /m/ sounds in line 12 and 15 calls attention to ideas about magic in fairy tales and how they contrast with the speaker's favorite but less flashy story about a nightingale. The alliteration emphasizes the meaning between the words, expressing the idea of a thread linking this line of stories in the fairy tale or myth tradition. The repetition of the /g/ sound (disguised/grandmas) in line 13 emphasizes the contrast between the disguised wolf and the grandmother. The sounds call attention to an idea of things not being what they seem. The many repeated sounds help create a rhythm of stressed syllables.*)

MAKE CONNECTIONS

Point out that the content of the story "The Nightingale" is found in lines 14–16 of the poem. The speaker tells what the story is about, then names it in line 17, then lists other stories with a similar theme in the rest of the stanza. (**Answer:** *The speaker tells of how the bird in this story uses its beautiful voice to soothe an emperor who is sad. The author alludes to other stories with similar themes, saying these were her favorites. Perhaps to the author, being a poet also means helping people feel better with the music of beautiful words.*)

For **speaking support** for students at varying proficiency levels, see the **Text X-Ray** on page 458D.

ANALYZE THE EFFECTS OF METER AND STRUCTURAL ELEMENTS IN POEMS

Annotate: Mark the alliteration and repeated sounds in stanza 3 (lines 12–16).

Infer: How do these elements contribute to rhythm and meaning?

MAKE CONNECTIONS

Annotate: Mark references to music and song in the poem.

Infer: What can you infer about the meaning of music and song, especially in "The Nightingale," to the poet?

Instead of magic beanstalks and man-eating giants
or wolves disguised as gentle grandmas
I chose the tale of a bird with a voice that could soothe
15 the melancholic³ spirit of an emperor
helpless despite his wealth and power.

Of all tales, only The Nightingale⁴ felt
like a story I knew before I was born
about Orpheus⁵ calming wild beasts with his lyre⁶
20 King David's harp easing Saul's despair⁷
Saint Francis with his curious flocks of birds⁸
singing back and forth in a language of wishing
that even the wolf understood.

³ **melancholic** (mĕl´ən-kŏl´ĭk): affected with sadness or depression.
⁴ **The Nightingale:** in this fairy tale by Hans Christian Andersen, the Chinese emperor prefers a mechanical nightingale until the real nightingale saves him with her song.
⁵ **Orpheus** (ôr´-fē-əs): a hero from Greek mythology who played the lyre and soothed animals and trees, causing them to sway or dance.
⁶ **lyre** (līr): a stringed instrument of the harp family, used to accompany a singer or speaker of poetry, especially in Greek mythology.
⁷ **King David's harp easing Saul's despair:** tale from the Bible in which David played the harp to soothe Saul from the evil spirit that bothered him.
⁸ **Saint Francis with his curious flocks of birds:** Saint Francis is the patron saint of animals and nature in the Catholic Church; the allusion refers to the legend of how Francis preached to birds and other animals about divine love.

462 Unit 6

IMPROVE READING FLUENCY

Targeted Passage Have students work with partners to read lines 1–16 of "Archetype." First, use lines 1–4 to model how to read a poem with a conversational tone that sounds natural but pays attention to the rhythm of the lines. Have students follow along in their books as you read the text with appropriate phrasing and emphasis, including the use of a questioning tone at the question mark. Then, have pairs read lines 1–16 aloud together. Remind students to pace their reading so an audience could understand the sense of the ideas in this poem.

 Go to the **Reading Studio** for additional support in developing fluency.

© Houghton Mifflin Harcourt Publishing Company • Image Credits: ©yzarabibrahim/Moment/Getty Images

CHECK YOUR UNDERSTANDING

Answer these questions about "Archetype" before moving on to the next poem.

1 The speaker in the poem questions whether —

A a favorite story reveals something about yourself

B fairy tales are real

C a person can have a "secret heart"

D fairy tales are scary or strange

2 The line <u>of the sorrowful evening news</u> does what in the poem?

F Makes the poem into a news story

G Connects qualities of fairy tales to the present day

H Shows the mood of the poem is sad

J Expresses what the poem is really about

3 What story means the most to the speaker of the poem?

A Jack and the Beanstalk

B Myth of Orpheus

C The Nightingale

D Hansel and Gretel

✏️ CHECK YOUR UNDERSTANDING

Have students answer the questions independently.

Answers:

1. *A*

2. *G*

3. *C*

If they answer any questions incorrectly, have them reread the text to confirm their understanding. Then they may proceed to the next poem on page 464.

 ENGLISH LEARNER SUPPORT

Oral Assessment Use the following questions to assess students' comprehension and speaking skills:

1. What does the author think can tell you something important about yourself? *(what your favorite story is)*

2. Does the author think the story of Hansel and Gretel is similar to or different from the news of today? *(similar)*

3. The speaker of the poem mentions many stories. Which story means the most to her? *(The Nightingale)*
   SUBSTANTIAL/MODERATE

BACKGROUND

After students read the Background note, ask them to consider the statement "That you have something impossible up your sleeve,. . . the will to do whatever must be done." Ask: *Does this description match the favorite story you chose during the Quick Start activity? Who, in your story, has the will to do what must be done?*

PREPARE TO COMPARE

Direct students to use the Prepare to Compare prompt to focus their reading.

MAKE CONNECTIONS

Point out to students that it is always important to read a question or direction carefully. They are not being asked to list impossible tasks here. They are not being asked to identify impossible tasks in the poem. They are being asked to find lines that comment on impossible tasks. This means they need to look for lines that say something about impossible tasks, not the tasks themselves. **(Answer:** *These lines connect to the larger idea of overcoming something that seems impossible. The poem uses the details and actions in fairy tales as a list of items between these statements about being asked to do the impossible.)*

BACKGROUND

A. E. Stallings *(b. 1968) is an award-winning poet. Her book of poetry, Archaic Smile (1999), won the Richard Wilbur Award. She also has won fellowships through the Guggenheim Foundation and the MacArthur Foundation for her poetry and translations. Stallings has studied Greek and Latin, and Greek mythology has influenced her poetry. She writes in sonnet form, as shown in "Fairy-tale Logic," as well as in a variety of other poetic forms. "Fairy-tale Logic" first appeared in* Poetry *Magazine in 2010.*

FAIRY-TALE LOGIC
by A. E. Stallings

Notice & Note

Use the side margins to notice and note signposts in the text.

MAKE CONNECTIONS

Annotate: This poem lists some "impossible tasks." Mark lines that comment on, rather than merely list, these tasks.

Interpret: How does the author use these comments to share ideas with the reader?

PREPARE TO COMPARE

As you read, note how the sounds, rhyme, and meter affect your reading and understanding of the poem.

Fairy tales are full of impossible tasks:
Gather the chin hairs of a man-eating goat,
Or cross a sulphuric lake[1] in a leaky boat,
Select the prince from a row of identical masks,
5 Tiptoe up to a dragon where it basks[2]
And snatch its bone; count dust specks, mote by mote,[3]
Or learn the phone directory by rote.
Always it's impossible what someone asks—

---

[1] **sulphuric lake** (sŭl-fyŏŏr´ĭk): a lake of sulfur, which is a pale-yellow, nonmetallic element occurring widely in nature and used to make gunpowder, rubber, medicines, etc.
[2] **bask** (băsk): to expose oneself to pleasant warmth.
[3] **mote** (mōt): a very small particle; a speck.

ENGLISH LEARNER SUPPORT

Analyze Meter and Structure Write the word *alliteration* on the board. (Spanish cognate: *aliteracion*) Review that alliteration is when the same consonant sound is repeated at the beginning of several different words. Ask students to read lines 5–7 silently. Then read the lines aloud, strongly emphasizing the /t/ sounds and asking students to follow along.

1. Ask students to point to and say the words that jumped out to them. (*tiptoe, dust, mote, rote*) Ask: *What do you notice when you read a poem aloud?* (*repeated sounds*)

2. Tell students that translating these words into a different language would lose the power of sound as the syllables and sounds would be different: *Rote* is *rota* in Spanish and *mote* is *rutina* so there would be no alliterations, rhyme, or snappy sounds.

3. Ask students to take turns reading these lines aloud while emphasizing the sounds of the double consonants at the ends of words. Are any of these sounds repeated? (*ks*) **MODERATE/LIGHT**

You have to fight magic with magic. You have to believe
10 That you have something impossible up your sleeve,
The language of snakes, perhaps, an invisible cloak,
An army of ants at your beck, or a lethal⁴ joke,
The will to do whatever must be done:
Marry a monster.⁵ Hand over your firstborn son.⁶

---

⁴ **lethal** (lē´thəl): causing or capable of causing death.
⁵ **Marry a monster:** perhaps a reference to Beauty and the Beast.
⁶ **Hand over your firstborn son:** in the popular fairy tale "Rumpelstiltskin,"
  a queen promises her firstborn son in exchange for straw spun into gold.

 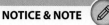
ANALYZE THE EFFECTS OF METER AND STRUCTURAL ELEMENTS IN POEMS

Annotate: Mark any alliteration or other repetition of sounds or words in lines 9–11.

Analyze: How do these elements affect your understanding of the poem?

CHECK YOUR UNDERSTANDING

Answer these questions about "Fairy-tale Logic" before moving on to the **Analyze the Texts** section on the following page.

1 In the first stanza, the speaker gives —

 A ways to overcome hard obstacles

 B remedies for the bad things that happen in fairy tales

 C lessons people can learn from stories

 D examples of tasks given in fairy tales

2 The line The will to do whatever must be done emphasizes what idea?

 F People should be brave when in danger.

 G People should not be scared to read fairy tales.

 H Fairy tales show characters taking big risks.

 J Fairy tales have characters that study a lot.

3 What is an important idea in the poem?

 A The impossible is actually possible.

 B It is easy to use magic.

 C Fairy tales are popular stories.

 D Fairy tales are for children.

ANALYZE THE EFFECTS OF METER AND STRUCTURAL ELEMENTS IN POEMS

Point out that this poem, unlike "Archetype," uses a rhyme scheme, or pattern. Both use alliteration. Have students read the lines aloud with a partner, listening for the repeated and rhyming sounds. (**Answer:** *The repetition of "you have to" and the word* magic *plus the alliteration of the /m/ sound in* magic *gives a ping-pong effect, or a back-and-forth feeling, so the reader gets the sense of a magic duel happening in this manner. The repetition of the /s/ sound evokes a snake which is a classical trickster in stories, and often related to bad events. Because of the allusion to Harry Potter, though, it creates a connection to Harry's use of "Parseltongue," or the language of snakes. It also helps make the text more memorable.*)

For **listening support** for students at varying proficiency levels, see the **Text X-Ray** on page 458C.

CHECK YOUR UNDERSTANDING

Have students answer the questions independently.

Answers:

 1. *D*

 2. *H*

 3. *A*

If they answer any questions incorrectly, have them reread the text to confirm their understanding. Then they may proceed to ANALYZE THE TEXTS on page 466.

ENGLISH LEARNER SUPPORT

Oral Assessment Use the following questions to assess students' comprehension and speaking skills:

 1. What types of examples does the speaker list in the first stanza? *(The speaker gives examples of some impossible tasks in fairy tales.)*

 2. What does "the will to do what must be done" mean? *(It means being able to take big risks when something hard needs to be done.)*

 3. What is one important idea in the poem? *(People can actually do the impossible.)* **SUBSTANTIAL/MODERATE**

APPLY

ANALYZE THE TEXTS

Possible answers:

1. **DOK 4:** *The question asks us to think about how we can know what is inside a person's "secret heart" (line 2). The author then uses examples from her own life to answer the question.*

2. **DOK 2:** *The breaks allow for space between thoughts and better understanding. Lines 12 and 14 allow for a thought to be started and finished; it begins, "Instead of . . . I chose . . . " Images pop up in between, for example, "man-eating giants" and "wolves disguised."*

3. **DOK 4:** *The end rhymes follow a pattern: A B B A A C C A. The stressed syllables and end rhymes give the poem its regular structure, typical of sonnets.*

4. **DOK 4:** *Both refer to impossible sacrifice or ruthlessness. Sacrifice is found all over the world. Soldiers, families, and many other people face impossible tradeoffs and sacrifices.*

5. **DOK 4:** *The contrast is between what other people like about stories and what the speaker likes. The speaker doesn't have a lot of patience for fairy-tale "archetypes," such as princesses, dragons, or giants. The speaker likes a story about a bird with a soothing voice. This shows how the speaker is unique.*

RESEARCH

Remind students to use reputable sources when conducting research. They may find quality information for filling in the chart in encyclopedias, biographies of these authors, or at websites for universities that have literature and/or folklore departments.

Extend Suggest that students make a two-column graphic organizer that uses "The text says . . . " as its first heading and "That reminds me of . . . " as its second heading. Encourage students to use this chart to record information about the connections they are able to make.

 RESPOND

ANALYZE THE TEXTS

Support your responses with evidence from the texts.   NOTEBOOK

1. **Synthesize** Review stanza 1 of "Archetype." Why do you think the author began with this particular question? What does the question reveal about the poem's speaker?

2. **Interpret** Read aloud lines 12–16 of "Archetype." Notice the line breaks and line lengths. What effects do these structural elements have on how you read and understand the poem?

3. **Analyze** Read lines 1–8 of "Fairy-tale Logic" aloud quietly. Notice the words and syllables that you seem to stress naturally, as well as the end-rhyming words in each line. What is the effect of these elements? What ideas are emphasized by this structure?

4. **Connect** Reread lines 13–14 of "Fairy-tale Logic," along with the footnotes. What idea or theme do the allusions help reveal? Explain.

5. **Notice & Note** Reread stanza 2 of "Archetype." What thoughts and ideas surprise you? What do these contrasts and contradictions reveal about the poem's speaker and theme?

RESEARCH

RESEARCH TIP
When you conduct online research, start by searching with key words, or in this case, the names of the writers you are researching. Often there are official sites dedicated to famous writers, which are good sites to begin your research. Once you complete background reading, extend your search using the information you learned.

"Archetype" and "Fairy-tale Logic" allude to, or refer to, other texts, especially to fairy tales. The Brothers Grimm and Hans Christian Andersen are among the most recognized writers of fairy tales. Complete the chart below with details about these writers and their works.

QUESTION	ANSWER
Which sources did the Grimm brothers use for their first collection of fairy tales?	*folktales from Germany's oral tradition*
Which Grimm brothers stories have you read or do you recognize?	*"Snow White" and "Cinderella"*
How did Hans Christian Andersen influence other writers?	*His writing influenced A.A. Milne and Beatrix Potter.*
Which stories by Hans Christian Andersen are most familiar to you?	*"The Ugly Duckling" and "The Little Mermaid"*

Extend Read an unfamiliar story by the Brothers Grimm or Hans Christian Andersen. Discuss the story with your partner and make connections to other stories or to your personal experiences.

CREATE AND DISCUSS

Paraphrase Lines in a Poem Choose a set of lines in either "Archetype" or "Fairy-tale Logic" to paraphrase.

❑ Carefully reread the lines you selected, and then write your paraphrase of the lines.

❑ Be sure to capture the meaning of the lines, rephrase the meaning in your own words, and present the paraphrase in logical order.

Have a Group Discussion In a small group, discuss the meanings and messages of your favorite fairy tales or stories from childhood. The following points will help your group discussion:

❑ Discuss the possible purposes for the stories you discuss.

❑ Make connections to the stories, drawing on your own personal experience and knowledge.

❑ Make connections to other stories and their role in society.

❑ Listen attentively during the discussion, take notes, and discuss points of agreement and disagreement in a constructive and respectful way.

RESPOND TO THE ESSENTIAL QUESTION

? What hidden truths about people and the world are revealed in stories?

Gather Information Review your annotations and notes on "Archetype" and "Fairy-tale Logic." Then, add relevant details to your Response Log. As you determine which information to include, think about:

• what these poems reveal about stories
• what the poems reveal about society and the world
• how stories affect your own life

At the end of the unit, use your notes to write a short story or folktale.

RESPOND

 Go to **Using Textual Evidence: Summarizing, Paraphrasing, and Quoting** in the **Writing Studio** for more on paraphrasing.

 Go to **Participating in Collaborative Discussions** in the **Speaking and Listening Studio** for more on having a group discussion.

ACADEMIC VOCABULARY
As you write and discuss what you learned from the poems, be sure to use the Academic Vocabulary words. Check off each of the words that you use.

❑ **emphasize**
❑ **occur**
❑ **period**
❑ **relevant**
❑ **tradition**

CREATE AND DISCUSS

Paraphrase Lines in a Poem Point out to students that the word *paraphrase* contains the Greek prefix *para-*, which means "alongside" or "side by side." To paraphrase is to put a new phrase side by side with the first phrase. Both phrases should basically mean the same thing. Point out that teachers often ask students to put things in their "own words." This does not mean to rearrange the original words, but to describe the *meaning* of the words in their own way.

For **writing support** for students at varying proficiency levels, see the **Text X-Ray** on page 458D.

Have a Group Discussion Remind students that when they do not understand a comment made by another group member, they should ask questions to clarify meaning. The process of asking and answering questions can help everyone understand an issue more clearly and can lead to new ideas.

EL ENGLISH LEARNER SUPPORT

Use Cognates Tell students that the word *paraphrase* and several of the Academic Vocabulary words have Spanish cognates: *paraphrase/parafrasis, period/periodo, tradition/tradicion.* The Spanish word for *relevant* is *pertinente,* and in English, the word *pertinent* is a synonym for *relevant.* **ALL LEVELS**

RESPOND TO THE ESSENTIAL QUESTION

Allow time for students to add details from "Archetype" and "Fairy-tale Logic" to their Unit 6 Response Logs.

INFER THEMES WITHIN AND ACROSS TEXTS

Before groups begin to fill in the Comparison Chart, suggest that they take a moment to work together to identify what they think are the main ideas in each poem and what evidence supports these big ideas. Note that reviewing the main ideas in a poem can give them clues as to its overall theme.

ANALYZE THE TEXTS

Possible answers:

1. **DOK 3**: *Both authors appear to be expressing what they personally feel and think about fairy-tales. In "Archetype," the author thinks these stories can reach into our hearts if we hear the right story that speaks to us as individuals.*

2. **DOK 2**: *"Fairy-tale Logic" mentions situations in fairy tales or other stories without specific names of characters or stories so students must have background knowledge and may need reminders. The most direct scenes, such as references to Harry Potter (lines 3 and 11) or to Beauty and the Beast and the Moses story (line 14) move the "story" to a sound conclusion with the final line. The more implicit references are not as obvious and will require students to make inferences. "Archetype" references many characters and stories by name, so there are explicit connections, and yet, more subtle references provide movement of the "story" in the poem by adding layers of meaning to the explicit references.*

3. **DOK 4**: *I like "Fairy-tale Logic." The poem reminded me of Dorothy's "impossible task" of getting the witch's broom in The Wizard of Oz.*

4. **DOK 4**: *I think the indirect references are more effective, because they cause the reader to become curious and dig deeper if they don't understand the reference.*

 RESPOND

Collaborate & Compare

ARCHETYPE
Poem by Margarita Engle

FAIRY-TALE LOGIC
Poem by A. E. Stallings

INFER THEMES WITHIN AND ACROSS TEXTS

Poems may have similar topics but express different themes. A **topic** is the work's subject. The work's **theme** is its message about life or human nature. Look at the following examples:

> Statement of topic: **The poem is about two friends who fight a lot.**

> Statement of theme: **Friendships can be difficult when personalities clash.**

The first example tells what the poem is about, so it states a topic, not a theme. The second example states a theme because it expresses general ideas about human nature and experience.

When you compare two texts' themes, you can draw on **explicit** (stated directly) or **implicit** (stated indirectly, or implied) information. Then you can identify similar or contrasting themes suggested in the two selections. Always use evidence from the poems to support your stated themes. Work in a small group to complete a Comparison Chart like the one that follows.

	ARCHETYPE	FAIRY-TALE LOGIC
Inferences about Theme		
Text Evidence		

ANALYZE THE TEXTS

Discuss these questions in your group.

1. **Compare** In what ways are the poems similar and different?

2. **Interpret** Both poems mention fairy tales and other stories. How does each poem use these references to reveal ideas?

3. **Connect** Which poem do you connect with more? Why?

4. **Evaluate** The poem "Archetype" names specific characters from other stories, while "Fairy-tale Logic" indirectly refers to other characters. Which use do you find more effective? Why?

© Houghton Mifflin Harcourt Publishing Company • Image Credits: (t) Library of Congress Prints & Photographs Division

WHEN STUDENTS STRUGGLE . . .

Infer Themes Within and Across Texts Have students look at the poem "Archetype" and reread line 17–18: "Of all tales, only The Nightingale felt like a story I knew before I was born" Ask: *How could you paraphrase those lines? Have you ever met someone for the first time or heard or read a story and felt a shock of recognition? How did you react?* Ask students whether they have heard a speech and felt like the speaker was speaking to them alone. Ask them how that feeling helps support the idea that if a story seems to speak to us personally, then we can learn about ourselves through that story.

COMPARE THEMES

Your group will continue to explore the themes in these poems, using evidence to support your inferences. Follow these steps:

1. **Review** In your group, review the comparison chart you created for the poems.

2. **Write Theme Statements** Use information from the chart to write a theme statement for each poem. Be sure to state each theme in a complete sentence.

Theme Statements:

"Archetype"

_____

_____

"Fairy-tale Logic"

_____

_____

3. **Compare and Contrast** Discuss similarities and differences in the themes you've identified.

4. **Connect** Share your personal opinions about these themes based on your knowledge and experience.

5. **Identify** Take notes on what others say. Do you agree or disagree? Identify points of agreement and disagreement and discuss.

6. **Share** Share your ideas with the larger group.

Go to the **Speaking and Listening Studio** for help with having a group discussion.

COMPARE THEMES

1. *As students review their charts, remind them that they need to refer to evidence that will support their inferences. In this case, evidence would be a quotation from the text.*

2. ***Theme Statement Possible Answers:***

   "Fairy-tale Logic": Like in stories, people do impossible things when they must.

   "Archetype": A person's deepest self can be found in a childhood story.

3. *Ask students to draw a Venn diagram in their notes with "Archetype" on the left and "Fairy-tale Logic" on the right. In the center list, possible notes include: Both are poems; allude to fairy tales; describe making a personal connection to fairy tales. Under "Archetype," students may note: free verse; about finding a character pattern that reveals the reader's "secret heart"; favorite characters may serve as role models. Under "Fairy-tale Logic," students may note: sonnet; rhyme; about fairy tales serving as a model for accomplishing impossible tasks.*

4. *Answers will vary.*

5. *Have students make a graphic organizer to capture thoughts as students discuss. Head one column with "Agree" and the other with "Disagree."*

6. *Remind students that when they do not understand a comment made by another group member, they should ask questions to clarify meaning. The process of asking and answering questions can help everyone understand an issue more clearly and can lead to new ideas.*

ENGLISH LEARNER SUPPORT

Practice Plurals Vietnamese, Cantonese, Hmong, and Korean speakers are used to speaking a language in which nouns do not change form to name plurals. Provide students with practice pronouncing plurals in English. List singular and plural forms of nouns on the board, such as: *princess/princesses, dragon/dragons, grandma/grandmas, task/tasks*. Then provide students with a frame to complete for each pair: *One ____. Many ____.* Listen to students speak and correct pronunciation of plurals as needed. **SUBSTANTIAL/MODERATE**

THE BOATMAN'S FLUTE

Folktale retold by Sherry Garland

GENRE ELEMENTS
FOLKTALE

A **folktale** begins when a story people like to hear is shared aloud throughout a certain area or culture and is retold again and again over several generations. It takes place in the distant past and has simple powerful themes and messages. It focuses on human nature and common strengths and weaknesses.

LEARNING OBJECTIVES

- Cite evidence to support analysis of plot and point of view.
- Conduct research about folktales.
- Discuss elements of plot.
- Rewrite the narrative from a different point of view.
- Expand knowledge of vocabulary.
- **Language** Identify and discuss with a partner the characters in a text, using the term *character*.

TEXT COMPLEXITY

Quantitative Measures	The Boatman's Flute	Lexile: 1050L
Qualitative Measures	**Ideas Presented** Simple, literal, explicit, and direct; some supported symbolism.	
	Structures Used Clear, chronological, conventional.	
	Language Used Mostly explicit, some figurative or allusive language; some meaning is implied.	
	Knowledge Required Situations and subjects familiar or easily envisioned; some cultural references.	

RESOURCES

Online **Ed**

- Unit 6 Response Log
- 🔊 Selection Audio
- 📖 Reading Studio: Notice & Note
- ▤ Writing Studio: Writing Narratives
- 💬 Speaking and Listening Studio: Giving a Presentation
- ⚛ Vocabulary Studio: Analyzing Word Structure
- ❗ Grammar Studio: Module 13: Lessons 1–2: Using Quotation Marks
- ✅ "The Boatman's Flute" Selection Test

SUMMARIES

English

In this Vietnamese folktale, the beautiful daughter of a wealthy mandarin is confined to her room. A boatman skilled on the flute passes by, and the daughter creates an elaborate fantasy about meeting and marrying him. He sees her at the window and dreams of her, but he is told he will never have her and stops passing the mansion. The daughter falls ill, and the mandarin brings her the boatman. When she sees he is ugly, she rejects him. He dies of a broken heart, which turns to jade and is made into a cup. When the daughter drinks from the cup, she sees her mistake, and the boatman's soul is freed.

Spanish

En este cuento folklórico vietnamita, la hermosa hija de un mandarín adinerado es confinada en su cuarto. Un barquero experimentado en la flauta pasa y la hija crea una elaborada fantasía en la cual conoce al barquero y se casan. Él la ve en la ventana y sueña con ella, pero le dicen que ella nunca será suya y por esto deja de pasar por la mansión. La hija se enferma y el mandarín la lleva adonde el barquero. Cuando ella ve que es feo, lo rechaza. Él muere despechado y su corazón roto se convierte en una piedra de jade con la que luego hacen una taza. Cuando la hija bebe de la taza, ve su error y el alma del barquero es liberada.

SMALL-GROUP OPTIONS

Have students work in small groups to read and discuss the selection.

Somebody Wanted But/So/Then

Challenge groups to summarize, not retell, the plot of this folktale as a short, yet fully descriptive summary.

1. Write the phrase "Somebody Wanted . . . " on the board. Ask students to work together to finish the sentence multiple times and change the "somebody" to each of the main characters.

2. Have students share their sentences. Then add *but, so*, and *then* to the board and tell students to use these words to finish their sentences.

3. Have students rearrange as needed to put all the sentences into one summary paragraph.

Three Before Me

When students finish their summaries of the story and their retelling in a different point of view, ask students to self-edit and then peer edit their own writing before turning it in.

1. Have students check their own work for any "non-negotiables" that have been established in the classroom, such as spelling commonly misspelled words that are posted on the wall.

2. Ask each student to have three other students edit the work, make written suggestions, and initial it.

3. Have students turn in revised work and the edited and initialed copy.

Text X-Ray: English Learner Support
for "The Boatman's Flute"

Use the Text X-Ray and the supports and scaffolds in the Teacher's Edition to help guide students at different proficiency levels through the selection.

INTRODUCE THE SELECTION
DISCUSS THE HIDDEN TRUTHS OF FOLKTALES

Folktales often have a "moral to the story" or a message about human nature to remind the listener or reader to look carefully within themselves for wisdom and avoid common errors that sometimes have devastating consequences. The Essential Question asks what hidden truths are revealed in stories, and "The Boatman's Flute" explores this theme through mistakes made and regretted by its main characters.

Provide the following English idiom: "You should not judge a book by its cover." Have students discuss the meaning. (*Do not judge the inside of someone by how the outside looks.*) Tell students that in general conversation, this idiom is often meant to suggest a book might be good on the inside while being unappealing on the outside. Ask students to discuss moments in their lives or in stories they have come across in which it turned out that what was beautiful on the surface was not sincere or truly beautiful underneath. This discussion can expand to include anything that is not what it seems to be.

CULTURAL REFERENCES

The following words or phrases may be unfamiliar to students:

- *the Land of Small Dragon* (paragraph 1): Vietnam
- *ballads of old* (paragraph 2): old stories that are sung
- *dewy* (paragraph 3): moist with water droplets condensed from the air
- *dappled shade* (paragraph 3): shade spotted with filtered sunlight
- *knew . . . by heart* (paragraph 10): memorized
- *pour his heart and soul* (paragraph 12): put all his energy and enthusiasm into

LISTENING

Understand Point of View

Point out the use of pronouns in these paragraphs and where they are placed in English sentences. For instance, remind speakers of Spanish and Vietnamese that it is not, "the boatman, he . . . " Tell students that, when writing a story, an author needs to decide who will tell it, and that this decision determines the pronouns that will be used.

Have students listen as you read aloud paragraphs 4–5. Have them repeat sentences and fragments that have pronouns. Use the following supports with students at varying proficiency levels:

- Tell students that you will ask yes or no questions about what you just read. Ask: *Is the daughter telling the story?* (no) *Is the servant telling the story?* (no) *Is a narrator telling the story?* (yes) **SUBSTANTIAL**
- Ask students whether the narrator is describing the daughter's actions alone or also her thoughts and feelings. (*actions, thoughts, and feelings*) **MODERATE**
- Ask students to summarize the boatman's actions in their own words and say whether the narrator suggests he knew the daughter was paying attention. (*He stopped his tasks, went to deeper water, and played the flute. It does not say he knew.*) **LIGHT**

SPEAKING

Discuss Characters

Have students discuss the characters in this narrative. Circulate around the room to make sure students are using the term *character* and can identify and describe aspects of these characters.

Use the following supports with students at varying proficiency levels, and have students share with the class when done:

- Provide a sentence frame: *Paragraph 1 says the mandarin's daughter was _____.* **SUBSTANTIAL**
- Ask students to identify and describe how the mandarin treated his daughter. Then ask students to explain why they think he acted as he did. **MODERATE**
- Have students work together to find two to three descriptions of the characters in order to cite text evidence when explaining to the class who the characters in this folktale are. **LIGHT**

READING

Read Dialogue

Draw students' attention to the use of prose descriptions in the story and ask them to add additional dialogue. Point out that the dialogue should be punctuated correctly and should not be random. It should reflect what the character *might* say in that moment.

Work with students to read paragraphs 26–27 aloud (choral reading). Use the following supports with students at varying proficiency levels:

- Model first and then ask students to highlight all the dialogue. **SUBSTANTIAL**
- Have students retell the content of the dialogue as prose when the daughter rejects the boatman. Ask: *How would you describe what she said, rather than using a quotation?* (*The girl thanked the boatman politely for . . .*) *Which do you like better?* **MODERATE**
- Have students work in pairs to retell paragraphs 22–24 (1 paragraph per group) as prose and compare the impact of each approach. Ask: *Which is better? Why?* **LIGHT**

WRITING

Write with Dialogue

Draw students' attention to the use of dialogue in a tale or narrative. Note that adding quoted lines from the characters brings their perspectives to life, allowing the reader to hear their actual words, rather than a summary provided by a narrator.

Use the following supports with students at varying proficiency levels:

- Write on the board and have students copy: *She asked the boatman to forgive her. "Please forgive me," she said.* Have students identify which sentence uses quoted dialogue. **SUBSTANTIAL**
- Put students into small groups. Ask students to look at the part of the story where the daughter imagines going down the river with the boatman. Ask students to add dialogue that would fit and punctuate it correctly. Then have them exchange their dialogue with another group to edit it for pronoun agreement and punctuation. Example: *She said, "The orchids are beautiful!"* **MODERATE**
- Have students continue adding dialogue, but focus on creating the boatman and daughter's imaginary conversations with more detail. **LIGHT**

? Connect to the
ESSENTIAL QUESTION

Read the Essential Question aloud. Tell students that in the folktale "The Boatman's Flute," all the characters learn something about themselves. Point out that this is true in most stories. Tell them that traditional stories that are passed on from generation to generation reveal important and often very basic truths all generations need to learn or be reminded about. These stories are meant to make listeners and readers put themselves in the character's places and think about their own beliefs, choices, and hidden truths.

COMPARE THEMES

Point out to students that both stories they will be reading are folktales. This means the stories have probably been around for hundreds of years and been shared from village to village in their country of origin. For the first story, it is possible that some of the storytellers played the flute at key moments in the story.

Write the words *Plot, Point of view*, and *Characters* on the board. Draw a blank Venn diagram with ovals containing the names of each tale to remind students what they will be comparing.

FOLKTALE
THE BOATMAN'S FLUTE

retold by **Sherry Garland**
pages 473–479

COMPARE THEMES

As you read, notice how the authors use plot structure and point of view to share their ideas. Pay attention to how the characters in each tale think, behave, and grow. Look for ideas and other ways that the two stories are similar to and different from each other. After you read both selections, you will work with a small group to complete a project.

 ESSENTIAL QUESTION:

What hidden truths about people and the world are revealed in stories?

FOLKTALE
THE MOUSE BRIDE

retold by **Heather Forest**
pages 487–495

470   Unit 6

The Boatman's Flute

QUICK START

Think of stories you've read that reveal a hidden truth. How did the writers reveal the truths about the world or the people involved? List a few of these stories and discuss their messages with a partner.

ANALYZE PLOT

A **plot** is a series of events in a story that center on a **conflict**—a struggle of opposing forces faced by the main character. Characters' **external** and **internal responses** to conflict, including their actions, decisions, and thoughts and feelings, help develop the plot. As you read, use the chart to identify the different stages of the plot.

PLOT STAGE	DESCRIPTION
Exposition	the first stage of plot that introduces setting and characters and provides background information
Rising Action	the events and complications that increase conflict
Climax	the point of greatest interest, where the conflict results in an important decision or action
Falling Action	the events that happen as a result of the climax
Resolution	the presentation of how the central conflict is solved

GENRE ELEMENTS: FOLKTALE

- originates in the oral tradition of a culture
- is often set in the culture of origin
- takes place in the distant past
- includes simple but powerful themes
- focuses on human strengths and weaknesses

IDENTIFY POINT OF VIEW

The **narrator** is the voice that tells the story. A writer's choice of narrator establishes **point of view.** Use the chart to help identify the point of view of the story. As you read, think about how the point of view affects your understanding of the story.

FIRST-PERSON POINT OF VIEW	THIRD-PERSON POINT OF VIEW
The narrator is a character in the story.	The narrator is not a character in the story.
The narrator uses the pronouns *I, me,* and *my.*	The narrator uses the pronouns *he, she,* and *they* to refer to the characters.
The narrator does not know what other characters are thinking and feeling.	A **third-person limited** narrator knows the thoughts and feelings of just one character, usually the main character. A **third-person omniscient** narrator knows what all of the characters think and feel.

The Boatman's Flute   471

QUICK START

Have students read the Quick Start question and work with a partner. Invite a few students to share the stories and hidden truths they reveal.

ANALYZE PLOT

Ask students to number the plot stages 1–5 and draw a graphic organizer with a plot diagram with the numbers in the correct places. Have them rewrite the plot stages with descriptions at the bottom of their note as a key. Then, as they read, ask them to put keywords related to the action of the story on the line under or next to the correct number.

Example Answers:

1. **Exposition:** *mansion, river, "Once," daughter in room*

2. **Rising Action:** *daughter hears flute, boatman notices daughter*

IDENTIFY POINT OF VIEW

Review the Point of View chart on page 471 with students. Ask students to identify different points of view from examples.

Example:

Say: *Since I was a small boy, I worked on the river in the family boat with my father. At night, he would teach me how to play his flute. After my father died, I worked on the river alone. One day as I was playing my flute, I noticed a girl at a window high on a hill looking out. I wondered if she heard my flute!*

Ask students if that is a first- or third-person point of view. *(first)* Then ask whether the narrator is a character in the story or a narrator telling a story about other people. *(He is a character in the story.)* Go through each of the point of view descriptions on the chart in this manner.

 ENGLISH LEARNER SUPPORT

Analyze Plot   Point out that the names of the stages of the plot have Spanish cognates: *esposition/exposicion, action/accion, climax/climax, resolution/resolucion.* The word *rising* is *creciente* in Spanish, which is related to the English, and Spanish, word *crescendo.*

- Point to *Rising Action* and *Falling Action* and mimic an up-and-down movement with your hand, having students say *rising action* and *falling*

action to name each part of the action. Then point to *Climax* and say *climax.* Ask students to practice pronouncing the words.

- Ask students to work in small groups to develop a plot diagram illustrating the stages of the plot and the story.
  SUBSTANTIAL/MODERATE

TEACH

CRITICAL VOCABULARY

Encourage students to read all the sentences before deciding on a word or phrase that will best complete each one. Remind them to look for context clues that match the meaning of each word.

Answers:

1. *local woman who sews*
2. *enclosed inner area*
3. *get agreement from*
4. *make*
5. *authentic and honest*
6. *consideration and respect*

■ English Learner Support

Use Cognates Tell students that *sincere/sincero* are cognates. Also similar are the words *convince/convencer* and *commit/cometer*. Point out that the word *seamstress* has an interesting Spanish partner in the word *costurera*, which is related to the English word *costume* and the French word *couture*. **SUBSTANTIAL/MODERATE**

LANGUAGE CONVENTIONS

Emphasize that the appearance of quotation marks in text signals that the words that follow are exactly what was said by a speaker or in another text. Note that the marks come in sets, indicating the beginning and ending of the section of quoted text, whether it is a line or dialogue or the specific title of a work. As students are reading, have them pay particular attention to what comes just before and just after the quotation marks in the tale.

✎ ANNOTATION MODEL

Remind students that they can underline important details and circle words that signal how the text is organized. Point out that they can also invent and use their own system for marking up the selection in their write-in text. They may want to color-code their annotations by using highlighters. Their notes in the margin may include questions about ideas that are unclear or topics they want to learn more about.

CRITICAL VOCABULARY

seamstress   courtyard   convince   commit   sincere   politeness

To preview the Critical Vocabulary words, replace each boldfaced vocabulary word with a word or words that have the same meaning.

1. He took the torn shirt to the (**seamstress**) _____ for repairs.

2. The museum had a (**courtyard**) _____ on the ground floor.

3. I tried to (**convince**) _____ my friend to walk with me.

4. If you (**commit**) _____ too many fouls, you will be removed from the game.

5. Her sister didn't think she was (**sincere**) _____ in her apology.

6. She thinks (**politeness**) _____ is important.

LANGUAGE CONVENTIONS

Quotation marks are used to set off a speaker's exact words. They are also used to set off the title of a story, an article, a short poem, an essay, a song, or a chapter. Punctuation marks, such as commas, question marks, and periods, appear inside the quotation marks.

ANNOTATION MODEL

NOTICE & NOTE ✎

As you read, mark evidence that indicates plot and point of view in the folktale. You can also mark words and phrases that support your own ideas. Here are one reader's notes on the beginning of "The Boatman's Flute."

> 1 Once, in the Land of Small Dragon, a wealthy mandarin lived in a large mansion on top of a hill overlooking a peaceful river. The mandarin had only one daughter, and her face was as beautiful as lotus blossoms in pale moonlight that floated atop the river.

I think this is the exposition because it introduces the story, setting, and characters.

BACKGROUND

Sherry Garland *(b. 1948) is an award-winning author of more than thirty books for children, teens, and adults. She has written several books focusing on the people and country of Vietnam, where she has traveled and done research. In her home state of Texas, she has worked with Vietnamese immigrants, helping them to relocate. The selection "The Boatman's Flute" is a folktale that she retold in her book* Children of the Dragon: Selected Tales from Vietnam *(2001).*

THE BOATMAN'S FLUTE

Folktale retold by Sherry Garland

PREPARE TO COMPARE

As you read, pay attention to what the characters think they want in the beginning of the folktale. Does what they want change during the course of the story?

1   Once, in the Land of Small Dragon, a wealthy mandarin[1] lived in a large mansion on top of a hill overlooking a peaceful river. The mandarin had only one daughter, and her face was as beautiful as lotus blossoms[2] in pale moonlight that floated atop the river.

2   The mandarin loved his daughter dearly and feared for her safety so much that all her life he had never allowed her to leave the mansion. She spent her days and nights in her room, high above the river, watching the world below. Servants brought her the most delicious dishes, and talented

---

[1] **mandarin** (măn′də-rĭn): a member of an elite group, especially a person having influence or high status in intellectual or cultural circles.
[2] **lotus blossoms:** flowers of the lotus, symbolic of purity.

NOTICE & NOTE

Notice & Note

Use the side margins to notice and note signposts in the text.

ANALYZE PLOT

Annotate: In paragraph 2, mark what you learn about the mandarin's relationship with his daughter.

Predict: How do you think the mandarin's actions might influence the plot?

BACKGROUND

After students read the Background note, explain that writers often find inspiration in cultures other than their own. In this case, the author is interested in Vietnamese culture and people, and has learned about their folktales. Ask students whether they are drawn to any particular culture or country and suggest that they research stories from that culture.

PREPARE TO COMPARE

Direct students to use the Prepare to Compare prompt to focus their reading.

 ANALYZE PLOT

Point out to students that the mandarin's daughter spent all her days and nights watching the world and not participating in it. Ask students how they think that would affect someone. For instance, she might live more in her dreams than reality. She has not accomplished anything nor failed at anything, so she might not have a good sense of her own heart and mind. (**Answer:** *Students may say that keeping someone locked up turns them into a prisoner. This introduces the conflict in the plot and defines the daughter's character and, therefore, the choices she may make in the plot.*)

For **speaking support** for students at varying proficiency levels, see the **Text X-Ray** on page 470D.

🔵 ENGLISH LEARNER SUPPORT

Analyze Plot   After students have been directed to annotate evidence of plot and point of view, use this strategy to provide further support:

1.   Ask students to revisit the plot diagrams and posters that they made through the activity on p. 471 and add the more complex plot stage evidence to their diagrams.

2.   Put students in small groups and have them take turns presenting their plot diagrams to the other members of their groups. **MODERATE/LIGHT**

IDENTIFY POINT OF VIEW

Explain to students that the word *omniscient* contains the Latin root *omni-* , which means "all" or "total," and *-sciens,* which means "to know." A third-person omniscient narrator, therefore, "knows all" or can tell what any character is thinking and feeling. Have them ask themselves whether that is true of this narrator based on the evidence in paragraphs 5–8. (**Answer:** *The pronouns used are* she, he, her, him, *or* they. *This is third person. I think the point of view is third-person omniscient because the narrator can see inside all the characters.*)

■ English Learner Support

Identify Point of View Point to the person or persons the pronouns refer to in each case. Example: Have students say *I* and *me* and point to themselves. As they do that, say, *First Person.* **SUBSTANTIAL**

For **listening support** for students at varying proficiency levels, see the **Text X-Ray** on page 470C.

CRITICAL VOCABULARY

seamstress: Point out that today, we usually call a person who sews a *sewer* or *tailor*, not a *seamstress*.

ASK STUDENTS what they can guess about the roots of this word from how it sounds and the context. (*When people sew, they sew seams together. The ending -ess indicated a woman held the job, like* actress *or* authoress.) Note that in English today, the words *sewer, actor,* and *author* are non-gender specific.

courtyard: Some homes and schools have these today, and as in the case of this mansion, the building is built around an open space that has trees and grass and even fountains. This is more common in public buildings, warm climates, and among the wealthy.

ASK STUDENTS to hypothesize the reasons for creating an enclosed courtyard rather than a simple yard. (*to protect the family and their possessions; to create privacy*)

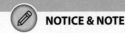

seamstress
(sēm´strĭs) *n.* A *seamstress* is a woman who sews, especially one who earns a living sewing.

courtyard
(kôrt´yärd´) *n.* A *courtyard* is an area enclosed by walls and open to the sky.

IDENTIFY POINT OF VIEW

Annotate: Review paragraphs 5–8 and mark pronouns that help you identify the folktale's point of view.

Analyze: What kind of narrator uses this point of view? How does this point of view affect your understanding? Explain.

---

seamstresses sewed her the finest gowns of silk. Musicians and poets sang to her the ballads of old.

3   But never had the beautiful girl walked barefoot on the dewy green grass nor plucked ripe fruit from a tree nor run along the banks of the river, flying kites and laughing like other children. The only sunlight that ever touched her fair skin was the few pale beams that peeked through the dappled shade in the walled-in **courtyard.**

4   One day the mandarin's daughter sat beside her window looking at the small boats and sampans[3] gliding over the peaceful blue waters below. Some were loaded with fresh fruit from the mountains, others with bags of rice or baskets of fish, and some ferried passengers back and forth across the river.

5   As she watched the activity below, one small *ghe*[4] caught her eye. The boatman stood up and skillfully steered the *ghe* out into deeper water with a long bamboo pole, then he sat down. He placed a bamboo flute to his lips and soon the most haunting, beautiful melody the girl had ever heard drifted up to her window. It was the sound of rippling waters and cool breezes, of tall bamboo and the night bird's song, all woven together. She watched the boatman, and as she listened to the sweet notes rise and fall, she imagined how young, strong, and handsome he must be.

6   All that day the mandarin's daughter stayed beside the window, until the sun began to set over the western mountain and the boatman steered his *ghe* away out of sight.

7   That night she dreamed of the strange melody and imagined herself stepping into the boat beside the young man, whose strong arms lifted her aboard with grace and ease. In her dream they drifted along the peaceful river by the light of a full moon. The boatman explained to her all the strange and wonderful sights that unfolded before them. She experienced things that she had only heard about from the poets — the sweet touch of the cool river waters on her hands trailing beside the boat, the gentle kiss of the night wind against her flushed cheeks, and the tingling fragrance of wild orchids hanging from trees in the nearby jungle.

8   A smile flickered across her lips, even as she slept. She dreamed of climbing out of the boat and running barefoot through the thick green grass and plucking wild berries that

---

[3] **sampans:** flatbottom Asian boats usually propelled by two oars.
[4] **ghe:** a small boat.

burst with a sour, tangy taste on her tongue. And when a green-eyed tiger roared deep in the jungle, the boatman held her tight.

9   The girl awakened to the sound of a brass gong. Without even stopping to taste the tray of delicacies laid out before her by her devoted handmaiden, the mandarin's daughter walked to the window and looked below. Her heart beat faster when she spotted the little boat and heard the haunting music floating up to the window once again.

10   All day she remained by the window, until she knew the tunes he played by heart. Whenever the boat came close to the foot of the hill, she dropped flower petals, hoping the wind would carry them to the boatman. If ever he looked in her direction, she waved her long silk scarf. She became **convinced** that he played the tunes just for her.

11   Every day the mandarin's daughter listened to the boatman's melodies, often making up her own words to sing along. Or she danced with her shadow, pretending it was the strong, young boatman. Every night she dreamed of riding down the peaceful river by his side. She knew that her father was planning for her to marry soon and prayed that somehow the boatman was really a lord in disguise who would be the one her father chose.

12   As for the boatman, he had seen a tiny figure at the window and had caught the petals floating down from above. He could only guess what the girl might look like or who she might be, but just knowing that she was listening made him pour his heart and soul into the melodies.

convince
(kən-vĭns´) *v.* To *convince* is to use argument or evidence to get someone to believe or be certain about something.

The Boatman's Flute   475

ENGLISH LEARNER SUPPORT

Spell Compound Words This story uses compound words such as *boatman* and *handmaiden*. Point out familiar items in the room that are compound words. Explain that a compound word is made of two smaller words. Help students spell these compound words using flashcards with the words *book, shelf, chalk, board, lunch, box, class,* and *room*.

- Display the flashcard *book*. Help students identify the card that completes the compound word *bookshelf*. *(shelf)* Then have small groups match the word cards that spell the remaining compound words. **SUBSTANTIAL/MODERATE**

- Have students work in pairs to select the cards that spell each compound word and write the compound words they form in sentences. **LIGHT**

CRITICAL VOCABULARY

convince: In this case, the daughter convinced herself. She made up reasons and "evidence" to believe what she wanted to be true: that the boatman was a secret handsome prince who loved her.

ASK STUDENTS to describe a time when they, or someone they knew, convinced themselves of something that probably wasn't true. This tendency is a hidden—or not so hidden—truth about human nature. *(Answers will vary.)*

LANGUAGE CONVENTIONS

Point out that the sentence preceding the quoted lines of dialogue identify the speaker in each paragraph. (**Answer:** *The dialogue signals that the plot will be about the boatman's feelings for the mandarin's daughter. The dialogue also reveals the that the boatman and the daughter are from different classes, which could be an obstacle.*)

ANALYZE PLOT

Have students review the parts of the plot from the chart on page 471. Note that the reader has already been introduced to the boatman, and these thoughts reveal new information about him. (**Answer:** *Rising Action; the thoughts explain to the reader why the boatman chooses to start avoiding this part of the river.*)

IDENTIFY POINT OF VIEW

Asking students to shift to what they would know about the plot and relationships if the narrators' point of view changed is a good way to reveal the writer's craft. (**Answer:** *We wouldn't know about the boatman's conversation with the gentleman and why he decided not to return. We would not know for sure whether the daughter dreamed about the boatman. Instead, we would have to guess from her actions in the presence of the handmaiden.*)

CRITICAL VOCABULARY

commit: The boatman convinced himself no mandarin would talk to him at all unless he had committed a crime. To "commit "often means to decide on a course of action. In this case, the boatman feared he had committed an action that broke a law he did not know about.

ASK STUDENTS whether they have ever felt guilty about something even though they didn't know what they might have done. (*Answers will vary.*)

 NOTICE & NOTE

LANGUAGE CONVENTIONS
Annotate: Mark the quotation marks in paragraphs 13–15.
Predict: What does the introduction of dialogue signal about the plot? What conflict does the dialogue reveal?

ANALYZE PLOT
Annotate: Mark the words that the boatman thinks to himself in paragraph 16.
Analyze: Which part of the plot is this? How does the storyteller use this view into the boatman's thoughts—his internal response to events—to develop the plot?

IDENTIFY POINT OF VIEW
Annotate: In paragraph 20, mark the sentence or sentences that focus on the handmaiden's role in this part of the story.
Analyze: How does the story's point of view affect your understanding of why the handmaiden acts as she does?

commit
(kə-mĭt´) *v.* To *commit* is to do or perform an action.

---

13   One day a gentleman he was ferrying across the river noticed the fine quality of the music. "Boatman, for whom do you play your little bamboo flute with such love and feeling? I see no maidens nearby."

14   The boatman smiled timidly and looked upward. "I do not know her name, but she comes to the window in that house high above the river every day and often drops flowers to show her approval."

15   The gentleman looked up toward the window, then laughed aloud. "You are a fool, young boatman. That is the mandarin's daughter—the most beautiful girl in all our land and one who is sought after by the most wealthy and powerful men, including myself. How could you be so foolish to think she would ever love a common, plain boatman like yourself?"

16   The boatman said nothing but sadly put away his flute and steered the boat down the river, for it was growing dark. *Better that I should leave now, while she is but a vision in my mind,* he told himself. *If ever I see her face, I will never have peace again.*

17   So it was that the boatman decided not to go to that part of the river anymore.

18   The next morning, when she went to the window, the mandarin's daughter did not see the small *ghe.* She thought of ten thousand excuses why the boatman might be late. As the day wore on, he still did not come. The girl's heart grew heavy and tears dropped from her dark, sad eyes. She refused to lie on her bed that night but instead knelt beside the window, staring at the dark river below.

19   Another day passed and the boatman did not come, and by nightfall the girl was weak from hunger and weeping. She soon fell ill. The servants placed her on her bed and summoned her father. The mandarin called in the best physicians, but they could find nothing wrong with her. As another day passed, the mandarin grew distraught.

20   Seeing the mandarin weep over his daughter, the girl's handmaiden could not hold her tongue another moment. She told the mandarin about the boatman who played tunes on his flute that seemed to make the girl very happy. The mandarin ordered his servants to search the river for a man in a small *ghe* playing a bamboo flute.

21   Soon the men returned with the boatman and his flute. He trembled before the wealthy mandarin, wondering what crime he had **committed.**

22   "Are you the young man who has been passing under my window playing tunes upon your flute for many days past?" the mandarin demanded.

23   "Yes, but I meant no harm. If I have broken a law, it was in complete ignorance. I only played the tunes to pass the long day and because it seemed to please the girl in the window. If I disturbed your household, I beg forgiveness and promise to never bother you again."

24   "It is no bother," the mandarin replied, as he studied the **sincere** young boatman. "It seems that your simple music has charmed my daughter. Now she is deathly ill, and I pray that your tunes will restore her spirit. I have been searching the lands for the finest husband for my daughter, but if fate has something else in store, who am I to question? Play your flute again, and if my daughter chooses you above all others, then so be it."

25   The boatman stood amazed. Never in his wildest dreams had he imagined that he might become the husband of this girl so rare in beauty that no man had ever been allowed to gaze upon her face. With a surge of hope in his heart, he raised the flute to his lips with trembling fingers, and he began to play his favorite melody. Soon the tender, warm notes filled the empty halls of the grand house and reached the bed where the girl lay. In a moment she opened her eyes and a smile touched her lips.

26   "He has returned," she whispered, and she begged the handmaiden to help her to her feet. With renewed energy, the girl walked through the house to the source of the music. At first her heart pounded as she saw the strong, young man from afar. But as she came nearer and saw his face, her eyes grew cold. Though his body was young and strong, the boatman's face was ugly. Out of **politeness**, she gave a slight bow.

27   <u>"Thank you for playing the lovely music on your flute. I feel much better now. Father, please pay the boatman for his kindness and do not worry about me. I am over my illness."</u> Quickly she returned to her room and once again looked out the window at the boats coming and going on the river below, wondering how she could have been so foolish to dream about a simple boatman.

28   But the boatman's heart was torn apart. He had gazed on a face that men see only in their dreams. He refused to take the bag of gold the mandarin offered, and left the mansion with heavy footsteps. No longer did he have the desire to play his flute, for the music reminded him of the beautiful girl. Neither

sincere
(sĭn-sîr′) *adj.* Something or someone *sincere* is genuine or heartfelt.

politeness
(pə-līt′nəs) *n.* Politeness is respectful behavior.

> **CONTRASTS AND CONTRADICTIONS**
>
> **Notice & Note:** How does the girl's attitude toward the boatman change? Mark and read aloud the dialogue spoken by the girl in paragraph 27.
>
> **Analyze:** Why does the girl act this way? What does the change reveal about her?

The Boatman's Flute   477

ENGLISH LEARNER SUPPORT

Use Graphic Organizers Ask students to draw a graphic organizer to illustrate how the daughter changes through the development of the plot.

MODERATE/LIGHT

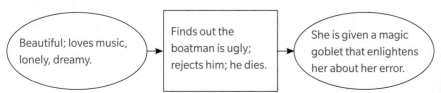

EL ENGLISH LEARNER SUPPORT

Understand Dialogue

- Write on the board the words *It is no bother, the mandarin replied* from paragraph 24. Model for students how to add quotation marks to set apart the dialogue, and have students copy the corrected sentence. **SUBSTANTIAL**

- Have students review paragraphs 22–24. Ask: Does a new paragraph start when the speaker changes? *(yes)* Who is speaking in paragraph 23? *(the boatman)* **MODERATE**

- Ask students to examine the dialogue in other places in the story and find evidence that a new paragraph begins when the speaker changes. **LIGHT**

▶ CONTRASTS AND CONTRADICTIONS

Discuss how the girl's cold reponse emphasizes the contrast between how we look and who we are. She was beautiful, and he was ugly, but only on the outside. Inside it was the opposite. It also contrasts the dream and the reality. (**Answer:** *When the boatman's looks did not match her fantasy, she lost interest. She was in love with a perfect dream, not a real human being.*)

For **reading support** for students at varying proficiency levels, see the **Text X-Ray** on page 470D.

CRITICAL VOCABULARY

sincere: The words of the boatman in paragraph 23 seemed genuine and heartfelt to the mandarin. He believed that the boatman was being truthful about his feelings.

ASK STUDENTS how they think they get a feeling—even if it may turn out to be wrong—that someone is being sincere or insincere. (*body language, facial expression, tone of voice*)

politeness: The daughter's nonverbal language is described as "cold," but her words are polite and civil. She is behaving in a socially acceptable way. She does *not* say, "You are too ugly for me."

ASK STUDENTS if the daughter was being sincere when she gave the bow out of politeness. (*no*)

TEACH

MEMORY MOMENT

Point out to students that because this is a folktale, the daughter's memory is not triggered by something that reminds her of the boatman directly, like a cup from which they both drank. The moment is more dramatic than that. When the daughter and boatman meet, and the boatman dies and is transformed, that is the climax. The goblet is, in fact, the boatman's heart transformed in a magical or supernatural way. (**Answer:** *As the daughter changes, the resolution phase of the plot begins and then continues until the end of the story.*)

 ANALYZE PLOT

Point students to the chart on p. 471 that explains the different plot stages. Tell them that the question is asking about the girl's monologue in paragraph 33. (**Answer:** *This is the climax. The girl has realized that she should not have rejected the boatman.*)

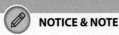 **NOTICE & NOTE**

did he have the spirit to work on the peaceful river, for it, too, reminded him of the girl. Everything he saw or did caused his heart to ache with great longing for the girl that he knew could never love him. Finally, many months later, he lay down and died of a broken heart.

29 When friends and relatives prepared to send the boatman's body down the river in a farewell voyage, they saw that it was gone. But in its place, where his heart would have been, lay an exquisite piece of green jade.[5] A relative took the jade to a carver, who shaped it into a beautiful drinking goblet.

30 Sometime later the relative sold the goblet to the mandarin, who gave it to his daughter. That night the girl's handmaiden served her cool water in the new gift. As the girl lifted the jade goblet to her lips she thought she heard a melancholy tune that she had not heard for a very long time — something that was both sad and lovely. Then, as she sipped the water, she saw in the bottom of the cup the image of a small *ghe* and the young boatman steering it down the peaceful river.

31 Suddenly the girl remembered the boatman's sweet music. She thought about all the happy hours she had spent listening to his flute and the wonderful dreams she had dreamed because of him. Since he had left, no one, not even the most handsome suitors[6] in the land, had made her feel such warmth and happiness. Now, it seemed her days and nights were even longer and more empty than before.

32 Her heart ached with remorse, and tears filled her eyes.

33 "Dear boatman, your love was the truest I have ever known. You were good and kind, and I made a terrible mistake. Wherever you are, please forgive me," she whispered. A single teardrop slid down the girl's petal-smooth cheek into the goblet. When the tear touched the water, the goblet burst into pieces and a breeze suddenly rushed in through the window. The girl saw a thin wisp of fog rise from the shattered goblet and sail out into the night. The sound of a flute blended with the sound of the night bird's song, but this time the tune was full of joy. The boatman's soul was free at last to go in peace.

MEMORY MOMENT

Notice & Note: What triggers, or sets off, memories for the girl? In paragraphs 30–31, mark her memories.

Evaluate: How do the girl's memories at this time in the story affect its plot?

ANALYZE PLOT

Annotate: Mark the words that the girl speaks in paragraph 33.

Analyze: Which part of the plot is this? How have the story's events affected the girl?

---

[5] **green jade:** a type of jade, a precious stone, believed to promote wisdom, balance, and peace.
[6] **suitor** (sōō′tər): someone who tries to gain the love and attention of another person.

478 Unit 6

IMPROVE READING FLUENCY

Targeted Passage Have students work as a class to choral read the last part of this folktale. First, use paragraphs 32–33 to model how to read a folktale. Have students follow along in their books as you read the text with appropriate pacing, intonation, and expression. Point out how you change your voice to read the girl's dialogue with emotion, emphasizing the most important words, and how you pause for punctuation. Then invite the class to read these paragraphs aloud together twice, volunteering feedback to one another after they have read these paragraphs for the first time.

 Go to the **Reading Studio** for additional support in developing fluency.

CHECK YOUR UNDERSTANDING

Answer these questions before moving on to the **Analyze the Text** section on the following page.

1 The mandarin's daughter dreams of riding in a boat with the boatman of the *ghe*. In her dream she —

  A traveled across a wide and stormy lake

  B experienced nature the way it had been expressed by poets

  C heard a strange bird song that was new to her

  D received a tray of delicacies to eat with the boatman

2 The boatman decides not to return to the part of river where he played to the mandarin's daughter because —

  F a gentleman he ferried across the river tells him he will report him to the mandarin

  G he learns that the mandarin's daughter is married

  H he knows if he sees her face again he'll never have peace

  J he has fruit and rice that he needs to deliver downriver

3 When the mandarin's daughter drinks from the jade cup —

  A she realizes she should have married the boatman

  B she decides to go in search of the boatman

  C she remembers the boatman's music and the dreams she had

  D she drops the goblet and it shatters

The Boatman's Flute **479**

© Houghton Mifflin Harcourt Publishing Company • Image Credits: ©View Stock/Getty Images

✎ CHECK YOUR UNDERSTANDING

Have students answer the questions independently.

Answers:

  1. *B*

  2. *H*

  3. *C*

If they answer any questions incorrectly, have them reread the text to confirm their understanding. Then they may proceed to ANALYZE THE TEXT on page 480.

 ENGLISH LEARNER SUPPORT

Oral Assessment   Use the following questions to assess students' comprehension and speaking skills:

  1. Did the daughter dream about nature? *(yes)*

  2. Did the boatman believe he could marry the beautiful woman? *(no)*

  3. What happens when the daughter drinks from the jade cup? *(She hears a tune that reminds her of the boatman's music.)* **SUBSTANTIAL/MODERATE**

ANALYZE THE TEXT

Possible answers:

1. **DOK 2:** *The writer introduces the wealthy gentleman who also wants to marry the mandarin's daughter. He tells the boatman he's a fool, informing him he has no chance. This introduces more conflict. The third-person narration shows the reader the conflict between the thoughts of the boatman and the mandarin's daughter.*

2. **DOK 4:** *Internal: the boatman is totally discouraged and gives up. External: he stops passing the mansion. In response, the girl is deeply saddened. Everything changes from happy to sad.*

3. **DOK 4:** *When the father gives his blessing, we think it might end happily, but the girl rejects the ugly boatman. This is the major turning point of the story. Because of that moment, the boatman dies. From there, the plot has falling action.*

4. **DOK 2:** *The resolution begins in paragraph 29 with the boatman's heart turning into green jade, which is made into a goblet, sold to the mandarin, and given to the daughter. After she drinks from the goblet, the girl hears the tune, sees a vision of the boatman, and asks forgiveness. The story resolves with her remorse and his soul's release.*

5. **DOK 4:** *The daughter was living in a fantasy based on the idea of a perfect mate. When the reality did not look like the dream, the daughter rejected it.*

RESEARCH

Remind students they can try ordering words differently as they put them into search engines to see whether they get differing results. Have them try both with and without the quotation marks. Point out that quotation marks make the words one topic rather than separate, possibly unrelated, keywords.

Connect Suggest that students use a compare-contrast graphic organizer to help them identify similarities and differences between the folktales they researched and "The Boatman's Flute."

RESPOND

ANALYZE THE TEXT

Support your responses with evidence from the text. NOTEBOOK

1. **Summarize** How does the writer build the action in paragraphs 13–18? Describe how the writer uses the narrator's point of view to create conflict in this part of the rising action.

2. **Analyze** Reread paragraphs 16–17. How do the boatman's internal and external responses to conflict—his thoughts and actions—affect the development of the plot?

3. **Evaluate** Reread paragraphs 24–27. Consider the role of conflict at the climax of a story. In what ways can you identify this passage as the story's climax?

4. **Interpret** Reread from paragraph 28 to the end of the story. Describe the falling action in the story's plot. At what point does the falling action become the story's resolution?

5. **Notice & Note** Contrast the behavior of the mandarin's daughter in paragraph 18 with her behavior in paragraph 27. Why did the character act so differently in these two parts of the story?

RESEARCH

RESEARCH TIP
If you are searching for a phrase, put the words in quotation marks. For example, search "folktale structure" to bring up more targeted results.

"The Boatman's Flute" is a folktale from Vietnam. Folktales are stories from a culture's oral tradition—in other words, they were told aloud and were often passed down from one generation to another.

In a small group, research common elements of folktales. Find two or three examples of stories from different parts of the world. Use a chart like the one below to record each story's topic, structure, and tropes, or figures of speech. For example, "beautiful as lotus blossoms in pale moonlight" is a trope, or figure of speech, particular to this Vietnamese folktale.

COUNTRY OF ORIGIN	TITLE	TOPIC	STRUCTURE	TROPES
Russia	Vasilisa	Beautiful daughter of a wealthy man is noticed by Tsar and marries	Narrative	Daughter as prisoner; Love at first sight

© Houghton Mifflin Harcourt Publishing Company

Connect With a small group, discuss how the discoveries you made in your folktale research connect to the story "The Boatman's Flute."

WHEN STUDENTS STRUGGLE . . .

Focus on Figurative Language Explain that the word *trope* has several meanings that apply to folktales. A trope is the use of common figures of speech, but it also means common elements, devices, and ideas that occur again and again in many stories. In fact, American readers will recognize the trope of the beautiful daughter wanting to marry the man of her choice and the trope of love at first sight, but these same readers may have expected the story to end differently because they are also used to the trope of the "handsome prince," or stories that end usually with the trope "happily ever after."

For additional support, go to the **Reading Studio** and assign the following LEVEL UP **Level Up tutorial: Myths, Legends, and Tales.**

CREATE AND DISCOVER

A Different Point of View Reread the story's ending, starting at paragraph 28. Imagine you are the boatman and tell the ending from his point of view.

❏ Rewrite the last paragraphs of the story from the boatman's point of view, in the first person, beginning with "My heart was torn apart."

❏ Be sure to include dialogue.

❏ Edit your work to make sure you use quotation marks correctly.

❏ If you stall or get stuck, try reading the last paragraphs aloud, as if you are telling the story as the boatman, using "I."

Share Your Writing Gather in a small group to share your writing. When everyone has shared, discuss how the shift in point of view affects the story and its plot.

❏ Maintain eye contact as much as possible when presenting your story ending.

❏ Speak clearly, at a rate and volume that allows everyone to hear you.

❏ Speak at a pace that allows your listeners to follow you easily.

❏ Use an appropriate stance and gestures while speaking.

❏ Listen actively to each presenter and ask questions to help clarify understanding.

RESPOND TO THE ESSENTIAL QUESTION

 What hidden truths about people and the world are revealed in stories?

Gather Information Review your annotations and notes on "The Boatman's Flute." Then, add relevant details to your Response Log. As you determine which information to include, think about:

• the plot elements

• how the internal and external responses of the characters affects the development of the plot

• whether or not you were surprised by the story's resolution

At the end of the unit, use your notes to write a short story or folktale.

Go to **Writing Narratives: Point of View and Characters** in the **Writing Studio** for more on writing narrative texts, or stories.

Go to **Giving a Presentation: Delivering Your Presentation** in the **Speaking and Listening Studio** for help with presenting your writing.

ACADEMIC VOCABULARY
As you write and discuss what you learned from the selection, be sure to use the Academic Vocabulary words. Check off each of the words that you use.

❏ emphasize

❏ occur

❏ period

❏ relevant

❏ tradition

CREATE AND DISCOVER

A Different Point of View Point out that the checklist on p. 481 is a list of very specific steps of what to check and what to include. Also note that an example of changing the point of view for paragraph 28 would be "I could feel my heart ripping apart . . . "

For **writing support** for students at varying proficiency levels, see the **Text X-Ray** on page 470D.

Share Your Writing As everyone shares their writing, stop and discuss how this point of view changes the story. Ask students whether hearing the boatman's point of view puts the focus on him rather than on the daughter, and do we change how we want the story to end? Do we understand the daughter or dislike her more, or both, or neither?

RESPOND TO THE ESSENTIAL QUESTION

Allow time for students to add details from "The Boatman's Flute" to their Unit 6 Response Logs.

APPLY

CRITICAL VOCABULARY

Possible answers:

1. I could **convince** them that everyone would enjoy and appreciate it.

2. I could find a sewer or **seamstress** to fix it.

3. A **courtyard** would be safe place for a basketball hoop.

4. When interacting with others, **politeness** can help to ease conflict.

5. A person who is **sincere** is not deceptive.

6. Drivers might get tickets if they **commit** offenses such as speeding or failing to stop at a red light.

VOCABULARY STRATEGY:
Word Structure

- **seamstress** — *seam* from Norse and German for "*sew.*" Latin for "*sew*" is *suere.* Suffix *-ess* is a feminine form of a noun.

- **courtyard** — *court* from Latin *cortem; yard* from Old English and German *geard/gaard* Latin *hortus* for "*garden*"

- **sincere** — from the Latin *sincerus*

RESPOND

WORD BANK

seamstress	commit
courtyard	sincere
convince	politeness

Go to **Analyzing Word Structure** in the **Vocabulary Studio** for more on bases, roots, and affixes.

CRITICAL VOCABULARY

Practice and Apply Answer each question using a Critical Vocabulary word in a complete sentence.

1. How can you get your parents to agree to take you and your friends out for dinner?

2. If you don't know how to sew and you tear your coat, how can you repair it?

3. Where might you find a safe place to set up a basketball hoop in a busy neighborhood with lots of street traffic?

4. What characteristic is valuable in avoiding an argument?

5. What is the opposite of being deceptive?

6. Why do drivers receive traffic violations, or tickets?

VOCABULARY STRATEGY:
Word Structure

The **base** of a word is the part of the word that can stand alone. For example, the base of the word *politeness* is *polite.*

Many words in the English language have Greek or Latin **roots.** You can check a print or digital dictionary to learn about the roots of words. The entry for a word often gives details about the word's origin, or etymology. If you can identify a Greek or Latin root, such as *hydro* ("water") or *bio* ("life"), in a word you don't know, you have a clue to what the word means.

An **affix** is a letter or group of letters that changes a word's meaning. Affixes can take the form of **prefixes** added to the beginning of a root or base, or **suffixes** added to the end of a root or base. The word *convince,* for instance, comes from Latin. Its affix is the Latin prefix *con-,* which means "with." The Latin base is *vincere,* meaning "to conquer."

Use a dictionary to complete the chart.

WORD	BASE OF THE WORD	PREFIX OR SUFFIX	LATIN OR GREEK ROOT
seamstress			
commit			
sincere			

© Houghton Mifflin Harcourt Publishing Company

482   Unit 6

ENGLISH LEARNER SUPPORT

Use Critical Vocabulary

Have students use the Critical Vocabulary words to finish the following sentences:

Work hard to _____(convince) your parents to allow you to go see a movie.

I need a tailor or _____(seamstress) to fix the rip in my coat.

My school has a_____(courtyard) surrounded by walls where we plant vegetables. **SUBSTANTIAL/MODERATE**

When I have a conflict with a friend, _____(politeness) keeps our friendship together.

I told her the truth, but she did not think I was being _____(sincere).

When I finally make a decision, I am very _____(committed) to a course of action. **MODERATE/LIGHT**

482   Unit 6

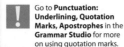
LANGUAGE CONVENTIONS:
Quotation Marks

Quotation marks are punctuation used to set off a speaker's exact words. Quotation marks are helpful in distinguishing narration from dialogue. For example, "The Boatman's Flute" begins with narration, and later includes dialogue between characters. The dialogue—set off with quotation marks—offers a break from the narration and brings variety and life to the writing. Use quotation marks whenever you want to express exactly what a person or character is saying.

Follow these basic rules when writing dialogue.

Insert a question mark or exclamation mark inside the end quotes, or final quotation marks:

"How are you?" I asked.

Insert a comma before the end quotes and name the speaker after the end quotes:

"I'm hungry," said Henry.

To write a line of dialogue without naming the speaker, place the period, question mark, or exclamation point within the end quotes:

"Let's eat!"

In dialogue, begin a new paragraph each time the speaker changes.

Practice and Apply Reread the dialogue between the mandarin and the boatman in paragraphs 22–24 and study the punctuation. Then add quotations and punctuation to the following dialogue between these characters: a mother and her two daughters. The mother is unnamed, and the two daughters are Lila and Lala.

Bring the wood in for the fire and hurry up, Lila! My arms are full already, yelled Lila. Lala, help your sister unload her basket and bring the wood in before it rains! Do I have to do it now? Lila whined to her mother. Her mother yelled impatiently, Yes!

Go to **Punctuation: Underlining, Quotation Marks, Apostrophes** in the **Grammar Studio** for more on using quotation marks.

LANGUAGE CONVENTIONS:
Quotation Marks

Remind students that you need to start a new line each time a new person speaks. Point out that a paragraph may include only dialogue, as in paragraph 23, or a combination of dialogue and narration, as in paragraph 26.

Practice and Apply

Possible answer:

"Bring the wood in for the fire and hurry up, Lila!"

"My arms are full already," yelled Lila.

"Lala, help your sister unload her basket and bring the wood in before it rains!"

"Do I have to do it now?" Lala whined to her mother.

Her mother yelled impatiently, "Yes!"

 ENGLISH LEARNER SUPPORT

Use Quotation Marks

Write the following sentences on the board without punctuation. Then ask volunteers to add the punctuation and explain their choices.

- "Bring me a pencil, David," said Jen.
- "Get your own!" yelled the boy.
- The mother yelled, "Stop fighting!"
  SUBSTANTIAL/MODERATE

MENTOR TEXT
THE MOUSE BRIDE
Folktale retold by Heather Forest

> This folktale serves as a **mentor text,** a model for students to follow when they come to the Unit 6 Writing Task: Write a Short Story.

GENRE ELEMENTS
FOLKTALE

Remind students that a **folktale** is a story, usually told orally, that represents the traditions of the culture in which it was originally told. Most folktales are set in the distant past and involve characters that are usually very good or very bad. Many folktales have a hero and a heroine who are kind, honorable, and courageous. Folktales usually convey a universal theme, or big idea, about the importance of people's behavior. Many folktales feature the rule of three—where characters and events occur in groups of three.

LEARNING OBJECTIVES

- Cite evidence to support an analysis of the textual elements of folktales.
- Conduct research about some of the common themes of folktales from around the world.
- Write an analytical essay about the themes in a folktale.
- Participate in a small-group discussion about the themes identified in a folktale.
- **Language** Discuss author's purposes, using the term *purpose*.

TEXT COMPLEXITY

Quantitative Measures	The Mouse Bride	Lexile: 780L
Qualitative Measures	**Ideas Presented** Simple ideas about human values.	
	Structures Used Simple chronological sequence of events	
	Language Used Direct with virtually no figurative language.	
	Knowledge Required A basic understanding of the folktale genre will be helpful.	

Online Ed

RESOURCES

- Unit 6 Response Log
- 🔊 Selection Audio
- 📖 Reading Studio: Notice & Note
- 🖥 Writing Studio: Using Textual Evidence
- 💬 Speaking and Listening Studio: Participating in Collaborative Discussions
- ⚛ Vocabulary Studio: Context Clues
- ❗ Grammar Studio: Module 2: Lesson 3: Adjectives; Module 3: Lesson 5: Adverbs
- ☑ "The Mouse Bride" Selection Test

SUMMARIES

English

In the folktale "The Mouse Bride," three sons (at the request of their father) go in search of brides. The two older sons seek out brides from areas nearby, and the youngest son goes into the forest, where he meets a magical mouse with whom he falls in love. Just when he thinks he has lost her to drowning, she emerges from the water, and his love transforms her into the beautiful princess she really is.

Spanish

En el cuento folklórico "La novia ratona", tres hijos (por petición de su padre) van en busca de novias. Los dos hijos mayores buscan novias de zonas cercanas y el hijo menor se va al bosque, donde conoce a una ratona mágica de la cual se enamora. Justo cuando piensa que la ha perdido al ella haberse ahogado, ella emerge del agua y su amor la transforma en la bella princesa que realmente es.

 ## SMALL-GROUP OPTIONS

Have students work in small groups to read and discuss the selection.

Three-Minute Review

During the discussion, pause and direct students to work with a partner.

- Set a timer for a three-minutes.
- During this time, have partners re-read the text and write clarifying questions.
- After the three minutes are up, ask students: *What have you noticed about the text you just read? What questions did you want to know the answers to?*
- Have volunteers share their clarifying questions. Hold a brief discussion with the class about answers to each.

Think-Pair-Share

Have students work with a partner.

After students have read "The Mouse Bride," pose this question: *What do you think is the main message of this folktale?*

- Have students think about the question individually and take notes.
- Then, have pairs discuss their ideas about the question.
- Finally, ask pairs to share their responses with the class.

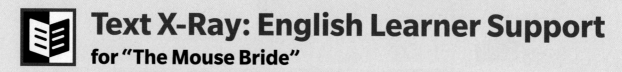

Text X-Ray: English Learner Support
for "The Mouse Bride"

Use the Text X-Ray and the supports and scaffolds in the Teacher's Edition to help guide students at different proficiency levels through the selection.

INTRODUCE THE SELECTION

DISCUSS PATTERNS IN FOLKTALE

This selection is a traditional folktale—a story told by a group of people from a single culture and usually passed on orally from one generation to the next. Most folktales include characters that try to thwart the actions or success of a good person.

Folktales often involve some form of magic in which things are not what they appear to be. The problem faced by the main character is overcome by an act of kindness, courage, or intelligence. Folktales exhibit basic story structure with a beginning that establishes a conflict or problem to be solved by the hero or heroine, unfolding plot events and character development during the middle section, and a happy ending during which the conflict is resolved. Invite students to discuss other folktales they know that follow this pattern.

CULTURAL REFERENCES

The following words or phrases may be unfamiliar to students:

- *maiden* (paragraph 3): girl or unmarried young woman
- *sarcastically* (paragraph 26): When someone says, "That was really funny" sarcastically, they mean the opposite—that the thing wasn't actually funny at all.
- *looks* (paragraph 27): how a person appears to others
- *empty-handed* (paragraph 29): not bringing anything
- *gown* (paragraph 72): a fancy dress

LISTENING

Listen for Adjectives and Adverbs

Remind students of the similarities and differences between adjectives and adverbs. Point out that while both are modifiers, adjectives modify nouns and pronouns and adverbs modify verbs.

Use the following supports with students at varying proficiency levels:

- Read aloud paragraph 1. Ask: *When does the story happen?* (*long ago*) **SUBSTANTIAL**
- Ask: *In paragraph 46, the mouse says, "I do hope your heart brings you here tomorrow." What question does the adverb "here" answer?* (*where*) **MODERATE**
- Note that many adverbs end in -ly. Ask: *What is an example of an adverb in paragraph 13?* (*Certainly*) Have students practice forming adverbs by adding the ending -ly to the following adjectives: *proud/proudly, beautiful/beautifully, happy/happily.* **LIGHT**

SPEAKING

Analyze Purpose and Structure

Remind students of the difference between an author's purpose and the theme of a text. Review the four basic purposes of writing, encouraging students to use the term *purpose* in their discussion.

Use the following supports at varying proficiency levels:

- Name possible purposes of the story: entertain, inform about a topic, teach a lesson, persuade, explain an idea. Have students raise a hand when you name a purpose of this story. **SUBSTANTIAL**
- Discuss folktales that students may have already read or animated versions they may have seen. Ask: *What do you think is the main purpose of a folktale?* Discuss the idea that folktales not only entertain, they also teach lessons. **MODERATE**
- After reading paragraphs 28–34, ask: *What prediction can you make about the ending of the folktale based on this passage? For what purpose do you think the author wrote a folktale with this ending?* **LIGHT**

READING

Identify a Theme

Emphasize that the theme of a literary work is the central idea the author wishes to convey to the reader. Explain that the theme of a literary work is often implied, that is, it is not directly stated.

Use the following supports with students at varying proficiency levels:

- Remind students that the topic of a text is different from its theme. Ask: *Is the topic of this story about finding a bride?* (yes) *Is the theme of this story about finding a bride?* (no) **SUBSTANTIAL**
- Ask: *What is the ending of "The Mouse Bride"? What lesson does this ending teach?* (*A singing mouse turns out to be a princess in disguise. This teaches that people are not always what they seem to be.*) **MODERATE**
- Ask: *How would you summarize the theme of "The Mouse Bride"?* (*The theme is "Look beneath the surface of people to find who they really are."*) **LIGHT**

WRITING

Write an Analytical Essay

Work with students to read the writing assignment on page 497.

Use the following supports with students at varying proficiency levels:

- Provide students with frame sentences to help them focus on a thesis statement for their analytical essay: *The brother falls in love with _____. The mouse is really _____.* **SUBSTANTIAL**
- Work with students to create a graphic organizer to record their suggested themes and evidence from the selection that supports their thesis statement. **MODERATE**
- Remind students that folktales often have more than one theme. Encourage students to identify two or more themes and explain their connection to each other. **LIGHT**

 Connect to the
ESSENTIAL QUESTION

In this text, a young man goes in search of a bride and falls in love with what appears to be a mouse, but he is eventually surprised to learn that his loved one is actually a princess who had been transformed until a kindhearted man could truly love her.

COMPARE THEMES

Point out that "The Boatman's Flute" and "The Mouse Bride" are both folktales from foreign places. Although they come from different cultures, they share similarities and differences in the structure of their plots and their characters. As students read, tell them to think about the following questions: *How are the main male characters in the story similar? How are they different? How are the plots of the two folktales alike? How are they different? In what ways are the themes of the folktales alike and different?*

MENTOR TEXT

At the end of the unit, students will be asked to write a short story. "The Mouse Bride" provides a model for how a writer can deliver a message about life or human nature.

FOLKTALE
THE MOUSE BRIDE

retold by **Heather Forest**
pages 487–495

COMPARE THEMES

Now that you've read "The Boatman's Flute," read "The Mouse Bride" to see how the characters and plot of this folktale from Finland compare to those in the folktale from Vietnam. Think about the stories' themes and how they are alike and different.

 ESSENTIAL QUESTION:

What hidden truths about people and the world are revealed in stories?

FOLKTALE
THE BOATMAN'S FLUTE

retold by **Sherry Garland**
pages 473–479

484   Unit 6

The Mouse Bride

QUICK START

Do you know someone who has been taunted or teased for making an unpopular choice? Would you let the possibility of being teased affect how you decide something? Discuss your thoughts with a partner.

INFER THEME

A text's **theme** is its message or big idea about life or human nature. Folktales often contain more than one theme; they may contain **multiple themes.** Some stories reveal their themes directly, but readers usually must **infer,** or make logical guesses about, a work's message based on evidence. In folktales, writers often use the thoughts, words, and actions of their characters to convey theme. To make inferences about theme in folktales, ask yourself:

- What do the characters want and how do they get what they want?
- How well do they succeed and why?
- How do the characters in the story compare to one another?

As you consider these questions, think about what the answers reveal about each character. Then, consider how the writer uses characterization to develop conflict and plot while expressing theme.

ANALYZE PURPOSE AND TEXT STRUCTURE

Author's purpose is the main reason an author writes a text. The purpose may be to inform, entertain, persuade, or express thoughts and feelings. Often the purpose of a folktale is to teach some sort of lesson about an aspect of life. To avoid confusing purpose with theme, remember that *purpose* is why the author decided to write, while *theme* is the message the author shared. You can analyze purpose by examining what happens at key points in the plot; then, ask yourself: Why is the author telling me this?

This chart shows how to use exposition to help you analyze the author's purpose. Use a chart like this to think about what the rising action, climax, falling action, and resolution reveal about purpose.

PLOT ELEMENT	WHAT HAPPENS	HINT ABOUT PURPOSE
Exposition	*I am introduced to one kind brother and two mean brothers.*	*The contrast between brothers may teach me something.*

GENRE ELEMENTS: FOLKTALE

- includes universal themes
- often features the "rule of three"—characters or events happen in groups of three
- may include supernatural events
- may feature animals or superhuman beings as characters

QUICK START

Before students begin the task, discuss the idea of peer pressure and its effects on personal decision making. Emphasize that students should avoid examples that might cause embarrassment. Encourage them to discuss problems that they or their partners may have seen in movies or TV shows, or may have read about in works of literature.

INFER THEME

Discuss the difference between the topic of a selection and its theme. Note that the topic is what the story is about, or its subject, whereas the theme is the message about life of human nature that is conveyed by the whole story. Note that themes are almost never stated directly in a text. Review the questions presented in the text that will enable a reader to infer the implied theme of a story.

ANALYZE PURPOSE AND TEXT STRUCTURE

Discuss the main reasons, or purposes, for which an author writes a text. Ask: *What do you think might be the author's main purpose for writing a folktale? Could an author have more than one purpose in writing? What might they be?*

Have students read the text. Emphasize that the way an author structures or presents the events in a story can affect the way the reader understands its theme, or message.

TEACH

CRITICAL VOCABULARY

Encourage students to read all the sentences before deciding which word best completes each one. Remind them to consider the context clues that the other words provide.

Answers:

1. *regal*
2. *elegant*
3. *amazement*
4. *enchanting*
5. *deceptive*

■ English Learner Support

Use Cognates Tells students that some of the Critical Vocabulary words have Spanish cognates: *regal/regio, elegant/elegante,* and *enchanting/encantador.*
ALL LEVELS

LANGUAGE CONVENTIONS

Emphasize the basic meaning of the word *modify*—"to make a change" in something. Read aloud and discuss a model sentence such as the following:

- With a few lessons, Jeff was able to modify his puppy's bad chewing behavior.

Read aloud the text that discusses the two common types of modifiers in English. Explain that a good way to distinguish adjectives and adverbs is to think about the question the word or phrase answers. Adjectives generally answer the questions: *Which? What kind of? How many?* Adverbs answer the questions: *How? When? Where? Why?*

ANNOTATION MODEL

Remind students to think about the skills listed on page 485 of the lesson when making annotations. Encourage students to include comments or questions about the plot and characters that might help them infer the theme of the folktale. Remind students of the different tools available to mark up the text as they read.

 **GET READY**

CRITICAL VOCABULARY

| amazement | enchanting | deceptive | regal | elegant |

To see how many Critical Vocabulary words you already know, use them to complete the sentences.

1. Playing the part of a king, the actor's costume was _____ .

2. The _____ gift came in a tasteful box tied with velvet ribbon.

3. The spectacular colors of the sunset fill me with _____.

4. The story was so _____ that I could not stop reading it.

5. To hide his identity, the thief responded with a _____ answer.

LANGUAGE CONVENTIONS

A **modifier** changes or modifies the meaning of another word in a sentence. **Adjectives** and **adjective phrases** or clauses modify nouns and pronouns. For example, the adjective phrase in boldface modifies *matter:*

Dark matter, **which is still unexplained,** is a subject of research.

Adverbs and **adverbial phrases** indicate time, place, manner, or cause. For example, the adverbial phrase in boldface modifies *waiting:*

I've been waiting for the bus to arrive **for 25 minutes.**

As you read, look for how the author uses modifiers to clarify ideas.

ANNOTATION MODEL   **NOTICE & NOTE**

As you read, mark any words and phrases that might help you infer the folktale's theme. Mark useful information about the characters and plot events. Here are one student's notes on the beginning of "The Mouse Bride."

| 1 | Long ago, when the world was filled with wonder, there was a farmer who had three sons. The two older sons took pleasure in teasing their youngest brother, who was so kindhearted he could not even sweep a spider from the cobwebs in the corner. | Introduction = Exposition

The story seems to be using the rule of three. Details about the brothers: two are mean and one is kind. |

BACKGROUND

Heather Forest (b. 1948) is an award-winning author, storyteller, and musician. In her storytelling, she incorporates many different elements, including poetry, prose, guitar, and song. When she begins working on a story to tell, she starts by singing the story until she gets just the right rhythm and feeling she is after. She lives on a small family farm in Huntington, New York, with her husband. The selection "The Mouse Bride" is a folktale from Finland that she retold in her book Wonder Tales from Around the World (1995).

THE MOUSE BRIDE

retold by Heather Forest

PREPARE TO COMPARE

As you read, pay attention to the father character in this story and consider how he compares with the father in the "The Boatman's Flute." Notice any similarities or differences between point of view in these two stories.

Notice & Note

Use the side margins to notice and note signposts in the text.

1   Long ago, when the world was filled with wonder, there was a farmer who had three sons. The two older sons took pleasure in teasing their youngest brother, who was so kindhearted he could not even sweep a spider from the cobwebs in the corner.

2   Now one day the farmer brought his sons to a field where three trees stood. "It is time for you to be wed," he said. "Each of you must cut down a sapling.[1] When it falls, walk forward in the direction it points, and you will find your sweetheart."

---

[1] **sapling:** a young tree.

BACKGROUND

Many folktales from around the world incorporate the idea of an unexpected or magical transformation of a character from ugliness or deformity to nobility and beauty. In this tale, the mouse becomes a beautiful princess. The idea of magical transformation continues to enthrall audiences today, as seen by the popularity of Harry Potter, X-Men, and other print and cinematic series involving magic.

PREPARE TO COMPARE

Direct students to use the Prepare to Compare prompt to focus their reading.

▶ NOTICE & NOTE

Review annotation tools such as underlining, circling, and highlighting. Emphasize that marginal notes often include comments or questions about important ideas expressed in the text.

 ENGLISH LEARNER SUPPORT

Establish Time and Place Have students echo read the opening phrase of the folktale, "Long ago, when the world was filled with wonder." Point out this is a typical opening to many folktales, including cinematic ones, such as *Star Wars*, which begins, "A long time ago, in a galaxy far, far away." Provide other examples of opening lines that set the time and place of a fantasy, folktale, or legend. **SUBSTANTIAL**

TEACH

 ## ANALYZE PURPOSE AND TEXT STRUCTURE

Remind students that after the exposition, or introduction of important story information, the writer begins developing the story's rising action. (**Answer:** *This paragraph represents the rising action in the story. The author is contrasting the behavior of the two self-centered and cruel brothers with the youngest brother, who is accepting of what life has to offer. The author uses the taunts of the older brothers to increase conflict and move the plot forward.*)

For **speaking support** for students at varying proficiency levels, see the **Text X-Ray** on page 484D.

▶ TOUGH QUESTIONS

Remind students of the importance of asking and answering tough questions as they read a text. Discuss why the young man may have found it difficult to respond to the mouse's question. (**Answer:** *To answer the mouse's question truthfully, the young man may have to hurt her feelings. We know that the young man is caring and sensitive because the text says he is kind even to spiders. Perhaps this question is another way to reveal the young brother's character or to say something about the theme of the story. The answer will probably move along the plot of the story.*)

CRITICAL VOCABULARY

amazement: The young man is staring in amazement because he has been surprised by the mouse.

ASK STUDENTS why the young man feels amazement from meeting the mouse. (*Mice can't really talk, so he is surprised that she can speak to him.*)

enchanting: The mouse's song is enchanting because the young man finds it charming.

ASK STUDENTS how they can tell that the young man finds the mouse's song enchanting. (*Instead of leaving, as he meant to, he stops at the door to listen to her sing.*)

488   Unit 6

 NOTICE & NOTE

3   The oldest son cut the largest sapling and it fell pointing north. "What luck!" he shouted, "I know of a fine maiden who lives in a house just north of here. I will go and ask for her hand in marriage."

4   The next oldest son cut a sapling and it fell pointing south. "I too shall live in happiness," said the second son, "for there is a delightful young woman who lives in a house just south of here. I will go and ask her to be my bride!"

5   But when the youngest son cut his sapling, it pointed towards the forest where there were no houses at all.

6   "You'll find a pointy-eared sweetheart with sharp teeth in that forest," laughed his two brothers.

7   "I will trust fate and my chances," said the youngest son. He carved a beautiful walking stick from the tree and set off in the direction of the woods.

8   The young man had not gone far into the forest when he came upon a cottage made of gray logs. He knocked on the door. A pleasant voice said, "Enter, please."

9   When he walked inside, he looked everywhere but saw no one.

10 "Here I am!" said the voice, "I am so glad to have company. I have been very lonely."

11 The young man stared in **amazement**. There on the table was a dainty blue-eyed mouse with its gray fur as sleek as velvet.

12 "You can speak!" the young man said.

13 "Certainly I can speak, but I prefer to sing," she said gaily, and she began a lively tune. The young man applauded her song, amazed. Then she curtsied² and asked, "What brings you here?"

14 "I am searching for a sweetheart," he replied.

15 "Well then, how about me?" said the mouse.

16 "You are not exactly the type of sweetheart I was seeking," said the young man politely as he turned to leave.

17 "Oh," she sighed, "I am sad to hear that, for I have longed to meet someone just like you." She began such an **enchanting** love song, the young man stood motionless at the door.

18 "Please don't stop," he pleaded when she finished her song. "I want that song to go on and on ... Strange as it seems, perhaps you could be my sweetheart."

ANALYZE PURPOSE AND TEXT STRUCTURE

Annotate: Mark the statement the youngest son makes in paragraph 7.

Interpret: Describe what element of the plot this paragraph represents and what it might tell you about the author's purpose.

amazement
(ə-māz´mənt) n. *Amazement* is a state of extreme surprise or wonder.

TOUGH QUESTIONS

Notice & Note: Why might the young man have difficulty answering the mouse's question in paragraph 15?

Infer: Consider what you know about the young man and the story so far. Why might the author have the mouse pose such a question?

enchanting
(ĕn-chăn´tĭng) *adj.* Something or someone *enchanting* is charming.

---

² **curtsied:** from *curtsy*, a gesture of respect made by bending knees with one foot forward and lowering the body.

488   Unit 6

APPLYING ACADEMIC VOCABULARY

☑ **emphasize**   ❏ **occur**   ❏ **period**   ☑ **relevant**   ❏ **tradition**

Write and Discuss   Have students turn to a partner to discuss the following questions. Guide students to include the Academic Vocabulary words *emphasize* and *relevant* in their responses. Ask volunteers to share their responses with the class.

- What words does the narrator use to **emphasize** how attractive the mouse is?

- How is it **relevant** that the mouse longed to meet someone like the brother?

© Houghton Mifflin Harcourt Publishing Company • Image Credits: ©Rudmer Zwerver/Shutterstock

19   "Then come to visit me at this time tomorrow," she said with a smile and a twitch of her silken whiskers.

20   "I promise I will return," said the young man as he left. And all the way home, his heart quickened as he thought about the mouse and her beautiful song.

21   When he arrived at the farm that evening his two brothers were bragging to their father.

22   "The woman I met has beautiful rosy cheeks," said the oldest son.

23   "The lovely maiden I met," bragged the next oldest son, "is the fairest in the countryside. Her hair is as black as a raven's wing."[3]

24   But they teased the youngest brother before he could speak a word, saying, "Who could you find in the woods but a pointy-eared, sharp-toothed beast!"

25   "I met the most enchanting singer," said the lad hesitantly, "and I cannot stop thinking about her. She has a captivating voice, sky-blue eyes, a beautiful smile, and she dresses in the very finest gray velvet. She even invited me to return tomorrow!"

26   "A princess no doubt!" the brothers shouted sarcastically. "He is making this up! Who could love him?"

27   "Congratulations to each of you on meeting sweethearts," said their father. "But attractive looks alone do not make for a happy hearth.[4] Tomorrow, I should like to see the kind of bread your sweethearts bake."

---

[3]   **as black as a raven's wing:** a raven is a large bird with glossy black feathers.
[4]   **a happy hearth:** a hearth is a fireplace, which at one time represented the center of family life.

LANGUAGE CONVENTIONS
Adverbial clauses act like adverbs to modify verbs, adjectives, or adverbs. Explain what the phrase "before he could speak a word" modifies in paragraph 24.

The Mouse Bride   489

LANGUAGE CONVENTIONS

Discuss the difference between a phrase and a clause. Explain that a clause is a group of words that has a subject with a noun or pronoun and a predicate with a verb. A phrase is a group of words lacking either a subject or a verb. Adverbial clauses, like adverbs, modify verbs. **(Answer:** *The adverbial clause "before he could speak a word" modifies the verb "teased"—that is, telling when this teasing takes place.)*

■ English Learner Support

Use Adverbs Have students complete the frame sentences with adverbs or adverbial clauses: *The mouse sang _____. The young man listened _____. The young man spoke _____.*

Have students repeat the completed sentences aloud.
SUBSTANTIAL/MODERATE

For **listening support** for students at varying proficiency levels, see the **Text X-Ray** on page 484C.

ENGLISH LEARNER SUPPORT

Read Dialogue Remind students that dialogue is a conversation between two or more characters. Point out that in the story, every time the speaker shifts, the writer begins a new line. Ask students to read aloud a section of dialogue, using different pitch and tone to represent the two characters. **SUBSTANTIAL/MODERATE**

TEACH

AGAIN AND AGAIN

Discuss the importance of time words and phrases in helping to move along the plot of a story. (**Answer:** *By repeating this image whenever the young man visits the mouse, the writer indicates that something special—timeless—is happening between the young man and the mouse. Perhaps, the author is saying that love itself is timeless.*)

NOTICE & NOTE

28   The next morning, the youngest son set out at dawn. When he arrived at the cottage the mouse greeted him eagerly, saying, "I am delighted that you have kept your promise to return!"

29   The lad blushed with embarrassment and said, "I told my father and brothers that ever since we met, I have not been able to stop thinking about you. But I did not tell them that you are a mouse! Now my father would like to see the kind of bread you bake! Oh," he moaned, "my cruel brothers will certainly ridicule me when I arrive home tonight empty-handed!"

30   "I cannot bear to think of them mocking you! You will not go home empty-handed!" said the mouse. "Of course I can bake bread!" She clapped her paws and one hundred gray mice appeared as she commanded, "Bring me the finest grains of wheat from the field!"

31   Fascinated, the young man stayed all day watching the marvelous effort as the little mouse directed the baking of a fine loaf of wheaten bread. She sang as she worked and enraptured the young man's ears with her music. The afternoon passed so quickly with their cheerful conversation and laughter, the young man hardly noticed that the sun was setting.

32   "I must hurry and leave," he said.

33   "Please take this loaf as a gift to your father," said the mouse, waving him goodbye. "I hope that you will come again tomorrow."

34   "Of course I'll return," assured the young man, "I would rather be here than anywhere else." He traveled back home with the loaf under his arm.

35   That night around the dinner table, the oldest brother proudly handed the farmer a loaf of rye bread made by his sweetheart and boasted, "See how hearty and well-baked it is!"

36   The second oldest brother handed the farmer some barley bread made by his sweetheart and bragged, "My sweetheart's bread is crusty and healthy to eat!"

37   But when the youngest brother handed his father the fine loaf of wheaten bread the farmer exclaimed, "Wheat bread! Only the richest among us eat wheat bread!"

38   The two older brothers bickered over who was to get the biggest piece of wheat bread and said, as they stuffed their mouths, "But there's no house in that woods for miles! What kind of sweetheart could you have found?"

39   "One whose conversation can make me forget the time of day," replied the lad.

40   "I am pleased that your sweethearts bake such fine bread!" said the farmer. "Skillful hands add comfort to a

AGAIN AND AGAIN

Notice & Note: Why is the youngest brother's experience of time in paragraphs 31, 39, and 45 important? Mark each reference to time.

Connect: Why might the author keep repeating this particular image of time?

home. Tomorrow, I should like to see the kind of cloth they can weave."

41   The next morning the lad set out again to visit the mouse in the woods.

42   "Come in!" said the little mouse when she heard him knock. She sang him a tune and a smile spread across his face.

43   "I wish you could weave as well as you bake and sing. But how could that be possible?" said the lad with a sigh. "My father would like to see the kind of cloth you make."

44   "Love makes everything possible," said the mouse, clapping her paws. Once again, one hundred mice appeared as she said, "Fetch me strands of the finest flax."[5]

45   Each mouse quickly returned with one strand of flax. The little mouse spun the flax into thread on a tiny spinning wheel.[6] The young man stared in amazement as she wove a fine piece of linen on a miniature loom.[7] They kept company all afternoon, talking and laughing while she worked. The time sped by so quickly, the sun was setting before the young man realized it.

---

[5] **flax:** a plant whose fiber is used for making linen cloth.

[6] **spinning wheel:** a device with a foot- or hand-driven wheel and single spindle, or rod, used to make thread and yarn.

[7] **wove a fine piece of linen on a miniature loom:** fine linen fabric was woven using a loom, an apparatus for weaving strands of yarn together at right angles.

The Mouse Bride   491

ENGLISH LEARNER SUPPORT

Spelling Suffixes –*ing*, -*en* Remind students that suffixes are word parts added to the ends of base words. Then explain that if a one-syllable word ends with a single consonant that follows a single vowel, then the final consonant is doubled: *sit* + *ing* = sitting. If a word ends with two consonants, then the final consonant is not doubled: *hard* + *en* = harden. Have students work in pairs to write the correct spellings for the following base words and suffixes. Then have them check their work using a dictionary.

soft + en = _____ *(soften)*

flat + en = _____ *(flatten)*

trap + ing = _____ *(trapping)*

belong + ing = _____ *(belonging)*

ALL LEVELS

WHEN STUDENTS STRUGGLE . . .

Time Phrases and Transitions Have students read paragraph 35 and identify the time phrase that indicates when the action is taking place. (*that night*) Then have students read aloud paragraph 37. Ask: *What words indicate time in the paragraph?* (*but when*)

Discuss other words and phrases used in paragraphs 40, 41, and 44 that indicate time. (*tomorrow, the next morning, and once again*)

Model reading these sentences aloud so students can hear the time phrases in context. Then invite students to use these time phrases to make up and share their own sentences.

TEACH

INFER THEME

Discuss how the statement, "Appearances can be deceptive," is reflected in the story so far. Discuss the youngest brother's response and compare it to the responses of the other two brothers. **(Answer:** *The youngest brother is talking about how the tiny nut might hold something that can't be imagined by just seeing a nut. The obvious appearance that is deceptive is the mouse who is really a princess. A possible theme is: Look deeper than at what people might seem like on the surface. Instead, consider their actions and your feelings in their presence.)*

For **reading support** for students at varying proficiency levels, see the **Text X-Ray** on page 484D.

CRITICAL VOCABULARY

deceptive: The nut's appearance is deceptive because its smallness gives a false impression of its contents.

ASK STUDENTS why the mouse's appearance is deceptive. *(She looks like a mouse, but she is actually a human.)*

492   Unit 6

---

46   "It's done!" she finally said, folding the small patch of delicate cloth in a walnut shell. "Take it to your father as a gift and I do hope your heart brings you here tomorrow."

47   The lad left for home with the walnut shell tucked carefully in his pocket.

48   That night around the hearth fire, each brother brought forward the cloth made by their sweethearts.

49   "Here is some coarse but sturdy cotton made by my love," boasted the first brother proudly.

50   "Here is some cotton and linen weave made by my love, and it is fancier than yours!" bragged the second brother.

51   "Here is a walnut," said the youngest brother as his older brothers howled.

52   "He has no sweetheart! He's brought a forest nut instead of some cloth!" they squealed.

53   "Appearances can be **deceptive**," said the lad. "Open the nut, Father."

54   The two older brothers stopped laughing and gawked in silence as the farmer opened the shell and held up the fine web of linen. "I have never seen such delicate work," said the farmer, admiring the cloth. "Sons, I must meet your sweethearts! Bring them home tomorrow so that I may see your brides-to-be," he said.

55   The lad's face flushed red as he imagined himself presenting the little mouse to his father and brothers as his bride. "This is ridiculous!" he thought. "I cannot marry a mouse! I must seek deeper in the forest for a proper human sweetheart."

56   But in the morning, as the young man approached the cottage he could not resist stopping for a moment. He thought, "I will tell her politely that I won't be visiting anymore. I need to find one of my own kind. But then, surely I will hurt her feelings! She is the most delightful companion I've ever met. Oh, I have never been more confused!"

57   As he nervously stood at the cottage door wondering what to do, the little mouse called out, "Welcome! Come in! I have composed a love song for you!"

58   The moment he entered the room she began to sing her beautiful song. His heart swelled with joy and every doubt he had about presenting her to his family disappeared with the first tones of her sweet voice.

59   "My Father wishes to meet you," he simply said. "Please come with me to visit him."

INFER THEME

Annotate: Mark the lad's response to his brothers in paragraph 53.

Infer: What is the meaning of this response, and how might you use the response to infer a theme?

deceptive
(dĭ-sĕp´tĭv) *adj.* Something *deceptive* is giving a false impression.

IMPROVE READING FLUENCY

Targeted Passage   Have students work in groups of five as they read paragraphs 48–55. Have one student read the text of the narrator and the others read the lines spoken by the three brothers and the father. Remind students that when reading aloud they should speak clearly and expressively.

 Go to the **Reading Studio** for additional support in developing fluency.

60   "Very well, I shall travel in the finest style!" replied the mouse.

61   She clapped her paws and six black mice appeared, pulling a tiny coach made of a chestnut burr with a toadstool for a canopy.[8]

62   The mouse, **regal** as a queen, climbed into the coach. With the youngest son walking alongside, they set out for his home.

63   When they arrived at the river, a hunter passed them on the bridge. He looked down at the mouse, coach, and six and exclaimed, "Ho! What is this! A pack of vile rodents! I hate rats."

64   "If you please, sir," said the lad, "these are not vile rodents. I'll not allow you to call them so!"

65   "I've killed every rodent that has crossed my path!" said the bully, looming dangerously over the lad.

66   "Open your eyes and look more carefully," said the young man bravely. "Here before you rides the most delightful creature one could chance to meet."

67   "Disgusting rats!" glowered the man and with his heavy boot he kicked the coach and six into the swift water below the bridge!

68   "Heartless cruel man!" screamed the lad as he jumped into the river to save the mouse.

69   "I've rid the world of some useless pests!" the hunter shouted and continued on his way.

70   The lad desperately tried to reach the sinking coach. But as the raging water swirled around the little mouse, she vanished in the rushing river.

71   Exhausted and almost drowned, the lad made his way to the riverbank. He climbed out of the water and wept. "Now that you are gone," he wailed, "I regret even one moment's doubt that you were indeed my true love."

72   Suddenly, with a great splash and spray of mist, out of the water came six black horses pulling a fine golden carriage. In the carriage was a beautiful woman with sparkling blue eyes, wearing a gray velvet gown.

73   "Who are you?" the lad asked, rubbing his eyes to be sure he was seeing clearly.

74   "Don't you recognize me?" she asked. Her lovely musical voice cheered his heart.

---

[8] **a chestnut burr with a toadstool for a canopy:** a burr is the fruit of the chestnut; a toadstool is an inedible or poisonous mushroom; and a canopy is an umbrella-like shelter.

regal
(rē′gəl) *adj.* Something *regal* appears to be royal, magnificent, or splendid.

ANALYZE PURPOSE AND TEXT STRUCTURE
Annotate: Mark the character's response to events in paragraph 71 and the resulting action in paragraph 72.

Analyze: Explain what the plot element is here and how this plot element might help reveal the author's purpose.

The Mouse Bride   493

© Houghton Mifflin Harcourt Publishing Company

ANALYZE PURPOSE AND TEXT STRUCTURE

Remind students that the way a story is structured can help reveal the author's purpose. (**Answer:** *The plot element here is the resolution. It reveals the author's purpose, which is to teach a lesson about life and love: Love can transform what we see on the surface into something much deeper than ordinary appearances.*)

ENGLISH LEARNER SUPPORT

Use Noun Phrases with Modifiers   Point out the phrases "sparkling blue eyes" and "lovely musical voice." Have students identify *eyes* and *voice* as the nouns. Explain that writers often provide details in the form of adjectives and adverbs that come before the noun they modify. Remind speakers of Spanish and Vietnamese that adjectives usually come before the noun they modify. Ask students to suggest other phrases from the text or ones they make up that contain modifiers before nouns. **SUBSTANTIAL/MODERATE**

CRITICAL VOCABULARY

regal: The narrator says that the mouse is as regal as a queen.

ASK STUDENTS why the narrator might describe the mouse as regal. (**Answer:** *She is really a beautiful princess.*)

NOTICE & NOTE

INFER THEME

Discuss how a careful reader makes connections between the text and its implied theme by using text evidence to make inferences. **(Answer:** *When the princess was a mouse, the youngest son saw beyond the surface reality and loved her for who she was—a kind and thoughtful being who could sing beautiful songs and who was wonderful to be around.)*

INFER THEME

Annotate: Mark the youngest son's response to the mouse in paragraph 76.

Analyze: How does this statement connect with the theme or themes you've already identified?

elegant
(ĕl´ĭ-gənt) *adj.* Someone *elegant* appears to be refined and tasteful, having a beautiful manner, form, or style.

75   She explained, "I am a royal princess. A Lapland witch,[9] jealous of my beauty, enchanted me to be a mouse until such time as a kindhearted man could truly love me for myself. You broke the spell when you risked your life and declared your love. I am your mouse bride if you will have me," she said with a shy smile.

76   "I loved you before when we were of different worlds," he said. "How could I love you less now?"

77   He climbed into the coach and together they rode to his father's house. His brothers tumbled over one another to greet the **elegant** guest at their gate. "But it's our brother!" they gawked as he stepped out of the coach holding the princess's hand.

78   After a day of celebration, the young man and the princess traveled back to the forest. Instead of finding the small cottage made of gray logs, they found a great gray stone castle filled with one hundred servants. And it was there that they dwelt in happiness for the rest of their lives.

---

[9] **Lapland witch:** witch characters and references appear in many traditional stories from Lapland, which is a region of extreme northern Europe within the Arctic circle that includes Finland (where this story originates), Norway, Sweden, and the Kola peninsula of Northwest Russia.

CRITICAL VOCABULARY

elegant: Now that the mouse is transformed into a princess, the narrator describes her as elegant.

ASK STUDENTS how the brothers react to meeting their elegant guest. **(Answer:** *They gawk at their brother because they are so surprised to see him with someone so elegant.)*

CHECK YOUR UNDERSTANDING

Answer these questions before moving on to the **Analyze the Text** section on the following page.

1 Which of the following statements by the father helps you infer a theme of the folktale?

A *Each of you must cut down a sapling.*

B *Congratulations to each of you on meeting sweethearts.*

C *Attractive looks alone do not make for a happy hearth.*

D *I should like to see the kind of bread your sweethearts bake.*

2 When the youngest brother learns he has to bring the mouse home to meet his father and brothers, he decides that he can't marry a mouse. What stops him from telling the mouse goodbye?

F He is curious to see what else the mouse and her 100 mouse helpers can make.

G He thinks he might hurt her feelings.

H He loves the wheat bread she baked.

J He wants to learn the beautiful songs she sang to him.

3 Which passage most likely begins the plot transition from falling action to a resolution?

A *"Here before you rides the most delightful creature one could chance to meet."*

B *"I've rid the world of some useless pests!" the hunter shouted and continued on his way.*

C *"Now that you are gone," he wailed, "I regret even one moment's doubt that you were indeed my true love."*

D *"I loved you before when we were of different worlds," he said. "How could I love you less now?"*

The Mouse Bride 495

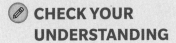

CHECK YOUR UNDERSTANDING

Have students answer the questions independently.

Answers:

1. C

2. G

3. C

If they answer any questions incorrectly, have them reread the text to confirm their understanding. Then they may proceed to ANALYZE THE TEXT on page 496.

 ENGLISH LEARNER SUPPORT

Oral Assessment Use the following questions to assess students' comprehension and speaking skills:

1. What did the father send his sons to find? *(brides)*

2. The mouse is different from other mice because she can do what? *(speak and sing)*

3. When does the brother realize he loves the mouse? *(when he thinks she has drowned)* **SUBSTANTIAL/MODERATE**

ANALYZE THE TEXT

Possible answers:

1. **DOK 2:** *The older brothers do not respect their youngest brother. They constantly make sarcastic, teasing comments toward him.*

2. **DOK 2:** *The father's comments indicate that the theme has something to do with looking under the surface of people to find their true beauty.*

3. **DOK 3:** *These paragraphs express the idea that people can be cruel, but it is possible to find the courage to fight against cruelty. In paragraph 66, the young man also repeats an important idea—the need to look "more carefully" than what you see on the surface. The author's purpose is to teach a lesson about the value of looking beneath appearances to find real truth and beauty.*

4. **DOK 3:** *The young man believes that the mouse has died, and he feels great regret that he ever doubted she was his true love. This is a moment of transformation, for now he understands the value of love. His love for her in this moment undoes the spell by the witch, and the mouse regains her human form. The author uses a transition in the plot to emphasize the lesson about the meaning of love and beauty.*

5. **DOK 4:** *With each task, the two older brothers brag and tease the youngest brother. The youngest brother remains steady in his character and shows kindness toward the mouse.*

RESEARCH

Discuss how all folktales try to teach moral principles, offering guidelines to right conduct. Kindness and sacrifice lead to positive outcomes, whereas selfishness and cruelty lead to negative outcomes. Although the settings are different, the story themes are similar. Gender models seem to be characteristic of earlier times when men and women were expected to fulfill different roles.

Connect Encourage students to identify characteristics common to folktales from many places around the world.

RESPOND

ANALYZE THE TEXT

Support your responses with evidence from the text. **NOTEBOOK**

1. **Summarize** Describe in your own words the two older brothers' attitudes toward their younger brother in paragraphs 24–26.

2. **Infer** Reread paragraph 27. What can you infer about the story's theme from the father's comments to his sons?

3. **Draw Conclusions** What ideas about human nature are expressed in paragraphs 65–70? Explain how they might reveal the author's purpose for telling this folktale.

4. **Evaluate** Reread paragraphs 70–76. How does the author use a transition in the plot to help characterize the young man? Explain how this moment in the plot contributes to the author's purpose.

5. **Notice & Note** Review paragraphs 2, 27, 40, and 54. Why do you think the father gives his sons and their sweethearts one task after another? What insights about the brothers do you gain with each task accomplished?

RESEARCH

Investigate common themes for folktales. What messages about life or human nature are common to folktales around the world? Do you notice any significant differences between countries? For example, are themes from Indian or Chinese folktales similar to or different from the Finnish folktale "The Mouse Bride"?

RESEARCH TIP
Keep track of the sources you use in your research. Copy and paste the URL for the reference into a new document. Copy the title and author if one is given. When doing research on topics such as folktales, university websites are often reliable sources of information.

FOLKTALE TITLE	COUNTRY OF ORIGIN	THEME OR THEMES
	Answers will vary	

Connect How does your research connect and build upon the research you did when reading "The Boatman's Flute"?

CREATE AND DISCUSS

Write an Analytical Essay Analyze "The Mouse Bride" to identify at least one theme. Refer to your notes as you work. Then, write a three- to four-paragraph analytical essay supporting your ideas.

❏ Include at least one theme in your analysis. Remember that folktales and other stories sometimes have multiple themes.

❏ Provide text evidence to support your ideas about theme.

❏ Revise your work. Look for ways to enhance your writing with modifiers such as adverbs, adjectives, and modifying phrases.

Present and Discuss Present your ideas about theme to your group.

❏ Support your ideas with evidence.

❏ Ask for questions and listen carefully to what is asked.

❏ Respond with care, referring to the text for examples.

After each member has presented, have a small group discussion about which theme or themes seem most relevant to your own lives and why.

 Go to the **Writing Studio** for more on using textual evidence.

 Go to the **Speaking and Listening Studio** for help with having a group discussion.

ACTIVE PARTICIPATION

❏ **Ask clarifying questions.**

❏ **Maintain eye contact.**

❏ **Speak at a natural rate.**

❏ **Be loud and clear.**

❏ **Gesture naturally.**

❏ **Take notes as necessary.**

RESPOND TO THE ESSENTIAL QUESTION

? What hidden truths about people and the world are revealed in stories?

Gather Information Review your annotations and notes on "The Mouse Bride." Then, add relevant details to your Response Log. As you determine which information to include, think about:

• what hidden truths the story revealed
• how and why some characters changed
• how and why some characters did not change

At the end of the unit, use your notes to write a short story or folktale.

ACADEMIC VOCABULARY

As you write and discuss what you learned from the folktales, be sure to use the Academic Vocabulary words. Check off words that you use.

❏ **emphasize**

❏ **occur**

❏ **period**

❏ **relevant**

❏ **tradition**

CREATE AND DISCUSS

Write an Analytical Essay Remind students that the purpose of a literary analytical essay is to examine the theme or some other element of a text. Emphasize that a good analytical analysis introduces a thesis statement that expresses the main point or claim of the essay. Remind students that the thesis statement should be part of the introductory paragraph.

 For **writing support** for students at varying proficiency levels, see the **Text X-Ray** on page 484D.

Present and Discuss Before making their presentations, encourage students to discuss the difference between the main idea and the theme of a work of fiction such as this folktale. Stress that the main idea is what the story is about, and the theme is the message or lesson the author wants the reader to take away. Remind students that the theme of a story is rarely stated directly and usually must be inferred from the text. Emphasize the importance of encouraging others to contribute to the discussion by listening respectfully to what they have to say.

RESPOND TO THE ESSENTIAL QUESTION

Allow time for students to add details from "The Mouse Bride" to their Unit 6 Response Logs.

CRITICAL VOCABULARY

Possible answers:

1. **elegant;** *Elegant* goes with *stylish,* which means "fashionably elegant."

2. **amazement;** *Wonder* goes with *amazement,* which means "great surprise."

3. **regal;** *Royal* goes with *regal,* which means "fit for a king or queen."

4. **deceptive;** *False* goes with *deceptive,* which means "misleading."

5. **captivating;** *Captivating* goes with *enchanting,* which means "charming."

VOCABULARY STRATEGY:
Context Clues

Words appear in bold in the text and are defined in the margin. Guessed answers may vary.

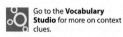 **RESPOND**

WORD BANK
amazement
enchanting
deceptive
regal
elegant

CRITICAL VOCABULARY

Practice and Apply With a partner, discuss and then write down an answer to each of the following questions. Then work together to write a sentence for each vocabulary word.

1. Which vocabulary word goes with *stylish?* Why?

2. Which vocabulary word goes with *wonder?* Why?

3. Which vocabulary word goes with *royal?* Why?

4. Which vocabulary word goes with *false?* Why?

5. Which vocabulary word goes with *captivating?* Why?

VOCABULARY STRATEGY:
Context Clues

 Go to the **Vocabulary Studio** for more on context clues.

Context clues are the words and phrases surrounding a word that provide hints about its meaning. The following are three types of context clues to look for when you come across an unfamiliar word.

Example clue: The writer uses words that are examples of the unknown word.

> The baker brought home three <u>loaves</u> to his children—rye, wheat, and barley—and they made French toast for breakfast.

Definition clue: The writer defines the unknown word directly in the sentence or in surrounding sentences.

> A <u>sapling</u> is a young tree.

Analogy clue: The writer pairs items that are related in some way.

> The <u>carriage</u> was like a stagecoach, only much fancier.

Practice and Apply Find the following words in the selection and identify clues to each word's meaning. Then check the definition.

WORD	CONTEXT CLUES	MEANING, ACCORDING TO CLUES	DEFINITION
amazement			
enchanting			
deceptive			
regal			
elegant			

EL ## ENGLISH LEARNER SUPPORT

Use Context Clues Give students additional practice opportunities to determine meaning based on context clues. Read about the three types of context clues and discuss the model sentences. Have pairs of students discuss the meaning of the underlined word after identifying the context clues. Tell students to write a clear definition of each word and use it correctly in an original sentence. **SUBSTANTIAL**

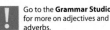
LANGUAGE CONVENTIONS:
Adjectives and Adverbs

An **adjective** is a part of speech that modifies a noun or a pronoun. It describes *what kind, which, how many*.

An **adverb** is a part of speech that modifies or describes verbs, adjectives, or other adverbs. Adverbs provide details about *time, place, manner*, and *cause*.

A **clause** is a group of words with a subject and a predicate — the two main parts of a complete sentence. An **adjectival clause** acts like an adjective to modify a noun or pronoun in the rest of the sentence.

> **Now one day the farmer brought his sons to a field where three trees stood.**

In this sentence, *where three trees stood* modifies the noun *field*.

An **adverbial clause** acts like an adverb to modify verbs, adjectives, or adverbs. It helps convey meaning by answering the questions *when, where, why, how*, or *to what degree*. Adverbial clauses typically appear at the beginning or end of a sentence.

> **The young man had not gone far into the forest when he came upon a cottage.**

In this sentence, *when he came upon a cottage* modifies the verb *gone*.

Practice and Apply Mark and identify the adjectival and adverbial clauses in these sentences from the story, along with the words they modify. When you have finished, compare your work with a partner's and explain how you decided which clauses were adjectival and which were adverbial.

1. When he arrived at the farm that evening his two brothers were bragging to their father.

2. But they teased the youngest brother before he could speak a word. . . .

3. The second oldest brother handed the farmer some barley bread made by his sweetheart. . . .

4. The mouse, regal as a queen, climbed into the coach.

Go to the **Grammar Studio** for more on adjectives and adverbs.

LANGUAGE CONVENTIONS:
Adjectives and Adverbs

Remind students of the difference between a phrase and a clause. Emphasize that both are groups of related words, but that a phrase lacks a noun or a verb, while a clause has both. Distinguish the two by noting that an adjective or adjective clause modifies a noun or pronoun, and an adverb or adverbial clause modifies a verb. Review and discuss the model sentences before students attempt the Practice and Apply items.

Practice and Apply

1. <u>When he arrived at the farm that evening</u> his two brothers were bragging to their father. *adverbial*

2. But they teased the youngest brother <u>before he could speak a word</u>. *adverbial*

3. The second brother handed the farmer some barley bread <u>made by his sweetheart</u>. *adjectival*

4. The mouse, <u>regal as a queen</u>, climbed into the coach. *adjectival*

ENGLISH LEARNER SUPPORT

Use Adjectives and Adverbs Provide students with focused practice using adjective and adverbial clauses.

- Have students find other sentences in the text that use adjective and adverbial clauses.
- Have students work with partners to write original sentences with adjective and adverbial clauses.
- Have students read their original sentence to a partner, who should identify the clause and the word it modifies. **MODERATE/LIGHT**

COMPARE THEMES

Before groups of students work on completing the chart, emphasize that they are comparing the key statements, key decisions, and lessons learned in two folktales. Emphasize that the goal of the activity is to determine ways the themes of the folktales are similar and different.

ANALYZE THE TEXTS

Possible answers:

1. **DOK 2:** *Both fathers love their children very much and want them to have lasting happiness.*

2. **DOK 4:** *The daughter learns to really see and appreciate the boatman for who he is rather than her fantasy of who she wants him to be. She learns humility and to ask forgiveness for being so unkind. The son learns to trust his fate and to take chances. He learns that courage has the power to transform what looks like a tragedy. The daughter's lesson is in some ways harder because she loses everything to gain her insight. The son appears to have lost everything, but through his courage, he regains love and happiness.*

3. **DOK 2:** *The girl drinks from the jade cup in paragraph 30 and hears the boatman's flute. She reflects on how happy his music makes her and how she felt such warmth and happiness from his actions. She feels remorse and asks forgiveness, and her teardrop sets the boatman's soul free. The mouse is set free from the spell by the youngest son's love for her, despite her mouse form, and by his courage in trying to save her.*

4. **DOK 4:** *The theme of "The Boatman's Flute" cautions against getting trapped by our images and fantasies of physical beauty rather than looking to someone's heart and actions to find inner beauty. The theme of "The Mouse Bride" focuses on ignoring what other people think and trusting your heart, instead.*

RESPOND

Collaborate & Compare

THE BOATMAN'S FLUTE
folktale retold by
Sherry Garland

THE MOUSE BRIDE
folktale retold by
Heather Forest

COMPARE THEMES

"The Boatman's Flute" from Vietnam and "The Mouse Bride" from Finland are both folktales that address the topic of love. You can infer the stories' themes by noting how each character makes decisions and responds to events, and in doing so, develops the plot. Recall that character responses may be internal (thoughts and feelings) or external (statements and actions). You can also infer themes by the lessons a folktale teaches. Making personal connections to these lessons may help you infer themes.

With your group, complete the chart by citing text evidence. As you work, remember that a folktale may have multiple themes.

	"THE BOATMAN'S FLUTE"	"THE MOUSE BRIDE"
Key statements		
Key decisions		
Lessons learned		

ANALYZE THE TEXTS

Discuss these questions in your group.

1. **Compare** Reread paragraphs 2, 20, and 24 in "The Boatman's Flute," and paragraphs 2, 27, 40, and 54 in "The Mouse Bride." What similarities do you see between the fathers in these tales?

2. **Analyze** Reread paragraphs 31–33 in "The Boatman's Flute" and paragraphs 56 and 75–76 in "The Mouse Bride." How did the mandarin's daughter and the farmer's youngest son learn important lessons, and how do these lessons differ?

3. **Infer** Both folktales feature a character who is freed. What do you infer about what actually sets the boatman and the princess free?

4. **Synthesize** What have your comparisons revealed about possible themes in each folktale?

© Houghton Mifflin Harcourt Publishing Company • Image Credits: (t) ©Delpixel/Shutterstock;

 ENGLISH LEARNER SUPPORT

Ask Questions Use the following questions to help students compare main themes across the texts:

- What are the most important statements the main characters in each folktale make? Why are these important?

- What decisions do characters make? Which are most important? Why do you think so?

- What do characters learn in each story? **MODERATE/LIGHT**

COMPARE AND PRESENT

In your group, review the ideas about themes from your discussion, and determine a central theme for each story. Follow these steps:

1. **Review the lessons learned.** Thinking about lessons learned by the main characters can help you to identify a central theme.

2. **Choose a central theme for each folktale.** Discuss which of the themes in each story is most important and why. Record the themes for each story in the chart below.

3. **Record details and evidence to support each theme.** Locate specific evidence in the stories to support the themes you choose. Be sure to include specific statements made by the characters, who said it, the paragraph number, and why the statement supports the theme.

ACTIVE PARTICIPATION
- ❏ Contribute your own ideas.
- ❏ Consider the ideas of others.
- ❏ Ask clarifying questions.
- ❏ Take notes as necessary.
- ❏ Maintain eye contact.
- ❏ Speak at a natural rate.
- ❏ Be loud and clear.
- ❏ Gesture naturally.

FOLKTALE THEMES	
"The Boatman's Flute" Central Theme: Evidence:	"The Mouse Bride" Central Theme: Evidence:

4. **Present your ideas to the class.** Present the themes you've selected to the class. Explain similarities you found in the two folktales, and present any significant differences in meaning that you found. Make sure to support all of your ideas with specific evidence from the texts.

Collaborate & Compare 501

COMPARE AND PRESENT

Discuss the goal of this group activity: to compare and contrast ways the themes of "The Boatman's Flute" and "The Mouse Bride" are alike and different.

1. **Review the lessons learned.** Remind students to use their Response Logs and selection annotations as they think about the lessons learned by the main characters in the two folktales.

2. **Choose a central theme for each folktale.** Emphasize that the folktales have multiple themes, but that the students' job is to determine which of these is most important and why. Encourage students to reach a consensus about which themes they think are most important if they cannot come to a unanimous decision. Remind students that they should listen carefully, ask questions when they don't understand a comment, and always be respectful of what others in their group have to say.

3. **Record details and evidence to support each theme.** Emphasize the importance of identifying evidence to support the themes the students have chosen. Explain that evidence must be found in the text and not in their discussion of it. Review the set-up of the chart and, if necessary, model an example of evidence from each text to help students understand the task. Remind students to use their notes and annotations as they work.

4. **Present your ideas to the class.** Discuss the elements that go into making a good presentation. Emphasize the importance of maintaining eye contact with the audience, as well as speaking in a loud, clear voice. Encourage class discussion of questions after each presentation.

ENGLISH LEARNER SUPPORT

Prepare a Presentation Provide support for students as they prepare to present:
- Guide them to make detailed notes, and make an outline of their key points, writing key phrases or entire sentences according to proficiency level.
- Have students practice in front of a small group before making their presentation.
- Follow up practice sessions with a discussion of ways to improve delivery, such as pronouncing all words correctly and being able to speak at length without hesitation.
ALL LEVELS

READER'S CHOICE

Setting a Purpose Have students review their Unit 6 Response Log and think about what they've already learned about how stories reveal hidden truths about people and the world. As they select their Independent Reading selections, encourage them to consider what more they want to know.

NOTICE NOTE

Explain that some selections may contain multiple signposts; others may contain only one. And the same type of signpost can occur many times in the same text.

 LEARNING MINDSET

Grit Remind students that our brains are muscles that become stronger the more we work them. Encourage students to adopt flexible thinking patterns so they will begin to see opportunities instead of problems. Invite them to select their Independent Reading selections as opportunities for hard work that leads to success. Offer praise to students who make an effort or use strategies as they read.

INDEPENDENT READING

? ESSENTIAL QUESTION:

What hidden truths about people and the world are revealed in stories?

Reader's Choice

Setting a Purpose Select one or more of these options from your eBook to continue your exploration of the Essential Question.

- Read the descriptions to see which text grabs your interest.
- Think about which genres you enjoy reading.

Notice Note

In this unit, you practiced asking **Big Questions** and noticing and noting two signposts: **Word Gaps** and **Quoted Words.** As you read independently, these signposts and others will aid your understanding. Below are the anchor questions to ask when you read literature and nonfiction.

Reading Literature: Stories, Poems, and Plays		
Signpost	**Anchor Question**	**Lesson**
Contrasts and Contradictions	Why did the character act that way?	p. 3
Aha Moment	How might this change things?	p. 3
Tough Questions	What does this make me wonder about?	p. 172
Words of the Wiser	What's the lesson for the character?	p. 2
Again and Again	Why might the author keep bringing this up?	p. 92
Memory Moment	Why is this memory important?	p. 93

Reading Nonfiction: Essays, Articles, and Arguments		
Signpost	**Anchor Question(s)**	**Lesson**
Big Questions	What surprised me?	p. 246
	What did the author think I already knew?	p. 420
	What challenged, changed, or confirmed what I already knew?	p. 332
Contrasts and Contradictions	What is the difference, and why does it matter?	p. 247
Extreme or Absolute Language	Why did the author use this language?	p. 247
Numbers and Stats	Why did the author use these numbers or amounts?	p. 333
Quoted Words	Why was this person quoted or cited, and what did this add?	p. 333
Word Gaps	Do I know this word from someplace else?	
	Does it seem like technical talk for this topic?	p. 421
	Do clues in the sentence help me understand the word?	

ENGLISH LEARNER SUPPORT

Develop Fluency Select a passage from a text that matches students' reading abilities. Pair students with a peer who is at a similar reading level.

- Read aloud the passage while students follow silently. Then have partners echo read the passage to each other. **SUBSTANTIAL**
- Have students look through the text together, looking for unfamiliar words. Then have students partner read, taking turns with each page. **MODERATE**

- Allow more fluent pairs to select their own texts. Set a specific time for students (for example, 15 minutes). Then have each pair discuss what they have read. **LIGHT**

  Go to the **Reading Studio** for additional support in developing fluency.

You can preview these texts in Unit 6 of your eBook.

Then, check off the text or texts that you select to read on your own.

FABLE

The Golden Serpent
retold by Walter Dean Myers

A quest to find the golden serpent uncovers truths about a kingdom and the king.

MYTH

Echo and Narcissus
retold by Lancelyn Green

Goddesses prevent a beautiful nymph and her true love from ever meeting face to face.

FOLKTALE

The Fisherman and the Chamberlain
retold by Jane Yolen

A fisherman outwits a greedy bully and is royally rewarded.

INFORMATIONAL TEXT

Urban Legends, Suburban Myths
Robert T. Carroll

Beware! Which reveal truths and which spread hoaxes: urban legends or suburban myths?

Collaborate and Share   With a partner, discuss what you learned from at least one of your independent readings.

- Give a brief synopsis or summary of the text.

- Describe any signposts that you noticed in the text and explain what they revealed to you.

- Describe what you most enjoyed or found most challenging about the text. Give specific examples.

- Decide if you would recommend the text to others. Why or why not?

 Go to the **Reading Studio** for more resources on **Notice & Note**.

INDEPENDENT READING

MATCHING STUDENTS TO TEXTS

Use the following information to guide students in choosing their texts.

The Golden Serpent   Lexile: 470L
  Genre: fable
  Overall Rating: Accessible

Echo and Narcissus   Lexile: 1100L
  Genre: myth
  Overall Rating: Challenging

**The Fisherman and the
Chamberlain**   Lexile: 620L
  Genre: folktale
  Overall Rating: Accessible

Urban Legends, Suburban Myths   Lexile: 1060L
  Genre: informational text
  Overall Rating: Challenging

Collaborate and Share   To assess how well students read the selections, walk around the room and listen to their conversations. Encourage students to be focused and specific in their comments.

Online
 for Assessment

- Independent Reading Selection Tests

Encourage students to visit the **Reading Studio** to download a handy bookmark of **NOTICE & NOTE** signposts.

WHEN STUDENTS STRUGGLE . . .

Keep a Reading Log As students read their selected texts, have them keep a reading log for each selection to note signposts and their thoughts about them. Use their logs to assess how well they are noticing and reflecting on elements of the texts.

Reading Log for (title)		
Location	**Signpost I Noticed**	**My Notes About It**

UNIT ⑥ Task

• WRITE A SHORT STORY

MENTOR TEXT

THE MOUSE BRIDE

Folktale retold by HEATHER FOREST

LEARNING OBJECTIVES

Writing Task

- Tell a story with an exposition, rising action, a climax, falling action, and a resolution.
- Sequence plot events to create suspense and lead to a resolution.
- Include a conflict that can unfold and be resolved in an interesting way.
- Use vivid language to make the setting and characters come alive.
- Use a point of view that suits the purpose of the story.
- Develop the characters through dialogue and interesting details.
- Clearly express the theme of the story.
- **Language** Write about character and setting using vivid words.

Assign the Writing Task in **Ed.**

Online
Ed

RESOURCES

- Unit 6 Response Log
- Reading Studio: Notice & Note
- Writing Studio: Writing Narratives
- Grammar Studio : Module 1: Lesson 10: Kinds of Sentences

Language X-Ray: English Learner Support

Use the instruction below and the supports and scaffolds in the Teacher's Edition to help you guide students at different proficiency levels.

INTRODUCE THE WRITING TASK

Explain that a **short story** contains all the elements of a novel, but is told in less space. Point out that the word *story* is related to the Spanish noun *historia*, which means "an account." Make sure students understand that a short story includes characters, setting, narrator, plot, conflict, and a theme.

Remind students that the selections in this unit discuss how stories reveal hidden truths about human nature. Work with students to plan their stories, encouraging them to use story elements with which they are familiar. Provide sentence frames to help them articulate their ideas. For example: *My setting will be _____. The theme will be _____.*

Brainstorm words and phrases related to the topic, and write them on the board. Then, have students work with a partner to complete the graphic organizer to plan their stories.

WRITING

Use Vivid Language

Tell students that vivid language helps make their characters and setting come alive for the reader. This, in turn, allows the reader to feel more involved in the story.

Use the following supports with students at varying proficiency levels:

- Work with students to create a list of vivid synonyms for common words, such as *good, run, walk,* and *pretty,* that they can use in their writing. **SUBSTANTIAL**
- Have students select three sentences in their drafts, then revise the sentences to incorporate vivid language. **MODERATE**
- Allow students to work with a partner when writing their drafts to revise for vivid language. **LIGHT**

WRITING

Vary Sentence Types

Tell students that varying the types of sentences they use makes their writing more interesting to read and leads to developing a personal writing style.

Use the following supports with students at varying proficiency levels:

- Provide students with sample simple, compound, and complex sentences. Explain each sentence type. Work with students to write compound and complex sentences. If necessary, have students dictate their sentences to you. **SUBSTANTIAL**
- Review conjunctions and how to use them to write compound and complex sentences with students. **MODERATE**
- Allow students to work with a partner when writing their drafts and work together to add compound and complex sentences to their writing. **LIGHT**

WRITING

WRITE A SHORT STORY

Introduce students to the Writing Task by reading the introductory paragraph with them. Remind students to refer to the notes they recorded in the Unit 6 Response Log as they plan and draft their short stories. The Response Log should contain ideas about how stories reveal hidden truths about human nature from a variety of perspectives. Drawing on these different perspectives will make their writing more interesting and well informed.

 For **writing support** for students at varying proficiency levels, see the **Language X-Ray** on page 504B.

USE THE MENTOR TEXT

Point out that their short stories will be similar to the folktale "The Mouse Bride" in that they will have a theme, setting, characters, narrator, conflict, and plot. However, their short stories will be shorter and less complicated.

WRITING PROMPT

Review the prompt with students. Encourage them to ask questions about any part of the assignment that is unclear. Make sure they understand that the purpose of their writing is to tell a story or folktale that delivers a message about life or human nature.

 WRITING TASK

Write a Short Story

 Go to the **Writing Studio** for help writing narratives.

This unit focuses on how hidden truths are revealed through stories. For this writing task, you will write a short story or a folktale that delivers a message about life or human nature. For an example of a well-written story that you can use as a mentor text, review the folktale "The Mouse Bride."

As you write your story or folktale, you can use the notes from your Response Log, which you filled out after reading the texts in this unit.

Writing Prompt

Read the information in the box below.

> *This is the topic or context for your story.*

> In their stories, authors often express messages or hidden truths about life and human nature.

Think carefully about the following question.

> *This is the essential question for the unit. How would you answer this question, based on the readings in this unit?*

> What hidden truths about people and the world are revealed in stories?

> *Now mark the words that identify exactly what you are being asked to produce.*

Write a short story or folktale that expresses a clear theme or message about life or human nature.

Be sure to—

> *Review these points as you write and again when you finish. Make any needed changes.*

- ❑ tell a story with an exposition, rising action, a climax, falling action, and a resolution
- ❑ sequence plot events to create suspense and lead to a resolution
- ❑ invent a conflict, or a problem, that can unfold and be resolved in an interesting way
- ❑ use vivid language to make your setting and characters come alive
- ❑ use a clear point of view that suits the purpose of your story
- ❑ develop your characters through dialogue and interesting details
- ❑ clearly express your theme, or message, about life or human nature

© Houghton Mifflin Harcourt Publishing Company

504   Unit 6

 LEARNING MINDSET

Asking for Help Encourage students to ask peers, teachers, and parents for help, as needed, with any part or element of their stories. Explain that asking for help from others can help students get "unstuck" and move forward. Reinforce that asking for help does not equal failure. Rather, seeking help is a way of "trying smarter."

1 Plan

Before you start writing, plan your short story or folktale. Begin by thinking about what theme, or message, you would like to express in your story. Then invent a conflict, or a problem, that can unfold in an interesting way. A story usually centers on a conflict faced by the main character.

Decide who will tell your story. Are you going to create a first-person narrator or tell the story from the third-person point of view? Think about who the characters in the story are and where the story takes place. What do the characters look like? How do they act and what do they say? When and where will the story events take place? What are the sights and sounds of this place? Use the chart below to assist you in planning your draft.

Story Planning Chart	
Theme, message, or hidden truth	
Conflict or problem	
Narrator	
Characters	
Setting	
Plot events	

Background Reading Review the notes you have taken in your Response Log after reading the texts in this unit. These texts are the background reading you will use to formulate the key ideas and storytelling techniques that you will explore in your story.

Go to **Writing Narratives: Introduction** for help planning your story.

Notice & Note

From Reading to Writing

As you plan your short story, apply what you've learned about signposts to your own writing. Remember that writers use common features, called signposts, to help convey their messages to readers.

Think about how you can incorporate **Words of the Wiser** into your story.

Go to the **Reading Studio** for more resources on **Notice & Note.**

Use the notes from your **Response Log** as you plan your story.

1 PLAN

Allow time for students to discuss their story ideas with partners or in small groups and then to complete the planning table independently.

■ English Learner Support

Understand Academic Language Make sure students understand words and phrases used in the chart, such as *theme, conflict, narrator, characters, setting,* and *plot.* Work with students to develop their ideas for their stories and write the information in the chart. **SUBSTANTIAL**

▶ NOTICE & NOTE

From Reading to Writing Explain to students that the **Words of the Wiser** signpost is often used to identify a text's theme. Encourage students to include a scene or two in their story in which a wiser character offers the main character some advice related to the story's theme.

Background Reading As they plan their stories, remind students to refer to the notes they took in the Response Log. They may also review the selections to find additional examples of short stories and folktales.

TO CHALLENGE STUDENTS . . .

Explore Narrative Perspectives Challenge students to tell the same story from a first-person perspective and then from a third-person perspective. Encourage them to be creative in exploring the different ways they can present the same theme depending upon the perspective from which they narrate their story.

WRITING

Organize Your Ideas Tell students that their planning chart lists the elements they need to include in their short stories or folktales. Explain that the next step in planning their story is to organize their ideas for the plot. Suggest that they use an outline to think about what events will happen in each part of the plot. For example:

I. Introduce Setting and Characters

II. Conflict and Rising Action

III. Rising Action

IV. Climax

V. Conclusion

Remind students that a short story is organized chronologically around the main events. Each event builds on the one before it. The conclusion should then wrap up the story with a satisfying end.

② DEVELOP A DRAFT

Remind students to follow their charts of story elements and plot events as they draft their short stories. Point out that they can still make changes to their writing plan during this stage. As they write, they may discover that they need different character development or plot points to best support their story.

■ English Learner Support

Use a Word Wall Allow students to use a word wall, dictionary, or other print resources when writing their short stories. **MODERATE**

Go to the **Writing Studio: Narrative Structure** for help organizing your ideas.

Organize Your Ideas The series of events in a story is called the **plot.** The plot usually centers on a conflict faced by the main character. List the key events of your story in chronological, or time, order. When you write, you do not need to tell the events in the order in which they occurred—in fact, it helps to build suspense if you don't. However, having a "map" of the events will help you organize your story.

Place a star next to the point of highest tension—for example, the point at which a key decision determines the outcome of events. This point is called the **climax.** At this point, or shortly afterward, the problem in a story is usually resolved.

Plot Events in Chronological Order
1.
2.
3.
4.
5.

② Develop a Draft

You might prefer to draft your story online.

Once you have completed your planning activities, you will be ready to begin drafting your story. Refer to your planning charts, as well as to any notes you took as you studied the texts in the unit. Together, these will provide a kind of map for you to follow as you write.

Using a word processor or online writing application makes it easier to make changes or move sentences around later when you are ready to revise your first draft.

© Houghton Mifflin Harcourt Publishing Company

WHEN STUDENTS STRUGGLE . . .

Draft the Short Story Remind students that a detailed chart of events will help make it easier to write their short story. Students can then incorporate the notes from their chart into complete sentences to create the first drafts of their short stories. Remind students that a first draft is not meant to be perfect. At this stage, they are just getting their ideas down on paper (or on the computer screen). They will have time to revise and edit their writing later.

Use the Mentor Text

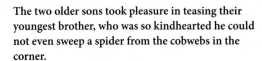

Character Development

The way a writer creates and develops characters is known as **characterization.** One method of characterization is for the writer to make direct comments about a character through the voice of the narrator. The writer may also describe the character's actions, allowing the reader to make inferences about the character. Authors use specific descriptions to develop their characters. Note the way the writer develops character in "The Mouse Bride."

> The two older sons took pleasure in teasing their youngest brother, who was so kindhearted he could not even sweep a spider from the cobwebs in the corner.

The narrator gives a specific description of the brother's kindness: he can't even kill a spider.

Apply What You've Learned To develop your characters, show their traits through their actions. How does a brave person act? How does a timid person act?

Dialogue

Dialogue is written conversation between characters. Writers use dialogue to bring characters to life and to give readers insights into characters' qualities and traits. Note the way the writer uses dialogue to reveal insights into the mouse's character.

> ". . . Oh," he moaned, "my cruel brothers will certainly ridicule me when I arrive home tonight empty-handed!"
> "I cannot bear to think of them mocking you! You will not go home empty-handed!" said the mouse.

Through dialogue the writer reveals that the mouse is confident and cares deeply about the son.

Apply What You've Learned Reveal your characters' strengths and weaknesses through dialogue. Place hints about your characters' personalities in the statements they make and the questions they ask.

Write a Short Story   507

WHY THIS MENTOR TEXT?

The excerpts from Heather Forest's "The Mouse Bride" provide good examples of incorporating character development and dialogue into a short story or folktale. Use the instruction below to help students use the mentor text as a model for creating characterization and using dialogue in their short stories.

USE THE MENTOR TEXT

Character Development Ask a volunteer to read aloud the top paragraph from "The Mouse Bride" on p. 507. Discuss how the author uses direct comments and description to develop the characters. Then invite students to write some examples of direct description that they could use in their short stories.

Dialogue To help students understand how dialogue can bring characters to life, have them read the bottom paragraph from "The Mouse Bride" on p. 507. Point out that the author uses dialogue to reveal aspects of the characters' personalities. Invite students to write some examples of dialogue that they could use in their short stories.

 ## ENGLISH LEARNER SUPPORT

Use the Mentor Text Use the following supports with students at varying proficiency levels:

- Write the words *characters* and *dialogue* on the board. Remind students that *characters* are the people or animals in a story and *dialogue* is the words they say. Look through the mentor text with students to identify examples of character description and dialogue. **SUBSTANTIAL**

- Have students work in pairs to read the mentor text and identify where and how the author effectively uses description and dialogue to enhance characterization. **MODERATE**

- Have students work in small groups or pairs to write dialogue that they can use in their short stories. **LIGHT**

WRITING

③ REVISE

On Your Own Have students answer each question in the Revision Guide to determine how they can improve their drafts. Invite volunteers to model their revision techniques.

With a Partner Have students ask peer reviewers to evaluate their descriptive details and character development by answering the following questions:

- How well is vivid vocabulary used to reveal the characters' traits?

- How well do the details help the reader understand the characters?

Students should use the reviewer's feedback to add descriptive details that aid the character development.

 Go to the **Writing Narratives: Point of View and Characters** in the **Writing Studio** for help revising your story.

③ Revise

On Your Own Once you have written your draft, go back and look for ways to improve your story or folktale. As you reread and revise, think about whether you have achieved your purpose. The Revision Guide will help you focus on specific elements to make your writing stronger.

Revision Guide		
Ask Yourself	**Tips**	**Revision Techniques**
1. Is my theme expressed clearly?	**Mark** sections that hint at the theme.	**Add** sentences that help the reader understand the theme, or message, about life or human nature.
2. Is my narrator consistent throughout the story?	**Mark** point-of-view words such as *I, she,* or *them*.	**Replace** words that express an inconsistent point of view.
3. Are my plot events organized effectively?	**Mark** each event.	**Reorganize** events to build suspense and serve the plot. Use transitions to make the meaning of each plot event clear.
4. Are my characters developed with descriptive details?	**Mark** words that reveal character traits.	**Add** interesting details that help expand the reader's understanding of the characters.
5. Is the story's climax the turning point and moment of greatest tension?	**Mark** the point in the story where the climax occurs.	**Add** words, phrases, or sentences that strengthen or signal the climax.
6. Does my story have its own style reflected in word choice, sentence variety, and dialogue?	**Mark** words and phrases that reflect the style of the story.	**Add** more descriptive word choices and dialogue to develop the distinctive style and feel of the story.

ACADEMIC VOCABULARY
As you conduct your **peer review,** be sure to use these words.

- ❑ emphasize
- ❑ occur
- ❑ period
- ❑ relevant
- ❑ tradition

With a Partner Once you and your partner have worked through the Revision Guide on your own, exchange papers and evaluate each other's draft in a **peer review.** Focus on providing revision suggestions for at least three of the items mentioned in the chart. Explain why you think your partner's draft should be revised and what your specific suggestions are.

When receiving feedback from your partner, listen attentively and ask questions to make sure you fully understand the revision suggestions.

 ## ENGLISH LEARNER SUPPORT

Use Vivid Vocabulary Explain that writers use vivid vocabulary to help readers form a picture in their minds of the characters and events in a story. Suggest that students first write or express aloud interesting details about their characters or plot events in their home language to a partner. Then have partners work together to revise their short stories to incorporate these details in English. **SUBSTANTIAL/MODERATE**

4 Edit

Once you have addressed the organization, development, and flow of ideas in your story, you can improve the finer points of your draft. Edit for the proper use of standard English conventions and correct any misspellings or grammatical errors.

Language Conventions: Style, Word Choice, Sentence Variety

Good writing has a particular style. A **style** is a manner of writing; it involves *how* something is said rather than *what* is said. Style is shown through elements such as the following:

- **word choice**—the author's use of powerful, vivid, and precise words, including descriptive adjectives and adverbs, to express ideas
- **sentence variety**—the author's use of a variety of sentence structures for different effects
- **dialogue**—conversation between characters, which helps to describe and reveal character traits
- **tone**—the author's attitude toward the subject, which might be serious, playful, mocking, or sympathetic

Notice how descriptive word choices, sentence variety, and revealing dialogue in "The Mouse Bride" capture your interest as a reader.

> ! Go to **Simple and Compound Sentences** in the **Grammar Studio** to learn more about sentence types and variety.

Style Element	Example
Descriptive Word Choice	Suddenly, with a great splash and spray of mist, out of the water came six black horses pulling a fine golden carriage.
Sentence Variety	His heart swelled with joy and every doubt he had about presenting her to his family disappeared with the first tones of her sweet voice. He climbed out of the water and wept.
Dialogue	"You'll find a pointy-eared sweetheart with sharp teeth in that forest," laughed his two brothers.

5 Publish

After you give your story its finishing touches, choose a way to share it with your audience. Consider these options:

- Present your story as a dramatization to the class.
- Post your story or folktale as a blog on a classroom or school website.

Write a Short Story   509

WRITING

4 EDIT

Suggest that students read their drafts aloud to assess how clearly and descriptively they have constructed their short stories. If the story feels hard to follow, students should check that they have effectively organized the plot to build to a climax followed by a resolution of the conflict. Reading aloud will also help students check for standard English conventions, misspellings, and grammatical errors.

LANGUAGE CONVENTIONS

Style, Word Choice, Sentence Variety Review the style elements of word choice, sentence variety, dialogue, and tone with students. Then discuss the example sentences in the chart, asking students to discuss how each one captures the interest of the reader. To emphasize the importance of word choice and sentence variety, rewrite the sentences with nondescript words and no variation in sentences. Read the sentences aloud so students can see and hear the difference. Then have students review their word choices and sentence variety in their short stories, making any changes in descriptive style elements where needed.

■ English Learner Support

Use Pronouns Have students work in pairs to locate pronouns used in their short stories. Have students work together to check that the pronouns agree in number and gender with the associated nouns. **MODERATE**

5 PUBLISH

Have students publish their short stories on the classroom blog. Additionally, allow time for students to share and discuss their short stories in small groups.

WHEN STUDENTS STRUGGLE . . .

Identify Tone Some students may have difficulty identifying the tone of a short story. Remind students that tone reveals the author's attitude toward a character or story. Allow students to highlight the words that reveal the tone of their stories. Some students may benefit from working with a partner or adult helper to identify the descriptive vocabulary and the tone of their short stories.

WRITING

USE THE SCORING GUIDE

Have students read the scoring guide. Invite them to ask questions about any words, phrases, or ideas that are unclear. Then form students into groups of three. Assign one student to score the organization/progression, one to score the development of ideas, and one to score the use of language and conventions. Have students exchange their narratives to score the assigned portion, using the scoring guide. Each student should write a paragraph explaining the reasons for the score awarded in each category.

 WRITING TASK

Use the scoring guide to evaluate your short story or folktale.

Writing Task Scoring Guide: Short Story		
Organization/Progression	**Development of Ideas**	**Use of Language and Conventions**
4 • The sequence of events is effective at building the plot and creating suspense. • The organization and pace keep the reader curious about the next plot event. • The well-designed plot begins with an intriguing conflict, builds to a climax, and the falling action leads to a satisfying resolution.	• The exposition vividly introduces the setting and main character and establishes the conflict in an engaging way. • Description and dialogue effectively develop characters and events. • The well-developed story reveals a significant theme. • The story ends satisfactorily and resolves the loose ends.	• The point of view is effective and consistent throughout. • Strong, descriptive word choices reveal the setting and characters. • Sentences vary in structure and have a rhythmic flow. • Dialogue reveals characters' personalities. • Spelling, capitalization, and punctuation are correct. • Grammar and usage are correct.
3 • The sequence of events is mostly effective at building the plot and creating suspense. • The organization is adequate, but the pace is somewhat slow or uneven. • The plot includes an interesting conflict, builds to a climax, and the falling action leads to a reasonable resolution.	• The exposition introduces the setting, a main character, and a conflict. • Description and dialogue develop characters and events. • The plot is adequately developed; the story suggests a theme. • The story resolves the conflict but needs more details to bring the plot to a satisfying resolution.	• The point of view is mostly consistent. • Setting and character need more description. • Sentence structure varies somewhat. • Dialogue is somewhat helpful in revealing personalities of the characters. • Spelling, capitalization, and punctuation mistakes occur. • Grammatical and usage errors occur.
2 • Confusion in the sequence of events weakens the plot and sense of suspense. • The organization is unclear and the pace often lags. • The story lacks thoughtful elements of plot; it does not build to a climax or include falling action ending with a resolution.	• The exposition is not engaging; it identifies a setting and a main character but only hints at a conflict. • More description and dialogue are needed to develop characters and events. • The plot development is uneven in places; a theme is only hinted at. • The story resolves some parts of the conflict.	• The point of view shifts confusingly. • Few descriptive words are used. • Sentence structures lacks variation. • Dialogue between characters is infrequent and does not provide information about the characters. • Spelling, capitalization, and punctuation are often incorrect. • Grammatical and usage errors occur often.
1 • The sequence of events and the plot are confusing; there is no sense of suspense. • The story is disorganized and the pace varies ineffectively. • The plot does not exist or does not progress to a climax and then lead to a resolution.	• Critical information about the setting and main character is missing; a conflict is not set. • Description and dialogue is missing. • The plot is barely developed and lacks a theme. • The story lacks a clear resolution.	• A clear point of view is lacking. • Unimaginative word choices and repetitive sentence structure create a dull story. • Dialogue is confusing or nonexistent. • Spelling, capitalization, and punctuation are mostly incorrect. • Grammar and usage errors occur throughout.

Reflect on the Unit

By completing your short story or folktale, you have created a writing product that pulls together and expresses your thoughts about the reading you have done in this unit. Now is a good time to reflect on what you have learned.

Reflect on the Essential Question

• What hidden truths about people and the world are revealed in stories? In what ways has your understanding of how to uncover hidden truths in stories changed since you started this unit?

• What are some examples from the texts you've read of hidden truths about people and the world?

Reflect on Your Reading

• Which selection reveals a hidden truth that you'd never thought about before?

• Which selection reminds you of a fairy tale, folktale, or nursery rhyme that you enjoyed as a young child? Does the selection lead you to reconsider what that story from your childhood was really about?

Reflect on the Writing Task

• Which hidden truth were you thinking about as you wrote your story or folktale?

• How did you come up with your plot and characters?

• What strategies did you use to create a specific style for your story?

UNIT 6 SELECTIONS
• *Storytelling*
• *The Prince and the Pauper*
• "Archetype"
• "Fairy-tale Logic"
• "The Boatman's Flute"
• "The Mouse Bride"

REFLECT ON THE UNIT

Have students reflect on the questions independently and write some notes in response to each one. Then have students meet with partners or in small groups to discuss their reflections. Circulate during these discussions to identify the questions that are generating the liveliest conversations. Wrap up with a whole-class discussion focused on these questions.

LEARNING MINDSET

Self-Reflection Explain to students that an important part of developing a learning mindset is the ability to recognize strengths and weaknesses. As students reflect on the unit, encourage them to ask themselves these questions: Did I ask questions if I needed help? Did I review my work for possible errors? Am I proud of the work I turned in?

HMH

Student Resources

 Online **Ed** *your friend in learning*

HMH *Into Literature* Studios
For more instruction and practice,
visit the HMH *Into Literature* Studios.

 Reading Studio

 Writing Studio

 Speaking & Listening Studio

 Grammar Studio

 Vocabulary Studio

UNIT 1
RESPONSE LOG

Use this Response Log to record your ideas about how each of the texts in Unit 1 relates to or comments on the **Essential Question.**

? **Essential Question:**
How do you find courage in the face of fear?

from The Breadwinner	
Life Doesn't Frighten Me	
Fears and Phobias	
Wired for Fear	
Embarrassed? Blame Your Brain	
The Ravine	

UNIT 2
RESPONSE LOG

? **Essential Question:**
What can you learn by seeing the world through an animal's eyes?

from Pax	
Zoo	
from Animal Snoops: The Wondrous World of Wildlife Spies	
Animal Wisdom	
The Last Wolf	
Wild Animals Aren't Pets	
Let People Own Exotic Animals	

UNIT 3
RESPONSE LOG

Use this Response Log to record your ideas about how each of the texts in Unit 3 relates to or comments on the **Essential Question.**

? **Essential Question:**
What does it take to be a survivor?

from A Long Walk to Water	
Salva's Story	
Chapter 21: Into the Lifeboat *from* Titanic Survivor	
from After the Hurricane	
from Ninth Ward	

UNIT 4
RESPONSE LOG

Use this Response Log to record your ideas about how each of the texts in Unit 4 relates to or comments on the **Essential Question.**

? **Essential Question:**
What are the ways you can make yourself heard?

from Selfie: The Changing Face of Self-Portraits	
from Brown Girl Dreaming	
What's So Funny, Mr. Scieszka?	
A Voice	
Words Like Freedom	
Better Than Words: Say It with a Selfie	
OMG, Not *Another* Selfie!	

UNIT 5
RESPONSE LOG

Use this Response Log to record your ideas about how each of the texts in Unit 5 relates to or comments on the **Essential Question.**

? **Essential Question:**
What keeps people from giving up?

A Schoolgirl's Diary *from* I Am Malala	
The First Day of School	
Speech to the Young: Speech to the Progress-Toward	
from Into the Air	
from The Wright Brothers: How They Invented the Airplane	

© Houghton Mifflin Harcourt Publishing Company

UNIT 6
RESPONSE LOG

Use this Response Log to record your ideas about how each of the texts in Unit 6 relates to or comments on the **Essential Question.**

 Essential Question:
What hidden truths about people and the world are revealed in stories?

from Storytelling	
The Prince and the Pauper	
Archetype	
Fairy-tale Logic	
The Boatman's Flute	
The Mouse Bride	

Using a Glossary

A glossary is an alphabetical list of vocabulary words. Use a glossary just as you would a dictionary—to determine the meanings, parts of speech, pronunciation, and syllabification of words. (Some technical, foreign, and more obscure words in this book are defined for you in the footnotes that accompany many of the selections.)

Many words in the English language have more than one meaning. This glossary gives the meanings that apply to the words as they are used in the selections in this book.

The following abbreviations are used to identify parts of speech of words:

adj. adjective   *adv.* adverb   *n.* noun   *v.* verb

Each word's pronunciation is given in parentheses. A guide to the pronunciation symbols appears in the Pronunciation Key below. The stress marks in the Pronunciation Key are used to indicate the force given to each syllable in a word. They can also help you determine where words are divided into syllables.

For more information about the words in this glossary or for information about words not listed here, consult a dictionary.

Pronunciation Key

Symbol	Examples	Symbol	Examples	Symbol	Examples
ă	pat	m	mum	ûr	urge, term, firm, word, heard
ā	pay	n	no, sudden* (sud´n)	v	valve
ä	father	ng	thing	w	with
âr	care	ŏ	pot	y	yes
b	bib	ō	toe	z	zebra, xylem
ch	church	ô	caught, paw	zh	vision, pleasure, garage
d	deed, milled	oi	noise	ə	about, item, edible, gallop, circus
ě	pet	ŏŏ	took	ər	butter
ē	bee	ōō	boot		
f	fife, phase, rough	ŏŏr	lure		
g	gag	ôr	core		
h	hat	ou	out	**Sounds in Foreign Words**	
hw	which	p	pop	KH	*German* ich, ach; *Scottish* loch
ĭ	pit	r	roar	N	*French,* bon (bôn)
ī	pie, by	s	sauce	œ	*French* feu, œuf; *German* schön
îr	pier	sh	ship, dish	ü	*French* tu; *German* über
j	judge	t	tight, stopped		
k	kick, cat, pique	th	thin		
l	lid, needle* (nēd´l)	*th*	this		
		ŭ	cut		

*In English the consonants *l* and *n* often constitute complete syllables by themselves.

Stress Marks

The relative emphasis with which the syllables of a word or phrase are spoken, called stress, is indicated in three different ways. The strongest, or primary, stress is marked with a bold mark (´). An intermediate, or secondary, level of stress is marked with a similar but lighter mark (´). The weakest stress is unmarked. Words of one syllable show no stress mark.

GLOSSARY OF ACADEMIC VOCABULARY

achieve (ə-chēv´) *v.* to succeed in accomplishing something; to bring about by effort

appropriate (ə-prō´prē-ĭt) *adj.* suitable for a particular person, occasion, or place

authority (ə-thôr´ĭ-tē) *n.* an accepted source, such as a person or text, of expert information or advice

benefit (bĕn´ə-fĭt) *n.* something that provides help or improves something else

circumstance (sûr´kəm-stăns´) *n.* a condition, or set of conditions, that affects an event

consequence (kôn´sĭ-kwĕns´) *n.* something that logically follows from an action or condition

constraint (kən-strānt´) *n.* something or someone that limits or restricts another's actions

distinct (dĭ-stĭngkt´) *adj.* easy to tell apart from others; not alike

element (ĕl´ə-mənt) *n.* an essential part of something

emphasize (ĕm´fə-sīz´) *v.* to give prominence or emphasis to

environment (ĕn-vī´rən-mənt) *n.* the natural world surrounding someone or something; surroundings

evident (ĕv´ĭ-dənt) *adj.* easily seen or understood; obvious

factor (făk´tər) *n.* someone or something that contributes to an accomplishment, result, or process

illustrate (ĭl´ə-strāt´) *v.* to show, or clarify, by examples or comparison

impact (ĭm´păkt´) *n.* something striking against another; also, the effect or impression of one thing on another

indicate (ĭn´dĭ-kāt´) *v.* to point out; also, to serve as a sign or symbol of something

individual (ĭn´də-vĭj´ōō-əl) *n.* a single human being apart from a society or community

injure (ĭn´jər) *v.* to hurt or cause damage

instance (ĭn´stəns) *n.* an example that is cited to prove or disprove a claim or illustrate a point

justify (jŭs´tə-fī´) *v.* to demonstrate or prove to be just, right, reasonable, or valid

occur (ə-kûr´) *v.* to take place; happen

outcome (out´kŭm´) *n.* a natural result or consequence

period (pîr´ē-əd) *n.* a particular length of time, often referring to a specific time in history or culture

principle (prĭn´sə-pəl) *n.* a rule or standard, especially of good behavior

relevant (rĕl´ə-vənt) *adj.* important to, connected to, or significant to an issue, event, or person in some way

respond (rĭ-spŏnd´) *v.* to make a reply; answer

significant (sĭg-nĭf´ĭ-kənt) *adj.* meaningful; important

similar (sĭm´ə-lər) *adj.* alike in appearance or nature, though not identical

specific (spĭ-sĭf´ĭk) *adj.* concerned with a particular thing; also, precise or exact

tradition (trə-dĭsh´ən) *n.* the passing down of various elements of culture from generation to generation; a custom

GLOSSARY OF CRITICAL VOCABULARY

accurate (ăk′yər-ĭt) *adj.* Something *accurate* is correct.

activate (ăk′tə-vāt′) *v.* To *activate* something means to cause it to start working.

adversity (ăd-vûr′sĭ-tē) *n. Adversity* is misfortune or hardship.

agonizing (ăg′ə-nīz′ĭng) *adj.* To be in an *agonizing* state means to feel great mental suffering and worry.

amazement (ə-māz′mənt) *n. Amazement* is a state of extreme surprise or wonder.

amplify (ăm′plə-fī′) *v.* To *amplify* something is to make it stronger or more intense.

angular (ăng′gyə-lər) *adj.* Something that is *angular,* such as a peaked roof, has two sides that form an angle.

anonymous (ə-nŏn′ə-məs) *adj.* Someone who is *anonymous* has an undisclosed or unknown name.

anxiety (ăng-zī′ĭ-tē) *n. Anxiety* is a feeling of uneasiness, fear, or worry.

anxiously (ăngk′shəs-lē) *adv.* To think of something *anxiously* means that you dread it.

apology (ə-pŏl′ə-jē) *n.* An *apology* is an expression of regret or a request for forgiveness.

apparatus (ăp′ə-răt′əs) *n.* An *apparatus* is a piece of equipment.

calculate (kăl′kyə-lāt′) *v.* To *calculate* is to figure out an answer by using math.

cascade (kăs-kād′) *v.* Something that can *cascade* will fall, pour, or rush in stages, like a waterfall over steep rocks.

celebrity (sə-lĕb′rĭ-tē) *n.* A *celebrity* is a famous person.

chastise (chăs′tīz′) *v.* To *chastise* is to punish or criticize.

collapse (kə-lăps′) *v.* When something is said to *collapse,* it falls down.

commit (kə-mĭt′) *v.* To *commit* is to do or perform an action.

constantly (kŏn′stəntlē) *adv. Constantly* means something that is regularly occurring.

convince (kən-vĭns′) *v.* To *convince* is to use argument or evidence to get someone to believe or be certain about something.

courtyard (kôrt′yärd′) *n.* A *courtyard* is an area enclosed by walls and open to the sky.

debate (dĭ-bāt′) *v.* To *debate* is to discuss opposing points or ideas.

deceptive (dĭ-sĕp′tĭv) *adj.* Something *deceptive* is giving a false impression.

defeat (dĭ-fēt′) *v.* To *defeat* a person or his or her efforts is to prevent his or her success.

defy (dĭ-fī′) *v.* To *defy* someone is to oppose him or her or refuse to cooperate with that person.

demonstration (dĕm′ən-strā′shən) *n.* A *demonstration* is a presentation meant to show how something works.

dictate (dĭk′tāt′) *v.* To *dictate* something is to require it to be done or decided.

discourage (dĭ-skûr′ĭj) *v.* To *discourage* is to take away hope or confidence.

discreetly (dĭ-skrēt′lē) *adv.* To act *discreetly* means to act with self-restraint; attracting little notice.

displease (dĭs-plēz′) *v.* To *displease* someone is to cause annoyance or irritation.

eavesdrop (ēvz′drŏp′) *v.* To *eavesdrop* is to listen secretly to others′ private conversations.

edict (ē′dĭkt′) *n.* An *edict* is a command or pronouncement enforced as law.

elegant (ĕl′ĭ-gənt) *adj.* Someone *elegant* appears to be refined and tasteful, having a beautiful manner, form, or style.

embrace (ĕm-brās′) *v.* To *embrace* someone is to hug or hold the person close.

enchanting (ĕn-chăn′tĭng) *adj.* Something or someone *enchanting* is charming.

GLOSSARY OF CRITICAL VOCABULARY

endure (ĕn-dŏŏr´) v. To *endure* is to carry on despite difficulty or suffering.

essential (ĭ-sĕn´shəl) adj. Something *essential* is so important that you can't do without it.

etch (ĕch) v. To *etch* is to cut or carve a drawing into a surface such as wood or metal.

eternity (ĭ-tûr´nĭ-tē) n. *Eternity* refers to infinite time, without beginning or end.

exempt (ĭg-zĕmpt´) adj. A person who is *exempt* is freed or excused from following a law or duty that others must obey.

exotic (ĭg-zŏt´ĭk) adj. Something that is *exotic* is from another part of the world.

experiment (ĭk-spĕr´ə-mənt) n. An *experiment* is a test to determine if an idea is true or to see if a device works.

fascinate (făs´ə-nāt´) v. To *fascinate* someone means to capture the interest or attention of that person.

focus (fō´kəs) v. When you *focus* on something, you keep attention fixed on it.

foil (foil) v. If you *foil* someone, you stop that person from being successful at something.

fortitude (fôr´tĭ-tōōd) n. To have *fortitude* is to show strength of mind and face difficulty with courage.

fume (fyōōm) v. To *fume* about something is to feel or show displeasure or resentment.

generate (jĕn´ə-rāt´) v. To *generate* is to create and develop something.

hesitate (hĕz´ĭ-tāt´) v. To *hesitate* is to pause or wait in uncertainty.

history (hĭs´tə-rē) n. *History* is a chronological record of events of a person or institution.

horizon (hə-rī´zən) n. The *horizon* is the intersection of the earth and sky.

humiliation (hyōō-mĭl´ē-ā´shən) n. A feeling of *humiliation* is even more intense than a feeling of embarrassment.

illuminate (ĭ-lōō´mə-nāt´) v. To *illuminate* means to brighten or give light.

immaturity (ĭm´ə-tyŏŏr´ĭ-tē) n. *Immaturity* is the state of not being fully developed or grown.

incorrect (ĭn´kə-rĕkt´) adj. Something *incorrect* is faulty or wrong.

indulgent (ĭn-dŭl´jənt) adj. *Indulgent* means excessively permissive. *Self-indulgent* is when one is overly permissive with oneself.

injury (ĭn´jə-rē) n. An *injury* is damage or harm done to a person or thing.

integral (ĭn´tĭ-grəl) adj. Something that is *integral* is necessary or essential for completeness.

intercept (ĭn´tər-sĕpt´) v. To *intercept* is to stop or interrupt something.

interplanetary (ĭn´tər-plăn´ĭ-tĕr´ē) adj. *Interplanetary* means existing or occurring between planets.

intimacy (ĭn´tə-mə-sē) n. *Intimacy* means close friendship and familiarity.

invariably (ĭn-vâr´ē-ə-blē) adv. Something that happens *invariably* occurs again and again or constantly.

jest (jĕst) v. To *jest* means to make playful remarks.

lament (lə-mĕnt´) v. If you *lament*, you are wailing or crying as a way of expressing grief.

linger (lĭng´gər) v. To *linger* means to leave slowly and reluctantly, not wanting to go.

microphone (mī´krə-fōn´) n. A *microphone* is an instrument that is often used to amplify the voice.

murky (mûr´kē) adj. Something *murky* is dark, obscure, and gloomy.

narcissist (när´sĭ-sĭst´) n. A person who is preoccupied with his or her looks is a *narcissist*.

nurture (nûr´chər) v. To *nurture* is to provide love, affection, nourishment, or something else necessary for development.

passion (păsh´ən) n. *Passion* means boundless enthusiasm.

pause (pôz) v. To *pause* is to hesitate or suspend action.

perplexed (pər-plĕkst´) adj. When you are *perplexed*, you are puzzled.

GLOSSARY OF CRITICAL VOCABULARY

poised (poizd) *adj.* To be *poised* means to be calm and assured, showing balanced feeling and action.

politeness (pə-līt′nəs) *n. Politeness* is respectful behavior.

portrait (pôr′trĭt) *n.* A *portrait* is a person's likeness, especially one showing the face, which may be painted, photographed, or otherwise represented.

precipice (prĕs′ə-pĭs) *n.* A *precipice* is an overhanging or extremely steep area of rock.

predator (prĕd′ə-tər) *n.* A *predator* is an animal that survives by eating other animals.

prediction (prĭ-dĭk′shən) *n.* When someone makes a *prediction*, they make a guess about something that has not yet happened.

prepare (prĭ-pâr′) *v.* To *prepare* is to get ready for an event or occasion.

preserve (prĭ-zûrv′) *v.* To *preserve* something is to keep it or save it.

pseudonym (sōōd′n-ĭm′) *n.* A *pseudonym* is a fictitious name, particularly a pen name.

reassure (rē′ə-shŏŏr′) *v.* To *reassure* someone is to give comfort or confidence to that person.

reflection (rĭ-flĕk′shən) *n.* A *reflection* is an image shown back, as from a mirror.

regal (rē′gəl) *adj.* Something *regal* appears to be royal, magnificent, or splendid.

regulate (rĕg′yə-lāt′) *v.* If you *regulate* something, you control or direct it according to a rule, principle, or law.

reluctance (rĭ-lŭk′təns) *n.* Showing *reluctance* to do something means you are unwilling.

resentment (rĭ-zĕnt′mənt) *n.* If you feel *resentment*, you feel anger or irritation.

responsibility (rĭ-spŏn′sə-bĭl′ĭ-tē) *n.* A *responsibility* is a duty, obligation, or burden.

rivulet (rĭv′yə-lĭt) *n.* A *rivulet* is a small brook or stream.

rueful (rōō′fəl) *adj.* To be *rueful* is to show sorrow or regret.

saturated (săch′ə-rāt′tĭd) *adj.* Something that is *saturated* is filled until it is unable to hold or contain more.

scurry (skûr′ē) *v.* Something that can *scurry* will run with quick, light steps.

seamstress (sēm′strĭs) *n.* A *seamstress* is a woman who sews, especially one who earns a living sewing.

sensitive (sĕn′sĭ-tĭv) *adj.* Something *sensitive* is able to perceive small differences or changes in the environment.

serene (sə-rēn′) *adj.* If you are *serene*, you are calm and unflustered.

shoulder (shōl′dər) *v.* To *shoulder* something is to carry it on one's shoulders.

sincere (sĭn-sîr′) *adj.* Something or someone *sincere* is genuine or heartfelt.

solution (sə-lōō′shən) *n.* A *solution* is a way of handling a problem.

span (spăn) *v.* To *span* is to extend over a period of time.

stake (stāk) *n.* A *stake* is something that can be gained or lost in a situation, such as money, food, or life.

stammer (stăm′ər) *v.* To *stammer* is to speak with involuntary pauses or repetitions.

stealthily (stĕl′thə-lē) *adv.* To do something *stealthily* means doing it quietly and secretly so no one notices.

terror (tĕr′ər) *n. Terror* is extreme fear of something.

trance (trăns) *n.* When someone is in a *trance*, he or she is in a daze or daydreaming.

trigger (trĭg′r) *v.* To *trigger* something means to cause it to begin.

turbulence (tûr′byə-ləns) *n.* In flying, *turbulence* is an interruption in the flow of wind that causes planes to rise, fall, or sway in a rough way.

universal (yōō′nə-vûr′səl) *adj.* Something that is *universal* affects every member of a group.

unrestrainedly (ŭn′rĭ-strā′nĭd-lē) *adv.* Doing something *unrestrainedly* means doing it without control.

veer (vîr) *v.* Something that can *veer* will swerve, or suddenly change course or direction.

wistfully (wĭst′fəl-ē) *adv.* When you think of something *wistfully*, you do so with sadness and longing.

Index of Skills

INDEX OF TITLES AND AUTHORS

ACKNOWLEDGMENTS

Excerpt from "After the Hurricane" by Rita Williams-Garcia from *Free? Stories About Human Rights* by Amnesty International. Text copyright © 2009 by Rita Williams-Garcia. Reprinted by permission of Rita Williams-Garcia.

Excerpts from *The American Heritage Dictionary of The English Language, Fifth Edition.* Text copyright © 2016 by Houghton Mifflin Harcourt Publishing Company. Reprinted by permission of Houghton Mifflin Harcourt Publishing Company.

Excerpt from *Animal Snoops: The Wondrous World of Wildlife Spies.* Text copyright © 2010 by Peter Christie, published by Annick Press Ltd. Reprinted by permission of Annick Press Ltd. All rights reserved.

"Animal Wisdom" from *Sacred Fire* by Nancy Wood. Text copyright © 1998 by Nancy Wood. Reprinted by permission of the Nancy Wood Literary Trust.

"Archetype" by Margarita Engle. Text copyright © 2005 by Margarita Engle. Reprinted by permission of Margarita Engle.

"The Boatman's Flute" from *Children of the Dragon: Selected Tales from Vietnam* by Sherry Garland. Text copyright © 2001 by Sherry Garland. Reprinted by permission of Sherry Garland.

Excerpt from *The Breadwinner* by Deborah Ellis. Text copyright © 2000 by Deborah Ellis. First published in Canada by Groundwood Books Ltd. Reprinted by permission of Groundwood Books Ltd., Oxford University Press, Allen & Unwin Pty. Ltd., and Penguin Random House LLC. All rights reserved. Any third party use of this material, outside of this publication, is prohibited. Interested parties must apply directly to Penguin Random House LLC for permission.

"Embarrassed?" by Jennifer Connor-Smith from *Odyssey* March 2015 copyright © 2015 by Carus Publishing Company. Reprinted by permission of Carus Publishing Company. All Cricket Media material is copyrighted by Carus Publishing Company d/b/a Cricket Media, and/or various authors and illustrators. Any commercial use or distribution of material without permission is strictly prohibited.

"Fairy-Tale Logic" from *Olives* by A. E. Stalling. Text copyright © 2006 by A. E. Stallings. Reprinted by permission of Northwestern University Press.

"Fears and Phobias" from *kidshealth.org*. Text copyright © 1995-2012 by The Nemours Foundation/KidsHealth*. Reprinted by permission of The Nemours Foundation.

"The First Day of School" from *The Happy Marriage and Other Stories* by R.V. Cassill. Text copyright © 1966 by R.V. Cassill. Reprinted by permission of the Estate of R.V. Cassill.

Excerpt from *I Am Malala* by Malala Yousafzai. Text copyright © 2014 by Salarzai Limited. Reprinted by permission of Little, Brown and Company.

Excerpt from "Into the Air" by Robert Burleigh, Illustrated by Bill Wylie. Text copyright © 2002 by Robert Burleigh and illustrations copyright © 2012 by Bill Wylie. Reprinted by permission of Robert Burleigh and Bill Wylie.

"The Last Wolf" by Mary TallMountain. Text copyright © 1994 by the TallMountain Estate. Reprinted by permission of the TallMountain Estate. All rights reserved.

"Let People Own Exotic Animals" by Zuzana Kukol from *USA Today* October 20, 2011. Text copyright © 2011 Gannett-USA Today. Reprinted by permission of PARS International on behalf of Gannett-USA Today. All rights reserved. Protected by the Copyright Laws of the United States. The printing, copying, redistribution, or retransmission of this Content without express written permission is prohibited. www.usatoday.com

"Life Doesn't Frighten Me" from *And Still I Rise: A Book of Poems* by Maya Angelou. Text copyright © 1978 by Maya Angelou. Reprinted by permission of Random House, an imprint and division of Penguin Random House LLC, Penguin Random House Audio Publishing Group, a division of Penguin Random House LLC, and Little, Brown Book Group, Ltd. All rights reserved. Any third party use of this material, outside of this publication, is prohibited. Interested parties must apply directly to Penguin Random House LLC for permission.

Excerpt from *A Long Walk to Water* by Linda Sue Park. Text copyright © 2010 by Linda Sue Park. Reprinted by permission of Houghton Mifflin Harcourt.

"The Mouse Bride: A Folktale from Finland" from *Wonder Tales from Around the World* retold by Heather Forest. Text copyright © 1995 by Heather Forest. Reprinted by permission of Marian Reiner on behalf of the publisher August House, Inc.

Excerpt from *Ninth Ward* by Jewell Parker Rhodes. Text copyright © 2010 by Jewell Parker Rhodes. Reprinted by permission of Little, Brown and Company.

Excerpt from *Pax* by Sara Pennypacker. Text copyright © 2016 by Sara Pennypacker. Reprinted by permission of Blazer + Bray, an imprint of HarperCollins Publishers.

The Prince and the Pauper by Mark Twain, as adapted by Joellen Bland from *Plays: The Drama Magazine for Young People* and from *Stage Plays from the Classics* by Joellen Bland. Text copyright © 1987, 2012 by Joellen Bland. Reprinted by permission of the publisher Plays. This play is for reading purposes only.

"The Ravine" by Graham Salisbury from *On the Edge: Stories at the Brink* edited by Lois Duncan. Text copyright © 2000 by Graham Salisbury. Reprinted by permission of Jennifer Flannery Literary Agency.

Excerpts from *Selfie: The Changing Face of Self-Portraits* by Susie Brooks. Text copyright © 2016 by Wayland Publishers. Reprinted by permission of Wayland Publishers.

"Speech to the Young, Speech to the Progress-Toward" from *Blacks* by Gwendolyn Brooks. Text copyright © 1945, 1949, 1953, 1960, 1963, 1968, 1969, 1970, 1971, 1975, 1981, 1987 by Gwendolyn Brooks. Reprinted by permission of Brooks Permissions.

Excerpt from *Storytelling: An Encyclopedia of Mythology and Folklore* by Josepha Sherman. Text copyright © 2008 by M.E. Sharpe, Inc. Reprinted by permission of Taylor & Francis Group.

ACKNOWLEDGMENTS

Excerpt from *Titanic Survivor* by Violet Jessop. Text copyright © 1997 by Sheridan House. Reprinted by permission of Rowman & Littlefield Publishers, Inc.

"A Voice" from *Communion* by Pat Mora. Text copyright © 1991 by Pat Mora. Reprinted by permission of the publisher Arte Público Press - University of Houston.

"What's So Funny, Mr. Scieszka? from *Knucklehead: Tall Tales and Almost True Stories of Growing Up Scieszka* by Jon Scieszka. Copyright © 2005, 2008 by Jon Scieszka. Illustrations, Photographs, and Text reprinted by permission of Viking Children's Books, an imprint of Penguin Young Readers Group, a division of Penguin Random House LLC. All rights reserved. Any third party use of this material, outside of this publication, is prohibited. Interested parties must apply directly to Penguin Random House LLC for permission.

"Wild Animals Aren't Pets" from *USA Today* October 23, 2011. Text copyright © 2011 Gannett-USA Today. Reprinted by permission of PARS International on behalf of Gannett-USA Today. All rights reserved. Protected by the Copyright Laws of the United States. The printing, copying, redistribution, or retransmission of this Content without express written permission is prohibited. www.usatoday.com

"writing #1," "late autumn," "the other woodson," "reading," "stevie and me," and "when i tell my family" from *Brown Girl Dreaming* by Jacqueline Woodson. Text copyright © 2014 by Jacqueline Woodson. Reprinted by permission of Nancy Paulsen Books, an imprint of Penguin Young Readers Group, a division of Penguin Random House LLC, and William Morris Endeavor Entertainment. All rights reserved. Any third party use of this material, outside of this publication, is prohibited. Interested parties must apply directly to Penguin Random House LLC for permission.

"Words Like Freedom" from *The Collected Poems of Langston Hughes* by Langston Hughes, edited by Arnold Rampersad with David Roessel, Associate Editor. Text copyright © 1994 by the Estate of Langston Hughes. Reprinted by permission of Alfred A. Knopf, an imprint of the Knopf Doubleday Publishing Group, a division of Penguin Random House LLC, and Harold Ober Associates Incorporated. All rights reserved. Any third party use of this material, outside of this publication, is prohibited. Interested parties must apply directly to Penguin Random House LLC for permission.

Excerpt from *The Wright Brothers: How They Invented the Airplane* by Russell Freedman. Text copyright © 1991 by Russell Freedman. Reprinted by permission of Holiday House, Inc.

"Zoo" by Edward D. Hoch. Text copyright © 1958 by King-Size Publications, Inc., copyright renewed © 1986 by Edward D. Hoch. Reprinted by permission of Sternig & Byrne Literary Agency.